PUBLIC PAPERS OF THE PRESIDENTS OF THE UNITED STATES

PUBLIC PAPERS OF THE PRESIDENTS
OF THE
UNITED STATES

Ronald Reagan

1984

(IN TWO BOOKS)

BOOK I—JANUARY 1 TO JUNE 29, 1984

UNITED STATES GOVERNMENT PRINTING OFFICE
WASHINGTON : 1986

Published by the
Office of the Federal Register
National Archives and Records Administration

For sale by the
Superintendent of Documents
U.S. Government Printing Office
Washington, DC 20402

Foreword

1984 was a special year for America. The last year of our first term brought continued prosperity to our people and increased stability in the world.

We made great strides in improving the quality of education in the United States, giving our children a strong foundation for their futures. We redoubled our efforts on behalf of missing and exploited children, whose sad plight tugs at our hearts and whose lives take on new meaning as we seek earnestly for ways to rejoin them with their loved ones. Inflation continued its downward trend, and our Americans joined the work force in record numbers.

As a world leader, America continued its march for freedom. We stood firm for democracy in Central America, never wavering in our dedication to the courageous freedom fighters who risked their lives for the God-given right to control their own destinies. In April, we journeyed to the People's Republic of China and held important talks with leaders there, strengthening an ever-increasingly solid relationship with a valued friend. And at the London Economic Summit, we joined with our partners from France, the United Kingdom, Italy, the Federal Republic of Germany, Canada, and the European Economic Community in our continuing discussions about ways to find solutions to common problems.

The first half of 1984 was a time of great pride for America. Our economic revival continued full speed, our domestic agenda had an appropriate emphasis on our young people, our democracy-loving neighbors received our support, the people of China opened their hearts to us, and our partnership with our European allies was stronger than ever.

These pages are an important and exciting record of this special time in our history.

Ronald Reagan

Preface

This book contains the papers and speeches of the 40th President of the United States that were issued by the Office of the Press Secretary during the period January 1-June 29, 1984. The material has been compiled and published by the Office of the Federal Register, National Archives and Records Administration.

The material is presented in chronological order, and the dates shown in the headings are the dates of the documents or events. In instances when the release date differs from the date of the document itself, that fact is shown in the textnote. Every effort has been made to ensure accuracy. Tape recordings of Presidential remarks are used to protect against errors in transcription, and signed documents are checked against the original to verify the correct printing. Textnotes, footnotes, and cross references have been provided by the editors for purposes of identification or clarity. Speeches were delivered in Washington, DC, unless indicated. The times noted are local times. All materials that are printed full-text in the book have been indexed in the subject and name indexes.

The Public Papers series was begun in 1957 in response to a recommendation of the National Historical Publications Commission. An extensive compilation of messages and papers of the Presidents covering the period 1789 to 1897 was assembled by James D. Richardson and published under congressional authority between 1896 and 1899. Since then, various private compilations have been issued, but there was no uniform publication comparable to the Congressional Record or the United States Supreme Court Reports. Many Presidential papers could be found only in the form of mimeographed White House releases or as reported in the press. The Commission therefore recommended the establishment of an official series in which Presidential writings, addresses, and remarks of a public nature could be made available.

The Commission's recommendation was incorporated in regulations of the Administrative Committee of the Federal Register, issued under section 6 of the Federal Register Act (44 U.S.C. 1506), which may be found in Title I, Part 10, of the Code of Federal Regulations.

A companion publication to the Public Papers series, the Weekly Compilation of Presidential Documents, was begun in 1965 to provide a broader range of Presidential materials on a more timely basis to meet the needs of the contemporary reader. Beginning with the administration of Jimmy Carter, the Public Papers series expanded its coverage to include all material as printed in the Weekly Compilation. That coverage provides a listing of the President's daily schedule and meetings, when announced, and other items of general interest issued by the Office of the Press Secretary. Also included are lists of the President's nominations submitted to the Senate, materials released by the Office of the Press Secretary that are not printed full-text in the book, and acts approved by the President. This information appears in the appendixes at the end of the book.

Volumes covering the administrations of Presidents Hoover, Truman, Eisenhower, Kennedy, Johnson, Nixon, Ford, and Carter are also available.

The Chief Editor of this book was Wilma Prudhum Greene, and William K. Banks was Associate Editor.

White House liaison was provided by Larry M. Speakes, Assistant to the President and Principal Deputy Press Secretary. The frontispiece and photographs used in the portfolio were supplied by the White House Photo Office.

John E. Byrne
Director of the Federal Register

Frank G. Burke
Acting Archivist of the United States

Contents

Administration of Ronald Reagan

1984

Statement on the Release by Syria of Navy Lieutenant Robert O. Goodman, Jr.
January 3, 1984

All Americans must be pleased that the Government of Syria has told our Ambassador that they have agreed to release Lieutenant Goodman as a result of the efforts of the Reverend Jesse Jackson. We are delighted that this brave young man will soon be united with his family and that his ordeal is over.

We hope the Syrian Government will continue to work for peace in Lebanon so that all foreign forces—Syrian, Israeli, and the multinational force—can come home and allow that country to be united, independent, and sovereign once more.

Note: Lieutenant Goodman was captured on December 4, 1983, during a bombing raid against Syrian antiaircraft positions in Lebanon.

Exchange With Reporters on the Release by Syria of Navy Lieutenant Robert O. Goodman, Jr.
January 3, 1984

Q. Mr. President, does Goodman's release change anything?

The President. No. I was just going to make a statement on that.

All of us here are delighted, of course, and very happy that this has taken place. I have been in touch with and been talking with Reverend Jackson and our Ambassador there and with Lieutenant Goodman, who is, of course, pleased that he is coming home. And we, as I say, are very pleased with this. And now Ambassador Rumsfeld will be leaving this evening for Lebanon. And we will, with renewed spirit, continue our efforts and our negotiations to advance the cause of peace in Lebanon.

Q. Do you think this is a peace gesture on the part of the Syrian Government?

The President. I'm not going to place any interpretation on it. I just am pleased that this action was taken.

Q. How did Goodman sound to you, sir?

The President. Just fine—but then I expected that. In the conversation I had with his wife earlier, while he was still a prisoner, to keep her up to date on our own efforts in trying to bring about his release, she told me a little about her husband. And it was that she had great faith in his ability to meet the circumstances there and what he was undergoing. And it evidently is true. He's a fine man.

Q. Did Reverend Jackson do a good job?

Q. [*Laughing*] Of course.

The President. You don't quarrel with success. [*Laughter*] Yes.

Q. Are you going to see the Reverend Jackson——

The President. Yes.

Q. ——tomorrow?

The President. Yes. I'm looking forward to it.

Q. Here?

The President. Yes.

Q. Thank you.

Note: The exchange began at 10:51 a.m. in the Oval Office at the White House, where the President met with Ambassador Donald H. Rumsfeld, the President's Personal Representative in the Middle East, and Secre-

1

tary of State George P. Shultz. Following that meeting, the President held a full session with his foreign policy advisers to discuss the Middle East situation.

Prior to the first meeting, the President spoke by telephone with the Rev. Jesse Jackson, Lieutenant Goodman, and U.S. Ambassador to Syria Robert P. Paganelli.

Statement on the Situation in Lebanon
January 3, 1984

This morning the National Security Council examined the Lebanon situation in some detail and how best to achieve our goals. This evening Ambassador Rumsfeld is returning to the Middle East to continue U.S. diplomatic initiatives in Lebanon and the Middle East. I have today written to President Assad regarding the release of Lieutenant Goodman. I expressed my appreciation for this action and suggested that this is an opportune moment to put all the issues on the table and work with the United States to bring greater stability to Lebanon and withdrawals of foreign troops.

Our support for Lebanon remains firm. Progress has been made toward achieving their twin goals of national reconciliation and troop withdrawals. We are continuing our support for these efforts. The work ahead is difficult, but with determined international effort and the good will of all the parties, we believe that continued progress will be made.

Proclamation 5143—Alaska Statehood Day, 1984
January 3, 1984

By the President of the United States of America

A Proclamation

The Territory of Alaska was admitted to the Union on January 3, 1959, as the forty-ninth State. In the twenty-five years since then, the sturdy inhabitants of our largest State have continued with distinction the work of developing this vast storehouse of abundant resources, while preserving its special environment. As a result of their efforts, Alaska now produces one-eighth of the Nation's gold, one-fifth of its petroleum, and two-fifths of its harvested fish. Ten of the sixteen strategic minerals vital to our Nation's security are produced in Alaska. The millions of dollars worth of minerals, forest and food products, and energy resources produced each year have long since repaid many times over the $7,000,000 paid by the United States to purchase Alaska in 1867.

The people of Alaska constitute a special resource, one which has made possible the wise use of all the other abundant resources of this important State. Native Alaskans and immigrants from every State, as well as foreign countries, have worked together to build the cities, pipelines, rail, water, air, and ground transportation facilities which are the basis of Alaska's prosperity. Their hard work and dedication are an example to the rest of our people as we work to maintain America's greatness.

In recognition of the importance of Alaska's people and its scenic and natural resources to the United States and in honor of the twenty-fifth anniversary of the admission of Alaska into the Union, the Congress, by Senate Joint Resolution 42, has authorized and requested the President to proclaim January 3, 1984, as "Alaska Statehood Day."

Now, Therefore, I, Ronald Reagan, President of the United States of America, do hereby proclaim January 3, 1984, as Alaska

Statehood Day and call upon the people of the United States and the Federal, State, and local governments to observe that day with appropriate ceremonies.

In Witness Whereof, I have hereunto set my hand this 3rd day of Jan., in the year of our Lord nineteen hundred and eighty-4, and of the Independence of the United States of America the two hundred and eighth.

RONALD REAGAN

[*Filed with the Office of the Federal Register, 10:38 a.m., January 4, 1984*]

Proclamation 5144—National Consumers Week, 1984
January 3, 1984

By the President of the United States of America

A Proclamation

The American consumer has been blessed by the freedom to participate in a social, economic, and governmental system that is unparalleled in any other land. Since the founding of this country, Americans have benefitted from the fruits of a free society. We are free to learn, free to choose a vocation, free to produce, and free to purchase. These fundamental freedoms and the willingness of our people to work hard have helped make America great. Americans are prosperous and enjoy a standard of living that is the envy of the world. It is appropriate to focus special attention on consumers and the important role they play in our economic and social system.

We have emerged from a recession on a wave of consumer optimism that dramatically proves the truth of this year's slogan—"Consumers Mean Business." Our economic recovery program has dramatically lowered inflation and interest rates, giving buyers more disposable income. Consumers are reacting to the Nation's resurgent economy by purchasing homes, automobiles, durable goods, and those products or services which enhance the quality of life. With greater purchasing power, it is important that consumers have access to the latest information.

Consumers need to understand the market economy, both here and abroad, and their options for earning, spending, saving, and investing income. Increased consumer and economic education in schools, workshops, the media, and the distribution of informative materials from government and business give consumers a greater appreciation of their rights and responsibilities in our incomparable American economy.

Those who are sensitive to consumer needs and services and recognize that well-informed consumers mean business—repeat sales and sound market relationships—can expect to be rewarded with continuing opportunities to serve and profit. Wise consumers, properly informed and working with business representatives at all levels, can assure that our marketplace operates on mutual trust and fairness.

By working together in the voluntary spirit that has always distinguished the character of Americans in all walks of life, we strengthen our free enterprise system and secure basic consumer rights for all.

Let us show appreciation during National Consumers Week for our many freedoms and work together to enhance the consumer's economic equity in the marketplace.

Now, Therefore, I, Ronald Reagan, President of the United States of America, do hereby proclaim the week beginning April 23, 1984, as National Consumer's Week.

In Witness Whereof, I have hereunto set my hand this 3rd day of Jan., in the year of our Lord nineteen hundred and eighty-4, and of the Independence of the United States of America the two hundred and eighth.

RONALD REAGAN

[*Filed with the Office of the Federal Register, 11:24 a.m., January 4, 1984*]

Proclamation 5145—Small Business Week, 1984
January 3, 1984

By the President of the United States of America

A Proclamation

America's strength lies in the ingenuity and perseverance of its people. No other group of Americans better exemplifies these qualities than the Nation's small business owners, who contribute daily to our economic well-being.

The willingness of these individuals to embrace the challenges of competition and independence ensures that our lives are enriched with new opportunities and innovations. When their resourcefulness and resilience are melded with an economic system that allows them to pursue their goals and harness the dynamic forces of the marketplace, new products and technologies are developed, jobs are created, and the young and unskilled are trained for more productive lives. With each new opportunity our commitment to liberty is strengthened; with each new accomplishment our faith in ourselves is reaffirmed.

Entrepreneurs are the standard-bearers of economic progress and the stalwarts of the energizing forces of the free market. As we embark upon a new era of economic growth and development, we should encourage small business owners by acknowledging their tremendous importance as the mainsprings of continued economic and individual progress for our Nation.

Now, Therefore, I, Ronald Reagan, President of the United States of America, do hereby proclaim the week beginning May 6, 1984, as Small Business Week. I call upon the American people to join with me in saluting the small business owners of our Nation during this week with appropriate ceremonies and activities.

In Witness Whereof, I have hereunto set my hand this 3rd day of Jan., in the year of our Lord nineteen hundred and eighty-4, and of the Independence of the United States of America the two hundred and eighth.

RONALD REAGAN

[*Filed with the Office of the Federal Register, 11:25 a.m., January 4, 1984*]

Executive Order 12457—President's Commission on Industrial Competitiveness
January 3, 1984

By the authority vested in me as President by the Constitution and laws of the United States of America, including the Federal Advisory Committee Act, as amended (5 U.S.C. App. I), and in order to increase the membership and extend the life of the President's Commission on Industrial Competitiveness, it is hereby ordered that Executive Order No. 12428 of June 28, 1983, as amended, is further amended as follows:

(a) The second sentence of Section 1(a) shall read: "The Commission shall be composed of no more than thirty-five members

appointed or designated by the President.".

(b) Section 4(b) shall read: "The Commission shall terminate on December 31, 1984, unless sooner extended.".

RONALD REAGAN

The White House,

January 3, 1984.

[*Filed with the Office of the Federal Register, 2:26 p.m., January 4, 1984*]

Note: The text of the Executive order was released by the Office of the Press Secretary on January 4.

Remarks to Reporters Following a Meeting With Navy Lieutenant Robert O. Goodman, Jr.
January 4, 1984

The President. Well, today is a homecoming celebration, and all of us are delighted to see Lieutenant Robert Goodman free, safe, and reunited with his family. This young naval officer was flying a mission of peace, and both during and after, he exemplified qualities of leadership and loyalty— qualities of so many fine men and women in our military that we're all proud of. Reverend Jackson's mission was a personal mission of mercy, and he has earned our gratitude and our admiration.

Lieutenant Goodman's release affords us a unique opportunity to—well, I took advantage of the opportunity to write to the President of Syria and call for Syrian cooperation in securing peace in Lebanon. Last night Don Rumsfeld left to seek diplomatic solutions to the problems of the region. And today, on this happy occasion, let all of us unite in a renewed determination to achieve a lasting stability and the withdrawal of all foreign forces from Lebanon.

As I say, this is a homecoming and a very welcome and a happy one here. Thank you all for recording it for posterity.

[*Speaking to Lieutenant Goodman*] Welcome home.

Lieutenant Goodman. Thank you, sir. Thank you.

I would just like to once again thank all of the people involved—Reverend Jackson, Ambassador Paganelli, the ministers in his delegation—for their diligent work and the ability to get me home a little bit earlier than I had envisioned. Thank you very much, and I appreciate all the support.

Reverend Jackson. Let me express thanks to the ecumenical body of ministers, led by Dr. Howard, who took this risky mission of mercy on faith. I want to express thanks to the Goodman family, Mrs. Marilyn Goodman and Bob and Terry, who prayed with us and gave us so much moral support and gave us the necessary inspiration; to the people around this nation who wore their blue ribbons as a measure of solidarity as we prayed together and fasted together, trying to rise above the everydayness of our lives that we might be able to secure the release of Lieutenant Robert Goodman and to gain his freedom and have a breakthrough for peace. We want to thank Almighty God, who heard our sincere and earnest prayers during this hour of crisis and this hour of opportunity.

It was especially meaningful to us that once we got our telegram back from President Assad, we then called Senator Charles Percy, chairman of our Foreign Relations Committee, which we thought was the appropriate thing to do. He then got us in contact with the State Department—Ambassador Murphy and Mr. Lawrence Eagleburger. It was the support of our State Department, within the law, that gave us the latitude that we needed to feel that we were doing the right thing within the law.

The fact that we left this country, and the Ambassador from Syria, Rafic Jouejati, escorted us to the airport, and when we arrived in Damascus, Syria, Ambassador Paganelli met us there, meant that we were without the portfolio of either government, but with the respect of both of them. President Reagan had the option to stop our mission. He had the option to interfere or to intervene. He did neither. And we felt that the fact that he made the choice to not intervene or interfere was significant to us.

The fact that Ambassador Paganelli met us in Syria was a signal that our government had reasonable doubt, because missions like this are not that successful often. But that was all that we needed, was a reasonable assurance and the support. I would hope that the cycle of pain is now broken and that this mission of peace will take us to an everlasting peace.

Lastly, it is significant that we were in Damascus, for one reason that many of us identify with Damascus is that a man traveling along that road many years ago fell off of a horse and was knocked unconscious. When he awakened, he saw a new light. It was the Apostle Paul, and because he saw that new light, the world has never been the same since. As it were, December of this past year, Lieutenant Robert Goodman was knocked from a plane and knocked unconscious. The Syrians had the right to kill him; they did not. They nursed him back to good health. And in due time, they released him. And thus we see another light on this day.

President Assad used this opportunity to seize an initiative, and we want to express our thanks to him. The fact that President Reagan has already sent him a letter is a sign that when the minds of leaders come together and their hearts agree, that we do have the capacity to save this generation from disaster.

Thank you very much.

Q. Mr. President, sir, would you be willing to meet with President Assad personally if it would advance the cause of peace in the Mideast?

The President. Of course.

Q. Are there any such plans, sir?

The President. Well, we have opened—as the Reverend just said and as I said in my remarks—we have opened communications with him, and we hope it'll lead to that.

Q. What about the Lebanese plan for reconciliation, Mr. President?

The President. That's going forward.

Q. Do we think that there's a breakthrough now? Gemayel's——

The President. We think we've made progress, yes.

Note: The President spoke at 10:56 a.m. in the Rose Garden at the White House.

Earlier, the President met in the Oval Office with Reverend Jackson and members of his party to discuss his trip to Damascus, Syria. Present at that meeting were the Vice President, Secretary of State George P. Shultz, Secretary of Defense Caspar W. Weinberger, Deputy Assistant to the President for National Security Affairs John M. Poindexter, Counsellor to the President Edwin Meese III, and Assistants to the President James A. Baker III and Michael K. Deaver. Following the discussion, they were joined by Lieutenant Goodman and members of his family.

Letter Accepting the Resignation of Paul Thayer as Deputy Secretary of Defense
January 4, 1984

Dear Paul:

It is with regret that I accept your resignation as Deputy Secretary of Defense.

During the period when you have served as the Pentagon's second-ranking civilian official, we have undertaken a major program to modernize every element of our military forces and prepare them to meet the challenges of the coming decade and beyond. You have played a key role in planning and putting into effect this crucially important project and especially in increasing the administrative efficiency of the large bureaucracy under your supervision. This is a task that cannot be accomplished overnight, but I know your successor will build on the solid foundations you have laid, and I want to thank you personally for a job well done.

Nancy and I send you our best wishes for every future success and happiness.

Sincerely,

RONALD REAGAN

[The Honorable Paul Thayer, Deputy Secretary

of Defense, The Pentagon, Washington, D.C. 20301]

Dear Mr. President:

For four decades—beginning as a naval aviator in the Pacific in World War II—I have been associated with some aspect of our national defense. When you took office and began to move to strengthen and revitalize our military, I shared with many Americans your sense of urgency and dedication. It was, therefore, without hesitation that I accepted your invitation to come to Washington and to be a part of this mission.

I believed then, as I do now, that your most important contribution to our country and to the world is your dedication to world peace and it has been rewarding to be able to support directly this endeavor. It had been my hope to continue to work with you and Secretary Weinberger on such vital projects as the recently completed Department of Defense budget—a budget which will continue to rebuild our military capability.

However, I have been advised that the Securities and Exchange Commission intends to file a civil complaint against me alleging that I improperly divulged insider information concerning certain securities.

This alleged activity took place before my joining the Department of Defense.

This allegation against me is entirely without merit. I intend to vigorously defend this matter in the courts with every confidence that I will ultimately be exonerated. Participation in and preparation of this case will require a substantial amount of my time and attention. I will not and cannot perform my duties as Deputy Secretary of Defense unless I can do so to the fullest of my abilities and without distraction. Accordingly, with the deepest regret, I hereby submit to you my resignation as Deputy Secretary of Defense to be effective on 12 January 1984.

I wish to express my gratitude to you and Secretary Weinberger for giving me the opportunity to share in the important work of the Department of Defense. I leave with every confidence that the progress which this Administration has made will continue under your leadership and that of Secretary Weinberger, with the dedicated assistance of the men and women of the Department of Defense.

Respectfully,

PAUL THAYER

[The President, The White House, Washington, D.C. 20301]

Nomination of William Howard Taft IV To Be Deputy Secretary of Defense
January 5, 1984

The President announced today his intention to nominate William Howard Taft IV to be Deputy Secretary, Department of Defense. He would succeed W. Paul Thayer, who has resigned.

Since April of 1981 Mr. Taft has been serving as General Counsel of the Department of Defense. From 1977 to 1981, Mr. Taft was an attorney with the firm of Leva, Hawes, Symington, Martin and Oppenheimer of Washington, DC. Prior to this, Mr. Taft worked in government for 7 years in various capacities. In April 1976 Mr. Taft was appointed by President Ford to be

General Counsel of the Department of Health, Education, and Welfare. For 3 years, from 1973 to 1976, Mr. Taft served as the Executive Assistant to the Secretary of Health, Education, and Welfare. From 1970 to 1973, he was the principal assistant to Caspar W. Weinberger, who was Deputy Director, then Director, of the Office of Management and Budget. Mr. Taft served as attorney adviser to the Chairman of the Federal Trade Commission in 1970.

Mr. Taft earned his Ph.D. in English from Yale College in 1966 and his J.D. from Harvard Law School in 1969. He resides in Lorton, VA, with his wife, Julia, and their three children. He was born in Washington, DC, on September 13, 1945.

Nomination of Richard A. Derham To Be an Assistant Administrator of the Agency for International Development
January 5, 1984

The President today announced his intention to nominate Richard A. Derham to be an Assistant Administrator of the Agency for International Development (Bureau for Program and Policy Coordination), U.S. International Development Cooperation Agency. He would succeed John R. Bolton.

Since August 1983 Mr. Derham has been serving as Acting Assistant Administrator of the Agency for International Development. He was a member of the law firm of Davis, Wright, Todd, Riese & Jones in 1965–1983 and served as managing partner in 1977–1982. He was director of Transducers, Inc., in 1977–1983 and served as legal counsel to the House of Representatives in Olympia, WA, in 1969 and 1971.

He graduated from Harvard College (A.B., 1962) and Columbia Law School (J.D., 1965). He was born May 29, 1940, in Seattle, WA.

Appointment of Ted A. Smits as a Member of the International Pacific Salmon Fisheries Commission
January 5, 1984

The President today announced his intention to appoint Ted A. Smits to be a member, on the part of the United States of America, of the International Pacific Salmon Fisheries Commission. He will succeed Donald R. Johnson.

Since 1976 Mr. Smits has served as vice president of Pacific Seafood Processors Association in Seattle, WA. Previously, he was assistant director of the Washington Department of Fisheries (Olympia, WA) in 1975; executive director of the Puget Sound Gillnetters Association (Seattle, WA) in 1974; and district representative (Western AA) for the United States House of Representatives in 1969–1972.

He is married, has three children, and resides in Edmonds, WA. He was born February 12, 1933, in Zeist, The Netherlands.

Radio Address to the Cuban People on the 25th Anniversary of Their Revolution
January 5, 1984

On behalf of the people of the United States, I would like to extend New Year's greetings to the people of Cuba.

We know you're marking an historic anniversary on your island. Twenty-five years ago, during these early January days, you were celebrating what all of us hoped was the dawn of a new era of freedom. Most Cubans welcomed the prospects for democracy and liberty which the leaders of the

Cuban revolution had promised.

Such a free and democratic Cuba would have been warmly welcomed by our own people. We're neighbors in a hemisphere that has been characterized by the quest for human freedom. Government which rests upon consent of the governed is a cardinal principle that enshrines the dignity of every individual. We share many of the same ideals, especially a common longing for a world of peace and justice. We are both proud peoples, proud of what we've achieved through our own efforts.

But tragically, the promises made to you have not been kept. Since 1959 you've been called upon to make one sacrifice after another. And for what? Doing without has not brought you a more abundant life. It has not brought you peace. And most important, it has not won freedom for your people—freedom to speak your opinions, to travel where and when you wish, to work in independent unions, and to openly proclaim your faith in God and to enjoy all these basic liberties without having to be afraid.

Cuba's economy is incapable of providing you and your families your most elementary needs, despite massive subsidies from abroad. But your leaders tell you, "Don't complain, don't expect improvement, just be ready for more sacrifice."

In the meantime, over half a million of your fellow citizens have migrated to the United States, where their talents and their hard work have made a major contribution to our society. We welcomed them, and we're proud of their success. But we have to wonder, what would Cuba's economy be like today if those people had been allowed to use their great talent, drive, and energy to help you create prosperity on your island?

The most important question remains: Where is Cuba heading? If it were heading toward greater welfare and freedom for your people, that would be wonderful. But we know prisoners of conscience convicted for their political activities have been languishing in Cuban prisons, deprived of all freedom, for nearly a quarter of a century. Never in the proud history of your country have so many been imprisoned for so long for so-called crimes of political dissent as

during these last 25 years. Others convicted of political crimes this past year can expect to be in prison well into the 21st century if the present system in Cuba survives that long.

You may not be aware of some of these things I've just told you or will tell you in this brief message. You may also be unaware of many other things you have the right to know. That's because you are systematically denied access to facts and opinions which do not agree with your government's official view. But why are your leaders so unwilling to let you hear what others think and say? If the power of truth is on their side, why should they need to censor anyone's views? Think about that.

Yet, while they supervise every word you hear, every picture you see, your authorities have free access to our news services in the United States and around the world. We don't believe in censorship. So, to correct this injustice, the Congress of the United States has authorized the startup soon of a new radio service on the Voice of America named for your great Cuban patriot, Jose Marti.

The objective of the Radio Marti program will be simple and straightforward: Tell the truth about Cuba to the Cuban people. We want you to know what you haven't been told, for example, about the situation in Grenada. When Grenada's Prime Minister Bishop was killed, the Governor General, as well as the majority of the English-speaking Caribbean, asked for our assistance in protecting them. Why didn't they ask for Cuba's assistance? Well, the sad truth is, they wanted to be protected from the Cuban Government.

The United States and other Caribbean forces were welcomed by Grenadians as liberators. The rest of the world has seen the evidence of the popular outpouring of support for our action. Cuban lives could have been saved if your government had respected the will of the Grenadian people and not ordered your soldiers to fight to the death. Fortunately, the great majority of your personnel in Grenada did not obey those orders.

One of your government officials said, in September 1982, that 120,000 Cubans have carried out international missions through the revolutionary armed forces alone. They have been sent to countries in four continents. You're never told how many of them are killed, how many families lose loved ones for a cause they have no right to resist. What mission or vital interest does Cuba have which can possibly justify this loss of life in such faraway lands?

These are not pleasant questions, but they deserve answers. I hope you'll contemplate them with care. At the beginning of this new year, let us pray that the future will be kinder than the past. And may that better future begin soon for all of you in Cuba.

Feliz Año Nuevo y que Dios los bendiga. [Happy New Year and God bless you.]

Note: The President recorded the address at approximately 5 p.m. at the White House for later broadcast on the Voice of America.

Statement Following a Meeting With the Chief of the United States Delegation to the Conference on Confidence and Security Building Measures and Disarmament in Europe
January 6, 1984

Today I met with Ambassador James E. Goodby, the Chief of the United States Delegation to the Conference on Confidence and Security Building Measures and Disarmament in Europe, generally known as the CDE. This new conference involves the United States, Canada, and 33 nations of Western and Eastern Europe. It is part of the East-West dialog growing out of the Conference on Security and Cooperation in Europe (CSCE), which produced the Helsinki accords of 1975.

Secretary of State Shultz joined us today. He and other NATO Foreign Ministers will participate in the CDE opening session in Stockholm on January 17. Their presence will underline the importance which the West attaches to the CDE and to a productive East-West dialog.

I reviewed with Ambassador Goodby the instructions to the U.S. delegation and gave my final approval. I emphasized to him my strong support for the Western objectives at CDE of reducing the risk of surprise attack in Europe and of inhibiting the use of arms for war or intimidation.

The strength and unity of the West have preserved the peace in Europe since World War II, and Western diplomacy in the "Helsinki process" has been crucial in advancing the East-West dialog. All of us wish Ambassador Goodby and his European and Canadian counterparts success and Godspeed in carrying forward this vital undertaking.

Remarks and an Informal Exchange With Reporters on Foreign and Domestic Issues
January 6, 1984

Unemployment Figures

The President. I just wanted to say one thing about the economy, and I think all of us can look forward to 1984 with even more confidence in view of the unemployment figures that we were handed this morning: that unemployment figures went down again in the month of December; 335,000 more people were working in December than were working in the month before. And it means that about 4 million more people are at work now than were at work a year ago in December.

And I think this is—the rate, counting in

the military, which I think is the only way to count it—total unemployment is now 8.1 percent. And, as I say, I think it's encouraging news for all of us, and we're going to keep on.

Central America

Q. Mr. President, do you think if we spend $1 billion more on Central America that that would somehow stop the Sandinistas from doing what they've been doing?

The President. Andrea [Andrea Mitchell, NBC News], I don't know. I've only known this—and I have spoken of this several times before—I think that we haven't been doing all that should be done. That was one of the reasons for having a commission. I have not yet obtained their report. But solving the social and economic problems or helping them solve them, themselves, down there is essential, just as it's essential that we help provide for their security while they're instituting those reforms. And we haven't been allowed to do as much as we should do.

Q. So, is the Kissinger group calling for a lot more money? Is that what your understanding is—that the Kissinger group will call for a lot more money?

The President. That I don't know. And, of course, the definition of what "a lot more" is could be subject to interpretation.

Charles Z. Wick

Q. Mr. President, do you condone the taping on the telephone by Charles Wick?

The President. I'm not going to comment further other than to say that I don't think that Charles Wick is a dishonorable man in any way. And the nature of the things that he was recording and that—I can understand his forgetting sometimes when he was talking to people particularly that he knew—but the purpose of that was different than it is from someone that is trying to keep a record on other people's conversations. What he was actually trying to do was be able to immediately transcribe so that he could provide the suggestions that were being discussed to the people that would have to implement them.

And I've heard there are some rumors around. Let me just say this. He has done a splendid job. I think the Voice of America, the whole United States Information Agency is far superior to anything that has ever been, and he's going to continue there.

Q. Mr. President, the New York Times claims he lied to them about the taping.

Q. Did he lie to them?

The President. That's their statement.

Note: The President spoke at 3:15 p.m. on the South Lawn of the White House as he was leaving for a weekend stay at Camp David, MD.

Appointment of General Robert H. Barrow as a Member of the President's Foreign Intelligence Advisory Board
January 6, 1984

The President today announced his intention to appoint Gen. Robert H. Barrow to be a member of the President's Foreign Intelligence Advisory Board.

General Barrow was commissioned as an officer of marines in 1943 and served over 40 years of active service. His last assignment was as Commandant of the Marine Corps, from which he retired in July 1983. During his career, he served seven tours of duty in the Far East. His most recent assignments included: Assistant Commandant

of the Marine Corps in 1978–1979; Commanding General, Fleet Marine Force, Atlantic, in Norfolk, VA, in 1976–1978; Deputy Chief of Staff for Manpower, Headquarters Marine Corps, in 1975–1976; Commanding General, Marine Corps Recruit Depot, Parris Island, SC, in 1972–1975; and Commanding General, Marine Corps Base, in Okinawa, in 1969–1972.

His personal United States decorations include the Navy Cross, the Army Distinguished Service Cross, the Silver Star, three

Legions of Merit, two Bronze Stars, and the Joint Service Commendation Medal.

General Barrow attended Louisiana State University, the University of Maryland (B.S., 1956), and graduate school at Tulane University. In addition, he attended two Marine Corps schools and the National War College. He is married, has five children, and resides St. Francisville, LA. He was born February 5, 1922, in Baton Rouge, LA.

Recess Appointment of Frieda Waldman as a Governor of the United States Postal Service
January 6, 1984

The President today recess appointed Frieda Waldman to be a Governor of the United States Postal Service for a term expiring December 8, 1992. She will succeed Robert L. Hardesty.

Since 1950 Mrs. Waldman has served as administrator of the Forrest Day School in Montclair, CA. She is also the author of several publications dealing with education.

Mrs. Waldman graduated from Northwestern University (A.A.), La Verne College (B.A.), and California Polytechnic University (M.A.). She is married, has seven children, and resides in Claremont, CA. She was born February 9, 1922, in Chicago, IL.

Informal Exchange With Representatives of Le Figaro, Together With Written Responses to Questions Submitted by the Newspaper
December 22, 1983

REMARKS DURING A MEETING WITH LE FIGARO REPRESENTATIVES

Q. The question—[*inaudible*]—this is the question I want to ask you: What definition does the President give for Reaganism to the Americans, the foreigners, and for the French?

The President. Well, I am not addicted to giving it labels, but what we've tried to do here—and I think we have been reasonably successful—is, first of all, to bring about an economic recovery. I think it is taking place. I think it not only benefits our country, but I think our country, just as it can export recession and economic troubles, a recovery here, I think, can benefit the world, certainly our long-time, good friend, France, in helping economic recovery in those places.

When we came here we felt that the United States had retreated from a position of strength that I think is important to, certainly, the free world, the Western World. I believe that we've succeeded in restoring our strength to the place that we have a real deterrent. We've had the longest period of peace in Europe now that we've had for many years among the major nations, and we're going to continue on that line. And the goal, internationally, is—and must be—peace. And we're dedicated to that.

We're going to continue with our efforts to bring about some realistic reduction, particularly nuclear weapons. And I believe that the course that we've followed so far has made that more possible.

There have been 19 efforts since World War II to persuade the Soviets to join the reduction of weapons. They have resisted every time—until this time. And even though there is a temporary lull, which I think is part of the bargaining process, they have actually proposed themselves reducing the number of their weapons, which is the first time they have ever done that. So, we're going to keep pressing for that.

I think that's—I hope that's an answer to your question.

Q. Mr. President, I met you 3 years ago, immediately after the inauguration ceremonies. You haven't changed, and you seem even younger. Do you feel in shape to start again for a new 4 years? [*Laughter*]

The President. Well, I'm going to be making an announcement about my decision January 29th as to what it will be.

Let me say that my physical condition won't even have to be a consideration in whatever I decide. No, I feel fine. I don't think I've ever felt better.

Q. Mr. President, can I ask a small question concerning what you answered to the first question? What do you think of the high frontier? It's a great problem, and I think you're going to present that project in order to be ready for this space war.

The President. Well, without restricting myself to that particular approach, I have asked for a complete study and for research into trying to develop a defensive weapon against the nuclear weapons. But again, I'm proposing that in the interest of hopefully being able to eliminate those weapons. If we could succeed and bring about a realistic defensive weapon against them, then my next step would be to inform the Soviet Union that we had this and now we were prepared to join them in eliminating all such weapons in the world.

Q. Mr. President, thank you very much. You've been generous with your time, and I hope it's near the end of another hard day.

The President. Well, listen, I'm so grateful for these, I'm going to take them up and look at the pictures. [*Laughter*]

You know, with your having to interpret for me [1] is something of a reflection on my early education, because when I was a schoolboy, I studied French for a couple of years. And then, 1949—the first time I ever set foot in your country—found myself with a couple, a married couple. The three of us were driving down across France in the Mediterranean. And I discovered that even

---

[1] *An interpreter was present to translate the questions for the President and to translate his responses into French.*

though they were English and just 20 miles away, they had never been to France. They did not know one word of French. And I was going to be the only thing between us and silence. [*Laughter*]

We were coming to a town for lunch. And I started trying to remember—that was a long time ago—so I could remember some of what I'd learned in my French study. So, we came to the town, and I mentally figured how I'm going to find—where do we have lunch? So, it was a *gendarme*. And I rolled down the window of the car, and I said: *"Pardon, monsieur, j'ai grand faim. Où est le meilleur café?"* And he told me where was the best cafe.

And my friend that was driving says: "What did he say?" And I said, "I haven't the slightest idea." [*Laughter*] I memorized the questions, never the answers. [*Laughter*]

Thank you all very much.

Q. Thank you very much, Mr. President.

The President. And thank you for these.

Q. Mr. President, thanks very much.

Q. Thank you very much, good luck, and Merry Christmas, Mr. President.

The President. Thank you. Merry Christmas to you.

Q. Merry Christmas, and a Happy New Year.

WRITTEN RESPONSES TO QUESTIONS SUBMITTED BY LE FIGARO

Soviet Military Budget

Q. The Romans used to say: "If you want peace, prepare war." How do you explain the fact that the U.S.S.R., a poor country, has such great military powers, whereas the wealthy United States remains so far back?

The President. No one is more conscious than I that the Soviet Union devotes more than twice as much of its economic resources to the military as the U.S. does, and has been doing so over the past two decades despite relative restraint on the part of the West. Other sectors of the Soviet economy, particularly those devoted to consumer production, suffer as a result.

If the Soviet people had a voice in the matter, the Soviet defense budget would probably be a lot smaller. But the people have no voice in the allocation of national resources. We in the West face the more demanding task of maintaining adequate military strength with the consent of our free peoples.

I would add that, while the continuing Soviet military buildup is a course of concern and requires a substantial U.S. and allied response, talk of the United States being "far back" suggests an alarming state of military weakness in the West that the facts do not warrant. While more still needs to be done, we and our allies have made important strides in the last few years toward restoring the military balance.

NATO Nuclear and Conventional Forces

Q. For example, General Rogers told me recently that NATO had acquired 400 of the latest tanks, whereas the Russian Army had got 1,000 that very same year. Is the free world incapable of arming itself?

The President. I am confident that the Atlantic alliance has the resources necessary to maintain an effective deterrent if they wish. The Warsaw Pact's continuing buildup of both nuclear and conventional forces is of major concern to the alliance. We are responding. The deployment of INF missiles is part of our coordinated response to that threat. The modernization of America's strategic deterrent is another element of our response.

The improvement of NATO's conventional forces is extremely important. In the face of the Soviet Union's relentless military buildup, all of us must do more to strengthen our conventional forces. America's conventional force modernization program is in high gear and involves equipment modernization and improvements in organization and training. America cannot do the job alone, and it is very important for each alliance partner to make every effort to strengthen their own forces.

East-West Arms Balance

Q. You have begun construction of MX super powerful rockets, but the Russians are also coming out with rockets as powerful. How are you planning to catch up with the U.S.S.R.'s military power or even talking of leaving them behind?

The President. Our policy is to create a more stable international balance and, through negotiations with the Soviets, reduce the numbers of arms, especially nuclear weapons, on both sides. Now, for many years, throughout the 1970's, the Soviets pursued a massive arms buildup at a time when the United States was exercising restraint. It became clear that the only way to get the Soviets to exercise restraint was to demonstrate that we would restore the balance. The increases in military procurement which this administration has undertaken are meant to restore and preserve an East-West arms balance as we pursue the other half of our policy—to seek deep reductions of arms on both sides through negotiations.

Soviet Compliance With Agreements

Q. You are always talking about negotiating seriously with the Russians whilst we have constant evidence of their breaking off treaties: SALT agreements, Helsinki agreements, United Nations Charter (i.e., Afghanistan's invasion), so why speak of negotiations with such a country?

The President. You are quite right in singling out the issue of Soviet compliance with agreements as a negotiating problem for the West. We have been concerned by evidence of Soviet actions that are inconsistent with existing agreements. One notable example of this is the use of chemical and biological weapons in Southeast Asia and Afghanistan in clear violation of existing international treaties.

Therefore, we insist that any new agreements contain strong verification procedures to ensure Soviet compliance, and we have looked at some existing agreements to see if their verification provisions can be strengthened. Agreements without adequate procedures for verifying compliance are dangerous because they invite violations. But negotiations leading to verifiable agreements are essential if we are to build a safer and more stable world.

Trade With the Soviets

Q. Retaliation measures against Moscow have been thought of here and there. You have in this line criticized the Franco-Soviet deal on gas, but at the same time you

14

are continuing to feed the Soviet Union by selling it excess wheat. Is it of such great importance to deal with the Russians?

The President. Our decision to negotiate a new grain agreement with the U.S.S.R. was based on our view that grain sales can best take place under the framework of a long-term agreement without cheap credit and subsidies. From past experience, we knew that if we did not sell grain to the Soviets, others would quickly take our place in the market. When we negotiated the new agreement, I made clear that this was an economic move and not a foreign policy gesture.

Regarding purchases of Soviet natural gas, the allies have agreed that our bilateral economic relations with the U.S.S.R. must be consistent with broad allied security concerns. This includes avoiding undue dependence on any one source of natural gas.

President's Foreign Policy Advisers

Q. American experts are often making wise international policy analysis but then they make capital mistakes: 20 years in Vietnam in a war finally lost; betraying the Shah of Persia to lose Iran; doing absolutely nothing to prevent the Russian invasion of Angola and further, the invasion of Afghanistan and then not even helping Afghan resistance. Do you consider yourself wisely advised?

The President. Well, I haven't been advised to do any of the things you mention, if that's what you mean!

I wouldn't agree with many of your characterizations—which, in any case, refer to events which occurred before this administration. There have obviously been mistakes as well as successes in the history of American foreign policy. And this is true of Soviet and even French foreign policies as well.

But I consider myself well-advised in terms of both interpretation of world events and recommendations for our foreign policy. The best you can do is try to get the best advice you can, listen carefully to many different views, make your decision and implement it with care, and keep testing your judgment to see if you need to make adjustments. This is what we've tried to do. I believe it's working pretty well.

U.S. Commitment to NATO

Q. In February 1981 you declared to Figaro magazine that the American people would consider any attack on Europe as an attack on the United States. But since, we have often heard from across the Atlantic statements according to which America was not to risk in any way its survival in war against Russia just to help European troublemakers. What is your opinion on this point today?

The President. My opinion remains completely unchanged: The United States would consider an attack on its NATO allies as an attack on itself. This is a commitment which is enshrined in the North Atlantic Treaty. It is a commitment which the United States has reiterated many times and enjoys broad support in the U.S. Congress and among the American people. We share common values, a common heritage, and parallel dreams. Europe's security is indivisible from our own. I can hardly think of another aspect of U.S. foreign policy on which there is broader consensus than our commitment to defend our allies against attack.

Q. I will insist, if I may, Europe is becoming more and more "pinkish", i.e., more and more socialist or more and more socio-communist. Don't you think that a new American President would be inclined to leave Europeans to themselves in order to look towards more promising areas such as Asia, Latin America, and let Russia paddle in Europe?

The President. I can only speak for myself. But in my view, there is no possibility of America's reducing its ties to Western Europe or its commitment to its NATO allies, let alone abandoning its European friends. We know that our security and that of Europe are bound together. Our friendships and alliances in other parts of the world are also very important—to our European friends as well as to ourselves. These ties are not in any way incompatible with our relationship with Europe.

Central America

Q. In this trend of mind, is it correct to think that a number of European countries are dealing directly against you in Central

America by supporting Marxist revolution?

The President. I don't think that's quite the problem. What we have in Central America is a Communist offensive that takes advantage of the longstanding inequities in the region. Many people saw only the local problems and not the Communist involvement. Over the last couple of years things have gotten a lot clearer. I think most everyone now realizes that we have a big task ahead—to foster democracy and to help resolve basic social and economic problems. We must help build democratic systems that are strong enough to meet their peoples' aspirations and to defend themselves. On this fundamental approach there is ample room for U.S. and European cooperation with the countries of Central America.

Lebanon

Q. How are you going to deal with the Middle East question? Don't you consider it immoral to allow tiny Lebanon to be destroyed by foreign forces with impunity at the same time G.I.'s and French paras get killed, apparently for nothing?

The President. The policy objectives of this administration have remained consistent. It is a policy we share with the Government of Lebanon. We seek the reestablishment of a stable, representative, and fully sovereign Lebanese Government, committed to national reconciliation and which can control all Lebanese territory. We also seek arrangements that will assure the security of Israel's northern border. If Lebanon is to have a chance, all external forces must leave.

The multinational force is in Lebanon because its presence has been requested by the Lebanese Government to support that government's efforts to consolidate that authority. The MNF helps provide the support and confidence the Government of Lebanon needs in moving forward to strengthen the fragile cease-fire, to achieve political reconciliation, and to secure the withdrawal of foreign forces.

Persian Gulf

Q. The creation of a rapid intervention force able to jump immediately into the Persian Gulf in the case of any threat to the Western World's petro supplies has been announced. What is the case exactly today?

The President. We are concerned that the longer the Iran-Iraq war lasts, the greater the danger of escalation and the greater the threat to commercial shipping and to neighboring Gulf States.

We support U.N. Security Council Resolution 540, which calls for cease-fire in the Gulf and urges all states, especially the two belligerents, to avoid action which would threaten freedom of navigation in the international waters of the Persian Gulf. We want a cease-fire and a negotiated settlement.

U.S. Economy

Q. Now, concerning economy, you have completely straightened the economic situation in your country. How did you manage to do so?

The President. It is too soon to say we have completely straightened out the economic situation in the U.S. But we have made significant strides. We anticipate that economic recovery in the U.S. will continue to benefit our major trading partners, particularly in Europe.

Our success in the economic field rests on three principles—monetary discipline, spending discipline, and greater reliance on market forces for economic adjustment. We are encouraged that other industrial countries have followed our example and are now following policies aimed at sustained, noninflationary growth.

U.S. Dollar

Q. You are of course aware that the dollar at the rate of 8.30 francs weighs heavily upon your allies economies. How do you plan to get rid of this difficulty?

The President. The strong dollar is, in part, a function of capital inflows which reflect the role of the United States as a safe haven for investment. We do not think that a high dollar necessarily poses difficulties for Europe. In fact, it can be argued that the locomotive effect of U.S. economic growth and the competitive advantage enjoyed by European exporters because of the high U.S. dollar are positive gains for Europe. While our trading partners are unhappy with the current strength of the dollar, we expect they would like it even less if the value of the dollar were to fall sharply.

Economic Recovery Program

Q. When you first took your Presidency, American media were most skeptical on your plans for economic recovery. Today you have won your bet on this whilst most statesmen have lost theirs.

The President. Our plans have worked because by giving priority to the reduction of inflation, and by reducing the burdens of overregulation and excessive taxation we have enabled the underlying natural vigor of our economy to reassert itself. I might add that other countries following a similar strategy have generally been most successful in reestablishing the preconditions for recovery. The strength of the U.S. recovery is now spreading abroad to those countries.

Q. You have succeeded in reducing taxes and in starting off your country's economy. Doesn't this seem contradictory?

The President. This is not at all contradictory—far from it. Reduction in the burdens of taxation has been, as I have said, a key element in our successful strategy for recovery. Excessive taxation distorts market signals and weakens the economic incentives on which our continued prosperity must depend.

Q. You have reduced the States' part as much as possible in order to favor initiatives and private effort and you have in this line also cut down social restraints. Do you not fear that having done so you might be hindering social justice?

The President. The economic welfare of all our people must ultimately stem not from government programs but from the wealth created by a vigorous private sector. What is more just than allowing individuals to benefit from their work and talent? Nothing is more unfair than the tax imposed by inflation, which hits those least able to protect themselves. Our policies reducing inflation and favoring growth are in fact the most efficient—and the only sus-

tainable—way of achieving widespread economic opportunity and prosperity.

Western European Socialist Governments

Q. Now, concerning politics, don't you think West European Socialist countries help Communist undermining?

The President. Many of our staunchest allies have democratic Socialist governments: France is one of them. Among friends there can be differences in economic philosophy, but this is not so important when we share basic values such as respect for democracy, individual liberties, and human dignity.

Pacifism

Q. Do you believe in the motto: "rather red than dead?" Is pacifism a real danger to the free world or is it only a flash in the pan?

The President. I think a better slogan would be "better alive and free." Our strength lies in our democratic principles and in the liberties which characterize our societies. When a free people decides to do what is necessary to stay secure, then no adversary can prevail. So, we will be neither dead nor red. In fact, it is freedom which is infectious and democracy which is the wave of the future. The tide of history is a freedom tide. Pacifism is not a danger to the free world, but it may be a danger to those that cannot tolerate dissidence. We in the free world can accommodate many points of view, because we know that the common sense of our people will support policies necessary to defend the liberties we all enjoy.

Note: The President met with the representatives from Le Figaro at 5:06 p.m. in the Oval Office at the White House. Among those attending the meeting were Robert Lacontre, editor in chief, and Alain Griotteray, chief editorial commentator, Le Figaro.

The transcript of the remarks at the meeting and the written questions and answers were released by the Office of the Press Secretary on January 7.

Radio Address to the Nation on School Violence and Discipline
January 7, 1984

My fellow Americans:

This is my first radio talk in 1984, so Happy New Year.

My prayer for you this new year is that you and your families will prosper in health and happiness. When I spoke to you last Saturday, on New Year's Eve, I made one request to everyone: When we drive, let's drive sober. Well, I was delighted to hear some very heartening news from Transportation Secretary Elizabeth Dole. Last New Year's weekend was the safest on our highways in 35 years. Our efforts to keep drunk, violent drivers off the road are beginning to show progress.

Today I want to talk about a subject which also deals with violence and is on our minds as the holidays end and our children go back to school—the problem of classroom discipline. The sad truth is, many classrooms across the country are not temples of learning, teaching the lessons of good will, civility, and wisdom important to the whole fabric of American life; many schools are filled with rude, unruly behavior, and even violence.

According to a 1978 report by the National Institute of Education, each month 3 million secondary school children were victims of in-school crime. I don't mean ordinary highjinks; I mean crime. Each month some 2½ million students were the victims of robberies and thefts, and more than 250,000 students suffered physical attacks. In large cities, the problem was so bad that almost 8 percent of urban junior and senior high school students missed at least 1 day in the classroom per month because they were afraid to go to school.

Well, now, maybe you're thinking that was back in 1978. Well, a study released in 1983 indicates this 1978 report probably understates the problem today.

Just as school violence affects our sons and daughters, it also affects their teachers. That 1978 National Institute of Education study found that each month some 6,000 teachers were robbed, about 125,000 a month were threatened with physical harm, and at least 1,000 teachers each month were assaulted with violence so severe they required medical care. One psychiatrist who treats teachers says many of them suffer symptoms identical to those of World War I shellshock victims. It's that bad.

Today American children need good education more than ever. But we can't get learning back into our schools until we get the crime and violence out. It's not a question of anyone asking for a police state. It's just that, as Albert Shanker of the American Federation of Teachers put it, "We're not going to get people interested in English or mathematics or social studies and languages, unless we solve discipline problems and take out of our schools those students who prevent teachers from teaching."

Today I'm asking Americans to renew our commitment to school discipline. Here at the national level, we're directing the Federal Government to do all it can to help parents, teachers, and administrators restore order to their classroom.

The Department of Education will study ways to prevent school violence, publicize examples of effective school discipline, continue its joint project with the National Institute of Justice to find better ways for localities to use their resources to prevent school crime.

The Department of Justice will establish a National School Safety Center. This center will publish handbooks informing teachers and other officials of their legal rights in dealing with disruptive students and put together a computerized national clearinghouse for school safety resources. I've also directed the Justice Department to file court briefs to help school administrators enforce discipline.

But despite the importance of these efforts, we can't make progress without help from superintendents and principals, teachers, parents, and students themselves.

I wish I could tell you all the stories I've heard of schools that have been turned around by determined local efforts. At Southwestern High in Detroit, once one of the city's most violent schools, firm discipline has raised the attendance rate from 53 to almost 87 percent.

In my home State of California at Sacramento's El Camino High, a discipline compact between parents and the school has helped achievement levels soar. And in the Watts section of Los Angeles, George Washington Preparatory High School recently established a policy of strict discipline with impressive results. Just 5 years ago, only 43 percent of the school's seniors expressed an interest in going to college. Well, last year,

80 percent of the seniors did go to college.

So, please, if you have discipline problems at your school, find out what you can do to help. By working together we can restore good order to America's classrooms and give our sons and daughters the education they deserve.

Till next week, thanks for listening, and God bless you.

Note: The President spoke at 12:06 p.m. from Camp David, MD.

Nomination of Jim J. Marquez To Be General Counsel of the Department of Transportation
January 9, 1984

The President today announced his intention to nominate Jim J. Marquez to be General Counsel of the Department of Transportation. He would succeed James Burnley IV.

Since 1981 Mr. Marquez has been serving as U.S. attorney for the District of Kansas. Previously he was a self-employed attorney in 1979–1981; secretary of corrections, Kansas Department of Corrections, in 1977–1979; pardon and extradition attorney

and legal adviser to the Governor of Kansas in 1975–1977; assistant district attorney, Johnson County, KS, district attorney's office, in 1973–1975; and an attorney for the National Labor Relations Board in 1973.

Mr. Marquez graduated from the University of New Mexico (B.A., 1965) and Washburn School of Law (J.D., 1972). He is married and resides in Lawrence, KS. He was born March 10, 1941, in Los Lunas, NM.

Remarks at the Welcoming Ceremony for Premier Zhao Ziyang of China
January 10, 1984

The President. It gives me great pleasure to welcome you, Premier Zhao, to the United States.

Your visit recalls an old Chinese saying which asks: Is it not delightful to have friends come from afar? Well, yes, it is delightful to have you with us. Your presence symbolizes the growing trust and cooperation between our two countries.

For a decade, relations between the United States and the People's Republic of China have been building. Today we know it is within our grasp to reap enormous re-

wards from the courage and foresight of those who opened the doors of Chinese-American friendship.

One of your predecessors, Premier Zhou Enlai, said in the early stages of our new relationship, "China places high hopes on the American people." Well, it is up to us, on both sides of the Pacific, to see to it that those high hopes become reality. For our part, we recognize the differences between our two countries, but we stand ready to nurture, develop, and build upon the many areas of accord to strengthen the ties between us.

China is now embarked on an exciting experiment designed to modernize the economy and quadruple the value of its national economic output by the year 2000. Premier Zhao, you eloquently described a key to achieving that end when you said that progress, and I quote, "lies in our efforts to emancipate our thinking in a bold way—to carry out reform with determination, to make new inventions with courage, and to break with the economic molds and conventions of all descriptions which fetter the development of productive force." These are words of vision. Our people understand and appreciate such vitality. We welcome the opportunity to walk at China's side in this endeavor.

Great strides of cooperation have already been made. In the last few years, each of our countries has tried to help the other build a better life. Our trade has flourished. The United States is now China's third largest trading partner. American investment in China exceeds that of all other countries. We're making available technology that will help open new horizons for your country.

Our citizens travel, study, and live in our respective countries in growing numbers. There are more than 10,000 Chinese students enrolled in American universities and more than a hundred Chinese delegations arrive here each month. And more than a hundred thousand Americans now visit China each year. These exchanges between our countries, especially among our young people in the universities, are a source of joy for today and optimism for tomorrow. Only countries determined to be friends would be so open themselves.

The numerous cultural and educational efforts between us recognize the truth of another Chinese saying. This one, found in the Book of Songs, written some 3,000 years ago, says, "The stones of yonder mountain may be used to polish gems."

We have much to learn from each other. Your visit, Mr. Premier, provides a welcome opportunity to continue the open dialog that embodies the new spirit between our countries. We have much to discuss—matters of bilateral, regional, and global importance. We share many concerns, especially in the arena of international peace and sta-

bility. We stand on common ground in opposing expansionism and interference in the affairs of independent states. We are united by our commitment for international peace and our desire for economic progress.

I look forward to returning the honor of your visit when I travel to your country in the spring.

Mr. Premier, you have an active week ahead of you, and I look forward to getting to know you better. We're pleased that you'll have the opportunity to see something of our land and our people beyond Washington. And we're happy that our people will have the opportunity to meet you and let you know that you are indeed among friends.

Premier Zhao, welcome to the United States.

The Premier. Mr. President and Mrs. Reagan, ladies and gentlemen, at the beginning of the new year, I have brought the American people the cordial greetings and good wishes of the 1 billion Chinese people. I would like to thank President Reagan for his kind invitation, which has offered me this opportunity to visit your great country.

As a friendly envoy of the Chinese people, I have come to visit your country for the purpose of seeking increased mutual understanding, stabilizing the relations between our two countries, enhancing Sino-U.S. friendship, and helping to preserve world peace. I believe this is not only the common aspiration of the Chinese and American peoples but also the expectation of the people of the world.

This year marks the 200th anniversary of the long sail to China by the American merchant ship *Empress of China*. That historic voyage started contacts between China and the United States. The history of Sino-U.S. relations over the past two centuries has witnessed both periods of friendly coexistence and exchanges, and of confrontation and conflict. However, the seas of friendship have always existed among the Chinese and American peoples.

This traditional friendship between our two peoples and the political foresight of the leaders of the two countries help to put an end to a long period of estrangement and confrontation between our two countries, and to bring about the normalization of our relations.

Since the establishment of diplomatic relations, the relations between China and the United States have, in the aggregate, made considerable progress. The friendly exchanges between our two peoples have greatly increased and their mutual understanding further deepened. Our exchanges and cooperation in the political, economic, cultural, scientific, technological, and other fields, have markedly expanded, but it should be considered that the growth of the Sino-U.S. relations is far below the level it should have attained. There have been ups and downs in the course of development, and there still exist difficulties and obstacles.

China has always attached importance to its relations with the United States and hopes to see their growth. U.S. Government leaders have also indicated on more than one occasion that they value Sino-U.S. relations and wish to see their development on a durable and stable basis.

I believe there is such a possibility. In order to turn the possibility into reality, it is necessary for both sides to show mutual respect and for each other, to take into account the national interests of the other side as well as his own country in handling the problems before them.

So long as both China and the United States strictly abide by the principles as confirmed by both sides in the joint communiques, perform the obligations each undertook, it is possible for Sino-U.S. relations to leave behind doubts and uncertainties and embark on a smooth path.

Five years ago, Chinese leader Ding Xiao Ping said at this podium that "great possibilities lie ahead for developing amicable cooperation between China and the United States." This remains our faith. Sino-U.S. relations are now at an important juncture. As Americans would say, "They're faced with big challenges and great opportunities as well." We should bravely accept the challenges and make full use of the opportunities.

The world situation is at present more turbulent. The people of all countries are deeply worried about the future of the world. The United States and China, both being big countries, should be aware of their heavy responsibility for the maintenance of world peace.

In the next few days, I shall hold talks with President Reagan and other leaders of your government and exchange views with them on ways to develop Sino-U.S. relations and on international issues of common interest.

We never construe the significance of Sino-U.S. relations as being limited to ordinary bilateral relations, but regard them as an important affair affecting the overall world situation. We stand for peace, not only because China needs peace, friendship, and economic development but also because people of all countries want peace, friendship, and development.

The amicable coexistence of China and the United States is a major factor for maintaining world peace and stability. As long as the peoples of the world take their destiny into their own hands, it will be possible to maintain world peace and prevent a new world war.

Mr. President, at this solemn podium I feel that hundreds of millions of people are watching us. They expect us to make contributions to the development of Sino-U.S. relations and to the cause of maintaining world peace. We should not disappoint them.

As I said just now, this year is the bicentenary of the beginning of contacts between China and the United States. This is an occasion for reviewing the past and looking ahead to the future. I believe that with the study of history we will learn to live together better in amity. I wish happiness to the American people and steady and sustained development of the Sino-U.S. relations.

Thank you.

Note: The President spoke at 10:10 a.m. on the South Lawn of the White House, where the Premier was accorded a formal welcome with full military honors. The Premier spoke in Chinese, and his remarks were translated by an interpreter.

Following the ceremony, the President and the Premier, together with U.S. and Chinese officials, met in the Oval Office.

They then met in the Cabinet Room, where additional U.S. and Chinese officials joined the discussions.

Nomination of William A. Wilson To Be United States Ambassador to the Holy See
January 10, 1984

The President today announced his intention to nominate William A. Wilson to be Ambassador to the Holy See.

Mr. Wilson has been serving since February of 1981 as the President's Personal Representative to the Holy See.

A registered mechanical and metallurgical engineer in California, Mr. Wilson was the president of Web Wilson Oil Tools, Inc., until 1960, and thereafter he was active in real estate development. Among his civic activities, Mr. Wilson is a member of the board of trustees of St. John's Hospital in Santa Monica, CA, serving on various committees. He is also a member of the board of regents of the University of California. He served as a member of the California Post Secondary Education Commission and the Commission of the Californias, an organization for the promotion of better understanding between California and Baja California.

Born in Los Angeles, CA, Mr. Wilson attended Stanford University and graduated with a degree in mechanical engineering. During World War II he served in the U.S. Army Ordnance Corps as a captain. Mr. Wilson is married to the former Elizabeth Johnson, and they have two children and six grandchildren.

Nomination of Charles G. Hardin To Be an Assistant Secretary of Transportation
January 10, 1984

The President today announced his intention to nominate Charles G. Hardin to be an Assistant Secretary of Transportation (Governmental Affairs).

Since 1981 Mr. Hardin has been serving as chief clerk and staff director (majority) for the Subcommittee on Transportation and Related Agencies, Committee on Appropriations, U.S. Senate. Previously, he was a member of the professional staff of the Committee on Appropriations, U.S. House of Representatives, in 1973–1980; and an administrative budget and management analyst, Bureau of Planning and Budget, Wisconsin Department of Administration, in 1970–1973.

He graduated from Florida State University (B.A., 1969) and the University of Wisconsin (M.A., 1970). He is married, has two children, and resides in Annapolis, MD. He was born April 10, 1947, in St. Louis, MO.

Statement on Receiving the Report of the President's Task Force on Food Assistance
January 10, 1984

This afternoon I met with the Task Force on Food Assistance and received its report. The report reflects months of thoughtful and diligent work by Chairman Clay La Force and his task force members, and I want to give them all my heartfelt thanks. They've made a major contribution to our understanding of why and how hunger exists in our country. But more important, they've made recommendations to help us in assisting Americans truly in need.

I have directed the members of our administration to examine closely the recommendations of this report and to determine what can be done to incorporate them in our policies.

God has blessed our great country with rich abundance. By reminding us that in this land of plenty, there can be no excuse for hunger, the Task Force on Food Assistance has presented us with a challenge. We will meet that challenge through public and private resources—and we will do so with intelligence, prudence, and compassion.

Once again, to the members of the Task Force on Food Assistance: Your work will help many of our countrymen. On behalf of all Americans, thank you, and God bless you.

Nomination of Jane E. Newman To Be an Assistant Secretary of Commerce
January 10, 1984

The President today announced his intention to nominate Jane E. (Bonnie) Newman of Durham, NH, to be an Assistant Secretary of Commerce (Economic Development Administration). She will succeed Carlos C. Campbell.

A native of Lawrence, MA, Ms. Newman presently serves as Associate Director of Presidential Personnel at the White House. Prior to joining the White House she was chief of staff for Congressman Judd Gregg (R-NH). Before that she was executive director of the Forum on New Hampshire's Future, a citizen participation program for industrial development and community planning. From 1972 to 1978, she held the position of dean of students at the University of New Hampshire.

Ms. Newman has served on numerous boards, including Indian Head Banks, Inc., the Center for New Hampshire's Future, the Governor's Economic Development and Land Use Committee, and the State of New Hampshire's Future Food Policy Committee.

She graduated from St. Joseph's College, Maine (B.A., 1967) and Pennsylvania State University (M.Ed., 1969). The degree of doctor of humane letters was conferred by River College in 1983. She was born June 2, 1945.

Nomination of Carlos C. Campbell To Be Alternate United States Executive Director of the Inter-American Development Bank
January 10, 1984

The President today announced his intention to nominate Carlos C. Campbell to be Alternate United States Executive Director of the Inter-American Development Bank. He would succeed Hugh W. Foster.

Mr. Campbell is currently Assistant Secretary of the Economic Development Administration, Department of Commerce. Prior to this appointment he was a management consultant. In 1974–1976, he served at the U.S. Department of the Interior in the American Revolution Bicentennial Administration. He was at the Department of Housing and Urban Development in 1969–1972. He served with the U.S. Navy as a commissioned officer.

He graduated from Michigan State University (B.S., 1959) and Catholic University of America (M.A., 1968). He is married, has two children, and resides in Reston, VA. He was born July 19, 1937, in New York, NY.

Toasts of the President and Premier Zhao Ziyang of China at the State Dinner
January 10, 1984

The President. Premier Zhao and distinguished guests, this house has been the scene of many an historic occasion, and tonight we celebrate another milestone. Premier Zhao, you are the first Chinese head of government to visit the United States, and we're honored to welcome you.

The magnitude of America's esteem and respect for Chinese civilization may not be fully understood in China today. As a boy going to school in a small town in our Midwest, I learned of the venerable Chinese culture, and it seemed then that China was a million miles away. Today our children are still taught about the great contributions China has made, and yet as we approach the 21st century, our young people think of your country as only hours away by jet plane. Technology has made us neighbors. It's up to us to make certain that we're also friends.

Mr. Premier, your visit gives me the opportunity to express the great value I place on the positive and expanding ties between our two countries. Our cooperation helps the well-being of both our peoples to blossom and serves the cause of world peace. Good will and friendship do not always, as we've found, bring agreement on every issue. But friendship gives us the freedom to disagree, even to criticize without fear of lessening cooperation in our many areas of mutual interest.

Let us always remember that open and frank dialog is the foundation that supports the bridge between us.

Mr. Premier, I remember well our last discussions in Cancún 2 years ago. I am grateful for the progress that we've made since then and look forward to even greater cooperation in the years ahead. I'm particularly pleased with the wide-ranging and constructive discussions that we enjoyed today. It was certainly a promising omen for the future and a positive way to begin a new year. Of course, the Chinese new year will not come for several weeks, but this past Year of the Pig has proven that we can feast together at the table of cooperation.

There's reason for optimism, but we must look past tomorrow and the day after and prepare with mutual trust and confidence for the next century. The bonds between our two proud and independent nations can be made a wellspring of hope and progress, of security and prosperity.

We've been watching with interest and

admiration your efforts to modernize by offering incentives to your people in stimulating economic competition. We have been pleased to contribute what we could as you expand the vistas of economic opportunity for the Chinese people.

Tonight we congratulate you, Premier Zhao, for the part that you're playing in the rebirth of China's economy. Before ascending to your current position, you were a leading force in turning around the economic decline of Sichuan. Under your guidance, the province went from stagnation to vibrancy, from hunger and food importation to abundance and the export of grain. In fact, I understand that because of the work you did there it is said in China, "If you want rice, go see Zhao." [*Laughter*]

Ladies and gentlemen, to give you an idea of the significance of the Premier's economic achievements, Sichuan Province, which the Premier managed for 4 years before moving to Beijing, has a hundred million people, making it the most populous province in China and bigger than all but seven of the countries of the world. The Premier is now putting that same creativity to work on a national basis.

Premier Zhao is also known for his personal commitment to vigorous physical exercise. Tonight I would ask all of you to join me in a toast to his health and to the health of China's other distinguished leaders and to peace, prosperity, and friendship between the Chinese and American people.

The Premier. Mr. President and Mrs. Reagan, ladies and gentlemen, from the very beginning of my visit to your country, I have been warmly received. I am greatly honored to be invited to this grand state dinner tonight. Please allow me, on behalf of my colleagues and in my own name, to express our hearty thanks to the President and Mrs. Reagan, to the U.S. Government, and friends from all circles.

Five years ago, the normalization of Sino-U.S. relations gave the people of both our countries great joy and made a far-reaching impact on the world situation. Over the past 5 years, Sino-U.S. relations have gone through twists and turns, with both advances in many fields and difficulties and obstacles cropping up along the way. The jolts and uncertainties in Sino-U.S. relations

do not serve the interests of the two peoples, nor those of world peace. We hope that this disturbing situation will soon be brought to an end.

Our two sides share the desire to develop Sino-U.S. relations. I appreciate what President Reagan said, to the effect that China and the United States are destined to grow stronger through cooperation, not weaker through division. I believe that both the Chinese and American peoples hope to see advances in our friendship through joint efforts and not the undermining of our friendship by aggravation of our differences. The Taiwan issue is the major difference between China and the United States, or in other words, the principal obstacle to the growth of Sino-U.S. relations. I hope that our two sides will strictly abide by the principles guiding our bilateral relations, which we jointly established in the Sino-U.S. communiques, and fulfill the commitments each of us has undertaken, so that our differences may be resolved.

The world today is still in turbulence. The confrontation between the two military blocs has become sharper, while the North-South contradictions are not yet resolved. Before the flames of one aggressive war are extinguished, those of another have started raging. The grim reality constrains everybody to worry about the future of the world. It also heightens the sense of responsibility and urgency of all the peace-loving countries and people for the maintenance of world peace. China will work in concert with them to ease international tension, stop the arms race, oppose power politics, and maintain world peace.

China has always been opposed to arms race, particularly nuclear arms race, and stands for the complete prohibition and thorough destruction of nuclear weapons. We have long declared that China will never be the first to use nuclear weapons. We are critical of the discriminatory Treaty on the Non-Proliferation of Nuclear Weapons, but we do not advocate or encourage nuclear proliferation. We do not engage in nuclear proliferation ourselves, nor do we help other countries develop nuclear weapons. We actively support all proposals that are truly helpful to realizing nuclear disarmament, terminating the nuclear arms race and eliminating the threat of nuclear war.

[*At this point, the Premier paused, and his interpreter addressed the dinner guests as follows.*]

Interpreter. Ladies and gentlemen, there's some changing in the last paragraph, so I have to translate it.

"Today I have had talks with President Reagan and some of his Cabinet members in a friendly and candid atmosphere. These talks have helped to enchance our mutual understanding, and both sides have expressed a desire to further develop Sino-U.S. relations. We both agreed that there are great potentials for economic and technological cooperation between our two countries, and are willing to take a positive attitude to further increase our cooperation.

"I sincerely hope that my visit and President Reagan's visit to China in April will help to promote steady and durable growth of Sino-U.S. relations on the basis of the five

principles of mutual respect for sovereignty and territorial integrity, mutual nonaggression, noninterference in each other's internal affairs, equality and mutual benefit, and peaceful coexistence. This will serve the interest of our two peoples and that of world peace."

The Premier. Allow me to propose a toast to the health of the President and Mrs. Reagan, to the health of the Vice President and Mrs. Bush, to the health of all our friends present here, to the happiness of the American people, to the friendship between the Chinese and American peoples, and to world peace!

Note: The President spoke at 10 p.m. in the State Dining Room at the White House. The Premier spoke in Chinese, and a translation of his remarks was provided to the dinner guests. As printed above, the remarks follow that text, except where modifications were made by the Premier's interpreter, as indicated.

Remarks to Reporters on Receiving the Report of the National Bipartisan Commission on Central America
January 11, 1984

The President. Ladies and gentlemen, I have just been hearing a report on this Commission. It's been 6 months now of the most arduous work, and work that has been extremely well done. And I want to express to all and each of them not only my thanks but the thanks on behalf of all the people of America for the service that they have performed for our country.

The report—while I have just received it and have not had time to read all of it, I have had an opportunity to have some summations and then to be present here for a discussion and a report by the individuals. And I believe that from what I've seen already, it is the most comprehensive and detailed review of the issues as they affect our national security that I have ever seen.

I'm impressed with the depth of the analysis and the creativity of the recommendations. And Henry has told me that this was

a diverse, but not a divisive group, and they worked in a bipartisan manner throughout. And I'm especially grateful to Lane Kirkland, to Bob Strauss, to others of the loyal opposition for this and for the fact that we have a consensus recognition of the urgent nature and the complexity of the crisis in Central America and the implications for our fundamental interests.

I believe that the Members of Congress, when they study this report, will share my belief that we must urgently seek solutions, solutions to the problems that are outlined in this study. I think that they will fully share our belief when they do look at it that it is time for us to go to work.

We've set forward a program that will achieve the goals the members of this Commission have set forth for us. And again, I can only say that I think all America is indebted to them for a job that I don't think has ever been surpassed with regard to the particular problem we face. And it's a challenge that I intend to do everything I can, and I'm sure the Congress will, too, to see that we meet.

Q. Mr. President, is this going to get bogged down in a fight over conditionality? The Commission calls for a conditionality, and some of your advisers say it's been counterproductive.

The President. No, no, it is not. And I have heretofore not said anything about this. I've been waiting until the time when

I had the report before me which, as I say, I will study and read. And I would think that it behooves the Congress, and it certainly behooves the administration, to try and come together in the same bipartisan way that this Commission has been together over these last 6 months.

Note: The President spoke at 11:50 a.m. in the Cabinet Room at the White House, where he had met with Dr. Henry A. Kissinger, Chairman, and other members of the Commission.

Appointment of Roy Martin Brewer as Chairman and Member of the Federal Service Impasses Panel
January 11, 1984

The President today announced his intention to appoint Roy Martin Brewer to be Chairman and member of the Federal Service Impasses Panel, Federal Labor Relations Authority, for a term expiring January 10, 1989. He will succeed Robert G. Howlett.

Mr. Brewer has been serving as a member of the Federal Service Impasses Panel since July 1983. He also serves as labor relations consultant for Walt Disney Productions, Inc., and consultant to Local No. 695, Sound Technicians. He has spent over 50 years in the field of labor. His past positions include: vice president of the Personnel & Industrial Relations Association

(District No. 5); director of industrial relations for Technicolor, Inc.; manager, branch operations, Allied Artists Corp.; president of the Motion Picture Industry Council; president of the Hollywood A.F. of L. Film Council; international representative for the International Alliance of Theatrical Stage Employees; chief, plant and community facilities, Office of Labor Production, War Production Board; and president of the Nebraska State Federation of Labor.

Mr. Brewer is married, has two children, and resides in Tarzana, CA. He was born August 9, 1909, in Cairo Hall County, NE.

Remarks of the President and Premier Zhao Ziyang of China on Signing Two United States-China Agreements
January 12, 1984

The President. Good morning. Thank you for joining us.

We've been delighted with all that's been accomplished as a result of Premier Zhao's visit. His trip has solidified the good will between us, and this morning we will sign two agreements that represent measurable steps forward in the relations between our countries.

In China the difference in time zones makes it almost tomorrow. Today we sign two agreements aimed at making China's tomorrow, as well as our own, a better day.

The first is an extension of our agreement on cooperation in science and technology. Cooperation between our two countries in the area of science and technology not only contributes to the scope of human knowledge and to China's own modernization; it also cements the ties between our governments and our peoples.

The joint science and technology commission overseeing this part of our relations has done a tremendous job. Today's extension is a tribute to the successful and growing cooperation that we're already experiencing in this vital area.

Signing this first accord will be our science adviser, Dr. Jay Keyworth, and his counterpart, Mr. Zhao Dongwan.

The Premier. I fully agree with President Reagan. The two agreements we are going to sign—one of them is an extension of the existing agreement; the other a new one. The signing symbolizes that we should preserve what we have already achieved and open up new areas in our bilateral relations. It shows that there are broad vistas for the development of Sino-U.S. relations. Let us continue our efforts to achieve new successes in our cooperation in the economic and technological fields.

Thank you.

[At this point, Mr. Keyworth and Mr. Zhao signed the Agreement To Extend the Agreement Between the Government of the United States of America and the Government of the People's Republic of China on Cooperation in Science and Technology.]

The President. Next, Premier Zhao and I will affix our signatures to an accord on industrial and technological cooperation.

China is now engaged in a vast modernization program, and this agreement will encourage further cooperation between our countries, especially in those industrial sectors on which China has placed a top priority. American know-how and investment should prove invaluable in these endeavors, and this accord will stimulate participation by our private sector in China.

Premier Zhao, any business deal that makes sense is based on mutual benefit. By signing this document, we are helping ourselves by helping each other. That should be the basis of our friendship.

[At this point, the President and the Premier signed the Accord on Industrial and Technological Cooperation Between the United States of America and the People's

Republic of China.]

The President. Well, ladies and gentlemen, I've come away from my working sessions with Premier Zhao more convinced than ever the importance of good U.S.-China relations and more determined than ever to ensure that our relationship is placed on a stable and enduring footing.

Our talks covered a broad spectrum of global and bilateral issues. China is a leading nation on the international scene, and I appreciated hearing directly from the Premier on his views. It was clear during our discussions that China and the United States agree on a number of questions and that the leaders of our two nations should come together regularly to compare notes.

Even on matters of disagreement, the Premier and I were able to clarify our respective positions. Though our strategies sometimes converge and sometimes differ, our goals remain the same. We both are committed to peace and stability in the world so that we can concentrate our energies and resources on improving the well-being of our people.

With respect to our bilateral relations, I think that Premier Zhao would agree that we've made considerable progress. Our economic cooperation, despite occasional problems, is healthy and holds enormous promise.

Several months ago, we expanded the potential for the transfer of American technology to China. Our scientific and student exchanges are flourishing. Building on this positive trend are the two specific agreements that we signed here today. Our agreements and understandings underscore my conviction that a modern, economically developing, and politically stable China is in the best interest of all peace-loving peoples.

Nancy and I will journey to China in April. We were delighted to get to know Premier Zhao before our visit to his country, and we now look forward all the more to our trip, knowing that friends will be there to meet us. So, let me wish Premier Zhao a happy continuation of his travels in the United States. I know that he'll be warmly welcomed everywhere.

And I won't say goodbye, Mr. Premier. I will only—and try to say correctly—*Tsai jen,* which I'm told means "See you again soon."

The Premier. Mr. President, the visit to the United States by the head of government of the People's Republic of China itself fully shows that there's some progress in Sino-U.S. relations.

Since I set foot on your land, I've been deeply impressed by the American people's warm friendship for the Chinese people. I personally feel the American people want Sino-U.S. relations to develop, not to stand still; to advance, not to retrogress. Therefore, I think there is, indeed, the basis for the amicable coexistence between China and the United States, and such a basis is very deep-rooted.

My colleagues and I have held friendly, candid, and serious talks with the American President and other leaders of the American Government. Through these talks, we enhanced our mutual understanding. It undoubtedly is useful to the promotion of the Sino-American relations on the road of steady development.

Of course, much remains first to be done to really solve the outstanding problems between us and implement the cooperation

we have already committed to.

Mr. President, before I leave you, I should like to thank you once again for your gracious hospitality. I would also like to thank Mrs. Reagan. I know it was her thoughtful arrangement that made our stay in Washington so pleasant.

Mr. President, I look forward to seeing you and Mrs. Reagan in Beijing this spring when it is warm and beautiful so as to reciprocate your hospitality here. What is more important is that I look forward to more substantial content in our future talks in Beijing to continue on the talks we have already started in Washington. Then we'll be able to show to both the Chinese and the American peoples how important these mutual visits are.

Thank you.

Note: The President spoke at 8:42 a.m. in the East Room at the White House. The Premier spoke in Chinese, and his remarks were translated by an interpreter.

Earlier, the President and the Premier attended a working breakfast in the State Dining Room. They were accompanied by U.S. and Chinese officials.

Message to the Congress Reporting Budget Deferrals
January 12, 1984

To the Congress of the United States:

In accordance with the Impoundment Control Act of 1974, I herewith report seven new deferrals of budget authority totaling $1,832,465,000 and seven revised deferrals of budget authority totaling $2,734,156,870.

The actions affect programs in Funds Appropriated to the President, the Departments of Agriculture, Commerce, Defense (Military and Civil), Health and Human

Services, Justice, State and the United States Information Agency.

The details of the deferrals are contained in the attached reports.

RONALD REAGAN

The White House,
January 12, 1984.

Note: The attachments detailing the deferrals are printed in the Federal Register *of January 16, 1984.*

Statement by Principal Deputy Press Secretary Speakes on the Nicaraguan Attack on an Unarmed United States Helicopter
January 12, 1984

The President today condemned the shooting down of an unarmed American helicopter by the Nicaraguan military. The fatal attack on the American and his two U.S. passengers occurred after the aircraft was downed in Honduran territory and after the pilot had left the helicopter. This we regard as reckless and unprovoked.

A brave American was killed, Chief Warrant Officer Jeffrey C. Schwab, of Joliet, Illinois, the pilot of the helicopter. The President offers his deepest condolences to his family.

The incident was protested immediately in the strongest terms to the Nicaraguan Government, and we are awaiting its explanation of the event. We have put the Nicaraguans on notice that this action is unacceptable.

Note: Larry M. Speakes read the statement to reporters assembled in the Briefing Room at the White House during the daily press briefing, which began at 12:35 p.m.

Proclamation 5146—National Fetal Alcohol Syndrome Awareness Week, 1984
January 12, 1984

By the President of the United States of America

A Proclamation

Fetal Alcohol Syndrome (FAS) is one of the major known causes of birth defects with mental retardation and the only one which, at present, is totally preventable.

FAS can result in many serious health problems including prenatal and postnatal growth retardation; developmental disabilities that may cause an infant to experience delays in activities such as walking and speaking; mental retardation; and other organ abnormalities such as heart defects.

In addition, in cases where FAS is not fully present, infants may suffer other alcohol-related birth effects—a series of health risks and problems that include low birthweight; increased prenatal infections; irritability or hyperactivity during the newborn period; birth defects and problems associated with mental impairment. Learning deficits may also occur, although these may not be apparent for a number of years.

Although some questions remain unanswered on consumption of alcohol during pregnancy, research over the past 10 years has established that prenatal alcohol exposure can pose a threat to the health of the unborn child. This knowledge led the Surgeon General of the United States, in 1981, to issue an advisory strongly encouraging women who are pregnant or considering pregnancy to avoid the use of alcohol. In addition, the medical and scientific community, many public and private agencies, and institutions and concerned citizens have, over the years, undertaken valuable efforts to promote public awareness of FAS and related health concerns.

In recognition of the potential for serious consequences of fetal alcohol exposure, and in the interest of increasing public awareness that these consequences are preventable, the Congress, by House Joint Resolution 324 (Public Law 98–188), has designated the week beginning January 15, 1984, as "National Fetal Alcohol Syndrome Awareness Week" and has requested the President to issue a proclamation in observance of that week.

Now, Therefore, I, Ronald Reagan, President of the United States of America, do hereby proclaim the week of January 15 through January 21, 1984, as National Fetal Alcohol Syndrome Awareness Week.

I invite the Governors, the chief officials of local governments, and all Americans to observe this week with appropriate activities, particularly those which seek to protect the health of children through heightened awareness of the consequences of alcohol use during pregnancy.

In Witness Whereof, I have hereunto set my hand this 12th day of January, in the year of our Lord nineteen hundred and eighty-four, and of the Independence of the United States of America the two hundred and eighth.

RONALD REAGAN

[Filed with the Office of the Federal Register, 10:51 a.m., January 13, 1984]

Announcement of the Conferral of the Presidential Medal of Freedom on Carlos P. Romulo, Foreign Minister of the Philippines
January 12, 1984

The President has conferred the Presidential Medal of Freedom on Carlos P. Romulo, Foreign Minister of the Philippines. General Romulo has announced that he will be retiring from public life on January 14, his 85th birthday. The award was given in recognition of Foreign Minister Romulo's long and distinguished career, which has spanned the better part of this century.

In addition to his long tenure as Philippine Foreign Minister, Carlos Romulo served as an aide-de-camp to General MacArthur during the Second World War. He was the Philippine delegate to the U.S. Congress during the Commonwealth period and later Philippine Ambassador to the United States, and he was a signatory of the United Nations Charter. Throughout his career, Foreign Minister Romulo has been a steadfast friend of the United States, and he devoted unstinting efforts to fostering good relations between our countries.

The medal was presented in Manila today by Ambassador Michael Armacost.

The text of the award reads as follows:

"As parliamentarian, soldier, educator, U.N. Charter signatory, diplomat, and foreign minister, Carlos P. Romulo's statesmanship and promotion of international accord add up to a remarkable record of achievement. His more than fifty years of public service embody the warm relationship between the United States and the Philippines from the colonial period through the Commonwealth, wartime, and independence to the present. In tribute to his long and close association with the United States, this medal is gratefully conferred."

Nomination of Richard H. Imus for the Rank of Ambassador While Serving as United States Negotiator on Textile Matters
January 13, 1984

The President today announced his intention to nominate Richard H. Imus for the rank of Ambassador during his service as United States Negotiator on Textile Matters in the Office of the United States Trade Representative. He would succeed Peter Otto Murphy.

In 1962 Mr. Imus entered the Foreign Service as vice consul in Sydney. He was consular officer in Tel Aviv from 1965 to 1967. From 1967 to 1969, he was on detail to the Department of Commerce as international economist. He attended Arabic language training in Beirut from 1969 to 1970. He was economic and commercial officer in Dhahran (1970–1972) and in Kuwait (1972–

1973). From 1973 to 1974, he was personnel officer in the Department. He attended economic studies at the Foreign Service Institute from 1974 to 1975. From 1975 to 1977, he was international economist in the Bureau of East Asian and Pacific Affairs in the Department. He was counselor for economic affairs in Wellington from 1977 to 1981. In the Department he was Chief of the Textiles Division in the Bureau of Economic and Business Affairs from 1981 to

1983. Since 1983 he has been on detail as United States Negotiator on Textile Matters in the Office of the United States Trade Representative.

Mr. Imus graduated from Stanford University (B.A., 1960) and the University of California at Berkeley (M.A., 1961). In 1958 he attended the University of Vienna in Austria. His foreign languages are German, Arabic, and French. He was born August 12, 1938, in San Francisco, CA.

Remarks and a Question-and-Answer Session With Elected Republican Women Officials
January 13, 1984

The President. Before I get into anything besides "good afternoon" and "welcome," I think I ought to point out that today is the birthday—someone, I believe I have it right, from St. Louis, Missouri—Bonnie Sue Cooper. Where is she? Oh, there! Happy birthday! [*Laughter and applause*]

Ms. Cooper. Thank you.

The President. Well, it's a pleasure to have you all here and a real delight for me to see so many good friends and to have a chance to make, I hope, some new ones. And I'm glad the Vice President and Barbara Bush and Secretaries Elizabeth Dole, Don Regan, Terrel Bell, Margaret Heckler, were able to be with us. And I hope that you're all as happy as I am that we have with us two of the most important women in my life—Nancy and Maureen.

And we also have with us some of the many extraordinarily capable women on the White House staff. I have seen, looking around the room, women here from the White House Personnel and Legislative offices. And I must mention Trudi Morrison, who runs a program close to my heart—the Fifty States Project.

I also see we've been joined by a few of the men on our staff, and in this crowd they sort of stand out. [*Laughter*] I don't have time to recognize everyone, but special thanks to Jim Baker for inviting you all here.

Now, before I say anything else, let me give you Republican officeholders my heartfelt thanks for all the time and labor each of you have given to the cause that unites us. When all is said and done, it's not gloss and glitter but effort and determination from people like you who make it possible for us to put our beliefs into practice. And all of you are especially important because you demonstrate the Republican commitment to American women.

I was thinking on the way over about a story I like to tell. And if you've heard it before, pretend you haven't, because I'm going to tell it. [*Laughter*]

There was an accident; a man lying out there on the pavement. There was a women bending over him and trying to help him, and a crowd gathered around. And then a man elbowed his way through the crowd, shoved the woman aside, and said, "I've studied first aid. Let me at him." And she meekly stepped back, and he went to work with the things that he'd learned. And then there came one point in which she tapped him on the shoulder and she said, "When you come to that part about calling the doctor, I'm right here." [*Laughter*]

As women have taken on new roles in society, the Republican Party has given them, I think, firm support. First, it was the GOP that gave its backing to women suffrage. And then our party became the first to elect a woman to the United States Congress and the only party ever to elect women to the United States Senate who were not first just filling out unexpired terms.

Today the two women in the Senate, my friends, Nancy Kassebaum and Paula Hawkins, are Republicans. And we have nine outstanding Republican women in the House of Representatives. And I'd just like to ask Paula right now, "Wouldn't you like to have more company?" [*Laughter*] All right.

In our administration, we've appointed many women to positions of top responsibility—women like our United Nations Ambassador Jeane Kirkpatrick, our Secretary of Health and Human Services Margaret Heckler, our Secretary of Transportation Elizabeth Dole, and the many women on the White House staff who are with us here today.

One of my proudest days in office was when I appointed Sandra Day O'Connor as the first woman Justice on the United States Supreme Court. And, believe me, I've had many reasons to cheer that appointment.

But just as important, today there are thousands of able Republican women like you serving in public office outside Washington. You, in State legislatures and other State and local offices, are on the frontlines of democracy. You have a chance to put your beliefs into practice close to the people, closer than Washington can, and Washington can't match your ability to do that.

We look on you as our eyes and ears, as leaders who truly know what the American people think and need. And just as we're eager to see the number of Republican women officeholders grow at the national level, we're also determined to see those numbers grow in every American town, city, and State. And together, we Republicans are working to reshape America's destiny. And when historians write the story of these years, they'll find that skilled and talented women played vital roles.

Now, I know you've already had a number of briefings today and that this afternoon you'll hear about the women's program run by the Small Business Admin-

istration, projects at the Department of Agriculture and the Women's Bureau at the Department of Labor. But if I could just take a moment, I'd like to give you an overview of what this administration has been doing.

Just 3 years ago we inherited the worst economic mess in decades. Big taxing and spending had led to soaring inflation and interest rates, government redtape had smothered productivity. In January of '81 inflation was in double digits, the prime interest rate was at its highest peak since the Civil War, and growth in industry and productivity was disappearing.

When I think of what the Democrats had done to our economy, I feel a little bit like the little boy that came to his mother and asked her, he said, "You know that jug that we have that you say has been passed down from generation to generation in our family?" And she said, "Yes, what about it?" He said, "I just broke it."

Well, I think the broken economy hit women especially hard. The majority of elderly Americans living on fixed incomes are women, and they found their purchasing power eaten up by inflation. Working women saw jobs become more and more scarce. Homemakers found that 12½-percent inflation made it harder and harder to buy groceries and pay the bills. And the thousands of women who wanted to start their own businesses saw 21-percent prime rates slam shut the doors of opportunity. The American people were fed up, and they did a little house cleaning.

Our administration moved in, and with Republicans in control of the Senate we went to work to make a new beginning. Believe me, little of any of what we've accomplished could have been done if we had not held one House of the Congress.

We reduced the growth of Federal spending, we pruned needless regulations, we reduced personal income tax rates and passed an historic reform called "tax indexing" that means government can never again use inflation to profit at the people's expense.

Incidentally, we had a report just the other day on publications. We have reduced them by the thousands. These were publications that were being put out all over the

Government here, useful things like how to buy eggs, and we figured that you could figure that out for yourselves. [*Laughter*]

To help all Americans achieve economic equality, we reduced the marriage tax penalty, almost doubled the maximum childcare credit, increased the limits for IRA and Keogh contributions, and eliminated estate taxes on family farms and businesses for surviving spouses.

Today, less than 3 years since we set our policies in place, our nation has one big program to help every American—man, woman, and child. It's called economic recovery.

The prime rate is almost half what it was when we took office. Inflation has plummeted by three-fourths to only 3 percent for the past year, and this morning we received a golden piece of news that I want to share with you. It was announced early this morning. The producer price index increased by only two-tenths of 1 percent last month and by only six-tenths of 1 percent for all of 1983. And that's the lowest it's been in 19 years.

Now I remember when our critics were insisting that our tax cuts would make— somebody's wanted on the phone [1]—[*laughter*]—oh, all right—would make inflation and interest rates soar, but just the opposite has happened.

And of course we know that factory orders, retail sales, housing starts are up. The stock market has come back to life. And the American worker's real wages are rising, and that's the first time that that's happened in a few years.

Unemployment is still too high, but it's dropping fast. Last year more than 4 million Americans found jobs. It was the steepest 12-month drop in unemployment in more than 30 years.

Since we took office, women have begun finding the economic opportunities they've deserved all along. With this recovery, you'll be glad to hear the unemployment rate among adult women has dropped from 9.1 percent to 7.1 percent. And today, more

women have jobs than ever before in our nation's history. The jobs women hold are getting better and better. In 1983 women filled almost three-quarters of all the new jobs in managerial, professional, and technical fields. The number of women-owned businesses is growing four times faster than those owned by men.

And just as we're turning the economy around, we're bringing a new sense of purpose and direction to American foreign policy. Today the world knows once again that America stands for the political, religious, and economic freedom of humankind.

In Grenada, we set a nation free. With the help of the National Bipartisan Commission on Central America, we've worked to develop a new consensus to support democracy in that region.

The peace process in Lebanon has been slow and painful, but there's been a genuine progress toward the goals of internal stability and the withdrawal of all foreign forces.

In Europe, the NATO alliance has held firm despite months of Soviet bluster. Sooner or later the Soviets will realize that arms reductions are in their interest, too. And when they do, we'll be at the table waiting for them, ready to go on negotiating from strength and in good faith.

I'm convinced that because we've strengthened our defenses and shown the world our willingness to negotiate the prospects for lasting world peace are better than they have been in many years. And I don't care how many Presidential candidates are out there yelling that we're threatened by imminent war. We have never been as far removed from that possibility as we have today, in the last several years. And that is because of our deterrent power. And we're going to continue on that.

All of us share a dream. It's a dream of a broad and open land that offers prosperity to all. It's a dream of a great country that represents a force for peace and goodwill among nations. It's a dream of a land where every citizen is judged not according to color, religion, or sex, but on the sole basis of individual merit; a land where every

---

[1] *The President was referring to the sound of an audience member's telephone paging device.*

woman and man is free to become all that she or he can. And come to think of it, I wouldn't be surprised if one day, one of you had my job.

All of us are laboring in the name of that dream. Yes, we'll suffer setbacks and, yes, others will do all they can to place obstacles in our path. But if we have the courage to do all that we can to make our dream come true, then we will achieve great good in this world and do our duty by our country.

And I don't know what—I'm not going to look at my clock, but I know that they've scheduled it very close and tight, but I've wanted to do this. And I know I only have a few minutes because we're going to have a chance to meet individually and shake hands and have our pictures taken. But maybe I've got time for a few questions. So, if someone has one—yes?

State of the Union Address

Q. I'm Joan Hastings from Oklahoma. In the State of the State speech will there be any new initiatives for women? I know your record on women is very good, but in the State of the State speech will there be any new initiatives particularly recognized?

The President. Any new initiatives that we'll propose? Well, we haven't put that speech together, and I can't speak in too great a detail about it, but I can tell you one that's going to be in there: I want line-item veto.

But we'll have to wait a little bit while we find out how much we can get into that speech on other details. But we will be talking about our program for the future and the deficits and how to control them. And I think the deficits are caused because the Government is taking too big a share out of the general—or the gross national product out of the private economy. And Government has got to be cut back to size.

Q. Mr. President, Pat Friebert from Kentucky. I'd like to thank you for this opportunity and to tell you how proud we are of you for your concern and your caring attitude towards women and women's issues.

The President. Well, thank you very much. That was an answer, not a question. [*Laughter*] Thank you very much.

Yes?

U.S. Immigration Policy

Q. Mr. President, I was told to ask you about the immigration policy. I'm from Miami, Florida, and we're quite concerned down there about immigrants.

The President. Well, we have what we think is a sensible program for immigration. There's no question but that our country has really, in fact, lost control of its own borders. And we have a program, and it's up there before the Congress, and so far they haven't let it out of committee, I understand. And we're going to keep pressing for it until we get it. And we're going to have, I think, policies in that legislation that are consistent with the words on the base of the Statue of Liberty and yet will give us control.

National Security

Q. Mr. President, I'm Mary Thompson from Las Cruces, New Mexico—State representative. I work at White Sands, and among the people that I work with at White Sands there's a great deal of concern about security in this country and of the information that's leaving our borders. And we wondered what plans you have to strengthen our security and to retain the information in this country that we wish to keep here.

The President. I think you're talking about security having to do with things that would be of aid to an adversary—technical information and so forth. Well, we have done much. Some of the things that were so widely hailed in the media as quarrels between us and our friends in Europe, our allies and so forth, actually were negotiations that have resulted in more unity than we've ever had with regard to joint control of that kind of sales or dissemination of information and the actual hardware. And we have a basic agreement with all of them.

We're very firm about that here, but security is one problem no matter how much you try to police something. We have just intercepted, as you know, a great shipment that was almost on its way through another country to the Soviet Union. And fortunately, our intelligence apparatus worked well enough that we intercepted and caught it there. It would have been of great assistance to anyone in improving their military capabilities. And we are working at that, and I think that our net is getting tighter and tighter in that regard. But we're very much aware of the problem, and we're not going to throw away any of these advantages.

My, it's a whole new world, isn't it, with technology? I remember when we were talking about scrap iron coming back to us in World War II as shrapnel.

Plans for Reelection

Q. Mr. President, Representative Jan McKenna from Fort Worth, Texas. A lot of us in Texas were wondering if you're planning on seeking reelection. [*Laughter*]

The President. I think I heard the magic words. [*Laughter*] You'll forgive me if I just stall a little about answering that, and I'll give you the word on January 29.

Communist Aggression in Central America

Q. Illeana Ros from Miami, Florida—State representative. We all applaud your efforts in trying to decrease the Communist aggression throughout the world. I wanted to know your opinion of the Kissinger report as it relates to Central America policies and the Communist takeover of many of those countries.

The President. It is a magnificent report. That Commission, which was truly bipartisan—and not just bipartisan in label, but bipartisan in philosophic belief—I know that many of them went, started on that Commission with the idea that we were all wrong in what we were trying to do.

It is a magnificent report, and it substantiates the positions that we have been taking down there: There is a challenge to us to eliminate what has been going on for hundreds of years, the economic and social differences that make them vulnerable to this kind of takeover, but also the fact that you can't have social reforms while you're having your head shot off by guerrilla forces that are armed and supported by the Soviet Union and Cuba. And they confirmed that this is true. And so, we're going to follow up on this.

I think that one of the things they said in the report made so much sense. We have been trying to help El Salvador. El Salvador has the first effort at a democratic government in 400 years. Now, sure, they've got some rightists who didn't want that democratic government—the so-called murder squads. But they're being assailed by thousands of left-wing guerrillas who also don't want a democratic government.

Now, we can't let either one of those factions destroy that effort at democracy. But because of limitations that have been imposed on us as to how much we can do in the line of helping them, actually what we've been doing is letting them slowly bleed to death. We have been helping, but not helping enough to rectify the wrongs or to give them the military capacity to be successful.

So, in that report—it was very eloquently stated—they said you can make a case for us doing nothing. Okay, walk away and leave them. Or you can make a case for us vastly increasing the help so they can bring about an answer. You cannot make a case for just helping them too little, and that's what we've been doing up until now. And we're really behind it. I think it's a magnificent report.

Efforts To Combat Drug Abuse

Q. Senator Stockton from Colorado. Mr. President, I wanted to take this opportunity to thank you for supporting Mrs. Reagan in her efforts to combat the drug scene. And I hope that your administration will continue to let her do that and will support her.

The President. Yes. You bet we're helping in that. And we're making great progress. We had one task force in Florida because that was the great entry point from out of the country, and in the South particularly, of drugs. And we've collected quite a fleet of yachts and cabin cruisers and airplanes and trucks and—I saw for the first time in my life—only time in my life—something else we'd confiscated from these drug runners, and that was on one table—$20 million in cash.

But now that's been so successful that we have expanded to 12 such task forces all around the country, because as we closed or partially closed one door, they started coming in in other places; and with our thousands of miles of coastline, we're pretty vulnerable to that. But they are having great effect.

But the main thing, and what Nancy's more interested in is this: I don't think there's any real way that you can totally shut off the flow of the drug itself. The best thing you can do is take the customers away from the sellers by talking them out of it. And that's what the programs that she's interested in—and so many of you are—are doing around the country, is convincing, particularly our young people, that that's not the road to go.

Ms. Reagan. Mr. President, are you deliberately not calling on me? [*Laughter*]

The President. I thought you were waving to tell me my time was up.

Ms. Reagan. Whatever you say. Thank you, Mr. President. [*Laughter*]

The President. I thought so. Sharper than a serpent's tooth. [*Laughter*]

All right. Thank you all. Thank you all, and God bless you. And I know we're going in the other room, and then I'm going to see you all individually again. Thank you all very much.

Note: The President spoke at 1:12 p.m. at a luncheon for the officials in the State Dining Room at the White House.

In his closing remarks, the President was speaking to his daughter Maureen.

Proclamation 5147—National Sanctity of Human Life Day, 1984
January 13, 1984

By the President of the United States of America

A Proclamation

The values and freedoms we cherish as Americans rest on our fundamental commitment to the sanctity of human life. The first of the "unalienable rights" affirmed by our Declaration of Independence is the right to life itself, a right the Declaration states has been endowed by our Creator on *all* human beings—whether young or old, weak or strong, healthy or handicapped.

Since 1973, however, more than 15 million unborn children have died in legalized abortions—a tragedy of stunning dimensions that stands in sad contrast to our belief that each life is sacred. These children, over tenfold the number of Americans lost in all our Nation's wars, will never laugh, never sing, never experience the joy of human love; nor will they strive to heal the sick, or feed the poor, or make peace among nations. Abortion has denied them the first and most basic of human rights, and we are infinitely poorer for their loss.

We are poorer not simply for lives not led and for contributions not made, but also for the erosion of our sense of the worth and dignity of every individual. To diminish the value of one category of human life is to diminish us all. Slavery, which treated Blacks as something less than human, to be bought and sold if convenient, cheapened human life and mocked our dedication to the freedom and equality of all men and women. Can we say that abortion—which treats the unborn as something less than human, to be destroyed if convenient—will be less corrosive to the values we hold dear?

We have been given the precious gift of human life, made more precious still by our births in or pilgrimages to a land of freedom. It is fitting, then, on the anniversary of the Supreme Court decision in *Roe v. Wade* that struck down State anti-abortion laws, that we reflect anew on these blessings, and on our corresponding responsibility to guard with care the lives and freedoms of even the weakest of our fellow human beings.

Now, Therefore, I, Ronald Reagan, President of the United States of America, do hereby proclaim Sunday, January 22, 1984, as National Sanctity of Human Life Day. I call upon the citizens of this blessed land to gather on that day in homes and places of worship to give thanks for the gift of life, and to reaffirm our commitment to the dignity of every human being and the sanctity of each human life.

In Witness Whereof, I have hereunto set my hand this 13th day of January, in the year of our Lord nineteen hundred and eighty-four, and of the Independence of the United States of America the two hundred and eighth.

RONALD REAGAN

[*Filed with the Office of the Federal Register, 10:24 a.m., January 16, 1984*]

Radio Address to the Nation on Recommendations of the National Bipartisan Commission on Central America
January 14, 1984

My fellow Americans:

Last April I addressed a joint session of the Congress and asked for bipartisan cooperation on behalf of our policies to protect liberty and democracy in Central America. Shortly after that speech, the late Senator Henry Jackson encouraged the appointment of a blue-ribbon commission to chart a course for democracy, economic improvement, and peace in Central America. I appointed 12 distinguished Americans to the National Bipartisan Commission on Central America and asked former Secretary of State Henry Kissinger to serve as its Chairman. This week the members of that group delivered to me their report on the crisis confronting our Latin neighbors.

I believe the Commission has rendered an important service to all Americans—all of us from pole to pole in this Western Hemisphere. The members of this Commission represented both political parties and a wide cross section of our country. They reached agreement on some very key points. They agreed that the crisis is serious and our response must include support for democratic development, improved living conditions, and security assistance.

They agreed that the United States has a vital interest in preventing a Communist Central America because if our own borders are threatened, then our ability to meet our commitments to protect peace elsewhere in the world—in Europe, the Middle East, and Asia—would be significantly weakened.

The members also agreed that Nicaragua's regime has violated its promise to restore democracy. And they warned that

Nicaragua's export of subversion could undermine the stability of neighboring countries, producing waves of refugees—perhaps millions of them—many of whom would seek entry into the United States.

The Commission concluded, "The crisis is on our doorstep." The report of this distinguished body presents no quick fix to ease the pain and suffering of tomorrow. There is none. Nor can we alone bring peace to this or any other part of the world. As the report notes, solutions to Central American problems must primarily be the work of Central Americans. But we can and must help, because it is in our interest to do so and because it's morally the right thing to do.

The Commission did present us positive recommendations to support democratic development, improve human rights, and bring the long-sought dream for peace to this troubled region so close to home. The recommendations reinforce the spirit of the administration's policies that help to our neighbors should be primarily economic and humanitarian. And since this report does present a bipartisan consensus, I will send to the Congress when it reconvenes a comprehensive plan for achieving the objectives set forth by the Commission. I urge the Members of Congress to respond with the same bipartisan spirit that guided the Commission in its work.

This Central American democracy, peace, and recovery initiative, which I call the Jackson plan, will be designed to bring democracy, peace, and prosperity to Central America. It won't be easy, but it can be done. I believe peace is worth the price.

There may be an argument for doing much and, perhaps, an argument for doing nothing. But there is no valid argument for doing too little. Well, I opt for doing enough—enough to protect our own security and enough to improve the lives of our neighbors so that they can vote with ballots instead of bullets.

The Government of Nicaragua must also understand this. They cannot threaten their peaceful neighbors, export subversion, and deny basic human freedom to their own people as the Commission has so rightly observed.

Now, you may have heard that there's a controversy between the administration and the Congress over human rights and military aid to beleaguered El Salvador. Well, I agree completely with the objective of improving prospects for democracy and human rights in El Salvador. I am also com-

mitted to preventing Cuban and Nicaraguan supported guerrillas from violently overthrowing El Salvador's elected government and others in the region; so is the bipartisan Commission; so, too, I believe, is our Congress.

Our administration will continue to work closely with the Congress in achieving these common goals. As we move to implement the recommendations of the bipartisan Commission, we will be offering the promise of a better tomorrow in Central America. But we must oppose those who do not abide by the norms of civilized behavior, whether they be of the extreme right or extreme left. Senator Henry Jackson would have had it so.

Until next week, thanks for listening, and God bless you.

Note: The President spoke at 12:06 p.m. from Camp David, MD.

Executive Order 12458—Delegation to the Secretary of State Concerning Foreign Assistance
January 14, 1984

By the authority vested in me as President by the Constitution and statutes of the United States of America, including Section 621 of the Foreign Assistance Act of 1961, as amended (22 U.S.C. 2381), and Section 301 of Title 3 of the United States Code, and in order to delegate certain functions concerning foreign assistance to the Secretary of State, it is hereby ordered as follows:

Section 1. Section 1–201(a) of Executive Order No. 12163, as amended, is further amended by inserting the following new subparagraphs at the end thereof:

"(23) Section 512 of the Foreign Assistance and Related Programs Appropriations Act, 1982;

"(24) Chapter 8 of Part II of the Act, except that such functions shall be exercised consistent with Section 573(d)(3) thereof;

"(25) The functions vested in the President by Section 101(b) of the Joint Resolution "Making further continuing appropriations for the fiscal year 1984" (Public Law

98–151), insofar as they relate to unnumbered paragraphs concerning El Salvador and Haiti.".

Sec. 2. Section 1–301 of Executive Order No. 12163, as amended, is further amended as follows:

(a) In subsection (a), by striking out "(except chapters 4 and 6 thereof)" and inserting in lieu thereof "(except chapters 4, 6 and 8 thereof)"; and

(b) in subsection (c), by striking out "(except chapters 4 and 6 thereof)" and inserting in lieu thereof "(except chapters 4, 6 and 8 thereof)".

Sec. 3. Section 1–801 of Executive Order No. 12163, as amended, is further amended as follows:

(a) In subsection (b), by striking out "(except chapters 4 and 6 thereof)" and inserting in lieu thereof "(except chapters 4, 6 and 8 thereof)"; and

(b) in subsection (c), by striking out "chapter 6" and inserting in lieu thereof "chapters 6 and 8".

RONALD REAGAN

The White House,
January 14, 1984.

[*Filed with the Office of the Federal Register, 10:25 a.m., January 16, 1984*]

Address to the Nation and Other Countries on United States-Soviet Relations
January 16, 1984

During these first days of 1984, I would like to share with you and the people of the world my thoughts on a subject of great importance to the cause of peace—relations between the United States and the Soviet Union.

Tomorrow the United States will join the Soviet Union and 33 other nations at a European disarmament conference in Stockholm. The conference will search for practical and meaningful ways to increase European security and preserve peace. We will be in Stockholm with the heartfelt wishes of our people for genuine progress.

We live in a time of challenges to peace, but also of opportunities to peace. Through times of difficulty and frustration, America's highest aspiration has never wavered. We have and will continue to struggle for a lasting peace that enhances dignity for men and women everywhere.

I believe that 1984 finds the United States in the strongest position in years to establish a constructive and realistic working relationship with the Soviet Union. We've come a long way since the decade of the seventies, years when the United States seemed filled with self-doubt and neglected its defenses, while the Soviet Union increased its military might and sought to expand its influence by armed forces and threat.

Over the last 10 years, the Soviets devoted twice as much of their gross national product to military expenditures as the United States, produced six times as many ICBM's, four times as many tanks, twice as many combat aircraft. And they began deploying the SS–20 intermediate-range missile at a time when the United States had no comparable weapon.

History teaches that wars begin when governments believe the price of aggression is cheap. To keep the peace, we and our allies must be strong enough to convince any potential aggressor that war could bring no benefit, only disaster. So, when we neglected our defenses, the risks of serious confrontation grew.

Three years ago, we embraced a mandate from the American people to change course, and we have. With the support of the American people and the Congress we halted America's decline. Our economy is now in the midst of the best recovery since the sixties. Our defenses are being rebuilt, our alliances are solid, and our commitment to defend our values has never been more clear.

America's recovery may have taken Soviet leaders by surprise. They may have counted on us to keep weakening ourselves. They've been saying for years that our demise was inevitable. They said it so often they probably started believing it. Well, if so, I think they can see now they were wrong.

This may be the reason that we've been hearing such strident rhetoric from the Kremlin recently. These harsh words have led some to speak of heightened uncertainty and an increased danger of conflict. This is understandable but profoundly mistaken.

Look beyond the words, and one fact stands out: America's deterrence is more credible, and it is making the world a safer place—safer because now there is less danger that the Soviet leadership will underestimate our strength or question our resolve.

Yes, we are safer now, but to say that our restored deterrence has made the world safer is not to say that it's safe enough. We're witnessing tragic conflicts in many parts of the world. Nuclear arsenals are far too high, and our working relationship with the Soviet Union is not what it must be. These are conditions which must be addressed and improved.

Deterrence is essential to preserve peace and protect our way of life, but deterrence is not the beginning and end of our policy toward the Soviet Union. We must and will engage the Soviets in a dialog as serious and constructive as possible—a dialog that will serve to promote peace in the troubled regions of the world, reduce the level of arms, and build a constructive working relationship.

Neither we nor the Soviet Union can wish away the differences between our two societies and our philosophies, but we should always remember that we do have common interests and the foremost among them is to avoid war and reduce the level of arms.

There is no rational alternative but to steer a course which I would call credible deterrence and peaceful competition. And if we do so, we might find areas in which we could engage in constructive cooperation. Our strength and vision of progress provide the basis for demonstrating with equal conviction our commitment to stay secure and to find peaceful solutions to problems through negotiations. That's why 1984 is a year of opportunities for peace.

But if the United States and the Soviet Union are to rise to the challenges facing us and seize the opportunities for peace, we must do more to find areas of mutual interest and then build on them.

I propose that our governments make a major effort to see if we can make progress in three broad problem areas. First, we need to find ways to reduce, and eventually to eliminate, the threat and use of force in solving international disputes.

The world has witnessed more than 100 major conflicts since the end of World War II. Today there are armed conflicts in the Middle East, Afghanistan, Southeast Asia, Central America, and Africa. In other regions, independent nations are confronted by heavily armed neighbors seeking to dominate by threatening attack or subversion. Most of these conflicts have their origins in local problems, but many have been exploited by the Soviet Union and its surrogates. And, of course, Afghanistan has suffered an outright Soviet invasion.

Fueling regional conflicts and exporting violence only exacerbate local tensions, increase suffering, and make solutions to real social and economic problems more difficult. Further, such activity carries with it the risk of larger confrontations. Would it not be better and safer if we could work together to assist people in areas of conflict in finding peaceful solutions to their problems? That should be our mutual goal.

But we must recognize that the gap in American and Soviet perceptions and policy is so great that our immediate objective must be more modest. As a first step, our governments should jointly examine concrete actions that we both can take to reduce the risk of U.S.-Soviet confrontation in these areas. And if we succeed, we should be able to move beyond this immediate objective.

Our second task should be to find ways to reduce the vast stockpiles of armaments in the world. It's tragic to see the world's developing nations spending more than $150 billion a year on armed forces—some 20 percent of their national budgets. We must find ways to reverse the vicious cycle of threat and response which drives arms races everywhere it occurs.

With regard to nuclear weapons, the simple truth is America's total nuclear stockpile has declined. Today we have far fewer nuclear weapons than we had 20 years ago, and in terms of its total destructive power, our nuclear stockpile is at the lowest level in 25 years.

Just 3 months ago, we and our allies agreed to withdraw 1,400 nuclear weapons from Western Europe. This comes after the withdrawal of 1,000 nuclear weapons from Europe 3 years ago. Even if all our planned intermediate-range missiles have to be deployed in Europe over the next 5 years— and we hope this will not be necessary—we will have eliminated five existing nuclear weapons for each new weapon deployed.

But this is not enough. We must accelerate our efforts to reach agreements that will greatly reduce nuclear arsenals, provide greater stability, and build confidence.

Our third task is to establish a better working relationship with each other, one marked by greater cooperation and understanding. Cooperation and understanding are built on deeds, not words. Complying with agreements helps; violating them hurts. Respecting the rights of individual citizens bolsters the relationship; denying these rights harms it. Expanding contacts across borders and permitting a free exchange or interchange of information and ideas increase confidence; sealing off one's people from the rest of the world reduces it. Peaceful trade helps, while organized theft of industrial secrets certainly hurts.

Cooperation and understanding are especially important to arms control. In recent years we've had serious concerns about Soviet compliance with agreements and treaties. Compliance is important because we seek truly effective arms control. However, there's been mounting evidence that provisions of agreements have been violated and that advantage has been taken of ambiguities in our agreements.

In response to a congressional request, a report on this will be submitted in the next few days. It is clear that we cannot simply assume that agreements negotiated will be fulfilled. We must take the Soviet compliance record into account, both in the development of our defense program and in our approach to arms control.

In our discussions with the Soviet Union, we will work to remove the obstacles which threaten to undermine existing agreements and a broader arms control process. Examples I've cited illustrate why our relationship with the Soviet Union is not what it should be. We have a long way to go, but we're determined to try and try again. We may have to start in small ways, but start we must.

In working on these tasks, our approach is based on three guiding principles—realism, strength, and dialog. Realism means we must start with a clear-eyed understanding of the world we live in. We must recognize that we are in a long-term competition with a government that does not share our notions of individual liberties at home and peaceful change abroad. We must be frank in acknowledging our differences and un-

afraid to promote our values.

Strength is essential to negotiate successfully and protect our interests. If we're weak, we can do neither. Strength is more than military power. Economic strength is crucial, and America's economy is leading the world into recovery. Equally important is our strength of spirit and unity among our people at home and with our allies abroad. We're stronger in all these areas than we were 3 years ago. Our strength is necessary to deter war and to facilitate negotiated solutions. Soviet leaders know it makes sense to compromise only if they can get something in return. Well, America can now offer something in return.

Strength and dialog go hand in hand, and we're determined to deal with our differences peacefully through negotiations. We're prepared to discuss the problems that divide us and to work for practical, fair solutions on the basis of mutual compromise. We will never retreat from negotiations.

I have openly expressed my view of the Soviet system. I don't know why this should come as a surprise to Soviet leaders who've never shied from expressing their view of our system. But this doesn't mean that we can't deal with each other. We don't refuse to talk when the Soviets call us imperialist aggressors and worse, or because they cling to the fantasy of a Communist triumph over democracy. The fact that neither of us likes the other system is no reason to refuse to talk. Living in this nuclear age makes it imperative that we do talk. Our commitment to dialog is firm and unshakeable, but we insist that our negotiations deal with real problems, not atmospherics.

In our approach to negotiations, reducing the risk of war, and especially nuclear war, is priority number one. A nuclear conflict could well be mankind's last. And that is why I proposed over 2 years ago the zero option for intermediate-range missiles. Our aim was and continues to be to eliminate an entire class of nuclear arms. Indeed, I support a zero option for all nuclear arms. As I've said before, my dream is to see the day when nuclear weapons will be banished from the face of the Earth.

Last month the Soviet Defense Minister

stated that his country would do everything to avert the threat of war. Well, these are encouraging words, but now is the time to move from words to deed. The opportunity for progress in arms control exists. The Soviet leaders should take advantage of it.

We have proposed a set of initiatives that would reduce substantially nuclear arsenals and reduce the risk of nuclear confrontation.

The world regrets—certainly we do—that the Soviet Union broke off negotiations on intermediate-range nuclear forces and has not set a date for the resumption of the talks on strategic arms and on conventional forces in Europe. Our negotiators are ready to return to the negotiating table to work toward agreements in INF, START, and MBFR. We will negotiate in good faith. Whenever the Soviet Union is ready to do likewise, we'll meet them halfway.

We seek to reduce nuclear arsenals and to reduce the chances for dangerous misunderstanding and miscalculations, so we have put forward proposals for what we call confidence-building measures. They cover a wide range of activities. In the Geneva negotiations, we proposed to exchange advance notification of missile tests and major military exercises. Following up on congressional suggestions, we also proposed a number of ways to improve direct channels of communications. Last week, we had productive discussions with the Soviets here in Washington on improving communications, including the hotline.

Now these bilateral proposals will be broadened at the conference in Stockholm. We're working with our allies to develop practical, meaningful ways to reduce the uncertainty and potential for misinterpretation surrounding military activities and to diminish the risk of surprise attack.

Arms control has long been the most visible area of U.S.-Soviet dialog. But a durable peace also requires ways for both of us to diffuse tensions and regional conflicts.

Take the Middle East as an example. Everyone's interest would be served by stability in the region, and our efforts are directed toward that goal. The Soviets could help reduce tensions there instead of introducing sophisticated weapons into the area. This would certainly help us to deal more positively with other aspects of our relationship.

Another major problem in our relationship with the Soviet Union is human rights. Soviet practices in this area, as much as any other issue, have created the mistrust and ill will that hangs over our relationship. Moral considerations alone compel us to express our deep concern over prisoners of conscience in the Soviet Union and over the virtual halt in the emigration of Jews, Armenians, and others who wish to join their families abroad.

Our request is simple and straightforward: that the Soviet Union live up to its obligations. It has freely assumed those obligations under international covenants, in particular its commitments under the Helsinki accords.

Experience has shown that greater respect for human rights can contribute to progress in other areas of the Soviet-American relationship. Conflicts of interest between the United States and the Soviet Union are real, but we can and must keep the peace between our two nations and make it a better and more peaceful world for all mankind.

Our policy toward the Soviet Union—a policy of credible deterrence, peaceful competition, and constructive cooperation—will serve our two nations and people everywhere. It is a policy not just for this year, but for the long term. It's a challenge for Americans; it is also a challenge for the Soviets. If they cannot meet us halfway, we will be prepared to protect our interests and those of our friends and allies.

But we want more than deterrence. We seek genuine cooperation. We seek progress for peace. Cooperation begins with communication. And, as I've said, we'll stay at the negotiating tables in Geneva and Vienna. Furthermore, Secretary Shultz will be meeting this week with Soviet Foreign Minister Gromyko in Stockholm. This meeting should be followed by others, so that high-level consultations become a regular and normal component of U.S.-Soviet relations.

Our challenge is peaceful. It will bring out the best in us. It also calls for the best in the Soviet Union. We do not threaten the Soviet Union. Freedom poses no threat. It is the language of progress. We proved this 35 years ago when we had a monopoly on nuclear weapons and could have tried to dominate the world, but we didn't. Instead, we used our power to write a new chapter in the history of mankind. We helped rebuild war-ravaged economies in Europe and the Far East, including those of nations who had been our enemies. Indeed, those former enemies are now among our staunchest friends.

We can't predict how the Soviet leaders will respond to our challenge. But the people of our two countries share with all mankind the dream of eliminating the risk of nuclear war. It's not an impossible dream, because eliminating these risks are so clearly a vital interest for all of us. Our two countries have never fought each other. There's no reason why we ever should. Indeed, we fought common enemies in World War II. Today our common enemies are poverty, disease, and above all, war.

More than 20 years ago, President Kennedy defined an approach that is as valid today as when he announced it. "So let us not be blind to our differences," he said, "but let us also direct attention to our common interests and to the means by which those differences can be resolved."

Well, those differences are differences in governmental structure and philosophy. The common interests have to do with the things of everyday life for people everywhere. Just suppose with me for a moment that an Ivan and an Anya could find themselves, oh, say, in a waiting room, or sharing a shelter from the rain or a storm with a

Jim and Sally, and there was no language barrier to keep them from getting acquainted. Would they then debate the differences between their respective governments? Or would they find themselves comparing notes about their children and what each other did for a living?

Before they parted company, they would probably have touched on ambitions and hobbies and what they wanted for their children and problems of making ends meet. And as they went their separate ways, maybe Anya would be saying to Ivan, "Wasn't she nice? She also teaches music." Or Jim would be telling Sally what Ivan did or didn't like about his boss. They might even have decided they were all going to get together for dinner some evening soon. Above all, they would have proven that people don't make wars.

People want to raise their children in a world without fear and without war. They want to have some of the good things over and above bare subsistence that make life worth living. They want to work at some craft, trade, or profession that gives them satisfaction and a sense of worth. Their common interests cross all borders.

If the Soviet Government wants peace, then there will be peace. Together we can strengthen peace, reduce the level of arms, and know in doing so that we have helped fulfill the hopes and dreams of those we represent and, indeed, of people everywhere. Let us begin now.

Thank you.

Note: The President spoke at 10 a.m. in the East Room at the White House.

Remarks on Receiving the Final Report of the President's Private Sector Survey on Cost Control in the Federal Government
January 16, 1984

You know, I can't resist—I'm accused, and certainly some elements accuse me of too much of telling anecdotes and so forth. But I think it'd be appropriate before I say anything else, that one of my favorite stories about government had to do with an

employee who sat at a desk. And papers came to his desk; he read them and determined where they were to go and initialed them and sent them on. And one day a classified document came there. But it came to him, so he read it, initialed it, and sent it on. Twenty-four hours later it came back to him with a note attached that said, "You weren't supposed to see this. Erase your initials, and initial the erasure." [*Laughter*]

But, ladies and gentlemen, it isn't often that we gather here in the East Room to honor Washington lobbyists and publicly accept their recommendations. But with pride, interest, and gratitude, that's exactly what we're doing today.

This ceremony marks the formal acceptance of an extraordinary group of recommendations from an extraordinary group of lobbyists. You don't want more government; you want less. And you do not represent a small special interest group, but the largest of them all, 94 million American taxpayers.

Back in 1967, when I was Governor of California, I asked a group of highly motivated private sector executives to survey the State bureaucracy and to identify potential savings. They made about 2,000 recommendations, and we implemented the majority of them. Their work helped return fiscal integrity to a State that had been spending a million dollars a day more than it was taking in.

Now, some of you may also remember that throughout the campaign of 1980 I spoke of waste and fraud and mismanagement in government and what it was doing to the American taxpayer. In my first State of the Union message, I also referred to this problem as an unrelenting national scandal, one that must be fought at every level and in every agency of the Federal Government. To some, of course, the mere mention of this issue suggests only empty political rhetoric, mere words about a problem that in their view is either exaggerated or so ingrained in government that nothing will be done about it. But your work established once and for all how serious a problem waste, fraud, and mismanagement is and how much can be done to eliminate it.

The reports of the Grace commission are remarkable documents. They dare us to think the unthinkable, and they urge us to do the undoable. They show us the price tag future generations must face because of so much government excess in our time, and they make 2,478 recommendations

from 36 task forces which could produce savings, as you've been told, of hundreds of billions of dollars a year.

The historic nature of these documents and the work of the commission should be obvious. The Grace commission has confronted the issues that so many government officials, academic experts, and professional consultants have ignored. The commission has pointed out that unless we face up now to the legacy that was left us by the years of tax and tax and spend and spend, we will be staring at even greater deficits and an impossible burden of taxes and spending.

This commission has given us a warning for the future. But you have also presented us with a program for action, a blueprint that can make government responsive to the needs of the less fortunate, while lifting the economic burden already carried by millions of Americans who are overtaxed and overregulated by government.

Now there are two tasks remaining. The first is to turn your recommendations into reality. You've given every member of this administration, every Member of the Congress, and every would-be President a chance to support your recommendations and show the American people that we do care how their money is spent. And with this support we can end the reckless, destructive abuse of hard-earned tax dollars, get control of runaway bureaucracy, and return this nation to fiscal integrity.

As all of you know by now, our Cabinet Council on Management and Administration will be studying your recommendations closely, and then we'll work with the departments and the Congress to implement them.

You know, I keep a sign on my desk that says, "It CAN be done," and the "can" is spelled out in capital letters. For me, that's the bottom line of your report, and that is the spirit in which I receive it today. I pledge to you not just talk but aggressive action on your recommendations.

Our second task is also very important and very pleasant. And this occasion gives me a chance to thank you. I really am aware of the enormous personal sacrifices you made. Those of you serving on this task force were away from your work and family for weeks at a time. I can understand the moments of frustration that you have had, the reluctance or opposition you encountered inside and outside the bureaucracy, the doubts you yourselves may have had as to whether your work would ever really bear fruit. Well, I hope that when historians look back on our time, they will see your report as a turning point on the domestic front.

Throughout history—Rome in ancient times, the French and Spanish empires in the 16th and 17th centuries, the Weimar Republic in this century—many great nations toppled and fell in large part because their economic policies failed to anticipate how their populace was being overburdened with taxes, spending, and debt. I pray your work will be seen as a major event that kept America from going that route. It's a route that revived the belief— or what you've done revived the belief that government is the servant of the people and not the other way around.

As so often happens with any great achievement, there's one person whose contributions stand out. His patience with bureaucracy, his insistence on bringing the best people into this enterprise, and his vision and drive for excellence made all this possible. Despite the fact that he is straightforward and outspoken, everybody still seems to like Peter Grace. [*Laughter*] Maybe because we all sense in Peter a man who is selfless and patriotic, a man who has with this commission's work left his nation a great legacy. I think he was just fed up with people "robbing Peter to pay Paul." [*Laughter*]

Peter, I know you and the other members of this commission will be working with us in the future. But to you personally and to all of you here today, I want to thank you for the hard work and sacrifice. Every American owes you a debt of gratitude. Not all of them will get a chance to say thank you, but on their behalf I want to do that today, from the bottom of my heart, to thank you.

We'll take it from here, and we'll do our very utmost. So, thank you, and God bless you.

Note: The President spoke at 1:40 p.m. at a ceremony in the East Room at the White House. Prior to his remarks, he received a two-volume summary of the survey's findings from its Chairman, J. Peter Grace.

Memorandum on Federal Paperwork Reduction
January 16, 1984

Memorandum for the Heads of Departments and Agencies

At a Cabinet Council on Management and Administration on January 5, 1984 we approved the Administration's Information Collection Budget for Fiscal Year 1984. This is the third government-wide "paperwork budget." It sets precise goals for limiting the number of hours that individual citizens, businesses, and State and local governments must spend filling out forms and reports for the Federal government.

Under this budget, Federal departments and agencies are expected to reduce paperwork by a total of over 130 million hours by the end of FY 1984—a reduction of 6.5 percent from last year. Reduction goals for each department and agency are described in the budget, and will be provided in individual allowance letters from the Director of the Office of Management and Budget.

We have already surpassed our goal of cutting Federal paperwork by over 300 million hours. This means that Americans now have well over 150,000 work-years available every year for activities of their own choosing, time that had previously been spent filling out unnecessary government forms. We can all take pride in this impressive accomplishment, which demonstrates the success of our efforts to reduce government meddling in the affairs of private citizens.

Without your support, and the hard work of those involved in the paperwork control program, our achievements to date would not have been possible. I want to express my congratulations to each of you for a job well done.

We still have a great deal to do in reducing Federal paperwork, and our attention to this critical effort must be constant and unflagging. The goals established for FY 1984 are high, but I am certain they can be attained or surpassed as they were last year. I am counting on each of you to devote your personal attention to meeting your agency's paperwork-reduction goal for the current year, as part of the Administration's commitment to minimizing the burdens and intrusions of government.

RONALD REAGAN

Executive Order 12459—Amending the Generalized System of Preferences
January 16, 1984

By virtue of the authority vested in me by the Constitution and statutes of the United States of America, including Title V of the Trade Act of 1974 (19 U.S.C. 2461 *et seq.*), as amended, section 604 of the Trade Act of 1974 (19 U.S.C. 2483), and section 503(a)(2)(A) of the Trade Agreements Act of 1979 (93 Stat. 251), and as President of the United States of America, in order to modify, as provided by section 504(a) of the Trade Act of 1974 (19 U.S.C. 2464(a)), the limitations on preferential treatment for eligible articles from countries designated as beneficiary developing countries, and to adjust the original designation of eligible articles, it is hereby ordered as follows:

Section 1. In order to subdivide and amend the nomenclature of existing items for purposes of the Generalized System of Preferences (GSP), the Tariff Schedules of the United States (TSUS) (19 U.S.C. 1202) are modified as provided in Annex I to this Order, attached hereto and made a part hereof.

Sec. 2. Annex II of Executive Order No. 11888 of November 24, 1975, as amended, listing articles that are eligible for benefits of the GSP when imported from any designated beneficiary country, is amended as follows:

(a) by deleting TSUS items 654.02, 654.03, 654.06, 654.09, 654.11, 654.14, 654.15, and 654.20; and

(b) by inserting in numerical sequence TSUS items 654.16, 654.25, 654.35, 654.45, 654.50, 654.65, 654.70, and 654.75.

Sec. 3. Annex III of Executive Order No. 11888, as amended, listing articles that are eligible for benefits of the GSP when imported from all designated beneficiary developing countries except those specified in general headnote 3(c)(iii) of the TSUS, is amended as follows:

(a) by deleting TSUS items 654.04, 654.07, 654.12, and 654.13; and

(b) inserting in numerical sequence TSUS items 654.08, 654.30, 654.40, 654.55, and 654.60.

Sec. 4. General headnote 3(c)(iii) of the TSUS, listing articles that are eligible for benefits of the GSP except when imported from the beneficiary developing countries listed opposite articles, is modified as follows:

(a) by inserting in numerical sequence the TSUS item number and country "654.08 . . . Taiwan"; and

(b) by deleting the TSUS item numbers and countries "654.04 . . . Republic of Korea and Taiwan", "654.07 . . . Taiwan", "654.12 . . . Taiwan", and "654.13 . . . Hong Kong" and by inserting in lieu thereof "654.30 . . . Republic of Korea and Taiwan", "654.40 . . . Taiwan", "654.55 . . . Taiwan", and "654.60 . . . Hong Kong", respectively.

Sec. 5. In order to provide staged reductions in the rates of duty for the new TSUS items created by Annex I to this Order, Annex III to Proclamation No. 4707 of December 11, 1979, is amended by Annex II to this Order, attached hereto and made a part hereof.

Sec. 6. Whenever the column 1 rate of duty in the TSUS for any item specified in Annex I to this Order is reduced to the same level as, or to a lower level than, the corresponding rate of duty inserted in the column entitled "Rates of Duty LDDC" by Annex I to this Order, the rate of duty in the "Rates of Duty LDDC" column for such item shall be deleted from the TSUS.

Sec. 7. The amendments and modifications made by this Order shall be effective with respect to articles both: (1) imported on and after January 1, 1976, and (2) entered, or withdrawn from warehouse for consumption, on and after January 17, 1984.

RONALD REAGAN

The White House,
January 16, 1984.

[Filed with the Office of the Federal Register, 10:51 a.m., January 17, 1984]

Note: The annex to the Executive order is printed in the Federal Register *of January 18, 1984.*

Letter Accepting the Resignation of David R. Gergen as Assistant to the President for Communications
January 16, 1984

Dear Dave:

It is with great reluctance that I accept your resignation as Assistant to the President for Communications, effective January 15, 1984.

For the past three years, you have served me with exceptional creativity, skill and dedication. As two of my predecessors learned, you also bring with you to the White House an unswerving commitment to open, honest and decent government. Over a period stretching back to the early 1970s, you have achieved a remarkable record of service to the country and to the Presidency.

During these first three years of my term, I have especially appreciated the assistance that you and members of your staff have given me in the field of communications. The steady stream of ideas that you have contributed and your energetic execution of those ideas have helped greatly in conveying to millions of people, both here and abroad, the policies and philosophy of this Administration. Your understanding of the modern media, your skills as a writer, and your sensitivity to the needs of the disadvantaged, minorities and women—all these have been an important part of your contribution to my Presidency.

Since the early days of the Administration, you have also been one of the leading advocates within the staff for open, accountable government and for good relations with the national press corps. Your hope has been that we might leave behind a much higher level of civility and professional respect between the White House and journalists who covered it. I share that goal, and with the help of you and others on the staff, I believe we have made progress toward its fulfillment.

Nancy and I know how much of a personal sacrifice these past three years have been for you, Anne and your children, Christopher and Katherine, and we join in wishing you all the best in the years ahead.

Thank you and God bless you.

Sincerely,

RONALD REAGAN

[The Honorable David R. Gergen, Assistant to the President for Communications, The White House, Washington, D.C. 20500]

January 12, 1984

Dear Mr. President:

I herewith submit my formal resignation as Assistant to the President for Communications, effective January 15, 1984.

It is with a mixture of pride and sadness

that I leave your ranks. Three years ago, you came to the White House when both the country and the Presidency were in decline. For more than a decade, the American economy had been on a roller coaster of higher and higher inflation and deeper and deeper recessions. Overseas, the experience of Vietnam left us in retreat as a world power and we were no longer certain of either purpose or will. As a people, we seemed to be abandoning one set of values and were unable to find new ones.

Moreover, the tides of history were running against the Presidency itself. No one since Dwight Eisenhower had successfully served two full terms, and a series of men had left the office with their hopes and dreams shattered. Serious students of the Presidency were becoming pessimistic about our ability to govern ourselves and were asking whether we should restructure our democratic institutions.

You have shown that what was needed was not a change of Constitution but a change of leadership. In just three years, you have begun to re-energize the American spirit. Our economy is climbing out of recession and with wise policies, inflation can remain under better control than anyone dared imagine a short time ago. The values that once served us so well as a people are undergoing fresh examination and are again being embraced. Our nation has ended its withdrawal from responsibilities overseas. We are better prepared to defend ourselves and others are again looking to the United States for world leadership. In short, largely because of your leadership, we have hope that the decade of the 80s can begin a new era of re-surgence for the country and the Presidency. I feel proud to have been a part of all this.

There are many reasons, if I may suggest, for the progress you have made in these past three years. Your devotion to principle and to putting the nation on a fresh course has been critical. So, too, has been your commitment to bipartisanship and to open government. And certainly, your ability to rally the nation behind your leadership has been indispensable. All these and more have been at the core of your success.

It has been my special privilege to work with you and learn from you as you have earned your reputation as "The Great Communicator." Your speeches, both in quality and quantity, are setting a higher standard for your office. Through the television screen, you have reached out to the American people more frequently and effectively than any of your predecessors. You have understood as well the power of radio, and you have broken important new ground in teleconferencing, electronic graphics, and filmed tapings. In your travel overseas and in your use of communication satellites, you have also shown that vigorous public diplomacy can be an important asset for the American government in the international competition of ideas. Indeed, no President since Franklin Roosevelt has mastered the arts of modern communication as well as you, and I count myself very fortunate to have had a supporting role.

As you know from many years in public life, staff members come and go. Now it is my turn to go. Over the past thirteen years, I have had eight years of service to an institution that I greatly love, the Presidency. As I have in two previous White Houses—those of Presidents Nixon and Ford—I have tried to serve you as completely, loyally and honorably as I know how. There have been mistakes along the way, battles lost and hopes dashed, but there have been triumphs, too, and I shall always savor the good moments. I leave with the memories of many, many fine people who have served you so well during these years.

Mr. President, you are making an extraordinary contribution to our national life. My family and I wish both you and Nancy all the best in the years ahead. You certainly deserve it.

With warmest best wishes,
Sincerely,

DAVE
DAVID R. GERGEN
Assistant to the President for
Communications

[The President, The White House, Washington, D.C. 20500]

Note: The text of the letters was released by the Office of the Press Secretary on January 17.

Nomination of Thomas W.M. Smith To Be United States Ambassador to Nigeria
January 17, 1984

The President today announced his intention to nominate Thomas W.M. Smith, of Maine, a career member of the Senior Foreign Service, Class of Minister-Counselor, as Ambassador to the Federal Republic of Nigeria. He would succeed Thomas R. Pickering.

Mr. Smith served in the United States Marine Corps in 1953–1956 as first lieutenant. He entered the Foreign Service in 1956 as an exchange program officer in the Department. In 1958–1960 he was economic officer in Tunis and attended economic studies at the University of Wisconsin in 1960–1961. He was finance officer in Paris (1961–1966) and economic officer in Lagos (1966–1968). In the Department he was Chief of the Division of United Nations Economic Affairs in 1968–1971. In 1971–1972 he attended the National War College. He was Deputy Chief of the Economic Section in London in 1972–1975 and Director of the Office of West African Affairs in the Department in 1975–1979. In 1979–1983 he was Ambassador to Ghana.

Mr. Smith graduated from Harvard College (A.B., 1951), Cambridge University (B.A., 1953; M.A., 1956), and the University of Wisconsin (M.A., 1970). His foreign language is French. He was born April 18, 1930, in Boston, MA.

Nomination of John D. Bossler To Be a Director of the National Ocean Service and a Member of the Mississippi River Commission
January 17, 1984

The President today announced his intention to nominate Capt. John D. Bossler to be Director of the Charting and Geodetic Services, National Ocean Service, National Oceanic and Atmospheric Administration, in the grade of rear admiral, and as a member of the Mississippi River Commission. He would succeed Herbert R. Lippold, Jr.

Captain Bossler has been with the National Oceanic and Atmospheric Administration (NOAA) since 1959 and is currently serving as Acting Director of the Charting and Geodetic Services. Previously he was Director of the National Geodetic Survey at NOAA in 1980–1983; project manager and Deputy Director of the National Geodetic Survey in 1975–1980; project manager for the new adjustment of the North American horizontal geodetic datum in 1973–1975; and executive officer of the NOAA ship *Davidson* in 1969–1971.

He serves as vice president of the American Congress on Surveying and Mapping and secretary of the American Geophysical Union, Geodesy Section. He is past chairman of the American Society of Civil Engineers.

Captain Bossler graduated from the University of Pittsburgh (B.S., 1959) and Ohio State University (M.S., 1964; Ph.D., 1972). He is married, has one child, and resides in Olney, MD. He was born December 8, 1936, in Johnstown, PA.

Nomination of Bessie Boehm Moore To Be a Member of the National Commission on Libraries and Information Science
January 17, 1984

The President today announced his intention to nominate Bessie Boehm Moore to be a member of the National Commission on Libraries and Information Science for a term expiring July 19, 1988. This is a reappointment.

Mrs. Moore has been on the National Commission on Libraries and Information Science since 1971 and has served as Vice Chairman since 1972. She served as executive director of the Arkansas State Council on Economic Education in 1962–1979; State coordinator, environmental education, Arkansas Department of Education, in 1970–1974; State supervisor, economic education, Arkansas Department of Education, in 1962–1974; and as a consultant to the U.S. Office of Education on economic education in 1966–1967.

Mrs. Moore served as a member of the National Board of Governors of the American Association for the United Nations in 1950–1957 and the United States Committee for UNICEF in 1958–1970.

She graduated from the University of Central Arkansas (B.S.E., 1942) and the University of Connecticut (M.A., 1962). She was born August 2, 1902, in Owensboro, KY, and now resides in Little Rock, AR.

Nomination of Daniel F. Bonner To Be an Associate Director of ACTION
January 18, 1984

The President today announced his intention to nominate Daniel F. Bonner to be Associate Director of the ACTION Agency (Domestic and Anti-Poverty Operations). He would succeed Lawrence F. Davenport.

Mr. Bonner joined ACTION in 1982 to manage the Agency's private sector liaison and to conduct a series of national workshops on voluntarism sponsored by the White House and ACTION. He was named Acting Associate Director for Domestic and Anti-Poverty Operations in July 1983. Prior to his ACTION service, Mr. Bonner was development officer for the Law and Economics Center at Emory University. In 1981 he was with the Ethics and Public Policy Center in Washington, DC. Previously he was with the Chase Manhattan Bank.

He graduated from Fordham University (B.A., 1970) and New York University (M.A., 1973). He is married, has three children, and resides in Rockville, MD. He was born August 10, 1937, in New York, NY.

Statement on the Assassination of Malcolm Kerr, President of the American University of Beirut
January 18, 1984

It was with the greatest shock and sadness that we learned early this morning of the death of Dr. Malcolm Kerr, the president of the American University of Beirut. He was a highly respected member of the academic world who, as president of the American institution in Lebanon, worked tirelessly and courageously to maintain the principles of academic freedom and excellence in education. His work strengthened the historical, cultural, and academic ties between the United States and Lebanon and other countries of the Middle East. Dr. Kerr carried on a family tradition—he himself was born in Beirut to parents also dedicated to the service of mankind.

Dr. Kerr's untimely and tragic death at the hands of these despicable assassins must strengthen our resolve not to give in to the acts of terrorists. Terrorism must not be allowed to take control of the lives, actions, or future of ourselves and our friends.

Remarks of the President and Prime Minister Mahathir bin Mohamad of Malaysia Following Their Meetings
January 18, 1984

The President. Well, it was my pleasure to meet today with Prime Minister Mahathir of Malaysia.

The Prime Minister and I had a valuable exchange of views on international and bilateral issues and found ourselves in agreement to a remarkable degree. We both attach the highest importance to the global economic recovery and believe a more open system of international trade and investment is essential. Our economic upsurge in the United States is helping spark new economic growth worldwide.

Part of our discussion focused on trade and commodities, which is significant to the well-being of Malaysia. Prime Minister Mahathir's creative leadership has been instrumental in developing the U.S.-ASEAN understanding of tin.

Malaysia shines as an example in many areas. Its vibrant economy, complemented by balanced social development and flourishing democratic institutions, should serve as an inspiration to developing nations.

On the international scene we discussed the situation in the Middle East. Although we have differing views on certain aspects of this complicated situation, we both seek an end to the turmoil that has engulfed the area for too long.

We also reviewed the situation in Southeast Asia, where Malaysia is playing a vital role in maintaining the region's peace and stability. Malaysia deserves the world's respect for its continuing efforts on behalf of the many refugees that are fleeing Communist persecution.

The United States applauds ASEAN's determination in these troubled times. We wholeheartedly support, for example, the program for a resolution of the Kampuchean problem. The unity among the member states of ASEAN is an inspiration for all of us.

After my very pleasant meeting with the Prime Minister, I'm confident that ties between Malaysia and the United States are strong and friendly. We can expect increased opportunities for contact between our two peoples on both the official and private level.

For our part, we look forward to continuing the dialog begun today and appreciate very much the Prime Minister's visit. We are pleased to have you here, Mr. Prime Minister.

The Prime Minister. Mr. President, ladies and gentlemen, my delegation and I are pleased with the very frank discussions we had this morning with you and your Cabinet colleagues. We regard this as a part of a continuing useful and constructive dialog.

Quite clearly, there exists a substantial measure of agreement on a variety of areas. I'm particularly happy to note the encouraging signs of economic recovery in the United States, which we consider significant, if not crucial, in assuring a healthy global economy. In fact, if you were to ask me what is it I would want the United States to do with regard to economic policy, my honest and simple response is for the U.S. economy to get ahead and regain its strength, for the healthier and more vibrant the U.S. economy becomes, the better it will be, not only for the United States and

Malaysia but all the developing countries in the world.

The overall relations between Malaysia and the U.S. are excellent, with both our countries sharing similar values and concerns. And where we differ in respect to perception or policy, I'm gratified to note that there is a willingness on the part of the United States to achieve closer understanding and cooperation such as our present round of meetings.

In our discussions, among other things, we conducted a comprehensive and forthright review of the relations between the U.S. and Malaysia. And I'm happy to find that there is a higher level of cooperation and respect between our two countries. We pledge to continue this friendly and cooperative relationship for mutual benefits.

We also took a closer look at a number of important developments and trends in the world in both the political and economic context and discussed what could be done to safeguard and promote global peace, economic development, and political stability. We discussed at length major global economic issues. I'm pleased to note that both our governments recognize that, in the interest of global peace and stability, it is important for both the industrially advanced and the developing countries to make progress on these major issues.

We do not expect handouts in our search for a better tomorrow. Quite clearly, of the many issues that we have been discussing, aid placed a minor or even an insignificant role. What we look for are new areas of cooperation and collaboration, particularly in the area of economy and trade interchange to help us in the realization of our aspirations to be a more self-relying and progressive nation.

Mr. President, I would like to thank you very much for the time that you have given me and my colleagues, and also for the time that members of your Cabinet have spent with us this morning. And I would like to thank you for the friendly discussions that we have had.

Thank you very much.

Note: The President spoke at 1:20 p.m. in the East Room at the White House.

Earlier, the President and the Prime Minister met, together with U.S. and Malaysian officials, in the Oval Office. They then held a working luncheon in the State Dining Room.

Appointment of Three Members of the Advisory Committee for Trade Negotiations
January 18, 1984

The President today announced his intention to appoint the following individuals to be members of the Advisory Committee for Trade Negotiations for terms of 2 years:

Owen Bieber would succeed Douglas A. Fraser. Mr. Bieber is president of the International Union of United Auto Workers (UAW) in Detroit, MI. He has been with the UAW for many years and has served as director of the union's General Motors department, director of UAW Region 1D, and as international representative. He is married, has five children, and resides in Southfield, MI. He was born December 28, 1929, in North Dorr, MI.

Roger J. Baccigaluppi would succeed Robert Barrie. Mr. Baccigaluppi has been with the California Almond Growers Exchange in Sacramento since 1961 and now serves as president and chief executive officer. He is also chairman of the board of the National Council of Farmer Cooperatives and director of the Agricultural Council of California. He is married, has four children, and resides in Sacramento. He was born March 17, 1934, in New York, NY.

Eleanor Lyons Williams III would succeed Stanton D. Anderson. Ms. Williams is presently serving as vice president of Environmental Energy Systems, Inc., in Washington, DC. Previously she was vice president of the American International Trade Group, Inc., in 1983 and vice president of Fraser/Associates in Washington, DC, in 1981–1982. Ms. Williams was born November 22, 1922, in Norfolk, VA, and now resides in Washington, DC.

Appointment of Nine Members of the President's Commission on Industrial Competitiveness
January 19, 1984

The President today announced his intention to appoint the following individuals to be members of the President's Commission on Industrial Competitiveness. These are new positions. The Commission's next meeting will be in Pittsburgh, PA, on February 2–3, 1984.

Robert H. B. Baldwin is chairman and managing director of Morgan Stanley Company, Inc., in New York, NY. He is married, has five children, and resides in New York City. He was born July 9, 1920, in East Orange, NJ.

Donald F. Ephlin is international vice president of United Auto Workers in Detroit, MI. He is married, has three children, and resides in Dearborn Heights, MI. He was born October 11, 1925, in Framingham, MA.

Samuel A. Hardage is chairman of the board of Hardage Enterprises, Inc., in Wichita, KS. He is married, has two children, and resides in Wichita. He was born March 14, 1939, in Jackson, IL.

Howard M. Love is chairman and chief executive officer of National Steel Corp. in Pittsburgh,

PA. He is married, has five children, and resides in Pittsburgh. He was born April 5, 1930, in Pittsburgh.

William H. Morris, Jr., is vice president for international marketing of P & C Bituminous Coal, Inc., in Brentwood, TN. He is married, has two children, and resides in Franklin, TN. He was born January 5, 1929, in Memphis, TN.

Robert N. Noyce is vice president of Intel Corp. in Santa Clara, CA. He is married, has four children, and resides in Los Altos, CA. He was born December 12, 1927, in Burlington, IA.

Howard D. Samuel is president of the Industrial Union Department of the AFL–CIO in Washington, DC. He is married, has three children, and resides in Chevy Chase, MD. He was born November 16, 1924, in New York City.

Randolph B. Stockwell is president and chief executive officer of Community Bank in Los Angeles, CA. He is married, has three children, and resides in Pasadena, CA. He was born May 21, 1946, in Los Angeles.

Edward V. Regan is comptroller of the State of New York in Albany. He is married, has three children, and resides in Katonah, NY. He was born May 14, 1930, in Plainfield, NJ.

Remarks at a White House Reception for the President's Council on Physical Fitness and Sports
January 19, 1984

We're delighted to have you here at the White House today. And this is obviously a good week to talk about physical fitness with Sunday's game coming up. [*Laughter*]

You know, I've been asked a few times who I'm rooting for. Since both teams playing are from my current hometowns— [*laughter*]—and since none of the Democrats that are interested in this job have declared their preferences, I see no reason to be recklessly courageous. [*Laughter*] May the best team win. [*Laughter*]

You'd never guess this was an election year, would you? [*Laughter*]

Well, what I have to say to all of you

today is brief, but heartfelt. The work of your Council, the growth of its membership, the tremendous accomplishments that you've been responsible for have been heartwarming and inspiring. Since George Allen has been your Chairman, the number of special advisers has quintupled. And it's that leadership, along with the tremendous efforts of you here today, that made this Council's work a success and will make the new fitness academy in Indianapolis a reality.

Attention to physical fitness is one of those things that says something about a nation and its people. It's an important indication of America's level of energy, competitiveness, and vigor. So, your work and sacrifice is an act of patriotism.

You're helping America keep strong and youthful. And on that point, let me stress the importance of your work with regard to the young people of America. I think you're aware of the attention that I've been giving to the education issue lately. It's one reason I think it's especially important that physical education continue to play a strong and a vital role in our schools. If it doesn't start

there, I don't know where it's going to start.

And finally, let me say that it's especially pleasing that your progress in keeping America physically fit has in large part been done through the private sector and the unselfish voluntary efforts of people like yourselves. And that, too, is most important.

So, again, I thank you from the bottom of my heart.

Note: The President spoke at 5 p.m. in the State Dining Room at the White House.

Remarks to the Reagan Administration Executive Forum
January 20, 1984

I don't know what the thermometer says, but I think we've just had a January thaw. [*Laughter*]

You know, I can't help but—with all of you here and with all of the reputation that this area has for trouble in transportation when we have snow and the weather is such, you've proven you're entirely different than the young man in the story. He was talking to his sweetheart, and he told her that he loved her so much that he could climb the highest mountain, he would swim the deepest ocean to be by her side. He'd be over Thursday night, if it didn't rain. [*Laughter*]

But I know you join me in thanking this wonderful Marine Band and the Drum and Bugle Corps. They sound better every year. And you'll never hear me criticizing any organization that's as old as the Marine Corps. [*Laughter*] That patriotic music, I think, is a reminder of how much God has blessed this great and beautiful land of ours.

But it's up to us to keep her prosperous and free. And all of you have devoted yourselves to that task. Whether in the White House, the departments, or the agencies, everyone in this hall and on this stage has worked with skill and diligence and heart. I can tell you that you have my deepest personal gratitude. But more important, you have the gratitude, I think, of the American people.

And something else: When historians

write the story of these years, they'll find that hundreds of skilled and talented women played vital roles—women like Transportation Secretary Elizabeth Dole; women like Health and Human Services Secretary Margaret Heckler. And, by the way, I just noticed that HHS has announced that there have been new gains in life expectancy for Americans. I'm happy about that. [*Laughter*] I've already lived about 20-odd years longer than my life expectancy when I was born. That's a source of annoyance to a number of people. [*Laughter*]

And then we have women like the finest, as George said,[1] U.N. Ambassador ever to serve our nation, Ambassador Jeane Kirkpatrick. And, Jeane, I must say, after the downing of the Korean airliner and on so many other occasions, the way you've spoken out for human freedom, democracy, and civilized behavior has thrilled and inspired the world. And on behalf of all Americans, I want to thank you.

As I stand here, I can't help thinking about, well, back to this date 3 years ago. It was a winter day like this one—only colder, because on that day we held the meeting outdoors. But as I look back on that January 20th 3 years ago, I can't help thinking we have made a new beginning.

In 1980 America faced a crisis. The

---

[1] *The Vice President had addressed the forum prior to the President's remarks.*

month when George and I took our oaths of office, inflation stood in double digits; the prime interest rate hit the highest point since the Civil War; and economic growth was disappearing. It didn't matter where you came from, whether you were a man or woman, or black or white. If you had scrimped, struggled, and saved to send your children to college, 21½—or 12½-percent, I should say, inflation rate was slamming shut the doors of opportunity. And if you had dreamed of owning your own home, inflation and interest rates were closing those doors of opportunity. And for working men and women who needed loans to start their own business, 21½-percent prime interst rates were closing the doors on their dreams, too.

At the same time, our defenses had grown weak. Real spending on defense had dropped, and research and development had been cut back. The Navy had fallen from nearly a thousand battle-ready ships to under 500—nearer 400. And as real military pay declined and respect for our Armed Forces eroded, morale among our men and women in uniform hit a low.

Overseas, American influence—always the strongest force for peace in the world—was shrinking. We Americans watched, seemingly helpless, as the Soviets amassed vast military might, then intimidated our allies, fueled regional conflicts, and propped up dictators around the world.

I'm convinced that in 1980 America faced one of those historic choices that come to a nation only a few times a century. We could continue our decline, perhaps comforting ourselves by calling it inevitable, or we could realize that there is no such thing as inevitable, and choose instead to make a new beginning. The American people chose the way of courage, and on this January day 3 years ago, this administration and all of you began to make a new beginning.

We cut the growth of spending; we pruned needless regulations; we reduced personal income tax rates; and we passed an historic reform called tax indexing. Government can no longer use inflation to profit at the people's expense. And today, less than 3 years since we set our policies in place, our nation has one big program to help every American man, woman, and child. And it's called economic recovery.

Inflation has plummeted to about 3 percent—3.2 if we want to be exact—during the past year. That's the lowest rate in more than a decade-and-a-half. The prime rate is almost half what it was when we took office. Factory orders, retail sales, and housing starts are up; the stock market has come back to life; and the American worker's real wages are rising. Unemployment is dropping at the fastest rate in more than 30 years. Last year alone 4 million Americans found jobs, and more people are working than ever before in our history.

And at the same time that we've moved ahead on the economy, we've moved against waste and fraud in the Federal Government, saving billions of dollars. We've taken aim at crime, increasing drug-related arrests, more than doubling organized crime convictions, and setting up drug task forces across the country. And we've moved education to the very top of the national agenda. When we took office, only a handful of States had task forces on education. Today that number is 50.

And just as our administration is curing our domestic ills, we're restoring respect for our Armed Forces and giving a new sense of purpose to our foreign policy.

In the military, morale has soared. The percentage of new recruits with high school diplomas has risen throughout our Armed Forces, and since 1980 the reenlistment rate has gone up almost a quarter. We all remember when so many pundits claimed that we could only attract recruits when the economy was weak. But today we're filling our ranks with better recruits than ever before. They know that America is giving our men and women in uniform better pay, better equipment, and the respect they've always deserved.

I just have to tell you something—I wasn't going to do this, but you're so nice. [*Laughter*] I wasn't going to do it because I've told so many of the people here on the stage this, and they've had to listen to it several times. But if you don't know, recently, one of our young lieutenants—marine lieutenant flying a Cobra was off Grenada and then went on to Beirut. And from there he wrote back to the Armed

Forces Journal something that he had been doing. He said that he noticed that every news story about the Grenada rescue mission contained a line—every story—that Grenada produces more nutmeg than any other place in the world. And he decided that was a code, and he was going to break the code. [*Laughter*] And he did.

He wrote back and said, "Number one, Grenada produces more nutmeg than any place in the world. Number two, the Soviets and the Cubans are trying to take Grenada. Number three, you can't make good eggnog without nutmeg." [*Laughter*] "And number four, you can't have Christmas without eggnog." [*Laughter*] "Number five, the Soviets and the Cubans are trying to steal Christmas." [*Laughter*] "And number six, we stopped them." [*Laughter*]

But in foreign policy, we've let the world know once again that America stands for the political, religious, and economic freedom of mankind. In Grenada, we did set a nation free. And with the help of the National Bipartisan Commission on Central America, we've worked to develop a new consensus to support democracy in that region. The peace process in Lebanon has been slow and painful. But there has been genuine progress toward the goals of internal stability and the withdrawal of all foreign forces.

In Europe, the NATO alliance has held firm, despite months of Soviet bluster. Sooner or later the Soviets are going to realize that equitable and verifiable arms reductions are in their interest, too. And, as I made clear in my address earlier this week, when they do, we'll be at the table, waiting for them, ready to go on negotiating real arms reductions. And we'll be determined that they will abide by the agreements that they have made. By strengthening our defenses and showing the world our willingness to negotiate, we have laid the foundation for a lasting world peace.

We still have a lot to do: wringing out more waste and fraud in government, putting more Americans back to work, attacking the Federal deficit, getting inflation and interest rates down still further—these and other great labors lie before us.

And I have to say to you that—and I think it's time we remind ourselves, be-

cause you know, it's easy to when you're in Rome do as the Romans do, and now we're in Washington. [*Laughter*] There's been a tendency in the past every time someone raised a voice about reducing government cost, reducing extravagance and so forth or spending, that then there were voices raised with special interests in mind who would say, "All right. You want to cut government spending. Which program do you want to eliminate?" And that usually wins the argument until we think through to something else.

Most government programs are well intentioned, and they serve a purpose. And it isn't necessary to eliminate some of government's legitimate functions in order to bring down government spending. What we came here to do, we must remind ourselves and remind those others in and out of government, is to run all those programs efficiently and more economically than they have ever been run before. And it can be done.

Now, one thing also that I want to make plain: For this administration, it isn't going to matter that this is a political year. We'll do what is best for the people and let politics take care of themselves. And won't some of the people in this town be surprised when they find out that doing what's good for the people also turns out to be good politics.

You may remember that verse in the Bible that says, "Your old men will dream dreams; your young men will see visions." Well, I deeply believe that this is just such a time of reawakening in America, a time when our country is healing the wounds of the past and beginning to look with courage and confidence to the future. Yes, we are making a new beginning.

The dream we share is a great dream—perhaps the greatest dream in all history. It's a dream of broad and open land that offers opportunity to all. It's a dream of a magnificent country that represents a force for peace and good will among nations. All of us have been laboring in the name of that dream. Today let us rededicate ourselves to that great work.

Yes, we'll suffer setbacks, and yes, others will do all they can to place obstacles in our path. But if we have the courage to do all that we can to make our dream come true, then we will achieve great good in this world, and we'll do our duty to our fellow men, to our beloved country, and to our God.

Thank you, and God bless you all.

Note: The President spoke at 11:39 a.m. to the Presidential appointees assembled in Constitution Hall.

Statement Following the Opening Session of the Conference on Confidence and Security Building Measures and Disarmament in Europe
January 20, 1984

Secretary of State Shultz has just returned from Stockholm, Sweden, where he represented the United States at the opening of the European Security Conference, known as the CDE. Together with the Foreign Ministers of 34 other countries, he discussed East-West relations and, in particular, peace and security in Europe.

The primary purposes of the Stockholm Conference is to reduce the risk of surprise attack or war by accident or misunderstanding. The historical justification is clear. Twice in this century, Europe has been the scene of terrible conflict.

We must never allow this to happen again. Therefore, to strengthen the prospects for peace and security in Europe, the United States and our NATO allies will propose a package of practical and concrete measures at the CDE. We will suggest that all states of Europe, East and West alike, agree:

—to exchange information about their military forces and provide annual previews of military exercises;

—to give advance notification of significant military activities and invite observers to those activities;

—to enhance the capacity for rapid communications among our governments; and

—to provide for verification of compliance with the commitments made at the conference.

At the same time, we recognize that these steps alone cannot safeguard the peace in Europe and the United States cannot succeed alone. We can only do so in concert with our friends and allies. A hall-mark of our foreign policy has been to build consensus among our partners in Europe and Asia—a consensus covering the full range of political, economic, and military issues.

The Atlantic alliance is demonstrating once again in Stockholm that it remains the keystone of peace and security in Europe. Because we and our allies stand together, we are better able to meet our common challenges we face.

None of these challenges is more important than the need to establish a constructive relationship with the Soviet Union. Last Monday, I proposed that we and the Soviet Union make a major effort to secure progress in three vital areas:

—first, to find ways to reduce, and eventually do away with, the threat and use of force in international affairs;

—second, to find ways to reduce the vast stockpiles of armaments in the world;

—third, to establish a better working relationship with each other, one marked by greater cooperation and understanding.

The meetings this past week in Stockholm helped us toward these ends. Secretary Shultz and Foreign Minister Gromyko had a full and serious exchange of views on key global questions. Of course, they did not resolve our differences. But the important thing is that despite those differences, we are determined to continue our efforts to make Europe and the world a safer and more secure place in which all of us may live in peace and dignity.

Note: The White House also announced that on the same day Secretary of State George P. Shultz met with the President in the Oval Office to discuss the Conference and the meeting with Soviet Foreign Minister Andrey A. Gromyko.

Radio Address to the Nation on the Economic Recovery Program
January 21, 1984

My fellow Americans:

It's that time again when we're deluged by a blizzard of economic facts, figures, and predictions. I hope you'll keep in mind that economic forecasting is far from a perfect science. If recent history is any guide, the experts have some explaining to do about what they told us had to happen but never did.

When our economic program first began in late 1981, many of the doom-criers had warned it would push inflation and interest rates through the roof. It hasn't quite worked out that way. We inherited 12.4-percent inflation in 1980; today it's 3.2. And the prime interest rate has dropped from over 21 percent to 11 percent.

Last year, those pessimists were back again. They told us bad times would go on and on and on. One forecaster said we were on the brink of a major collapse. Another one of Wall Street's favorites made headlines when he said the recovery would be "one of the weakest on record."

I'm not trying to belabor a point, but these predictions just aren't panning out. Far from being weak, this recovery has been one of the strongest since the 1960's. More people are on the job than ever before in our history. From solid growth in housing to new frontiers in high technology, from a healthy recovery in real wages to a big improvement in productivity, and from record increases in venture capital to new highs in the stock market, America is moving forward, getting stronger, and confounding everyone who said it can't be done. Well, like "The Little Engine That Could," it is being done.

I only wish this would convince the naysayers to let up a little, but they don't seem willing. This year we're hearing a new variation of their gloomy refrain, not about in-flation or interest rates taking off, not about the recovery that won't happen, but about the recovery that can't last. Government deficits, we're told, will kill the recovery by draining capital needed by business to keep the economy expanding.

Well, I happen to believe those who underestimated the strength of this recovery may be wrong about the size of future deficits, too. But let's be clear: The deficits do matter. The problem is they were created by a pattern of overspending that began 50 years ago and that's been hard to break. We must bring deficits down and work toward a balanced budget. The question is: How? By spending cuts and economic growth or by tax increases? I don't think you need to be an economist to understand the evidence. We don't face large deficits because you're not taxed enough; we face those deficits because government spends too much.

Even with our tax reductions now in place, families are still being taxed at near record peacetime levels. Yet, as fast as taxes have gone up, spending has gone up even faster. In the past, raising taxes simply encouraged government to spend more. And since people had less money in their pockets to spend or save, economic growth was hurt. So fewer people were employed and able to pay taxes. Deficits went up, not down.

The World Bank has released a study showing that countries with lower tax burdens have consistently enjoyed higher growth rates. Japan, where I recently visited, has had the lowest tax burden and the highest growth rates of all the developed nations.

We must try harder to reduce spending. Back in 1967, as Governor of California, I asked a group of business executives to survey the State bureaucracy and identify potential savings. They made about 2,000 recommendations, and we implemented most of them. Their work helped return fiscal integrity to a State that had been spending a million dollars a day it didn't have.

Now, we're trying the same approach in Washington, because believe me, there's plenty of fat to cut. The Grace commission, comprised of nearly 2,000 leaders from private industry, has just presented us a blueprint for reducing wasteful spending. The commission recommended that the Federal Government upgrade its computer systems. This could save $4 billion. Tracking certain incorrect pension payments could save $4 billion. These are but two of some 2,500 examples that could save taxpayers billions and billions of dollars. And, as the late Senator Everett Dirksen said, "A billion here, a billion there—pretty soon you're talking about real money."

We should prepare for strong protests from Washington-based representatives of the many special interest groups. They will fear that implementing such management reforms means cuts for their favorite programs. What we're really talking about is doing things more efficiently without hurting people in need and without compromising America's security.

Yes, we have a deficit problem. But let's be sensible about it. When warnings about deficits seem to be hysterical, just remember the lessons of recent history. Predictions are often wrong. Some may be using predictions to mask their favorite pastime—raising your taxes; others may underestimate our ability to cut government down to size over time.

Like death and taxes, the doom-criers will always be with us. And they'll always be wrong about America until they realize progress begins with trusting the people. With your support, we'll make this year's batch of pessimists as wrong as last year's.

Till next week, thanks for listening, and God bless you.

Note: The President spoke at 12:06 p.m. from Camp David, MD.

Recess Appointment of Maureen E. Corcoran as General Counsel of the Department of Education
January 21, 1984

The President has recess appointed Maureen E. Corcoran to be General Counsel, Department of Education. She will succeed Daniel Oliver. This appointment is effective January 20, 1984.

Ms. Corcoran is an associate counsel with the law firm of Weissburg and Aronson, Inc., in San Francisco, CA. Previously, she was a Special Assistant to the United States Attorney in Washington, DC, in 1983; Special Assistant to the General Counsel at the Department of Health and Human Services in 1981–1983; attorney with the firm of Hassard, Bonnington, Rogers & Huber, San Francisco, CA, in 1979–1981; and a California Supreme Court Extern in 1978.

She graduated from the University of Iowa (M.A., B.A.) and Hastings College of Law (J.D., 1979). She was born February 4, 1944, in Iowa City, IA, and now resides in San Francisco, CA.

Recess Appointment of Two Members of the Board of Directors of the Legal Services Corporation
January 21, 1984

The President today recess appointed the following individuals to be members of the Board of Directors of the Legal Services Corporation:

Albert Angrisani would succeed Frank J. Donatelli. Mr. Angrisani recently served as Assistant Secretary of Labor (Employment and Training) (1981–1983). Previously he was with the Chase Manhattan Bank as vice president (1978–1981), assistant vice president (1977–1978), investments and product manager (1974–1977), and investment assistant (1972–1974). Mr. Angrisani graduated from Washington and Lee University (B.A., 1971), Fairleigh Dickinson University (M.B.A., 1974), and New York University

(A.P.C., 1978). He is married and resides in New Jersey. He was born August 26, 1949.

Peter Joseph Ferrara would succeed William F. Harvey. Mr. Ferrara is currently associate attorney with the firm of Shaw, Pittman, Potts & Trowbridge (1983–present). Previously, he was in the Office of Policy Development at the White House (1982–1983), in the Office of Policy Development at the Department of Housing and Urban Development (1981–1982), and an associate attorney with the firm of Cravath, Swain & Moore (1979–1981). Mr. Ferrara graduated from Harvard College (B.A., 1976) and from Harvard Law School (J.D., 1979). He is married and resides in Washington, DC. He was born April 26, 1955.

Interview With Lou Cannon, David Hoffman, and Juan Williams of the Washington Post on Foreign and Domestic Issues
January 16, 1984

Administration Accomplishments

Mr. Cannon. Mr. President, as you may know, we're preparing a story for this Sunday's Post on the third anniversary—right after the third anniversary of your inauguration, that's going to try to look at what's been accomplished and what might lie ahead.

We'd like to ask you, what is it you feel that you've achieved as President—as a central achievement? What do you think there's—do you still think there's left to do? And assuming on our part that you intend to seek a second term—we're not going to step on your announcement, but if that should happen, why is it you would want to run again? What would you want to accomplish in that second term?

The President. Well, let's start out with the situation as of 3 years ago: skyrocketing interest rates, higher than they've been in a hundred years; inflation in double digits; a continued decline in business; and a continued increase in unemployment. And today we're in the midst of a recovery. While the

interest rates are still too high, they're only about half of what they were. We have returned to economic growth without inflation. In fact, we've brought inflation down to about a fourth or so of what it was. It's 3.2 for the year. Personal earnings, after taxes, increased last year about 5 percent—real income, about 5 percent.

All of this turnaround, this economic turnaround, I think, is one of the great accomplishments, because a great many economists are suggesting that it not only is a recovery from the recession but that it is the beginning of growth and expansion. Prior to this time, we were told that we might—you'll remember, voices were saying that we might have to give up the idea that there's any future growth in America, that it would be a no-growth society. Voices were saying that inflation was institutionalized and it would take a decade at least of great effort before it could ever be brought under control.

We have about 4 million more people working today than we had working a year

61

ago at this time, and that's one of the biggest increases—or decreases, I should say, in unemployment in a great many years.

Mr. Cannon. What do you still think there's left to do, then? You seem to have done so much.

The President. Well, no, there is much to do. But, on the other hand, there were other things.

I said repeatedly—and long before I was ever a candidate for this job—in recent years there's been a growing hunger in our land for what I called a spiritual revival. A feeling again of people with a belief in themselves and in our country, a belief in our institutions.

We know that, in the defense field, that our national security had been badly eroded. We know that we didn't have the approval or respect of many of our neighbors and allies and certainly of our adversaries. All of this has changed also.

But now, you just say, why? Well now, without saying what I'm going to say on the 29th, one way or the other, no, the job isn't finished. Not with those deficits out there that have to be brought under control. We haven't gotten all of the economic improvements that we asked for. And no one ever wants to walk away from a job unfinished.

Mr. Cannon. If there was to be a second Reagan administration, a second term, what would be your central purpose in it? What would you want most to accomplish in that second term?

The President. To continue on the same economic path to where we did have not only just a recovery but a return to a growth economy in this country. To continue what I think we have started, and that is a real, viable search for peace, particularly by way of disarmament. And that is the goal above all that—must meet.

I remember as a small boy the war to end all wars, World War I. But I also remember coming out of World War II and coming out of uniform with the firm conviction, this must never happen again. And I still have that conviction.

We've only begun in the area of trying to better international relations and bring about reduction of armaments, and particularly a reduction of nuclear weapons, and, hopefully, one day, the total elimination of

them. All that remains to be done.

There are other things on the social side here in our own system, apart from the economic things, legislative matters. There are things like reforms in our budgetary system, the adoption of constitutional amendments to require a balanced budget as so many of our States do, line-item veto power for a President to help curb spending and keep it under control. But then, in the social area, restoration of prayer in schools, treatment of the problems of abortion. There are things of that kind that I haven't fallen back from or retreated from and we still haven't made much progress with.

Mr. Cannon. When you took office, some of those things that you mentioned were items like the line-item veto, which you have in Sacramento. And there were people in your administration who described Washington kind of as a big Sacramento and said that you could deal with the problems here much the way you did there. Has that turned out to be true, and has there been anything that you've learned from being here in the White House specifically that you didn't bring when you came from Sacramento?

The President. Well, of course, there is one phase and one facet of this job that no one has at the State level, and that is foreign policy. I think I was surprised at how much a part of the job that is, how much, what percentage of your time and effort and thinking is devoted to the international situation.

But with regard to domestic policies—and I never referred to it as just a big Sacramento—but the same situation—it's a very funny thing—prevailed. When I became Governor of California, California was in a desperate economic strait. It was spending a million dollars a day more than we were taking in. I know the figures are a little different at the State level than they are at the Federal level. California is about 10 percent of the population of the Nation. But we had to deal with that, and there we had a time consideration in dealing with it, because California does have a constitutional provision that you cannot have a deficit. And you come into office in the middle of the fiscal year. So, a deficit had already been piled up, and we only had 6 months to treat with that problem.

But that and the other part of the situation is I had a legislature the majority of which belonged to the other party, in that case, in both houses. Here, at least, we have a majority in one House. So, it'd be difficult for there to be too many surprises. I was kind of geared—the only experience I'd had was dealing with that kind of a situation.

Foreign Policy

Mr. Cannon. When you entered office here you were preoccupied, as you said, with the problems of the economy——

The President. Yes.

Mr. Cannon. ——and 3 months into your term you're the target of an assassination attempt and are wounded. Looking back on it, do you think that in the first year you left, perhaps of necessity, foreign policy issues too much to your subordinates, or how do you feel about that period now?

The President. Oh, no. No, from the very first, as a matter of fact, lying in that hospital bed after that assassination attempt, I wrote a letter to Leonid Brezhnev on our relationship and sent it to him in longhand as I had written it.

No, you can't be here very long without realizing that that is very much an important part of this job. When I expressed earlier my surprise, I guess it was just that, as I say, I hadn't anticipated that it was that much of a daily problem.

From my own experience in California, it is true I came here with my attention fixed on the great economic problems that faced us. At the same time, I had declared over and over again that I was going to see if we couldn't embark on a refurbishing of our defensive capability, which had been allowed to decline so much. It didn't take me long, as I say, to find out that the international situation was very much a part of the daily schedule.

Mr. Cannon. How much does the President—you, any President—control this international situation? I mean, as a President do you feel you can effect control of these foreign situations from the Oval Office, or are you pretty well governed by events over which neither you nor anybody

else has any control?

The President. Well, with a great big wide world out there, there are always going to be events and surprises. But you have to deal with those, and you have to deal very definitely with the problem of your relations with the friendly nations of the world, as well as the adversarial ones. And you'd better start right in doing that, which I did.

Let me, just if I could, illustrate a surprise, a real physical surprise that came to me. Getting in the helicopter on the South Lawn to go someplace across—out of the District—about a half-an-hour flight—to a luncheon invitation. And that was my first awareness, leaving the White House just that distance, to discover that now, wherever a President of the United States goes, phones have been installed, all the communication equipment and so forth, that keeps you in touch with every corner of the world. And I was. I was overwhelmed to discover that, that I couldn't do something of that kind without having that kind of preparation take place.

Mr. Cannon. This just a few days after you became President?

The President. Yes. And it brought home to you that—and when you stop to think about it, I had to say to myself, I understand the necessity for this. This isn't something in which I could say, "Well, this is foolish. Isn't this excessive?" No. It isn't excessive. And you know that there's one person, yourself, who must be available for instant communication worldwide.

U.S.-Soviet Relations

Mr. Cannon. You said in a recent interview that you would not use the phrase now "focus of evil" to apply to the Soviet Union. Your language today in this speech was obviously very careful. Do you think that some of your own rhetoric, phrases like "evil empire" and so forth have—whether or not those are accurate descriptions, do you think those phrases have contributed to the difficulty of negotiating, dealing with the Soviets?

The President. No. And really, I think they have been overplayed and overexaggerated in much of the talk about the present international situation. We are not in greater danger. We are not closer to a war than we were a few years ago. The rhetoric—and all you have to do is look back at the pattern of Soviet rhetoric, no matter who is in the White House, and what has been going on for years, that we're "imperialists," we're "aggressors," we're all of these things that they've been saying about us. No, I'm not repeating some of those things simply because I said them, and what I felt was necessary was for the Soviet Union to know that we were facing reality and that there was some realism on our part with regard to them and their style.

Lou, let me take advantage of this to straighten something out, that ever since the first press conference, there has been a distortion of an answer of mine to a question there that has become just accepted, and that is that I called the Soviets a lot of names, gave an answer to a question about dealing with the Soviets. And everyone seems to have forgotten that I was quoting them with regard to lying, cheating, and so forth. I didn't say that, that that was my opinion of them. I made it very plain that they themselves, in their writing and speaking over the years, have said that anything of this kind that furthers socialism is moral. They do not view it as immoral if it furthers their cause. Lenin's famous line that "Treaties are like pie crusts. They're made to be broken." So——

Mr. Cannon. Well, even if they said it, do you think it was wise of you to bring it up?

The President. Yes. I thought that it was necessary that they know. Now, I did not volunteer that as a statement. It was an answer to a question. But I think it was necessary for them to know that we were looking at them realistically from here. There was an end to what, I think, maybe has been prevalent in some dealings for several years, and that is the idea that, well, they were just a mirror image of ourselves, and you could shake hands on someone's word and walk away confident that a deal had been made. That, no, we were aware of the differences between our two societies in our approach to things, and we intended to deal with that realism.

Mr. Cannon. You said—you touched on this today in your speech—and you said

today that we're safer than we were when, I think, when you took office.

The President. Yes.

Mr. Cannon. With the negotiations broken off and a pretty good stream of rhetoric from the other side, what's the evidence that we're safer and that this defense buildup which you advocated and achieved has made this country safer than it was?

The President. Because—with realism on their part—we have a deterrent capacity we didn't have 3 years ago. Now, you are in danger if a possible adversary thinks that an action of his would not lead to unacceptable punishment. And I think the very fact that we have proceeded on this path would require them, with their realism, to say, this, it would be unacceptable, the damage to ourselves.

Mr. Williams. Excuse me, can I just interject here to ask you if you think that the American people haven't heard that message from you, and do you really think that they feel safer today than they did when you were elected?

The President. I have to say that, from all the reports that I'm getting, and from all the contact that I, myself, have—whether it's through mail or personal meetings or meeting new people, as well as old friends—that, yes, there is a new feeling on the part of the American people. They have a confidence that they didn't have just a short time ago when they knew that the Soviet Union had engaged in this massive arms buildup and they saw evidences that we hadn't.

Not only the decline in quality, as well as in quantity, the restiveness of our NATO allies about whether we were dependable as an ally—I think there's a great change in the feeling of our people now. I think a little evidence of that—granted, this wasn't any great military operation, but I think the reaction of our people to the success of our rescue mission in Grenada was an indication.

Lebanon

Mr. Hoffman. Mr. President, speaking of Grenada, and turning to another foreign policy issue, when we sent American forces to Grenada, they were welcomed. When you sent American forces to Lebanon, they've been shot at. What, in your mind, accounts for the difference in that reception?

The President. Oh, well, let me put two things out. For one thing, there was no question that we rescued some people that—not just Americans. The Grenadians, themselves, made it plain that they were not happy with the form of government that they saw being imposed on themselves.

But let's go back to when we first sent the marines to Beirut. And remember, they went in answer to a request from the Lebanese Government. But Beirut was a battlefield. Thousands and thousands of civilians were being killed, were being wounded and maimed because a battle—a war was being fought right within the streets of the city.

We arrived and were well received by the people there. As a matter of fact, our American marines in a typical American military fashion, pretty soon were organizing helpful things for kids, teaching them to play ball, and all the sort of things of this kind in the city. I have mail that indicates that the people felt that finally they had a chance to live relatively normal lives.

Now, granted, that very much divided society is a place where you're never quite sure that there isn't going to be a sniper in the street, some terrorism of some account. But all this went on, and a great deal of progress was made: the agreement between Lebanon and Israel, Israel's withdrawal, the beginning of communications between some of the internal factions and the Lebanese Government; the progress in the Lebanese—in building their own military, in which we were very much a part. Our training, our provision of weapons built that army up to about 35,000, as it is right now, and it's continuing to build up. And it has conducted itself well in the battles that it has been engaged in. It's proven that it is a capable military.

Now, all of this—I have a letter from a young man—actually, he's Greek, but his job and his life is in Lebanon. And this letter didn't come to me; it was sent to his girlfriend, who doesn't live in Lebanon. And she thought I would like to see this letter. And he was telling her of the experiences and what the marines meant, and

telling her what the slaughter would have been if it was not for the presence of marines.

But now, a few months ago, this started, the thing that you've mentioned—this attack not only on our marines but on the others of the multinational force. And it started, I think, for one reason, and it's very obvious, one reason only. There are terrorist elements who know that they cannot succeed in their cause while the multinational force is there. And they are trying to take advantage of what they see as criticism here, lack of public support in the hope that public opinion will force the withdrawal of the multinational force. And it would be disaster if they succeeded.

But what we should see is that the very fact they're doing that is proof of the fact that the multinational force was being successful in its purpose.

Mr. Hoffman. Given that these terrorist attacks began, do you agree with the Long commission that the mission of the marines changed while they were there and that they were unwisely deployed, specifically at the Beirut Airport?

The President. Well, I've read that report very carefully. And, frankly, I thought it was a fine report. I thought they had great understanding in everything that they were criticizing there. I don't interpret their suggesting a change in the mission as meaning that they had one purpose when they went there and now, suddenly, they've changed and have a different purpose.

The only incident that could be interpreted as them participating in a military action, say, in alliance with the Lebanese forces had to do with one in which the decision was very carefully considered and before it was made, and that is at Suq al-Gharb, the little village of Suq al-Gharb, which looks down the throat of our forces there, as well as others. It's about the situation of Capitol Hill with regard to the White House, geographically. It's that much proximity. And the Lebanese Armed Forces were in an engagement, and this was at a period before they were as well built-up as they are now, to retake and preserve Suq al-Gharb from being possessed by the same forces that are creating the terror and so forth.

Well, we believed that if we were going to have the marines at the airport there, that we had a stake in their security and safety. And so, we joined in during that engagement with naval offshore artillery, in support of the Lebanese Armed Force.

Now, I don't think that that makes us as presently changing our purpose or our mission. The decision was made based on the fact that our marines would be in an untenable position if that area in the hills looking down on them fell into those hostile hands. So, we helped in the preservation of it as a neutral territory.

No, the mission is still what it was, and that is that—remember that the main goal was the departure from Lebanon of foreign forces. We helped in the evacuation of the PLO, which was definitely one of the hostile foreign forces. Granted, many of them then came back in by way of Syria and other places, but that was out.

We had had the word previously that both Israel and Syria would withdraw when the Lebanese Government was able to take over the policing of its own territory. The multinational force was to be there, you might say, behind the Lebanese Army, helping preserve order in that divided land while they went out and restored sovereignty. Well, Israel withdrew to much closer to their own borders. They're not fully withdrawn, but because Syria then balked and said no, they would not withdraw. And so, the mission still remains to enable the Lebanese Armed Forces and the Lebanese Government to resume control over their own sovereignty, their own territory.

Mr. Hoffman. That remains the mission, but, Mr. President, you're well known for your optimism. Do you think, in retrospect, you were just too optimistic in believing that sending the marines there could bring about a prompt diplomatic solution, given what's happened in the past year?

The President. No, I never set any timetable on it, never thought it was something that was going to happen in 48 hours. We had—remember, with Phil Habib, the long time and before any marines were ever, anything of that kind ever sent there—his shuttle diplomacy and the successes that he had. Incidentally, this was at a time when Israel had invaded, and all the way into Beirut, and was battling the PLO in Beirut. If you look at what has been achieved, and if you look at the difference in spite of the still ongoing fire and fighting that's going on, there has been great progress made.

No, I don't think we were over-optimistic. This was part of our whole, overall peace plan for the Middle East. We did not feel since a fair, legitimate settlement of the PLO problem—the Palestinian problem must be a part of the peace proposal that I made a year ago September—that it could not go forward while you had that war going on in Lebanon. So, Lebanon, which is not really, you might say, the primary part of what we're trying to achieve, which is finally a peace between the Arab nations and Israel. To date, other than Lebanon, the only peace treaty that we have is between Egypt and Israel.

What we're aspiring to are more Egypts, more Arab nations that will drop that claim that Israel has no right to exist, will recognize their right to exist, will come into peace negotiations with them. But it seemed that you could not move on that until you settled this Lebanon issue and then proceeded on. And we still think there is movement. Maybe now it has reached a point that we can begin to proceed with the broader peace initiatives. All of this is part of the diplomatic exchanges that are going on.

Mr. Cannon. We have two questions. Could we ask them both? Do you have time? We'll make it quick. You go first and——

Mr. Speakes.[1] Does it have something to do with the article on Sunday?

Mr. Cannon. Yes. They both do.

The Federal Budget

Mr. Hoffman. Mr. President, in 1980 you—is this not the one——

Mr. Cannon. Yeah—No, that's fine.

Mr. Hoffman. In 1980 you expressed a lot of confidence that you could balance the budget, build up the defense budget, and

---

[1]*Larry M. Speakes, Principal Deputy Press Secretary to the President.*

cut taxes, and you could accomplish all three of these. In retrospect—and one of your officials said last week that it was good that you accomplished two out of the three—do you think you promised too much in terms of reducing the deficit?

The President. No, but, again, with all of this having to project economic situations 5 years ahead and so forth, which I don't believe in—I think the best of economists aren't very much good beyond the first year, and most of them will privately admit it to you. The thing was no one—there had been no prediction of the sudden deepening of the recession. That caught everyone by surprise. And that has had a lot to do with the fact that only two out of three so far. We have not balanced the budget.

Fifty percent of the deficit is occasioned by the recession, the fact that people, instead of being employed and paying taxes, suddenly became dependents, you might say, of government because they were no longer working and paying taxes—the great increase in unemployment that took place. That was one.

There was one other thing that none of us could foresee, and again it comes down to projections. None of us ever dreamed that we could be as successful in lowering inflation as we were. And you must realize that inflation accounts for some of your tax revenue—the bracket-squeeze that takes place on people. And our tax revenues dropped below what had been projected by us because of the effect of the reduced inflation. So, we had to readjust our projections based on how far down we had brought inflation. So, we did not foresee that.

I still believe that, in spite of this setback, that we can—and with the cooperation of Congress, proceeding on the same lines involving both further spending, getting the spending measures or the cuts that we asked for and have not yet gotten. Remember, our deficits would be considerably smaller if Congress had given us all the cuts in spending that we asked for. They didn't. But we're going to continue on that path.

And we're going to continue looking at the longer range on planning and reviewing those things that you might say are structural changes in government that have not

been dealt with as yet, so that you don't have a built-in increase in spending that is—well, as Congress itself refers to it—as "uncontrollable." You know, if you pass something that guarantees a constant increase in spending, and you've passed the measure, and then you never have to lay hands on it again, it just automatically keeps increasing. That is uncontrollable only to the sense that you and Congress and the government are not willing to deal with it and change what you did that was wrong.

Mr. Cannon. Juan, do you want to take the last question?

Mr. Williams. Yeah.

Mr. Cannon. I guess we overstayed our time. Thank you, Larry, for your patience here.

Civil Rights

Mr. Williams. Martin Luther King's birthday was Sunday. And many people celebrate that because of the efforts he put into bringing about changes in the laws in the country—put in civil rights laws so that blacks and whites would have equal treatment under the law. Do you think there's anything more to be done now by the government, by anyone, to bring about equality between the races?

The President. Oh, yes, although I do think that—you know, you can't, I guess, ever totally erase anyplace in the world among human beings, bigotry and prejudice, one way or the other. Hatreds go both ways.

But, having lived longer than anybody in this room, I have firsthand memories of the situation as it was, and I sometimes wonder if some of you who are younger realize how far we have come, how totally different this country is than what it was then. But that doesn't mean that you quit. No, there are heritages left over from that time. Occupations, let's say, and jobs and so forth that were once denied to a segment of our society and now are open to them, but they don't have a past history and tradition going way back in them. So that, you have to be alert, and you have to continue making sure that we don't fall back into any of the other patterns.

Mr. Williams. Well, as a followup to that,

if you were a young—let's say that Ronald Reagan was a young black woman in Dixon, Illinois, today, trying to make it in America, and Ronald Reagan was the President, do you think that that young black woman would prosper?

The President. Yes. And I think that much of what we've done in our economic recovery has been more beneficial at the bottom of the economic ladder. And we have to admit that because of past practices, that a disproportionate number of blacks and other minorities are in that segment of the population, at the bottom of the ladder. But there are also a great many whites that are in that too. But the things that we have done in the economic recovery benefited them first and most of all.

Let's take someone who only had an income of $5,000, which is way below the poverty line, as we know, at the beginning of 1979. By the end of 1980, in just those 2 years, that $5,000 had lost 20 percent in purchasing power. It would only buy $4,000 worth of food and shelter and clothing.

Now, the very fact of inflation alone, look what it has done for those same people. Today, the person at the—the average family, the median income has $3,300 more in purchasing power than they would have had if we had stayed at the same tax and inflation rates of 1980.

The very fact that now the—even with the unemployment—the fact that there are more people working than have ever worked before in our history, and not just more in numbers, that you could say, "Well, it's accounted for by the growth in our population." No, a higher percentage of all the people between 16 and 65, which is taken as the work force in—the potential work force; a higher percentage of those people are actually employed today, even with our continued, above-normal unemployment, than at any time in our previous history. And the truth is that for both women and for minorities, the percentage of decline in unemployment is greater for both women and minorities than it has been for the adult male—or white male.

So, I think we have done those things. I'm going to be referring to this young lady in a speech. She was on the air the other night; a story of—she didn't come from Dixon, Illinois, but 90 miles away—Chicago, out of a ghetto. Raised by a grandmother. And today runs a tremendously successful, multimillion-dollar advertising agency in the city of Chicago.

Mr. Williams. That's wonderful.

The President. And she happens to be black. And she's the sole head and proprietor of this successful operation.

Mr. Williams. And it's not the case that that person would get the breaks only because of tax breaks given to the rich or something like that?

The President. No. As a matter of fact, that again—that, too, is a distortion, that our tax program gave the breaks to the rich. Let me just draw a contrast with numbers so I won't have to try and convince you by rhetoric.

John F. Kennedy had a tax reduction program somewhat similar to ours back in the early sixties. Some of his own party opposed him very much on this, but he went forward with it and said it will stimulate the economy. It'll actually increase, eventually, revenues, more than decrease them. And it did.

Now, 29 percent of his tax relief went to business; only 23 percent of ours did. And he gave greater cuts to the top five tax brackets than we did with ours; our greater percentage of ours is below the top brackets in this 25 percent across the board that we put in. But in addition to that, we put in some other things, like giving working mothers more tax credit or deduction for child care that they might have to provide; like giving the working wives—there's a tax penalty on them in the income tax. We reduced that very sizably. Now most two-earner families are two earners because they are at the lower end of the earning scale. We did a number of things which has benefited at the lower level more than at the upper level.

Yes, I think there's a greater opportunity for young people today in this country than there's been for a long, long time. And, well, when I was a sports announcer after I got out of college—just let's look at one difference. You push that button and you look at pro football and you look at pro baseball, you look at pro basketball. Well, when I was a sports announcer, blacks were not allowed to play in any of those games— organized games. And there were a lot of us at that time that editorialized like hell against that and said that was wrong. And it was wrong, and it's all been changed.

Messrs. Cannon, Hoffman, and Williams.

Thank you, Mr. President.

Note: The interview began at 2:37 p.m. in the Oval Office at the White House.

The transcript of the interview was released by the Office of the Press Secretary on January 22.

Remarks by Telephone With Coach Tom Flores of the Los Angeles Raiders Following Super Bowl XVIII
January 22, 1984

The President. Coach Tom Flores?

Coach Flores. Yes, Mr. President.

The President. Congratulations. That was a wonderful win tonight. I just think you ought to know, though, that you've given me some problems. I have already had a call from Moscow. They think that Marcus Allen is a new secret weapon and they insist that we dismantle it. [*Laughter*] Now, they've given me an idea about that team that I just saw there of yours. If you'd turn them over to us, we'd put them in silos and we wouldn't have to build the MX missile. [*Laughter*] But it's been great. You proved tonight that a good defense can also be a pretty good offense.

Coach Flores. Well, thank you, Mr. President. I really appreciate it. We played a good game tonight. Our players were just tremendous in every phase. We totally dominated. I think we proved to the whole world that the silver and black is the best

team.

The President. Well, you certainly were from what we saw out there on the field tonight. And, again, my congratulations to you. God bless all of you. And there isn't anything that I could say that would make you any happier than you all must be.

Coach Flores. Well, thank you. I wish you were here to enjoy it with us, but I appreciate your call. Thank you very much.

The President. You bet.

Note: The President spoke at 8:30 p.m. from the Diplomatic Reception Room at the White House. The conversation with Coach Flores was broadcast live on the CBS network following the Raiders 38 to 9 victory over the Washington Redskins in Tampa, FL.

The President also spoke with Jack Kent Cooke, owner, and Joe Gibbs, coach, Washington Redskins.

Letter Accepting the Resignation of William French Smith as Attorney General of the United States
January 23, 1984

The President today accepted with deepest appreciation and regret the resignation of Attorney General William French Smith, effective upon the confirmation of his successor.

The President announced his intention to appoint William French Smith, upon his

resignation as Attorney General, to the President's Foreign Intelligence Advisory Board.

The text of the exchange of letters follows:

Dear Bill:

It is with deep regret that I accept your

resignation as Attorney General, effective upon the confirmation of your successor.

You have served in a fine tradition with extraordinary distinction. You may take justifiable pride in your contribution to the public good through your many accomplishments at Justice.

Particularly noteworthy among these have been: the strengthening of Justice as a Department through reorganization and improved management procedures; the consolidation of the FBI and the Drug Enforcement Agency in the increased attack on organized crime drug trafficking; the establishment of Law Enforcement Coordinating Committees to promote maximum cooperation among Federal, state and local authorities; the successful international negotiation of important mutual law assistance and extradition treaties; the development and promotion of an historic legislative reform of our criminal laws; the vigorous enforcement of civil rights laws through more productive and effective remedies; the emphasis on economic realism in antitrust policy combined with a more vigorous attack on anti-competitive activities than ever before; and the development of a comprehensive reform of the Nation's immigration laws.

You have indeed enforced the laws fully, effectively, and impartially—while advancing beneficial changes through the Congress and urging proper restraints upon the courts.

While I will deeply miss your continued participation as a member of the Cabinet, I appreciate your offer to participate in the 1984 campaign. And I am especially pleased that you have agreed to serve as a member of the President's Foreign Intelligence Advisory Board. We will all benefit from your continued wise counsel.

Nancy and I extend to you and Jean our very best wishes. We of course look forward to many years of continuing close friendship.

Again, let me express—on my own behalf, and on behalf of the American people—profound appreciation for your contribution to the Nation and for a job well done.

Sincerely,

RON

[The Honorable William French Smith, Attorney General, Department of Justice, Washington, D.C. 20530]

Dear Mr. President:

Surely public service is the greatest confidence that can be bestowed in a democracy. For me—building upon so many years of close friendship and personal association—service in your Cabinet has been both a great honor and a personal pleasure. However, it is now time for me to return to private life. Among the several reasons why I must do so is the strong conviction that the interests of the country require that you run and be re-elected. I have been involved in that process since 1966, and I do not want 1984 to be an exception. This would not be possible in my present position.

As your Attorney General, I have continually kept in mind the words of our first President in offering this post to the Nation's first Attorney General. George Washington wrote to Edmund Randolph that "the due administration of justice is the firmest pillar of good government." With your support and the assistance of the exceptionally fine appointees you named to posts in this Justice Department, we have done our utmost to enforce the laws fully, effectively, and impartially—and to urge beneficial changes upon the Congress and proper restraints upon the courts. I hope that our efforts have indeed provided one of the firm pillars in this Administration—a pillar that can be built upon by you and my successor.

I will leave with the deepest gratitude for the opportunity you provided me to serve the public and with the greatest pride in having served you.

With continuing admiration, respect and affection,

BILL

WILLIAM FRENCH SMITH

[The President, The White House, Washington, D.C. 20500]

Nomination of Edwin Meese III To Be Attorney General of the United States
January 23, 1984

The President today announced his intention to nominate Edwin Meese III to be Attorney General. Mr. Meese would succeed William French Smith.

In announcing Mr. Meese's appointment, the President said that, "While I deeply regret the resignation of a close friend and long-time adviser who has served as one of the nation's very finest Attorneys General, I am delighted to be able to nominate Ed Meese as his successor.

"Ed is not only my trusted Counsellor, he is also a person whose life and experience reflect a profound commitment to the law and a consistent dedication to the improvement of our justice system. I know of no one better able to continue in the fine tradition so well represented by the service of Bill Smith."

Edwin Meese's professional career has spanned 25 years as a lawyer, public official, business executive, and educator.

Since January 1981 he has been Counsellor to the President and a member of the President's Cabinet and National Security Council. He has had management responsibility for those White House units involved in policy development, planning and evaluation, and the administration of the Cabinet.

Starting as a lawyer in 1959, Mr. Meese was appointed a deputy district attorney in Alameda County, CA, where he served as a trial attorney for 8 years, handling major litigation and investigations. During this time he was also legal adviser to the county grand jury and represented the State District Attorney's and Peace Officer's Association before the California Legislature.

Newly elected Governor Reagan selected him to be his legal affairs secretary in 1967. In this position Mr. Meese had responsibility for all legal matters in the Governor's office and for liaison with the judiciary, law enforcement organizations, and the legal profession of California.

From 1967 to 1974, Mr. Meese served as executive assistant and chief of staff to Governor Reagan. In this capacity he directed all activities of the Governor's office and had management responsibility for the Office of Criminal Justice Planning and several other State agencies involved in emergency service.

Entering business in 1975, Mr. Meese was named vice president for administration of Rohr Industries, Inc., an aerospace and transportation company located in Chula Vista, CA. He returned to the private practice of law in 1976, engaging primarily in business and corporate law in San Diego County.

In 1977 Mr. Meese became professor of law at the University of San Diego and served also as director of the law school's Center for Criminal Justice Policy and Management.

He has been active in numerous civic and professional organizations. During 1977–1980 he was vice chairman of California's Organized Crime Control Commission. He is a member of the American Bar Association and its criminal law section's "Committee on the Future." He is a member of the State Bar of California, where he has served on the Criminal Justice and Criminal Law and Procedure Committees. From 1965 to 1967, he was a part-time faculty member at the School of Law at the University of California at Berkeley. He has also lectured widely on legal topics including "The Responsibility of the Legal Profession to Provide Services to the Poor" and "Reform of the Justice System."

Mr. Meese is a life member of the California Police Association and an associate member of the International Association of Chiefs of Police. He is also an honorary member of the National Sheriffs' Association and the National Organization of Black Law Enforcement Executives.

He received his B.A. degree in public administration from Yale University in 1953 and his J.D. degree from the University of California School of Law at Berkeley in 1958. He has also received honorary degrees of doctor of laws from several educational institutions. He served in active duty in the United States Army during 1954–1956, and is currently a colonel in the Army Reserve.

Mr. Meese and his wife Ursula reside in McLean, VA, with their daughter Dana, a high school student. A son, Mike, is an Army officer living with his wife, Ramona, at Fort Ord in California.

Message to the Congress Transmitting a Report and a Fact Sheet on Soviet Noncompliance With Arms Control Agreements
January 23, 1984

To the Congress of the United States:

If the concept of arms control is to have meaning and credibility as a contribution to global or regional stability, it is essential that all parties to agreements comply with them. Because I seek genuine arms control, I am committed to ensuring that existing agreements are observed. In 1982 increasing concerns about Soviet noncompliance with arms control agreements led me to establish a senior group within the Administration to examine verification and compliance issues. For its part the Congress, in the FY 1984 Arms Control and Disarmament Act, asked me to report to it on compliance. I am herewith enclosing a Report to the Congress on Soviet Noncompliance with Arms Control Agreements.

After a careful review of many months, and numerous diplomatic exchanges with the Soviet Union, the Administration has determined that with regard to seven initial issues analyzed, violations and probable violations have occurred with respect to a number of Soviet legal obligations and political commitments in the arms control field.

The United States Government has determined that the Soviet Union is violating the Geneva Protocol on Chemical Weapons, the Biological Weapons Convention, the Helsinki Final Act, and two provisions of SALT II: telemetry encryption and a rule concerning ICBM modernization. In addition, we have determined that the Soviet Union has almost certainly violated the ABM Treaty, probably violated the SALT II limit on new types, probably violated the SS–16 deployment prohibition of SALT II, and is likely to have violated the nuclear testing yield limit of the Threshold Test Ban Treaty.

Soviet noncompliance is a serious matter. It calls into question important security benefits from arms control, and could create new security risks. It undermines the confidence essential to an effective arms control process in the future. It increases doubts about the reliability of the U.S.S.R. as a negotiating partner, and thus damages the chances for establishing a more constructive U.S.-Soviet relationship.

The United States will continue to press its compliance concerns with the Soviet Union through diplomatic channels, and insist upon explanations, clarifications, and corrective actions. At the same time, the United States is continuing to carry out its own obligations and commitments under relevant agreements. For the future, the United States is seeking to negotiate new arms control agreements that reduce the risk of war, enhance the security of the United States and its Allies, and contain effective verification and compliance provisions.

We should recognize, however, that ensuring compliance with arms control agreements remains a serious problem. Better verification and compliance provisions and better treaty drafting will help, and we are working toward this in ongoing negotiations. It is fundamentally important, however, that the Soviets take a constructive attitude toward compliance.

The Executive and Legislative branches of our government have long had a shared interest in supporting the arms control process. Finding effective ways to ensure compliance is central to that process. I look forward to continued close cooperation with the Congress as we seek to move forward in negotiating genuine and enduring arms control agreements.

RONALD REAGAN

The White House,
January 23, 1984.

Fact Sheet

Commitment to genuine arms control requires that all parties comply with agreements. Over the last several years the U.S.S.R. has taken a number of actions that have prompted renewed concern about an expanding pattern of Soviet violations or possible violations of arms control agreements. Because of the critical importance of compliance with arms control agreements, about one year ago the President established an interagency Arms Control Verification Committee, chaired by his Assistant for National Security Affairs, to address verification and compliance issues. In addition, many members of Congress expressed their serious concerns, and the Congress mandated in the FY 84 Arms Control and Disarmament Act Authorization that "The President shall prepare and transmit to the Congress a report of the compliance or noncompliance of the Soviet Union with existing arms control agreements to which the Soviet Union is a Party."

The President's Report to Congress covers seven different matters of serious concern regarding Soviet compliance: chemical, biological, and toxin weapons, the notification of military exercises, a large new Soviet radar being deployed in the Soviet interior, encryption of data needed to verify arms control provisions, the testing of a second new intercontinental ballistic missile (ICBM), the deployment status of an existing Soviet ICBM, and the yields of underground nuclear tests. Additional issues of concern are under active study.

Soviet violations of arms control agreements could create new security risks. Such violations deprive us of the security benefits of arms control directly because of the military consequences of known violations, and indirectly by inducing suspicion about the existence of undetected violations that might have additional military consequences.

We have discussed with the Soviets all of the activities covered in the report, but the Soviets have not been willing to meet our basic concerns which we raised in the Standing Consultative Commission in Geneva and in several diplomatic demarches. Nor have they met our requests to cease these activities. We will continue to pursue these issues.

The Findings

The Report examines the evidence concerning Soviet compliance with: the 1972 Biological Weapons Convention (BWC) and the 1925 Geneva Protocol and customary international law, the 1975 Helsinki Final Act, the 1972 ABM Treaty, the unratified SALT II Treaty, and the unratified Threshold Test Ban Treaty (TTBT) signed in 1974. Preparation of the Report entailed a comprehensive review of the legal obligations, political commitments under existing arms control agreements, and documented interpretations of specific obligations, analyses of all the evidence available on applicable Soviet actions, and a review of the diplomatic exchanges on compliance issues between the U.S. and the Soviet Union.

The findings for the seven issues covered in the Report, as reviewed in terms of the agreements involved, are as follows:

1. *Chemical, Biological, and Toxin Weapons*

—*Treaty Status:* The 1972 Biological and Toxin Weapons Convention (the BWC) and the 1925 Geneva Protocol are multilateral treaties to which both the U.S. and U.S.S.R. are parties. Soviet actions not in accord with these treaties and customary international law relating to the 1925 Geneva Protocol are violations of legal obligations.

—*Obligations:* The BWC bans the development, production, stockpiling or possession, and transfer of: microbial or other biological agents or toxins except for a small quantity for prophylactic, protective or other peaceful purposes. It also bans weapons, equipment and means of delivery of agents or toxins. The 1925 Geneva Protocol and related rules of customary international law prohibit the first use in war of asphyxiating, poisonous or other gases and of all analogous liquids, materials or devices; and prohibits use of bacteriological methods of warfare.

—*Issues:* The study addressed whether the Soviets are in violation of provisions that ban the development, production, transfer, possession and use of biological and toxin weapons.

—*Finding:* The Soviets, by maintaining an offensive biological warfare program and capabilities and through their involvement in the production, transfer and use of toxins and other lethal chemical warfare agents that have been used in Laos, Kampuchea and Afghanistan, have repeatedly violated their legal obligations under the BWC and customary international law as codified in the 1925 Geneva Protocol.

2. *Helsinki Final Act—Notification of Military Exercises*

—*Legal Status:* The Final Act of the Conference on Security and Cooperation in Europe was signed in Helsinki in 1975. This document represents a political commitment and was signed by the United States and the Soviet Union, along with many other states. Soviet actions not in accord with that document are violations of their political commitment.

—*Obligation:* All signatory states of the Helsinki Final Act are committed to give prior notification of, and other details concerning, major military maneuvers, defined as those involving more than 25,000 ground troops.

—*Issues:* The study examined whether notification of the Soviet military exercise Zapad–81, which occurred on September 4–12, 1981, was inadequate and therefore a violation of their political commitment.

—*Finding:* With respect to the Helsinki Final Act, the U.S.S.R. by its inadequate notification of the Zapad–81 military exercise, violated its political commitment under this Act to observe the Confidence-Building Measure requiring appropriate prior notification of certain military exercises.

3. *ABM Treaty—Krasnoyarsk Radar*

—*Treaty Status:* The 1972 ABM Treaty and its subsequent Protocol ban deployment of ABM systems except that each party can deploy one ABM system around the national capital or at a single ICBM deployment area. The ABM Treaty is in

force and is of indefinite duration. Soviet actions not in accord with the ABM Treaty are therefore a violation of a legal obligation.

—*Obligation:* In an effort to preclude a territorial ABM defense, the Treaty limited the deployment of ballistic missile early warning radars, including large phased-array radars used for that purpose, to locations along the national periphery of each party and required that they be oriented outward. The Treaty permits deployment (without regard to location or orientation) of large phased-array radars for purposes of tracking objects in outer space or for use as national technical means of verification of compliance with arms control agreements.

—*Issue:* The study examined the evidence on whether the Soviet deployment of a large phased-array radar near Krasnoyarsk in central Siberia is in violation of the legal obligation to limit the location and orientation of such radars.

—*Finding:* The new radar under construction at Krasnoyarsk almost certainly constitutes a violation of legal obligations under the Anti-Ballistic Missile Treaty of 1972 in that in its associated siting, orientation, and capability, it is prohibited by this Treaty.

SALT II

—*Treaty Status:* SALT II was signed in June 1979. It has not been ratified. In 1981 the United States made clear its intention not to ratify the Treaty. Prior to 1981 both nations were obligated under international law not to take actions which would "defeat the object and purpose" of the signed but unratified Treaty; such Soviet actions before 1981 are violations of legal obligations. Since 1981 the U.S. has observed a political commitment to refrain from actions that undercut SALT II as long as the Soviet Union does likewise. The Soviets have told us they would abide by these provisions also. Soviet actions contrary to SALT II after 1981 are therefore violations of their political commitment.

Three SALT II concerns are addressed: encryption, SS–X–25, and SS–16.

4. *Encryption—Impeding Verification*

—*Obligation:* The provisions of SALT II

ban deliberate concealment measures that impede verification by national technical means. The agreement permits each party to use various methods of transmitting telemetric information during testing, including encryption, but bans deliberate denial of telemetry, such as through encryption, whenever such denial impedes verification.

—*Issue:* The study examined the evidence whether the Soviets have engaged in encryption of missile test telemetry (radio signals) so as to impede verification.

—*Finding:* Soviet encryption practices constitute a violation of a legal obligation prior to 1981 and a violation of their political commitment subsequent to 1981. The nature and extent of encryption of telemetry on new ballistic missiles is an example of deliberate impeding of verification of compliance in violation of this Soviet political commitment.

5. *SS–X–25—2nd New Type, RV Weight to Throw-weight Ratio, Encryption*

—*Obligation:* In an attempt to constrain the modernization and the proliferation of new, more capable types of ICBMs, the provisions of SALT II permit each side to "flight test and deploy" just one new type of "light" ICBM. A new type is defined as one that differs from an existing type by more than 5 percent in length, largest diameter, launch-weight and throw-weight or differs in number of stages or propellant type. In addition, it was agreed that no single reentry vehicle ICBM of an existing type with a post-boost vehicle would be flight-tested or deployed whose reentry vehicle weight is less than 50 percent of the throw-weight of that ICBM. This latter provision was intended to prohibit the possibility that single warhead ICBMs could quickly be converted to MIRVed systems.

—*Issue:* The study examined the evidence: whether the Soviets have tested a second new type of ICBM (the SS–X–25) which is prohibited (the Soviets have declared the SS–X–24 to be their allowed one new type ICBM); whether the reentry vehicle (RV) on that missile, if it is not a new type, is in compliance with the provision that for existing types of single RV missiles, the weight of the RV be equal to at least 50 percent of total throw-weight; and whether

encryption of its tests impedes verification.

—*Finding:* While the evidence is somewhat ambiguous, the SS–X–25 is a probable violation of the Soviets' political commitment to observe the SALT II provision limiting each party to one new type of ICBM. Furthermore, even if we were to accept the Soviet argument that the SS–X–25 is not a prohibited new type of ICBM, based on the one test for which data are available, it would be a violation of their political commitment to observe the SALT II provision which prohibits (for existing types of single reentry vehicle ICBMs) the testing of such an ICBM with a reentry vehicle whose weight is less than 50 percent of the throw-weight of that ICBM. Encryption on this missile is illustrative of the impeding of verification problem cited earlier.

6. *SS–16 ICBM—Banned Deployment*

—*Obligation:* The Soviet Union agreed in SALT II not to produce, test or deploy ICBMs of the SS–16 type and, in particular, not to produce the SS–16 third stage, the reentry vehicle of that missile.

—*Issue:* The study examined the evidence whether the Soviets have deployed the SS–16 ICBM in spite of the ban on its deployment.

—*Finding:* While the evidence is somewhat ambiguous and we cannot reach a definitive conclusion, the available evidence indicates that the activities at Plesetsk are a probable violation of their legal obligation not to defeat the object and purpose of SALT II prior to 1981 during the period when the Treaty was pending ratification, and a probable violation of a political commitment subsequent to 1981.

7. *TTBT—150 kt Test Limit*

—*Treaty Status:* The Threshold Test Ban Treaty was signed in 1974. The Treaty has not been ratified but neither Party has indicated an intention not to ratify. Therefore, both Parties are subject to the obligation under international law to refrain from acts which would "defeat the object and purpose" of the TTBT. Soviet actions that would defeat the object and purpose of the TTBT are therefore violations of their obligation. The U.S. is seeking to negotiate improved verification measures for the Treaty.

Both Parties have each separately stated they would observe the 150 kt threshold of the TTBT.

—Obligation: The Treaty prohibits any underground nuclear weapon test having a yield exceeding 150 kilotons at any place under the jurisdiction or control of the Parties, beginning March 31, 1976. In view of the technical uncertainties associated with predicting the precise yield of nuclear weapons tests, the sides agreed that one or two slight unintended breaches per year would not be considered a violation.

—Issue: The study examined whether the Soviets have conducted nuclear tests in excess of 150 kilotons.

—Finding: While the available evidence is ambiguous, in view of ambiguities in the pattern of Soviet testing and in view of verification uncertainties, and we have been unable to reach a definitive conclusion, this evidence indicates that Soviet nuclear testing activities for a number of tests constitute a likely violation of legal obligations under the TTBT.

Conclusions

The President has said that the U.S. will continue to press compliance issues with the Soviets through confidential diplomatic channels, and to insist upon explanations, clarifications, and corrective actions. At the same time we are continuing to carry out our obligations and commitments under relevant agreements. We should recognize, however, that ensuring compliance with arms control agreements remains a serious problem. Improved verification and compliance provisions and better treaty drafting will help, and we are working toward this in ongoing negotiations. It is fundamentally important, however, that the Soviets take a constructive attitude toward compliance.

Nomination of Sidney Lewis Jones To Be an Under Secretary of Commerce
January 23, 1984

The President today announced his intention to nominate Sidney Lewis Jones to be Under Secretary of Commerce for Economic Affairs. He would succeed Robert G. Dederick.

Since 1979 Dr. Jones has been a research scholar at the American Enterprise Institute. Previously he was an assistant to the Board of Governors of the Federal Reserve System in 1978; fellow at the Woodrow Wilson International Center for Scholars in 1977–1978; Assistant Secretary for Economic Policy at the Department of the Treasury in 1975–1977; Counselor to the Secretary of the Treasury in 1975; Deputy Counselor for Economic Policy, the White House, in 1974–1975; Assistant Secretary for Economic Affairs at the Department of Commerce in 1973–1974; Minister-Counselor for Economic Affairs, United States Mission to NATO, Brussels, Belgium, in 1972–1973; and senior economist and special assistant to the Chairman, Council of Economic Advisers, in 1969–1971.

Dr. Jones graduated from Utah State University (B.S., 1954) and Stanford University (M.B.A., 1958; Ph.D., 1960). He is married, has five children, and resides in Potomac, MD. He was born September 23, 1933, in Ogden, UT.

Appointment of Two Special Assistants to the President for National Security Affairs
January 23, 1984

The President today announced his intention to appoint the following individuals to be Special Assistants to the President for National Security Affairs:

Kenneth E. deGraffenreid joined the National Security Council staff in March 1981 and is currently Senior Director of Intelligence Programs. He served from 1977 to 1980 on the professional staff of the Senate Intelligence Committee and then participated on the Reagan transition team at the Central Intelligence Agency. Mr. deGraffenreid also served for 10 years in the U.S. Navy as an aviator and intelligence officer with the Defense Intelligence Agency and is presently a commander in the Naval Reserve. He is a 1967 graduate of Purdue University and received his M.A. in national security studies from Catholic University. Mr. deGraffenreid has written and lectured widely on intelligence and national security issues. He is married, has two children, and resides in Severna Park, MD. He was born July 18, 1944, in Chicago, IL.

Constantine C. Menges has served since 1983 as Senior Director of Latin American Affairs at the National Security Council. Previously he served as the national intelligence officer for Latin America with the Central Intelligence Agency (1981–1983). Until September 1981 he was senior associate with the Washington office of the Hudson Institute. His professional work on foreign policy has included experience as a faculty member at the University of Wisconsin (1964–1967), as a professional staff member at the Rand Corp. (1967–1970), and as a subcabinet official (1975–1977). Dr. Menges also has worked on domestic policy issues as an official of the Department of Health, Education, and Welfare (1970–1975), including service as Deputy Assistant Secretary for Education. He received his A.B. degree from Columbia College in New York and his Ph.D. in political science from Columbia University. Dr. Menges has lectured and published extensively on international politics and Latin American issues, including coauthorship of Politics in Europe (1965) and authorship of Spain: The Struggle for Democracy Today (1978). He was born September 1, 1939, in Ankara, Turkey.

Remarks Following a Performance Reopening the National Theatre
January 23, 1984

I know I speak for Nancy when I say this has been an evening of thrills from the moment that we walked through the theater doors. The show we've just seen is one of those big, bright Broadway productions that starts on a peak and then keeps on going up. [*Laughter*]

And before I say anything else, I want to thank the very talented "42nd Street" cast. Watching them sing and dance as they did made me wonder if I was seeing the reason why my own career in show business took a different turn. [*Laughter*]

The National Theatre opened, as you were told, on this site in 1835 when the occupant of the White House was Andrew Jackson. Americans perched on the roof and peered through the windows of this build-

ing to watch the horseback inaugural parades of McKinley and Teddy Roosevelt. They saw the face of the National when they watched newsreels of the inaugural parades of Wilson, Coolidge, and F.D.R.—parades that took place when American admirals still wore cockeyed hats. And through all those years, the National was staging productions that entertained and delighted the people of this city.

In recent years, though, the National fell on hard times. Some even talked of tearing her down. And then a year and a half ago, an army of designers, electricians, and carpenters went to work to save it. They cleaned the exterior. They've refurbished the interior, as we have been able to see tonight, installed a new lighting and a sound system, and added a whole new building four stories high for dressing rooms and storage. And they did it all without a penny of government money. [*Laughter*]

And tonight we're among the lucky first to enjoy the results. A special thanks to J. Adams, the chairman of the National Theatre, to the Schuberts, Gerald Schoenfeld and Bernard Jacobs, and, of course, to Carol Laxalt and Betty Wright, the cochairmen of tonight's gala. I know we want to applaud everyone who had a hand in this wonderful restoration. With this reopening, downtown Washington has a splendid theater and a living link with the past.

And speaking as two who live in the neighborhood—[*laughter*]—we're all delighted. One more thing: Now that the National has reopened, even those of us in Washington will be able to hear "The Lullaby of Broadway."

Thank you. God bless you all.

Note: The President spoke at 9:25 p.m. at the theater.

Letter to the Speaker of the House and the Chairman of the Senate Foreign Relations Committee Reporting on the Cyprus Conflict
January 24, 1984

Dear Mr. Speaker: (Dear Mr. Chairman:)

In accordance with Public Law 95–384, I am submitting herewith a bimonthly report on progress toward a negotiated settlement of the Cyprus problem.

Since the previous report (November 7, 1983) the Turkish Cypriot community declared its statehood. The declaration of November 15, 1983 was condemned by the Administration as unhelpful to the process of finding solutions. We urged reversal of the Turkish community's moves and called on all states of the world not to recognize the self-proclaimed entity. On November 18, 1983 we joined a nearly unanimous U.N. Security Council in passing resolution 541 which also called for reversal of the declaration and for no international recognition of the self-proclaimed entity.

Following the November 18, 1983 Security Council action, Cypriot President Kyprianou came to Washington where Secretary Shultz and I met with him to assure him of our opposition to the Turkish Cypriot move and of our continuing determination to see the Cyprus question settled fairly and finally. We also met with (then) Turkish Foreign Minister Turkmen to whom we explained these same points. With both the Cypriot and Turkish government officials we urged flexibility in reacting to any opportunities for progress which may present themselves.

The Secretary of State made a similar presentation to Greek Foreign Minister Haralambopoulos.

In early December, 1983 State Department Counselor Edward Derwinski visited Greece and Cyprus to meet with Government leaders and private individuals for discussions of the situation on Cyprus. Several additional visits to Cyprus by members of the Congress took place during the period.

On December 15, 1983 the U.N. Security Council renewed the mandate for the U.N. Forces in Cyprus (UNFICYP) for another six months. (Secretary General's report of December 1 is attached.) The Turkish Cypriot community did not support the terms of this renewal but its leaders have said they will continue to cooperate with U.N. forces in their peacekeeping role.

On January 2, 1984, the Government of Turkey announced its intention to remove 1500 of its troops from Cyprus. On the same day Mr. Denktash, leader of the Turkish Cypriot community, announced a series of "goodwill" measures designed to settle some of the outstanding issues between the communities. Included among these were proposals to turn over the city of Varosha and the Nicosia airport to U.N. administration, reactivation of the Committee on Missing Persons, and several other confidence-building measures. The Administration welcomed these proposals as being movement in the right direction.

On January 9, 1984, President Kyprianou again visited Washington during a private visit to the U.S. and discussed with Secretary Shultz and others his Government's ideas on how to achieve progress toward a comprehensive settlement.

The Secretary of State's Special Cyprus Coordinator Richard Haass and other Department officials have maintained close liaison with U.N. officials involved with the Cyprus question. We continue to support the Secretary General's good offices role.

During the period, the Administration has encouraged the parties to the Cyprus question to be forthcoming with new ideas for progress and not to reject out of hand any proposals for progress. We believe the January 2, 1984 proposals from the Turkish side and the plans discussed with President Kyprianou in November and in January constitute positive results. We intend to continue our strong support for the U.N. Secretary General's role in the search for solutions to the Cyprus problem.

Sincerely,

RONALD REAGAN

Note: This is the text of identical letters addressed to Thomas P. O'Neill, Jr., Speaker of the House of Representatives, and Charles H. Percy, chairman of the Senate Foreign Relations Committee.

Remarks at a Luncheon Sponsored by the Senate Republican Policy Committee
January 24, 1984

It's a pleasure for me to be here this afternoon. This is the third time that I've had lunch with you, and today's occasion, I know, will be just as informative and enjoyable as the first two.

By the way, Howard Baker and Senator Tower called to remind me to bring $5. [*Laughter*] Leave it to them to make sure we show the rest of the Congress there's no such thing as a free lunch. [*Laughter*]

But I want to thank Howard and John and all of you for your vital work in the Senate. Howard is not only the first Republican majority leader in more than a quarter of a century; I think we all agree he's one of the most effective majority leaders in history.

If I was still in the business I used to be in, I'd sit down now. [*Laughter*]

But your chairman, John Tower, has always advocated discipline for government and freedom for the individual. And in all the long history of our Republic, no one has ever done more to see that America has the defense that she required.

Time and again, Howard and John have given me the benefit of their knowledge, judgment, and understanding of the Senate.

And whatever successes our administration has enjoyed, these two Senators deserve a big slice of the credit.

This January makes it 36 months since our party won the Senate and regained the White House. Thirty-six months—that's just a short span in the life of a nation, but I deeply believe that together we've changed American history.

Think back to that crisp January day, back 36 months ago: inflation in double digits, prime interest rates at the highest level since the Civil War, economic growth disappearing. At the same time our defenses were weak. As John has pointed out so often, from 1970 to 1980 real defense spending dropped more than 20 percent. Military equipment was growing obsolete; real military pay was too low; and morale among our uniformed men and women was sagging.

In foreign policy America had become known the world over for hesitation, vacillation, and self-doubt. And our great nation stood by as if paralyzed while the Soviets amassed a vast military might, then began to intimidate our allies, fuel regional conflicts, and prop up tyrannies. And when Americans looked to their leaders for encouragement, they only heard about a so-called national malaise.

Well, in the past 36 months, the world has seen an American miracle. Time has marched on, but instead of growing older and more tired—I'm not talking about me now—[*laughter*]—our country has recaptured the vitality, self-confidence, and courage of the youthful nation that she still is.

Last month the Producer Price Index increased by only two-tenths of 1 percent, and by only six-tenths of 1 percent for all of 1983. That's the best record in 19 years. And just this morning we had more good news. For calendar year 1983 the Consumer Price Index went up only 3.8 percent, and that's the best record in more than a decade.

The prime interest rate is barely half what it was when we took office. Factory orders, retail sales, and housing starts are up. The stock market has come back to life—a little nervous at times, but back to life. Real wages are rising, and America is leading the world in technological revolution, even more far-reaching and profound than the Industrial Revolution of a century ago.

Unemployment is dropping at the fastest rate in more than 30 years. Last year alone, more than 4 million Americans found jobs. And today, some 103 million Americans are at work; that's more than ever before in our history.

In the military, morale has soared as we've been giving the men and women in our Armed Forces good pay, good equipment, and the respect they deserve.

In foreign policy, the world knows once more what America stands for: the freedom of mankind. From Central America to Africa to the Middle East, we're working to support democracy and produce peace. In Lebanon, the peace process has been slow and painful, but we've made genuine progress. In Europe the NATO alliance has held firm. In our dealings with the Soviets, by strengthening our defenses and showing the world our willingness to negotiate, we've laid the foundations for a lasting world peace. And on an island in the Caribbean, we set a nation free.

Now, there's a story, and it's a true story and I know I've told it to some of you, but I know not all, and I hope the rest of you haven't heard it because I want to tell it. It comes from Grenada. A young first lieutenant marine who pilots a Cobra was in Grenada and then moved on to Beirut. And he sent a message back to the Armed Forces Journal not too long ago. He said that in Grenada, every news story he noticed contained the words and the phrase that Grenada produces more nutmeg than any place in the world. And this was so regular in all the stories he decided that it was a code. And he was going to break the code. And he wrote back to say he'd succeeded.

He had broken the code, six points in breaking that code. Number one, Grenada does produce more nutmeg than any other place on Earth. Number two, the Soviets and Cubans were trying to take Grenada. Number three, you can't make eggnog without nutmeg. [*Laughter*] Number four, you can't have Christmas without eggnog. Number five, the Soviets and the Cubans were trying to steal Christmas. [*Laughter*] And, number six, we stopped them. [*Laughter*]

Well, a moment ago, I called the turnaround in America a miracle. And, now, I don't mean a miracle like a magic trick; I mean a miracle of determination, hard work, and teamwork. All that has been accomplished, we've accomplished together. Believe me, down on Pennsylvania Avenue, Capitol Hill sometimes looks more like a mountain. And I don't like to think how hard it would have been to push our programs over the top without Republican control of the Senate. In fact, I think it would have been impossible.

In 1984 nothing matters more than keeping the Senate. And I pledge to do all within my power to see that we do just that. In the meantime, we still have plenty of work cut out for us: attacking the Federal deficit, getting inflation and interest rates down still further, wringing waste and fraud out of government, and so much more. Where we have honest differences you can count on me to be a willing listener and a genuine partner.

Of course, there'll always be room for improvement in the way we do our job. But for the sake of the country, we must get the job done. Working together, we will.

And I thank you, and God bless you all. And, now, Howard, here's my $5. Let's

eat. [*Laughter*]

Note: The President spoke at 12:33 p.m. in Room S-207 of the Capitol.

Nomination of Ann Dore McLaughlin To Be an Under Secretary of the Interior
January 24, 1984

The President today announced his intention to nominate Ann Dore McLaughlin to be Under Secretary of the Interior. She would succeed J.J. Simmons III.

Since 1981 Mrs. McLaughlin has been serving as Assistant Secretary for Public Affairs at the Department of the Treasury. She was president of McLaughlin & Co. of Washington, DC, and Washington manager of Braun and Co. of Los Angeles, CA, in 1977–1981.

In 1974–1977, she was with the Union Carbide Corp. She was Director, Office of Public Affairs, Environmental Protection Agency, in 1973–1974. Mrs. McLaughlin was assistant to the chairman and press secretary, Presidential Inaugural Committee, in 1972–1973. In 1971–1972, she was direc-

tor of communications, Presidential Election Committee. Previously she served as an account executive with Myers-Infoplan International, Inc., of New York City. Mrs. McLaughlin was a consultant and literary agent with Perla Meyers International Kitchen in 1970–1971; director, alumnae relations, Marymount College, in 1966–1969; and supervisor, network commercial scheduling, American Broadcasting Co., in 1963–1966.

Mrs. McLaughlin graduated from Marymount College (B.A., 1963) and attended the University of London, Queen Mary College in 1961–1962. She is married and resides in Washington, DC. She was born in Chatham, NJ, on November 16, 1941.

Executive Order 12460—Amendments to the Manual for Courts-Martial, United States, 1969 (Revised Edition)
January 24, 1984

By the authority vested in me as President by the Constitution of the United States and by Chapter 47 of Title 10 of the United States Code (the Uniform Code of Military Justice), in order to prescribe amendments to the Manual for Courts-Martial, United States, 1969 (Revised edition), prescribed by Executive Order No. 11476, as amended by Executive Order No. 11835, Executive Order No. 12018, Executive Order No. 12198, Executive Order No. 12233, Executive Order No. 12306, Executive Order No. 12315, Executive Order No. 12340, and Executive Order No. 12383, it is

hereby ordered as follows:

Section 1. Paragraph 75 of the said Manual for Courts-Martial is amended by adding, after paragraph 75*f,* the following:

"*g. Capital cases.*

"(1) *In general.* Death may be adjudged only when:

"(*a*) Death is expressly authorized under the code and this Manual for an offense of which the accused has been found guilty or is authorized under the law of war for an offense of which the accused has been found guilty under the law of war; and

"(*b*) The requirements of 75*g* (2) and (3)

have been met.

"(2) *Procedure.* In addition to the other provisions in 75, the following procedures shall apply in capital cases—

"(a) *Notice.* Before arraignment, trial counsel shall give the defense written notice of which aggravating circumstances under 75g(3) the prosecution intends to prove. Failure to provide timely notice under this subsection of any aggravating circumstances under 75g(3) shall not bar later notice and proof of such additional aggravating circumstances unless the accused demonstrates specific prejudice from such failure and that a continuance or a recess is not an adequate remedy.

"(b) *Evidence of aggravating circumstances.* Trial counsel may present evidence in accordance with 75b(4) tending to establish one or more of the aggravating circumstances in 75g(3).

"(c) *Evidence in extenuation and mitigation.* The accused shall be given broad latitude to present evidence in extenuation and mitigation.

"(d) *Necessary findings.* Death may not be adjudged unless the members find:

"(i) Beyond a reasonable doubt that one or more of the aggravating circumstances under 75g(3) existed; and

"(ii) That any extenuating or mitigating circumstances are substantially outweighed by any aggravating circumstances including such circumstances under 75g(3) as the members have found existed.

"(e) *Basis for findings.* The findings in 75g(2)(d) may be based on evidence introduced before the findings on the issue of guilt, during the sentencing proceeding, or both.

"(f) *Instructions.* In addition to the instructions required under 76b(1), the military judge shall instruct the members on such aggravating circumstances under 75g(3) as may be in issue in the case and on the requirements and procedures under 75g(2)(d), (e), (g), and (h). The military judge shall instruct the members that they must consider all evidence in extenuation and mitigation before they may adjudge death.

"(g) *Voting.* In closed session, before voting on a sentence, the members shall vote by secret written ballot separately on each aggravating circumstance under 75g(3)

on which they have been instructed. Death may not be adjudged unless all members concur in a finding of the existence of at least one such aggravating circumstance. After voting on all the circumstances on which they have been instructed, the members shall vote on a sentence in accordance with 76b(2) and (3).

"(h) *Announcement.* If death is adjudged, the president shall, in addition to complying with 76c, announce which aggravating circumstances under 75g(3) were found by the members.

"(3) *Aggravating circumstances.* Death may be adjudged only if the members find, beyond a reasonable doubt, one or more of the following aggravating circumstances:

"(a) That the offense was committed before or in the presence of the enemy, except that this circumstance shall not apply in the case of a violation of Article 118 or 120;

"(b) That in committing the offense the accused intended to:

"(i) cause substantial damage to the national security of the United States; or

"(ii) cause substantial damage to a mission, system, or function of the United States, provided that this subparagraph shall apply only if substantial damage to the national security of the United States would have resulted had the intended damage been effected;

"(c) That the offense caused substantial damage to the national security of the United States, whether or not the accused intended such damage, except that this circumstance shall not apply in the case of a violation of Article 118 or 120;

"(d) That the offense was committed in such a way or under circumstances that the lives of persons other than the victim, if any, were unlawfully and substantially endangered, except that this circumstance shall not apply to a violation of Article 120;

"(e) That the accused committed the offense with the intent to avoid hazardous duty;

"(f) That, only in the case of a violation of Article 118 or 120, the offense was committed in time of war and in territory in which the United States or an ally of the United States was then an occupying power or in which the armed forces of the United States were then engaged in active hostilities;

"(*g*) That, only in the case of a violation of Article 118(1):

"(i) The accused was serving a sentence of confinement for 30 years or more or for life at the time of the murder;

"(ii) The murder was committed while the accused was engaged in the commission or attempted commission of any robbery, rape, aggravated arson, sodomy, burglary, kidnapping, mutiny, sedition, or piracy of an aircraft or vessel, or was engaged in flight or attempted flight after the commission or attempted commission of any such offense;

"(iii) The murder was committed for the purpose of receiving money or a thing of value;

"(iv) The accused procured another by means of compulsion, coercion, or a promise of an advantage, a service, or a thing of value to commit the murder;

"(v) The murder was committed with the intent to avoid or to prevent lawful apprehension or effect an escape from custody or confinement;

"(vi) The victim was the President of the United States, the President-elect, the Vice President, or, if there was no Vice President, the officer next in the order of succession to the office of President of the United States, the Vice-President-elect, or any individual who is acting as President under the Constitution and laws of the United States, any Member of Congress or Member-of-Congress elect, or any judge of the United States;

"(vii) The accused then knew that the victim was any of the following persons in the execution of office: a commissioned, warrant, noncommissioned, or petty officer of the armed services of the United States; a member of any law enforcement or security activity or agency, military or civilian, including correctional custody personnel; or any firefighter;

"(viii) The murder was committed with intent to obstruct justice;

"(ix) The murder was preceded by the intentional infliction of substantial physical harm or prolonged, substantial mental or physical pain and suffering to the victim; or

"(x) The accused has been found guilty in the same case of another violation of Article 118;

"For purposes of this paragraph, 'national security' means the national defense and foreign relations of the United States and specifically includes: (*a*) a military or defense advantage over any foreign nation or group of nations, (*b*) a favorable foreign relations position, or (*c*) a defense posture capable of successfully resisting hostile or destructive action from within or without, overt or covert. Examples of substantial damage to the national security of the United States may include: impeding the performance of a combat mission or operation; impeding the performance of an important mission in a place subject to hostile fire or imminent danger pay (*see* 37 U.S.C. section 310(a)) and disclosing military plans, capabilities, or intelligence such as to jeopardize any combat mission or operation of the armed services of the United States or its allies or to materially aid an enemy of the United States.

"(*h*) That only in the case of a violation of Article 118(4), the accused was the actual perpetrator of the killing;

"(*i*) That, only in the case of a violation of Article 120:

"(i) The victim was under the age of 12; or

"(ii) The accused maimed or attempted to kill the victim; or

"(*j*) That, only in the case of a violation of the law of war, death is authorized under the law of war for the offense.

"(4) *Spying.* If the accused has been found guilty of spying under Article 106, 75*g*(1)(*b*), (2), and (3), and 76 shall not apply. Sentencing proceedings in accordance with 75*a* through *f* shall be conducted, but the military judge shall announce that by operation of law a sentence of death has been adjudged."

Sec. 2. Paragraph 76*b*(1) is amended by adding in the first sentence after the language "in 76*b*(2) and 76*b*(3)," the following language:

"and, in capital cases, 75*g*(2) (*g*)."

Sec. 3. Paragraph 76*b*(3) is amended by adding after the first sentence the following language:

"*See* 75g(2)(g)."

Sec. 4. Paragraph 126*a* is amended by adding after the third sentence in the second paragraph the following language: "*See* 75g."

Sec. 5. Paragraph 126*b* is amended by adding after the language "by the code" the second time it appears, the following language:

"and this Manual"

Sec. 6. These amendments shall be effective immediately. These amendments shall apply in trials of capital offenses committed on or after this date.

Sec. 7. The Secretary of Defense, on behalf of the President, shall transmit a copy of this Order to the Congress of the United States in accord with Section 836 of Title 10 of the United States Code.

RONALD REAGAN

The White House,
January 24, 1984.

[*Filed with the Office of the Federal Register, 11:52 a.m., January 25, 1984*]

Note: The text of the Executive order was released by the Office of the Press Secretary on January 25.

Letter Accepting the Resignation of Edward C. Schmults as Deputy Attorney General
January 25, 1984

Dear Ed:

It is with regret that I accept your resignation as Deputy Attorney General, effective February 3, 1984.

I know that you have been a strong right hand for Bill Smith as the Department of Justice has kept our promise to the American people to wage unremitting war against crime. You have played a leading role in our counterattack against those who terrorize innocent victims, and especially against organized crime, which can only be defeated by resolute action at the Federal level. Your experience and knowledge in this and many other areas will be sorely missed, but I know that your successor will build on the solid foundations you have laid. I want to thank you personally for a job well done.

Nancy and I send you our best wishes for every future success and happiness.

Sincerely,

RONALD REAGAN

[The Honorable Edward C. Schmults, Deputy Attorney General, Washington, D.C. 20530]

———

January 23, 1984

My Dear Mr. President:

For three years, it has been my privilege to be the Deputy Attorney General of the United States. Every day I have had a keen sense of accomplishment and pride in working with Bill Smith to serve the cause of justice and carry out your policies here at the Department of Justice. Thus, it is not easy for me to tender my resignation, which I do by this letter, effective on February 3, 1984.

Because of your unswerving leadership and strong support, the Federal effort against crime is being fought more effectively than at any time in our Nation's history. The law enforcement community knows it has a President who respects and supports what it is doing, and the results are now apparent to the American people.

My deepest thanks for the opportunity of helping you to further your goals. As I return to private life, I stand ready to do whatever you ask as you seek a second term, knowing that the American people will reelect a President who has served them so well.

Respectfully,

/s/EDWARD C. SCHMULTS

[The President, The White House, Washington, D.C. 20500]

Nomination of Irving P. Margulies To Be General Counsel of the Department of Commerce
January 25, 1984

The President today announced his intention to nominate Irving P. Margulies to be General Counsel of the Department of Commerce. He would succeed Sherman E. Unger.

Mr. Margulies is presently serving as Acting General Counsel of the Department of Commerce. He was Deputy General Counsel of the Department of Commerce in 1981–1983. He was an Associate General Counsel with the Department of Housing and Urban Development in 1977–1981. Prior to 1977 Mr. Margulies served as Associate General Counsel for Equal Opportunity and Administration; Associate General Counsel for Equal Opportunity, Litigation, and Administration; Assistant General Counsel for Legislation; and senior attorney, legislation, at the Department of Housing and Urban Development. In 1956–1961 he served as a legislative attorney at the Department of Labor.

Mr. Margulies graduated from Wayne University (A.B., 1948) and Wayne University Law School (LL.B., 1950). He is married, has four children, and resides in Gaithersburg, MD. He was born June 9, 1925, in New York, NY.

Appointment of Three Members of the President's Advisory Committee on Women's Business Ownership
January 25, 1984

The President today announced his intention to appoint the following individuals to be members of the President's Advisory Committee on Women's Business Ownership. These are new positions.

Corlene Hobbs Cathcart is vice president and controller of Majo Ranch, Inc., in Cody, WY. She was president of the women's board of the Art Institute of Chicago in 1976–1979. She is married, has five children, and resides in Cody, WY. She was born September 30, 1926, in Chicago, IL.

Clara Giordano owned and operated a restaurant in Lincoln Park, MI, in 1959–1975. She is married, has three children, and resides in Wyandotte, MI. She was born October 10, 1924, in Piney Fork, OH.

Malcolm A. MacKillop is senior vice president for corporate relations at Pacific Gas and Electric Co. in San Francisco, CA. He has been with Pacific Gas and Electric Co. since 1955 and has served as attorney, assistant general counsel, and vice president for governmental relations for the firm. He has two children and resides in San Francisco, CA. He was born August 1, 1922, in San Francisco.

Excerpt of Remarks During a Meeting With Network Anchors on United States-Soviet Relations
January 25, 1984

Q. Does the Andropov interview published today mean any fine-tuning of phrase here and there?

The President. I think—I welcome it and am willing to join them if they're—want to talk. That's all we've been waiting for and wanting. So, I welcome that, and I think that it is a reply to all this feeling that we have no communications with them. We do have and——

Q. Do you see it as a conciliatory message from Andropov or not? Do you see it as a conciliatory response?

The President. Well, I saw it as that he, himself, expressed what we have; that he believes there should be a dialog on some of the problems confronting us. So do I.

Note: The luncheon meeting was held in the Roosevelt Room at the White House.

As printed above, this item follows the text of the White House press release.

Proclamation 5148—Centennial of the Birth of Harry S Truman
January 25, 1984

By the President of the United States of America

A Proclamation

May 8, 1984, marks the one hundredth anniversary of the birth of Harry S Truman, the thirty-third President of the United States and one of this Nation's most respected statesmen.

First elected to the United States Senate from Missouri in 1934, Mr. Truman gained national recognition during World War II, when his investigating committee saved the taxpayers large amounts of money by exposing waste and extravagance in the procurement process. In November 1944, the voters elected Mr. Truman Vice President. He served only 83 days in that office and succeeded to the Presidency in April 1945, upon the death of President Roosevelt.

In his first months in office, President Truman guided the country through the end of World War II and made the difficult decisions that ushered in the nuclear age. In the postwar years, he oversaw America's transition from a wartime to a peacetime economy and began an era of growth and stability. In foreign affairs, President Truman established the cornerstones of the policy of containment in dealing with the communist threat to Europe. Through the Truman Doctrine and the Marshall Plan he stalwartly assisted free peoples in their efforts to stem the tide of totalitarian subversion. In applying the principles of collective security, President Truman assisted in the formation of the North Atlantic Treaty Organization to help European nations respond to this threat.

In 1948, Mr. Truman was elected to the Presidency, battling from behind to overtake Governor Thomas Dewey. President Truman responded to the invasion of South Korea by utilizing United Nations as well as American forces in dealing with that crisis.

Although confronted with a series of major challenges throughout his tenure, President Truman responded with courage, humanity, decisiveness, and a wit which have secured his place in the Nation's history as one of our most respected Presidents.

Now, Therefore, I, Ronald Reagan, President of the United States of America, do hereby proclaim May 8, 1984 to be the "Centennial of the Birth of Harry S Truman." I call upon the people of the United States to observe that day with appropriate ceremonies and activities in remembrance of his many accomplishments and dedication to freedom and democracy.

In Witness Whereof, I have hereunto set my hand this 25th day of January, in the year of our Lord nineteen hundred and eighty-four, and of the Independence of the United States of America the two hundred and eighth.

RONALD REAGAN

[Filed with the Office of the Federal Register, 11:05 a.m., January 26, 1984]

Address Before a Joint Session of the Congress on the State of the Union
January 25, 1984

Mr. Speaker, Mr. President, distinguished Members of the Congress, honored guests, and fellow citizens:

Once again, in keeping with time-honored tradition, I have come to report to you on the state of the Union, and I'm pleased to report that America is much improved, and there's good reason to believe that improvement will continue through the days to come.

You and I have had some honest and open differences in the year past. But they didn't keep us from joining hands in bipartisan cooperation to stop a long decline that had drained this nation's spirit and eroded its health. There is renewed energy and optimism throughout the land. America is back, standing tall, looking to the eighties with courage, confidence, and hope.

The problems we're overcoming are not the heritage of one person, party, or even one generation. It's just the tendency of government to grow, for practices and programs to become the nearest thing to eternal life we'll ever see on this Earth. [*Laughter*] And there's always that well-intentioned chorus of voices saying, "With a little more power and a little more money, we could do so much for the people." For a time we forgot the American dream isn't one of making government bigger; it's keeping faith with the mighty spirit of free people under God.

As we came to the decade of the eighties, we faced the worst crisis in our postwar history. In the seventies were years of rising problems and falling confidence. There was a feeling government had grown beyond the consent of the governed. Families felt helpless in the face of mounting inflation and the indignity of taxes that reduced reward for hard work, thrift, and risk-taking. All this was overlaid by an ever-growing web of rules and regulations.

On the international scene, we had an uncomfortable feeling that we'd lost the respect of friend and foe. Some questioned whether we had the will to defend peace and freedom. But America is too great for small dreams. There was a hunger in the land for a spiritual revival; if you will, a crusade for renewal. The American people said: Let us look to the future with confidence, both at home and abroad. Let us give freedom a chance.

Americans were ready to make a new beginning, and together we have done it. We're confronting our problems one by one. Hope is alive tonight for millions of young families and senior citizens set free from unfair tax increases and crushing inflation. Inflation has been beaten down from 12.4 to 3.2 percent, and that's a great victory for all the people. The prime rate has been cut almost in half, and we must work together to bring it down even more.

Together, we passed the first across-the-board tax reduction for everyone since the Kennedy tax cuts. Next year, tax rates will be indexed so inflation can't push people into higher brackets when they get cost-of-living pay raises. Government must never again use inflation to profit at the people's expense.

Today a working family earning $25,000 has $1,100 more in purchasing power than if tax and inflation rates were still at the 1980 levels. Real after-tax income increased 5 percent last year. And economic deregulation of key industries like transportation has offered more chances—or choices, I should say, to consumers and new changes—or chances for entrepreneurs and protecting safety. Tonight, we can report and be proud of one of the best recoveries in decades. Send away the handwringers and the doubting Thomases. Hope is reborn for couples dreaming of owning homes and for risktakers with vision to create tomorrow's opportunities.

The spirit of enterprise is sparked by the sunrise industries of high-tech and by small businesspeople with big ideas—people like Barbara Proctor, who rose from a ghetto to build a multimillion-dollar advertising agency in Chicago; Carlos Perez, a Cuban refugee, who turned $27 and a dream into a successful importing business in Coral Gables, Florida.

People like these are heroes for the eighties. They helped 4 million Americans find jobs in 1983. More people are drawing paychecks tonight than ever before. And Congress helps—or progress helps everyone—well, Congress does too—*[laughter]*—everyone. In 1983 women filled 73 percent of all the new jobs in managerial, professional, and technical fields.

But we know that many of our fellow countrymen are still out of work, wondering what will come of their hopes and dreams. Can we love America and not reach out to tell them: You are not forgotten; we will not rest until each of you can reach as high as your God-given talents will take you.

The heart of America is strong; it's good and true. The cynics were wrong; America never was a sick society. We're seeing rededication to bedrock values of faith, family, work, neighborhood, peace, and freedom—values that help bring us together as one people, from the youngest child to the most senior citizen.

The Congress deserves America's thanks for helping us restore pride and credibility to our military. And I hope that you're as proud as I am of the young men and women in uniform who have volunteered to man the ramparts in defense of freedom and whose dedication, valor, and skill increases so much our chance of living in a world at peace.

People everywhere hunger for peace and a better life. The tide of the future is a freedom tide, and our struggle for democracy cannot and will not be denied. This nation champions peace that enshrines liberty, democratic rights, and dignity for every individual. America's new strength, confidence, and purpose are carrying hope and opportunity far from our shores. A world economic recovery is underway. It began here.

We've journeyed far, but we have much farther to go. Franklin Roosevelt told us 50 years ago this month: "Civilization can not go back; civilization must not stand still. We have undertaken new methods. It is our task to perfect, to improve, to alter when

necessary, but in all cases to go forward."

It's time to move forward again, time for America to take freedom's next step. Let us unite tonight behind four great goals to keep America free, secure, and at peace in the eighties together.

We can ensure steady economic growth. We can develop America's next frontier. We can strengthen our traditional values. And we can build a meaningful peace to protect our loved ones and this shining star of faith that has guided millions from tyranny to the safe harbor of freedom, progress, and hope.

Doing these things will open wider the gates of opportunity, provide greater security for all, with no barriers of bigotry or discrimination.

The key to a dynamic decade is vigorous economic growth, our first great goal. We might well begin with common sense in Federal budgeting: government spending no more than government takes in.

We must bring Federal deficits down. But how we do that makes all the difference.

We can begin by limiting the size and scope of government. Under the leadership of Vice President Bush, we have reduced the growth of Federal regulations by more than 25 percent and cut well over 300 million hours of government-required paperwork each year. This will save the public more than $150 billion over the next 10 years.

The Grace commission has given us some 2,500 recommendations for reducing wasteful spending, and they're being examined throughout the administration. Federal spending growth has been cut from 17.4 percent in 1980 to less than half of that today, and we have already achieved over $300 billion in budget savings for the period of 1982 to '86. But that's only a little more than half of what we sought. Government is still spending too large a percentage of the total economy.

Now, some insist that any further budget savings must be obtained by reducing the portion spent on defense. This ignores the fact that national defense is solely the responsibility of the Federal Government; indeed, it is its prime responsibility. And yet defense spending is less than a third of the total budget. During the years of President Kennedy and of the years before that, defense was almost half the total budget. And then came several years in which our military capability was allowed to deteriorate to a very dangerous degree. We are just now restoring, through the essential modernization of our conventional and strategic forces, our capability to meet our present and future security needs. We dare not shirk our responsibility to keep America free, secure, and at peace.

The last decade saw domestic spending surge literally out of control. But the basis for such spending had been laid in previous years. A pattern of overspending has been in place for half a century. As the national debt grew, we were told not to worry, that we owed it to ourselves.

Now we know that deficits are a cause for worry. But there's a difference of opinion as to whether taxes should be increased, spending cut, or some of both. Fear is expressed that government borrowing to fund the deficit could inhibit the economic recovery by taking capital needed for business and industrial expansion. Well, I think that debate is missing an important point. Whether government borrows or increases taxes, it will be taking the same amount of money from the private sector, and, either way, that's too much. Simple fairness dictates that government must not raise taxes on families struggling to pay their bills. The root of the problem is that government's share is more than we can afford if we're to have a sound economy.

We must bring down the deficits to ensure continued economic growth. In the budget that I will submit on February 1st, I will recommend measures that will reduce the deficit over the next 5 years. Many of these will be unfinished business from last year's budget.

Some could be enacted quickly if we could join in a serious effort to address this problem. I spoke today with Speaker of the House O'Neill, Senate Majority Leader Baker, Senate Minority Leader Byrd, and House Minority Leader Michel. I asked them if they would designate congressional representatives to meet with representatives of the administration to try to reach prompt agreement on a bipartisan deficit reduction plan. I know it would take a long, hard struggle to agree on a full-scale plan. So, what I have proposed is that we first see if we can agree on a downpayment.

Now, I believe there is basis for such an agreement, one that could reduce the deficits by about a hundred billion dollars over the next 3 years. We could focus on some of the less contentious spending cuts that are still pending before the Congress. These could be combined with measures to close certain tax loopholes, measures that the Treasury Department has previously said to be worthy of support. In addition, we could examine the possibility of achieving further outlay savings based on the work of the Grace commission.

If the congressional leadership is willing, my representatives will be prepared to meet with theirs at the earliest possible time. I would hope the leadership might agree on an expedited timetable in which to develop and enact that downpayment.

But a downpayment alone is not enough to break us out of the deficit problem. It could help us start on the right path. Yet, we must do more. So, I propose that we begin exploring how together we can make structural reforms to curb the built-in growth of spending.

I also propose improvements in the budgeting process. Some 43 of our 50 States grant their Governors the right to veto individual items in appropriation bills without having to veto the entire bill. California is one of those 43 States. As Governor, I found this line-item veto was a powerful tool against wasteful or extravagant spending. It works in 43 States. Let's put it to work in Washington for all the people.

It would be most effective if done by constitutional amendment. The majority of Americans approve of such an amendment, just as they and I approve of an amendment mandating a balanced Federal budget. Many States also have this protection in their constitutions.

To talk of meeting the present situation by increasing taxes is a Band-Aid solution which does nothing to cure an illness that's been coming on for half a century—to say nothing of the fact that it poses a real threat to economic recovery. Let's remember that a substantial amount of income tax is presently owed and not paid by people in the underground economy. It would be immoral to make those who are paying taxes pay more to compensate for those who aren't paying their share.

There's a better way. Let us go forward with an historic reform for fairness, simplicity, and incentives for growth. I am asking Secretary Don Regan for a plan for action to simplify the entire tax code, so all taxpayers, big and small, are treated more fairly. And I believe such a plan could result in that underground economy being brought into the sunlight of honest tax compliance. And it could make the tax base broader, so personal tax rates could come down, not go up. I've asked that specific recommendations, consistent with those objectives, be presented to me by December 1984.

Our second great goal is to build on America's pioneer spirit—[*laughter*]—I said something funny? [*Laughter*] I said America's next frontier—and that's to develop that frontier. A sparkling economy spurs initiatives, sunrise industries, and makes older ones more competitive.

Nowhere is this more important than our next frontier: space. Nowhere do we so effectively demonstrate our technological leadership and ability to make life better on Earth. The Space Age is barely a quarter of a century old. But already we've pushed civilization forward with our advances in science and technology. Opportunities and jobs will multiply as we cross new thresholds of knowledge and reach deeper into the unknown.

Our progress in space—taking giant steps for all mankind—is a tribute to American teamwork and excellence. Our finest minds in government, industry, and academia have all pulled together. And we can be proud to say: We are first; we are the best; and we are so because we're free.

America has always been greatest when we dared to be great. We can reach for greatness again. We can follow our dreams to distant stars, living and working in space for peaceful, economic, and scientific gain. Tonight, I am directing NASA to develop a permanently manned space station and to do it within a decade.

A space station will permit quantum leaps in our research in science, communications, in metals, and in lifesaving medicines which could be manufactured only in space. We want our friends to help us meet these challenges and share in their benefits. NASA will invite other countries to participate so we can strengthen peace, build prosperity, and expand freedom for all who share our goals.

Just as the oceans opened up a new world for clipper ships and Yankee traders, space holds enormous potential for commerce today. The market for space transportation could surpass our capacity to develop it. Companies interested in putting payloads into space must have ready access to private sector launch services. The Department of Transportation will help an expendable launch services industry to get off the ground. We'll soon implement a number of executive initiatives, develop proposals to ease regulatory constraints, and, with NASA's help, promote private sector investment in space.

And as we develop the frontier of space, let us remember our responsibility to preserve our older resources here on Earth. Preservation of our environment is not a liberal or conservative challenge, it's common sense.

Though this is a time of budget constraints, I have requested for EPA one of the largest percentage budget increases of any agency. We will begin the long, necessary effort to clean up a productive recreational area and a special national resource—the Chesapeake Bay.

To reduce the threat posed by abandoned hazardous waste dumps, EPA will spend $410 million. And I will request a supplemental increase of 50 million. And because the Superfund law expires in 1985, I've asked Bill Ruckelshaus to develop a proposal for its extension so there'll be additional time to complete this important task.

On the question of acid rain, which concerns people in many areas of the United States and Canada, I'm proposing a research program that doubles our current funding. And we'll take additional action to restore our lakes and develop new technology to reduce pollution that causes acid rain.

We have greatly improved the conditions

of our natural resources. We'll ask the Congress for $157 million beginning in 1985 to acquire new park and conservation lands. The Department of the Interior will encourage careful, selective exploration and production on our vital resources in an Exclusive Economic Zone within the 200-mile limit off our coasts—but with strict adherence to environmental laws and with fuller State and public participation.

But our most precious resources, our greatest hope for the future, are the minds and hearts of our people, especially our children. We can help them build tomorrow by strengthening our community of shared values. This must be our third great goal. For us, faith, work, family, neighborhood, freedom, and peace are not just words; they're expressions of what America means, definitions of what makes us a good and loving people.

Families stand at the center of our society. And every family has a personal stake in promoting excellence in education. Excellence does not begin in Washington. A 600-percent increase in Federal spending on education between 1960 and 1980 was accompanied by a steady decline in Scholastic Aptitude Test scores. Excellence must begin in our homes and neighborhood schools, where it's the responsibility of every parent and teacher and the right of every child.

Our children come first, and that's why I established a bipartisan National Commission on Excellence in Education, to help us chart a commonsense course for better education. And already, communities are implementing the Commission's recommendations. Schools are reporting progress in math and reading skills. But we must do more to restore discipline to schools; and we must encourage the teaching of new basics, reward teachers of merit, enforce tougher standards, and put our parents back in charge.

I will continue to press for tuition tax credits to expand opportunities for families and to soften the double payment for those paying public school taxes and private school tuition. Our proposal would target assistance to low- and middle-income families. Just as more incentives are needed within our schools, greater competition is needed among our schools. Without standards and competition, there can be no champions, no records broken, no excellence in education or any other walk of life.

And while I'm on this subject, each day your Members observe a 200-year-old tradition meant to signify America is one nation under God. I must ask: If you can begin your day with a member of the clergy standing right here leading you in prayer, then why can't freedom to acknowledge God be enjoyed again by children in every schoolroom across this land?

America was founded by people who believed that God was their rock of safety. He is ours. I recognize we must be cautious in claiming that God is on our side, but I think it's all right to keep asking if we're on His side.

During our first 3 years, we have joined bipartisan efforts to restore protection of the law to unborn children. Now, I know this issue is very controversial. But unless and until it can be proven that an unborn child is not a living human being, can we justify assuming without proof that it isn't? No one has yet offered such proof; indeed, all the evidence is to the contrary. We should rise above bitterness and reproach, and if Americans could come together in a spirit of understanding and helping, then we could find positive solutions to the tragedy of abortion.

Economic recovery, better education, rededication to values, all show the spirit of renewal gaining the upper hand. And all will improve family life in the eighties. But families need more. They need assurance that they and their loved ones can walk the streets of America without being afraid. Parents need to know their children will not be victims of child pornography and abduction. This year we will intensify our drive against these and other horrible crimes like sexual abuse and family violence.

Already our efforts to crack down on career criminals, organized crime, drugpushers, and to enforce tougher sentences and paroles are having effect. In 1982 the crime rate dropped by 4.3 percent, the biggest decline since 1972. Protecting victims is just as important as safeguarding the rights of defendants.

Opportunities for all Americans will increase if we move forward in fair housing and work to ensure women's rights, provide for equitable treatment in pension benefits and Individual Retirement Accounts, facilitate child care, and enforce delinquent parent support payments.

It's not just the home but the workplace and community that sustain our values and shape our future. So, I ask your help in assisting more communities to break the bondage of dependency. Help us to free enterprise by permitting debate and voting "yes" on our proposal for enterprise zones in America. This has been before you for 2 years. Its passage can help high-unemployment areas by creating jobs and restoring neighborhoods.

A society bursting with opportunities, reaching for its future with confidence, sustained by faith, fair play, and a conviction that good and courageous people will flourish when they're free—these are the secrets of a strong and prosperous America at peace with itself and the world.

A lasting and meaningful peace is our fourth great goal. It is our highest aspiration. And our record is clear: Americans resort to force only when we must. We have never been aggressors. We have always struggled to defend freedom and democracy.

We have no territorial ambitions. We occupy no countries. We build no walls to lock people in. Americans build the future. And our vision of a better life for farmers, merchants, and working people, from the Americas to Asia, begins with a simple premise: The future is best decided by ballots, not bullets.

Governments which rest upon the consent of the governed do not wage war on their neighbors. Only when people are given a personal stake in deciding their own destiny, benefiting from their own risks, do they create societies that are prosperous, progressive, and free. Tonight, it is democracies that offer hope by feeding the hungry, prolonging life, and eliminating drudgery.

When it comes to keeping America strong, free, and at peace, there should be no Republicans or Democrats, just patriotic Americans. We can decide the tough issues not by who is right, but by what is right.

Together, we can continue to advance our agenda for peace. We can establish a more stable basis for peaceful relations with the Soviet Union; strengthen allied relations across the board; achieve real and equitable reductions in the levels of nuclear arms; reinforce our peacemaking efforts in the Middle East, Central America, and southern Africa; or assist developing countries, particularly our neighbors in the Western Hemisphere; and assist in the development of democratic institutions throughout the world.

The wisdom of our bipartisan cooperation was seen in the work of the Scowcroft commission, which strengthened our ability to deter war and protect peace. In that same spirit, I urge you to move forward with the Henry Jackson plan to implement the recommendations of the Bipartisan Commission on Central America.

Your joint resolution on the multinational peacekeeping force in Lebanon is also serving the cause of peace. We are making progress in Lebanon. For nearly 10 years, the Lebanese have lived from tragedy to tragedy with no hope for their future. Now the multinational peacekeeping force and our marines are helping them break their cycle of despair. There is hope for a free, independent, and sovereign Lebanon. We must have the courage to give peace a chance. And we must not be driven from our objectives for peace in Lebanon by state-sponsored terrorism. We have seen this ugly specter in Beirut, Kuwait, and Rangoon. It demands international attention. I will forward shortly legislative proposals to help combat terrorism. And I will be seeking support from our allies for concerted action.

Our NATO alliance is strong. 1983 was a banner year for political courage. And we have strengthened our partnerships and our friendships in the Far East. We're committed to dialog, deterrence, and promoting prosperity. We'll work with our trading partners for a new round of negotiations in support of freer world trade, greater competition, and more open markets.

A rebirth of bipartisan cooperation, of economic growth, and military deterrence, and a growing spirit of unity among our people at home and our allies abroad underline a fundamental and far-reaching change: The United States is safer, stronger, and more secure in 1984 than before. We can now move with confidence to seize the opportunities for peace, and we will.

Tonight, I want to speak to the people of the Soviet Union, to tell them it's true that our governments have had serious differences, but our sons and daughters have never fought each other in war. And if we Americans have our way, they never will.

People of the Soviet Union, there is only one sane policy, for your country and mine, to preserve our civilization in this modern age: A nuclear war cannot be won and must never be fought. The only value in our two nations possessing nuclear weapons is to make sure they will never be used. But then would it not be better to do away with them entirely?

People of the Soviet, President Dwight Eisenhower, who fought by your side in World War II, said the essential struggle "is not merely man against man or nation against nation. It is man against war." Americans are people of peace. If your government wants peace, there will be peace. We can come together in faith and friendship to build a safer and far better world for our children and our children's children. And the whole world will rejoice. That is my message to you.

Some days when life seems hard and we reach out for values to sustain us or a friend to help us, we find a person who reminds us what it means to be Americans.

Sergeant Stephen Trujillo, a medic in the 2d Ranger Battalion, 75th Infantry, was in the first helicopter to land at the compound held by Cuban forces in Grenada. He saw three other helicopters crash. Despite the imminent explosion of the burning aircraft, he never hesitated. He ran across 25 yards of open terrain through enemy fire to rescue wounded soldiers. He directed two other medics, administered first aid, and returned again and again to the crash site to carry his wounded friends to safety.

Sergeant Trujillo, you and your fellow service men and women not only saved innocent lives; you set a nation free. You inspire us as a force for freedom, not for despotism; and, yes, for peace, not conquest. God bless you.

And then there are unsung heroes: single parents, couples, church and civic volunteers. Their hearts carry without complaint the pains of family and community problems. They soothe our sorrow, heal our wounds, calm our fears, and share our joy.

A person like Father Ritter is always there. His Covenant House programs in New York and Houston provide shelter and help to thousands of frightened and abused children each year. The same is true of Dr. Charles Carson. Paralyzed in a plane crash, he still believed nothing is impossible. Today in Minnesota, he works 80 hours a week without pay, helping pioneer the field of computer-controlled walking. He has given hope to 500,000 paralyzed Americans that some day they may walk again.

How can we not believe in the greatness of America? How can we not do what is right and needed to preserve this last best hope of man on Earth? After all our struggles to restore America, to revive confidence in our country, hope for our future, after all our hard-won victories earned through the patience and courage of every citizen, we cannot, must not, and will not turn back. We will finish our job. How could we do less? We're Americans.

Carl Sandburg said, "I see America not in the setting sun of a black night of despair . . . I see America in the crimson light of a rising sun fresh from the burning, creative hand of God . . . I see great days ahead for men and women of will and vision."

I've never felt more strongly that America's best days and democracy's best days lie ahead. We're a powerful force for good. With faith and courage, we can perform great deeds and take freedom's next step. And we will. We will carry on the tradition of a good and worthy people who have brought light where there was darkness, warmth where there was cold, medicine where there was disease, food where there was hunger, and peace where there was only bloodshed.

Let us be sure that those who come after will say of us in our time, that in our time we did everything that could be done. We finished the race; we kept them free; we kept the faith.

Thank you very much. God bless you, and God bless America.

Note: The President spoke at 9:02 p.m. in

the House Chamber of the Capitol. He was introduced by Thomas P. O'Neill, Jr., Speaker of the House of Representatives. The address was broadcast live on nationwide radio and television.

Message to the Congress Transmitting the United States-Bulgaria Fishery Agreement
January 26, 1984

To the Congress of the United States:

In accordance with the Magnuson Fishery Conservation and Management Act of 1976 (Public Law 94–265; 16 USC 1801), I transmit herewith a governing international fishery agreement between the United States and the People's Republic of Bulgaria, signed at Washington on September 22, 1983.

This agreement is one of a series to be renegotiated in accordance with that legislation. I urge that the Congress give favorable consideration to this agreement at an early date.

RONALD REAGAN

The White House,
January 26, 1984.

Message to the Congress Transmitting the Proposed United States-Norway Agreement on Nuclear Energy
January 26, 1984

To the Congress of the United States:

I am pleased to transmit to the Congress, pursuant to section 123 d. of the Atomic Energy Act of 1954, as amended (42 U.S.C. 2153(d)), the text of the proposed revised Agreement for Cooperation Between the United States of America and Norway Concerning Peaceful Uses of Nuclear Energy with an accompanied annex and agreed minute. The Agreement is accompanied by my written approval, authorization and determination concerning the agreement and the memorandum of the Director of the United States Arms Control and Disarmament Agency with the Nuclear Proliferation Assessment Statement concerning the Agreement. The joint memorandum submitted to me by the Secretaries of State and Energy, which includes a summary of the provisions of the Agreement, and the views and recommendations of the Director of the United States Arms Control and Dis-

armament Agency and the Members of the Nuclear Regulatory Commission are also enclosed.

The proposed revised agreement with Norway has been negotiated in accordance with the Nuclear Non-Proliferation Act and in order to strengthen the basis for continuing and close cooperation between our countries. In my judgment, the proposed revised agreement for cooperation, together with its accompanying agreed minute, meets all statutory requirements.

I am pleased that this agreement is with Norway, one of the strongest supporters of the Non-Proliferation Treaty and of international non-proliferation efforts generally. We have a long history of close cooperation with Norway, particularly in nuclear research and in the critical area of reactor safety work. The agreement reflects our deep interest in strengthening international nuclear safety and in supporting Norway's important work in that area. The agreement will, in my view, further the non-proliferation and other foreign policy interests of the United States.

I have considered the views and recommendations of the interested agencies in reviewing the proposed agreement and have determined that its performance will promote, and will not constitute an unreason-

able risk to, the common defense and security. Accordingly, I have approved the agreement and authorized its execution, and urge that the Congress give it favorable consideration.

RONALD REAGAN

The White House,
January 26, 1984.

Message to the Congress Transmitting the Proposed United States-Sweden Agreement on Nuclear Energy
January 26, 1984

To the Congress of the United States:

I am pleased to transmit to the Congress, pursuant to section 123 d. of the Atomic Energy Act of 1954, as amended (42 U.S.C. 2153(d)), the text of the proposed Agreement for Cooperation Between the United States of America and Sweden Concerning Peaceful Uses of Nuclear Energy and accompanying annexes, agreed minute, and exchange of notes; my written approval, authorization and determination concerning the agreement; and the memorandum of the Director of the United States Arms Control and Disarmament Agency with the Nuclear Proliferation Assessment Statement concerning the agreement. The joint memorandum submitted to me by the Secretaries of State and Energy, which includes a summary of the provisions of the agreement, and the views and recommendations of the Director of the United States Arms Control and Disarmament Agency and the Members of the Nuclear Regulatory Commission are also enclosed.

The proposed revised agreement with Sweden has been negotiated in accordance with the Nuclear Non-Proliferation Act, which sets forth certain requirements for new agreements for peaceful nuclear cooperation with other countries. In my judgment, the proposed agreement for coopera-

tion between the United States and Sweden, together with its accompanying agreed minute, meets all statutory requirements.

The proposed bilateral agreement between Sweden and the United States reflects the desire of the Government of the United States and the Government of Sweden to establish and confirm a framework for peaceful nuclear cooperation between our two countries in a manner which recognizes both the shared non-proliferation objectives and the friendly and harmonious relations between the United States and Sweden. The proposed agreement will, in my view, further the non-proliferation and other foreign policy interests of the United States.

I have considered the views and recommendations of the interested agencies in reviewing the proposed agreement and have determined that its performance will promote, and will not constitute an unreasonable risk to, the common defense and security. Accordingly, I have approved the agreement and authorized its execution, and urge that the Congress give it favorable consideration.

RONALD REAGAN

The White House,
January 26, 1984.

Message to the Congress Transmitting the United States-Canada Agreement on Social Security
January 26, 1984

To the Congress of the United States:

Pursuant to section 233(e)(1) of the Social Security Act (42 U.S.C. 433(e)(1)), I transmit herewith the Agreement between the United States of America and the Government of Canada which consists of five separate instruments negotiated and signed over a period of several years.

The U.S.-Canada agreements are similar in objective to the social security agreements already in force with Italy, the Federal Republic of Germany, and Switzerland and to proposed agreements with Belgium and Norway which were recently submitted to Congress for review. Such bilateral agreements, generally known as totalization agreements, provide for limited coordination between the United States and foreign social security systems to overcome the problems of gaps in protection, and of dual coverage and taxation for workers who move from one country to the other.

I also transmit a comprehensive report prepared by the Department of Health and Human Services. This report explains the provisions of the Agreements and provides data on the number of persons affected by the Agreements and the effect on social security financing as required by the same provision of the Social Security Act.

The Department of State and the Department of Health and Human Services join with me in commending the U.S.-Canada Social Security Agreement and related documents.

RONALD REAGAN

The White House,
January 26, 1984.

Message to the Congress Transmitting the Annual Report of the National Science Board
January 26, 1984

To the Congress of the United States:

I am pleased to submit to the Congress the 15th report of the National Science Board, entitled *Science Indicators—1982.* This report is the sixth in a continuing series in which important aspects of the status of American science and engineering are examined.

The importance of scientific and engineering research and development to the well-being of our Nation is widely recognized. The science and technology policies which our Administration is implementing will ensure the continued preeminence of the United States in the various measures of national scientific and technological vigor reported here. We have provided for significant increases in Federal R&D support, especially in basic research, and encouraged scientific and engineering education. These will provide the basis for continued investments by both government and industry, which will strengthen our national security and our international competitiveness.

I commend *Science Indicators—1982* to the attention of the Congress. It will provide a useful reference to all who are involved with this Nation's R&D enterprise.

RONALD REAGAN

The White House,
January 26, 1984.

Note: The report is entitled "Science Indicators—1982, An Analysis of the State of U.S. Science, Engineering, and Technology, National Science Board, 1983" (Government Printing Office, 344 pages).

Appointment of Charles A. Black as a Member of the National Advisory Committee on Oceans and Atmosphere
January 26, 1984

The President today announced his intention to appoint Charles A. Black to be a member of the National Advisory Committee on Oceans and Atmosphere for a term expiring July 1, 1986. He will succeed Sharron Stewart.

Mr. Black is president of Mardela Corp. in Woodside, CA. He founded the Mardela Corp., which is engaged in marine and freshwater aquatic resource scientific development, in 1968. He served as a member of the National Advisory Committee on Oceans and Atmosphere in 1973–1976. He was a cofounder of Pacific Mariculture, Inc.,

in 1965. He was with the Ampex Corp., Redwood City, CA, in 1957–1965 and Stanford Research Institute in 1952–1957.

He is a corporate member of the Woods Hole Oceanographic Institution and of the Oceanic Institute in Hawaii. He was adviser to the Indian Ocean Programme (FAO) of the Indian Ocean Fisheries Commission in Rome, Italy, in 1973–1975.

Mr. Black graduated from Stanford University (B.A., 1940; M.B.A., 1945). He is married, has three children, and resides in Woodside, CA. He was born March 6, 1919, in Oakland, CA.

Nomination of Six Members of the Federal Council on the Aging
January 26, 1984

The President today announced his intention to nominate the following individuals to be members of the Federal Council on the Aging:

Ingrid Azvedo, for a term expiring June 5, 1985. She would succeed Charles J. Fahey. She serves on California State Senator John Doolittle's Advisory Committee on Aging. She is married, has two children, and resides in Elk Grove, CA. She was born February 28, 1934, in West Germany.

The following individuals to serve for terms expiring June 5, 1986. These are reappointments:

Nelda Ann Lambert Barton is president and chairman of the board of Health Systems, Inc., in Corbin, KY. She is married, has five children, and resides in Corbin. Mrs. Barton was born May 12, 1929, in Providence, KY.

Edna Bogosian is principal insurance examiner

for the Department of Banking and Insurance of the Commonwealth of Massachusetts. She was born November 17, 1913, in Boston, MA, and now resides in Watertown, MA.

James N. Broder is senior resident partner with the law firm of Thaxter, Lipez, Stevens, Broder & Micoleau in Washington, DC. He is married, has two children, and resides in Rockville, MD. He was born October 2, 1946, in Hartford, CT.

Tony Guglielmo is owner of Penny-Hanley & Howley Co. in Stafford Springs, CT. He is married, has three children, and resides in Stafford Springs. He was born October 13, 1940, in Stamford, CT.

Frances Lamont is a State senator from South Dakota who has authored and passed legislation dealing with the aging. She has twice served on the White House Conference on Aging. She has four children and resides in Aberdeen, SD. She was born June 10, 1914, in Rapid City, SD.

Remarks at a Spirit of America Rally in Atlanta, Georgia
January 26, 1984

There's someone from the old days. [*Laughter*] Well, if you'd done this a few years ago when I was making "Bedtime for Bonzo," I'd still be there. [*Laughter*]

Well, thank you very much, Jay. Governor Harris, Senator Mattingly, Congressmen Gingrich and Levitas, and the many sponsoring organizations and ladies and gentlemen:

May I say, this is a tonic to be in Georgia with so many thousands of America's finest. I believe that I'm looking at citizens who don't consider themselves Democrats or Republicans so much as just deeply patriotic Americans.

You are concerned about your country and determined to do all you can to make tomorrow better. And you are doing that. It's people like you who show us the heart of America is good, the spirit of America is strong, and the future of America is great. You give meaning to words like entrepreneur, self-reliance, personal initiative and, yes, optimism and confidence. And you will lead America to take freedom's next step.

Perhaps you heard my speech to the Nation last night on the state of our Union. What I said before that joint session I certainly can see and feel here this afternoon: Energy, optimism, and progress are surging through our land. America is back, as I said last night, and standing tall. And we're looking to the eighties with courage, confidence, and hope.

Together, we've charted a new course since 1980. And because we took those bold steps, I believe America is stronger, more prosperous, and more secure today than 3 years ago. It seems like only yesterday we were hearing that our country was doomed to decline and the world would slide into disaster no matter what we did. Like death and taxes, the doom-criers will always be with us, and they'll always be wrong.

They're wrong because they lack faith in the American people. They just can't understand that there is no limit to what proud and free citizens can do. But you understand, and you always have. It was

you who reminded Washington that we are a government of and by the people, not the other way around. And it's you who told us that it was time to put earnings back in the hands of the people, time to put trust back in the hands of the people, and time to put America back in the hands of the people.

And that's what we've been trying so very hard to do, trying to change just one little two-letter word—control *by* government to control *of* government.

Our economic program is guided by a spirit of enterprise that encourages risk-taking, rewards innovation, and involves millions of Americans making their own decisions. We have one policy intended to benefit Americans from every walk of life— it's called economic recovery, one of the best recoveries in the decade.

In just 6 days, a brand new airline, Air Atlanta—it's headed by Michael Hollis and primarily black-owned and managed—will begin service to Memphis and New York. We salute the spirit of entrepreneurship in the black community, and I'm pleased to say we're getting the Federal Government out of the way so they can compete.

Deregulation of the transportation industry has created new opportunities for small business while holding down costs for consumers. And we haven't cut back on safety.

Women have begun finding the economic opportunities they've always deserved. In 1983 they filled almost three-quarters of all the new jobs in managerial, professional, and technical fields. And the number of women-owned businesses is growing four times faster than those owned by men.

But we can do better. We can build a new era of lasting economic expansion filled with greater opportunities for all our people. You know something?—that'll be quite an improvement from what we inherited, because in 1981, as I said last night, we inherited the worst economic crisis in postwar history. There was only one thing fair about those policies of the past—and we hear a lot about fair today—they didn't discriminate. They made everyone miserable.

Would you agree that by reducing inflation from 12.4 percent in 1980 to just 3.2 in 1983 that we're helping all Americans and we should stick with it? [*Applause*]

Would you agree that by knocking down the prime rate from over 21 percent in 1981 to 11 percent today that we're helping small business and we should stick with it? [*Applause*]

Would you agree that by refusing to balance the budget on your backs, but insisting that government spend less, that we're doing what's right and fair for the people and we should fight on? [*Applause*]

And would you agree that by building a recovery which has created 4 million jobs and employed more people than any time in our history, that together we can and will save the American dream? [*Applause*]

Well, then, I have one more question. Would you tell the people in Washington what you just told me? [*Applause*] Thank you.

I know this is an election year. But I believe responsible Republicans and Democrats can still cooperate and put good government over politics. To those who say we must turn back to tax and tax and spend and spend, I can only reply: Not on your life. The best view of big government is in the rearview mirror as we leave it behind. [*Laughter*]

I know the intentions were good, but we paid a terrible price for those government excesses of prior years. Americans endured a long and terrible ordeal lasting more than a decade and filled with one economic disappointment after another. Despite an increase in American incomes of 140 percent during the seventies, a 112-percent increase in inflation and personal tax rates that nearly tripled left them feeling worse off than before. But we're seeing a new dawn of hope for our people. As the passage says in Psalms, "Weeping may endure for a night, but joy cometh in the morning."

From solid growth in housing to new frontiers in high technology, from a healthy recovery in real wages to a big improvement in productivity, and from record increases in venture capital to new confidence in the stock market, America is moving forward and getting stronger.

I believe our challenge of building a permanently manned space station within the next decade can open up an entire—well, open up new industries, not just an industry for space-based entrepreneurs.

Our work is far from finished. Too many of our fellow countrymen are still out of work or down on their luck. They include workers and would-be workers in areas that depend heavily upon one company or industry. Many of them have been displaced by changes in the way things are produced.

If the dream of America is to be preserved, we must not waste the genius of one mind, the strength of one body, or the spirit of one soul. We need all our people—men and women, young and old, individuals of every race to be healthy, happy, and whole. This is our goal. We will not rest until all Americans can reach as high as their vision and God-given talents take them. And that's why I've been asking the Congress for 2 years to get off the dime and pass our enterprise zones proposal. If they do, we can prove that areas of chronic unemployment need not be areas of permanent unemployment. But the Congress must act. Now, present company is excepted when I say this. I know where they stand.

And as I said last night, we need the cooperation of the Congress for structural reforms that will ensure continued progress for years to come. First and foremost, we must insist on common sense in Federal budgeting.

We face large deficits, and there's no disagreement about the need to bring those deficits down. The disagreement is over how we do it—with spending cuts and economic growth or through tax increases. Well, I happen to believe responsible budgeting does not mean routing more and more of your earnings to Washington, DC. Responsible budgeting means government spending no more than government takes in.

People should have freedom to keep more of the money they earn to spend the way they want to and not have the government taking more and more of their money to spend the way it wants to.

Our critics sometimes forget that even after our tax cuts, the American people are shouldering a near-record peacetime tax burden. The other problem with raising taxes, as we've seen in the past, is that it simply encouraged government to spend more. And since people had less money in their pockets to spend or save, economic growth was hurt, so fewer people were employed and able to pay taxes. Deficits went up, not down. Tax revenues doubled between 1976 and 1981, but deficits increased. A recent study shows that countries with lower tax burdens have higher rates of economic growth and employment.

Of course, this shouldn't come as a surprise to anyone who understands incentives: We don't face large deficits because you're not taxed enough; we face those deficits because government still spends too much.

We've already cut spending growth by more than half from its 17.4-percent rate in 1980. And in the area of waste, fraud, and abuse, the diligence of our Inspectors General has saved taxpayers over $30 billion and improved the use of funds. I sent them out—we put them all together into a kind of a task force, the Inspector Generals, and sent them out through government. And for the last year and a half they've been out there, and they report to me every 6 months. And the only thing I told them to do was, I said, I just want you to be as mean as junkyard dogs. [*Laughter*] And they have been.

Now a recent poll has revealed—and I'm surprised—that fewer than 10 percent of our people know what the Grace commission report is. We must change that. I asked an American industrialist, Peter Grace, to put together a task force of citizens from the world of commerce and industry to find ways that government could become more businesslike. Mr. Grace organized an executive committee of 161 such experts from the business world—the private sector— then nearly 2,000 others like themselves. They went into every area of government and, incidentally, financed the whole operation themselves.

The Grace commission's report has come up now. We have it in hand with nearly 2,500 recommendations that could save billions of dollars in wasteful Federal spending. I'm asking the members of our administration to study those recommendations

with a fine tooth comb to see how many we can put in place.

Beyond that, I'm convinced that we need improvements in the budget process itself. Some 43 of our 50 Governors have the right to veto individual items in appropriation bills without having to veto the entire bill. When I was Governor of California we used that line-item veto to very good effect. Isn't it time to bring the Federal Government into the 20th century by enacting the same fiscal controls the States have been using for years? [*Applause*] Mr. Mattingly, sitting on this platform, is undertaking the task of getting this started up there on Capitol Hill.

Most of our States also have provisions in their constitutions requiring balanced budgets. Indeed, Thomas Jefferson, way back in the beginning of our country, said there was one thing lacking in the Constitution, and he said this right after it had been adopted. He said, "It should have additionally a clause that forbids the Federal Government from borrowing money."

Well, my dream is to see the day when a constitutional amendment requiring the Federal Government to balance its budget, as well, will be adopted.

A balanced budget amendment is no panacea, because it would take several years of continued effort to achieve it. But it would force the leaders in the Congress and the executive branch to sit down to work out a long-term plan for spending restraint. And I believe we owe this to the people. It's what you sent us to Washington to do.

In addition to long-term reforms for spending, I believe we should make our tax system more simple, fair, and rewarding for all the people. Would you believe I've been told that even Albert Einstein had to ask the IRS for help on his 1040? [*Laughter*] Now if we could broaden the tax base, then personal tax rates could come down, rather than go up. And I think that's one change the American people want and our economy needs.

Spending and regulations guided by common sense and fairness, a monetary policy that ensures lasting price stability, and a tax system anchored by incentives that reward personal initiative, risk taking, and economic growth—these are keys to a society of opportunities offering a better life for our people with no barriers for bigotry or discrimination.

The trouble is when tough but necessary decisions to restrain spending are made, they're described usually in negative terms—how much less government will spend. How many fewer benefits will be given away? How many fewer programs will survive? This is an old trap we shouldn't fall into. The spenders always say, "All right, if you want to cut spending, what programs will you do away with?"

Well, most of us agree that government does have legitimate functions it must perform. Our answer must be we believe government's tasks can be performed more economically and efficiently. Cutting back a runaway government which stifles the spirit of enterprise can be profoundly positive, like performing surgery on a patient to save his life.

That's why the ultimate and overwhelmingly positive goal of our administration is to put limits on the power of government. Yes, but do it in a way that liberates the powers and the real source of our national genius—you, the people, in your families, neighborhoods, and places of work.

We are a nation under God. I've always believed that this blessed land was set apart in a special way, that some divine plan placed this great continent here between the oceans to be found by people from every corner of the Earth who had a special love for freedom and the courage to uproot themselves, leave homeland and friends, to come to a strange land. And coming here they created something new in all the history of mankind—a land where man is not beholden to government, government is beholden to man.

George Washington believed that religion, morality, and brotherhood were the pillars of society. He said you couldn't have morality without religion. And yet today we're told that to protect the first amendment, we must expel God, the source of all knowledge, from our children's classrooms. Well, pardon me, but the first amendment was not written to protect the American people from religion; the first amendment was written to protect the American people from government tyranny.

Indeed, there is nothing in the Constitution at all about public education and prayer. There is, however, something very pertinent in the act that gave birth to our public school system—a national act, if you will. It called for public education to see that our children—and quoting from that act—"learned about religion and morality."

Well, the time has come for Congress to give a majority of American families what they want for their children—a constitutional amendment making it unequivocally clear that children can hold voluntary prayer in their schools.

Within our families, neighborhoods, schools, and businesses, let us continue reaching out, renewing our spirit of friendship, community service, and caring for the needy—a spirit that flows like a deep and mighty river through the history of our nation. But to lawbreakers and drug peddlers who would harm and prey on innocent citizens, who make our family and friends live in fear, we will demand justice with swift and sure punishment for the guilty.

We are a people who seek peace within us, within our communities, and around the world. The United States has no higher mission than to build a lasting peace that enshrines liberty, democracy, and dignity for individuals everywhere. And I believe that what we've accomplished together—restoration of economic and military strength and a growing spirit of unity at home and with our allies abroad—put America in its strongest position in years to seize the opportunities for peace.

Sooner or later the Soviets will realize they have nothing to gain by waiting. Good-faith negotiations are in their interest, because the West could offer them many benefits their people now lack. People don't make wars; governments do. And if the Soviet Union wants peace, there will be peace.

People don't want confrontation; they want a better life. And that's what the spirit of America does best—it builds the future. And we've always been willing to share the fruits of our success with others.

We see it in a person like John Shepherd. His hard work, vision, and determination helped him rise from poverty in Chicago to build thriving enterprises that have taken scores of families off welfare. Shepherd said, "This is the greatest country in the world. And it does offer opportunity to those who have the guts to get in there and fight for it."

In these last 3 years, we've made a new beginning, a dramatic and far-reaching step toward a much better tomorrow. Thank you for keeping the faith. Thank you all for your strength and support. I believe we've come too far, struggled too hard, and accomplished too much to turn back now. With your help we can put strong wings on weary hearts. We can make America stronger not just economically and militarily, but also morally and spiritually. We can make our beloved country the source of all the dreams and opportunities she was placed on this good Earth to provide. We need only to believe in each other and in the God who has so blessed our land.

A short time ago, I had the pleasure and honor of awarding the Presidential Medal of Freedom to that great friend of our nation and a great statesman, physically a small man, but so great in so many ways, who for many years was the Philippine Ambassador to the United States, General Romulo. He addressed a farewell message to America as he left to return to his own country. He ended his message saying, "Thank you, America, and farewell. May God keep you always, and may you always keep God."

Thank you, and God bless you.

Note: The President spoke at 4:55 p.m. in Omni Coliseum. He was introduced by Jay Van Andel, chairman of the board of the Amway Corp. and chairman of the rally, which was a gathering of business people from the southeastern United States and the Atlanta area.

Following his remarks, the President met at the coliseum with representatives of the host committee of the rally.

Remarks at the Southern Republican Leadership Conference in Atlanta, Georgia
January 26, 1984

Audience. [*Chanting*] Four more in '84! Four more in '84!

The President. Thank you. I'll take that under consideration until Sunday night. [*Laughter*] Well, I thank you Mack and Bill Harris, Bob Bell, and Members of the Congress, Newt Gingrich, and ladies and gentlemen.

I have to tell you a little something here that's just reminded me of a story—two things have reminded me. First of all, I understand that many of you heard me last night, and then I happened to hear that a great many of you heard me on television just a little while ago. And the other thing is that when two gentlemen came in here, that left me backstage with their wives. [*Laughter*] And that also helped remind me of the story—[*laughter*]—that the fact that you heard me twice also—it happens to be a story of an older preacher who was talk-

ing to a young preacher who hadn't had as much experience.

And he said to him, "You know, sometimes on Sunday morning, they begin to nod off." And he says, "I've found a way to wake them up." He says, "Right in my sermon when I see them beginning to doze, I say, 'Last night I held in my arms a woman who is the wife of another man.'" And he says, "That wakes them up." [*Laughter*] And he says, "Then, when they look at me startled, I say: It was my dear mother." [*Laughter*]

Well, the young preacher took that to heart. And a few weeks later, sure enough, there some of them were, dozing off. So, he remembered what had been told him, and he said. "Last night I held in my arms a woman who is the wife of another man." And they all looked at him, and everyone was awake. And he says, "I can't remember who it was." [*Laughter*]

But it's wonderful to be here with all of you in Georgia. It wasn't that long ago, yes, when the South was a stronghold for the Democratic Party. But from the spirit I sense here, those days are long gone. Today it's the Republican Party that reflects the progress and the vibrance of the new South.

And I think—having been a Democrat myself, as I'm sure many of you were also and made the change, and you know what it is like to make that change—but I think that many of us look back—I know I do— and say, did I really change? Or was it that the party of my father and the party that I had belonged to, it changed? It no longer stood for the things that it had stood for, for so many years.

I, once as a new Republican, tried to talk the Republican Party into using the 1932 Democratic platform. [*Laughter*] It called for a 25-percent reduction in government spending, a return to the States and local communities autonomy that had been confiscated by the Federal Government, a reduction and elimination of useless boards and bureaus and departments in government. And I thought, that's still a brand new platform. At least they've never used it. [*Laughter*]

Hundreds of Republicans have been elected through the South. Your own Senator, Mack Mattingly, Congressman Newt Gingrich, Bill Young, Macon's mayor, George Israel, and others who couldn't be with us—they represent the kind of courageous leadership of which southerners and all Republicans are rightfully proud. And I'm especially grateful, because I relied heavily on them for the last 3 years. And all I ask is, "Send me more."

You here today are proof of a new solid South about to emerge on the American political scene. And only this time, it'll be a Republican South. I predict that in this coming election, we're not only going to hold our own; we're going to make gains throughout the region.

The new South will not, for political expediency, be tying itself to political bosses and big spenders in other parts of the country. Those days are over. The new South is concerned about economic growth and expanding opportunity for everyone. The new South is concerned about a strong America and about maintaining the values and the strength of character that made this country the richest and the greatest in history. And now is the time to reach out to our Democratic friends as never before and to tell them how good the water is over on this side. [*Laughter*]

Voting Republican isn't half bad. As I told you, I know how hard it is to make that first move, but it wasn't me or it wasn't you who have made the same change that moved. As I say, the party moved.

Now, once Democratic candidates encouraged people to work for the country. I remember, as a matter of fact, a young President at his inaugural who said, "Ask not what your country can do for you—ask what you can do for your country." And within a matter of weeks, they had introduced 29 new spending programs of what the country could do for the people. [*Laughter*]

Today, we see candidates who are trying to buy support by telling people what the country will do for them and making promises to interest groups. Just a while ago, there was a debate up in New Hampshire. [*Laughter*] And there were so many candidates on the platform, there weren't enough promises to go around. [*Laughter*]

But I just don't believe the people can be bought with promises anymore that have to be paid for out of the Treasury. They know who eventually ends up paying for all of those promises. I feel sorry for some of those Democratic Congressmen, though, at the same time. Can you imagine what it must be like, worn out after a day at the office? They go home. They try to go to sleep. And the first thing you know, they're having nightmares that the money they're spending is their own. [*Laughter*]

Calvin Coolidge once said that "Patriotism is easy to understand in America. It means looking out for yourself by looking out for the country." Well, the Republican message to voters this year is just that: When we vote, we should do it for America. When we choose on election day, we should think of the future of our children. It'll require hard work on our part. We have to get our message out, and that isn't so easy in America. There just does seem to be more attention paid to things other than what we have to say.

For example, right now that whole thing about that all of our problems could be solved if we would just take that defense budget and whittle it down to size. We're so extravagant with defense spending. Well, would you like to know that in 1962 the defense budget under a Democratic administration was 48 percent? Would you like to know also that our budget—that was 48 percent of the whole budget for defense. Our budget last year was 27.6 percent— 27.6 percent. And this year, the budget we're asking for will be 28 percent of the total budget. So, no, it isn't that. But, again, the distortions keep on coming out.

The other day, I just heard one of them on television, and he referred to the recent recession as my recession. [*Laughter*] Well, now, as I recall with those double-digit interest rates and inflation rates and everything, and unemployment up there pretty high and climbing, and it'd been climbing since 1979, we proposed our economic recovery program. But when we fell off into the big dip called the recession—which was really a continuation of the recession that had started in 1979—but when we fell off into that big dip of unemployment, and the housing industry folded because of the high interest rates, and the automobile companies and the steel companies all shut down, and it spread—nothing of our economic recovery program had been put in place yet. It wasn't there. We were still operating on the last budget of theirs, which we had to inherit when we came into office.

Audience member. Georgia apologizes! [*Laughter*]

The President. Well, but seriously— [*laughter*]—these are economic matters that a great many people don't understand. For example, right now, the whole talk about the deficits—no one wants more than we do—for years we've been complaining about them. But we started deficit spending 50 years ago. And for 46 of those 50 years, the Democrats had a majority in both Houses of the Congress—to say nothing of how many times they also had the White House. And it is the Congress that spends money. There's nothing in the Constitution that gives the President any right to spend any money. Not a penny.

But they—if you'll remember back—they told us that deficit spending didn't matter because we owed it to ourselves. [*Laughter*] And they said it was necessary for prosperity that we have a little deficit spending too—and a little inflation also—and that we could keep on going with that. And now the pattern has been set to which the deficits are caused by what they call the uncontrollables, meaning programs that they created, adopted, and built in an automatic increase in spending every year so they don't have to go back and increase it themselves, it just automatically increases.

Well, these are the things—why we need more in the Congress of the people like are on this platform, more so that we can get the job done of getting government back down to where it should be and proving that nothing is uncontrollable if a Congress is willing to undo the mistake that it made.

There's one thing—I don't think any of us should be afraid in the coming election year of asking our friends and our Democratic friends: "Are you worse or better off than you were 4 years ago? Is America better off than it was 4 years ago?"

We'd permitted our military strength— going back to the defense budget—to erode. And as it declined, so did our prestige and our national security. How many of you have heard some friend who's back from going abroad in those days and comes back and the feeling that he got over there of the disdain that so many people felt for this country? But we reversed that trend in the last 3 years. And I think today every citizen of the United States is safer and the United States is more respected and more secure because of what we've done.

And right here, I've got to interrupt and tell a little story. I enjoy telling it. [*Laughter*] Those guys of ours, those young men and women in uniform, when you see one of them on the street anymore, remember what it was like back in the war, if you're old enough to remember then? Why don't you—don't just pass them by. Kind of smile and maybe stick out a hand and tell them you're glad they're doing what they're doing.

What I wanted to—the story I want to tell, I've been telling it all over the Capital, and I hope it hasn't gotten here yet. [*Laughter*] It comes from a young first lieutenant, a marine lieutenant who flies a Cobra. He was at Grenada, and now he's in Beirut. He moved on when the relief force moved over there. And he wrote back and said that while he was in Grenada, he noticed that every news story about Grenada contained one line that never varied, that Grenada produced more nutmeg than any other place on Earth. And he decided that was a code. [*Laughter*] And he was going to break the code. And so he wrote back to say he did.

In six steps he had broken the code. Number one, Grenada does produce more nutmeg than any other place on Earth. Number two, the Soviets and the Cubans are trying to take Grenada. Number three, you can't have Christmas—or you can't make eggnog—you can't make eggnog without nutmeg. Number four, you can't have Christmas without eggnog. Number five, the Soviets and the Cubans were trying to steal Christmas. [*Laughter*] And, he wrote, number six, we stopped them. [*Laughter*]

Listen, I've kept you standing there longer than I intended to, and I just want to again thank you for all the support that you've given and the way you've rallied. And all of the polls show that the things that we want so badly and that are being denied by the majority today in Congress, the polls show they're the things that the American people overwhelming want.

Eighty-three percent of the most recent poll of the people said, yes, they want the deficits reduced, but they don't want them reduced by raising taxes. They want them reduced by cutting spending—83 percent. Over 70 percent in all the polls that I've seen say they want the President to have the line-item veto. By the same numbers, they want the constitutional amendment to balance the budget.

So, we're going to try to talk, and we're going to try to negotiate in a bipartisan fashion, dealing with the deficit. But I can tell you now I am dead set against raising taxes to do it.

So, again, thank you all——

Audience member. Are you going to run?

The President. What? [*Laughter*]

Audience member. Are you going to run?

The President. Tune in Sunday night. Don't miss it.

Thank you all very much. God bless you.

Note: The President spoke at 6 p.m. in the International Ballroom at the Omni Hotel. Prior to his remarks, he met with southern Republican leaders at the hotel.

Following his appearance at the conference, the President returned to Washington, DC.

Remarks at a White House Meeting With Republican Congressmen
January 27, 1984

Just going to say a few words in here—that it's a pleasure for me to welcome you here this morning, as one who knows first-hand the good work that you've been doing up on the Hill. And a special thanks to Bob Michel and Trent Lott, who are two of the most skilled and articulate legislators that I've ever known.

And I want to share with you a quotation that I came across recently in my unofficial reading. It comes from a man who was a celebrated speaker, a journalist, a soldier, an historian, and a statesman. His name was—you've maybe heard it before—Winston Churchill. Some say that if he wanted to, he could even have been a great character actor. [*Laughter*] He once said that Americans did not cross the ocean, cross the mountains, and cross the prairies because we're made of sugar candy.

Well, I believe Sir Winston had a point. I think back to the opening days of this administration. Many observers predicted that we couldn't work together, that the economic and social problems that had piled up over 50 years had been insurmountable. Well, I think we've proved the critics wrong. And we did it by working together, by building coalitions, and by daring to chart a new course.

Inflation, as we said the other night, has plummeted to 3.2 percent during the last year. That's the lowest rate in over a decade. The prime interest rate is nearly half what it was when we took office. Factory orders, retail sales, and housing starts are up. The stock market has come back to life. Real wages are rising, and America's leading the world in a technological revolution that is even more far-reaching and profound, as I said the other night, than the Industrial Revolution of a century ago.

Unemployment—dropping at the fastest rate in more than 30 years. Last year alone, more than 4 million Americans found jobs, and today 103 million Americans are at work. And that's more than ever before in our history.

In the military, morale has soared as we've begun giving the men and women in our Armed Forces good pay and good equipment and the respect they deserve.

In foreign policy, the world knows once more again what America stands for: the freedom of mankind. From Central America to Africa to the Middle East, we're working to support democracy and promote peace. In Lebanon, the peace process has been slow and painful, but we've made genuine progress.

In Europe, the NATO alliance has held firm. In our dealings with the Soviets, by strengthening our defenses and showing the world our willingness to negotiate, we've laid the foundations for a lasting world peace. And on an island in the Caribbean, we set a nation free.

There's no doubt that we're changing the course of American history, and we're doing it together. Believe me, I know how tough this has been for many of you, but you can be proud of all that we've accomplished. There's no better place to sit than the Oval Office to see how important and effective you all are.

In 1984 nothing matters more than increasing your numbers, and I pledge to do all within my power to see that we do just that.

And in the meantime, we have our work cut out for us. We have to get on with the job of bringing the budget under still better control. To contain special interest spending we must pass the line-item veto. We must bring inflation and interest rates down still further without loading new burdens on the backs of the American taxpayer. We must maintain a strong defense and face our world responsibilities squarely. And we must continue to return resources and responsibilities to the American people that will mean more savings, more freedom, more economic opportunity, and more jobs for all Americans.

I want you and your Democratic colleagues to know that I'm serious about negotiating a downpayment on the deficit. This is not a political posturing, as some have suggested. I'm not ruling anything out as beyond the bounds of legitimate debate. But I do think that we should try to concentrate on the less contentious issues. If we all focus on what's doable, we can get something done for the American people.

That'll mean more hard work, but I believe it'll be worth it for our party and, more importantly, for America. So, let us strive together to make it work.

Thank you, God bless you. And now, let's eat.

Note: The President spoke at 9 a.m. in the East Room at the White House.

Message to the Senate Transmitting the Convention for the Protection and Development of the Marine Environment of the Wider Caribbean Region
January 27, 1984

To the Senate of the United States:

I transmit herewith, for the advice and consent of the Senate to ratification, the Convention for the Protection and Development of the Marine Environment of the Wider Caribbean Region. The Department of the State has prepared a report with respect to the Convention which is attached. I also transmit to the Senate, for its information, the Protocol to the Convention Concerning Cooperation in Combating Oil Spills in the Wider Caribbean Region and the Final Act of the Cartagena Conference which adopted the Convention and Protocol.

The Convention for the Protection and Development of the Marine Environment of the Wider Caribbean Region will create general legal obligations to protect the marine environment of the Caribbean Sea, the Gulf of Mexico and areas of the Atlantic Ocean immediately adjacent thereto. It covers a variety of forms of marine pollution including pollution from ships, pollution by dumping, pollution from land-based sources, pollution from seabed activities, and airborne pollution. It includes provisions on specially protected areas, cooperation in emergency situations, and environmental impact assessment. The Convention also contains an annex outlining non-compulsory procedures for the peaceful settlement of disputes arising under the Convention.

The Convention, which was concluded within the framework of the United Nations Environment Program's Regional Seas Program, is intended to be supplemented, where necessary, by the development of specific protocols to it, such as the Protocol Concerning Cooperation in Combating Oil Spills in the Wide Caribbean Region (which extends to other hazardous substances as well), providing for more concrete obligations. In areas where there are existing international agreements, such as on marine pollution from ships and by dumping, the Convention provides for the application of the relevant international rules and standards developed under those agreements.

The entry into force of the Convention, augmented by its Protocol, will be an important step in creating, in the region, marine pollution standards which are generally higher, more uniform, consistent in character, and closer to our own than presently exist. Consequently, the Convention and its Protocol will provide new protection for United States territory, the Gulf States, as well as the Commonwealth of Puerto Rico and the Virgin Islands.

The United States played a leading role in the negotiation of the Convention for the Protection and Development of the Marine Environment of the Wider Caribbean Region. Expeditious United States ratification of the Convention would demonstrate our concern for the protection of the marine environment of the Caribbean region and our commitment to the region as a whole. It is my hope that the United States will also play a leading role in the effective implementation of the Convention, which we expect to enter into force in a short period of time. To this end, it is important that the United States be represented at the first meeting of the Contracting Parties, which will be held no later than two years after entry into force of the Convention, following the deposit of the ninth instrument of ratification, acceptance, approval, or accession.

I recommend that the Senate give early and favorable consideration to the Convention and give its advice and consent to ratification.

RONALD REAGAN

The White House,
January 27, 1984.

Message to the Senate Transmitting the United States-South Africa Consular Convention
January 27, 1984

To the Senate of the United States:

I am transmitting for the Senate's advice and consent to ratification the Consular Convention between the United States of America and the Republic of South Africa which was signed at Pretoria on October 28, 1982. I am also transmitting for the information of the Senate the report of the Department of State with respect to the Convention. This Convention will establish firm obligations on such important matters as free communication between a national and his consul, notification of consular officers of the arrest and detention of their nationals and permission for visits by consuls to nationals who are under detention.

I welcome the opportunity through this Convention to improve the relations between the two countries and their nationals. I urge the Senate to give the Convention its prompt and favorable consideration.

RONALD REAGAN

The White House,
January 27, 1984.

Radio Address to the Nation on the Space Program
January 28, 1984

My fellow Americans:

Three days ago in my State of the Union Message I spoke to you about taking on the challenge of America's next frontier, space, as one of four great goals for the eighties. Well, today I'd like to tell you more about that challenge, about how we can advance America's leadership in space through the end of this century and well into the next, and how, by reaching for exciting goals in space, we'll serve the cause of peace and create a better life for all of us here on Earth.

For a quarter of a century, we've moved steadily forward in the exploration and utilization of space, extending our knowledge of our solar system, our galaxy, and our universe. The space shuttle, our most recent advance in space technology, gives us routine access to space.

Just as the Yankee Clipper ships of the last century symbolized American vitality, our space shuttles today capture the optimistic spirit of our times. Our many achievements have proven that we can do much in space and that there's much more we must do to ensure that America lives up to her description—a land of hope and opportunity.

Our space goals will chart a path of progress toward creating a better life for all people who seek freedom, prosperity, and security.

Our approach to space has three elements. Let me discuss each of them briefly. The first is a commitment to build a permanently manned space station to be in orbit around the Earth within a decade. It will be a base for many kinds of scientific, commercial, and industrial activities and a stepping-stone for further goals.

Scientists from NASA, universities, and private industry will do research in and around the space station—research that's only possible in the zero-gravity and vacuum of space. As needed, private industry will fund expansions of the NASA facility where companies can manufacture new products and provide new services.

But most importantly, like every step forward, a space station will not be an end in itself but a doorway to even greater progress in the future. In this case, a space station will open up new opportunities for expanding human commerce and learning and provide a base for further exploration of that magnificent and endless frontier of space.

International cooperation, the second element of our plan, has long been a guiding principle of the United States space program. The tricentennial of the first German immigration to America was celebrated last year with a joint space effort. Just as our friends were asked to join us in the shuttle program, our friends and allies will be invited to join with us in the space station project.

The third goal of our space strategy will be to encourage American industry to move quickly and decisively into space. Obstacles to private sector space activities will be removed, and we'll take appropriate steps to spur private enterprise in space.

We expect space-related investments to grow quickly in future years, creating many new jobs and greater prosperity for all Americans. Companies interested in putting payloads into space, for example, should have ready access to private sector launch services.

Transportation Secretary Elizabeth Dole will work to stimulate the private sector investment in commercial, unmanned space boosters. We need a thriving, commercial launch industry. NASA, along with other departments and agencies, will be taking a number of initiatives to promote private

sector investment to ensure our lead over current and potential foreign competitors. So, we're going to bring into play America's greatest asset—the vitality of our free enterprise system.

We've always prided ourselves on the pioneer spirit that built America. Well, that spirit is a key to our future as well as our past. Once again, we're on a frontier. Our willingness to accept this challenge will reflect whether America's men and women today have the same bold vision, the same courage and indomitable spirit that made us a great nation.

The peaceful use of space promises great benefits to all mankind. It opens vast new opportunities for our industry and ingenuity. The only limits we have are those of our own courage and imagination. When President John Kennedy challenged America to go to the Moon, he said it would not be one person going but an entire nation putting him there.

Our space program has done so much to bring us together because it gives us the opportunity to be the kind of nation we want to be, the kind of nation we must always be—dreaming, daring, and creating.

Until next week, thanks for listening, and God bless you.

Note: The President spoke at 12:06 p.m. from the Oval Office at the White House.

Address to the Nation Announcing the Reagan-Bush Candidacies for Reelection
January 29, 1984

My fellow Americans:

It's been nearly 3 years since I first spoke to you from this room. Together we've faced many difficult problems, and I've come to feel a special bond of kinship with each one of you. Tonight I'm here for a different reason. I've come to a difficult personal decision as to whether or not I should seek reelection.

When I first addressed you from here, our national defenses were dangerously weak, we had suffered humiliation in Iran,

and at home we were adrift, possibly because of a failure here in Washington to trust the courage and character of you, the people. But worst of all, we were on the brink of economic collapse from years of government overindulgence and abusive overtaxation. Thus, I had to report that we were "in the worst economic mess since the Great Depression."

Inflation had risen to over 13 percent in 1979 and to 19 percent in March of 1980. Those back-to-back years of price explosions were the highest in more than 60 years. In the 5 years before I came here, taxes had actually doubled. Your cost-of-living pay raises just bumped you into higher tax brackets.

Interest rates over 21 percent, the highest in 120 years; productivity, down 2 consecutive years; industrial production down; actual wages and earnings down—the only things going up were prices, unemployment, taxes, and the size of government. While you tightened your belt, the Federal Government tightened its grip.

Well, things have changed. This past year inflation dropped down to 3.2 percent. Interest rates, cut nearly in half. Retail sales are surging. Homes are being built and sold. Auto assembly lines are opening up. And in just the last year, 4 million people have found jobs—the greatest employment gain in 33 years. By beginning to rebuild our defenses, we have restored credible deterrence and can confidently seek a secure and lasting peace, as well as a reduction in arms.

As I said Wednesday night, America is back and standing tall. We've begun to restore great American values—the dignity of work, the warmth of family, the strength of neighborhood, and the nourishment of human freedom.

But our work is not finished. We have more to do in creating jobs, achieving control over government spending, returning more autonomy to the States, keeping peace in a more settled world, and seeing if we can't find room in our schools for God.

At my inaugural, I quoted words that had been spoken over 200 years ago by Dr. Joseph Warren, president of the Massachusetts Congress. "On you depend the fortunes of America," he told his fellow Americans. "You are to decide the important question on which rests the happiness and liberty of millions yet unborn." And he added, "Act worthy of yourselves."

Over these last 3 years, Nancy and I have been sustained by the way you, the real heroes of American democracy, have met Dr. Warren's challenge. You were magnificent as we pulled the Nation through the long night of our national calamity. You have, indeed, acted worthy of yourselves.

Your high standards make us remember the central question of public service: Why are we here? Well, we're here to see that government continues to serve you, not the other way around.

We're here to lift the weak and to build the peace, and most important, we're here, as Dr. Warren said, to act today for the happiness and liberty of millions yet unborn, to seize the future so that every new child of this beloved Republic can dream heroic dreams. If we do less, we betray the memory of those who have given so much.

This historic room and the Presidency belong to you. It is your right and responsibility every 4 years to give someone temporary custody of this office and of the institution of the Presidency. You so honored me, and I'm grateful—grateful and proud of what, together, we have accomplished.

We have made a new beginning. Vice President Bush and I would like to have your continued support and cooperation in completing what we began 3 years ago. I am, therefore, announcing that I am a candidate and will seek reelection to the office I presently hold.

Thank you for the trust you've placed in me. God bless you, and good night.

Note: The President spoke at 10:55 p.m. from the Oval Office at the White House. His address was broadcast live on nationwide radio and television. It was paid for by the Reagan-Bush '84 Committee.

Interview With Thomas DeFrank and Eleanor Clift of Newsweek on the 1984 Presidential Election
January 27, 1984

The President's Candidacy

Mr. DeFrank. Obviously, Mr. President, we appreciate the chance to chat with you very much. Thank you.

It probably will come as no surprise that we asked to talk with you on the presumption that on Sunday night you'll be telling us that you're going to announce for reelection. Now, obviously, this is off the record until Monday, so before we get into this, we're hoping you might tell us, off the record, whether we're right about that.

The President. Well, I don't think so. I will do it on the supposition that you're interviewing me on the assumption that I am going to run, and I'll answer accordingly.

Mr. DeFrank. Fair enough, all right. On that basis——

Ms. Clift. You don't want to say the three little words, though?

The President. No.

Ms. Clift. No?

The President. No.

Mr. DeFrank. Okay.

Ms. Clift. Well, all right, we'll imagine that that is the—that you have made a "go" decision, though. And I guess we want to ask you when you finally did make up your mind?

The President. Well, making up my mind as to what the decision would be was left to the latest possible moment. I've always believed, for one thing, that campaigns are too long. But I also—in the event that the answer was to be yes—I've always felt that it's too easy to find yourself making decisions on the basis of the political ramifications, rather than on what's right or wrong with the decision that has to be made. And if I'd informed—when I was Governor of California I would not let a Cabinet discuss with me any political ramifications of any issue. I won't let my Cabinet now do that. We will only discuss things on the basis of are they, or are they not, good for the people.

But to nurse a decision, then, it's a little bit like having seen the other fellow's card in a cardgame. You may be the most honest person in the world, but you can't take it out of your mind that you know where that card is.

Ms. Clift. Right. But you must have, at some point, made an emotional commitment to running again. Was that, like, a month ago? Or just 2 days ago or a week ago? Is there any——

The President. Well, either way, it's an emotional commitment——

Ms. Clift. ——set point?

The President. ——as to whether you're going to walk away or whether you're going to keep on trying. I can only say it has been—what I guess I'm trying to say is that I tried very definitely in my own mind to not even consider what that decision was going to be for as long as I could and until I finally had to with all the ramifications that go with it, as to whether other people have enough advance notice, what they may want to do and so forth, and then I did it. And it has been fairly recently.

Mr. DeFrank. When did you begin confiding with your staff, Mr. President, or with the Vice President, or other people in whom you've confided the decision? Some people say that happened over Christmas— or began happening over Christmas.

The President. They had to come to me as to whether they were going to do the physical job of putting together an organization, and that was done without any declaration from me, one way or the other. And to this moment, none of them have ever been told what that decision is going to be.

Mr. DeFrank. Even now?

Ms. Clift. What about your wife? Have you——

The President. Yes, there——

Ms. Clift. ——told her what you're going to do?

The President. Yes, because whatever we do, it's "we." It's always been that way with us, so obviously I would never make any important decision without her being very much a part of it.

Mr. DeFrank. Did she have any reservations, Mr. President?

The President. No. I think normal wifely concerns for my welfare. Other than that, what is it the—there's a man, writer, some many years ago—Robert Burton—who wrote that "there is no joy, there is no comfort, there is no pleasure like to that of a good wife."

Mr. DeFrank. Was this decision ever a close call on your mind, Mr. President? Or did you always assume, more or less, that you would run unless something major intervened along the way?

The President. No, as I say, it was what I firmly believed, have always believed, that you get an indication from the people as to whether you should or not. And you can't get that too early at all.

Ms. Clift. Have you enjoyed the fact that you've been able to keep this air of mystery around this decision?

The President. I never thought of it much from a standpoint of pleasure. It hasn't been a game or anything with me. It's just been a deeply held conviction that, oh, stems from a lot of things. I think campaigns are too long. I would welcome a limitation on them. I think one of the reasons for the increasingly low turnout in voters is not a lack of interest; I think it's that we've bored them to death. They're never free of something political going on.

You couple that with the other things that I've told you already, about how I feel about not letting your mind dwell on those subjects, for fear it might affect your decisions on other things, and—so it wasn't a game. No. I had enough on my desk without that.

Mr. DeFrank. Now that you have decided, Mr. President, what were the principal factors in deciding this?

The President. Well, on the assumption that you're going—it would be, number one, I think I have heard some encouragement from the people. But it would be the desire to finish what I think is well started—the economic recovery, to get this country back into a growth pattern. To stop having these recurrent recessions, which we've had eight times since World War II, where we just go from one and then, in a

temporary cure that distorts the economy and sets the stage for another one even worse 2 or 3 years beyond—to really have a solid recovery. And I think we have made a good start on that.

In the international area, to really carry forward the effort to achieve real reduction of weapons. To set the stage for real negotiations with the Soviet Union, leading to peace in the world. To complete something that I started early on in my administration with regard to our neighbors south of the border, that I don't think we've ever carried out properly, and that is a friendship and a pattern of partnership in all these countries of the Americas that are so unique in this hemisphere. All of these things that remain unfinished.

Ms. Clift. What is it that would have prevented you from running? Did you have a set of guidelines in your mind that you might——

The President. That would prevent it?

Ms. Clift. That would have prevented it.

The President. Well, suppose I came to the feeling that I could not accomplish these things that we were trying—this recovery that has taken place, that it was beyond my capacity to get done? Suppose the people made it very evident that they didn't like the course that we were on?

Ms. Clift. Well, you're riding very high in the polls right now, so I guess you got the message that you wanted from the people. Did you seek anyone's counsel in making this decision, or was it totally a private——

The President. I thought it was something I had to do. Not counsel, but facts, such as polling and so forth.

Mr. DeFrank. I think we're going to move on to another category here, Mr. President. But before we do, it sounds like you really did not spend a lot of time struggling with this in your own mind. And it also sounds like you have more or less sensed the decision in your own mind for an awful long time. Are we wrong about that?

The President. Well, no, other than what I said about not having it in mind, or not playing with that in my mind until recently, because I felt that what we were doing was what my mind had to center on, not what effect it might have on someone.

Mr. DeFrank. Okay.

1984 Presidential Campaign

Ms. Clift. Going into a campaign, what do you see as your biggest political hurdle?

The President. Biggest political hurdle? Well, frankly, I have to say that some misperceptions that have been carefully crafted by a certain amount of demagoguery on the part of opponents of what we've been trying to do here. Issues that would have me uncaring for certain groups of our citizenry—and they're not true at all. And they've probably been the most frustrating thing that I personally have felt. And yet they have—the polls indicate—they have been able to create this perception.

Let me take one. I won't get into the fairness thing or anything else, which I think is very unfair, that what they're talking about. But let's take the one of the polls showing that people have an image of me that I might recklessly get us into a war, I go for violence. I came here believing that one of the greatest challenges was to bring us closer to peace.

All through the campaign, it is true, I did not support agreements like SALT II, and I didn't support them because they were simply placing limits on how many more weapons could be built, that you could continue to expand militarily, but within certain limits. And what I said over and over again was the time has come to sit down and talk about reducing the number of weapons in the world.

Ms. Clift. But when you have troops in Lebanon and you have military involvement in Central America, how do you—and you did go into Grenada, and while that was a success, how do you then dispel the impression that you are a warmonger, I guess is the phrase that's used?

The President. Well, because I've lived long enough to remember that there was a World War I. And after 4 years of trying to avoid it on the part of President Wilson—what he called his policy of watchful waiting—we found ourselves embroiled in that war and unprepared for it because someone on the other side, namely the Kaiser, over and over again expressed his belief that America wouldn't fight no matter what was

done. And finally, they did those things to where there was no choice but to fight.

Now, you come to World War II, and the same thing was true again. I know that military men of ours, after the war was over, when they could talk to their counterparts in Japan and they could talk about and rehash things, and their question was, "Why Pearl Harbor?" Why would they have done that? And these officers said, "Why not Pearl Harbor? You were holding military games in Louisiana, and your soldiers were carrying wooden guns, and you were using cardboard tanks to simulate armored warfare."

Ms. Clift. Mr. President, you're not shy about mentioning your longevity, and you kid about your age. But do you think that your age is a potential political problem in the campaign?

The President. No. I think somebody tried to make it one 4 years ago, and it didn't work. And I've never heard it mentioned, or I don't—most of the time now they don't even ask about it in the polls. And I've tried to start a rumor that I'm really not that old, that they mixed up the babies in the hospital. [*Laughter*]

Mr. DeFrank. Mr. President, your speech in Atlanta yesterday seemed to suggest, at least to us, that you think Walter Mondale might be your potential opponent in the fall. Is that a fair reading of some of the things you said yesterday?

The President. Well, you can't deny the fact and your understanding that he's out ahead. But I will tell you, I was most surprised when a number of you—well, not you or any magazines, but a number in the daily press—the media interpreted me at aiming a line at him. I hadn't even thought about it. I was talking about them as a group.

Ms. Clift. Oh, Democrats in general.

The President. Yes.

Mr. DeFrank. What do you think about Walter Mondale?

The President. Frankly, I think he has tried to be all things to all people, and I think he's made more promises than can probably—can possibly be kept, because as soon as he keeps one promise he has made it impossible to keep another that he's made to someone else.

I've asked our people to do a little arithmetic here and find out, with all of his expressed concern about the deficit, which didn't seem to bother him in all those years he was voting on spending bills in the Senate, to see just how much they add up. And the figure's pretty high already that his promises, if all kept, would give us a budget that, as one of his opponents in the Democratic contest said of him, would make the deficits $400 billion.

Mr. DeFrank. He did come out with a proposed deficit reduction package yesterday, I think of about $60 billion. Have you had a chance to look at that?

The President. Only slightly. One thing that's been called to my attention is that we probably wouldn't have a military defense for our country if we cut what he wanted to cut.

Mr. DeFrank. Okay. Regardless of whether he is or isn't the nominee, are you prepared to debate a campaign opponent in the fall?

The President. I've always, in principle, supported that. I think it's too early to talk about or speculate as to terms of debate or any mechanics of that kind. But I have always supported the idea.

Ms. Clift. You've given the image of being somewhat of a reluctant candidate. And I'm wondering whether you're a reluctant campaigner, or are your juices starting to flow for another campaign?

The President. I don't know about those juices in a campaign. I don't know of anyone, really, that comes out of a campaign without being amazed that you could take it—[*laughing*]—that long.

I must say that it has been kind of pleasant to look at the news with regard to those candidates that have been out there for the better part of a year now and be kind of glad that you're not in it.

Ms. Clift. Do you dread it—to——

The President. What?

Ms. Clift. Do you dread it somewhat?

The President. Oh, no. No. No, there's one part about it that you can't dread at all, and that is the opportunity to meet again the people of this country that I think are so wonderful. I love them.

Ms. Clift. Okay.

Views on the Presidency

Mr. DeFrank. We're going to switch back in another direction now. Somebody in this room—we won't tell you who—said that it might be useful to try a couple of introspective questions on you. So, we'll give that a shot.

One of the first things you said when you came to Washington was that—you used to complain about living over the store——

The President. Yeah.

Mr. DeFrank. ——being a bird in a gilded cage. Have you made your peace with that?

The President. Oh, sure. You have to, or you'd be very unhappy about it. But I will say this—and I think every President before me has found it this way—that you really look forward to those weekends at Camp David. You know, the walk to here, the elevator up, and once you're there, you're there. And that's it until the weekend comes, and so you have those things to look forward to. So, you fit it all in.

And it's—I must say—the quarters are very comfortable. I have no quarrel with that.

Ms. Clift. Well, some people say that you seem to handle the burdens of the Presidency so well that you ought to teach a course in stress management. What is your secret? I mean, you do seem very at ease in the office.

The President. Well, maybe I learned it early on as Governor of California when, for a time, I found myself becoming a victim of stress. And then I just sat down with myself—and it also had to do with this thing we talked about earlier, with regard to political considerations—and I said that the best that I can do is get all the viewpoints and all the advice I can get from staff and Cabinet, and then make a decision on what I honestly believe in my own mind is the right thing to do for the people. And I found that I started sleeping better.

Mr. DeFrank. All the polls, Mr. President, for a very long time, have shown that your personal popularity has always exceeded your job rating. What is it about you that the American people seem to like?

The President. [*Laughing*] I don't know of anyone that can answer that—a question like that. [*Laughter*]

Mr. DeFrank. That's why we're trying.

The President. No, I'll tell you. Maybe if there is anything, maybe they sense that I like people. I like them.

Ms. Clift. The public thinks of you as a very gregarious person, yet the people that work with you here say you're really quite private and reserved and that you don't reveal your feelings easily and that you don't have many close friends.

The President. I thought they were *all* my friends.

Ms. Clift. Well——

The President. No, I don't think that. Oh, I think there are certain things that you don't babble or blab about, but I think I'm gregarious. I like to be with people and with the group and to socialize.

Ms. Clift. I guess the fact that you've played "I've Got a Secret" so long with this decision made people realize that you were able to be more of a private person than people thought.

The President. Well, yes, that, of course, had to be kept private because of my desire not to let political thinking be an influence.

Mr. DeFrank. Second term.

Ms. Clift. Second term.

Mr. DeFrank. Just briefly on a second term: Do you worry at all that going into a second term you might become an immediate lameduck, or do you see some advantages to a second term that you didn't have this time around?

The President. Oh, yes, and based on experience, because, as I say, there's one thing—I don't think there is any training for this job that is better than serving as a Governor. Granted, it is infinitely smaller in the whole thing, and it doesn't have a foreign relation——

Ms. Clift. That's what Jimmy Carter thought, too, though.

The President. Yeah. But it is that type of job. And I know in California that, really, the things that were completed and the great achievements were done in the second term. And I didn't find that there was any sense—till right toward the very end and similar to the situation I'd been in for 3 years, although we have a majority in one House. There I had a majority of the other party in both houses. So, it was an 8-year struggle—well, with the exception of 1 year, when we got a bare lead, due to a couple of special elections. But I found there it was the same struggle that you'd had in the first term.

And I don't think that—as I say, toward the end, yes. Where it comes to ratification of appointees who may be for term appointments that will be longer, or judicial appointments—then you find there are some people that want to take advantage of the fact that maybe they can hold out and stall until you're gone.

Ms. Clift. What's going to be different about a second Reagan term?

The President. I'm trying to think in terms of those memories of the other time. Well, for example, in the first term there, we had laid the groundwork for the great comprehensive welfare reforms that were unlike anything that had been done anyplace in this country before. I never mentioned them in the campaign for reelection, never made them an issue, never held them up as something to look forward to. I didn't want to politicize it. And immediately after the reelection, we went to work on them, and we achieved them. And they had a terrific impact.

Ms. Clift. Is there a comparable issue——

Mr. DeFrank. Is there a parallel here? Do you feel that, perhaps, in a second term you would be able to do something about the runaway cost of entitlements?

The President. I think that—let me put it this way: I believe that there have to be some structural changes in our government, things that presently you can't get at. I would think that those would be—you'd have a better opportunity in a second term. And this is part of the—getting at the deficit problem over the long haul—that I look forward to doing.

Ms. Clift. Some analysts think a second Reagan term would be more conservative and far less pragmatic than the first, particularly since you've pledged to fight hard on the social issues like abortion and school prayer. Is that a fair assessment?

The President. No. Let me say what everyone's calling "pragmatic"—maybe I interpret pragmatic differently. I had this same run-in with some diehard people when I was Governor, and who thought, because I had compromised on something and settled for less than I'd asked for, they would have jumped off the cliff holding the flag. Well, you do that, and you're never around to get anything more. If this is pragmatic, then I'm pragmatic.

My belief is that in this democratic process, which entails compromise, you seek what you think should be done. And if you can only get half of it, three-quarters of it, whatever, and politically it is impossible to get beyond that, I don't think it makes any sense to dig in your heels and say then, "I won't play." No, you take what you can get and tuck it away in your mind that you'll wait and come back another time and try to get the next bite.

And that hadn't been my interpretation of "pragmatic." I know what the goal is. And suppose even at the very end you've only gotten 70 or 75 percent of the goal. Well, that's a lot better than being back where you started.

Mr. DeFrank. Do you think it's going to be a close election, Mr. President?

The President. I'm a pessimist about that. I've never been one of those fellows that says, "I'll take him in the third round." No, I think you jinx yourself if you do that. I'm superstitious.

Mr. DeFrank. Yeah, but everybody calls you the designated optimist around here. This is something that we don't usually hear from you—pessimism.

The President. Oh, I am on other things but that. But I always think that if you declare you're going to win—maybe that comes from having been a sports announcer and in athletics, myself. You know, when I was a sports announcer broadcasting major league baseball and I'd be calling a game in which a pitcher has not given a hit and you're getting up there at the sixth or sev-

enth, I never mentioned it, because there's an old superstition in baseball that if anyone mentions that he's pitching a no-hitter, you'll jinx him and he won't pitch the no-hitter.

So, I kind of feel the same way about campaigning. As I've said so many times, just take the advice of President Dewey: Don't get overconfident.

Ms. Clift. Right. You're in better shape politically than any President since Eisenhower in his second term. Do you consider yourself lucky, exceptionally lucky? Irish luck is something that a lot of people seem to tag you with. Is that something you've thought about?

The President. Well, luck is one name for it or not. Let me just say I think I've been blessed with good fortune in achieving some of the things that we have. When you stop to think that just 3 short years ago, there were an awful lot of people in this country that overwhelmingly believed that the good days for our land were over, that we would never again see the type of thing we'd had.

In fact, we had people in Washington before we got here who said that we should give up any dreams of future growth for America. And we have it—the growth.

Mr. DeFrank. Mr. President, we appreciate the chance to chat very much. Thank you, sir. We'll see you out there on the trail, I suppose.

Ms. Clift. Right.

The President. All right.

Note: The interview began at 3:04 p.m. in the Oval Office at the White House.

The transcript of the interview was released by the Office of the Press Secretary on January 30.

Informal Exchange With Reporters on the 1984 Presidential Election
January 30, 1984

Q. How about a news conference?

The President. What's that?

Q. How about a news conference?

The President. The people will just fall all over in shock if I——

Q. We want to talk to the candidates, the candidates who run for the Presidency. We always want to talk to them, sir. [*Laughter*]

The President. You'll throw me off my whole schedule. "Big Brother" is watching there—Larry. [*Laughter*]

Q. How do you feel this morning? Are you going to win?

Q. Do you feel any differently now that you're a candidate as well as President?

The President. [*Inaudible*]

Q. Well, what about the Democrats—[*inaudible*]—on you now, really going after you very strongly.

The President. When have they not been? [*Laughter*]

Q. Oh, they haven't been. This is a whole new thing.

The President. I think we'll have some interesting discussions.

Q. Do you have any answers? Mondale says that you represent the special interests of the wealthy.

The President. Well, the actual facts and figures reveal that our tax program actually benefits more at the lower range than even the Kennedy tax program back in the sixties; that a higher percentage of his tax relief went to those in the top five brackets than has been true of ours; a higher percentage went to big business than was true of ours. Our tax program was fair. It was fair across the board.

Q. Do you think Lebanon will be an issue? Getting the troops out of Lebanon will be a major issue?

The President. It depends on how long they're there, doesn't it?

Q. Sir, will you debate your Democratic opponent this fall?

The President. I said that in principle I support debates, yes.

Q. You'll debate—a television debate—with your Democratic opponent?

The President. Well, yes. It's too early to say anything about this case or how it will work out, but, yes, I favor that idea.

Q. Are you going to win the election?

The President. What?

Q. Are you going to win the election?

The President. Now, Helen [Helen Thomas, United Press International], you know me. I never say anything like that—too superstitious.

Note: The exchange began at 9 a.m. in the Rose Garden at the White House.

In his remarks, the President referred to Larry M. Speakes, Principal Deputy Press Secretary to the President.

Remarks at the Annual Convention of the National Religious Broadcasters
January 30, 1984

Thank you, Brandt Gustavson, Dr. Ben Armstrong, and ladies and gentlemen, distinguished guests. Thank you all very much.

I'm going to depart from what I was going to say, or begin with here, for just a moment to tell a little story. And I hope Pat Boone won't mind. I'm going to tell it on him. [*Laughter*]

Some years ago when there was a subversive element that had moved into the motion picture industry and Hollywood, there were great meetings that were held.

There was one that was held in the Los Angeles Sports Arena—16,000 people were there, and thousands of them up in the balcony were young people.

And Pat Boone stood up, and in speaking to this crowd he said, talking of communism, that he had daughters—they were little girls then—and he said, "I love them more than anything on Earth." "But," he said, "I would rather"—and I thought, "I know what he's going to say and, oh, you must not say that." And yet I had underestimated him. He said, "I would rather that they die now believing in God than live to grow up under communism and die one day no longer believing in God."

There was a hushed moment, and then 16,000 people, all those thousands of young people came to their feet with a roar that you just—it thrills you through and through.

Well, I thank you all very much. This is a moment I've been looking forward to. I remember with such pleasure the time we spent together last year. Today I feel like I'm doing more than returning for a speech; I feel like I'm coming home.

Homecoming—I think it is the proper word. Under this roof, some 4,000 of us are kindred spirits united by one burning belief: God is our Father; we are His children; together, brothers and sisters, we are one family.

Being family makes us willing to share the pain of problems we carry in our hearts. But families also come together in times of joy, and we can celebrate such a moment today. Hope is being reborn across this land by a mighty spiritual revival that's made you the miracle of the entire broadcasting industry.

I might say your success and my celebrating another birthday about this time of year are both a source of annoyance to a number of people. [*Laughter*]

Let me set the record straight on your account: The spectacular growth of CBN and PTL and Trinity, of organizations that produce religious programs for radio and television, not to mention the booming industry in Christian books, underlines a far-reaching change in our country.

Americans yearn to explore life's deepest truths. And to say their entertainment—their idea of entertainment is sex and vio-

lence and crime is an insult to their goodness and intelligence. We are people who believe love can triumph over hate, creativity over destruction, and hope over despair. And that's why so many millions hunger for your product—God's good news.

In his book, "The Secret Kingdom," Pat Robertson told us, "There can be peace; there can be plenty; there can be freedom. They will come the minute human beings accept the principles of the invisible world and begin to live by them in the visible world." More and more of us are trying to do this. George Gallup has detected a rising tide of interest and involvement in religion among all levels of society.

I was pleased last year to proclaim 1983 the Year of the Bible. But, you know, a group called the ACLU severely criticized me for doing that. Well, I wear their indictment like a badge of honor. I believe I stand in pretty good company. [*Laughter*]

Abraham Lincoln called the Bible "the best gift God has given to man." "But for it," he said, "we could not know right from wrong." Like that image of George Washington kneeling in prayer in the snow at Valley Forge, Lincoln described a people who knew it was not enough to depend on their own courage and goodness; they must also look to God their Father and Preserver. And their faith to walk with Him and trust in His word brought them the blessings of comfort, power, and peace that they sought.

The torch of their faith has been passed from generation to generation. "The grass withereth, the flower fadeth, but the word of our God shall stand forever."

More and more Americans believe that loving God in their hearts is the ultimate value. Last year, not only were Year of the Bible activities held in every State of the Union, but more than 25 States and 500 cities issued their own Year of the Bible proclamations. One schoolteacher, Mary Gibson, in New York raised $4,000 to buy Bibles for working people in downtown Manhattan.

Nineteen eighty-three was the year more of us read the Good Book. Can we make a resolution here today?—that 1984 will be the year we put its great truths into action?

My experience in this office I hold has

only deepened a belief I've held for many years: Within the covers of that single Book are all the answers to all the problems that face us today if we'd only read and believe.

Let's begin at the beginning. God is the center of our lives; the human family stands at the center of society; and our greatest hope for the future is in the faces of our children. Seven thousand Poles recently came to the christening of Maria Victoria Walesa, daughter of Danuta and Lech Walesa, to express their belief that solidarity of the family remains the foundation of freedom.

God's most blessed gift to His family is the gift of life. He sent us the Prince of Peace as a babe in a manger. I've said that we must be cautious in claiming God is on our side. I think the real question we must answer is, are we on His side?

I know what I'm about to say now is controversial, but I have to say it. This nation cannot continue turning a blind eye and a deaf ear to the taking of some 4,000 unborn children's lives every day. That's one every 21 seconds. One every 21 seconds.

We cannot pretend that America is preserving her first and highest ideal, the belief that each life is sacred, when we've permitted the deaths of 15 million helpless innocents since the Roe versus Wade decision—15 million children who will never laugh, never sing, never know the joy of human love, will never strive to heal the sick, feed the poor, or make peace among nations. Abortion has denied them the first and most basic of human rights. We are all infinitely poorer for their loss.

There's another grim truth we should face up to: Medical science doctors confirm that when the lives of the unborn are snuffed out, they often feel pain, pain that is long and agonizing.

This nation fought a terrible war so that black Americans would be guaranteed their God-given rights. Abraham Lincoln recognized that we could not survive as a free land when some could decide whether others should be free or slaves. Well, today another question begs to be asked: How can we survive as a free nation when some decide that others are not fit to live and should be done away with?

I believe no challenge is more important

to the character of America than restoring the right to life to all human beings. Without that right, no other rights have meaning. "Suffer the little children to come unto me, and forbid them not, for such is the kingdom of God."

I will continue to support every effort to restore that protection including the Hyde-Jepsen respect life bill. I've asked for your all-out commitment, for the mighty power of your prayers, so that together we can convince our fellow countrymen that America should, can, and will preserve God's greatest gift.

Let us encourage those among us who are trying to provide positive alternatives to abortion—groups like Mom's House, House of His Creation in Pennsylvania, Jim McKee's Sav-A-Life in Texas, which I mentioned to you last year. Begun as a response to the call of a conscience, Sav-A-Life has become a crisis counseling center and saved 22 children since it was founded in 1981.

I think we're making progress in upholding the sanctity of life of infants born with physical or mental handicaps. The Department of Health and Human Services has now published final regulations to address cases such as Baby Doe in Bloomington. That child was denied lifesaving surgery and starved to death because he had Down's Syndrome and some people didn't think his life would be worth living.

Not too long ago I was privileged to meet in the Oval Office a charming little girl—tiny little girl—filled with the joy of living. She was on crutches, but she swims, she rides horseback, and her smile steals your heart. She was born with the same defects as those Baby Does who have been denied the right to life. To see her, to see the love on the faces of her parents and their joy in her was the answer to this particular question.

Secretary Heckler and Surgeon General Koop deserve credit for designing regulations providing basic protections to the least among us. And the American Academy of Pediatrics and the National Association of Children's Hospitals have now affirmed a person's mental or physical handicap must not be the basis for deciding to withhold medical treatment.

Let me assure you of something else: We want parents to know their children will not be victims of child pornography. I look forward to signing a new bill now awaiting final action in a conference committee that will tighten our laws against child pornography. And we're concerned about enforcement of all the Federal antiobscenity laws.

Over the past year, the United States Customs Service has increased by 200 percent its confiscation of obscene materials coming in across our borders. We're also intensifying our drive against crimes of family violence and sexual abuse. I happen to believe that protecting victims is just as important as safeguarding the rights of defendants.

Restoring the right to life and protecting people from violence and exploitation are important responsibilities. But as members of God's family we share another, and that is helping to build a foundation of faith and knowledge to prepare our children for the challenges of life. "Train up a child in the way he should go," Solomon wrote, "and when he is old he will not depart from it."

If we're to meet the challenge of educating for the space age, of opening eyes and minds to treasures of literature, music, and poetry, and of teaching values of faith, courage, responsibility, kindness, and love, then we must meet these challenges as one people. And parents must take the lead. And I believe they are.

I know one thing I'm sure most of us agree on: God, source of all knowledge, should never have been expelled from our children's classrooms. The great majority of our people support voluntary prayer in schools.

We hear of cases where courts say it is dangerous to allow students to meet in Bible study or prayer clubs. And then there was the case of that kindergarten class that was reciting a verse. They said, "We thank you for the flowers so sweet. We thank you for the food we eat. We thank you for the birds that sing. We thank you, God, for everything." A court of appeals ordered them to stop. They were supposedly violating the Constitution of the United States.

Well, Teddy Roosevelt told us, "The American people are slow to wrath, but when their wrath is once kindled, it burns like a consuming flame."

I think Americans are getting angry. I think they have a message, and Congress better listen. We are a government of, by, and for the people. And people want a constitutional amendment making it unequivocally clear our children can hold voluntary prayer in every school across this land. And if we could get God and discipline back in our schools, maybe we could get drugs and violence out.

I know that some believe that voluntary prayer in schools should be restricted to a moment of silence. We already have the right to remain silent—[*laughter*]—we can take our fifth amendment. [*Laughter*]

Seriously, we need a new amendment to restore the rights that were taken from us. Senator Baker has assured us that we will get a vote on our amendment. And with your help, we can win, and that will be a great victory for our children.

During the last decade, we've seen people's commitment to religious liberty expressed by the establishment of thousands of new religious schools. These schools were built by the sacrifices of parents determined to provide a quality education for their children in an environment that permits traditional values to flourish.

Now I believe that some of you met with my advisers to discuss the situation of religious schools in Nebraska. We have all seen news accounts of the jailing of a minister, the padlocking of a church, and the continuing imprisonment of fathers of students. This issue of religious liberty has arisen in other States. The question is how to find the balance between assuring quality of education and preserving freedom for churches and parents who want their schools to reflect their faith.

These cases have mostly proceeded in State courts. A number of State supreme courts have reached decisions that moderated the effect of State regulations on religious schools. Last week, a panel appointed by the Governor of Nebraska concluded that the State's regulations violate the religious liberties of Christian schools.

I'm a firm believer in the separation of powers, that this nation is a federation of sovereign States. But isn't it time for the

Nebraska courts or legislature to solve this problem by a speedy reconsideration? I hope some way can be found to resolve the legal issues without having people in jail for doing what they think is right.

Within our families, neighborhoods, schools, and places of work, let us continue reaching out, renewing our spirit of friendship, community service, and caring for each other—a spirit that flows like a deep and powerful river through the history of our nation.

I made a point last year which some of our critics jumped on, but I believe it has merit. Government bureaucracies spend billions for problems related to drugs, alcoholism, and disease. How much of that money could we save, how much better off might Americans be if all of us tried a little harder to live by the Ten Commandments and the Golden Rule? I've been told that since the beginning of civilization millions and millions of laws have been written. I've even heard someone suggest it was as many as several billion. And yet, taken all together, all those millions and millions of laws have not improved on the Ten Commandments one bit.

Look at projects like CBN's "Operation Blessing," Moody Bible Institute's "Open Line" radio program, Inner City—or the radio program, "Inner City," I should say, in Chicago, and the work of Dr. E.V. Hill of Mt. Zion Baptist Church in Los Angeles. They show us that America is more than just government on the one hand and helpless individuals on the other. They show us that lives are saved, people are reborn and, yes, dreams come true when we heed the voice of the spirit, minister to the needy, and glorify God. That is the stuff of which miracles are made.

Our mission stretches far beyond our borders; God's family knows no borders. In your life you face daily trials, but millions of believers in other lands face far worse. They are mocked and persecuted for the crime of loving God. To every religious dissident trapped in that cold, cruel existence, we send our love and support. Our message? You are not alone; you are not forgotten; do not lose your faith and hope because someday you, too, will be free.

If the Lord is our light, our strength, and our salvation, whom shall we fear? Of whom shall we be afraid? No matter where we live, we have a promise that can make all the difference, a promise from Jesus to soothe our sorrows, heal our hearts, and drive away our fears. He promised there will never be a dark night that does not end. Our weeping may endure for a night, but joy cometh in the morning. He promised if our hearts are true, His love will be as sure as sunlight. And, by dying for us, Jesus showed how far our love should be ready to go: all the way.

"For God so loved the world that He gave His only begotten Son, that whosoever believeth in Him should not perish but have everlasting life." I'm a little self-conscious because I know very well you all could recite that verse to me. [*Laughter*]

Helping each other, believing in Him, we need never be afraid. We will be part of something far more powerful, enduring, and good than all the forces here on Earth. We will be a part of paradise.

May God keep you always, and may you always keep God. Thank you very much.

Note: The President spoke at 2:20 p.m. in the Grand Ballroom at the Sheraton Washington Hotel.

In his opening remarks, the President referred to Brandt Gustavson, president, and Ben Armstrong, executive director, National Religious Broadcasters.

Interview With David Hartman of ABC News on the 1984 Presidential Election
January 30, 1984

The President's Candidacy

Mr. Hartman. Was there ever a moment when you really thought, "No, I am not going to run the second time," and, if so, why?

The President. No, I can't say that. But I believe what I've said so often, that the people let you know whether you should or not. And I just resisted allowing myself to think about it too early. I think campaigns are too long anyway. And I just waited as things went on and doing what had to be done here on the job and finally came to a decision that there was a belief in what we're trying to accomplish here and that I wanted to see if we couldn't finish it.

Mr. Hartman. How about Mrs. Reagan—because ever since you were shot, she has been afraid for you, and she has expressed that in different ways many times. The discussions between the two of you, how difficult was it for her? How difficult were the discussions? What was the substance of those?

The President. No, the funny thing is, both of us felt pretty much the same way. Several times, when the thing would come up in talk or articles or conversation or anything and—or something like, should we let this organizational effort go forward even without my being an announced candidate—but we both had the attitude of saying that there would come a time when we would sit down and talk about it. And then there did come a time when we sat down and I——

Mr. Hartman. When did you do it? When did you sit down?

The President. Oh, not too long ago. I'd have to say it was this fall. And there wasn't any disagreement about it. We both had the feeling that it should be done.

Mr. Hartman. Most people are saying this is going to be a close election. Whoever the nominee is for the Democrats, it's going to be a close election. You're an old political pro. Honestly, could you lose this election?

The President. Yes, I happen to be some-one who—I've never done this, in all the times I've done it, without feeling I'm one vote behind.

1984 Presidential Compaign

Mr. Hartman. What one, either perception or issue or question or political concern have you at the moment—that one thing, whatever it is, that could lose this election for you?

The President. Oh, I don't know that I could pick winning or losing the election on one thing. Frankly, I believe that there have been great misperceptions that have been created about me and this adminstration, what our positions are and where we stand. The fairness issue, for example—I don't think anything could be farther from the truth about that.

Mr. Hartman. You're talking about fairness to whom? The poor?

The President. To—yes.

Mr. Hartman. The disenfranchised.

The President. Yes, and supposed that we rigged our programs and our tax breaks and so forth for the rich and for business. These are absolute falsehoods. Anyone who looks at it, I defy them to go back a long way in some of the tax relief programs, such as Kennedy's tax cut program in the sixties, and you will find that there were more benefits for the top five brackets, the income tax payers, and for business in those bills than there were in ours.

Mr. Hartman. But, Mr. President, there are people across this country, the truly needy, the down-and-out, the poor, who look at you, and they say, "Yeah, he is the nicest man, and we like him; but his policies are causing misery. They're hurting us. We're hungry." And they don't understand. They say, "If he cares that much, why are we hurting?" What do you say to them?

The President. Dave, I'll tell you, what I would like to be able to say to them or have a chance to say to them is that, sure, when someone is down on his luck and is having hard times and they'd like to have someone to blame, they have heard a steady drumbeat. Now, they've been told over and over again that because we're trying to hold down government spending that somehow we're taking it out of their hides.

We are spending more on food for the hungry, more on the needy, more on health care than has ever been spent in the history of this country. If there are people that are falling through the cracks when we're spending more than has ever been spent on programs for them, more on food stamps and more people are getting food stamps, then we want to find out. And this was what the commission was to do, to find out why—if this is true that this is widespread, then is this caused by inefficiency at the administrative level, that in the distribution of these programs? Is it caused by people who maybe don't know how or where to apply for them, don't have the knowledge they should have? What is the reason? Well, the commission reported that they did not find it that widespread.

What we have found in this country, and maybe we're more aware of it now, is one problem that we've had, even in the best of times, and that is the people who are sleeping on the grates, the homeless who are homeless, you might say, by choice. Now, this has been aggravated somewhat by some things at local or State levels, where there have been changes made in committing people with mental problems to institutions, and they've suddenly been turned out, willing to go. They want out. But they had no place to go.

Mr. Hartman. Mr. President, in the interest of time, let me—I want to cover a number of very important points, and I know they're important to you as well, so let's——

The President. You ask questions that I have to answer too long. [*Laughter*]

Mr. Hartman. Absolutely.

Lebanon

Lebanon. More and more people are saying, "Let's get our marines out." Will they be out by election time, by November of this year?

The President. Well, as to a timing when they will get out, election time won't have anything to do with that. In other words,

there will be no decision made for political expediency.

I don't know when they will get out. The mission remains the same. We are studying right now things that we can do to hopefully see that no tragedies of the kind we've had happen again.

U.S.-Soviet Relations

Mr. Hartman. Let me move to the Soviet Union. You have said for a long time, the only way to negotiate arms reduction is to do somewhat from a position of strength——

The President. Yeah.

Mr. Hartman. ——that the Soviets respect strength. You're rebuilding our military and our defenses at the present time. However, tensions are at their greatest with the Soviet Union since the early sixties. The Soviets have left the negotiating table, and quite frankly, people across this country are more afraid than they have been in many, many years that we might be going to war. How long do the people of our country, right now, have to wait for your philosophy of negotiate from strength to pay off, because right now they're frightened, Mr. President.

The President. Well, what they need to find out—and maybe in the campaign ahead we'll have an opportunity to tell them—we're not in more danger. We are safer and more secure than we were several years ago.

Mr. Hartman. How do you prove it to them?

The President. Well——

Mr. Hartman. How do you prove it to us?

The President. The proof is several years ago the United States had allowed its own defensive strength to decline to the point that you could look and say we weren't too far from a point of weakness in which the enemy could be tempted because we didn't have the strength.

There have been four wars in my lifetime. None of them started because the United States was too strong.

Mr. Hartman. Will you make concessions to get the Soviets back to the negotiating table?

The President. We have been more flexible. They are the ones who have been adamant. They have not come back when we meet some terms of theirs and say, "All right, let's negotiate on this." They have nothing to offer.

Now, we're——

Mr. Hartman. You're saying, no, we won't make further concessions——

The President. No.

Mr. Hartman. ——to get them back to the negotiating table?

The President. No. We're saying, "We'll be at the table; come on back." They made a statement on the START talks. They made one statement about something of— well, they were willing to discuss a certain number of missiles, a certain number of planes, a certain number of missiles and submarines. And we've said, "We're ready to talk on that. We'd like to then throw in some limitations on the number of warheads"—total warheads, because each missile carries more than one warhead. They haven't come back.

Federal Budget

Mr. Hartman. Deficits. Most people of knowledge say it's the biggest single problem facing the economic free world. You have suggested bipartisanship over in the Congress. Let's take a look at it late this year or sometime next year in '85. Why should people vote for you or anybody in Congress who are willing to put on hold for a year the biggest single problem facing the economic free world today?

The President. That isn't what we've said, Dave. What we have said to the Congress— we have to submit a budget—and we said something that they first broached. Their leadership, Congressman Jim Wright and others said——

Mr. Hartman. They say it's your leadership. They say——

The President. No, they said——

Mr. Hartman. ——you're the President.

The President. ——"Why don't you get together with us?" They've been saying this all through the fall. "Why don't you get together and we start talking about this deficit problem?" All right. We've offered to. Now——

Mr. Hartman. Why not do it now, Mr. President?

The President. What?

Mr. Hartman. Why not do it now instead of waiting——

The President. But we are talking now. What we've said is you can't solve the whole thing in this one year. We've talked about our budgeting and a program that we can agree on that won't be made a political football in the campaign, that they will come and meet with us on some provisions to start this string of deficits on a downward path and then, at the same time, to agree that having started this, as we called it, downpayment on that, we then take up the structural problems.

Mr. Hartman. Few seconds left. Scale of 1 to 10. Everybody's—every pollster is calling everybody in America and saying, "What do you think of Ronald Reagan as President of the United States?" What if your phone rang today and they said, "Scale of 1 to 10, how good a President are you?" 1 to 10.

The President. Well—*[laughing]*—I think I would answer them that I'd be a lot better President if I had a majority of my own party in both Houses instead of having to buck the opposition in the House of Representatives.

Note: The interview was taped at 3:30 p.m. in the Oval Office at the White House for broadcast on January 31.

Mr. Hartman is cohost of ABC News "Good Morning America."

Appointment of Three Members of the Architectural and Transportation Barriers Compliance Board
January 31, 1984

The President today announced his intention to appoint the following individuals to be members of the Architectural and Transportation Barriers Compliance Board for the term expiring December 3, 1986:

Vito P. Battista will succeed Paul Muldawer. He is director of the Institute of Design and Construction in Brooklyn, NY. He served as a member of the Assembly for New York State in 1969–1975 and was chairman of the Committee on Neighborhood Preservation. He is married, has two children, and resides in Brooklyn, NY. He was born September 7, 1908, in Bari, Italy.

Elizabeth M. Hanicke will succeed Hale Joseph Zukas. She has been secretary-treasurer of P. W. Hanicke Manufacturing Co. in Kansas City, MO, since 1946. She is past national director and past president of the women's auxiliary of the American Orthotic & Prosthetic Association. She is married and resides in Shawnee Mission, KS. She was born January 27, 1925, in Pleasant Hill, MA.

David W. Myers is a reappointment. He is executive director of the Louisiana Commission for the Deaf and program administrator for service for the deaf and hard of hearing at the Office of Rehabilitation Services in Baton Rouge, LA. He was born October 17, 1936, in Winston-Salem, NC, and now resides in Baton Rouge.

Remarks at the Annual Convention of the Concrete and Aggregates Industries Associations in Chicago, Illinois
January 31, 1984

I was just trying to learn here for just a second whether the weather was as bad here yesterday as it looked last night on television, in Washington. I understand it wasn't that bad.

Thank you, Bill. Members of Congress, distinguished guests, and ladies and gentlemen, I appreciate this chance to be with you. Over the years we've stood shoulder to shoulder on the major issues of the day. I remember when it was in style to say that no growth would improve the quality of life. Well, we can be grateful no one's falling for that anymore. The folks in your industry are today, as you have always been, working not to keep America the same but building to make it better.

Your group was one of the first I addressed after becoming Governor of California back in 1967. I also spoke at one of your luncheons in San Francisco in 1971. And while preparing for today, I looked over that 1971 speech. It began with the words, "I just returned from a trip to Washington, DC, and have to say it's a great place to visit, but I wouldn't want to live there." [*Laughter*]

Now, I still have some of the same feelings today, but—[*laughter*]—I think maybe I'll stretch the visit out for a few more years, if I can, and then I'll head home. [*Applause*] Thank you very much. [*Applause*] Well, thank you. Thank you very much. Be careful. I may decide not to go on after that. [*Laughter*]

I appreciate this opportunity to give you an update on what we've been accomplishing during our 36-month tenure in Washington. Of course it's what you and people like you outside of Washington are doing that makes all the difference. Too often government is given a lion's share of the credit. And that's a pretty good excuse for a story here about the old farmer who took over a parcel of land down near the creek bottom. It had never been cleared, it was covered with rocks, brush, all rutted, and he just determined to make it flourish. And he went to work and he hauled away the rocks and he cleared away the brush, cultivated the ground and fertilized and so forth, and then planted his garden and before long just had a very beautiful garden.

And he was so proud of what he'd accomplished that one Sunday after church he asked the minister to drop by and see his place. Well, the reverend came out and he was impressed. He said, "That's the tallest corn I've ever seen. The Lord certainly has blessed this land." And then he said, "Those melons! I've never seen any any bigger than that. Praise the Lord." And he went on that way—tomatoes, squash, the beans, everything, and what the Lord had done with that land. And the old farmer was getting pretty edgy. And finally he couldn't take it anymore and he said, "Reverend, I wish you could have seen it when the Lord was doing it by Himself." [*Laughter*]

We Americans have always been grateful to God for the blessings bestowed on this land. One of our greatest blessings was freedom that unleashed the creative energy of our people. That energy took an undeveloped land with vast stretches of wilderness and desert and turned it into an economic dynamo that has provided a better quality of life and a greater degree of freedom for people than any other in history.

There are many explanations for the American miracle, but government planning isn't one of them. I can't help but think that had Chicago faced modern Federal regulations, we'd still be stepping over the burned-out wrecks left by that great fire. Of course, back in those days, no one waited for help from Washington. They just rolled up their sleeves and went to work.

Chicago's resilience reflected the spirit of a free people. The key word is "free." The prevalent notion in this country was that progress is the result of unleashing people's talents and energies to achieve goals as established by the people, themselves.

Now, this was contrary to another concept that has had a degree of acceptance in the latter half of the 20th century, especially in the Nation's Capital. This theory supposes that progress is a product of harnessing the people's energy and focusing it on predetermined goals. Planners would determine the goals to be targeted. The planners, invariably, are people with whom the espousers of this philosophy agree.

The latter theory didn't take hold here because—and this is something of which we can all be proud—it is pretty darn hard to harness an American. Thank God for that.

The American character is proud and independent. It's one of this country's greatest assets. We came here from every land. We're the product of every culture and race. We came to be free and to better our lives and the lives of our families. And yet, we are all Americans. Our love of liberty and the values that flow from it unite us as a nation and a people.

An aspect of American history, distasteful to some, is the important role played by the profit motive. Well, I, for one, have no trouble with the profit motive. When people are free to work for themselves they work longer and harder. They'll do a better job because they're not just following orders, they're doing what they want to do. Profit motive unleashed an explosion of energy in America.

The young Frenchman, Alexis de Tocqueville, traveled to America back in the 1830's and he observed that, "America is a land of wonders in which everything is in constant motion and every change seems an improvement." He wrote that, "No natural boundary seems to be set to the efforts of man, and in his eyes what is not yet done is only what he has not yet attempted to do."

Well, those who are uncomfortable with profits may not understand something that you folks in business know well. In a competitive economy, making a profit means filling other people's needs and doing it efficiently, courteously, and at as low a rate as possible.

Because our business men and women have been working for profit, the American people pay less of their income for food and necessities of life than people anywhere else. Of course, mistakes sometimes happen. There's a story of a fellow whose friend was so successful that he was opening up a new branch office and a floral arrangement was ordered for the occasion. He was upset when he got to the opening to find a wreath reading, "Rest in peace." [*Laughter*] Well, on the way home, he was so upset he went by and stopped by the flower shop to complain. And after he ranted for a little bit the owner of the flower shop said, "Well, calm down. Things aren't all that bad." He said, "Just think, somewhere today someone was buried under a flower arrangement inscribed, 'Good luck in your new location.'" [*Laughter*]

It hasn't been perfect and, yes, our country has made mistakes. But with freedom and a profit motive we've achieved greatness as a nation. And don't let anyone tell you that because our people are working for themselves and their families it is contrary to community spirit and the spirit of human kindness and generosity. The frontier spirit of pulling together is legendary. And today people voluntarily donate hundreds of millions of hours and billions of dollars to charitable and community projects each year.

This, too, is inherent in the spirit of America. After all, when people are free the choice of helping others becomes meaningful. The choice of doing something to better one's community becomes a source of pride because it reflects the character of the donor and not the product of legal coercion.

It's time to reject the notion that advocating government programs is a form of personal charity. Generosity is a reflection of what one does with his or her own resources and not what he or she advocates the government to do with everyone's money.

Calls for more and more government may reflect a lack of understanding of the American character. Our values as a people are strong. We believe in work, yes, but also in family, faith, and neighborhood. We're optimistic people who believe we can overcome adversity and accomplish great things.

Four years ago it was clear that something had gone wrong. There was a growing feeling of pessimism and a sense of hopelessness inconsistent with the American character. For the first time the refrain was heard that America's best days were behind her.

Economic stagnation held us in a vise-like grip while double-digit inflation picked our pockets. Sky-high interest rates knocked the construction and automobile industries right off their feet. Now, I know this isn't a political gathering, but does anyone really want to go back to those days?

The woes from which we're now emerging were not the result of some uncontrollable cycle, nor were they the result of personality defects in our political leaders. We simply strayed too far from those truths which serve as the basis of American progress. Government was spending too much, draining away any chance for growth in the private sector. Federal taxes were too high, undercutting the incentive to work or invest. Federal regulation was beyond all

reason, tying our hands and threatening our freedom.

Getting this situation straightened out and putting this country back on the right road has not been easy, and the job is not yet done, but we have made a beginning. I want to take this opportunity to thank you for all your support over the last 36 months. What we've accomplished couldn't have been done without the active support of you and good folks like you.

Together, we've put the inflation monster in a cage, and we've broken the inflation mentality. Together, we've cut the growth in Federal spending more than in half. More progress can be made here, but we've made a good start. The prime interest rate has come down from 21½ percent to 11 percent. Here, too, those rates can and must come down more.

I think there are just some people that aren't quite sure that what's going on now is for real. Well, maybe a little bit longer and they'll realize it is for real.

Federal regulatory reform has reduced the growth of Federal redtape by more than 25 percent. This initiative, led by Vice President Bush, has cut over 300 million man-hours of needless, government-required paperwork each year and will save more than $150 billion for you over the next 10 years.

Through across-the-board tax rate reductions and indexing, to begin in 1985, we're preventing people from being mangled by built-in tax increases.

As the political rhetoric heats up this year, there'll be those trying to appeal to greed and envy. Make no mistake, that is what they're trying to do. They suggest our tax program favors the rich. Well, this is the same antibusiness, antisuccess attitude that brought this country to the brink of economic disaster. The finger-pointers and hand-wringers of today were the policymakers of yesterday, and they gave us economic stagnation and double-digit inflation. There was only one thing fair about their policies: They didn't discriminate; they made everyone miserable. [*Laughter*] Today 10 percent of the people—10 percent—pay 50 percent of the income tax. And 50 percent of the workers in America, and earners, pay 93 percent.

Teddy Roosevelt once said, "It ought to be evident to everyone that business has to prosper before anybody can get any benefit from it." Well, together, we're restoring progress, and every American will benefit.

We're turned stagnation and decline into robust growth—6 percent in 1983. Productivity is up; consumer spending is up; factory use is up; housing starts and auto sales are up; and, most encouraging, venture capital, which lays the foundation for a better tomorrow, is way up. During 1983, $4.1 billion was raised. That was four times more than in 1980.

Working people are already seeing results. More people are, in fact, working today than ever before in our history. Last year unemployment took its biggest drop in 33 years. Real wages went up last year and the year before that. When we got to Washington, real wages were going down. And one statistic of which I'm most proud: A working family earning $25,000 has $1,500 more in purchasing power than if tax and inflation rates were still at the 1980 levels.

Just this morning we received two gems of good news. The leading economic indicators, forecasting the direction of the economy, posted a solid increase in December, the 15th increase in the last 16 months, and home sales in December jumped to their highest level in more than 5 years.

America's economy is strong and, yes, I do believe the American people are better off than they were before. We inherited despair, and we're turning it into hope. With hard work and common sense, we're turning the era of limits into an era of opportunity.

We've come a long way, but much remains for us to do. Turning the economy around was priority number one. Now we can turn to the equally difficult task of streamlining government, making it more efficient and responsive. We've made a start here, too. We've transferred a host of programs back to the State and local levels, programs that never should have been the Federal Government's responsibility in the first place.

We also put to work a team of experts from the private sector to determine where changes can be made to eliminate waste and make the Federal Government more cost-effective. The Grace commission came up with some 2,500 recommendations that are being studied right now throughout the departments and agencies. This was all done by some 2,000 of your companions in the business world who volunteered and even put up the money to fund their activity.

We, of course, still must come to grips with the deficit. My only caution is to watch out for those offering easy answers. I have attempted to keep this issue from being politicized by supporting the creation of a bipartisan working group from the Congress. The group will work with the administration on making a down payment on the deficit. More substantial measures will still be required. But one thing is certain: Raising taxes and threatening the recovery is no answer. This problem was long in the making. It'll require more than band-aid solutions.

I've sometimes compared government to that unkind definition of a baby: It's an alimentary canal with an appetite at one end and no sense of responsibility at the other. [*Laughter*] One of the first steps that we can take to make our system more responsible is providing the Chief Executive with a line-item veto. It's working in 43 States and I think it should be put to use in Washington, DC.

The American people want this reform. And they and I also want a constitutional amendment mandating a balanced Federal budget. Now, this isn't a new idea. At the adoption of the Constitution, 1787, Thomas Jefferson noted that the Constitution needed one additional article. He said it should contain one that would prohibit the government from borrowing money.

Well, in addition to long-term reforms, I believe we should make our tax system more simple, fair, and rewarding for all the people. If we could broaden the tax base, then personal rates could come down rather than go up. And I think tax simplification is an historic change the people want and our economy needs.

In closing, just let me express that I have every confidence that we can control government spending, taxing, and in doing so, ensure a lasting era of growth and opportunities for all our people. Although the rhetoric gets thick at times, especially during election years, the leaders of both political parties are individuals of good will, individuals who want what's best for this country. Nobody should ever sell America or Americans short.

We are today recapturing much of the spirit of enterprise about which that Frenchman, de Tocqueville, wrote. Your industry, more than most, reflects this spirit. You've proven that those who are willing to take a chance, willing to work hard and live right, can accomplish great things. You need only look around you to find successful individuals at the head of impressive companies who started with a pick or shovel or driving a truck.

This magnificent theater in which we're meeting today is part of the legacy of an individual who started in the sand and gravel industry, Colonel Henry Crown. His father, Arie—I hope I have the name, pronounced the name right—after whom this theater is named, was a Lithuanian immigrant. From the humblest of beginnings, Henry Crown became one of the most successful men in the American business world. Reflecting the good and decent values at the heart of this country, he's been one of this country's leading philan-

thropists. Colonel Crown, thank you for all you've done.

Colonel Crown's story is not unique among this group. You are powerful forces for good in your communities across our country. Walt Whitman once wrote, "O, America, because you build for mankind I build for you."

Today American liberty shines brightly, offering proof to a mankind plagued with tyranny and deprivation: There is a better way. Together, we can keep America the blessed land of freedom and opportunity God meant it to be.

Thank you, and God bless you.

Note: The President spoke at 12:38 p.m. in the Arie Crown Theatre at McCormick Place. He was introduced by William Jenkins, chairman of the board of the National Ready Mixed Concrete Association. Following the President's remarks, he was presented with a plaque bearing a replica of the convention badge.

Before returning to Washington, DC, the President met at McCormick Place with a group of Illinois labor leaders.

The event was the combined annual convention of the National Ready Mixed Concrete Association, the National Sand and Gravel Association, and the National Crushed Stone Association.

Message to the Congress Transmitting the Annual Report of the United States Arms Control and Disarmament Agency
January 31, 1984

To the Congress of the United States:

I am pleased to transmit the 23rd Annual Report of the United States Arms Control and Disarmament Agency. The report reviews the important role that arms control and the men and women of the Agency play in strengthening our country's national security.

The United States Arms Control and Disarmament Agency has primary responsibility for leading the Administration's efforts to reduce the world's nuclear arsenals, to

negotiate a complete ban or reductions in chemical weapons, to reduce conventional forces in Europe, and to reinforce the barriers against war through confidence-building measures.

Soviet actions in the area of arms control in 1983 were a disappointment. We developed several sound positions, demonstrated our willingness to be flexible, and consistently invited the Soviets to walk through the door to serious negotiations. We hope that the Soviet Union will be willing to do this in 1984.

For its part, the United States will leave no stone unturned in its pursuit of reductions in nuclear arsenals. In 1984 we will renew our efforts to use the arms control process in ways that enhance our national security and improve global stability.

The Arms Control and Disarmament Agency's 1983 report testifies to this Nation's continuing search for a peaceful and more stable world.

RONALD REAGAN

The White House,
January 31, 1984.

Note: The report is entitled "United States Arms Control and Disarmament Agency— 1983 Annual Report."

Appointment of William Henkel as Deputy Assistant to the President and Director of the Presidential Advance Office
February 1, 1984

The President today announced the appointment of William Henkel to be Deputy Assistant to the President and Director of the Presidential Advance Office.

In addition to his current responsibilities for Presidential Advance, Mr. Henkel will assume a greater role in the area of schedule coordination. He will also assist Michael A. McManus, Assistant to the President and Deputy to the Deputy Chief of Staff, in his role as White House Coordinator for the 1984 Republican Convention.

Since September 1982 Mr. Henkel has been a Special Assistant to the President and Director of the Presidential Advance Office. Prior to joining the White House, Mr. Henkel was associated with the Merrill Lynch Capital Markets Group in New York City between 1977 and 1982. He was manager of corporate financial services for the Capital Markets Group. He served as Deputy Assistant Secretary of Commerce for Economic Development Operations in 1975–1977.

Mr. Henkel served previously in the White House in several related positions. In 1970 he joined the White House staff as a staff assistant to the President, serving as a Presidential Advance Representative. In November 1972 he was named Director of the White House Advance Office. He was appointed Special Assistant to the President and Director of Advance in 1973 and served in that position until January 1975.

From 1965 to 1970, Mr. Henkel served as an account executive in a Merrill Lynch New York City branch office. He joined Merrill Lynch in 1963 as a junior executive trainee.

Mr. Henkel graduated from St. Lawrence University (B.S., 1963). He is married to the former Alice O'Brien, has six children, and resides in Arlington, VA. He was born June 19, 1941.

Message to the Congress Transmitting the Fiscal Year 1985 Budget
February 1, 1984

To the Congress of the United States:

In the past year, the Nation's prospects have brightened considerably. The economy has grown strongly—beyond expectation. Inflation has been reduced to its lowest rate in 16 years. Unemployment has declined faster than at any other time in 30 years. We are well on our way to sustained long-term prosperity without runaway inflation.

Our national security is being restored. Our domestic programs are being streamlined to reflect more accurately the proper scope of Government responsibility and intervention in our lives. Government operations are being made more effective and efficient, as steps are taken to reduce costs.

These developments are the result of the program I proposed 3 years ago to correct the severe economic and political problems caused by previous short-sighted and misguided policies and priorities. That program focused on long-range real growth. My tax proposals were designed to provide badly needed incentives for saving and productive investment. I supported the Federal Reserve in its pursuit of sound monetary policy. I worked with the Congress to reverse the growth of Government programs that had become too large or had outlived their usefulness, and as a result, domestic programs, which had been growing rapidly for 3 decades, have finally been contained. I worked to eliminate or simplify unnecessary or burdensome regulations.

To the Nation's great good fortune, the preceding Congress appreciated the fundamental soundness of this program and joined with my administration in helping to make it a reality. Frequently, because of entrenched constituency special interests, the political risks involved in doing so were great. I thanked Members then, and continue to be grateful, for the crucial support my program received. The Nation is now beginning to reap the solid fruits of our joint perseverance and foresight.

The economy's response has fully vindicated my economic program. During the past 2 years the percentage rise in consumer price index has been no more than it was during the first 6 months of 1980. Economic recovery has been vigorous during the past year, with real GNP rising over 6% and industrial production by 16%. Unemployment, though still unacceptably high, has declined by a record 2½ percentage points in a single year. Capacity utilization in American plants has risen dramatically. Business investment in new plant and equipment has risen 11½% in the past year, in real terms. American productivity, stagnant from 1977 to 1981, climbed 3.7% between the third quarter of 1982 and the third quarter of 1983. Interest rates declined substantially in mid-1982, followed by a major, sustained rally of the stock market that added half a trillion dollars to the net financial worth of American households. Real disposable personal income rose 5.1% in 1983. After a substantial decline, the U.S. dollar has rallied powerfully to its highest level in more than a decade.

We are not, however, out of the woods yet. Despite our success in reducing the rate of growth of nondefense spending in the last three budgets, spending in 1985 will exceed 1981 levels by 41%, reflecting continued increases in basic entitlement programs, essential increases in defense spending, and rapid growth of interest costs. Clearly, much remains to be done. The task of rebuilding our military forces to adequate levels must be carried to completion, and our commitment to provide economic and military support to small, poor nations that are struggling to preserve democracy must be honored. At the same time, further action is required to curb the size and growth of many programs and to achieve managerial efficiencies throughout Government, wherever the opportunity is present.

Three Years of Accomplishment

Last year, I reviewed the dramatic improvements during the preceding 2 years in Government operations, and in the way they affect the economy. I am happy to report that these improvements continued through a third year.

- Where the growth rate of spending was almost out of control at 17.4% a year in 1980, it will decline to 7.3% this year.
- Where spending grew 64% over the 4 years from 1977 to 1981, it will rise by only 41% over the 4-year period from 1981 to 1985, despite legislated cost-of-living adjustments and the needed defense buildup.
- The Federal tax system has been significantly restructured. Marginal income tax rates have been substantially reduced, greatly improving the climate for saving and investment. Depreciation reform has been enacted, restoring the value of depreciation allowances eroded by inflation. Tax loopholes have been closed, making the tax

131

structure more equitable. Efforts have been made to shift to financing Government programs through user fees commensurate with benefits and services provided.

- Our military strength is being restored to more adequate levels.
- Domestic spending, which grew nearly 3-fold in real terms in a little more than 2 decades, will actually be lower this year than it was in 1981.
- The rapid growth of means-tested entitlement programs has been curbed. Eligibility criteria have been tightened to target benefits more to the truly needy, and significant steps have been taken to improve the efficiency and effectiveness of these programs. Unnecessarily frequent cost-of-living adjustments were pared back.
- The social security system has been rescued from the threat of insolvency raised by rampant inflation, excessive liberalizations, and lagging growth of its tax base.
- Unnecessary or excessive Federal credit activities have been eliminated or cut back. Improvements in the management and control of Federal credit activities are being pursued. The administration has supported the basic intent of proposed legislation that would move off-budget lending onto the unified budget, in order to provide better budgetary control over Federal lending.
- Proliferation of regulations and red tape has been stopped. The number of new Federal rules has fallen by over a quarter during the past three years, and hundreds of unnecessary old rules have been eliminated. For the first time, the *Federal Register* of new regulatory actions has grown shorter for three consecutive years; it is now one-third shorter than in 1980. Federal paperwork requirements have been cut by well over 300 million hours annually, and will be reduced even further in 1984. This has saved the American public over 150,000 work-years that had been spent every year filing out unnecessary Federal forms and reports.

Our regulatory reform efforts to date will save individual citizens, businesses, and State and local governments over $150 billion over the next decade.
- Major management improvement initiatives are underway that will fundamentally change the way the Federal Government operates. The President's Council on Integrity and Efficiency has reported $31 billion in cost reductions or funds put to better use.
- The Federal nondefense work force has been reduced by 71,000 employees since I took office.

These are impressive accomplishments—accomplishments to be proud of and to build on. And together we can build on them. With this budget I call on all Members of the Congress once again for additional steps to ensure the firmness of our foundations and overcome the Nation's budget problem.

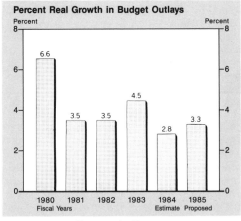

Percent Real Growth in Budget Outlays

Maintaining Economic Recovery

Before us stands the prospect of an extended era of peace, prosperity, growth, and a rising standard of living for all Americans. What must we do to ensure that that promise shall be realized and enjoyed in the years to come? What must we do to ensure that the high price of adjustment to this new era paid by the Nation in recent years shall not have been paid in vain?

All signs point to continued strong economic growth, vigorous investment, and rising productivity, without renewed inflation—all but one. Only the threat of indefinitely prolonged high budget deficits threatens the continuation of sustained non-inflationary growth and prosperity. It raises the specter of sharply higher interest rates, choked-off investment, renewed recession, and rising unemployment.

This specter must be laid to rest: just as fears of rampant inflation and its attendant evils are being laid to rest; just as fears of helplessness before growth in Soviet military might and all it threatens are being laid to rest; just as fears that the Nation's social security system would "go under" have been laid to rest. A number of actions will be required to lay it to rest. This budget requests these actions of Congress; it calls for measures to continue to curb the upward momentum of Federal spending and to increase Federal receipts. Other actions involve such fundamental reform of our fiscal procedures that they will require that the Constitution be amended.

Congress has each year enacted a portion of my budget prosposals, while ignoring others for the time being. It is moving slowly, year by year, toward the full needed set of budget adjustments. I urge the Congress to enact this year not only the proposals contained in this budget, but also constitutional amendments providing for a line-item veto and for a balanced budget—rather than the fitful policy of enacting a half-hearted reform this year, another one next year, and so on.

Where Congress lacks the will to enforce upon itself the strict fiscal diet that is now necessary, it needs the help of the Executive Branch. We need a constitutional amendment granting the President power to veto individual items in appropriations bills. Forty-three of the fifty States give this authority to their governors. Congress has approved a line-item veto for the District of Columbia, Puerto Rico, and the trust territories. It is now time for Congress to grant this same authority to the President. As Governor of California, I was able to use the line-item veto as a powerful tool against wasteful government spending. It works, and works well, in State government. Every number in this document bears testimony to the urgent need for the Federal Government to adopt this fundamental fiscal reform.

Let us also heed the people and finally support a constitutional amendment mandating balanced Federal budgets and spending limits. I encourage our citizens to keep working for this at the grassroots. If you want to make it happen, it will happen.

We must seek a bipartisan basis for fundamental reforms of Government spending programs. We need to reexamine just what, how, and how much the Federal Government should be doing—given our need for security and well-being and our desire to leave power and resources with the people. The President's Private Sector Survey on Cost Control (Grace Commission) has already come up with some interesting suggestions in this regard that, with the help of the Congress, will be adopted wherever possible.

To those who say we must raise taxes, I say wait. Tax increases pile unfair burdens on the people, hurt capital formation, and destroy incentives for growth. Tax cuts helped sustain the recovery, leading to faster growth and more jobs. Rather than risk sabotaging our future, let us go forward with an historic reform for fairness, simplicity, and growth. It is time to simplify the entire tax code so everyone is on equal footing.

The tax system must be made simpler and fairer; honest people should not pay for cheaters; the underground economy should come back into the sunlight; and everyone's tax rates should be reduced to spark more savings, investment, and incentives for work and economic growth. This is the blueprint for a brighter future and a fairer tax system. Therefore, I am directing the Department of the Treasury to complete a study with recommendations by the end of the year.

With these changes completed and the necessary fiscal tools in place, I am confident that we can devise a sweeping set of fiscal policy changes designed to reduce substantially the persistent Federal deficits that cloud our otherwise bright economic future. The plan must be based on these cardinal principles:

- It must be bipartisan. Overcoming the deficits and putting the Government's house in order will require everyone's best efforts.

- It must be fair. Just as all Americans will share in the benefits that are coming from recovery, all should share fairly in the burden of transition to a more limited role of Government in our society.
- It must be prudent. The strength of our national defense must be restored so that we can pursue prosperity in peace and freedom, while maintaining our commitment to the truly needy.
- Finally, it must be realistic. Government spending will not be curbed by wishful thinking.

In the meantime, the proposals in this budget provide important additional steps toward reducing the deficit.

Meeting Federal Responsibilities

My administration seeks to limit the size, intrusiveness, and cost of Federal activities as much as possible and to achieve the needed increase in our defense capabilities in the most cost-effective manner possible. This does not mean that appropriate Federal responsibilities are being abandoned, neglected, or inadequately supported. Instead, ways are being found to streamline Federal activity, to limit it to those areas and responsibilities that are truly Federal in nature; to ensure that these appropriate Federal responsibilities are performed in the most cost-effective and efficient manner; and to aid State and local governments in carrying out their appropriate public responsibilities in a similarly cost-effective manner. The Nation must ask for no more publicity-provided services and benefits than the taxpayers can reasonably be asked to finance.

Education.—I have devoted considerable time this year to the problems of our schools. The record of the last two decades is not good, though relieved in places by the efforts of many dedicated teachers, administrators, parents, and students. It has been extremely gratifying to observe the response all across the country to my call for a renewed commitment to educational excellence. Excellence in education will only happen when the States and school districts, parents and teachers, and our children devote themselves to the hard work

necessary to achieve it. Federal money cannot buy educational excellence. It has not in the past and will not in the future. What we will do in this budget is seek resources to help the States plan and carry out education reforms. My budget includes $729 million, about 50% more than Congress appropriated for 1984, for the education block grant and discretionary fund. States and localities will receive this increase in resources and be able to use the funds for education reform without Federal prescription and interference.

The budget also provides for stabilizing funding for almost all major education State grant programs at the 1984 level and in the future allows room for modest growth for most of these programs.the budget reflects continued support of several more important initiatives that will strengthen American education:

- Enactment of tuition tax credits for parents who send their children to qualified private or religiously-affiliated schools.
- Establishment of education savings accounts to give middle- and lower-income families and incentive to save for their children's college education and, at the same time, to encourage a real increase in saving for economic growth.
- Reorientation of student aid programs to ensure that students and families meet their responsibilities for financing higher education.
- Permission for States or localities, if they so choose, to use their compensatory education funds to establish voucher programs to broaden family choice of effective schooling methods for educationally disadvantaged children.
- Assistance to States to train more mathematics and science teachers.

Training and employment.—While the economic forecast predicts continuing improvement in the economy and further steady declines in the unemployment rate, I recognize that there are those who lack the skills to find and hold steady jobs. This is particularly true for some of our youth. In the past, Federal training and employment programs have not always helped these people gain the skills needed for success in the job market. Instead the Government spent precious tax dollars funding temporary, dead-end, make-work jobs that did little, if anything, to prepare these people for holding real jobs in the private sector. My administration worked with the Congress to change that. The Job Training Partnership Act, which I signed into law in 1982, involves private industry in the design and delivery of job training programs. Each year it will train 1.5 million disadvantaged adults and youths, dislocated workers, and welfare recipients in skills needed for private sector jobs. Additional work experience for over 700,000 disadvantaged youths will be provided during the summer months. What is needed now is not more Government programs, but removal of Government-created barriers that make it difficult for youths who want to work to find jobs. It has long been acknowledged that the minimum wage is a barrier to job finding for youths, especially minority youths who lack skills. Therefore, I am again asking the Congress to authorize a wage of 75% of the minimum wage for youths newly hired for jobs during the summer months. This will let employers lower their costs to levels more in line with the skills youths possess, and it will help many young people find jobs and gain valuable work experience. The legislation I have proposed includes protections for adult workers.

Research.—Recognizing the Federal responsibility to maintain and strengthen U.S. leadership in science and technology, the budget proposes further increases of more than 10% in Government-wide funding for basic research. The $8 billion planned for support of such research represents a relatively small share of the budget, but it is a critical investment in the Nation's future. Basic research lays the foundation for a strong defense in the years to come and for new technologies and industries that will maintain U.S. industrial leadership, create new jobs, and improve our quality of life.

Space.—Our civilian space program has made remarkable progress in the past year. The space shuttle, the world's most advanced space transportation system, has made eight pathbreaking trips into space and is progressing rapidly towards achieving routine operational status.

We can not look forward confidently to the next major challenge in space—a space station. The space station, to be placed in permanent Earth orbit in the early 1990's, is intended to enhance the Nation's science and application programs, to help develop advanced technologies potentially useful to the economy, and to encourage greater commercial use of space. The budget provides planning money to initiate this program.

National defense.—During the past 3 years, we have also taken decisive measures to increase our military strength to levels necessary to protect our Nation and our friends and allies around the world. At the same time, we have vigorously pursued diplomatic approaches, such as arms reduction talks, in an effort to ensure the principles of security and freedom for all.

The improvement in our defense posture has been across the board. Long-overdue modernization of our strategic forces is proceeding, while our conventional forces are also being modernized and strengthened. Successful recruiting and retention over the past 3 years have resulted in all of our armed services being more fully manned with capable, high-caliber men and women.

Energy.—My administration has significantly reoriented the country's approach to energy matters toward reliance on market forces—instead of Government regulation and massive, indiscriminate Federal spending. This has resulted in greater energy production, more efficient use of energy, and more favorable energy prices. For example:

- The U.S. economy currently is using 30% less oil and gas per dollar's worth of output than it did 10 years ago when energy prices began to rise.
- Heating oil prices have been lower this past year than they were in January 1981, when I removed oil price controls. Gasoline prices have fallen to levels which, after adjustments for general inflation and sales taxes, are within 5% of those that prevailed in the U.S. in the 1950's.

Energy programs proposed in the budget

are designed to complement market forces by focusing resources on limited but appropriate responsibilities of the Federal Government and by managing these programs well. Thus, for example, the budget proposes increased spending for basic and other long-term energy research. In addition, the administration continues its commitment to filling the strategic petroleum reserve. The reserve has more than tripled in size in the last three years.

Health care.—Progress has been made in slowing the explosive growth of health costs. As part of the Social Security Amendments of 1983, Congress enacted the Administration's proposed fixed price prospective payment system for hospital care. This replaced the previous Medicare hospital reimbursement system under which hospitals were reimbursed for their costs. The new prospective payment system has altered incentives and should lessen the rate of increase in hospital costs.

Under the proposals in this budget, physicians will be asked to maintain present fee levels for medicare through the next fiscal year. Tax incentives prompting overly-costly employee health insurance benefits would be revised to make users and providers more sensitive to costs. Finally, resources for biomedical research will increase.

Transportation.—My administration has sought to shift much of the costs of transportation from the general taxpayer to those who use transportation services and facilities. I signed into law several administration-backed proposals to increase excise taxes on aviation and highway users and thereby provide funding needed to revitalize and modernize these important segments of the Nation's transportation system. The proportion of the Department of Transportation's budget financed by user fees has risen from 49% in 1982 to 72% in 1985. The budget reflects the administration's continued commitment to the "users pay" principle by including receipts proposals for nautical and aviation aids, the inland waterway system, and construction and maintenance of deep-draft ports.

Recognizing the importance of safety in our transportation systems, the budget provides for significant improvements in this area. In addition, my administration secured passage of legislation designed to rebuild the Nation's highway and public transportation facilities. This legislation substantially increased funds available to the States and local communities to complete and repair the aging interstate highway system, to rehabilitate principal rural and urban highways and bridges, and to improve mass transit systems. The budget also provides for improvements in the safety of our transportation system.

Improved ports and channels will help to make U.S. coal exports competitive in world markets. My administration will work with the Congress to provide for timely and efficient port construction. A system that recovers a significant portion of the cost of existing port maintenance and new port construction must be enacted prior to any new construction. In the last 3 years, my administration has sent several reasonable proposals to the Congress, and progress is being made. It is time for action on this important issue.

Reducing the Federal presence in commercial transportation, currently regulated by the Interstate Commerce Commission, the Civil Aeronautics Board, and the Federal Maritime Commission, will improve the efficiency of the industry. Authority for the Civil Aeronautics Board will expire next year, and its residual functions will be assumed by other agencies. The administration will continue to seek legislation to deregulate ocean shipping, and will propose legislation to deregulate oil pipelines and natural gas. Experience since the adoption of initial transportation deregulation legislation has shown clearly that both consumers and industry benefit from reduced Federal involvement in these activities.

Criminal justice.—My administration has continued to strengthen the Federal criminal justice system by seeking major legislative changes in immigration policy, sentencing, and bail procedures, and by seeking increased funding for law enforcement activities. An additional organized crime drug enforcement task force will be established in Florida, bringing the total number of task forces to 13. The budget proposes to bolster immigration control by strengthening border enforcement and improving the effectiveness of border inspection programs. Additional attorneys will be sought for the Internal Revenue Service and the Justice Department, underscoring my administration's determination to tackle the serious problem of tax protesters and evaders. The administration will enhance its efforts to identify, neutralize, and defeat foreign agents who pose a threat to the Nation.

International affairs.—Our foreign policy is oriented toward maintaining peace through military strength and diplomatic negotiation; promoting market-oriented solutions to international economic problems; telling the story abroad of America's democratic, free-enterprise way of life; and reducing barriers to free trade both here and abroad.

• The security assistance portion of the international affairs program has been increased to assist friendly governments facing threats from the Soviet Union, its surrogates, and from other radical regimes.

• Development aid emphasizes encouraging the private sectors of developing nations and increasing U.S. private sector involvement in foreign assistance.

• The budget provides for continuing the major expansion of international broadcasting activities started last year. Television, exchanges of people, and other programs to improve communications with foreign countries are included.

• My administration will continue to work with the Congress to strengthen the management and coordination of the Government's international trade functions by consolidating them in a Department of International Trade and Industry.

The United States faces threats to its interests in many parts of the world. The Middle East, with its vital energy resources, is still in turmoil. In Central America, Marxist forces continue to threaten democratic governments, exploiting temporary economic dislocations and the continuing poverty of less developed countries. In Africa, the poorest nations of the world are facing

the prospect of great privation, accentuated by drought. This budget addresses each of these concerns:

• It continues military and economic support for Israel and Egypt, with improved financial terms.

• It provides for a significant increase in assistance to Central America, the specific nature of which will be defined after our review of the recommendations of the National Bipartisan Commission on Central America.

• It provides special humanitarian aid to counter the immediate effects of African drought and proposes a longer-term program aimed at the root causes of Africa's economic problems.

Although now less than 2% of the budget, international programs are critical to American world leadership and to the success of our foreign policy.

Civil service retirement.—There is growing recognition that civil service retirement has far more generous benefits and is much more costly than retirement programs in the private sector or in State and local governments. Accordingly, the administration continues its strong support of the civil service reform proposals advanced in last year's budget. In 1985, the administration will focus its legislative effort on three of those proposals, in modified form: cost-of-living adjustment (COLA) reform, a high 5-year salary average for the benefit formula, and increased employee and agency retirement contributions.

GI bill rate increase.—The budget proposes legislation to provide a 15% increase in the rates of educational assistance and special training allowances to GI bill trainees and disabled veterans receiving vocational rehabilitation assistance, effective January 1985. The increase will offset increased costs since GI bill benefits were last raised in 1981. It will provide an increase in monthy education benefit checks to 544,000 veterans and their dependents and survivors.

Continuing Reform of our Federal System

The overall efficiency of Government in the United States can also be improved by a more rational sorting out of governmental responsibilities among the various levels of government in our Federal system—Federal, State, and local—and by eliminating or limiting overlap and duplication.

In 1981, the Congress responded to my proposals by consolidating 57 categorical programs into nine block grants. In 1982, a block grant was created for job training in the Jobs Training Partnership Act.

The administration is improving the management of intergovernmental assistance by providing State and local elected officials with greater opportunity to express their views on proposed Federal development and assistance actions before final decisions are made. Under Executive Order 12372, Intergovernmental Review of Federal Programs, which I signed in July 1982, Federal agencies must consult with State and local elected officials early in the assistance decision process and make every effort to accommodate their views. The Order also encourages the simplification of State planning requirements imposed by Federal law, and allows for the substitution of State-developed plans for federally required State plans where statutes and regulations allow.

Controlling Federal Credit Programs

Federal credit in all its forms imposes costs on the U.S. economy that must be weighed against its benefits. Federal intervention through guarantees and direct loans may misdirect investment and preempt capital that could be used more efficiently by unsubsidized, private borrowers. Because federally assisted borrowers are frequently less productive than private borrowers, large Federal credit demands, and the degree of subsidy involved in Federal credit activity, must be reduced if we are to improve prospects for economic growth.

The administration continues its strong commitment to control Federal direct loans and loan guarantees. It has supported the basic intent of proposed legislation to move off-budget Federal lending into the unified budget. It seeks other basic reforms in the way in which direct loans and loan guarantees are presented and controlled.

In the coming year, my administration will issue a directive establishing Government-wide policies on credit. This directive will be both an explicit statement of the administration's goals in providing credit assistance and a means of controlling the manner in which that assistance is provided.

Regulatory Reform

Federal regulation grew explosively throughout the 1970's. Whether well or poorly designed, whether aimed at worthy or dubious objectives, these rules have one thing in common: they "tax" and "spend" billions of dollars entirely within the private sector of the economy, unconstrained by public budget or appropriations controls.

My administration has taken steps to correct this problem. Under Executive Order 12291, all Federal regulations must be reviewed by the Office of Management and Budget before being issued to determine whether their social benefits will exceed their social costs. As a result of this review process, we have reversed the rate of growth of Federal regulations. Hundreds of ill-conceived proposals have been screened out, and hundreds of existing rules have been stricken from the books because they were unnecessary or ineffective. Equally important, numerous existing regulations have been improved, and new rules have been made as cost-effective as possible within statutory limits. We are steadily winding down economic controls that regulate prices, form barriers to entry for new firms, and other anti-competitive regulations. At the same time we are increasing the effectiveness of our programs promoting health, safety, and environmental quality.

Our regulatory reform program has been open and public. New rules and changes to existing rules now require public notice and comment. My Executive Order requires regulatory agencies to consider the interests of the general public as well as special interest groups in rulemaking proceedings. The Task Force on Regulatory Relief and the Office of Management and Budget have issued regular reports detailing the progress of regulatory reform efforts. *The Unified Agenda of Federal Regulations,* issued twice each year, describes all planned and pending regulatory changes in virtually all Federal agencies. The administration's *Regula-*

tory Policy Guidelines, published in August 1983, is the first comprehensive statement of regulatory policy ever to be issued.

I believe it is time the policies and procedures of Executive Order 12291 were enacted into law. Individual regulatory decisions will always be contentious and controversial, but surely we can all agree on the general need for regulatory reform. Making each Government rule as cost-effective as possible benefits everyone and strengthens the individual regulatory statutes. Regulation has become such an important role of the Federal Government that strong and balanced central oversight is becoming a necessity and a bi-partisan objective. The Laxalt-Leahy Regulatory Reform Act, which passed the Senate unanimously in 1982, would have accomplished this reform. I strongly urge the Congress to take up and pass similar legislation this year. In addition, my administration continues to support measures to deregulate financial institutions.

Improving the Efficiency of Government

It is important to continue to reduce the size of Government. It is equally important to use the remaining resources as efficiently and effectively as possible. My administration has begun to make great strides in doing exactly that.

During the past 3 years, we have initiated several Government-wide management improvement efforts under the guidance of the Cabinet Council on Management and Administration. They are:

—Reform 88;

—Personnel management reform;

—Federal field structure reform; and

—The President's Private Sector Survey on Cost Control.

These management improvement and cost reduction programs focus on 4 objectives:

—Reducing fraud, waste, and mismanagement;

—Improving agency operations;

—Developing streamlined Federal Government management systems; and

—Improving the delivery of services.

Reducing fraud, waste, and mismanagement.—This objective seeks better use of appropriated dollars. The President's Council on Integrity and Efficiency (PCIE) was formed in early 1981 and is made up of 18 department and agency Inspectors General. They recently reported $8.4 billion in cost reductions or funds put to better use in the last 6 months of 1983 and a total of $31 billion since they were appointed. The PCIE is beginning to direct its efforts toward preventing problems before they occur, through improved technology and better audit processes, as described in their latest report.

The PCIE also found that enormous waste was occurring because the Federal Government had never established an effective cash management system—despite the fact that it handles almost a trillion dollars in cash annually. This is currently being corrected by installing sophisticated, up-to-date systems that the Department of the Treasury estimates could save as much as $3½ billion a year.

When my administration came to office we found delinquent debt owed the Government rising at a rate of over 40% per year—with a total debt outstanding of over $240 billion. After only 2 years' effort, this annual growth rate has been reduced to 2%. A credit pre-screening system is now being put in place, and automated collection centers are being installed.

Federal procurement involves annual expenditures of $170 billion. Procurement was an overly complex process with only 50% of our contract dollars awarded under competitive bid. My administration has replaced three sets of regulations with one, and we are now setting up a new pro-competitive policy to cut costs.

We have extended our fight to reduce waste and mismanagement to a direct attack on that nemesis that has always characterized the Federal Government: red tape and paperwork. We have already reduced the paperwork burden placed on the private sector by the Federal Government by well over 300 million hours. In this current fiscal year we intend to reduce the burden by another 130 million hours.

Further savings and improvements are possible. The President's Private Sector Survey on Cost Control (Grace Commission) developed numerous recommendations for savings and cost avoidance. These recommendations range from reducing costs of Federal employee retirement programs to upgrading the Government's seriously outdated and inefficient management and administrative systems. I have already included many of these ideas in this budget and will include more in future budgets. My administration will develop a tracking system to make sure they are carried out.

These are but a few of the efforts underway to make sure that appropriated funds go further and are used for the purposes for which they were intended.

Improving agency operations.—I am directing Federal agencies to coordinate their administrative activities so that they reduce their current operating costs immediately, rather than wait for future improvements in systems and technologies. Savings resulting from these efforts are reflected in this budget. These efforts include: (1) consolidating headquarters and regional administrative services; (2) requiring service centers to meet minimum productivity standards for processing documents; (3) using private sector contractors to provide support services where appropriate and economical; (4) reducing Federal civilian employment by 75,000 by the beginning of 1985, reducing higher graded staff, and improving personnel planning; (5) reducing office space by 10%; (6) reducing printing plants by 25% and publications by 25%; and (7) eliminating the processing of documents altogether for most small agencies, by requiring them to obtain services from larger agencies that have efficient centers.

Developing streamlined Federal Government management systems.—As we are reducing the size of Government and reducing fraud, waste, and abuse, we also need to change fundamentally the way the Federal Government is managed. When I came into office, we found that the Federal Government lacked a well-planned compatible management process, so we set about developing one. This effort involves five major projects: (1) planning and budgeting, (2) financial management and accounting, (3) personnel management and payroll, (4) personal and real property, and (5) automatic data processing and telecommunications management. Responsibilities and resources

for the development of each of these management systems have been assigned to those agencies that have or are capable of developing the most advanced management system in each category. Without this effort, the Federal Government would continue to operate in an inefficient manner that does not serve our citizens well.

Improving the delivery of services.—My administration is looking seriously at the way the delivery of Federal services is handled across the country. The objective of this effort is to achieve improved service at lower cost, through improved technology and management techniques such as pre-screening, computer matching, adjusted payment schedules, contractor and grantee performance incentives, and a streamlined field structure.

All of these efforts are being planned and coordinated centrally as part of the budget process. The results of these efforts will be reported to the Congress together with resulting savings and proposals to upgrade management of the Federal Government.

Conclusion

Vigorous, noninflationary economic recovery is well underway. The long winter of transition from the misguided policies of the past, with their inflationary and growth-deadening side-effects, is now yielding to a new springtime of hope for America. The hope of continued recovery to long-term noninflationary prosperity can be realized if we are able to work together on further deficit reduction measures. Bold, vigorous fiscal policy action to break the momentum of entrenched spending programs, together with responsible and restrained monetary policy, is essential to keep the recovery on track; essential to the Nation's future economic health and vitality. Limited measures to increase receipts will also be necessary to make our tax system fairer and more efficient. But it is important—more than important, *crucial*—to get the mix of spending restraint and receipts increases right. There must be substantial reductions in spending and strictly limited increases in receipts.

I call urgently upon the Congress, therefore, to take the actions proposed in this budget. Far too much is at stake to permit casual dismissal of these essential belt-tightening measures. The Nation has paid a high price for the prospect of a secure, prosperous, noninflationary future; that prospect must not be sacrificed to a sense of complacency, to an expedient ducking of the issues.

With confidence in the ultimate beneficial effects of our actions, let us seize the high ground and secure, for ourselves and our posterity, a bright and prosperous future—a future in which the glory that was America is again restored.

RONALD REAGAN

February 1, 1984.

Note: The President's message is printed in the report entitled "Budget of the United States Government, Fiscal Year 1985" (Government Printing Office).

Message to the Congress Reporting Budget Rescissions and Deferrals
February 1, 1984

To the Congress of the United States:

In accordance with the Impoundment Control Act of 1974, I herewith report nine rescission proposals totaling $634,711,454, thirteen new deferrals of budget authority totaling $143,595,000 and five revised deferrals of budget authority totaling $68,152,365.

The rescissions affect programs in the Departments of Housing and Urban Development and Interior, the Corporation for Public Broadcasting, the Delaware and Susquehanna River Basin Commissions, the Panama Canal Commission, and two Department of Agriculture off-budget revolving funds.

The deferrals affect the Departments of Agriculture, Education, Energy, Interior, State, and Transportation, and the Tennessee Valley Authority. The details of the rescission proposals and deferrals are contained in the attached reports.

RONALD REAGAN

The White House,
February 1, 1984.

Note: The attachments detailing the proposed rescissions and deferrals are printed in the Federal Register *of February 7, 1984.*

Remarks of President Reagan and President Mika Spiljak of Yugoslavia Following Their Meetings
February 1, 1984

President Reagan. It's been a great pleasure for me and for all of us to have—or to be able to welcome President Spiljak of Yugoslavia and to confer with him on issues of importance to both our countries.

Relations between Yugoslavia and the United States are good. President Spiljak's visit follows a long and well-established tradition of consultation and cooperation. The United States strongly supports Yugoslavia's independence, unity, and territorial integrity. Further, we respect its policy of nonalignment. Further, we respect this man who has done so much in these recent years for his country.

Despite understandable differences, consultations between us provide a unique and valuable perspective, and today's meeting was no exception. I expressed to the President our continued support for his government's efforts to meet its serious economic challenges. We'll do our part to help in cooperation with other Western governments, international financial institutions, and commercial banks. Vigorous economic recovery in the United States will itself help Yugoslavia by creating new opportunities for mutually beneficial commercial activity and the strengthening of bilateral trade.

Yugoslavia, like other nations of Europe, hopes for progress in arms control negotiations between the United States and the Soviet Union. I conveyed to President Spiljak our deeper commitment to reach equitable, verifiable agreements with the Soviet Union. Such agreements would be in our interest, the Soviet Union's interest, and in the interest of all mankind. We're flexible and realistic in pursuit of this goal and share the President's hope that the negotiations will resume in the near future.

Today, we also discussed the serious menace of international terrorism and underscored our intention to cooperate in opposing it wherever it occurs and for whatever reasons. The United States deplores all terrorist attacks against Yugoslav diplomatic counsellor and other representatives, and we will not tolerate such attacks on our territory.

The American people join me in conveying our best wishes to the people of Yugoslavia for the success of this year's Winter Olympic Games, which will begin next week in Sarajevo. Like our Los Angeles Olympic Organizing Committee, the Yugoslav Olympic Committee has invested tremendous human and material resources in putting the games together. As the two host countries for the 1984 games, we have reason to be proud of these endeavors.

It's especially fitting that in this Olympic year, we're signing a U.S.-Yugoslav tourism agreement. We hope that the agreement to be signed tomorrow will lead to an increase in tourism and good will between our two countries.

President Spiljak has been an especially welcome guest, and I look forward to frequent consultations with him. And I'm confident that our bilateral relations will continue to grow and flourish. It's been good to have you here.

President Spiljak. First of all, I would like to express my pleasure with the opportunity to visit the United States of America and exchange views with President Reagan on the possibilities for promoting further our bilateral cooperation and on some important international issues.

I would like to point out that the talks with President Reagan were held in a friendly and candid atmosphere of full, mutual respect which characterizes the relations between our two countries and peoples. President Reagan and I share the view that a practice of dialog in meetings between the highest representatives of our two countries, regardless of the well-known differences in our positions and views in some international issues, continues to greatly contribute to a better mutual understanding and stable cooperation in all fields of mutual interest. The principles of equality, independence, and noninterference as a mutually accepted basis for bilateral relations and cooperation were reaffirmed in our talks today.

I'm glad to note that our talks confirmed once again that the overall Yugoslav-American relations have been developing successfully and that there exist ample possibilities for their even more comprehensive promotion in the long run.

As President Reagan displayed the interest, I briefed him on the essence of the Yugoslav long-term program for economic stabilization. The achievement of our targets will offer a broader basis for an overall economic cooperation with all countries and in which United States of America is one of the most significant partners. In this context, I would like to emphasize that we attach great importance to the results achieved, as well as to the prospects to further develop mutual, economic cooperation in all areas. In this respect, special attention should be devoted to industrial, technological, financial cooperation as well as joint ventures.

President Reagan reiterated the resolve of the United States administration to prevent the terrorists and other hostile activities against Yugoslavia which are, at the same time, directed against the good Yugoslav-American relations and cooperation.

I had a very useful exchange of views

with President Reagan on pressing international issues. Thus we acquired a greater knowledge of, and gained a better insight in, the positions and activities of our two countries on the international scene. We share the concern over the present dangerous developments and further deterioration of the situation in the world.

We agreed that the policy of the release of international tensions in negotiation has no alternative. We, for our part, pointed in particular to the need for strengthening international confidence and creating an atmosphere favorable for the renewal of dialog as a precondition for the settlement of the acute international political and economic problems.

I also informed President Reagan of our assessments of the East-West relations, the situation in Europe, and of our deep concern over the continuation of the arms race, in particular. We presented our views on the problems of the relations between the developed and the developing countries, as well as our assessments of some acute hotbeds of crisis such as the Middle East and Near East, southern Africa, and others. We find it to the need of resolving them by peaceful means in compliance with the principles and purposes of the Charter of the United Nations. In this context, we pointed to the activities and initiatives of the nonaligned countries at solving the outstanding international problems.

I'm confident that my visit and the fruitful and meaningful talks I had with President Reagan will give a fresh boost to an even more comprehensive development of cooperation between our two countries, thus contributing to international understanding in general.

Note: President Reagan spoke at 1:30 p.m. to at the South Portico of the White House. President Spiljak read the opening and closing portions of his departure statement in Serbo-Croatian; his interpreter read the complete statement in English.

Earlier, the two Presidents, together with U.S. and Yugoslavian officials, met in the Oval Office. They then held a working luncheon in the State Dining Room.

Remarks on Signing the National Tourism Week Proclamation
February 1, 1984

Welcome to the White House. We're here for the signing of a proclamation that is designating the week beginning May 27th as National Tourism Week. I know I speak for the entire travel and tourism industry in thanking the Congressional Tourism Caucus for making this event possible.

For Nancy and me, your industry's pretty close to home. The White House is part of our national inheritance, and last year alone, more than a million people came to visit. So, if you suddenly hear a lot of shuffling feet out there, it's just another tour group. Don't turn around. [*Laughter*]

Travel and tourism is an important industry. It's good business, and it's great for America. And to borrow a line, your industry does it in the old-fashioned way, through the hard work of thousands of small businesses. All Americans benefit from your profession, your calling. As our second largest retail industry, employing 4½ million workers, you help bring about one of the best economic recoveries in decades. And it's going to get even better.

Now, today a working family earns $25,000 and has $1,500 more in purchasing power than if tax and inflation rates were still at their 1980 levels. Real after-tax income has increased—well, last year, increased by 5 percent. With inflation down from 13.5 to 3.2 percent and the prime rate cut almost in half, more and more Americans can afford to travel and see our beautiful country.

But I think the importance of travel and tourism goes far beyond economics. Experiencing America firsthand provides outstanding educational opportunities and is terrific for personal growth. And where in the world is there a more beautiful place to travel, have fun, and relax than in America? From our mountains, our beaches, our islands and plains, to our great cities and towns and to God's wonderful creations like the Grand Canyon, the redwoods of California, the great Smokey Mountains, America is "America the Beautiful."

It's no wonder that travel and tourism is such a growth industry. You're just selling the best product in the world. You make it possible for people all over the world to discover America. Foreign visitors may come for the Olympics or a World's Fair, a business conference, or just to enjoy our nation's beauty and its heritage. Whatever they do, or whenever they do, they come to know our values and vision, our system of government, and they can feel the spirit of a good and great country.

There's no better way to promote international understanding and good will, or to explain freedom and democracy, than through travel and tourism. And when you celebrate National Tourism Week, I hope you'll celebrate your achievements and use the opportunity to highlight what you are doing for America.

And now I'm going to sign that proclamation, and when I do, I'm also recognizing that travel and tourism is a partnership—a partnership of industry, labor, the Congress, and the administration. And we'll do everything we can to keep it that way. There's no doubt that the golden days of tourism are yet to come.

I can't quit without telling you a little story before I sign that—about the recent summit at Williamsburg. I was all set, I couldn't wait for my companions, the leaders of the other several states to come there. And then, when we gathered as we always do, the first meeting is at dinner the night before the conference actually starts. And I was waiting till the first moment of silence as we sat down. And then, I had planned to say to Margaret Thatcher, "Margaret, if one of your predecessors had been a little more clever, you would be hosting this gathering." [*Laughter*]

But never try to top a lady. As I said, the moment came, and I said, "Margaret, if one of your predecessors had been a little more clever——" She said, "Yes, I know. I would have been hosting this gathering." [*Laughter*]

[*At this point, the President signed the proclamation.*]

Thank you very much.

Note: The President spoke at 2:48 p.m. in the East Room at the White House.

Proclamation 5149—National Tourism Week, 1984
February 1, 1984

By the President of the United States of America

A Proclamation

The tourism industry is extremely important to the United States, contributing to our employment, economic prosperity, and international trade and understanding.

Each of us benefits from the effects of tourism. It substantially enhances our personal growth and education. Tourism also promotes intercultural understanding and appreciation of the geography, history and people of the United States. Now that inflation has been reduced and the economy is growing, personal incomes and leisure time will increase more rapidly. Tourism therefore can be expected to play an even greater role in the lives of the American people.

In recognition of the significance of the tourism industry to the enhancement of international trade, understanding and goodwill, the Congress, by House Joint Resolution 168, has designated the week beginning May 27, 1984, as "National Tourism Week" and has authorized and requested the President to issue a proclamation in observance of that week.

Now, Therefore, I, Ronald Reagan, President of the United States of America, do hereby proclaim the week beginning May 27, 1984, as National Tourism Week, and I call upon the people of the United States to observe such week with appropriate ceremonies and activities.

In Witness Whereof, I have hereunto set my hand this 1st day of February, in the year of our Lord nineteen hundred and eighty-four, and of the Independence of the United States of America the two hundred and eighth.

RONALD REAGAN

[*Filed with the Office of the Federal Register, 11:53 a.m., February 2, 1984*]

Remarks at the Annual National Prayer Breakfast
February 2, 1984

Thank you, Mark, and thank all of you ladies and gentlemen. Before I say what I was planning to say this morning, Senator Javits, you concluded your readings with a prayer, and so, of course, I know, understood that we are—all of us—accustomed not to applauding prayer. But I can't help but think that all of us here have a hunger within us to applaud you for your presence here and what you have meant to this gathering. [*Applause*]

And, Barbara, I had a terrible fear there for a few moments that you were going to make anything I had to say redundant. [*Laughter*] But I think that maybe the two fit together.

We all in this room, I know, and we know many millions more everywhere, turn to God in prayer, believe in the power and the spirit of prayer. And yet so often, we direct our prayers to those problems that are immediate to us, knowing that He has promised His help to us when we turn to Him. And yet in a world today that is so torn with strife where the divisions seem to be increasing, not people coming together, within countries, divisions within the people, themselves and all, I wonder if we have ever thought about the greatest tool that we have—that power of prayer and God's help.

If you could add together the power of prayer of the people just in this room, what would be its megatonnage? And have we maybe been neglecting this and not thinking in terms of a broader basis in which we pray to be forgiven for the animus we feel towards someone in perhaps a legitimate dispute, and at the same time recognize that while the dispute will go on, we have to realize that that other individual is a child of God even as we are and is beloved by God, as we like to feel that we are.

This power of prayer can be illustrated by a story that goes back to the fourth century. The Asian monk living in a little remote village, spending most of his time in prayer or tending the garden from which he obtained his sustenance—I hesitate to say the name because I'm not sure I know the pronunciation, but let me take a chance. It was Telemacmus, back in the fourth century. And then one day, he thought he heard the voice of God telling him to go to Rome. And believing that he had heard, he set out. And weeks and weeks later, he arrived there, having traveled most of the way on foot.

And it was at a time of a festival in Rome. They were celebrating a triumph over the Goths. And he followed a crowd into the Colosseum, and then there in the midst of this great crowd, he saw the gladiators come forth, stand before the Emperor, and say, "We who are about to die salute you." And he realized they were going to fight to the death for the entertainment of the crowds. And he cried out, "In the name of Christ, stop!" And his voice was lost in the tumult there in the great Colosseum.

And as the games began, he made his way down through the crowd and climbed over the wall and dropped to the floor of the arena. Suddenly the crowds saw this scrawny little figure making his way out to the gladiators and saying, over and over

145

again, "In the name of Christ, stop." And they thought it was part of the entertainment, and at first they were amused. But then, when they realized it wasn't, they grew belligerent and angry. And as he was pleading with the gladiators, "In the name of Christ, stop," one of them plunged his sword into his body. And as he fell to the sand of the arena in death, his last words were, "In the name of Christ, stop."

And suddenly, a strange thing happened. The gladiators stood looking at this tiny form lying in the sand. A silence fell over the Colosseum. And then, someplace up in the upper tiers, an individual made his way to an exit and left, and others began to follow. And in the dead silence, everyone left the Colosseum. That was the last battle to the death between gladiators in the Roman Colosseum. Never again did anyone kill or did men kill each other for the entertainment of the crowd.

One tiny voice that could hardly be heard above the tumult. "In the name of Christ, stop." It is something we could be saying to each other throughout the world today.

Now, several days ago while I was very concerned about what I was going to say here today and trying to think of something to say, I received through diplomatic channels a message from far out across the Pacific. Sometime ago, our Ambassador presented to General Romulo of the Philippines the American Medal of Freedom. Not only had he been a great friend of the United States in our time of war, but then he had spent 17 years as an Ambassador here in Washington, from his country to ours. And for whatever reason, he sent this message of thanks to me for the medal that had been given, and then included the farewell statement that he had made when he left Washington, left this country, after those 17 years.

And I had to confess, I had never been aware that there had been such a farewell message, and I'm quite sure that many of you hadn't. And so, I'm going to share it with you. I think it fits what we're talking about today. He said, "I am going home, America. For 17 years, I have enjoyed your hospitality, visited every one of your 50 States. I can say I know you well. I admire and love America. It is my second home. What I have to say now in parting is both tribute and warning.

"Never forget, Americans, that yours is a spiritual country. Yes, I know you're a practical people. Like others, I've marveled at your factories, your skyscrapers, and your arsenals. But underlying everything else is the fact that America began as a God-loving, God-fearing, God-worshiping people, knowing that there is a spark of the divine in each one of us. It is this respect for the dignity of the human spirit which keeps America invincible.

"May you always endure and, as I say again in parting, thank you, America, and farewell. May God keep you always, and may you always keep God."

Thank you.

Note: The President spoke at 9:16 a.m. in the International Ballroom at the Washington Hilton Hotel. He was introduced by Senator Mark O. Hatfield of Oregon. Among those participating in the breakfast program were Jacob Javits, former U.S. Senator from New York, and Barbara Jordan, former U.S. Representative from Texas.

Message to the Congress Transmitting the Annual Economic Report of the President
February 2, 1984

To the Congress of the United States:

I have long believed that the vitality of the American economy and the prosperity of the American people have been diminished by inappropriate policies of the Federal Government: unnecessary government regulations that discouraged initiative and wasted scarce capital and labor; an inefficient and unfair tax system that penalized effort, saving, and investment; excessive government spending that wasted taxpayers' money, misused our Nation's resources, and created budget deficits that reduced capital formation and added to the burden of the national debt; and monetary policies that produced frequent business cycles and a path of increasing inflation.

I came to Washington to change these policies. The needed reforms are far from complete, but substantial progress can already be seen: the burden of regulation has been reduced, tax rates have been lowered and the tax structure improved, government spending on a wide range of domestic programs has been curtailed, and a sound monetary policy has been established.

Although the full favorable effect of those reforms on our Nation's rate of economic growth will take time to develop, some of the benefit of our economic policies is already visible in the current recovery. The economy's performance in 1983 was very gratifying to me. The 3.2 percent rise in consumer prices between 1982 and 1983 was the lowest rate of inflation since 1967. The recovery produced a sharp drop in unemployment and a substantial increase in the income of American families. The number of people at work increased by more than 4 million and the unemployment rate fell from a high of 10.7 percent in December 1982 to 8.2 percent in December 1983. The 6.1 percent rise in real gross national product (GNP) last year means that real annual income per person in the United States rose $700.

Reducing Unemployment

Despite the substantial reduction in unemployment, the number of unemployed workers remains unacceptably high. Continued economic recovery will mean millons of additional jobs in the years ahead and further declines in the rate of unemployment. In 1984 alone, the American economy is expected to add more than 3 million additional jobs. By the end of the decade, we will need 16 million new jobs to absorb a growing labor force. Only a strong and expanding economy can provide those jobs while achieving a progressively lower level of unemployment over the next 6 years.

Although economic growth is by far the most important way to reduce unemployment, special policies to help the structurally unemployed and particularly disadvantaged groups can also be helpful. To assist these individuals in developing job-related skills that will lead to productive careers in the private sector, I proposed the Job Training Partnership Act that I signed into law in 1982. Last year I proposed additional measures to increase opportunities for training and retraining. Although the Congress has enacted some of my employment proposals, I am still waiting for congressional action on others.

Of particular concern to me is the unemployment among teenagers. Such unemployment is not only a problem in itself, but is also indicative of lost opportunities to acquire on-the-job training and job-related skills. It is widely recognized that the minimum wage law is a substantial barrier to the employment of teenagers, especially minority teenagers. I have proposed that during the summer months the minimum wage for teenagers be reduced to 75 percent of the regular minimum wage. This reform would give many teengagers the opportunity to get a first job and acquire the skills needed to help them with subsequent employment and would not hurt adult employment. With an unemployment rate of nearly 50 percent among black teenagers and with only about 20 percent of black teenagers employed, we must act. The Federal Government must not be the source of barriers to employment.

Inflation and Monetary Policy

Reducing the rate of inflation was my most immediate economic goal when I arrived in Washington. In the preceding 24 months, the consumer price level had increased more than 27 percent. Many people feared the U.S. Government had lost its ability to control inflation. Until inflation was brought under control, a healthy recovery could not get under way.

The inflation rate has declined dramatically over the past 3 years. Between 1982 and 1983, the consumer price index rose only 3.2 percent. Americans can again have confidence in the value of the dollar, and they can save for the future without fearing that the purchasing power of these savings will be destroyed by inflation. I am firmly committed to keeping inflation on a downward path. We must never relax in our pursuit of price stability.

The basic requirement for a continued moderation of inflation is a sound monetary policy. I continue to support the Federal Reserve in its pursuit of price stability through sound monetary policy. Last year was a particularly difficult time for monetary policy because of the substantial changes in financial regulations. I am pleased that, in spite of these difficulties, the monetary aggregates at the end of the year were within their target ranges. I expect that in 1984 the Federal Reserve will expand the money stock at a moderate rate that is consistent with both a sustained recovery and continuing progress against inflation.

There are those who advocate a fast rate of money growth in an attempt to depress interest rates. Experience shows, however, that rapid money growth inevitably leads to an increased rate of inflation and higher interest rates. The only monetary policy that can bring interest rates down, and keep them down, is one that promotes confidence that inflation will continue to decline in the years ahead.

The Dollar and the Trade Deficit

The high interest rates in the United States and our low rate of inflation continue to make dollar securities an appealing investment for individuals and businesses around the world. In addition, the United States has been an attractive place for stock market investment and for direct business investment. The result has been a continued rise in the dollar's exchange value relative to other currencies of the world.

The sharp rise in the value of the dollar since 1980 has made it cheaper for Americans to purchase products from overseas, thereby helping us fight inflation. But the dollar's sharp rise has made it difficult for American businesses and farmers to compete in world markets. The decline in U.S. exports and the substantial rise in our imports has resulted in record trade deficits in 1982 and 1983. The trade deficit has been

temporarily exacerbated by the international debt problems and by the more advanced stage of recovery in the United States than in the world at large.

Despite these problems, I remain committed to the principle of free trade as the best way to bring the benefits of competition to American consumers and businesses. It would be totally inappropriate to respond by erecting trade barriers or by using taxpayers' dollars to subsidize exports. Instead, we must work with the other nations of the world to reduce the export subsidies and import barriers that currently hurt U.S. farmers, businesses, and workers.

I am also firmly opposed to any attempt to depress the dollar's exchange value by intervention in international currency markets. Pure exchange market intervention cannot offset the fundamental factors that determine the dollar's value. Intervention in the foreign exchange market would be an exercise in futility that would probably enrich currency speculators at the expense of American taxpayers. A combination of exchange market intervention and expansionary monetary policy could reduce the dollar's exchange value, but only by causing an unacceptable increase in the rate of inflation. The dollar must therefore be allowed to seek its natural value without exchange market intervention.

Regulation

One of the four key elements of my program for economic recovery is a far-reaching program of regulatory relief. Substantial progress has been made during the last 3 years. The growth of new regulations has been reduced by more than a third. The demands on the private sector of government paperwork have been reduced by several hundred million hours a year. The Congress approved legislation that has led to substantial deregulation of financial markets and intercity bus transportation. The Federal Communications Commission, with our support, has reduced the regulation of broadcasting and of new communications technology, and the Interstate Commerce Commission and the Civil Aeronautics Board have gone far down the path of deregulation of competitive transportation markets. The benefits of these and other deregulation measures are now increasingly apparent to American consumers and businesses.

It is also apparent that substantial further deregulation and regulatory reform will require changes in the basic regulatory legislation. I urge the Congress to act on the several measures that I proposed last year on natural gas decontrol, financial deregulation, and reform of private pension regulation. I remain confident that there is a basis for agreement on measures that would reduce the burden of Federal regulations, while protecting our shared values and not jeopardizing safety.

Tax Reforms

The final installment of the 3-year personal tax cut took effect in July, giving a helpful boost to the economic recovery. The income tax rate at each income level has been reduced by about 25 percent since 1980. In 1984 a median income four-person family will pay about $1,100 less than it would have without these tax reductions. And, beginning in 1985, the tax brackets will be adjusted automatically so that inflation will no longer push taxpayers into higher brackets and increase the share of their income taken in taxes.

The Economic Recovery Tax Act of 1981 went beyond reducing tax rates to establish important reforms in the structure of the tax system. For businesses, the Accelerated Cost Recovery System increased the after-tax profitability of investments in plant and equipment. The sharp fall in inflation has also increased after-tax profitability. As a result, investment in business equipment has recently been quite strong despite the high real interest rates.

For individuals, the Economic Recovery Tax Act reduced the marriage tax penalty, the estate tax burden, and tax discrimination against saving. The response to the universal eligibility of Individual Retirement Accounts (IRAs) has been far greater than was originally expected. It is estimated that more than 15 million individuals now use IRAs to save for their retirement. Last year, I proposed to expand the opportunity for all married couples to use IRAs fully by allowing them to contribute up to $2,000 each per year to an IRA even if only one has wage income.

Further improvement and simplification of our tax system are sorely needed. The burden of taxation depends not only on the quantity of tax revenue that is collected but also on the quality of the tax system. I have asked the Secretary of the Treasury to develop a plan of action with specific recommendations to make our tax system fairer, simpler, and less of a burden on our Nation's economy. By broadening the tax base, personal tax rates could come down, not go up. Our tax system would stimulate greater economic growth and provide more revenue.

Government Spending

One of my principal goals when I came to Washington was to reverse the dramatic growth of Federal spending on domestic programs and to shift more resources to our Nation's defense. Although many doubted this could be done, both goals are being achieved. We must do everything that we can to avoid waste in defense as in other areas of government. But we must also be willing to pay the cost of providing the military capability to defend our country and to meet our responsibilities as the leading Nation of the free world. Outlays for defense had declined to only 5.2 percent of GNP in 1980, less than one-fourth of total government outlays. By the current fiscal year, defense outlays have increased to 6.7 percent of GNP and 28 percent of total outlays. Real defense outlays have grown 39 percent since 1980. Our spending on defense, however, remains a far smaller percentage of our national income than it was in 1960, when defense outlays took 9.7 percent of GNP.

Real spending has been cut on a wide range of domestic programs and activities. Many wasteful bureaucratic activities have been eliminated and the number of nondefense employees on the Federal payroll has been reduced by 71,000. We have examined every area of Federal Government spending, and sought to eliminate unnecessary and wasteful spending while protecting the benefits needed by the poor and the aged. As a result, total nondefense spending now takes a smaller share of our GNP than it did in 1980. Moreover, under present law, nondefense spending will continue to take a declining share of our GNP in the years ahead.

This reduction has been accomplished without any decrease in existing social security benefits or any change in the medicare benefits for the elderly. Spending on all other nondefense activities and programs has actually declined over 12 percent in real terms since 1980. Even with no further reductions in these activities and programs, their share of GNP in 1986 will be nearly back to the level of 1965.

I am committed to continuing the search for ways to reduce government spending. The budget that I am submitting to the Congress identifies significant savings in entitlement programs and reductions in outlays for other programs that are excessive or that are not the proper responsibility of the Federal Government. The Grace Commission has given us some 2500 ways to reduce wasteful spending that could save billions of dollars in the years ahead.

Budget Deficits

I have long believed that our Nation's budget must be balanced. A pattern of overspending by the Federal Government has produced a deficit in 22 of the last 23 years. My most serious economic disappointment in 1983 was therefore the failure of the Congress to enact the deficit reduction proposals that I submitted last January in my budget for fiscal 1984. We would be much closer to a balanced budget today if the Congress had enacted all of the spending cuts that I have requested since assuming office, and if the long recession and the sharp decline in inflation had not substantially reduced real tax revenue. In last year's budget I proposed changes in outlays and revenues that could put the deficit on a sharply declining path that, by 1988, would have been less than 2 percent of GNP and on its way to a balance of revenues and outlays.

The unwillingness of the Congress to accept the proposals that I offered has made it clear to me that we must wait until after this year's election to enact spending reductions coupled with tax simplification

that will eventually eliminate our budget deficit. But we cannot delay until 1985 to start reducing the deficits that are threatening to prevent a sustained and healthy recovery. I have therefore called on the Democratic and Republican leaders in the Congress to designate representatives to work with the Administration on the development of a "downpayment" deficit reduction program.

I believe that this bipartisan group could develop a package that could be enacted this spring which would reduce the deficit by about $100 billion over the next 3 fiscal years. The package could include a number of the less contentious spending cuts that are pending before the Congress plus additional outlay savings based on the proposals of the Grace Commission. Additional revenue could be provided by measures to close certain tax loopholes—measures that the Department of the Treasury has previously said are worthy of support.

These deficit reductions can increase the public's confidence in our economic future and their faith in the ability of the political system to deal satisfactorily with the deficit. The downpayment package can be a first step toward full elimination of the remaining deficits. Even with a 3-year $100 billion package, the deficits projected for fiscal 1986 and beyond are totally unacceptable to me. They would be a serious threat to our Nation's economic health and a heavy burden to future generations. I am committed to finding ways to reduce further the growth of spending and to put the budget on a path that will lead to a balance between outlays and receipts. In 1985 I will submit a budget that can achieve this goal. But we must go further and make basic structural reforms in the budgetary process—including the line-item veto and the balanced budget amendment—that will keep spending under control and prevent deficits in the future.

Looking Ahead

As I look ahead, I am very optimistic about the prospects for the American economy. Substantial progress has been made in reforming the economic policies that will shape our economic future. If we continue to develop and pursue sound policies, our Nation can achieve a long period of strong economic growth with low inflation, and the American people can enjoy unprecedented prosperity and economic security.

RONALD REAGAN

February 2, 1984.

Note: The President's message is printed in the report entitled "Economic Report of the President, Transmitted to the Congress, February 1984—Together With the Annual Report of the Council of Economic Advisers" (Government Printing Office, 343 pages).

Statement on United States Participation in the 40th Session of the United Nations Human Rights Commission
February 2, 1984

On February 6 in Geneva, the United Nations Human Rights Commission will open its 40th session. This important world forum, which authored the Universal Declaration of Human Rights in 1948, will meet once again to focus on allegations of human rights violations around the world. It will address a number of important human rights concerns, including the situations in Central America, Afghanistan, and Poland, as well as Soviet abuse of psychiatry. Those deprived of their human rights must have the support of all of us who cherish freedom.

We Americans are bound together not by common ancestry, but by our common blessing of freedom. But too often we forget the price that was paid to win that freedom. Sometimes only a person who has experienced tyranny can fully appreciate freedom's blessings. Such a person is the U.S. Representative to the Human Rights Commission, Richard Schifter, who briefed me today on the Commission's work.

Dick Schifter came to this country as a very young man fleeing Nazi tyranny. Many members of his family, including his father and mother, perished in the Holocaust.

From bitter personal experience, Dick understands the meaning of human rights. He knows that the difference between a free and an unfree society can be the difference between life and death. And he also knows that the struggle for human rights is a solemn responsibility and a moral duty of all who love freedom.

As our Representative to the Commission, Dick Schifter has spoken with eloquence and pride of America's commitment to liberty, democracy, and human rights. And he has always insisted on standards of fairness and balance in the U.N. treatment of human rights.

The great struggle in the world today is not over oil or grain or territory, but over freedom. We believe every man, woman, and child on this Earth is born with God-given rights that are theirs by virtue of their humanity.

That is the American dream, and in articulating it so forcefully and effectively, Dick Schifter has become a spokeman for a more civilized world. As he prepares once again to head our delegation to the U.N. Human Rights Commission in Geneva, I wish him Godspeed and all success.

Message on the Observance of the Chinese New Year
February 2, 1984

Nancy and I are pleased to send warmest greetings to all those celebrating this Lunar New Year, 4682, the Year of the Rat.

This is a special time for Chinese, Korean, and Vietnamese Americans—a time for reflection on the accomplishments of the past year and planning for continued success in the year to come. All of us should look to the future with renewed hope, ready to dream new dreams for the betterment of all peoples.

I commend you for preserving your rich cultural heritage by participating in this joyous festival. You have given much to our country. Your talent, hard work, and intitiative helped build this nation and have rewarded you with success and prosperity.

We wish you the very best for an enjoyable season and for peace and happiness in the year to come.

RONALD REAGAN

Nomination of Woodward Kingman To Be an Associate Director of the United States Information Agency
February 2, 1984

The President today announced his intention to nominate Woodward Kingman to be an Associate Director (Management) of the United States Information Agency. He would succeed James T. Hackett.

Mr. Kingman is presently serving as a consultant to Crocker National Bank in San Francisco, CA. He was executive vice president of the Crocker National Bank in 1974–1983. Previously, he was President and Chief Executive Officer of the Government National Mortgage Association at the U.S. Department of Housing and Urban Devel-

opment in 1969–1974; assistant to the executive vice president for finance, International Telephone and Telegraph Corp., in 1966–1969; assistant to the vice president of the national division of the First National City Bank in New York City in 1956–1966; and was with Cowles magazine in 1951–1956.

He graduated from Amherst College (B.A., 1949) and Harvard Business School (M.B.A., 1951). Mr. Kingman was born September 5, 1925, in Minneapolis, MN, and now resides in San Francisco.

Remarks at a Republican Congressional Luncheon
February 2, 1984

Thank you, Howard. I could have listened right through lunch. And I want to thank all of you, and after that kind of a welcome, I don't see how I can possibly get by with less than 42 minutes. [*Laughter*]

No, I'm delighted we're all able to be here today. In our jobs we work together day in and day out, but it's too seldom we get a chance to relax for a moment together like this.

Permit me to begin by giving every man and woman in this room my heartfelt thanks. For 3 years now, you've been giving me just what I needed—advice at critical moments and support during some tough times and balanced judgment all the time. Howard and Dick and Ted and Paul and—well, I'd better stop naming names, because I'll go on—Bob Michel and Guy, Trent Lott—all of you are among the most skilled legislators that I have ever known. And George, I believe that—very firmly—you're the best Vice President in our history.

I once said sometime after my marriage that Nancy's mother had ruled out, as far as I was concerned, had made it impossible to tell any mother-in-law stories. And I feel the same way about Vice President stories after watching him work for 3 years. [*Laughter*]

But, as Howard said, they told us 3 years ago, it couldn't be done and that Members of the Congress would never again work together to produce a program that would benefit not the special interests, but the American people. And we all remember the mess the country was in—the soaring inflation, the high interest rates, the weakened defenses, and the loss of respect for our nation abroad. Just after the inauguration, I came across a quotation that summed it all up. "When we got into office," President Kennedy once said, "the thing that surprised me most was to find that things were just as bad as we'd been saying they were." [*Laughter*]

Well, I think in these 3 short years there has been a great deal accomplished here. Just before I came over here this morning, I was meeting with someone—the title of Ambassador, but who serves in one of our—the international organizations overseas, and on his way back to that particular assignment. And he told me how one—I won't name the country, but one of his colleagues there from another country came up to him when he was newly appointed and just asked him whether he thought things were going to be different now. And our Ambassador said, "Yes, they are." "Well," he said, "in what way?" He said, "When you kick us in the shins, we're not going to say 'thank you' anymore." [*Laughter*]

But we still have our work cut out for us. We must use our restored strength to put world peace on a more secure footing. And soon I will forward a plan based on the recommendations of the National Bipartisan Commission on Central America, just one example of how we can promote democracy in these troubled regions. And here at home we must attack the deficits and simplify the tax code and make constitutional

changes like the line-item veto and the balanced budget amendment. I think these are the Republican goals for 1984 and beyond.

And now let's take a moment to consider the Democrats. Tip O'Neill always complains about the way we cut taxes. But if the Democrats had been in charge, there wouldn't have been any tax cut—none at all. They opposed the very idea of a tax cut again and again throughout the 1980 campaign. But if you look back over the years, the American people—and maybe this campaign is a good time to remind them—look back over the years, and you will find they aren't tax cutters at all. The tax cutting that has been done back through the years has been done by the Republican Party.

If they had been running the show, American families would still be suffering sky-high inflation and interest rates. The stock market wouldn't have set new records. The gross national product wouldn't have started growing again. And the American workers' real wages wouldn't have started climbing.

With them in control, our defenses would still be growing weaker while the Soviets grew bolder. Troops would have landed on Grenada, that's for sure. They just wouldn't have been American troops. And the Grenadians wouldn't have been applauding.

So, let's approach this election year with the high spirits and the sense of challenge that's such an important part of American politics. We can tell the people that, yes, America is back, but we're not satisfied with that. We're not resting on our laurels. Our challenge is to take freedom's next step, and this nation's future is at stake.

If we keep the Senate and the White House and remain strong in or even with the House, then America will go on to a new birth of freedom and prosperity, and all the world will benefit. If we lose, then all that we've worked so hard to accomplish will be undone.

We all know the elections will be hard-fought and close. Since a campaign flounders without ideas or intensity, let's make certain that we take the offensive. We must challenge our opponents on the line-item veto, push them on the balanced budget amendment, and challenge them on tax simplification. We must force them to stop gathering special interest endorsements and go to the American people. And we must make it clear that they don't want to cut spending; they want to raise taxes.

I promise to do all I can to see to it that we keep the Senate and gain strength in the House. And for the sake of our cause, let's all pledge to work together in a spirit of firm unity. For the good of the country, we must win. And I'm convinced that working together, we will.

Thank you, and God bless you. And now the words you've been waiting to hear from me: Let's eat. [*Laughter*]

Note: The President spoke at 12 noon in the Senate Caucus Room at the Russell Senate Office Building. He was introduced by Senate Majority Leader Howard H. Baker, Jr.

Message on the Observance of National Afro-American (Black) History Month, February 1984
February 2, 1984

On February 1st we began the Fifty-eighth Annual Black History Month, a national celebration of the role of Black Americans in all segments of life in this nation and in Black culture around the globe.

Launched in 1926 by Dr. Carter Godwin Woodson, founder of the Association for the Study of Afro-American Life and History, Inc., Black History Month provides opportunities for our nation's schools, institutions of higher learning, and the public to gain a deeper understanding and knowlege of the diverse contributions of Black Americans to our country and the world.

This year's Black History Month theme, "Black Americans and the Struggle for Excellence in Education," is particularly timely, coinciding with efforts across the land to reexamine public education and reinforce excellence for all students.

It is a very special privilege for me to call on the people of the United States to join in this important time of exploring, learning, appreciating, and saluting all that Black Americans have done to help build this great nation.

As we celebrate Black History Month, 1984, let us also share a prayerful thought for the memory of Dr. Martin Luther King, Jr. Dr. King was brutally gunned down by an assassin in 1968, his life cut short at the age of 39. But his leadership and devotion in the cause of human rights changed America forever. In this, the fifty-fifth year since his birth, may Black History Month be an especially meaningful and productive time for all of us.

RONALD REAGAN

Remarks at a White House Ceremony Marking the Observance of National Afro-American (Black) History Month
February 2, 1984

Welcome to the White House, the house that belongs to all of us.

Today we mark the 58th annual Black History Month, a celebration of the part that black Americans have played in building our great country. The story of black Americans is one of valor in the face of hardship. The first blacks were brought to America against their will, kidnaped by the thousands from their homelands, and when they reached our country, they encountered prejudice and servitude.

Until only a few decades ago, black Americans lived lives that were separate and unequal. Most were taught in segregated schools. Too many could find only poor jobs, toiling for low wages. Blacks were barred from hotels and restaurants and made to use separate facilities and even forced to drink at separate water fountains. In a nation that proclaimed liberty and justice for all, too many black Americans were living with neither.

I remember some years ago, before we were freed from that kind of custom, a friend of mine telling me of having to tell his small son who couldn't understand why on a hot day he could not drink from the fountain and how his little son was crying. And hearing that story, I made up my mind then that anything I could ever do to help in seeing that no parent in this country ever again would have to tell a child they were denied something because of some difference in their complexion. And I think all of us are resolved, and we've made marvelous strides in seeing that that isn't going to happen again in this land.

In the 1920's Carter G. Woodson, a great black educator, came to realize that if black Americans were to regain their dignity they would have to begin by regaining their past. And he founded the Association for the Study of Afro-American Life and History. And in 1926 he launched the first Black History Month.

In the years since, the ASALH and annual Black History Months have enriched our country by fostering a sense of pride among black Americans and by teaching all of us about black contributions to American life. And just yesterday, the U.S. Postal Service issued a Carter G. Woodson stamp as part of their Black Heritage Series.

We'll remember great black lawyers like Charles Hamilton Houston and William H. Hastie. We'll honor black physicians like Dr. Daniel Hale Williams, who performed the first open-heart surgery in the world in 1893, and physicians like Dr. Charles Drew, who discovered a method of storing blood plasma that enabled it to be used in emergencies.

This month we'll honor the black Americans who achieved so much in sports: the courageous Jackie Robinson, the great Hank Aaron. Here again I interject a personal note. I was a sports announcer, broadcasting major league baseball. And at that time, shamefully enough, I didn't have a Jackie Robinson or a Hank Aaron or a Willie Mays or any of the others to talk about. And there were some of us in the sports world at that time that editorialized and campaigned that that should be changed. And thank God, it has been.

We celebrate the black musicians who combined elements of African and Western music to produce something completely new and distinctly American—jazz. And as we remember that Louis Armstrong, Duke Ellington, Lionel Hampton, and so many other black musicians began their careers playing in hotels where they were forbidden to take a room, we'll promise never to allow such injustice again.

This Black History Month will remind Americans that again and again, blacks have taken up arms to defend our country with their courage and, in thousands of cases, their lives. In the Revolutionary War, some 5,000 black Americans joined the fight for independence. The first American to die in that war was named Crispus Attucks; he was black. In this century, thousands of black Americans fought in World War I, World War II, Korea, and Vietnam.

I tell you that this Black History Month brings back a personal memory. During World War II, I narrated a film about black pilots trained at Tuskegee Institute. I remember how impressed I was by the skill and bravery of those fliers. One of those brave men was Chappie James, who went on to become a great aviator and the first black four-star general in the Air Force. And a few months ago in the Oval Office, I had the privilege, I should say, months— moments ago, I had the privilege of presenting Tuskegee officials with a grant to help build the Chappie James Center for Aerospace Science and Health Education on the Tuskegee campus. It is a fitting monument to a true patriot.

Hero in two wars, fighter against discrimination, champion of equal opportunity, believer in personal responsibility—Chappie wore four stars on his shoulder and 50 stars in my heart. This man, who did fight discrimination and who had the bitter memories of that, has still left words, and written words about his love for this land, for this country that should inspire every American who can read those words.

This month will remind us most of all of the great black struggle for equal rights. And just 13 weeks ago, it was my privilege to sign into law a national holiday marking the birthday of Dr. Martin Luther King, Jr.

"I have a dream," Dr. King said, "that one day on the red hills of Georgia the sons of former slaves and the sons of former slaveowners will be able to sit down together at the table of brotherhood." He spent his life combating bigotry so that his dream might come true. And he gave his life to that noble cause. So, this month, let us rededicate ourselves to that great dream of brotherhood.

The theme of Black History Month this year is "Black Americans and the Struggle for Excellence in Education." Our country's come a long way since the days when men and women were jailed for teaching blacks to read. Today black Americans are in virtually every school and university in the country, and they're breaking new ground in every field of endeavor. And black Americans, like astronauts Guy Bluford and Ronald McNair, who's blasting off in a space shuttle tomorrow, are teaching black children—and all our children—to really reach for the stars.

Martin Luther King and others often said that black Americans must assert a sense of their own worth. Well, this Black History Month will remind all of us that the story of black Americans adds up to just that—a truly majestic sense of worth.

I've got one more little story I just have to tell—dates back to World War II—or, I'm sorry, back to Vietnam. In a warehouse there, a shipment of ammunition, a captain with his platoon in there stacking this ammunition. And the platoon was typical of our military. They were black, brown, and white. And suddenly, a box of grenades was dropped, rolling all over the floor. And the captain ordered everyone out immediately. And they fled. And then they waited—and no explosion—nothing had happened.

So, the captain told them all to wait, and he went back inside. And then he gingerly picked up a grenade and with scotch tape tied down the pin so that it couldn't fire— did it to a few more—and then called the platoon inside and told them what he had done and showed them how to do it—and to do this to stop what could have been a terrible disaster.

He had behaved in the highest tradition of an officer of our Armed Forces. He did the dirty job that had to be done to make sure it could be done before he called his men in to do it. And I will regret forever—I know that story, but I don't have his name. The captain was black. And, as I say, no officer has ever shown more faithfulness to the principles that should govern all officers in the military.

So, again, I thank all of you for being here. God bless you all.

Note: The President spoke at 3:14 p.m. in the East Room at the White House.

Statement by Principal Deputy Press Secretary Speakes on the President's Weekly Radio Addresses to the Nation During the 1984 Presidential Campaign
February 2, 1984

Prior to the President's announcement of his candidacy for reelection, various radio broadcasters were carrying his weekly Saturday morning broadcasts as a public service and also providing an opportunity for the airing of opposing views. Now that the President is a candidate, however, it has become apparent that the continued broadcast of these public service talks has caused some concern to the broadcasters because of a number of complicated questions under existing Federal communications statutes and regulations.

Although the President does not believe that his weekly talks have been partisan in nature, to avoid creating confusion and potentially cumbersome legal issues for broad-casters who wish to continue to carry the President's weekly radio talks, the President has directed his campaign committee (Reagan-Bush '84) to purchase sufficient broadcast time to ensure the continued broadcast of those talks during the period of his campaign.

Interview With Robert L. Bartley and Albert R. Hunt of the Wall Street Journal on Foreign and Domestic Issues
February 2, 1984

The Federal Budget

Mr. Hunt. Why don't we start, if we could, sir, with a budget question. Speaker O'Neill says that your offer of a downpayment on deficit reduction is disingenuous, because you're not willing to put either your defense budget or proposed tax increases on the table. Is that so?

The President. Well, when you invite people to come in as negotiators from both sides and with varying views, there's no restriction on what can be put on the table. And everything's subject to discussion and negotiation there. What we've thought we could do in this political season, instead of going along with the thought that election years are ruled out for any kind of progress or anything, is to see if we cannot discuss the noncontentious issues and find some agreement that will whittle at this deficit.

Mr. Hunt. Taxes and defense would probably be part of any package if you were to reach an agreement then?

The President. Well, if anyone—as I say, no subject is ruled out for discussion. I feel very strongly, myself, with regard, for example, to taxes. We had a tax increase last year, premised on the idea that we were going to get three dollars in spending cuts for every dollar of increased revenue. We never got the three dollars in spending cuts. We think we're owed something.

Mr. Bartley. Mr. President, in drawing up the budget you've obviously made an explicit decision not to ask for very much in the way of cuts—only $5 billion, I think. Can you tell us why you didn't do more?

The President. Yes, it's pretty much the cuts we got last year. And we discussed this at great length. We know there are more cuts, and we know we need more cuts. But rather than polarize and have no result, we've come in with about, as I say, those cuts that we didn't get.

And, again, the noncontentious ideas—to see if we can come together in a bipartisan package for the Congress, and we think that there are more cuts than we have put in there. But we know that if we had done everything that we thought we could get, we couldn't get it. Not when the voices we were getting from the opposition were calling for more spending even than we've suggested in this budget.

Mr. Bartley. Could we look forward to what might happen in a second term? When this budget was released, Dave Stockman was talking about structural reforms and tough bullets to bite. If you're reelected, would you try to reduce the big middle-class entitlements? And if so, what would be the prime targets?

The President. Well, yes, I've read something about supposedly the middle class and their entitlements. I don't think we've aimed anything at any class or any group. This misconception that has been quite a drumbeat from—resulted from the drumbeat from the other side, that somehow we've penalized the poor and the needy— we are taking care of more people, better, and spending more on this than any other— well, than any time in our previous history. And so, we don't think that any of our economic program has penalized particularly those people at the lower level.

157

Actually, if there are individuals who suffer from our economic program, they are people who've been dropped from various things like food stamps because they weren't morally eligible for them. Maybe some instances technically, but even, in many cases, weren't even technically eligible for those programs. We have tried to redirect the effort toward the people with the greatest need.

Mr. Bartley. But if there are more budget cuts there that haven't been proposed, they have to be in some program. What about veterans benefits, for example?

The President. About what?

Mr. Bartley. Veterans benefits? Do you think that could be cut, and maybe in a second term?

The President. I'm not going to discuss things like that and what we may do in a second term. But this is only a downpayment on what must be done at getting government back to within its means.

Now, let me just give as an example that takes you 3,000 miles away from here, is the type of thing that I think is more prevalent in government.

In California, we succeeded with the most comprehensive welfare reforms that have ever been attempted in this country. We saved there at a State level $2 billion for the taxpayers. We were able to increase the grants to the needy by 43 percent. And they hadn't had—this was in 1971 and '2—they hadn't had a raise in their grant since 1958, in spite of all of the inflation.

Now, I guess what I'm saying is that everytime over the years that people have tried to curb government spending, those who defend it—the special interest groups—have come back and said, all right, what program do you want to do without? Well, that is a trap that no one should let themselves get pulled into.

Maybe there are some programs that government shouldn't be performing or conducting—if so, why those should be eliminated whether there's a deficit or not simply because then there's something that's a needless expense. But, basically, government has some programs that are government's legitimate function. What those of us who have advocated savings are saying is, government can be run more effi-ciently and more economically than it has been run. And I think we've proved that in the cuts so far.

Mr. Bartley. A lot of people think that if you want a mandate for cutting the budget, you ought to send up the cuts now—before the election.

The President. No, in a political season, I have some idea of what's going to happen in the politicizing the things of that kind. We had an example. It had to do with a program that needed reforming because the program was going broke in 1981, would have been broke by 1983. In 1982, because we suggested correcting that and preventing bankruptcy of the program, nothing was done. We were kicked from every side. And it became the political issue of 1982. But after the election of 1982, a bipartisan group came together and came in with a plan that restored fiscal integrity to that program.

Now, this is pretty much what we have in mind now. Let us deal now with the less contentious issues that can further reduce this present deficit as we have estimated, say, by a hundred billion dollars over the next 3 years—knowing that that is not enough; we must go farther. On the other hand, I don't think that the score is in yet on the half of the deficit which is caused cyclically by the recession.

Our economic program and reforms, first of all, on reducing spending have been implemented less than half of what we proposed. But on the tax program—and as I say, we compromised a year ago and gave those who demanded that, a chunk, I think, of what they were asking for—but we haven't really felt for a long enough period the full impact of what the tax cuts that we've made have done.

Monetary Policy

Mr. Hunt. But, sir, another important element here is going to be monetary policy. Are you satisfied right now with the Federal Reserves' current monetary policy?

The President. If we're talking about the increase in the money supply, right now I am. I am not going to deny that there have been volatile changes in that in the past and that there has been a period in which they fell below even their own track, and in which the string was pulled too tightly on the money supply which, I think, had an effect on the interest rates not coming down after they had started to come down several stages.

I have to say that the monetary policy has certainly been most helpful in getting a handle on inflation, from double digits down to 3.2 for last year. But now I do know that they are in their track, that they have deemed is, and is apparently, pretty much in the context of our growth, what our requirements are.

Mr. Hunt. Let's look ahead for a minute. Some people on Wall Street worry that the Fed might ease too much, that it might rekindle a burst of inflation by the end of the year. On the other hand, some of your allies, like Congressman Jack Kemp, have said, no, that the problem is just the opposite; they're going to tighten up too much. They should focus on bringing interest rates down. Which do you think is the greatest concern if you look 6, 7 months ahead?

The President. I think either one of them is wrong. Let me point something out. If we had a chart here in front of us of the increase in the money supply between '79, 1980: the steepest increase in the money supply in the history of this country and double-digit inflation for 2 years in a row, interest rates, the prime rate at 21½. At one point inflation touched 19 percent here in this country. And then, realizing—and that chart, if we were looking at it, would have a peak going up like that.

Then, when they did pull the string at the end of 1980 and on into 1981, they came down so steeply that I feel it probably had something to do with the additional depth of the recession that took place. I know they call it two recessions, that we had one '79 and '80 and then we had reprieves and then we had one again in '81, in July when the bottom fell out. Of course, politically in this season they're saying that it was our economic program that did it in 1981, only our economic program wasn't in place until October and then only a small fraction of it. But there with the string pulled that tightly, there is no question, it had a salubrious effect on inflation. But it also kept the interest rates high. Now——

Mr. Hunt. Sir, I have a question, that does it worry you that the Fed may repeat that again?

The President. Well, I don't think they're going to. We have reason to believe that their policy—and not just that great dip—there has been a time recently, as I say, when they got below. It isn't——

Mr. Hunt. [*Inaudible*]—happen now?

The President. It's a kind of a clumsy tool. There isn't a fine-tuning that they can always be exact. You have to take what they're doing over a little longer period of time than just month to month.

But I do know that their track is set and they're apparently in that track now. It's my understanding that they intend to stay in that range.

Nuclear Arms Reduction

Mr. Bartley. Mr. President, could we turn to foreign affairs for a moment?

The President. I'd be relieved. [*Laughter*]

Mr. Bartley. Your administration is obviously anxious to resume the arms negotiations with the Soviet Union.

The President. Yeah.

Mr. Bartley. And yet at the same time you're saying the Soviets are violating existing arms treaties. And we don't seem to be able to do very much about it. Do you think it might be misleading to let people believe that this kind of negotiation on this kind of a treaty is going to solve any of our problems?

The President. You're talking about our reporting to the Congress on supposed violations or apparent violations. That is required of us by an act of Congress. We didn't just go running out and say, "Hey, let's blow the whistle on the Soviets if they're doing something." They demanded that. And we gave them as exactly as we could the evidence that we had as to whether there were things that were actually apparent violations of an agreement. There were some that were ambiguous and that gave the appearance of that. And we presented that evidence, their evaluation, whatever they wanted to evaluate. But we also said——

Mr. Bartley. [*Inaudible*]—about it?

The President. Yes, we said that this only

strengthens our position of insisting that a major part of any future treaties must be verification, the ability to verify whether the treaties are being kept.

Mr. Bartley. But after you've decided they aren't being kept, as you have in some cases here, what do you do then?

The President. Well, we call them to the attention—and have—to the Soviet Union. But, as I say, I think that in the negotiations that we hope will resume, that this is our evidence as to why we're justified in seeking full verification.

Mr. Bartley. You've proposed a big research program for what everyone calls a Star Wars missile defense. Do you agree that actually deploying that kind of a system would require the renunciation of the SALT I treaty? And are you ready to do that, if you have to?

The President. My ambition, or my dream, for—if there is a defensive weapon—you see, here's a new weapon in the world and for the first time it is a weapon that has no defense against it, except deterrence, that we each have it. It's like two fellows with a gun pointed at each other, both of them cocked and both with their fingers on the trigger, and we're going to stand, spend the rest of our life doing that.

My dream was that if we could find a weapon that offered a defense against those, we could then immediately take the next step and say, "Now, doesn't common sense dictate that we eliminate these weapons?" And that would include our own. If we had the defensive weapon and no one else had it, but we also had the missiles, wouldn't it be the proof of our sincerity if we said, "Look, we've got it made. We've got both now. And we tell you we will eliminate ours, along with everyone else."

Dwight Eisenhower wrote a letter to a publisher in his closing days in office, and he said, "We are coming to a point at which for the first time in history we have weapons that render obsolete any of the previous notions we've ever had about victory or defeat in war, that there can be with these weapons no defeat or victory as we have known it, only the destruction of mankind." Now, he said, "Reaching that point, isn't it time that we sat down together and figured out a better way to settle disputes than by war?"

Well, I feel that way very definitely. And I think that the—my hope is that if we can continue, resume the negotiations with regard to nuclear weapons—we are going to; the date is set for the MBFR negotiations—but the others, that starting down that road, everyone will see the wisdom of total elimination.

Mr. Hunt. Mr. President, let me just try one more arms control question. I remember being with you time and time again in 1980, in which you basically argued that the reason we had to build up our defenses was to persuade the Soviets that it was futile for them to think that they could outdo us in this area and that if we built up our defenses, that sooner or later the Soviets would realize this and out of self-interest they would become more reasonable.

The President. Yes.

Mr. Hunt. Now, we've certainly built up our defenses. Do you see signs that the Soviets have become more reasonable?

The President. Well, I think that what we're seeing is a part of negotiations. And I think that what we've accomplished here is what I had talked about. And I said then, also in that campaign over and over again, that I would stay at a table—well, meaning our country, our negotiators stay at a table as long as was necessary to bring about a reduction in arms.

The SALT treaties—and the reason I've never been enthusiastic about them, they were simply trying to set caps on how many more you could have. And I was shocked when a knowledgeable person in that field told me shortly after I arrived in this office, that had we ratified SALT II, under the terms of that treaty, the Soviet Union would have been able to add the equivalent of the megatonnage that we dropped on Hiroshima—every 11 minutes since the treaty was ratified.

Now, the reason for negotiating, I feel, must be to reduce the weapons. Now, you're asking about—I think that it is too early to say this. We do know this. We know that they are pretty much at their maximum of output and have been for a long time. We also know that we have been unilaterally disarming over a period of years.

They didn't have to demand that we eliminate a B–1 bomber. Even without going to a negotiating table we canceled it. And we were doing this with weapons. We were reducing our Navy. We were unilaterally disarming. Now, it seemed to me that the only way that we were going to convince them that common sense called for reduction of arms was to build our own defenses to where we had a deterrent capacity, but to make it evident that we were going to maintain a deterrent policy. They would then have to look and say, how much would they have to build to try and get a sufficient advantage over us, and I don't think they can. And I think then they know that. They know the industrial might of this nation.

Lebanon

Mr. Hunt. Let me turn you to Lebanon, if I may, sir. As you know, House Speaker O'Neill provided the crucial support for the bipartisan consensus on the war powers resolution 3 months ago. He now says that your policy in Lebanon is a failure. The House next week is expected to pass a resolution which would call on you to bring the marines home. How are you going to respond to that?

The President. Well, I'm going to respond that he may be ready to surrender, but I'm not. As long as there is a chance for peace, the mission remains the same. And the very fact that since, along about last August, for the first year that they were there—and it's not just the marines; there is a multinational force—we have three allied powers who feel as strongly as we do who are in there.

The multinational force was sent in at a time when Lebanon, after years of civil war, literally in which there virtually was no government—certainly they did not have authority over their own territory—the Israelis, because of the threats to their northern border and the actual assaults on their northern border, had finally advanced and gone all the way to the edge of Beirut. The PLO, with its terrorist bands, was widespread throughout the country. They were less refugees than they were an occupying force. The Syrians had moved in for

their own purposes. Beirut was the battlefield. The casualties were mainly civilian.

The idea was, and I had proposed, that we take up where Camp David left off and try to bring about overall peace through negotiations between the Arab nations and Israel. You couldn't do that as long as this situation prevailed in Lebanon. The idea was that if the other international forces or the other countries could be made to withdraw, then the Lebanese Government would have to have the authority and then have the military capability of taking over the areas previously occupied by these other forces, but which now would be in the hands of the same militant Lebanese forces who had been in a state of civil war—and that the multinational force would be a stabilizing force while Lebanon strengthened itself and then moved out to do this.

When we went in, the understanding was that both Israel and Syria had agreed that they would withdraw, both saying, when the other—we will withdraw together. The PLO had been taken out, removed from the country. Great progress was made. With the removal of the PLO, the Israelis signed an agreement and have already made phased withdrawals back toward their own border, Syria, for whatever reason of their own, reneged and has now said they won't withdraw. This is a stumbling block, and this is——

Mr. Hunt. President Assad yesterday was quoted as saying you have two choices. He said, you either have to increase, you have to escalate the number of troops over there, or you have to get them out. Is that pretty much the size of the dilemma, do you think?

The President. Well, what he was really admitting was the fact that they reneged because Syria is bent on territorial conquest. It wants Lebanon, or a large part thereof, to be Syria. They are an occupying force, in violation of what they had previously agreed to.

But we look at the progress that had been made. We look now that there is a Government of Lebanon, and due to our own training of their military force—we have an army unit; everyone's so busy talking about the marines, they don't notice this—that the army has been in there training. We have been equipping them. They are, really, a first rate military force. They don't have the numbers yet. By April, however, there'll be double the number of brigades that they presently have. Of course, Syria's got some 57,000 armed—or military—on Lebanese soil. But as long as there is a chance for victory, for peace, I don't know of any of the multinational forces that are in there, the four nations in there, that are desirous of leaving.

We are not just sitting here with our fingers crossed. We are studying and planning on where we can be more effective and where we can resist, because—as I started to say a moment ago about last August—the terrorist attacks that are being leveled against the multinational forces are being leveled because of the success of this plan. And now they want to drive us out because they can't recognize their territorial ambitions as long as we're there.

Now, can the United States, in the face of this, can the United States suddenly up and—regardless of our allies in the multinational force or anything else—say, "Well, we're going to get out"? And if we get out, that means the end of Lebanon. And if we get out, it also means the end of any ability on our part to bring about an overall peace in the Middle East. And I would have to say that it means a pretty disastrous result for us worldwide.

Mr. Hunt. You mentioned the terrorist attacks, sir. You said after the Beirut attack last October—your administration said basically that it appeared to be the fault of the Iranians, abetted by the Syrians, and that—I believe you used the term, or the administration used the term—those who directed this atrocity must be dealt justice, and they will be. My question is, why haven't you retaliated? And do you plan to?

The President. Well, you have seen us retaliate in the event of when we've had artillery targets to fire back at.

Mr. Hunt. Is that justice? Is that dealing them justice?

The President. No, but let me say this also with regard to that. Enough civilians have been the targets in this war. It is true that these terrorist groups and the Syrians and

others and the Druze make use of civilians and launch their assaults by rocket or artillery or whatever from civilian enclaves and residential areas where to fire back you are a threat to civilian targets.

On the matter of the terrible tragedy and the terrorist group, we set out with the best ability we had of reconnaissance and intelligence to make sure that we could locate the perpetrators, their stronghold, so that we would not just be killing somebody without knowing who in revenge, you might say, whether they had anything to do with the dastardly deed or not. And we had some feelings that we had located, but there was additional information we wanted that the people involved were still there. And someone else evidently knew more than we did or was not as careful as we were and took that target out before we could get to it. It was as simple as that.

Mr. Bartley. So, you don't expect to do anything more about that pledge on the marines?

The President. Well, unless we continue trying to the best of our ability intelligence-wise to get evidence on the locale of these-type terrorists and where they might be. And we have, as I said the other night in my speech, we are contacting our own allies and friends worldwide as to how we can together combat this new kind of warfare.

I don't think any country, modern times has ever been prepared for this kind of assault. And you don't fight it the way you take a Grenada, for example.

El Salvador

Mr. Bartley. If we could shift to another hotspot——

Mr. Speakes.[1] We'll have to make this the last question, because the President has someone at 2:50 in here—[*inaudible*].

Mr. Bartley. [*Inaudible*]—going to have an election next month in El Salvador, and one of the leading candidates is Roberto D'Aubuisson who—recently the State Department wouldn't give him a visa even to visit the United States. And I'm wondering,

---

[1] *Larry M. Speakes, Principal Deputy Press Secretary to the President.*

if he's elected down there, whether you'll be able to support his government.

The President. Well, that's going to depend a lot on what kind of a government and what kind of policies he follows. We are determined—and I think George Shultz and, before him, Vice President Bush, who brought a letter from me down there expressing my views, and then expressed his own and very forcefully and appropriately, that made it plain, we have very definite feelings about the violence and the violation of human rights, whether from the left or right.

I think the thing that we have to recognize, though, is that the left and the right are literally together on their goals. The guerrillas—we know what they're after, the destruction of a democratic government, the first such government that, I think, that country's had in 400 years. But those from the right who are opposed to the democratic principles and policies that this government is implementing, they have the same goal as the left. They're trying to destroy that same democratic government.

Now——

Women's Issues

Mr. Hunt. Mr. President, I would never ignore Larry Speakes, I promise you. But before we go, I just want to ask you quickly one, somewhat different question. And that is about women. We're all sort of products of our environment. And occasionally when you have made references to "gals" or something like that, it's tended to offend women, particularly younger women. Has that surprised you?

The President. I think to the extent that things that we've had and that actually are even affectionate terms, and that are not meant in any derogatory manner, are suddenly seized upon by, let's say, certain factions as being violations now of what they believe must be the new acceptance. Well, I always have accepted women, frankly.

When I was assailed by that one woman in the businesswomen's meeting over there for my story about us and what we might do, I wasn't joking. I really meant it. I think they have and are a magnificent civilizing influence. But I also think you can't look around the world and—their belief that

women can be entrusted with certain professions and jobs that they have never or not often had before does not surprise me.

I had the greatest esteem for a Golda Meir; I have, too, for a Margaret Thatcher. But I also think that if England wants to look back in its history, they did pretty well with Queen Victoria. And we forget——

Mr. Hunt. Does your daughter ever give you a hard time about those remarks?

The President. What?

Mr. Hunt. Does your daughter Maureen ever give you a hard time about those remarks?

The President. No, because she knows how I feel. But, really, this is—I think, it's like lacking a sense of balance or humor for some people to get so imbued with something that they set standards that are a little extreme.

I certainly, as I said, had never meant anything derogatory. I spoke with great admiration when I've sometimes used the term—I'm a little more careful now, because if they're going to offend someone, I don't want to do that. But I don't know whether I should tell this story or not——

Mr. Hunt. Oh, go ahead.

Mr. Baker. Mr. President, you're due in the East Room in 6 minutes, and you've got another group in here before that, so——

The President. Oh.

Mr. Hunt. Can't you just tell that one story? [*Laughter*]

The President. Oh, well, I'll tell you, if they'll shut off the tape.

Mr. Hunt. Okay.

The President. I'll tell it off the record, because it might not be diplomatic.

Mr. Hunt. Okay.

Note: The interview began at 2:23 p.m. in the Oval Office at the White House. Those attending the interview were Warren H. Phillips, chairman and chief executive, Peter R. Kann, vice president/associate publisher, Norman Pearlstine, managing editor, Robert L. Bartley, editor, and Albert R. Hunt and Rich Jaroslovsky, staff reporters.

James A. Baker III is Assistant to the President and Chief of Staff.

The transcript of the interview was released by the Office of the Press Secretary on February 3.

Remarks Announcing a Proposed Initiative for Central America
February 3, 1984

Good morning to all of you, and welcome to the White House.

Before discussing the positive initiative that we'll propose for the region of Central America, I'd like to share some wonderful news with you. We have just learned that total unemployment has dropped to 7.9 percent, and another 250,000 Americans found jobs last month. Now, I'm just beginning to wonder if the best thing we could do for Central America would be to export our own economic recovery program. [*Laughter*] But I think, in a way, that's what we're talking about.

As I was about to say, in the coming days we'll send legislation to the Congress based on a remarkable bipartisan consensus of the National Bipartisan Commission on Central America. And I urge prompt congressional action and support.

Last April, in an address to a joint session of the Congress, I spoke to the American people about what is at stake in Central America and asked for bipartisan cooperation in our efforts to help make a better life for the people of that region. Shortly after that speech, the late Senator Henry Jackson called for the appointment of a bipartisan commission to chart a long-term course for democracy, economic improvement, and peace in Central America. And as Scoop Jackson so rightly observed, "Whatever policy options might be available to us, ignoring threats to the stability of Central America and refusing to engage ourselves in the problems of the region are not among them."

It was against this background that I did establish the National Bipartisan Commission on Central America. Its mission was to recommend a long-term policy appropriate to the economic, social, political, and military challenges to the region.

The distinguished Americans who served on that Commission have performed a great service to all Americans. All of us—when I say *all* Americans—*all* of us from Point Barrow to Tierra del Fuego. Henry Kissinger and the Commission members and senior counselors: My appreciation for a tough job well done.

Our proposed legislation, the Central America democracy, peace, and development initiative act, is based on the Commission's analysis and embodies its recommendations, and it's in the spirit of Senator Jackson who first proposed the idea of a bipartisan commission and served until his death as one of its senior counselors. He represented something very special in American politics. Scoop Jackson stood for national security and human rights because he knew that one without the other is meaningless. He said what he believed and stuck to it with vision, integrity, and grace.

The legislation does not offer a quick fix to the crisis in Central America; there is none. Our plan offers a comprehensive program to support democratic development, improve human rights, and bring peace to this troubled region that's so close to home.

The approach is right. It includes a mix of developmental, political, diplomatic, and security initiatives, equitably and humanely pursued. We either do them all, or we jeopardize the chance for real progress in the region. The plan responds to decades of inequity and indifference through its support of democracy, reform, and human freedom. It responds to the economic challenges of the region.

The legislation calls for $400 million in supplementary economic assistance for fiscal year 1984. And during the next 5 years, economic assistance will amount to $5.9 billion in appropriated funds and $2 billion in insurance and guarantees.

To support the security of the region's threatened nations, the legislaton will provide $515 million over the next 2 years. At the same time, it will require semiannual reports to the Congress assessing El Salvadoran policies for achieving political and economic development and conditions of security.

To support dialog and negotiations both among the countries of the region and within each country, the legislation provides guidance for cooperation with the Central American countries in establishing, then working with, the Central American Development Organization.

Our plan is for the long haul. It won't be easy, and it won't be cheap. But it can be done. And for strategic and moral reasons, it must be done. I ask the Congress to study the Commission report and to give our legislative proposal its urgent attention and bipartisan support. It is not an impossible dream. We have the resources to do it. This initiative serves the interest of the United States and of the Western Hemisphere. The beleaguered people in Central America want our help. Our enemies, extremists of the left and the right, would be delighted if we refused to give it. And if we don't help now, we'll surely pay dearly in the future.

With the support of the Congress, we will not let down all those in Central America who yearn for democracy and peace. And in so doing, we'll not let ourselves down.

So, I thank you all very much for being here. And, again, I thank the Commission for their outstanding work. Thank you all.

Note: The President spoke at 10:48 a.m. in the East Room at the White House to Members of Congress, members of the diplomatic community, and administration officials. Prior to his remarks, the President met in the Cabinet Room with the bipartisan congressional leaders to discuss the proposed initiative.

Remarks at a White House Luncheon for Elected Republican Women Officials
February 3, 1984

I'm delighted to welcome you here and see so many good friends and to have a chance to make some new ones.

It's always a special occasion when I can be joined by two of the most important women in my life—Nancy, and my daughter, Maureen. And I'll let you have a little secret: Even though I go to work and come home from work in an elevator—[*laughter*]—this is about the only time we get to have lunch together. [*Laughter*] And we're also pleased to have the Vice President and Barbara Bush with us, as well as some of the women on the White House staff.

Now, before I say anything else, I want to give you my heartfelt thanks for all the time and effort that each of you has given to the cause that unites us. When all is said and done, what really counts is drive and energy and determination. And that's what makes it possible to put our beliefs into practice. It's you, officeholders in communities throughout our land, who demonstrate the deep Republican commitment to American women.

On the way over here, I remembered a story that made me think of all of you. And if you've heard it before, pretend you haven't. I know my own people have heard it before—[*laughter*]—because you've got to remember that when you—life not only begins at 40, but so does lumbago and the tendency to repeat the same story. [*Laughter*]

But this is a story about—it was an automobile accident, and there was a man stretched out there, and a woman was bending over him, trying to give some aid. And a crowd had begun to gather, and a n elbowed his way through the crowd, shoved the lady aside, and said, "Let me at him. I've had first aid training." And she meekly stepped back, and he went to work with all the things that he learned. And then at one point she tapped him on the shoulder and said, "When you come to that part about calling the doctor, I'm right here." [*Laughter*]

Women have increasingly taken on new roles in society, and the Republican Party has given them solid support. It was the GOP that gave its backing to women's suffrage. And then our party became the first to elect a woman to the United States Congress—and I think I'm indebted to Maureen for a little research on this—and that was before women were allowed to vote. And we're the only party ever to elect women to the United States Senate who were not first just filling out an unexpired term.

Today our party is building on that tradition. The only two women in the Senate, Nancy Kassebaum and Paula Hawkins, are Republicans. And there are nine outstanding Republican Congresswomen, including Marge Roukema, Claudine Schneider, who are with us today.

In our administration, we've appointed many women to important positions of top responsibility—women like Ambassador Jeane Kirkpatrick, Secretary of Health and Human Services Margaret Heckler, Secretary of Transportation Elizabeth Dole, and right here at the White House, Faith Whittlesey. And one of my proudest days was when Sandra Day O'Connor became the first woman Justice on the Supreme Court. And believe me, I've had many reasons to cheer her appointment ever since.

But just as important is the fact that there are thousands of able Republican women like you serving in public office all over the country. Whether it's in the legislatures or in other State and local offices, you're on the frontlines of democracy. You're making the difference. And what I want to see is the number of Republican women officeholders grow here in Washington and in every American town, city, and State like they did in Rhode Island last year, when eight Republican women won State senate seats. The minority leader of the senate is here at my table.

And together, we Republicans are working to reshape America's destiny. When historians write the story of these years, they'll find that very skilled and very talented women played vital roles.

Three years ago this week, in my first address to the Nation, I reported on the state of our economy. I told the American people they wouldn't like the news, but that we had to face the truth if we were going to turn the economy around. The Federal budget was careening out of control, and we faced the worst economic crisis since the Great Depression. Our economy was broken, and women were hit especially hard. The majority of elderly Americans living on fixed incomes are women, and double-digit inflation was destroying their purchasing power. Homemakers found it harder and harder to pay bills. And the thousands of women who wanted to start their own businesses saw 21 percent interest rates slam shut the doors of opportunity.

With Republicans in control of the Senate, we made a new beginning. And believe me, if we didn't control one House of the Congress, we wouldn't have been able to get the job done.

We can be proud of the results. Inflation—I know you've been told already, and I'm plowing plowed ground here—but down to 3.2 percent; the prime rate—knocked nearly in half; 4 million new jobs last year alone; personal income tax rates reduced; and indexing, beginning next year, which means government can no longer use inflation to profit at the people's expense. And thanks to the hard work of the Vice President, we've reduced the growth of government regulations by 25 percent and cut well over 300 million hours of government-required paperwork, taken it off the backs of the people. And that's 300 million hours each year.

Now, to help all Americans achieve economic equality, we reduced the marriage tax penalty. We almost doubled the maximum child care credit. We increased the limits for IRA and Keogh contributions, and we've eliminated estate taxes on family farms and businesses for surviving spouses. And our work is continuing to ensure women's rights, provide for equitable treatment in pension benefits and IRA's, to facilitate child and dependent care, and to enforce delinquent parent support payments.

From solid growth in housing to new frontiers in high technology and from a healthy recovery in real wages to the sharpest drop in unemployment in nearly 33 years, America is moving forward and getting stronger.

Have we made a new beginning? You bet we have. Today our nation has one big program to help every American man, woman, and child—it's called "economic recovery." Maybe the eight Democratic candidates still haven't heard about it—[*laughter*]—they're still talking doom and gloom.

Well, good news might not always make news. But today we've got more good news. I think someone has indicated that to you; I hope they haven't given all the news away. Last month, total unemployment dropped again to 7.9 percent. And among adult women, the unemployment rate is 7.1 percent. And that's down from 9 percent in the past year. And the jobs are getting better and better. Last year, women filled 73 percent of all the new jobs in managerial, professional, and technical fields.

But there's still work to be done. Unemployment is still too high, and I'm not going to be satisfied until everyone who wants a job can find one. We need basic budget and tax reforms, like the line-item veto, a constitutional amendment mandating a balanced budget, and tax simplification—reforms that can ensure the progress that we're enjoying will continue for our children and even our children's children.

And just as we've turned the economy around, there's a new sense of purpose and direction to American foreign policy. Back in 1981 we had an uncomfortable feeling that we'd lost respect overseas. Some questioned whether we had the will to defend peace and freedom. Well, 3 years later, the world knows once more what America stands for: freedom for mankind. From Central America to Africa to the Middle East, we're working hard to support democracy and to build peace.

In Lebanon, the peaceful process has been painfully slow, but we have made gen-uine progress. In Europe, the NATO alliance has remained united and strong. Our relations in the Far East have never been better. In our relations with the Soviet Union, by strengthening our defenses and making clear our determination to negotiate, we have laid the foundation for meaningful agreements and a safer, more peaceful world. On an island in the Caribbean, we rescued Americans and set a nation free.

All of us share a dream. It's a dream, I think, of a world at peace, and it's a dream of a broad and open land that offers opportunity and prosperity to all. It's a dream of a land where every citizen is judged only on merit, a land where every woman and man is free to become all that she or he can. And I'm sure that one day one of you may have this job, my job. And I think the only thing we have to worry about is to be sure she's a Republican. [*Laughter*]

All of us are laboring in the name of that dream, and there's a lot of work yet to be done. But if we have the courage to continue the good fight, we'll get it done, and we'll achieve great good at home and throughout the world.

And I can't close for dessert here for a moment without mentioning—I don't know whether she's been introduced or you've met her or not. But we have here a visitor we're very proud to have who was closely aligned with us in the recent rescue mission in Grenada, Prime Minister Charles of Dominica.

Note: The President spoke at 12:48 p.m. in the State Dining Room at the White House.

Designation of Hoyt D. Gardner as Alternate United States Representative on the Executive Board of the World Health Organization
February 3, 1984

The President today announced his intention to designate Hoyt D. Gardner to be the Alternate Representative of the United States of America on the Executive Board of the World Health Organization. He would succeed Dr. Benjamin D. Blood.

Dr. Gardner has been a general surgeon in private practice since 1958. He is a fellow of the American College of Surgeons and a member of the board of the National

Blue Cross Blue Shield Association. He was on the board of trustees of the American Medical Association (1974–1981) and served as president in 1979–1980. He was a member of the U.S. Delegation, World Health Assembly, in Geneva, Switzerland (1975).

Dr. Gardner attended Westminster College (1942–1946) and graduated from the University of Louisville School of Medicine (1950). He is married, has three children, and resides in Louisville, KY. He was born on August 2, 1923, in Paragould, AR.

Radio Address to the Nation on the Budget Deficit, Central America, and Lebanon
February 4, 1984

My fellow Americans:

As you know, last Sunday I announced my candidacy for reelection to this office. I asked for your support to help finish what we began 3 years ago—getting government spending firmly under control, encouraging growth in our economy, and strengthening peace so we can provide opportunities for the liberty and happiness of our citizens today and for millions still unborn.

I wasn't surprised that my announcement set off some pretty sharp rhetoric from the other side, but I'd like to think that with some good will and common sense Republicans and Democrats could rise above election-year politics for the good of our country. Certainly there are important areas— and three come immediately to mind— where we could and should be working together.

For example, I believe there's basis for agreement on a downpayment on projected budget deficits. I think we could reduce projected deficits by at least $100 billion over the next 3 years. So, frankly, I was a bit puzzled why those new converts to concern about looming deficits held back on joining a bipartisan working group.

Now, I understand they will be prepared to meet next week. I urge them to approach the negotiations in the same spirit as we will. Let's try to put the partisan issues aside. I repeat that all issues can be on the table for discussion. But, obviously, we cannot compromise the principles of our tax program without compromising our economic recovery and America's future.

I simply can't agree to increase taxes on families already pinching pennies to pay their bills. We want to reduce the deficit, not the recovery. And it would be foolhardy, indeed, to compromise America's defense rebuilding program just as we're beginning to restore the credibility that was so recklessly squandered.

Yet this does not mean that there aren't areas in which to find bipartisan agreement. We could focus on the less contentious spending cuts still pending before the Congress. These could be combined with measures to close certain tax loopholes that the Treasury Department has indicated it believes worthy of support.

If we focus on what we might agree on, we can get something done for the people. And the Grace commission has come up with some 2,500 recommendations for reducing wasteful government spending. We should examine them together.

Uniting to promote democracy, peace, and prosperity in the troubled region of Central America is a second area where Republicans and Democrats should work together. Last July I appointed 12 distinguished Americans to the National Bipartisan Commission on Central America and asked former Secretary of State Henry Kissinger to serve as its Chairman. Three weeks ago, the members of that Commission delivered to me their report on the crisis confronting our Latin neighbors. Their recommendations are the basis of legislation that I will soon present to the Congress.

I should point out that the late Senator Henry Jackson first proposed the idea of the

Bipartisan Commission on Central America, and he served until his death as one of its senior counselors. All his life, Scoop said what he believed and stuck to it. He believed in freedom, dignity for the individual, and a strong America. And he believed Republicans and Democrats should leave politics at the water's edge on important questions of national security. Senator Jackson's wisdom is the guiding spirit of our legislation. It offers a balance of political, economic, diplomatic, and security initiatives that can bring stability and a better life to our neighbors and ultimately greater security to our own country. This plan deserves the bipartisan support of the Congress. We have a responsibility to act.

Continued support for the peace process in the Middle East is a third critical area where Republicans and Democrats must rise above politics. We're working closely with Lebanon's President Gemayel to find a political solution. Support for his government is broadening among the different groups. And just as important, our efforts to strengthen the Lebanese Army and its ability to keep the peace are making sure and steady progress.

Yes, the situation in Lebanon is difficult, frustrating, and dangerous. But that is no reason to turn our backs on friends and to cut and run. If we do, we'll be sending one signal to terrorists everywhere: They can gain by waging war against innocent people.

The men and women who patrol our streets here at home also face great dangers every day. But the greatest danger of all would be to yank those police officers off the streets and to leave our neighborhoods and families at the mercy of criminals. If we're to be secure in our homes and in the world, we must stand together against those who threaten us. This is a time for unity, not partisan politics.

Till next week, thanks for listening, and God bless you.

Note: The President spoke at 12:06 p.m. from Camp David, MD.

Remarks During a Homecoming and Birthday Celebration in Dixon, Illinois
February 6, 1984

Thank you for those very generous words. And I can't help but digress, being bathed in nostalgia as I am. That line back there that you just read, actually, I have to tell you how that came about.

I was in England making a picture called "The Hasty Heart." It was a story in which we were all in a field hospital in Burma—India in World War II, and talking about things like home. And the line in the script from—it was a famous Broadway play—had me saying that everybody has a place to go back to and for me it's Boston. Well, after almost 4 months of an English winter, I was so homesick.

Now, the funny thing is, I'd lived a great many years away from Dixon by that time, in California. But I found myself saying to the director, "I would like to change the line." And I changed the line—"Dixon, place on the Rock River." Some of the people in the publicity department were a little upset about that, because Boston's bigger than Dixon. [*Laughter*] But, anyway, the line went in the picture that way.

Now, Nancy and I have been looking forward to this day for a long time, and your warm welcome, believe me, touches our hearts. And before I say anything else, let me express my sincere thanks to everyone who made this terrific day possible.

Mayor Jim Dixon, Governor Jim Thompson, Senator Chuck Percy, Congresswoman Lynn Martin, distinguished guests, and may I add with great pride and pleasure, my fellow Dixonians, it's great to be back home. And, you know, if our old house on Hennepin Avenue looked as good in 1924 as it does now—[*laughter*]—I might never have left.

Incidentally, Moon and I—his name is Neil, but Moon since he was here in Dixon—we've been asking everyone on this committee connected with that house undertaking up there one thing, though, that has fooled us. How did they shrink it? [*Laughter*] We remembered it as much bigger.

But anyway, my heart is still here. I know his is, and it always will be.

Birthdays are special moments, and you've given me one today. But I must tell you, even though this is the 34th anniversary of my 39th birthday—[*laughter*]—those numbers don't faze me at all. I believe Moses was 80 when God first commissioned him for public service. [*Laughter*] And I also remember something that Thomas Jefferson once said. He said, "We should never judge a President by his age, only by his works." And ever since he told me that—[*laughter*]—I've stopped worrying. There are those who say I've stopped working. [*Laughter*]

But back in 1951, another Illinois native returned to his hometown for a short visit. Carl Sandburg was also 73 years old when he spent a day on his cousin's farm in Galesburg, just about a hundred miles or so down the road from here.

And later, he reflected on America's future. He thought about the three wars and the two depressions that he had lived through. He reminisced about the pain and the suffering he'd seen on so many faces. But Carl Sandburg didn't forecast a dark future for America. When he came back to the prairies of Illinois he felt the spirit of a strong and worthy people, and that made him an optimist. He said, "I see great days ahead . . ." for "men and women of will and vision." And then he tipped his hat as a way of offering his favorite toast: "To the storms to come and the stars coming after the storms."

Carl Sandburg understood that our greatest strength is not bullets or balance sheets, but the mighty spirit of a free people under God. And our spirit has never waned. The heart of America is strong, it's good, and it's true. We look forward to the future. We know we were never meant to be second best, and we never will be.

Like Carl Sandburg, I also remember those depression years. Times were tough. But what I remember most clearly is that Dixon held together. Our faith was our strength. Our teachers pointed to the future. People held on to their hopes and dreams. Neighbors helped neighbors. We knew—my brother, Moon, and I, our mother and father, Nelle and Jack, saw to that—saw that we knew we would overcome adversity and that after the storm, the stars would come.

Dixon has changed a lot since then. But in many ways, it hasn't changed at all. And I'm not talking about Lowell Park or St. Luke's or the Memorial Arch. What I'm really referring to are the values and traditions that made America great.

Our values bring us together as a nation. They help us go just as far as our God-given talents will take us. Americans are the most charitable people in the world. We reach out to the needy. We're a nation of volunteers. We seek community service. It's so easy to have faith in America. I know of the volunteer effort that it's taken from so many to bring about not only this day but the restoration of that house. And it's so easy to have faith in America.

When you're talking about the character of America, you're also talking about the small business community, about the owners of that store down the street, the faithful who support their churches and their civic organizations, all the brave men and women with faith to invest in the future to build a better America.

Only when individuals are given a personal stake in deciding their own destiny, in benefiting from their own risks, do societies prosper, grow, and remain free. To those who would stifle personal initiative through more and more government, I ask them to read the Constitution. As a matter of fact, just read the first three words. It says, "We the People." It doesn't say, "We the Government."

It's everyday people with big ideas that count—people like Father John Dixon, who arrived here in 1830 with his wife, five children, and a dream. His ferry service provided the only means of crossing the Rock River for travelers to Galena coming from Peoria, Fort Dearborn, and Fort Armstrong.

But he didn't stop there. Through his efforts, he lived to see Dixon's Ferry become the county seat and a thriving community of 8,000, and now you've doubled that.

You know, I must say, that if Father Dixon had to fill out environmental impact statements, report to regulatory agencies in Washington, or wait for an area redevelopment plan, Dixon would probably still be known as Dixon's Ferry. [*Laughter*] And our town might never have seen people like John Deere and the Walgreens, people with ingenuity, audacity, and vision.

That's why we're working so hard to limit the size and the scope of the Federal Government. We've already reduced the growth of Federal regulations by more than 25 percent. We've cut well over 300 million man-hours of government-required paperwork that was laid on the people each year. And we're going to reduce it even more. We just want to give today's pioneers the same chance that Father Dixon had.

And there's something else. When you stop to think, it's easy to understand why America's back on her feet and moving forward with confidence. Our rebirth began right here, in our homes, schools, churches, and neighborhoods. From the grocery store to the football field, from the service clubs to the Chamber of Commerce, America has recaptured her drive, energy, and determination.

There's a new spirit of community building. You can feel it everywhere. We see so many acts of courage and downright heroism—like an 11-year-old in Hampton, Virginia, who was seriously burned recently while rescuing his elderly neighbor from a serious house fire. I talked to him—Tim Diakis—11 years old. He'll be out of the hospital in a few weeks, and he's going to be okay. It'll take a number of operations because of his severe burns. And now his community is chipping in to help cover the cost of his hospitalization.

And you showed how much you care in Dixon when you raised $37,000 for special medical care needed by young Jason Hiner-icks. God bless you, Jason.

Well, this community spirit responds to our desire for cooperation and brotherhood, and it makes our hometown a better place to live. If anybody wants to know about community and what community is all about, come to Lee County and Dixon, Illinois.

Come take a look at the Hometown Heritage Foundation, a community alumni organization dedicated to future development of the local area. By working together—individuals, businesses, civic organizations, and local government—Dixon is building a brighter future.

So, you see, the reason I came home today was not to celebrate my birthday, but to celebrate Dixon and America. Honor, integrity, and kindness do exist all across our land. There is a zest for life and laughter.

Another Illini, Adlai Stevenson, kind of put it all together when he said, "America is much more than a geographical fact. It is a political and moral fact—the first community in which men set out in principle to institutionalize freedom, responsible government, and human equality." And that's what we're really celebrating today.

And all I can say, again, to all of you is God bless you; thank you very much. And God bless America.

Thank you very much.

Note: The President spoke at 1:31 p.m. in the Dixon High School gymnasium. He was introduced by Dean Harrison, cochairman of the Hometown Coordinating Committee.

Earlier, after arriving in Dixon, the President and his brother, Neil, and their wives toured and lunched at one of the homes the Reagan family had lived in during the President's boyhood. The home had been renovated by the Ronald Reagan Home Restoration Foundation. They then viewed a homecoming parade from the Nachusa House Hotel.

Following his remarks to the citizens of Dixon, the President met at the high school with a small group of local residents.

Remarks at Eureka College in Eureka, Illinois
February 6, 1984

Mr. Grunwald, thank you very much. Governor Thompson, President Gilbert, distinguished guests here, the faculty, the administration, the trustees who might be present, fellow citizens, and students of this wonderful college:

I want you to know that this has been a day that—if I said, Neil, you wouldn't know who I was talking about—my brother, Moon, and I will long remember. It's a day of warmth and memory, a day when the good things that have happened in our lives all seem very close and very real again.

We've just come from Dixon, where I attended my biggest birthday party ever. It was the 34th anniversary of my 39th birthday. [*Laughter*] And I had what every man who has that many candles on his birthday cake needs around him—a large group of friends and a working sprinkler system. [*Laughter*]

And now we're here for Eureka's birthday. Legend has it that after Ben Major led a wagon train here, he sunk an ax into the first tree he felled and said, "Here we'll build our school." And that was, as you've been told, more than 129 years ago. And just to end any speculation going on among the undergraduates, no, I was not a part of that original wagon train. [*Laughter*]

It's always wonderful to return to Eureka. People ask me if I'm looking back at my college years, if I can remember any inkling that I would someday run for President. Well, actually, the thought first struck me on graduation day, when the president of the college handed me my diploma and asked, "Are you better off today than you were 4 years ago?" [*Laughter*]

Besides being wonderful, coming back to Eureka is also a great temptation. Sitting in a college audience can sometimes be dangerous duty. Something about your youthfulness and the bright, fresh hope it symbolizes makes guest speakers like myself very free with their reminiscenses and very reluctant to sit down.

You've heard, I'm sure, that I like to tell an anecdote or two. Well, life not only begins at 40; so does lumbago and the tendency to tell the same stories over and over again. [*Laughter*] But, I promise I'll try to be brief today, so rest easy. You're lucky. I have to be in Nevada tonight.

But I don't want to miss this opportunity to share with you some thoughts on the changes that have happened to America in the 50-odd years—and some of them were odd—since I left this campus and to offer too some thoughts on how we can shape those changes to serve the cause of human freedom—to inspire, not burden, those who come after us. I can't think of a better occasion for such reflections.

In addition to Founder's Day here at Eureka, we're also marking the first in a series of speeches sponsored by Time magazine to commemorate its 60th anniversary. For 60 years, Time has lived up to what Henry Luce and Briton Hadden envisioned when they founded the magazine in 1923: a weekly digest of news, put together with much more care and perspective than is usually possible under the deadline pressure of daily journalism. Well, if it's important for news organizations like Time to keep in mind the value of perspective, you can imagine how important it is for those of us in public life to remember that proximity to daily events can be as much a handicap as an advantage in understanding their meaning.

And that's what struck me when I was thinking about what I wanted to say here today: the ease, the unknowing grace with which my generation accepted technological and political changes that so radically transformed our world. We didn't know then that ours was to be one of those infrequent generations that would preside over a great transition period. We went in a single lifetime literally from horse and buggy to space travel.

In 1932, for example, I graduated from Eureka and landed a job in radio. Though I didn't realize it at the time, I had become part of the communications revolution that was shrinking the dimensions of my world even more than radio's successor, television, would shrink your own. Already my generation's sports idols, celebrities, newsmakers, and heroes had come in large measure from the world of radio. It seemed a perfect career choice.

Yet if I'd only stopped to think about it, I would have remembered back in my boyhood days, just a few short years before, when my friends and I followed our neighborhood genius around town in Dixon trying to pick up radio signals with his jury-rigged crystals, aerial, and headphones. Can you imagine our sense of wonder when one Sunday afternoon, down by the river there in Dixon, we heard the sounds of radio for the first time, an orchestra playing over KDKA several hundred miles away in Pittsburgh?

And yet it took only a few years for that sense of wonder to dissolve. Radio, which was heard in only 60,000 households in 1922, was heard in almost 18½ million households by 1932, my graduation year.

By that time, of course, the market had crashed, the depression years were upon us, and over those radio sets now sitting in every parlor and living room in the nation came the rich, reassuring tones of Franklin Roosevelt. All of us who lived through those years can remember the drabness the depression brought. But we remember, too, how people pulled together, that sense of community and shared values, that belief in American enterprise and democracy that saw us through. It was that engrained American optimism, that sense of hope Franklin Roosevelt so brilliantly summoned and mobilized.

It was a time of economic emergency, and there seemed a certain logic to arguments that the National Government should take onto itself new and sweeping prerogatives. In the grip of that emergency, many of us could not see the enormous and sometimes harmful—oftentimes harmful political changes that this expanded role for the government would bring.

Once again, as I look back, the rapidity of that political change was as astonishing as the change brought by technology. At the start of that era, government collected in taxes a dime out of every dollar earned. Two-thirds of that dime went to State and local governments, with only one-third to Washington. Today government at all levels is collecting more than 40 cents out of every dollar, and the proportion is completely reversed, with two-thirds of that going to the Federal Government and only one-third for State and local governments.

My generation was a bit surprised to realize that the Federal Government, called upon in an economic emergency, was becoming an obstacle to economic progress. In addition to damaging the autonomy of local and State governments, usurping the rights of the people, the public sector had grown so large it was consuming our national wealth, discouraging energy and initiative, and suffocating the spirit of enterprise and resourcefulness that had always been at the heart of America's economic miracle.

In the depression years and their aftermath, we forgot that first founding lesson of the American Republic: that without proper restraints, government the servant becomes quickly government the master. I call it an American lesson, but actually it's much older. Cicero believed that the budget should be balanced, the treasury should be refilled, the public debt should be reduced, the arrogance of officialdom should be tempered and controlled. And since that time, many nations that failed to heed the words of that wise Roman have been brought to their knees by governments that borrowed and taxed their citizens into servitude.

But some peoples, like our Founding Fathers, revolted under such oppression. No one would understand better the danger of unchecked government power than those men. "I am not a friend to a very energetic government. It is always oppressive," Jefferson said.

I remember quoting a few of these warnings long after I had left radio for films, television, and after-dinner speeches. And by that time, this reformed New Dealer could add one of his own: that a government agency is the nearest thing to eternal life we'll ever see on this Earth. [*Laughter*] And yet even as the decades of the fifties and sixties went by, and more Americans shared my concern, government grew like Topsy. In the decade of the seventies, Federal spending tripled, taxes doubled, and the national debt reached almost a trillion dollars. Government bureaus, agencies, and employment rolls kept multiplying. It had become too easy for politicians to promise more to win more, to spend their way to election victories.

Fortunately, that juggernaut of big government has now been slowed. During the last 3 years, we've brought skyrocketing spending back to Earth and reduced that enormous momentum toward big government. It wasn't easy, but measure the results by our ability to achieve what people once said was impossible. Federal spending growth has been cut by more than half. Government regulations have been cut by more than a quarter. And taxes on working Americans have actually been reduced and indexed to the rate of inflation. A working family earning $25,000 has $1,500 more in purchasing power today because of the cut in taxes and the lowered rate of inflation.

Today economic recovery is in full swing. But I hope we can use these moments of reflection today to understand the hard lessons we've learned since the depression about the growth of government. We need some basic reforms that will protect us against government's all too powerful tendency to grow and grow.

For one thing, it's time for the Federal Government, in the best federalist tradition, to learn something from successful experiments in the State and local laboratories of governments. The evidence from States and many municipalities is overwhelming. The executive branch needs a powerful weapon to cut out porkbarreling and special interest expenditures buried in large, catchall appropriation bills. It is time the Congress gave the President the authority to veto single-line items in the Federal budget, as Governors can do in 43 of our 50 States.

And second, politicians at the national level must no longer be permitted to mortgage your future by running up higher and higher deficits. The time has come to force government to live within its means. And I repeat my call today for making a balanced budget a constitutional amendment. When the Constitution was ratified, Thomas Jefferson voiced a regret that it did not contain a clause prohibiting the Federal Government from borrowing.

And finally, our tax system is now a nightmare of tangled requirements and twisted priorities. The American people want and deserve a tax code that is fair, rewarding, and simple enough to be understood by someone other than an army of green-shaded accountants and lawyers.

Now—you know, I've been told that Einstein had to have help filling out his 1040. [*Laughter*] But now, in addition to the technological revolution marked by inventions like radio, and the political revolution brought on by the sweeping new scope of Federal power, there has been an additional development worth noting. That is the emergence of America's international role—our sudden designation as the champion of peace and human freedom in the struggle against totalitarianism.

We didn't seek this leadership. It was thrust upon us. In the dark days after World War II when much of the civilized world lay in ruins, Pope Pius XII said, "The American people have a genius for splendid and unselfish action, and into the hands of America, God has placed the destinies of afflicted humanity."

Throughout World War II and most of the postwar era, though the adversaries changed—from Hitler to Stalin—there was still basic agreement on the moral imperative of defending freedom and the self-evident differences between totalitarian and democratic governments.

But that broad consensus of the Truman, Eisenhower, Kennedy years began to break down in the sixties and seventies. Partly in response to the Vietnam tragedy, an era of paralyzing self-doubt ruled out just and legitimate uses of American power—even acts of self-defense.

The consequences of America's retreat were not long in coming. All of you can remember a few years back when the tragedy of the Iranian hostages was fresh in our minds; when around the world, especially in Afghanistan and Central America, Soviet expansionism proceeded unchecked; when our defenses had declined dramatically and some nations thought they could threaten or harm the United States with impunity.

We've changed this. We're trying to see to it that American citizens—and it doesn't matter whether they're navy pilots in the Gulf of Sidra or medical students in Grenada—can no longer be attacked or their lives endangered with impunity.

You know, Jeane Kirkpatrick, our Ambassador to the United Nations, has a wonderful story to explain how fundamental this reversal has been. She says that when she arrived at the U.N., someone asked her what would be different about our administration's foreign policy. "Well," she said, "we've taken off our 'Kick Me' sign."

And she was asked, "Does that mean if you're kicked, you'll kick back?"

"Oh, not necessarily," she replied, "but it does mean that if we're kicked, at least we won't apologize."

Yet, it goes beyond just self-defense. When I spoke to the British Parliament a year and a half ago, I said our cause was human freedom; and so it has been—in Europe, in Lebanon, in Central America. We've tried to bring a new honesty and moral purposefulness to our foreign policy, to show we can be candid about the essential differences between ourselves and others while still pursuing peace initiatives with them.

As I've said before, the democracies have their own serious injustices to deal with. But this should not prevent us from making the crucial moral distinctions between pluralist systems which acknowledge their own wrongs and shortcomings and systems that excuse their defects in the name of totalitarian ideology.

Our willingness to speak out on these distinctions is the moral center of our foreign policy. For us, human freedom is a first principle, not a bargaining chip. To fail to publicly enunciate the differences between totalitarian and democratic systems of government would be to forsake this moral high ground.

Peace remains our highest aspiration, and that's why arms control isn't enough. Arms reduction is our goal. And may I interject right here—I, a few years ago, stood in this exact spot and made the announcement then that we were going to ask for arms reduction meetings with the Soviet Union to reduce the number of strategic nuclear weapons we both held. But then, as we have tried to communicate to the people of the Soviet Union, would it not be better to do away with nuclear weapons entirely? I think our new realism is an important means to this end.

Just as important, it reestablishes the basis of that broad foreign policy consensus that existed in the pre-Vietnam era when we understood the moral imperatives of defending freedom and the importance of taking totalitarian powers seriously.

You know, I've heard mentioned an observation by a distinguished French intellectual, Jean François Revel, on this point. Mr. Revel points out that some people are embarrassed to call the struggle between democracy and totalitarianism by its own name and prefer euphemisms like the "competition between East and West" or "the struggle between superpowers."

And here I want to point out that the political revolutions we've seen in America in domestic and international policy are only a reflection of a deeper trend, a trend that directly concerns the world that you have been part of here at Eureka, the world of ideas.

There has been a dramatic turnabout among the intellectuals. For most of my adult life, the intelligentsia has been entranced and enamored with the idea of state power, the notion that enough centralized authority concentrated in the hands of the rightminded people can reform mankind and usher in a brave new world. Well, I remember hearing one commonly held view of the Roosevelt era that all societies were moving toward some modified form of communism.

Well, we know now that the trend in America and the democracies has been just the other way. In the political world, the cult of the state is dying; so, too, the romance of the intellectual with state power is over. Indeed, the excitement and energy in the intellectual world is focused these days on the concerns of human freedom, on the importance of transcendent and enduring values.

In economics, for example, as the recent Nobel Prizes to Fredrick von Hayek, Milton Friedman, and George Stigler attest, the free market is again becoming the focal point. In political philosophy, a whole generation of intellectuals led especially by French thinkers like Revel, Jean Marie Benoit, Guy Sorman are rejecting the old cliches about state power and rediscovering the danger such power poses to personal freedom. Russian intellectuals ranging from majestic figures like Aleksandr Solzhenitsyn to noble crusaders like Vladimir Bukovsky have brought new attention to the horrors of totalitarian rule and to the spiritual desert that is communism.

Here in America, this revolution has been spearheaded for 30 years by intellectual presences like William F. Buckley's National Review. It's been supplemented recently by what's called the neoconservative revolution led by Irving Kristol, Midge Decter, Norman Podhoretz, and others.

In many ways, this counterrevolution of the intellectuals was predated by one of the most vivid events of my time, an event whose meaning is echoed in today's disenchantment with communism.

It involved, coincidentally, an editor of Time magazine, Whittaker Chambers, who in public testimony in 1948 named former high U.S. Government officials as spies. He was not believed at first, but the inexorable power of the truth was slowly felt, and overwhelming evidence led a jury to convict one of those former officials of perjury.

In Chambers' autobiography, "Witness," he added a sequel. Chambers marked the beginning of his personal journey away from communism on the day that he was suddenly struck by the sight of his infant daughter's ear as she sat there having breakfast. And then, he said, he realized that such intricacy, such precision could be no accident, no freak of nature. He said that while he didn't know it at the time, in that moment, God—the finger of God had touched his forehead.

And that is why Chambers would write that faith, not economics, is the central problem of our age and that "the crisis of the western world exists to the degree in which it is indifferent to God." The western world does not know it, but it already possesses the answer to this problem, he said, but only provided that its "faith in God and the freedom He enjoins" is as great as communism's belief in material power.

Chambers' story represents a generation's disenchantment with statism and its return to eternal truths and fundamental values. And if there is one thought I would leave with you today, it is this: For all the momentous change of the last 50 years, it is still the great civilized truths—values of family, work, neighborhood, and religion—that fuel America's technological and material progress and put the spark to our enduring passion for freedom.

We're lucky to live in a time when these traditional values and faith in the future—this sense of hope has been reawakened in our country. Yet, we have so much more to achieve, from assuring continued economic growth to developing space, America's next frontier, to keeping the peace and extending the borders of freedom. You in this room can play a personal part in these next chapters of human progress.

Now, I know you have a sense of excitement about all of this, and that's why it strikes me as odd that some people say today that college students are too conservative. Well, I think the truth is that you've discovered early in life what it took another great American writer, Scott Fitzgerald, many tumultuous years to discover.

Toward the end of his life he would write to his daugher in college about the importance of what he called the fundamental decencies. "My generation of radicals and breakers-down," he said, "never found anything to take the place of the old virtues of work and courage and the old graces of courtesy and politeness."

I hope you'll remember that and something else F. Scott Fitzgerald once said, that America is "a willingness of the heart." In the past half century, America has had its flirtation with statism, but we're returning now to our roots: limited government, the defense of freedom, faith in the future and in our God. With these values as guides, the future can be even more breathtaking than the last 50 years, because it will hold out not only the promise of sweeping improvements in mankind's material conditions but progress in the spiritual and moral realm as well. And that's why I hope that 50 years from now, should Time magazine ask you for your reflections, you'll be able to recall an era exciting beyond all your dreams. Believe me, there are great days ahead for you, for America, and for the cause of human freedom.

Thank you very much. God bless you, and may God bless this campus 'neath the elms. Thank you.

Note: The President spoke at 3:44 p.m. in the Reagan Physical Education Center gymnasium. In his opening remarks, the President referred to Henry Grunwald, editor in chief of Time magazine, who introduced the President; and Dr. Daniel D. Gilbert, president of Eureka College.

Following his remarks, the President attended a reception for donors to Eureka College. He then traveled to Las Vegas, NV, and the Sands Hotel, where he remained overnight.

Statement on the Situation in Lebanon
February 6, 1984

Once more the news from Lebanon is filled with scenes of indiscriminate killing and suffering. I know that men and women of good will throughout the world share my deep concern over the renewed violence. They join me in deploring the continued shelling of innocent civilians and the actions of those who would destroy the legitimate Government of Lebanon.

I call on the Government of Syria, which occupies Lebanese territory from which much of the shelling of civilian centers originates and which facilitates and supplies instruments for terroristic attacks on the people of Lebanon, to cease this activity.

President Gemayel is now hard at work trying to form a new government. I welcome his efforts to stop the fighting and to resume the talks in Geneva aimed at achieving national reconciliation. He has set forth a specific agenda of reforms and reconciliation and demonstrated again his openness to a dialog on all the issues. He has demonstrated his strong desire to bring all factions together to develop equitable and durable political and economic arrangements for his country.

All responsible Lebanese political leaders should take this opportunity to bring into being the more broadly representative government they say they want and which we have continually supported. I urge all parties to answer President Gemayel's call. It is time for all Lebanese to rise above their confessional or factional affiliations and join together as citizens of one nation united and sovereign.

The commitment of the United States to the unity, independence, and sovereignty of Lebanon remains firm and unwavering. We will continue to support the Government and the people of Lebanon in their efforts to achieve these goals. With good will and hard work, the dream of a rebuilt and reunited Lebanon can still be made a reality. We remain committed to help in that task.

Remarks at the Annual Convention of the National Association of Secondary School Principals in Las Vegas, Nevada
February 7, 1984

Thank you very much for a very warm reception, although in my past I've had some warm receptions from principals. [*Laughter*]

I'm really taken aback. I'm glad there wasn't a knife; I wouldn't have known where to start with that first good-luck or good-wish slice of that cake. It's just magnificent, very beautiful.

And I must say, with regard to that honorary membership, you have now given me a new sense of guilt, because about 25 years after I left Eureka College, graduated from there, they gave me an honorary degree. And that only compounded a sense of guilt that I had nursed for some 25 years, because I thought that the first one they gave me was honorary. [*Laughter*]

But I'm delighted to join the National Association of Secondary School Principals here in Las Vegas for your 68th annual convention. Nothing is younger—or older than I am! [*Laughter*]

And a special welcome to the principals that I met with at the White House in September. It was a pleasure to be with you then and to give awards on behalf of your outstanding schools. But I have to admit, I have mixed emotions. When I was a boy going to see the principal meant I'd done something wrong. And today the principals are coming to see me. [*Laughter*] I don't know whether I can handle that or not. [*Laughter*]

By the way, did some of you have training as math teachers? Because on the way in, I thought I spied a few of you at the machines doing fieldwork in probability. [*Laughter*]

Before I say anything else, I'd like to recognize three outstanding gentlemen—Robert Howe, the president of this association, Dale Graham, your president-elect, and Scott Thomson, your executive director. Secretary Bell has told me how much assistance these men have given us as we've worked to improve our nation's schools. And I want to thank them and all of you for the help that you've already given and ask you to keep the help coming. It means a great deal to those of us in Washington, but more important, it means a great deal to America's sons and daughters.

You know, principals and Presidents have jobs that are very much alike. Both of us have to keep a lot of people happy. You have school boards; I have the Cabinet. You have the PTA; I have the voters. You have unruly children; well, I better not name any names. [*Laughter*]

But, if your fine Representatives and Senators won't mind—from Nevada here—let me put it this way: When Congress leaves

town, it's no accident that we call it recess. [*Laughter*]

But I am honored to be with you today. Every man and woman in this room could rightly follow President Truman's example and keep a sign on his desk that says, "The Buck Stops Here." Education is one of the most important issues facing our country, and that makes you principals among the most important people in America.

All of us remember all too painfully the crisis our country faced just a few years ago. Big taxing and spending had led to soaring interest rates and inflation, and our defenses had grown weak. All over the world America had become known not for strength and resolve but for vacillation and self-doubt.

Our schools, too, showed unmistakable signs of crisis. From 1963 to 1981, scholastic aptitude test scores underwent a virtually unbroken decline. Science achievement scores of 17-year-olds showed a similar drop. And most shocking, the National Commission on Excellence in Education reports that more than one-tenth of our 17-year-olds can be considered functionally illiterate.

In the face of all this bad news, our free and hard-working people began for a time to feel almost helpless. It seemed as though our nation, her schools included, was undergoing a protracted and inevitable decline.

Well, on this Earth there's no such thing as inevitable; only men and women building our nation's destiny one day at a time. The American people decided to put a stop to that long decline, and in the past few years our country has seen a rebirth of energy and freedom—a great national renewal. And as I said in my State of the Union Address just 2 weeks ago, "America is back, standing tall, looking to the eighties with courage, confidence, and hope."

We've knocked inflation down, and we can keep it down. The prime rate is about half what it was when our administration took office. All across this vast land of ours, a powerful economic recovery is gaining strength. Morale in the military has soared. And once again America is respected throughout the world as a force for peace and freedom.

Just as our schools were in decline during

the bad days, today they're playing their part in the national renewal. Since our administration put education at the top of the American agenda we've seen a grassroots revolution that promises to strengthen every school in the country. From Maine to California, parents, teachers, school administrators, State and local officeholders, and principals like you have begun vital work to improve the fundamentals—not fancy budget structures, not frills in the curriculum, but basic teaching and learning. In the words of Secretary Bell, "There is currently in progress the greatest, most far-reaching, most promising reform and renewal of education we have seen since the turn of the century."

When our administration took office only a handful of States had task forces on education. Today they all do. In addition, 44 States are increasing graduation requirements, 42 are studying improvements in teacher certification, and 13 are establishing master teacher programs. With school reform, as with so many other challenges again and again in our nation's history, the American people are showing it can be done.

We've traveled far in improving our schools, but I don't believe there's one principal in this room who wouldn't agree that our journey has just begun.

Now, some insist there's only one reform that would make any real difference—more money. But that's been tried. Total expenditures in our nation's schools this year, according to the National Center for Educational Statistics, will total $230 billion. That's up almost 7 percent from last year, about double the rate of inflation, and more than double what we spent on education just 10 years ago.

So, if money alone were the answer the problem would have been shrinking, not growing. And those who constantly call for more money are the same people who presided over two decades of unbroken education decline.

James Coleman, a top education expert, argues in his recent book, "High School Achievement," that we need to focus on the factors that truly matter. He states, "Characteristics of schools [that] are related to achievement can be divided into two

areas: academic demands and discipline."

Well, I think he's right, and I'd like to talk to you today about these two school characteristics—academic expectations and discipline.

On academic expectations, it's clear that we must expect our students to perform to higher standards. Our children need to do more work and better work, and that includes homework. Indeed, in her well-known study, Barbara Lerner found that the amount of homework assigned in a school is the single most reliable predictor of how well the students in that school will perform on national tests.

Now, none of this is a prescription for gloomy students. We've learned that when students know their parents and teachers have confidence in their abilities the students gain self-esteem, enjoy their work, and live up to those high expectations.

We must also expect our students to learn the basics. Too many are allowed to abandon vocational and college prep courses for general ones, so when they graduate, they're prepared for neither work nor higher education. Stories abound of students who leave school unable to read and write at an adult level. In 1980, 35 States required only 1 year of math for a high school diploma; 36 required only 1 year of science.

Compare that to the case in other industrialized countries. In Japan, specialized study in mathematics, biology, and physics starts in sixth grade. In the Soviet Union, students learn the basic concepts of algebra and geometry in elementary school. So, it's not surprising that Japan, with a population only about half the size of ours, graduates from college more engineers than we do, while the Soviet Union graduates from college almost five times more engineering specialists than we do.

We cannot allow our children to continue falling behind. Instead, we must insist that all American students master the basics— math, science, history, reading, and writing—that have always formed the core of our civilization.

If I can interject, there is an article recently put out by Benjamin Stein. And it seems that he has made contact with a number of young, not only high school graduates, but now enrolled in some of our better universities—and has regular contact with them. And it was almost horrifying to read his article, when he found that most of those students—as high as juniors in universities—did not know when World War II was fought or who was the enemy whom we were fighting. There were other examples that were equally glaring of the lack of knowledge of our nation's history.

But no learning can take place without good order in the classroom, and that means restoring good old-fashioned discipline. In too many schools, teachers lack authority to make students take tests, hand in homework, or even quiet down in class. And in some schools, teachers suffer verbal and even physical abuse.

According to a 1978 report by the National Institute of Education, each month over 2 million secondary schoolchildren were victims of in-school crime. Not ordinary highjinks—crime. In 1981, during a 5-month period in California, there were at least 100,000 incidents of violence. A study of Boston high schools showed that during 1982 more than one-sixth of female students and more than one-third of male students carried weapons to school. And a 1983 survey of Michigan schools shows that one in five Michigan teachers has been struck by a student.

As long as one teacher is assaulted, one classroom is disrupted, or one student is attacked, then I must and will speak out to give you the support you need to enforce discipline in our schools. For too long, courts and others have concentrated on protecting the rights of the disruptive few. Well, it's high time we paid some attention to the rights of the well-behaved students who want to learn.

I can't say it too forcefully: To get learning back into our schools, we must get crime and violence out. [*Applause*]

Thank you.

Now, I'm not talking about establishing order only in our classrooms and hallways, but in our students' hearts and minds. We're training our children for life in a democracy, so we must teach them not only discipline but self-discipline. And if it's sometimes difficult to assert rightful adult authority, we must ask: "Who should correct the child's arithmetic? His math teacher? Or years later, his boss? Who should teach the child respect for rules? His principal? Or some day, law officers?"

We must teach our sons and daughters a proper respect for academic standards, for codes of civilized behavior, and for knowledge itself—not for the sake of those standards, not for the sake of those codes, not even for the sake of that knowledge, but for the sake of those young human beings.

Now, the Federal Government can support these reforms and do so without recycling still more tax dollars or imposing still more regulations. And our administration is doing just that. We're working to restore our nation's parents, State and local officials, teachers, school administrators, and principals to their rightful place in the educational process.

Our administration has replaced 29 narrow categorical education programs with one broad block grant to give State and local officials greater freedom. And in the budget I submitted to Congress last week I called for that grant to be increased by $250 million. We've instituted major regulatory reforms to dig educators out from under mountains of redtape. And because parents should have the right to choose the schools they know are best for their children, we've proposed education vouchers and tuition tax credits—concepts the American people support overwhelmingly.

In October I signed a proclamation that named this school year the National Year of Partnerships in Education. The proclamation urged businesses, labor unions, and other groups of working people to form partnerships with schools in their communities. Since then, partnerships in education have increased around the country dramatically. And in December, I announced a new program to recognize outstanding students—the President's Academic Fitness Awards.

To promote good order in our schools, the Department of Education is studying ways to combat school violence, and the Department is continuing its joint project with the National Institute of Justice to find better ways for localities to use their resources to prevent school crime.

The Department of Justice is establishing a National School Safety Center to inform teachers and other officials of their legal rights and to provide a computerized national clearinghouse for school safety resources. In addition, the Justice Department will file friend-of-court briefs in appropriate cases to support the rights of school administrators to enforce discipline. And right now, the Department of Justice is studying possible amendments of Federal law that would help principals and others reestablish good order in our schools.

Now there's one more effort that we're making at the Federal level that I want to mention, and I'm absolutely determined to see it through even though it may be sneered at in some supposedly sophisticated circles. The God who blessed us with life, gave us knowledge, and made us a good and caring people should never have been expelled from America's schools. [*Applause*]

You don't know how happy I am to hear that from you.

As we struggle to teach our children the fundamental values we hold so dear, we dare not forget that our civilization was built by men and women who placed their faith in a loving God. If the Congress can begin each day with a moment of prayer and meditation, so then can our sons and daughters.

I'll try hard now not to be tempted to tell the story of the father and son in the gallery of the Congress one day, and the son asked who that was. And it was the chaplain. And the father explained. And the boy said, "He's praying for the Congress?" And he said, "No, he's praying for the people." [*Laughter*]

Despite the importance of these initiatives at the national level, the main responsibility for education rests with our States and communities, and they're moving ahead. State by State, the success stories are mounting.

Indiana has increased high school graduation requirements and initiated a basic skills program for early grades. In Iowa the State is putting together a program of incentives for students who take upper-level math and science courses. States from Tennessee to Florida have begun work on pay incentives

for instructors because they know that to promote good teaching we must reward good teachers. And polls show that merit pay for teachers has the support of 61 percent of the NEA teachers, 62 percent of the AFT teachers, and 70 percent of independent teachers.

At the local level parents have begun to give schools new support in ways that range from helping out on field trips to raising money for special projects. School boards have begun to write stricter discipline codes and rewrite curriculums to stress the basics. And in community after community, principals have turned schools around.

I don't have time to tell you all the stories I've heard about principals who've made a critical difference, but there is one that I want to share. Just 5 years ago, George Washington High School suffered from all the ills that afflict so many inner-city schools—drugs, violence, gangs. The school had a 28-percent absentee rate and one of the lowest academic ratings in Los Angeles County. Then George McKenna became principal.

He designed this compact for both applicants and their parents to sign. It states in part: "Defiance of the authority of school personnel, either by behavior, verbal abuse, or gestures, is not permitted. Homework is given every day, and students are expected and required to complete all assignments. Parents are expected to participate in workshops, conferences, meetings, and cooperate with the school in supporting specific activities."

Today the absenteeism rate at Washington High School has been cut to 11 percent, and enrollment has risen from 1,700 to 2,600 plus a waiting list. Five years ago, 42 percent of Washington High's students said they might go on to college. Last year 80 percent did go on to college. And all this because of one determined principal, a hero with faith in the commonsense values which have never failed us when we've had the courage to live up to them.

As principals you have an enormous responsibility. Perhaps more than any other Americans, you hold our nation's future in your hands. I know that you're determined to go on with the great work of making certain our schools give our sons and daughters the quality education they deserve. And I'm convinced that with your help America's future will be bright beyond our dreams.

Thank you, and God bless you all.

Note: The President spoke at 10:53 a.m. in the Rotunda at the Las Vegas Convention Center. He was introduced by Robert Howe, president of the association.

Remarks at a Nevada Republican Party Fundraising Luncheon in Las Vegas
February 7, 1984

Paul, look, I'd be very happy to relinquish my time to you. I was enjoying everything you were saying. [*Laughter*]

Reverend Kurhey, Toastmaster Tom Weisner, Wayne Pearson, Marilyn Gubler, Curtis Patrick, and ladies and gentlemen:

It's certainly a pleasure for me to be with you here today, and you've made it even more of a pleasure since I've been in this room. And I'm especially glad to see Senators Laxalt and Hecht. Chic, I can't tell you how great it was the last election night when the word came in from Nevada. Your victory and that of Congresswoman Vucanovich made our evening. And since he got to Washington, Chic has made himself indispensable to the Republican team.

Congresswoman Vucanovich couldn't be with us today, but she's up for reelection this year. And if there's one thing you folks of Nevada can do for your country, it's to keep her on the job. She's been a strong and creative leader for responsible government. She's been playing an important part in our efforts to revive the economy and strengthen America's defenses. We can't afford to lose her. So, please, do me a personal favor: Don't just vote for her, make sure your friends and neighbors vote for her, too.

And, Paul Laxalt, it is no secret to anyone in this room or anyone in the country how much I've relied on you since coming to Washington 3 years ago. We got to know each other when I was Governor of California and he was Governor of Nevada. And Nancy and I both cherish the friendship we have with Paul and with Carol, and now with Chic and Gail. And Paul and I both like to ride. And knowing how to deal with a horse comes in mighty handy sometimes

up on—[*laughter*]—when you're dealing with Capitol Hill. [*Laughter*] Paul, I deeply appreciate the guidance, advice, and moral support that you've given me.

Senators Laxalt and Hecht have been stalwart examples of how Republicans can stick to their principles even when the going gets rough. In the last 3 years we've stuck to our principles rather than trying to be everything to everybody. The opposition kept telling us it wouldn't work, but sometimes I don't think there's anything that they believe will work.

Well, today the roar of economic recovery is drowning the naysayers and the hand-wringers. But we can't take it for granted that recovery will be translated into votes in the elections. As in the past, the Republicans' biggest challenge is how to get our message out. Some of our finest accomplishments, I think, are some of the best kept secrets in the Nation's Capital. If there's one word that we must repeat to our friends and neighbors, one word that will carry the cause for our day, that word is "remember." It's fair that we be judged on what we've accomplished. However, we should be compared not to what our opponents say that they will do, but instead, to what we remember our opponents did.

In the 4 years prior to this administration our critics had total control of both Houses of the Congress, the Presidency, and all of the departments and agencies of the Federal Government. And what they did is what we must make certain the American people remember. They gave the country double-digit inflation that ravaged the elderly, the poor, and the middle class. They gave us economic stagnation from which we're just now recovering. They gave us interest rates that knocked the automobile and home-building industries right off their feet. They gave us high taxes, big spending, and government that didn't work. they gave us pessimism and national self-doubt as never before experienced in this country.

There was only one thing "fair" about their policies—and they love to use that word—and I must say, they have been fair. They didn't discriminate; they made everybody miserable. [*Laughter*]

Now we've brought double-digit, near-runaway inflation down to 3.2 percent for all of 1983. We've cut the 21½-percent prime interest rate that we inherited almost in half. We've cut the growth in Federal spending and cut that about in half. And we've prevented the people from being mangled by built-in tax increases by passing a 25-percent across-the-board tax cut and by indexing their tax rates starting next year.

Now, I don't think any Republican should hesitate to ask the people if they think they're better off than they were 4 years ago.

Of course, we should help them remember what it was like. I get letters every day from all over America, and I must tell you that I don't think anyone is going to pull the wool over your eyes in the coming election. One letter was from a working mother in Oklahoma, and she wrote: "I like going shopping for food or clothing for my children and not seeing the prices go up every week the way it was when inflation was so high. I like getting a letter from my mortgage company telling me that more of my payment will be applied to my loan principal because of a lower interest rate. I like having more take-home money from my paycheck because of lower income taxes. I like having hope that my sons won't have to go to war because you're helping to keep our country strong. My husband and I are not rich. But we are making ends meet, mostly by our own hard work. But I feel your policies are helping."

Well, a letter like that makes my day, I can tell you. And if what we've done in these last 3 years has turned despair into hope, self-doubt into confidence, then the American people will judge for themselves what we've achieved.

I believe we have a solid record of achievement and accomplishment to offer. Nevertheless, we must be aware that most people are more concerned about what we offer for the future than what we've achieved in the past, even the near past. We must make certain that the public is keenly aware that it is Republicans who have a bold vision of the future.

We're the ones who will push to simplify the tax code. For 30 years the liberals have controlled the House where tax bills originate. As a matter of fact, for 27 of these last 30 years the Democratic Party has controlled both Houses of the Congress, and then for these 3 years, we have had the one House, the Senate. And believe me, nothing of what we've accomplished could have been done if we did not have the majority in that one House. If the public wants real tax reform, we're the ones that will give it to them.

And we're the ones who offer institutional reform to bring responsibility to government spending. We'd start by amending the Constitution to require a balanced Federal budget. We'd also give the Chief Executive a line-item veto which would prevent the worst kind of porkbarrel projects from passing simply because they're attached to very necessary and vital legislation.

We're the ones who would strengthen the social institutions that are the foundation of our society and our freedom. Fundamental American values have been under attack for too long, and it's about time we stand up and say enough is enough.

We can start by letting our children have the right to call on a little help from God at the beginning of their school day. As far as I'm concerned, He never should have been kicked out of school in the first place. [*Laughter*]

Education, of course, is something that demonstrates the difference in approach between the two parties. And here, too, we're the ones with enough courage to call for basic reform. We know that just throwing money at a problem isn't the answer. And certainly more Federal controls and regulations—something that is a byproduct of looking to Washington as a solution to local problems—is not the answer. No, we must reinvigorate education from the bottom up or real change will not happen.

Here in Nevada you're showing what can be accomplished when people set their mind to it. A cross section of community leaders has gotten together to establish private sector funding and support for State contributions for a school of engineering at the University of Nevada, Las Vegas. Once established, the school will provide a necessary link in preparing today's students for the new and emerging fields of high technology that will carry Nevada and the United States from the eighties to the 21st century. This is the kind of initiative that fosters progress. It represents a grassroots momentum emerging all over the country.

People now understand that they can't wait for the Federal Government to do what needs to be done. And I think we can all be proud that we put the future back in the hands of the people. You know, sometimes when those other fellows start talking about the necessity of as much government as they would like, some of us here in the West should remind them—we did all this out here without an area redevelopment plan. [*Laughter*]

During the coming elections, I'm confident that people will recognize the significance of the choices that they'll make. Now there's a little story that I like to tell, and, you must remember, since you've been so kind as to sing Happy Birthday, that life not only begins at 40, but so does lumbago and the tendency to tell the same story over and over again. [*Laughter*] So, if you've heard it, just be polite and pretend you haven't. [*Laughter*]

It's about a little boy who was selling some puppies that he had to get rid of. And he set up shop right outside a Democratic fundraiser. And when the people began coming out, and one couple stopped and looked, and then, joshingly, the man said, "Are those Democrat puppies?" And he said, "Oh, yes, sir." Well, the couple wound up buying one.

Well, the next week the Republicans were having a fundraiser, and he set up shop again—same location and some of the same pups. And out came the people and, sure enough, somebody asked him if they were Republican pups. And he said, "Yes." And he sold one. And a newspaper reporter who was nearby and had been present the week before said, "Hey, kid, wait a minute. Last week you said those were Democrat pups. Now you're saying they're Republicans." And the kid says, "Yeah." And he says, "Well, how come?" He says, "That's easy." He says, "This week they got their eyes open." [*Laughter*]

Well, we've got to make certain that the American people go into the next year with their eyes open, and that's going to depend on you and Republican activists around the country. And I can't tell you how proud I am to have participated in this gathering here today and to learn that it has been as successful as it has. But, let me remind you, President Dewey told me to remind you— [*laughter*]—don't get overconfident. [*Laughter*]

We've got a job to do, and one of the best things that we can do—we know what you can do for us—it's that mouth-to-mouth, that hand-to-hand contact, and that telling about the difference in the record. And so we're going to try to see if we don't provide the information that you'll need to convince your friends and neighbors and to straighten out—I read the other day where they were going to follow us through the campaign with truth squads. Well, that will make those the slowest truth squads in the world, because we're going to be circling around behind them telling the truth on them. [*Laughter*] And I doubt that they would be really telling the truth.

But we must have faith in the people of this country and faith in our principles. And I thank you from the bottom of my heart for all that you've done. God bless you all. Thank you.

Note: The President spoke at 12:45 p.m. in the Herbst-Collins Executive Hangar at the McCarron International Airport. He was introduced by Senator Paul Laxalt.

In his opening remarks, the President also referred to Thomas N. Weisner, Republican Party supporter; Wayne Pearson, Republican Party fundraiser; Marilyn Gubler, chairman, Clark County Republican Central Committee; and Curtis Patrick, chairman, Nevada State Republican Committee.

Following the luncheon, the President left Nevada and went to Rancho del Cielo, his ranch near Santa Barbara, CA, where he stayed for the remainder of the week.

Statement by Principal Deputy Press Secretary Speakes on the Situation in Lebanon
February 7, 1984

At the President's direction, the Vice President convened a meeting at the White House today to review the current situation in Lebanon with national security advisers. The meeting began at 11 a.m. EST and lasted 2 hours. This meeting was a follow-on to meetings and conference telephone calls yesterday and Sunday, including a meeting chaired by the President Sunday afternoon at the White House.

After being briefed on the current situation in Beirut and the results of today's meeting, the President directed further vigorous diplomatic efforts on the part of Ambassador Rumsfeld and Ambassador Bartholomew. These efforts will be aimed at maintaining a cease-fire and working with the Government of Lebanon to form a broad-based representative government under the constitution of Lebanon. Ambassador Rumsfeld will meet with President Gemayel at the earliest opportunity. The President directed all appropriate measures be taken to ensure American interests, including the safety of American citizens in Lebanon.

The President has consulted with leaders of other multinational force countries and is continuing those consultations. The aim of the United States remains to seek a peaceful solution for Lebanon.

The President this morning directed the Vice President to delay his departure for Europe, which was scheduled for Wednesday morning, so that he may continue to coordinate the activities in Washington.

Statement on the Situation in Lebanon
February 7, 1984

The bloodshed we have witnessed in Lebanon over the last several days only demonstrates once again the lengths to which the forces of violence and intimidation are prepared to go to prevent a peaceful reconciliation process from taking place. If a moderate government is overthrown because it had the courage to turn in the direction of peace, what hope can there be that other moderates in the region will risk committing themselves to a similar course? Yielding to violence and terrorism today may seem to provide temporary relief, but such a course is sure to lead to a more dangerous and less manageable future crisis.

Even before the latest outbreak of violence, we had been considering ways of reconcentrating our forces and the nature of our support in order to take the initiative away from the terrorists. Far from deterring us from this course, recent events only confirm the importance of the decisive new steps I want to outline for you now. Thus, after consultation with our MNF partners and President Gemayel, and at his request, we are prepared to do the following:

First, to enhance the safety of American and other MNF personnel in Lebanon, I have authorized U.S. naval forces, under the existing mandate of the MNF, to provide naval gunfire and air support against any units firing into greater Beirut from parts of Lebanon controlled by Syria, as well as against any units directly attacking American or MNF personnel and facilities. Those who conduct these attacks will no longer have sanctuary from which to bombard Beirut at will. We will stand firm to deter those who seek to influence Lebanon's future by intimidation.

Second, when the Government of Lebanon is able to reconstitute itself into a broadly based representative government, we will vigorously accelerate the training, equipping, and support of the Lebanese Armed Forces, on whom the primary re-

185

sponsibility rests for maintaining stability in Lebanon. We will speed up delivery of equipment; we will improve the flow of information to help counter hostile bombardments; and we will intensify training in counter-terrorism to help the Lebanese confront the terrorist threat that poses such a danger to Lebanon, to Americans in Lebanon, and indeed to peace in the Middle East.

Third, in conjunction with these steps, I have asked Secretary of Defense Weinberger to present to me a plan for redeployment of the marines from Beirut Airport to their ships offshore. This redeployment will begin shortly and will proceed in stages. U.S. military personnel will remain on the ground in Lebanon for training and equipping the Lebanese Army and protecting the remaining personnel. These are traditional functions that U.S. personnel perform in many friendly countries. Our naval and marine forces offshore will stand ready, as before, to provide support for the protection of American and other MNF personnel in Lebanon and thereby help ensure security in the Beirut area as I have described.

These measures, I believe, will strengthen our ability to do the job we set out to do and to sustain our efforts over the long term. They are consistent with the compromise joint resolution worked out last October with the Congress with respect to our participation in the multinational force.

Statement by Principal Deputy Press Secretary Speakes on the Situation in Lebanon
February 8, 1984

The President this morning at 8:50 a.m. convened a conference call that included the Vice President, Bud McFarlane in Washington, Admiral Poindexter and Mike Deaver in Santa Barbara, the President being at the ranch. They spoke for 15 minutes. During the conference call, the President received an extensive briefing and update on the situation in Beirut on the ground. In addition, he received a report through the Vice President and McFarlane from Ambassador Rumsfeld which dealt with Ambassador Rumsfeld's meeting today with President Gemayel in Beirut.

The conference call this morning here followed an extensive discussion that the Vice President had by telephone with other foreign policy advisers in Washington. The Vice President, as you know, over the past several days—Monday and Tuesday—had been conducting either meetings in the White House Situation Room or having the meetings by conference call. This morning's meeting was by conference call in Washington.

The President subsequently talked to the Vice President again about 9:25 a.m. for about 5 minutes to provide further guidance for the Vice President as a result of the phone call.

Overnight, the President received a decision paper from his foreign policy advisers and made a number of specific decisions that were designed to implement the plan that he announced yesterday afternoon.

Note: Larry M. Speakes read the statement to reporters assembled in the Vista Mar Monte Room at the Sheraton Hotel in Santa Barbara, CA, during his daily press briefing, which began at 10:17 a.m.

Nomination of J.J. Simmons III To Be a Member of the Interstate Commerce Commission
February 8, 1984

The President today announced his intention to nominate J.J. Simmons III to be a member of the Interstate Commerce Commission for the remainder of the term expiring December 31, 1985.

Since 1983 Mr. Simmons has been serving as Under Secretary of the Interior. Previously he was a member of the Interstate Commerce Commission. He was vice president for government relations for the Amerada Hess Corp., New York City, in 1970–1982; Administrator, Oil Import Administration, Department of the Interior, in 1969–1970; Deputy Administrator, Oil Import Administration, in 1968–1969; Assistant Director, Office of Oil and Gas, Department of the Interior, in 1961–1968; and vice president, secretary-treasurer, and geologist with Simmons Royalty Co., Muskogee, OK, in 1949–1961.

He graduated from St. Louis University (B.S., 1949) and attended the University of Detroit. He is married, has five children, and resides in Washington, DC. He was born March 26, 1925.

Remarks by Telephone to Crewmembers on Board the Space Shuttle *Challenger*
February 9, 1984

The President. Commander Brand, I'd like to say a good morning to you and your crew. I'm talking to you from California. I don't know exactly where you are. I know you're up there someplace. But you're all doing a fine job on this historic mission.

And I'd like to say hello to Bruce McCandless and Bob Stewart who are sending us this spectacular television coverage of man's historic walk in space. Let me ask you, what's it like to work out there unattached to the shuttle and maneuvering freely in space?

Astronaut McCandless. Well, we've had a great deal of training, sir, so it feels quite comfortable.

The view is simply spectacular and panoramic. And we believe that—maneuvering units first time working unattached—we're literally opening a new frontier in what man can do in space, and we'll be paving the way for many important operations on the coming space station, sir.

The President. Well, that is just great. You've really opened a new era for the world in space with this mission. You've shown both our commercial partners and our foreign partners, who play an important role in this and other missions to come, that man does have the tools to work effectively in space.

I understand you had an opportunity this morning—an unexpected or unscheduled thing—maneuvering the shuttle and making the recovery of an object in space.

Commander?

Commander Brand. Yes, sir.

The President. What do you and Hoot Gibson and Ron McNair do while Bruce and Bob are working outside?

Commander Brand. Well, we're pretty busy in here just keeping track of them. They have a lot of tests to go through and, of course, it is the first check out of something that's rather futuristic, the backpack, the man-maneuvering unit. So, we're just monitoring them, making sure that we don't lose sight of them.

The President. That's good. [*Laughing*]

Say, Hoot, I understand you must have a special interest in making sure everything's working right up there, since your wife will be making the trip on board the shuttle this summer. Do you have any tips to pass along to her?

Astronaut Gibson. That's true, Mr. President, she is. She's going up about in August, and that's why, as you say, I've been trying to check everything out and make sure it's going to work well when she goes. The thought of myself going up doesn't bother me, but I think I'll be nervous when she goes.

The President. I can understand that. Do you think she'll enjoy it?

Astronaut Gibson. I know she'll enjoy it.

The President. Well, now, could I ask, how are the experiments on board the shuttle working out? I understand that you have one dealing with arthritis and other experiments on board that may lead to advances in manufacturing and various kinds of material processing.

Astronaut McNair. Mr. President, the experiments are working out very well. We're very pleased with the results we're seeing, and there's a lot of promise being demonstrated in all the areas you've just mentioned. And we look forward to getting them back on the ground and analyzed and make some good use of these results.

The President. Well, let me again congratulate all of you on board the space shuttle *Challenger.* You're doing a fine job. Your commitment and courage on this historic flight, I think, are an inspiration to all of us.

And I know that you have things to do much more important than getting a telephone call from Earth, so let me just say to you, have a safe journey home, and God bless you all.

Commander Brand. Thank you very much for calling, sir. We really appreciate it.

The President. That's my pleasure. All right.

Astronaut McCandless. We're all proud to be part of this mission.

The President. All right. Goodbye.

Note: The President spoke at 7:32 a.m. from Rancho del Cielo, his ranch near Santa Barbara, CA.

Appointment of Two Members of the President's Commission on White House Fellowships
February 9, 1984

The President today announced his intention to appoint the following individuals to be members of the President's Commission on White House Fellowships. These are new appointments.

Garrett D. Pagon is president of Snohomish Commercial Realty, Inc., in Snohomish, WA. Previously he was assistant vice president of the Winmar Co., Inc., in 1976–1979 and assistant vice president of the Seattle First National Bank in 1975–1976. He graduated from Stanford University (B.A., 1967) and Harvard Business School (M.B.A., 1972). He is married, has four children, and resides in Snohomish, WA. He was born November 12, 1945, in Washington, DC.

Bishop William Milton Smith is Senior Bishop of the African Methodist Episcopal Zion Church. He is also on the national board of directors and steering committee of the NAACP. He received his B.S. degree from Alabama State University and has studied at Tuskegee Institute, Hood Seminary (Livingstone College), and Perkins School of Theology (Southern Methodist University). He is married, has one child, and resides in Mobile, AL. He was born December 18, 1918, in Stockton, AL.

Nomination of Edward Noonan Ney To Be a Member of the Board for International Broadcasting
February 9, 1984

The President today announced his intention to nominate Edward Noonan Ney to be a member of the Board for International Broadcasting for a term expiring April 28, 1985. He would succeed Charles David Ablard.

Mr. Ney is chairman and chief executive officer of Young and Rubicam, Inc., in New York City. He has been with Young and Rubicam, Inc., since 1951 and served as president of the international division in 1968–1970; executive vice president in 1967–1968; senior vice president in 1963–1967; and vice president in 1959–1963. He serves as a director on the Warner Communications, Inc., board of directors and as a member of the executive committee of Radio Free Europe.

He graduated from Amherst College (B.A., 1947). He is married, has three children, and resides in New York City. He was born May 26, 1925, in St. Paul, MN.

Letter to the Chairmen of the Senate and House Armed Services Committees Reporting on the Recommendations of the President's Commission on Strategic Forces
February 9, 1984

Dear Mr. Chairman:

I am pleased to report that over the past eight months significant progress has been made toward implementing the recommendations of the Scowcroft Commission. Such progress has been possible only because of bipartisan cooperation and support from both Houses of Congress. The attached report is submitted pursuant to the provisions of section 1231(e) of Title XII of the Department of Defense Authorization Act, 1984, enacted as part of Public Law 98–94. The attached document addresses the topics set out in section 1231(e).

This effort has provided a unique opportunity for Republicans and Democrats to work together for our common goal of equitable, verifiable arms control and a more stable peaceful world. I trust that the attached report provides you the information necessary for your continued support in implementing fully the recommendations of the Scowcroft Commission.

Sincerely,

RONALD REAGAN

Note: This is the text of identical letters addressed to John Tower, chairman of the Senate Armed Services Committee, and Melvin Price, chairman of the House Armed Services Committee.

The text of the letter was released by the Office of the Press Secretary on February 10.

Nomination of Fred T. Goldberg, Jr., To Be an Assistant General Counsel at the Department of the Treasury
February 10, 1984

The President today announced his intention to nominate Fred T. Goldberg, Jr., to be an Assistant General Counsel in the Department of the Treasury (Chief Counsel for the Internal Revenue Service). He would succeed Kenneth W. Gideon.

Mr. Goldberg presently serves as a partner with the law firm of Latham, Watkins & Hills (tax department) in Washington, DC. He served as Assistant to the Commissioner of Internal Revenue in 1981–1982 and Acting Director, Legislation and Regulations Division, Office of Chief Counsel, Internal Revenue Service, in 1982. Previously he was with Latham, Watkins & Hills as a partner in 1981 and an associate in 1973–1981. He was an instructor at Yale University in 1971–1973.

He graduated from Yale University (B.A., 1969; J.D., 1973). He is married, has four children, and resides in Bethesda, MD. He was born October 15, 1947, in St. Louis, MO.

Nomination of Robert H. Conn To Be an Assistant Secretary of the Navy
February 10, 1984

The President today announced his intention to nominate Robert H. Conn to be Assistant Secretary of the Navy (Financial Management). This is a new position.

Since 1981 he has been serving as Deputy Under Secretary of the Navy (Financial Management). Previously he was manager of the Federal liaison division of Arthur Andersen & Co. in 1972–1981. He served in the United States Navy in 1943–1972 in various positions, including Assistant Director, Budget and Reports, Office of the Navy Comptroller (1969–1972); Director, Fleet Resources Office, Headquarters Naval Material Command (1968–1969); and Assistant Director in the Chief of Naval Operations Budget Office (1967–1968). He retired from the Navy as captain on January 1, 1972.

He graduated from the University of Mississippi (B.A., 1956) and the University of Rochester (M.S., 1962). He is married, has five children, and resides in Kilmarnock, VA. He was born June 8, 1925, in Boonton, NJ.

White House Statement on the Situation in Lebanon
February 10, 1984

The President this afternoon spoke with the Vice President and Robert C. McFarlane, Assistant to the President for National Security Affairs, to receive an update on the situation in Lebanon and receive their recommendations on Secretary Weinberger's withdrawal plan and the composition of the United States delegation to the funeral services for Yuriy Andropov. They spoke at 1:30 p.m. PST (4:30 p.m. EST) for 15 minutes.

The President this afternoon received the plan for the redeployment for the United States multinational force in Lebanon from Secretary Weinberger. The report remains under review. The President has directed that consultations take place with the Government of Lebanon and other members of the multinational force. A decision will not be made until those consultations are complete, and we do not expect a final decision until the first of next week.

Statement by Principal Deputy Press Secretary Speakes on the Death of President Yuriy V. Andropov of the Soviet Union
February 10, 1984

The President has sent a message expressing his condolences to Mr. Kuznetsov, the Acting Soviet Chief of State, on the death of Chairman Andropov. In his message the President emphasized to the people and Government of the U.S.S.R. his desire for cooperation between the two countries in the search for a more peaceful world.

As the President reaffirmed in his address of January 16, the United States has sought and will continue to seek a constructive and realistic dialog with the Soviet Union aimed at building a more productive and stable relationship. Our objective is not dialog for its own sake, but a dialog that produces real solutions to the many concrete problems that divide us.

There are, to be sure, fundamental differences between the American and Soviet systems and our respective political beliefs. But the American and Soviet peoples have a common interest in the avoidance of war and the reduction of arms. It is this need to preserve and strengthen the peace that is at the heart of U.S. policy.

The President's policy toward the Soviet Union seeks to achieve progress in three broad areas: developing ways to eliminate the use and the threat of force in international relations; significantly reducing the vast arms stockpiles in the world, particularly nuclear weapons; and establishing a better working relationship with Moscow, characterized by greater cooperation and understanding and based on mutual restraint and respect.

At this time of transition in the Soviet Union, our two nations should look to the future in order to find ways to realize these goals. In the nuclear age, there is no alternative to dialog.

The United States hopes that the Soviet leader will work with us in this spirit and take advantage of the opportunities at hand to find common ground and establish a mutually beneficial relationship.

Note: Larry M. Speakes read the statement to reporters assembled in the Vista Mar Monte Room at the Sheraton Hotel in Santa Barbara, CA, during his daily press briefing, which began at 10 a.m.

Radio Address to the Nation on United States-Soviet Relations
February 11, 1984

My fellow Americans:

I'd like to speak to you about a subject always on the minds of Americans, but of particular interest today in view of the death of Soviet leader Yuriy Andropov: our relations with the Soviet Union.

Changes of leadership have not happened often in the Soviet Union. Yuriy Andropov was only the sixth Communist Party leader in the 66 years since the Russian Revolution. In recent months, he'd been totally absent from public view, so his death did not come as a shock to the world. Nevertheless, the importance of the U.S.-Soviet relationship makes his passing away a time for reflection on where that relationship is heading.

The changes in Moscow are an opportunity for both nations to examine closely the current state of our relations and to think about the future. We know that our relationship is not what we would like it to be. We've made no secret of our views as to the reasons why. What is needed now is for both sides to sit down and find ways of solving some of the problems that divide us.

In expressing my condolences to Mr. Andropov's family and to the Soviet Government, I emphasized once again America's desire for genuine cooperation between our two countries. Together we can help make the world a better, more peaceful place. This was also the message for the Soviet people in my address on Soviet-American relations last month. In that speech, as in my private communications with the late Chairman Andropov, I stressed our commitment to a serious and intensive dialog with the Soviet Union, one aimed at building a more constructive U.S.-Soviet relationship.

This commitment remains firm, and Vice President Bush will lead our delegation to Moscow for Mr. Andropov's funeral. He will be accompanied by Senate Majority Leader Howard Baker and our Ambassador in Moscow, Arthur Hartman. I hope there will be an opportunity for the Vice President to meet with the new General Secretary.

As we engage in discussions with Soviet leaders, we recognize the fundamental differences in our values and in our perspectives on many international issues. We must be realistic and not expect that these differences can be wished away. But realism should also remind us that our two peoples share common bonds and interests. We are both relatively young nations with rich ethnic traditions and a pioneer philosophy. We have both experienced the terrible trauma of war. We have fought side by side in the victory over Nazi Germany. And while our governments have very different views, our sons and daughters have never fought each other. We must make sure they never do.

Avoiding war and reducing arms is a starting point in our relationship with the Soviet Union, but we seek to accomplish more. With a good-faith effort on both sides, I believe the United States and the Soviet Union could begin rising above the mistrust and ill will that cloud our relations. We could establish a basis for greater mutual understanding and constructive cooperation, and there's no better time to make that good-faith effort than now.

At this time of transition in the Soviet Union, our two nations should look to the future. We should find ways to work together to meet the challenge of preserving peace. Living in this nuclear age makes it imperative that we talk to each other, discuss our differences, and seek solutions to the many problems that divide us.

America is ready. We would welcome negotiations. And I repeat today what I've said before: We're prepared to meet the Soviets halfway in the search for mutually acceptable agreements. I hope the leaders of the Soviet Union will work with us in that same spirit. I invite them to take advantage of the opportunities at hand to establish a more stable and constructive relationship. If the Soviet Government wants peace, then there will be peace.

In recent days, millions of citizens inside the Soviet Union, the United States, and countries throughout the world have been brought together by one great event, the winter Olympics. The competition is fierce, and we cheer for the men and women on our respective teams. But we can and should celebrate the triumphs of all athletes who compete in the true spirit of sportsmanship and give the very best of themselves. And when each race or event is done and our teams come together in friendship, we will remember that we are meant to be one family of nations.

We who are leaders in government have an obligation to strive for cooperation every bit as hard as our athletes, who reach within for the greatest efforts of their lives. If the Soviet Government would join us in this spirit, then together we could build a safer and far better world for the human family, not just for today but for generations to come.

Till next week, thanks for listening. God bless you.

Note: The President spoke at 9:06 a.m. from Rancho del Cielo, his ranch near Santa Barbara, CA.

Message on the Observance of Lincoln Day, 1984
February 12, 1984

Lincoln Day provides us with an opportunity to remember the life of a man widely admired for his beliefs and love for the people and the Union of the United States.

Abraham Lincoln guided his country through one of the most difficult periods of its history, when bloodshed decided whether two regions would remain united, or separate, because of unresolved differences. It was his belief that that struggle would ultimately determine the fate of democracy throughout the world. With a strong, patient, and sometimes weary hand, he led the American people from the most devastating war in our history to the pathway of greatness. Indeed, just as he envisioned, America remains the last, best hope for freedom in the world.

In the annals of every great nation there are leaders whose legacy will endure through the ages. Lincoln was one of those leaders. Generations have looked up to him as the man who not only preserved the Union, but helped us realize that true democracy is an evolving process. He once said the American Revolution "was the germ which has vegetated, and still is to grow and expand into the universal liberty of mankind." Since his time our democratic system has evolved and made great strides in righting the wrongs that existed. Today, all of us have the chance to reap the rich benefits of liberty and opportunity. Lincoln would be proud of how far we have come. He would be pleased with this country and what its people stand for.

In this year of hope for a better future, may we remember his words to an army regiment in 1865: "With malice toward none, with charity for all, with firmness in the right as God gives us to see the right, let us . . . achieve and cherish a just and lasting peace among ourselves and with all nations." Americans have good reason to celebrate the life of Abraham Lincoln. And as Republicans, we remember him as one of the founders of our Party—the Party of peace, freedom, and equality for all.

Ronald Reagan

Remarks of the President and King Hussein I of Jordan Following Their Meetings
February 13, 1984

The President. King Hussein and I met today in the spirit of good will and cooperation that characterizes the relationship between the United States and the Hashemite Kingdom of Jordan. Cooperation between us is increasingly vital in the face of the tragic violence in Lebanon, a growing terrorist threat, and the ominous cloud of war that hovers over much of the Middle East.

Today we witness bloodshed and conflict between Iran and Iraq, in Chad, in the Western Sahara, and Lebanon. And now, as never before, it behooves people of good will to work together for peace and stability.

King Hussein has led Jordan with strength and wisdom these last three decades. He's an experienced statesman, and his insights are valuable to us as well as to the people of Jordan. His Majesty was an important force behind the U.N. Resolution 242, which continues to be the starting point for tangible Middle East peace efforts, including my own peace initiative of September 1, 1982.

King Hussein has proven himself a responsible leader and a reliable friend on many occasions. His support for friends in the Gulf region has demonstrated his capacity for deeds as well as words. The economic progress of his people, the political equality and the religious tolerance found in

Jordan are a tribute to the benevolence of his reign, and I am grateful for his counsel.

His Majesty's visit strengthens the bonds of friendship that link Jordan and the United States. America's commitment to help Jordan meet its security needs remains firm and unwavering.

Today we spoke of a number of bilateral concerns, but the focus of our meeting was on the issues affecting regional peace. We both believe that while the challenges remain formidable, the opportunities for a broader peace are still present. We also agree that terrorism cannot be tolerated and that the leaders of all states must stand together against this new barbarism that threatens civilization.

States that condone terrorism undermine their own legitimacy. In these times of trial, disillusionment would be easy. But my meeting today with King Hussein has reaffirmed to me that the good and decent people of this world can and will work together and that progress can be made toward the perplexing problem of peace in the Middle East.

Your Majesty, it's good to have you here.

The King. Thank you very much, sir.

Mr. President, once again, sir, it's a privilege and a pleasure for me to have the opportunity to meet with you as the leader of the United States of America, as a man I respect and admire, as a friend. And I would like to say that these feelings are shared by my government and my people— the feelings of pride in our friendship, the feelings of pride in the fact that our goals and aims are one and the same; our ideas, our principles, our belonging to the family of free people throughout the world.

The challenges before us are indeed tremendous, but the determination is there to strive for a better tomorrow. This is a cause to which we are dedicated in Jordan—the cause of a stable area, the cause of establishing, eventually, a just and lasting peace in the area, the cause of a better future for generations to come.

On all the subjects, sir, that you were kind enough to address, I could not in all honesty say that I could have presented my views any differently. I thank you for the opportunity and the chance, sir, to discuss problems of the moment and to share with you the vision of the future and to reaffirm our commitment to our common goals of a better future within our area and within the world and for the establishment of a just and durable peace.

We are proud of our friendship, and we will do all we can to see it grow and flourish in every way and in every area. Thank you once again, sir, for the wonderful opportunity of meeting with you. God bless you, and thanks again for all your kindnesses to me.

Note: The President spoke at 1:06 p.m. at the South Portico of the White House.

Earlier, the President and the King met in the Oval Office and then attended a working luncheon, together with U.S. and Jordanian officials, in the State Dining Room.

Proclamation 5150—Save Your Vision Week, 1984
February 13, 1984

By the President of the United States of America

A Proclamation

Every day we rely on vision to provide us with a clear, vivid picture of our surroundings and the people we care about. Although we use our eyesight in virtually all activities, we often take it for granted until it is endangered by disease or injury. This is unfortunate because there are steps we can take to protect our eyes and to safeguard the precious gift of sight.

As a sight-saving precaution, everyone should have regular, professional eye examinations. Most people who have these checkups will get the reassuring news that their eyes are healthy. But a few people will receive an early warning of some serious eye disease requiring prompt treatment. An eye examination revealing the need for treatment of glaucoma or some other sight-destroying disease could spare thousands of Americans visual loss each year.

People with diabetes should be particularly aware of the need to have their eyes examined regularly to prevent the blindness that sometimes stems from the disease. This is especially important because there now is a sight-saving treatment which is highly effective if applied early enough in the course of the disease.

Regular eye checkups are also of special importance for older people because many serious eye diseases tend to strike in the later years. With early warning of a need for treatment, people can obtain the required medical care and give themselves the best possible chance of retaining good vision throughout their lives. Children also need regular eye examinations in order that readily treatable problems which otherwise could needlessly affect them in school and at play may be detected.

Protecting our eyes against injury is another way to preserve vision. In work with chemicals or machinery which might be dangerous to the eyes, safety glasses, goggles, or a face mask should be worn. Protective eyewear is also important for people participating in sports.

In looking to the needs of others, we can arrange to donate our eyes after death and, in this way, offer the gift of sight to a person who needs corneal transplant surgery. We also can support the many fine organizations which are devoted to research, sight conservation, and rehabilitation of the visually handicapped.

To encourage the American people to cherish the gift of sight and take steps to protect it, the Congress, by joint resolution approved December 30, 1963 (77 Stat. 629, 36 U.S.C. 169a), has requested the President to proclaim the first week in March as "Save Your Vision Week."

Now, Therefore, I, Ronald Reagan, President of the United States of America, do hereby proclaim the week beginning March 4, 1984, as Save Your Vision Week, 1984. I urge all Americans to participate in appropriate observances and activities and to make eye care and eye safety an important part of their lives.

In Witness Whereof, I have hereunto set my hand this thirteenth day of February, in the year of our Lord nineteen hundred and eighty-four, and of the Independence of the United States of America the two hundred and eighth.

RONALD REAGAN

[*Filed with the Office of the Federal Register, 11:53 a.m., February 14, 1984*]

Note: The text of the proclamation was released by the Office of the Press Secretary on February 14.

Proclamation 5151—National Surveyors Week, 1984
February 13, 1984

By the President of the United States of America

A Proclamation

In the development of our country, the role of the surveyor has been of vital importance. In colonial days, surveyors were among the leaders in the community—statesmen, influential citizens, and shapers of cultural standards, including people such as George Washington and Thomas Jeffer-

son. It was the surveyor's work that determined the boundaries of land, the greatest economic asset in the colonies. Thomas Jefferson chaired a committee in 1784 to devise a plan for disposing of lands west of the Thirteen Colonies. He argued that surveying before sale was necessary to prevent overlapping claims and to simplify deeds and registers. He reportedly wrote a plan which was debated in Congress, and in modified form was adopted as the Land Ordinance of May 20, 1785. The ordinance established the Public Land Survey System (PLSS)—the rectangular system that continues in effect today in 30 midwestern and western states.

Since 1785, the nature of surveying has changed dramatically. No longer is surveying limited to the description and location of land boundaries. Today, hydrographic surveys are important to the use of all our bodies of water; engineering surveys are utilized in the study and selection of engineering construction; geodetic surveys determine precise global positioning for such activities as aircraft and missile navigation; and cartographic surveys are used for mapping and charting, including the use of photogrammetry, the science of using aerial photographs for measurement and map production. Many services are provided through the use of sophisticated equipment and techniques, such as satellite-borne remote sensing devices and automated positioning, measuring, recording, and plotting equipment.

In recognition of the significant contribution made by surveyors to the United States, the Congress, by Senate Joint Resolution 44, has authorized and requested the President to designate the week beginning on March 11, 1984, as "National Surveyors Week."

Now, Therefore, I, Ronald Reagan, President of the United States of America, do hereby proclaim the week beginning March 11, 1984, as National Surveyors Week. I urge the people of the United States to observe this week with appropriate ceremonies and activities paying tribute to professional surveyors and their contribution to society. I invite all Americans to look back at the historic contributions of surveying and look ahead to the new technologies which are constantly modernizing this honored and learned profession.

In Witness Whereof, I have hereunto set my hand this 13th day of Feb., in the year of our Lord nineteen hundred and eighty-four, and of the Independence of the United States of America the two hundred and eighth.

RONALD REAGAN

[*Filed with the Office of the Federal Register, 11:54 a.m., February 14, 1984*]

Note: The text of proclamation was released by the Office of the Press Secretary on February 14.

Proclamation 5152—National Agriculture Day, 1984
February 13, 1984

By the President of the United States of America

A Proclamation

The United States produces nearly one-twelfth of the total output of the world's major agricultural commodities. This abundant production enables us to feed not only our own population, but tens of millions of other people throughout the world.

Our remarkable food and fiber production links together 23 million Americans who are involved in growing, processing, and marketing hundreds of United States agricultural commodities. Our farmers and ranchers produce a wide variety of meat, fruits, vegetables, food grains, flowers, dairy products, fibers, fish, and livestock. Maintaining such production requires natural resources, fertilizers, chemicals, credit, specialized equipment, processing, transporting, marketing, and State and national policies that strengthen the system. This vast integration of production and labor—an outgrowth of our free enterprise system—has transformed agriculture into the Nation's largest industry, with assets exceeding one trillion dollars.

To honor the working men and women of agriculture in America and to achieve a greater understanding of the stake each American has in maintaining the strength of the Nation's most basic industry, the

Congress, by House Joint Resolution 311 (Public Law 98–206), has authorized and requested the President to proclaim March 20, 1984, as "National Agriculture Day."

Now, Therefore, I, Ronald Reagan, President of the United States of America, do hereby proclaim March 20, 1984, as National Agriculture Day, and I call upon the people of the United States to observe this day with appropriate ceremonies and activities.

In Witness Whereof, I have hereunto set my hand this 13th day of Feb., in the year of our Lord nineteen hundred and eighty-four, and of the Independence of the United States of America the two hundred and eighth.

RONALD REAGAN

[Filed with the Office of the Federal Register, 11:55 a.m., February 14, 1984]

Note: The text of the proclamation was released by the Office of the Press Secretary on February 14.

Proclamation 5153—Municipal Clerk's Week, 1984
February 13, 1984

By the President of the United States of America

A Proclamation

The municipal clerk is the oldest of public servants and a critical part of efficient and responsive local government. The accurate recording, careful safeguarding, and prompt retrieval of public records are vital functions, without which effective local government could not exist.

As local government has grown in responsibility and importance through the Nation's history, so has the role of the municipal clerk. The clerk provides a direct link between past, present, and future by preserving records for posterity and implementing governmental decisions. Municipal clerks also seek better and more effective ways to perform these critical responsibilities in light of the rapid technological advances of today's world.

In recognition of the outstanding and vital services performed by municipal clerks and their dedication to public service, the Congress, by Senate Joint Resolution 92, has designated the week beginning May 13, 1984, as "Municipal Clerk's Week," and has authorized and requested the President to issue a proclamation in observance of that week.

Now, Therefore, I, Ronald Reagan, President of the United States of America, do hereby proclaim the week beginning May 13, 1984, as Municipal Clerk's Week. I call upon the people of the United States to observe that week with appropriate ceremonies and activities.

In Witness Whereof, I have hereunto set my hand this 13th day of Feb., in the year of our Lord nineteen hundred and eighty-four, and of the Independence of the United States of America the two hundred and eighth.

RONALD REAGAN

[Filed with the Office of the Federal Register, 11:56 a.m., February 14, 1984]

Note: The text of the proclamation was released by the Office of the Press Secretary on February 14.

Memorandum on Soybean Product Exports From Brazil
February 13, 1984

Memorandum for the United States Trade Representative

Subject: Memorandum of Determination Under Section 301 of the Trade Act of 1974

Pursuant to Section 301(a)(1) of the Trade Act of 1974, as amended (19 U.S.C. 2411(a)(1)), I have determined that the action described below is appropriate and feasible to enforce United States rights under the Agreement on the Interpretation and Application of Articles VI, XVI and XXIII of the General Agreement on Tariffs and Trade (the Subsidies Code) with respect to the subsidy practices of the Government of Brazil concerning exports of soybean oil and meal. With a view toward eliminating or reducing the harmful effects of the Brazilian subsidies on soybean oil and meal exports, I am directing the United States Trade Representative to pursue the dispute settlement procedures which have already been initiated under the Subsidies Code.

This determination, together with the Statement of Reasons, shall be published in the *Federal Register.*

RONALD REAGAN

Statement of Reasons

The United States Trade Representative (USTR) initiated an investigation under Section 301 on May 23, 1983 (48 FR 23947), on the basis of a petition filed by the National Soybean Processors Association. The petitioner alleged that Brazil has acted inconsistently with its obligations under the Subsidies Code by granting subsidies on the production and exportation of soybean oil and meal. These subsidies include: 1) the provision of preferential loans to oil and meal exporters for operating funds and for the purchase of raw materials to be processed and exported; 2) the partial exemp-

tion from income tax of profits from oil exports; and 3) the exemption from tax of gains from foreign hedging operations. The petitioner further alleged that as a result of the Brazilian subsidy programs, Brazilian exports of oil and meal have increased and have displaced United States exports in third country markets.

In an effort to resolve this problem, the United States held consultations with Brazil on November 21, 1983. Those consultations focussed on the United States complaint and on a subsequent Brazilian complaint against United States programs as they relate to the production and export of soybean oil and meal. During the consultation process it was learned that Brazil had suspended the application of two of its subsidy programs to soybean products. Both parties agreed to a further exchange of information regarding their respective programs which is scheduled to occur within the next month. If a resolution to the problem is not reached through consultations, the United States will continue the dispute settlement process as set forth in the Subsidies Code.

While it is disappointing that the dispute settlement process has not moved more expeditiously, I believe that the process is moving smoothly and that United States interests would be best served by following that process to its conclusion. I expect the USTR to pursue a resolution of this issue in a diligent and expeditious manner.

[Filed with the Office of the Federal Register, 2:06 p.m., February 14, 1984]

Note: The memorandum is printed in the Federal Register *of February 16, 1984.*

The text of the memorandum was released by the Office of the Press Secretary on February 14.

Interview With the Knight-Ridder News Service on Foreign and Domestic Issues
February 13, 1984

Ms. Small.[1] Mr. President, the three gentlemen opposite you—Saul Friedman and Bob Boyd, the bureau chief, and also Owen Ullmann—were going to ask most of the questions. The others might have a few questions, and we thought, perhaps, Saul would like to ask the first one.

The President. All right.

U.S.-Soviet Relations

Q. I'd like to ask the first question about what's happening in the Soviet Union. And since it's fresh, and news, my colleagues would never forgive me if I didn't ask the question. Is there something you can tell us about the new Soviet leader and how it might affect relations with the Soviet Union—his appointment might affect our relations with the Soviets?

The President. Well, the only thing that I can say is that in this case you have to wait and see what the position's going to be. I do think that when there is a change of leadership, the new individual hasn't been on record with any positions that might cause him problems in shifting position or with regard to discussions and so forth. So, the message that I've sent with Vice President Bush is one in which we should begin to talk and negotiate on the problems that, at the moment, lie between us.

Q. There was some speculation, some reports out at Santa Barbara, that you might be willing to meet with him in what was called a get-acquainted session that wouldn't necessarily have all the trappings of a summit. Is that a possibility?

The President. Well, I think just to get acquainted—obviously you'd get acquainted if you had a summit meeting, but, no, I think it still remains that you should have an agenda to have such a meeting that lays out the issues that we need to discuss.

There has been one example in our

recent history about a kind of get-acquainted meeting, and it was under President Johnson. And, if you'll recall, there was a kind of great letdown when that's all they did was, really, get acquainted, and the world was waiting for maybe a solution to some of the problems.

Q. I assume you're talking about Glassboro?

The President. I don't recall exactly the details of where it was, but I do remember that thing and the result of it. No, I think that—and we're certainly ready—I think that to have an agenda of the things that right now concern us: the arms talks, a number of other issues of that kind. And it isn't—some have suggested that we want to be able to claim that we can win something or other—no, that isn't a guarantee that you want. You want to know that there's some substantive issues that we can really get down to talking about.

Q. Mr. President, in your radio talk Saturday, you said you were willing to meet them halfway and to try to get a more stable and constructive relationship. What, more specifically, do you mean by meeting them halfway? Are there some adjustments we might make on our side in our positions?

The President. Well, that—you see, so far in the disarmament talks, for example, we have put the positions on the table. They have not come back, in reality, with any substantive positions of their own. And, in one set of negotiations where they did, we met them halfway. We proposed, then, a change in our original position. And this is what we mean: that to negotiate, one side just can't sit silent and say, "We don't like your first proposal, make another one." Well then, they could sit there forever while we try to think up new proposals. No, they've got to come back with something that they think meets whatever objections they had to our proposal, and then we discuss those points to see if there's a common meeting ground. And we're willing to do that.

But it's not only just the disarmament thing where they've walked away from the table. I think all the things that have them feeling that it is necessary to keep the world in kind of armed camps—they would be far better off, the world would be far better off, if we would find those areas where we could be a family of nations and settle our disputes and get along.

Q. Wouldn't it be—I'm thinking about what Eisenhower said when he said he'd go anywhere, anytime, in search of peace. And wouldn't it, at this point—could there be some gesture on the part of the United States towards this new Soviet leader, short of changing a position—a negotiating position, but some gesture, either an offer of you to get acquainted with the new General Secretary or something other—something symbolic, perhaps, that you might have in mind?

The President. Well, I think that George is taking a message that makes that plain, that the time has come or has long since passed for talking about a number of the contentious issues between us. And, again, this comes down to where there's a—the world kind of assumes that if there is a halt in our discussions or if there's some strain, it must be our fault. Well, we didn't walk away from the table, they did. And we have, over and over again, said, "We'll be waiting. Come back to the table."

Q. Is there anything new, though, in what the Vice President is sending to them aside from the fact that you'd want a summit that's carefully prepared, which is what you've been saying?

The President. Well, communications can be opened at many levels, and we want to have communication with them.

Q. Would you think the new leadership holds hopes for them meeting you halfway for any change in position or more responsiveness at the negotiating table?

The President. Well, let me—again, if I understand your question correctly, let's take the INF talks. I proposed what I think is a very commonsense idea, that in the intermediate-range weapons—more than a thousand of which are poised on their side against the European allies, and we, at the request of the allies, a request that was made in 1979 and approved by the Government—then Government of the United States, and of which we are implementing—that a far more sensible proposal would be to agree on zero; no intermediate-range weapons in Europe on either side. They refused to even discuss such a thing. So, we came back and said, "All right then, let us meet and discuss whatever reduced number you are willing to settle for." And the negotiations started, and those are the negotiations that have broken off. So, I think this demonstrated some flexibility on our part.

In the START talks, we found that our proposal to start by discussing the land-based ballistic missiles and then discuss the submarine-launched, airborne, and so forth. But in our thinking, the land-based were the most destabilizing to the people—the thought that someone pushes a button, and then there's no retrieval; it's on its way, and 20 minutes later, 30 minutes later, something blows up. And they had objections to that because of their own standpoint. We immediately countered, because we saw some merit in their objection, and we said, "All right, we'll put them all in, and we'll talk about them all at once, not in stages."

So, I think that we have demonstrated a flexibility; but when they walked away, they left nothing on the table. We had made a new proposal and left it on the table, and they walked away from it.

Q. I wonder if you think the Soviets would be more flexible or change their position in any way under a new regime.

The President. At least come back and start telling us if they didn't like it, what they didn't like and what they would prefer.

Q. How do you size up Chernenko? Do you think that he might be more flexible than they have been, Mr. President?

The President. I don't know. I've seen all the speculation on that that has appeared in the media as to quoting previous statements that he has made or not. I hope that we could have a change in approach.

The Middle East

Q. Maybe we could switch the subject a bit to the Middle East and to your conversations this morning with King Hussein. As a result of your conversations, do you see any more chance that he may be able or willing to help you revive your September 1st peace plan?

The President. King Hussein has been, I must say, most cooperative and has taken a great deal of courage to be that way in the situation as it is, with his border with Syria and all. And, yes, he is as determined as I am to find a way to pursue the problem of overall peace in the Middle East.

And tomorrow I will be meeting with him and President Mubarak of Egypt.

Q. Did he have to ask you to help him in some way—for example, by making some more moves on the Israeli settlements on the West Bank?

The President. No, he knows that we have urged the Israelis to stop the settlements in the West Bank, because I think that whole West Bank—that is one of the principal areas for negotiation in an effort to bring about peace in the Middle East. I've described it as a willingness to exchange territory for security.

Q. On the issue of Lebanon, it seems to me that you said that if our policy—if our troops cannot sustain themselves in Lebanon and our policy in Lebanon fails, so the Middle East peace initiative fails. Could you give us a report on the Middle East peace initiative that you made on September 1st, 1982? Is it not affected by what has happened lately in Lebanon?

The President. Well, it has been delayed, because after proposing that, suddenly Lebanon became the scene of open warfare. The PLO headquartered themselves and their military in the very heart of Beirut. The Israelis, who had—their border was being used—the terrorist PLO groups shelling across the border and so forth, they advanced, war being fought there, which prompted us to do what we've done with regard to the multinational force in order to get at the overall problem of peace in the Middle East.

Basically, that peace as we, I think, can all recognize, depends on peace between the Arab world and Israel. And, as you know, the Arab position for a long time had been that Israel did not have a right to exist as a nation and this was why the successive

wars that have been fought there. But you couldn't get on with that while the strife was going on in Lebanon. It was literally war between Syria and Israel, to say nothing of the internecine war and the various factions within Lebanon itself.

Now, the function of the multinational force was predicated on the other forces, foreign forces, leaving Lebanon and the multinational force providing something of a stability while a Government of Lebanon, which had not existed to any purposeful extent for a dozen years, then could reorganize their military—and we have helped in the training, incidentally, of their military—could then assume sovereignty over their own soil, at which point the multinational force could go home. But in the meantime, we could get on with the resumption of the peace talks.

Now, one faction, the Syrians—we did get the PLO out. The Israelis withdrew from their positions—not all the way to their border, but certainly well back toward it. And I could understand their stopping short, because there still was no guarantee of safety of that border until everyone else left. The Syrians then reneged and refused to leave.

But progress has been made—the talks in Geneva. We have trained and equipped the Lebanese forces to where it is really a capable military force. They need more. They need to be bigger, have more men than they have. There have been some setbacks, as we know, all along the line, but I think that progress was made. And that was why last August, those who don't want progress there began the terrorist acts against the multinational force and particularly our marines there at the airport. I think that that was an indication that we were being successful in this trying to find—or secure a stable Lebanon in peace.

We, from the time of the great tragedy over there—the explosion—we have been trying to find a more practical and a more viable deployment in which our presence still would be felt and we would not be bugging out or abandoning the original purpose. We haven't abandoned it, although I'm afraid that some have treated this deployment, in spite of all we've tried to say, as a leaving, and it isn't. We think that they will be—the fleet has been there for a long time; it will remain; they will remain on shipboard—they will remain able to go ashore if there is any reason to bring them ashore. And in the meantime we are sending in a force for additional training in certain specialties, training of the Lebanese Armed Forces. So, there is no leaving at all.

Some of the confusion about the announcements and all that were because the usual thing that happens here in Washington of leaks coming out, which were only part of the information. Everything that we had planned we had to check in with our multinational force allies, with the Government of Lebanon, and while all that was going on, the leaks began. So, some people thought that they were being betrayed, that we had an announcement to make and hadn't consulted with them.

Q. Is the timetable still as it was outlined by a senior administration official the other day to a group of reporters; that is to say, the troops out, redeployed within a month, save 200 left behind? Is that still——

The President. Well, I understand that Secretary Weinberger said that that was something they were looking at. We had not set any time for this. It was to be a phased withdrawal. The marines that would be left in there are the marines that normally protect the Embassy, which has come under attack recently and has necessitated our responding. And then there will be, as I say, these additional forces that will be going in for this specialized training.

Q. But will it be a month before most of them are out?

The President. I honestly can't tell you.

Q. We don't——

The President. It's feasible that it could be done within 30 days.

Q. Wasn't it a little bit unfair, Mr. President, to say that the Democrats' call for an orderly and prompt withdrawal was ill-founded when you yourself were planning to do something very much like that at the same time?

The President. Well, no, the question that was asked of me was with regard to a statement of the Speaker—and maybe I shouldn't have given a throwaway answer, as I did——

Q. Couple of Irishmen.

The President. ——but it sounded as if what, no, he was advocating was bugging out, out and go home. And as long as there is a chance for peace, we're going to continue striving for what we originally set out to achieve.

Q. Mr. President, you mentioned some forces would be going in for training purposes in Lebanon. Could you give us an idea of the size of those forces and the role they'll perform on the ground?

The President. They will be there training the Lebanese Armed Forces. They will be Army personnel, not Marine, and they will be specialists in certain areas having to do with terrorism and that sort of thing.

Q. Will they participate in the field with Lebanese Army forces?

The President. No, they'll be trainers.

Q. And you said that the marines will be offshore to be called in if they're needed. There was some ambiguity about that, and so I'd like to ask you, will they be there to go back in if, say, the Syrians make a move or if——

The President. No, it isn't that. It's as if—well, just the same as if they were at the—when they were at the airports. If they could contribute to their mission by moving from there or deploying into additional territory, they would have moved. The same thing is true with them on the vessels.

Remember that the multinational force was not there in a combat role or to be allied with any of the factions engaged in this internecine warfare. As I say, they were there to permit the limited Lebanese forces, once they were ready, to move out into the areas that had once been occupied by Syria and Israel. And I think this mission still prevails. And if that mission can be better served, if there is a development in what is going on that it can be better served by them coming back and taking over some area, they would do that. Or if it's necessary for our own security, they would.

Q. So, they could get back on land. Do you foresee that?

The President. I can't—it would be hypothetical to try and imagine what situation would, but, yes. They are there—if they weren't there and available for any such action, we'd bring them home.

Q. How many army trainers might there be, sir?

The President. You asked that question, and I didn't answer it. I can't speculate on that. I don't really have that much information about the size of the detachment. It would not be as extensive as the marine presence that has been there.

Q. When will we make the decision on whether the feasibility of bringing them all out in a month turns into the reality? I know that Secretary Weinberger is supposed to report to you on a plan. I just wonder when you will know when they're going to be able to come out and on what this will depend?

The President. Well, all I can do is repeat what he said before the Congress the other day when he made a statement—I think he's already made one today—that it is feasible that we could have them on board a ship within 30 days. But he wasn't making any guarantees, so I'm not going to.

1985 Federal Budget

Q. Okay.

Q. Should we move to domestic——

Q. Yes.

Q. Well, I'd like to ask about the recent drop in the stock market. A lot of people read that as a vote of no confidence on your budget and the lack of any action on reducing deficits either by your administration or Congress. And there is this increasing worry around the country that perhaps there will be no action on reducing the deficit for at least a year until after the election and that it's a very large risk and gamble with the economy. I'm wondering if you think there's anything to this risk and if you think perhaps the economy could falter before any major reduction of the deficit is accomplished.

The President. Well, since I was given an estimate sometime ago that the stock market could fall as much as from a hundred to two hundred points and the reason for it had nothing to do with forebodings of evil up ahead, but had to do simply with the fact that the continuing interest rates were making bonds much more attractive from a revenue standpoint than equities—

that this was what we were going to see, was a shift of money into bonds because of the return. And the interest rates didn't fall; the interest rates have stayed where they are. And we're seeing exactly what I was told we could look forward to. So, I don't think that this is any pushing a panic button at all. I think this is just plain earning capability.

Q. I should ask who your broker is, but I'll—[*laughter*]——

The President. What?

Q. I should ask who your broker is.

The President. [*Laughing*] No, I wouldn't be able to tell you, because anything I own is in a blind trust.

Q. How goes the downpayment negotiations?

The President. Well, the negotiators have gone home on a 10-day recess. That's why I hastened to come back. I didn't want to be out of Washington with them gone. It's too pleasant here. [*Laughter*]

Q. No, really, do you think that the Democrats are negotiating seriously?

The President. They haven't appeared to be. They were the ones who first conceived of this idea. And we bought the idea, and we proposed this and proposed immediate negotiations, even before we had submitted a budget and all. And they kept stalling. And finally they came up with a date—and a date in which they knew, I'm sure, that I was due to be in Dixon, Illinois, and Eureka and Las Vegas, the 6th of February. We offered them the dates of February 2, 3, and 4 or 8, and we finally had one meeting.

And now they have gone home, as I say, on recess. And they're talking about maybe something more than a month away—or at least a month away from when we had suggested the first meeting—to get together again. I'm disappointed in that, because we took them at face value on their proposal.

And the budget that we submitted was a budget based on the cuts that we'd tried to get a year ago and which they refused to consider. But at the same time, we were aware that if we're really going to be serious about the deficits, we need more cuts. And so we made the proposal. All right, here is this budget, and if they still feel the way that they felt a year ago, we'll have to battle over that one. But we do have a plan for additional savings that could amount to about a hundred billion dollars over 3 years, and they're the less contentious issues—and to see if we couldn't get together on those. And so far, they haven't made anything that's a realistic——

Q. Well, are the negotiations now at a standstill? Are they done for? Are they——

The President. Until they come back. Jim, I don't know of any proposal for setting a date.

Mr. Baker.[2] They've suggested, Saul, that we wait until after the 22d of February to get together again. They suggested that in a letter they sent down here to us.

Q. Well, one issue, Mr. President, has been your defense budget. And I'm not sure it would be defined as among the less contentious issues, but the Democrats have been saying repeatedly that it should be on the table. And I'm wondering, are you prepared to agree to some reductions in your defense budget to achieve a compromise on this downpayment?

The President. When you invite negotiations, everything went on the table. We put all three things there: the cuts in domestic spending, we put defense on the table, and we put the matter of revenues on the table. All three are in the present budget proposal we made.

Now, I think that budget proposals are based on what is a function of government and what is essential to—well, in a matter of security. You don't go at the defense budget on the matter of dollars and cents; you go at the defense budget on what do we believe is essential to our national security. And before the figure that is in the present budget, before we arrived at that, here within our own ranks, $16 billion was knocked out of that. I remember one point joking with Cap, and I said, "You ought to leave it in there so that they could take it out." But we didn't. We got down to what we thought was a realistic defense budget.

They have claimed and made some wild proposal with regard to defense spending as being the source of reducing the deficit, but

_____
[2] *James A. Baker III, Assistant to the President and Chief of Staff.*

again, as I say, you don't start with money; you start with what is necessary. Now, what we mean by putting that on the table is if they have a figure and they believe that they have a defense program that would meet the necessities and for their figure, bring it out on the table and let us discuss it, and let us negotiate on that. And this they've refused to do.

Now, they were a little like what I said about the Russians a little bit earlier in disarmament. They sit there and say, you know, "We don't like that figure. Give us another one." Well, that's not negotiating.

Q. So, you're inviting them to come back with a specific proposal?

The President. That's right. Yes.

Q. Well, they came back with this hundred billion dollars in defense.

The President. Yes, and without one thing as to how you could achieve that and still have a defense package or program that would meet our needs. That's what I say: They were just talking numbers of dollars; they weren't talking about national defense and what you could or could not do without.

Q. Well, how do you assess the chances of reaching an agreement on this downpayment plan this year—or this spring?

The President. Well, I'll tell you. We take very seriously the deficits. As a matter of fact, we've taken them seriously for the last half-century. It has been their plan and their proposal, and we believe that we have got to deal with the problem of deficits. And the principal way is to reduce government spending. That's why I asked for the Grace commission—that task force of hundreds and hundreds of business leaders in this country and experts in every field to come in. And they've come in with more than 2,500 recommendations for making government more economic and more efficient, and we now are just starting in on those.

But I would think if they're going to insist on talking about the deficits now as if it's something that they had never heard of before, when they had much to do with building the government structure that has made those deficits a way of life, I would think that they would want to meet us in an attempt, in a bipartisan way, without getting politics into it, to find out how we can achieve the goal of a balanced budget.

Q. Do you think that's possible this year—in an election year?

The President. A balanced budget? No, I think a balanced budget—I think what is possible in what we're trying to get at is a declining level that will point down here to a point down the road in which we can have, achieve a balanced budget.

Q. Can other people ask a couple of questions here toward the end now?

Grenada

Q. Mr. President, let me ask a question on another subject. If you had to do Grenada over again, or you have a situation like that in the future, do you see there is a way that you would trust the press to come in on the first wave?

The President. Well now, with all the attacks that have been leveled against us, we didn't have anything against the press at all in the Grenada invasion. It wasn't an invasion, actually, it was a rescue mission. And it was more of a commando operation. And we felt so seriously—it was such a short time when the request came to us from those other six island nations to head off what was happening—and our own concern about a possible hostage situation with those several hundred young people that were down there, those students of ours.

In fact, before that request came in, we had our replacement force on its way to Beirut. And I called Secretary Weinberger and asked him if, with the turmoil down there, with the murder of Bishop and all, where was the location of that flotilla, and could it possibly change its course a little and be—while it was still traveling toward Beirut—be closer to Grenada if there should come a threat to those young people and, as I say, a hostage situation. Then when we received in that one eventful weekend the request—and I okay'd it—we recognized that we only had a very short time. And knowing, again, the danger of leaks, we didn't even take our own press department into our confidence. Only the few of us that were involved turned over to the Joint Chiefs, and the first mission, of course, was the rescue of our young people,

their security. The second essential was to minimize the casualties.

Now, what we knew about the Cuban presence there, we knew that there was some ability to fight back. We also knew that Cuba was a lot closer than we were, and we knew—we did not even confirm to those other nations that had asked for our help the absolute decision because of this concern. And we didn't see—they only had 48 hours to plan that operation—we didn't see how we could run the risk of having to notify people that something was going to take place. And for once we did have something that was absolutely secure, and no word was out until we ourselves called the Cubans and the Russians and told them—guaranteed the safety of their people. They didn't resist.

Q. Do you think in the next such situation, should it happen, that there is a way to work out so that representatives of the press are there?

The President. Right now the Defense Department has invited press representatives in and to conceive of a plan on how that we can do this. But in that particular decision—that was not made here in the White House or anything else—I said that because of the short planning, the necessity for secrecy, the press was never mentioned; I said this time we won't look over the shoulders of the commanders in the field. They're going to be in full charge. They're on the ground; they're going to be the ones that know what is needed. And there won't be any political opinions given to them of any kind. And so, the decision, I guess, was made by them that they saw no way that they could do this, but by the second day after the·landing, as you know, a pool went in, and then, the third day, a larger pool, and then finally it was wide open.

But, no, we don't want that to happen again. And that's why they're meeting, to see if we cannot draw up plans in which we wouldn't be faced with the same problem.

Q. Thank you, sir.

Cuba

Q. Mr. President, on the issue of Cuba, from time to time they make sounds that they would like to enter into discussions about various issues between the two nations. What set of signals would you require in order to enter into those kinds of discussions with Cuba?

The President. Well, we tried early on. There were some noises of that kind made early in my administration, and we immediately picked up on them and then found that they evidently didn't mean it; we got no place. And they're making something of the same kind of noises now. We don't think that they're really serious.

Q. What would convince you that they were serious?

The President. Well, perhaps a change of tone and maybe if they were willing to get out of Nicaragua and stop interfering in other people's lives and other countries, we might think that they really meant it. And, believe me, I would like it. I think that Cuba and the Cuban people would be so much better off if Cuba would remember that it's a member of the Western Hemisphere and rejoin the family of nations over here instead of tying themselves so closely to the Soviet Union.

Farm Policy

Q. Mr. President, on farm policy. You've stood, obviously, for free market and little government interference. And on farm policy, you've had to go 180 degrees the other direction and, in fact, have done more than any other administration in farm support. If you were reelected, which direction do you think you'd be going on farm policy?

The President. Well, I have always believed in the free market, but it's got to be a fair market. The only problems we have had is where competitors have been subsidizing and permitting selling in our market or the international market at below production costs. And this was one of the main issues we dealt with at the summit conference in Williamsburg, where we set up the GATT Organization and COCOM and got a great deal of agreement—more than we've had previously—with our allies about fair trade.

There still is a problem with regard to agricultural products and some subsidy and subsidizing of sales in those. But I'm optimistic about all of our problems. We've been making great progress on that.

Lebanon

Q. Mr. President, I'd like to return to what you said about Lebanon a moment, and the army trainers that you said—of whom you said would be sent in there. Do you have a timetable for that? Do you know when that will begin to happen?

The President. I think that's going to happen very quickly. I can't give you the exact time, but they will be going in simultaneous with the withdrawal.

Religion

Q. Mr. President, I'd like to ask you—turn a little bit to politics, if I may, and ask you a question about something that may be a little delicate, but it's nevertheless been on my mind and on the minds of several people.

I was at your speech to the National Association of Broadcasters, and as others have commented, you've never been much to wear religion on your sleeve one way or the other. But I wonder if the comments to the National Association of Religious Broadcasters and other such speeches in which what seemed to me what you were doing was preaching the Gospel of Christ, as it were, isn't a little bit divisive and whether it might not be wise, especially since there are a heck of a lot of people in this country who are not of the same persuasion. It just doesn't seem like you in the past, and that's why I'm asking.

The President. Maybe others haven't listened to me in the past. I remember once, long before I was even the Governor of California, when I was just out of the mashed-potato circuit, I was invited to speak to a national meeting of military chaplains. They'd been having a 3-day meeting in California. And afterward, one of them came up to me and told me that— he shook my hand and said that I was the first person in their 3-day meetings of chaplains who had mentioned the name of Christ.

No, it isn't easy for me to talk about this, or to talk about it here, but I do believe that there is, and has been—and I've talked about it many times in speeches over the years—that there is a great hunger for a kind of a spiritual revival in this country, for people to believe again in things that they once believed in—basic truths and all. And, obviously, if I was speaking to those religious broadcasters, I was going to speak more on that subject than I would, say, to the Chamber of Commerce.

But I do believe and have grown up believing that these two great continents were placed here—you can call it mystical if you want—but were placed here between the oceans to be found by people who had a love for freedom, a courage, and that there was a divine purpose in that. And today, there's no place in the world like it. We've come from—even around this table, if we started tracing our heritage, we would find we—not perhaps from every corner in the world around this table, but Americans are from every corner of the world. We have respected every other religion. They're free to practice in our country, I guess, unless they go for human sacrifice. We wouldn't allow it. [*Laughter*]

But I just—I feel—and I've also felt—I've been a history buff for a number of years— that if you look back at the fall of any empire, any great civilization, it has been preceded by their forsaking their gods. And for a country that started as ours has and with a belief that we are a nation under God, I have sensed that maybe this hunger I mentioned is because we have under the guise of the first amendment, things of that kind, we have strayed from that. And I don't want us to be another great civilization that began its decline by forsaking its God.

And I also feel that there is a responsibility in this position also—as Teddy Roosevelt called it, "a bully pulpit"—to do those things. I was criticized for speaking about school prayer in the House Chamber at the State of the Union address, but am I not correct that above my head, engraved in the wall above my head was "one nation under God"?

Q. I'm speaking of a specific kind of religion. The allusions to the Christian Gospel and to Christ as coming from a President who is a man in a nonsectarian office.

The President. Yes. But may I recall that at the lighting of the Christmas tree that I said that on that birthday the man from Galilee—that there are those in our land who recognized him as a prophet or a great teacher—but a man, and just a teacher. And there are others of us who believe that he was of divine origin and the Son of God. And whichever, we celebrated his birthday with respect for the man.

Q. Thank you for the answer, Mr. President.

Q. We'd better end on that note, Mr. President. You can't get much higher than that. [*Laughter*]

Mr. Speakes. That's right. We've got a few minutes before you go to the Soviet Embassy.

Q. Are you signing the book today?

The President. Yes

Q. Sounds like a full day.

The President. What?

Q. Sounds like a full day.

The President. Yeah, a little bit.

Note: The interview began at 3:40 p.m. in the Cabinet Room at the White House.

Larry M. Speakes is Principal Deputy Press Secretary to the President.

The transcript of the interview was released by the Office of the Press Secretary on February 14.

Appointment of Two Members of the International Private Enterprise Task Force
February 14, 1984

The President today announced his intention to appoint the following individuals to be members of the International Private

Enterprise Task Force:

Milton Fredman will succeed Nicolas M. Salgo. Mr. Fredman is president of Fredman, Silverberg & Lewis, Inc., in San Diego, CA. He also serves as president of San Pasqual Vineyards in San Diego County. He was Deputy Commissioner General of the United States at the World's Fair in Montreal, Canada, in 1966–1967. He graduated from the University of Wisconsin (A.B.). He is married, has two children, and resides in Del Mar, CA. He was born July 20, 1920, in Minneapolis, MN.

Myer Rashish will succeed Henry T. Wilfong, Jr. Mr. Rashish is consulting economist and president of Rashish Associates, Inc., in Washington,

DC. He served at the White House as assistant for international trade policy in 1961–1963; as Special Assistant to the Under Secretary of State for Economic Affairs in 1961; and as chief economist and staff director, Subcommittee on Foreign Trade Policy, Committee on Ways and Means, U.S. House of Representatives, in 1956–1960. He graduated from Harvard University (A.B., 1944; A.M., 1947). He is married, has three children, and resides in Washington, DC. He was born November 10, 1924, in Cambridge, MA.

Remarks of President Reagan, President Mohammed Hosni Mubarak of Egypt, and King Hussein I of Jordan Following Their Meetings
February 14, 1984

President Reagan. I have been honored today to welcome and confer with King Hussein and President Mubarak. Their visit highlights the friendship between the United States and the two important countries they lead. Our countries share common interests in developing practical solutions to the problems of the Middle East. The good will and trust between us promise a solid foundation for overcoming the formidable obstacles to peace and progress in the region.

Our discussions today have reaffirmed that Egypt and Jordan will remain leaders in efforts to bring peace and security to the Middle East. King Hussein and President Mubarak have demonstrated foresight, realism, and resolve, which are essential if the peace process is to succeed.

We discussed in detail the opportunities for progress in the Middle East. Recent events in the area make it even more urgent to keep the broader peace process moving. The tragic events in Lebanon show that the occupation of territory by outside forces does not lead to peace, but rather to continued conflict and turmoil. I wish today, therefore, to reaffirm my commitment and that of our government to the principles I set forth in September of 1982, and in particular to the principle that the Arab-Israeli conflict must be resolved

through negotiations involving an exchange of territory for peace.

The Egyptian-Israeli treaty proves what can be accomplished when states have the will to take risks for peace. And I'm confident that further steps toward peace in the Middle East are possible. For our part, the United States is ready to do all it can to keep the process moving forward.

King Hussein, President Mubarak are men I greatly admire, and I'm grateful to them for having come here to speak as friends and to reconfirm our common purposes in the enduring struggle for peace.

King Hussein. Mr. President, my good brother and oldtime friend, President Mubarak, I'd like to thank you, sir, for your great kindness in enabling me and my brother, President Mubarak, to meet with you today and to discuss all aspects of the problems which we face in our area of the world; and our common goals and objectives for a better future for all in that area—of establishment of a just and comprehensive peace for greater stability and for a better life for generations to come.

I'm very grateful for the opportunity to have had this chance to hear your views, sir, and the views of President Mubarak on all matters and to contribute what I could for the purpose of achieving better understanding of our respective positions as we move ahead with hope and determination and with a commitment to do our utmost for a better future in the area from which we come and for a just and comprehensive peace. I will carry back with me, the impressions I gained of your determination and that of the United States to contribute its full share to help all concerned achieve their objectives.

We are proud of our friendship. It is of long standing. We are hopeful that this friendship will develop and evolve and that, based on trust and confidence and with determination, we shall overcome what appear and have appeared to be for a long period of time insurmountable obstacles. After all, the cause we are striving to serve is the cause of people, their future, their rights, human dignity, and, at the same time, their freedom and a better life, which is their right.

I thank you once again, sir, for many kindnesses, and I thank you, my brother, President Mubarak, and wish you every continued success. And I would like to say that this has been a visit I shall always remember. I'll treasure the memories of this visit and the wonderful opportunity it has given me to meet with you both. Thank you very, very much indeed for your many courtesies and kindnesses and the warmth of your welcome.

Thank you.

President Mubarak. I was very pleased to meet once again with our good friend, President Reagan, and discuss with him issues of great concern to our nations. We did so in the spirit of friendship and cooperation that dominates the relationship between Egypt and the United States.

I find it most rewarding to consult regularly with President Reagan and exchange views with him on matters of mutual interest. He is a statesman of great courage and wisdom. He has a profound sense of mission and responsibility. Our bilateral relations constitute a shining model for understanding and the cooperation among nations. We are determined to strengthen the bonds of friendship that link our peoples. The talks we held today will certainly add to this evergrowing friendship and mutual understanding.

I would like to seize this opportunity to thank the American people for cooperating with us in the vigorous efforts we are exerting to improve the quality of life for our masses. We are striving to reform our economic system and increase production and productivity. We are struggling to restore security and stability to the Middle East and Africa. Egypt has a pivotal role to play and a mission to fulfill. It is determined to do so with vigor and dedication. We are devoted to strengthening the structure of peace in our region and throughout the world.

The situation in Lebanon today is intolerable. The escalation of violence and the bloodshed is a threat to us all. Every nation is called upon to help. The peacekeeping role of the U.N. must be expanded and reinforced. The partition of this war-torn country should be prevented at any cost. The Lebanese people have a right to live and prosper like all other nations.

The key to a viable solution is the prompt and unconditional withdrawal of Israeli forces. The Israeli invasion is the root and the cause of the present sad situation in the area. No problem can be solved through foreign intervention and the use of force.

The Lebanese crisis is a stark reminder of the centrality of the Palestinian problem. That question must be addressed frontally and without delay. Our purpose is to create the necessary conditions for coexistence and the mutual recognition between the Palestinians and the Israelis. This coexistence must be based on justice and the recognition of rights. First and foremost, the right of the Palestinian people's self-determination should be honored and exercised. This is the clue to peace and security for all nations, including Israel.

The Palestinian people are entitled to your support and understanding. There is no substitute for a direct dialog with them through their chosen representative, the PLO. Such dialog will immensely serve the cause of peace to which we are both committed. Mr. Arafat is a responsible leader who has demonstrated tremendous courage under the most difficult circumstances. A dialog with him would reassure the Palestinian people and rekindle their hope for a better future.

No other nation can speak for the Palestinians. No other entity has a mandate to lay out their requirements for peace, and no other nation is more qualified than the American people, lending their support and backing.

The war between Iran and Iraq is another sad chapter in the history of the Middle East. We should spare no effort to bring it to an end immediately. No one can possibly benefit from the continuation of bloodshed between peoples who are linked together through the strongest cultural and spiritual bonds. To restore peace between these neighbors, certain concrete steps should be taken by those who are genuinely concerned. The mere expression of good will is no help in the face of continued fighting and escalated tension.

I came here also to plead the case for Africa. The African people need your attention and understanding. They are struggling against formidable odds. Economic crises and natural disasters are strangling their efforts for development and social transformation. Helping them is not only a moral obligation; it is a practical necessity for building a better world in which all nations live in peace and cooperate for their common good.

We are seeking your help in order to secure the unconditional independence of Namibia. The continuation of the present situation is unacceptable to all African nations. The minority regime of South Africa

must know that the United States cannot support its policy of aggression and violation of human rights.

It was a happy coincidence that I met here with His Majesty King Hussein and pursued with him our ongoing consultation. We believe that Jordan has an important role to play in solidifying the structure of peace. It is an element of stability and security in the Middle East. Therefore, we support the dialog between Jordan and the PLO. This is a positive step towards peace. In the months ahead, we will be intensifying our contents with our partners in the peace process with a view of accelerating progress.

I have extended an invitation to President Reagan to visit Egypt at the earliest possible date. This will give our people an opportunity to demonstrate the depth of their sentiments towards the President and every American.

Thank you.

Note: President Reagan spoke at 1:51 p.m. in the East Room at the White House.

Earlier, the two Presidents met, together with U.S. and Egyptian officials, in the Oval Office. They then held an expanded meeting in the Cabinet Room.

Later in the Oval Office, King Hussein joined the two Presidents. Then, together with their advisers, they held a working luncheon in the State Dining Room.

Letter to the Speaker of the House and the President Pro Tempore of the Senate Reporting on United States Participation in the Multinational Force in Lebanon
February 14, 1984

Dear Mr. Speaker: (Dear Mr. President:)

I am providing herewith a further report with respect to the situation in Lebanon and the participation of the United States Armed Forces in the Multinational Force. This report, prepared by the Secretaries of State and Defense and covering the period from December 12, 1983 to February 13, 1984, is consistent with Section 4 of the

Multinational Force in Lebanon Resolution. This report also includes the information called for by the House version of the Resolution and is submitted consistent with its more restrictive time limits.

Congressional support for our continued participation in the Multinational Force remains critical to peace, national reconciliation, and the withdrawal of all foreign forces from Lebanon. We will continue to keep you informed as to further developments with respect to this situation.

Sincerely,

RONALD REAGAN

Note: This is the text of identical letters addressed to Thomas P. O'Neill, Jr., Speaker of the House of Representatives, and Strom Thurmond, President pro tempore of the Senate.

Remarks at a White House Ceremony Marking the Observance of National Crime Prevention Week
February 15, 1984

The President. Welcome to the White House. We want you to enjoy yourselves, so I hope that all the police chiefs here can sit back and relax and stop worrying about what your deputies are doing back at headquarters. [*Laughter*]

I'm delighted to have the opportunity to help recognize National Crime Prevention Week and to tell you that crime prevention is a top priority on the national agenda. Americans should have the right and the opportunity to walk our streets without being afraid, to feel safe in our own homes, and to be confident that when our children leave the house they'll return safely.

For too many years, crime and the fear of crime robbed the—or eroded the strength and vitality of our neighborhoods. We're finally making some headway. In 1982—or maybe you've already been told and know that the crime rate dropped by 4.3 percent, and that's the biggest drop since 1972.

And just last week the Senate under the able leadership of our Judiciary Committee chairman, Strom Thurmond, overwhelmingly passed our comprehensive crime control initiatives. Now, if the House would act—and for the life of me I don't know what they're waiting for—we could finally put a comprehensive and long-overdue anticrime package on the books. Clay,[1] we'll be working with you to try to get them moving on this.

We know that formidable challenges remain, and meeting them is what Crime Prevention Week is all about. This year the

spotlight is on the Neighborhood Watch. But crime prevention is much more than that, and it's a nationwide movement. All across the country people are working together with law enforcement agencies to protect themselves, their loved ones, and their neighborhoods.

The National Exchange Club started the movement 37 years ago. And today its nearly 1,300 service clubs nationwide are working hard to promote crime preventive activities. The American Association of Retired Persons is helping the elderly. The National Crime Prevention Council and its spokesdog, McGruff, are leading a nationwide anticrime education program. The National Sheriffs Association has a key role in the Neighborhood Watch program.

Even sports teams are getting into the act. The Kansas City Chiefs, supported by local business, distribute football cards to local police departments, which in turn give them away to neighborhood children. The cards have a color, action picture of a player on one side and a crime prevention tip on the other. The only way to get a card is to ask a policeman, which reinforces positive communications between the cop on the beat and the neighborhood children.

In the past 3 years, 16 million cards have been given away. And now several other teams, including the Washington Redskins, are following suit.

And, of course, our nation's law enforcement officers are on the frontlines performing a tough job under enormous pressure. They're expected to be administrators, social workers, public relations experts, at times, philosophers and politicians, and still

---

[1] *Representative E. Clay Shaw, Jr., of Florida.*

somehow always be an officer of the law. And I thought my job was tough. [*Laughter*] Well, let me assure police officers everywhere of our firm support and unfailing gratitude. If we can get our comprehensive crime control act through the House, I think your job will become a little bit easier.

And now, let me commend the Neighborhood Watch Program. It's a program that I really like. In preparing for this ceremony, we did a little research and discovered that, using conservative estimates, of course—no other kind—[*laughter*]—that one in six live in a community with a citizen anticrime program. Watch programs in nearly 30,000 communities involve about 10 million volunteers. The best news is that they're doing a great job. Fairfax County, Virginia, reported a 44-percent drop in burglary over the last 3 years. Each day and night a thousand citizens watch out for their neighbors. Chief Buracker estimates that it would cost the taxpayer $30 million a year to replace this volunteer effort.

In Florida's Dade County, a youth crime watch program is credited for much of the 25-percent decline in school crime and 20-percent drop in narcotics use since 1983—pardon me, 1981. That would have been a sudden drop. We're seeing the same positive results with watch programs all over the country, from Seattle to Las Vegas to Jackson, Mississippi. And what we're really witnessing is a reaffirmation of American values: a sense of community and fellowship, individual responsibility, caring for family and friends, and a respect for the law.

I hope we can mark our observance of National Crime Prevention Week by redoubling our efforts. We'll continue cracking down on career criminals, organized crime, drug pushers, and pornographers. We'll continue working to protect the interests of victims. But the strongest guardian against crime is the American people and the institutions that bind us together as a free society. Together we can turn the tide on crime and make it permanent. And with your help, we will.

And now, it gives me great pleasure to award the George Washington Honor Medal to PACT, Police and Citizens Together, for their fine efforts in law enforcement. And I am delighted to present this award to Chief Maurice Turner of the District of Columbia Police Department and Officer Kenneth Perry of the U.S. Park Police.

Gentlemen, it's a pleasure to present this to you.

Attorney General Smith. Mr. President, I would like at this time, if I can find him, to present to you, McGruff, our national crime dog.

The President. I've got a kibble right in my pocket. [*Laughter*]

Attorney General Smith. And, Mr. President, one further item.

Chief Turner. Mr. President, from the Washington area law enforcement officers, we would like to present you with your own McGruff.

The President. Thank you all. God bless you, and thank you for being here.

Note: The President spoke at 10:55 a.m. in the East Room at the White House. Attorney General William French Smith also attended the ceremony.

Nomination of David Campbell Mulford To Be a Deputy Under Secretary of the Treasury
February 15, 1984

The President today announced his intention to nominate David Campbell Mulford to be a Deputy Under Secretary of the Treasury (International Affairs). Upon confirmation the President will designate Mr. Mulford as an Assistant Secretary of the Treasury. He would succeed Marc Leland.

Since 1974 Mr. Mulford has been senior

investment adviser for the Saudi Arabian Monetary Agency, director of Merrill Lynch, Pierce, Fenner, and Smith, and managing director of Merrill Lynch White Weld Capital Markets Group. Previously, he was head of White Weld International Finance Group in New York (1970–1974) and was with White, Weld & Co., Inc., international investment banking in New York and London (1966–1974). He was a White

House fellow in 1965–1966 and served as a special assistant to the Secretary of the Treasury.

Mr. Mulford graduated from Lawrence University (B.A., 1959), Boston University (M.A., 1962), and Oxford University, St. Anthony's College (Ph.D., 1965). He is married, has two children, and resides in Rockford, IL. He was born June 27, 1937, in Rockford.

Appointment of Kathleen M. Bennett as a Member of the Acid Precipitation Task Force
February 15, 1984

The President today announced his intention to appoint Kathleen M. Bennett to be a member of the Acid Precipitation Task Force. She will succeed Ellis Cowling.

Mrs. Bennett is presently serving as director of regulatory affairs for Champion International Corp. in Stamford, CT. Previously, she was Assistant Administrator for Air, Noise, and Radiation, United States Environmental Protection Agency, in 1981–

1983; Federal affairs representative for the Crown Zellerbach Corp. in 1977–1981; and director of legislative affairs for the American Paper Institute in 1974–1977.

She graduated from Manhattanville College (B.A., 1970). She is married, has three children, and resides in Alexandria, VA. She was born May 11, 1948, in Staten Island, NY.

Remarks at a Fundraiser for Republican Women Candidates on the Occasion of Susan B. Anthony's Birthday
February 15, 1984

I'm delighted to be here and see so many good friends, and it's always a pleasure for me to be joined by two of the most important women in my life, Nancy and Maureen.

And warm greetings to those joining us by satellite across the country. At the Susan B. Anthony birthday party in Los Angeles the celebrations are being led by former First Lady Betty Ford, by the First Lady of California Gloria Deukmejian, and by Transportation Secretary Elizabeth Dole. And also present is a longtime friend, Carol Burnett.

In Washington State, Republican women are hosting a party at the Governor's mansion, and among the distinguished guests

are Health and Human Services Secretary Margaret Heckler and a very active Republican woman, Jill Ruckelshaus. Thousands more are joining us by way of the C-Span television network, and I want to welcome all of you to this special party.

And now before I say anything else, let me give each of you my heartfelt thanks for all the time and labor that you've given to the Republican cause. In the end, it's not gloss and glitter but your determination and hard work that's made it possible for us to put our beliefs into practice—and will again in November. And all of you are especially important, because you demonstrate the Republican commitment to American women.

Tonight we mark the birthday, as we've been told, of a great American. Susan B. Anthony was born in 1820 in an America where women were virtually excluded from public life. In many States it was difficult for women to get a public education. Women were denied the right to control their own property and, worst of all, across the country women were denied the most fundamental democratic right, the right to vote.

Throughout her life Susan Anthony struggled to correct these injustices. She traveled the land, organizing women's groups, writing pamphlets, and speaking at conventions. To dramatize her cause in 1872 she registered and voted, and for that simple act she was arrested, tried, and fined. But her trial helped awaken our country's conscience.

By the turn of the century, the women's suffrage movement that Susan Anthony helped to create had begun making progress. Year by year States granted women improved legal status. Susan B. Anthony died in 1906, but the movement lived on. And in 1920 the 19th amendment finally gave women the right to vote.

We can all be proud that as women have taken on new roles in American society, the Grand Old Party has given them firm support. First, Republicans gave their backing to women's suffrage. Then our party became the first to elect a woman to the United States Congress. And we're the only party ever to elect women to the United States Senate who were not first filling unexpired terms.

Today the two women in the Senate, my friends Nancy Kassebaum and Paula Hawkins, are Republicans. We have nine outstanding Republican women in the House, and we're pleased to have three with us here tonight—Congressmen Nancy Johnson, Claudine Schneider, and Olympia Snowe. And this year our party faces no task more important than reelecting Senator Kassebaum and her colleagues in the House and sending still more skilled women to the Congress. To give an old phrase a new twist, "A woman's place is in the House—and the Senate." As a matter of fact, Republican women ought to increase their numbers at every level of elective office.

In the executive branch we've appointed women to positions of top responsibility, as you've been told here tonight, women like our U.N. Ambassador Jeane Kirkpatrick, our Secretary of Health and Human Services Margaret Heckler, and our Secretary of Transportation Elizabeth Dole. And I'm honored to have loyal and talented women like Ambassador Faith Whittlesey in the White House. And one of my proudest days in office was when I appointed Sandra Day O'Connor to be the first woman in history on the United States Supreme Court.

Together, we Republicans are working to reshape America's destiny. And when historians write the story of these years, they'll find that skilled and talented women played vital roles.

Think back to the mess that our country was in just 3 years ago. Big taxing and big spending had led to soaring inflation, and interest rates and government redtape had smothered productivity. You know, I have to—I just have to pause here and say that we've heard about some of the issues that the Gang of Eight are bringing up. [*Laughter*] Fairness is one. Well, I have to say this about our opponents: They didn't discriminate; they have been fair; they made everyone miserable. [*Laughter*]

But the broken economy hit women especially hard. The majority of elderly Americans are women, and they found their purchasing power eaten up by inflation. Working women saw taxes eat more of their paychecks. Homemakers found that double-digit inflation made it harder and harder to buy groceries and pay the bills. And the thousands of women who wanted to start their own businesses saw 21-percent prime interest rates slam shut the doors of opportunity.

And then our administration took office. And with Republicans in control of the Senate, we went to work to make a new beginning. We reduced the growth of Federal spending, pruned needless regulations, reduced personal income tax rates, and passed an historic reform called tax indexing that means government can never again use inflation to profit at the people's expense.

To help all Americans achieve economic

equality we reduced the marriage tax penalty, almost doubled the maximum child care credit, increased the limits for IRA and Keogh contributions, and eliminated estate taxes on family farms and businesses for surviving spouses. But our job is not complete.

We've asked the Congress to enact legislation designed to provide women with more equitable treatment in pension benefits and IRAs, to further increase child and dependent care tax credits for low- and middle-income workers, and to enforce delinquent parent support payments.

Today, less than 3 years since we set our policies in place, our nation has one big program to help every American man, woman, and child. It's called economic recovery.

The prime rate is only about half what it was when we took office. Inflation plummeted by three-fourths, to only about 3 percent last year. Auto sales were up 15 percent in 1983 to the highest level since 1979. Housing starts rose by a healthy 60 percent. Factory orders are up, and last month retail sales jumped 2.2 percent, the fifth straight monthly gain. And tomorrow morning, if you're out around 8:30—and I can't tell you any more than that—you're going to hear some good economic news in a couple of areas.

American workers' real wages are rising, and last year 4 million Americans found jobs. With this recovery, you'll be glad to hear that the unemployment rate among adult women has dropped from 9.1 to 7.1 percent, and today more women have jobs than ever before in our nation's history. Just as important, the jobs women hold are getting better and better. In 1983, women filled almost three-quarters of all the new jobs in managerial, professional, and technical fields. And the number of women-owned businesses is growing four times faster than those owned by men.

I believe that we must also move boldly to develop the potential of space, while preserving our resources here on Earth—our land, water, and air. And let us preserve our other resources which are just as precious—our values of faith, family, work, neighborhood, peace, and freedom, which make us a good and loving people.

Just as we're regaining our confidence at home, we're bringing a new sense of purpose and direction to American foreign policy. Today the world knows once again that America stands for freedom for humankind. Around the world we're working hard to support democracy and to build peace.

And that brings me to our relationship with the Soviet Union. We know it isn't what we want it to be. Time and again in public statements and in private communications to the Soviet leadership I've stressed our commitment to a serious and intensive dialog, one aimed at building a more constructive relationship, avoiding war, and reducing arms as a starting point. But we want to accomplish much more, and for that we need a good-faith effort on both sides. That's the message Vice President Bush carried to Moscow earlier this week.

In his meeting with General Secretary Chernenko, Vice President Bush emphasized once again America's desire for greater mutual understanding and genuine cooperation between our two countries. He also made clear our concerns over issues such as human rights and regional conflicts.

Let me share with you the Vice President's impressions of the new Soviet leadership that he passed to me following his meeting in the Kremlin. The atmosphere was positive. Although Secretary Chernenko did not depart from standard Soviet positions, he did appear ready to put our relationship on a more constructive basis. Vice President Bush and I have the impression that the new Soviet leadership is making an effort to downplay rhetoric and to explore ways to promote a more useful dialog.

America has always been willing to meet the Soviets halfway to find solutions to the many problems that divide us and to reach fair arms reduction agreements. If the new Soviet leadership decides to join us in a good faith effort we can accomplish much good together, and there's no better time to start than right now. If the Soviet Government wants peace, then there will be peace.

And finally, let me say a few words about recent events in Lebanon. We all know the peace process has been painfully slow, but we must continue to search for peace and stability in that deeply troubled country as long as there is the slightest chance to bring it about. You need only see the pain and suffering in the eyes of the Lebanese people, and particularly the children, to understand that we have a moral obligation not to abandon those people.

In recent weeks I have become increasingly concerned about the situation there. Should the various Lebanese factions fail to establish a basis for reconciliation, it would only encourage the radicals and extremists and put the Lebanese people in even more danger. And this would be more dangerous for the whole world.

The presence of the multinational force, the MNF, must never be an excuse for the Syrians and their clients to avoid a negotiated solution and reconciliation. So to use our diplomatic and military resources to the best advantage, and after consultation with President Gemayel, we have decided to shift our forces to an offshore deployment.

The recent outbreak of violence only re-

affirms the importance of the actions that we're taking. If a moderate government were overthrown because it had the courage to turn in the direction of peace, imagine the consequences for the future. We will remain steady. We will pursue every avenue in the search for peace and stability in that troubled region.

All of us share a dream of America as a great force for peace and goodwill among nations. And all of us share Susan B. Anthony's dream of America as a land where every citizen is judged not according to color or sex, but on the sole basis of individual merit; a land where every woman and man is free to become all they can be. I believe that, under God, we're making that great dream come true.

Thank you all, again, and God bless you all.

Note: The President spoke at 10:06 p.m. in the Hall of Flags at the U.S. Chamber of Commerce building.

Appointment of Two Members of the Federal Service Impasses Panel
February 16, 1984

The President today announced his intention to appoint the following individuals to be members of the Federal Service Impasses Panel, Federal Labor Relations Authority, for terms expiring January 10, 1989:

Robert G. Howlett would succeed Roy Martin Brewer. Mr. Howlett is currently a partner in the law firm of Schmidt, Howlett, Van't Hof, Snell and Vana in Grand Rapids, MI. Previously he was a member of the Federal Service Impasses Panel (1982–1984) and was appointed chairman of the Panel by President Ford in 1976 and served in that capacity until 1978. Mr. Howlett graduated from Northwestern

University (B.S., 1929; J.D., 1932). He is married, has three children, and resides in Grand Rapids, MI. Mr. Howlett was born November 10, 1906, in Bay City, MI.

Susan S. Robfogel is currently a member of the Federal Service Impasses Panel. She also is a partner in the law firm of Harris, Beach, Wilcox, Rubin and Levey. Previously she served as senior assistant corporation counsel to the city of Rochester, NY (1967–1970). Mrs. Robfogel graduated from Smith College (B.S., 1964) and Cornell Law School (J.D., 1967). She is married, has two children, and resides in Rochester, NY. She was born April 4, 1943, in Columbus, OH. This is a reappointment.

Message on the Observance of Brotherhood/Sisterhood Week, 1984
February 17, 1984

On this occasion, we mark the fiftieth anniversary of the celebration of Brotherhood/Sisterhood Week. For half a century this event has played a major role in encouraging greater understanding and communication among conflicting segments of society.

Brotherhood/Sisterhood Week furthers our awareness of the universal nature of the human experience. In promoting the spirit of brotherhood among the people of our nation, we strengthen our respect for the rich diversity of our country. By focusing on the importance of the dignity of the individual, we acknowledge the bonds of birth, hope, and freedom that gave meaning to our way of life.

In reaching out in brotherhood to our fellow citizens, we help stem the tide of historic challenges to mankind's advancement—starvation, disease, poverty, and war. Recognizing the precariousness of man's life on this planet, we strive to undergird the work of men and women of goodwill to bring about a world built upon the true values of fellowship and mutual respect.

RONALD REAGAN

Note: Brotherhood/Sisterhood Week will be observed February 20–26.

Nomination of Alfred Hugh Kingon To Be an Assistant Secretary of the Treasury
February 17, 1984

The President today announced his intention to nominate Alfred Hugh Kingon to be an Assistant Secretary of Treasury (Policy Planning and Communications). He would succeed Ann Dore McLaughlin.

Since 1983 Mr. Kingon has been serving as Assistant Secretary for International Economic Policy at the Department of Commerce. Previously he was with Macro Communications, Inc., in New York City, serving as editor in chief of Saturday Review (1980–1982), and Financial World (1973–1983) and editor of Money & Credit (1970–1973). He was portfolio manager for the Businessman's Fund in 1969–1971; security analyst, vice president and director of research for Scheinman, Hochstin & Trotta in 1967–1969; and investment adviser with Burnham & Co. in 1963–1967. He was a member of the Executive Committee of the President's Private Sector Survey for Cost Control Task Force and the President's National Productivity Advisory Committee.

Mr. Kingon graduated from Union College (B.S., 1953) and attended New York University Graduate School of Business Administration in 1956–1961. He is married, has one child, and resides in Chevy Chase, MD. He was born May 11, 1931, in Brooklyn, NY.

Appointment of Robert H. Snedaker, Jr., as a Member of the President's National Security Telecommunications Advisory Committee
February 17, 1984

The President today announced his intention to appoint Robert H. Snedaker, Jr., to be a member of the President's National Security Telecommunications Advisory Committee. He would succeed Robert M. Pirnie.

Mr. Snedaker is currently president of United Telephone System, Inc., and chairman of the board of directors of the United States Telephone Association. Previously, he was president of United Telephone Co. of Ohio (1971–1979); vice president and general manager of Ohio Bell in Columbus, OH (1964–1971); and staff director at AT&T (1962–1964).

Mr. Snedaker graduated from Dartmouth College (B.S., 1947; M.S., 1949). He is married, has four children, and resides in Prairie Village, KS. He was born February 13, 1926, in New York, NY.

Remarks at a White House Luncheon for Elected Republican Women Officials
February 17, 1984

I once learned that you're never supposed to open any remarks with an apology, but I must, because I am the reason for—of being delayed a little bit and it was late coming here. And I have to explain the reason I was late. I was getting connected to Yugoslavia so that I could congratulate on behalf of all Americans Scott Hamilton for winning the gold.

Now, about that introduction and that line that was used in introducing me the other night by Mrs. Reagan. I had always heard that an emcee was to be so dull in introducing those to follow that they would appear brilliant by contrast. [*Laughter*] She got the biggest laugh of the night. [*Laughter*]

But I'm delighted to welcome you here. And it's good to see so many friends and to have a chance to make some new ones. I want to thank all of you for what you're doing to advance the goals and ideals that unite us. It's you, the officeholders in State capitals and communities all across America, who are putting our beliefs into practice.

And I believe that America is moving forward again, and it's not because of any magic in Washington. The only magicians are on the other end of Pennsylvania Avenue—sleight-of-hand artists who have a way of taking your tax dollars and making them disappear. [*Laughter*] But it's your drive, energy, and determination that make the difference. And that's why America's future is looking better every day.

My spirits are high for another reason as well. I'm able to share these few moments with two of the most important women in my life—Nancy and Maureen. And, you know, I only work a few hundred feet from here, but I rarely get home for lunch. [*Laughter*]

Maureen did a little research for me, and I know that even before women had the right to vote, our party became the first to elect a woman to the United States Congress. Well, that's the Republican Party tradition, and I'm determined to build on it. The only women in the Senate, Nancy Kassebaum and Paula Hawkins, are Republicans, not to mention our nine outstanding Republican Congresswomen. Now, don't you think it's about time we gave them some more company?

We're calling on the talents and leadership of women in a big way. For the first time in history, three women are in the Cabinet at the same time—Ambassador Jeane Kirkpatrick, Secretary of Health and Human Services Margaret Heckler, and Secretary of Transportation Elizabeth Dole. Ambassador Faith Whittlesey has brought her talent to our White House staff.

And all told, more than a thousand women hold policymaking posts in our administration. And one of my proudest days was when Sandra Day O'Connor became the first woman justice in the history of the Supreme Court. In counting the votes sometimes and some of the issues in these last 3 years, I've had reason to cheer her being there.

But just as important, thousands of able Republican women like you are serving on the frontlines in public offices all across America. We want to see the number of Republican women officeholders growing here in Washington and in every American town and city and State. Someday a woman's going to have my job. Let's make sure it's a Republican woman.

When historians write about these years, they're going to find that very skilled and talented women played a key role in putting America back on her feet. Challenges are still before us, and together we Republicans can turn them into opportunities.

Three weeks ago in my State of the Union Address, I talked about how far we've come since those days in 1980 when we were hearing sorry excuses about some sort of malaise that the American people suffered. Well, I won't belabor the point, but have you figured out why our critics are going around the country moaning and groaning? Maybe we should speak a little louder about the one big program that is helping every man, woman, and child in America. It's called economic recovery.

By turning the economy around, we've helped everyone, and particularly women. The majority of elderly Americans are women. And double-digit inflation in 1979 and 1980 was destroying their purchasing power. Now inflation is only 3.2 percent.

Thousands of women who wanted to start their own businesses saw 21-percent prime interest rates slam shut the doors of opportunity. Well, those interest rates have been cut nearly in half. And if Congress will cooperate, we can do even better.

Personal income tax rates have been reduced, and indexing begins next year, meaning that government can no longer profit at the taxpayer's expense. We reduced the marriage tax penalty and almost doubled the maximum child care credit. We increased the limits for IRA and Keough contributions. And we've eliminated estate taxes on family farms and businesses for surviving spouses.

From solid growth in housing—new housing starts in January were at their highest since 1978—to new frontiers in high technology and from a healthy recovery in real wages to the sharpest drop in unemployment in nearly 33 years, we have good reason to be proud of what's been accomplished. For 13 months we have been putting an average of 300,000 people a month back into jobs and off the unemployment rolls.

Believe me, if we didn't control one House of the Congress, none of that could ever have been done. There's still so much to do, more to do in ensuring women's rights, providing for equitable treatment in pension benefits and IRAs, facilitating child and dependent care, and enforcing delinquent parent support payments. And we've introduced legislation in all these areas to accomplish these goals.

Unemployment is now down to 7.9 percent. The unemployment rate among adult women has dropped from 9.1 to 7.1 percent. And today more women have jobs than ever before in our nation's history. But I won't be satisfied until every American who wants a job can find a job.

We need basic budget and tax reforms like the line-item veto, a constitutional amendment mandating a balanced budget, and tax simplification, so that we can make sure the progress we're enjoying will continue for generations to come. And I believe we must also move boldly to develop the enormous potential of space while preserving our resources here on Earth—our land, water, and air. And let us preserve our other resources which are just as precious—our values of faith, family, work, neighborhood, peace, and freedom, the values that have made us a good and a loving people.

Just as we're turning the economy around, there's a new sense of purpose and direction to America's foreign policy. Back in 1981 we had an uncomfortable feeling that we'd lost respect overseas. Some questioned whether we had the will to defend peace and freedom. Well, 3 years later, the world knows once more what America stands for—freedom, dignity, and peace for everywhere, for people from Asia to Central and South America.

And that brings me to two final points. The first has to do with the Soviet Union. For the first time in years, we're on the way to restoring a constructive dialog, one that builds stability and is so essential for peace. Time and again, in public statements and in private communications to the Soviet leadership, I've stressed our commitment to a serious and intensive dialog, one aimed at building a more constructive relationship. Avoiding war and reducing arms is the starting point.

But I want to accomplish much more. And all that's needed is a good-faith effort on both sides. That's the message that Vice President Bush carried to Moscow earlier this week. And the Vice President emphasized once again America's desire for greater mutual understanding and genuine cooperation between our two countries.

America has always been ready to meet the Soviets halfway. To find solutions to the many problems that divide us and to reach fair arms reduction agreements. If the new Soviet leadership decides to join us in a good-faith effort, we can accomplish much good together. And there's no better time to start than right now.

Finally, let me say a few words about recent events in the Middle East. We all know the peace process has been painfully slow but we must continue to search for peace and stability as long as there's a chance to bring it about.

For the past 35 years, the United States has been working to build peace and stability in that troubled region. Most of that effort has been focused on resolving the conflict between Israel and her Arab neighbors. Lebanon's troubles are just part of the overall problem in the Middle East, and her internal strife has only made it worse. The most recent outbreak of violence reaffirms the importance of redoubling our efforts to find a peaceful solution to the fundamental problems of the region. And we're trying to do just that.

Earlier this week I met with King Hussein of Jordan and President Mubarak of Egypt. We discussed our September 1982 Middle East plan and ways to move the peace process forward—both of them in complete agreement that this should be done, and they want to be of help. We're pursuing every avenue in the search for peace and stability.

Well now, that's—I've gone on long enough. When you get back home, tell people what we stand for, what we've done, and how far, together, we can still go.

We can make our dreams come true. The Republican Party needs you, and so does America. So, temporarily, I'll say, "Good luck, and God bless you"—and we'll have dessert.

Note: The President spoke at 12:55 p.m. in the State Dining Room at the White House.

Message to the Congress Transmitting a Proposed Initiative for Central America
February 17, 1984

To the Congress of the United States:

I herewith transmit proposed legislation that embodies the consensus arrived at by the National Bipartisan Commission on Central America. Its unifying thread is the spirit of the late Senator Henry M. Jackson—to advance the twin purposes of national security and human development.

Peace and individual betterment are universal purposes. They are at the heart of the American dream. Yet, today in Central America these goals are not realized. Poverty and violence are widespread. As a consequence, democratic forces are not able to flourish, and those who seek to disrupt freedom and opportunity threaten the heart of those nations.

Throughout our history, our leaders have put country before party on issues in foreign affairs important to the national interest. The Commission identifies the situation in Central America as this kind of issue. The 12 Commissioners—Democrats and Republicans alike—conclude "that Central America is both vital and vulnerable, and that whatever other crises may arise to claim the nation's attention, the United States cannot afford to turn away from that threatened region."

We face an inescapable reality: we must come to the support of our neighbors. The democratic elements in Central America need our help. For them to overcome the problems of accumulated historical inequities and immediate armed threats will take time, effort, and resources. We must support those efforts.

As the Commission recommends, our policy must be based on the principles of democratic self-determination, economic and social improvement that fairly benefits all, and cooperation in meeting threats to the security of the region.

Accordingly, I propose the "Central America Democracy, Peace and Development Initiative Act of 1984." This Act calls for an increased commitment of resources beginning immediately and extending regularly over the next five years. This assistance is necessary to support the balance of economic, political, diplomatic, and security measures that will be pursued simultaneously.

I propose authorization for an $8 billion, five-year reconstruction and development program for Central America, composed of $6 billion in direct appropriations and $2 billion in insurance and guarantee authority. For fiscal year 1985 the figures are $1.1 billion and $600 million, respectively. In addition, the plan calls for $400 million in supplemental appropriations for an emergency economic stabilization program for fiscal year 1984.

These resources will support agricultural development, education, health services, export promotion, land reform, housing, humanitarian relief, trade credit insurance, aid for small businesses, and other activities. Because democracy is essential to effective development, special attention will be given to increasing scholarships, leadership training, educational exchanges, and support for the growth of democratic institutions.

Regional institutions such as the Central American Common Market (CACM) and the Central American Bank for Economic Integration (CABEI) made a major contribution to the region's economic growth in the 1960's and early 70's. I am proposing a substantial assistance program to revitalize these institutions and thereby stimulate intra-regional trade and economic activity.

To enable the countries of Central America to participate directly in the planning of these efforts, I shall explore the creation of a Central American Development Organization (CADO). This would enable political and private leaders from both the United States and Central America to review objectives and progress, and make recommendations on the nature and levels of our assistance efforts. The organization would, in effect, help to oversee and coordinate the major efforts that must be made. The legislation I am proposing sets out a series of principles to guide the negotiations for the establishment of this new regional institution. I intend to respect those principles in these negotiations and in our subsequent participation in CADO. As the Commission recognized, the ultimate control of aid funds will always rest with the donors. Consistent with the Constitution and this precept, final disposition of funds appropriated under this legislation will be subject to the ultimate control of the Congress and the President.

The National Bipartisan Commission specifically recommends significantly increased levels of military aid to the region, especially El Salvador. In the words of the Report, "the worst possible policy for El Salvador is to provide just enough aid to keep the war

going, but too little to wage it successfully."
I propose authorization for a $259 million
supplemental appropriation for the region
for fiscal year 1984 and a $256 million pro-
gram for fiscal year 1985.

U.S. military assistance is vital to shield
progress on human rights and democratiza-
tion against violence from extremes of both
left and right. I shall ensure that this assistance is provided under conditions necessary
to foster human rights and political and economic development, and our Administration will consult with the Members of the
Congress to make certain that our assistance is used fairly and effectively.

No new laws are needed to carry out
many of the Commission's recommendations. There is, for example, a consensus on
an integral part of our strategy in Central
America: support for actions implementing
the 21 Contadora objectives to help bring
about peace. The Contadora objectives are
in Central America's interest and in ours.
Similarly, we are urging other nations to

increase their assistance to the area.

I believe it is no accident that the Commission reached many of the same conclusions about comprehensive solutions to Central America's problems as have the participants in the Contadora process. As Dr. Kissinger noted in his January 10 letter to me,
"the best route to consensus on U.S. policy
toward Central America is by exposure to
the realities of Central America."

The National Bipartisan Commission on
Central America has done its work. Now it
is our turn. Unless we act—quickly, humanely, and firmly—we shall face a crisis
that is much worse for everyone concerned.
We owe it to our children to make sure that
our neighbors have a chance to live decent
lives in freedom.

I, therefore, ask that the enclosed legislation be given your urgent attention and
early and favorable action.

RONALD REAGAN

The White House,
February 17, 1984.

Message to the Congress Transmitting the Annual Report on United States International Activities in Science and Technology
February 17, 1984

To the Congress of the United States:

In accordance with the requirements of
Title V of the Foreign Relations Authorization Act for Fiscal Year 1979 (Public Law
95–426), I am transmitting the 1983 annual
report on the United States Government's
international activities in the fields of science and technology. As in the past, this
report has been prepared by the Department of State in collaboration with other
concerned agencies of the Federal government.

I would like to take this opportunity, first
of all, to express again my personal regret
on the passing of Congressman Clement J.
Zablocki. As Chairman of the House Foreign Affairs Committee and of the Subcommittee on International Security and Scientific Affairs, Congressman Zablocki made
many significant contributions to this Na-

tion's pursuit of foreign relations spanning
several administrations. None of these, however, was more important than his tireless
efforts to see that science and technology
play greater roles in the conduct of foreign
policy. Chairman Zablocki understood well
the benefits of scientific progress toward
economic growth both for our Nation and
others across the globe and incorporated
that understanding into the Title V legislation of which he was the prime architect.
On behalf of the people of the United
States, I want to express the gratitude of
the Nation for his many years of distinguished service.

Science and technology have been key to
the economic and social development of the
United States. Political liberty and free enterprise provide a fertile environment to
American scientists and engineers who have

given us a standard of living unequaled in the history of the world. We are certain that science and technology offer similar hope to all nations committed to the pursuit of realistic and sustained economic development. The United States has increasingly made cooperative scientific and technological arrangements important to our developmental assistance efforts to Third World countries and of strengthened bilateral relations with other industrialized nations.

During 1983 we were successful in our efforts to encourage international science and technology cooperation. There were many positive developments which are set out in detail in this report. Of particular importance, though, are several of our bilateral relations. It is important to develop a strong bilateral relationship with the People's Republic of China while maintaining our friendship with the democratic nations of Asia. Broad-based science and technology agreements are a vital part of our efforts to build this relationship. The role of science and technology plays a similar role in Latin America. This is particularly true in our bilateral relations with Brazil and Mexico. I am certain that these nations attach as much importance to scientific and technology cooperation as we do. We will continue to pursue the opportunities for increased cooperation.

Perhaps the most disturbing development of 1983 in the field of science and technology has been our reluctant, but necessary, decision to give notice of our intent to withdraw from participation in UNESCO. Our persistent efforts over the past three years to convince the UNESCO bureaucracy in Paris to address the Agency's serious problems of administrative and fiscal mismanagement and to reorient its direction to pursue once again only the mission envisioned in its charter have failed. We see no viable option but to sever our ties with this Agency if its overt hostility to American values and its increasing substantive impotence and procedural abuse are not satisfactorily corrected. We will strive to minimize any significant adverse effect on beneficial science and technology activities at UNESCO by making alternative arrangements for U.S. participation in such programs.

Our scientific and technological relations with the Soviet Union and Poland have been adversely affected by disappointing Soviet attitudes and actions. In our Title V Report for 1982, I made it clear that cooperation depends upon the steps the Soviet Government takes to comply with recognized norms of international behavior. Soviet behavior still falls far short of this standard, and our position remains unchanged. We will continue to carefully observe Soviet behavior and adjust our science and technology cooperation accordingly.

In the overall international arena, we can be proud of our scientific leadership. It can go a long way in helping the cause of freedom and economic growth around the world. The international programs described in this report benefit our Nation and our cooperative partners, and are a source of good will around the world.

RONALD REAGAN

The White House,
February 17, 1984.

Nomination of Fred William Alvarez To Be a Member of the Equal Employment Opportunity Commission
February 17, 1984

The President today announced his intention to nominate Fred William Alvarez to be a member of the Equal Employment Opportunity Commission for the term expiring July 1, 1988. He would succeed Armando M. Rodriguez.

Since 1980 he has been in the private practice of law with the firm of Sutin, Thayer & Browne in Albuquerque, NM. Previously he was a trial attorney with the

National Labor Relations Board in Oakland and San Francisco, CA, in 1976–1980; and was a law clerk to Chief Justice LaFel E. Oman, New Mexico Supreme Court, Santa Fe, in 1975–1976.

He graduated from Stanford University (B.A., 1972; J.D., 1975). He is married and resides in Albuquerque, NM. He was born June 1, 1949, in Las Cruces, NM.

Executive Order 12461—District of Columbia Police and Firefighters' Retirement and Disability System
February 17, 1984

Designating a Federal Retirement System Under Public Law 98–168

By the authority vested in me as President by the Federal Employees' Retirement Contribution Temporary Adjustment Act of 1983 (title II of Public Law 98–168) ("the Act"), it is hereby ordered as follows:

Section 1. The District of Columbia Police and Firefighters' Retirement and Disability System, insofar as it applies to Federal employees who are covered under section 203(a)(1) of the Act, is designated a covered retirement system under section 203(a)(2)(D) of the Act. The Secretary of the Treasury is designated the appropriate agency head with respect to such system, under section 205(a)(2)(D) of the Act. In discharging the responsibilities delegated by this Order, the Secretary shall be guided by the information and recommendations provided by the Mayor of the District of Columbia.

Sec. 2. This Order shall be effective as of January 1, 1984.

RONALD REAGAN

The White House,
February 17, 1984.

[*Filed with the Office of the Federal Register, 10:17 a.m., February 21, 1984*]

Executive Order 12462—President's Advisory Committee on Mediation and Conciliation
February 17, 1984

By the authority vested in me as President by the Constitution and statutes of the United States of America, including the Federal Advisory Committee Act, as amended (5 U.S.C. App. I), in order to create an advisory committee on methods of mediating and on the voluntary adjustment of labor disputes, it is hereby ordered as follows:

Section 1. Establishment. There is established the President's Advisory Committee on Mediation and Conciliation. The Committee shall be composed of not more than twelve members who shall be appointed or designated by the President from among persons with special knowledge and familiarity with labor relations problems. The Director of the Federal Mediation and Conciliation Service is hereby designated as Chairman of the Advisory Committee.

Sec. 2. Functions. (a) The Committee shall advise the President and the Director of the Federal Mediation and Conciliation Service on methods of improving the efficiency of arbitration of disputes arising under collective bargaining agreements, and on other matters, not involving particular labor disputes, of general significance to strengthening and increasing the effectiveness of bilateral dispute resolution mechanisms under such agreements.

(b) In performance of its advisory responsibilities, the Committee shall report to the President and the Director of the Federal Mediation and Conciliation Service from time to time as requested.

(c) The Committee will undertake a review of regulations promulgated by the Federal Mediation and Conciliation Service that affect established arbitration and mediation procedures, and offer their findings and recommendations in a report to the President and the Director of the Federal Mediation and Conciliation Service within nine months of the Committee's establishment.

Sec. 3. Administration. (a) The heads of Executive agencies shall, to the extent permitted by law, provide the Committee such information as it may require to carry out its functions.

(b) Members of the Committee shall serve without compensation for their work on the Committee. However, members appointed from among private citizens of the United States may be allowed travel expenses, including per diem in lieu of subsistence, as authorized by law for persons serving intermittently in the government service (5

U.S.C. 5701–5707).

(c) The Director of the Federal Mediation and Conciliation Service shall provide the Committee with such administrative services, facilities, staff and other support as may be necessary for the effective performance of its functions.

Sec. 4. General. (a) Notwithstanding the provisions of any other Executive Order, the responsibilities of the President under the Federal Advisory Committee Act, as amended, except that of reporting annually to the Congress, which are applicable to the Committee established by this Order, shall be performed by the Director of the Federal Mediation and Conciliation Service, in accordance with guidelines and procedures established by the Administrator of General Services.

(b) The Committee shall terminate on December 31, 1984, unless sooner extended.

Ronald Reagan

The White House,
February 17, 1984.

[*Filed with the Office of the Federal Register, 10:18 a.m., February 21, 1984*]

Radio Address to the Nation on Proposed Crime Legislation
February 18, 1984

My fellow Americans:

Shouldn't we have the right as citizens of this great country to walk our streets without being afraid and to go to bed without worrying the next sound might be a burglar or a rapist? Of course we should. But in reality we don't. The sad fact is too many of our friends and loved ones live in fear of crime. And there's no mystery as to why. For too many years, the scales of criminal justice were tilted toward protecting rights of criminals. Those in charge forgot or just plain didn't care about protecting your rights—the rights of law-abiding citizens.

We came to Washington determined to change that by restoring the proper balance to our criminal justice system and by assisting all of you who, through Neighborhood Watch-type programs, are trying to protect life, property, and security in your communities.

Common sense is beginning to pay off. In 1982 the crime rate dropped by 4.3 percent—the biggest decline since 1972. But we still face a tremendous challenge, and meeting that challenge is what I want to talk to you about today.

Since drugs are related to an enormous amount of violent crime, drug trafficking and organized crime are among our major targets. For the first time in this nation's history, we've thrown the resources of the FBI into drug enforcement. A new border interdiction program is underway. Task forces aimed at drug gangs cover the Nation, and they've indicted more than 1,300 persons in the last year.

In fact, since our administration came into office, the number of drug-related convictions has increased 33 percent. Since 1981 the number of enforcement agents, prosecutors, and the amount of funding and Federal cooperation with State and local agencies have all greatly increased. Even the military is providing assistance in the fight against drug traffickers. But we still need to do more. We need new laws to stop drug traffickers from harming our people, especially our young people. And we need tougher laws to fight other forms of crime so we can make the lives of all Americans more secure.

This issue should never turn into a prolonged partisan struggle, but it has. The Senate recently passed overwhelmingly our Comprehensive Crime Control Act. The House has done nothing and continues to wait. But wait for what? Bottling up long-overdue reforms that would provide you, the people, greater protection against dangerous criminals is a serious mistake you should not tolerate.

Let me give you some examples of what's at stake here. One of our bill's reforms would create tougher laws permitting Federal prosecutors to seize the profits and assets of organized crime and drug traffickers. This would be a severe blow to the crime czars. Why should any right-minded person oppose it?

Another reform, involving the so-called exclusionary rule, would allow evidence obtained reasonably and in good faith to be used in a criminal trial. How many times have we seen law enforcement officers handcuffed by the maze of technicalities that make collection and presentation of evidence so difficult?

Our bill also makes sentencing more uniform and certain. There's nothing complicated about this. The sentence imposed should be the sentence served, with no parole. Too many sentences today are inadequate and the time served too short.

Another important reform concerns bail.

It's hard to imagine the present system being any worse. Except in capital cases, Federal courts cannot consider the danger a defendant may pose to others if released. The judge can only consider whether it's likely the defendant will appear for trial if granted bail. Recently, a man charged with armed robbery and suspected of four others was given a low bond and quickly released. Four days later he and a companion robbed a bank, and in the course of the robbery a policeman was shot. This kind of outrage happens again and again, and it must be stopped. So, we want to permit judges to deny bail and lock up defendants who the government has shown pose a grave danger to their communities.

Our bill would also cut back on the misuse of insanity as a defense, strengthen child pornography laws, and provide greater financial assistance to State and local law enforcement programs. Independently of our crime package, we're mounting a major effort to combat crimes such as sexual assault and family violence. We're also working hard to improve the justice system treatment of our fellow citizens who were the innocent victims of crime.

These reforms make good sense, and there's no excuse for not passing them. The liberal approach of coddling criminals didn't work and never will. Nothing in our Constitution gives dangerous criminals a right to prey on innocent, law-abiding people. I would hope the Members of the House could remember this and bring up our bill for consideration without further delay. This is the most comprehensive anti-crime legislation in more than a decade. In the interest of true justice and in recognition of this past week, National Crime Prevention Week, it deserves full debate and a vote. Perhaps you might inquire from your Representative if he or she is ready to act, and if not, why not.

Till next week, thanks for listening, and God bless you.

Note: The President spoke at 12:06 p.m. from the Oval Office at the White House.

Written Responses to Questions Submitted by Oslobodjenje of Yugoslavia on the 1984 Winter Olympic Games
February 18, 1984

Q. Mr. President, this year Yugoslavia is host of the winter Olympic games and the United States of the summer Olympics. We are looking forward to it as an opportunity for strengthening of friendships and understanding among youth of the world. Children in Yugoslav schools even sent a message to the world leaders asking them to stop all wars in Olympic year as was the case in ancient Greece. How important are in today's world such events as Olympic games?

The President. I believe that the Olympic games show the human race at its best. We judge the best athletes in the world according to standards of excellence and sportsmanship, not political and economic doctrine, race, or religion. The Olympics show us what we can achieve when we agree on our goals and pursue them in a spirit of cooperation and understanding. Leaders in government have an obligation to strive for cooperation every bit as hard as our athletes who reach within for the greatest efforts of their lives. Together we should build a safer and far better world for the human family, not just for today but for generations to come. The United States has no higher priority than peace, as exemplified by the Olympic spirit.

Q. How do you see Yugoslavia as a first nonaligned country that will be host of such an event?

The President. As I told President Spiljak during his visit to the United States earlier this month, we greatly admire the effort and care that went into the preparation of the Olympic games in Sarajevo. Athletes, visitors, and Olympic officials have commented that they have never seen a better organized Olympics, and the hospitality of the people of Sarajevo is unsurpassed.

Q. The United States will host the summer Olympic games in Los Angeles this year. What does it mean to you?

The President. It is a great honor. California is my home State, and I know that the Los Angeles Olympic Organizing Committee has spared no effort to offer the world's Olympic athletes and visitors to the games the best possible facilities. All Americans are anxious to welcome the people of the world with the same warm hospitality that was extended to our athletes in Sarajevo.

Q. What is your opinion, Mr. President, about some previous attempts to make the Olympics a stage for political confrontation?

The President. In ancient Greece, the Olympic games were a celebration of human excellence, not of nation states or political systems. That is the great tradition that has brought about the popularity of the modern Olympic movement. We must do everything we can to honor that tradition.

Q. Were you watching the games? Which ones in particular? Were you satisfied with what you saw—the spirit, the atmosphere?

The President. The Olympic events I have seen on TV have been exciting and inspirational. The competition is fierce and requires great stamina, spirit, and skill. Obviously, we cheer for the men and women on our respective teams. But we can and should celebrate the triumphs of all athletes who compete in the true spirit of sportsmanship and give the very best of themselves. So, while we were thrilled at the victories of our American skiers, we cheered with you when Jure Franko skied to a silver medal in the men's giant slalom. It's been a great event.

Note: As printed above, the questions and answers follow the text of the White House press release.

Toasts of the President and Prince Rainier III of Monaco at a Benefit Gala for the Princess Grace Foundation
February 18, 1984

The President. Thank you very much. Your Serene Highness, Prince Albert, Princess Caroline, Princess Stephanie, Mr. Casiraghi, members of the Kelly family, and distinguished guests:

Tonight we're gathered to honor a woman who touched our lives deeply and to inaugurate the foundation to support in her name the arts she loved so much.

Princess Grace was a woman of great beauty—one of the greatest beauties of our time. Yet she possessed not only outward beauty but inward character, sincerity, strength of purpose, and loving kindness. Throughout her life Princess Grace had a passion for the performing arts. As a young woman she became an actress, and no one will ever forget Grace Kelly in "Rear Window" or "High Society." As a princess, she constantly worked to support the arts in her own Monaco and in America. And now it falls on us to carry on her work.

The Princess Grace Foundation will dedicate itself to the encouragement of emerging artists, the young performers who need support to succeed in their work. The foundation will concentrate on two of the fields that the Princess loved best—the theater and the dance. And the foundation will conduct its work with the same dignity and commitment to excellence that were so characteristic of Princess Grace.

Princess Grace once said that "each individual always has opportunities to do good and, in doing good, to repay the kindness of God who gives us life." So, Princess Grace led her life doing good, spreading joy, uplifting the spirits of so many, and now it's our turn to follow her example. And I just have to believe that by establishing this foundation we, in our small way, will be thanking God for giving us Princess Grace.

Would you please join me in a toast to the memory of our beloved Princess Grace and to the good work of the foundation that bears her name.

The Prince. Thank you, Mr. President. Allow me to express to you and to Mrs. Reagan, not only in my name but also in the name of my children, our deep gratitude and true appreciation for your presence here tonight.

I fully measure the special meaning and value of your gesture as President of the United States of America and, may I add, as a friend of my dear wife. My children and I are indeed honored and pleased to be here with you and Mrs. Reagan on this very special occasion.

We are all gathered here to continue what Grace had begun and do all we possibly can to turn her wish into reality. Many of us know how deeply and genuinely concerned she was in the support and help to emerging young artistic talent. It is certainly wonderful that her many friends and loved ones are here not only to witness but also to take part in this inauguration of the Princess Grace Foundation.

None better than you all can feel and know how important it is for the foundation to continue the legacy of the patronage of the arts that Grace set herself to assure with such care and heart. Most of you share in Grace's great passion for the theater and dance, and your presence here this evening demonstrates to me and to the world that her commitment to the arts will be continued. For this, my children and I are profoundly grateful.

Grace's two great loves were her family and the artistic world that beckoned her from an early age. Her personal endeavors as an artist not only taught her great appreciation of the art but also imbued her in an empathy for the tremendous dedication all artists make to bring light, love, music, and laughter into the world.

This is not just another gala evening, but because it is gratified by your presence, Mr. President, on the occasion of this inauguration, it is an evening to remember. The launching of the Princess Grace Foundation has most certainly a special significance for us all. As of now, we and all those who wish to can actively take part in the fostering of new talents in this country who will one day thrill the world with their art and skill.

As Grace is the inspiration for this great impulse, so the foundation will be the inspiration for countless people who may otherwise be prevented from sharing their talents with those who love theater and dance. It will strive to maintain the same commitment to beauty and excellence that are the hallmarks of Grace's life.

The foundation created in her name has a mission: to encourage and assist aspiring young artists in the fields of theater and dance. To fulfill that mission, the Princess Grace Foundation will provide scholarships and awards to outstanding young theater and dance students or professionals. And, of course, as time goes by, other ways and

means of helping and encouraging talents may be discovered to fulfill the mission of this foundation.

And it is not without emotion that I wholeheartedly give my support to the work of the Princess Grace Foundation, confident as I am that it will achieve its goals. For you, Grace's friends and admirers, I express my most sincere gratitude for your unswerving support and the honor you bring to her name.

Thank you.

Note: The President spoke at 10:22 p.m. following the dinner at the Departmental Auditorium. In his opening remarks, the President referred to Stefano Casiraghi, the husband of Princess Caroline.

Remarks at an Iowa Caucus Rally in Waterloo
February 20, 1984

The President. Thank you very much, Governor Terry Branstad, and members of the Iowa delegation, and my old friend, the conscience of the Congress, H.R. Gross. Thank you all for your very warm welcome.

And may I say it's a tonic to be in this beautiful place. And if I can remember the way we used to do the call letters, "Where the West begins in the State where the tall corn grows." And it's good to be back with hard-working people who share an abiding love for God and family. You don't listen to the worldly cynics; you're too busy making America's future better.

It's wonderful to see so many of you here. There are almost as many of you as there are Democratic Presidential candidates. [*Laughter*] You know, I'm a little curious about some of the things those fellows have been saying. Now, correct me if I'm wrong, because you're closer to the situation than I am. But aren't these people who talk so much about fairness for all Americans the same ones who can't see you unless you belong to a special interest group? And don't you get a little nervous when those born-again budget balancers tell us there's only one way to reduce deficits, and it

begins with raising your taxes?

But let's be fair. This is one area where all our liberal friends are willing to cut spending. There is one area. They'll cut what America needs to protect her national security. Oh, they say they're for a strong national defense. But ask them if we should build the B-1 bomber or the MX missile or the Trident submarine or the cruise missile or the aircraft carriers or the M-1 tank or rebuild the battleship *Iowa*—but that's another story.

I don't know how they feel about slingshots—[*laughter*]—but I do know that with them in control our defenses would still be growing weaker. Oh, troops would have landed in Grenada all right; they just wouldn't have been American troops.

The Grenadians wouldn't have been applauding, and our American students might not have been saved. You know, I'm going to interrupt right here, because—I wasn't going to tell you this, but I have to.

One of our young men, a lieutenant in the Marine Corps, pilots a Cobra, was in Grenada, and then he went on to Beirut. And this young lieutenant wrote back to the Armed Forces Journal at the Pentagon.

And he said that in every story about Grenada, in every paper, he read in every one of them the same line: Grenada produces more nutmeg than any other spot on Earth. And he had come to the conclusion that that was being repeated so often, it was a code. And so he wrote back to say he had broken the code.

Six stages. Number 1: Grenada produces more nutmeg than any other spot on Earth. Number 2: The Soviets and the Cubans are trying to take Grenada. Number 3: You cannot make good eggnog without nutmeg. [*Laughter*] Number 4: You can't have Christmas without eggnog. [*Laughter*] Number 5: The Soviets and the Cubans were trying to steal Christmas. And Number 6: We stopped them.

Audience. [*Chanting*] U.S.A.! U.S.A.! U.S.A!

The President. You bet. Thank you.

What we're talking about are questions of values, judgment, and courage. Our administration did not answer a problem of national security by slapping an unfair grain embargo on Iowa's farmers. We removed that grain embargo and began rebuilding America's defenses. And now we're doing our best to help farmers work their way back, strengthen their prices, increase their exports, and regain their reputation as reliable suppliers.

We can do better. But we must never shy from telling the truth. And we have some important truths to tell between now and November 6, election day 1984.

The first truth is the old reliable: People who live in glass houses should never throw stones. Or, to put it another way: The liberals who had total control over government but who saddled America with double-digit inflation, record interest rates, huge tax increases, too much regulation, credit controls, farm embargoes, no growth at home, weakness abroad, and phony excuses about you having a malaise are the last people who should be giving sermonettes about fairness and compassion.

Now, I have to say there was one thing fair about their policies. They didn't discriminate; they made everybody miserable. And now these critics say that we can do nothing right. The spending and tax cuts were too big, all their special interests have been hurt, and the recovery can't last. If pessimism was an Olympic event, they'd win a gold medal for sure.

You know, their attitude reminds me of a comment that a great American leader made about a similar situation. He said, "Those who are frightened by boldness and cowed by the necessity for making decisions complain that all we have done is unnecessary and subject to great risks. Now that these people are coming out of their storm cellars, they forget that there ever was a storm." Those words were spoken by President Franklin Delano Roosevelt in the fall of 1934—which brings me to the second truth we must tell between now and November: America *is* better off today than we were 3 years ago. We're better off because we're through placing faith in more government programs. We're restoring our faith in the greatest resource this nation has—the mighty spirit of free people under God.

It was you at the grassroots who reminded Washington that we are a government of and by and for the people, not the other way around. And it was you who said it is time to put earnings back in the hands of the people, time to put trust back in the hands of the people, time to put America back in the hands of the people.

And that's why America is moving forward with confidence again. We're seeing a new dawn of hope for our people. As the psalm says, "Weeping may endure for a night, but joy cometh in the morning." We're still not where we want to be, but look how far we've come. We don't have 12½-percent inflation anymore; inflation is less than 4 percent and has been for 2 years. We don't have interest rates over 21 percent; the prime rate is now down to 11. We don't have taxes doubling in 5 years; we cut everyone's tax rates. And next year, your taxes will be indexed so that government can no longer use inflation to profit at your expense. And we eliminated estate taxes for spouses, so that Iowa families won't have to sell the family farm just to pay the government a tax.

In 1980 we had economic stagnation; in 1984 we have a sparkling recovery that is reducing unemployment by the fastest rate in nearly 33 years. America *is* back.

But if the dream of America is to be preserved, we must not waste the genius of one mind, the strength of one body, or the spirit of one soul. We need all our people—men and women, young and old, individuals of every race—to be healthy, happy, and whole. And I assure your fine Governor and all of you here today, we must not and will not be satisfied until every person who wants to work can find work. This is our goal. And for each of the last 13 months, an average of 300,000 people a month have found jobs here in this land of ours.

Recovery in the farm community has been more difficult. The worldwide recession, large crops in other countries, last summer's drought, East-West tensions, and unfair trade practices have all contributed to cash flow problems for our producers, and they've made it harder for us to correct the legacy of the past. But make no mistake: We are working our way back from despair to hope. We've made a commitment to help, and we're doing our darn level best to carry it out.

We said we would lift the grain embargo, and we did. We said we would help restore the reputation of American farmers as reliable suppliers, and we negotiated a new long-term grain agreement with the Soviets. We promised to lift the burden of surpluses off the back of agriculture, and most surpluses have been cut. Prices are still too low, but they're stronger than they were, and this year farm costs will decline.

As proof of our commitment to expand exports, I recently approved a $1 billion increase for agricultural export credit guarantees in fiscal year 1984. The new total of $4 billion is almost twice what the previous administration made available in any year.

Let me interject some words here about a person who's been a rock of support in Washington for Iowa's farmers. He reflects the values of your people, and he represents you well. His Joint Economic Committee hearings on the next generation of agricultural policy were among the most important ever held in Congress. He's been a leader in controlling government spending and reducing taxes. He doesn't leave any doubt that he's Iowa's Senator. And if all of us work together, Roger Jepsen will be reelected as Iowa's Senator.

The third district of Iowa can also be proud of their Representative, Cooper Evans.

Audience. [*Chanting*] Coop! Coop! Coop!

The President. I must say, a moment ago you scared me when you started yelling for Coop. [*Laughter*] I have a little problem with one ear; I thought you were booing. [*Laughter*] Roger informed me of what you were saying—[*laughter*]—that it was all right.

But Cooper sits on the House Agriculture Committee and the House Select Committee on Aging. He serves his district well. He's been a strong voice in both his committees, and he's carried on the great Republican tradition begun by Senator Grassley before you elected to send Chuck to the Senate. These men, along with your other Iowa Republicans—Jim Leach, who is with us today, and Tom Tauke, who will join me in Des Moines—make an important contribution to the country.

We had a plan to rescue this nation in 1980, and that plan is working. Now it's time to take freedom's next step, to make sure that the progress that we've made will continue—not just through the next election, but through the next generation. And once again we're the ones with the clear idea of what must be done. In the coming months we must build a great coalition of Republicans, Independents, and disenchanted Democrats around our bold vision of an opportunity society for the future.

Let others appeal to greed and envy, pit group against group, treat people as helpless victims, and seek to weaken our national defense. Let them promise the Moon—they'll deliver green cheese. Their first promise begins with taking back all the tax reductions that we were able to pass with your help. They're captives of an anti-growth, dinosaur mentality that offers nothing for the future but repeating their failures of the past. For 44 of the last 50 years they controlled both Houses of Congress. They gave us annual deficits and a national debt of nearly a trillion dollars. But far from objecting then, they said this was good for us. Well, big government wasn't good for us then, and it isn't good for us now.

We have a positive vision of our citizens and our country: America moving confidently forward, her people united by shared values of faith and, as the Governor said, family and work and neighborhood and peace and freedom. We seek to bring out the best in every person, because we know every man and woman carries the spark of greatness.

As an opportunity society begins, it begins with growth, and we know how to create it. Our tax incentives spurred this recovery, but tax increases can destroy it. We are on the side of the little taxpayers, not the big tax spenders. I consider stopping them from taking more of your earnings an economic responsibility and a moral obligation. If the big spenders get their way, they'll charge everything on your taxpayer's express card and, believe me, they never leave home without it. [*Laughter*]

That's why we're urging needed reforms to bring greater responsibility to government spending. The Congress should stop fiddling and pass a constitutional amendment requiring a balanced Federal budget. Do you know who first started that idea and how long ago? And he's been touted as a Democrat hero ever since. I don't think he'd be happy with them. Thomas Jefferson in 1787, looking at the Constitution, says, "It lacks one thing. It lacks an article preventing the government from being able to borrow."

We also seek a line-item veto to prevent pork barrel projects from passing just because they're attached as amendments to important legislation. And if this Congress won't pass these reforms—and I'm excepting present company—then let's elect men and women who will.

Greater growth will also come from simplifying the tax code. We want to make the tax system more fair and easier to understand. And we want you to have the incentives of personal tax rates coming down, not going up. Along with these reforms, we will encourage growth by continuing to modernize our industries, expand our import markets—or export markets, I should say, and develop the new frontiers of high technology and space.

But America can only move forward if the foundation of our society and freedom is secure. Our families and communities must be able to live and work without fear of being mugged, robbed, and raped. We have a comprehensive crime bill that would provide long-overdue protection to law-abiding citizens. It would put an end to the liberal era of coddling criminals. The Senate with its Republican majority has passed that bill, but the House with its Democratic majority is sitting on it. Maybe it's time they felt some pressure from the grassroots. You know, you don't have to make them see the light; just make them feel the heat. [*Laughter*]

Building an opportunity society also means providing our children the best possible education. And here, too, we're the ones with courage to call for basic reforms. Overall spending on education soared by 600 percent over two decades, but the test scores—the SAT scores—went down, down, down. So, what do our critics want? More money for more programs. What America's schools really need are tougher standards, more homework, more discipline, merit pay for teachers, and our parents finally in charge.

Now there's one other reform that I hope you'll help us on—an amendment making it clear that the God who loves us be welcomed back into our children's classrooms. [*Applause*] I thank you, because as far as I'm concerned, He never should have been expelled in the first place. And just maybe, just maybe, speaking for nationwide, if we can get God and discipline back in our schools, we could get drugs and violence out.

Ben Franklin asked the Constitutional Convention in 1787—and he was speaking of the Lord—he said: "Have we now forgotten this powerful Friend? Or do we imagine we no longer need His assistance?"

An opportunity society, reaching for its future with confidence, sustained by faith, fair play, and a conviction that good and courageous people will flourish when they're free—this is our vision of a strong and prosperous America, at peace with itself and the world.

Just as America has always been synonymous with freedom, so, too, should she become the symbol of peace all over the

Earth. I'm confident that we can keep faith with that mission.

Peace is our highest aspiration. A lasting peace must be anchored by courage, realism, and unity. We must go beyond the control of nuclear weapons to actual reductions. And my dream is to see a day when nuclear weapons will be banished from the Earth all together. We remain flexible in our bargaining. I've repeatedly stressed this to the Soviets, and we're beginning to see some positive signs. But I must make one thing plain: As Commander in Chief, I have an obligation to protect this country, and I will never allow political expediency to influence these crucial negotiations.

I believe with all my heart that America is more prosperous, safe, and secure today than 4 years ago. Hope has been reborn, confidence is rising, a spirit of optimism is spreading across our land. We have made a new beginning, a dramatic and far-reaching step toward a much better future.

I urge you: Take our message, the Republican message, to the people. Remind them where we were, what we've done, and how far, together, we can still go. You—you have always been our greatest strength. You made the difference before; you can do it now. With your talent, your drive, and your heart, we can make history again. We can make 1984 the next great wave of a Republican renaissance. And in doing that, we can make our beloved country the source of all the dreams and opportunities she was placed on this good Earth to provide. We need only to believe in each other and in the God who has so blessed our land.

Thank you. God bless you all, and God bless America.

Note: The President spoke at 3:03 p.m. in the McElroy Auditorium. He was introduced by Gov. Terry Branstad.

Interview With Jim Zabel of WHO Radio in Des Moines, Iowa
February 20, 1984

Mr. Zabel. My name is Jim Zabel. I've been sports director of WHO Radio since 1944. And obviously we're honored and excited today to have the President of the United States, Ronald Reagan, who sat behind this microphone on many occasions from 1933 to 1937 when he had my job. He was sports director here at WHO. President, great to have you here. And, of course, your friend, and a great friend of WHO's, Charlie Gross—H.R. Gross, the former news director here.

The President. Yes.

Mr. Zabel. Now, the memories that this microphone right here evokes in you—what are they?

The President. Oh, my goodness. [*Laughter*] There are so many. It's like a film montage there of everything, the various events and the—I remember probably one outstanding occasion—the microphone of that kind—out at Birdland Park, and they were having the Olympic tryouts out there, the AAU tryouts for the Olympic team. And we were feeding network—going to feed the NBC network, and that was really tops. We had half an hour to fill. And some of the Olympic officials got in an argument, and I was on the air for 30 minutes, nationwide—[*laughter*]—and they did not run off one single swimming event.

I think I described every drop of water in the pool—[*laughter*]—everyone that was warming up, and what they were doing, and talking about, what events were going to be held. Went off the air and 2 minutes after we were off the air, they had the first event.

Mr. Zabel. But your adlib ability was really put to a super test with that machine right there, the old Western Union ticker-tape that used to bring in the Chicago Cubs re-creations to you.

The President. Yes.

Mr. Zabel. And you had a stick one time—in that famous story—you fouled it off 34 times, 35 times——

The President. [*Laughing*] Yes. It was—

you sat—there was a window here. Curly Waddel was the operator, sat on that side with the headphones, and he would type and slip it under the window to me. And they used to keep track—because there'd be seven or eight stations competing and broadcasting, and most of them live, right at the park—and we were within half a pitch of right up with the live ballgame all the time.

Mr. Zabel. Sure.

The President. To do that, he had to abbreviate things down, like in would come the paper, and it would say, "Out 4–3." Well, that meant out from second base to first base, that meant it had to be a grounder. So, you'd take it, and you'd say, "And Dean comes out of the windup, and here comes the pitch, and it's a hard hit ground ball down toward second base. So-and-so going over after the ball, picks it up, flips it over to first, just in time for the out." And by this time you're waiting for the next one. Or he would send you "S–1–C." And that meant strike one called. So, you'd say, "He's got the sign, comes out of the windup, here's the pitch, and it's a called strike, breaking over the outside corner just"—[*laughter*]—"above the knees." And all of that.

But the thing that you're talking about was the time that—it was the ninth inning, the Cards and the Cubs, tied up 0–0, and he was typing, and I thought there's a play coming. And he kept shaking his head when I had—and it was Dean on the mound—and I had Billy Jurgess at the plate. And I had him getting a sign from the catcher, and finally here comes the slip of paper, and it said, "The wires have gone dead." And I knew in that ninth inning if I suddenly said, "Well, we'll have a little interlude of music while we get back connected with the ballpark," we'd lose every—they'd all turn on some of those other stations. So, I thought, "There's only one thing that can get in the—doesn't get in the score book: foul ball."

So, I had Jurgess foul one, and then I had him foul another. And then I had him foul one that missed a homerun by a foot. Then I described two kids down back of third base that—[*laughter*]—were in a fight over the ball that had gone into the stands there.

And pretty soon I know I'm beginning to set a world record for somebody standing at the plate and hitting successive fouls, if anyone ever kept those figures. And I was beginning to sweat a little, because I knew now that if I told them we'd lost the wire they'd know I hadn't been telling the truth.

Mr. Zabel. Who finally did get the hit in that game?

The President. Well, just—pretty soon, Curly started typing. And I had him throw another pitch, and in came the slip, and then I started giggling. I had trouble getting it out, because the slip said Jurgess popped out on the first ball pitched. [*Laughter*]

Mr. Zabel. That's good.

Charlie Gross, let's bring you in here. You were known as kind of a meticulous perfectionist at the time. Here was a young sportscaster. Did he live up to your standards when you were here?

Representative Gross. The young sportscaster?

Mr. Zabel. Yes.

Representative Gross. Oh, yes, sir. Yes, sir.

Mr. Zabel. You kind of made him toe the line?

Representative Gross. This was the source of all sports news around here—that is, by way of radio—this gentleman here, the President.

Mr. Zabel. Did you project in him at that time, when he was 22, 23 years old, the qualities that enabled him to become President of the United States?

Representative Gross. No, I never—he was a Democrat. He belonged to the wrong party—[*laughter*]—at this time, but——

The President. Yeah, but I outgrew that.

Representative Gross. Yes, but he outgrew it. That's right. [*Laughter*] No, I never thought, of course, that he would become President of the United States and that I would be here at his side tonight.

Mr. Zabel. Mr. President, this microphone brings back—you were selected Wheaties Sportscaster of the Year one time. You did——

The President. Yeah.

Mr. Zabel. ——the Wheaties commercial, you did the Kentucky Club commercial——

The President. Yeah, they sponsored an

awful lot of baseball, Wheaties did.

Mr. Zabel. And when you came into Des Moines today, down Fleur Drive from the airport did you notice some changes about the city of Des Moines?

The President. Well, long about the time we got here—by the time that I got here, I was just prepared to turn right and go to 914 Walnut Street. And here I am in a whole new institution.

I've got to tell you one about——

Mr. Zabel. I want to hear one that you've got down here——

The President. ——Charlie Gross. Well, let me just tell you, he is a pioneer, and a true pioneer. Under the Fair Trade Practices Act back in the those depression days, radio was not allowed to do news, because it would be unfair. They thought that you could just go and put it in a microphone instead of having to have it put in print and out on the streets. And B.J. Palmer, who was then the head of the central broadcasting, decided that he was going to challenge that and we were going to have news. And only one news service would provide us with a newswire. And Charlie was the whole news department, including the writing and rewriting of the stories. And we went on the air with news, and it was a first in radio. It became a daily twice-a-day feature for his news.

And then, of course, he was a pioneer in another thing, as you know—when he went to Congress. It was no surprise to those of us that knew him that he would be known as the conscience of the Congress, that his colleagues would go to him because they knew he had read the bills, and they'd go to him before they voted to find out.

Representative Gross. You're being overly generous.

The President. No, I'm not.

Mr. Zabel. Okay, Charlie. Mr. President, you told me when I did an interview with you in 1974 on the 50th anniversary of WHO Radio that the 5 years you spent here were 5 of the happiest years of your life.

The President. Oh, yes.

Mr. Zabel. Do you still look back on those that fondly?

The President. Oh, yes. They were really—those were foundation years, and I think everything that happened came out

of this.

Mr. Zabel. Well, it's the true American hero story—hitchhiking to Davenport, I believe, to get the job in the first place.

The President. Yes. Had a rather unusual audition from Pete McArthur, who was the program director then.

I had been told that in looking for a job in those depression days—and I'd hitchhiked all the way around the country quite a bit—I'd been told that you should ask an employer not for what you wanted to be—a sports announcer—just tell him you'd take any job to get in the station and then take your chances on moving up from there. So, I made my usual pitch of that kind after a number of turndowns to Pete. And this time, the turndown was really disappointing because he said, "Where were you last week? We auditioned 90 people and hired an announcer." And on my way out the door, I said, "How do you ever get to be a sports announcer if you can't get in a station?", and went on down to the elevator, which, fortunately, wasn't there.

And Pete, who was badly handicapped with arthritis and on two canes—I didn't know until I heard him thumping down the hall yelling at me—and he asked me what that was I said about sports. And I told him that's what I'd like to be. And he said, "You know anything about football?" And I said, "I played it for 8 years." He said, "Do you think you could tell me about a game and, if I was sitting there listening, I could see the game?" And I said, "I think so." And he took me in a studio, put me in front of one of these. No, they weren't even this one then—this was a modern one. This was the old carbon mike.

Mr. Zabel. Right.

The President. And he put me in front of that, and he said, "When the red light goes on, you start broadcasting an imaginary football game." And I did for about 15 minutes. It wasn't really imaginary. I knew I had to have names. So, I picked a game that I'd played in—in college, the previous fall—which we'd won in the last 20 seconds by a 65-yard touchdown run—I did not make the run. So, I chose that game and said, when the light came on, started—that we were in the 4th quarter. You know, I had everything. I had the long, blue shadows settling over the field——

Mr. Zabel. The famous long, blue shadows—[*laughter*]——

The President. Yes—the chill wind coming in through the end of the stadium— we didn't have a stadium, we had bleachers. [*Laughter*] And I did it for about the 15 minutes and made that winning touchdown. One thing I did put in. As a running guard, coming out and around and leading the interference—on that play, that day, Eureka College, I missed my man, the first man in the secondary. And I don't know how Bud Cole got by and reversed the field, because I missed him. In the broadcast, I nailed him. [*Laughter*] It was a magnificent block—[*laughter*]—key to the whole success of the play.

And he came in and told me to be there on Saturday, that I was broadcasting the Iowa-Minnesota game, and he would give me $5 and bus fare.

Mr. Zabel. The price hasn't changed any. [*Laughter*] No, I'm saying that facetiously. Well, Mr. President, obviously we're just thrilled and happy to have you here to reminisce about the old—let me ask you one question, from sportscaster to sportscaster—would you have stayed a sportscaster if the telegram had not come from Warner Brothers, do you think?

The President. I think so, yes. There had always been a sneaking lust in my heart for it—[*laughter*]—the theatric end of the business.

Mr. Zabel. Well, we have about eight to ten thousand people, I think, a full house waiting up at the auditorium. Can you tell us what you're going to tell them up there tonight?

The President. Well, I don't think anything that I say has been said by any of the eight other candidates who've been running around the State. [*Laughter*] I might have a little different twist on things than that. But I'm going to talk about this recovery that we have going and what I think is needed to keep it going.

Mr. Zabel. How does it feel to be back in Des Moines?

The President. Oh, great. It's too short, as always, but give me another 7½ minutes, and I'd be so far down nostalgia lane— [*laughter*]——

Mr. Zabel. Let me ask you one question a lot of people ask of me about you. What type of sportscaster were you? I mean, how do you categorize your style? What was it?

The President. Oh, I don't know. I always thought—I always had in mind a listener out there, and I thought that I was painting a word picture. If I was in the stadium over at University of Iowa broadcasting an Iowa football game, I always tried to use references like saying not just that they're on the 20-yard line, 15 yards in from the side of the field; I would say, "They're down here to the right on their own 20-yard line, 15 yards in from this side of the field" or place them. I always figured that he—that viewer out there—he or she must be able to get a picture in their minds of what it looked like.

Mr. Zabel. Well, you gave them a lot of pictures, Mr. President. A thrill to have you here at WHO today.

The President. I rambled on, but you shouldn't have turned me loose.

Mr. Zabel. Well, the fans love it, I'm sure. Thank you very much. Good luck to you tonight.

The President. Well, thank you.

Mr. Zabel. Congressman Gross, thank you for being here with us.

Representative Gross. Not at all. A pleasure to see you, sir.

Mr. Zabel. Thank you.

Note: The interview began at 5:21 p.m. at the WHO broadcasting studio.

Remarks at an Iowa Caucus Rally in Des Moines
February 20, 1984

Thank you very much. And Governor Terry Branstad, what a surprise! This is the first time that I have seen Melba since that night. [*Laughter*] So, it's the first time I've had a chance to tell you—the gun was empty; I didn't have any cartridges. [*Laughter*] If he hadn't of run when I told him to, I was going to have to throw it at him. [*Laughter*] [1]

Well, I tell you—Senator Jepsen and Mrs. Jepsen, Congressman Tauke and former Congressman Gross and Mrs. Gross, my good friend, Senator Paul Laxalt—coming here from Washington, DC, is a little like landing in the real world after an extended visit to the twilight zone. [*Laughter*]

On the way from the airport to here, I stopped and was on the air on WHO Radio. And if I don't get going on the remarks I'd intended to make, you're going to have a warm nostalgic bath, because I am being carried away by nostalgia.

I know and appreciate the people of Iowa. I know and respect your values, your love of God and family, your belief in the dignity of work, and your honest patriotism. I learned about this when I lived and worked here many years ago. And during that time I came to know and work with an Iowan who was destined to one day be called "the conscience of the United States Congress." His name was H.R. Gross. And long before either of us had any thought of

---

[1] *The President was referring to an incident in 1933 when he lived in Des Moines. Melba King, then a nursing student, was accosted on a sidewalk by a robber who grabbed her purse and suitcase. The President, then a sportscaster for WHO Radio, saw the attempted robbery from his second floor apartment. He pointed an automatic pistol at the would-be robber, who dropped the purse and suitcase and fled. The President then escorted Melba to the nursing school.*

In his introductory remarks, Governor Branstad related the story and introduced Mrs. King.

a political career, H.R. and I worked at WHO Radio. And that was where I had, among other things, some lessons in the words—or in the economy of words.

One day Ed Reimers—you remember Ed Reimers—you're in good hands. Ed was an announcer on the staff there, and he and I were in the studio. And Ed had just done the station break. It takes about 20 seconds before you went back to the network program. And not having a commercial or anything to fill the time, he said, "This is radio station WHO, Des Moines, Iowa." And in a few minutes the studio door opened and our boss came in, B.J. Palmer. And he said, "I heard the station break, Ed." Ed said, "Yes, B.J." He said, "You know, advertisers pay a lot to get their messages on the air. We should eliminate as much unnecessary conversation as we can." And then he said, "You don't need to say, 'This is.' [*Laughter*] If they're listening, they know 'this is.'" [*Laughter*] Ed said, "Yes, B.J." And he says, "And, Ed, you don't need 'radio station.' That's all their sets can get." [*Laughter*] And, again, Ed said, "Yes, B.J." Now he's down to "WHO, Des Moines, Iowa." And B.J. started to leave, got halfway through the door, and then turned back and over his shoulder said, "Ed, there's only one Des Moines, and it's in Iowa." [*Laughter*] From then on, we knew the station break would be, "WHO, Des Moines."

Well, in the coming election the political rhetoric is going to be pretty thick. You've had about a year of it already. Our biggest challenge as Republicans is to focus public attention on what is behind the words and promises and not get lost in the excess words.

The candidates in the other party have already laid out a strategy of promising everything to everybody. You've had a gang of them swimming all over the State in the past few weeks. They've got so many candidates vying for votes in today's caucuses that there haven't been enough promises to go around. [*Laughter*]

Yes, we Republicans make promises, but

not to special interest groups to be paid from the public treasury and not promises that cancel each other out, because if you keep one promise to one group you'll have to break the promise you made to another group.

Four years ago, the inflation monster was loose in this land, mangling the middle class, destroying the value of the lifelong savings of older Americans, and hitting the poor and minorities hard. A family on a fixed income of $10,000 at the beginning of 1979, by the end of 1980, he had lost $2,000 in purchasing power just because of that inflation. The experts were telling us it would take a decade to wring inflation out of the economy.

We promised to put that monster back in a cage, and that's just what we've done. We took runaway, double-digit inflation and brought it down to less than 4 percent last year, and it's been that way for 2 years now.

Government spending was growing at a rate of 17 percent per year when we got to Washington. We have cut that more than half. To pay for that Federal growth, the tax system we inherited was siphoning off an ever-increasing share of the people's money. The Federal tax take doubled just between 1976 and 1981.

We promised an across-the-board tax rate reduction. And that's exactly what we provided. We're also indexing tax rates beginning in 1985, so that government will no longer be able to make a profit from inflation at the people's expense.

And there's one tax reform of which I'm particularly proud. The inheritance tax had gotten to the point where it was destroying the right of hard-working people to pass their family farm or family business to their children or their widows. We were restoring that right by increasing the inheritance tax exemption for the children and eliminating it altogether for surviving spouses. As far as I'm concerned, we should never have been taxing widows like that in the first place.

We inherited a prime interest rate that was going through the roof at 21½ percent when we got to Washington. We promised to bring the prime rate down.

[*At this point, the President was interrupted by a heckler. Others in the audience booed the heckler. The President then resumed speaking.*]

Don't tell me one of the eight is here? [*Laughter*]

We have cut that prime rate down, almost in half. And we can and must make more progress in reducing interest rates.

Now, we also inherited economic stagnation. Productivity was actually falling. Major industries were just hanging on with little hope in sight. We promised to turn this situation around, to reinvigorate the economy and get America moving again.

It's taken time to put our program in place and for it to take hold. And, my, aren't we happy we stuck to our guns? This year no Republican should hesitate asking people if they're better off than they were 4 years ago.

We're in the first phase of a recovery that has astounded the experts. The gross national product was up a healthy 6.2 percent last year. Unemployment is dropping sharply. Retail sales are soaring. Housing starts and auto sales are up. Last month, new housing starts were at the highest level since 1978. Productivity, after falling in the 2 years before we took office, rose 3½ percent last year. Venture capital, which was under a billion dollars in 1980, was $4 billion last year. Because of progress in controlling inflation and our tax cuts, real take-home pay has been rising during the past 2 years after having dropped significantly in the 4 previous years.

This recovery is going to benefit everyone, especially the less fortunate, by creating——

[*At this point, the President was again interrupted by heckling from a section of the audience.*]

Is there an echo in here? [*Laughter*]

By creating more jobs and providing all Americans with more opportunity, we're going to benefit everyone. And those who suggest that somehow our policies are unfair are the same ones who gave this country economic stagnation and ruinous inflation. The only thing fair about their program was that they didn't discriminate;

they made everybody miserable.

Listen carefully when you hear screeching accusations about fairness. Just below the surface, you'll hear an appeal to greed and envy totally inconsistent with the American spirit. I predict when given the chance, the American people will choose opportunity and economic growth over greed and envy any day of the week.

The opposition will try to sell the American people the same old idea of Federal control and regulations, only this time it'll be packaged in a bright new box.

One regulation being promoted is a domestic content law, which would be interpreted by our trading partners in Japan and Europe as another restriction on international commerce. This is just the kind of tinkering that can backfire on the American farmer. We should be trying to open up markets and stimulate trade between nations, not protect special interests by throwing monkey wrenches into the works.

If history suggests anything, it is that government, even when directed by well-meaning individuals, usually causes more problems than it solves.

How many of you can remember the howls of anguish from the liberals when one of my first acts as President was to decontrol the price of oil? They ranted and raved that the consumer would be taken to the cleaners. Well, instead, by freeing the market, we unleashed a stampede of exploration. Production went up, contributing to a developing world glut of oil, and today the price of oil and gas at the pump is lower than it was 3 years ago.

Now, one more thing. If the inflation we inherited had continued, the price of gasoline would be $1 a gallon more than it is today, just by virtue of inflation. The cost of doing business and the price of energy are now substantially less. And that's what I call "Republican fairness."

Over these last 3 years we've proven that we can be trusted to keep our word. Now, we must let it be known that we're not expecting people to vote for us because of what we've done, but for what we will do. We, as Republicans, have a bold vision for the future, and unlike our opposition, it's not based on increasing government taxing, spending, regulating, or inflating. Real

progress comes not from expanding the power of government, but, instead, in increasing freedom and opportunity.

Nowhere is this more clear than in one of America's biggest industries—agriculture. I don't have to tell you how the inflationary spiral and economic uncertainty of the last decade devastated the American farmer. The interest rates, the incredible rise in the cost of doing business, and the high taxes were bad enough. Then, to add insult to injury, your own government cut your legs out from under you by making you bear the full burden of a grain embargo against the Soviet Union.

Well, during the 1980 campaign, we promised to end that ill-conceived embargo. And that's another promise we kept. We went one step further. We negotiated a new long-term grain agreement with the Soviet Union that requires the Soviets to buy 50 percent more U.S. grain than they did under the old agreement.

These last 3 years we've been trying to keep American farmers going till they, like our economy, recover from the destructive liberal policies of the past. It's a long and arduous process. Sometimes progress comes step by step. But we've been doing our best to open new markets for our farmers and make certain they aren't undercut by unfair competition. Given open and free markets, along with stable economic conditions at home, I have faith that our farmers can produce more, sell more, and do it more efficiently than anyone else in the world.

You know, there are other parts of the world where farming is done on a different basis than here. And I happen to have a new hobby. I've taken to collecting jokes that I can confirm from defectors and refugees that are actually told by the Russian people among themselves, and that sort of display a lack of respect or some cynicism for their own government. And one of the latest that I heard had to do with a Commissar in the Soviet Union who went out to one of those state collective farms, grabbed the first worker he came to, and said, "Comrade, are there any complaints?" And he said, "Oh, no, Comrade Commissar, no complaints. I've never heard anyone complain." And he said, "Good. How are the crops?" "Oh," he said, "the crops, never been better, just wonderful." And he said, "How about potatoes?" "Oh," he said, "Comrade Commissar, if we could put the potatoes in one pile they would reach the foot of God." And the Commissar said, "This is the Soviet Union. There is no God." And he said, "That's all right, there are no potatoes." [*Laughter*]

Creating stable economic conditions has been the reason that we've fought so hard to get spending and taxes under control these last few years. It's been one of the pivotal economic battles of our time. And I just want you to know how proud I've been to have Congressmen Evans, Tauke, and Leach at my side. All I have to ask is, send me more like them. And on election day, don't just go out and vote for them, tell your friends and neighbors to get out and vote for them, too.

And then there is Senator Jepsen, who works side by side with your other fine Republican Senator, Chuck Grassley. I don't have to tell you how important Republican control of the Senate has been to the progress we've made. We couldn't have done any of it without controlling that one House. Senator Jepsen has been a mighty force for responsible government and the farmers best friend in Washington. We couldn't have accomplished what we did

without him. Senator Jepsen and his lovely wife, Dee, reflect all the good qualities for which the people of Iowa are so admired. And you should all be proud of the job he's doing as your United States Senator. He deserves all our support for reelection.

When you leave here, those of you who are going to your Republican caucuses, keep in mind that in a free country like ours the future will be determined not only by what we believe but by what we do. Iowans have much of which to be proud. Together, we can keep America the decent land of freedom and opportunity that God intended it to be.

I thank you, all of you, for what you've done and what you will do. God bless you. Thank you very much.

Note: The President spoke at 6 p.m. in the Veterans Auditorium. He was introduced by Gov. Terry Branstad.

Prior to his remarks, the President met at the auditorium with Republican Party officials and Reagan-Bush campaign leaders. Following the rally, he met with Kathryn Graf, Governor Branstad's liaison for the Fifty States Project, and Sue Fallon, executive director of the project, to receive Iowa's report on the project. The President then left Des Moines and returned to Washington, DC.

Statement on the Murder of Leamon (Ray) Hunt
February 21, 1984

The cowardly murder of Ray Hunt is another painful reminder of the reality of terrorism. In the 1980's terrorism is more and more used by governments as a weapon of policy. It is a challenge to all of us and to everything we believe in.

American personnel abroad are targets because they represent us. America is a target because those who commit such crimes are directing their fire at our country's most basic interests, policies, and values. Ray Hunt was a target because as head of the multinational force and observers in the Sinai, he was helping to imple-

ment the peace treaty between Egypt and Israel. Our role in helping bring peace to the Middle East is one of our country's proudest achievements; for this very reason it is bitterly opposed by the enemies of peace.

There is another message here. Ray Hunt exemplified the best in America. He represented in his career the talent, dedication, and decency of so many other men and women who do their country's work abroad—helping others, keeping the peace, serving their country.

We remember our gallant soldiers, sailors,

airmen, and marines who made the supreme sacrifice throughout our history defending freedom. We owe our gratitude as well to the thousands of Americans who serve in a civilian capacity—in the Foreign Service or as attachés or international civil servants or in other essential jobs—because they, too, are on the frontlines. Many of them, too, have taken the risks or paid the price of being an American.

They did it for us, and we should never forget it.

Announcement of the Recipients of the Presidential Medal of Freedom
February 21, 1984

The President today announced his intention to award the Presidential Medal of Freedom, the highest civilian award of our government, at a luncheon to be held at the White House on March 26, 1984. The following individuals will be awarded this prestigious award by the President:

Senator Howard Baker, for his contribution in the field of government service;

James Cagney, for his contribution in the field of entertainment and the arts;

Whittaker Chambers (posthumous), for his contribution in the field of public service;

Leo Cherne, for his contribution in the field of government service and humanitarianism;

Dr. Denton Cooley, for his contribution in the field of medicine and surgery;

Tennessee Ernie Ford, for his contribution in the field of entertainment and the arts;

Dr. Hector Garcia, for his contribution in the field of humanitarianism;

Gen. Andrew Goodpaster, for his contribution in the field of international affairs;

Lincoln Kirstein, for his contribution in the field of dance and the arts;

Louis L'Amour, for his contribution in the field of literature and the arts;

The Rev. Norman Vincent Peale, for his contribution in the field of theology;

Jackie Robinson (posthumous), for his contribution in the field of sportsmanship;

Egyptian President Anwar Sadat (posthumous), for his contribution in the field of world affairs and peace; and

Eunice Kennedy Shriver, for her contribution in the field of mental retardation.

Remarks on Receiving the Report of the Commission on Security and Economic Assistance
February 21, 1984

Secretary of State Shultz. Mr. President, I want to thank you for giving us a chance to present you with a copy of the report of the Commission on Security and Economic Assistance.

I think this is an extremely important report on a subject of tremendous moment. I asked Frank Carlucci to be Chairman of it, and Larry Silverman, Lane Kirkland, and Cliff Warden to be Cochairmen, and many others to take part. It's notable that nine of the Commission members are from the Congress. You can see that by looking around. They served as members and members ex officio; joined in very strongly in the discussions.

Others on the Commission, many of whom are sitting here, are representatives of business, of labor, of private voluntary organizations, the university world, and others professionally interested in our foreign policy. And they produced a thoughtful and bipartisan statement.

The last time there was a comprehensive

review of our security and economic assistance programs was in 1970. I think we all know, Mr. President, that there have been profound changes since then in the world out there that we're working with. There are countries in the family of free nations today who can point to our security assistance as a key ingredient in their struggle to remain free. And we can similarly point with pride to many countries where our assistance is promoting economic development and is essential for that end.

Our efforts in science and technology have contributed to such successes as the Green Revolution. Still, Mr. President, as you are only too aware, threats to the security of friendly countries are around us throughout the world. Some are military in nature; others stem from their inability to meet the aspirations of their peoples. So, it is very much in the interest of the United States—and this report emphasizes this—to help these countries grow into free, open, and self-sustaining societies.

Mr. President, I've reviewed this report and talked with Frank and other members of the committee a great deal about it, and I commend it to you. It's the collective insight of a most knowledgeable and distinguished group of people, and its recommendations will help us design a more effective program. In fact, they already have done that. As we were working through the budget process, as you know, we had the benefit of seeing these recommendations evolving. So we will have an improved program, grounded in our national interest, and meriting the full support of the American people.

I think among the things that they call for that's especially important and welcome—which we've been trying to do—is to emphasize the importance of a close integration between the security assistance and security needs that we're trying to serve, the problems of economic development, and the political aspirations of the countries that we're working with. We can see that all around the world and, most notably, it sounds like a refrain of the bipartisan Kissinger commission—the same kind of emphasis.

A number of the recommendations in this report are already being carried out. We

are asking in your fiscal '85 budget—or you are—for more resources. We proposed some new initiatives in Africa and in the Caribbean Basin, with particular emphasis on reform in economic policy and private sector growth. We've sought greater flexibility in the terms of military assistance where circumstances warrant, and we're increasing our emphasis on training, science, and technology and institutional development. And we want to make all of this go by working with the congressional leadership in a bipartisan spirit to put across this very important program of foreign assistance.

The Commission has made a number of other major concerns and recommendations, and we're reviewing them and giving everything a great deal of thought.

Mr. President, finally, I'd like to thank very much Frank Carlucci, who is one of those enduring public servants. I first knew him when he was running the poverty program. I got him to come over and help me run the Office of Management and Budget. Then he worked with Cap over in HEW and had a great hand in the CIA and then in the Defense Department. And he's no sooner in the private sector when we call him back. And when you say, "Frank, there's something important for you to do to serve your country," he says, "Yes." And that's the kind of public servant that we really need in the private sector or public sector.

So, I want to thank Frank and, also, all the other members of the Commission. But Frank gave it the leadership, and I appreciate it very much.

Frank also has the copies of this report, and so here is a copy, Mr. President, of this report. And just so the Vice President doesn't fail to read it, I want to be sure he has a copy, too. [*Laughter*] I understand he's a very influential guy around here. [*Laughter*]

The President. Yes, he is.

Well, George, I thank you very much. And many thanks to you, Frank Carlucci, and to all the people who put this together.

When economic misfortune creates instability or external threats endanger our friends, our response can make the difference between peaceful development or chaos and violence. And that's why we've put such emphasis on our own defense and on foreign assistance programs.

The Commission's concern regarding the significant decline in support for foreign assistance is well-founded. Our assistance program is not an end in itself. Yes, we seek to help people build better lives economically and across the whole spectrum of human needs and aspirations. Americans can be proud of our tradition of helping others in need. Whether it be humanitarian aid in response to natural disasters, economic support for struggling countries, or security assistance to friends threatened by external aggression, America has always been there.

Economic and security assistance are not just a moral duty; they also serve our national interests. When conceived and administered well, assistance programs strengthen our foreign policy and enhance the security of our nation. By promoting economic development in needy countries, we bolster the vitality and security of the free world. Well-conceived assistance programs create stronger partnerships, establish mutual confidence, and make for a safer world.

When our friends face threats to their security, investors shy away and economic growth weakens. So, we must work hard to provide the right balance of both economic and military assistance. The key to success, as it is with all elements of our foreign policy, rests in our ability to forge a bipartisan consensus.

This Commission has searched for reasonable ways to better use our scarce resources and to generate greater congressional and public support for foreign assistance programs. It's now up to all of us to take advantage of what the Commission has done. We will—if we go forward in the same spirit—strengthen our national security and offer the promise of a safer, brighter future to millions of people all over the world.

I thank all of you very much for being here and, again, I thank the Commission for their fine work. Sometimes when the going is rough and sometimes when we wonder with our own problems whether we can keep on doing this help, maybe we should all read the words again of a former Prime Minister, some years ago, of Australia. And I can't quote him exactly, although I have the quote in a drawer upstairs, but where he said he wondered if the smaller nations of the world had ever thought where they would be if it were not for this United States, so willing to come to their aid and to help wherever help was needed. And it was a beautiful tribute, delivered very sincerely, by someone saying what maybe sometimes we forget about ourselves and something that should be a great source of pride to all of us.

So, again, I thank you all very much. Frank, thank you.

Note: Secretary Shultz spoke at 1:34 p.m. in the East Room at the White House.

Message to the Senate Returning Without Approval the Water Resources Research Bill
February 21, 1984

To the Senate of the United States:

I am returning herewith without my approval S. 684, an act "To authorize an ongoing program of water resources research, and for other purposes."

Title I would authorize appropriations totalling $36 million annually for the fiscal years 1985–1989 for a variety of water resources research activities throughout the nation, including a new, separate authorization of grants for the development of water technology, which is not an appropriate Federal activity.

Title II would convey desalting test facilities that are no longer in Federal use to Wrightsville Beach, North Carolina, and Roswell, New Mexico. The Administration has supported these conveyances. I would be pleased to sign a bill that provides only for them.

For some twenty years, the Federal government has provided "seed money" for the type of water research that would be authorized by Title I. This Federal support has produced a number of successful State water research institutes. I believe that these State institutes are now at a point where further Federal involvement in their research activities is not necessary. They can stand and continue to succeed on their own.

Moreover, the water research that S. 684 would promote can be characterized as mostly local or in some cases regional in nature. The focus of such research will of course vary from State to State because water problems and needs often differ by region. The States and private industry should be fully responsible for financing research necessary to deal with their own particular problems and needs.

If we are to truly succeed in reducing Federal spending we must sort out those responsibilities which are appropriately Federal from those which can be more effectively and fairly implemented at the State and local level.

Accordingly, I feel constrained to disapprove S. 684.

RONALD REAGAN

The White House,
February 21, 1984.

Note: The Senate and the House of Representatives voted to override the President's veto on March 21 and 22, respectively. As enacted, S. 684 is Public Law 98-242.

Nomination of David B. Rohr To Be a Member of the United States International Trade Commission
February 22, 1984

The President today announced his intention to nominate David B. Rohr to be a member of the United States International Trade Commission for the remainder of the term expiring December 16, 1985. He would succeed William R. Alberger.

Mr. Rohr is currently staff director, Subcommittee on Trade, Committee on Ways and Means, U.S. House of Representatives. Previously, he was professional staff member, Subcommittee on Trade, Committee on Ways and Means, U.S. House of Representatives (1974–1980); Director, Trade Negotiations and Agreements Division, Office of International Trade Policy, U.S. Department of Commerce (1970–1974); international economist, Office of Commercial and Financial Policy (1961–1970); and supervisor, master scheduling staff, Stanley Aviation Corp. (1959–1960).

Mr. Rohr graduated from Colorado State University (B.S., 1958; M.S., 1963). He was a National Institute of Public Affairs Fellow at Stanford University (1967–1968). He is married, has two children, and resides in Laurel, MD. He was born April 18, 1933, in Hartford, CT.

Message to the Congress Reporting Budget Deferrals
February 22, 1984

To the Congress of the United States:

In accordance with the Impoundment Control Act of 1974, I herewith report seven new deferrals of budget authority totaling $28,960,700.

The deferrals affect the Departments of Interior, Justice and Transportation. The details of the deferrals are contained in the attached reports.

RONALD REAGAN

The White House,
February 22, 1984.

Note: The attachments detailing the deferrals are printed in the Federal Register *of February 28, 1984.*

Appointment of Two Members of the President's Advisory Committee on Women's Business Ownership
February 22, 1984

The President today announced his intention to appoint the following individuals to be members of the President's Advisory Committee on Women's Business Ownership. These are new positions.

Paula Brown is currently president of Brown and Associates in Washington, DC. She graduated from Southern Methodist University (B.A., 1979). She was born June 25, 1959, in Dallas County, TX.

Donald Vincent Seibert is currently on the board of directors of J.C. Penney Co. in New York, NY. He attended the University of Cincinnati. He was born August 17, 1923, in Hamilton, OH.

The President's News Conference
February 22, 1984

Legislative Priorities

The President. I have a short statement— good evening.

The Congress has returned, as you know, from its recess. Important business is pending, and I'll be commenting on much of this in the weeks ahead. But tonight I want to highlight three matters at the top of the domestic agenda for the next 10 days.

First is crime. The Senate is completing its work on the most sweeping anticrime bill in more than a decade. Our legislation provides a long overdue protection to law-abiding Americans, and it would help put an end to the era of coddling criminals. The security of our people should take precedence over partisan politics, so I ask the House to stop dragging its feet and to act promptly.

Second, prayer in schools. The Senate will begin debate shortly on whether to permit voluntary prayer again in our nation's schools, our children's schools. And a huge majority of Americans favor restoring this long-cherished tradition of religious freedom. I urge the Senate to reaffirm that voluntary prayer in school is indeed a basic right of our people, and I hope the House will follow suit.

Third are deficits. It's been almost a month since I called for negotiations to reach agreement on a downpayment on the projected deficits. We've sought to schedule meetings almost every day, but Democratic representatives have begged away from all but one meeting. It's ironic that those who demanded negotiations have been so reluctant to negotiate. Be that as it may, it's time to get down to business. If we don't act soon, we'll lose another year to fruitless political posturing and legislative stalemate.

So, I'm pleased to announce they have agreed to attend their second meeting tomorrow. We'll be prepared to comment on their suggestions on defense spending. I trust they'll be prepared to answer our specific proposal for a hundred billion dollars in deficit reduction measures over the next

3 years, so that together we can get something constructive done.

And now, Mike [Michael Putzel, Associated Press], I'm sure you have something on your mind.

U.S. Involvement in Lebanon

Q. Mr. President, the marines you sent to Lebanon 17 months ago are now being withdrawn on your orders. Considering their inability to achieve their peacekeeping mission and the casualties they suffered, has the United States lost credibility in the region? Has Syria won? And where do we go from here?

The President. Well, in the first place, no, I don't think, first of all, that you can say we have lost as yet. I know that things don't look bright, as bright as they have at some times in this last year and a half since they've been there, but I think it's time to review a little history here and what this mission was and is.

A year and a half or so ago, we and some of our allies—the United Kingdom, France, and Italy—decided on this idea of a multinational force, all of us to contribute troops to go there on a stabilizing mission, not a combat mission at all. And I would like to recall what the situation was. There've been five wars in the last 36 years between Syria and Israel. Israel had crossed the Lebanese border because of terrorist attacks across her northern border, attacks on her civilians, and Israel had advanced all the way to Beirut.

There were somewhere between ten and fifteen thousand PLO terrorists in Beirut, and a pitched war was being fought right there in the streets with thousands of casualties among civilians. Syria was also on Lebanese soil. Since 1975 Lebanon had been fighting a kind of civil war among its own people. There was very little in the way of a government in Lebanon by this time. The PLO—finally there was an indication that they would be willing to depart from Lebanon, but they were fearful of stopping fighting for fear that they would then, if they tried in an orderly way to get out, they would be massacred. This, again, was one of the reasons for our stabilizing force going in from the four countries.

We went in with the idea that as they left, then the other two countries, Syria and Israel, could withdraw. Then, as a government was put in place in Lebanon—and we helped and intended from the beginning to help them restore their military capability not only with weapons but with training and all—that then, as Lebanon with a government was able to move out into the areas that had been occupied by Syria and Israel and where were the factions that had been part of the internecine warfare, the force put in by ourselves and the allies would have constituted behind their advance a stabilizing force there.

Now, that was the mission. We wanted to prevent a war between Syria and Israel. It was a part and brought about by our proposal for an overall peace settlement in the Middle East, where we were going to try and bring, once and for all, the Arab nations and Israel together, to do what Egypt before them had done.

Great progress was made in the first year. First of all, the PLO did leave. The Israelis did start a phased withdrawal and evidenced their intention to move back toward their own borders. Syria then reneged—having said that it would leave—and refused to leave, even though they were asked by the present Government of Lebanon. The first President was the brother of this present President. He was assassinated shortly after he took office, and a number of his Cabinet officials were murdered. He was elected, this President, as was his brother, under the laws of that country.

A few months ago, late summer or early fall, because of the progress—remember the talks that had started in Geneva about broadening the base of the government, to take in those factions that had been fighting against Lebanon and bring them in to be a part of the government, so that it was broad-based and gave every element in the country representation. Those meetings went on. I think there was progress in that.

The Government of Lebanon then arrived at an agreement with Israel for peace between them and a withdrawal of Israel and protection of the northern border so that the terrorist attacks that had prompted their invasion would no longer exist. As this much success came to be, terrorist attacks began against the members of the multinational force on the part of those who don't want a peaceful settlement and who don't want a solution to the problem. And I think this is an indication of the success that this stabilizing force was having, that the efforts were made and the great tragedy took place with our marines with the suicide attack there.

Now, we still have an Ambassador at Large there that is commuting between Damascus and Beirut, Tel Aviv, trying to help wherever we can in bringing about a peaceful settlement. I have no hesitation in saying that I have no regret of the fact that we went in there with the idea of trying to bring peace to that troubled country.

We are redeploying, because once the terrorist attacks started, there was no way that we could really contribute to the original mission by staying there as a target just hunkering down and waiting for further attacks. So, the forces have been moved, redeployed—ours as well as others, and ours are going to be on the vessels offshore.

But as long as there's a chance for a peaceful solution, we're going to try and see if there's any contribution we can make to achieving that. And as long as that chance exists, I'm not going to give up and say, "Well, it's all over." And we're not bugging out; we're just going to a little more defensible position.

Q. If I may follow up, Mr. President, you said that the terrorist attacks were a factor in the withdrawal. Does this mean that terrorist attacks like that can succeed in the Middle East and elsewhere?

The President. No, I had said that about those who urged us to simply bug out and come all the way home, and I said that that would be an admission. But I don't think that simply redeploying to a more defensible position, because terrorist attacks—no one has still found a truly foolproof defense against these surprise attacks, particularly when the attackers are willing to give their own lives.

So, no, we're on hand. We still will have marines there defending, as is customary of the marines, defending our Embassy and our Embassy personnel there. And we have been discussing with the Gemayel forces

sending some training teams in that have been specializing in things like terrorism for further training of their forces.

Q. Mr. President, on February 2, you told the Wall Street Journal that if we pulled out of Lebanon it would be disastrous results worldwide for us. And you also said you weren't going to cut and run even though there is a widespread perception that that's what we're doing. My question, sir, is, do you think we will have now disastrous results worldwide because of this pullout? And I'd like to follow up.

The President. Helen [Helen Thomas, United Press International], I don't think so, because I think that those people who make decisions and so forth, and who have to make them based on what is going on, they're not going to see this as cutting and running, because, as I say, they are on the ships and that naval task force is going to stay where it is. And so, I don't think that they're going to view this in the disastrous way that I had—because when I was speaking then, I was talking in reply to those who were urging us to just pick up and go home without any regard to whether our allies were to do the same thing or not. We've stayed in consultation with them. We're acting together and in sync with them.

Q. Under what circumstance would you send the marines back in?

The President. Well, that's a hypothetical that I don't know whether I could answer. If—let me say this—if they could improve the possibility of carrying out their mission, then, yes, that would be a reason for sending them in.

Andrea [Andrea Mitchell, NBC News]?

Q. Mr. President, when our marine compound was bombed, a lot of the parents of those young men said that they wondered what was the reason for the mission, and you've tried to explain the mission tonight. But can you say to those parents, now that you've withdrawn the marines to the ships, why more than 260 young men died there?

The President. Andrea, I have talked to a great many of the families, the widows, and the parents of the men who died there in that one terrible holocaust, and I have been amazed at their attitude, which was one of complete confidence that it was a worthwhile mission. And most of them based that on the letters that they were receiving from their sons and husbands, who said they believed in the mission, that they were there, that it was a worthwhile mission. And many of them expressed a pride in being there.

I'm sure that now some of the younger men that are not really aware that this is a redeployment more than a coming home thing and have been quoted as saying that they're sorry that they were not able to complete their mission. Well, I don't see their mission as being over yet. And I don't think people knowledgeable over there with what's going on see it as over yet.

Q. Well, sir, the Secretary of State has been one of those who is said to be very discouraged and has said that in Lebanon the light at the end of the tunnel can be the train coming at you. Can you tell us whether you share that discouragement? And would you accept a resignation from George Shultz, who, some people feel, has failed in this policy?

The President. No, I wouldn't. And he has not failed. And I have seen that talk, and I think it's disgraceful, frankly. I think he has done a splendid job. And I have every confidence in the world in him. And I hope he doesn't have any thoughts about leaving us at this point.

The idea for the mission happened to be mine—sitting in the Situation Room in a meeting with all of the people that are concerned in these affairs. And he and our Ambassadors, beginning with Phil Habib, and then Bud McFarlane, and now Don Rumsfeld—all of these have been doing a splendid job there. And we're going to continue, as I say, as long as there is a chance.

You. You—Pat [Patrick McGrath, Metromedia News]. [*Laughter*] My finger must not aim right. [*Laughter*]

Q. Someone jumping in the back.

Mr. President, our policy on naval shelling has been that it's in response to attacks against our marines on the ground. Now that the marines are being withdrawn to the safety of ships, does this mean that there will be an end to U.S. shelling of Lebanon?

The President. Well, there hasn't been some shelling for quite a while. But remember, the most recent shelling was not because of attacks on the marines at the airport; it was because of shelling of our Embassy. Now, that's United States territory. And our Embassy personnel for a number of days were living in the basement. And for whatever protection that could be— there was one direct hit on, I think it was the residence, I'm not sure whether it was that or the Embassy headquarters—and that's what we were responding to.

But we are behaving with restraint now. We are flying reconnaissance flights, and there have been some instances of firing on them—without result, I'm pleased to say. And we have not responded, because we think this is a time for restraint and for hoping to cool things down.

Q. Mr. President, if I may follow up. Did you say earlier—or suggest earlier—that there may now be some question about whether U.S. troops will be sent in to train the Gemayel government forces?

The President. Well, this has been one of the things that we're planning. And we're watching developments here as to when that might be—they might be too busy right now to being trained. We're waiting until we can coordinate with them.

Yes?

U.S. Oil Exports

Q. Back home, Mr. President. This week the Senate will consider amendments to the Export Administration Act. One will be to lift the ban on the export of Alaskan oil, allowing it to be sold to markets in the Far East. If a change in the law were to take place, it would reduce our trade deficit with Japan; it would reduce the Federal deficit by generating new revenues from increased domestic exploration and production; provide safer and cheaper transportation instead of going through the Panama Canal—and there are many other things. Your administration has privately supported this. Will you campaign aggressively when it's being considered by Congress?

The President. Well, we're still looking and studying at this. There are still some problems about it. And, I share the view that it would be an asset to the United States to do this.

Q. May I ask you if one of your problems in making a final decision is the opposition that the maritime unions have expressed?

The President. Well, I have to say that consideration of our merchant marine, the maritime force, has to be one, because they are essential to our national defense and as an adjunct to the Navy. And we want to make sure that there is a merchant marine in existence in this country.

Bill [Bill Plante, CBS News]?

Lebanon; President's Leadership

Q. Mr. President, why did you not initiate some action sooner on withdrawing the marines from Beirut? And what's your response to the people who have suggested, a number of critics, that it takes too long for you to hear the debate between your advisers and arrive at a consensus, and who ask, therefore, whether you are in fact really running things and whether you are a full-time President? What do you say?

The President. Well, Bill, I think—and I've read a little of the fiction that's been going around about that, also. I can tell you, no, there was certainly thorough discussion, and for a long time, ever since the suicide bombing, as to whether there was a way in which we could keep our forces there, not only ourselves but, again, as I say, in sync with the other nations' forces and that might reduce the possibilities of and the vulnerability from terrorist attacks.

And we were looking at everything. And from the very first, one of the alternatives was putting them on the ships. We held out for a while, because—the very thing that Helen brought up—we were concerned that people over there might see that as leaving, as abandoning the mission, and we didn't want that.

We finally did arrive in the belief that we could do this. We talked to the Gemayel government; we talked to our allies; and we had made a decision that this looked like the most logical thing to do, a phased withdrawal to the ships, keeping our training detachment there that has been working with the Lebanese Army and all. And so, it wasn't a case of delay; it was a case of looking at the situation and wanting to make the right decision.

Now, as to that other fiction about wheth-er I sit back and then somebody tells me what to do: That's a lack of understanding of how our system has been working here. And I will admit I don't think any administration, to my knowledge, has ever exactly worked with the Cabinet and the staff the way we have.

First of all, I think we've got one of the finest staffs and one of the finest Cabinets that has been in this city in many, many years. And I want people around me who are independent-minded. I want to hear all sides of everything. We have regular Cabinet meetings and things we call the Cabinet Council meetings, where it's a portion of the Cabinet based on the particular issue where it wouldn't particularly be of interest to the others.

Now, in those meetings, I hear all sides. It could best be compared to a board of directors or a board of regents or governors of an institution other than business. And the debate rages, and it isn't just limited to one Cabinet officer who thinks that the problem is in his particular area. I hear and get the input, and the debate sometimes rages. And many times—it's nice if you can get a consensus, that's easy—but many times, I have to make a decision in which I come down, obviously, against some of the advocates in the Cabinet and on the side of others. But it goes back and forth. The loser this week may be the winner next week. But this is the way the decisions are made.

The only difference between a board of directors then and our Cabinet meetings is, when it comes time for decision, we don't take a vote. The decision is mine, and I make it on the basis of the information that I have heard. And if they haven't given me enough information, I make them come back again, and we talk some more.

Q. Well, sir, what's your response to those who suggest that you don't spend enough time at the job of being President?

The President. My answer to them is they don't know what they're talking about. And I almost made that a little more blunt right then, but decided——

Q. Go ahead. [*Laughter*]

The President. ——no, it would be unseemly if I did. But they don't know what they're talking about. I have never gone upstairs from that office once that I have not carried an entire evening full of homework with me. And I could tell you about the sniping that takes place at so-called vacations, like the 4 days I spent at the ranch, one of which was a weekend day.

I have to tell you, Presidents, I've learned, don't take vacations. They just get a change of scenery.

Federal Budget

Q. Mr. President, are you still confident that there will not be a clash this year between borrowing by the Federal Government and borrowing by the private sector of a type that could abort the recovery? And if so, why?

The President. Well, right now, I think that I could safely say that there won't. The amount of savings has been such—and we know about the proportion of that, the percentage that would be the government—but there has also been an increase in profits, and a number of companies have already gone forward with modernizing and so forth out of their own earnings. And that, of course, is one of the—over the long term that you look at—is one of the problems that you want to solve.

I'm not underestimating deficits. I've been talking for a quarter of a century against them. I am a little struck by these born-again budget-balancers who, for 40 out of the last 44 years, have controlled both Houses of the Congress and who have religiously had a policy of deficit spending and never raised their voices about it while others tried to talk spending within our limits. And now, suddenly, they want to discover deficits. Well, I'm as determined as they are to get them down, but I'm not going to get them down the way they want them down.

Sam [Sam Donaldson, ABC News]?

President's Leadership

Q. Sir, Walter Mondale is one of those who's attacking you on the so-called leadership issue, but he goes beyond the things that you told Bill about. He says you're intellectually lazy and you're forgetful—so forgetful that he says you're providing leadership by amnesia. What do you say to that?

The President. I'm surprised he knew what the word meant. I haven't any comment to make at that. If that's all he has to talk about out there on the trail to his audiences, why, let him go. I'm going to be talking about the things we're doing and the things we intend to do. And what we intend to do is build for the kind of a future that this country and the people of this country have always wanted, and we're going to try to give it to them.

Q. Well, do you think those kind of personal attacks are fair comment, or do you think that's sort of hitting below the belt?

The President. Well, as I say, he doesn't know what he's talking about because—I think through the process we have of discussing all issues in the Cabinet, I probably have a better store of information on the issues confronting us than a President normally has.

Q. Sir?

The President. No.

Q. This man?

Interest Rates

Q. Mr. President, you take justifiable pride in bringing the inflation rate down, but interest rates—real interest rates haven't really come down the way you would like them to. I wonder, as you see yourself moving into the campaign season, what steps you might take, working with the Federal Reserve, so that people who are buying homes and cars can get a better rate of interest.

The President. Well, I think that the Federal Reserve right now is on a path of the money-supply increase that is consistent with a sound recovery without inflation. To go one way in excess, they could cause more inflation, and I don't think they're planning on that. They could go the other way, tighten the strings too much and interfere with the recovery, and I don't think they're going to do that.

I think that one of the reasons the interest rates have stayed where they are is still out there in the money market. After seven previous recessions since World War II in which the artificial cure has only brought on another and worse recession each time, I think they're not quite convinced yet that we mean it and that we are going to hold inflation down. And so, they're trying to guard against getting caught again by lending their money at a lower interest rate. I think as they see that we're determined to follow the course—stay the course, if I could coin an expression—I think that we will see a further decline in the interest rates.

Now, listen, I've got to come over here. Yes?

Israeli Settlements in the West Bank

Q. Last week you said the Arab-Israeli conflict must be resolved through negotiations involving an exchange of territory for peace. Were you telling Israel to reverse its settlement activity in the West Bank?

The President. No, from the very beginning—and the Israelis know this—I have told them that I thought with an effort that must be made out there for an overall peace in the area, that it was not helpful to go forward with what they were doing. I think that the peace process that we envision is based on the Camp David process, the U.N. Resolutions 242 and 338. And I had never referred to them as illegal, as some did. But I did say that I thought they were not helpful, because obviously the peace process, when the negotiations come between the Arab States and Israel, it is going to have to involve territorial changes in return for secure, peaceful borders. And so, no, I just think that we would've had a better chance.

Jerry [Jeremiah O'Leary, Washington Times]?

Oil Shipments From the Middle East

Q. Mr. President, the war between Iraq and Iran is heating up in a rather perilous way, and I'd like to ask what the depth of your concerns are about the possibility that this war would lead to the closing of the Straits of Hormuz and cut off the supply of oil to Japan, Western Europe, and ourselves, and to what lengths you're prepared to go to keep the Straits open.

The President. Jerry, what you have just suggested—Iran, itself, had voiced that threat some time ago, that if Iraq did certain things, they would close the Straits of Hormuz. And I took a stand then and made a statement that there was no way that

we—and I'm sure this is true of our allies—could stand by and see that sealane denied to shipping, and particularly, the tankers that are so essential to Japan, to our Western allies in Europe, and, to a lesser extent, ourselves. We're not importing as much as they require. But there's no way that we could allow that channel to be closed.

And we've had a naval force for a long time, virtually permanently stationed in the Arabian Sea, and so have some of our allies. But we'll keep that open to shipping.

U.S.-Soviet Relations

Q. Mr. President, do you have anything different to say to Mr. Chernenko in Moscow than you had to say to his predecessor, Mr. Andropov? Anything new to encourage them to talk with the United States?

The President. Yes, and on the reports that the Vice President brought back after a very fruitful meeting there. We're very hopeful in this latest announcement that he had made that he was willing to agree to onsite inspection with regard to chemical warfare. We think this is a good sign, and we have let him know that we want better relations. We want to sit down and try to resolve some of the problems that we have.

Gary [Gary Schuster, Detroit News]?

Federal Budget Deficits

Q. Mr. President, going back to your opening statement, with your nearly $200 billion deficit budget getting such a cool response on the Hill, would you sit still for a bipartisan budget written by Congress that, one, raised taxes, and two, made a sizable cut in the defense spending?

The President. Gary, we are trying to do a bipartisan thing that they, themselves, on the other side of the aisle first suggested. And I responded in my State of the Union address to the idea of a bipartisan group getting together to go beyond the budget that we have submitted with regard to additional savings. We've put everything on the table and said we'll discuss everything with them.

I don't mind saying that my own belief is that it would be counterproductive to talk an increase in taxes. About half your deficits are created by the recession; they're cyclical. And our recovery is reducing that part of the deficit. Raising taxes doesn't reduce a deficit. Raising taxes creates more government spending.

May I give two examples? We've not only cut down the rate of increase in spending that we inherited and that we found when we came here, but no one has added up the proposed spending increases that we have denied. For example, $3 billion program to stimulate the housing industry. It would have taken months and months before such a program could be put into effect, and we turned it down because the signs were already there that the housing industry was coming back. And it is back. It's the highest point of new starts in housing that we've known in 5 years. So, $3 billion would have been spent to do what is already being done by the recovery. $3½ billion was proposed in a job training—or a job program to put 300,000 people to work in some kind of makework jobs—300,000; $3½ billion. We turned that down, because our recovery for 13 months has been putting more than 300,000 people to work every month instead of this big program.

When a budget resolution was passed a year ago in defiance of mine over in the House, that budget proposal contained an increase in taxes and actually contained as many increased spending ventures as the revenue would have brought in.

I believe that we still have a lot further to go in reducing government spending, and we have 2,478 proposals by the Grace commission. These are things that have been researched by some of the finest business leaders and leaders of institutions in our country who volunteered and who even contributed the money to pay for the undertaking, who came up with those proposals that can make government more economical and more efficient. And until we can study and see what can be implemented there, I don't think we should be talking about new revenues.

Ms. Thomas. Thank you, Mr. President.

Q. What about the defense cuts, Mr. President?

The President. Defense cuts?

Q. Defense cuts.

The President. Oh, yes, you did ask about that. Helen, I'll just answer that one.

You don't decide to spend a certain amount of money on defense. You look at what you believe is necessary to do in order to ensure national security, and then you add up how much that's going to cost. On the other side, these attacks that are coming on the other side of the aisle on the defense spending—incidentally, in the figure that we've submitted in this budget, we, ourselves, and the Defense Department, under the Secretary, reduced that budget by $16 billion before it was submitted by taking things out that would have been worthwhile, would have increased our security ability, but which we believed we could do without for a time and settled on this particular thing.

Now, if the Democrats in this meeting that will take place tomorrow—and they're constantly talking cutting defense, all they talk about is cut dollars—well, our idea is that if they've got a plan in which they can come in and say what they would eliminate in the defense budget and how much money that would then save and we could study and see what would that do to our national security, how far would it reduce it, how far would it increase the window of vulnerability that we're trying to close, that is the way you negotiate on defense.

I happen to believe that we've submitted a most reasonable defense budget, in view of the several years' decline in spending that had taken us down to the very dangerous state we were in by 1980. In the last few years, before we came here, there was a 21-percent reduction in defense spending; entire weapons systems were canceled. And I think the world is a safer and more secure place, and we're further removed from a possible war by what we have done with the defense budgets that we have introduced, than we've been in a number of years.

Helen said the time was up. I'm sorry. I know there were more hands and more of you that I—[*inaudible*].

Note: The President's 22d news conference began at 8 p.m. in the East Room at the White House. It was broadcast live on nationwide radio and television.

Remarks at a Meeting With Asian and Pacific-American Leaders
February 23, 1984

Good morning, and welcome. I'm very pleased to have this opportunity to be with you, if only for a few minutes, and I've had that kind of morning. Everything that I've been in, someone is telling me, "You're due someplace else in *x* number of minutes."

But whenever I get a chance to speak to a group like yours, I'm tempted to talk about the one program that is helping every American—every ethnic group and every nationality across our nation—and it's called "economic recovery." But I know that you've been spoken to by others here this morning, including Don Regan, and all, and so maybe I'd be plowing ground that's already been plowed.

But for more than a year, I would like to say, if it hasn't been said already, an average of 300,000 people a month have found jobs for the last 13 months. Inflation is staying down. Factory orders are rising. All Americans can be proud, I think, of what we've accomplished together.

And last week's news about the continuing surge in housing starts and rise in personal income indicates confidence that the recovery will be strong and sustained. And did anyone this morning tell you that as of 8:30 this morning, they announced the figures for January in the sale of durable goods and they are up substantially?

But today I'd like to also talk about something else; you might call it "the spirit of America." Back in the fall of 1980 I attended a rally that I will always remember. It was held in the shadow of the Statue of Liberty. And there were many nationalities and ethnic groups there, all reminding us of America's rich and diverse heritage. They reminded us that we're all descendants from immigrants, most of whom came here looking for freedom and opportunity. And while our country had its flaws—and we still have them—the American dream was real.

Asian and Pacific Americans have helped preserve that dream by living up to the bedrock values that make us a good and a worthy people. I'm talking about principles that begin with the sacred worth of human life, religious faith, community spirit, and the responsibility of parents and schools to be teachers of tolerance, hard work, fiscal responsibility, cooperation, and love.

It's no wonder that the median income of Asian and Pacific American families is much higher than the total American average. After all, it is values, not programs and policies, that serve as our nation's compass. They hold us on course. They point the way to a promising future. And I'm pleased that Americans of Asian and Pacific ancestry are now eligible to receive business development assistance from the Commerce Department's Minority Business Development Agency.

And when we look toward that great and grand Pacific Basin, there's a promising future there, as well. You may not hear much about our Pacific and Asian foreign policy, but then there's a lot of good news that you don't seem to hear about. [*Laughter*] I think some of the things we've been doing here are very well-kept secrets, and we would rather they weren't.

But our relations with our Pacific and Asian friends and allies have never been better. First of all, it's not all foreign policy; America is part of the Pacific. There's Hawaii, American Samoa, Guam, the soon-to-be commonwealth status of the Northern Mariana Islands, and our special relationship with the Federated States of Micronesia and the Republics of Palau and the Marshall Islands. These countries are America's partners.

Partnership is also the starting point for our relations in the Far East and South Asia. From Japan and the Republic of Korea in the north to the ASEAN [Association for South East Asian Nations] countries and India in the south, our partnerships are getting stronger, and mutual trust and cooperation are increasing.

I couldn't have been more pleased with the results of our trip to Japan and Korea. We're making progress on security issues and trade and financial matters. The same is true with the ASEAN countries. Prime Minister Mahathir of Malaysia and I had a very useful meeting here at the White House just last month. And I'm pleased to note that Indo-American relations are good.

Our ties with the People's Republic of China are positive and expanding. Premier Zhao's visit in January points the way to increased trade, greater exchanges, and cooperation in various science and technology fields. Our trip in April will help broaden this spirit of good will and friendship. And remember, friendship gives both countries the freedom to disagree, even to criticize, without fear of lessening cooperation and understanding. I remember one head of state once that was accused of there being some divisions of that kind and he said, "Our relationship is like a happy marriage. Sometimes there are quarrels, but we're still married." [*Laughter*]

And while we're strengthening our relationship with the People's Republic, we maintain very close economic and cultural ties with the people of Taiwan. In a conversation on this subject with Premier Zhao, I told him that I thought that he would be encouraged that in making new friends, we don't discard the old. We will continue to support their needs and requirements in accordance with the 1979 Taiwan Relations Act.

America needs our Asian and Pacific American citizens. You've enriched our national culture and our heritage. You've upheld the beliefs that account for so much of our economic and social progress. You've never stopped striving for excellence, despite times not long ago when you experienced terrible discrimination. And let me add that we will continue to fight against discrimination wherever there are any vestiges of it remaining, until we've removed such bigotry from our entire land.

We need your energy, your values, your hard work, and we need them expressed at the polls and within our political system. Those who escaped oppression have a special appreciation for America's freedom, and those who fled poverty cherish America's opportunity. So I urge you to get involved, stay involved, and run for public office. That is another way of helping in this land of ours.

On this point, I'd like to say a few words about Anna Chennault. Anna is a great leader of our Chinese American community and a greatly valued resource for this White House. Because of her long years of hard work in the American political system, she is that.

America provides many opportunities for economic, social, and political participation. Those who participate in the political process can reap the rewards of their hard work. If you follow your hopes and aspirations, all of us will benefit.

And now I know that my time is up, and I'm going to have to leave, and I don't want to. But I don't have much choice. They tell me I'm the most powerful man in the world. I don't believe that. [*Laughter*] Over there in that White House someplace there's a fellow that puts a piece of paper on my desk every day that tells me what I'm going to be doing every 15 minutes. He's the most powerful man—[*laughter*]—in the world.

But thank you all, and God bless you for being here. Thank you.

Note: The President spoke at 11:45 a.m. in Room 450 of the Old Executive Office Building.

Letter to the Speaker of the House and the President of the Senate on Nuclear Cooperation With EURATOM
February 23, 1984

Dear Mr. Speaker: (Dear Mr. President:)

The United States has been engaged in nuclear cooperation with the European Community for many years. This cooperation was initiated under agreements concluded over two decades ago between the

United States and the European Atomic Energy Community (EURATOM) which extend until December 31, 1995. Since the inception of this cooperation, the Community has adhered to all its obligations under those agreements.

The Nuclear Non-Proliferation Act of 1978 amended the Atomic Energy Act to establish new nuclear export criteria, including a requirement that the United States have a right to consent to the reprocessing of fuel exported from the United States. Our present agreements for cooperation with EURATOM do not contain such a right. To avoid disrupting cooperation with EURATOM, a proviso was included in the law to enable continued cooperation until March 10, 1980, and negotiations concerning our cooperation agreements.

The law also provides that nuclear cooperation with EURATOM can be extended on an annual basis after March 10, 1980, upon determination by the President that failure to cooperate would seriously prejudice the achievement of United States nonproliferation objectives or otherwise jeopardize the common defense and security and after notification to the Congress. President Carter made such a determination four years ago and signed Executive Order 12193, permitting continued nuclear cooperation with EURATOM until March 10, 1981. I made such determinations in 1981, 1982 and 1983 and signed Executive Orders 12295, 12351 and 12409 permitting continued nuclear cooperation through March 10, 1984.

The United States has engaged in five rounds of talks with EURATOM regarding the renegotiation of the US–EURATOM agreements for cooperation. These were conducted in November 1978, September 1979, April 1980, January 1982 and November 1983. The European Community is now considering U.S. proposals relating to our cooperation agreements, and progress in the talks appears to be possible.

I believe that it is essential that cooperation between the United States and the Community continue and likewise that we work closely with our Allies to counter the threat of nuclear explosives proliferation. A disruption of nuclear cooperation would not only eliminate any chance of progress in our talks with EURATOM related to our agreements, it would also cause serious problems in our overall relationships. Accordingly, I have determined that failure to continue peaceful nuclear cooperation with EURATOM would be seriously prejudicial to the achievement of United States nonproliferation objectives and would jeopardize the common defense and security of the United States. I intend to sign an Executive Order to extend the waiver of the application of the relevant export criterion of the Nuclear Non-Proliferation Act for an additional twelve months from March 10, 1984.

Sincerely,

RONALD REAGAN

Note: This is the text of identical letters addressed to Thomas P. O'Neill, Jr., Speaker of the House of Representatives, and George Bush, President of the Senate.

Executive Order 12463—Nuclear Cooperation With EURATOM
February 23, 1984

By the authority vested in me as President by the Constitution and statutes of the United States of America, including Section 126a(2) of the Atomic Energy Act of 1954, as amended (42 U.S.C. 2155(a)(2)), and having determined that, upon the expiration of the period specified in the first proviso to Section 126a(2) of such Act and extended by Executive Order Nos. 12193, 12295, 12351 and 12409, failure to continue peaceful nuclear cooperation with the European Atomic Energy Community would be seriously prejudicial to the achievement of the United States non-proliferation objectives and would otherwise jeopardize the common defense and security of the United States, and having notified the Congress of this determination, I hereby extend the duration of that period to March 10, 1985.

RONALD REAGAN

The White House,
February 23, 1984.

[*Filed with the Office of the Federal Register, 10:30 a.m., February 24, 1984*]

Executive Order 12464—Award of the Purple Heart
February 23, 1984

By the authority vested in me as President and as Commander in Chief of the armed forces by the Constitution and laws of the United States of America, Executive Order No. 11016 of April 25, 1962, as amended, is further amended as follows:

Section 1. Paragraph 1 is amended as follows:

(a) In clause (d), delete "or" at the end thereof.

(b) In clause (e), delete the period and substitute therefor a semicolon.

(c) At the end of such paragraph, add the following new clauses:

"(f) after March 28, 1973, as a result of an international terrorist attack against the United States or a foreign nation friendly to the United States, recognized as such an attack for the purposes of this Order by the Secretary of the department concerned, or jointly by the Secretaries of the departments concerned if persons from more than one department are wounded in the attack; or

"(g) after March 28, 1973, as a result of military operations, while serving outside the territory of the United States as part of a peacekeeping force.".

Sec. 2. Paragraph 2 is amended to read as follows:

"The Secretary of a military department, or the Secretary of Transportation, shall, in the name of the President of the United States, award the Purple Heart, with suitable ribbons and appurtenances, posthumously, to any person covered by, and under the circumstances described in,—

(a) paragraphs 1 (a)–(e) who, after April 5, 1917; or

(b) paragraphs 1 (f)–(g) who, after March 28, 1973,

has been, or may hereafter be, killed, or who has died or may hereafter die after being wounded.".

RONALD REAGAN

The White House,
February 23, 1984.

[*Filed with the Office of the Federal Register, 10:31 a.m., February 24, 1984*]

Note: The President signed the Executive order in an Oval Office ceremony attended by Members of Congress and representatives of veterans groups.

Remarks on Signing an Executive Order on Commercial Expendable Launch Vehicle Activities
February 24, 1984

Thank all of you for being here, and welcome to the White House. George and I were both a little astonished at the new decorations, but certainly they're in keeping. [*Laughter*] You see, we even provide the atmosphere for the occasion.[1]

But it is space that brings us here today. And on the way over, I was thinking back to how thrilled we all were when men first walked on the Moon. For thousands of years when people gazed into the night sky, they looked at the Moon with wonder. The Moon controlled the ocean tides; it lighted the fields at harvest times, exerted an irresistable pull on the human imagination— and I won't go into some of the more exotic ideas that had to do with the Moon. [*Laughter*]

When an American spaceship landed on the Moon, the moment represented centuries of advances in navigation and exploration. It seemed the crowning achievement of human ingenuity and courage. And today we know that that first landing on the Moon was not just a crowning achievement but a great beginning. The dream of regular space travel, the use of space to enrich life on Earth is becoming a reality, a working part of our everyday lives.

Five centuries ago, America was the new world. Today space is the new world. And just as Columbus' discovery marked the beginning of growing ties between the old world and the new, we're beginning to create more and more ties between Planet Earth and outer space.

Our approach to space has three elements. First, we're determined to put a permanently manned space station into orbit and to do so within a decade. The space station will serve as a base for a wide range of scientific research and industrial work, and it will point the way to further goals.

Second, we're committed to ongoing international cooperation, long a principle of the American space program. Last year, for example, we celebrated the tricentennial of the first German immigration to America with a joint American-German space project. And such cooperation will grow in importance as more and more activities take place in space.

Third, we're doing all we can to encourage space work by American industry. Private enterprise made America great. And if our efforts in space are to show the same energy, imagination, and daring as those in our country, we must involve private enterprise to the full. And that's where today's important event comes in.

Elizabeth Dole, when I sign this Executive order, your Department of Transportation will become the Government agency with primary responsibility for expendable launched vehicles, or ELV's, the powerful rockets that carry satellites into orbit. The Executive order directs the Department to encourage, facilitate, and coordinate the development of commercial expendable launch vehicle operations by private American enterprise.

Until today, private industries interested in ELV's have had to deal with 17 Government agencies. From now on, they'll only have to get in touch with the Department of Transportation, and the Department will clear away what Secretary Dole has called "the thicket of clearances, licenses, and regulations that keep industrial space vehicles tethered to their pads." With Elizabeth and her team in charge, private enterprises interested in space won't see redtape; they'll see blue sky.

As private concerns begin to supply and launch ELV's, we'll see a vital new industry take shape. The new space industry will foster the launching of telecommunications satellites, and there satellites will expand TV coverage and improve telephone and data transmission around the world. The

---

[1] *Behind the President and Vice President was a large picture of the Earth as it appears from space and several small models of U.S. rockets.*

space industry will help us to take the first steps toward processing materials at zero gravity, and this could open dramatic new possibilities for producing alloys and crystals. And producing compounds in zero gravity could increase their purity by 5 or 10 times and drastically reduce the cost of many pharmaceuticals, an exciting new opportunity for medicine.

Perhaps most important, the new space industry will launch satellites with capabilities for remote sensing. These satellites can look down on Earth the way a plane pilot looks down on a neighborhood. They'll help us identify the sources of water and air pollution, forecast crop growth, measure and guard against insect infestation, assist in mineral exploration and land use manage-

ment, and monitor weather conditions both on land and at sea—all saving countless dollars and untold lives.

I want to thank everyone here, for you've all had a hand in supporting this Executive order. And I know that you'll take a keen interest as American private enterprise literally blasts off.

By working to expand our involvement in space, we'll enhance life on this beautiful blue and green globe called Earth. So, I thank you, and God bless all of you for all that you've helped accomplish.

And I shall now sign the Executive order.

Note: The President spoke at 10:48 a.m. in the East Room at the White House.

Executive Order 12465—Commercial Expendable Launch Vehicle Activities
February 24, 1984

By the authority vested in me as President by the Constitution and laws of the United States of America, and in order to encourage, facilitate and coordinate the development of commercial expendable launch vehicle (ELV) operations by private United States enterprises, it is hereby ordered as follows:

Section 1. The Department of Transportation is designated as the lead agency within the Federal government for encouraging and facilitating commercial ELV activities by the United States private sector.

Sec. 2. Responsibilities of Lead Agency. The Secretary of Transportation shall, to the extent permitted by law and subject to the availability of appropriations, perform the following functions:

(a) act as a focal point within the Federal government for private sector space launch contacts related to commercial ELV operations;

(b) promote and encourage commercial ELV operations in the same manner that other private United States commercial enterprises are promoted by United States agencies;

(c) provide leadership in the establishment, within affected departments and agencies, of procedures that expedite the processing of private sector requests to obtain licenses necessary for commercial ELV launches and the establishment and operation of commercial launch ranges;

(d) consult with other affected agencies to promote consistent application of ELV licensing requirements for the private sector and assure fair and equitable treatment for all private sector applicants;

(e) serve as a single point of contact for collection and dissemination of documentation related to commercial ELV licensing applications;

(f) make recommendations to affected agencies and, as appropriate, to the President, concerning administrative measures to streamline Federal government procedures for licensing of commercial ELV activities;

(g) identify Federal statutes, treaties, regulations and policies which may have an adverse impact on ELV commercialization efforts and recommend appropriate changes to affected agencies and, as appropriate, to the President; and

(h) conduct appropriate planning regarding long-term effects of Federal activities related to ELV commercialization.

Sec. 3. An interagency group, chaired by the Secretary of Transportation and composed of representatives from the Department of State, the Department of Defense, the Department of Commerce, the Federal Communications Commission, and the National Aeronautics and Space Administration, is hereby established. This group shall meet at the call of the Chair and shall advise and assist the Department of Transportation in performing its responsibilities under this Order.

Sec. 4. Responsibilities of Other Agencies. All executive departments and agencies shall assist the Secretary of Transportation in carrying out this Order. To the extent permitted by law and in consultation with the Secretary of Transportation, they shall:

(a) provide the Secretary of Transportation with information concerning agency regulatory actions which may affect development of commercial ELV operations;

(b) review and revise their regulations and procedures to eliminate unnecessary regulatory obstacles to the development of commercial ELV operations and to ensure

that those regulations and procedures found essential are administered as efficiently as possible; and

(c) establish timetables for the expeditious handling of and response to applications for licenses and approvals for commercial ELV activities.

Sec. 5. The powers granted to the Secretary of Transportation to encourage, facilitate and coordinate the overall ELV commercialization process shall not diminish or abrogate any statutory or operational authority exercised by any other Federal agency.

Sec. 6. Nothing contained in this Order or in any procedures promulgated hereunder shall confer any substantive or procedural right or privilege on any person or organization, enforceable against the United States, its agencies, its officers or any person.

Sec. 7. This Order shall be effective immediately.

RONALD REAGAN

The White House,
February 24, 1984.

[*Filed with the Office of the Federal Register, 3:25 p.m., February 24, 1984*]

Remarks of the President and Prime Minister Robert D. Muldoon of New Zealand Following Their Meetings
February 24, 1984

The President. I am delighted that Prime Minister Sir Robert Muldoon has once again come to Washington. I value the wise counsel of such a good friend, and it was a real pleasure to confer with Sir Robert on issues of importance to both our countries.

The Prime Minister's thoughts on the international economic situation have been most helpful. His breadth of experience in international finance as Finance Minister and as Prime Minister is matched by very few people. And I sincerely appreciate his insights on these important international issues.

I also want to thank Sir Robert and all

New Zealanders for the key role they play in the South Pacific, a region which should serve as a model for the rest of the world. The South Pacific is tranquil, respects human rights, and has peacefully developed democratic institutions and self-government. These accomplishments would not have been possible without New Zealand's development assistance programs.

New Zealand's contributions to stability and security extend far beyond the South Pacific. We see them as far away as the Sinai Desert and in Singapore. And we have special appreciation for, Sir Robert, your commitment to ANZUS, an alliance which has assured our mutual security in the Pacific for more than 30 years.

I might mention that our ANZUS partners, New Zealand and Australia, are our only allies who have been at our side in all four major conflicts of this century. The strong bonds between our two nations reflect our common values, shared history, and mutual interests.

We are more than good friends. And I am especially grateful to Sir Robert for his untiring efforts to further strengthen our close ties. We will stay in close touch in the future. And, Sir Robert, I thank you for coming to Washington, and on behalf of our countrymen, wish you Godspeed during your visit to America and a safe journey home.

The Prime Minister. Mr. President, I last stood here at the White House with you 30 months ago. The friendship between our countries, as you've said, goes back a long way and, through difficult times for the West, was attested to then by the warmth of your welcome and your hospitality as it has been again today.

July 1981 was the midpoint of the first year of your administration. The economic and political tasks that you had set yourself were of global significance. Among these was a determination to place greater emphasis on consultation with America's allies by being good listeners wherever possible. New Zealand is one ally which welcomed that undertaking as a renewal of the concept which lies at the heart of the ANZUS Treaty.

Mr. President, you've been as good as your word. The period of your first term has been marked by a frequency and closeness of contact which has made New Zealand, geographically your most distant security partner, feel that its voice is listened to in your administration, whether on issues of bilateral concern or wider issues affecting regional and global security. We've not had to shout to be heard.

Much of that is due to the regularity of contact at the Cabinet level between our governments, highlighted, of course, by the

visit of Vice President Bush to New Zealand in May 1982. We look forward in July to seeing our good and valued friend, George Shultz, back in the South Pacific region once again.

Political visits are not the sole measure of the relationship and its durability. Rather, it's a matter of the way our citizens relate to each other as people. You've often spoken about the desires of ordinary Americans to live free, in peace and well-being. New Zealanders share that view of the world. It is why, when we've had to, we've acted together with you to preserve such values for ourselves and other peoples. That hasn't changed.

New Zealanders are not isolationists, in spite of our relative geographic isolation. Nor are New Zealanders among those fair-weather friends who are only too ready to attack American motives and policies. In an uncertain world, you need have no doubt about where the New Zealand Government and people stand. Your citizens—private, official, and military—remain more than welcome in our country.

Mr. President, our discussions today have touched upon New Zealand's own trade concerns, your government's aspirations at home and abroad, and the concern of many nations for a new stability in international economic affairs. Our exchanges have been characterized by the easy give and take of ideas which is the hallmark of close friends and allies.

I thank you warmly for your hospitality and that of Mrs. Reagan for my wife. The coming year brings new challenges of government and political life for both of us and our families. I wish you and the First Lady well in all that lies ahead.

Note: The President spoke at 1:21 p.m. at the South Portico of the White House.

Earlier, the President and the Prime Minister, together with their advisers, met in the Oval Office. They then attended a working luncheon in the State Dining Room.

Nomination of Donald D. Engen To Be Administrator of the Federal Aviation Administration
February 24, 1984

The President today announced his intention to nominate Donald D. Engen to be Administrator of the Federal Aviation Administration, Department of Transportation. He would succeed J. Lynn Helms.

Since 1982 Mr. Engen has been serving as a member of the National Transportation Safety Board. Previously he was senior associate for professional development and training for Ketron, Inc., in Arlington, VA. He was general manager, Piper Aircraft Corp., Lakeland Division, in Lakeland, FL, in 1978–1980. He served in the U.S. Navy as Deputy Commander in Chief, U.S. Atlantic Command and U.S. Atlantic Fleet, Norfolk, VA, in 1976–1978. He was commissioned ensign in the U.S. Navy in 1943 and progressed through the ranks to vice admiral in 1976. He retired from the Navy in 1978.

He graduated from George Washington University with a B.S. in business administration. In addition, he graduated from the U.S. Naval War College. He is married, has four children, and resides in Alexandria, VA. He was born May 28, 1924.

Radio Address to the Nation on Prayer in Schools
February 25, 1984

My fellow Americans:

From the early days of the colonies, prayer in school was practiced and revered as an important tradition. Indeed, for nearly 200 years of our nation's history, it was considered a natural expression of our religious freedom. But in 1962 the Supreme Court handed down a controversial decision prohibiting prayer in public schools.

Sometimes I can't help but feel the first amendment is being turned on its head. Because ask yourselves: Can it really be true that the first amendment can permit Nazis and Ku Klux Klansmen to march on public property, advocate the extermination of people of the Jewish faith and the subjugation of blacks, while the same amendment forbids our children from saying a prayer in school?

When a group of students at the Guilderland High School in Albany, New York, sought to use an empty classroom for voluntary prayer meetings, the 2d Circuit of Appeals said, "No." The court thought it might be dangerous because students might be coerced into praying if they saw the football captain or student body president participating in prayer meetings.

Then there was the case of the kindergarten class reciting a verse before their milk and cookies. They said, "We thank you for the flowers so sweet. We thank you for the food we eat. We thank you for the birds that sing. We thank you, God, for everything." But a Federal court of appeals ordered them to stop. They were supposedly violating the Constitution of the United States.

Teddy Roosevelt told us, "The American people are slow to wrath, but when their wrath is once kindled it burns like a consuming flame." Up to 80 percent of the American people support voluntary prayer. They understand what the Founding Fathers intended. The first amendment of the Constitution was not written to protect the people from religion; that amendment was written to protect religion from government tyranny.

The amendment says, "Congress shall make no law respecting an establishment of religion or prohibiting the free exercise thereof." What could be more clear?

The act that established our public school system called for public education to see that our children learned about religion and morality. References to God can be found in the Mayflower Compact of 1620, the Declaration of Independence, the Pledge of Allegiance, and the National Anthem. Our legal tender states, "In God We Trust."

When the Constitution was being debated at the Constitutional Convention, Benjamin Franklin rose to say: "The longer I live, the more convincing proofs I see that God governs in the affairs of men. Without His concurring aid, we shall succeed in this political building no better than the builders of Babel." He asked: "Have we now forgotten this powerful Friend? Or do we imagine we no longer need His assistance?" Franklin then asked the Convention to begin its daily deliberations by asking for the assistance of Almighty God.

George Washington believed that religion was an essential pillar of a strong society. In his farewell address, he said, "Reason and experience both forbid us to expect that national morality can prevail in exclusion of religious principle." And when John Jay, the first Chief Justice of the United States Supreme Court, was asked in his dying hour if he had any farewell counsels to leave his children, Jay answered, "They have the Book."

But now we're told our children have no right to pray in school. Nonsense. The pendulum has swung too far toward intolerance against genuine religious freedom. It's time to redress the balance.

Former Supreme Court Justice Potter Stewart noted if religious exercises are held to be an impermissible activity in schools, religion is placed at an artificial and state-created disadvantage. Permission for such exercises for those who want them is necessary if the schools are truly to be neutral in the matter of religion. And a refusal to permit them is seen not as the realization of state neutrality, but rather as the establishment of a religion of secularism.

The Senate will soon vote on a constitutional amendment to permit voluntary vocal prayer in public schools. If two-thirds of the Senate approve, then we must convince the House leadership to permit a vote on the issue. I am confident that if the Congress passes our amendment this year, then the State legislatures will do likewise, and we'll be able to celebrate a great victory for our children.

Our amendment would ensure that no child be forced to recite a prayer. Indeed, it explicitly states this. Nor would the state be allowed to compose the words of any prayer. But the courts could not forbid our children from voluntary vocal prayer in their schools. And by reasserting their liberty of free religious expression, we will be helping our children understand the diversity of America's religious beliefs and practices.

If ever there was a time for you, the good people of this country, to make your voices heard, to make the mighty power of your will the decisive force in the halls of Congress, that time is now.

Until next week, thanks for listening, and God bless you.

Note: The President spoke at 12:06 p.m. from Camp David, MD.

Toasts at a White House Dinner Honoring the Nation's Governors
February 26, 1984

The President. Well, Nancy and I are delighted to welcome you to the White House. We're pleased and honored to have all of you here tonight.

This room is often used for state dinners honoring visiting heads of state, and it's fitting that we, too, share this room in recognition that you are also heads of sovereign States. Our Federal system of sovereign States is today as vital to the preservation of freedom as it was in the time of Jefferson and Adams and those other farsighted individuals we revere as our Founding Fathers.

They envisioned a system that would secure the greatest degree of liberty, while at the same time be functional and efficient. They knew well that if too much power and authority were vested in the central government, even if intended for a noble purpose, not only would liberty be threatened but it just wouldn't work.

Jefferson warned, "Were we directed from Washington when to sow and when to reap, we should soon want for bread." [*Laughter*] I think during the last decade and before, we've gotten a taste of just what it was that Jefferson was warning us about. So much power had centralized in Washington that frustration and stagnation ruled the day. The Federal Government taxed away the available revenue and set up a confusing web of regulations and bureaucratic controls to be complied with in order to get these resources back. Furthermore, the rules and restrictions, to a large degree, were coming from faraway, unelected officials. This neither worked, nor was it consistent with principles of American freedom.

Over the last 3 years, we put a stop to this ever-increasing centralization of power. Through our block grant programs, through our efforts to get control of Federal spending and taxing, we've halted what I consider to be a very ominous trend. People are no longer looking to Washington to solve every problem. As a result, we're seeing a renaissance of direct involvement—whether in the local schools or in neighborhood-watch programs—and the reemergence of State and local government as significant forces in determining the future of our country and the quality of life of our people.

This has been accomplished with close consultation and cooperation with you and with other State and local officials. I want each of you to know I deeply appreciate the responsible and, in most cases, nonpartisan way that we have worked together to ensure progress in the area of federalism. There's still much to be done, and I hope we can build on the working relationship that we've already established.

Technology today is opening up new opportunities at the State and local level. State government has some of the most competent and hard-working employees to be found in government at any level. And in the last few years, we've seen creativity and

innovation as never before in the state-houses throughout the country. Today that vision of our Founding Fathers of a federal system of States is as viable, if not more so, than at any time in our history. So, let us continue working together to keep faith with that dream.

And now, would you please join me as I toast you, the Governors of the States of the Union, and you can toast each other. And we can toast also to our freedom and to strong and efficient State government.

Governor Thompson. Mr. President, Mrs. Reagan, the members of your Cabinet and staff, my fellow Governors and their spouses, we are honored to be in this home this evening.

A year ago when we were here, and my wife was able to be with me, on the way in through the door I kind of nudged her and I said, "Hey, not bad for two kids from the west side of Chicago." [*Laughter*] I think probably all of us here tonight, despite the fact that we are called Governor, and no matter how far we may have traveled, nor no matter what we may have done or accomplished or hope yet to do, feel a rare sense of privilege at being within these walls and being with each other and being with you and Mrs. Reagan.

Tonight, party, philosophy, region, and interest are irrelevant. We are all very proud Americans. This is our house. Every time that I come to Washington and see the lines of tourists stretched around the building with fathers and mothers, particularly young fathers and mothers, holding the hands of the children, I know they're saying, "Be patient. Once inside, you'll see something extraordinary, and you'll remember it. You'll tell the class. You'll tell your brother and sister. You'll tell your grandmother, grandfather." This is an American privilege.

Our session went very long today, Mr. President. Tomorrow, we'll report to you formally on what we have accomplished thus far in our meeting, though we have much to do. We expended many passions today, especially in our committee—issues involving the budget and the deficit, acid rain, and all those controversies which swirl around us in public office—in your office, in ours, at the other end of the avenue in the legislative branch, and sometimes in the judicial branch.

Those passions have dissipated tonight. Because we're good at our jobs, they'll be back tomorrow morning full steam. And when you see us in the East Room tomorrow morning, we'll probably have some pretty good questions for you and for the members of your staff and your Cabinet. That's why we're here. But tonight we join you as brother.

You were a Governor—a good Governor, a proud Governor. And you share with us many common experiences.

Now you hold the position that we elected you to. And though you are formally now engaged in a contest to retain that office, we still look upon you as brother. And we're glad of the opportunity to come with you once a year in this formal setting. And I must say, in my experience and perhaps in the experience of every Governor in this room, you have extended the hospitality, the warmth and, most importantly the interest of your office to us, your brothers, on so many more occasions, whether in the Oval Office or in our States, than we might reasonably expect, for we know you have to deal with mayors—[*laughter*]—and legislators, county executives, business people and labor people, and just all sorts of people that it's somewhat remarkable how much time you spend with Governors. I think, perhaps, there's a bias there. At least, we hope so.

The issues which concern us, Mr. President, and about which even we differ among ourselves and within our States are only as good as the men and women who enliven them. There is justice or no justice, depending upon the passions and the caring of men and women, not just on the pages of a book or in the words on those pages.

There will be a better education for our children than we had for ourselves not only because that is important but because it is necessary, but only achievable if we care to make it so and invest the time and the resources to achieve it. And whether it's the infrastructure of our country—our roads, our highways, our bridges, our dams, our buildings, sewer systems, our water systems—or it's our responsibility for the safety and well-being of our fellow citizens through law enforcement, for public health, or care for abused or neglected children, or infant mortality rates, words are words, pages are pages, and laws are laws unless we, the Governors, infuse them with our care.

We know how hard it is to be a President and a First Lady, because all of us in this room have experienced at least a portion of that which you live. We know there are many nights where you must feel frustrated, tired, mad, but many more where you feel satisfied, glad, challenged. We do, too, or we would not be with you tonight. When we leave this city and go back to our States and try and infuse our political, governmental, and personal lives with renewed vigor and caring, in part because we were here, we will remember you and Mrs. Reagan and wish for you the same. And we know it will be achieved.

And so tonight, Mr. President, from your brothers—and I am pleased to say, from one sister who has now joined the ranks—on behalf of the Governors, I propose a toast to the lady who guides you, sustains you, passionately loves you, and to the President of the United States.

Note: The President spoke at 9:50 p.m. in the State Dining Room at the White House. Gov. James R. Thompson of Illinois is chairman of the National Governors' Association.

Nomination of Jack L. Courtemanche To Be Administrator of General Services
February 27, 1984

The President today announced his intention to nominate Jack L. Courtemanche to be Administrator of General Services. He would succeed Gerald P. Carmen.

Since October 1983 Mr. Courtemanche has been serving as Deputy Assistant to the President and Deputy Director of the Office of Public Liaison. Previously, he was Executive Director of the White House Conference on Productivity in 1983; president of Crown Coach Corp., Los Angeles, CA, in 1980–1983; president of the Seven Corp., Los Angeles, 1977–1980; and vice president of Mack Trucks, Inc., in Allentown, PA, in 1974–1979.

Mr. Courtemanche is married, has six children, and resides in Washington, DC. He was born March 9, 1935, in McMinnville, OR.

Appointment of Frank J. Donatelli as Deputy Assistant to the President for Public Liaison
February 27, 1984

The President today announced his intention to appoint Frank J. Donatelli to be Deputy Assistant to the President for Public Liaison. He will succeed Jack L. Courtemanche.

Mr. Donatelli is presently serving as Assistant Administrator of the Agency for International Development (African Affairs). Previously, he was an attorney with the law firm of Patton, Boggs & Blow in Washington, DC, in 1981–1983; with the Reagan-Bush transition in 1980–1981; regional political director for the Reagan for President Committee during the primary and general elections in 1979–1980; campaign manager for the Baker for attorney general campaign in Texas in 1978; and executive director of Young Americans for Freedom in 1973–1977.

Mr. Donatelli graduated from the University of Pittsburgh (B.A., 1967) and American University Law School (J.D., 1976). He is married, has one child, and resides in Alexandria, VA. He was born July 5, 1949, in Pittsburgh, PA.

Proclamation 5154—Cancer Control Month, 1984
February 27, 1984

By the President of the United States of America

A Proclamation

The news about cancer is getting brighter. While three out of ten Americans will develop cancer at some time in their lives, half of those who do will live five years or more and are considered curable. For some of the major cancers, more than two-thirds of patients survive beyond the five-year mark.

Physicians treating cancer patients anywhere in the United States now have access to the latest treatment information through a new computerized database. In addition, there are in 34 States new community cancer programs which are affiliated with 200 hospitals and designed to bring the latest and best treatment to cancer patients in their own communities.

We have learned more about the basic nature of cancer in the past ten years than in the entire history of science. The new technologies developed through research now give us the tools to examine the intricate steps that occur when cancer begins to form. We expect these tools to give us even better diagnosis, treatment, and prevention.

The best news of all about cancer today is that we are developing clear ideas about how to prevent it. Cancer researchers believe that two-thirds of all cancers in this country are linked with our lifestyles so we can now make daily choices that may decrease our odds of developing cancer. The single most important step which can be taken is to avoid smoking. Evidence also shows that some dietary components may not only prevent cancer, but even act to reverse a cancer-causing process which has already begun.

Thus we are reaping important benefits from the billions of dollars and the years of work this country has invested in the all-out effort to control cancer. With the continued advance of medical science to improve treatment and prevention, it may be possible to reduce by fifty percent the national death rate from cancer by the year 2000.

In 1938, the Congress of the United States passed a joint resolution (52 Stat. 148; 36 U.S.C. 150) requesting the President to issue an annual proclamation setting aside the month of April as "Cancer Control Month."

Now, Therefore, I, Ronald Reagan, President of the United States of America, do hereby proclaim the month of April 1984 as Cancer Control Month, 1984. I invite the Governors of the fifty States and the Commonwealth of Puerto Rico and the appropriate officials of all other areas under the United States flag to issue similar proclamations. I also ask that health care professionals, the communications industry, and all other interested persons and groups unite during this appointed time to reaffirm publicly our Nation's continuing commitment to control cancer.

In Witness Whereof, I have hereunto set my hand this 27th day of Feb., in the year of our Lord nineteen hundred and eighty-four, and of the Independence of the United States of America the two hundred and eighth.

RONALD REAGAN

[*Filed with the Office of the Federal Register, 4:28 p.m., February 27, 1984*]

Executive Order 12466—Reimbursement of Federal Employee Relocation Expenses
February 27, 1984

By virtue of the authority vested in me as President by the laws of the United States of America, including Public Law 98–151 and Section 301 of Title 3 of the United States Code, it is hereby ordered as follows:

Section 1. Executive Order No. 11609 of July 22, 1971, as amended, is further amended by designating the present text of subsection (7) as subsection 7(a), and by adding the following new subsections 7(b) and 7(c):

"(b) In consultation with the Secretary of the Treasury, the authority of the President under 5 U.S.C. 5724b to prescribe the regulations provided for therein relating to reimbursement of Federal, State, and city income taxes for travel, transportation, and relocation expenses of employees, transferred at Government expense, furnished in kind or for which reimbursement or an allowance is provided.

"(c) The authority of the President to prescribe guidance pursuant to which each agency shall carry out its responsibilities under 5 U.S.C. 5724c.".

Sec. 2. This order shall be effective as of November 14, 1983.

RONALD REAGAN

The White House,
February 27, 1984.

[*Filed with the Office of the Federal Register, 4:29 p.m., February 27, 1984*]

Appointment of Four Members of the National Advisory Council on Adult Education
February 28, 1984

The President today announced his intention to appoint the following individuals to be members of the National Advisory Council on Adult Education:

Abraham Shemtov, to serve for the remainder of the term expiring July 10, 1985. He will succeed Michael Marino. Rabbi Shemtov is national director for the American Friends of Lubavitch in Philadelphia, PA. He is married, has six children, and resides in Philadelphia. He was born February 16, 1937, in Wilno, Poland.

Mary Sellman Jackson, to serve for a term expiring July 10, 1986. This is a reappointment. She is owner/manager of Davidsonville Diversified Services in Davidsonville, MD. She is married,

has four children, and resides in Davidsonville. She was born March 7, 1939, in Edgewater, MD.

Rawlein G. Soberano, to serve for a term expiring July 10, 1986. This is a reappointment. He is associate professor, division of history and sociology, at Our Lady of Holy Cross College in New Orleans, LA. He is married, has three children, and resides in New Orleans. He was born April 19, 1941, in Barcolod, Philippines.

Patric Dorsey, to serve for a term expiring July 10, 1986. This is a reappointment. She is owner/manager of Mulberry, Inc., in New Bern, NC. She is married, has three children, and resides in New Bern. She was born August 30, 1924, in El Reno, OK.

Appointment of Betty T. James as a Member of the National Voluntary Service Advisory Council
February 28, 1984

The President today announced his intention to appoint Betty T. James to be a member of the National Voluntary Service Advisory Council. She will succeed C. William Verity.

Mrs. James is a homemaker in New York City. Before moving to New York, she was

active in community affairs and fundraising for various private institutions in southern California.

She graduated from San Jose State University (B.A., 1955). She is married and resides in New York City. Mrs. James was born August 19, 1933, in Amarillo, TX.

Remarks at the Welcoming Ceremony for President Rudolf Kirchschläger of Austria
February 28, 1984

President Reagan. Mr. President, Mrs. Kirchschläger, Ministers Lanc and Fischer, honored guests, Nancy and I are delighted to welcome you and your party to the

United States. I take special pride in greeting you, since this is the first time an American President has had the privilege of hosting an Austrian state visit.

Americans have deep admiration for Austria, her industrious people, and her rich culture. When we think of Austria, we picture snowcapped mountains and deep, fertile valleys, and churches, museums, and monuments of cities like Salzburg and Vienna. Austria is truly a nation of breathtaking beauty and noble history. And Americans have a deep respect for Austria's part in foreign affairs.

We recognize the crucial role your nation has played in maintaining peace in central Europe and working for peace throughout the world. But we are drawn to you by more than admiration and respect. We revere shared values of democracy, personal freedom, human dignity, and the rule of law—values as ancient as Salzburg Cathedral and as soaring and noble as the Austrian Alps.

Your reconstruction of your society from the physical and political rubble of World War II and your creative use of neutrality to create a pluralistic society and political system stand as an inspiration for the rest of the world. As a signatory of your state treaty and, therefore, a guarantor of your sovereignty, the United States salutes your accomplishments and supports your active neutrality.

Looking to the future, we want to make certain that the understanding between our two peoples is passed on to the younger generation of Austrians and Americans. And toward that end, we will begin this year a pilot program of youth exchanges with plans to expand the program in future years. Allowing young Austrians and Americans to spend time in each other's countries will multiply the ties of firsthand knowledge and friendship so important to our close and warm relations. It will mean that many young Austrians and Americans will forever carry something of the other's country in their hearts.

In addition to promoting these new youth exchanges, your visit will help cement our ties through enhanced cooperation in science and research. Minister Fischer and my science adviser, Dr. Keyworth, will be exchanging letters this afternoon which will give a new impetus to mutually beneficial cooperation on basic research. Scientists and researchers from both our countries will now have new reasons to increase their joint research projects, pooling their knowledge for the benefit of Austrians, Americans, and all mankind.

Mr. President, in your meetings today and in your visits to many parts of the United States, I know that you will experience the depth of the good will that we Americans feel toward Austria. I'm delighted that you will have the opportunity to meet Americans across our land and experience the variety of our culture and the warmth of our hospitality. The people of the cities that you'll visit eagerly await the opportunity to share this, the first state visit by an Austrian President, with you. And together all Americans are proud to say, *Wir heissen Sie herzlich willkommen.* [We bid you a warm welcome.]

We welcome you, Mr. President, and we cherish your friendship. May God bless you and Mrs. Kirchschläger.

President Kirchschläger. Mr. President, Mrs. Reagan, Mr. Vice President, Mr. Secretary of State, ladies and gentlemen:

Thank you very much for your warm words of welcome, and thank you very much for your kind invitation to officially visit this great country.

Your invitation was more appreciated since this is for me and for all of Austria a truly historic event. It is indeed the first official visit of an Austrian head of state to the United States since the establishing of relations between Vienna and Washington about 200 years ago.

In the heart and in the mind of the Austrian people the relations between our two countries are inviolably anchored by two facts. First, we feel closely linked through our mutual adherence to the fundamental values of democratic western pluralism. Second, we have not forgotten how much the American people have contributed through the Marshall plan to the rebuilding and to the building of our economy after World War II.

Reflecting this basic attitude of the Austrian people, I came here today, Mr. President, as a true friend, advocating the promotion of friendship between Western Europe and the United States, but also advocating the dialog between East and West.

The history of my country has proven that it is only through a constructive dialog that our living with each other in peace is ensured. Recent messages from across both sides of the ideological borderlines seem to give hope for mutual understanding and co-existence.

I'm looking forward with great interest to an exchange of views with you, Mr. President, with Vice President Bush, and with Secretary Shultz, concerning the present political and economic global situation. For me, as an Austrian, it is of particular value to see the American perspectives in direct contact.

Also being a small country, Austria is situated geopolitically in a sensitive area, and her historical ties with the peoples across the borders have also a particular political importance. Consequently, Austria has a role to play in demonstrating to all of our neighbors a living and well-functioning, free democracy with all of its principles America

stands for.

Mr. President, I'm truly happy to be your guest in your great country, and I'm confident that my visit will bring our two peoples even closer together. It is particularly the young people we have to turn to in our efforts to ensure our values also for the future. I am, therefore, very pleased that it is planned, as you stated today, to include Austria in the youth exchange program, which you, Mr. President, decided to intensify to the benefit of international relations in general, and of Austro-American friendship in particular.

Thank you very much.

Note: President Reagan spoke at 10:10 a.m. President Kirchschläger was accorded the formal welcome in the East Room at the White House, rather than on the South Lawn, because of inclement weather.

Following the ceremony, the two Presidents met, together with U.S. and Austrian officials, in the Oval Office.

Remarks of President Reagan and President Rudolf Kirchschläger of Austria at the State Dinner
February 28, 1984

President Reagan. Mr. President, Mrs. Kirchschläger, Ministers Lanc and Fischer, honored guests, I said this morning, and I would like to say again, how happy and proud that Nancy and I are to welcome you to the United States for the first state visit by an Austrian President. I consider your visit a celebration of our common bonds and our common purpose.

Before I say anything else, Mr. President, I want you to know that one of the best loved of all Austrian Americans is with us tonight, Baroness von Trapp.

The Baroness and her family fled Austria shortly before the outbreak of World War II, and their story has become known to millions in the wonderful play and film "The Sound of Music." Since arriving in the United States, the Baroness has come to stand for Austrian integrity, wit, and charm. And perhaps more than any other single

American, she's contributed to the deep friendship that our two nations enjoy. So, Baroness, on behalf of the American people, I thank you.

Mr. President, as a neutral country between East and West, Austria has played a constructive role in international and human relations and earned the respect of all nations. During World War II, thousands of people like the von Trapps were forced to flee Austria, but today, your nation offers asylum to those who are fleeing tyranny and human suffering. Austria is a shining example of compassion and courage.

Our countries, united not by military alliance, but by shared beliefs, have a common conviction that there are basic values which transcend every system of government. Among these are the dignity of man, liberty and justice, and the cornerstone of all of our values, an unshakable belief in God. Mr.

President, we have deep respect for your neutrality. We are proud to guarantee your sovereignty, and we take great comfort in the knowledge that Austria is a steadfast member of the community of Western democracies.

Given your history and geography, Austria is vitally interested in the state of East-West relations. From the beginning of my tenure in office, Mr. President, I have emphasized that in our dealings with the Soviet Union, we should be guided by realism, proceed from a position of strength, and be ready at all times to engage in efforts to reach equitable and verifiable agreements. Your country's very existence as a free and independent nation proves what patient, persistent negotiations with the Soviets can produce. We welcome the wisdom of your counsel and rest assured that we will continue this policy in the hope that it will yield the results for which the world yearns.

This morning, I spoke about creating a new tie between our peoples. In the past year, Vice President Bush's visit to Vienna, the reopening of our consulate in Salzburg, and the appointment of Helene von Damm to be our Ambassador to Austria have shown our commitment to build stronger and more vital links between our governments and our peoples. But the bonds of true friendship can never be too many or too strong. And we will create still more through your exchanges—youth exchanges, I should say, and enhanced cooperation in scientific and technological research.

Mr. President, we're grateful for your visit. The people of America look forward to hosting you and your party across our country. Your visit is a celebration of something real, tangible, and enduring: the friendship between the people of Austria and the people of the United States. At one point in "The Sound of Music," the character who plays Baron von Trapp sings a song about the edelweiss, an Austrian flower. And before the song ends, the lyrics become a prayer for Austria itself. It is a prayer Americans join in—"Blossom of snow, may you bloom and grow—and bless your homeland forever."

Ladies and gentlemen, would you please join me in a toast to the President of Aus-

tria and Mrs. Kirchschläger and to the friendship and freedom that our two peoples enjoy.

President Kirchschläger. Mr. President, Mrs. Reagan, distinguished ladies and gentlemen, it is indeed a great privilege, Mr. President, to be your guest today here in the White House. And believe me, it is a moving evening for all Austrians present here—a moving evening by the words, your address to us, and by the music you offered to us.

I would like to thank you most sincerely for this gracious and warm hospitality you are extending to us and for all the friendship we felt here in Washington and in the United States. I express this thanks also in the name of my wife and on behalf of the members of the Austrian Government in my company as well as in the name of the other Austrian guests today. And I am joining you to express my real pleasure that Baroness Trapp is here with us. In Austria, too, you have a wonderful reputation. You know it, I hope.

It's true—and I may repeat what I said this morning—I'm profoundly appreciative, Mr. President, that you have invited me to pay this official visit to the United States. For me and for all of Austria, this is a truly historic event. It is indeed the first official visit of an Austrian head of state to the United States since relations between Vienna and Washington were established formally 146 and informally 200 years ago.

This should not lead to wrong conclusions. The relations between our two countries have been always very good, considering the fundamentally different structures of our countries until 1918. It was on the model of your Supreme Court, for instance, as established under your Constitution, that the Austrian Empire in 1869 established its own *Reichsgericht*. And again, in 1919, Austria was the first country in Europe to adopt, on the example of the United States, the principle of full judicial review.

But it was during World War II, and especially in the period after the war, that the hearts of the Austrian people went out to America and the image of the United States in my country was forged by the Marshall plan, which played such a decisive part in the rebuilding of Austria and with which it has remained linked ever since. Only recently we celebrated in Vienna the 35th anniversary of the signing of the agreement on American temporary assistance to Austria and on economic cooperation, and we will never forget this event.

In those years, the trust between Austria and the United States was strengthened by 10 years of tough negotiations over the Austrian state treaty and the strong commitment of the Austrian people to democratic ideals. The conclusion of the state treaty and the recovery of Austria's full freedom in 1955 have led to a long-lasting period of excellent relations, which has continued to this day.

In the late thirties, freedom and democratic life and America's willingness to offer asylum to political and racial refugees attracted many of Austria's best sons and daughters, who have found a new home in your great country but have also helped as pioneers to build it up. Most Americans will be surprised to learn that at the middle of this century, only four countries had supplied more distinguished Americans listed in "Who's Who in America" than the small country of ours, Austria. It may indeed be unexpected that a land-locked country of central Europe, speaking a different language from that of America—you see it in my speaking—as small as the State of Maine and less populous than the city of New York should have been one of the major contributors to American life and culture. But to us, it is additional proof of our community of interests.

Mr. President, you exercise your high office at a time of global political tension and crisis, many of which are also of vital importance to my country. Austria, as a permanently neutral country, makes every effort to contribute towards the maintenance of world peace by promoting understanding in the geopolitical area in which

history has placed us. And by trying to secure friendly relations with all our neighbors, we are trying to remain an element in Europe's stability and security, to be a haven for refugees as well as a clear voice in support of human rights.

As a small country we have a vested and, indeed, a vital interest in upholding the rule of law in world politics and the principle of universality in international organizations. In all these respects, the world can continue to count on us in the future.

Our two countries are and will remain closely linked through their mutual adherence to the fundamental values of democratic Western pluralism to which the Austrian people has dedicated itself in all elections since 1945. In my view, this is the best basis for a mutual interest in a long-lasting friendship. Our common pledge for an increased support to youth exchange programs will additionally promote mutual understanding and help to deepen our relations also in the next generation.

As an expression of this hope, and as a token of our heartfelt friendship, I would like to extend to you, Mr. President, and to Mrs. Reagan a cordial invitation to pay a visit to Austria, be it officially or unofficially, whatever is more convenient to you. [*Laughter*]

With repeated cordial thanks for your hospitality and with my sincere good wishes for the prosperity of the United States and the American people, I invite you all to join me in a toast to the President of the United Nations of America and Mrs. Reagan.

Note: President Reagan spoke at 9:45 p.m. in the State Dining Room at the White House.

In his opening remarks, the President referred to Erwin Lanc, Austrian Foreign Affairs Minister, and Heinz Fischer, Austrian Science and Research Minister.

Nomination of Edward Sulzberger To Be a Member of the Board of Directors of the National Corporation for Housing Partnerships
February 29, 1984

The President today announced his intention to nominate Edward Sulzberger to be a member of the Board of Directors of the National Corporation for Housing Partnerships for the term expiring October 27, 1986. This is a reappointment.

Mr. Sulzberger is currently serving as president of Sulzberger-Rolfe, Inc., in New York City. He is also president of the Association for Government Assisted Housing. He has been the president of the Metropolitan Fair Rent Committee since 1962. He is a member of the National Association of Real Estate Boards, Real Estate Board of New York, and the International Federation of Real Estate Agents. He is a member of the board of directors of the Realty Foundation of New York and the Realty Advisory Board on Labor Relations.

He graduated from Brown University (B.A., 1929). He is married, has one child, and resides in New York City. He was born November 30, 1907, in New York City.

Remarks at a White House Briefing for the National Alliance of Senior Citizens
February 29, 1984

Good afternoon, and welcome to Washington. I'm delighted to have you here today, because I'm a long-time admirer of the National Alliance of Senior Citizens. Under the fine leadership of your president, Mrs. Virginia Aubrey; your national vice president, Colonel Barry Taylor; your board members, and you, the State and regional leaders. The National Alliance of Senior Citizens skillfully represents its 1.4 million members and works tirelessly to make this a better country for senior citizens and for all Americans. You've given this administration your firm support, and I want to let you know how grateful we all are.

You know, I've been around awhile myself. [*Laughter*] One of my favorite quotations about age comes from Thomas Jefferson. He said that we should never judge a President by his age, only by his work. And ever since he told me that—[*laughter*]—I've stopped worrying. And just to show you how youthful I am, I intend to campaign in all 13 States. [*Laughter*]

But in our society, senior citizens play a vital role. Senior citizens provide invaluable skill, talent, and wisdom that can come only with years. I always remember that Winston Churchill was almost 65 when World War II broke out, but he carried England through all those bitter years and on to victory. And I think, if I remember correctly, that Adenauer, when he was bringing about economic recovery in West Germany after the war, was 80 or better.

Now, I know you're having a number of briefings today, but if I could take just a moment, I'd like to speak about some of our accomplishments. And maybe some of those who are going to do the briefing here will have to scratch things out if I say them first. [*Laughter*] Don't do it. It bears repetition.

Just 3 years ago, we inherited the worst economic mess in decades. Big taxing and spending had led to soaring inflation and interest rates. In January of 1981 inflation was in double digits, the prime rate hit its highest peak since the Civil War, and growth was disappearing.

The broken economy hit senior citizens especially hard. Many live on fixed incomes and found the purchasing power was eaten up by inflation. Like all Americans, senior citizens found jobs becoming more and more scarce. And senior homemakers found that 12½-percent inflation made it harder to buy groceries and pay bills.

Our administration went to work, as we said, to make a new beginning. We reduced the growth of Federal spending. We pruned needless regulations. We reduced personal income tax rates and passed an historic reform called tax indexing, a reform that means that government can never again use inflation to profit at the people's expense. And now, today, less than 3 years since we set our policies in place, our nation has one big program to help every American, young and old. It's called economic recovery.

The prime rate is almost half of—[*applause*]—thank you—of what it was when we took office. Inflation has plummeted by two-thirds to about 4 percent during the past year. And that lower inflation rate makes the average retired person's private pension benefits worth about a thousand dollars more in purchasing power than if inflation had stayed at the 1980 levels.

But all the economic indicators—factory orders, retail sales, and housing starts—are up. The stock market has come back to life, and the American worker's real wages are rising. Unemployment is still too high but is dropping fast. Last year more than 4 million Americans found jobs, the steepest 12-month drop in unemployment rate in 30 years.

And just this morning we saw a picture of the future of our economy, and it looks good. A strong gain in January's leading economic indicators means this recovery isn't about to fizzle; it'll keep going strong—just like America's senior citizens. The index of leading indicators is a combination of different activities in the economy, and it rose by 1.1 percent. The index shows the direction the economy is headed in future months. So, send away the hand-wringers, because today's good news marks the 16th rise in the last 17 months of those indicators.

Now, there are those that claim that we've cut social security and medicare benefits, and I have to tell you whenever I hear that, it sort of touches my temperature control. [*Laughter*] Nothing could be further from the truth. Our budget for this year provides for $238 billion in programs that affect the elderly, which averages out to $17,000 for every senior couple in America.

Since we took office social security benefits for the average retired couple have gone up about $180 a month. Medicare benefits are higher than ever before. Even after adjusting for inflation, our administration is giving America's senior citizens more social security, medicare, and other benefits than they've ever received, and we will not betray those entitled to social security or medicare benefits. And just as we put social security on a firm footing, we'll also put medicare on a sound financial basis. So, the next time you hear someone claim otherwise, you tell them an Irishman named Reagan says they're full of blarney. [*Laughter*]

Just as we're turning the economy around, we're bringing a new sense of purpose and direction to American foreign policy. In Grenada we've set a nation free. In Central America we're working to defend democracy and advance economic development. Events in Lebanon have been painful, but we're determined to do all we can to promote stability and peace in the Middle East. And one thing's for certain: Our presence in Lebanon has prevented far greater destruction and loss of life than would have otherwise taken place.

In Europe the NATO alliance, which was kind of trembling for a while, has held firm. And as for arms talks, we hope the Soviets will come back to the negotiating table soon. And when they do, they'll find American negotiators waiting for them, ready to come to equitable and verifiable agreements. In the meantime, we and our NATO allies will remain steadfast in the defense of our freedom and the protection of world peace.

Permit me to close by mentioning two vital matters that are now before the Congress. The first is a subject of special concern to senior citizens—crime.

Every American should be able to walk the streets unafraid and go to bed at night without worrying that the next sound might be the footsteps of a burglar or a rapist. But, tragically, we still can't do that. Think of all the senior citizens who don't visit their families or see a doctor because

273

they're afraid they might get robbed or mugged on the way.

The reason crime is so bad is no mystery. For too many years the scales of criminal justice were tilted in favor of the criminals themselves. Those in charge forgot, or just plain didn't care, about protecting the rights of law-abiding citizens. We came to Washington determined to restore the proper balance to our criminal justice system. And we've begun to get results.

In 1982 the crime rate dropped by 4.3 percent, and that was the biggest decline in a decade. But we still face a tremendous challenge. One of the most important steps we've proposed is the comprehensive control act and the most sweeping anticrime bill in more than 10 years. Recently, the Senate passed the crime control act and several important related crime bills. But in the House, instead of giving those bills the priority they deserve, the leadership has bottled them up in committee.

Now, let me give you some examples of the reforms the House leadership is blocking. One reform would widen the powers of Federal prosecutors to go after mobsters and drug traffickers by seizing their profits. It could be a knockout blow against the drug syndicates that are poisoning our country. Why should any right-minded person oppose this?

Another reform involving the so-called exclusionary rule would allow evidence obtained reasonably and in good faith to be used in a criminal trial. It'd be a big step toward making sure criminals don't go free on technicalities. Who in good conscience could object to that?

Let me give you an example, because I know a great many people aren't completely familiar with the exclusionary rule and how it employs. Several years ago in California, San Bernardino, on the suspicion that a couple living in a home were peddling heroin, narcotics agents got a warrant and had enough evidence to get that, went to this house and then searched the house for the heroin, and they couldn't find any. And on the way out, just on a hunch, one of them turned back to the baby in the crib and took off its diapers, and there was the heroin. It was thrown out of court and couldn't be used, because they said the

baby hadn't given its permission to be searched.

Well, these crime bills that we're talking about should be above partisan politics. And I urge you to help me tell the American people what the House leadership is doing. If we hold a few feet to the fire, certain Members of the Congress might finally realize that the American people want action. I've said repeatedly, you don't have to make them see the light; just make them feel the heat. [*Laughter*]

Now, the second issue is school prayer. From the early days of the American colonies, prayer in school was practiced and revered as an important tradition. Indeed, for nearly 200 years of our history, it was considered a natural expression of our religious freedom. And then in 1962, the Supreme Court expelled God from America's classrooms. Well, I happen to believe that if the Congress can begin its day with prayer, then so can our children. And along with you, all the people, or most of them, agree. Polls show that by a margin of 4 to 1 Americans want prayer back in our schools.

The Senate will soon vote on a constitutional amendment to permit voluntary vocal prayer in our schools. If the amendment passes in the Senate, we'll have to work to get a vote in the House. But neither will happen without our support. If ever there was a time for the people of this country to make their voices heard, the time is now. I urge you to support the school prayer amendment in your home States and to tell your Senators and Representatives where you stand. I think it would be nice to show the world that America is still one nation under God.

Strength in the economy, a firm sense of purpose in foreign affairs, the will to combat crime and seek God's help—it all adds up to a great national renewal, a reaffirmation of the fundamental American values of hard work, family, freedom, and faith.

And I have to interject something here. You know, our generation—and I don't think many of us realize it—is a very unusual one in the history of man. Only occasionally back through history have there been single generations that presided over a great period of transition and saw a great change, and ours was one. We literally in our lifetimes have gone from the horse and buggy to space travel and landing on the Moon. And we've seen four wars in our lifetime. We've seen a Great Depression that certainly made us look on the recent recession with a little more ease than some of the people who had never experienced that Great Depression.

And I have to just tell you a little experience. When I was Governor, back in those days of the riots on the campus and all that was going on, I wanted more than anything to be able to go to the campus and talk to some of those young people, but if I went I started a riot. I was the establishment. And one day some of the student leaders in our university system in California demanded a meeting with me. Well, I was delighted.

And they came in and, as was the custom of some in that day, in torn tee-shirts and some of them barefoot, slouched into their chairs, and then one of the spokesmen teed off, and he started in on me. And he said, "You know, Governor, it's impossible for you to understand your own children." He said, "Your generation cannot understand

ours at all." Well, I tried to pass it off. I said, "We know more about being young than we do about being old." [*Laughter*]

And he said, "No, I'm serious." He said, "When you were our age, when you were growing up," he said, "you didn't have instant electronics, computers figuring in seconds what it used to take months and weeks or days to compute." He said, "You didn't have jet travel. You didn't have space exploration." And he went on like that. And, you know, usually you only get the right answer after it's over and you've gone home, but he talked just long enough that the Lord blessed me, and I thought of the answer. [*Laughter*] And when he paused for breath, I said, "You're absolutely right. We didn't have those things when we were your age. We invented them." [*Laughter*]

So now, among other things, there's one more thing we can do and that is build an America to pass on to our children and grandchildren with pride.

Thank you. God bless you all.

Note: The President spoke at 1:03 p.m. in Room 450 of the Old Executive Office Building.

Remarks at a White House Reception for Members of the United States Winter Olympic Team
February 29, 1984

The President. Good afternoon, and welcome to the White House. Nancy and I just want you to know how proud all of us—your families, your friends, and countrymen—how proud we are of the job that you did representing us in Sarajevo. And we were all watching and we were by your side, in spirit at least, during the entire competition. We're aware of the enormous commitment of time and effort that your participation in the winter Olympics represents.

It's said that in sports, it's not just the will to win, but the will to prepare to win that makes the difference. And it took enormous preparation for you to compete, and we're grateful for your dedication. Whether you

won or lost, you're now part of that elite group of citizens who represented our country in the Olympic games. It's a distinction that will be yours for the rest of your lives.

For those of you who won medals, we have a special word of thanks. The competition was fierce and your achievement was well-deserved. You've proven that a free country like ours, where support for the Olympics is totally voluntary, can hold its own against societies which subsidize their athletes.

Debbie Armstrong, you not only won our first gold medal at the games, you're also the first American woman to win a gold medal in Olympic skiing competitions since

1972. Your victory was especially sweet. So, congratulations to you and many thanks for giving us all a big lift in spirit.

And Scott Hamilton, the image of you skating a victory lap waving the Red, White, and Blue is now fixed in the memory of this nation. Your battle against a childhood illness and your commitment to the years of practice and training needed to excel on the ice now—well, they're indeed an inspiration. And now you hold three world championships and a fresh Olympic gold medal.

Kitty and Peter Carruthers, you've taken another step up from your showing at Lake Placid 4 years ago. Your silver medal in the pairs competition adds another accomplishment to a great career that's included many national titles and world team appearances for our country.

And Rosalyn Sumners at the young age of 19 took home a silver medal for figure skating. And you add that to the world and national championships you've been winning—no wonder you're the honorary mayor of your hometown—Edmonds, Washington. [*Laughter*] If the burden gets too heavy, just get in touch and we'll talk things over. [*Laughter*] I know there *are* days like that. [*Laughter*] But I'm sure they're all very proud of you.

And, Rosalyn, with you, Scott Hamilton, the rest of the fine skaters, America is well represented on the ice. And that goes for all our medal winners—the Mahre brothers, Phil and Steve, Bill Johnson, who smoked them—[*laughter*]—Christen Cooper, too.

All of you here who competed and those who couldn't be with us: You gave your country thrills beyond description. Most important, you reminded us that the qualities of personal commitment—courage, character, and heart—are the mark of greatness in sport. You have your country's thanks and best wishes. And believe me, all Americans—Republicans, Democrats, Independents, from whatever race, religion, or creed—we're all on the same team in this, cheering you on.

This year's winter contests were in the finest tradition of the Olympics. I've read of the warmth and enthusiasm with which the citizens of Sarajevo greeted athletes and visitors from around the world. I'm sure

that the people of our country will be equally as friendly and hospitable, particularly those in southern California, who will actively host the summer Olympic games.

I was out in California not too long ago—you undoubtedly read that—[*laughter*]—and they're leaving no stone unturned in preparation for the games. The city of Los Angeles has rolled out the welcome mat, and I'm certain that the teams and visitors from around the world are going to feel as welcome as all of you did in Sarajevo.

In closing, I'd like to offer a special note of congratulations to two other American medal winners in winter Olympic sports—Mike May and Ron Salviolo. Mike skis better blind than most sighted skiers. And your skill and your spirit are doing much to encourage others who might otherwise needlessly limit their own expectations. Mike, you and the other competitors here are a testimony to all young people that they should never be afraid to dream big dreams, and they should never hesitate to try to make those dreams a reality.

I participated in sports quite awhile ago. And today, I work a little bit upstairs in the gym at staying fit. Then my other favorite exercise is exercising a horse. But my experience in high school and college athletics—I know, as the years go by and I look back, more and more I see them as providing just as much education and as much benefit for me at later life than any of the things that happen in a classroom or a lecture hall.

And I know in the years ahead all of you will feel the same way about your experience in the Olympics. So, thank you all for being such fine representatives of our country. And thank you especially for being here today. And now let's get behind the summer team for the next round of the Olympics in Los Angeles. And, again, God bless you all.

Mr. Hamilton. Hmmmm. [*Laughter*] Well, I've been elected on behalf of the athletes to say a few words. And it's really a thrill and an honor for me to be able to address the President directly. I—my heart—again—[*laughter*]——

First, personally, I'd like to thank you for calling me after I won my medal. I'm sorry if I was short with you—[*laughter*]—but I'm short with most people. [*Laughter*]

I know as President of the United States you're also the honorary president of the Olympic Committee. But I don't think that's enough. And I just hope I'm speaking the hearts of all the athletes here. We would like you to be a member of the Olympic team with all of us, and we have some gifts for you.

First, we have this plaque with all the different disciplines of all the sports and their pins, their official pins, and we'd like you to have this.

The President. Well, thank you very much.

Mr. Hamilton. Secondly, what kind of team member would you be if you couldn't be recognized in the street as an Olympic athlete? [*Laughter*] We have this jacket, our official jacket, from Levi's, and we'd like

you to have that. And also these pins, Mrs. Reagan——

The First Lady. Thank you.

Mr. Hamilton. ——and President Reagan.

The President. Thank you.

Mr. Hamilton. And thank you from all of us for sharing your afternoon with us and for having—I know it's an extreme honor and a thrill for all of us to finally meet you. Thank you very much.

The President. Well, thank you very much. Thank you all very much. We're very greatly honored. And I have to confess to you that I once *did* have some dreams myself. But it was before the water froze; I was going to do it in swimming. [*Laughter*] So, finally, I've made the Olympic team. [*Laughter*]

Note: The President spoke at 2:11 p.m. in the State Dining Room at the White House.

Remarks at an Event Sponsored by the American Legion Auxiliary
March 1, 1984

Madam President, I'll be sure and just keep that one hat on—[*laughter*]—not wear the other one here today.[1]

But it's wonderful to be here and to see so many of you from out there in the heartlands of America here in Washington. I'm sure the city isn't looking its best for you, but it's just a little too chilly for the cherry blossoms yet. And most of the heated air that's normally found in Washington has moved out on the campaign trail. [*Laughter*]

There's one good thing about a political year, though. It's the chance to meet with so many of you who are not part of the permanent Washington establishment. And you should be commended for being part of the American Legion Auxiliary's Awareness Assembly and participating in the briefings that you'll be getting this week from gov-

---

[1] *In introducing the President, Anna Gear asked the audience to welcome him "not as a candidate for reelection, but as President."*

ernment officials. But I hope that you'll keep in mind something that I've learned in the past few years. The conventional wisdom in this town isn't always on target.

There's one informal survey I could give as an example that's mentioned in the book "The Real Campaign." And that was taken at almost exactly this same time 4 years ago during the height of the Presidential primary season. Members of the Washington Press Club were asked to predict who would be the President of the United States in 1981. One candidate—and I won't mention any names—got 197 votes. Another got 65. And there were two others with 19 each. And then there was one other candidate whose vote total was so insignificant that it wasn't even reported. But I didn't let that discourage me. [*Laughter*]

When we came to Washington 3 years ago—3 years and a month or so ago—we came having announced that we'd challenge the conventional wisdom and show that campaign promises could be kept. We wanted to reverse a domestic policy of tax and tax and spend and spend and end a foreign policy of watching the chances for peace with freedom, democracy, and dignity steadily retreat. So, one by one, we dealt with the critical problems that faced our people.

First it was inflation, once at 12.4 percent, now down to around 4 percent. Then Federal spending growth, cut more than in half. Now, we'd been told this couldn't be done. Then the prime interest rate—21½ percent, the highest since the Civil War— cut nearly in half to 11 percent. And then the unemployment rate. This one really shocked Washington's doomsayers. It's been dropping faster than during any recovery in the last 30 years. For 14 months, we have averaged 300,000 people a month going back to work.

And on the foreign front, America is restoring her strength in words and in deeds. The decay in our military ships that couldn't leave port and aircraft that couldn't take off, a rapid deployment force that was neither rapid, deployable, or much of a force—all of that's behind us now.

That same uniform that so many of your fathers, brothers, husbands, sons, and daughters brought such honor to is being worn today with pride by millions of young Americans. And all of you know far better than most how important it is that these young men and women, poised and ready, are equipped with the best that we can give them. Their readiness and resolve are the greatest guarantee that we have that our young people will never again see the face of battle, bear the burden of war that we've had to do in the past. There've been four wars in my lifetime. None of them started because America was too strong.

We're seeing to it that America stands proud again, that American citizens, whether they're navy pilots in the Gulf of Sidra or medical students in Grenada, can no longer be attacked or their lives endangered with impunity. And about that Grenada rescue mission—wasn't it nice for a change to see graffiti on foreign walls that read, "God bless America," not "Yankee go home"?

I have to interrupt to tell you, I just received a phone call a little while ago— about 2:30 this morning, Cap Weinberger arrived back from his trip to Europe and the Middle East. He had been out there on the vessels talking to our marines and telling them how proud we all were—those who have been taken offshore in Beirut. This is the same unit that was also at Grenada. And then later he was walking through and among the marines there and talking to some of them, and he came to one who seemed a little smaller than the rest. He was pretty short. And Cap asked him, he said, "Tell me. Which do you think was the best and the most important mission—Grenada or Beirut?" And the kid just looked at him for a second and then said, "Both."

Across the globe, Soviet expansionism, once unchecked, has now been blunted. And for the first time in a long while, an American administration is leveling with the American people and the rest of the world about the crucial nature of the struggle between democracy and totalitarianism.

Yet even as we've been candid about our adversaries, we've pushed forward a series of negotiating initiatives which, I believe, will eventually lead to not just arms control but arms reductions. And we must continue working until that day arrives when nuclear weapons have been banished from the face of the Earth.

Three years then—the direction of our domestic and foreign policies has been fundamentally changed. At the same time we were dealing with the pressing problems of our economy and national security, the problem of crime and the career criminal has remained among our top priorities. The 8-point program that I announced over a year ago is beginning to show some gratifying results.

Drug-related arrests are averaging a thousand a month and convictions 800 a month, and Federal law enforcement has taken out of circulation 2⅓ million pounds of illicit drugs and 20 million doses of prescription drugs. FBI organized crime convictions are up from 515 in fiscal '81 to 1,331 in 1983. After years of decline in our investigative forces, more than a thousand new investigators and 200 new prosecutors joined the fight last year against crime.

We've improved State and local cooperation through local law enforcement coordinating committees and the Justice Department's Governors Project. We've added prison space and improved training opportunities for local and State police. We've brought the FBI in on major drug cases. Our 12 new regional drug task forces are bringing in the big cases against major drug traffickers. And we've stepped up our educational efforts so we can take potential drug customers away from the dealers, because just reducing the supply of drugs isn't good enough. We can't solve the problem until we turn off the customers.

Our organized crime commission, headed by Judge Irving Kaufman, will put the menace of organized crime, well, where it belongs: front and center on the American agenda. Our goal is a frontal assault on criminal syndicates in America. We mean to cripple the mobsters' organization, dry up their profits, and put their members behind bars where they belong.

Through our victims of crime task force and the family violence task force, we have launched major initiatives to improve the treatment of innocent victims of crime and solve the problem of violence in American households.

In all these things, we're doing our best to deliver on our promises and keep faith with the American people. We've shown that America's problem wasn't a great national malaise at all, but a failure of leadership in the Nation's Capital.

Yet even all this progress—progress we've won together—hasn't satisfied some of the doomcriers who even now are saying that our country's on the wrong course. I just wish that those who were so pessimistic about America's future would remember the record of the last 3 years.

You know, if you'll forgive me—a little story from show-business world—some of these cynical, professional pessimists remind me of the story of a young performer who was auditioning for a hard-bitten theatrical agent. He wanted to get into vaudeville. And the agent's sitting out there in the theatre all by himself with his cigar, said to the—"Okay, kid, let's see what you can do." Well, the young fellow walked up on the stage and then suddenly just took off. And he flew up and over the balcony, circled a couple of times, flew around the ceiling, came back to a perfect landing on the stage, and took a bow. And the agent took the cigar out of his mouth and said, "Okay, kid, what else do you do beside bird imitations?" [*Laughter*]

We have come a long way, and success is in sight. The 3-year record of this administration shows how dramatically we broke with the legacy of an awful, immediate past. This administration has a strong record, a hopeful record. It's open to scrutiny; we welcome it.

You know, there are old rules in politics—for example, in a campaign year: Don't get over confident. President Dewey told me about that one. [*Laughter*] And then there's a very pertinent one, namely that the people don't want to hear so much about where we've been, but about where we're going; not so much about what's been done, but what needs to be done.

And the issue before the American people is the issue of the future. Will America return to the days of malaise and confusion? Will we go back to double-digit inflation, skyrocketing interest rates, and economic stagnation and decline? Will we return to self-delusion about our adversaries and retreat in the face of provocation and aggression, to the days of decaying defenses and shattered prestige? Or will we get on with the unfinished agenda of the eighties? This is the real issue before us.

Will we continue America's progress toward a strong economic recovery at home, a strong defense abroad, a return to discipline and excellence in our schools, a crackdown on criminal elements in our society, and a renaissance of traditional values?

Now, I'm sure you've heard some who are out of step with the American public on all these issues using words like "fairness" and "compassion," possibly because they're stuck for something meaningful to say. I think it's time for these experts on fairness and compassion to answer a few questions.

Let these experts on fairness explain to working Americans why it is fair to oppose tax cuts and tax indexing and why they want to take those tax breaks away from the American people.

Or let them explain why, when the overwhelming majority of Americans favor a balanced budget amendment, they think it's fair to bitterly oppose it.

And on another important constitutional amendment, favored overwhelmingly by the American people, will somebody get them to tell us why it is compassionate to deny schoolchildren a right even the Members of the United States Congress have and that is to open each day with a simple prayer?

And can they explain why they're so bitterly opposed to tuition tax credits and why they think it's fair for one parochial or private school parents to be forced to pay twice for their children's education?

And why these fairness experts and compassion crusaders have bottled up effective anticrime legislation on Capitol Hill for 2 years in a row? Where's the compassion in forgetting the victims of crime? What is fair about holding up urgently needed reform of our bail and parole systems, about refusing to revise the exclusionary rule or reinstitute the death penalty? The Senate has adopted a significant package of these very anticrime measures. Now it's time for the House to act.

And, you know, if I could interject something here, I mentioned the exclusionary rule, and I've discovered that a great many people aren't quite aware what we're talking about. We're talking about technicalities that are invoked in court to deny the introduction of legitimate evidence. And I'll give you an example. Happened in our own State of California several years ago. Two narcotics agents, based on evidence suggesting that a man and woman, living in a home there, were peddling heroin. They got from a judge a search warrant, legally and legitimately, to go in and search that house to see if they could find the heroin. Well, they searched, and they couldn't find it. And then, as they were leaving, on a hunch, one of them turned back to the baby in the crib and took off its diapers, and there was the heroin. The evidence was thrown out of court because the baby hadn't given its permission to be searched. That became known as the diaper case. And of course, the word was out, that's where you can hide heroin, and no one can touch you.

Well, I believe those who are so quick to find fault with what we and the American people have achieved during the past 3 years owe an accounting to the American people. Perhaps they can explain how under the guise of compassion and fairness those who once stood for the working people have now divorced themselves from the concerns of everyday Americans and turned themselves over to the trendy politics of the special interest groups. Maybe they could explain why they're opposed to tax cuts, to the balanced budget amendment, to the prayer amendment, to tuition tax credits, to anticrime legislation, to adequate defense spending.

I think the debate now getting underway in America is an especially important one, that these days are momentous ones for our country, that the choices we make will have much to do with the fate of freedom and prosperity for the rest of this century. And I've often thought that the worst legacy of those grim years at the end of the seventies was the loss of self-confidence by our leaders in our institutions and people. More than a few of those leaders openly blamed their own inadequacies on our system of government and on you, our people as a whole.

Well, the last 3 years have shown just how wrong they were, just how resourceful the American people still are, and just how resilient our system is, and how willing the heart of America remains. Those of you here today from, as I said, the heartlands know what I'm talking about. Your organization and the dedication you bring to it is one of the many examples of America's enduring vitality and energy.

You know, during the days of World War I, not long before the American Legion was founded in Paris, some of the allied commanders doubted whether the green American troops were really up to the job. And then during a great offensive in the Argonne Forest, the allies and the enemy found out just how very quickly these young Americans—they found out what they were made of.

Now, some of you may remember the story in that war of the Lost Battalion, a group of American soldiers trapped behind enemy lines who joined together, fought for days with incredible gallantry against over-whelming odds. And then when the surren-der demand finally came, the reply came from the throats of those young Americans who united and shouted, "Come on over and get us!" Well, the enemy came over, and they got nothing except defeat.

Twenty-six years later, not far away from that same World War I battlefield, another group of American soldiers would cheer when their commander responded to a sur-render demand by an overwhelming enemy with one immortal word: "Nuts!"

In both instances, the challenge then before Americans was to win a war. Today the challenge before Americans is to pre-vent a war.

You know far better than most how im-portant this work is, how high the price of war really is, and how great the heartbreak that it brings. But you also know that an America, strong at home and strong abroad, will never again pay that price or know that heartbreak.

Only the strong are free, and peace comes only through strength. With your continued support and help we can keep America strong, free, prosperous, and at peace. America is moving forward again. Let's keep her there.

Thank you, God bless you, and God bless America.

Note: The President spoke at 10:55 a.m. in the International Ballroom at the Washington Hilton Hotel.

Remarks on Signing an Agreement With Morocco To Modernize the Voice of America Relay Station in Tangier
March 1, 1984

The President. Well, good afternoon. We've just had a meeting in the Oval Office. And I am delighted to welcome you all to the White House to witness the sign-ing of our agreement on modernizing the Voice of America relay station in Tangier.

I'm pleased to call on Director Wick and Minister Filali[1] to sign this agreement, an important step towards strengthening the signal of the Voice of America.

[At this point, the agreement was signed.]

Secretary of State Shultz. I didn't know Charlie Wick could sign something with such a flourish. [*Laughter*]

The President. Now, if that station ever needs a sports announcer—[*laughter*]——

We come together today as people of two free nations, bound by common ideals and aspirations. And one of the most important ideals that we share is our belief in the power of truth. Truth is mankind's best

hope for a better world.

The Voice of America has been a strong voice for truth, and despite problems of an-tiquated equipment and Soviet jamming, the Voice of America has been able to spread its message of truth around the world.

Were it not for many years of neglect, the Voice of America could be heard more clearly by many more people around the globe. And that's why our administration has made the same kind of commitment to modernizing the Voice of America that President Eisenhower and President Ken-nedy brought to the space program. It's our firm commitment to Voice of America mod-ernization which brings us here today.

Millions of people who long to hear the truth will benefit from this agreement. And by increasing the direct flow of information to the people and allowing them to make up their own minds about the major issues of the day, we'll be serving the cause of peace and human rights.

America's ties with Morocco go back more than 200 years—long before the advent of international broadcasting. Our

---

[1] *Charles Z. Wick, Director of the United States Information Agency, and Abdellatif Filali, Moroccan Minister of Foreign Af-fairs, respectively.*

relations are warm and close, and we share many of the same values. The cooperation between our two countries is symbolized by this agreement. And I want to say how much I, as well as Ambassador Reed, Charles Wick, Ken Tomlinson, and others at the Voice of America appreciate the cooperative spirit that has characterized the negotiating between our two countries.

I would particularly like to express my gratitude to His Majesty, King Hassan II for his role in this negotiation. His involvement and wise counsel were critical to its success-ful conclusion, and we owe him a debt of gratitude.

So, thank you all very much.

Note: The President spoke at 1:45 p.m. in the Roosevelt Room at the White House. The ceremony was attended by Moroccan and U.S. officials.

In his closing remarks, the President referred to Joseph Verner Reed, Jr., U.S. Ambassador to Morocco; and Kenneth Y. Tomlinson, Associate Director for Broadcasting, United States Information Agency.

Message to the Senate Transmitting the United States-France Convention on Penal Sentences
March 1, 1984

To the Senate of the United States:

With a view to receiving the advice and consent of the Senate to ratification, I transmit herewith the Convention Between the United States of America and France on the Transfer of Sentenced Persons, which was signed at Washington on January 25, 1983.

I transmit also, for the information of the Senate, the report of the Department of State with respect to the treaty.

The Convention would permit citizens of either nation who had been convicted in the courts of the other country to serve their sentences in their home country; in each case the consent of the offender as well as the approval of the authorities of the two Governments would be required.

This Convention is significant because it represents an attempt to resolve a situation which has inflicted substantial hardships on a number of citizens of each country and has caused concern to both Governments. The treaty is similar to those currently in force with Bolivia, Canada, Mexico, Panama, Peru, and Turkey. I recommend that the Senate give favorable consideration to this Convention at an early date.

RONALD REAGAN

The White House,
March 1, 1984.

Statement by Principal Deputy Press Secretary Speakes on United States Assistance in the Completion of the Airport in Grenada
March 2, 1984

We are pleased to announce today that the United States will assist the Government of Grenada in its efforts to complete the airport at Point Salines. Following a detailed feasibility study, commissioned by USAID, and after considering the Grenadian Government's request, the President determined that the airport is vital to the revival of Grenada's economy, which was left in shambles following 4½ years of mismanagement under the Cuban-supported Bishop regime.

In a February 27, 1984, letter to Nicholas Brathwaite, Chairman of the Advisory Council of Grenada, the President said that the United States is "committed to the timely completion" of the airport "as quickly as possible." The airport is expected to boost tourism in Grenada, generating badly needed hard currency to enable the private sector oriented economy to revitalize itself.

While the United States plans to contribute a substantial part of the estimated $24 million to finish the project, other countries have indicated they are prepared to participate in the financing of the airport as well.

Remarks at a White House Luncheon for Elected Republican Women Officials
March 2, 1984

Good afternoon, and welcome. It's good to see so many old friends and have a chance to make new ones. And a warm welcome to Congresswomen Olympia Snowe and Claudine Schneider. Where are you? There you are. All right.

And it's always a pleasure to be joined by two of the most important women in my life—Nancy and Maureen. I want you to know Nancy warmed my heart recently when she introduced me at the Susan B. Anthony birthday celebration. She said that I had helped her and Maureen quite a lot through the years, and then she said, "because, as we all know, behind every successful woman there's a dedicated man." [*Laughter*]

And my special congratulations are in order for one person here—Connecticut State Senator Adela Eads. Happy birthday.

I'm pleased that we have with us some of our outstanding women from the White House Personnel and Legislative Offices, and I also notice we've been joined by a few of the men on our staff. They do sort of stand out. [*Laughter*] But many thanks to Jim Baker for inviting all of you here.

And permit me to begin by giving each of you high praise and heartfelt thanks for all you've done for our Republican cause. Politics has its share of fun and glamour, but in the end it's sheer, unrelenting hard work from people like you that makes it possible for us to put our beliefs into practice. And the role you play is especially important because you demonstrate the Republican commitment to American women.

The GOP commitment to women runs deep, from its support of women suffrage to

when it was first to elect a woman to the United States Congress and the only party to ever elect women to the United States Senate who were not first filling unexpired terms. Today, the two women in the Senate—my friends, Nancy Kassebaum and Paula Hawkins—are Republicans. And we have nine outstanding Republican women in the House of Representatives. Now, isn't it time we give them more company?

In this administration, we've appointed women to positions of top responsibility—women like our United Nations Ambassador, Jeane Kirkpatrick, our Secretary of Health and Human Services, Margaret Heckler, our Secretary of Transportation, Elizabeth Dole, Assistant to the President for Public Liaison, Faith Whittlesey, and many other women on the White House staff who are with us today. And one of my proudest days in office was when I appointed Sandra Day O'Connor to be the first woman in history on the United States Supreme Court.

But just as important, today there are thousands of able Republican women like you that are serving in public office outside Washington. You in State legislatures and other State and local offices are on the frontlines of democracy, putting your beliefs into practice close to the people. We look on you as leaders who truly know what the American people think and need.

And just as we're eager to see the number of Republican women officeholders grow at the national level, we're determined to see those numbers grow in every American town, city, and State. And together, we Republicans are working to reshape

America's destiny. Everyone who takes part, from stuffing envelopes to running for town council to holding national office, is making history.

And I know you're having briefings all day, but if I could just take a moment I'd like to give you an overview of some of our accomplishments. And if you've heard it before, please don't stop me—[*laughter*]—I enjoy saying it so much.

Just 3 years ago, we inherited a mess: soaring inflation and interest rates and declining productivity. And the month that I stood on the steps of the Capitol to take my oath of office, inflation was in double digits and the prime interest rate had hit the highest peak since the Civil War.

The economic crisis struck women hard. The majority of elderly Americans living on fixed incomes are women, and they found their purchasing power eaten up by that inflation. Working women saw jobs become more and more scarce. Homemakers found that 12½-percent inflation made it a nightmare to try and buy groceries and pay the bills. And the thousands of women who wanted to start their own businesses saw 21-percent prime rate slam shut the doors of opportunity.

When we took office, the economy was job one. And with Republicans in control of the Senate, we moved quickly to set our program in place. And believe me, if we had not had one House of the Congress, we couldn't have achieved what we've achieved so far.

We reduced the growth of Federal spending. We pruned needless regulations. George Bush was in charge of that, and we hacked them out by the score. We reduced personal income tax rates, passed an historic tax reform called indexing, which means that government can never again use inflation to profit at the people's expense. We reduced the marriage tax penalty, almost doubled the maximum child care credit, increased the limits for IRA and Keogh contributions, and eliminated estate taxes on family farms and businesses for surviving spouses.

Now today, from Maine to California, a powerful economic recovery is taking place. The prime rate is almost half what it was when we took office. Inflation has plum-

meted by two-thirds, to about 4 percent. Factory orders, retail sales, and housing starts are up. Speaking of housing, this morning the news was released for January: 688,000 new houses were sold in America and, except for December of 1983, that was the highest figure for any month since 1979.

The American worker's real wages are rising. The stock market has come back to life, providing new funds for growing sectors of the economy and raising the value of pension funds where millions of workers have their retirement savings. The best news of all is that last year more than 4 million Americans found jobs. That's the steepest 12-month drop in the unemployment rate in more than 30 years.

The economic crisis hit women hard, but today's recovery is giving women new opportunities. The unemployment rate among adult women has dropped from 9.1 to 7.1 percent. And today, more women have jobs than ever before in our Nation's history. And the jobs women hold are getting better and better. In 1983 women filled over 60 percent of all the new jobs in managerial, professional, and technical fields. And the number of women-owned businesses is growing twice as fast as those owned by men.

In foreign policy, we're acting with a new firmness and sense of purpose. From Central America to Western Europe to an island called Grenada, we've worked to defend freedom and peace. And while events in Lebanon have been painful, our presence there has prevented far greater destruction and loss of life than would otherwise have taken place. In our dealings with the Soviets, the prospects for world peace stand on a new and firm footing.

Let me take just a moment to mention two vital matters now that are before the Congress, and the first is crime. For too many years the scales of justice have been tilted in favor of the criminals, with devastating results. Rising crime rates, a flood of illegal drugs, billions of dollars worth of property stolen or destroyed each year, and, worst of all, millions of Americans living their daily lives in fear. We were determined to restore balance to our criminal justice system, and I think we've made genuine progress.

In 1982 the crime rate dropped by 4.3 percent, and that was the sharpest decline in 10 years. But we still have much to do. Recently the Senate passed our comprehensive crime control act and several other related crime bills. But in the House, the Democrats have stalled these vital bills by bottling them up in committee.

Now let me give you some examples of the reforms the House Democrats are blocking. One reform makes sentencing more uniform and certain. There's nothing complicated about this. The sentence imposed should be the sentence served. Why should any right-minded person oppose that reform? Another reform involving the so-called exclusionary rule would allow evidence obtained reasonably and in good faith to be used in a criminal trial. It would help keep criminals from going free on technicalities. Now, who could object to that in good conscience?

I have a favorite story I like to tell as an example of the exclusionary rule at work. It was in California, San Bernardino, several years ago. Two narcotics agents with a legitimate warrant, obtained in the legal way, to search a house where they believed heroin was being sold, searched the house and couldn't find the heroin. A man and woman lived there. And they were starting out the door when one of them, on a hunch, just turned back to the crib where the sleeping baby lay and took off its diapers and there was the heroin. Evidence thrown out of court; they went free because the baby had not given its permission to be searched.

Well, we think these crime bills should be

above partisan politics, and I urge you to join in pressing for action.

The second issue is school prayer. I deeply believe that the loving God who gave us this land should never have been expelled from America's classrooms. If the Congress can begin its day with prayer, children can, too. Not that Congress maybe doesn't need it more than the children do— [*laughter*]—present company excepted. [*Laughter*]

But I think the country agrees with this. The polls show that by a majority of 80 percent, the American people want voluntary prayer back in our schools. Soon the Senate will vote on a constitutional amendment to permit voluntary vocal prayer in our schools. If the amendment passes the Senate, we'll have to work to get a vote in the House. But neither one will happen without our support. If ever there was a time for the people of this country to make their voices heard, that time is now.

Please support the school prayer amendment in your home States, and tell your Senators and Representatives here in Washington where you stand. Passage of the amendment would reaffirm one of the most fundamental American values—faith.

President Lincoln's portrait hangs above the fireplace in this room. And more than a century ago, he said America was the last, best hope of Earth. Well, today the light of that hope is once again aglow. Together, we can make it a shining beacon for all mankind.

Thank you, and God bless you. And let's have dessert. [*Laughter*]

Note: The President spoke at 12:53 p.m. in the State Dining Room at the White House.

Proclamation 5155—Women's History Week, 1984
March 2, 1984

By the President of the United States of America

A Proclamation

In countless ways, both recorded and un-

recorded, women have played a vital role in the development of this Nation. The greatness of the United States reflects the accomplishments of American women throughout our history.

Today, whether single or married, with children or other dependents, women continue to assume critically important leadership positions in our Nation's economic, cultural, and social life. They are contributing substantially to the character and growth of the economy and permanently influencing the development of our political, commercial, judicial, and legal institutions.

Although women have always constituted a significant portion of America's labor force and, in fact, represent nearly half of it today, more and more of them are serving in demanding and rewarding professional jobs. Women are university presidents, astronauts, military officers, corporate officials, labor leaders, business owners, and members of innumerable other professions. They serve in State and local governments as well as in the Federal government and the United States Congress. They are members of the President's Cabinet, the diplomatic corps, and, making more history in 1981, a woman is now a Justice of the Supreme Court of the United States.

Women who work in the traditional roles of mothers and homemakers continue to be a wellspring of our Nation's strength, helping us to maintain our social and spiritual values. They have fostered unity and stability in our families, which are the cornerstone of American life. They serve as the backbone of our volunteer movement, which certainly is one of the most powerful forces for good anywhere on the earth. The vision of women has made them leaders in many causes which have brought important social reform in such areas as abolition, health care, child labor laws, temperance, voting rights, and improvement of industrial labor conditions.

It is appropriate that all Americans recognize the outstanding achievements of women and celebrate their continuing contributions to our Nation and its heritage.

The Congress, by H.J. Res. 422, has designated the week beginning March 4, 1984, as "Women's History Week" and has requested the President to issue a proclamation in observance of that week.

Now, Therefore, I, Ronald Reagan, President of the United States of America, do hereby proclaim the week beginning March 4, 1984, as Women's History Week. I encourage all individuals, governmental agencies, and private institutions and associations throughout the country to observe this occasion by participating in appropriate ceremonies and activities.

In Witness Whereof, I have hereunto set my hand this 2nd day of March, in the year of our Lord nineteen hundred and eighty-four, and of the Independence of the United States of America the two hundred and eighth.

RONALD REAGAN

[*Filed with the Office of the Federal Register, 4:32 p.m., March 2, 1984*]

Executive Order 12467—International Boundary and Water Commission, United States and Mexico
March 2, 1984

By virtue of the authority vested in me as President by the Constitution and laws of the United States of America, including Section 1 of the International Organizations Immunities Act (59 Stat. 669, 22 U.S.C. 288), it is hereby ordered as follows:

Section 1. The International Boundary and Water Commission, United States and Mexico (hereinafter referred to as "the Commission"), in which the United States participates pursuant to 22 U.S.C. 277 *et seq.,* and *inter alia,* the 1889 International Boundary Convention (26 Stat. 1512, 9 Bevans 877), and the 1944 Treaty Relating to the Utilization of the Waters of the Colorado and Tijuana Rivers and of the Rio Grande (59 Stat. 1219, 9 Bevans 1166), is hereby designated as a public international organization entitled to enjoy the privileges, exemptions, and immunities conferred by the International Organizations Immunities Act. This designation shall not be deemed to abridge in any respect the privileges, exemptions or immunities which the Commission may have acquired or may acquire by international agreement or by Congressional action.

Sec. 2. This designation shall not extend to the United States Section of the Commission in respect of matters within its exclusive control, supervision or jurisdiction, or within the sole discretion of the United States Commissioner, pursuant to international agreements in force with the United Mexican States, statute or other authority.

RONALD REAGAN

The White House,
March 2, 1984.

[Filed with the Office of the Federal Register, 4:33 p.m., March 2, 1984]

Statement on Signing the Veterans' Compensation and Program Improvements Amendments of 1984
March 2, 1984

I am very pleased to sign S. 1388, the Veterans' Compensation and Program Improvements Amendments of 1984. This bill will provide a 3.5-percent cost-of-living increase in the monthly compensation checks of some 2.3 million veterans with service-connected disabilities. It will also provide the same percentage cost-of-living increase to approximately 319,000 widows and children of veterans whose deaths were service-connected. These increases will be effective on April 1, 1984.

Compensation benefits to our disabled veterans and their survivors are a reflection of the deep gratitude of all Americans to those men and women who suffered injuries or died in the service of their country. This legislation demonstrates the Nation's continuing commitment and support for these men and women, and their survivors.

S. 1388 will also benefit our veterans in many other ways. For instance, this legislation increases the maximum rate of disability compensation payable to hearing-impaired blinded veterans and liberalizes eligibility for compensation of certain other groups. It improves the Veterans Administration's education, home loan, and medical construction programs, in a number of respects. It extends the State veterans cemeteries grant program for 5 years. And, finally, it increases the membership of the Board of Veterans Appeals in order to improve timeliness in processing appeals from veterans.

I am gratified that the 3.5-percent increase in compensation benefits, as well as other provisions contained in S. 1388 that I proposed in my fiscal year 1984 budget, will now become a reality.

Chairman Alan Simpson and Chairman Sonny Montgomery and the other members of the Senate and House Veterans' Affairs Committees are to be commended for their skillful and dedicated stewardship of this bill.

Note: As enacted, S. 1388 is Public Law 98–223, approved March 2.

287

Appointment of Henry A. Kissinger as a Member of the President's Foreign Intelligence Advisory Board
March 2, 1984

The President today announced his intention to appoint Henry A. Kissinger to be a member of the President's Foreign Intelligence Advisory Board. This is an initial appointment.

Dr. Kissinger is chairman of Kissinger Associates, Inc. He is a consultant to Goldman Sachs & Co. and is chairman of the international advisory committee for the Chase Manhattan Bank. Dr. Kissinger serves at Georgetown University as counselor to the Center for Strategic and International Studies and professor of diplomacy at the School of Foreign Service at Georgetown University. He is also a senior fellow of the Aspen Institute, a member of the board of trustees of the Metropolitan Museum of Art in New York City, and chairman of the board of the International House. He serves as a contributing analyst to the American Broadcasting Co.

He served as Secretary of State in 1973–1977. Previously he served at the White House as Assistant to the President for National Security Affairs in 1969–1974. From 1951 to 1969, he held various positions at Harvard University including lecturer, professor of the department of government, and director of the defense studies program. He was awarded the Nobel Peace Prize in 1973 and the Presidential Medal of Freedom in 1977.

Dr. Kissinger graduated from Harvard University (A.B., 1950; M.A., 1952; Ph.D., 1954). He is married, has two children, and resides in New York City. He was born May 27, 1923, in Fürth, Germany.

Appointment of William A. Schambra as a Member of the National Historical Publications and Records Commission
March 2, 1984

The President today announced his intention to appoint William A. Schambra to be a member of the National Historical Publications and Records Commission for a term expiring December 26, 1987. He will succeed Norbert Brockman.

Dr. Schambra is a resident fellow at the American Enterprise Institute. Previously, he was assistant director of the Project to Study the Constitution at the American Enterprise Institute in 1979–1983, associate editor of Public Opinion magazine in 1977–1979, and instructor at Northern Illinois University in 1976–1977.

He graduated from Michigan State University (B.S., 1971) and Northern Illinois University (M.A., 1973; Ph.D., 1983). He is married, has one child, and resides in Alexandria, VA. He was born March 27, 1949, in Freeport, TX.

Remarks at the Annual Conservative Political Action Conference Dinner
March 2, 1984

Thank you very much for those kind words, Lew. Mr. Vice President, Members of the Congress, members of the Cabinet, and distinguished ladies and gentlemen:

I just want to say thank you to Mickey Edwards. I'm honored to stand beside this fine Congressman from Oklahoma and ACU's great leader.

Seeing the size of your gathering here this evening, the exciting program that you've planned, and the media attention you're drawing, and seeing and feeling the drive, energy, and intellectual force that's coming to our cause from the American Conservative Union, Young Americans for Freedom, Human Events, and National Review, I believe the proof is undeniable: The conservative movement is alive and well, and you are giving America a new lease on life.

It is true that many of you are helping now in our administration. And we're going to add one more in the next few days, because coming to the West Wing, there on our staff, will be the man that organized the first four of these dinners—Frank Donatelli.

We've been together through many struggles. We've known the agony of defeat. And recently, we've seen public support begin to swell behind our banner. What we worked so long and hard to win was good, but hardly good enough. So, in expressing my pride and affection for this good family, for our family, may I say not only Happy Anniversary, ACU, but also, long live the revolution.

The mission of this conference is a mission of principle: It is a mission of commitment, and it must and will be a mission of victory. Color our cause with courage and confidence. We offer an optimistic society. More than 200 years after the patriots fired that first shot heard 'round the world, one revolutionary idea still burns in the hearts of men and women everywhere: A society where man is not beholden to government; government is beholden to man.

The difference between the path toward greater freedom or bigger government is the difference between success and failure; between opportunity and coercion; between faith in a glorious future and fear of mediocrity and despair; between respecting people as adults, each with a spark of greatness, and treating them as helpless children to be forever dependent; between a drab, materialistic world where Big Brother rules by promises to special interest groups, and a world of adventure where everyday people set their sights on impossible dreams, distant stars, and the Kingdom of God. We have the true message of hope for America.

In "Year of Decision, 1846," Bernard DeVoto explained what drove our ancestors to conquer the West, create a nation, and open up a continent. If you take away the dream, you take away the power of the spirit. If you take away the belief in a greater future, you cannot explain America—that we're a people who believed there was a promised land; we were a people who believed we were chosen by God to create a greater world.

Well, I think we're remembering those bedrock beliefs which motivate our progress. A spirit of renewal is spreading across this land. We even have a pro-conservative newspaper in the Nation's Capital. [*Laughter*] And, if I may just interject, I understand that Jim Whalen will be honored by your group tomorrow night, and that's wonderful news and well deserved.

I think America is better off than we were 3 years ago because we've stopped placing our faith in more government programs. We're restoring our faith in the greatest resource this nation has—the mighty spirit of free people under God. It was you who reminded Washington that we are a government of, by, and for the people, not the other way around. It was you who said it is time to put earnings back in the hands of the people, time to put trust back in the hands of the people, time to put America back in the hands of the people.

And this is what we're trying to do. Our critics are not pleased, but I hope we'll be forgiven this small observation: The spendthrifts who mangled America with the nightmare of double-digit inflation, record interest rates, unfair tax increases, too much regulation, credit controls, farm embargoes, gas lines, no-growth at home, weakness abroad, and phony excuses about "malaise," are the last people who should be giving sermonettes about fairness and compassion.

Their failures were not caused by erratic weather patterns—[*laughter*]—unusual rotations of the Moon—[*laughter*]—or by the personality of my predecessor. [*Laughter*]

They were caused by misguided policies and misunderstanding human nature. Believe me, you cannot create a desert, hand a person a cup of water, and call that compassion. You cannot pour billions of dollars into make-work jobs while destroying the economy that supports them and call that opportunity. And you cannot build up years of dependence on government and dare call that hope.

But apparently nothing bothers our liberal friends. The same expertise that told them their policies must succeed, convinced them that our program spelled economic Armageddon. First they blamed the recession on our tax cuts. The trouble is, our tax cuts hadn't started yet. [*Laughter*] They also warned that when our tax program passed, America would face runaway inflation, record interest rates, and a collapse of confidence. Well, at least they got part of it right. Our program passed, and we witnessed a collapse all right. A collapse of inflation from 12.4 down to about 4 percent; a collapse of the prime interest rate from over 21 percent to 11; and a new surge of confidence in stocks and bonds.

They warned that decontrolling the price of oil would send the cost of gas at the pumps skyrocketing. We decontrolled, and the price is lower today than it was 3 years ago when we decontrolled.

And then they said that recovery couldn't come, or would be too feeble to notice. Well, from strong growth in housing to autos, construction, and high technology, from a rebirth of productivity to the fastest drop in unemployment in over 30 years, we have one of the strongest recoveries in decades. And we'll keep it strong if they'll get out of the way.

Pardon me if I add something here. You know, I did get a kick out of watching on TV the door-to-door campaigning in New Hampshire. I got to see some of the homes the people have been able to buy since we brought interest rates down. [*Laughter*] Incidentally, I'm sure all of you have read or seen on the air that in the month of January our sale of new houses dropped, and dropped to a great percent—about a 9-percent drop below what it was the previous month. Only 688,000 new homes were sold in January. But they didn't add that that

drop was only from the sales in December, and beyond that it was the highest number that had been sold since 1979 in a single month.

But our critics moan the recovery can't last. Those awful tax cuts haven't sparked business investment; private borrowers are being crowded out of the capital markets. Well, if that's true, how did the venture capital industry raise four times as much capital in 1983 as it did in 1980? How could real, fixed business investment increase by a 13-percent rate last year, the fastest rate in any recovery in the past 30 years? And how could funds raised in the equity markets zoom from $16.8 billion in 1983—or in 1982, to $36.6 billion in 1983? Still another record. Now, all this means more growth, more jobs, more opportunities, and a more competitive America.

Now, lately, the pessimists have been sounding a new alarm: The dollar is so strong, they say, that exporters can't export, and we'll have no chance for lasting growth. Well, the facts are—as Secretary Don Regan has pointed out—the dollar is strong because of people's confidence in our currency, our low rate of inflation, and the incentives to invest in the United States. No American should undermine confidence in this nation's currency. A strong dollar is one of our greatest weapons against inflation. Anyone who doubts the value of a strong currency should look at the postwar performances of Japan, Switzerland, and West Germany.

Yes, we have a trade deficit, but this isn't entirely new. The United States had a merchandise trade deficit in almost all of the years between 1790 and 1875. I remember them well. [*Laughter*] Of course, I was only a boy at the time. [*Laughter*] But that was when our economy grew into one of the largest and strongest in the world. Rising incomes have given us the ability to increase purchases from abroad. The U.S. economy is serving as an engine for worldwide recovery, and this will translate into greater demands for our own goods. But even with our current trade deficits, exports of goods and services have made a greater contribution to this recovery than to any previous recovery in the postwar period.

The critics were wrong on inflation, wrong on interest rates, wrong on the recovery, and I believe they'll be wrong on the deficit, too, if the Congress will get spending under control. If optimism were a national disease, they'd be immune for life. [*Laughter*] Isn't it time that we've said no to those who keep saying no to America? If the sourpuss set cannot believe in our nation and her people, then let them stand aside and we will get the job done.

In fairness, I'll admit our critics are worried sick about the future of the economy. They're worried it might keep getting better and better. [*Laughter*]

Now, those who deal in a world of numbers cannot predict the progress of the human mind, the drive and energy of the spirit, of [or] the power of incentives. We're beginning an industrial renaissance which most experts never saw coming. It started with the 1978 capital gains tax reduction—passed over the objections of the last administration—and which was then made greater by our own tax reductions in 1981.

Incentives laid the seeds for the great growth in venture capital which helped set off the revolution in high technology. Sunrise industries, such as computers, microelectronics, robotics, and fiber optics—all are creating a new world of opportunities. And as our knowledge expands, business investment is stimulated to modernize older industries with the newer technologies.

Dr. Robert Jastrow, chairman of the first NASA lunar exploration committee, believes the potential in our high-tech industries for new jobs and economic growth is mind-boggling. A year ago, he predicted the computer industry would double in size by 1986, becoming America's biggest business. And now we're seeing the knowledge and benefits of high technology being put to use in medicine, bringing new hope to millions who suffer handicaps and disabilities.

Visionaries see infinite possibilities for new economic growth in America's next frontier—space. Our challenge of building a permanently manned space station, and of further exploration, can open up entire new industries. Products from metal alloys to lifesaving medicines—these can immensely improve our environment and life on Earth.

All space-related activities must begin with the transportation to get there. This is an area of American technological leadership, and I intend to make sure we keep that edge. That's why I've asked Transportation Secretary Elizabeth Dole to start immediately promoting private sector investment in commercial, unmanned space boosters—the powerful rockets that carry satellites into orbit. With those boosters, and a thriving commercial launch industry, American private enterprise will be blasting off toward new horizons of hope, adventure, and progress—a future that will dazzle our imaginations and lift our spirits.

An opportunity society awaits us. We need only believe in ourselves and give men and women of faith, courage, and vision the freedom to build it. Let others run down America and seek to punish success. Let them call you greedy for not wanting government to take more and more of your earnings. Let them defend their tombstone society of wage and price guidelines, mandatory quotas, tax increases, planned shortages, and shared sacrifices.

We want no part of that mess, thank you very much. We will encourage all Americans—men and women, young and old, individuals of every race, creed, and color—to succeed and be healthy, happy, and whole. This is our goal. We see America not falling behind, but moving ahead; our citizens not fearful and divided, but confident and united by shared values of faith, family, work, neighborhood, peace, and freedom.

An opportunity society begins with growth, and that means incentives. As I told the people of Iowa last week, my sympathies are with the taxpayers, not the taxspenders. I consider stopping them from taking more of your earnings an economic responsibility and a moral obligation. I will not permit an antigrowth coalition to jeopardize this recovery. If they get their way, they'll charge everything on your "Taxpayers Express Card." And believe me, they never leave home without it. [*Laughter*]

As good conservatives, we were brought up to oppose deficits. But sometimes I think some have forgotten why. We were against deficit spending. Those who would be heroes trying to reduce deficits by raising taxes are not heroes. They have not addressed the point I made in the State of the Union: Whether government borrows or increases taxes, it will be taking the same amount of money from the private economy and, either way, that's too much.

We must bring down government spending to a level where it cannot interfere with the ability of the economy to grow. The Congress must stop fiddling and pass a constitutional amendment requiring a balanced Federal budget. With strong support from many of you here, we nearly scored a great victory in 1982. It's time to try again. We also seek a line-item veto to prevent pork barrel projects from passing just because they're attached to otherwise good legislation. I'm sure we're united by one goal. The Grace commission identified billions of dollars in wasteful government spending. And I believe the Congress has a responsibility to work with us and eliminate that waste wherever it exists.

Combining these spending restraints with another key reform will make America's economy the undisputed leader for innovation, growth, and opportunity. I'm talking about simplification of the entire tax system. We can make taxes more fair, easier to understand and, most important, we can greatly increase incentives by bringing personal tax rates down. If we can reduce personal tax rates as dramatically as we've reduced capital gains taxes, the underground economy will shrink, the whole world will beat a path to our door, and no one will hold America back. This is the real blueprint for a brighter future and declining deficits.

But economic opportunities can only flourish if the values at the foundation of our society and freedom remain strong and secure. Our families, friends must be able to live and work without always being afraid. Americans are sick and tired of law-abiding people getting mugged, robbed, and raped, while dangerous criminals get off scott-free.

We have a comprehensive crime bill to correct this. It would put an end to the era of coddling criminals, and it's been passed by the Senate. But the legislation is bottled up in the House. Now, maybe it's time they heard from a few of you—a few million of

you. You know, you don't have to make them see the light; just make them feel the heat. [*Laughter*] I hope you realize that in my comments about some of the shortcomings of the Congress, believe me, tonight, present company is excepted.

Strengthening values also demands a national commitment to excellence in education. If we are to pioneer a revolution in technology, meet challenges of the space age, and preserve values of courage, responsibility, integrity, and love, then we can't afford a generation of children hooked on cocaine and unable to read or write. Conservatives have pointed out for years that while Federal spending on education was soaring, aptitude scores were going steadily down. Look at the case of New Hampshire. It ranks dead last in State spending on education, but its students have the highest SAT scores among those States where at least half the students take the test. And they've maintained that honor for more than 10 years. America's schools don't need new spending programs; they need tougher standards, more homework, merit pay for teachers, discipline, and parents back in charge.

Now there's another important reform to be voted on soon in the Senate—possibly by Monday. Let us come together, citizens of all faiths, to pray, march, and mobilize every force we have so the God who loves us can be welcomed back into our children's classrooms. I'm gratified that Congressman Newt Gingrich is organizing a rally Monday night on the Capitol steps in support of our prayer in school amendment. Please be there if you can, and please send the message loud and clear that God never should have been expelled from America's schools in the first place. And maybe if we can get God and discipline back in our schools, we can get drugs and violence out. Now, let me make it plain that we seek voluntary vocal prayer, not a moment of silence. We already have the right to remain silent; we can take the fifth amendment. [*Laughter*]

But as we go on, we must redouble our efforts to redress a national tragedy. Since the Roe versus Wade decision, 15 million unborn children have been lost—15 million children who will never laugh, never sing, never know the joy of human love, will never strive to heal the sick or feed the poor or make peace among nations. They've been denied the most basic of human rights, and we're all the poorer for their loss.

Not long ago I received a letter from a young woman named Kim. She was born with the birth defect, spina bifida, and given little chance to live. But her parents were willing to try a difficult and risky operation on her spine. It worked. And Kim wrote me: "I am now 24 years old. I do have some medical problems due to my birth defect. I have a lot of problems with my legs. But I'm walking. I can talk. I went to grade and high school, plus 1 year of college. I thank God every day for my parents and my life." And Kim said, "I wouldn't change it if I could."

Life was her greatest opportunity, and she's made the most of it. An opportunity society for all, reaching for its future with confidence, sustained by faith, fair play, and a conviction that good and courageous people flourish when they're free—this is the noble vision we share, a vision of a strong and prosperous America, at peace with itself and the world. Just as America has always been synonymous with freedom, so, too, should we become the symbol of peace across the Earth. I'm confident we can keep faith with that mission.

Peace with freedom is our highest aspiration—a lasting peace anchored by courage, realism, and unity. We've stressed our willingness to meet the Soviets halfway in talks on strategic weapons. But as Commander in Chief, I have an obligation to protect this country, and I will never allow political expediency to influence these crucial negotiations.

We should remember that our defense capability was allowed to deteriorate for many years. Only when our arms are certain beyond doubt can we be certain beyond doubt that they will never be used. President John F. Kennedy spoke those words in 1961. Too many who admired him have forgotten that the price of peace is dear. But some members of his party have not, and I am proud to have one of them, a brilliant patriot, Jeane Kirkpatrick, by my side.

And I deeply appreciate your patriotic support for rebuilding our defenses. We're just beginning to restore our capability to meet present and future security needs. I am open to suggestions for budget savings, but defense is not just another Federal program. It is solely the responsibility of the Federal Government. It is its prime responsibility. So, our first responsibility is to keep America strong enough to remain free, secure, and at peace, and I intend to make sure that we do just that.

America's foreign policy supports freedom, democracy, and human dignity for all mankind, and we make no apologies for it. The opportunity society that we want for ourselves we also want for others, not because we're imposing our system on others but because those opportunities belong to all people as God-given birthrights and because by promoting democracy and economic opportunity, we make peace more secure.

Democratic nations do not wage war on their neighbors. But make no mistake, those who would hang a "Do Not Disturb" sign on our shores, those who would weaken America or give Castro's terrorists free rein to bring violence closer and closer to our borders, are doing no service to the cause of peace.

Fellow citizens, fellow conservatives, our time has come again. This is our moment. Let us unite, shoulder to shoulder, behind one mighty banner for freedom. And let us go forward from here not with some faint hope that our cause is not yet lost; let us go forward confident that the American people share our values, and that together we will be victorious.

And in those moments when we grow tired, when our struggle seems hard, remember what Eric Liddell, Scotland's Olympic champion runner, said in "Chariots of Fire." He said, "So where does the power come from to see the race to its end? From within. God made me for a purpose, and I will run for His pleasure."

If we trust in Him, keep His word, and live our lives for His pleasure, He'll give us the power we need—power to fight the good fight, to finish the race, and to keep the faith.

Thank you very much. God bless you, and God bless America.

Note: The President spoke at 9:30 p.m. in the Sheraton Ballroom at the Sheraton Washington Hotel. He was introduced by Lewis E. Lehrman, chairman of the dinner.

Radio Address to the Nation on Taxes and on the Budget Deficit
March 3, 1984

My fellow Americans:

If you had to choose between shrinking the size of government or shrinking the size of your paycheck, which would it be? Chances are you think you're paying enough taxes already. And I agree with you.

The trouble is, your opinions don't always count for much in Washington, DC. It seems to be taken for granted here that the Federal Government has an automatic right to grow at your expense. Listening to people talk, you'd almost think government owns your earnings. So, please be a little skeptical when you hear the moaning from Washington's born-again deficit fighters. The truth is, these are the same people who brought us big and bloated government in the first place, and they haven't changed a bit.

The Democrats use foggy language like "recovering revenue" or "stopping the revenue drain," but you don't need a Ph.D. in bureaucracy to know what they're offering: a choice between a tax increase, a tax increase, or a tax increase.

In the downpayment deficit reduction talks at the White House, suggestions were made on behalf of liberal House Democrats—suggestions for making you pay more taxes. They added up to $100 billion or more. Some examples: Liberal Democrats want very badly to eliminate indexing; that's the historic reform that will tie your tax brackets to the rate of inflation. Starting next year, you will no longer be pushed into a higher tax bracket just because you're receiving a cost-of-living raise. Keep in mind that indexing doesn't help the wealthy; they're already in the highest tax brackets. Indexing helps those who need help, but it deprives government of the automatic increase in its allowance, so the spenders

want to get rid of it. I don't intend to let them.

Another suggestion of theirs is a 3-year postponement in additional estate tax reductions. This would be a cruel blow to surviving spouses of family-owned farms and businesses. Hasn't the farm community suffered enough with the last administration's grain embargo? And the liberals would raise personal tax rates on millions of families and small businesses. These tax increases are neither wise nor compassionate. And they wouldn't reduce the deficit, they'd just reduce the recovery. And none of us should want that.

Yes, deficits are a problem. I've been saying so for more than a quarter of a century now. But the problem is not the size of the deficit, it's the size of government's claim on our economy. Whether government borrows or increases taxes, it will be taking the same amount of money from the private economy. So, if we raise taxes before cutting spending, the money will just be spent, the deficit won't be reduced, and government will grow bigger.

Now, that's what the House Democrats tried to do last year. Their budget resolution would have raised your taxes, then squandered that money on new programs. Well, we have a better way to cut deficits—cut the growth of government by cutting out the waste. This will reduce government's claim on the people's earnings, leaving more money for you to borrow, spend, invest, and to help our economy grow.

Don't let anyone tell you it can't be done. We've already cut spending by more than $300 billion on a 5-year basis. Contrary to what you've heard, we haven't done this by hurting the needy. Total spending on social programs has increased by $71 billion during these last 3 years.

To cite two examples frequently misrepresented, social security and Medicare benefits to America's senior citizens are higher than ever before, even after adjusting for inflation. We've been cutting the growth of government by eliminating waste. My Inspectors General have identified nearly $31 billion in agency fraud, waste, and abuse; and we're going after it.

For example, we've almost stopped the growth of delinquencies on amounts owed the Federal Government. And we boosted collections by $12½ billion last year. As part of its new "get tough" policy, the Department of Education is cracking down on people who defaulted on their student loans, and they're recovering $390,000 a day. And believe me, there's plenty more

waste to cut.

Those $300 billion in budget savings I mentioned are barely half of what we asked for from the Congress. And the Grace commission made some 2,500 recommendations for reducing billions of dollars in wasteful government spending and subsidies.

I'll be speaking out on this topic in future radio talks, but one thing is clear: Raising taxes is a cop-out; cutting waste in government is the right way to go. And this is what we're doing and what we'll continue to do. With your support, we can shrink government and stop the spendthrifts from shrinking your paychecks.

Till next week, thanks for listening, and God bless you.

Note: The President spoke at 12:06 p.m. from the Oval Office at the White House.

Proclamation 5156—National Beta Club Week, 1984
March 5, 1984

By the President of the United States of America

A Proclamation

On a cold January day 50 years ago in Landrum, South Carolina, 15 quiet citizens led by John West Harris founded the Beta Club and dedicated themselves to the promotion of leadership, honesty, achievement, and community service among high school students throughout the United States. The motto that was adopted by that infant club was: "Let us lead by serving others."

The six words in that motto tell a proud story. The Beta Club grew from "three handfuls" of citizens to a current membership of 200,000 high school students, alumni numbering over 1.5 million, and 4,500 chapters in 36 states.

From its small beginnings, the Beta Club sought to recognize high school students who displayed leadership abilities, personal integrity, academic achievement and a demonstrated willingness to serve one's fellow citizens.

The original Beta Club members were

opportunity innovators. They literally had the brashness to create and run the risk of failure. They had the toughness to experiment and were honest enough to learn from experience. Above all, they were willing to be judged on what they contributed to the well being of others.

The best growth generators are those persons who have the inner moral fiber to accept new ideas, concepts, machines and technology. The Beta Club founders had the ability to convince others that productive change was necessary in revitalizing high school youth to widen their spiritual and intellectual horizons. In recognizing the outstanding achievements of the Beta Club, we pay homage to a vital part of our Nation's heritage.

In recognition of the accomplishments of the Beta Club for its significant accomplishments toward the development of the youth of our Nation, the Congress, by Senate Joint Resolution 184, has designated the week beginning March 4, 1984 as "National Beta Club Week."

Now, Therefore, I, Ronald Reagan, President of the United States of America, do hereby proclaim the week beginning March 4, 1984, as National Beta Club Week, and call upon the people of the United States to observe the week with appropriate programs, ceremonies, and activities.

In Witness Whereof, I have hereunto set my hand this fifth day of March, in the year of our Lord nineteen hundred and eighty-four, and of the Independence of the United States of America the two hundred and eighth.

RONALD REAGAN

[*Filed with the Office of the Federal Register, 12:10 p.m., March 5, 1984*]

Remarks of the President and Chancellor Helmut Kohl of the Federal Republic of Germany Following Their Meetings
March 5, 1984

The President. Mr. Chancellor, Mr. State Secretary, and ladies and gentlemen, we've been honored to have Chancellor Kohl as a guest today. German-American partnership remains a positive, dynamic, and vital force in the free world's struggle for peace, security, and prosperity. The personal relationship between the Chancellor and myself exemplifies the close ties between our two countries.

Today I was most pleased to discuss with him issues of bilateral and international significance. Our talks focused on the need for Western leaderhip in dealing with the changing world of the 1980's.

We both agreed that 1983 was a crucial year for the NATO alliance. The leaders of the Western democracies stood firm in the face of an intense Soviet campaign of intimidation aimed at blocking NATO deployment of new intermediate-range missiles. To its common credit, the alliance demonstrated its determination to restore the military balance in Europe and maintain a credible nuclear deterrence and emerge stronger from the challenge. Thanks to the courage and vision of leaders like Chancellor Kohl, we can point to the past year with pride and look to the future with confidence.

Both Chancellor Kohl and myself would prefer to achieve a nuclear balance through arms reduction. Today I reconfirmed my willingness, eagerness to continue to effort to reach arms reduction agreements with the Soviet Union. Both Chancellor Kohl and I agreed that, with new leadership in the Kremlin, an opportunity exists for real progress in relations between East and West. However, in the face of Soviet intransigence at the negotiating table, a table which we remain ready to return to any time, the alliance will continue to strengthen its conventional and nuclear deterrent.

In the Declaration of Brussels last December, the NATO Foreign Ministers affirmed our offer to establish constructive contacts and dialog with the Soviets. I reafirmed to Chancellor Kohl today my personal commitment to explore every possible avenue for improvement of relations with the East. And I'm ready to meet personally with the Soviet leadership if such a meeting is well prepared and holds promise of fruitful results.

Chancellor Kohl and I also discussed the strengthening of Western economies and the peaceful cooperation between our peoples. We're especially optimistic about the increasing team effort our countries are demonstrating in the exploration of space. The November mission of the shuttle was the first to include a non-American astronaut, a German. And I was delighted that the communications hookup allowed Chancellor Kohl and myself to talk with each other and with the astronauts in space. It was an exciting achievement and a reflection of the good will upon which future progress can be built.

This morning I presented Chancellor Kohl with a plaque commemorating that mission, which bears photographs and the U.S. and German flags that were flown on that mission in space. As the inscription says on the plaque, we look toward future German-American cooperation to strengthen peace, build prosperity, and expand freedom in developing space—our next frontier.

I am particularly pleased with our success in expanding the human side of the German-American relationship. The tricentennial of German immigration to America heightened our awareness of the deep personal and family ties between our two peoples. The German-American Friendship Garden, established during the tricentennial, symbolizes this relationship. And the newly launched Congress-Bundestag Youth Exchange Program will assure that these important contacts continue unabated.

Mr. Chancellor, after only 17 months in office, you are in the forefront of leadership in the Western World. There's rarely an issue of international significance on which your views are not sought and where your influence is not felt. Chancellor Kohl, I count on your friendship as Americans count on the friendship of the German people, as we rise together to meet challenges of the coming decade.

Thank you for visiting us in Washington here today, and I look forward to our next get-together.

The Chancellor. Mr. President, ladies and gentlemen, first of all, I would like to extend to you—dear Mr. President and dear friend—very warmly for the extremely friendly welcome you extended to me and for the intensive and detailed conversations we had on that occasion.

In the last few months, I felt it with particular strength how important it was for us not only to agree on political issues but also on fundamental personal values. Well, for us, the Germans, in order to preserve peace and the liberty of our countries, we have to rely on two fundamental principles. First of all, they are the close ties with our friends in the United States of America, and the second issue—the second principle of equal importance is our close relations within the allies with our friends, the United States of America.

You, Mr. President, in particular, made special contributions towards this end, particularly as regards to friendship between our two governments—but when I think back on the tricentennial celebrations—also the contribution to the friendship between our two nations. We discussed thoroughly and in detail the perspective and prospects for future developments between East and West, and there is a far-reaching agreement concerning future developments.

Our two governments stand firmly by the proven and by the balanced concepts of the alliance. We would also in future assure the defense capability of the West by seeking military balance and equilibrium at as low a level as possible.

You referred to the statement in a declaration issued by the alliance on the 9th of December, 1983, and you, Mr. President, reaffirmed that declaration in the fundamental speech you made on the 16th of January, 1984. And we in Europe have considered that speech of yours as a great message of peace.

Mr. President, over the last 2 years, I have met in you a man who has always been aware of his personal responsibility for the peace in the world and who is also ready to bear and to shoulder that responsibility. And for that very reason, I again recommended to you, and in this very spirit, to seek, not as a propaganda coup, but as a political step, an early and a well-prepared meeting with the new Secretary General of the Soviet Union, Mr. Chernenko. And this meeting should not be a propaganda exercise. The Federal Government and I, as Federal Chancellor, do not consider ourselves to be mediators in that context. But nevertheless, if such a meeting is well prepared and if this opportunity is wisely used, we would consider such a meeting to be of great importance and helpful for shaping future East-West relations.

The President and I underlined the importance and the significance which attaches to the current arms control negotiations. And we were in agreement that the West should take the initiative in the negotiations about mutual and balanced forces reductions in Vienna and in the negotiations about a worldwide ban on chemical weapons and that it should make new proposals along these lines. And I was grateful to note, Mr. President, how much support you are giving to the proposals made by Secretary of State Shultz concerning a ban on chemical weapons.

We have also discussed questions of our national economies, questions which are of mutual concern and interest. We also discussed in that connection—in connection with the discussion of our economic—the state of our national economies, the fact that it is important for us to ensure that protectionism will not prevail and will not spread in our countries and in our continents, because protectionism is not a means to foster free economy. It's only free trade and free commerce which will ensure the future, which will ensure prosperity, and which will make for a free exchange of goods and ideas.

And of course, among friends there are also subjects on which one is not fully in agreement, on which one does not com-

pletely see eye to eye. A European who is here in the White House has got to speak about the high level of interest rates and the impact that has on the European economies. And it is quite clear this is a European problem.

Well, and even before that background, I would like to point out that these conversations once again showed to me the very strong foundations on which German-American partnership and friendship rest. This was a conversation among friends, and what better there you could say?

Note: The President spoke at 1:25 p.m. in the East Room at the White House. Chancellor Kohl spoke in German, and his remarks were translated by an interpreter.

Earlier, the President and the Chancellor met, together with U.S. and German officials, in the Oval Office. They then held a working luncheon in the State Dining Room.

Designation of Robert J. Lagomarsino as a Member of the Northern Mariana Islands Commission on Federal Laws
March 5, 1984

The President today announced his intention to designate Robert J. Lagomarsino as a member of the Northern Mariana Islands Commission on Federal Laws. He will succeed Phillip Burton.

Congressman Lagomarsino (R-CA) is currently serving his sixth term in the United States House of Representatives, having first been elected in 1974. He is a member of the Committee on Foreign Affairs and the Committee on Interior and Insular Affairs. For the 98th Congress he is the ranking Republican member of the Foreign Affairs Subcommittee on Western Hemi-

sphere Affairs and the Interior Subcommittee on Insular Affairs. He is also a member of the Interior Subcommittee on Public Lands and National Parks. Prior to his election to Congress he served 12 years in the California Senate.

He graduated from the University of California at Santa Barbara (1950) and the University of Santa Clara Law School (1953). He is married, has three children, and resides in Alexandria, VA, and Ventura, CA. He was born September 4, 1926, in Ventura.

Appointment of Four Members of the National Advisory Committee on Oceans and Atmosphere
March 5, 1984

The President today announced his intention to appoint the following individuals to be members of the National Advisory Committee on Oceans and Atmosphere:

Richard T. Leier, for a term expiring July 1, 1985. He will succeed Paul Bock. Mr. Leier is process engineer for Reserve Mining Co. in Silver Bay, MN. He is married, has two children, and resides in Silver Bay. He was born July 1, 1951, in St. Paul, MN.

John Norton Moore, for a term expiring July 1, 1985. He will succeed Robert M. White. Mr. Moore is the Walter L. Brown professor of law and director of the Center for Oceans Law & Policy at the University of Virginia. He is mar-

ried and resides in Charlottesville. He was born June 12, 1937, in New York City.

Burt Henry Keenan, for a term expiring July 1, 1986. This is a reappointment. He is chairman and chief executive officer of Offshore Logistics, Inc., in Lafayette, LA. He has three children and resides in Lafayette. He was born May 19, 1939, in New Orleans, LA.

Don Walsh, for a term expiring July 1, 1985. This is a reappointment. He is professor and director of the Institute for Marine and Coastal Studies at the University of Southern California. He is married, has two children, and resides in Palos Verdes Estates, CA. He was born November 2, 1931, in Berkeley, CA.

Remarks at the Annual Conference of the National League of Cities
March 5, 1984

Thank you very much for that, and thank all of you for a warm welcome, and good afternoon.

I'm delighted to have another chance to speak with the National League of Cities. As you probably remember—some of you at least—when we met in this room 3 years ago this week, I didn't have much good news to give you. The United States faced the worst mess since the Great Depression. Our national economy was nearing the breaking point, and so were our cities.

We'd paid a steep price for years of good intentions badly misdirected. Families felt helpless in the face of double-digit inflation, 21½-percent prime interest rates, and a virtual halt in economic growth.

Cities were especially hard hit. The eroding tax base had widened the cost-revenue gap of city budgets. As labor costs increased, services were cut. Doubling of tax exempt bond rates knocked local governments out of the bond market, so you had to delay your infrastructure projects. And the private sector couldn't provide much help because high taxes and the high cost of borrowing had drained them of money and

flexibility. Decades of Federal programs costing billions of dollars hadn't done the job. And the dramatic increase of Federal participation in local government complicated urban problems and threatened the foundation of our federal system.

We'd begun to lose sight of the fact of how our cities first became great, and that loss of vision may well have been our worst urban problem. Ingenuity and innovation built our cities and made them centers of commerce and education, of culture and communication, and of progress and opportunity. But the gradual shift of power toward the Federal Government moved us away from the very principles which kept our cities on a sound footing for most of our history.

Back when I was getting a degree in economics, taxes—Federal, State, and local— were taking a dime out of every dollar earned. And two-thirds of that went to State and local government. Today government is taking more than four times that much, and two-thirds of that is the Federal Government's share.

Communities had lost control of some of the most basic decisions affecting everyday life. Local policymakers became less able to respond to the needs of their community as the Federal Government became ever more intrusive. The growing burden of Federal oversight did little but put cities in handcuffs.

We knew America could not get back on its feet without—or with our cities flat on their backs. And that's why we appealed for your support to embark on a new course. Our compass would be those time-tested principles which have never failed us when we've lived up to them.

I think we're beginning to make headway both in addressing the causes of urban decline and in lifting your cities toward a new era of prosperity and stability. We believe there are four keys to success:

First, strong and steady economic growth. A healthy economy is our most powerful tool for revitalizing urban America.

Second, federalism. By sorting out who does what best, we can return power to levels of government closer to the people.

And third, public-private partnerships. We want to pool government and private sector resources through positive incentives and enterprise zones so that we can harness the power and creativity of the marketplace.

And fourth, a return to basic values. We seek to promote a renewal of community life and to strengthen the social fabric of the city—excellence in the classrooms, voluntarism, a sense of responsibility, and safety on the streets.

We should be confident. We are the same people who put our ambitions and skills to work and built the best cities in the world. If our program is fully enacted, today's problems can be overcome.

Now, I know that success will not come easy. It'll take great effort and patience. But it can and it will be done. Rebuilding cities begins with economic growth, and I believe our economic recovery is the most important urban renewal program in America today. The breadth and strength of this economic expansion are carrying fresh breezes of hope and opportunity to more and more urban areas.

Industrial production has increased for 14 straight months. Factory orders, factory utilization, and residential construction are all gaining strength. The growth of service industries continues to expand. Last year auto sales were at a 5-year high. More than 100,000 auto workers have been recalled. And with real, fixed business investment up by 13 percent—that was last year—the biggest gain of any recovery in the past 30 years, we see a bright future with more growth and jobs, and that's good news for the cities.

One example sums up the difference between the old policies of government pump-priming and our approach that begins with trusting people. Last year, there were demands for us to support an old-style, $3½ billion training program that was meant to place 300,000 people in make-work jobs. We turned it down so that economic recovery could do the job. Well, this recovery has put as many people back to work each month as they claimed their program would have done in a year. We have added 300,000 jobs every single month for the past 14 months. That's more than 4 million new workers on the job and paying taxes.

The second key to success is a renewed emphasis on federalism. We believe that when it comes to running cities, local officials can do a better job from city hall than bureaucrats can from Washington. [*Applause*] You tempt me to quit right there. [*Laughter*]

In our discussions, you said you wanted regulatory relief and reform, general revenue sharing, and block grants. Well, we agree. We want to make programs more responsible for the people that they're—and more responsive to the people that they're meant to help. And we want to put an end to cumbersome administration and spiraling costs at the Federal level.

Well, we're beginning to do this. We supported general revenue sharing and the surface transportation act which provides dedicated capital funding for mass transit. We've consolidated 56 narrow-purpose categorical grant programs into eight block grants, and we replaced two regulation-burdened programs—CETA and Title XX—with flexible block grants.

The cut in wasteful overhead has been dramatic: 647 pages of regulations have been eliminated. And your paperwork burden at State and local levels has been cut by 90 percent. We estimate that local governments were spared $2 billion in annual costs and between $4 billion and $6 billion in startup costs.

Our current budget proposes further grant consolidations to let State and local levels determine their own priorities, transfer funds to high priority areas, and further reduce overhead. This new flexibility for the States is now being felt at the local level. Six States have consolidated portions of their health block grants into mini-blocks for their local governments. Now, admittedly, that's only a start; we'd like to see more States doing the same thing. Federalism can't stop at the State capital.

Public-private partnerships are the third important key for sparking economic opportunity and development of urban areas. Partnerships can take advantage of every opportunity available, and they can use these opportunities in a most efficient and productive way to meet local needs. No single sector of our nation—government, business, labor, or nonprofit organizations—can solve our urban problems alone. But by working together, pooling our resources, and building on our strengths, we can accomplish great things.

Starting with a $2 million CDBG grant, Columbus, Ohio's partnership with lending institutions, a community housing group, and a local management company revitalized a neighborhood that was threatened with displacement. The project generated over $24 million in private investment. And the neighborhood of low- and moderate-income families was saved.

In Wilkes-Barre, Pennsylvania, a public economic development agency used its $1.7 million grant to create a revolving loan fund. The fund generated over $12 million in private capital to revive the downtown area and begin development of the city's industrial park. Nearly a thousand jobs have been either created or saved, and Wilkes-Barre's tax revenues have increased by more than $500,000.

Long Beach, California, used its CDBG and UDAG grants for a major downtown redevelopment program. And the private sector contributed $100 million to build a regional shopping center. City leaders tell us this partnership has sparked $1.2 billion in new commercial and residential development, 1,200 new jobs, and a major increase in tax revenues.

Partnerships produce jobs. The Job Training Partnership Act gives local government new flexibility, and by using private industry councils it matches local needs with sensible training. The program will train over a million permanently displaced blue-collar workers per year for productive jobs. CETA did just the opposite. It spent $53 billion to find private sector jobs for only 15 percent of the participants. Well, CETA's days are over. Our commitment is to a genuine partnership for real jobs with a real future.

While I'm talking about jobs, let me mention that more and more people recognize the minimum wage puts unskilled young people at a disadvantage in finding that crucial first job. Our youth employment opportunity wage bill will give a much needed boost to those looking for their first summertime job, and it deserves your support.

There's one more initiative that could mean exciting renewal for urban areas of hardcore unemployment and blight. Fifteen months ago, at your annual convention in Los Angeles, I talked about our enterprise zone legislation. Well, it's been on Capitol Hill now for more than 2 years. The Senate has passed it. The House continues to bottle it up. How in the world can some people give speeches about creating jobs and hope when they refuse to take action on a bill that's designed to provide just that? Enterprise zones encourage growth where we need it most—in areas of high youth and minority unemployment, in urban areas where the tax base has been hit the hardest. And our legislation will give cities the flexibility they need to make this innovative idea work.

Twenty-one States have already passed their own enterprise zone programs, and the results are very encouraging. Success stories are coming in from cities nationwide. And I'm told that after your unanimous endorsement of this initiative last December, you placed it on your 1984 priorities list. Well, now, all of you will be on Capitol Hill this week. Permit me to make one request. Please tell those people to look at the evidence and give our enterprise zones bill a chance. I've said it before and I'll say it again: They don't have to see the light; they have to feel the heat. [*Laughter*]

The fourth and final key to a stronger, more prosperous, and stable urban America is a strengthening of basic values through renewal of community life. People coming together in a spirit of neighborhood is what makes cities worth living in. It's what keeps businesses and attracts new ones. And it's what keeps faith with the fine traditions of the past while enabling us to build the future with confidence. Shakespeare said, "The people are the cities." And if our cities can create thriving neighborhoods that offer excellence in education, efficiency and affordability, safety on—but drugs and crime off—our streets, then they can become great centers of growth, diversity, and excitement, filled with sound, colors, warmth, and delight.

For too many years, crime and the fear of crime robbed our cities of their strength and vitality and frightened away the business community. Well, common sense is beginning to pay off. In 1982 the crime rate dropped by 4.2 percent—the biggest decline in a decade. And all over the country people are banding together and working with law enforcement agencies in thousands of crime prevention programs. We're cracking down on habitual criminals, organized crime, and the drugpushers. Federal task forces are stepping up the pressure. And we're working hard to improve the criminal justice treatment of the innocent victims of crime.

But formidable challenges remain. The scales of criminal justice are still tilted toward protecting the rights of criminals. I believe it's high time we restore a proper balance and start doing more to protect our law-abiding citizens. Lenient judges are only lenient on crooks; they're very hard on society.

The way to get along—or to get long overdue reform begins with passage of our comprehensive crime control act. It passed the Senate last month. But here again, the

House continues to wait. When you're on Capitol Hill this week, maybe you could give our friends in the House another message. When it comes to putting dangerous criminals behind bars, when it comes to keeping our people safe in their homes and neighborhoods, there should be no Republicans or Democrats, only Americans working for the common good.

We should also work together to improve the quality of American education. The report by the Commission on Excellence in Education made it clear that nothing short of a grassroots revolution would bring back quality education to our classrooms. Total expenditures for our schools rose more than 600 percent between 1960 and 1980, but Scholastic Aptitude Test scores were in a steady decline, and 13 percent of our 17-year-olds were functional illiterates.

We should take a lesson from New Hampshire. In fact, I'm a little—not just what happened recently—[*laughter*]. In fact, I'm a little surprised so few people noticed, during all the time they spent there in recent weeks, New Hampshire ranks 50th, dead last in State aid to education. But New Hampshire ranks first in Scholastic Aptitude Tests in those States where at least half the students take the test. And it's maintained that honor for more than 10 years. Very simple, why: In New Hampshire control of education remains in the hands of the people at the community level.

I believe that education already is playing its part in America's renewal. Parents, teachers, administrators, local officeholders, and school boards are finally getting back to fundamentals. They're providing leadership, working harder, and thinking smarter.

Today all 50 States have education task forces, and major reforms are being adopted in academic standards, discipline, curriculum, and basic values. We're seeing signs of improvement in test scores. Excellence in education is on its way back.

This spirit of renewal is the American spirit, and we see that spirit everywhere we look, from the healthy rise in corporate and private giving to thousands of exciting private sector initiatives, and from neighbors helping neighbors to a welcome return to our basic values.

Now, I know that over the last 3 years we've had to make some tough decisions, and there are still some tough ones to come. I appreciate that the cities you represent have felt the pain of reducing the growth of Federal spending. But to continue down that path that America was on would have meant disaster. We all want what is best for those who live in our cities.

They deserve no less. And together we can make it happen. And with your leadership, and with our partnership, it will happen.

Thank you, and God bless you all.

Note: The President spoke at 3:12 p.m. in the International Ballroom at the Washington Hilton Hotel.

Nomination of Gerald P. Carmen To Be the United States Representative to the United Nations European Office
March 6, 1984

The President today announced his intention to nominate Gerald P. Carmen, of New Hampshire, as the Representative of the United States of America to the European Office of the United Nations, with the rank of Ambassador. He would succeed Geoffrey Swaebe who is now Ambassador to Belgium.

Mr. Carmen was with Carmen Automotive, Inc., in Manchester, NH, in 1944–1959 beginning as stock clerk and advancing to vice president. In 1959–1979 he was the owner of Car-Go Home and Auto Centers,

Inc., and in 1979–1982 was in consulting and real estate with Mach I, Inc., in Manchester. In 1980 he served as transition team leader at the Department of Housing and Urban Development in Washington, DC, and since 1981 has been Administrator of the General Services Administration.

Mr. Carmen received his B.A. in 1952 from the University of New Hampshire. He is married, has two children, and resides in Washington, DC. He was born July 8, 1930, in Quincy, MA.

Nomination of Thomas H. Anderson, Jr., To Be United States Ambassador to Barbados
March 6, 1984

The President today announced his intention to nominate Thomas H. Anderson, Jr., of Mississippi, as Ambassador to Barbados, and to serve concurrently as Ambassador to the Commonwealth of Dominica, to Saint Lucia, to Saint Vincent and the Grenadines, to Antigua and Barbuda, and to St. Christopher and Nevis. He would succeed Milan D. Bish.

Mr. Anderson was assistant to the vice president of Hancock Bank in Gulfport, MS, in 1969–1972. Since 1973 he has been ad-

ministrative assistant to the United States House of Representatives Minority Whip Trent Lott (R-MS). He serves on the board of directors of Southern Federal Savings and Loan Association in Gulfport, MS.

Mr. Anderson graduated from the University of Mississippi (B.A., 1968). He is married to the former Katherine Milner and they are residents of Gulfport and Alexandria, VA. He was born March 17, 1946, in Gulfport.

Proclamation 5157—Frozen Food Day, 1984
March 6, 1984

By the President of the United States of America

A Proclamation

The United States is blessed with an impressive array of agricultural products that make our food production and distribution system the envy of the world. One significant aspect of that system is the frozen food industry, which in March 1984 celebrates its fifty-fourth year of service to the people of America and the world.

Throughout history, one of the primary goals of human effort has been the production of food. The farm-to-city migration created a great demand for food supplies in dense population centers in which such supplies could not be grown. The frozen food industry has made great strides in recent decades to respond to consumer needs.

The international frozen food industry started in the United States. Frozen vegetables, fruit, meat, and fish were first packaged and offered to consumers in 1930, contributing greatly to the convenience of life and freeing consumers permanently from the cycle of limited seasonal availability of many foods.

Between 1935 and 1940, frozen foods became available to the public on a large scale. During World War II, ration point values posted in stores and carried in newspapers focused public attention on frozen food. Frozen food became a part of the space age when Apollo XII astronauts took frozen meals on board. Seventy-two frozen food items were stored on the Skylab for a five hundred-day supply of meals for the crew.

The American frozen food industry, in close cooperation with producers, has continued research and development for the purpose of seeking better ways to bring the nutrition, quality, and taste of American agricultural products to consumers.

In recognition of the significant contribution which the frozen food industry has made to the nutritional well-being of the American people, the Congress, by Senate Joint Resolution 193, has designated March 6, 1984, as "Frozen Food Day" and authorized and requested the President to issue a proclamation upon this occasion.

Now, Therefore, I, Ronald Reagan, President of the United States of America, do hereby proclaim March 6, 1984, as Frozen Food Day, and I call upon the American people to observe such day with appropriate ceremonies and activities.

In Witness Whereof, I have hereunto set my hand this sixth day of March, in the year of our Lord nineteen hundred and eighty-four, and of the Independence of the United States of America the two hundred and eighth.

RONALD REAGAN

[*Filed with the Office of the Federal Register, 11:38 a.m., March 6, 1984*]

Remarks at the Annual Convention of the National Association of Evangelicals in Columbus, Ohio
March 6, 1984

Thank you all very much. [*Applause*] A speaker devoutly prays that that's what will greet him when he *finishes* speaking. [*Laughter*] But Members of the Congress, distinguished members of the clergy here, and you in the audience, I'm delighted to join you here in Columbus—the 42d annual convention of the National Association of Evangelicals and the 150th anniversary of this great city, Mr. Mayor. It's always a pleasure for me to return to the heartland of America.

Talking to a church audience like this reminds me a little of a church in a little town in Illinois—Dixon, Illinois—that I used to attend as a boy. One sweltering Sunday morning in July, the minister told us he was going to preach the shortest sermon he had ever given. And then he said a single sentence. "If you think it's hot today, just wait." [*Laughter*]

And, of course, there was the minister—and I know I'm taking a chance here because I tell stories about your profession, your calling; you probably know them all. But this was the minister who put his text on the pulpit a half an hour before every service. And one Sunday a smart aleck hid the last page. And the minister preached powerfully, but when he got to the words, "So Adam said to Eve," he was horrified to discover that the final sheet was gone. And riffling through the other pages, he stalled for time by repeating, "So Adam said to Eve"—and then in a low voice he said, "There seems to be a missing leaf." [*Laughter*]

But it is an honor to be with you today. For more than four decades, the National Association of Evangelicals has ministered to the people of this country in the name of God's word. And today, the NAE has some 38,000 member churches representing some 4 million Americans, as you well know. You provide Christian education, foreign missions, religious broadcasting, and as you were just told, the provision of a very worthwhile safety net—a host of other services. In doing so, you are leaders in promoting fundamental American values of hard work, family, freedom, and faith. And on behalf of a grateful nation, I thank you.

In keeping with your convention theme, "Leadership with Integrity," I'd like to talk to you today about religious values in public life.

Any serious look at our history shows that from the first, the people of our country were deeply imbued with faith. Indeed, many of the first settlers came for the express purpose of worshiping in freedom. The historian Samuel Morison wrote of one such group, "doubting nothing and fearing no man, (they) undertook to set all crooked ways straight and create a new heaven and a new earth. If (they) were not permitted to

do that in England, (they) would find some other place to establish (their) city of God." Well, that other place was this broad and open land we call America.

The debates over independence and the records of the Constitutional Convention make it clear that the Founding Fathers were sustained by their faith in God. In the Declaration of Independence itself, Thomas Jefferson wrote that all men are ". . . endowed by their Creator with certain unalienable rights. . . . ." And it was George Washington who said, "Of all the dispositions and habits which lead to political prosperity, Religion and Morality are indispensable supports."

So, the record is clear. The first Americans proclaimed their freedom because they believed God himself had granted freedom to all men. And they exercised their liberty prayerfully, avidly seeking and humbly accepting God's blessing on their new land.

For decades, America remained a deeply religious country, thanking God in peacetime and turning to him in moments of crisis. During the Civil War, perhaps our nation's darkest hour, Abraham Lincoln said, "I have been driven many times upon my knees by the conviction that I had nowhere else to go." Believe me, no one can serve in this office without understanding and believing exactly what he said.

During World War II, I remember a rally to promote war bonds that was held at Madison Square Garden in New York. The rally featured the great figures from government; great stars of the theater entertained the audience, and many times those people proclaimed that God was on our side. And then it remained for a $54-a-month buck private who spoke nine words that no one there that day will ever forget. His name was Joe Louis—yes, the Joe Louis who had come from the cotton fields to become the world heavyweight prize-fighting champion. Now, this $54-a-month private walked out to center stage after all those other celebrities had been there, and he said, "I know we'll win, because we're on God's side." There was a moment of silence, and then that crowd nearly took the roof off.

During the civil rights struggles of the fifties and early sixties, millions worked for equality in the name of their Creator. Civil rights leaders like Dr. Martin Luther King based all their efforts on the claim that black or white, each of us is a child of God. And they stirred our nation to the very depths of its soul.

And so it has been through most of our history. All our material wealth and all our influence have been built on our faith in God and the bedrock values that follow from that faith. The great French philosopher Alexis de Tocqueville, 150 years ago is said to have observed that America is great because America is good. And if she ever ceases to be good, she will cease to be great.

Well, in recent years, we must admit, America did seem to lose her religious and moral bearings, to forget that faith and values are what made us good and great.

We saw the signs all around us. Years ago, pornography, while available, was mostly sold under the counter. By the midseventies it was available virtually on every magazine rack in every drugstore or shop in the land. Drug abuse used to be confined to limited numbers of adults. During the sixties and seventies, it spread through the Nation like a fever, affecting children as well as adults and involving drugs that were once unheard of, drugs like LSD and PCP, ironically nicknamed "angel dust."

But perhaps most important, years ago, the American family was still the basic building block of our society. But then families too often found themselves penalized by government taxation, welfare policies that were spinning out of control, and the social mores of our country were being undermined. Liberal attitudes viewed promiscuity as acceptable, even stylish. Indeed, the word itself was replaced by a new term, "sexually active." And in the media, what we once thought of as a sacred expression of love was often portrayed as something casual and cheap.

Between 1970 and 1980, the number of two-parent families dropped while the number of single-parent families almost doubled. Teenage pregnancies increased significantly. And although total births declined during the decade between 1970 and 1980, the number of illegitimate births rose about a quarter of a million.

At the same time that social standards seemed to be dissolving, our economic and governmental institutions were in disarray. Big taxing and spending had led to soaring interest rates and inflation. Our defenses had grown weak. Public officials at the highest levels openly spoke of a national "malaise." All over the world America had become known not for strength and resolve, but for vacillation and self-doubt. It seemed for a season as though our nation was in permanent decline and that any sense of justice, self-discipline, and duty was ebbing out of our public life.

But the Almighty who gave us this great land also gave us free will, the power under God to choose our own destiny. The American people decided to put a stop to that long decline, and today our country is seeing a rebirth of freedom and faith, a great national renewal. As I said in my State of the Union address, "America is back. . . ."

We've begun tackling one problem after another. We've knocked inflation down, and we can keep it down. The prime rate is about half what it was when our administration took office. All across the country, a powerful economic recovery is gaining strength. As we've begun rebuilding our defenses in the name of freedom, morale in the military has soared. And once again, America is respected throughout the world as a great force for freedom and peace.

But this renewal is more than material. America has begun a spiritual awakening. Faith and hope are being restored. Americans are turning back to God. Church attendance is up. Audiences for religious books and broadcasts are growing. On college campuses, students have stopped shunning religion and started going to church. As Harvard theologian Harvey Cox put it— and I quote—"Rather than the cynical, careerist types who supposedly have filled the campuses, I see young people who are intensely interested in moral issues, in religious history and beliefs."

One of my favorite Bible quotations comes from Second Chronicles: ". . . if My people who are called by My name humble themselves and pray and seek My face, and turn from their wicked ways, then will I hear from heaven, and forgive their sin and heal their land." Today Americans from Maine to California are seeking His face. And I do believe that He has begun to heal our blessed land.

As this special awakening gathers strength, we must remember that many in good faith will hold other views. Let us pledge to conduct ourselves with generosity, tolerance, and openness toward all. We must respect the rights and views of every American, because we're unshakably committed to democratic values. Our Maker would have it no less.

So, please use your pulpits to denounce racism, anti-Semitism, and all ethnic or religious intolerance as evils, and let us make it clear that our values must not restrict, but liberate the human spirit in thought and in deed.

You may remember, but I'm sure you don't agree with, a very cynical quote that got wide circulation, from H.L. Mencken. He said puritanism "is the haunting fear that someone, somewhere, may be happy." [*Laughter*] Well, some suspect that today's spiritual awakening reflects such narrow-mindedness. We must show that faith and traditional values are the things that give life human dignity, warmth, vitality, and yes, laughter and joy.

Sometimes we all must think when we look at ourselves—the Lord must have a sense of humor. [*Laughter*]

Now, although millions of Americans have already done so much to put our national life back on the firm foundation of faith and traditional values, we still have far to go.

In foreign affairs I believe there are two fundamental tasks that we must perform. First, we must make certain our own country is strong, so we can go on holding out the hope of freedom for all the world. When I took office, I made rebuilding our defenses a top priority. Although we still have a great deal to do, we've already made dramatic headway. And since American forces are the cornerstone in the global defense of liberty, that's good news for all the world.

Second, in this age when electronics beam messages around the globe, we must keep telling the truth, including the truth about the difference between free and totalitarian societies.

This month it will be my honor to award a posthumous medal of honor—a Medal of Freedom, I should say—to Whittaker Chambers, a man of courage and wisdom. Chambers understood the struggle between totalitarianism and the West. He, himself, had turned to communism out of a sense of idealism in which he thought that might be the answer. And then he wrote, all the great visions of the free world "have always been different versions of the same vision: the vision of God and man's relationship to God. The Communist vision is the vision of man without God."

I don't know whether you've ever read his line of when he first began to awaken. They had a new baby, a little girl. And he was looking at her one morning as she sat in her highchair. And he said he found himself looking at the delicate convolutions of that tiny ear. And that was when he said to himself, "That cannot be just an accident of nature, a freak of nature." And he said he may not have realized it at the moment, but he knows that in that moment, God had laid His finger on his forehead.

When men try to live in a world without God, it's only too easy for them to forget the rights that God bestows—too easy to suppress freedom of speech, to build walls to keep their countrymen in, to jail dissidents, and to put great thinkers in mental wards. We will deal with the Communist world as we must with a great power: by negotiating with it, from strength and in good faith.

And if the new Soviet leadership is willing, we will renew our efforts to ease tensions between East and West. And while we will never accept for ourselves their system, we will never stop praying that the leaders, like so many of their own people, might come to know the liberating nature of faith in God.

In our own hemisphere, the Communist Sandinista regime in Nicaragua has systematically violated human rights, including the freedom to worship. Threats and harassment have forced virtually all Nicaraguan

Jews to flee that country. Catholic clerics have been attacked by government-instigated mobs. Protestant religious leaders have been arrested, beaten, and deported. Dozens of Protestant churches have been burned. And today, the Sandinistas are trying to spread Communist subversion throughout Central America. If they succeed, millions of Central Americans will suffer. And our own security and economy, especially in our own southern States, would be threatened by significantly increased numbers of refugees that might stream toward the United States.

There is hope for Central America if America acts now with wisdom. Last month I sent to the Congress the Jackson plan, a plan that embodies the overall recommendations of the Bipartisan Commission on Central America. The plan calls for a 5-year program of increased political, economic, and military aid to the region with some three out of four dollars going to the direct improvement of living conditions for the Central American people. It is essential to freedom in Central America and around the world that the Congress pass this bipartisan plan. I would like to ask you to join me in urging your Senators and Members of Congress to approve that plan swiftly.

Here at home, I believe there are three basic tasks that we must accomplish. First, we must do our duty to generations not yet born. We cannot proclaim the noble ideal that human life is sacred, then turn our backs on the taking of some 4,000 unborn children's lives every day. This as a means of birth control must stop.

In a recent speech to the National Religious Broadcasters, I stated that as abortions are performed, the unborn children that are being killed often feel excruciating pain. And, oh, immediately, that statement prompted sharp criticism and denials. Well, just the other day, I received a letter signed by 24 medical doctors, including such eminent physicians as Dr. Bernie Pisani, president of the New York State Medical Society, and Dr. Anne Bannon, former chief of pediatrics at the St. Louis City Hospital. The letter explained that in recent years medical techniques have "demonstrated the remarkable responsiveness of the human fetus to pain, touch, and sound." "Mr. Presi-

dent," the letter concluded, "in drawing attention to the capability of the human fetus to feel pain, you stand on firmly established ground."

Many who seek abortions do so in harrowing circumstances. Often, they suffer deep personal trauma. Just as tolerance means accepting that many in good faith hold views different from our own, it also means that no man or woman should sit in judgment on another. If we could rise above bitterness and reproach, if Americans could come together in a spirit of understanding and helping, then we could find positive solutions to the tragedy of abortion—and this we must do.

Second, we must restore education in basic value to America's schools. Since our administration put education at the top of the national agenda, we've seen a grassroots revolution that promises to strengthen every school in the country. Across the land, parents, teachers, school administrators, State and local officeholders have begun work to improve the fundamentals—not frills in the curriculum, but basic teaching and learning. As this great educational reform takes place, we must make certain that we not only improve instruction in math and science, but in justice, religion, discipline, and liberty, for to guide America into the 21st century, our children will need not only technical skills but wisdom.

And because parents know best what schools are right for their children, our administration has proposed education vouchers and tuition tax credits—concepts that the American people overwhelmingly support. And I intend to keep pressing for those reforms until they're passed.

And third, school prayer. From the early days of the American colonies, prayer in schools was practiced and revered as an important tradition. Indeed, for nearly two centuries of our history it was considered a natural expression of our religious freedom. Then in 1962 the Supreme Court declared school prayer illegal. Well, I firmly believe that the loving God who has blessed our land and made us a good and caring people should never have been expelled from America's classrooms. And the country agrees. Polls show that by a majority of 80 percent, the American people want prayer back in our schools.

We stand on firm historical and constitutional ground. During the Constitutional Convention, Benjamin Franklin rose to say that—he said, "The longer I live, the more convincing proofs I see that God governs in the affairs of men. Without His concurring aid, we shall succeed in this political building no better than the builders of Babel." And he asked, "Have we now forgotten this powerful Friend? Or do we imagine we no longer need His assistance?" And then Franklin moved that the Convention begin its daily deliberations by asking for the assistance of Almighty God.

Today prayer remains a vital part of American public life. The Congress begins each day with prayer, and the Supreme Court begins each sitting with an invocation. Now, I just have to believe that if the Members of Congress and the Justices can acknowledge the Almighty, our children can, too.

And it's not just public prayer that the courts have moved against. Today, courts are preventing students from using school premises for Bible study groups, prayer meetings, or just getting together to talk about their faith. When students at the Guilderland High School near Albany, New York, sought to use an empty classroom for a voluntary prayer meeting, the Second Circuit Court of Appeals said no. The court claimed that it could be a bad influence on other students if they were "to see the captain of the football team or the student body president or the leading actress in a dramatic production participating in communal (school) prayer meetings." The court ruled that the "symbolic inference" that a school approves of prayer is "too dangerous to permit." Well, as far as I'm concerned, it's rulings like this that are dangerous, not school prayer. [*Applause*] Thank you.

Hasn't something gone haywire when this great Constitution of ours is invoked to allow Nazis and the Ku Klux Klan to march on public property and urge the extermination of Jews and the subjugation of blacks, but it supposedly prevents our children from Bible study or the saying of a simple prayer in their schools? In 1952 a prominent jurist wrote a legal opinion that I be-

lieve still holds true. "We are a religious people," he wrote, "whose institutions presuppose a Supreme Being. We guarantee the freedom to worship as one chooses. We make room for as wide a variety of beliefs and creeds as the spiritual needs of man deem necessary . . . . To hold that (government) may not (encourage religious instruction) would be to find in the Constitution a requirement that the government show a callous indifference to religious groups. That would be preferring those who believe in no religion over those who do believe . . . ." Well, the name of that jurist was Supreme Court Justice William O. Douglas. And the situation we face today is just what Justice Douglas was warning about: government hostility to religion. We must change it and change it now.

Senator Denton and Congressman Lott have proposed legislation to make certain that students who seek to use school premises in the name of their faith receive equal access. Well, I intend to support some of this legislation, and I urge you to join me in doing so, too.

But most important, in a matter of days, the Senate will vote on an amendment to the Constitution to allow voluntary vocal prayer in America's schools. Our amendment explicitly states that no child must ever be forced to recite a prayer, nor would it allow any State to compose the words of a prayer. But under this amendment the Federal Government could not forbid voluntary vocal prayer in our schools. And by reasserting our children's freedom of religious expression, the amendment would help them to understand the diversity of America's religious beliefs and practices.

If this amendment receives a two-thirds of the vote in the Senate, it can come to a vote in the House. But neither will happen without our support. In recent weeks the school prayer amendment has received a groundswell of backing across the country. And last night in Washington, many Americans gathered for an all-night prayer vigil at the Capitol. It was a most moving event and a clear expression of the will of the people.

I'm convinced that passage of this amendment would do more than any other action to reassert the faith and values that made America great. I urge you and all those listening on television and radio to support this amendment and to let your Senators and Members of Congress know where you stand. And together we can show the world that America is still one nation under God.

Saint Paul wrote a verse that I've always cherished: ". . . now abide faith, hope, love, these three; but the greatest of these is love." May we have faith in our God and in all the good that we can do with His help. May we stand firm in the hope of making America all that she can be—a nation of opportunity and prosperity and a force for peace and good will among nations. And may we remain steadfast in our love for this green and gentle land and the freedom that she offers.

And thank you all for letting me be with you, and God bless you all.

Note: The President spoke at 1:57 p.m. in the Regency Ballroom at the Hyatt Regency Hotel.

Remarks at a New York Republican Party Fundraising Dinner
March 6, 1984

The President. Chairman George Clark, Chucky baby—[*laughter*]—reverend clergy, Senator D'Amato, Secretary Pierce, Members of the Congress, and ladies and gentlemen:

Nancy and I are happy to be a part of this magnificent gathering tonight. And let me begin by saying that we Republicans not only think New York is a top priority State; we Republicans are going to carry New York this fall. The Republican victory here in 1980 was no aberration. It marked a turning point in New York politics, and we're going to prove that in 1984.

This city and this State represent the hub of America's commercial and financial activity, and it's good to see labor also recognized or represented here tonight. And as one who was head of a union for six terms and is, I think, the first one in this job that's ever been able to say a lifetime member of an AFL–CIO union, I know that union and management have the same stake in a strong economy.

And believe me, all of us remember that those now asking for our trust are part of the same liberal crew that dominated the Presidency, all the departments and agencies, as well as both Houses of Congress. They had absolute control of our government. And whether from the Senate or from the executive branch or the House, their policies gave us runaway inflation, record interest rates, huge tax increases, economic stagnation, military weakness, and phony talk about a national "malaise."

Well, we've got some mighty important items to discuss this year. The American people deserve a chance to hear the issues, and as—God bless him—Al Smith used to say, "Let's look at the record."

As for the record, I think the Republicans shouldn't hesitate to ask loud and clear and over and over again this year whether the American people believe they are better off now than they were 4 years ago.

Let me ask you: Does anyone want to go back to that double-digit inflation nightmare of 4 years ago?

Audience. No!

The President. Does anyone want to go back to the stumbling, sputtering economic failure of 4 years ago?

Audience. No!

The President. And does anyone want to go back to that "your-money-belongs-to-Washington" era of 4 years ago?

Audience. No!

The President. I want to interrupt and just remind you of something here. In 1976 our opponents cooked up a thing they called the misery index. And that was that you added the rate of unemployment and you added the rate of inflation and that was the misery index. And then in 1976 they said of our President Ford, "He shouldn't even be allowed to run for reelection because his misery index was 12½ percent." Well, in 1980 they were running, and the misery index was just a fraction of a point under 20. Well, we're running again now, and the misery index is less than 12.

And as much as our opponents would like us to believe that the murderous inflation, the economic stagnation, and the crisis of confidence we suffered 4 years ago were part of a mysterious cycle or the result of my predecessor's personality, it doesn't wash. The economy is improving, America is growing stronger, moving forward, for one simple reason: We Republicans reversed the liberal policies of tax, spend, and inflate and put you, the American people, back in charge. It took time to put our program in place, and it's taken time for it to take effect. My goodness, aren't we happy we stuck to our guns?

We're in the first phase of a recovery that has already astounded the experts. The gross national product grew at a firm 6.2 percent last year. And January's hefty jump in the index of leading economic indicators suggests a healthy growth rate will continue. Employment is at the highest level in history, with unemployment dropping sharply. We have more people working today than we've ever had before in our history. Housing starts and auto sales are heavy. Housing starts—you probably saw the announcement a few days ago, and the way it was carried, that the sale of new houses in the month of January was 9 percent below the rate in December. And that's the way it was presented. Well, let me tell you the rest of the story. That's right; it was 9 percent below December. But that was because December just happened to be a little bigger than January. The January rate was also the highest rate of sales of new homes in the United States since 1979. They didn't put it that way when they told you about it.

Productivity, after falling in the 2 years before we took office, rose 3½ percent last year. Real take-home pay, thanks to our tax cuts and the progress we've made in controlling inflation, is rising. And a sign that even better days are ahead—venture capital rose $4 billion last year, and that's four times what it was in 1980.

Now that we've rebuilt America's confidence and got her back on the road to robust growth, no way are we turning back. The recovery now surging through this land will benefit each and every American. There's a lot of talk from our opponents that our program is somehow not fair or compassionate. Well, those who brutalized our people with inflation and stagnation, undercutting everyone's chance to improve their lot, should not be pointing fingers and preaching sermonettes about compassion. There was one thing fair, I will admit, about their policies. They didn't discriminate; they made everybody miserable. [*Laughter*]

Of course, it wasn't just our economy that seemed to be going haywire 4 years ago. The images of American hostages and burning American flags will not be forgotten. Our friends and adversaries alike seemed to be counting us out. And, this too, was not a result of some uncontrollable cycle. We were not, as some suggested, a nation in decline; instead, we were being led by a team with good intentions and bad ideas—people with all the common sense of Huey, Dewey, and Louie. [*Laughter*]

Real defense spending—and this was no accident—was permitted to erode by 20 percent in the last decade. Weapons systems like the B-1 bomber were unilaterally canceled. Members of left-to-liberal think tanks might have been impressed, but those who run the Kremlin weren't. As our level of power dropped, so did our influence. We were less secure and less respected.

In 1981 we went to work repairing the damage done by those who believe that a weaker America is a safer America. We continue to strive for realistic arms reduction negotiations with the Soviet Union. But, to be taken seriously, the Soviets must know that we're not going to simply give them what they want without concessions in return. Make no mistake, those who call for gutting the defense budget are undercutting our chances for arms reduction agreements with the Soviets. Those who condemn the United States any time a stand is taken against aggression are flirting with disaster.

In the coming campaign, Republicans should have no hesitation about bringing the issue of peace and security to the American people. There are many patriotic Democrats who will join us in supporting our efforts to rebuild our country's defenses, and we must reach out to them. They know that wearing love beads and touting our sincerity will not make for a safer world. Peace through strength is not a slogan, it's a fact of life. Four wars in my lifetime, and none of them came about because the United States was too strong.

I have to tell you, Nancy and I had—a few months ago—a unique reunion on the White House lawn. We brought together members of the Armed Forces, of the branches that had served in Grenada, representatives from each group, and hundreds of the American medical students that they had rescued there. It was a moment we'll always remember, especially those scenes when the students—and they were all about the same age, the students and the military—to see those students, some of them openly confessing that they had, once had a viewpoint where they did not respect the uniform—they couldn't keep their hands off those marines and soldiers and seamen and airmen. They were throwing their arms around them. They were telling them, "You saved our lives. You rescued us." And that heartwarming scene reconfirmed for me that Americans are still a great people who can accomplish great things. They'll accomplish great things if you, the people of this country, have a government that believes in you. And this government does.

I have to interrupt again and tell a little incident about Grenada. Some weeks after Grenada—and some of our troops that had gone there came home—I received a message from a marine lieutenant who flew a Cobra. He was at Grenada and then had gone on to Beirut. And the message that he sent back was to the Armed Forces Journal in the Pentagon. He said that in Grenada he realized that every news story spelled out, in some place in the story, that Grenada produced more nutmeg than any other place in the world. And he finally decided the regularity of this must have been a code, and he was going to break the code. So, he sent me the message that in six points he had broken the code. Number one: Grenada produces more nutmeg than

any other spot on Earth. Number two: The Soviets and the Cubans are trying to take Grenada. Number three: You cannot make good eggnog without nutmeg. [*Laughter*] Number four: You cannot have Christmas without eggnog. [*Laughter*] Number five: The Soviets and the Cubans were trying to steal Christmas. [*Laughter*] And number six: We stopped them. [*Laughter*]

If I could just impose something on you. I'm so proud of what's happened in these few years and these men and women of ours in uniform. When you see one of them on the street, kind of remember the wartime thing and say hello to them, with a smile, and tell them you're kind of grateful for what they're doing. They're wonderful young people. We can all be proud.

Our people want us to be a force for good in the world. We'll stand by our friends and protect our national interests. In Lebanon we were not a part of a military mission, but members of an international peacekeeping force. And while time and events—longstanding hatreds and mistrust—prevented the restoration of order, it was not from lack of trying or an absence of responsibility on our part. We have every reason to be proud that our marines, along with other members of the multinational force, attempted to bring peace and stability to that troubled country. It was a worthwhile mission. And furthermore, we remain near and ready to help if our efforts can serve the cause of peace.

During the latter half of the last decade, our country was paralyzed by its declining military power and a crisis of confidence. We were represented in bodies like the United Nations by people who seemed to spend more time apologizing than representing our interests. Well, we've turned this around, too. All Americans can be proud that we now have a person with courage and dignity representing us in the United Nations, a brilliant individual whose strength of character reflects the values of our great country. I think Jeane Kirkpatrick is a 10, and I'm mighty grateful for the magnificent job that she does every day.

After she'd been there awhile, I asked Jeane what was the biggest difference between things now and what they had been.

And she told me, she said, "Mr. President, we've taken off our 'Kick me' sign." [*Laughter*]

Sometimes democratic countries are singled out for abuse in the United Nations. Well, America will stand by her friends. And this is especially true concerning our commitment to the one Western-style democracy in the Middle East, the state of Israel. There have been moves afoot to kick Israel out of the United Nations. And let me say just one thing and make it very plain: If Israel is ever forced to leave the United Nations, we'll leave together.

The security of our country and its people is the paramount responsibility of American government at every level. Unfortunately, too many of our citizens are not even secure on the streets of their community or in their own homes. The epidemic of crime and violence that we experienced in the last two decades has been a national disgrace. You in New York know what a nightmare crime can be. What we suffered—the assaults, the murders, the rapes—was the manifestation of policies which bent over backward to defend the rights of thugs, but which had too little concern about the innocent people victimized by the criminals. Well, the Republican Party reaffirms that the purpose of the law is to protect the innocent.

The Republican Senate has passed a package of criminal justice reforms, reforms aimed at making the system more efficient and more capable of getting career criminals off our streets. As of yet we're waiting for the Democrat-controlled House to move on this vital legislation. If the leadership of the House refuses to act and continues jeopardizing the safety of the American people, it's time that we replace those liberal opponents of ours with some good, old-fashioned law-and-order Republicans. Some of the provisions of that program of ours were authored by your Senator D'Amato.

In these last 3 years, I've been grateful to New York for the fine Republican delegation that it has in Washington. Senator D'Amato has been a real plus in the Senate. Your 14 Republican Representatives have been a source of support vital to our efforts to get control of Federal spending and taxing and to reinvigorate the economy. All

I ask is that on election day, don't just vote for them, get all your friends and neighbors out to vote for them, too. And, yes, if you could, send us more just like them. We'd be able to put them to good use.

One member of your delegation of whom all of you can be rightfully proud is retiring after 20 years of frontline service. And even though Congressman Barber Conable couldn't be here tonight, I wanted to take this opportunity to thank him for all he's done for our country and for the Republican Party.

Real progress in this country can be traced to the work of conscientious and hard-working individuals like Congressman Conable. One such person is John Mariotta, who's providing jobs and training for the hardcore unemployed of the South Bronx. Born of Puerto Rican immigrants, and having served in the United States Army, Mr. Mariotta has had all the ups and downs associated with entrepreneurship. And today, through Wed-Tech, he not only has built a successful corporation, he's helping hundreds of people who would otherwise be condemned to menial jobs or a life on the dole. And what gave Mr. Mariotta the courage to keep going when others quit? He tells us it was his faith in God. Now his faith has moved mountains, helping hundreds of people who'd almost given up hope. People like John Mariotta are heroes for the eighties.

The future of our country, the direction that we go as a people, whether we move ahead to meet the challenges of the future or slide back into the irresponsible policies of the past, will be determined by those who get involved. By being here tonight, you're proving that you are willing to do your part. Together, with the other good and decent people of this country, we can make certain that America is the kind of place, the shining light of opportunity and freedom, that God intended it to be.

Thank you all, and God bless all of you.

Note: The President spoke at 8:38 p.m. in the Grand Ballroom at the Waldorf Astoria Hotel. He was introduced by George L. Clark, Jr., chairman, New York State Republican Party.

In his opening remarks, the President referred to Charles Gargano, chairman of the dinner, Senator Alfonse M. D'Amato, and Secretary of Housing and Urban Development Samuel R. Pierce, Jr.

Prior to the dinner, the President attended a reception for New York State Republican leaders at the hotel. Following the dinner, he returned to Washington, DC.

Proclamation 5158—35th Anniversary of NATO
March 6, 1984

By the President of the United States of America

A Proclamation

Thirty-five years ago, on April 4, 1949, the North Atlantic Treaty was signed in Washington. Established in the dark aftermath of the most destructive war the world had ever seen, the NATO Alliance represents a living commitment of the nations of the West to the defense of democracy and individual liberty. By uniting Europe and North America in this way, it has deterred war between NATO and the Warsaw Pact for three and a half decades and made possible the longest period of peace and prosperity in modern history.

This success has not been won without effort. Throughout its history, the NATO Alliance has been challenged by the military power and political ambitions of the Soviet Union. Yet, in every decade, the nations of the Alliance have consistently pulled together to maintain peace through their collective strength and determination. On the basis of that strength and unity, the nations of the Alliance also have taken the initiative to seek a more constructive relationship with the Soviet Union.

Over the years, NATO has grown from its original twelve members to include Greece, Turkey, the Federal Republic of Germany, and, most recently, Spain. It has demonstrated a capacity to adapt to evolving political and security challenges and to meet the changing needs of its members. The Alliance's commitment to collective security has been sustained through full democratic respect for the sovereign independence of each member.

I am proud to rededicate the United States to the ideals and responsibilities of our Alliance. In May, the United States will host in Washington the spring meeting of NATO foreign ministers. This will be a special opportunity to celebrate the thirty-fifth anniversary of our common enterprise and to consider the future challenges facing the transatlantic partnership. I call upon the Congress and people of the United States to join me in expressing our support for a bond which has served us so well over the years and which will continue to be essential to our welfare in the future.

Now, Therefore, I, Ronald Reagan, President of the United States of America, do hereby direct the attention of the Nation to this thirty-fifth anniversary of the signing of the North Atlantic Treaty, and I call upon the Governors of the States and upon the officers of local governments to facilitate the suitable observance of this notable event throughout this anniversary year with particular attention to April, the month which marks the historic signing ceremony, and May, the month which marks the meeting of the North Atlantic Council in Washington.

In Witness Whereof, I have hereunto set my hand this 6th day of March, in the year of our Lord nineteen hundred and eighty-four, and of the Independence of the United States of America the two hundred and eighth.

RONALD REAGAN

[*Filed with the Office of the Federal Register, 3:46 p.m., March 7, 1984*]

Note: The text of the proclamation was released by the Office of the Press Secretary on March 7.

Nomination of Richard Fairbanks To Be Ambassador at Large
March 7, 1984

The President today announced his intention to nominate Richard Fairbanks, of the District of Columbia, as Ambassador at Large. Mr. Fairbanks had previously served as Special Negotiator for the Middle East Peace Process for the past 2 years. Prior to that he was Assistant Secretary of State for Congressional Relations (1981–1982).

Mr. Fairbanks served in the United States Navy in 1962–1966 as lieutenant. He was an associate attorney in the law firm of Arnold and Porter in Washington, DC, in 1969–1971. In 1971 he was Special Assistant to the Administrator of the Environmental Protection Agency. He was with the President's Domestic Council as staff assistant (1971–1972), and Associate Director for National Resources, Energy and Environment (1972–1974). In 1974–1977 he was a member of the Citizen's Advisory Council on Environmental Quality. In 1974–1981 he was the founding partner in the law firm of Beveridge, Fairbanks and Diamond in Washington, DC.

Mr. Fairbanks received his A.B. (1962) from Yale University and J.D., magna cum laude, (1969) from Columbia University Law School. His foreign languages are reading knowledge of French and Spanish. He was born February 10, 1941, in Indianapolis, IN.

Note: Larry M. Speakes, Principal Deputy Press Secretary to the President, announced the nomination during his daily press briefing in the Briefing Room at the White House. He also read the following information about Mr. Fairbank's responsibilities:

Mr. Fairbanks will focus on two particular areas—nonnuclear energy issues and long-term United States strategy toward the Pacific Basin. He will engage in planning related to the potential interruption of oil supplies and the development of indigenous and other sources of natural gas. In addition, he will seek ways to protect United States interests in the Pacific region and to take advantage of trade opportunities. He will seek to support the Vice President's efforts to resolve our bilateral and capital-flow problems with Japan and also to work to expand opportunities for sale of nonnuclear energy to Japan.

Nomination of Marge Bodwell To Be a Member of the National Advisory Council on Women's Educational Programs
March 7, 1984

The President today announced his intention to nominate Marge Bodwell to be a member of the National Advisory Council on Women's Educational Programs for a term expiring May 8, 1986. This is a reappointment.

She is a teacher at the Yucca School in Alamogordo, NM. In 1975 she was awarded the Freedom Foundation's Teachers Medal Award which is the highest award given to a teacher. She has been actively involved in the PTA and the Girl Scouts.

Mrs. Bodwell has a degree in psychology. She has three children and resides in Alamogordo, NM. She was born September 19, 1920, in Xenia, OH.

Nomination of David Charles Miller, Jr., To Be United States Ambassador to Zimbabwe
March 8, 1984

The President today announced his intention to nominate David Charles Miller, Jr., of Pennsylvania, as Ambassador to Zimbabwe. He would succeed Robert V. Keeley.

Mr. Miller was a summer intern with the Department of Commerce in 1962 and with the Department of Justice in 1965. He was research associate with Simulmatics Corp. (for advanced research projects agency) in Vietnam in 1967–1968. In 1968–1969 he was a White House fellow at the Department of Justice and was Special Assistant to the Attorney General in 1969–1970. He was Director of the White House Fellows Commission in 1970–1971. In 1971–1981 he was with Westinghouse Electric Corp., serving successively in Pittsburgh, PA, as assistant to the executive vice

president for defense and public systems, director of planning of Westinghouse world regions, and director of corporate international relations. Following service in Lagos, Nigeria, as general manager of TCOM Corp. and Westinghouse country manager for Nigeria, he was deputy, international business operations, of Westinghouse Defense Group in Baltimore, MD. In early 1981 he served as Special Assistant to the Assistant Secretary of State for African Affairs in the Department of State. He was appointed Ambassador to Tanzania in October 1981, where he has been serving until the present time.

Mr. Miller was born July 15, 1942, in Cleveland, OH. He graduated from Harvard College (B.A., 1964) and the University of Michigan Law School (J.D., 1967).

Nomination of Barrington King To Be United States Ambassador to Brunei
March 8, 1984

The President today announced his intention to nominate Barrington King, of Georgia, a career member of the Senior Foreign Service, Class of Minister-Counselor, as Ambassador to Brunei. He would be the first accredited American Ambassador to Brunei.

Mr. King was a salesman with Goodyear Tire and Rubber Co. in Spartanburg, SC, in 1953–1955 and a field representative with the United States Social Security Administration in Charleston in 1955–1956. In 1956 he entered the Foreign Service as Foreign Service officer in the Department. He was administrative and political officer in Cairo in 1957–1959 and in 1959 attended French language training in Paris. In 1959–1961 he was administrative and political officer in Dar es Salaam. In the Department he was

officer in charge of Tanzania and Zanzibar affairs in 1961–1963. In 1963–1964 he attended Greek language training at the Foreign Service Institute. He was chief of the economic section in Nicosia (1964–1967) and economic and political officer in Athens (1967–1972). In 1972–1973 he attended Princeton University on a Woodrow Wilson fellowship. In the Department he was Chief of the Training and Liaison Staff in the Bureau of Personnel in 1973–1975. In 1975–1979 he was deputy chief of mission in Tunis and since 1979 has been deputy chief of mission in Islamabad.

Mr. King graduated from the University of Georgia (B.F.A., 1952). His foreign languages are Greek and French. He was born September 25, 1930, in Knoxville, TN.

Nomination of Four Members of the National Council on Educational Research, and Designation of Chairman
March 8, 1984

The President today announced his intention to nominate the following individuals to be members of the National Council on Educational Research for a term expiring September 30, 1986. These are reappointments. The President also intends to designate George Charles Roche III as Chairman upon confirmation.

J. Floyd Hall is superintendent for the school district of Greenville County, SC. He graduated from Auburn University (B.S., 1948; M.S., 1951; Ed.D., 1957). He is married, has two children, and resides in Greenville, SC. He was born August 11, 1925, in Langdale, AL.

Donna Helene Hearne is an insurance agent and broker and a fee agent for the Missouri Department of Revenue. She graduated from Washington University in St. Louis (B.A., 1962). She is married, has five children, and resides in St. Louis, MO. She was born April 16, 1940, in Detroit, MI.

Carl W. Salser is executive director and editor for the Educational Research Association in Portland, OR. He graduated from Oregon State University (B.S., 1947; M.S., 1956). He is married, has three children, and resides in Lake Oswego, OR. He was born August 16, 1921, in Emporia, KS.

George Charles Roche III is president of Hillsdale College in Hillsdale, MI. He graduated from Regis College (B.S., 1956) and the University of Colorado (M.A., 1961; Ph.D., 1965). He is married, has three children, and resides in Hillsdale. He was born May 16, 1935, in Denver, CO.

Proclamation 5159—Red Cross Month, 1984
March 8, 1984

By the President of the United States of America

A Proclamation

Since its beginning, the American Red Cross has been in the forefront of efforts to provide for the well-being of the American people. Its volunteers and staff have kept that tradition going during this past year. They brought needed relief to hundreds of thousands of our fellow citizens who suffered in disasters and spent a record-breaking amount for disaster assistance and preparedness. These dedicated people also implemented programs to improve the health of all Americans through life-style changes, kept our Nation's blood supply strong, and provided morale-building services to the men and women in uniform and their families.

The American Red Cross was founded in 1881 on the principle of service to others and has been sustained since then by millions of Americans who freely offer their time and talents for the benefit of their fellow citizens.

The American Red Cross pioneered in disaster relief, public health, assistance to veterans, and in efforts to enhance the spirits of our military services in war and peace. It also initiated the world's largest system for voluntary blood donations. And through Red Cross Youth Services, it helps our Nation's young people to learn the role of leadership and the value of service to others.

These efforts have been made possible by financial contributions from the public. Without this support, there would not be a Red Cross. It is the goodwill of all of us that perpetuates its efforts and provides such an inspiring example of what the private sector is capable of doing.

In the years ahead, there will be many opportunities for new endeavors as our Nation's social conditions change. The American Red Cross, as in the past, will respond to such challenges and will persevere in its efforts on behalf of human life and dignity.

Now, Therefore, I, Ronald Reagan, President of the United States of America, and Honorary Chairman of the American Red Cross, do hereby designate March 1984 as Red Cross Month and urge all Americans to generously support the work of their local Red Cross chapter.

In Witness Whereof, I have hereunto set my hand this 8th day of March, in the year of our Lord nineteen hundred and eighty-

four, and of the Independence of the United States of America the two hundred and eighth.

RONALD REAGAN

[*Filed with the Office of the Federal Register, 11:42 a.m., March 9, 1984*]

Note: The President signed the proclamation in a ceremony in the Oval Office at the White House.

Memorandum Urging Support of the American National Red Cross
March 8, 1984

Memorandum for Heads of Executive Departments and Agencies

Subject: Red Cross Month, 1984

I have just issued a proclamation which designates March 1984 as Red Cross Month.

This has been an especially tragic year for hundreds of thousands of our fellow countrymen left destitute by disasters. To assist these victims, the Red Cross has spent a record amount for help and for disaster preparedness. As a recipient of blood voluntarily donated through the Red Cross, I know the value of its Blood Services and its efforts to ensure that we constantly have supplies for the sick and injured. Also through the Red Cross, we help the men and women serving in our country's military forces, their families and veterans. Millions of us are trained in first aid, water and boat-

ing safety, and health care courses given by the Red Cross. Our Nation's young people, through the Red Cross in schools, obtain leadership skills and learn the value of being of service to their communities.

Within the Federal government, the Red Cross is part of the Combined Federal Campaign. During March, more than one-half of the Red Cross chapters will raise funds, while others will use the period to inform the public about Red Cross services and to recruit new blood donors.

As President of the United States of America and Honorary Chairman of the American Red Cross, I urge all civilian employees of the Federal government and members of the Armed Forces to support in every way possible this vital voluntary effort.

RONALD REAGAN

Nomination of Paul Henry Nitze To Be Special Representative for Arms Control and Disarmament Negotiations
March 9, 1984

The President today announced his intention to nominate Paul Henry Nitze, of the District of Columbia, as Special Representative for Arms Control and Disarmament Negotiations, United States Arms Control and Disarmament Agency, and to have the

rank of Ambassador while so serving.

Mr. Nitze was an accountant with Container Corp. of America in Bridgeport, CT, in 1928–1929, and vice president of Dillon, Read and Co. in New York, NY, in 1929–1938 and also in 1939–1941. In 1938–1939 he was president of P.H. Nitze and Co. in New York City. He was coordinator of Inter-American Affairs at the Department of State in Washington, DC, in 1941–1942. He was Chief of Bureau of the Board of Economic Warfare (1942–1943), Director of the Bureau of the Foreign Economic Administration (1943–1944), and Director of the Policy Planning Staff at the Department of State (1946–1953). In 1953–1961 he was president of the Foreign Service Educational Foundation in Washington, DC. He was Assistant Secretary of Defense for International Security Affairs (1961–1963), Secretary of the Navy (1963–1967), Deputy Secretary of Defense (1967–1969), and a member of the United States Arms Control

and Disarmament Agency as head of the United States delegation to the strategic arms limitation talks (1969–1974). In 1974–1981 he was a self-employed consultant in Washington, DC. In 1981 he was appointed to the United States Arms Control and Disarmament Agency as head of the United States delegation to the Intermediate-range Nuclear Force Negotiations, with the rank of Ambassador (1981–1984), and since January 1984 he has been Special Representative for Arms Control and Disarmament Negotiations.

Mr. Nitze received his A.B. (cum laude) in 1928 from Harvard University. His foreign languages are German and French. He was born January 26, 1907, in Amherst, MA.

Appointment of Three Members of the Advisory Committee to the Pension Benefit Guaranty Corporation, and Designation of Chairman
March 9, 1984

The President today announced his intention to appoint the following individuals to be members of the Advisory Committee to the Pension Benefit Guaranty Corporation for terms expiring February 19, 1987. These are reappointments. The President also intends to designate Roger F. Martin as Chairman upon appointment.

Joseph Geronimo is vice president of the pension products division of the employee benefit group for Bankers Trust Co. in New York City. He is married, has one child, and resides in Maplewood, NJ. He was born June 23, 1950, in Jersey City, NJ.

Perry Joseph is business manager for Carpet, Linoleum, Hardwood & Resilient Tile Layers' Local Union No. 1310 in St. Louis, MO. He has two children and resides in St. Louis. He was born April 28, 1922, in St. Louis.

Roger F. Martin is senior vice president for MGIC Investment Corp. in Milwaukee, WI. He is married, has four children, and resides in Mequon, WI. He was born December 16, 1927, in Cincinnati, OH.

Informal Exchange With Reporters on Foreign and Domestic Issues
March 9, 1984

Q. Mr. President, you've been wanting to talk to us for a long time. Come on over.

Q. What a surprise!

The President. Yes, I've restrained myself, though, haven't I?

Q. Mr. President, what do you think about the Meese hearings?

The President. Wait a minute. Helen [Helen Thomas, United Press International], what——

Q. What about the Meese situation?

The President. Same thing—the Meese situation. Well, I don't know of a nominee that is any more qualified than he is, and I am quite sure that the Senate is going to ratify him, as they should.

Q. Are you concerned at all about these loans?—and then the people who gave him the loans getting government appointments?

The President. No, I am not. I have complete confidence in his standards, and I don't think there was anything more than what he has answered fully on all of those questions—anything more to say about it.

Q. Did you appoint any of those people because they had helped Meese out?

The President. No. As matter of fact, I didn't even know about such things. I don't inquire into the private affairs of the people around me.

Q. Are you going to church this Sunday, sir? The Democrats say you talk about religion, but you don't go to church.

The President. Yes, I've noticed that, that they've been talking about that. I haven't bothered to check on their attendance, but I think they must be well aware of why I have not been attending. And frankly, I miss it very much. But I represent too much of a threat to too many other people for me to be able to go to church.

Q. Aren't you amazed at how Gary Hart has just come up and blasted Mondale out of it?

The President. No. No, I just——

Q. Why aren't you?

The President. Well, I don't pay too much attention to that. That's the Democrats' problem.

Q. But you must have thought about what the race in November could be like if it's you against Hart. Tell us what you think about it.

The President. No, I just—what does it matter who's running on the other side? I'm going to campaign on what I believe and on what I think we should still be doing and what we have been doing.

Q. He says that you're the old ideas and he's the new ideas.

The President. I haven't heard anything yet that you could say was a specific idea that he's had to say. But then, I haven't followed him that closely.

Q. Well, what do you think of what he's saying?

The President. Well, can anyone here tell me specifically what he's going to do?

Listen, all of these questions, and not one

of——

Q. Yes——

The President. ——not one of you have asked me one question about what I think is the biggest news of the day for the whole United States, and that is 400,000 more people went to work in February. The unemployment rate is down to 7.7. That's only three-tenths of a percentage point above where it was when I took office. 4,900,000 people have gone to work in the last 14 months in this country, and there were 700,000 actually more on the payroll in February than there were the month before.

Q. How much are you going to cut your defense budget?

The President. See, you change the subject, and I'm right in the midst of the biggest news of the day. [*Laughter*] We're having some productive meetings with the Senate, and we will come forth with a program with regard to the deficits.

Q. Are you willing to cut defense, though?

Q. You will have to cut defense—[*inaudible*].

The President. We had already cut it $16 billion before we presented the first figures.

Q. Well, how about some more?

The President. We're looking at everything.

Q. Why did you try to make an end run on the Senate for that $21 million for Nicaragua?

The President. We weren't trying to make an end run. When we realized that we could not bridge the gap until they're going to take action—which we hope they will take—on the Kissinger commission's report, that there was going to be a financial gap in there for both of those funds, we then thought in terms of going directly there with the proposal of a separate bill and were advised that this, too, would take too long. So, we thought we would do what so many of them do: ask them to put it onto a program that was already going through the legislature.

Q. How do you feel about the Republicans turning that down, sir?

The President. What?

Q. How do you feel about the Republicans on that committee? They voted it down.

The President. Well, there were three, three votes against it. But I think some of that had to do with the particular bill we wanted to amend.

Q. What are you going to do now?

Q. Do you think you're going to end up having to use your emergency authority—[*inaudible*]—aid to El Salvador at this point?

The President. Well, I certainly hope not. They're going to take it up next week, and I think that reason will prevail. I don't see how anyone could think it was responsible after all this time to actually envision the armed forces of Salvador running out of ammunition and materiel that is needed to defend the country against the guerrillas. And that's the situation as it will stand.

Q. [*Inaudible*]—Meese has got many memos that come across his desk—[*inaudible*]?

The President. Knowing how many come across my desk and I figure should go someplace else—yes. Anyone that's been involved in a career there—

But let me point out, again, those memos were dredged up from the Albosta committee record after they had been completely investigated by the FBI, and the FBI had said there was no evidence of wrong-doing at all. Now, this is all rehashed, old material. There's nothing new in this at all.

Q. [*Inaudible*]—at the moment says the Justice Department clouded the ethics—[*inaudible*]—and could move toward a special prosecutor. Are you going to appeal that ruling?

The President. I think that the FBI did a very thorough examination; including, I made myself available to them.

Q. There's a rumor that Charles Wick is going to leave the Government soon.

The President. What?

Q. There's a rumor that Charles Wick is going to leave the Government soon. Is that true?

The President. You classified it exactly, it's a rumor. No, it's not true.

Q. It is going to be Hart, or is it going be Mondale?

The President. That's up to those other people to decide.

Q. Which would be easier in a television debate?

The President. Let them decide. I'm not going to help them make their decision.

Q. Are you willing to debate, though, either one?

The President. What?

Mr. Speakes. That's enough.

Q. Will you debate either one?

The President. In principle, I've always supported the idea of debating, yes.

Mr. Speakes. Thank you. That'll do.

Q. But Hart comes across like Jack Kennedy!

Mrs. Reagan. He'd come across like Ronald Reagan. [*Laughter*]

The President. There!

Q. Saved by your wife!

Note: The exchange began at 2:52 p.m. at the South Portico of the White House as the President and Mrs. Reagan were leaving for a weekend stay at Camp David, MD.

Larry M. Speakes is Principal Deputy Press Secretary to the President.

Radio Address to the Nation on the Economic Recovery Program
March 10, 1984

My fellow Americans:

During the last 2 years the United States has risen from the depths of recession to one of the strongest recoveries in decades; from dark days of despair to a bright new dawn of promise and hope for all Americans.

I remember saying back when things looked the worst that too much pessimism could be deadly. Well, some people criticized me for trying to sugar-coat bad news. I merely wanted us to remember that there's a psychological factor in recession, and too much hammering at it makes recession worse.

What pulled us through that ordeal, I'm convinced, was our determination to stick to our program, believe in ourselves, and trust in our values of faith, freedom, and hard work—values that have never failed us when we've lived up to them.

And now we're seeing the payoff. 1983 was a banner year for America, notwithstanding voices of pessimism which always found the single dark cloud in every blue sky. Those voices come from many different areas of our society. Recently, the Wall Street Journal reported on a survey of one of them—the television networks' nightly news coverage of the economy during the last half of 1983. During that entire period there were 4 to 15 economic statistic stories a month telling us whether inflation, unemployment, interest rates, retail sales, or housing starts were up or down for a given month. The survey found nearly 95 percent of these reports were positive. However, of the 104 lengthy economic news stories in which the networks gave us their interpretation of what was happening, 86 percent were primarily negative. The survey found the economic news in the second half of 1983 was good. But the coverage on network television was still in recession.

Now please don't get me wrong, every administration must be held accountable. None of us can be excluded from the fury of a free press whenever that's right and proper. But true balance implies consistently showing all faces of America, including hope, optimism, and progress.

Our economy is stronger than practically anyone predicted. The index of leading economic indicators has been up 16 of the last 17 months. Industrial production has risen 14 straight months. Housing starts climbed 60 percent in 1983 to the highest level in 4 years. Retail sales surged. Auto sales registered their best year since 1979. And we had the steepest drop in the unemployment rate in more than 30 years. Yesterday we learned that unemployment for all workers in February dropped to 7.7 percent. More Americans are now at work than ever before in this nation's history.

Here's one example that sums up the difference between yesterday's policies of depending on government and our approach that begins with trusting people. Last year we were asked to raise taxes and appropriate money for a $3½ billion program to put 300,000 people in make-work jobs over a year. We said no, because incentives produce economic recovery, and strong, steady growth puts more people back to work than any government program. And it has.

Recovery has put as many people back to work each month as their program would in a year. We've added an average of 300,000 jobs every single month for the past 15 months, and almost 400,000 last month alone. That's 4.9 million additional workers working and paying taxes. Our economic recovery has become economic expansion. And the potential for new jobs and economic growth in the future is beyond our imagination.

The revolution in science and high technology is only beginning. Each time our knowledge expands, each time we push back frontiers of medicine, agriculture, and space, we will be creating entire new industries, modernizing older ones, and raising our standard of living.

The issue before America in 1984 is clear: Which direction will we go now—forward with optimism, faith, and confidence, continuing to build an opportunity society for all our people; or backward in pessimism and fear, surrendering to politicians who would dismantle our program because their agenda is to make government grow big and fat at your expense?

To serve that agenda, they need to dwell on bad news. So when good news comes, they're either dumbstruck or they pretend they didn't hear. Well, with your support, we'll keep our economy moving forward, and we'll keep America's rendezvous with an optimistic future.

Till next week, thanks for listening, and God bless you.

Note: The President spoke at 12:06 p.m. from Camp David, MD.

Remarks and a Question-and-Answer Session With Students at Congress Heights Elementary School
March 12, 1984

The President. This is like theater in the round. [*Laughter*] If I sit down any way, somebody's going to be behind me here.

Well, the last time we met we didn't really meet. Mr. Dalton and I were at the White House and you were all here, and we were beamed in here on television. And it was at that point that he learned for the first time that the White House wanted to adopt Congress School. And we're very happy that we did.

I know that some of our people have been here and have been in your classes. There have been field trips and all. And I have to tell you, they're learning as much from those meetings as you are, and maybe more at times. But they're all enjoying it. And we all are very interested in education and the importance of this school and what it's going to mean in all of your lives.

And it may seem strange to you, but years and years from now when you're as old as I am—if anyone could ever be that old—you're going to be surprised at how much you remember about these days right here in this school and how much they're going to mean to you.

But now I understand—you know, if you're going to be partners—and incidentally, this whole idea of partnership is spreading all over the whole country, all the way across. I'm almost afraid to tell you who are partners of the schools in San Diego, because then you'll probably wish that you had them instead of us. [*Laughter*] But the football team there and a baseball team there have adopted schools in San Diego. But this is going on.

Now, there has to be some kind of personal relationship when you're doing this. So, I'm going to—I want to have a student from here be a pen pal, and we'll exchange letters. And I understand that the young man who's going to do this is Rudolph Hines. Where is Rudolph Hines? He doesn't know this yet.

There. Rudolph, come on up here. [*Laughter*] Hi. My name's Reagan. Rudolph, the idea is that you and I will kind of exchange letters with each other. You write and I'll answer you, or I'll write and you'll answer me. And we'll kind of keep in contact that way. And maybe you can tell me some of the things that are going on here, and maybe sometimes in my letters, I'll complain about what's going on at the White House. [*Laughter*]

Rudolph. Thank you.

The President. There. Now, I understand that we've got a little time in which I can answer questions, and so I'm going to ask you, Rudolph, you'll have to keep watching them to see who raises their hand. And just for one, at least, would you pick the first one that I'm supposed to answer?

So, who has a question? I know there must have been times when you've said, "Boy, if I could ask him something I'd sure ask him this or that." So go ahead. Who has a question? That's you.

Q. What do you do at the White House? [*Laughter*]

The President. Well, there are a lot of people that have been asking that question. [*Laughter*] Let me just give you an idea of what's taken place so far today, and maybe that will explain it.

This morning, into the White House for what we call a staff meeting—that's catch-up with anything that's new or that we need to discuss for today. And then I went into the Cabinet Room and we had a number of Congressmen in there—leaders and chairmen of committees and so forth in the Congress. And I discussed with them plans for trying to reduce the Federal deficit. And we had a good meeting.

Then I went back to the Oval Office and two gentlemen[1] came in who are not part

---

[1] *At his daily press briefing, which was held later in the day, Larry M. Speakes, Principal Deputy Press Secretary to the President, identified the gentlemen as David Rockefeller and Archibald Roosevelt.*

of government but who have just come back from a trip to the Middle East. And they've been in several countries over there. They've been in Turkey and Saudi Arabia and Morocco and, well, a number of other—Egypt and Oman and those countries. And they wanted to tell me that they had met there with the heads of government in those states, and they reported to me on the things that they had discussed and that these heads of state had discussed with them as to things that we can do to be closer with them.

Then they left the office and in came two Foreign Ministers—the Foreign Minister of a country in Central America, Costa Rica, and the Foreign Minister of Honduras. Now these are both countries down there where we're trying to be helpful and where there is war going on and people are being killed. And we're hoping that we can find an answer that will end all that and allow them to live better and live the way we do and live in peace with each other.

And at about that time, somebody came into the office and just stood there staring at me until I knew that they were telling me that time was up, and I said goodbye to the Foreign Ministers because I had to get in the car and come over here to Congress School.

So, that's just an idea of what part of the day is. And pretty soon somebody's going to look at me or tap me on the shoulder and tell me I have to go back over to the Oval Office because I have another meeting over there.

Now I'm on my own, aren't I? Young lady. Yes?

Q. Mr. President, would you return to politics or go back to the movies when you leave the White House?

The President. [Laughing] No, I think that probably it's the time for me to retire from thinking about the movies. I have a hunch—we have a ranch which I miss very much. And I have a hunch that when this job is over that maybe I'll just go to the ranch and ride my horses and do the things that have to be done around the ranch. There's always a lot to be done. As a matter of fact, last summer I had a couple of weeks there, and we built some 400 feet of fence out of telephone poles, and there were just

three of us working at it. So I'd find things to do. But, no, I don't know what—I liked pictures, and I liked working in them, but I think that's all finished now.

You, yes.

Q. How did you get to become President?

The President. Oh! *[Laughing]* I think there are always some people that tell you whether you should try to do that or not, and this happened—I had been Governor of California for 8 years, and on the basis of that, there were people that thought that I should seek this particular job. And so I did, and was elected by the people to be President. And I have to tell you it's a hard job, but it's also a very challenging and fulfilling thing to have an opportunity to do something that you think might help the people of our country.

Now I think I better turn to the other side here, hadn't I? All right.

Q. Will the White House adopt our school again next year?

The President. Oh, I didn't know this was a yearly thing. We've adopted the school, and as long as I'm in the White House, you're our school.

Yes?

Q. Mr. President, how do you feel about Congress Heights as a whole since the adoption?

The President. Well, from everything that I've heard from all of our people who have been able to come here—and, incidentally, I know I've met some of you before, and not just on television, because there were some of you who visited the White House, and I saw you outside on the South Lawn there and got to say hello to a number of you—but from all that I've heard, everybody on our side is very happy that you're our adopted school.

Q. What do you like most about being the President?

The President. Visiting Congress School. *[Laughter]*

There are—may I just add to that, also, as you know—there are other things, too. I think it's being in a position where you can be of help to people, and I like people.

Yes?

Q. How has your business been going? *[Laughter]*

The President. Well, I can tell you business has been steady. [*Laughter*] I mentioned going to the ranch last summer and everything. And my wife, Nancy, told me after that vacation, she said that she's decided that Presidents don't get vacations, they just get a change of scenery.

Yes?

Q. What are your feelings about supporting a woman as a Presidential candidate in 1988? [*Laughter*]

The President. Well, I have to tell you this, that I am firmly convinced—I don't know that I can say about a particular year or not, who'd be supported—I am convinced that one day before too long there's going to be a woman holding this job. And among the heads of state that I have been able to meet, both when I was Governor and since I've been President, people like Golda Meir, when she was the head of government of Israel, Margaret Thatcher, who is the present Prime Minister of England, Indira Gandhi of India—I have found them to be really tremendous people, wonderful people and strong leaders. And I see no reason why the United States should not be able to do the same thing.

The little girl in red—yes?

Q. [*Inaudible*] [*Laughter*]

The President. Well—[*laughing*]—shall we try the one in green? Then I'll come back to you.

Q. How did you get to the White House?

The President. Does she mean to live in it?

Q. How did you get to be President at the White House?

The President. Well, I've asked myself the same question several times. But I think that it all came from when I was asked, and agreed, to become the Governor or seek the Governorship of California. And on the basis of the 8 years there as Governor, that led to this.

I have to tell you, though, I never had any idea in my life, prior to that time, that I would ever be doing anything like this. So don't be surprised, or don't be disturbed if all of you haven't made up your minds yet what you want to do with your future, with your life. I didn't really settle down to what I was going to do until I'd actually finished my total education.

Now, I said we'd turn to you.

Q. Why did you decide to adopt Congress Heights out of all the other schools?

The President. Well, we had looked at a number, and then between us, we all decided that this was the school we'd like to do. So we had a meeting on education over at the White House, and it was covered by television, and the television was being played also to your school here, as you know. And there, on television, we made the announcement that it was going to be your school. And Mr. Dalton, who was standing there beside me, didn't know that I was going to say that.

So, I think we just did it—that we believed that here was a school that we would like to have this relationship with, and get to know you and let you get to know us.

Mr. Dalton. Mr. President, I know that you have another appointment. I want to interrupt to say that the Congress Heights School appreciates being a partner with the White House, and your endeavors have been rewarding to the students. And before you go, we would like to make a small presentation to you from one of your schools.

Tammi Gardner will make a small presentation.

The President. Well, all right. Thank you very much.

Tammi. Mr. President, I would like to present this scroll to you from the family, from members of the Congress Heights family.

The President. Well, Tammi, thank you very much. You are partners. You've all signed this for us. Well, believe me, we're very proud to have this. Let me—well, of course you've seen it because you all signed it. [*Laughter*] Well, this is wonderful. And, Tammi, thank you, and thank all of you.

Now I know I didn't get to all the hands. But I think, as partners, there'll be other occasions when we can get together, and we'll answer the questions we missed today or, maybe, at that time, you'll have figured out some different ones you want to ask.

But again, this has been a great pleasure and—well, the principal says that I can't, that my time is up. He says that I can't take any more. It's the same way with the press there in the press conferences. There are always more hands than we have time for.

So again, just remember what you were going to ask, and I know I'll be back again. Thank you all very much. And, Rudolph, thank you.

Note: The President spoke at 10:57 a.m. at the elementary school in the District of Co- *lumbia. During the question-and-answer session, Annie Staton, a teacher, repeated the students questions for the benefit of the other participants and observers. William Dalton is the principal of the school.*

The White House adopted the school on October 13, 1983, as part of the National Partnerships in Education Program.

Nomination of Frank C. Casillas To Be an Assistant Secretary of Labor
March 12, 1984

The President today announced his intention to nominate Frank C. Casillas to be an Assistant Secretary of Labor (Employment and Training). He would succeed Albert Angrisani.

Since 1982 Mr. Casillas has been serving as vice president of business development and technology for the Bunker Ramo Corp. Previously, he was vice president for corporate development and technology with the Bunker Ramo Corp. in 1968–1982; manager of product planning and market research for General Electric-Computer Division in 1958–1968; systems analyst for the Rand Corp. in 1957–1959; and staff engineer for Standard Oil Co. of Indiana in 1953–1957.

Mr. Casillas served as a member of the President's Advisory Council on Minority Business Enterprise and as chairman of the board of directors of NEDA (National Economic Development Association).

He graduated from Purdue University (B.S., 1948). He is married, has six children, and resides in Downers Grove, IL. He was born April 19, 1926.

Nomination of Mario F. Aguero To Be a Commissioner of the Copyright Royalty Tribunal
March 12, 1984

The President today announced his intention to nominate Mario F. Aguero to be a Commissioner of the Copyright Royalty Tribunal for the unexpired term of 7 years from September 27, 1977. He would succeed Mary Lou Burg.

Mr. Aguero was owner-president of Havana East Restaurant in New York in 1972–1982. Previously, he was producer and sponsor of various events in the entertainment field (1961–1976); vice president and owner of Morimar, Inc., in 1964–1967; vice president and owner of Enterprises Latinos Corp. in 1960–1963; and president and owner of Caribe Artists Corp. in 1950–1961.

He is founder and president of the organization ARTE (Artists Radio Television Espectaculos) and is a New York member of the First Hispanic Council.

He is married, has one child, and resides in New York, NY. He was born May 1, 1924, in Camaguey, Cuba.

Accordance of the Personal Rank of Ambassador to Andrew E. Gibson While Serving as Special Envoy on International Labor Organization Matters
March 12, 1984

The President today announced his intention to accord the personal rank of Ambassador to Andrew E. Gibson, of New Jersey, in his capacity as Special Envoy on International Labor Organization Matters.

Mr. Gibson served in the United States Navy in 1951–1953 as lieutenant. In 1953–1971 he was assistant to the treasurer and advanced to senior vice president at Grace Line, Inc., in New York, NY. He was Assistant Secretary of Commerce in Washington, DC, in 1969–1972. In 1973–1974 he was president of Interstate Oil Transport in Philadelphia, PA, and chairman of General Dynamics Shipyard in Quincy, MA, in 1974–1975. He was president of Maher Terminals in Jersey City, NJ, in 1975–1977 and consultant at Harbridge House in Boston, MA, in 1978–1979. He was president of Delta Steamship Lines in New Orleans, LA, in 1979–1982. Since 1983 he has been chairman of American Automar, Inc., in Washington, DC. Since 1984 he has been Special Envoy on International Labor Organization Matters, Department of State.

Mr. Gibson graduated from Brown University (B.A., 1951) and New York University (M.B.S., 1959). He was born February 19, 1922, in New York, NY.

Remarks at a White House Luncheon for Elected Republican Women Officials
March 12, 1984

Good afternoon, and welcome to the White House. And it's good to see so many old friends and westerners to boot, and have the opportunity to make new ones—friends that is—not westerners. [*Laughter*]

And, of course, I have been introduced by one of my two favorite women. And she's explained to you why there's only one of them here. You've all heard that politics make strange bedfellows. Well, I found out that kind of works in reverse also—[*laughter*]—so, she's in Houston, and I'm in Washington.[1]

Well, I want to thank all of you for what you're doing to advance the ideals and the goals that unite us. We've journeyed far, I think, in these 3 years. But it never would have happened without the drive and the energy and determination of officeholders in State capitals and communities all across America. America's future looks bright, and you've made the difference.

Our economic recovery is bringing new hope and opportunity to our people. Inflation has plummeted by two-thirds to about 4 percent. The prime rate is almost half what it was when we took office. Three words describe our recovery program: Jobs, jobs, and jobs.

And last month alone, 700,000 more Americans were found on the payrolls. And we've had the steepest drop in the unemployment rate in over three decades. And I meant the 700,000 in just that 1 month—from the previous month. The overall unemployment rate is down to 7.7 percent, and among adult women, the rate has dropped from 9.1 to 6.9. Since the beginning of the dramatic upturn 15 months ago, nearly 5 million—4.9 million—people have

---

[1] *The President was introduced by his daughter Maureen. Mrs. Reagan was attending a luncheon hosted by the Houston Magic Circle Women's Republican Club in Texas.*

gone back to work in the United States. And more people are working than ever before in our history. But we can't rest until every American who wants a job has found one.

All the leading economic indicators suggest that our economic growth will continue. The failed policies of higher taxes, bigger government, soaring inflation, and runaway spending haven't disappeared. In fact, they're lurking not far away, as anyone who had time to watch the debate last night would know. Right now those failed policies are on the stump—just a few hundred miles south of here.

The Federal Government and the budget must be brought under better control. Deficits remain a problem, but the biggest problem is the size of the government's claim on our economy. I'm dead serious about negotiating a downpayment on the deficit. But common sense, not partisan politics, should govern the deliberations so that we can protect the interests of the American people.

The starting point is to cut out the waste in spending—and believe me, we've discovered there's still a lot of waste in spending. Personal tax rates have been reduced. We passed an historic tax reform indexing so that government will no longer be able to use inflation to profit at your expense. But those in government who have a stake in bigger government don't want you to have indexing. The billions in tax and spending increases that these spenders are pushing would not reduce the deficit; they just reduce the recovery.

We want to go forward, not backward. And America will go forward if we simplify the tax system and reduce tax rates further. Republicans want to build an opportunity society. We can all be proud that we're putting America's future back in the hands of the people and proud that we're working to strengthen our social institutions, the bedrock of our society and our freedom.

But important challenges remain. We can start by letting our children have the right to call on a little help from God at the start of the school day, if they so choose. When 80 percent of the people want voluntary prayer back in our schools, I think it takes a lot of gall to tell them they can't have it. Well, if enough of you make your voices heard, we can restore the right of voluntary prayer in the classroom.

Education is another area where we're the ones with the courage to call for basic reform. Excellence in education means getting back to fundamentals, working from the bottom up, providing local leadership, and thinking smarter. And I think our support for basic reform is starting to pay off. When our administration took office, only a handful of States had task forces on education. Today they all do. And reforms are being adopted in academic standards, discipline, curriculum, and basic values. For example, 44 States are increasing graduation requirements; 42 are studying improvements in teacher certification; and 33 are considering or have enacted legislation for master teacher type programs. So, it's up to us to make sure the momentum continues.

In connection with this whole thing on education, I just had a chore this morning that was most pleasant. You know, this partnership thing that is sweeping the Nation of various business firms or organizations or groups and labor unions—and even some of our professional athletic teams have formed partnerships with local schools, and they help and are going to field trips and going there to lecture, whatever they can do to help. Well, the White House adopted a school here in town—Congress Heights School—and I was out there this morning and was taking questions from the students there and meeting them.

The most humbling experience was in the kindergarten—[*laughter*]—the kindergarten computer class. [*Laughter*] I don't know the first thing about those things, but those 5-year-olds did. There they all sat in front of their computers. Finally, the one I was sitting beside said, "Well go ahead and push the button." I was scared to death. [*Laughter*]

But a third important challenge is to restore the proper balance to our criminal justice system. We came to Washington determined to crack down on habitual criminals, organized crime, and the drugpushers. And in 1982 crime went down 4.3 percent, and that's the biggest decline in 10 years. But too many law-abiding citizens are still being harmed or killed while dangerous criminals get off scot-free.

The long overdue reform that we need must begin with passage of our comprehensive crime control act, the most important anticrime legislation that's been introduced in more than a decade. It was approved by the Senate last month. You can imagine why—who has the majority there. But now the bill is being bottled up in committee by Democrats in the House. And I'm very disappointed in their attitude. When it comes to putting criminals behind bars, when it comes to keeping the American people safe, there should be no Republicans or Democrats—just Americans. Now, if they continue to refuse, then you and I not only have the right; we have the obligation to hold their feet to the fire.

And just as we're strengthening the basic values which made America great, there's a new sense of purpose and direction to America's foreign policy. Thirty-seven years ago today, President Truman addressed the American people before a joint session of the Congress. In the closing of that speech, which later would be known as the Truman Doctrine, he said, "The free peoples of the world look to us for support in maintaining their freedoms. If we falter in our leadership, we may endanger the peace of the world—and we shall surely endanger the welfare of this nation."

Well, back in the late seventies, some had lost sight of Mr. Truman's wisdom. We had an uncomfortable feeling that we'd lost respect overseas, and we no longer trusted our leaders to defend peace and freedom. Today the world knows once more that America can be counted on to defend freedom, peace, and human dignity. And, believe me, that makes the world safer for all of us.

Now let me say a few words about El Salvador, a new democracy that is struggling to protect itself from extremists of the right and the left. El Salvador will be holding elections at the end of this month. But if they're to succeed, they must take place in a climate of security. We know that Cuban-supported guerrillas plan to disrupt these elections, just as they tried and failed to do that 2 years ago when they held their first elections. But the Salvadorans are out of U.S. military aid assistance funds, because

my original request was not fully funded by the Congress. El Salvador—their army, trying to protect them against these guerrillas, will soon be out of ammunition, supplies, and funds for U.S. training support. As a matter of fact, shipments of medical supplies have already had to be stopped. Without these supplies and training support, El Salvador cannot hold secure elections or defend their country.

Therefore, I've asked the Congress to approve an emergency, short-term military assistance package to tide the situation over until the Congress acts on the recommendations of the Bipartisan Commission on Central America. This package is urgently needed, and I urge its rapid approval by the Congress. Democracy in El Salvador depends on it.

And to those who maybe question whether they really are achieving anything in democracy: Two years ago, observers from our Congress went down to observe those elections. Eighty-three percent of the people turned out. We haven't turned out 83 percent of the people for an election in years and years. And they actually saw—some of these Congressmen—and talked with a woman who was standing in the lines for hours waiting to vote, waiting her turn, had been shot, wounded by the guerrillas, and refused to leave the lines for medical attention until she had been allowed to vote. This is what we're trying to defend down there and protect, and I think they deserve our help after 400 years.

Two months ago that Bipartisan Commission submitted its report. They called on our government to substantially increase economic and military assistance to Central America. Between two-thirds and three-fourths of that assistance will be economic and social, not military. And although the region is vital to our national interest and the situation increasingly urgent, the Congress has not acted.

As a nation, we can't afford to let this issue drag on while people die in Central America. We can't afford to let political partisanship jeopardize our security interests or undercut the opportunity for El Salvador to build its democracy. The Bipartisan Commission gave us a formula which should be

329

acceptable to all. So, let's use it and get on with it.

When historians write about these years, they'll find that very skilled and talented women played a key role in putting America back on her feet. And here in Washington we're calling on the talents of women and the leadership of women in a big way. For the first time in history, three women are on the Cabinet at the same time—U.N. Ambassador Jeane Kirkpatrick, Secretary of Health and Human Services Margaret Heckler, Secretary of Transportation Elizabeth Dole. Ambassador Faith Whittlesey has brought her talent and skill to the White House staff. And all told, more than 1,400 women hold policymaking posts in our administration. And a number of them are here in the room today with you. We couldn't get all 1,400 in—[laughter]—but several others that are in here—and I won't try to name all of them. But I can just tell you, believe me, they are serving, and we are dependent on them. And I say that with one—my own "girl Friday" is sitting over there—Kathy Osborne—and she keeps me on track. [Laughter]

Well, one of my proudest days was when Sandra Day O'Connor became the first woman Justice in the history of the Supreme Court. That's the tradition of the Grand Old Party.

Even before women—maybe you don't know this—had a right to vote, our party became the first party to elect a woman to the United States Congress. And today the only women in the Senate are Nancy Kassebaum and Paula Hawkins—Republicans. And, of course, we have nine outstanding Republican Congresswomen, including Barbara Vucanovich, who is here with us today. Now, don't you think it's about time that we give them some more company? [Applause]

But just as important, thousands of able Republican women like you are serving in public offices all across America. We want to see the numbers grow. We want to see them grow here in Washington for sure—and here in Washington and in every American community. Someday, and I hope it's sooner rather than later, a woman's going to have my job. Our job is to make sure she's a Republican.

We have good reason to approach this election year in high spirits. We can be confident that the American people share our values. But we cannot afford to rest; there's too much that remains to be done. So, with your help, with your frontier spirit, we'll get the job done. And we'll make 1984 a great year for the Republican Party.

Now, I thank you all for being here, and God bless you all. And now the words you've been waiting to hear—let's have dessert. [Laughter]

Note: The President spoke at 12:47 p.m. in the State Dining Room at the White House.

Nomination of 11 Members of the Board of Directors of the Legal Services Corporation
March 12, 1984

The President today announced his intention to nominate the following individuals to be members of the Board of Directors of the Legal Services Corporation:

For the remainder of the term expiring July 13, 1986:

Lorain Miller would succeed Milton M. Masson. Mrs. Miller is a widow with eight children who has been active as a community worker, neighborhood volunteer, and worker with the local YMCA. She was born December 15, 1934, in Hazard, KY, and now resides in Detroit, MI.

Hortencia Benavides would succeed Ronald Frankum. Miss Benavides is currently employed by the El Paso Catholic Pentecostal Renewal Office. She was born October 10, 1931, in El Paso, TX, where she currently resides.

For the remainder of the term expiring July 13, 1984, and for the subsequent term expiring July 13, 1987:

Thomas F. Smegal, Jr., would succeed David E. Satterfield III. Mr. Smegal is a partner in the San Francisco law firm of Townsend & Townsend. He was born June 19, 1935, in Eveleth, MN, and currently resides in Piedmont, CA.

Basile Joseph Uddo would succeed Howard H. Dana, Jr. Mr. Uddo is a professor of law at Loyola University, School of Law, in New Orleans, LA. He was born April 22, 1949, in New Orleans, LA, where he currently resides.

The President also announced his intention to nominate the following individuals who were previously nominated: Robert A. Valois, Leaanne Bernstein, Claude Galbreath Swafford, Michael B. Wallace, William Clark Durant III, Paul B. Eaglin, and Pepe J. Mendez to be members of the Board of Directors of the Legal Services Corporation.

Appointment of Nackey Scripps Loeb as a Member of the Architectural and Transportation Barriers Compliance Board
March 12, 1984

The President today announced his intention to appoint Nackey Scripps Loeb to be a member of the Architectural and Transportation Barriers Compliance Board for a term expiring December 3, 1986. She will succeed William Reid Ralls.

Mrs. Loeb is publisher of the Union Leader in Manchester, NH. She has two children and resides in Goffstown, NH. Mrs. Loeb was born February 24, 1924, in Los Angeles, CA.

Nomination of Two Members of the Board of Trustees of the Harry S. Truman Scholarship Foundation
March 12, 1984

The President today announced his intention to nominate the following individuals to be members of the Board of Trustees of the Harry S. Truman Scholarship Foundation for terms expiring December 10, 1989.

Anita M. Miller is a consultant to Inside Edge in Sacramento, Calif. She served as chairperson of the California Commission on the Status of Women and was a member of the board of directors of the American Association of University Women Educational Foundation. She graduated from California State University (A.B.) and Stanford University (M.A.). She is married, has two children, and resides in Sacramento, CA. She was born May 19, 1928, in

Versailles, KY. This is a reappointment.

Elmer B. Staats is president of the Harry S. Truman Scholarship Foundation. He served as Comptroller General of the United States in 1966–1981. He serves as a member of the board of directors of the American Academy of Political and Social Science, the National Academy of Public Administration, and of the board of directors of Radio Free Europe/Radio Liberty. He graduated from McPherson College (B.A., 1935), the University of Kansas (M.A., 1936), and the University of Minnesota (Ph.D., 1939). He is married, has three children, and resides in Washington, DC. He was born June 6, 1914, in Richfield, KS. H would succeed John W. Snyder.

Interview With Southeast Regional Editors on Foreign and Domestic Issues
March 12, 1984

Presidential Campaign

Q. Do you want to venture a guess on who's going to come out on top tomorrow—Democratic field?

The President. No. I'll let them have that all to themselves and decide.

Q. Want to tell us who you would prefer to face in November?

The President. No, no—I'll offer no help in who they might want to select.

Q. Would you tell us if you've been at all surprised by Gary Hart's surge in the primaries so far?

The President. Well, maybe might not have picked that, and yet I think I can understand—a kind of a new face. But I still think that it's too early to really be naming any frontrunners or anything in that race. Having gone through a series of primaries, there's a long way to go.

Q. Mr. President, a lot of us pundits have been predicting that this race would turn into a generational conflict. I recall you in the past talking about how—finally how America needs to return to the stature and to the values of its past. Will you be adjusting that strategy if you are facing an opponent who talks about, compares himself—backing the future, as opposed to the policies of the past?

The President. No, I have always felt and based any campaigning or anything that I do on what we do, not what the other fellow says he's going to do—what we do and what we plan to do. And that's the way I would campaign. I don't see any need for any generational struggle in here, but if there is, maybe we can settle it with an arm wrestle. [*Laughter*]

Q. Is it true what Gary Hart says, that you and Walter Mondale represent the policies of the past?

The President. No. As a matter of fact—it might be in the past in that, to the extent that some of the things were principles that this country was based on—but I think that what we've done has been a departure, certainly from the past 40-odd years of Demo-cratic domination in the country in which they have held both Houses of the Congress.

Federal Budget Deficits

Q. Mr. President, can you give us some idea about what you would do in the next term to control the deficits? Are we talking—would you—are you considering possibly another increase, or an increase in taxes by changing the system, say, or would you make any further cuts in entitlement programs?

The President. We are looking at—and have been—and this is nothing new——

Q. Right.

The President. ——what we think are so-called loopholes that offer not quite fair benefits to some and not to all. We have also discussed and I've asked the Treasury Department to look into something that can't happen in this coming year, it's going to take more study than this, and that is a simplification of our tax structure. We need to look at ways to get the billions and billions of dollars that are not being paid in taxes—owed by people legitimately and not by way of loopholes; in this instance, just outright violations of the tax code. To that extent, yes, we're going to do that. But for the future, we have to bring down the percentage of the gross national product that government is taking in this country.

See, I have a degree in economics myself. Now, that doesn't make me an authority, because I don't think economists are authorities; it's an inexact science. But I do remember that when I was getting my degree, it was more or less a standard acceptance in economics that the business cycle, so called, and the lean periods previous to that are—what we now call recessions and depressions—when they did occur, that usually it was when the government had gone beyond a certain point in the percentage of gross national product that it was taking. And that was just more or less accepted as standard.

Well, I think it is very true today. And I think that after we get what we've called a downpayment, which is about all we can get in this year, with the limited time that Congress is going to be here, then I think, in a bipartisan way, we're going to have to continue to look at government, as to how, structurally, we can reduce the share that government is taking.

Q. Can you give us an idea, though—I mean, could you give us some specifics about what you might do? I mean, what——

The President. Well, let me give them to this extent. Some of them you could look at, and they could be contained in the Grace commission—or committee reports. Here was a look at government by almost 2,000 top business leaders in the private sector— not only from institutions and so forth but from the business and financial world—that looked at government as they would look at a business if they were thinking of merging or taking it over—as to things that are wrong or that could be changed. And we are really seriously looking at these recommendations, 2,478—or -28?—but anyway, it's almost 2,500 recommendations that they have made. And many of them would require legislative action, because they would result in changes in procedure in the processes of government.

Q. In the negotiations that have been going on in the last few weeks on this downpayment that you referred to, what concessions have you expressed willingness to make? And what concessions might you be willing to make for your part in these negotiations?

The President. Well, frankly, I've lost a little faith in the bipartisan approach to this, because the other side seemed more interested, I think, in politics than they did in meeting us in any way on trying to achieve this downpayment. So, I am and have been meeting with the leadership of our own in the House and in the Senate on that very thing, and will be willing, once we all come to agreement and have settled on a plan— and I can't go beyond that, because we haven't—but I will be willing then to go forward with our own proposal and hope that we can, with the support of the people, that we can get bipartisan support for it.

Q. So, you're saying you haven't even put forth a proposal yet?

The President. That what?

Q. You have not, even yet, put forth a proposal in these negotiations? I don't quite understand.

The President. Well, this is in our own discussions within, I might say, the family, meaning the Republican leadership, both the House and Senate and myself. We are discussing—and there are a number of viewpoints on figures having to do with spending reductions—and I think we're pretty much agreed on that tax revenues would be—if there are any—would be obtained from corrections in the tax program and not in any change in the rates.

Support From Blacks

Q. Mr. President, not too long ago your finance chairman in Mississippi, William Munger, was reflecting back on the Republican's defeat in the gubernatorial race in that State last year, and he said that in order for Republicans to do well in Mississippi, they had to attract black votes, but if they did the things necessary to attract black votes, they'd be going against Republican philosophy. Do you agree with that?

The President. No, I don't. No, I think everything that we've done in our economic approach is of benefit to everyone. I know that there are charges being made—I listened to the debate—that somehow our attempts at economies and all have penalized people who were dependent on government aid. That is a falsehood. The simple fact of the matter is we're spending more on help for the people and for the needy than has ever been spent before in history. Our budget cuts have been reductions in the increase planned in spending. We haven't come to some place where we're spending less than had been spent.

Q. But, sir, blacks in Alabama say that they're not going to vote for you. They say they're going to vote for the Democrat, whoever he is. How are you going to counter what they perceive to be an administration that doesn't have their interest at heart?

The President. Well, you said the key word, that they "perceive" to be. And I'm just going to hope that in the campaign we can reveal to them that they have not been given the truth, that they are the victims of a lot of demagoguery that has portrayed us as guilty of things we haven't done.

Presidential Campaign

Q. Do you think that all the campaigning among eight contenders for the Democratic nomination has changed public perception of you along those lines or along other lines on——

The President. Well, even before a campaign started, this has been pretty much the theme of the other side. I have been held up as eating my young, that we have been hostile to the poor and our tax program benefits the rich. How can a program that cuts taxes evenly, percentagewise, across the board—thus leaving the same rate of progression in our progressive tax system—how can that be beneficial to the rich and detrimental to the others?

How can it be unfair to the people of lower income or the poor to reduce inflation from double digits—12½ percent when we came here—down to a third of that or less, less than a third of that. When the people with the least—let's take someone with $10,000 of income between—through 2 years, 1979 and 1980—before we got here. By the end of 1980 that $10,000 would only buy $8,000 worth. He was getting $5,000 a year. He got a $1,000 cut in his ability to buy each year.

That was probably the worst tax on the elderly with fixed incomes, the worst tax on the poor who have to spend most of their earnings on subsistence, on the necessities. The person with luxury income who spends a minor portion of it on necessities and the rest on luxuries, they weren't really penalized as much by inflation.

So, I think everything we've done has been beneficial to everyone at every level.

Entitlement Programs

Q. You mention the elderly. If I could ask about that. The large elderly population of Florida—and they—many voters seem to be convinced that you, more than the Democrats, have been trying to restrain the growth or cut back entitlement programs such as social security and medicare. First of all, is that a correct perception? And is it possible in a second term that you would be advocating further cutbacks?

The President. I have said repeatedly that programs like that—there are things that need to be done, but we must never pull the rug out from those people presently receiving their payments from the program and dependent on it. You can't suddenly undermine them or break your contract with them. Reforms, if there are such to be made, must be made, looking toward the future, on people not yet dependent and who would have plenty of time and warning with regard to such changes.

Again, this was—if you will remember, that was the issue of the 1982 campaign. And nothing had been done. We were guilty of trying to tell the Congress and our opponents that social security was facing financial disaster and it could hit it as early as July 1983. They denied that. I remember hearing the Speaker of the House, himself, deny that that was true. And then after the election was over, we all got together in a bipartisan group and without any animus, came up with a plan to save social security because it would be broke by July of 1983. And we came up with that program. It wasn't a permanent answer to some of the problems, but it did buy us a great many years down the road before we would again be in the fiscal spot of that kind.

Now, as to what we've done in social security since we've been here, the average married couple on social security has had a $180-a-month increase. So, I, again, don't think that we were doublecrossing anyone.

Unemployment

Q. Mr. President, in 1980 West Virginia was one of, I think, half a dozen States that voted for Carter. And now, 4 years later unemployment is hovering around 15 percent, and the coal industry and the steel industry are ailing, and some Federal programs that West Virginians have depended on have been cut. What would you say to the guy in the street in West Virginia to convince him that he should vote for you in 1984?

The President. Well, first of all, we know that unemployment is never consistent with the national average. I described this to some of our own people a little while ago, that to think that it is like the man that drowned trying to wade across a river whose average depth was 3 feet. There are those pockets and certain areas that are going to be hit harder than others. But in the surge which—in reducing unemployment—which is greater than anything we've seen in the last 30 years—even those hard-hit areas are being benefited.

More will have to be done. This is why we have for a couple of years now been trying to get the enterprise zone legislation through the Congress. And it's been blocked.

This is a program—and I was amazed when one of the candidates in the debate last night started talking about we must look at tax incentives to help industry and so-forth put people back to work. Well, that's what the enterprise zones are all about, picking those hard-hit spots, both rural and urban, and generating employment through the use of tax incentives. And so far, a number of States have gotten tired of waiting for the Congress to act and do it at a national level, and have put in their own enterprise zone programs. And every one of them is proving tremendously successful.

But, knowing that you might get around to unemployment, I just decided some figures might be of interest to you. You represent two, four, six, eight States—and all in the same region. In every one of them the figures for the peak of unemployment, and the figures for—I can't give them to you except for one State now—but in December, as of the December level of the comeback, were considerably down from the peak. And in the State that you just mentioned, your own, at the peak, unemployment in West Virginia was 21. By December it was down to 15.7.

Now, I don't know what it is today. We won't know for awhile, because when the Labor Department gives you the overall statistics, they don't break it down to States at the present figure. It takes them awhile to break it down as to States. So, all I have are the November figures, except for Florida, and that's because they do break it down for the 10 most populous States earli-

er than they do for the rest.

Florida was 8.6 at its peak—or, wait a minute—Florida was 10.4 at its peak, and in December was down to 7.5. But to give you an idea of what the rest of the figures may look like when we get them—for the present, Florida is now down to 6.

Q. Ours was at 11.4 in December and in January was back up to 13.5. I mean, some of that has to do with seasonal——

The President. That's Arkansas?

Q. Alabama.

The President. Alabama. Alabama, yes.

Q. It's creeping back——

The President. Well, at the peak——

Q. It's creeping back up.

The President. Yes, but at the peak you were 16.7. In December you were 12.3. Now, I don't know what the present one is——

Q. Well, in January it was 13.5.

The President. 13.5. Well, I think there'll be these fluctuations. I'll be very interested in seeing what it comes out as from February.

Q. Is there anything else that you think that the States could do to help pull themselves up?

The President. Well, I think most States, as far as I can see, are doing all they can, just as we are. Maybe—and, you know, all of your States, particularly there in the Sunbelt, you're going to have to recognize also that your reduction in unemployment may be a little slower because of the migration to the Sunbelt. And that means that newcomers coming in, without jobs and looking for jobs, are temporarily going to distort the figures.

Economic Recovery Program

Q. Back on the economic issue for just 1 minute, back to the budgetary thing—when you campaigned for President, one of your promises, of course, was to balance the budget by 1984. Obviously, it's not balanced. I wonder what you look at as the main reason for that. What happened to Reaganomics that made it not work like you wanted it to?

The President. Nothing happened to Reaganomics. And I'm glad you asked this question.

Yes, I had the help of some of the finest economists in the country in working on the program that I call the economic recovery program. And toward the end of the summer, 1980, I announced that plan, and based our projections—that, yes, it could balance the budget by '83, based on all the projections that those economists at that time—before the election. Between that announcement and November, that projection was no longer valid, because the economy in 1980 was deteriorating so fast, and had not been projected to do so by any of these notable economists. No one had. So, it continued to worsen, and by the time of the Inaugural—then even a later time—was beyond any prediction; it had continued to get worse. That was when interest rates were 21½. Inflation, then, for '79 and '80 had been double digit both years.

Now, when I started—you've got to remember that the President comes in not with his own budget. You are still bound until the following October by the budget of the previous administration. Nor was my program in effect. We were still trying to get it. And in July of 1981 was when the further big dip came.

Now, some economists have said, well, we had a 1979, '80 recession, and then the thing that happened in July was another—a different recession. Well, I don't think so. Things were—it was a continuation. And the bottom fell out with the interest rates that stayed high, the automobile industry, the housing industry—either one of which can start a recession by itself. So, nothing of what happened and the great surge to 10.8 percent in unemployment—none of that could be attributed to our program, because our program hadn't started.

And then, as our program was implemented—and remember, it was only implemented in stages. It took 3 years to get the 25-percent tax cut. Other things that were implemented—and we never got all of the spending cuts. As a matter of fact, we got a little less than half of what we asked in spending cuts. And that's to this day.

Now, I could turn around and say that maybe the recovery might have been even better if we had gotten—remember that one stage of our tax cut—10 percent of it—was going to go into effect retroactively to

January of 1981, and we didn't get it then. And when we did get it, after the drop had occurred, it was only 5 percent, and it didn't go into effect until October, which meant that it was about 1¼ percent when it only went on for 3 years—or 3 months.

And so, I have to say that all of the recovery has taken place after our program went into effect, and none of our program was in effect when the bottom fell out.

Federal Budget Deficits

Q. Mr. President, I want to get clear on one thing. Are you—your comments earlier about this bipartisan—bipartisan meetings over the deficit—when you said you're now pursuing your own plan with other Republican leaders. Are you saying that you've abandoned altogether any hope of reaching any kind of compromise with the Democrats? Are you through talking with them?

The President. Well, I—no. I hope that maybe when we come forth with this plan and say, "Look, here's something now, we'll tell you, we're ready to go with; here is a plan"—I would like to have, because we can't get such a plan unless we have bipartisan support. I would like to think that they would do it. But what I meant was that to sit down with them and start from scratch to negotiate, they were very unwilling. We had great difficulty getting them to even meet.

And, finally, one meeting they just simply walked away on one issue and refused to talk. Then they came back. And it wasn't very encouraging to us.

Q. Can you still—you don't have any idea about how soon you might have a plan ready to put forward? Before, I mean—

The President. I'm hoping——

Q. ——before the elections, though.

The President. Oh, Lord, I'm hoping very soon, not the election. We've got to move on this deficit matter and move fast.

Q. Some of your economic advisers have been saying for some time now, and Wall Street analysts, that we've got to do something about the deficit. And you've just said it needs to be handled or taken by the horns as soon as possible. But you have been saying for some time that—or painting the picture that things are going to be fine, things are going to be okay. And that's not exactly the picture that's come from some of your advisers, if we don't take control of the deficit immediately. And I'm wondering——

The President. Well——

Q. ——how——

The President. ——it isn't an exact science. And some of the economists—and some of them, I think, are trying to scare the Congress into recognizing that we should be dealing with it. But let me just point some——

Q. Not scare you, but the Congress.

The President. Not scare me, no, because, look, I'm not one to underestimate the deficits. I've been talking about them for 30 years.

Is it impossible for us to—well, no, you can't remember; all of you're too young, so it would have to be history for you—but for almost half a century the other party has been in control, as I said earlier, of both Houses of the Congress. And Congress is the only one that can deal with these things. A President has a veto power, but a President cannot spend a single dime. There's nothing in the Constitution that gives the President the right to spend anything. But for almost this half-century we have every year run deficits. It was almost a trillion dollars by the time we came here. And there were many of us who opposed this. And we were told at the time that the national debt didn't matter because we owed it to ourselves. That was the explanation. We were told the deficit spending and a little inflation was necessary to maintain prosperity. Well, some of us didn't think that added up. And I can show you speeches I made 20, 25 years ago in which I said inflation cannot continue without going out of control eventually. You cannot go down this road. The deficit spending and the piling up of the debt that—it has never worked in history; it never will.

Well, now, suddenly, with the big dip that came in July in that recession, with millions more people added—the unemployed, who became wards of the government, which increased the spending, but who were no longer paying the taxes, which decreased that; the very fact that we improve the inflation figure also militated

against government revenues, because inflation is a source of tax increase. And we didn't get—we didn't think we could reduce inflation that fast. We thought that there would be higher revenues than there turned out to be because of licking inflation.

Well, all of this, for them now to suddenly become aware of deficits—and yet, when you try to talk to them, what is the only answer that they have for curbing the deficit? Increase taxes. Well—and they'll also agree to cut defense spending. Well, defense spending right now is down to a little more than a fourth of the budget. Defense spending, historically, the days of Jack Kennedy, was virtually a half of the budget. Under Jack Kennedy, it was 47.8 percent. So, the—and the increase in taxes—they doubled taxes in the 5 years before we got here. And the deficits increased, because when you increase taxes, they increase spending.

And may I point to the 1983 budget resolution passed by the Democratic majority in the House. And they really didn't think that it would ever amount to anything or be passed by anyone else. But, if you'll remember, they described it as a reaffirmation of Democratic principles. And it did call for somewhere around $70 billion in increased taxes. But it also called for that much increased spending for new programs, social programs.

So, this was where we philosophically just were in complete disagreement—that they think you can solve the budget deficit by increasing taxes. They don't even pay attention to the fact that this could subvert the recovery that we're now having and put us back where we were. But beyond that, they've made it plain, and, indeed, their own candidates talk of new spending programs.

School Prayer Amendment

Q. When you're on the campaign trail, how much of an issue are you going to make of the school prayer issue and the abortion?

The President. Well, I'm hoping that before I get out there that we'll have the school prayer amendment passed in the

Congress. And here again, the effort that is being made to portray that as someway, somehow we're talking compulsory prayer; we're going to compel the schools. I'm sure there would be some schools—all we're asking is that they have the right to if they want to. Now, there may be some schools that'll decide not to. There may be some that'll decide they will. But I think it's a right that we had for the bulk of our entire history in this country. And it didn't destroy the country at all. As a matter of fact, crime rates were lower, and we didn't have drug epidemics, and all sorts of things.

Illegal Drugs

Q. Let me ask a question about drugs. There's a lot of reports, including administration reports, that there are more illegal drugs coming into this country than ever, especially cocaine—much of it coming through Florida—despite intensified enforcement in Florida and elsewhere. Would you say that that represents a failure of that drug strategy? And what would you want to do to—would you be advocating anything——

The President. Well now, wait a minute—I'm going to have to ask, but—you know, I have to tell you something about this room. I don't know whether you've noticed it or not—out there in that center of the room under the dome, you kind of disappear a little on me.

Q. A mild-mannered reporter, I'd say. [*Laughter*]

Mr. Speakes.[1] [*Inaudible*]—last question—[*inaudible*].

The President. Oh, dear. I'm having so much fun. [*Laughter*]

Q. I was asking about the illegal drug shipments into the country.

The President. Oh.

Q. And the evidence is that there's more illegal drugs coming in than ever before—at least in recent years and despite intensified enforcement in Florida and other places. And what I'm wondering is whether you think that because of that that there's going to be a need to change the drug enforce-

ment strategy, and whether the drug enforcement strategy that you've employed has been a success?

The President. Oh, well, wait a minute. Then this—if this is a new figure that I haven't obtained—our task force in Florida, which is the first time that we have ever put the Federal Government, the State government, and the local authorities, the drug enforcement authorities, and the military involved in trying to head this off—this shipment from out of the country coming in—was so successful in Florida that this is where, why we went to 12 such task forces all around the country on our borders to try and have the same success. Of course, there's no question: When you've got the coastlines that we've got and the borders that we have, I don't think you will ever solve the problem totally by intercepting the drugs.

The answer is going to be the kind that has Nancy down in Houston. To really be successful, you're going to have to take the customer away from the pusher. The customer's going to have to start saying no. And this we're embarked on also, as you know, with great efforts all through the country.

But the figures that we have is that—and the reason for the rest of the other 11 task forces were—that we so slowed it down in Florida and reduced it in Florida, that they began seeking new entry points around the country. But we're the owner now of a fleet of cabin cruisers and yachts and airplanes and helicopters and trucks and cars. And down there, the last time I was in Florida I remember being taken into a big building there at the airport and shown what we had intercepted, but also on a table that was about the size of that desk, the first time in my life I saw $20 million in cash stacked up there in bills that had been taken away from the drugdealers. That had to hurt.

But, no, I think the program is being very successful. But we know that it's a wholesale business. It isn't just a fellow on a corner with something in his pocket to sell. It is coming in in freighters. It's coming in in airplanes and everything else. But we've stepped up our efforts and have been tremendously successful.

---

[1] *Larry M. Speakes, Principal Deputy Press Secretary to the President.*

Q. Do you think the military can be used to stop, like, particularly some of the drug smuggling that's coming in on that Mobile corridor? It's being flown inland.

The President. What we used was we used their radar facilities; also their air surveillance for information that we needed. I don't think they actually participated in any of the arrests, but they provided the surveillance and the information for us. If they can see an enemy coming in, I can see that.

Chemical Weapons

Q. I had just one final question for you related to defense. This year for the third year now you're requesting in your defense budget funds for chemical weapons production. And of course, Congress has narrowly defeated these proposals for the last 2 years. There's been a suggestion made in the last week by some Democratic House Members that any proposal for funding for chemical weapons should be tied to legislation requiring the administration to make a new initiative on talks with the Soviets on chemical weapons control. So, my question is, first, do you think that the United States is doing all it can in this area? Would you agree to a proposal like that? And also, do you see any reasons now why Congress might be willing to pass the chemical weapons appropriation when they haven't been?

The President. If they were responsible, they would, because the very thing that they're talking about we are going to be ready very shortly to table a treaty for discussion of banning chemical weapons. We know that's the way to go. But the reason why they would be more of help if they would okay the spending is, how better to get the other side, then, to agree to a treaty with us banning this; how much better able we'll be if they know that if they don't do that, they will have to face the fact that we have chemical weapons that we can use against them.

In other words, it's the same as in the nuclear field. It's a deterrent. So, this is exactly our own plan. Yes, we want to get them into a verifiable treaty banning chemical weapons.

Q. Mr. President——

Q. Would you agree to having it written into the legislation?

The President. What?

Q. Would you agree, then, to have it written into the authorizing legislation that the U.S. would have to do this?

The President. I don't know whether that would—I don't know whether that would help or not. There wouldn't be any reason why we shouldn't be willing since we, ourselves, are working on such a treaty.

Mr. Speakes. You've got a whole batch of Congressmen this afternoon, so we'd better break off.

The President. It serves them right. [*Laughter*]

Q. Thank you, Mr. President.

Charles Z. Wick

Q. Have you talked to Mr. Wick just lately about the possibility of his resigning? Has he sent you a letter of resignation or anything?

The President. No, not a kind—there's never been a hint of it. I don't know where that rumor came from. Not a word of it.

Q. So, he's not spoken to you——

The President. No.

Q. ——and you still think that he's—you still want him to stay on.

The President. I sure do. Yes, he's done a great job.

Unemployment Figures

Would you like to hear about your own States, since I talked about a few of them? Alabama: 16.7 down to 12.3. Arkansas: 11.3—and remember, these are December figures—down to 9.4. You know about Florida. You know about Georgia. Mississippi: 13.8 is down to 10. South Carolina: 11.6 is down to 7.9—only two-tenths of a point above the norm, or the average. 13.7 for Tennessee, down to 10.3. And 21 down to 15.7—and that was December. And we've done even better in January and February.

Edwin Meese III

Q. Are you going to continue to insist on Mr. Meese as your nominee for the Attorney General's spot?

The President. Heavens yes. Yes.

Q. Questions being raised now about the Carter papers and about his loans?

The President. All of that—we happen to know that they sent for those when they couldn't get him on anything else. They sent for those from the Albosta committee. Those are part of the record that the FBI said, as far as they're concerned, there was no criminal action, there was no misdeeds, and closed the investigation.

Q. But you don't believe any ethical questions have been raised at all?

The President. I don't think he violated them. I have every trust in his ethics, and have known him for a great many years. And I think he'd make a fine Attorney General.

Q. Do you think the American people would——

The President. What?

Q. Do you think the American people would be able to trust him as Attorney General?

The President. Yes. I trust him more than

some of the Senators that have been raising these issues.

Editor. Thank you very much, Mr. President.

Note: The interview began at 3:30 p.m. in the Oval Office at the White House. Participating in the interview were Carol Matlack of the Arkansas Gazette, Greg McDonald of the Atlanta Constitution/Journal, Olivia Barton of the Birmingham News, Mary Glass of the Charleston (South Carolina) News & Courier, David Greenfield of the Charleston (West Virginia) Daily Mail, William E. Gibson of the Fort Lauderdale News and Sun Sentinel, and Tom Opell of the Jackson (Mississippi) Clarion-Ledger.

The transcript of the interview was released by the Office of the Press Secretary on March 13.

Remarks at the Young Leadership Conference of the United Jewish Appeal
March 13, 1984

I'm delighted to be here. And special greetings to Steven Greenberg of the Young Leadership Cabinet and Mickey Baron of the Young Women's Leadership Cabinet.

For almost 45 years, the United Jewish Appeal has served as the main fundraising organization of American Jews, and you certainly have proven that to me this morning with the figures that we've just heard. Through the agencies it funds, the UJA provides vital social and economic assistance, including resettlement, rehabilitation, and development programs for Jews in Israel and more than 30 other countries. And through its Young Leadership Cabinet, the UJA trains the hundreds of young men and women for service positions of responsibility around the world. In recognition of your historic task and your great humanitarian achievements, I certainly commend you.

In your lives, you must overcome great challenges. I know you draw strength and inspiration from the well of a rich spiritual heritage, from the fundamental values of

faith and family, work, neighborhood, and peace.

Two centuries ago, those values led Americans to build democratic institutions and begin their Constitution with those courageous and historic words, "We, the people . . . ." And today our democratic institutions and ideals unite all Americans, regardless of color or creed. Yet as we enjoy the freedom that America offers, we must remember that millions on Earth are denied a voice in government and must struggle for their rights. They live under brutal dictatorships or Communist regimes that systematically suppress human rights.

Under communism, Jews, in particular, suffer cruel persecution. Here in our own hemisphere, the Communist Sandinista regime in Nicaragua has used threats and harassment to force virtually every Nicaraguan Jew to flee his country.

In the Soviet Union, Jews are virtually forbidden to teach Hebrew to their children, are limited to a small number of synagogues, and cannot publish books of

Hebrew liturgy. Emigration of Jews from the Soviet Union has been brought to a near standstill. Prominent Jews like Iosif Begun have been arraigned in mock trials and given harsh sentences. Hebrew scholars like Lev Furman have seen their teaching materials robbed and their homes ransacked. And Jewish dissidents like Anatoly Shcharanskiy have been put in mental wards or thrown in jail. We must support Soviet Jews in their struggle for basic rights, and I urge all Americans to observe the International Day of Concern for Soviet Jews this Thursday, day after tomorrow, March 15th.

In this world where so many are hostile to democracy, how can Americans best preserve and promote the democratic ideals that we hold dear, ideals which are the keys to the golden door of human progress?

Here at home, I believe we can move forward together toward a genuine opportunity society by meeting two important challenges.

First, we must teach tolerance and denounce racism, anti-Semitism, and all ethnic or religious bigotry, wherever they exist, as unacceptable evils. And down through our history, American Jews have been on the frontlines in our nation's great struggles for equal rights. A century ago, the 14th amendment proclaimed the full protection of the law for all. In the fifties and sixties, the struggle for civil rights stirred our nation's soul. Americans must continue that great tradition, because even today vestiges of racism and anti-Semitism remain. Synagogues are vandalized, Jews and others are harassed and mocked, and Nazis and the Ku Klux Klan have attempted to march through black and Jewish neighborhoods. Well, let us reject prejudice, turn our backs on bigotry, and stand shoulder to shoulder for equal rights.

Our second challenge is to promote economic growth. Throughout history, civil and economic rights have gone hand in hand. For centuries, rulers kept Jews down by limiting their occupational choices. In our own country, many blacks suffered from Jim Crow prejudice, denied all but the poorest of jobs. But in a strong and growing economy, all groups have the opportunity to advance through hard work, enterprise, and heart.

Just 3 years ago, our nation was an economic disaster area. Double-digit inflation, record interest rates, huge tax increases, and too much regulation were destroying growth, drying up opportunities, and freezing those at the bottom of our society into a bleak existence of dependency. And that's why economic recovery without inflation was our top priority. We cut taxes, reduced the growth of the Federal budget, eliminated useless regulations, and passed an historic reform called tax indexing. Indexing means government can never again profit from inflation at your expense.

Today America's economic engine is pulling this nation forward again. Inflation is down from more than 12 percent in 1980 to about 4 percent. The prime interest rate has fallen by almost half. New businesses are the biggest innovators and job producers, and from January to November 1983, more than 548,000 companies incorporated. That's nearly half again the yearly rate during the 1970's. It means more jobs and opportunities, so it's no accident that unemployment is down to 7.7 percent, the sharpest drop in more than 30 years. More Americans are holding jobs today than any other time in this nation's history.

Despite all we've accomplished, we must go forward to new goals to keep the nightmare of inflation from ever coming back. We must enact constitutional budget reforms like the line-item veto and the balanced budget amendment. And to make taxes more simple and fair and to provide greater incentives to our people, we must press for tax simplification—a sweeping and comprehensive reform of the entire tax code.

Could I interject something here? When we talk about simplification, it sounds awfully simple. But the other day I got a figure from the Treasury Department that astounded me. If you were a young lawyer deciding, maybe, to get into the area of tax counseling and advice and so forth, do you know how many books of regulations you would have on your shelves just to help you with the income tax? Well, you've heard of the Harvard Classics—5-foot shelf of books. You'd have to have a shelf of 31 feet of books just for that one subject.

Well, as we move ahead, we're determined to leave no one behind. Under this administration more funds go to needy Americans, even after adjusting for inflation, than ever before. And total spending on social programs has increased by $71 billion during these last 3 years.

And while I'm on this subject, I wonder if you who are intensely committed to social justice and Jewish charity would join us in questioning the relationship between greater Federal spending and a healthy, prosperous, and growing country. During the sixties and seventies, the Great Society and other Federal programs led to massive increases in social spending. Why, then, at the same time, did the number of Americans below the poverty line stop shrinking? Why did we see a drop in the number of males in the work force and a huge increase in births out of wedlock?

I believe the answer lies in the firm difference between the New Deal and the Great Society. The New Deal gave cash to the poor, but the Great Society failed to target assistance to the truly needy and made government the instrument of vast transfer payments, erecting huge bureaucracies to manage hundreds of social programs. The Great Society failed in two crucial aspects: It fostered dependence on government subsidies, and it made the transfer of money from Washington bureaucrats to those in need seem like a mission impossible.

I was a New Deal Democrat. And I still believe, today, that there is only one compassionate, sensible, and effective policy for Federal assistance: We must focus domestic spending on the poor and bypass the bureaucracies by giving assistance directly to those who need it. We must end dependency, eliminate quotas, and foster a vital, innovative economy that rewards all Americans according to their talent and hard work. If we do, we can enhance our democratic ideals and can make America a genuine opportunity society.

To promote our democratic ideals abroad, we must also meet great challenges, and I see three that are paramount.

First, we must keep America strong. During the seventies the United States made a conscious choice to restrict its military development, fervently hoping the Soviets would respond in kind. Well, during those 10 years our spending on defense dropped over 20 percent in real terms. We canceled major weapons programs, reduced our nuclear stockpile to its lowest level in 20 years, and slackened in the training of our Armed Forces. Between 1968 and 1978, we cut our Navy, the fleet, by more than half.

But far from responding to our good intentions with restraint, the Soviets launched the most massive military buildup in world history. From 1974 to 1980, they outproduced us in practically every category of weapons: 3 times more tanks, twice as many tactical combat aircraft, 5 times more ICBM's, and 15 times more ballistic missile submarines. By 1980 total Soviet military investment was more than 1½ times ours.

President Carter's Secretary of Defense, Harold Brown, put it very well. He acknowledged a bitter lesson about Soviet practice in saying, "When we build, they build. When we don't build, they build."

Since taking office, our administration has made significant headway in rebuilding our defenses and making America more secure. Perhaps you remember the 29th Psalm in which King David said, "The Lord will give strength to His people; the Lord will bless His people with peace." Well, today America once again recognizes that peace and strength are inseparable.

But we've only begun to repair past damage. Make no mistake: If we heed those who would cripple America's rebuilding program, we will undermine our own security and the security of our closest friends, like Israel, and I am not prepared to let that happen. After two decades of military expansion by the Soviet Union and a decade of neglect by the United States, we're struggling not to regain the superiority we once enjoyed, but simply to restore the military equivalence we need to keep the peace.

A second great challenge is to defend and promote human rights throughout the world. Aleksandr Herzen, the great Russian writer, warned, "To shrink from saying a word in defense of the oppressed is as bad as any crime. . . ." Well, we who are blessed by the fruits of liberty have a personal responsibility and a moral obligation to speak out in defense of our brothers and sisters. We must not and we will not remain silent.

Our administration has repeatedly and vigorously protested the persecution of Jews and others in the Soviet Union and other Communist nations. We're also using our influence with countries that receive American assistance to give human rights firm support. In El Salvador, we're insisting that the leaders take steps to end human rights abuse. And although El Salvador is far from perfect, we've seen marked progress.

In the United Nations, Iran's representative once called Israel, "a cancerous growth," and Libya's representative has referred to the people of Israel as "the most vile people upon Earth." Well, this so-called anti-Zionism is just another mask for vicious anti-Semitism, and that's something the United States will not tolerate.

As I wrote last month to Stanley Blend, the president of the Jewish Federation of San Antonio, ". . . the lesson of history is overwhelmingly clear. Silence is never an acceptable response to anti-Semitism."

U.N. Ambassador Jeane Kirkpatrick is our leader on this. And let me assure you of one thing about Jeane: She is a very tenacious woman. She has defended Israel and stood up for human rights with persistence and courage. But just so no one gets any ideas, I will be blunt: If Israel is ever forced to walk out of the U.N., the United States and Israel will walk out together.

Standing steadfast with our allies in support of greater economic growth and of peace with freedom is our third great challenge. Our administration is working hard to do just that. In Europe we and our NATO allies have shown the Soviets our willingness to negotiate and our unshakable resolve to defend Western Europe. In the Far East, we are strengthening our ties to the Asian democracies and developing our relations with China. In Central America we have supported democracy and fostered economic development. And in the Middle East we have strengthened our relations with a nation close to your heart and mine—the State of Israel.

Now, let me take a moment to describe our relations with Israel and our efforts in the Middle East. Israel and the United States are bound together by the ties of friendship, shared ideals, and mutual interests. We're allies in the defense of freedom in the Middle East. The United States was the first nation to recognize the State of Israel, and ever since, our support for Israel has remained unflinching. Today, when even our NATO allies vote with us in the United States [United Nations] only some 6 out of 10 votes, the alliance between the United States and Israel is so strong that we vote together more than nine times out of ten.

Since I took office, the U.S.-Israeli relationship has grown closer than ever before in three crucial ways.

First, the U.S.-Israeli strategic relationship has been elevated and formalized. This is the first time in Israel's history that a formal strategic relationship has existed. The new American-Israeli Joint Political-Military Group is working to decide how the U.S. and Israel can counter the threat that growing Soviet involvement in the Middle East poses to our mutual interests. Our cooperation adds to deterrence and improves and protects the prospects for peace and security. The negotiations have been positive, and they're moving forward.

Second, we're negotiating to establish a free trade area between the United States and Israel, and this will launch a new era of closer economic relations between our countries. By substantially eliminating duties and nontariff barriers between our nations, we will enable American producers to sell and compete in Israel while providing Israeli manufacturers unimpeded access to the free world's largest market.

Now, third, the United States will soon be giving Israel military aid on a grant, not a loan, basis. We have restructured our 1985 foreign aid package, and Israel will now receive economic aid totaling $850 million and a military grant of some $1.4 billion. This will ensure that Israel maintains its qualitative military edge.

All in all, the friendship between Israel and the United States is closer and stronger today than ever before. And I intend to keep it that way.

In the Middle East, as a whole, the United States has three aims.

First, we must deter the Soviet threat. As the crossroad between three continents and the source of oil for much of the industrialized world, the Middle East is of enormous strategic importance. Were the Soviets to control the region—and they have expanded their influence there in a number of ways, notably, by stationing 7,000 troops and advisers in Syria—the entire world would be vulnerable to economic blackmail. Their brutal war against the Afghan people continues with increasing ferocity. We must not allow them to dominate the region.

Second, we must prevent a widening of the conflict in the Persian Gulf which could threaten the sealanes carrying much of the free world's oil. It could also damage the infrastructure that pumps the oil out of the ground, and we must not permit this to happen.

Third, we seek to go on promoting peace between Israel and her Arab neighbors. In response to the growth of Syrian power and the rise of the Iranian threat, we must help to protect moderate Arabs who seek peace from the radical pressures that have done such harm in Lebanon.

Syria is trying to lead a radical effort to dominate the region through terrorism and intimidation aimed, in particular, at America's friends. One such friend we continue to urge to negotiate with Israel is King Hussein of Jordan. Today, Jordan is crucial to the peace process, and for that very reason, Jordan, like Israel, is confronted by Syria and faces military threats and terrorist attacks.

Since the security of Jordan is crucial to the security of the entire region, it is in America's strategic interest, and I believe it is in Israel's strategic interest, for us to help meet Jordan's legitimate needs for defense against the growing power of Syria and Iran. Now such assistance to Jordan does not threaten Israel, but enhances the prospects for Mideast peace by reducing the dangers of the radical threat.

This is an historic moment in the Middle East. Syria must decide whether to allow Lebanon to retain control over its own destiny or condemn it to occupation. Syria forced the Lebanese Government to re-nounce the May 17th agreement with Israel precisely because it was a good agreement. Now those who have chosen this course will have to find other ways to secure the withdrawal of Israeli forces. Arab governments and the Palestinian Arabs must decide whether to reach peace with Israel through direct negotiations. And if Arab negotiators step forward, Israel must decide if she will take the risks necessary to attain the real security that comes only with genuine peace. I have no doubt that given that choice, the Israelis will once again have the courage to choose peace.

I'm convinced that the initiative that I presented on September 1st, 1982, remains the best option for all the parties. It is squarely based on the Camp David framework and U.N. Security Council Resolution 242. It is time for the Arab world to negotiate directly with Israel and to recognize Israel's right to exist.

Now, we hope that the Government of Israel will understand that continued settlement activity in the West Bank and Gaza will make the peace process more difficult. Peace can only come about through the give-and-take of direct negotiations. These negotiations will deal with many issues, including the status of Jerusalem, voting rights, land use, and security. If there's to be any hope for these negotiations, however, we must preserve our credibility as a fairminded broker seeking a comprehensive solution. Only the United States can advance this process. And we must not undermine our role.

And permit me to reaffirm a longstanding American commitment: So long as the PLO refuses to recognize Israel's right to exist and to accept Security Council Resolutions 242 and 338, the United States will neither recognize nor negotiate with the PLO.

Only 2 weeks ago, terrorists planted hand grenades outside a store on a crowded street in Jerusalem. When they exploded, 21 shoppers and passers-by were injured, some seriously. Yasser Arafat, on behalf of the PLO, praised the attack on innocent civilians. He had the gall to call it a "military operation." Well, terrorism, whether by government or individuals, is repulsive, and peaceful coexistence can never come from indiscriminate violence.

If I could leave you with one thought today it would be this: Even though in the Middle East and elsewhere the world seems hostile to democratic ideals, it's the free men and women on this Earth who are making history.

Here in the United States we've only seen the beginning of what a free and a brave people can do. Today America is leading a revolution even more sweeping than the Industrial Revolution of a century ago. It's a revolution ranging from tiny microchips to voyages into the vast, dark spaces of space; from home computers that can put the great music, film, and literature at a family's fingertips to new medical breakthroughs that can add years to our lives, even helping the lame to walk and the blind to see.

In Israel free men and women are every

day demonstrating the power of courage and faith. Back in 1948 when Israel was founded, pundits claimed the new country could never survive. Well, today no one questions that Israel is a land of stability and democracy in a region of tyranny and unrest.

So, this Sunday, as Jews the world over observe Purim, they'll celebrate not only the ancient deliverance of Jews from the wicked but a modern joy as well—the miracle of the State of Israel.

Permit me to join you and all Jews—and I'm now going to demonstrate my own courage—[*laughter*]—your fervent and triumphant affirmation: *Am Yisrael Chai!* [The people of Israel live!]

Thank you, and God bless you.

Note: The President spoke at 11:12 a.m. in the International Ballroom at the Washington Hilton Hotel.

Appointment of Six Members of the National Commission for Employment Policy
March 13, 1984

The President today announced his intention to appoint the following individuals to be members of the National Commission for Employment Policy. These are new positions.

Walton E. Burdick is vice president of IBM for personnel. He is a member of the Business Roundtable, Employee Relations Committee and Planning Committee, and the board of trustees of the National Institute for Work and Learning. He graduated from Cornell University (B.S.). He is married, has five children, and resides in Mt. Kisco, NY. He was born May 16, 1932, in Scranton, PA.

Peter W. Dauterive is president and chief executive officer of Founders Savings & Loan Association in Los Angeles, CA. He has served as a director of the California Savings and Loan League and as director and president of the American Savings and Loan League. He graduated from the University of Southern California (B.A.). He was born February 2, 1919, in Olivia, LA, and now resides in Los Angeles, CA.

Juan Rangel is president and chief executive officer of Medcenter Bank National Association in San Antonio, TX. He is a director and vice president of the Laredo Health Facilities Corp. and the Laredo Development Foundation. He is married, has three children, and resides in Laredo, TX. He was born May 23, 1948, in Castroville, TX.

John Alexander Rocco is an assemblyman (district 6) for the State of New Jersey and serves as a member of the Assembly Education Committee and the Joint Committee on Public Schools. Since 1970 he has also been serving as an associate professor of education at Rider College. He graduated from West Chester State College (B.A.), Villanova University (M.A.), and Rutgers University (Ed.D.). He is married, has two children, and resides in Cherry Hill, NJ. He was born June 25, 1936, in Philadelphia, PA.

Max L. Rowe is an attorney with the firm of Kirkland & Ellis in Chicago, IL. He served as chairman of the advisory board, Department of Personnel, State of Illinois, and was a member of the Small Business Administration National Advisory Council. He graduated from the University of Illinois (A.B., J.D.). He is married, has four children, and resides in Wilmette, IL. He was born August 14, 1921, in Dallas City, IL.

Paula V. Smith is director of the Department of Labor and Industrial Relations in Jefferson City, MO. She also serves on the Missouri Job Training Coordinating Council and is a trustee of the Missouri Council on Economic Education. She is married, has three children, and resides in St. Louis, MO. She was born July 4, 1933, in Memphis, TN.

Appointment of Burleigh C.W. Leonard as Special Assistant to the President for Policy Development
March 14, 1984

The President today announced the appointment of Burleigh C.W. Leonard as Special Assistant to the President for Policy Development. He will also serve as Executive Secretary of the Cabinet Council on Food and Agriculture.

Mr. Leonard has been serving as Deputy Assistant Director for Energy, Natural Resources, and Agriculture in the Office of Policy Development and as Acting Executive Secretary of the Cabinet Council on Food and Agriculture.

Mr. Leonard received his B.A. degree cum laude from Princeton University in 1973 and did postgraduate study at Mansfield College, Oxford University. He received his J.D. degree from the Washington College of Law at American University in 1981 and was a member of the Jessup International Moot Court Team which placed second in the 1980 Mid-Atlantic Regional Competition.

Mr. Leonard served as a legislative assistant and as a professional staff member, U.S. Senate Agriculture Committee from 1977 to 1980. He was legislative coordinator for the Reagan transition team at the U.S. Department of Agriculture and served as legislative director for the U.S. Senate Agriculture Committee in 1981 before joining the Office of Policy Development staff.

He was born on March 30, 1951, in Cape Girardeau, MO. He is married and resides in Arlington, VA.

Remarks of the President and Prime Minister Mário Soares of Portugal Following Their Meetings
March 14, 1984

The President. It has again been an honor and a pleasure to welcome Mário Soares to the White House. He came here a year ago as Vice President of the Socialist International and now returns as Prime Minister of Portugal.

He's truly an international personality, a valiant supporter of Western values and ideals, and a man of great personal courage. As Prime Minister of Portugal, he represents a close and valued ally, one of the founding members of the North Atlantic alliance. We regularly seek his counsel, and again today we've had valuable and extensive discussions.

Prime Minister Soares and I examined economic matters of importance to both our peoples. I assured the Prime Minister that the United States will continue to do all that is feasible to assist Portugal in meeting its difficult economic challenges.

In another vital area of cooperation, we discussed the bilateral mutual security arrangements renewed last December. Under these arrangements, Portugal is playing a significant role in protecting the freedom of the Western democracies and maintaining world peace. The responsibilities he demonstrates reflects well on the character of Portugal's people and her leaders. And today I reaffirm to Prime Minister Soares that the United States stands ready to help modernize the Portuguese Armed Forces.

We applaud Prime Minister Soares' and Portugal's commitment to a strong and effective NATO alliance, and we wish them well as they move to join the European Communities.

The Prime Minister and I exchanged views on the present situation and outlook in the Middle East and Central America— regions in which he has a long and deep interest and concern. And certainly we benefited from his insights. We had an especially useful discussion of the outlook for peaceful settlements of the conflicts in southern Africa. Portugal's historic interests in Africa and her cultural, economic, and political ties of today add much weight to Prime Minister Soares' judgments in this area. We agreed that regular consultations between our two governments on African questions are useful for us both, and we will continue this practice.

I want to thank Mário Soares for his visit and our forthright exchange of ideas. He is a special friend, as well as an important leader, and I wish him Godspeed and look forward to our meeting again.

The Prime Minister. Mr. President, I would like, at the outset, to express my appreciation to the President of the United States for his invitation to make this official visit to Washington, and to say how pleased I am to have been afforded this opportunity to renew now, as head of the Portuguese Government, the contacts and friendly relationships which I established in the past with President Reagan and the American administration.

During this period, we have learned to respect your leadership qualities and the straightforward way in which you have handled delicate situations, while always keeping in mind the fundamental values of democracy. Contacts between the leaders of our countries, which should be considered normal between two NATO allies which have maintained close relations over a long period, now assume special importance in view of the readiness of both parties to imbue our relationship with a new dynamic

following the important impetus to our cooperation in the defense area provided by the renewal of the Lajes Base agreement.

The sound relations existing between the United States and Portugal are not the result of occasional identical positions or passing convergence of interests. They are, rather, the result of a sincere and profound sharing of values and ideals, such as freedom, democracy, and respect for human rights, principles in which we believe and which we practice. The Luso-American community residing in this country, which here bears witness to the affection in which the Portuguese hold the American people, greatly contributes to the friendship which unites us.

Among the issues which we have had the opportunity to address, I wish to emphasize those related to southern Africa, a region of the world where important steps on the road to peace are now being taken. Portugal, which maintains centuries-old ties of friendship with the people in this region, namely with those of Mozambique and Angola, has devoted particular attention to the problems of this area, following the process of decolonization carried out in 1974, and has spared no effort to contribute to the creation of a climate of dialog and peaceful solutions to the problems of the region.

We also considered the situation in Central and South America. I believe the initiatives of the Contadora group, as well as all those directed towards advancing the democratic process and establishing regimes guaranteeing true freedom in the countries of the region, are deserving of our support. The cultural ties existing between the Iberian countries and Latin America, stemming from a longstanding commonality of history and language, lead Portugal to take profound interest in the evolution of the situation in the countries of this region and to maintain close contacts with those forces seeking to uphold the principles of liberty in that part of the world.

It was very gratifying for me to note that the United States and Portugal share very similar points of view regarding East-West relations and the need to strengthen the Atlantic alliance in order to resist expansionist threats and contribute to peace.

Reporter. Mr. President, is the Meese nomination now in trouble, sir?

The President. Not as far as I'm concerned.

Q. Are you upset about the loan story?

The President. No.

Q. Should he withdraw his name, Mr. President? Should he take his name out?

The President. No.

Q. What about this latest loan? Did he forget?

The President. I'm not answering.

Q. Why didn't he declare the money? Why did he hide it?

The President. I don't think he hid it, and

I think he will make it clear when he testifies.

Q. So, you're not going to withdraw him?

The President. No.

Q. Do you think he'll be confirmed, sir?

The President. Yes.

Note: The President spoke at 1:13 p.m. at the South Portico of the White House. The Prime Minister spoke in Portuguese, and his remarks were translated by an interpreter.

Earlier, the President and the Prime Minister, together with U.S. and Portuguese officials, held meetings in the Oval Office and the Cabinet Room. They then held a working luncheon in the State Dining Room.

Message on the Observance of St. Patrick's Day, 1984
March 14, 1984

Nancy and I wish everyone a joyous St. Patrick's Day. For the Irish and all the sons and daughters of Erin the world over, this is truly a festive day filled with pride and renewed hope for the future. It gives us an occasion to acknowledge the special qualities brought to our shores by those who traveled from distant and lovely Ireland.

Like so many of the Irish before and after him, my great-grandfather, Michael Reagan, heard, in the words of a favorite song, ". . . a whisper of a country that lies beyond the sea, where rich and poor stand equal in the light of freedom's day." He and millions like him left home and family in Ireland to make their way to this country. While they came seeking the bounty of America, they

brought with them a rich Irish heritage, a strong faith in God, and a love of liberty. They came imbued with sustaining talents great enough to make them an integral part of their new home and to spark a nurturing and enduring friendship between the peoples of Ireland and America.

The annual observance of St. Patrick's Day provides a fine opportunity for all of us to warm our hearts in remembrance of the bonds of history, family, and tradition that have come to us from the Emerald Isle. We join Irish Americans throughout the land in celebrating their truly singular contribution to our way of life.

RONALD REAGAN

Statement on the International Day of Concern for Soviet Jews
March 15, 1984

Today is the International Day of Concern for Soviet Jews. It marks the seventh anniversary of the arrest of Anatoly Shcharanskiy for his activities on behalf of human rights in the Soviet Union. His courage and

determination to stand up for those rights have earned him the respect and admiration of countless people worldwide. But he would not want this day to be dedicated solely to him. Rather it is a day when men and women of good will reflect on all the aspects of the situation of Jewry in the U.S.S.R. That situation has deteriorated over the past year. Jewish emigration from the Soviet Union has fallen to its lowest levels since the late 1960's; officially tolerated anti-Semitism manifesting itself in broadcasts, articles, and the widely publicized formation of an "Anti-Zionist Committee of the Soviet Public" has increased; and individual refuseniks continue to be subjected to harassment.

All in all, this is a grim picture. But we will not be disheartened. Soviet Jews value the support of concerned individuals and organizations all over the world. In our country this support reflects the broad, grassroots concern which abuse of human rights elicits in the American public. Outrage where human rights are violated is one of the best American traditions. I endorse the International Day of Concern and the goals for which it stands.

The United States Government shares these goals. It has actively supported the right of Soviet Jews to practice their cultural traditions freely and to emigrate from the U.S.S.R. if they so choose. This point has been emphasized to the Soviet authorities in many fora and at all levels; it has been conveyed to the new Soviet leadership. It is our sincere hope that the Soviets will ease their repressive human rights policies and fulfill the solemn international obligations they have undertaken, including their commitment under the Helsinki accords. In our dialog with the Soviet authorities, we have no higher priority. Those who care about the fate of Soviet Jews should know that we are with them today and will be with them tomorrow.

Remarks During a Meeting With Puerto Rican Leaders
March 15, 1984

Vice President Bush, Governor Ferré, and ladies and gentlemen:

Good afternoon, and I know that the Vice President and I both bid you a very warm welcome. And let me say to each of you, *"Mi casa, su casa."* And it really is.

I'm delighted to have this opportunity to spend a few minutes with you, and an opportunity is what I'd like to talk about in those few minutes.

America has always been a magnet for people seeking freedom and peace and the opportunity to better their lot and to go as far as their God-given talents will let them. Pioneers came to our shores with the courage to start all over again because they knew America offered a hope for the future. Today our task is to make sure that even the most recent pioneers have good reason to dream the same great dreams as those who came before.

A promising future begins with a foothold on the economic ladder, and the recovery now surging through this land is providing millions of our people that chance. The eco-nomic recovery is helping every American and every ethnic group. And just this morning we received more good news. In February, industrial production rose another 1.2 percent. That is the 15th consecutive monthly increase. And just to put a little frosting on the cake, this morning when they gave us that news about February, the month of February, they also corrected the information they'd previously given us about January, and it was higher than had previously been announced.

Industrial production, of course, we know, is one of the most significant measures of economic health. And this means that 1984 is starting off very strong. And, of course, that means more jobs. Last month alone, 700,000 Americans found jobs. And we're experiencing the steepest drop in the unemployment rate in more than 30 years. Since the beginning of the recovery, nearly 5 million—well, actually, 4,900,000 Americans have found work. But we can't rest until every American who wants a job can find a job.

We want to build an opportunity society. And that means we cannot go back to the failed policies of big taxing and spending. The painful consequences of those policies haven't been forgotten. Too many dreams were shattered when double-digit inflation, record interest rates, economic stagnation knocked industries, small businesses, home-makers, and breadwinners off their feet. Inflation robbed us all, and the worst hardships were borne by those at the bottom of the economic ladder.

Nor did the explosion in social spending get crime and drugs off the street or give us a better education for our children. The disadvantaged became more dependent on Federal programs as work disincentives discouraged initiative. Urban America was going downhill, and solutions seemed farther and farther away. It is no wonder that Americans were losing confidence in their government. And now that we're regaining confidence, and now that America is back on the road to robust growth, I believe it's time to build even wider opportunities.

We must go forward to new goals to keep the nightmare of inflation from ever coming back. We must enact constitutional budget reforms like the line-item veto and the balanced budget amendment. And to make taxes more simple and fair and to provide greater incentives to our people, we must press for tax simplification, a sweeping and comprehensive reform of the entire tax code.

There are some in government who have a very simple tax proposal in mind. There will only be two lines on the tax form: How much did you make last year? Send it. [*Laughter*]

Now, I know that Secretary of Labor Ray Donovan and Secretary of Housing and Urban Development Sam Pierce and others are going to be speaking with you this afternoon. And at the risk of preempting them, I'd like to highlight several programs that offer exciting opportunities for urban America.

In the area of jobs, the Job Training Partnership Act gives communities new flexibility, and by using private industry councils, it matches local needs with sensible training. This program will train over a million workers a year for productive jobs. The old

job program, CETA, did just the opposite. It spent $53 billion to find private sector jobs for only 15 percent of the participants.

Well, those days are over, and the future is now a genuine partnership for real jobs with a bright future. And while I'm talking about jobs, let me mention that more and more people recognize that the minimum wage puts unskilled young people at a disadvantage when they're looking, particularly, for those first jobs or those summer vacation jobs. Our youth employment opportunity wage proposal would give our young people the opportunity to gain their first foothold on the economic ladder. And the proposal would protect current workers from displacement. It'll soon be before the Congress, and I'd like to appeal for your strong support.

Enterprise zones is another legislative initiative that would mean welcome renewal for urban areas of hardcore unemployment. Enterprise zones encourage growth and opportunity where we need it most—in areas of high unemployment and in areas that are hardest hit by urban decay. The legislation provides incentives for business firms and entrepreneurs to invest in blighted areas, create new jobs, and bring new life to distressed areas. This legislation has been on Capitol Hill for 2 years. The Senate has passed it, but the House continues to drag its feet. And, forgive me, but those who refuse to take action on a bill that's to create jobs and opportunity are the last people who should be giving speeches about their compassion for the unemployed.

And too many of those Members in the House are dragging their feet on another important piece of legislation—one that would get tough on criminals. For too many years, crime and the fear of crime robbed our cities of their strength and vitality, and inner cities suffered the most. Well, common sense is beginning to pay off. In 1982 the crime rate dropped by 4.3 percent, and that's the biggest decline in a decade. But we still need to do much more, and I am determined to do everything possible to get crime off our streets.

We need new laws to stop drug traffickers and tougher laws to fight the criminal elements in our society. And the way to get long-overdue reform begins with the passage of our Comprehensive Crime Control Act. This package will give more protection to our law-abiding citizens by cracking down on criminals, particularly organized crime and drug traffickers. It would enable authorities to keep people considered dangerous to the community behind bars, pending trial, and it would eliminate paroles. The legislation has, as I say, already passed the Senate. The House should stop delaying, put partisan politics aside, and do what's right for you, the law-abiding people of this country.

These programs—and they're only a sample—will help those who need help, and they'll promote stronger, more prosperous, and stable urban communities.

I sense a spirit of optimism spreading across our land, carrying hope and opportunity for more and more urban areas. And I think it's justified. America is moving forward again. I know much remains to be done. I know many of our fellow countrymen still wonder what will come of their hopes and dreams. Success will not come

easy, but it will come. And to make it happen, America needs the help of all Americans, including those from *la isla de encanto.*

You'll forgive me for stumbling on that one word there. [*Laughter*] It's so close to St. Patrick's Day, I've been rehearsing me Irish. [*Laughter*]

But you've enriched our national culture and our heritage. And we need your energy, your hard work, and your values. We need people like Antonio Monroig, Rita DiMartino, Reynaldo Maduro, and Rafael Capo—Puerto Ricans who are doing an outstanding job in leadership positions in our administration. If you follow their hopes and dreams, all of us will benefit.

So—I'll try to do better now—*muchas gracias* and *vaya con Dios.*

Note: The President spoke at 1:31 p.m. in the East Room at the White House.

In his opening remarks, the President referred to former Gov. Luis Ferré of Puerto Rico, head of the Commonwealth's Republican Party.

Proclamation 5160—World Trade Week, 1984
March 15, 1984

By the President of the United States of America

A Proclamation

America can be proud of its record in international trade. From the earliest days of the Republic, the Yankee trader was a familiar figure in all the great cities of the world. Merchants of every nation knew and respected these traders for the energy and resourcefulness that have always been so characteristic of the American people. By the middle of the nineteenth century, clipper ships from the United States had become the graceful symbols of our national determination to be first and best.

In each decade of our history, we have matched our trading strength with that of the strongest nations in the world. We have opened new markets, created new indus-

tries, and pioneered new technologies. In a competitive environment, we have succeeded and flourished. We have built the prosperity of this country on our confidence and on our own strength, ingenuity, and creativity.

Today, the United States is the greatest trading nation on Earth. We are the world's largest economy, its biggest market, and its leading exporter. American brand-names are household words in every market, and everywhere the words "Made in U.S.A." are accepted as an assurance of the highest quality and service.

The strength of our exports has meant a great deal to America. To industry, it has meant profits and added opportunities for growth. To labor, exports have meant jobs—more than five million in 1983. To the American consumer, free and fair trade has meant better products in greater variety and at lower prices.

There is no question that world trade is fiercely competitive nowadays. Few industries are unaffected by the pressure of foreign goods and services, whether competing for sales at home or abroad. This is a continuing challenge for us. Some would have the United States look to protectionist measures for the answer to competition. As we learned in the 1930's, protectionism in one country only provokes retaliation and invites protectionism in others. International tension grows, the flow of trade is diminished, and the world economy contracts.

Free and fair trade benefits all nations. For this reason, the United States is committed to policies promoting unrestricted trade and investment consistent with our security interests. Internationally, we are working with our trading partners for new negotiations in support of freer world trade, greater competition, and more open markets. At home we have urged American business to challenge foreign competition

with aggressive selling, research and development, improved management systems, and innovations. Above all, we must build on the surest foundation for this country's prosperity—our confidence in our own strength and abilities.

Now, Therefore, I, Ronald Reagan, President of the United States of America, do hereby proclaim the week beginning May 20, 1984, as World Trade Week, and I invite the people of the United States to join in ceremonies affirming the importance of trade to America and recognizing the need for increased export efforts.

In Witness Whereof, I have hereunto set my hand this 15th day of March, in the year of our Lord nineteen hundred and eighty-four, and of the Independence of the United States of America, the two hundred and eighth.

RONALD REAGAN

[*Filed with the Office of the Federal Register, 4:55 p.m., March 15, 1984*]

Remarks to Reporters Announcing a Deficit Reduction Plan
March 15, 1984

Ladies and gentlemen, in my State of the Union Message, I proposed a bipartisan negotiation to develop what I called a downpayment on the deficit. I urged Democrats and Republicans to come together on the less controversial issues to enact a deficit reduction program quickly that would reduce the deficit by a hundred billion dollars over 3 years.

To help get the process moving, I've had a series of meetings with the Republican leadership who are here with us today, except for two—Senator Dole, who is busy on the Hill, and Senator Mark Hatfield, but who are both in total agreement with this plan. Senator Hatfield is appearing at Harvard right now.

Our objective has been to reach agree-

ment on a deficit reduction package that could be passed by the Senate and that would be supported by the bipartisan group representing both Houses of Congress. I'm happy to announce that the congressional leadership and I have agreed on a balanced package that is comprised of three basic elements.

First, we have agreed to save $43 billion over 3 years from the nondefense portion of the budget. These savings can be achieved by passing the Senate Finance Committee's pending entitlement reforms and Grace commission savings, a farm program target price freeze, the pending reconciliation bill's Federal pay cap and COLA delays, and a freeze and cap on nondefense discretionary programs.

Second, we have agreed to close certain tax loopholes to raise revenues by $48 billion over 3 years. There would be no increase in tax rates. The changes in tax law would close certain loopholes of questionable fairness.

Third, we have agreed to further reductions in defense spending, which will slow our defense buildup somewhat but which will not seriously reduce our national security to a point of unacceptable risk. The changes we've made will amount to defense budget authority reductions over the next 3 years of approximately $57 billion and 3-year defense outlay savings of about 40 billion. This, I should note, is in addition to the reductions that we already made before submitting our budget to the Congress.

The enactment of all these proposals will save $18 billion in interest payments on the Federal debt. This would bring the 3-year total savings to some $150 billion, a substantial downpayment on the deficit.

For the 1985 budget, it would mean $9 billion in additional revenues, and I repeat, without increasing tax rates. Domestic spending will be reduced by 9 billion, and defense budget authority in 1985 by 14 billion. It is a fair and balanced package, one that can be easily implemented. It merits the support of all those who are responsibly concerned about deficits. It's worthy of prompt attention and positive action by the Congress.

And I want to thank the Republican leaders of the Senate and the House for their constructive effort and cooperation. I hope their Democratic colleagues will now join with them in enacting this downpayment on the deficit. And with that, I can tell you that Secretary Don Regan and Dave Stockman will be prepared to brief you as we leave here in the Press Room.

Q. Think the Democrats are going to go for it, sir?

Q. How is this different from what the Democrats propose?

The President. What?

Q. How is this different from what the Democrats proposed in your little conferences up to now?

The President. Ask that in the briefing in there.

Q. Why should the Democrats go along, sir?

The President. Why shouldn't they?

Q. Well, because——

The President. They've been complaining that they want the deficit reduced, and after 50 years of raising the deficits, here is a chance to start reducing it and going the other way.

Q. Do you have any indications that the Democrats are going to go along? Have you been talking to them?

The President. No. We had to find out that we were all agreed ourselves.

Q. Didn't know whether you were going to go along yet, right?

The President. All of us have worked out what we think is a responsible plan, and we're going to submit it to them.

Q. Do you have anything to say now that King Hussein has rejected your peace plan firmly and finally?

The President. I'm not going to suggest another news item here other than what we've been talking about. We'll talk about that at a time when there's no more news. [*Laughter*]

Q. How about tomorrow?

Q. How about at 6:35?

Q. Are you still behind Mr. Meese?

The President. I've just opened myself up to a charge of manipulating.

Q. Guilty.

Q. Mr. President, are you going to talk to us on your way to Camp David tomorrow about Hussein?

The President. What's that?

Q. Are you going to talk to us about Hussein tomorrow on the way to Camp David?

The President. Let me see how well you treat this. [*Laughter*]

Note: The President spoke at 4:51 p.m. in the Rose Garden at the White House.

Statement on Resumption of the Mutual and Balanced Force Reductions Negotiations
March 16, 1984

I am pleased to note the resumption in Vienna today of the negotiations on conventional force reductions in Europe, known as the MBFR talks. The U.S. Representative, Ambassador Morton Abramowitz, and his NATO colleagues will be working closely together in seeking early progress toward an agreement to reduce NATO and Warsaw Pact forces in Central Europe to a substantially lower and equal level.

The Western participants in MBFR are united in their pursuit of positive results. I call upon the Soviet Union and the other nations of the Warsaw Pact to join us in a good-faith effort to achieve real progress.

The MBFR talks are an important part of the East-West security and arms control dialog. The resumption of MBFR coincides with the conclusion today of the first round of the CDE talks in Stockholm, which deal with military confidence-building measures in Europe. Here, too, the Western nations are working closely together. During the initial round, we have tabled a comprehensive package of proposed measures to reduce the risk of war.

I welcome these developments and sincerely hope that General Secretary Chernenko and other members of the new Soviet leadership will approach these negotiations in a similarly positive spirit. I also urge the Soviet Union to return to the INF and START negotiations, where very important work in the cause of building a more secure and peaceful world has been suspended by them. These crucial negotiations can succeed if the Soviet Union wants them to succeed. We are certainly ready to do our part. It is in the interest of all mankind that these vital efforts be resumed now.

Nomination of Harry E. Bergold, Jr., To Be United States Ambassador to Nicaragua
March 16, 1984

The President today announced his intention to nominate Harry E. Bergold, Jr., of Florida, a career member of the Senior Foreign Service, class of Minister-Counselor, as the Ambassador to the Republic of Nicaragua. He would succeed Anthony Cecil Eden Quainton.

Mr. Bergold served in the United States Army in 1954–1956. In 1957 he entered the Foreign Service as an international economist in the Department. He was economic officer in Tegucigalpa (1959–1962) and political officer in Mexico, D.F. (1962–1964). In the Department he was international re-

lations officer, then foreign affairs officer in 1964–1967. He was political officer in Madrid (1967–1972) and in Panama (1972–1973). He was on detail to the Department of Defense as Deputy Assistant Secretary of Defense in 1973–1976. In 1977–1979 he was on detail to the Department of Energy as Assistant Secretary of Energy for International Affairs. In 1980–1983 he was Ambassador to Hungary.

Mr. Bergold graduated from Yale University (A.B., 1953; M.A., 1957). His foreign language is Spanish. He was born November 11, 1931, in Olean, NY.

Nomination of John P. McTague To Be an Associate Director of the Office of Science and Technology Policy
March 16, 1984

The President today announced his intention to nominate John P. McTague to be an Associate Director of the Office of Science and Technology Policy. He would succeed Ronald B. Frankum.

Since 1982 he has been serving as chairman of the National Synchrotron Light Source Department at Brookhaven National Laboratory. He is also adjunct professor of chemistry at Columbia University. Previously he was a professor of chemistry and member of the Institute of Geophysics and Planetary Physics at UCLA. In 1964–1970 he served as a member of the technical staff at the North American Rockwell Science Center.

He is the author of numerous articles on physics and chemistry. He is a member of the American Chemical Society and a fellow of the American Physical Society, and has served as associate editor of the Journal of Chemical Physics. He received the A.P. Sloan, John Simon Guggenheim, and NATO Senior Fellowships.

He graduated from Georgetown University (B.S., 1960) and Brown University (Ph.D., 1975). He is married, has four children, and resides in Santa Monica, CA. He was born November 28, 1938, in Jersey City, NJ.

Nomination of Daniel Raul Lopez To Be a Commissioner of the United States Parole Commission
March 16, 1984

The President today announced his intention to nominate Daniel Raul Lopez to be a Commissioner of the United States Parole Commission, Department of Justice, for a term of 6 years. He would succeed Benjamin J. Malcolm.

Since 1974 Mr. Lopez has been hearing representative to the Board of Prison Terms. Previously he served as a member of the Adult Authority for the California Parole Board in 1970–1974. He was with the Department of Human Resources in 1966–1970, serving as chief deputy director for the department in 1969–1970. He was a special agent for the California Department of Corrections in 1964–1966 and correctional captain at the California Rehabilitation Center in 1962–1964.

Mr. Lopez attended the University of Southern California and the University of the Pacific McGeorge School of Law. He is married and resides in Oceanside, CA. He was born July 11, 1918, in Oxnard, CA.

Toasts of the President and Prime Minister Garret FitzGerald of Ireland at a White House Luncheon
March 16, 1984

The President. There'll be a question about me being Irish since I came up here without this [1]—*[laughter]*—the day before

---

[1] *The President was referring to his glass for the toast.*

St. Patrick's Day.

Well, I know we all enjoyed Mr. Dowling, and I wish he hadn't had to shorten the program.

Mr. Prime Minister, Mrs. FitzGerald, and ladies and gentlemen:

I want to say how delighted that Nancy and I are to have you and Mrs. FitzGerald here today. I know you've been to America a good deal, and you're acquainted with us. But we're very proud that you could be our guest on your first visit here as Prime Minister. And we're especially happy to have you visiting at such an appropriate moment. Tomorrow is a great day in America, a day of bagpipes and shamrocks and a day when everyone is Irish or, as the saying has it, wishes they were. [*Laughter*]

In the United States, especially, the impact of the Emerald Isle on our culture and history is enormous. America is today, because of the Irish, a richer, brighter, freer, and, yes, a bit noisier country than it otherwise would have been. Virtually all Americans feel a surge of pride when they hear expressions like the "Fighting 69th," or the "Fighting Irish of Notre Dame."

I have to pause for a second. I've already told this to some of you, but I have to tell the rest because I know that Father Hesburgh is here in the room someplace from Notre Dame. Back in the days of the great Knute Rockne when Notre Dame was the giant of the football world, it was between halves one day at a game, when the officials came into the locker room and said to Rockne that the other team was complaining that the Notre Dame players in the pile-ups were biting them. [*Laughter*] And he said, "We can't fine them, of course, and, Rock, what do you think we should do?" And Rock says, "Tell them next year to play us on Friday." [*Laughter*]

But so many of our great public figures are of Irish ancestry, from the man considered by many as the father of the American Navy, John Barry, to our first heavyweight champion, John L. Sullivan, to the great tenor, John McCormack, to a couple of Presidents of the United States and, yes, even to the current Speaker of the House.

In fact, the secret wish disclosed the other day by my friend, Tip O'Neill, is an indication of the hold that Ireland has on all of us here in the States. This is a nation where the Speaker of the U.S. House of Representatives aspires to someday be Ambassador to Ireland. Tip, what about day after tomorrow? [*Laughter*]

Mr. Prime Minister, I was explaining to Tip only a few moments ago, though, seriously, why I thought that appointment was impossible, and perhaps, knowing your countrymen as you do, you'll agree with me. Tip, the Irish aren't looking for Speakers, they're looking for listeners. [*Laughter*]

Well, Mr. Prime Minister, the joshing we do here is in the best Irish tradition. It makes light of what are sometimes serious political differences. But I think there's one point on which the Speaker, Senator Kennedy, myself, and the other Irish American leaders here are united—our admiration for the efforts that you are making to bring peace and stability to Ireland. We support your personal mission in America to end the tragically misguided support of some here for terrorist elements in Northern Ireland.

Now, you know, Mr. Prime Minister, I've been told by one of your countrymen that the Reagan family line goes back as far as the great 11th century warrior king, Brian Boru. If it's true, I'm exceedingly proud. But sometimes, like you, I wonder what our brave ancestors—those who fought so gallantly over so many centuries against such hopeless odds—what they would say about the valor of people who commit acts of violence and prey on the innocent, sometimes maiming and killing innocent women and children.

Your words have been very direct on this point, Mr. Prime Minister. You've reminded those in this country who provide assistance to Northern Ireland's terrorists that they are assisting in violence and murder. Let me assure you that the vast majority of Irish Americans join you today in condemning support for those who preach hatred and practice violence in Ireland.

But there's another part of your mission to America, Mr. Prime Minister, which is perhaps more fitting to today's festive atmosphere and more important over the long run, and that is the message of hope that you bring us. We're especially heartened by your own efforts, as well as your colleagues', in the New Ireland Forum and the British Government as they seek a democratic and peaceful reconciliation of Ireland's diverse traditions. As we know, the high-level dialog between Ireland and Britain has been renewed, and the groups promoting reconciliation and economic cooperation—groups like Cooperation Ireland—are also bearing fruit. For our part, we shall continue to encourage American firms to invest in Ireland, north and south, in ways which promote prosperity and both traditions.

Some time ago, a former American Ambassador told me of a weekend retreat where politicians from the various Irish traditions met together for a frank discussion of the differences that separated them. And it was a good weekend. Those who'd never talked of such matters before were able to speak and listen to each other in a spirit of understanding. And on the bus back home, they laughed and sang songs. The spirit of friendship bloomed. And when they got off the bus, the spirit somehow seemed to evaporate. And after hearing this story, I told our Ambassador to take them a message, and I think it bears repeating.

Mr. Prime Minister, I express your sentiments, sir, and those of our own people and of the people of both parts of Ireland when we say to all those who struggle with the problem of peace in Ireland: "Please get back on the bus."

From my discussion with you this morning, Mr. Prime Minister, I know how deeply you're committed to this effort. I assure you the hopes and prayers of the American people go with you. Peace and good cheer have never left Irish hearts. And so we look to days of peace and harmony to come, when every day we may say what is said on St. Patrick's Day:

"O Ireland, isn't it grand you look
Like a bride in her rich adornin'?
And with all the pent-up love of my heart
I bid you top o' the mornin'."

But now, may I ask all of you here to join me in a toast to our friends, Prime Minister and Mrs. FitzGerald, and to the warmest and best friendships—Ireland and the United States.

The Prime Minister. Thank you, Mr. President, for those warm, encouraging, and heartening words which I think will bring comfort and, as you said, cheer to all our people in Ireland.

Joan and I and all of us from Ireland are very grateful to you and Mrs. Reagan for your warm welcome, your splended hospitality in this beautiful and historic setting, provided by an Irish architect, James Hoban.

There's always a special friendliness about the American welcome that makes the visitor, and especially the Irish visitor, feel very much at home. We like to think that this is an aspect of the American character that derives from the Irish part of your heritage. [*Laughter*] No other country has a warmer place in Irish hearts than the United States, nor is any people prouder than we are of the contribution our forebears have made to the development of this great nation—and has been made, indeed, by the 43.7 million of them who are still working hard at it. [*Laughter*]

It's sometimes forgotten that the Irish ethnic tradition in American society historically has had two strands. The better known today is the predominantly Roman Catholic tradition of the immigration that swelled to huge proportions after the great famine of the 1840's. A strong tradition, indeed, it was, and still is the deep and positive influence in American society.

But it was not the only, nor the earliest tradition which the Irish brought to these shores. Most of the early Irish immigrants were Protestants, very many of them from what is now Northern Ireland. Such were eight of the nine men of Irish birth or descent who signed the Declaration of Independence. And such were the great majority—and here I beg leave, sir, in our own house to correct you—the great majority of the dozen American Presidents—I think you said "a couple,"—[*laughter*]—of established Irish origin. I know that the rest of them just never got around to tracing their roots properly. [*Laughter*]

In America, Irishmen of these two great traditions of Ireland have worked together to shape this wonderful country. We in Ireland hail them all with equal pride. But in one part of Ireland these two traditions have not yet come to terms with each other. Within Northern Ireland the two Irish traditions are sharpened into separate identities which have confronted one another in mutual, and sometimes violent antagonism.

With this tragic situation, we in the south cannot remain unconcerned. For these people—Catholic and Protestant, Nationalist and Unionist alike—are our own people. Their troubles are ours. And in the solution of their problems we have a crucial role to play, one that must be undertaken in the spirit of openmindedness and generosity. To reconcile the conflicting identities of the two traditions in Ireland and to suggest new political structures that could accommodate both of them are the main tasks to which we, in the four political parties of Irish Constitutional Nationalism, north and south, representing 70 percent of the people of Ireland, have dedicated ourselves through the unique deliberations of the New Ireland Forum.

In undertaking this task, Mr. President, let me say how much we in Ireland value the encouragement that in your own words today you, yourself, have given to this cause of Irish reconciliation, together with the support of other great Irish American political leaders, some of them with us today here—Speaker O'Neill, Senator Kennedy, Senator Moynihan, so many others, who have given us comfort and heart and courage to continue with our work.

It was the great Abraham Lincoln, who wrote, "Among free men, there can be no successful appeal from the ballot to the bullet." He answered a century and more ago the claim by certain violent men in our Ireland to take power with a ballot box in one hand and an armalite rifle in the other.

When the Irish people come together, it will be in one way only—in peace, by agreement, under structures devised for the security of all the island's people and for the advancement of all their interests. And we know, and you've made it explicit today, Mr. President, that in our efforts to promote that process, we have your support and encouragement.

May I turn to your forthcoming visit with your wife to Ireland. Already this visit is the subject of conversation and excitement throughout the length and breadth of the land. We know how much you cherish your Irish heritage and how much you are looking forward to setting foot in that tiny village in County Tipperary—which, as I said to you, fortunately has a wide main street to accommodate all the people who'll be there when you come—[*laughter*]—from which your great grandfather stepped out bravely one day to face the world, as my own grandfather did, also, to the same place, London, a decade later, from a place not 7 miles away from Ballyporeen.

My father returned to Ireland half a century later to take part with my mother in the movement for Irish freedom. It's because they came back 70 years ago that I shall be there with Joan to welcome you and your wife on the 2d of June next, when you return for this visit to the land of your ancestors—the first of several—the last—not the last—one of a number of such visits. [*Laughter*] There have been others before and there will, I hope, sir, be others in the future also. Believe me, you'll receive a warm Irish welcome on that day and the succeeding days that you spend with us.

A *Céad Míle Fáilte*—as we say in Ireland—"a hundred thousand welcomes."

Mr. President, I've already presented you with some shamrock. We had a little difficulty. I tried pinning it on, but partly because of my concern to make sure I didn't actually physically assault the President of the United States by sticking a pin in him—[*laughter*]—I totally failed. The President took over the job himself and did it very neatly and quickly. [*Laughter*] But if I might formally present you with a bowl of our shamrocks so there will be some to go around to the whole family.

The President. I have something for you.

The Prime Minister. Something for me? Oh, good. [*Laughter*]

[*The President gave the Prime Minister a green cap.*]

The Prime Minister. Do I put this on? [*Laughter*]

The President. Well, you don't have to. There! [*Laughter*]

The Prime Minister. How does it look? I

take my hat off to you now. [*Laughter*]

Now, I've done precisely what the President did, only he remembered in time. I left my glass behind. I wonder if you'd just let me have the glass for the toast. This is the absentmindedness which gets me into trouble occasionally. [*Laughter*]

Now I want us all to raise our glasses to that happy day on the 2d of June next, to Irish-American friendship, and to the President and Mrs. Reagan.

Note: The President spoke at 1:27 p.m. in the State Dining Room at the White House. Vincent Dowling, former artistic director of the Irish National Theatre in Dublin and current artistic director of the Shakespeare Company in Stamford, CT, provided the entertainment prior to the exchange of toasts.

Prior to the luncheon, the President and the Prime Minister met in the Oval Office.

Proclamation 5161—National Employ the Older Worker Week, 1984
March 16, 1984

By the President of the United States of America

A Proclamation

Older workers today represent a national resource of incomparable knowledge, judgment, and experience. In the coming decades, it is likely that older workers will constitute an increasing percentage of our population. Therefore, it is vital to the future prosperity of this Nation that these workers be encouraged to continue to make their considerable contributions by remaining in the work force or by serving their communities in voluntary roles.

Many employers have already recognized the potential contributions of older workers and have initiated hiring, retraining, second career, and job retention programs. In addition to these significant private initiatives, the Federal government has been active in promoting opportunities for older workers through a variety of efforts, including the recently implemented Job Training Partnership Act. These various private and public sector efforts have successfully demonstrated that, if sufficient opportunities are available, older workers can continue to make useful and valuable contributions which enhance the quality of life for their communities and which develop a renewed sense of their accomplishment and self-worth.

The Congress, by Senate Joint Resolution 205, has called for the designation by the President of the second full week in March, 1984 as "National Employ the Older Worker Week." Recognition of this special week presents an invaluable opportunity to focus public attention on the accomplishments of older workers.

Now, Therefore, I, Ronald Reagan, President of the United States of America, do hereby designate the week beginning March 11, 1984, as National Employ the Older Worker Week, and I call upon the people of the United States to observe this week with appropriate programs, ceremonies, and activities. I urge all Governors, Mayors, and other public officials, leaders in business and labor, voluntary organizations, and private citizens to give special consideration to older workers with a view toward expanding the opportunities available to them.

In Witness Whereof, I have hereunto set my hand this 16th day of March, in the year of our Lord nineteen hundred and eighty-four, and of the Independence of the United States of America the two hundred and eighth.

RONALD REAGAN

[*Filed with the Office of the Federal Register, 12:03 p.m., March 16, 1984*]

Radio Address to the Nation on the Economic Recovery Program
March 17, 1984

My fellow Americans:

Happy St. Patrick's Day to all of you. You know, this is a day when those of us of Irish descent have an opportunity to boast a little and, like good Irishmen, celebrate a lot. Because of the Irish, America today is a richer, brighter, freer, and, yes, a bit noisier land than it otherwise would have been.

But today all Americans can take pride in the rich diversity of America's ethnic heritage—especially the Irish American contribution to that heritage. It's one reason why Nancy and I were delighted to host a lunch here at the White House yesterday for Prime Minister FitzGerald of Ireland. We all had a roaring good time, but there was some important business done as well.

The Prime Minister and I urged all Americans not to give support of any kind to the terrorist IRA elements in Northern Ireland. Believe me, it was a call heartily endorsed by all the Irish American political leaders who were present.

And second, the Prime Minister brought us a message of hope about peace and reconciliation of the problem of Northern Ireland. After all the tragedy in Northern Ireland, it was cheering to hear about groups who are working toward mutual tolerance, and peaceful and democratic solutions.

Here at home, as we prepare to greet the first days of spring, there is also reason for confidence and cheer. Good economic news is bursting out all over, and America's economy seems to be saying, "This is celebration time." Optimism is being bolstered by vigorous new growth, continued low inflation, and better prospects for reducing budget deficits.

Just yesterday we learned that the Producer Price Index rose only four-tenths of 1 percent in February, a smaller rise than in January, and a solid sign that inflation remains in check. We're determined to keep the nightmare of runaway inflation from ever coming back. Housing starts reached 2.2 million units in February, the highest level in nearly 6 years. That's an 11-percent increase from the January level, which was

revised up to 1.9 million units. And building permits, a signal of builders' intentions, also registered a strong increase, so that means continued housing strength in the months to come.

Combine these signs of economic confidence with a strong recovery in one industry after another—15 consecutive monthly increases in industrial production, business investments stronger than expected, growing research in science and technology, and a welcome rebirth of productivity growth, and we can understand how the United States economy created nearly 5 million jobs in the last 15 months and has become the engine for a new era of worldwide economic expansion.

We're also making progress towards reducing projected budget deficits. For one thing, the sheer strength of America's economic growth, as measured by all those new jobs created in the last 15 months, means more people are supporting themselves and paying taxes, and fewer people need government assistance. As I've said again and again, strong and steady economic growth is the best way to reduce deficits.

And as you may have heard, I've just reached agreement with the Republican leadership in the Congress on a deficit reduction package totaling some $150 billion over the next 3 years. Just Thursday night, shortly after we reached agreement, the Senate Finance Committee concluded its work on a major portion of our package. I'm hopeful the entire package will be passed promptly by the Senate.

This $150 billion downpayment deserves strong bipartisan support in the House because it will reduce the deficit in a way that's effective, responsible, and fair, by targeting $43 billion of savings in nondefense spending, $57 billion in defense authority reductions, and by raising some $48 billion in revenues, primarily from closing certain tax loopholes of questionable fairness.

Now, make no mistake. The defense cuts will slow our defense buildup somewhat, but not to a point of unacceptable risk.

There will be no increase in tax rates on American families and no tax increases that would threaten the economic recovery. Continued strong growth with the prospect of deficits coming down and without renewed inflation spells a brighter future for America's economy, provided the Congress will just stick with our program.

Some might attribute our success to the "luck o' the Irish." Well, maybe we have enjoyed a bit of luck. But believe me, the real reason is an economic recovery program based on common sense.

Until next week, thanks for listening, and God bless you.

Note: The President spoke at 12:06 p.m. from Camp David, MD.

Interview With Agence France Presse on Foreign and Domestic Issues
March 15, 1984

U.S.-France Relations

Q. Mr. President, you're going to meet President Mitterrand next week, and what are the main issues you are going to raise with him and—for instance, are you going to talk about the need for reform in NATO to prevent a drift between Europe and the U.S., as many have suggested? The need—do you think there is a need for such reforms?

The President. For——

Q. In NATO.

Q. Restructuring NATO, you know, everybody talking about that now.

The President. Well, I'd be very happy to talk with him about it. I think right now that we and our—all our Western allies and certainly our relationship with France is on a very strong footing. But I'd be glad to hear any views about whether a restructuring or not could benefit the alliance and see what we'll be talking about.

We've got a host of things to talk about from trade and the Middle East and some other things of that kind. I think we'll be mainly in agreement, remembering back to the summit conference here. But still, it'll be worthwhile to have a discussion. I'm looking forward to it.

There are a few things where we may have some slight differences which maybe some conversation can straighten out—having to do with Central America, things of that kind. I know we'll be discussing trade problems and the progress that we have made and continue to make, not only bilaterally but through the European market with regard to freer trade and more cooperation and things of—the kind of—

And also I will be discussing with him the East-West relations and what our goals are, because we are determined to bring about arms reductions and to get conversations restored with the Soviet Union to where we can discuss face to face the problems that only we can solve.

Q. Did you see the story that President Mitterrand wrote for Parade this week, coming out this week?

The President. Oh, no.

Q. I wanted to ask you what you thought of that phrase there: "Within the Alliance, the U.S. and France know that in time of need they can rely on each other——"

The President. Yes. We are really the oldest allies.

Q. You and President Mitterrand came into office at about the same time 3 years ago; you with a conservative agenda, him on a socialist platform. Given this contrary background, how have you been able to develop a good rapport and maintain the cooperation between your two governments?

The President. Well, while it is true that there are differences in our political philosophies, there are a greater number of things we have in common. We have spent a fair amount of our lives in politics, worked hard to become Presidents, and entered office at approximately the same time. Since then we have been together on several occasions—at three summit meetings, at

Yorktown and Cancún, as well as in each other's capital. Finally, we are both leaders of major Western nations with a set of global interests and concerns which, while not always identical, are almost always compatible.

What we share the most is a common commitment to the Atlantic alliance. We have both worked to strengthen that alliance. I think it fair to say that today there is an unusual degree of transatlantic consensus and security cooperation. President Mitterrand played a significant role in helping achieve this. He and I also share a desire for a renewed and improved East-West dialog, including the resumption of arms reduction talks to reduce world tensions.

I will be discussing this and a whole range of global issues with President Mitterrand. I am looking forward to his visit, which comes at a time when U.S.-French relations have seldom been better than they are today.

Q. Your Ambassador to Paris, Mr. Evan Galbraith, has been widely criticized recently for intervening in French domestic affairs by publicly criticizing the role of Communist Ministers in the French Government. At the time, the White House said he had your full confidence. Does that mean that you approve of his views and the way he expressed them?

The President. The matter was successfully resolved some weeks ago, and I see no good reason to reopen it. I look forward to seeing Van Galbraith again—and as you have noted, he enjoys my full confidence—when he is here for the state visit of President Mitterrand.

European Unity

Q. Some Europeans are again talking about a common European defense effort. So far, your government's reactions to that have been mixed. Are you afraid that such a trend would weaken the defense links between Europe and the United States within NATO?

The President. We regard, as do all other of its members, the Atlantic alliance as the essential framework of our common security. Within that framework, we have consistently urged a greater defense contribution from our European partners. We note with pleasure the steps which have been taken in this regard in recent years. As always, our attitude toward any specific initiatives for enhanced European defense will depend on the contribution that can be made to the overall strength and cohesion of the Atlantic alliance.

U.S. Troops Abroad

Q. Several Democratic hopefuls have picked up the old idea of reducing the level of American troops in Europe as a way to cut U.S. defense spending. Is that your intention?

The President. As I have said on several occasions, U.S. troops in Europe are there to defend our vital national interests. Unilateral reductions in the number of U.S. troops in Europe will not reduce the threat to these interests. On the contrary, it would increase that threat.

I am committed to maintain the American contribution to the defense of Europe; indeed, we have made major efforts to strengthen that contribution. This commitment is shared, I believe, by the vast majority of the American people.

Third World Countries

Q. On the Third World, the French sometimes criticize your analysis and policies on Central and Latin America. On your part, how do you assess France's role in Africa, in general, and Chad, in particular.

The President. France plays a constructive role in Africa, through its economic and security assistance programs. We maintain a constant and frank dialog with the French Government on African developments. We seek to work with France in a complementary fashion.

Both the United States and France have a particular concern about Africa's worsening economic crisis, and both countries are taking steps to be of assistance. I plan on seeking Mr. Mitterrand's views on this subject when we meet.

As for Chad, the response of the French Government has been laudable. France has taken the lead in providing assistance to the legitimate government of that country in withstanding Libyan aggression. We are proud to be associated with France in that assistance effort.

And I'm glad you mentioned Central America. We share with all the nations of Europe a firm belief that peace needs to be restored in Central America. As you know, we are working actively to assure that El Salvador's new democracy is allowed to develop without violence or guerrilla harassment. And we are determined in our view that Nicaragua and Cuba should not succeed in the export of revolution elsewhere in the region.

Central America and the Caribbean are of the utmost strategic importance to the United States. What we are witnessing to the south is a power play by Cuba and the Soviet Union, pure and simple. Cuba, after nearly 25 years of so-called revolution, is an economic basket case. It cannot supply even its own needs without massive and costly Soviet subsidies. Like a roving wolf, Cuba looks to its peace-loving neighbors with hungry eyes. We want to avert a crisis before it happens—to help our neighbors build strong economies and democratic governments and to counter Soviet-backed insurgency. The way to end hostilities in El Salvador, for example, is through free elections. But we see those who oppose democracy now trying, through violence, to disrupt the March 25 elections there.

What the United States is doing on behalf of freedom in Central America is minimal, considering what is at stake. We have a vital interest, a duty, and a responsibility— and I ask you, why should the United States and France, two of the great democracies of history, not want to see democracy prevail in Central America?

Federal Budget Deficit

Q. Many French and European officials complain that the huge Federal deficits are responsible for high interest rates and an overvalued dollar which jeopardize their economic recovery and increase protectionist pressures. Are you prepared to take concrete steps to alleviate such fears before the November election?

The President. As to your specific question, yes, I am prepared to take concrete steps before the November election and have just done so. I am asking the Democratic and Republican leaders in the Congress to work with the administration on the development of a downpayment deficit reduction program. A program of spending cuts and tax measures to close certain loopholes could, I believe, be enacted this spring that would reduce the deficit by some $150 billion over the next 3 fiscal years. I see this as a first step toward full elimination of the remaining deficits.

As to the fears of some Europeans that the U.S. budget deficit, high interest rates, and strong dollar jeopardize their recovery, may I say that the strong performance of the U.S. economy has given a significant push to European recovery, and the strong dollar of which they complain has given Europe a substantial export advantage which is further contributing to their recovery.

I have great confidence in our own economic recovery, and I am looking forward to discussing it with your President. As spring begins here in Washington, I think President Mitterrand will find a lot of optimism about the future.

Note: The interview took place in the Oval Office at the White House. Participating in the interview were Claude Moisy, Gilbert Grellet, and Pierre Rousselin.

As printed above, this item follows the transcript released by the Office of the Press Secretary on March 19.

Proclamation 5162—National Energy Education Day, 1984
March 17, 1984

By the President of the United States of America

A Proclamation

America's vast energy resources are among its greatest assets. Intelligent use of our existing energy supplies together with prudent conservation measures and development of alternative sources of supply will allow this country to maintain its position of world leadership and help ensure a higher standard of living and greater prosperity for all our people.

The shift in Government policy away from artificial controls to an emphasis on free market forces has produced adequate supplies of energy at affordable prices. The impact of this policy shift was clearly demonstrated by deregulation of petroleum prices, which resulted in greater production of energy, more efficient use of energy, and lower energy costs for consumers. We anticipate a similar experience with the move toward a freer market in natural gas.

Fundamental changes in the energy future of the United States and moves toward even greater energy security require that all grade levels of the American educational system prepare our youth for the new demands and challenges that lie ahead. In recognition of this fact and to bring together students, teachers, school officials, and community officials to focus on the need for a greater understanding of energy issues, Congress has, by Senate Joint Resolution 146, requested the President to proclaim March 23, 1984, as "National Energy Education Day."

Now, Therefore, I, Ronald Reagan, President of the United States of America, do hereby proclaim March 23, 1984, as National Energy Education Day. I call upon educational institutions, Federal agencies, and all Americans to participate in appropriate ceremonies and activities on that day.

In Witness Whereof, I have hereunto set my hand this seventeenth day of March, in the year of our Lord nineteen hundred and eighty-four, and of the Independence of the United States of America the two hundred and eighth.

RONALD REAGAN

[*Filed with the Office of the Federal Register, 11:23 a.m., March 19, 1984*]

Note: The text of the proclamation was released by the Office of the Press Secretary on March 19.

Proclamation 5163—National Organ Donation Awareness Week, 1984
March 17, 1984

By the President of the United States of America

A Proclamation

One of the most meaningful gifts that one human being can bestow upon another is the precious gift of life. It can be given simply by making arrangements to donate our organs or those of our loved ones after death. Donation of our corneas would give others the gift of sight; donation of our kidneys, hearts, lungs, livers, and pancreata could save the lives of many people who might otherwise die.

On several occasions during the last year, I have asked the American people to be aware of the opportunities to donate their organs, and I have made special pleas for small children in need of liver transplants. The response proved to be overwhelming. Tragically, however, many desperately ill persons, including small children, have died while awaiting a suitable organ.

Ironically, recent surveys indicate that about 93 percent of all Americans have heard about organ transplants, but the need for organs far surpasses the number donated each year. Our organ procurement system is being managed effectively by the private sector but can be improved to meet a larger portion of the need. For these reasons, I supported the establishment of the American Council on Transplantation. The primary goal of this national umbrella organization is to increase the availability of organs for transplantation.

It is appropriate that we as a Nation encourage organ donation and increase public awareness of the need for such donations. By filling out a uniform donor card carrying it, and by making our wishes of donation known to our families, we may give the gift of life to people who so desperately need solid organs for transplantation, an exceedingly scarce resource.

Americans are a caring and giving people. I have heard from many Americans who have lost their loved ones in tragic accidents, but who have found solace in knowing that through their loss other lives were saved.

The Congress, by House Joint Resolution 229, has authorized and requested the President to issue a proclamation designating the week beginning April 22, 1984, as "National Organ Donation Awareness Week."

Now, Therefore, I, Ronald Reagan, President of the United States of America, do hereby designate the week of April 22 through April 28, 1984, as National Organ Donation Awareness Week. I urge all citizens, health care professionals, educators, the media, and the public and private organizations concerned with organ donation and transplantation to join me in supporting this humanitarian action.

In Witness Whereof, I have hereunto set my hand this seventeenth day of March, in the year of our Lord nineteen hundred and eighty-four, and of the Independence of the United States of America the two hundred and eighth.

RONALD REAGAN

[Filed with the Office of the Federal Register, 11:24 a.m., March 19, 1984]

Note: The text of the proclamation was released by the Office of the Press Secretary on March 19.

Remarks on Signing the Annual Report on the State of Small Business
March 19, 1984

Good morning. It's a real pleasure to welcome Jim Sanders, the head of the Small Business Administration, Frank Swain, SBA's Chief Counsel for Advocacy, and you, the representatives of small business across America.

You know, the White House is a lot like small business—Nancy and I live above the store. [*Laughter*]

Small business plays a vital role in American life. Many businesses—well, they make everything from ice cream to shoes to computers. Small businesses are the biggest providers of new jobs, give the most employees the freedom to work part time, hire the

most women, young people, and senior citizens. They embody innovation, provide economic diversity, and chart our path toward the products, markets, and jobs of the future.

And to remain engines of hope and prosperity, small businesses need a healthy economy. Just 3 years ago, the American economy was, as we all know, anything but healthy. We all remember those days. Government was growing like Goliath, wrecking the economy with punishing inflation and interest rates, a growing tax burden, and government regulations that were smothering economic growth. When an enterprising man or woman wanted to borrow money to start their own business, 21½-percent prime interest rates shut the door in their faces. When a small business wanted to buy a new plant or materials to expand, 12.4-percent inflation put opportunity beyond its reach.

When we took office, we made restoring economic vitality our top priority. We reduced the growth rate of government spending, pruned needless regulations, cut taxes, and passed an historic reform called tax indexing.

I always liked—when I think about regulations, I always remember one of the favorite stories I had about bureaucracy long before I was here in Washington. And that was a fellow here in Washington that sat at a desk, and papers came to him, and he looked at them and decided where they should go, initialed them, and sent them on. And one day a classified document arrived at his desk. Well, he accepted it, saw where it should go, initialed it, sent it on. Twenty-four hours later, it came back to him. It said, "You weren't supposed to see this. Erase your initials and initial the erasure." *[Laughter]*

Well, one of our reforms, also, was tax indexing. It means the government can never again profit from inflation at your expense. And today, we're seeing a surging economic recovery from Maine to California. Housing starts, factory orders, and real income are all up. The stock market has come back to life. Between the end of 1982 and the end of 1983, net private savings shot up nearly 50 percent to over $230 billion, making more funds available to the risk-takers and innovators who give small business their drive.

Small businesses have led the way in creating new jobs, and today more Americans have jobs than ever before in our history. Since the beginning of the recovery 15 months ago, nearly 5 million Americans have found work. And the unemployment rate has fallen to 7.7 percent, marking the steepest drop in more than 30 years.

Now, this isn't a Keynesian recovery produced by big-spending bureaucrats tinkering with aggregate demand. In fact, I don't know of a single Keynesian who predicted it. Instead, this recovery was created by the incentives of tax rate reductions, which shifted resources away from government back to American producers, savers, and investors.

Small business has responded to the recovery with new vigor. Last year alone, there were almost 600,000 new business incorporations, virtually all of them small business. That's an all-time high, and half again as many incorporations that there were each year during the early 1970's. At the same time, bankruptcies declined some 30 percent in the second half of '83, compared with the same period in 1982. And small business income, as measured by proprietorships and partnerships, grew by a remarkable 18 percent.

But we must go forward toward new goals so we can keep the nightmare of inflation from ever coming back. We must enact constitutional reforms like the line-item veto—and, oh, do I want that—*[laughter]*—and the balanced budget amendment. And to make taxes more simple and fair and to provide greater incentives for growth in our people, I believe that we must press for tax simplification, a sweeping comprehensive reform of the entire tax code—and not the kind of simplification that was sent to me the other day. Someone sent me a new tax form. It had two lines. Fill in—"What did you make last year?" The second line said, "Send it." *[Laughter]*

And, as you may have heard, I've just reached agreement with the Republican leadership in the Congress on a deficit reduction package totaling some $150 billion over the next 3 years. Just Thursday night, shortly after we reached agreement, the Senate Finance Committee concluded its work on a major portion of our package. I'm hopeful the entire package will be passed promptly by the Republican Senate. This $150 billion downpayment deserves bipartisan support because it will reduce the deficit in a way that's effective, responsible, and fair, by targeting $43 billion of savings in nondefense spending, $57 billion in defense authority reductions, and by raising some $48 billion in revenues primarily from closing certain tax loopholes of questionable fairness.

Now, make no mistake: The defense cuts

will slow down our defense buildup somewhat, but not to a point of unacceptable risk. There will be no increase in tax rates on American families, and no tax increases that would threaten the economic recovery.

Permit me to mention a few of the inspiring small business success stories that I've heard, now, at this point. Back in 1978, Ginnie Johansen of Dallas—she was in college and needed a belt to wear with casual slacks. And since she didn't like anything she saw in the stores, she made a few belts of her own. Several students offered to buy several belts, and soon Ginnie decided to try her hand at business. Today Ginnie's company grosses $8 million in annual sales, manufactures 57 different accessories and, best of all, employes 65 people, most of them young women. By the way, Ginnie is now 24 years old.

Roberto Ruiz of Tucson was born in Mexico, moved to the United States as a teenager. In 1977 he founded a construction company and an engineering corporation. Between 1979 and 1983, sales for Roberto's companies grew from $1.4 million to $7.2 million, an increase of more than 500 percent. Roberto's companies do a great deal of work in the Arizona border area, a section of the country hard hit by the devaluation of the peso. And Roberto has always made an effort to hire local workers. Last year alone he hired 100 employees, and today his firms account for more than 200 jobs.

And then there are Frank Huggins and Dean Robinson of Champaign, Illinois. Less than 2 years ago, they founded DISK-TEC—a firm that makes components for computer disc drives. From March 1983 to February 1984, DISK-TEC recorded $3 million in sales, and the company projects sales of $15 million for the calendar year 1984. And today DISK-TEC employs about 230 people—that's 230 jobs created by two talented entrepreneurs in less than 2 years.

Cervantes once said, "Many littles make a much." And as small businesses spring up across the country, they add up to products we've never dreamed of, new standards of excellence, and jobs for millions. It's small business people like you who remind us of the enterprise that made our nation great. You show us that Americans have just as much pluck as ever, and you prove that our country's best days are still to come.

On behalf of all Americans, I commend you, and I thank you. God bless you.

And now, I'm going to sign the report. Speaking of small business, now there's an idea: Produce pens that would only write one word for bill signing ceremonies. [*Laughter*]

[*At this point, the President signed copies of the report for transmittal to the Senate and House of Representatives.*]

There we are. And there it is.

Note: The President spoke at 11:05 a.m. in Room 450 of the Old Executive Office Building, where he was presented with the report prepared by the Small Business Administration, with the assistance of the Council of Economic Advisers, for transmittal to the Congress. The ceremony was attended by representatives of the small business community.

Annual Report to the Congress on the State of Small Business
March 19, 1984

To the Congress of the United States:

I am pleased to submit to the Congress my third annual report on the state of small business. The year 1983 was an excellent year for the economy in general, and especially for small business. At last, we are succeeding in establishing economic conditions which recognize and promote the vital role small business performs in our economy. And small business has responded with record business formation, employment, and activity.

Small business optimism and faith in the future have been demonstrated not only in polls and surveys, but in the economic record this report details. In the first three quarters of 1983 new business starts were up 13 percent from the same period in 1982. There was a significant decline in business bankruptcies in 1983—over 10 percent. The strengthening of the recovery is seen in more recent figures—in the last half of 1983 business bankruptcies were 30 percent lower than during the last half of 1982.

Income from partnerships and proprietorships—which comprise most small business—increased in 1983 by 18 percent over the previous year. In addition, as the report details, the opportunity for business ownership and activity is reaching great numbers of minorities, women and other members of our society. To encourage that activity among women entrepreneurs, I have directed the Small Business Administration (SBA) to begin a National Initiatives Program. This series of regional conferences is designed to provide managerial and technical assistance to women business owners and women entrepreneurs.

The reason for the success of small business in 1983 is no mystery. The economy reflects the growing confidence of private sector decisionmakers to invest capital and take risks. Business decisions can be made more confidently with an inflation rate of 4 percent instead of 12 percent. Small business, which relies more heavily on borrowed capital, is better off with prime interest rates at 11 percent rather than 21 percent. And small business has done far more than most to provide employment for members of our work force. During 1983 total employment increased by four million jobs. Small business contributed significantly to this growth, continuing the strong trend shown during 1981 and 1982, when small business contributed 2.6 million new jobs to the economy.

This Administration's goal has been to achieve stable and favorable economic conditions, and in 1983 we came a long way toward reaching that goal. We are promoting a number of specific Government policies that have a major, favorable impact on small business. It has been my desire to ensure that, whenever possible, our policies reflect the importance of small business to the economy as a whole.

The cuts in individual and estate taxes in 1983 are part of our efforts. These important changes in the tax law directly benefit the more than 85 percent of small businesses that pay taxes through the personal income tax returns of their owners. Tax policies that sustain the cash flow of small firms will continue to be a major goal of this Administration. More reasonable and understandable tax regulations are important and necessary policy goals for small business. In this regard, the action of the Internal Revenue Service to withdraw its proposed rule and reexamine the issue of classifying small business investments as debt or equity is notable.

Progress in relieving small firms of unnecessary regulation and paperwork continued in 1983. Many Federal agencies developed a positive working relationship with small business. Regulation, when it is necessary, is increasingly achieved with a maximum of flexibility and common sense and a minimum of extraneous costs and burdens. The Task Force on Regulatory Relief has established the momentum and the Office of Management and Budget (OMB) is continuing the effort. Agencies are utilizing the Regulatory Flexibility Act to scrutinize new and old rules for their effect on small business.

The OMB and the SBA's Office of Advocacy have continued to work with agencies to achieve better regulation for small business. Together they have managed to cut 300 million hours of Federally imposed paperwork burden. Hearings held by SBA on small business paperwork confirm that this is significant progress, but that we must redouble our efforts to attack those forms which still vex and confuse small business owners. The opportunity this Nation offers for individual entrepreneurial effort ought not to be diminished by outdated or overzealous regulation.

Many small businesses recognize that the Government can be an important customer. Annual Federal purchases of goods and services, excluding employee compensation, represent approximately 20 percent of Federal expenditures. It has been my consistent conviction that the taxpayer and the Government are well served by strong small business participation in the procurement process. We need to utilize the wealth of technological capability, experience, and efficiency present in the small business sector. To this end, we have significantly increased the amount of Federal purchases from small and minority businesses. In addition, to further open the procurement process to small business in 1983, I signed the Commerce Business Daily Act (Public Law 98–72) which requires Federal agencies to allow longer periods for responses to bid requests.

The first year of the Small Business Innovation and Research (SBIR) program demonstrated the critical role played by small research and development companies. The SBIR program resulted in ten Federal agencies making over 800 research awards to small firms. The $40 million committed in 1983 will expand to $120 million in 1984, creating new opportunities for small business and increasing Federal agencies' utilization of small business' technological expertise. In an important related development, the SBA, the Department of Justice, and the Federal Trade Commission approved the first joint research and development company for small firms under Section 9 (d) and 11 of the SBA Act.

Small business progress in 1983—whether in terms of new business starts, creation of new jobs, efficient sales to the Government, or new innovations—cannot be sustained without continued, favorable Federal policies toward small businesses. We intend to act on upcoming issues to ensure that our Nation's policies continue to be favorable to small business.

First and foremost, we must preserve the individual tax cuts and tax indexing enacted over the past three years. It would be unwise to roll back the progress small business has made as a result of these 1981 reforms.

We must take other actions to maintain a healthy economy. We need to ensure that Federal activities are as efficient and cost effective as possible. We will vigorously implement policies against unfair competition with the private sector from the Government or other tax-advantaged sectors of the economy.

The procurement process must continue to be simplified and made more accessible to small firms, especially in the important area of spare parts for Government and military purchases. The major Federal procurement agencies have committed to reduce procurement paperwork by 10 percent in Fiscal Year 1984. I intend to pursue policies that ensure that necessary procurement by the Government results in wise and effective use of our tax dollars.

There are several specific areas of business where we look forward to positive Congressional action in 1984. This Administration recognizes the spirit and capabilities of small and minority businesses in its support of Federal Enterprise Zones and urges Congressional action on this important issue.

The potential liability of many small manufacturers and distributors in product liability tort actions governed by a myriad of state laws is of continuing concern. Simple reform of this legally complicated area is needed. The Congress should recognize problems that affect small manufacturers and enact a fair bill reforming product liability.

The condition of our Nation's immigration laws is a matter of national concern and specific concern to the small business community. Legislation on this issue is in the Congress and has been carefully debated by many participants, including representatives of the small business community. Enactment of legislation would immediately provide significant predictability and reform of a difficult national issue.

The Equal Access to Justice Act should be reauthorized. This law provides an important tool for the small business faced with unjust Government action. From my perspective, there is an equally important influence upon potentially overzealous regulatory agencies which have an impact upon small business. The statute needs improvement, however, and we will work with the Congress to produce legislation which resolves unanswered questions regarding the scope of the law.

The necessity to keep our national leadership role in technological development is a responsibility shared by small and large business. This Administration has proposed legislation which would clarify and ease the procedure for firms to form joint research and development companies. Enactment of this legislation will be an important step to increase our technological development through use of the best minds and resources in capable firms of all sizes.

We should be mindful of the important role played by small business in our Nation as employer of many of our citizens, as job creator, and as innovator. Our job in Government is to continue to create an economic environment where creativity and hard work pay dividends. With the im-

proved conditions in 1983, small business has adapted and thrived. There is every reason to feel confident that this prosperity will continue.

RONALD REAGAN

The White House,
March 19, 1984.

Note: The report is entitled "The State of Small Business: A Report of the President, Transmitted to the Congress, March 1984" (Government Printing Office, 485 pages).

Text of the President's Remarks During a Meeting With Cuban-American Leaders
March 19, 1984

Cuban Americans, perhaps better than others, appreciate what opportunity and economic freedom mean to people who are struggling to better themselves. Many of you arrived here in the early 1960's when America was enjoying high growth and low inflation. In that environment, everyone had the chance to better themselves.

But during the 1970's this shining land of opportunity, once so vibrant and vital, was ravaged by inflation and economic stagnation. By 1980 it was painfully clear to all Americans that something was seriously wrong.

So we set out to make some long-overdue changes. By reversing unwise policies of over-taxing and spending, we've put America back on track. And I'm mighty proud that when the heat was on, and the advocates of the failed policies of the past tried to get us to reverse course before our program had a chance to take hold, we stuck to our principles; we stayed the course. I think the country is beginning to understand why we did.

I firmly believe what's best for all Americans, especially those who want to improve their condition, is a policy of low inflation and strong growth. America needs jobs and opportunity, not make-work and handouts.

The Cuban community, especially in Florida and other Gulf Coast States, has

become a center for commercial activity, much of it with Latin America. This has boosted our economic potential and has been a boon to our neighbors to the south. I'd like to thank you for the vital role you are playing.

You know how significant our struggle is, not only for our neighbors to the south but for the United States, as well. I can assure you today that our administration fully recognizes the vital importance of the economic, political, and military struggle going on in Central America and the Caribbean. We do not intend to let the Soviet Union, through its Communist Cuban proxies, take over that region.

Central America and the Caribbean are of the utmost strategic importance to the United States. If we don't give friends so close to home the means to defend themselves against Soviet-supported insurgents, who will trust us anywhere in the world, especially in the faraway Middle East and Europe?

To those who would spend time focusing on the flaws of our friends—and they are far from perfect—let me just say we all are concerned about human rights. But I believe it is being either naive or downright phony to profess concern for human rights, while pursuing policies that lead to the overthrow of less-than-perfect democracies by Marxist dictatorships which systematically crush all human rights. We've seen it happen in countless countries, including Afghanistan, Vietnam, and, yes, Cuba. In these countries there are no human rights nor any debates about human rights. There is only brutal suppression by the Communist Party. Because such regimes are at war with the basic laws of human nature, invariably they inflict great economic misery on their people. That is why it's both logical and necessary for them to conquer other lands to obtain the resources they cannot produce themselves.

What we are witnessing to the south is a power play by Cuba and the Soviet Union, pure and simple. Cuba, after nearly 25 years of so-called revolution, is an economic basket case. It cannot supply even its own needs without massive and costly Soviet subsidies. Like a roving wolf, Castro's Cuba looks to its peace-loving neighbors with hungry eyes and sharp teeth. Our challenge is to avert a crisis before it happens—to help our neighbors build strong economies, democratic governments, and give them weapons to counter Soviet-backed insurgency.

A few months ago, we saw this very process unfolding on a small island in the Caribbean—Grenada. Massive stores of military supplies were being stacked high in the warehouses there. The island was living under virtual Cuban occupation. The lives of American students, as well as the islanders and, indeed, Grenada's peaceful, freedom-loving neighbors, were all being put in jeopardy. We had no choice but to join with our neighbors, at their request, and to free the people of Grenada. And that's exactly what we did.

I just have to tell you, one of my most heartwarming memories will always be of a reunion we had on the White House lawn. Students, many of whom had negative attitudes about the military before, threw their arms around the young soldiers, sailors, and marines who risked their lives to save them. Then the students introduced these military men to their parents as heroes.

Americans are a great people, and nobody should ever sell us short. And when I say Americans, I mean all of us, because from the tip of Tierra del Fuego to the North Pole, we are all Americans.

We have every reason to be confident. But if freedom is to prevail, if peace is to be preserved, we cannot be complacent. Our greatest strength is truth, because truth is on our side and with it we can and will turn the tide. Saint John said you shall know the truth and the truth shall make you free. I am very proud that we are making steady progress in our efforts to put Radio Marti on the air.

Note: The President met with the leaders in the East Room at the White House.

As printed above, this item follows the text of the President's prepared remarks as released by the Office of the Press Secretary.

Nomination of Bruce E. Thompson, Jr., To Be a Deputy Under Secretary of the Treasury, and Designation as an Assistant Secretary of the Treasury
March 19, 1984

The President today announced his intention to nominate Bruce E. Thompson, Jr., to be a Deputy Under Secretary of the Treasury (Legislative Affairs). He would succeed W. Dennis Thomas. Upon confirmation, the President will designate Mr. Thompson to be an Assistant Secretary of the Treasury.

Since June 1983 Mr. Thompson has been serving as Assistant Secretary for Business and Consumer Affairs at the Department of the Treasury. Previously he was Deputy Assistant Secretary of the Treasury for Legislative Affairs. Before joining the Department of the Treasury, he was legislative assistant to Senator William V. Roth, Jr. (1974–1981). He was senior policy analyst for Government Research Corp. in 1971–1974.

Mr. Thompson graduated from Georgetown University (B.S., B.A., 1971) and has done graduate work at George Washington University. He is married, has two children, and resides in Chevy Chase, MD. He was born June 5, 1949, in Cleveland, OH.

Message to the Congress Reporting on the Continuation of Export Control Regulations
March 19, 1984

To the Congress of the United States:

This report is submitted pursuant to section 204 of the International Emergency Economic Powers Act (50 U.S.C. 1703) and section 401(c) of the National Emergencies Act (50 U.S.C. 1641(c)) to account for government expenditures attributable to the national economic emergency that I declared following the lapse of the Export Administration Act of 1979, as amended (50 U.S.C. App. 2401 *et seq.*) (EAA) on October 14, 1983. On that date, I issued Executive Order No. 12444 to continue in effect the system of controls that had been established under the EAA. In view of the extension by Public Law 98–207 (December 5, 1983) of the authorities contained in the EAA, this emergency authority was no longer needed, and on December 20, 1983, I issued Executive Order No. 12451, a copy of which is attached, rescinding the declaration of economic emergency and revoking Executive Order No. 12444.

The EAA export controls were not expanded during the emergency period, and the administration of the system of controls continued in the normal course. Accordingly, the government spent no funds over and above what would have been spent had the EAA remained in force without interruption.

RONALD REAGAN

The White House,
March 19, 1984.

Statement on Signing a District of Columbia Courts Bill
March 19, 1984

I am pleased to approve H.R. 3655, a bill that will create seven new judgeships on the Superior Court of the District of Columbia and also raise the mandatory retirement age from 70 to 74 for judges on that court and on the District of Columbia Court of Appeals.

The Superior Court is a unique Federal court with important judicial responsibilities in the Nation's Capital. The growing backlog of criminal and civil litigation in the Superior Court is accordingly a matter of both local and Federal concern, and this legislation will help alleviate the backlog. It is my hope that the District of Columbia Judicial Nomination Commission will act promptly in submitting lists of qualified individuals for nomination to these judgeships so that the new judges can be in place, reducing the backlog, as soon as possible.

While this legislation will ease the caseload problem in the Superior Court, it does not provide a cure for that problem or the similar problems plaguing most of our nation's courts. The staggering increase in litigation has strained the capacity of our courts and threatened their ability to settle disputes. One of America's greatest lawyers, Abraham Lincoln, once said: "Discourage litigation. Persuade your neighbors to compromise whenever you can. Point out to them how the nominal winner is often a real loser—in fees, expenses, and waste of time." We must continue to search for alternative means of settling disputes. If we fail to do so, the costs and delays of litigation in our overcrowded courts will effectively close the courthouse doors to all but the wealthy and those that seek to use delay to their advantage. We must not permit meritorious claims deserving of prompt judicial resolution to become lost in a sea of frivolous suits or disputes that could more quickly and efficiently be resolved in other forums.

Note: As enacted, H.R. 3655 is Public Law 98–235, approved March 19.

Nomination of John F. Scruggs To Be an Assistant Secretary of Health and Human Services
March 19, 1984

The President today announced his intention to nominate John F. Scruggs to be an Assistant Secretary of Health and Human Services (Legislation). He would succeed Thomas R. Donnelly, Jr.

Since 1982 Mr. Scruggs has been serving as Special Assistant to the President for Legislative Affairs. Previously, he was floor assistant to the Republican Whip, U.S. House of Representatives, in 1981–1982; minority counsel, Subcommittee on the Rules of the House, U.S. House of Representatives, in 1980–1981; and staff assistant to the Committee on Rules in 1978–1980.

He graduated from Biola College (B.A., 1978) and is presently attending the Washington College of Law at American University. He is married and resides in Alexandria, VA. He was born January 14, 1955, in Salinas, CA.

Proclamation 5164—Import Fees on Certain Sugars, Sirups and Molasses
March 19, 1984

By the President of the United States of America

A Proclamation

By Proclamation 4887 of December 23, 1981, and Proclamation 4940 of May 5, 1982, I imposed, on an emergency basis, import fees on certain sugars, sirups and molasses. These fees were to be effective pending my further action after receipt of the report of findings and recommendations of the United States International Trade Commission after its investigation with respect to this matter pursuant to section 22 of the Agricultural Adjustment Act of 1933, as amended (7 U.S.C. 624). The Commission has made its investigation and reported its findings and recommendations to me.

On the basis of the information submitted to me, I find and declare that:

(a) Sugars classified under items 155.20 and 155.30 of the Tariff Schedules of the United States (TSUS) (19 U.S.C. 1202) are being or are practically certain to be imported into the United States under such conditions and in such quantities as to render or tend to render ineffective, or materially interfere with, the price support operations being conducted by the Department of Agriculture for sugar cane and sugar beets.

(b) The imposition of the import fees hereinafter proclaimed is necessary in order that the entry, or withdrawal from warehouse for consumption, of such sugars will not render or tend to render ineffective, or materially interfere with, the price support operations being conducted by the Department of Agriculture for sugar beets and sugar cane.

Now, Therefore, I, Ronald Reagan, President of the United States of America, by the authority vested in me by section 22 of the Agricultural Adjustment Act of 1933, as amended, and the statutes of the United States, including section 301 of Title 3 of the United States Code, do hereby proclaim until otherwise superseded by law:

A. Headnote 4 of part 3 of the Appendix to the TSUS is continued in effect and amended, effective 12:01 a.m. Eastern Standard Time of the day following the date of the signing of this proclamation, by changing paragraph (c) to read as follows:

(c)(i) The quarterly adjusted fee provided for in items 956.05 and 957.15 shall be the amount of the fee for item 956.15 plus one cent per pound.

(ii) The quarterly adjusted fee provided for in item 956.15 shall be the amount by which the average of the adjusted daily spot (domestic) price quotations for raw sugar for the 20 consecutive market days immediately preceding the 20th day of the month preceding the calendar quarter during which the fee shall be applicable (as reported by the New York Coffee, Sugar and Cocoa Exchange) expressed in United States cents per pound, in bulk, is less than the applicable market stabilization price: *Provided,* That whenever the average of the daily spot (domestic) price quotations for 10 consecutive market days within any calendar quarter (1) exceeds the market stabilization price by more than one cent, the fee then in effect shall be decreased by one cent per pound, or (2) is less than the market stabilization price by more than one cent, the fee then in effect shall be increased by one cent per pound. The adjusted daily spot (domestic) price quotation for any market day shall be the daily spot (domestic) price quotation for such market day less the amount of the fee for item 956.15 that is in effect on that day. For any market day for which the New York Coffee, Sugar and Cocoa Exchange does not report a daily spot (domestic) price for raw sugar, then

the Secretary of Agriculture (the Secretary) shall use such other price as he determines appropriate.

(iii) The market stabilization price that shall be applicable to each fiscal year (October 1–September 30) shall be determined and announced by the Secretary in accordance with this headnote no later than 30 days prior to the beginning of the fiscal year for which such market stabilization price shall be applicable. The market stabilization price shall be equal to the sum of: (1) the price support level for the applicable fiscal year, expressed in cents per pound of raw cane sugar; (2) adjusted average transportation costs; (3) interest costs, if applicable; and (4) 0.2 cent. The adjusted average transportation costs shall be the weighted average cost of handling and transporting domestically produced raw cane sugar from Hawaii to Gulf and Atlantic Coast ports, as determined by the Secretary. Interest costs shall be the amount of interest, as determined or estimated by the Secretary, that would be required to be paid by a recipient of a price support loan for raw cane sugar upon repayment of the loan at full maturity. Interest costs shall only be applicable if a price support loan recipient is not required to pay interest upon forfeiture of the loan collateral.

(iv) Notwithstanding the provisions of paragraph (iii) hereof, if the Secretary determines that there is a significant change in any one or more of the elements comprising the market stabilization price during the fiscal year, the Secretary shall adjust the market stabilization price within the fiscal year to reflect such change. The Secretary shall announce any such adjusted market stabilization price and file notice thereof with the *Federal Register.* This adjusted market stabilization price will become effective the first calendar quarter following its announcement or, if the Secretary announced it less than 30 days before the beginning of a new calendar quarter, then it will become effective the second calendar quarter following its announcement. Any adjusted market stabilization price, once effective, shall remain in effect through the remainder of the fiscal year unless it is adjusted further in accordance with this paragraph.

(v) The Secretary shall determine the amount of the quarterly fees in accordance with this headnote and shall announce such fees not later than the 25th day of the month preceding the calendar quarter during which the fees shall be applicable. The Secretary shall certify the amount of such fees to the Commissioner of Customs and file notice thereof with the *Federal Register* prior to the beginning of the calendar quarter during which the fees shall be applicable. The Secretary shall determine and announce any adjustment in the fees made within a calendar quarter in accordance with the proviso of paragraph (ii) hereof, shall certify such adjusted fees to the Commissioner of Customs, and shall file notice thereof with the *Federal Register* within 3 market days of the fulfillment of that proviso.

(vi) If an adjustment is made in the fee in accordance with the proviso of paragraph (ii) hereof, any subsequent adjustment made within that quarter shall only be made on the basis of the average spot price for any 10 consecutive market day period following the effective date of the immediately preceding fee adjustment. No adjustment shall be made in any fee in accordance with the proviso of paragraph (ii) hereof during the last 15 market days of a calendar quarter.

(vii) Any adjustment made in a fee during a quarter in accordance with the proviso of paragraph (ii) hereof shall be effective only with respect to sugar entered or withdrawn from warehouse for consumption after 12:01 a.m. (local time at point of entry) on the day following the filing of notice thereof with the *Federal Register: Provided,* That such adjustment in the fee shall not apply to sugar exported (as defined by Customs in accordance with 19 CFR 152.1) on a through bill of lading to the United States from the country of origin before such time. The exemption contained in the preceding proviso shall apply regardless of whether the adjustment in the fee is upward or downward.

B. Items 956.05, 956.15 and 957.15 of part 3 of the Appendix to the TSUS are continued in effect and the "Rates of Duty (Section 22 Fees)" are amended to read as follows:

Item	Articles	Rates of duty (section 22 fees)
	Sugars, sirups and molasses derived from sugar cane or sugar beets, except those entered pursuant to a license issued by the Secretary of Agriculture in accordance with headnote 4(a):	
	Principally of crystalline structure or in dry amorphous form, provided for in item 155.20, part 10A, schedule 1:	
956.05	Not to be further refined or improved in quality. . . .	An amount determined and adjusted in accordance with headnote 4(c), but not in excess of 50% ad val.
956.15	To be further refined or improved in quality......	An amount determined and adjusted in accordance with headnote 4(c), but not in excess of 50% ad val.
957.15	Not principally of crystalline structure and not in dry amorphous form, containing soluble nonsugar solids (excluding any foreign substance that may have been added or developed in the product) equal to 6% or less by weight of the total soluble solids, provided for in item 155.30, part 10A, schedule 1.	An amount determined and adjusted in accordance with headnote 4(c) per pound of total sugars, but not in excess of 50% ad val.

C. The Secretary of Agriculture, in consultation with other appropriate agencies, shall review the fee system established by this Proclamation on a quarterly basis and shall submit to me any recommendations for any changes determined to be necessary or appropriate.

D. The provisions of this proclamation shall terminate upon the filing of a notice in the *Federal Register* by the Secretary of Agriculture that the Department of Agriculture is no longer conducting a price support program for sugar beets and sugar cane.

E. The provisions of Proclamation 4940 of May 5, 1982, are hereby terminated, except that the import fees on items 956.15, 956.05 and 957.15 presently in effect and the market stabilization price determined and announced by the Secretary of Agriculture for fiscal year 1984 (October 1, 1983–September 30, 1984) shall remain in effect,

unless adjusted by the Secretary of Agriculture in accordance with paragraph (c) of Headnote 4 of part 3 of the Appendix to the TSUS, as modified herein.

F. This proclamation shall be effective as of 12:01 a.m. Eastern Standard Time on the day following the date of its signing, and shall apply to articles entered, or withdrawn from warehouse for consumption, on or after such effective date.

In Witness Whereof, I have hereunto set my hand this 19th day of March, in the year of our Lord nineteen hundred and eighty-four, and of the Independence of the United States of America the two hundred and eighth.

RONALD REAGAN

[Filed with the Office of the Federal Register, 4:08 p.m., March 19, 1984]

Remarks at a White House Ceremony Marking the Observance of National Agriculture Day
March 20, 1984

Good morning, and welcome to the White House. I'm delighted you could be with us on this first day of spring. Here in Washington, it means the advent of cherry blossoms and lots of tourists, and, hopefully, some congressional action on the budget. [*Laughter*] But for all of you, the beginning of spring signals the time to pull equipment out of the sheds and to turn attention to the fields.

This is also National Agriculture Day, a day set aside to express our appreciation to the working men and women of agriculture for the bounty of food and fiber you provide and for the strength that you give us. It's a fitting time to honor America's bedrock industry, and I encourage the American people, both on and off the farm, to participate in the special activities that are taking place all across our nation.

National Agriculture Day is also a special day for me because, as I've told Jack Block on many occasions, I'm a bit of a rancher

myself, and he's never seen fit to tell me otherwise. [*Laughter*] I remember once, some years ago, having an experience that you'd all understand. I decided with all that space and everything out there, why didn't we have our own fresh eggs every morning? So, I put in a battery of chickens. And we did—we had our own fresh eggs every morning. They only cost $1.65 apiece. [*Laughter*]

Well, today we pay tribute to an industry whose record of productivity is unmatched by any other in the world. Our farmers and ranchers produce the most wholesome and varied range of foodstuffs known anywhere. In fact, our agricultural community has been so successful, it's too often been taken for granted. Few advances in modern technology can surpass the miracle of American agriculture. In 1820 a farmer in this country produced enough food to feed four people. By 1940 one American farmer fed 11 people. Today the same farmer can produce enough food for himself and 75 other people.

This unparalleled productivity enables us to feed our own population and tens of millions of people throughout the world. The United States is the world's leading exporter of agricultural products. Our food travels to every corner of the Earth. In 1982 nearly one-fifth of the world's agricultural products was shipped from American ports. And let me assure you, now that we've regained our reputation as a reliable supplier, we're going to keep it that way.

Some would say that American agriculture is nothing short of magic. Well, it's not magic; it's the miracle of freedom. Millions of individuals, each representing a single farming operation, yet linked together so effectively that agriculture is the largest business in the United States—an enterprise of 23 million people with assets equal to about 70 percent of those held by all manufacturing corporations in the United States.

I'm delighted to be with those of you who make American agriculture work so well. And I believe part of the reason for your great success is your partnership with the Department of Agriculture and agencies like the Agricultural Stabilization and Conservation Service, the ASCS. The county ASCS office is the place where you're likely to see a neighbor's pickup truck outside and have some good conversation inside. And that's the way government works best—at the grassroots, where programs are responsive to the people they're meant to help.

I want all of the ASCS State committeemen and directors with us this morning to know that I appreciate what you've done to make our Payment-In-Kind program a success. Thanks to your fine efforts we've cleared away many price-depressing surpluses, and we've moved closer to the point where the market, not the government, will be sending the production signals to our producers. I'm sure that you're approaching this year's farm program with the same dedication. For our part, we'll take into account the hard lessons of recent years as we work toward the resolution of farm problems.

And so—missed me.[1] And so—[laughter]—so, let me take this opportunity to congratulate the Jaycee award winners with us today. They have recently been honored for their outstanding contributions to American agriculture. We're proud of your achievements. We're proud of all that you've done.

And we heard some pretty good stories at breakfast this morning. You know what it's like—all of you—to watch a hailstorm destroy a year's labor, how it feels to witness a dreaded fever spread through your livestock. But you also know the value of free enterprise and what it means to have a personal stake in deciding your future.

You know the exhilaration of opportunity and the accomplishments of scientific research. We now have many disease-resistant crops and stronger livestock, and we're on the threshold of even greater scientific and technological breakthroughs. The work being done at places like USDA's Beltsville Agricultural Research Center is bringing exciting new advances.

National Agriculture Day is a celebration of America, and when we talk about our farm community, we're talking about the values and traditions that made America great: hard work, faith, family, neighbors helping neighbors, freedom, and independence. We can touch the spirit of America in our farm communities.

Ladies and gentlemen, your contributions keep our great nation strong, prosperous, and free. And we thank you for that, and God bless you all.

And now I'd like to ask the families of the Jaycee award winners to join us here on the platform. And then we had the pleasure of starting the day with breakfast with these fine people, and here are the four winners: Pete Bontekoe, Rollie Moore, Gary Veenstra, and John Belter.

Now, the schedule calls and Nancy and I are going to move on, and I will turn you over to Jack Block. But with all these wonderful-looking people up here on the platform, these fine young families here, and

---

[1] *The President was reacting to a noise which came from the area where members of the press were gathered.*

what I was saying about freedom being the basis of our agriculture, I can't resist telling just one little story. I happen to collect stories that I get from defectors from some of the Warsaw bloc nations, of the stories that the people in those countries tell among themselves about their own system—shows a little cynicism too, at times.

And one has to do with a commissar, the Soviet Union, visiting a collective farm, grabbed the first fellow he saw, and he said, "Tell me, comrade, any complaints?" "Oh," he said, "I've never heard anyone complain. No, sir, everything's just fine." "Well," he said, "How are the crops?" He said, "Crops never been better. They're just wonderful."

He said, "Potatoes?" He said, "If we could pile the potatoes in one pile, they would reach the foot of God." And the commissar said, "Comrade, this is the Soviet Union. There is no God." He said, "That's all right. There are no potatoes." [*Laughter*]

Note: The President spoke at 9:15 a.m. in the East Room at the White House.

Earlier, the President hosted a breakfast for the U.S. Jaycees 1984 National Outstanding Young Farmers award winners and their families in the Family Dining Room. Also attending the breakfast was Secretary of Agriculture John R. Block.

Appointment of Karna Small as Deputy Assistant to the President and Senior Director for Public Affairs at the National Security Council
March 20, 1984

The President today announced his intention to appoint Karna Small to be Deputy Assistant to the President and Senior Director, Public Affairs, National Security Council.

Since November 1981 Ms. Small has been serving as Director of Media Relations and Planning for the White House Office of Communications. From January 1981 to November 1981, she served as White House Deputy Press Secretary.

From 1978 to 1981, Ms. Small was writer and moderator of a public affairs television program on economic, political, and foreign policy issues which aired in Washington on WJLA–TV (ABC) and was syndicated in 135 cities nationwide. She also hosted a 3-hour radio program on WRC (NBC).

From 1976 to 1978, she anchored the 10 p.m. news on WTTG–TV in Washington, DC. From 1972 to 1976, she anchored the early evening news on KGO–TV (ABC) in San Francisco, and from 1968 to 1972, she was featured on three newscasts per day on KRON–TV (NBC). During that time, she also commuted to Los Angeles once a week to appear on the 6 p.m. news on KNBC–TV (NBC).

Ms. Small received her B.A. degree, with honors, from the University of Michigan and studied journalism and television news in the graduate school at San Francisco State and Stanford Universities.

Ms. Small is a native of Wilmette, IL. She resides in Washington, DC.

Appointment of Pamela Giles Bailey as Special Assistant to the President and Director of the White House Office of Communications Planning
March 20, 1984

The President today announced his intention to appoint Pamela Giles Bailey as Special Assistant to the President and Director of the White House Office of Communications Planning.

Mrs. Bailey joined the White House Staff in April of 1983 as Special Assistant to the President for Public Affairs and Deputy Director of the White House Office of Public Affairs.

From 1981 to 1983, Mrs. Bailey served as Assistant Secretary of Health and Human Services (Public Affairs). From 1975 to 1979, Mrs. Bailey was with American Hospital Supply Corp. as director, government relations. From 1970 to 1975, she was a member of the White House staff. She was Assistant Director of the Domestic Council in 1974–1975; Staff Assistant to the President and Director of Research in 1973–1974; and Research Assistant to the President in 1970–1973.

Mrs. Bailey was assistant director of the office of personnel, office of the President-elect, in 1980. She was a member of the Reagan-Bush Campaign Advisory Task Force on Welfare Reform.

She graduated from Mount Holyoke College (A.B., 1970). She is married to William W. Bailey and has four children. Mrs. Bailey was born in Reading, PA, on May 24, 1948. She resides in Annandale, VA.

Appointment of Merrie Spaeth as Special Assistant to the President and Director of the White House Office of Media Relations
March 20, 1984

The President today announced his intention to appoint Merrie Spaeth to be Special Assistant to the President and Director of the White House Office of Media Relations.

Since May 1982 Ms. Spaeth has been serving as Director of Public Affairs for the Federal Trade Commission in Washington, DC. Previously she was Special Assistant to the Director of the Federal Bureau of Investigation, Judge William H. Webster.

In 1979 she produced segments for ABC's weekly show, 20/20. In 1978 she was the host and producer of a nightly television show in Columbus, OH, for Warner-Amex Cable. Between 1970 and 1978, she wrote for numerous print publications and was a reporter for several local television stations. She also started her own cable production company.

Ms. Spaeth received her B.A. degree, with honors, from Smith College in 1970, and from the Columbia Graduate School of Business in 1980. She serves on the Alumnae Association's board of directors.

Ms. Spaeth was born August 23, 1948, in Philadelphia, PA. She now resides in Rosslyn, VA.

Nomination of James W. Fuller To Be a Director of the Securities Investor Protection Corporation
March 20, 1984

The President today announced his intention to nominate James W. Fuller to be a Director of the Securities Investor Protection Corporation for the term expiring December 31, 1986. This is a reappointment.

Mr. Fuller has been a Director of the Securities Investor Protection Corporation since 1982. He is partner and chief executive officer for Presidio Management—James Fuller & Co. in San Francisco, CA. Previously, he was senior vice president, marketing, for the Charles Schwab Corp. in 1980–1983; senior vice president, marketing and public information, for the New York Stock Exchange in 1977–1980; manager, investment industries program for SRI International in 1974–1977; and vice president of Shields & Co. in 1972–1974.

He graduated from San Bernardino Valley College (A.A., 1960), San Jose State University (B.S., 1962), and California State University (M.B.A., 1969). He is married, has two children, and resides in San Francisco, CA. He was born April 3, 1940, in Rochester, IN.

Proclamation 5165—Afghanistan Day, 1984
March 20, 1984

By the President of the United States of America

A Proclamation

For much of the world spring is now beginning. It is a time of new life, renewal, freshness, and hope.

For the people of Afghanistan, March 21 is the traditional celebration of the New Year, the beginning of the cycle of life. It is a period of rejoicing and celebration for life's regeneration as a gift of God.

But today, for most of the people of Afghanistan, the March 21 New Year brings only the renewal of fighting, destruction, and death. For more than four years, the armed forces of the Soviet Union have occupied Afghanistan. More than 100,000 Soviet soldiers now occupy that beleaguered country. The overwhelming majority of the Afghan people are struggling against the Soviet occupation troops and the puppet regime headed by Babrak Karmal. It is a regime that is maintained only by Soviet force.

Afghan resistance to Marxist rule grew dramatically after the Soviet invasion, and it has now spread throughout the country. A solution to the Afghanistan problem must begin with the removal of the Soviet troops. A negotiated political settlement can be achieved if the Soviet Union agrees to withdraw its military forces of occupation.

The goal of United States policy remains clear and consistent. We seek the removal of Soviet military forces so that the Afghan people can live freely in their own country and are able to choose their own way of life and government.

Hope, it is said, springs eternal. We continue to hope that a negotiated settlement can be found, a settlement which fulfills the conditions spelled out five times in resolutions resoundingly endorsed by the General Assembly of the United Nations.

These resolutions, passed by the overwhelming majority of the world's nations, call for the immediate withdrawal of foreign troops from Afghanistan; reaffirm the right of the Afghan people to determine their own form of government and to choose their economic, political, and social system; reiterate that the preservation of the sovereignty, territorial integrity, political independence, and nonaligned character of Afghanistan is essential for a peaceful solution of the problem; and call for the creation of the conditions which would enable the Afghan refugees to return voluntarily to their homes in safety and honor.

We stand in admiration of the indomitable will and courage of the Afghan people who continue their resistance to tyranny. All freedom-loving people around the globe should be inspired by the Afghan people's struggle to be free and the heavy sacrifices they bear for liberty.

Afghanistan Day will serve to recall the fundamental principles involved when a people struggles for the freedom to determine its own future and the right to be free of foreign interference. Let us therefore resolve to pay tribute to the brave Afghan people by observing March 21, 1984 as Afghanistan Day. Let us pledge our continuing admiration for their cause and for their perseverance, and lend our support to the Afghan refugees in Pakistan.

Let us redouble our determination to help find a negotiated settlement that will enable the Afghan people to again welcome spring without the suffering brought by war, but with celebration and joy.

Now, Therefore, I, Ronald Reagan, President of the United States of America, do hereby proclaim March 21, 1984, as Afghanistan Day.

In Witness Whereof, I have hereunto set my hand this 20th day of March, in the year of our Lord nineteen hundred and eighty-four, and of the Independence of the United States of America the two hundred and eighth.

RONALD REAGAN

[*Filed with the Office of the Federal Register, 3:02 p.m., March 20, 1984*]

Appointment of Two Members of the Board of Visitors of the United States Naval Academy
March 20, 1984

The President today announced his intention to appoint the following individuals to be members of the Board of Visitors to the United States Naval Academy for the terms expiring December 30, 1986.

C. *Fred Chambers* is owner, president, and chief executive officer of Chambers Exploration, Inc., in Houston, TX. He graduated from the University of Texas at Austin (LL.B., 1941). He is married, has eight children, and resides in Houston, TX. He was born March 22, 1918, in Dallas, TX. Mr. Chambers will succeed Evelyn Gandy.

Lando William Zech, Jr., is former Deputy Chief of Naval Operations and Chief of Naval Personnel (Manpower, Personnel and Training), Department of the Navy. He graduated from the United States Naval Academy (B.S., 1944) and George Washington University (M.S., 1971). He is married, has five children, and resides in Falls Church, VA. He was born June 29, 1923, in Astoria, OR. He will succeed Blu Middleton.

Statement on Senate Action on the Proposed Constitutional Amendment on Prayer in Schools
March 20, 1984

I am deeply disappointed that, although a majority of the Senate voted for it, the school prayer amendment fell short of the special two-thirds majority needed to win in the Senate today.

I would like to express my heartfelt gratitude for the unprecedented outpouring of support from citizens who made their views known to their Senators on this issue. And I want to thank Senators Baker, Thurmond,

Helms, and Hatch for their valiant efforts to restore this revered American tradition.

This has been an important debate revealing the extent to which the freedom of religious speech has been abridged in our nation's public schools. The issue of free religious speech is not dead as a result of this vote. We have suffered a setback, but we have not been defeated. Our struggle will go on.

The courts themselves can restore a more balanced view of the first amendment, as we have seen in some recent cases. My administration will continue our efforts to allow government to accommodate prayer and religious speech by citizens in ways that do not risk an establishment of religion. I urge the Congress to consider the equal access legislation before both Houses so that voluntary student religious groups can meet on public school property on the same terms as other student groups.

Written Responses to Questions Submitted by Le Monde of France
March 19, 1984

East-West Relations

Q. The French head of state seems to be one of the Western leaders whose views regarding the East-West relations you most value. However, when the Socialists assumed power in 1981 and included Communists in the cabinet, your administration showed a clear apprehension. Is this concern now alleviated?

The President. Let me start by saying that you are right—President Mitterrand is one of the Western leaders whose views regarding East-West relations I value most. And despite differences in our political philosophies, there are a greater number of things we have in common. In particular, we find ourselves pursuing many mutually supportive national security policies. Our goals are congruent, because we are determined to bring about arms reductions and to get meaningful conversations going with the Soviet Union so that we can solve East-West problems. But the composition of the French Government is an internal French concern, and I don't feel that I should comment.

U.S.-Soviet Relations

Q. The U.S. welcomed Mr. Chernenko's first statements with some optimism. Does this feeling still prevail? Is it realistic to expect a resumption of the two Geneva negotiations and a summit meeting between yourself and Mr. Chernenko before November's elections?

The President. Clearly, words alone are not enough to bring about meaningful improvement in relations between our two countries. Dialog between the Soviet Union and the United States, if it is to have meaning, must lead to deeds—specific actions and changes in policy that address some of the basic issues between our two countries. For our part, we would welcome that opportunity. We are more than ready to meet the Soviets halfway if they are willing to do the same.

As in the Middle East, this will not be an easy process. Some of the rhetoric coming out of Moscow is less than encouraging. Nonetheless, I remain hopeful. Better relations are in the interest of both our peoples, and Mr. Chernenko will eventually have to acknowledge that the United States is not the intransigent party. We're ready and willing to talk, and if agreement can be reached, to act.

There is, for instance, no real reason why our negotiators should not be able to return immediately to the table in Geneva to continue discussion of nuclear arms reductions in both START and INF. We continue to urge the Soviets to do so.

As for a summit, I remain, as always, willing to meet with the leader of the Soviet Union to discuss a full range of issues. But I also believe—as the Soviets apparently do as well—that such a meeting would have to be carefully prepared in order to be useful and to have the prospect of meaningful results.

Q. In order to help resume the Geneva talks, would you be ready to consider merging the INF and START negotiations? In that case, can France and Europe expect the American stand on the Euromissiles to be as firm as on the question of the strategic armaments?

The President. As I indicated, we think the best way to make progress in reducing nuclear arms is for the Soviet Union to return to the INF and START talks. In both negotiations, we have made good proposals with built-in flexibility which the Soviets ought to explore. If they have serious ideas for other ways to resume talks, we will listen. The Soviets have never indicated an interest in merging the two negotiations.

Last year President Mitterrand, myself, and the other leaders of the Western democracies met at Williamsburg and reconfirmed our resolve to do what is necessary to preserve peace.

We agree on the absolute necessity of maintaining an effective nuclear deterrent and reestablishing a balance of power. We also agreed that pursuing fair, verifiable arms control agreements is of utmost importance. Any such arms control agreement must meet two standards: It must safeguard Western security, and it must reduce the risks of war. On this we are all agreed.

Atlantic Alliance

Q. Mr. President, several leading American political figures have recently urged Europe to assume a greater responsibility in Western defense. What is your position in this respect, and will you initiate a discussion of this matter with Mr. Mitterrand?

The President. The Atlantic alliance is healthy, its structure sound, and its strategy valid and viable. The strength and resilience of the alliance has most recently been demonstrated by the first initiation of INF deployments aimed at reestablishing the nuclear balance in Europe. The allies moved forward despite unprecedented Soviet threats and intimidation. Hopefully, they learned that negotiation will better serve their interests than trying to frighten the Western democracies into submission. I would hope all the Western allies would do more to strengthen their defenses. I'm pleased at the steps being taken in this

regard and hope that some day it will convince the Soviets that arms reduction agreements are the way to a better, more secure world.

As for the United States, our commitment to the defense of Europe remains steadfast. Indeed, we have taken and will continue to take steps to strengthen it. President Mitterrand and I have had numerous discussions about the Western defenses, and I applaud his courageous leadership, independent and strong sense of responsibility.

We'll be discussing this and a number of other significant issues, including the forthcoming economic summit in London, and international economic concerns this week.

The Middle East

Q. Yourself, as well as the highest ranking officials in your administration, have repeatedly warned that withdrawing the marines from Beirut under Syrian pressure would seriously jeopardize world peace, Western influence, and vital interests in the Middle East. Now that you have redeployed the marines on board American ships, how do you assess the situation in the region?

The President. The bloodshed in Lebanon and the continuing stalemate of the Arab-Israeli peace process remain a threat to the peace and stability of the Middle East and the world. It is in the interests of Arab nations, Israel, the United States, and for Europe as well to restore order in Lebanon and get on with the peace process. The United States, France, and the other nations which committed troops to the peacekeeping force in Lebanon have not given up even though longstanding hatreds prevented us from reaching our immediate goal.

The United States has three principal aims in the Middle East. First, we must continue to promote peace between Israel and her Arab neighbors. Second, we must prevent a widening of the conflict in the Persian Gulf, which might disrupt the flow of oil to the free world. Third, we must deter any Soviet threat to this vital and strategically important region. The conflicts in this region are numerous and intense. They are complicated by historical animosities and deadly power now in the hands of extremists and terrorists. Yet we must try to do what we can.

In the case of Lebanon, the United States will continue to pursue its long-term goals: the restoration of a sovereign, independent, unified nation; the removal of all foreign forces; and the security of Israel's northern border. Peace must be restored to this troubled land, and Lebanon itself must remain intact as one country. The partition of Lebanon would solve nothing and in the long run would led to even greater instability.

Our efforts to bring peace to Lebanon are something of which our countries can be proud. It is a humanitarian endeavor, taken at great risk. It reflects well on the character of the American and French people— and of Italians and British as well—that we would undertake risk and hardship for the people of a faraway land.

Q. Do you think that the September 1982 peace plan is likely to be accepted? And if so, where can you now find the necessary support to promote it?

The President. The positions contained in my September 1, 1982, peace initiative are the most realistic, workable, and promising approach to a just and lasting peace settlement between Israel and its neighbors. Furthermore, our proposal is the only one on the table. If there is a better plan, let's hear it.

The first step is direct negotiations among the parties in conflict based upon United Nations Security Council Resolutions 242 and 338. It is up to them. We can't walk that road for them. There is no possibility of progress on the many complex issues in the Middle East without talks. Nothing will be achieved by more fighting. Five wars in 36 years have proven that.

We remain ready to offer our support and assistance, to walk that road alongside those in conflict. However, only the effort and commitment of those directly involved bring real progress.

Nicaragua

Q. Under what precise terms and conditions would the American Government be prepared to ease the economic and military pressure it is now, directly or indirectly, exerting on the Nicaraguan authorities?

The President. The Government of Nicaragua is under considerable pressure to modify its aggressive foreign policy and repressive internal rule. The pressure comes not only from the U.S. but also from its neighbors, other Western countries, the regional negotiations of the Contadora group, and, of course, the armed and unarmed Nicaraguan opposition. The United States is deeply concerned about the continuing crisis in Central America, especially events in and around Nicaragua. Our objectives vis-a-vis that country are simple.

There should be an end to Nicaraguan support for insurgents attempting to overthrow the government of neighboring countries. We would like to see a severance of Nicaraguan military and security ties to Cuba and the Soviet bloc. A reduction of Nicaragua's military strength to levels that would restore military equilibrium in the area. Finally, there should be a fulfillment of the original Sandinista promise to support democratic pluralism.

These are legitimate concerns, and, as of yet, there is no convincing evidence that the Sandinistas are willing to address them. We have made our views known through private and public diplomacy, and we have made clear that we will respond in kind to meaningful, concrete steps taken by the Sandinistas.

Early on, the United States reached out in friendship to the new Government of Nicaragua, providing them large amounts of direct aid and assuring them of our good will. Nevertheless, for ideological reasons, the Sandinistas moved rapidly to establish a Marxist dictatorship, a militarized state closely tied to the Soviet Union and bent on undermining neighboring governments. This is unacceptable to the United States and other countries of the hemisphere.

El Salvador

Q. The State Department has until now considered Mr. D'Aubuisson as persona non grata in the United States apparently because of the strong presumptions of involvement with the death squads resting on him. In your opinion, what consequences would his election to the Salvadoran Presidency have?

The President. Normally, I wouldn't answer a hypothetical question like that.

But let me try to explain my government's position.

Our interest in the election is in the electoral process itself. The freedom of the Salvadoran people to choose their own leader is our basic concern. As far as the candidates, we are neutral and will respect the results of any free and fair election in which the people express their views. We do not base our relationships with other nations on personalities, but rather on their institutions and policies.

Our position on visits is consistent with this approach. In the closing days of the Salvadoran election campaign, we prefer that none of the Presidential candidates visit and bring the Salvadoran campaign to the United States.

We are deeply alarmed about political violence in El Salvador, from whatever source. It is tragic to note that the violent left, which opposes democracy in El Salvador, has escalated the level of bloodshed in an apparent effort to disrupt the March 25 election—something their leaders said they would not do. This violence from the left often does not receive the same attention in the world press as when such acts are committed by the violent right. But from whatever source, the United States wants to end the killing and to develop democratic institutions that will provide a peaceful means of settling disputes.

The United States has vital interests in Central America. Our objectives in the region are to reduce external influence and restore peace and stability through political, social, and economic reform. Much of what happens in the region hinges on what happens in El Salvador. A bipartisan commission from the United States endorsed a policy of ending hostilities in Central America through free elections, and that is our guiding principle—one that a democracy like France can well appreciate.

The urgency of promoting the democratic process and social justice in Central America will be one of many issues that President Mitterrand and I will discuss this week. I will be listening attentively to what President Mitterrand has to say on these matters. France is our oldest ally and a champion on liberty. We greatly value the warm relationship between our two countries—a relationship deeply rooted in a mutual respect for democratic traditions and humanitarian principles.

Presidential Campaign

Q. According to the polls, Mr. Hart would be for you a much stronger adversary than Mr. Mondale in the November's election. What is your own feeling on this question?

The President. Well, I think I can understand interest in a new face. But it's too early to really be naming a front runner in that race. Having gone through a series of primaries myself, I know they have a long way to go.

Anyway, I have always felt we should discuss our own record and not base our campaign on who the other fellow is or what he says. I think Americans will see the difference and make sound judgments about what's best for our country.

Note: As printed above, the questions and answers follow the text of the White House press release, which was released by the Office of the Press Secretary on March 21.

Interview With Midwest Regional Reporters on Foreign and Domestic Issues
March 20, 1984

Presidential Campaign

Q. Mr. President, a recent poll showed you beating Mondale among independent voters, but losing to Hart. Given the fact the independents possibly can be expected to decide the next election, why do you think that Hart has this advantage among independents at this time? And how do you propose to counter it, assuming he's the nominee?

The President. Oh, I think that we're seeing a contest that is going on over there and that is very much in people's minds, in the press and in the media, so that, as I've always said, I think polls are pertinent to when they're taken. And there've also been several polls that have shown the reverse—that I'm doing all right. So, I'm just going to wait for that poll that takes place next November.

Q. Do you care to tell us what the chief vulnerability seems to be for Hart and Mondale?

The President. No, I'd rather not comment on their problems. I enjoy watching it.

Q. Mr. President, next November you plan to win reelection, I know. I'm wondering whether you think the prize will be worth it. We're facing huge deficits, possibilities of tax increases. A second Reagan administration may not be able to come up with many new, exciting initiatives for the American people. Do you think it's going to be a terrible chore in the second term, or are you going to be able to excite the public somehow?

The President. Well, to a certain extent it's always quite a chore, but, no, one of the reasons why I would like to run is the job is unfinished. And I think we've made a tremendous start on getting things corrected that have needed correcting for decades. And it just isn't possible to get the job done in these few years.

Q. But will there be a possibility of any new initiatives when we're facing these kinds of problems—the deficits and the possibility of tax increases and so forth?

The President. Well——

Q. I mean, how do you start new programs if you don't have money to pay for them?

The President. Well, maybe if we continue on the course we're on, I am convinced that we will reduce the cost of government, certainly the rate of increase in government spending. We have already—we've about cut it in two, and we're doing the things that I think needed doing. We are bringing unemployment down at a faster rate than it's been brought down in more than 30 years. The growth in gross national product and productivity and retail sales—all of those economic indicators are up.

And, yes, it is going to take some time, but I'd like to recall to you that I said a couple of years ago that this wouldn't be done in months, and it wouldn't even be done in just a few years, that it was—it's been coming on for a half a century. And so, I foresee getting some of the things that we've been refused so far. We've only obtained about half of what we asked in changes in government spending. So, we'll keep on going for the other half.

Q. What are some of those things, Mr. President?

The President. Well, they're—I'll tell you, a great many of them would be found, and will be found, in the recommendations of the Grace commission. Almost 2,000 top leaders in every facet of our economy volunteered their services to take a look at government and take a look from the standpoint of whether modern business practices could improve things, improve the way of doing things. And they now have given us almost 2,500 recommendations. And we have a task force of our own now that is working on those to see—because many of them, the bulk of them, will take legislation.

Q. I meant in terms of new initiatives in a second Reagan administration, not the things that are needed to cut the deficit, but new programs, perhaps. Do you have anything like that in mind?

The President. Well, if there are new programs that'll be beneficial to the people and proper to employ, why yes, you'd go that way. But right now, I think a great deal of our problem is that government has attempted to do a great many things that aren't government's proper prerogative.

Q. Mr. President, are some of those things entitlement programs affecting the middle class? And will those be off limit in a second term——

The President. Now, I think that the entitlement programs have to be looked at structurally. And that's got to be a very careful study, because there is no way that I would ever support pulling the rug out from under people that are presently dependent on programs such as social security. And contrary to what some of our opponents have said of me, there has never been a time when I have advocated pulling that rug out. As a matter of fact, the average married couple on social security today is getting $180 a month more than they were getting when I took office.

But I think that looking at the demography, looking at the statistics with regard to workers, earners, retirement ages, and so forth, you have to look at programs of that kind as to whether they need restructuring for people just coming into the work force and who one day will be depending on those programs.

Federal Budget Deficits

Q. Mr. President, in that general context, the Democratic leaders in the House this afternoon reached tentative agreement on a plan for budget deficit reduction, and it's not too different from the one you supported ahead of them, except for $50 billion difference. And I wondered whether you could see any give between those two plans that might bring a mutual agreement between the Democrats on the House side——

The President. Well, this has always been my hope. We have to have, under the situation with a majority of one party in one House and the majority of the other in the second House—we have to have bipartisan programs. But I haven't seen or heard what it is they've come out with today or what they've come together on, and I'd like to see it and study it with regard to ours.

Edwin Meese III

Q. Mr. President, Minority Leader Byrd said the other day that Ed Meese will always have a cloud over him because of the allegations and charges that have come to light over the last few weeks in his nomination hearing. Why do you continue to back Mr. Meese, and do you want to have an Attorney General, should he be approved or sanctioned by the Senate, who, when people see him, may bring forth those thoughts that here's a guy who trades jobs for loans?

The President. Well, Gary, that charge— let me just remind you of something about our administration, and during the campaign, something that I said. This idea of

jobhunters that could be purchased or something—let me point out, I said that we were going to try to get people in our administration who didn't want or need a government job. And we've done pretty much that. And so, the situation is a little distorted with regard to that.

No, we have an investigation now that's going forward. Ed Meese has supported the idea. He wants it. And so, I can't comment on particulars now, because there is such an investigation, but I have complete confidence in him. I've known him for a great many years, and I think he'd make an excellent Attorney General.

Q. Well, you have confidence in him, Mr. President, but the perception, as Senator Mathias of Maryland said the other day, is one that could cause a problem, not only with the Senate but with the American people as well.

The President. Well, perception is something that's always present in government and in politics, and there are an awful lot of wrong perceptions about many things having to do with this administration. And I think when the truth is known and an investigation is completed, then I think the American people are very fair and they can make their judgment.

Q. Have you——

Q. So, you don't think—let me just finish up, Jerry. So, you don't think, then, that he should step aside or withdraw, or you wouldn't ask him to do that?

The President. No, no, because then there would be a cloud over him because he would no longer have the means or there would no longer be investigations or anything by which he could be cleared.

Q. Sir, has he offered to step aside?

The President. No——

Q. Mr. President——

The President. ——and I wouldn't listen if he did.

Q. Were you aware of these loans and transactions at the time you nominated him?

The President. What's that?

Q. Were you aware of these loans and transactions at the time you nominated him?

The President. No, I hadn't delved into

his personal life. I do know that, like so many others that came into these government jobs, I knew that he had to make some pretty great economic sacrifices to come here and work for the Government.

Q. In a general sense, Mr. President, does it concern you that there may be an appearance of possible impropriety in a situation where there are six instances where people—whatever the reasons were—where people who provided financial help to Meese did receive jobs in the administration? I'm not impugning any wrong motives to anybody, but there is that factual situation.

The President. I know, but as I answered a moment ago, I think someone should take a look and see what did they have to give up in order to take that government job. And most of the people in our administration had to give up a great deal.

Q. Well, Mr. President, it's more than just a paycheck with the government; it's a whole question of influence and being able to get on the inside, in government agencies and so forth. It's more than just giving up a high-paying job in private industry for another job in government. The perception—again, without impugning any motives—to some people is buying influence in the Government.

The President. I don't know. I just have to tell you that there are more people who actually are public spirited enough, believed enough in what we were trying to do that they wanted to be of help in that, than anyone is giving them credit for.

Q. You know, Mr. President, a related problem that occurs in situations like this is that the situation itself may, in the end, be damaging to the administration or the President, whoever he may be. A situation of that type occurred in President Carter's administration with his good friend, Bert Lance. And Lance eventually withdrew from his position as head of the budget bureau, but it had damaged the administration. Are you—is there any concern on your part that there is that prospect of——

The President. No. If I thought that there was anyone who, in our administration, who was doing something that was contrary to the public interest and the interest of the people, I'd be the first one to take action to

oust them. On the other hand, I've never been one that wanted to throw the baby out of the sleigh to the wolves in order to lighten the load.

El Salvador

Q. Mr. President, on another subject if I might—Secretary Shultz said today that we must accept the results of the Salvadoran election, whatever those might be. But realistically, do you think that Congress would sanction continued aid to a regime headed by this fellow D'Aubuisson, who's suspected of involvement in murder? And, secondly, do you have any message for those Salvadoran military leaders who are rumored to be thinking about a coup?

The President. Well, certainly I would not support the idea of a coup. We have a democratic government there, probably for the first time in 400 years, that has been doing its best to institute democracy and democratic principles, practices. And I'm not going to say a word now about anyone who is a candidate there, because I think that the United States—I want to be of help and I think we should be of help down there, but I don't think we should say anything that indicates that we are taking sides in this election. I don't think that's our place.

Farm Programs

Q. Mr. President, in much of rural America, farmers have been beset by large crop surpluses, depressed prices, increased competition from abroad; they've seen their neighbors facing bankruptcy; they've had trouble getting their own operating capital. I wonder, with that set of circumstances, why rural America should support you for another term.

The President. Now, I miss—you know something, there's a terrible thing about this room here, and even in spite of my hearing problems—with that dome. When you get out there toward the center—at the beginning, you're——

Q. Much of rural America today is——
The President. Oh, farmers.
Q. Yes.
The President. Ah. Well, there's no question but that in the cost-price squeeze, the

inflationary spiral, and the high interest rates that reached their peaks in 1980, the farmers were probably hurt worse than any other segment of our society. Their costs skyrocketed at the same time that, in all of the inflation, the prices they could obtain were going down. And then they had the embargo thrown at them, which was a serious blow to a large segment of our farm economy. On the other hand, the bankruptcies that some people are talking about today—last year there were 270,000 loans out to farmers, and less than one-half of 1 percent resulted in bankruptcies. So, I don't think that that is a major problem there.

What we've been able to do is, by bringing down inflation, reduce the however increasing cost of operation for them. By our PIK program, we, by eliminating a great deal of the surplus, we have increased prices for their products. The other—that surplus hung over them and was an artificial cap on them. We are going to be—the Department of Agriculture is going to be lending some $4.6 billion this year in help to the farmers. We have now eliminated the embargo, opened up foreign trade for them. The new long-term agreement with the Soviets calls for 50 percent more than had been in the agreement.

So, the farmer will be the slowest in coming back—but is coming back, and there is improvement out there in the agribusiness.

Q. You're asking them to stay the course with you?

The President. Yes.

Q. Things will get better?

The President. Yes, they are getting better, and they are better.

Arms Sales to Jordan

Q. Mr. President, why do you insist that the sale of the Stinger planes go through to Jordan in light of what King Hussein said this past weekend and in light of what Secretary of State Shultz has said in the last couple of days? Are you still hanging in there for that sale, or are you willing to pull it back?

The President. Well, let me just say, I'm not going to talk about details of it other than to say that the whole basis for peace in the Middle East, and the thing that we

tried to help bring about and are going to continue to try and help bring about, is dependent on being fair and evenhanded in dealing with the moderate Arab States that I think also want peace—Israel, and we know our relationship with Israel and what it has always been and will continue to be. And we can't appear to be one-sided. Jordan—and King Hussein had the courage to participate and make himself available for the peace efforts, and he is in a position in which there was some risk entailed with the border that he has with Syria. And, therefore, I think that it is only fair. And if we don't make available the things that he needs for his own security, he's going to find them someplace else.

Q. Could I——

Q. Sir——

Q. Can I follow up on that, Mr. President?

The President. Yeah.

Q. One of the most damaging things— charges, though, it seems to me, that King Hussein made was to, in effect, say that your administration and some previous ones as well have not been honest brokers in the Middle East. How do you respond to that?

The President. Well, I read what he said in the interview, but then I also saw him on television last Sunday. And I thought that there was a sort of withdrawal from some of what had been cited as more extreme statements. But I do know this: We've had a friendship, and I think he and his country are essential to peace in the Middle East. And we're not going to give up that goal very lightly.

Superfund Program

Q. Mr. President, last week EPA Administrator Ruckelshaus said that, while in principle the administration supports reauthorizing Superfund, nothing would be done until after the election. I'm wondering why the delay, and can people in towns that are contaminated with various chemicals like dioxin, such as Times Beach, be assured that there will be government help?

The President. Well, I don't know of anyone here that thinks that the Superfund is going to await the taking place of an election. Bill Ruckelshaus had made it plain to me that he's determined to carry on with that program.

Q. So, there will be—is there a plan or a deadline when the administration plans to come out and say at what level you will reauthorize Superfund?

The President. Well, you caught me a little short on this one. Things have been going along over there—and very well—and I know that he's been establishing himself and getting these programs into operation. And so, I just don't know the basis for the question there, whether there's some——

Mr. Speakes.[1] Mr. President, I'm not familiar with it either. I think we'll have to check into it——

The President. Yeah.

Mr. Speakes. ——and get back to you then, because I don't—I'm not——

The President. Yeah.

Mr. Speakes. ——even familiar with Ruckelshaus' statement.

Q. Thank you.

Presidential Campaign

Q. Mr. President, have you given any thought to your campaign yet—I mean, whether you'll campaign differently against Mr. Mondale and Mr. Hart, should one or the other be the nominee?

The President. No, I don't think it'll make much difference who the other fellow is. I've always preferred campaigning on the basis of what we've done and what we intend to do, looking to the future with positive, new ideas.

Q. Who would you sooner face?

The President. What?

Q. Who would you sooner face?

The President. I won't answer that. I'm not going to help them out. [*Laughter*] They're going to have to make that choice themselves.

Q. "Looking to the future with positive, new ideas" sounds like Gary Hart.

The President. What? It did?

Q. Do you—[*laughter*]——

The President. I don't know.

Q. Do you envision a run against him more than Mondale at this point?

---

[1]*Larry M. Speakes, Principal Deputy Press Secretary to the President.*

The President. No, I was just talking—that my idea of a campaign is to give the balance sheet on what we've done, what we've accomplished, and what we intend to do if given the opportunity to go forward on this. And I think we've got a lot of things to be proud of, things that are drastically different. Very few of you have realized that for the last 3 years, unlike the last 50, there haven't been arguments going on in Washington about whether or not and what to spend additional money on. The arguments have been on where do we cut.

Q. Mr. President, you've called—to follow up with another political question, if I may—you've called Mondale, "Vice President Malaise" in the past, I believe. And if it's fair—I wonder if it is fair to blame him for the mistakes of the Carter administration, and if so, are there any mistakes in your administration that you'd attribute to George Bush?

The President. [*Laughing*] No, and believe me, George has been a working partner in this administration. I think probably more so than most other Vice Presidents that I can recall.

I don't recall actually tying his name to that. I have talked about that—all that talk of malaise back at a time when they were trying to explain our economic problems as being blamed on the people.

Q. He was the suspect target, I guess, of your——

The President. Oh, well, no, I haven't been targeting anyone. I've been talking about—we came here with a whole policy of government that we inherited: that had been on one path of growth in government, constant increasing of the amount of earnings that we took away from the people for government, government doing more and more things—and many of them that were not government's proper province. And we set out to streamline this somewhat. We set out to give the economy a chance and give the people a chance out there. And I think it's worked.

We have the greatest decline in unemployment in more than 30 years. I believe we have an economic improvement that is—it's on a solid basis and not just a temporary quick fix, an artificial stimulant, which has been characteristic of seven previous recessions since World War II.

I'm proud of what we've done with regard to the military. We have the highest percentage of high school graduates in our military today than we have ever had in the history of this country, and that includes back when we had the draft, which was an all-encompassing sweep that took in everybody. We have 91 percent of our personnel out there—are high school graduates. And there's a morale, there's a readiness that I think is something the people of this county have every reason and right to be proud of.

Domestic Programs

Q. Mr. President, I've often wondered, we see the charge made very often, and usually by opponents of yours, that your administration is the administration of the wealthy, that you don't have much sensitivity for poor folks, for minorities, and so forth. I'm sure you're familiar with all these charges; they've been made over and over again. I was just curious as to how does that make you feel? I mean, what do you feel about that? Does that disturb you, does that bother you, does that——

The President. It frustrates me, yes. And it is a part of what Gary was talking about a little while ago. It's a perception, and it's a perception that is based absolutely on falsehoods. We can turn to any area of the society we want to, and we will find out that none of those things are true.

Was reducing 12½-percent inflation and bringing it down to around 3 percent—was that more beneficial to the rich than it was to the lower income person who had to spend the bulk of his income, didn't have any to put aside? A fellow in 1979 that was making $5,000 a year, which would leave him pretty poor, by the end of 1980—in just those 2 years, his $5,000 would only buy what $4,000 would have bought before simply because of inflation.

We tripled the taxes in the decade or so before we got here. The personal earnings—well, let me give a figure, not just personal earnings. In the last several years before we got here, there were three increases in the grants to people on the program Aid for Dependent Children, and at the end of the three increases they were

poorer and had less purchasing power than they had before the increases went into effect—because of inflation. And, of course, the increase in taxes, as I say, well, they doubled in the last 4 or 5 years before we came here.

Q. But the priority was cutting government spending, was cutting programs. The administration wasn't saying, "We want to go out and help all these people." I mean it was——

The President. No, but we did——

Q. The emphasis——

The President. All right.

Q. Maybe the perception is because of the emphasis.

The President. Well, wait a minute. Here's what we did. Many of those programs had become so encrusted, the administration so big, that the Federal Government was paying a tremendous fee for every dollar that it delivered to a needy person. The things we were trying to cut was not the dollar to the needy person; it was the sometimes $2 it took to deliver that to him.

On the other hand, we also found people in these programs that had no justification for being there. When people were earning above 150 percent of the poverty level, as much as up to 180 percent, and still being declared eligible for these programs, we felt something had to be done. And we redirected those programs toward those who were truly needy. And today, we are feeding more people; we are taking care of more people; we are funding more students going to college than ever before in our history.

We are giving more food stamps to more people than we were ever giving in our history. And yet we got 800-and-some thousand people off of food stamps. But we increased the number—total number that were getting food stamps. But the 800,000 or more—it was around 860,000—those people were of an income that was above a level in which their neighbors should have been contributing to their welfare.

Q. I don't want to—but you say it frustrates you, and there has to be a way to counter this, to change it. How would you go about changing this perception?

The President. Well, I'm hopeful. As the campaign goes on, we'll tell the truth. And you see, so far, it's just been a constant drumbeat from the other side, the fairness issue, and that somehow our tax program benefited the rich, not those at the lower level of income. And yet the very people saying this have been fighting and fighting to get us to cancel indexing. Well, if you canceled indexing, the penalty for canceling it would run about 2-percent increase in taxes for the person at $100,000. It would be a 9-percent increase for the person at $10,000. Now, does that make us the administration of the wealthy or the rich?

The truth of the matter is in everything from college loans to grant programs to food stamps, we took programs that were benefiting people who really should not be dependent on government, and we redirected that money to the people of true need. And actually, with all of this supposed cuts in budgets, no, all we've done—all we've been able to do is reduce the rate of increase in spending. We're spending more. We're just not spending as much more.

And if we had stuck to the budgets of our predecessor, his—you know, how you have to project now under the law several years ahead—if we had stuck to his projected budgets, today's deficit would be $191 billion more than it is.

Q. There are 3 or 4 million more people below the poverty level now according to the Census Bureau's figures than there were when you took office. How does that——

The President. Not than when we took office. The recent survey that was widely touted was from 1979 to 1982.

Q. '82, right.

The President. Well, 1982 we'd just started—because when you take office in 1981, you take office inheriting the budget already in place and the programs already in place from your predecessor.

Now, our program for economic recovery had just begun in 1982 to be phased in, but we had that great further dip in the 1970 and '80 recession in July of 1981. Not one bit of our program was in place when that big fall into 10.8-percent unemployment and so forth, when that took place. So, of course, there are more people in poverty in

that particular year. But the decline—or the increase, I should say, in the number of people living in poverty that began back in '79 and '80—we weren't even here yet. And in '81 we were here, but as I say, the budget and the programs were already in place. So, it is frustrating to try and answer all these.

What I'm going to be interested in seeing is where is the—what is the number of people living in poverty in 1983 once the recovery was underway. The truth is, if they wanted to even go back farther, back in the sixties, the early sixties, we had fewer people living below the poverty line than we had in the later sixties after the great war on poverty got underway. And there has been from that moment on a steady increase in the level of poverty right on up to the figures that were used—the 1979, '82 figures.

Mr. Speakes. We've got time for one more. Take Jerry.

Federal Budget Deficit

Q. Thank you. Mr. President, could I ask a question on the deficit? You've proposed a downpayment on the deficit, but that still would leave you with pretty large budget deficits——

The President. Yeah.

Q. ——and I wonder if the choices on a second downpayment aren't going to become more difficult. Business Week magazine has proposed, and I wonder if you could react to their suggestions on how to reduce the deficit—I found them interesting—that some cuts in social security and medicare, which would be sensitive; slowing the defense buildup, which you'd rather not do; slashing farm supports, which could be politically dangerous; cutting State and city aid some more; cutting Federal pensions and raising taxes on the middle class. Do you reject all of those, or do you——

The President. [*Laughing*] Quite a few of them, yes, I do, quite a few. Now, we have, part of our own proposal is a freeze on farm payments, as you know. But that was because the 1981 farm bill, when it was passed, was based on what they had projected would be a much higher inflation rate. And so, we're spending in the farm program several times more than we should have been spending.

No, what I said, this is a downpayment, because the structural changes, the things such as the Grace commission, their recommendations, these are going to take really bipartisan approach and study, because these are—your deficit was made up of half recession and half structural; that structural thing was built in. That was the automatic increases that just took place, as every year went by; and the Congress didn't have to increase them, they were there.

Now, we need structural reform. The recovery has already had some reductions of our own estimates of the deficit. As you know, last summer we were estimating above $200 billion, and suddenly it is down sizably more than that—down around 180. That is the recovery that's doing that. Now, that will continue as the recovery continues—I've got to stop saying recovery. Some of the leading economists in the country have contacted me and said I should no longer use that word, because we're beyond recovery; we are now into expansion. So, the expansion will continue.

But the structural part will remain a threat until we deal with it. And this is where, as I say, I think that we, not only in those commission reports but everything else—we must look at structural reforms that can be made that will leave government doing what government is intended to do—for example, some of the savings that we made, by way of things we call block grants.

As Governor I came here knowing that in California the categorical grants, where the Federal Government gave the State of California x amount of money for a certain program, and then told us right down to the smallest "t" how we could use that money and what must be done with it. Well, it didn't meet our priorities. Maybe it met the next State's priorities, but ours were different, and then someone else's were different. And so, I came here conceiving this idea of let's put the money for general purpose in block grants and turn them over to the States and localities, and give them the ability to administer these as they know they will be most efficient. And this allowed—there again, the money that was

being saved in reducing these amounts—was the administrative overhead that was being eliminated. And we must do more of this.

Even when a mayor tells you that a program with regard to transportation for the handicapped, the way the government, the Federal Government, forced it on him—so costly that he, he could have sent taxicabs for every handicapped person that needed transportation and been money ahead—if he'd been allowed to do that. It wouldn't have cost as much as it did doing it the way the Federal Government said they had to do it.

So, these are the type of structural reforms that are just waiting to be implemented.

Q. In the second administration?

The President. What?

Q. In a second Reagan administration?

The President. Yes.

School Prayer Amendment

Q. Are you going to get a prayer amendment in the second administration?

The President. I'm going to try. And here again——

Q. We didn't ask you about that. Could you just tell us——

The President. What?

Q. The prayer amendment in the Senate—the defeat in the Senate——

The President. Well, we got a majority. A majority were for it, but we didn't get the two-thirds. But here again, could I take advantage of you—I know Larry says we're through—let me take advantage of you, though, for one thing. And maybe the media in some ways has helped with this—certainly in the editorial pages.

I've talked to Senators, and who voted against this—and so caused its not getting the two-thirds—and was amazed to find that their reason for voting against it was they felt that they were voting against where government was going to mandate school prayer on the schools. And there was nothing of the kind. That isn't what we had before the Supreme Court decision.

When I was going to six elementary—different elementary schools in 8 years, because my father moved around so much—

and it was taken for granted that there was no ban on prayer in schools. But we didn't have concerted prayer. Oh, I can remember a few times when some classmate was ill or some student's mother was very ill, and the teacher might say, "Let's all pray for the recovery," so-forth, things of that kind.

All the amendment we proposed would do would be to say, if the schools want to, that's up to them. It's permitted. The Constitution does not deny them the right. What we did specify was that, no, they couldn't write a prayer, and, no, they couldn't dictate a specific prayer or dictate a method of doing this. They didn't have to do it at all if they didn't want to—and many of the schools, as I say, that I attended didn't, other than in occasions of this kind. And for Senators who are up there in the debate to be so convinced that what they were voting against was an order, a mandate on the schools—we just wanted to give the authority back to the schools to do what they wanted to do.

Q. They missed the boat.

The President. So, we'll try to make it more—

Q. They missed the boat?

The President. What?

Q. They missed the boat?

The President. They just didn't understand it. And we got the majority vote this afternoon, but it wasn't a two-thirds, so—a constitutional amendment requires the two-thirds.

Q. Thank you, Mr. President.

Q. Thank you.

The President. All right.

Q. We didn't have those problems in my school. We prayed all the time—it was Catholic. [*Laughter*]

The President. Well, yes.

Note: The interview began at 4:45 p.m. in the Oval Office at the White House. Participating in the interview were Jerry Watson of the Chicago Sun-Times, Gary Schuster of the Detroit News, Andrew Miller of the Kansas City Star, Frank Aukofer of the Milwaukee Journal, David Phelps of the Minneapolis Tribune, Paul Bedar of the St. Louis Globe-Democrat, and Tom Ottenad of the St. Louis Post-Dispatch.

The transcript of the interview was released by the Office of the Press Secretary on March 21.

Remarks to the Senate Republican Caucus on the Budget Deficit
March 21, 1984

I have to explain something, confess to something, here, that I came around to the wrong side here where I was supposed to sit, and was directed over to this side, but coming in this short aisle, I realized that if I came directly this way, I had to turn left. [*Laughter*] So, I did it backward.

But I've come here and asked for permission to talk to you this morning—and I appreciate this opportunity—on the so-called downpayment that we have come together on, some of your colleagues and ourselves, and the importance of it.

As you know, in the State of the Union Address, I had asked for a possibility of a bipartisan group from both Houses of the Congress that we could get together, and

without polarizing or making it an election issue, that we could come to an agreement on a downpayment—called a downpayment because we realize that there is nothing that we can do, right now and in this short span, to completely resolve the ongoing deficit problem. But that doesn't mean there aren't things that we can do over the long range, looking to a date possible when we will have a balanced budget. And that's why I continue to hope that we can convince everyone of the need for a constitutional amendment that will make a balanced budget mandatory.

It seemed that we couldn't get the cooperation we sought in trying to come to that bipartisan position. So, with your leadership—Howard Baker, Ted Stevens, and John Tower, and Pete Domenici, and Bob Dole, Mark Hatfield, Jake Garn, and Paul Laxalt—we did, in a series of meetings, move to and come to agreement on this plan which would call for $43 billion over a 3-year period in savings in the domestic side of the budget, $57 billion in budget authority in the defense budget, and $48 billion in increased revenues, but without a tax increase as to rates. We believe that there are loopholes, there are provisions in the tax law that, in some instances, say, are unfair generally, or some can take advantage—unintended advantage of them. And in looking at these, we believe that this sum of money was possible.

Now, we know that there are others. Your colleagues on the other side of the aisle, who want—or profess to want—a reduction of the deficit, but they would put the major emphasis on defense and increasing taxes and increasing tax rates.

We believe that this is a good package. Let me just say that—I have to say that I believe the cuts that we're proposing in defense will mean a slowdown in what we're trying to accomplish. But I don't believe it's unacceptable—that it isn't enough to overcome the need for us to deal with this deficit problem.

Now, I know that we're hearing all sorts of things about the deficit, and I think it's wonderful that suddenly after all these 40-odd years in which our opponents had the majority in both Houses of the Congress, and during which time we virtually without exception had deficits, literally as a matter of policy—that they have now decided that we should share and that the deficits are ours. Well, we don't want them. So, what we're going to try to do is get rid of them.

I think that as an issue, it's going to be rather difficult for those who have, as I say, participated deliberately in a policy of deficit spending that accounted for virtually a trillion dollars in national debt before we got here, to now turn around and say to those of us who have been asking for reductions in spending in these last 3 years—and have only gotten about half of what we asked for—to now say that we are responsible for these, when, at the same time, we are the ones who are asking for a balanced

budget amendment, and they are the ones who are resisting that.

But I do hope that we can be bipartisan to the extent that there will be well-meaning legislators on the other side of the aisle who see the necessity for getting this downpayment. And then, as I indicated a moment ago, that there is further distance to go—then I believe that we must seriously study the structural changes that have to be made in government in order to come to that day of balanced budget.

About half of the deficit, this vastly increased deficit, came about because of the added dip in the recession that took place in July of 1981—10.8-percent unemployment and so forth. The other half was structural. Now, the half that was due to the deficit [recession] is going away. It's going away because I have been hearing from some very noted economists who have contacted me on their own to tell me I should stop calling it an economic recovery. They said we have passed the recovery stage; we are now in economic expansion. And some of the figures certainly bear that out—the most recent one, the flash estimate 7.2 percent for this quarter of growth in the gross national product; what has been happening with unemployment.

I just received some figures yesterday. The automobile industry, which was in such dire straits when we came here in 1981, has added some 83,000 more employees working today in the automobile industry than were working in 1981 in that industry when we came here. Their rate in the industry now of unemployment is 5.9 percent, which is well below the 7.1 percent national average. But there are figures—all of these things—the retail sales, the personal income, the housing starts—everything indicates this recovery that we're having. So, that part, that half of the deficit is being taken care of.

It is up to us now to face up to the structural, built-in causes of deficit and look toward a long-term change in that structure to where we can have government under control. Now, I know we want to run and say, "Stop the presses" or "I have a story that'll crack this town wide open" or something if I say what I'm going to say, and I will, and that is: I've dug in my heels on taxes. I want you to know that if—first of all and this third part of the downpayment, the $150 billion downpayment—the $48 billion in added revenue—if an effort is made and is successful enough to reach my desk, that attempts, first of all, to get that without keeping the promise for the spending cuts, I will veto. I will veto also if there's an effort made to increase rates.

But I will say at the same time, if when we have finally brought government down to the percentage of the gross national product that government is taking, and we believe ourselves and can honestly say this is the minimum—this is as far as we can go, and this is now the cost of government if we're to do the things that are required of us—and if that figure then is still above the percentage of gross national product we're taking in revenues, then I would be the first one to say we would have to adjust to meet this standard of government. I happen to believe that there's a good chance that will not be necessary if we do what we should do with regard to shrinking the cost of government.

So, I think I've covered the point here, except that I believe, in this year particularly, it is absolutely essential that we appear as—the group of us, your leadership and ourselves—that we appear united in our determination to get this package and stand together. And I think it will benefit all of us very much in every way. It will not only be good government; it will be good politics.

So, I know that we're going to have a chance to visit a little bit, so I'll sit down. I've said enough.

Note: The President spoke at 11:24 a.m. in the Old Senate Chamber of the Capitol.

Remarks to the House Republican Caucus on the Budget Deficit
March 21, 1984

The President. Well, Jack and Bob, I want to thank you very much for this opportunity and making it possible. I've come down here to talk to you about our $150 billion downpayment and try and—if I can—express the importance that we place on it, how essential I think it is that we all stand together in this particular time. And I would like to commend at the same time, Bob Michel, Trent Lott, and Silvio Conte and Barber Conable and Del Latta, and their colleagues in the Senate for our coming together as we have on this $150 billion downpayment—working together. And we did have consensus on this.

I think we have to remember with all that's going on where we were 3 years ago: the inflation rates, the interest rates, the economy that had faltered so badly. Everyone seemed to think that when the bottom kind of fell out a little further in July of 1981, that that was the recession. They're forgetting a little bit that some of us campaigned in 1980 in areas where employment—unemployment, was over 20 per-

cent. I remember being castigated by some because I referred to the situation then as a depression, not a recession. And when they took me on and said that technically it wasn't, if you will remember, I said that a recession is when your neighbor's out of work, and a depression is when you're out of work. And there were a lot of the people I was talking to who were out of work.

But I promise you that in this we're not going to play politics with the economy, and we're not going to take risks with our national security in what we do with regard to the defense budget. But today, the change that has come about in these 3 years, I've had some letters recently from well-known, nationally known economists who have criticized me for continuing to refer to what we have today as an economic recovery. They said, "We are past recovery. This is economic expansion."

Well, the latest figures for this quarter are 7.2-percent growth in the gross national product. There has never been a recovery in the seven preceding recessions since

World War II of that level. But at the same time, I don't think it's overheated. And I think it's a solid one because it has been based on solid practices. It hasn't been a quick fix with flooding the money market and artificial stimulants of spending programs and which we know seven times previously resulted in another and worse recession just 2 or 3 years after the one that we had come out of.

Our package calls for $43 billion in domestic savings. It calls for $57 billion in defense savings. This is in authority—I'm not talking, now, the outlays; I'm talking the budget authority. And it calls for $48 billion in increased revenues. Now let me hasten to say this does not represent a tax rate increase. This is finding provisions in the tax laws and some loopholes which we would be justified in closing even if there were no deficit to be handled.

But this is a downpayment, $150 billion over 3 years, at the same time that the Treasury Department is going forward with a study on how we might be able to simplify and broaden the tax base, and even be possible to reduce the rates at the same time; a tax program that possibly could catch that $100 billion in revenue that is now being denied us and that is legitimate revenue because it is people who actually owe the tax and are not paying it at all.

I will tell you now that if anyone sends to me the tax package of this $150 [billion] and has not given us at the same time the spending cuts, I will veto the tax package.

Now, we believe that all these things are possible. But we also believe that then, with the Grace commission reports that we have—and, incidentally, some of those Grace commission recommendations are responsible for some of the cuts that are in here, including in defense. As a matter of fact, Cap Weinberger and his team cut $16 billion out of their proposed budget—some of it was Grace commission findings that they found could be utilized—before he delivered the first budget to us, and which our group now—the Republican group of Representatives, Senators, and we of the administration—he had cut that much, and then we further reduced that, but with his—he was a part of the negotiations, and he agreed that we could do it. Now, we have

to say it does slow, somewhat, what we think is necessary for national security, but not to the point of an unavoidable—or to a risk that we can't take. It is not that much of a risk and with the necessity of getting control of the deficit.

Now, let me, if I can, just touch on something else with this deficit since it seems to be becoming a campaign issue already. And I'm a little astounded at how far out on a limb some of our opponents have gotten with this campaign use of the deficit. Because are we to forget that for more than 40 years they have dominated both Houses of the Congress, and for more than 40 years, deficit spending has been a deliberate part of their policy? How many of you, when you tried to protest, heard in the past that we didn't have to worry about the national debt, we owed it to ourselves?—and that deficit spending was necessary, and a little inflation was good for us, also; it maintained prosperity? And those of us who kept saying, "It will one day catch us, and the bottom will fall out," well, it has happened.

Now, about half the deficit, the estimated big deficits, were the result of that further dip, plus what had gone before in the economy, because half of the deficit is cyclical. Now, that is the part that is shrinking right now. The other half is structural, and you and I know it. It was built into government policy. You didn't have to each year increase spending or anything, it was automatic. And it'll be automatic and keep on going unless we do something about it.

So, once this downpayment gets in place, that doesn't mean we're finished. No. We're going to go to work. And I hope it'll be a bipartisan study of what can be done to make the structural changes that must be made to let us control deficits and deficit spending.

How can they claim that we are the ones that seemingly want deficit spending, when for 2 years we've been asking for a constitutional amendment to prohibit deficit spending by the Federal Government, require a balanced budget, and they are the ones who are opposed to it? Now, I still believe that we should have that amendment to the Constitution. Granted, we would have to point to a year of implementation that we could foresee with what we could legitimately do without causing chaos and disruption in bringing government spending down to the level of government revenues. And that we will proceed with.

And with the 2,500 recommendations of the Grace commission—they will be a part of our study, what we're going to try to do. But let me just point out some things. Recently, the figures were thrown at us that poverty has increased. And the period they chose to say that it increased was from 1979 to 1982. Well, we weren't here until 1981, and in 1981 we were still using their budget and their spending policies because you come in in the midst of a fiscal year.

The truth of the matter is we started an increase in the number of people living in poverty back in the late sixties and early seventies when the Great Society, the War on Poverty actually was implemented and got underway. And rather than decreasing poverty, it increased the number of people that were declared in poverty.

Nineteen seventy-four—and many of you participated in it—there was a budget process that was passed for us to get control of the budget. And from 1974 when that was passed until 1981, the deficits totaled $560 billion, on top of the almost—well, that made the almost trillion dollars that was here when we came.

Now, I'm saying all of this to you, and I know that you agree because——

Q. Mr. President, the mike has gone off.

The President. What?

Q. Did somebody touch the mike out there? I think somebody touched the microphone.

The President. You mean this went off?

Q. Yes. Is it back on?

The President. Well, I'll just talk louder, in case—there it is! [*Laughter*] All right.

Well, again, I think if we all stick together and if we recognize that we're not being unfair, that we're feeding more people today who are hungry than have ever been fed, we're providing more food stamps, we are sending more young people to college— 40 percent of the people going to college today are going there with the aid of Federal grants, loans, and so forth. In other words, all of this talk about fairness and unfairness, they who want to cancel—as an

aid to curing the deficit—want to cancel the tax indexing—and they say that would be fair—well, maybe you'd be interested in knowing that we figured out what would happen.

The tax penalty in canceling the index would only amount to 2 percent additional tax for people at $100,000 a year. It would amount to a 9-percent tax increase for people at $10,000 a year. If you're already in the upper brackets, indexing doesn't do anything for you.

We're trying to help the people that are down there. The cuts that we've made in many of the social programs have been cuts in administrative overhead. I came here with the knowledge, as previously having been a Governor, that there were a number of the social reforms here in which it cost the Federal Government $2 to deliver $1 to a needy person. And these are the things that—where we have been trying to cut and trying to bring some sense into government. And it's what we're continuing to try to do.

More people are getting food stamps today than have ever gotten them. But there are 860,000 people who were getting them that are not getting them because we found they morally had no right to them. Their income was above 150 percent of poverty.

So, we've got a story to tell, and I hope that we'll get out there and tell it to all of the people in this campaign. And it's a story in which 12.4-percent interest—or inflation rates, are not fair to people at the bottom of the economic ladder. But I think that—not completely out of it, but 3 percent, and right now, only around 4-percent rates are a little more fair than 12.4. And this is what we've been achieving here.

We have a solid recovery on its way. Let me just give you a couple more figures. I know I've gone over my time here, and I have to let you go, but let me just tell you that the automobile industry, the industry as a whole now has 83,000 more people working than were working in that industry when we came here in 1981. Their unemployment rate, believe it or not, in that industry is now only 5.9 percent, as contrasted to the general average of 7.1.

We could go on with the figures of that kind, of the housing starts, with the fact that on the cyclical part of the deficit, the further help that we're going to be—that in the last 15 months, we've put 4,900,000 more people into jobs in this country. Now, that hasn't had time to have, really, the impact—only the first ones for the first year—but from here on, to have almost 5 million more people, many of them no longer wards of the government, not getting unemployment insurance and food stamps and things of that kind, but working and paying taxes, we can see that the cyclical part of the deficit is being taken care of.

When we, last August, told you that it looked like the deficit was going to be a little over $200 billion, and now it comes down to about 185—do you know how that happened? We couldn't even project back then what the recovery was going to be, and then we found out that we got $15 billion more in tax revenues from the reduced rates than we had anticipated just a short a time ago as August to January.

So, if we will stick together on that other part—the structural reforms that are needed—I think we'll find it's not only good government, it's good politics.

Thank you very much.

Note: The President spoke at 12:05 p.m. in the Foreign Affairs Committee Room of the Rayburn House Office Building.

In his opening remarks, the President referred to Representatives Jack F. Kemp of New York and Robert H. Michel of Illinois.

Nomination of Robert Thomas Hennemeyer To Be United States Ambassador to The Gambia
March 21, 1984

The President today announced his intention to nominate Robert Thomas Hennemeyer, of Illinois, a career member of the Senior Foreign Service, Class of Minister-Counselor, as Ambassador to the Republic of The Gambia. He would succeed Larry Gordon Piper.

Mr. Hennemeyer served in the United States Army in 1944–1946. He was an instructor in the Chicago city high schools and Junior College in Chicago, IL, in 1948–1952. In 1952 he entered the Foreign Service as program officer, Division of Exchange of Persons, in the Department. He was Director of the United States Information Centers in Bremen (1952–1953), and principal officer in Bremerhaven (1953–1954). In 1954 he was Assistant United States Secretary to the Allied General Secretariat of the Allied High Commission in Bonn and economic officer in Munich in 1954–1958. In the Department he was Assistant Chief of Protocol (1958) and desk officer in the Bureau of African Affairs (1958–1960). In 1960–1961 he attended African area studies at Oxford University. He was deputy chief of mission in Dar es Salaam in 1961–1964 and faculty adviser at the Naval Academy in 1964–1965. In the Department he was Director of the Functional Personnel Program (1966–1967) and Special Assistant to the Director General of the Foreign Service (1967–1968). He was chief of the political section in Oslo (1968–1971) and consul general in Dusseldorf (1971–1975). In 1975–1976 he attended the senior seminar on foreign policy at the Foreign Service Institute, and was Senior Deputy Assistant Secretary of State for Consular Affairs in the Department in 1976–1978. He was consul general in Munich in 1978–1980. In the Department he was Senior Inspector (1981), Executive Director, in the Office of the Under Secretary for Management (1981–1983), and Executive Assistant to the Under Secretary of State for Management (1983–1984).

Mr. Hennemeyer graduated from the University of Chicago (Ph.B., 1947; M.A., 1950). His foreign language is German. He was born December 1, 1925, in Chicago, IL.

Nomination of Patricia A. Goldman To Be a Member of the National Transportation Safety Board
March 21, 1984

The President today announced his intention to nominate Patricia A. Goldman to be a member of the National Transportation Safety Board for the term expiring December 31, 1988. This is a reappointment.

Ms. Goldman was a member of the National Transportation Safety Board in 1979–1983 and served as Vice Chairman in 1982–1983. Previously she was executive director of the House Wednesday Group in 1971–1979. In 1964–1972 she served as a research assistant to the Joint Economic Committee of the Congress and later as legislative assistant on the Ad Hoc Subcommittee on the War on Poverty of the Education and Labor Committee of the U.S. House of Representatives. She also served as research consultant to the U.S. Chamber of Commerce and as director of the manpower and poverty programs of that organization. In 1971 she was legislative counsel for the National League of Cities and for the U.S. Conference of Mayors.

She graduated from Goucher College (B.A., 1964). She is married and resides in Washington, DC. She was born March 22, 1942, in Newton, NJ.

Proclamation 5166—National Single Parent Day, 1984
March 21, 1984

By the President of the United States of America

A Proclamation

Before they are eighteen, about half of our Nation's children will have lived part of their lives with a single parent who strives to fill the role of both mother and father.

Many single parents in America are making valiant efforts on behalf of their children under trying circumstances. Whether it is a deserted spouse forced to work and care for children simultaneously, or a spouse who is not receiving child support that has been awarded by a court, or an unwed mother who has bravely foregone the all-too-available option of abortion, or a widow or widower, single parents deserve our recognition and appreciation for their demonstrated dedication to their young.

At the same time, we should also recognize the vital and ongoing role a large percentage of non-custodial parents play in the nurturing process of their offspring. Their sacrifices, devotion, and concern reflect the bonds of caring for those they have brought into this world.

Single parents can and do provide children with the financial, physical, emotional, and social support they need to take their places as productive and mature citizens. With the active interest and support of friends, relatives, and local communities, they can do even more to raise their children in the best possible environment.

The Congress, by H.J. Res. 200, has designated March 21, 1984, as "National Single Parent Day" and has requested the President to issue a proclamation in observance of that day.

Now, Therefore, I, Ronald Reagan, President of the United States of America, do hereby proclaim March 21, 1984, as National Single Parent Day. I call on the people of the United States to recognize the contributions single parents are making, sometimes under great hardships, to the lives of their children, and I ask that they volunteer their help, privately or through community organizations, to single parents who seek it to meet their aspirations for their children.

In Witness Whereof, I have hereunto set my hand this twenty-first day of March, in the year of our Lord nineteen hundred and eighty-four, and of the Independence of the United States of America the two hundred and eighth.

RONALD REAGAN

[*Filed with the Office of the Federal Register, 11:13 a.m., March 22, 1984*]

Remarks at the Welcoming Ceremony for President François Mitterrand of France
March 22, 1984

President Reagan. Mr. President, Madame Mitterrand, Mr. Foreign Minister, and distinguished guests:

Nancy and I are pleased and honored to greet you and Madame Mitterrand. We welcome you as a head of state who has demonstrated courage and decisiveness in the face of international challenges that test the character of Western leadership. We welcome you, also, as the representative of the French people for whom all Americans share a special affection.

We look out over the White House grounds, and we see evidence that the bond between us is deep and has stood the tests of time. There in the distance is the Jefferson Memorial, a tribute to America's third President, a founder of our republic, an intellectual whose ideas were profoundly influenced by his exposure to French philosophy and culture. It is not mere coincidence that this giant of American freedom was one of our first representatives to France.

Mr. President, millions of people throughout the world admire and respect your country's historic legacy. Today, under your leadership, France continues to be a major contributor to world stability and peace. In this cause, we stand together as two peoples who cherish liberty and two peoples committed to humane and civilized values.

Ours is not an easy task. As you have astutely noted: "Peace, like liberty, is never given, and the pursuit of both is a continual one."

In Lebanon, we Americans are proud that we're part of a peacekeeping force working together at great risk to restore peace and stability to that troubled land. We will always remember that in this gallant and humanitarian effort we stood shoulder to shoulder with your brave countrymen.

Our nations, two great world powers, have responsibilities far beyond our own borders. Your influence is a force for good in the Middle East. You have drawn a line against aggression in Chad, and you've extended assistance to other African nations seeking to preserve their security and better the lives of their peoples. These are but a few examples of the constructive global role that France is playing.

Mr. President, the American people applaud you and the people of France for your diligence and your courage.

President Mitterrand, you come here fresh from a European Community summit meeting in Brussels. At this meeting and elsewhere you exerted your leadership as an advocate of greater European unity. I am most eager to discuss with you our bilateral concerns and also those economic, social, and political issues of significance to Europe as a whole. America continues to support a strong and united Europe. The European democracies are, through the North Atlantic alliance, anchoring the mutual defense of our common freedom. Today, as in years past, our own liberty relies heavily on the good will and shared sense of purpose among those people in the world who enjoy freedom. Victor Hugo's words still ring true. "It is through fraternity," he said, "that liberty is saved." Clearly, Mr. President, if those who love liberty stand together strong in resolve, freedom will not only survive, it will prevail.

Symbolic of our friendship, this summer America will greet the first contingent of French experts coming to New York to aid in the restoration of the Statue of Liberty.

This year we will begin celebrating the centennial of that lady of light. That magnificent gift, a beacon of liberty for all mankind, is a lasting reminder of that precious heritage that we, the French and American people, share.

Mr. President, I'm pleased that your visit will include travel to parts of America that, as President of France, you have not yet been able to visit. You've already seen a good part of our east coast, especially the tidewater section of Virginia which you visited during the celebration of the French and American alliance at Yorktown, and again when we met with summit colleagues at Williamsburg.

This week you will go further south to the dynamic city of Atlanta; later, north to Pittsburgh. Then you will also journey to America's heartland, the Midwest, the farm country, for a firsthand look at American agriculture. And you will travel to the American west coast and visit our home State of California. There, innovations in energy and electronics, spurred by tax incentives that reward personal initiative and risk-taking, are paving the road to the 21st century and a new era of high technology.

It's comforting to know that no matter what changes technology brings to our way of living, the good will between our peoples will remain solid and lasting. America is delighted that you have set this week aside to be with us as a friend.

During your visit to Washington, Nancy and I look forward to deepening our personal relationship with you and Madame Mitterrand and with your colleagues. We offer you a warm welcome and our best wishes for a rewarding and memorable visit.

President Mitterrand. Mr. President, Madame, ladies and gentlemen:

My visit today is taking place between two anniversaries—that of the Treaties of Versailles in Paris last September, and the anniversary of the Allied landings in Normandy in 2 months time. Now, I may say that this is perhaps a case where chance has been on our side, but I think that there is more than this. There is something symbolic. And, in fact, there is no such thing as chance in the history of peoples of the world. There is, however, something that is called destiny. And our destiny is indeed a common destiny.

And so, I think it is natural that my first thoughts should go to the Americans and the French, brothers in arms, who from Yorktown all the way through the ages to Beirut have, in fact, shed their blood together. And history shows that these sacrifices have never been made in vain, because their purpose was not to conquer nor to achieve power, but to defend freedom.

Now, despite all this, perhaps our two peoples do not yet know each other well enough. And so there is sometimes, shall we say, room for certain uncertainties. Now, after having had conversations with yourself, Mr. President, I will have the opportunity of spending 5 days traveling through the country in order to see again places that I've learned to know in the last 38 years since my first visit to this country, but also to get a better understanding of the dynamic qualities of the country, the great diversity of the United States, its culture and its modernness.

But my ambition is also to show you—during my visit and during our conversations on world affairs and the affairs that concern our two countries—I want you to see the true picture of France: France, which is, all right, a country of tradition, but is also a country of economic and technological power that is looking towards the future; and France that is preparing herself with determination for the world of the future that the next few years are going to bring to us; France, which is a constant ally that can be counted upon and which intends to bring her own original contribution to the quest for peace and the pursuit or the resumption of development, because relations between our two countries obviously cannot only be a matter of celebrating our glorious past.

Our main concern in 1984 must surely be the question of security in Europe and relations between the East and the West and also between the North and South, which we'll be talking about.

And here the firm and clear orientations that I have given to French diplomacy are known to yourself and to your administration and to our friends throughout the world and based on the basic idea of unfailing loyalty to our friends and the concept of the balance of forces worldwide and in Europe. Firmness and determination are indispensable qualities, but they must go together with keeping the dialog open, particularly with the Eastern bloc.

Now, France is strong, independent, and sure of herself and, therefore, is willing and prepared and determined to dialog with everyone on all subjects. And France, sure of her own citizens, is, as I say, open within her means to a discussion on all matters while being always loyal to her friends. But there are other important tasks that we have to tackle jointly and which are essential for the balance and the equilibrium of the world.

Now, it is true, we recognize that the upturn, the economic circumstances in the United States and the presence of American diplomacy worldwide—all this creates favorable conditions for a recovery of world affairs in all sense of the term. And it is true that the serious dangers that were threatening the international financial system last year have been able to be met. But our efforts must never be relinquished in such areas.

And yet, despite all this that we have achieved, I think the main task is still ahead of us. We must consolidate what has been achieved, which is still fragile. We must push back the frontiers of poverty, which remain in so many regions of the world the true, the genuine roots of war. And we must guard ourselves against too much indifference—any indifference towards the Third World, in particular. We must remember that the Third World is in the same universe, although in difficult condi-

tions, as ourselves. And what will happen, the future of the Third World is something that of course depends on them, but also on us.

So you appreciate, Mr. President, that we have so many tasks to perform together. I don't think, though, it is likely that our friendship will have much opportunity of remaining idle for very long. We have numerous tasks to perform.

Now, Mr. President, Madame, I am really happy to be here, in front of the White House, in this city of Washington, in this garden, in these places which mean so very much to all of us. For you and I this will be another of our meetings, and we have always been able to communicate among each other concerning our plans and projects. And it is my earnest wish that this visit should establish yet closer ties of friendship and fraternity between us, because I think that that would be the best way of ensuring even speedier progress towards that region of the heart, perhaps, where liberty exists. We're moving in that direction, but we still have some road to follow.

Now, Mr. President, how can I end these remarks, these first remarks that I'm making here on American soil? Well, I wish to say to all those who are here, all those who are present all over the United States, I wish to extend, and in English, my warmest greetings to the great American people.

Note: President Reagan spoke at 10:12 a.m. on the South Lawn of the White House, where President Mitterrand was accorded a formal welcome with full military honors. President Mitterrand spoke in French, and his remarks were translated by an interpreter.

Following the ceremony, the two Presidents met in the Oval Office. They then went to the Cabinet Room for a meeting with U.S. and French officials.

Statement on the Nomination of Edwin Meese III To Be Attorney General of the United States
March 22, 1984

I support Ed Meese's request to the Attorney General for the appointment of an independent counsel. I know that an impartial, prompt, and thorough inquiry will demonstrate the high level of integrity and dedication which have marked Ed's long career of public service. I will not withdraw his nomination for the position of Attorney General.

He has been my trusted colleague for 17 years. He will remain as my Counsellor to the President until confirmed. I am confi-

dent that the results of an independent inquiry will permit the Senate to confirm rapidly his nomination.

Note: On the same day, Mr. Meese sent a letter to Attorney General William French Smith requesting that the Attorney General recommend the appointment of an independent counsel to investigate the allegations raised before the Senate Judiciary Committee which relate to Mr. Meese.

Proclamation 5167—National Social Work Month, 1984
March 22, 1984

By the President of the United States of America

A Proclamation

It is appropriate that Americans express our appreciation to the many thousands of dedicated men and women in all parts of our Nation who have devoted their lives to helping those in need. For more than a century, social workers have been committed to the betterment and general welfare of all our society. They have helped implement social services with creativity, resourcefulness, and true professionalism.

It is within our local communities that the real contribution to the welfare of our citizens is made. Those closest to the problem—the social workers in State and local governments, area agencies, and private and voluntary organizations—are usually the most qualified persons to decide what help is needed and the best way to provide it. In this way, they carry on and enhance our proud American heritage of neighbors helping neighbors, and people helping

people.

In recognition of the many contributions of the social work profession to the welfare of our society, the Congress, by Senate Joint Resolution 112, has authorized and requested the President to proclaim the month of March 1984, as "National Social Work Month."

Now, Therefore, I, Ronald Reagan, President of the United States of America, do hereby proclaim the month of March 1984, as National Social Work Month. I ask all our citizens to join in this recognition and to search their hearts for ways in which they too can help their fellow Americans.

In Witness Whereof, I have hereunto set my hand this twenty-second day of March, in the year of our Lord nineteen hundred and eighty-four, and of the Independence of the United States of America the two hundred and eighth.

RONALD REAGAN

[Filed with the Office of the Federal Register, 4:29 p.m., March 22, 1984]

Proclamation 5168—National Safe Boating Week, 1984
March 22, 1984

By the President of the United States of America

A Proclamation

Americans increasingly look to the water for recreation and relaxation. This year, approximately one-quarter of us will enjoy boating in one or more of its many and varied forms. Therefore, it is important that all those involved in recreational boating observe proper safety practices, know and obey rules of safe boating, and show courtesy and consideration on the water.

In addition, all boaters should wear personal flotation devices while on the water. Seventy-five percent of those who died in boating accidents last year might have been saved had they worn these devices, according to United States Coast Guard instructions.

The theme of this year's "National Safe Boating Week" emphasizes the dangers of combining alcohol consumption with boat operation. The use of alcohol and other intoxicating substances is a major factor in boating accidents and fatalities. Boat operators who drink impair their ability to recognize and react to hazards and thereby endanger not only themselves but also others on the water. The use of even small amounts of alcohol can significantly reduce an operator's judgment and boat handling skills. This is particularly true as fatigue caused by sun, glare, noise, wind, and boat motion intensifies the effects of alcohol. Through the observance of "National Safe Boating Week, 1984," Americans should be alerted to these dangers.

In recognition of the need for boating safety, the Congress enacted the joint resolution of June 4, 1958 (36 U.S.C. 161), as amended, authorizing and requesting the President to proclaim annually the week commencing on the first Sunday in June as National Safe Boating Week.

Now, Therefore, I, Ronald Reagan, President of the United States of America, do hereby proclaim the week beginning June 3, 1984, as National Safe Boating Week.

I also invite the Governors of the States, Puerto Rico, the Northern Mariana Islands, the Virgin Islands, Guam, and American Samoa, and the Mayor of the District of Columbia to provide for the observance of this week.

In Witness Whereof, I have hereunto set my hand this twenty-second day of March in the year of our Lord nineteen hundred and eighty-four, and of the Independence of the United States of America the two hundred and eighth.

RONALD REAGAN

[*Filed with the Office of the Federal Register, 4:30 p.m., March 22, 1984*]

Toasts of President Reagan and President François Mitterrand of France at the State Dinner
March 22, 1984

President Reagan. Mr. President, Madame Mitterrand, Mr. Foreign Minister, honored guests, ladies and gentlemen:

Our evening together has rekindled some pleasant memories of warm June nights in the beautiful gardens of Versailles, of observing the colorful and moving commemoration of the union of French and American forces at Yorktown, of the many distinguished world leaders at Williamsburg just last year. Soon, I look forward to bringing home yet another memory in which President Mitterrand will be a major part.

We will meet later this year to commemorate the anniversary of the landing of Allied Forces on the Normandy beaches 40 years ago. That event tied the hearts of our people, and for all time sent a message to tyrants that free men are all citizens of the same land.

Mr. President, your visit to America this week is yet another milestone in the common heritage and close association of our two freedom-loving nations. France was America's first ally. The trust and confidence which have characterized our long relationship is undoubtedly an object of great envy throughout the world. France and America share many traditions. We have innumerable ties, cherished by our people, nurtured by our governments.

Foremost among our ties is a profound commitment to democracy and liberty, a heritage inscribed in the Constitution of both our countries. These values lie at the heart of the Atlantic alliance. And this commitment between the great democracies of Europe and North America has preserved peace for a longer period than any [other] in modern European history.

Tonight I would like to reemphasize that the United States remains thoroughly committed to the Western alliance and to the defense of Europe. We seek peace and security, and to that end, America also strives to achieve greater East-West dialog. We will continue to work for a more stable relationship with the Soviet Union—one that will lead to better understanding and a relaxing of existing tensions.

This evening, while savoring the memories of Lafayette and Rochambeau, of Jefferson and Franklin, we must also salute those contemporary figures who personify the richness of the bonds between us. I'm struck by how many of our guests here tonight share close ties to France and to French culture. Both our nations can be proud of our citizens whose work and creativity have contributed so much to the quality of our lives and who are recognized on both sides of the Atlantic.

We share strong links of culture and commerce. We engage in extensive scientific cooperation. And every day, we reap the harvest of social, cultural, and educational interchanges.

I'm particularly pleased that France and the United States are engaging in two new endeavors—an artists exchange program and a cooperation in environmental affairs. These agreements will greatly contribute to the cultural and scientific enrichment of our societies.

Mr. President, today we had a frank discussion of bilateral issues and also of those concerns of the European Community as a whole. And such dialog between us can only serve the interests of both our countries. In the years ahead, Americans and Frenchmen will be as they always have been—proud and independent, but united together in the cause of freedom, security, and economic progress. All Americans are grateful for your friendship and appreciate the courageous stands France has taken throughout the world in the cause of liberty.

When you return to your country, please take that message of our gratitude and admiration with you. In the meantime, we wish you a pleasant and worthwhile visit to the United States.

So, let us raise now a glass to the common purpose and the special friendship of France and the United States, and of President François Mitterrand and his lovely wife, Danielle, our guests and our friends.

President Mitterrand. Mr. President, Madame, ladies and gentlemen, dear friends:

The President of the United States has just used two words. He said that our meetings were pleasant and fruitful, and I think that no better words could be chosen.

Pleasant, our meetings have been, since this morning when we first got together from the very first moment. Thanks to yourself, Mr. President, and your wife, and all those who have contributed to make our visit so pleasant, we have enjoyed the warmest possible hospitality. And I'm speaking on behalf of myself and Mrs. Mitterrand and those accompanying me. At the same time, we have been able to engage in serious conversation, but in a climate of friendship. And you have been, I think, particularly, if I may say so, nice to France, and this is particularly due to you, Mr. President, and to you, Madame. You're responsible for this—for the warmth of our reception—and I want to thank you.

Now, I hope also that our meetings will

prove to be fruitful. We have, in fact, already started discussing a number of aspects of the life of this world we live in, and sometimes those aspects are somewhat tragic and, at any rate, dramatic. We have talked about war. We have tried to find ways of overcoming and preventing war and how it can be possible, perhaps, to develop the machinery to ensure that thing that is so difficult to achieve and is so mysterious, perhaps—peace.

We have, perhaps, not yet found the secret of the key to peace, but we are craftsmen working on the job, and we are looking and we are seeking for the secret and for the key. And I think our work will prove to be fruitful because, in any case, it is always fruitful and useful to compare the assessments of the world situation of two countries who are united by friendship, and such friendship that has existed for so long, for so many years, that it becomes just a natural way of life. And I think that that is the right way to talk together and, indeed, to do good work together.

Now we have reached the end of the day and not the least pleasant moment of this very pleasant day. We have reached a moment of rest and a pleasant moment of relaxation; at the same time, a rich and useful conversation which, at the same time, carries with it the great pleasure, the warmth of just being together and, for a moment, forgetting perhaps the requirements of our official ties and existence.

And yet the paradox is that this is still a state visit, as the diplomats call it, because President Reagan has invited the President of the French Republic. But all the same, tonight for a few hours we have perhaps been able to shed the mantle—the somewhat heavy mantle of protocol and official ties and relations which we will, of course, resume very seriously tomorrow. But for the moment, we have a few hours just to live our life, and to live our life in a pleasant environment and, also, in a few moments, in an artistic environment.

Now, I will not recall here all the moments of our common history that, of course, come to mind—the people, the events that have led our two nations throughout the years and centuries of history to the situation that we are in today in this world of turmoil, where the United States and France have managed to stay linked together, closely tied and united, and for the important things have always been able to work together for peace and for the defense of a few simple principles that do not need complex explanations, but which are merely the very essence of our civilization.

And so I wish to thank you, Mr. President, and you, Madame, for the exceptional warmth and quality of the way you have received us here today and particularly tonight, and I want to thank you on behalf of my country, on behalf of France. Life—everyday life is not always particularly easy. Washington and Paris—well, there is some distance between them, naturally. And we do not always—our eyes are not always turned in exactly the same direction. And that, in a way, is perfectly natural, in view of the fact that we aren't sitting in the same place. But when it is necessary, you are present and we are present. And we know that. You know it, and we know it. And that, I think, is the best assurance that when we are gone, our successors will be able to say that that friendship which was struck up at the end of the 18th century stood well the test of time until the end of the 20th century, and then, as far as the future is concerned, well, that will be their problem.

But I think that I would like to close, Mr. President, by raising my glass. And I would like to drink to your health, Mr. President. You are responsible for a great country whose tremendous diversity reflects so much charm and strength. And to you, Madame, to your own health, to the health of your family. And to you, ladies and gentlemen, I want to drink to your health and to your life, your work, and your hopes. In other words, your life, to coin a phrase. And I hope that your life will be a long and prosperous one. In other words, what I'm saying is that I'm raising my glass to the American people so admirably represented here tonight.

Thank you.

Note: President Reagan spoke at 9:50 p.m. in the State Dining Room at the White

House. President Mitterrand spoke in French, and his remarks were translated by an interpreter.

On the following day, the two Presidents held a breakfast meeting in the Blue Room at the White House.

Executive Order 12468—Presidential Advisory Council on the Peace Corps
March 22, 1984

By the authority vested in me as President by the Constitution and statutes of the United States, including the Federal Advisory Committee Act, as amended (5 U.S.C. App. I), it is hereby ordered as follows:

Section 1. Establishment. (a) There is established the Presidential Advisory Council on the Peace Corps.

(b) The Council shall be composed of no more than 15 persons, who shall be appointed by the President. The President shall designate a member to serve as Chairman of the Council and a member to serve as Vice Chairman. Members shall serve at the pleasure of the President.

Sec. 2. Functions (a) The Council shall advise the President and the Director of the Peace Corps on initiatives needed to promote the purposes of the Peace Corps Act and actions of the Peace Corps which do so.

(b) The Council shall submit simultaneously to the President and the Director of the Peace Corps an annual report on its review of Peace Corps activities, its recommendations concerning those activities, and the activities of the Council.

Sec. 3. Administration. (a) The heads of the Executive agencies shall, to the extent permitted by law, provide the Council with such information as may be necessary for the effective performance of its functions.

(b) Members of the Council shall not receive compensation for their work on the Council. While engaged in the work of the Council, members may be allowed travel expenses, including per diem in lieu of subsistence, as authorized by law for persons serving intermittently in the government service (5 U.S.C. 5701–5707).

(c) The Director of the Peace Corps shall, to the extent permitted by law and subject to the availability of funds, provide the Council with such administrative services, funds, facilities, and other support services as may be necessary for the effective performance of its functions.

Sec. 4. General Provisions. (a) Notwithstanding the provisions of any other Executive Order, the functions of the President under the Federal Advisory Committee Act which are applicable to the Council, except that of reporting annually to the Congress, shall be performed by the Director of the Peace Corps, in accordance with guidelines and procedures established by the Administrator of General Services.

(b) The Council shall terminate two years from the date of this Order, unless sooner extended.

RONALD REAGAN

The White House,
March 22, 1984.

[Filed with the Office of the Federal Register, 11:18 a.m., March 23, 1984]

Note: The text of the Executive order was released by the Office of the Press Secretary on March 23.

Proclamation 5169—Loyalty Day, 1984
March 22, 1984

By the President of the United States of America

A Proclamation

As Americans, we enjoy a rich heritage of freedom. How fortunate we are that the founders of this great country were committed to the ideal that all people share inalienable rights to life, liberty, and the pursuit of happiness. This ideal has been the inspiration for many generations of Americans in the building of what is today the greatest and most prosperous Nation in the world.

The people of the United States cherish their liberties and recognize that our freedoms of conscience and action are at the heart of the unique American tradition. To preserve this great tradition, it is important for us all to pause from time to time to rededicate ourselves to the democratic ideals which have served us so well.

For this purpose, the Congress, by joint resolution approved July 18, 1958 (72 Stat. 369, 36 U.S.C. 162), has designated May 1 of each year as Loyalty Day, a day for the reaffirmation of loyalty to the United States of America and for the recognition of the heritage of American Freedom.

Now, Therefore, I, Ronald Reagan, President of the United States of America, do hereby proclaim May 1, 1984, as Loyalty Day and call upon all Americans and patriotic, civic, and educational organizations to observe that day with appropriate ceremonies. I also call upon all government officials to display the flag of the United States on all government buildings and grounds on that day.

In Witness Whereof, I have hereunto set my hand this 22nd day of March, in the year of our Lord nineteen hundred and eighty-four, and of the Independence of the United States of America the two hundred and eighth.

RONALD REAGAN

[*Filed with the Office of the Federal Register, 11:38 a.m., March 23, 1984*]

Note: The text of the proclamation was released by the Office of the Press Secretary on March 23.

Letter to Mrs. Clarence M. Mitchell, Jr., on the Death of Her Husband
March 22, 1984

Dear Mrs. Mitchell:

Nancy and I were very sorry to learn of the death of your husband. Clarence Mitchell was without any doubt one of the most effective and respected men in Washington during his long career as a leading advocate for the NAACP.

The civil rights revolution that began in the '50s has been one of the most dramatic and beneficial events of our time. It would be hard to name anyone who made a larger contribution to the success of that revolution than your husband. His victories did not often gain him headlines, but his patient, behind-the-scenes effort shaped all the important civil rights legislation of that era. He changed the world we live in more rapidly and completely than perhaps even he imagined possible.

Although he faced great difficulties and experienced many disappointments in his battle, Clarence Mitchell himself was respected by all sides because of his idealism, generosity and goodwill. The nation truly shares your grief at his passing.

Nancy and I send our deepest sympathy to you and your family on this sad occasion. We are thinking of you and will keep you in

our prayers.
Sincerely,

RONALD REAGAN

[Mrs. Clarence M. Mitchell, Jr., 1324 Druid Hill Avenue, Baltimore, Maryland 21217]

Note: The text of the letter was made available by the Office of the Press Secretary on

March 23. On the same day, the White House announced that the President had asked Lee Verstandig, Assistant to the President for Intergovernmental Affairs, to represent the administration at funeral services for Mr. Mitchell. Mr. Verstandig delivered the President's letter of condolence to Mrs. Mitchell on March 23, the date of the services.

Nomination of Michael Hayden Armacost To Be an Under Secretary of State
March 23, 1984

The President today announced his intention to nominate Michael Hayden Armacost, a career member of the Senior Foreign Service, Class of Minister-Counselor, as Under Secretary of State for Political Affairs. He would succeed Lawrence S. Eagleburger.

Mr. Armacost has served as Ambassador to the Philippines since 1982. From 1980 to 1982, he was Deputy Assistant Secretary of State for East Asian and Pacific Affairs. In 1978–1980 he served as Deputy Assistant Secretary of Defense, and in 1977–1978 he was senior staff member for East Asia at the National Security Council. In 1972–1974 he was special assistant to the Ambassador to Japan in Tokyo. He was a member of the Policy Planning Staff at the Department of State in 1969–1972 and in 1974–1977.

Mr. Armacost was a lecturer at Georgetown University (1971–1972) and at Johns

Hopkins University (1970–1971). In 1968–1969 he was visiting professor of international relations at the International Christian University in Tokyo, Japan. He was assistant professor of government (1965–1968) and instructor in government (1962–1965) at Pomona College in Claremont, CA.

Included among his awards are the State Department's Superior Honor Award and the Department of Defense Distinguished Civilian Service Award. His distinguished academic career includes publications and commentaries on national security and foreign affairs. He is a member of the Council on Foreign Relations.

Mr. Armacost graduated from Carleton College (B.A., 1958) and Columbia University (M.A., 1961; Ph.D., 1965). He is married, has three children, and resides in Bethesda, MD. He was born April 15, 1937, in Cleveland, OH.

Nomination of Stephen Warren Bosworth To Be United States Ambassador to the Philippines
March 23, 1984

The President today announced his intention to nominate Stephen Warren Bosworth, of Michigan, as Ambassador to the Republic of the Philippines. He would succeed Michael Hayden Armacost.

Mr. Bosworth entered the Foreign Serv-

ice in 1961 and was principal officer in Panama from 1962 to 1964. He was Panama desk officer in the Department (1964–1967), economic officer in Madrid (1967–1971), and chief of the economic policy unit in Paris (1971–1973). From 1973 to 1974, he was an international economist at the Continental Illinois Bank under the auspices of the White House Executive Interchange Program. In the Department, he was Director of the Office of Fuels and Energy, Bureau of Economic and Business Affairs (1974–1976); and Deputy Assistant Secretary of State for International Energy, Raw Materials and Food Policy (1976–1979). He was Ambassador to the Republic of Tunisia from 1979 to 1981. In the Department he

was Senior Deputy Assistant Secretary of State in the Bureau of Inter-American Affairs from July 1981 to December 1982. Since December 1982 he has been chairman of the Policy Planning Council.

Mr. Bosworth received his A.B. in 1961 from Dartmouth College. He attended George Washington University from 1965 to 1967. His foreign languages are Spanish and French. He was born December 4, 1939, in Grand Rapids, MI.

Announcement Concerning Licensing and Enforcement Procedures Under the Export Administration Act
March 23, 1984

The President has recently made a number of decisions relating to the export control program under the Export Administration Act (EAA) to ensure that there is an appropriate balance between national security and export interests.

First, he has decided to grant Defense authority in principle to participate in the Commerce Department's review of distribution licenses that permit multiple shipments of goods to non-Communist countries. This review will be carried out in a phased manner and will depend on successful implementation of a Memorandum of Understanding between Defense and Commerce for Defense review of individual validated licenses for East-West trade for selected countries and commodities.

Second, the President has also determined that a dual capability to enforce export controls should be maintained in that both the Commerce and Treasury Departments bring important, complementary assets to this important problem. The President has also directed that the two Departments vigorously implement the January 16, 1984, Memorandum of Understanding which designates Customs as the agency responsible for liaison with foreign governments in the conduct of export enforcement investigations, with certain specific exceptions. In addition, the two agencies are to engage in a process of more complete information sharing.

Finally, the President reaffirmed his opposition to any statutory change relating to Defense review of licensing and to EAA enforcement. As Congress prepares for its conference on the export administration bills, the President hopes that the conferees will work towards developing a bill that maintains an appropriate balance between national security and export interests.

KEY ELEMENTS OF PRESIDENT'S DECISION ON DOD LICENSING REVIEW AND EAA ENFORCEMENT

DOD Licensing Review Decision

• The President affirmed the Memorandum of Understanding (MOU) that has been reached between DOD and Commerce on individual validated licenses, providing for Defense review of license applications for 12 countries and 7 commodity groups.

• The President has decided to grant Defense authority in principle to review distribution licenses.

• At the same time, the President has indicated that the greatest possible care must be taken to establish review arrangements that are efficient and not disruptive to the review process.

• The Defense review of distribution licenses will be carried out in a phased manner and will depend on successful implementation of the MOU on individual validated licenses.

411

• An NSC-chaired Monitoring Committee will be established immediately to set forth criteria to assure administrative efficiency in implementing the MOU and to assure that it is satisfactorily administered.

• Within 3 months of successful implementation of the MOU on validated licenses, the Monitoring Committee will recommend a plan and schedule for Defense review of a few carefully preselected commodity lines for one or two countries.

• After successful completion of the initial phase of distribution licensing review, the Committee will make recommendations for a gradual broadening of Defense review.

EAA Enforcement Issue Decision

• The President has determined that Commerce and Treasury bring important, complementary assets to the enforcement problem and that a dual enforcement capability should continue.

• The President has directed vigorous implementation of the January 16, 1984, Memorandum of Understanding (MOU) reached on EAA enforcement between Commerce and Treasury. This designates Customs as the lead agency responsible for liaison with foreign governments in cases under investigation, except for Austria, Belgium, India, Japan, Sweden, and Turkey, where the trade ministries are responsible for enforcing export controls.

• The President has instructed that both Commerce and Treasury engage in a process of more complete information sharing.

• A special monitoring group chaired by NSC will be established to review implementation.

Statutory Change to Existing Law

• The President reaffirmed his opposition to any statutory change relating to Defense review of licensing and to EAA enforcement.

• The President views with great concern efforts to radically curtail Presidential authority and discretion in the management and administration of export controls.

Current Law:

Defense Review of Licensing

Under Section 10(g) of the current EAA, Defense can review all applications for licenses to export goods or technology to any country to which exports are controlled for national security purposes. In general, only license applications for Warsaw Pact countries and the People's Republic of China have been referred to Defense. However, the EAA does not prohibit Defense review of any license application which may be referred from Commerce. The question of expanding Defense review to include shipments to non-Communist destinations results from concerns that tightened controls over direct exports to Communist countries have increased the incentive to divert shipments through friendly countries.

Enforcement

General authority for enforcement is given to any department or agency exercising functions under the EAA. The Department of Commerce has had the basic authority for EAA enforcement since 1949. The Secretary of Commerce, by regulation, has historically authorized the Customs Service (Treasury) to exercise certain enforcement-related functions.

Definition of Terms:

Individual Validated Licenses

Authorize individual shipments, and are used to control exports to Warsaw Pact countries and exports of sensitive items elsewhere.

Distribution Licenses

Authorize multiple shipments of a broad range of commodities for reliable exports to approved overseas consignees in non-Communist countries.

Radio Address to the Nation on Central America
March 24, 1984

My fellow Americans:

Tomorrow is an historic day for the beleaguered nation of El Salvador. Scores of international observers will watch as the people of El Salvador risk their lives to exercise a right we take for granted—the right to vote for their President.

This right of choice is not something that is common in all of Central America. It contrasts sharply, for example, with Nicaragua, where the Sandinistas staged a revolution in 1979 promising free elections, freedom of the press, freedom of religion. Despite these promises, the Sandinistas have consistently broken their word, and the elections that they've announced for November seemed designed only to consolidate their control.

Unlike El Salvador, the Nicaraguans don't want international oversight of their campaign and elections. When the members of the National Bipartisan Commission on Central America visited Nicaragua, the Sandinista dictators briefed them with Soviet intelligence and said the U.S. is the source of all evil.

In El Salvador the members heard appreciation for our country's efforts to promote peace, democracy, and development. El Salvador is an emerging democracy plagued by a Communist insurgency and human rights abuses which must stop, but a nation which is strongly pro-American and struggling to make self-government succeed.

Nicaragua is a Communist dictatorship armed to the teeth, tied to Cuba and the Soviet Union, which oppresses its people and threatens its neighbors.

The stability of our Latin friends—indeed, the security of our own borders—depends upon which type of society prevails—the imperfect democracy seeking to improve, or the Communist dictatorship seeking to expand.

The Bipartisan Commission warned that new Communist regimes could be expected to fall into the same pattern as Nicaragua; namely, expand their armed forces, bring in large numbers of Cuban and Soviet bloc advisers, and increase the repression of their own people and the subversion of their neighbors. And the Commission warned that a rising tide of communism would likely produce refugees, perhaps millions of them, many of whom would flee to the United States.

Now, these tragic events are not written in stone, but they will happen if we do nothing or even too little. Based on the recommendations of the Commission, I sent the Congress in February a proposal to encourage Democratic institutions, improve living conditions, and help our friends in Central America resist Communist threats. Three-fourths of our request is for economic and humanitarian assistance.

And that brings me to an important point: The people who argue that the root of violence and instability is poverty, not communism, are ignoring the obvious. But all the economic aid in the world won't be worth a dime if Communist guerrillas are determined and have the freedom to terrorize and to burn, bomb, and destroy everything from bridges and industries to power and transportation systems. So, in addition to economic and humanitarian assistance, we must also provide adequate levels of security assistance to permit our friends to protect themselves from Cuban and Soviet supported subversion.

Military assistance is crucial right now to El Salvador. The Salvadoran people repudiated the guerrillas when they last voted in 1982, but continued Soviet-Cuban-Nicaraguan support for the guerrillas, combined with the failure of our Congress to provide the level of military aid I've requested, have put El Salvador in an extremely vulnerable position. The guerrillas have been seizing the identification cards that allow citizens to vote. One of El Salvador's principal guerrilla commanders has pledged an all-out effort to disrupt the elections. And, should there be a need for an election runoff in late April or May, these same guerrillas, who have already assassinated elected congressmen in El Salvador, will do everything they can to disrupt that election as well.

We're looking at an emergency situation. So, I've asked Congress to provide immediate security assistance for El Salvador while the comprehensive bipartisan legislation makes its way through the Congress over the next several months.

This is the moment of truth. There is no time to lose. If the Congress acts responsibly, while the cost is still not great, then democracy in Central America will have a chance. If the Congress refuses to act, the cost will be far greater. The enemies of democracy will intensify their violence, more lives will be lost, and real danger will come closer and closer to our shores. This is no time for partisan politics.

Until next week, thanks for listening. God bless you.

Note: The President spoke at 12:06 p.m. from the Oval Office at the White House.

Remarks at the Presentation Ceremony for the Presidential Medal of Freedom
March 26, 1984

Thank you very much. We're delighted to welcome you to the White House. Over its history this room has been the site of many occasions honoring America's heroes, and today we carry on in that tradition.

During my inaugural address, I noted that those who say that we're in a time when there are no heroes, they just don't know where to look. A few months ago, we had a reception on the White House lawn for some of America's latest heroes: the soldiers, sailors, and marines who rescued the American medical students on the island of Grenada. It's a memory that we'll long cherish; seeing those medical students—some who once had admittedly negative feelings toward the military—throwing their arms around those brave young men who had rescued them, taking pictures of them, and introducing them to their parents as heroes. All of us can be proud of the courage and dedication of our military personnel in Grenada, in Beirut, wherever they're stationed, domestically or on foreign shores.

This is also a good opportunity to note the heroism of some other Americans who cherish freedom: the people of El Salvador. Yesterday those valiant people braved guerrilla violence and sabotage to do what we take for granted—cast their votes for President. While the final vote count is not yet in, it looks like the turnout is another victory for freedom over tyranny, of liberty over repression, and courage over intimidation.

We have already heard by phone from so many of our Congressmen who were down there as observers, both Democrat and Republican, and some who in their legislative activities have not looked with too much favor upon what we've been doing. But the calls we're getting back are, all of them, just complete enthusiasm of the heroism they saw there on the part of these people who, in spite of everything, insisted on going to vote.

But these are the very qualities that we're here to honor today in a group of our own heroes—individuals whose bravery, dedication, and creativity have enormously contributed to our quality of life and the cause of human freedom.

The Medal of Freedom is designed not to honor individuals for single acts of bravery, but instead, to acknowledge lifetime accomplishments that have changed the face and the soul of our country. The people we honor today are people who refused to take the easy way out, and the rest of us are better off for it. They're people who knew the risks and the overwhelming effort that could be required, but were undeterred from their goals. They are people who set standards for themselves and refused to compromise. And they're people who were not afraid to travel in unexplored territory.

By honoring them today, we, as a free people, are thanking them. Choices they made have enriched the lives of free men and women everywhere, and we're grateful.

Now, let me read the citations and present the medals to each recipient. And the first is Senator Howard H. Baker, Jr.

The citation:

As a Member of the United States Senate, one of the country's most powerful and influential citizens, and an individual whose character shines brightly as an example to others, Howard Baker has been a force for responsibility and civility on a generation of Americans. In his almost 20 years of service, he has earned the respect and admiration of his fellow citizens regardless of their political persuasion. As Majority Leader of the Senate, his quiet, cooperative style and keen legislative skills have honored America's finest traditions of enlightened political leadership and statesmanship.

Citation:

As a giant in the world of entertainment, James Cagney has left his mark not only on the film industry but on the hearts of all his fellow Americans. In some 60 years in entertainment, performing on stage and screen, he mastered drama and action adventure, as well as music and dance. One of his most remembered performances, as George M. Cohan in "Yankee Doodle Dandy," was a whirlwind singing and dancing film that inspired a Nation at war when it sorely needed a lift in spirit. James Cagney's professional and personal life has brought great credit to him and left unforgettable memories with millions who have followed his career.

Could I add something else? And this didn't have anything to do with the award. As a great star at the same studio where I started, he was never too busy to hold out a hand to a young fellow just trying to get underway.

Now, Mr. John Chambers will accept for his father, the late Mr. Whittaker Chambers.

At a critical moment in our Nation's history, Whittaker Chambers stood alone against the brooding terrors of our age. Consummate intellectual, writer of moving majestic prose, and witness to the truth, he became the focus of a momentous controversy in American history that symbolized our century's epic struggle between freedom and totalitarianism, a controversy in which the solitary figure of Whittaker Chambers personified the mystery of human redemption in the face of evil and suffering. As long as humanity speaks of virtue and dreams of freedom, the life and writings of Whittaker Chambers will ennoble and inspire. The words of Arthur Koestler are his epitaph: "The witness is gone; the testimony will stand."

Leo Cherne:

Although he has never held elected office, Leo Cherne has had more influence on governmental policy than many Members of Congress. Since the late 1930's, Leo Cherne has stepped forward and with brilliance, energy, and moral passion helped this Nation overcome countless challenges. His lifetime devotion to aiding his country and to serving the cause of human freedom, especially through his work on behalf of refugees, reflects the strong and generous character of a man who deserves the respect and gratitude of all Americans.

Dr. Denton Cooley:

In an outstanding professional career, Dr. Denton Cooley has distinguished himself time and again in the field of medicine. As one of this country's leading heart surgeons, he has charted new territory in his search for ways to prolong and enrich human life. His efforts have saved the lives not only of his own patients, but of those of many other doctors who have studied and mastered techniques developed by him.

As a heart surgeon and as a creative, independent thinker, Dr. Denton Cooley is a force for innovation in American medicine.

Ernest Jennings "Tennessee Ernie" Ford:

Through his musical talents, warm personality, and quick "down-home" wit Tennessee Ernie Ford won the hearts of the American people. Ford's music, which revealed his character and soul to all who listened, inspired as well as entertained his audiences. His respect for traditional values, his strong faith in God, and his unlimited capacity for human kindness have greatly endeared him to his fellow countrymen.

America is a Nation richer in spirit because of Tennessee Ernie Ford.

Dr. Hector Garcia:

Dr. Hector Garcia's patriotism and community concern exemplify the meaning of good citizenship. His many community-building endeavors included his work as a founder and first National Chairman of the American G.I. Forum, a veterans' organization which has done much to improve the lot of Americans of Mexican descent. Over the years, he has faithfully represented our government on numerous occasions, overseas and domestically. Dr. Hector Garcia is a credit to his family and community, and to all Americans.

Through his efforts, based on a deep belief in traditional American ideals, he has made this a better country.

General Andrew Goodpaster:

During his long service to his country, General Andrew Goodpaster shouldered heavy responsibility and worked tirelessly with the highest professional standards. His organizational and diplomatic skills helped shape the NATO Alliance and develop American military and foreign policy over three decades. As Supreme Allied Commander of the NATO Alliance, Presidential representative, and soldier, General Goodpaster has earned a well-deserved reputation as a thoughtful and diligent public servant. His work has contributed immensely to the security and freedom of his country and to the cause of peace.

Lincoln Kirstein:

Lincoln Kirstein is an author and entrepreneur who has honored and delighted Americans through his enormous contribution to ballet in our country. Through his commitment, two major institutions of American dance, the New York City Ballet and the School of American Ballet, were created and flourished. Developing and fostering appreciation for the arts have always depended on the energy, creativity, and commitment of individual citizens. Lincoln Kirstein stands tall as one of a select and treasured few in the world of American art.

Louis L'Amour:

Through his western novels, Louis L'Amour has played a leading role in shaping our national identity. His writings portrayed the rugged individual and the deep-seated values of those who conquered the American frontier. Starting out from humble beginnings, he has lived a fulfilling and adventurous life. An eminently successful writer, more than 100 million copies of his novels are in print, L'Amour's descriptions of America and Americans have added to our understanding of our past and reaffirmed our potential as an exploring, pioneering, and free people.

Dr. Norman Vincent Peale:

With a deep understanding of human behavior and an appreciation for God's role in our lives, Dr. Norman Vincent Peale helped originate a philosophy of happiness. Through the American Foundation of Religion and Psychiatry and his many books, Dr. Peale became an advocate of the joy of life, helping millions find new meaning in their lives. Few Americans have contributed so much to the personal happiness of their fellow citizens as Dr. Norman Vincent Peale.

Mrs. Jackie Robinson will accept for her late husband, Mr. Jackie Robinson.

As an individual of courage and conviction, and as a skilled and dedicated athlete, Jackie Robinson stood tall among his peers. His courage opened the door of professional sports to all Americans when, in 1947, he became the first black baseball player in the major leagues. He bravely demonstrated to all that skill and sportsmanship, not race or ethnic background, are the qualities by which athletes should be judged. In doing so, he struck a mighty blow for equality, freedom, and the American way of life. Jackie Robinson was a good citizen, a great man, and a true American champion.

Mr. Gamal el-Sadat will accept for his father, the late President Anwar el-Sadat.

President Anwar el-Sadat, as a soldier, led his country in war, but his greatest acts of courage came in pursuit of peace. He captured the imagination of people everywhere by taking the first great step toward achieving a lasting peace between Egypt and Israel. His humanity and sense of responsibility, even now that he is gone, remain a giant force for peace and stability in the world. Anwar el-Sadat was a peacemaker of monumental wisdom and tenderness who will remain forever a hero in the hearts of the American people.

Eunice Kennedy Shriver:

With enormous conviction and unrelenting effort, Eunice Kennedy Shriver has labored on behalf of America's least powerful people, the mentally retarded. Over the last two decades, she has been on the forefront of numerous initiatives on the behalf of the mentally retarded, from creating day camps, to establishing research centers, to the founding of the Special Olympics. Her decency and goodness have touched the lives of many, and Eunice Kennedy Shriver deserves America's praise, gratitude, and love.

Well, that concludes our presentations. And again, I offer my personal congratulations to the recipients. As a representative of the American people, I want to thank each of you for what you've done that has added so much to our lives.

Thank you, and God bless you all.

Note: The President spoke at 1:10 p.m. in the East Room at the White House following a luncheon for the recipients and their guests.

As printed above, the citations follow the texts of the citations which accompanied the medals.

Executive Order 12469—East-West Foreign Trade Report
March 26, 1984

By the authority vested in me as President by the Constitution and the statutes of the United States of America, including section 301 of Title 3 of the United States Code (3 U.S.C. 301), and section 411(c) of the Trade Act of 1974 (19 U.S.C. 2441(c)), in order to provide for more efficient reporting to the Congress, it is hereby ordered as follows:

Section 1. The reporting functions of the East-West Foreign Trade Board under section 411(c) of the Trade Act of 1974 (19 U.S.C. 2441(c)), as transferred to the President by section 5(c) of Reorganization Plan No. 3 of 1979 (19 U.S.C. 2171 note), are delegated to the United States Trade Representative.

Sec. 2. This order is effective upon publication in the *Federal Register.*

RONALD REAGAN

The White House,
March 26, 1984.

[*Filed with the Office of the Federal Register, 4:30 p.m., March 26, 1984*]

Message to the Congress Reporting Budget Deferrals
March 26, 1984

To the Congress of the United States:

In accordance with the Impoundment Control Act of 1974, I herewith report three new deferrals of budget authority totaling $42,632,000.

The deferrals affect the Departments of Justice and Transportation. The details of the deferrals are contained in the attached reports.

RONALD REAGAN

The White House,
March 26, 1984.

Note: The attachments detailing the deferrals are printed in the Federal Register *of April 2, 1984.*

Appointment of Four Members of the National Institute of Justice Advisory Board
March 26, 1984

The President today announced his intention to appoint the following individuals to be members of the National Institute of Justice Advisory Board for terms expiring November 11, 1986.

Donald L. Collins has been in the private practice of law for 25 years. He was a member of Congress from Alabama in 1962–1966. He is married, has four children, and resides in Mountain Brook, AL. He was born September 3, 1929, in Gadsden, AL. This is a reappointment.

George D. Haimbaugh, Jr., is serving as the David W. Robinson professor of law at the University of South Carolina School of Law. He is married and resides in Columbia, SC. He was born November 21, 1916, in Rochester, IN. This is a reappointment.

Priscilla H. Douglas is manager of Quality Systems, Pontiac Motor Division, General Motors Corp., in Pontiac, MI. She resides in Birming-

417

ham, MI. She was born November 1, 1947, in Cambridge, MA. She will succeed Mimi Halper Silbert.

Judy Baar Topinka is presently serving as State representative for the 43d district of Illinois. She has one child and resides in Riverside, IL. She was born January 16, 1944, in Chicago, IL. She will succeed Billy L. Wayson.

Statement on Signing the National Fish and Wildlife Foundation Establishment Act
March 26, 1984

I have signed today H.R. 2809, a bill to establish a National Fish and Wildlife Foundation. H.R. 2809 would establish the National Fish and Wildlife Foundation to encourage and administer donations of real or personal property, in connection with U.S. Fish and Wildlife Service programs and other activities to conserve fish, wildlife, and plant resources of the United States. The Foundation's governing board of nine directors would be appointed by the Secretary of the Interior. H.R. 2809 would also authorize the Attorney General to sue the Foundation if it should appear that the Foundation's actions are inconsistent with the purposes of the act.

I have signed H.R. 2809 because it promotes important conservation and preservation goals and encourages private sector initiative to aid us in attaining those goals. I must note my serious reservations about the approach taken in the bill. Before this bill was passed, the Department of Justice advised the Congress that the bill's provisions, taken together, create ambiguity about whether the Foundation is to be a private entity or an establishment within the executive branch. The statements in the bill to the effect that the Foundation shall be a nonprofit, charitable corporation and that it shall not be an agency or establishment of the United States are contradicted by the facts that the Foundation is established by Congress, funded by Congress, and endowed with the sole purpose of assisting and benefiting a Federal agency, the U.S. Fish and Wildlife Service; its property is made exempt from condemnation by State and local governments; and its Directors are all appointed by the Secretary of the Interior. Moreover, the bill exempts the Foundation from certain provisions of the United States Code which would be clearly inapplicable if the Foundation were truly nongovernmental.

Entities which are neither clearly governmental nor clearly private should not be created. The Supreme Court has recently warned against constitutional innovations merely because they seem to be expedient. Establishment of the Foundation under the terms of the bill is an unwise and dangerous precedent. I have, therefore, given serious consideration to vetoing the bill even though I support its laudable objectives. I have not done so because the Attorney General has advised that the bill can be given a constitutional construction.

I have been advised by the Attorney General that the governmental character of the Foundation predominates. Under the Supreme Court's cases, the character of an agency will be determined by its functions, not its label, *Buckley* v. *Valeo*, 424 U.S. 1 (1976). On this basis, the Foundation must be regarded as an establishment within the executive branch. The Directors of the Foundation, therefore, will be removable at the discretion of the Secretary of the Interior, because they are appointed by him and they exercise no powers which insulate them from removal at will. Accordingly, I will direct the Secretary to ensure compliance by the Directors of the Foundation with their statutory purposes through the exercise of the removal power. It will not be necessary to enforce compliance through suit by the Attorney General, an aspect of the bill which raises significant constitutional issues. In addition, I have directed the Attorney General and the Secretary to examine the other provisions of the bill to determine how they should be given effect

consistent with constitutional principles.

Note: As enacted, H.R. 2809 is Public Law 98–244, approved March 26.

Remarks at the National Legislative Conference of the Independent Insurance Agents of America
March 27, 1984

Thank you, Dick Teubner, Fred England, Frank Patterson, Larry Hite, ladies and gentlemen. Welcome to Washington. I know that you're here from all parts of the country, and after taking a look at some of the things going on here, you may think you took a wrong turn and ended up in the twilight zone. [*Laughter*]

You may be aware that I've got my own independent insurance agent, Jim Norris, a member of your California association. And I'm hoping I'll have to call on Jim about including our present residence on the homeowner policy on our ranch for about, say, another 4 years. [*Laughter*] But I appreciate this opportunity to be with you at this national legislative conference.

I understand some of you were briefed last night at the White House on economic and national security questions. And this morning you got another point of view from Congressman Jim Jones. One of the great cornerstones of our way of life is our right to disagree, to openly and critically discuss the policies of government.

You know, there's a story about a Russian and an American that were talking about the relative freedom in their countries. And the Yank proudly stated, "In our country, everyone is free to speak." And the Russian said, "That's true in the Soviet Union as well; the only difference is, after you speak, you're still free." [*Laughter*]

You'll be hearing many points of view during your visit to Washington. And we can all thank the Lord that we live in a country where citizens like yourselves can come, examine the facts, hear the arguments, make judgments, and then use your influence to be part of the decisionmaking process.

You make your living providing people with insurance for their lives and property. But the only insurance of good government is the involvement of solid citizens. For far too long, while you were focusing on your jobs and families and communities, special interests were hard at work in Washington. A political coalition of these interests and well-intentioned politicians of a liberal persuasion brought this country to the edge of economic catastrophe. They gave us out-of-control spending, oppressive taxation, near runaway inflation, sky-high interest rates, and economic stagnation. There was an adversary relationship between government and the business community.

The same people who created that mess now have the gall to lecture us about compassion and fairness. Well, the only thing fair about their policies is that they didn't discriminate; they made everybody miserable. [*Laughter*]

In these last 3 years, we've done our best to reverse the policies of tax and spend and inflate that wrought such havoc on our country. At first, we were told that turning the situation around would be impossible. We were told, for example, that it would take 10 years to wring inflation out of the system. Well, I just kept in mind something President Coolidge reportedly once said. "I have found it advisable," he said, "not to give too much heed to what people say when I'm trying to accomplish something of consequence. Invariably they proclaim it can't be done. I deem that the very best time to make the effort." Well, now, contrary to some reports on my age, Cal didn't tell me that personally. [*Laughter*] I read it.

We didn't let the pessimists hold us back, and today I'm proud to report that we've

419

taken inflation from double digits, eating away at our standard of living, and brought it down to about 4 percent. It was under 4 percent for the last year.

They said there was no way to get control of spending. It tripled during the decade of the seventies and was growing at 17 percent annually when we got here. We've cut that in half. And more progress can still and must be made on this front.

The prime interest rate was 21½ percent just before we got to Washington. It can be expected to fluctuate up or down a point, but it's way down from the outrageous prime rate we inherited. In the long run, if we go forward with our program, the prime will come down further.

I've often said that our country was in trouble because government was spending too much and taxing too much. Well, our 25-percent, across-the-board reduction in the tax rates have prevented the people from being further sapped by built-in tax increases. And we've indexed those rates so that starting next year government will no longer make a built-in profit off the taxpayers' misery.

You may have noticed that there's been considerable pressure to back away from our tax rate reductions. Clearly, the deficits remain a problem. But the answer is not undercutting economic recovery with higher and higher taxes. Recently we offered a balanced budget amendment, and we offered a 3-year deficit reduction package providing for a $150 billion cut in the projected deficit. The proposal is realistic and a good first step. We've started the process moving, but I have no intention of giving in to those whose only answer is taking the American people back into the poorhouse. We must have meaningful cuts in spending. As we look to the future, we can balance up with tax increases and lock ourselves into economic bondage, or we can balance down with lower tax rates and spending, permitting our economy to break free.

This is no time to go back to the failed policies of the past. It took time to put our program in place, and it took time for it to take effect. But we're now in the beginning phase of an economic renaissance that will touch the lives of all Americans.

I've been hearing from some pretty renowned economists lately, and they've criticized me for talking anymore about economic recovery. They said we've passed that stage; we are now in expansion.

So, from the ashes of pessimism, a stronger and more vibrant America is emerging. Productivity, after falling for 2 years before we took office, rose 3½ percent last year. The gross national product was up a healthy 6 percent, and it appears that the first quarter growth this year was even stronger—7.2 percent. Unemployment is dropping faster than anyone predicted. Housing starts, auto sales, and retail shopping are all up. Venture capital, which lays the foundation for a better tomorrow, rose less than $1 billion in 1980. It shot up over $4 billion last year.

And lo and behold, the deficit, which all the pessimists predicted would keep going up, is now coming down—and is being brought down by economic growth. I might say that in this same hotel just a few nights ago, we had the famous and traditional Gridiron in which you're supposed to say outrageous things. So I said one. I said that all this talk about the deficit, I just wasn't going to worry about it, that it's big enough to take care of itself. [*Laughter*] But I do worry about it.

In 1983 almost 600,000 new businesses were incorporated. That's an alltime high in our history. Now, most of those represent small business ventures, spearheaded by individuals like yourselves, proud and independent, taking risks and putting in long, hard hours to earn a living and be your own boss. Each one is just a minuscule part of our economy. But, taken together, small business represents a dynamo of energy and creativity that is catapulting our country toward new levels of opportunity and freedom.

John Naisbitt, futurist and author of "Megatrends," is saying that "1984 has arrived just in time to witness an explosion of bottom-up entrepreneurialism and the dawn of an era that may offer our best hope yet. . . ." Well, all of this is no accident. Instead of channeling an increasing percentage of working people's paychecks to Washington, we're letting people keep more of what they earn. Instead of centralizing power in the Federal bureaucracy, we're giving more autonomy to State and local government, transferring programs and resources to them in the form of block grants. We're freeing people from hundreds of millions of hours required to process needless Federal regulations and redtape, unleashing them for more productive endeavors.

In short, we're altering the basic direction of government. Ironically, historians may record that 1984 was the year Americans turned away from "big brother" and put their faith back in the people. And the American people are meeting the challenge, just as they have every time they've had a government that believes in them.

We've come a long way. Our next step is putting in place fundamental reforms that will prevent us from sliding back into the pit from which we've just emerged—reforms that will enable all Americans of every age, race, creed, and color to go forward together to build a true opportunity society. The first thing we need, which would take us a long way toward responsible spending, is what I mentioned earlier, a constitutional amendment requiring a balanced Federal budget. Now, many States already have such a requirement for their own budgets.

Along with a constitutional requirement for a balanced budget, we need to give the Chief Executive a line-item veto, so pork-barrel projects can't be attached to needed legislation. Now, this, too, is a tool that's available to many Governors that could be put to use in Washington. I had it when I was Governor of California. And I know that during those 8 years, I vetoed several hundred, almost a thousand, of those items in line-item veto and was never overridden once. They could vote for them when they were concealed in another package of legislation. When they had to vote to override the veto on that particular item, no one would stand up and vote to override, or not enough to override the veto.

At long last, we need to overhaul, also, our tax system. We need to make it more fair and provide greater incentives for everyone to work, save, and invest by broadening the base and bringing income tax rates down, not up. I'm not just suggesting

minor changes. What is needed is a sweeping, comprehensive reform, but certainly not like the proposed new tax form that was sent to me the other day. It had two lines on it. The first line said, "What did you make last year?" And the second line says, "Send it in." [*Laughter*]

Now, much of what we've done has been simply making up for the nonsense of the last few decades. Putting our economy back on the right track was priority number one. But there are other life or death issues confronting us.

Today, far too many of our citizens feel unsafe in their own neighborhoods and even in their own homes. Now, instead of just a lock, many of our citizens peer out of their dwellings, relying on bolts, chains, and even metal bars propped grotesquely against their door. They hire private security guards to patrol near their homes. They have dogs and burglar alarms. They find themselves behind barred windows. And even with all this, they do not feel safe. It's about time the American people start asking who's to blame for this.

The crime epidemic we suffered in the last two decades was no more a result of an uncontrollable cycle than were the inflation and stagnation that ravaged our people. It can be traced to policies that make it ever more difficult to convict the guilty, but have nothing to do with protecting society. The headlines in newspapers throughout the country tell the story. Our criminal justice system is long overdue for reform. It is about time we take the handcuffs off law enforcement and put them on the thugs and murderers where they belong.

The Senate has passed a package of criminal justice reform which, if enacted, will toughen up the system and make it more efficient and capable of getting vicious criminals off the streets. The liberal leadership of the House, ignoring the cries of victims throughout this country, has yet to move on this legislation. I think in this election every candidate, for whatever office, should be on record as far as this legislation is concerned. This is not a peripheral issue. People's lives are at stake, and politicians and the media should not dismiss it lightly. We must never reach the point in this country where Americans feel they have no alternative but to take the law into their own hands. So, maybe it's time to move some politicians out of office in order to get criminals off the streets. [*Laughter*]

Our national security is no less vital than our citizens' personal security and was no less ill managed in the last decade. Defense spending in real terms was permitted to erode by over 20 percent in the 1970's. Weapons systems were unilaterally canceled. The real pay of our military personnel dropped as inflation took off. The CIA was gutted, as longtime agents were let go. Those in charge seemed to be operating under the notion that a weaker America is a more secure America. Well, I don't buy that, and I don't think you do, either. Peace through strength is not a slogan; it's a fact of life.

But let's not kid ourselves, national security has a price tag. It's an expensive proposition, and it's been made even more so because we've been playing catchup—making up for the irresponsibility of the past. The ones you hear yelling the loudest these days are the ones who put us behind the eight ball in the first place. Many of them publicly oppose the modernization of our strategic systems, while at the same time loudly proclaiming their intent to negotiate arms control agreements with the Soviet Union. Well, it's about time to get serious and ask these would-be leaders what they expect to use as incentives with the Soviet Union. Good will and sincerity will get them a smile and a glass of vodka—[*laughter*]—and you can guess why the Soviets will be smiling.

We had two treaties—the SALT treaties—the SALT Treaty I, SALT Treaty II. And SALT Treaty II was not ratified by the Senate, I'm pleased to say. No one has paid any attention to the fact that under those two treaties—the Soviet Union under SALT I, from that time on, added 7,950 nuclear warheads to its arsenal, and 3,850 of those were added after everyone signed SALT II.

I recently agreed to scale down our planned increase in defense spending. It's played heavily on my mind. It was done only after great thought and regard to all factors. I've looked into the faces of the young people in our military, and as long as

I'm President, we're not going to ask these brave young men and women who defend this country to put their lives on the line using obsolete weapons and bargain-basement equipment. We as a people must have the courage to stand behind them.

Now, let me also—you have seen and heard for quite some time now a drumbeat about wrenches costing $12,000 or bolts that could be bought for 15 cents costing $3.50 and things of that kind. Now, all of that is true, but no one has added in the stories that we're the ones that have provided those figures. It is our Defense Department that has found this out and that it was going on and has gone to work to change it and so far has gotten back hundreds of millions of dollars in rebates and hundreds of convictions for fraud in this type of operation. And the rebates are still coming in, many voluntarily now, from businesses that have found out what was going on.

Our administration has proposed a modest investment promoting economic growth and the development of democratic institutions in Central America, as well as providing our friends the means to protect themselves against the attack of Soviet-backed insurgents. Being in the business you're in, I hope you can appreciate what we're asking the Congress to approve: Our program is an insurance policy to protect against the chaos that would result from allowing anti-American Marxists to shoot their way to power in Central America. We must not permit that to happen.

Like any insurance policy, there's a premium to pay, but it's cheaper now than to wait for a crisis, and there's no time to lose. The National Bipartisan Commission on Central America clearly warned that our own national security is at stake in this struggle.

And this last weekend, we witnessed dramatic confirmation by the people of El Salvador of their commitment to democracy. Intimidation and threats by Marxist guerrillas couldn't keep these brave, these courageous people from casting their vote for democracy. Many of them walked as far as 20 miles and stood in the hot sun for hours, braving the wrath of guerrillas to vote. The El Salvadorans are worthy of our support.

Let me just interject that yesterday the committee of observers in that election, consisting of Democratic and Republican Congressmen and Senators, added to them people from the private sector—from ranks of labor, ranks of business, a clergyman—had gone down to observe these elections. And yesterday they came into my office to report on what they had seen. Many of them admitted they went there with a different idea that maybe we were wrong about what we were doing there. They came back, all of them, totally converted.

They talked to the people who were waiting for hours, the sweat streaming from them in a hot sun, in line to go in and vote. You know how easy it is to vote here. How would you like it if your neighbor said to you, "If you vote, we're going to shoot you"? And then you had to go down and stand in the sun for several hours and then maybe find out you were in the wrong line and have to go someplace else for several hours. But they did it.

And over and over these observers asked, and they said, "Well, why? Why are you doing this?" And a little elderly lady standing in line said, "I'm voting for democracy." And another one said, "I'm voting for God and peace." And it went on this way. They found out that these people—there was nothing going to stop them. They frankly admitted, maybe this election alone won't do it—this is the second election—but we've been trying for democracy for a long time. We'll keep on having these until we have democracy. Everything that they heard down there convinced them: These are people that deserve the help and support of people that are as fortunate as we are.

Now, for the last 3 years we've been trying to build a strong America, not just militarily but economically and, yes, spiritually. We all appreciate the necessity of maintaining the military power to deter aggression and to prevent war. Yet we must also acknowledge that the greatest source of our strength is not weapons or laws, but, instead, the character of our people—our standards as individuals and our recognition of those values that transcend the politics of the moment.

Four years ago, a cloud of pessimism hung over this land. A negative and cynical attitude, totally inconsistent with our traditions, like a wet blanket, smothered that resilient spirit so long associated with America and Americans. I'm proud that this, too, is something else we've helped change. And I say "we" because this kind of transformation can't be from the top. It reflects a change of heart, not just a change of politics [policies].

I'd like to take this opportunity to thank each of you for what you've done, and continue to do, to keep this blessed land the good and decent place God intended it to be. And I want to congratulate you as an association. Your national, local, and State boards are, for example, in the forefront of the campaign against drunk driving, and at the same time, you're promoting highway safety programs throughout the country. You've also been involved in anticrime programs, especially concerning arson. But this doesn't even scratch the surface.

Independent insurance people are active in veterans and service clubs, in churches and PTA's, in charitable and community programs, in cities and towns across the width and breadth of America. Your own president-elect, Fred England, was designated an "Angel" last year by the Association of Retarded Citizens. The Massachusetts Independent Insurance Agents sponsor the ARC. The Insurance Women of Denver sponsor the Special Olympics, something in which my wife, Nancy, as you know, is also deeply involved.

Your vice president, Richard Taylor, is a national board member of the National Society for the Prevention of Blindness and speaks on their behalf across the country. Your national State director from Hawaii, Norm Westly, has, for years, devoted his personal time to drug rehabilitation programs. I know that these individuals are not unique. They represent thousands of people in your profession.

More than a century ago, a French philosopher came to this country, as he said, to find out the secret—then, a hundred years ago—of our greatness. And he said that he had looked everywhere, in our business, in our busy harbors, in our factories and industries, and then, he said, he discovered that

America is great because she is good. And if she ever ceases to be good, America will cease to be great. You are helping America to live up to its potential. Together we can keep America the shining light of liberty God intended it to be.

Thank you, and God bless you.

Note: The President spoke at 10:46 a.m. in the Presidential Ballroom at the Capital Hilton Hotel. In his opening remarks, he referred to Richard D. Teubner, president, Frederick J. England, Jr., president-elect, Frank J. Patterson, chairman of the Federal Affairs Committee, and Lawrence E. Hite, chairman of the NAPAC board of trustees, Independent Insurance Agents of America.

Statement by Principal Deputy Press Secretary Speakes on the Death of President Ahmed Sékou Touré of Guinea
March 27, 1984

The United States regrets the untimely death of Sékou Touré of the Republic of Guinea in Cleveland on March 26. Sékou Touré was an internationally respected statesman whose efforts on behalf of peaceful settlement of disputes had earned for him and his country an enviable reputation for peacemaking. He exercised a unifying role within the Organization of African Unity and in African affairs generally.

The United States valued his wise and prudent counsel. We expect to continue the close and cooperative relations between our two countries.

Note: Larry M. Speakes read the statement to reporters assembled in the Briefing Room at the White House during his daily press briefing, which began at 12:30 p.m.

Announcement Concerning the Annual Report on the Federal Information Security System and a Letter to the Director of the Information Security Oversight Office
March 27, 1984

On March 23, 1984, the President received the FY 1983 Information Security Oversight Office (ISOO) annual report on the information security system. In a letter to ISOO Director Steven Garfinkel, the President expressed his appreciation to those whose efforts have helped to make the information security system work.

The number of original classification decisions is the most important measurement of an information security program. During the first year of the President's Executive order on national security information (Executive Order 12356), government officials classified almost 200,000 (18 percent) fewer new secrets than they had in any of the previous 3 years. In addition, most of this reduction occurred in the higher classification levels, "Secret" and "Top Secret." These facts and many others about the Government's information security program are contained in a March 16, 1984, report from the ISOO, which is located in the United States General Services Administration and oversees the government-wide information security program.

In his letter to the President transmitting the FY 1983 annual report, ISOO Director Garfinkel stated: "This reduction [in original classification] is an unprecedented accomplishment, especially in the context of improved protection for national security information." Garfinkel also noted that to date the President's announced objective of "enhancing protection for national security information without permitting excessive classification" is being achieved.

Among the other accomplishments set out in the report are the following:

—Under the revised system in FY '83, classifiers marked documents for automatic declassification at a rate 3½ times as great as they had under the prior Executive order.

—The number of persons authorized to classify information originally continued to decline under the new Executive order and is down by almost 90 percent from the total number of classifiers in 1972.

—Over 90 percent of public requests for declassification under the mandatory review provisions of this order resulted in complete or partial declassification and disclosure of the information requested, the highest rate of disclosure ever achieved.

—The transition from the information security system under the prior Executive order to the revised system under the new Executive order resulted in no serious problems or abuses.

The report also addresses several areas of the information security program in which greater efforts are needed to meet the goals established by the President. These include the generating of additional classified documents deriving from original classification decisions, the program for systematic declassification review of the historically valuable classified records in the National Archives, the quantity and quality of agency self-inspections designed to detect security infractions, and delays in processing researchers' declassification review requests. The President has asked that the Information Security Oversight Office pay particular attention to these areas in the coming year.

March 23, 1984

Dear Mr. Garfinkel:

I was very pleased to review your FY 1983 Annual Report and to learn that the system we have established under Executive Order 12356 to provide better protection for national security information without excessive classification is working. While we anticipated that the revised information security system would improve credibility and efficiency of the program, its success is also dependent upon the outstanding oversight efforts of you and your staff and the thousands of other persons throughout the executive branch who are dedicated to making it work. Please convey my appreciation to all those whose efforts made these achievements possible.

I ask for the same commitment in the future to improving our performance even more. We must continue to insure that information is being classified only when this extraordinary protection is necessary; that those entrusted with access to national security information appreciate the seriousness of their responsibility to safeguard it; and that systematic review and other declassification efforts are made in accordance with the order's goal of making information no longer requiring security protection available to the public.

I trust that you and your staff will continue to work with responsible officials throughout the Government to address these and other issues that relate to the administration of the information security program. I look forward to future reports on the progress that has been made as a result of these efforts.

Sincerely,

RONALD REAGAN

[Mr. Steven Garfinkel, Director, Information Security Oversight Office, 18th and F Streets, N.W., Washington, D.C. 20405]

Note: The 27-page report is entitled "Annual Report to the President, FY 1983— Information Security Oversight Office."

Letter to the Speaker of the House and the President of the Senate on Soil and Water Conservation Programs
March 27, 1984

Dear Mr. Speaker: (Dear Mr. President:)

I am pleased to transmit this report on the extent to which programs and policies recommended in the 1985 budget meet the standards in the Statement of Policy and recommended program for soil and water conservation programs sent to Congress on December 21, 1982.

1985 budget policy is designed to maintain strong economic growth and promote vigorous investment and rising productivity without setting off renewed inflation. The 1985 budget requests Congress to take a number of actions to cut Federal spending. They are necessary to avoid the specter of higher interest rates, choked-off investment, renewed recession, and rising unemployment. These policy objectives are especially important for the long-term well-being of the agricultural sector of the economy.

In the Statement of Policy, I indicated that future budgets for conservation programs would be consistent with overall economic and fiscal policy requirements and the need for resources for other national goals and interests. The 1985 budget for conservation activities proposes new budget authority of $725 million, $10 million or one percent less than the lower level of the recommended program. It is consistent with overall fiscal policy. It provides adequate resources for the most important conservation activities, technical assistance, soil surveys, and research and analysis, while recommending reductions for other activities that might be postponed or carried out by State and local governments or landowners themselves.

A key feature of the recommended program was the plan to target a larger share of conservation resources to critical problem areas. 1985 will be the third year of the five-year program under which the Department has been allocating additional assistance for soil and water conservation in these critical problem areas. In 1985, 15 percent of all technical assistance will be so targeted. The goal for 1987 is to target 25 percent of all technical and financial assistance. This policy is producing results as total soil savings is expected to be considerably more in 1985 than in 1983. Significantly, a much higher portion of the soil savings in 1985 will be on land where erosion rates are at their highest and most serious levels.

Finally, I have asked the Cabinet Council on Food and Agriculture, which is chaired by Secretary Block, to conduct a comprehensive review and assessment of current food and agriculture problems. One of the important tasks for the Council will be to develop recommendations for farm programs that will achieve both price support and conservation objectives.

I look forward to working with the Congress as you consider the budget recommendations and other aspects of conservation policy in the coming months.

Sincerely,

RONALD REAGAN

Note: This is the text of identical letters addressed to Thomas P. O'Neill, Jr., Speaker of the House of Representatives, and George Bush, President of the Senate.

Nomination of Bohdan A. Futey To Be Chairman of the Foreign Claims Settlement Commission of the United States
March 28, 1984

The President today announced his intention to nominate Bohdan A. Futey to be Chairman of the Foreign Claims Settlement Commission of the United States, Department of Justice, for the remainder of the term expiring September 30, 1985. He would succeed J. Raymond Bell.

Since 1975 Mr. Futey has been a partner in the law firm of Bazarko, Futey & Oryshkewych in Parma, OH. Previously, he was executive assistant to the mayor of the city of Cleveland in 1974–1975; chief assistant police prosecutor for the law department of the city of Cleveland in 1972–1974;

partner in the law firm of Futey & Rakowsky in 1968–1972; and special counsel to the attorney general of Ohio in 1970.

Mr. Futey graduated from Western Reserve University (B.A., 1962; M.A., 1964) and Cleveland Marshall Law School (J.D., 1968). He is married, has three children, and resides in Parma, OH. He was born June 28, 1939.

Interview With Steven R. Weisman and Francis X. Clines of the New York Times on Foreign and Domestic Issues
March 28, 1984

The President. Before we get underway, I just have one question of my own—on the other side of the political fence and all. I found this, that my popularity had improved, but I had to turn to the second section on the 6th page to find it, that——

Mr. Weisman. Well, it's no longer news. [*Laughter*]

The President. I've heard that before.

Mr. Weisman. Well, it's a good answer. Shall we begin? Thank you very much for giving us this time.

The President. Well, pleased to do it— sorry we've kept you waiting.

Administration Goals

Mr. Weisman. No problem. The first question we'd like to ask you, Mr. President, is one that we've asked the Democratic Presidential candidates, and that is: What do you think is the most important problem facing the United States in the next decade, and what ideas do you have for dealing with it?

The President. Well, I think the problem remains—and it's a group of problems—and that is maintaining and continuing this expansion of our economy, so that we can provide jobs with a future and opportunity for all of our people. I think it is the problem of achieving a lasting peace, with the reduction, particularly, of nuclear weapons in the world, to reduce and, hopefully, one day eliminate that threat that hangs over

us. I think others—to help, as we can, those nations that are trying to establish democracies and become working members of the family of nations. And, I believe, the restoration of some traditional values of family and neighborhood. The distortion that's occurred down through the last few decades of the relationship within our own country of our different levels of government, and to restore authority and autonomy to those levels where the Federal Government has assumed too much of it. I'll probably think of several more answers to that later, but——

Mr. Weisman. Okay.

The President. ——but right now, I think that's covered basically: the economy, the economic expansion that is needed and that we have embarked on, and peace in the world and reduction of the tensions and the armaments.

Federal Budget Deficits

Mr. Clines. Sir, on the deficit question, I noticed yesterday you joked slightly about it and then emphasized how seriously you take the deficit problem. Could you be more specific? How serious a problem is it, and what would you do to deal with it?

The President. Well, that would be a part of the overall generic answer that I gave about the economy. Yes, the deficit is a problem; no one can ignore it. But it's been going on for some 50 years, and for most of that time, almost totally in that time, it has been a deliberate part of government policy. And some of us who complained about it back through the years always said that it would get literally out of control, that you could not go on that way without coming to a day of reckoning. And we now are at that day of reckoning. I think the basic part of that deficit is due to government itself and the excessive share of the people's earnings, the gross national product that the government is taking.

And so, we're going to continue. We've made a proposal for a downpayment over the next 3 years that is pretty evenly divided between some revenues, not by raising rates, but by eliminating some tax practices that we think aren't fairly distributed. And that, of course, is part of this temporary downpayment. But at the same time, I have ordered the Treasury Department to embark on a study of the entire tax structure—as to how we can collect the uncollected tax that is being evaded by people who owe it and don't pay, simplify the tax structure, broaden the base, hopefully reduce the rates on individuals.

Entitlement Programs

Mr. Clines. You—excuse me—you had mentioned last week in passing that you saw the need at some point to restructure social security for new workers coming into the program. Could you elaborate on that?

The President. Well, I think we have to— we've got to look at the whole governmental structure, and this includes the entitlement programs. There have been demographic changes that have been ignored that make some policies now leading inevitably toward another day of reckoning if we don't reorder those programs. About half of your deficit has been structural. About half of your deficit has been cyclical, the result of the recessions. And we are eliminating that half—the cyclical—by the recovery that has taken place. An evidence of that is that just between August and the first of the year our own projections of the deficit were reduced by $15 billion, because we obtained that much more tax revenue than we had anticipated due to the recovery in the economy.

Mr. Weisman. Mr. President, on the enti-

tlements, can you be more specific about how this restructuring—it is a year in which you're asking voters to return you to office. Can't you be more specific about what you would do for medicare and social security?

The President. No, not really, because this is something that is going to require thorough study to ensure that you do not pull the rug out from under anyone who is presently dependent on those programs. They must not be frightened as they have been by political demagoguery as they were in the '82 campaign, when our opponents took advantage of the fact that social security— the program was facing, and by our date as of July 1983—facing outright bankruptcy. And they denied this. And then they waged a political campaign that we were out—in some way we intended to take the payments—either reduce them or take them away from people dependent on them. And they caused panic among people who were in a—the senior citizens that are not in a position to defend themselves against this when someone says, "Oh, did you know that they're going to do this or this or that to you?"

Mr. Weisman. But you could be more specific——

The President. Well——

Mr. Weisman. ——and put some of these fears to rest, couldn't you?

The President. Well, I had tried—and everyone seemed to ignore it—I have said over and over again in talking about social security's problem, that nothing must be done to penalize those people who are now dependent on those checks. But what we need to do is a revamping of the program.

We finally, then, when the election was over and the demagoguery stopped——

Mr. Weisman. Yeah.

The President. ——then our opponents agreed to a bipartisan get-together to find an answer to the immediate problem.

Mr. Weisman. But isn't it risky now in an election year for you to say that we should revamp and restructure these programs without being specific?

The President. No. As long as they understand—and as long as you will print that what I said—that there is no intention on the part of anyone of taking away from those people now getting. And maybe also it would be well if you printed that the rebuttal to the demagoguery of the '82 campaign is the fact that today the average couple, married couple on social security is getting $180 a month more than they were getting before we came here.

So, these are our goals and our purposes. But there is no way to answer until you have gone into a study of the whole actuarial situation.

Now, I read in one of the interviews with one of the present candidates of the other party, where he was claiming that, "Well, there's no problem with social security at all because it's safe till the end of the century." Well, 1984 isn't too far away from the end of the century. Well, how can he so carelessly dismiss the fact that those same people out there, who, as you've said, can be frightened if someone is saying to them, "Yes, the program's going to run into another financial bind," but he doesn't offer any suggestion for solving it. I'm saying that what we must do now is more of what we did in that temporary fix——

Mr. Weisman. Right.

The President. ——is a bipartisan facing up to the fact that you ensure that those people are going to get their payments.

Mr. Weisman. But let me take one more pass at this. Do you think, then, in a second term, should you win reelection, that you will want to take another look at these structural problems in social security, as well as medicare?

The President. As long as it is in the context that we are not going to pull the rug out from anyone who's presently dependent on those programs.

Taxes

Mr. Weisman. Okay. May I ask you a question about the, what you mentioned a moment ago, about broadening the tax base, as being an objective in your tax simplification study? Would you accept a tax simplification that does lead to an, in effect, an increased tax burden on Americans? Or would your goal be to keep the tax burden the same as it is now?

The President. I am looking for a program that can bring about simplification, but I see no need to increase the burden on indi-

viduals. This is what—we set out to reduce that——

Mr. Weisman. Right.

The President. ——and simplification—what we are looking toward, and I can't answer now, because this is a study that has to be made, and it's a very complex subject—when you say "broaden the tax base," again, you're talking about involving, in the payment of taxes, people now who, for one reason or the other, have been able to, in many instances, remain totally tax free or remain well below what they should be paying. And thus it limits your ability to reduce the overall burden on individuals by tax rate cuts because of the lost revenue which, right now, is estimated around a hundred billion dollars a year.

Mr. Clines. Is that what you're basically after, the lost revenue, or would you, in effect, net more with a simplification program? That's——

The President. Well, when you look at a simplification program you are also looking at a way of making it impossible for those who are presently evading, to evade.

Mr. Weisman. When you say "evading," you don't mean evading illegally; you mean from unfair tax breaks, as well, right?

The President. Oh, no. An awful lot of outright evading.

Mr. Weisman. But in addition to that, you're also talking about loopholes, tax breaks, whatever you want to call it.

The President. I hesitate—I won't answer that now, as to what all will be in the study. We are, as I said before, in our present proposal, we are changing some that we believe—while they were undoubtedly well-intentioned, they have led to some taking an—getting an advantage that is denied to others. Where that is true, then that should be corrected, whether you have a deficit or——

Mr. Weisman. Right.

The President. ——have a tax reform or not.

Defense Programs

Mr. Clines. On the subject of defense spending, sir, you've accepted a reduction this time around in the budget fight, in the rate of defense growth. We wanted to know whether that's a real reduction, or are you just stretching it out? In other words, you'd have the same buildup at the same cost over a longer period of time.

The President. Well, obviously, to have such a—to be able to make such a reduction as we did involves some elements of stretching it out, which means that over a longer period of time the same amount of money is distributed so that you have people taking a longer time with their taxes to pay for it. But the defense budget is not determined by how much you want to spend. It's determined by what is necessary to guarantee our security and thus the ability to preserve the peace. And for those who approach the budget from the standpoint of, "Well, let's make it this percentage of the budget or let's cut this amount of money," how do you have national security on that basis?

Everything that you're going to cut from the defense budget, you have to say, "Does this reduce to an unacceptable point our ability to preserve our security or not?" And if it does, then you can't make that cut. If you can delay, if you can postpone some things and you look and say, "Well, in looking at the potential adversaries in the world, what emergencies might arise, this is not an unacceptable risk"—we can do this, particularly when it is to help bring about the economic strengthening.

Now, we have been doing this, and we have—we ourselves, with all of the talk about defense spending as being the source of added funds for reducing the deficit— and I've seen the terms used many times in the media that—"record defense spending." It's record if you take the number of dollars without regard to the value of those dollars. It is far below any record at all. There is no hint of such a thing if you take it as a percentage of the budget or as a percentage of gross national product. And in either one of those ratings, our defense spending is far below what was customary back through the years.

In the Kennedy era, 1962, I believe it was, the defense budget was about 47.8 percent of the total budget. It's down around 27 percent or so now of the budget. It is a smaller percentage of the gross national product than it was then. So, we

think that we are really tightening our belt to make this reduction that we're proposing.

Now, how do you arrive at lower defense spending ever? You arrive at it by the other thing that we're trying to bring about, and that is a reduction in armaments with those who could be considered possible adversaries. Then, if you have a reduction of the threat, you can have a reduction of the deterrent on our side. And that is a road toward lesser defense spending.

Mr. Weisman. We'd like to move on to that subject, but before I ask you about that, let me just ask once more if it's correct to assume that you see this reduction in the rate of growth that has been accepted now as primarily a postponement of the buildup, a deferral of the buildup, or do you see it as causing any elimination of anything that you had in mind?

The President. Not in the sense of weapons systems or reducing manpower. There are—let me be honest and say this whole thing is definitely not all postponement. We have been working and, as a matter of fact, had made $16 billion cut in the defense budget ourselves before we even, then, took this further step. But much of that was based on the things that we, ourselves, have been discovering, as we have in every other area of government, of government practices that could be changed. Some of that spending cut reflects the findings of the Grace commission that we're now implementing.

All of this thing that you all have had such a field day with, with regard to wrenches costing thousands of dollars and bolts costing $4½ when they should cost 4 cents and so forth—no one has published those are *our* figures. *We* found that that was going on, and we are the ones who have changed that. And already the savings are at hundreds of millions of dollars of rebates that have come back to us, to say nothing of the future savings now of correcting that practice. And there have been indictments, hundreds of them, for fraud and things of that kind.

Mr. Clines. Incidentally, how much of a shock was that for you——

The President. What?

Mr. Clines. How much of a shock was that for you to discover the amount of conniving that defense contractors might attempt?

The President. Well, it had to be quite a shock, when you first came up with a finding of some little gizmo that you could buy in a store off the shelf for about a tenth or less of what we were paying for it.

Mr. Weisman. Don't you wish you could have had some of those when you were campaigning?

The President. Yes—[*laughing*]—yes.

U.S.-Soviet Relations

Mr. Weisman. May I ask you about the East-West tensions, which you raised or mentioned a moment ago? Are there no further steps that the United States can take unilaterally, now, to reduce tensions with the Soviet Union or to persuade them to return to the negotiating table? For instance, submitting the threshold test ban treaty for ratification, which, I think, is on their list.

The President. We are in conversations with the Soviet Union on a number of things of this kind. And on things like—we'll soon be talking about a chemical warfare treaty—and with regard to their position, I think the tensions are, frankly, more evident in rhetoric than they are in actuality. I think that there is less tension today and less threat and danger with the rebuilding that we have done that makes us more secure than there was earlier when our defenses were so lax that there was a window of vulnerability.

No, we—and they have agreed now to come back into negotiations on one of the three treaties that they walked out on, the conventional weapons treaty, the multiple balanced force [mutual and balanced force reductions] MBFR treaty. We're hopeful that they will come back in the others.

We've made it plain that we're flexible, that while we have made a proposal, we have evidenced our willingness to negotiate in what may be differing views of theirs. An example of that in the intermediate-range weapons in Europe: My first proposal was—and I think it was a commonsense proposal—and that was zero on both sides, eliminate them all, and that type of weapon.

Well, the Soviets would not hear of that.

We said all right, then, granted that would be our goal—and we think it's a good goal—but we're willing, then, to talk whatever reduction in numbers that we can make that will be verifiable, that will be fair and even for both sides. And that still remains on the table.

Mr. Weisman. But the administration seems to have taken the position now that no new revisions or new revised proposals will be offered until they come to the negotiating table, and then you might have something. Is that a correct description?

The President. No, what we're saying is we're not going to sit here and negotiate with ourselves and while they sit out there not participating——

Mr. Weisman. Right.

The President. ——waiting to see what we'll finally come up with. That would be very poor negotiating strategy. We have said to them, we're flexible. We're willing to negotiate fair and verifiable agreements when they're ready to come back to the table.

Mr. Weisman. Do you think that by not negotiating or not going back to the table the Russians might be trying to influence the outcome of the American election?

The President. Oh, I don't think someone could rule that out. I'm not going to make the charge, but I'm not going to also guess at what might be their—part of their problems might simply be with the change now in leadership, that they're in a period of putting their shop together.

Mr. Clines. On an informal level, do you have a better reading of the new leader there, or have you been in touch with him in some way, in some oblique way—Chernenko?

The President. Well, the Vice President had an opportunity to meet with him when he was there. And, as I say, there is communication between our two governments, and we remain optimistic that we can arrive at agreements. In the first place, we want them, and they need them.

The Middle East

Mr. Weisman. Frank, do you want to ask about the Middle East——

Mr. Clines. The Middle East. In the last year it would seem that the Government—the United States Government might have misjudged the stability of Lebanon and the Lebanese Government and the effectiveness of its army and the willingness of Syria to cooperate with some of our stratagems. Are you satisfied with the basic information you've gotten on what—that was the underpinning for your strategy there? Were you misinformed in the first place or what?

The President. No, we knew that what we were attempting to help with was a very complex and complicated problem. And what we and our allies joined together to do was based on the necessity for a withdrawal of the foreign forces that were in there.

Remember that when this all started, Israel, because of the violations of its own northern border by the Palestinians, the PLO, had gone all the way to Beirut. War was being fought in the city streets there with the PLO. Casualties among civilians were probably exceeding those of the military. The Syrians, they were also on Lebanese soil. And we went in to help bring about the removal of the PLO, who felt that any effort to surrender could result in a massacre, and they were—some ten to fifteen thousand were removed from the country. Syria had indicated that it, too, would leave, the Israelis would leave, and then Syria changed its mind. That was unanticipated.

But even so, the purpose of the troops of Italy, the United Kingdom, France, and ourselves were there to more or less help maintain order while a government, a viable government of Lebanon was created and then to help train—which we did—their army to then go out and occupy the areas occupied by foreign forces—Syria and Israel—as they withdrew, because, also, in those areas were the militias, the unofficial armies that had been fighting each other and fighting the government, such as it was, in Lebanon.

Now, for quite some time, progress was made. And I still have to say right now the progress, the meetings that have taken place in Switzerland would not have taken place had all of us not done what we did. It is true that when Syria balked and began

supporting some of the rebel elements—but our whole idea was that for Libya—or for Lebanon to have a government, they were going to have to make peace with those militias and find some kind of a broad-based government. And they've set out and they've tried to do that. It didn't succeed.

But the very fact that all of us began to be subject to terrorist attacks and change the basing of our troops—us putting them on ships offshore and so forth—actually was evidence of the fact that we were succeeding. And those who didn't want success knew that one of the steps in having their way was to force the withdrawal of our own forces.

Mr. Clines. Was the level of success, as you describe it, worth the price that we paid, the dead marines?

The President. I don't know how you answer this thing that is becoming worldwide now, the terrorist method of suicide attacks and so forth. I'd like to say that there is no cause that's worth the life of any man, but we know that isn't true.

We did not succeed in what we thought could have gone forward. There has not been—they are still working at it there, the Lebanese Government. One thing, also: We did a good job of training their military and equipping it. What we couldn't anticipate then was at the instigation of Syria, on ethnic and religious bases, some of the elements of that trained army then refused to perform against the radical forces that the army had been trained to handle.

But that doesn't change the need for us to continue in the Middle East overall with what must take place. And we hope if we can be helpful that we can bring about, and that is a meeting of the moderate Arab States and Israel and the bringing about of peace just as Egypt and Israel brought about peace.

Mr. Clines. If the circumstances were the same, but, hypothetically, we were back 4 years and you were running against President Carter, wouldn't you be hammering him for the death of the marines in Beirut?

The President. For what?

Mr. Clines. For the death of the marines in the Beirut massacre.

The President. No, if I had all the knowledge that I presently have about the situation. There was one thing, whether it was campaigning or just making speeches in the past that I have always recognized, and that is that there are a number of areas in which only a President has the information, all the information, on a situation. And those who criticize are criticizing without having access to that same information.

Mr. Speakes.[1] You'd better do one more, if you can.

Mr. Weisman. Well, how about two more?

Mr. Speakes. Be quick.

Mr. Weisman. Would you—a quick one— would you veto the bill requiring the United States Embassy to be moved from Tel Aviv to Jerusalem?

The President. I am hoping I won't have to, but like the several previous Presidents before me, I think that that is a most unwise thing. It should never have been introduced in our Congress. The effort should never have been made, because if we are to have a negotiated peace that will end once and for all the literally—well, the hostility between the Arab world and Israel, then that would be one of the things that must be negotiated. The place of Jerusalem, the West Bank, things of this kind—these are all the matters that must be negotiated between these forces. And the United States has no right to put itself in a position of trying to lean one way or the other on those areas for negotiation.

Central America

Mr. Weisman. Why don't—I'd like to ask the final question about Central America, Mr. President. I wonder if I could ask you to explain or justify how the United States can go about assisting people who are, as you have called them, freedom fighters who are seeking to overthrow a government that we have diplomatic relations with, and answer, if you could, critics who are worried that this is increasing our involvement in Central America.

The President. Well, the answer to that is, first of all, this particular government of

---

[1] *Larry M. Speakes, Principal Deputy Press Secretary to the President.*

Nicaragua's is a government that was set up by force of arms. The people have never chosen it. It's a revolutionary government. And that government, in violation of its pledge to us at a time when it was a revolutionary force trying to become a government, had promised that it would not aid the guerrillas in El Salvador, who are attempting to overthrow a duly elected government and a democratic government. And they have violated that. The guerrillas are literally being directed from bases near Managua. They're being supplied by that government. And the other factor with regard—and why I have referred to them on occasion as freedom fighters is because many of them are elements of the same revolution that put the Sandinista government in force.

The revolution against the Somoza dictatorship—and our government, under the previous administration, sat back and never lifted a finger in behalf of Somoza and then, when the fighting was over, did start to give financial aid to the revolutionary government to help it install itself—and had to cancel that when it discovered what that government was doing. During the revolution against Somoza, the revolutionaries appealed to the Organization of American States—of which we're a member also—and appealed to that organization to ask Somoza to step down and end the bloodshed. And the Organization of American States asked for a statement of what were the goals of the revolution. And they were provided: democracy, a pluralistic government, free elections, free labor unions, freedom of the press, human rights observed—those were the goals of the revolution, submitted in writing to the Organization of American States.

After they got in, they followed the pattern that was followed by Castro in Cuba. Those other elements that were not Sandinista, other groups who wanted—and they thought all the same thing, democracy—to rid themselves of a dictatorship. Those elements were denied participation in the government. Arrests were made. There were some who were exiled. There were some, I'm afraid, were executed. And many of the people now fighting as so-called *contras* are elements of the revolution. And it is less an overthrow that they're fighting for as it is a demand that they be allowed to participate in the government and that the government keep its promises as to what it had intended for the people.

And I see no dichotomy in our supporting the Government, the democratic Government of El Salvador, and the *contras* here. And we've made it plain to Nicaragua— made it very plain that this will stop when they keep their promise and restore a democratic rule and have elections. Now, they've finally been pressured; the pressure's led to them saying they'll have an election. I think they've scheduled it for next November. But there isn't anything yet to indicate that that election will be

anything but the kind of rubberstamp that we see in any totalitarian government. How do you have—there aren't any rival candidates; there aren't any rival parties. And how would they campaign without a free press?

Mr. Weisman. Well, that's a good note for us to close on.

Mr. Speakes. End on the free press. [*Laughter*]

Mr. Weisman. Thank you very much, Mr. President.

Note: The interview began at 11:43 a.m. in the Oval Office at the White House.

The transcript of the interview was released by the Office of the Press Secretary on March 29.

Nomination of Chapman B. Cox To Be General Counsel of the Department of Defense
March 29, 1984

The President today announced his intention to nominate Chapman B. Cox to be General Counsel of the Department of Defense. He would succeed William H. Taft IV.

Mr. Cox is presently serving as Assistant Secretary of the Navy for Manpower and Reserve Affairs. Previously he was Deputy Assistant Secretary of the Navy (Logistics) in 1981–1983. He was an associate with the law firm of Sherman & Howard (Denver) in 1972–1981 and a partner in the firm of Adams, Duque & Hazeltine (Los Angeles) in

1968–1972. He is a member of the Department of Defense Reserve Forces Policy Board and the Department of the Navy Review and Oversight Council. He is also a member of the United States Naval Institute, the Navy League, and the Marine Corps Reserve Officers Association.

He graduated from the University of Southern California (B.A., 1962) and Harvard Law School (J.D., 1965). He is married, has two children, and resides in Arlington, VA. He was born July 31, 1940, in Dayton, OH.

Nomination of David T. Kingsbury To Be an Assistant Director of the National Science Foundation
March 29, 1984

The President today announced his intention to nominate David T. Kingsbury to be an Assistant Director (Biological, Behavioral and Social Science) of the National Science Foundation. He would succeed Eloise E.

Clark.

Since 1981 Dr. Kingsbury has been serving as scientific director of the Naval Biosciences Laboratory and professor of medical microbiology at the University of California (Berkeley). Previously, he was associate professor of microbiology and molecular biology biochemistry at the College of Medicine, University of California (Irvine), in 1976–1981; visiting scientist at the Laboratory of Central Nervous System Studies at the National Institutes of Health in 1978–1979; and assistant professor of medical microbiology and molecular biology and biochemistry at the University of California

(Irvine) in 1972–1976. He is the author of numerous publications on microbiology and biochemistry.

He graduated from the University of Washington (B.S., 1962; M.S., 1965) and the University of California at San Diego (Ph.D., 1971). He is married and resides in Berkeley, CA. He was born October 24, 1940, in Seattle, WA.

Interview With Ann Devroy of USA Today on the President's Health
March 29, 1984

Ms. Devroy. ——actually, that is the first question. How are you?

The President. Just fine.

Ms. Devroy. How is the general state of your health?

You know this is—I'm doing a story that relates to that——

The President. That's what I understand, yes. Have you talked to Dan [1] yet?

Ms. Devroy. Yes.

The President. I understand you were going to. Well, I don't know what he told you—[*laughing*]——

Ms. Devroy. I'll tell you after you tell me. [*Laughter*]

The President. No, I can tell you I feel— I've never felt better.

Ms. Devroy. Do you have any problems left relating to the shooting? Any physical problems?

The President. No. No, as a matter of fact, I'm amazed at how hard I have to look now to see the extensive scarring.

Ms. Devroy. You don't want to do a Lyndon Johnson and show them to us, do you? [*Laughter*]

The President. No. No, you can catch me, oh, come summer, in a swimming suit.

Ms. Devroy. How——

The President. See how old-fashioned I am? I still call trunks a swimming suit. [*Laughter*]

---

[1] *Dr. Daniel Ruge, Physician to the President.*

Ms. Devroy. How often do you see Dr. Ruge?

The President. Oh, well, I have to see him pretty frequently. Every couple of weeks or so, I stop in to get my sneeze shots. I still have my little hay fever allergy, and I've discovered that Sacramento and Washington have something in common. They must be the allergy capitals of the world.

Ms. Devroy. You get—[*inaudible*]—every couple of weeks?

The President. Yes.

Ms. Devroy. Someone said that you also have allergies to feathers and stuffing in some of the chairs. Is that——

The President. Yes. As a matter of fact, here I've been wondering if some of my problem isn't indoors as much as out. Because I can go up to [Camp] David or a few days at the ranch or anything and—well, you can hear my voice now—and it's just fine. I can come back here and within 24 hours——

Ms. Devroy. Start getting hoarse?

The President. ——I have, kind of have that little allergic stuffiness.

Ms. Devroy. I want to clear something up. The Times reported on your birthday that you haven't had a physical in 2 years. Is that the case? The last—basically, the last one was April when you went out to the hospital by helicopter?

The President. I guess so, yes. Although there have been oh, interim things, like because of trips and so forth, they do a blood test on me, something of that kind.

Ms. Devroy. Why is that? It's the first time—according to the—[*inaudible*]—the first time in like 20 years you haven't had an annual physical.

The President. Well, Dan doesn't happen to be a believer in those. After that length of time, he doesn't think they're that essential. Now, this year we will. He's told me that we'll do some testing when we clear the schedule here a little bit.

Ms. Devroy. Well, when you were considering whether to run again, weren't you curious as to how—that you were in top shape, that your health was in good shape to go another 5 years?

The President. Yes, but now that we've dwelled on those allergies for so long, let's get around to the good part of it. There's just no question, I honestly believe—I work out daily in that gym upstairs at the end of the day. I'm still, at every opportunity, when the weather permits, riding, as I always have. And——

Ms. Devroy. Well, out here, the weather never seems——

The President. What?

Ms. Devroy. Well, out here the weather never seems to permit——

The President. Yes, this has been the longest stretch, I think, of not being able to. But no, I honestly am in excellent shape. And, as I say, I think in——

Ms. Devroy. You didn't have——

The President. ——better shape——

Ms. Devroy. ——any curiosity about going through a full physical just to make absolute sure?

The President. No, because I felt so good. Part of my workout is I get on a treadmill and climb uphill on that treadmill—they have a set climb—and that's part of the workout. I do that every day. And I know how I feel.

Ms. Devroy. When you were campaigning in 1980, when some of your advisers thought that age might be an issue—it didn't turn out to be—you pledged to take regular physical and mental tests and release them to the public while you were in office.

The President. [*Laughter*]

Ms. Devroy. Now, whatever happened to those? I haven't seen one.

The President. Well, no, I said if ever——

Ms. Devroy. By the way, Larry[2] says press conferences—[*inaudible*]——

The President. Yes.

Ms. Devroy. [*Inaudible*]—subject. But—[*laughter*]——

The President. Yes. No, what I actually said that time—because everyone was asking, you know, my mental faculties were not going to be able to survive, and I said if I ever had any indication that I was drifting into something of that kind, I certainly would——

Ms. Devroy. Oh, it was conditioned on if you found yourself having memory problems or something, that you'd——

The President. Yes.

Ms. Devroy. Oh, it wasn't an actual——

The President. No, and nothing like that has happened.

Ms. Devroy. When you take this, the physical you're going to take this year, will you release that publicly?

The President. Will I what?

Ms. Devroy. Make that public?

The President. Oh, I'm sure. Dan has always—no, I was just gesturing.

Ms. Devroy. Oh. [*Laughter*]

The President. Occasionally, if I look out the windows, it's to see if the squirrels are still eating the acorns. I brought down a great big bag of acorns from Camp David, and I put them out there in the—[*inaudible*]——

Ms. Devroy. I remember reading about that.

The President. No, Dave—or, I mean Dan, does that and answers any queries. And there's never been any reason not to answer them.

Ms. Devroy. Well, when I spoke to him, he said that most of that information really isn't the public's business. It's between you and he as your doctor. And, as you know, we haven't seen a report like that. And I'm wondering, this being an election year and people perhaps wanting to be reassured, if you would make that public.

The President. Well, I'll venture to say that when the campaign gets underway, it

---

[2] *Larry M. Speakes, Principal Deputy Press Secretary to the President.*

will be the same as it's been all the way back to those years when I was traveling a mashed-potato circuit for the GE Theatre; and that is that I'll be still going when the rest are in a state of collapse. [*Laughter*]

I remember back in those years—on that theatre—that I'd go into a town, visit the plant, and then all the schedule that they'd have for me. And usually my leaving would be, as they said goodbye, they'd say, "We're glad you're getting out of town." [*Laughter*]

Ms. Devroy. I'm not implying anything other than the fact that we haven't seen an actual report like that, and some of the Democratic candidates are starting to release reports from their physicians. Do you think your age will become an issue? It didn't in '80.

The President. I can't believe that it will. If it does, I'll challenge him to an arm wrestle.

Ms. Devroy. One eminent psychologist recommended recently at the American Psychiatric Institute that a government—I know you're not going to like this—that a government panel be set up to examine all candidates for the President to report to the public on their health. Would you accept that?

The President. [*Laughing*] Well, certainly I would accept it if that was what they wanted, and everyone felt that's what should be done. But I just wonder if we haven't gone so far anymore in the restrictions that are being placed on people in government, in the suspicions that motivate so many things that are being done, not only to elected officials but to appointees in government, that pretty soon we're going to find that the best people won't seek government as a way to—service to their country.

I think that's as I've said. And if we run any checks or anything, I'll make sure that Dan knows it's all right with me to answer the questions.

But to get back to the health factor, at a time when an awful lot of people I know are worried because their belt size is changing, my worry is that I'm growing out of my coats because I've added an inch and a quarter around my chest.

Ms. Devroy. Are you still——

The President. Yes.

Ms. Devroy. Are you still doing that?

The President. Sure.

Ms. Devroy. I mean, is that——

The President. Every day. Well, 6 days a week. You take 1 day off.

Ms. Devroy. Do you——

The President. Two different sets of exercise—one 3 days, and the other one 3 days.

Ms. Devroy. Do you take any medicines?

The President. I take vitamins. Nancy's father was a surgeon, as you know, and got us in that habit a long time ago. And I don't know what effect it's had, but it must have done something right. And that was—he said that he always—he was not a great believer in a lot of vitamins or anything, but he said—and he prescribed a certain multiple vitamin—he said we're all of us so careless about our food. You know, lunch time is when you grab a sandwich or something, a cup of coffee and a roll, that sort of thing. And he said that he'd always believed that this one multivitamin every day would make up for any deficiencies in your diet.

And we both got in the habit of doing it. And, I suppose, if you have to call that a medicine, well, that's a medicine.

Ms. Devroy. Let me turn to one pretty serious subject. Have you considered or discussed what would happen here if you became impaired in your second term somehow?

The President. If I become——

Ms. Devroy. Impaired somehow? You know, constitutionally, if you were impaired, there's a procedure. Have you discussed that?

The President. No. I assume——

Ms. Devroy. The thought never occurred to you that——

The President. No. [*Laughing*]

Ms. Devroy. Well, I'll try—how about—everything I've read or know about you indicates that you are very optimistic. Do you ever go through periods when you're bothered by stress or—of the job—or depression about something that's happening?

The President. No. I think I do some reasonable worry about whether a decision that I have to make—the hardest decisions are the ones when there's so much right on both sides. They're not clean-cut this way or that way.

But, no. And I think maybe this comes from the previous experience of having been a Governor of the largest State in the Union—not in acreage, in population. I remember when I first started that job, yes, I discovered what stress was.

Ms. Devroy. Did it keep you awake or did you pace? I mean, how did it affect you?

The President. Well, it was just a tension that I had. We'd inherited a situation somewhat similar to what we inherited here—in California. And it seemed as if every day that I sat down at my desk, there was someone in front of the desk saying, "We've got a problem." And I found myself almost with a physical desire to look over my shoulder to see if there wasn't someone I could turn to and tell that to. And I just——

Ms. Devroy. That never—it never caused any real physical problem? I mean, it was just something you coped with and got used to?

The President. And I just said to myself one day, "Look, all I can do is make a decision based on what, to the best of my ability, is my belief in what is right for the people." I had already told the Cabinet and others, as I have here, that I don't want anyone suggesting things on the basis of the political context; that the decisions will be made on what's right or wrong for our people. And I haven't had that since.

Ms. Devroy. Well, what about anger? You have to have, in the past—this morning, I got up and saw the Meese stuff all over TV. It was all over TV last night. That sort of thing has to affect you in terms of anger. You must have to cope with that. How do you cope with that?

The President. Oh, sometimes I get mad. My fellows tell me—I wasn't even conscious of it—they tell me that once in a while, they watch. When I throw my glasses—[*laughter*]—they know I'm angry.

But, yes, I think that's something that is very frustrating. Look, I'm the guy they're after with their demagoguery. Well, all right, then, come after me. But quit picking on people who haven't done anything wrong and who actually have made a sacrifice in order to serve in government—and try to destroy human beings the way they are.

Now, why didn't someone—in that splash last night about those cufflinks—why didn't somebody bother to find out that there are at least nine people, including people at the State Department, who received those gifts from the Korean Government when we were there, but all were assured that the terms under which such gifts could be given and accepted had been met by the Korean Government? In other words, there is a financial limit below which it is proper. All of them had been told that these gifts came underneath that limit. Now, somebody——

Ms. Devroy. Larry was one with the——

The President. ——somebody went out and got a local estimate. Well, do you go by what an estimate is at our kind of inflated prices, or do you go by what they cost the Government over there?

Ms. Devroy. But what do you do when you see that, and you say to yourself, "This is really unfair"?

The President. Yes, I say that, and maybe I say some unprintable language for a minute or 2. But I also learned that you can eat yourself up with anger, and I'd rather eat them up. [*Laughter*]

Mr. Speakes. Mr. President, you're running late here. You've got the black college presidents.

The President. But we're having so much fun. [*Laughter*]

Mr. Speakes. Have you got one more?

Ms. Devroy. Well, I'll tell him one quick anecdote.

I was researching this story, and I talked to this doctor—when you had said you'd take these mental tests and put out the results. I was speaking to a doctor who's a specialist in that area and asked him if there's a simple test that you can give a President to assess that. And he said, "Sure, it's just three or four questions long. But it won't work in this case." And I said, "Why not?" And he said, "The first question is, 'Who's the President of the United States?'" [*Laughter*] So, that took care of that idea. [*Laughter*]

The President. Well, let me just——

Ms. Devroy. Thank you very much.

The President. On your way out, let me just show you something.

Ms. Devroy. Do you want to arm wrestle?

The President. No. [*Laughter*] Kathy[3] brought in today——

Ms. Devroy. Someone told me it was incredible.

The President. There. Now, does that look like I need to take a physical? And these are all very recent. These are from the last time out there.

Ms. Devroy. Is this the latest issue of National Geographic?

The President. I guess so, yes.

Ms. Devroy. Thanks.

The President. So, my only illness is, after looking at this, homesickness.

Ms. Devroy. Thank you, Mr. President.

The President. Well, thank you.

Note: The interview began at 2 p.m. in the Oval Office at the White House.

The transcript of the interview was released by the Office of the Press Secretary on March 30.

Letter to the Speaker of the House and the President of the Senate on Recommendations Pursuant to the Alaska National Interest Lands Conservation Act
March 30, 1984

Dear Mr. Speaker: (Dear Mr. President:)

Enclosed in accordance with section 1311 of the Alaska National Interest Lands Conservation Act (16 U.S.C. 3200) is the recommendation of the Secretary of the Interior and the Governor of Alaska with respect to the creation of a scenic highway along the routes described in that section.

The Secretary and the Governor recommend that no such scenic highway be established and, further, that the Congress move

immediately to repeal the public lands withdrawal from mining and mineral leasing imposed by section 1311. I concur in those recommendations.

Sincerely,

RONALD REAGAN

Note: This is the text of identical letters addressed to Thomas P. O'Neill, Jr., Speaker of the House of Representatives, and George Bush, President of the Senate.

Executive Order 12470—Continuation of Export Control Regulations
March 30, 1984

By the authority vested in me as President by the Constitution and laws of the United States of America, including section 203 of the International Emergency Economic Powers Act (50 U.S.C. 1702) (hereinafter referred to as "the Act"), and 22 U.S.C. 287c,

I, *Ronald Reagan*, President of the

United States of America, find that the unrestricted access of foreign parties to United States commercial goods, technology, and technical data and the existence of certain boycott practices of foreign nations constitute, in light of the expiration of the Export Administration Act of 1979, an unusual and extraordinary threat to the national security, foreign policy and economy of the United States and hereby declare a national economic emergency to deal with that threat.

---

[3] *Kathleen Osborne, Personal Secretary to the President.*

Accordingly, in order (a) to exercise the necessary vigilance over exports from the standpoint of their significance to the national security of the United States; (b) to further significantly the foreign policy of the United States, including its policy with respect to cooperation by United States persons with certain foreign boycott activities, and to fulfill its international responsibilities; and (c) to protect the domestic economy from the excessive drain of scarce materials and reduce the serious economic impact of foreign demand, it is hereby ordered as follows:

Section 1. Notwithstanding the expiration of the Export Administration Act of 1979, as amended (50 U.S.C. App. 2401 *et seq.*), the provisions of that Act, the provisions for administration of that Act and the delegations of authority set forth in Executive Order No. 12002 of July 7, 1977 and Executive Order No. 12214 of May 2, 1980, shall, to the extent permitted by law, be incorporated in this Order and shall continue in full force and effect.

Sec. 2. All rules and regulations issued or continued in effect by the Secretary of Commerce under the authority of the Export Administration Act of 1979, as amended, including those published in Title 15, Chapter III, Subchapter C, of the Code of Federal Regulations, Parts 368 to 399 inclusive, and all orders, regulations, licenses and other forms of administrative action issued, taken or continued in effect pursuant thereto, shall, until amended or revoked by the Secretary of Commerce, remain in full force and effect, the same as if issued or taken pursuant to this Order, except that the provisions of sections 203(b)(2) and 206 of the Act (50 U.S.C. 1702(b)(2) and 1705) shall control over any inconsistent provisions in the regulations with respect to, respectively, certain donations to relieve human suffering and civil and criminal penalties for violations subject to this Order. Nothing in this section shall affect the continued applicability of administrative sanctions provided for by the regulations described above.

Sec. 3. Provisions for the administration of section 38(e) of the Arms Export Control Act (22 U.S.C. 2778(e)) may be made and shall continue in full force and effect until amended or revoked under the authority of section 203 of the Act (50 U.S.C. 1702). To the extent permitted by law, this Order also shall constitute authority for the issuance and continuation in full force and effect of all rules and regulations by the President or his delegate, and all orders, licenses, and other forms of administrative action issued, taken or continued in effect pursuant thereto, relating to the administration of section 38(e).

Sec. 4. This Order shall be effective as of midnight between March 30 and March 31, 1984, and shall remain in effect until terminated. It is my intention to terminate this Order upon the enactment into law of a bill reauthorizing the authorities contained in the Export Administration Act.

RONALD REAGAN

The White House,
March 30, 1984.

[*Filed with the Office of the Federal Register, 3:07 p.m., March 30, 1984*]

Message to the Congress Reporting on the Continuation of Export Control Regulations
March 30, 1984

To the Congress of the United States:

Pursuant to section 204(b) of the International Emergency Economic Powers Act, 50 U.S.C. 1703, I hereby report to the Congress that I have today exercised the authority granted by this Act to continue in effect the system of controls contained in 15 C.F.R. Parts 368–399, including restrictions on participation by United States persons in certain foreign boycott activities, which heretofore has been maintained under the authority of the Export Administration Act of 1979, as amended, 50 U.S.C. App. 2401 *et seq.* In addition, I have made provision for the administration of Section 38(e) of the Arms Export Control Act, 22 U.S.C. 2778(e).

1. The exercise of this authority is necessitated by the expiration of the Export Administration Act on March 30, 1984, and the resulting lapse of the system of controls maintained under that Act.

2. In the absence of controls, foreign parties would have unrestricted access to United States commercial products, technology and technical data, posing an unusual and extraordinary threat to national security, foreign policy, and economic objectives critical to the United States. In addition, United States persons would not be prohibited from complying with certain foreign boycott requests. This would seriously harm our foreign policy interests, particularly in the Middle East. Controls established in 15 C.F.R. 368–399, and continued by this action, include the following:

National security export controls aimed at restricting the export of goods and technologies which would make a significant contribution to the military potential of any other country and which would prove detrimental to the national security of the United States;

Foreign policy controls which further the foreign policy objectives of the United States or its declared international obligations in such widely recognized areas as human rights, anti-terrorism, and regional stability;

Nuclear nonproliferation controls that are maintained for both national security and foreign policy reasons, and which support the objectives of the Nuclear Nonproliferation Act;

Short supply controls that protect domestic supplies; and

Anti-boycott regulations that prohibit compliance with foreign boycotts aimed at countries friendly to the United States.

3. Consequently, I have issued an Executive Order (a copy of which is attached) to continue in effect all rules and regulations issued or continued in effect by the Secretary of Commerce under the authority of the Export Administration Act of 1979, as amended, and all orders, regulations, licenses, and other forms of administrative actions under that Act, except where they are inconsistent with sections 203(b) and 206 of the International Emergency Economic Powers Act.

4. The Congress and the Executive have not permitted export controls to lapse since they were enacted under the Export Control Act of 1949. Any termination of controls could permit transactions to occur that would be seriously detrimental to the national interests we have heretofore sought to protect through export controls and restrictions on compliance by United States persons with certain foreign boycotts. I believe that even a temporary lapse in this system of controls would seriously damage our national security, foreign policy and economic interests and undermine our credibility in meeting our international obligations.

5. The countries affected by this action vary depending on the objectives sought to be achieved by the system of controls instituted under the Export Administration Act. Potential adversaries are seeking to acquire sensitive United States goods and technologies. Other countries serve as conduits for the diversion of such items. Still other countries have policies that are contrary to United States foreign policy or nuclear nonproliferation objectives, or foster boycotts against friendly countries. For some goods or technologies, controls could apply even to our closest allies in order to safeguard against diversion to potential adversaries.

6. It is my intention to terminate the Executive Order upon enactment into law of a bill reauthorizing the authorities contained in the Export Administration Act.

RONALD REAGAN

The White House,
March 30, 1984.

Message to the Congress Transmitting Proposed Legislation To Approve the Compact of Free Association Between the United States and the Trust Territory of the Pacific Islands
March 30, 1984

To the Congress of the United States:

There is enclosed a draft of a Joint Resolution to approve the "Compact of Free Association," the negotiated instrument setting forth the future political relationship between the United States and two political jurisdictions of the Trust Territory of the Pacific Islands.

The Compact of Free Association is the result of more than fourteen years of continuous and comprehensive negotiations, spanning the administrations of four Presidents. The transmission of the proposed Joint Resolution to you today marks the last step in the Compact approval process.

The full text of the Compact is part of the draft Joint Resolution, which I request be introduced, referred to the appropriate committees for consideration, and enacted. I also request that the Congress note the agreements subsidiary to the Compact. Also enclosed is a section-by-section analysis to facilitate your consideration of the Compact.

The defense and land use provisions of the Compact extend indefinitely the right of the United States to foreclose access to the area to third countries for military purposes. These provisions are of great importance to our strategic position in the Pacific and enable us to continue preserving regional security and peace.

Since 1947, the islands of Micronesia have been administered by the United States under a Trusteeship Agreement with the United Nations Security Council. This Compact of Free Association with the governments of the Federated States of Micronesia and the Republic of the Marshall Islands would fulfill our commitment under that agreement to bring about self-government. Upon termination of the Trusteeship Agreement, another political jurisdiction of the Trust Territory of the Pacific Islands, the Northern Mariana Islands, will become a commonwealth of the United States.

The Compact of Free Association was signed for the United States by Ambassador Fred M. Zeder, II, on October 1, 1982, with the Federated States of Micronesia, and on June 25, 1983, with the Republic of the Marshall Islands. It is the result of negotiations between the United States and broadly representative groups of delegates from the prospective freely associated states.

In 1983, United Nations-observed plebiscites produced high voter participation, and the Compact was approved by impressive majorities. In addition to approval in the plebiscites, the Compact has been approved by the governments of the Republic of the Marshall Islands and the Federated States of Micronesia in accordance with their constitutional processes.

Enactment of the draft Joint Resolution approving the Compact of Free Association would be a major step leading to the termination of the Trusteeship Agreement with the United Nations Security Council, which the United States entered into by Joint Resolution on July 18, 1947. Therefore, I urge the Congress to approve the Compact of Free Association.

RONALD REAGAN

The White House,
March 30, 1984.

Executive Order 12471—Amending the Generalized System of Preferences
March 30, 1984

By virtue of the authority vested in me as President by the Constitution and statutes of the United States of America, including Title V of the Trade Act of 1974 (the Trade Act) (19 U.S.C. 2461 *et seq.*), as amended, section 604 of the Trade Act (19 U.S.C. 2483), and section 503(a)(2)(A) of the Trade Agreements Act of 1979 (93 Stat. 251), in order to modify, as provided by sections 504(a) and (c) of the Trade Act (19 U.S.C. 2464(a) and (c)), the limitations on preferential treatment for eligible articles from countries designated as beneficiary developing countries; to adjust the original designation of eligible articles after taking into account information and advice received in fulfillment of sections 131–134 and 503(a) of the Trade Act (19 U.S.C. 2151–2154, 2463); to provide for the continuation, to the greatest extent possible, of preferential treatment under the Generalized System of Preferences (GSP) for articles which are currently eligible for such treatment and which are imported from countries designated as beneficiary developing countries, following changes to the Tariff Schedules of the United States (TSUS) (19 U.S.C. 1202) made by Proclamation 5140 (48 F.R. 56553); and to make technical changes in the identification of certain beneficiary developing countries, it is hereby ordered as follows:

Section 1. In order to subdivide and amend the nomenclature of existing items for purposes of the GSP, the TSUS are modified as provided in Annex I to this Order.

Sec. 2. Annex II of Executive Order No. 11888, as amended, listing articles that are eligible for benefits of the GSP when imported from any designated beneficiary developing country, is amended by substituting therefor the new Annex II to this Order.

Sec. 3. Annex III of Executive Order No. 11888, as amended, listing articles that are eligible for benefits of the GSP when imported from all designated beneficiary countries except those specified in General Headnote 3(c)(iii) of the TSUS, is amended by substituting therefor the new Annex III to this Order.

Sec. 4. General Headnote 3(c)(iii) of the TSUS, listing articles that are eligible for benefits of the GSP except when imported from the beneficiary countries listed opposite those articles, is modified by substituting therefor the General Headnote 3(c)(iii) set forth in Annex IV to this Order.

Sec. 5. In order to provide staged reductions in the rates of duty for those new TSUS items created by Annex I to this Order, Annex III to Proclamation 4707, and Annex III to Proclamation 4768, are amended as set forth in Annex V to this Order.

Sec. 6. Whenever the column 1 rate of duty in the TSUS for any item specified in Annex I to this Order is reduced to the same level as, or to a lower level than, the corresponding rate of duty in the column entitled "LDDC" by Annex I to this Order, the rate of duty in the column entitled "LDDC" for such item shall be deleted from the TSUS.

Sec. 7. Annexes III and IV of Proclamation 4707, Annexes II, III, and IV of Proclamation 4768, and Annex I of Executive Order No. 12413, are superseded to the extent inconsistent with this Order.

Sec. 8. General Headnote 3(c)(i) of the TSUS listing the designated beneficiary developing countries for purposes of the GSP is modified as provided in Annex VI to this Order.

Sec. 9. In order to clarify the eligibility of certain articles for benefits of the GSP, headnote 1 to subpart C, part 2 of the Appendix to the TSUS is modified by deleting "the Appendix to". This modification is effective with respect to articles both: (1) imported on or after January 1, 1976, and (2) entered, or withdrawn from warehouse for consumption, on or after January 1, 1984.

Sec. 10. Unless otherwise specified, the amendments made by this Order shall be effective with respect to articles both: (1)

imported on or after January 1, 1976, and (2) entered, or withdrawn from warehouse for consumption, on or after March 30, 1984.

RONALD REAGAN

The White House,
March 30, 1984.

[*Filed with the Office of the Federal Register, 4:11 p.m., March 30, 1984*]

Note: The annexes to the Executive order are printed in the Federal Register *of April 3, 1984.*

Letter to the Speaker of the House and the President Pro Tempore of the Senate on the Termination of United States Participation in the Multinational Force in Lebanon
March 30, 1984

Dear Mr. Speaker: (Dear Mr. President:)

Since the date of my last report to you on the participation of United States Armed Forces in the Multinational Force (MNF) in Lebanon, I have decided that the U.S. will terminate its participation in the MNF. In accordance with my desire that Congress be kept informed on these matters, and consistent with Section 4 of the Multinational Force in Lebanon Resolution, I am hereby providing a final report on our participation in the MNF.

U.S. foreign policy interests in Lebanon have not changed, and remain as stated in my last report to Congress on February 13. The U.S. is committed to the goals of the restoration of a sovereign, independent and united Lebanon, the withdrawal of all foreign forces, and the security of Israel's northern border. However, the continuation of our participation in the MNF is no longer a necessary or appropriate means of achieving these goals. We have discussed our decision with the Government of Lebanon and the other MNF participants, and the other MNF countries have made similar decisions.

The U.S. military personnel who made up the U.S. MNF contingent were earlier redeployed to U.S. ships offshore. Likewise, the MNF personnel of other national contingents have either already departed Lebanon or are in the process of departing.

As you know, prior to their earlier redeployment to ships offshore, U.S. MNF personnel had come under intermittent hostile fire as a result of continued fighting in the Beirut area, including the round of serious fighting that occurred in late February. On February 25–26, and again on February 29, U.S. warships returned fire against artillery and rocket positions in Syrian-controlled territory that had fired on U.S. military and diplomatic locations and on U.S. reconnaissance flights.

During the overall course of our participation in the MNF, U.S. forces suffered a total of 264 killed (of which 4 non-MNF personnel were killed in the April 1983 bombing of the U.S. Embassy), and 137 wounded in action. (Three of these were wounded in the period since my last report to Congress on February 13.) The estimated cost of U.S. participation in the MNF for FY 1984 was a total of $14.6 million for the U.S. Marine Corps deployment, $44.9 million for U.S. Navy support, and $243,000 for U.S. Army support.

These were heavy burdens and grievous losses for our country. We owe a great debt of gratitude to those military and diplomatic personnel of the United States and other MNF countries who served their countries so proudly to give the people of Lebanon a chance to achieve peace and national reconciliation.

The United States has not abandoned Lebanon. The U.S. Embassy in Beirut remains in full and active operation and a Marine detachment of approximately 100 personnel drawn from the Marine unit afloat remains to provide additional external security for our diplomatic mission. In addition, a limited number of U.S. military personnel (equipped with personal weapons for self-defense) will remain to provide military training and security assistance liaison to the Lebanese Armed Forces. These personnel will not be part of any multinational force; they will be deployed under the authority of the Foreign Assistance and Arms Export Control Acts, and my Constitutional authority with respect to the conduct of foreign relations and as Commander-in-Chief of U.S. Forces. I do not intend or expect, under present circumstances, that these personnel will become involved in hostilities; nonetheless, U.S. naval and air forces in the Mediterranean area, including the U.S. Marines redeployed from Lebanon, are available to protect our military and diplomatic personnel should that need ever arise.

I appreciate the support for this vital effort that Congress provided last October in adopting the Multinational Force in Lebanon Resolution. I hope that Congress will support the programs of economic and security assistance that are essential for the future of Lebanon and the Middle East. I will keep Congress informed on events in Lebanon, and on the U.S. role in encouraging peace and stability in the area.

Sincerely,

RONALD REAGAN

Note: This is the text of identical letters addressed to Thomas P. O'Neill, Jr., Speaker of the House of Representatives, and Strom Thurmond, President pro tempore of the Senate.

Appointment of Charlton Heston as a Member of the Board of Trustees of the John F. Kennedy Center for the Performing Arts
March 30, 1984

The President today announced his intention to appoint Charlton Heston to be a member of the Board of Trustees of the John F. Kennedy Center for the Performing Arts, Smithsonian Institution, for the remainder of the term expiring September 1, 1988. He will succeed Efrem Zimbalist, Jr.

Mr. Heston is an actor with over 50 starring roles in films to his credit in addition to many roles in the theater and television. He made his Broadway debut in 1948 in "Antony and Cleopatra." He received an Academy Award for his performance in "Ben-Hur" in 1959 and made his debut as a motion picture director in 1971 with the film version of "Antony and Cleopatra."

He served six terms as president of the Screen Actors Guild and was Chairman of the American Film Institute. He received the 1978 Jean Hersholt Humanitarian Award from the Academy of Motion Picture Arts and Sciences. He recently served as Cochairman for the arts on the Presidential Task Force on the Arts and Humanities.

Mr. Heston attended Northwestern University and served in the United States Air Force. He is married and has two children. A native of Evanston, IL, he now resides with his family in Beverly Hills, CA.

Radio Address to the Nation on Opportunities for Women
March 31, 1984

My fellow Americans:

A few weeks ago, George Gallup, who regularly surveys the pulse of America, released a poll with very upbeat news. Gallup

445

said the current mood of the American people is the brightest in 5 years. Our citizens still feel the burdens of everyday problems, but there's a feeling among us that we've finally turned the corner. Real progress is being made, and America is moving forward again.

Better days for America may be bad news for some, but even the most committed gloom mongers can't deny the truth forever. Our economy is strong, prices are stable, jobs are increasing, and our nation is at peace. We're building a true opportunity society, and this is especially true for today's women.

Women in the eighties are a diverse majority with varied interests and futures. Some seek to pursue their own careers; some run for political office; others focus on the home and family. Some seek to do all these things. They are members of a growing group called "working mothers," and sometimes their days resemble a script from "Mission Impossible."

Well, no role is superior to another. What's important is that every woman have the right and opportunity to choose the role she wishes—or, perhaps, try to fill them all. And whether the choice be homemaking, career, or both, our administration is trying to help in many different ways.

We've increased training opportunities through the Job Training Partnership Act so women can secure permanent, productive employment. For those whose former spouses are delinquent in child-support payments, we've strengthened the Federal child-support enforcement system, and we have additional proposals pending before the Congress.

For all women we've provided several forms of tax relief—relief, by the way, which could and should have been passed long ago by those in Washington who had a monopoly on power and who still claim a monopoly on compassion.

We've reduced personal income tax rates by 25 percent. We've greatly reduced the marriage tax penalty. We've almost doubled the maximum child care tax credit for working mothers. We've expanded IRA accounts, benefiting women whether they work at home or in paid jobs, and we're moving to bring even greater equity to those accounts. And we've eliminated the widow's tax, the estate taxes levied on a surviving spouse. This will help women who've been hard-working partners on family farms and small businesses.

We're also working with the Congress on historic legislation that reforms inequities against women in private pension plans. This legislation has passed the Senate, and we're waiting for final action in the House. I hope it will come soon. The reforms would lower the age employees can participate in company pension plans, protect spouses from losing death benefits without their knowledge, permit a break in service of up to 5 years without loss of pension credit, coordinate State and Federal laws so divorced spouses can collect court-awarded pension benefits more easily, and require private pension plans to survivor's benefits—offer survivor's benefits, I should say, protection to workers after they're 45.

I've always believed the greatest contribution we can make is to get our economy moving and keep it moving. Economic growth will provide more opportunities for women than if all the promises ever made in Washington, DC, were enacted into law.

Well, economic growth is very strong. And job opportunities for women are popping up like springtime tulips. Three million more women are working today in our economy than in January 1981. One exciting area of growth is that of women-owned businesses. The number of businesses owned by women is increasing four times faster than those owned by men.

Yesterday, I met some of the people whose dreams, intelligence, and hard work are making America in 1984 the most forward-looking and successful nation in the world. I had lunch at the White House with the members of my Advisory Committee on Women's Business Ownership—12 women and 3 men, all successful in the professional world. They're working with the Small Business Administration on conferences across the country to help women acquire skills to own businesses and compete effectively. They're also trying to identify problems business owners and potential business owners are meeting. Now, if you've had any, please write to me at the White House, and I'll share your thoughts with the Advisory Committee.

Next Thursday, I'll be traveling to New York to attend one of these conferences to meet with and to address women business owners of that great city.

All over this country the entrepreneur is changing the face and brightening the future of America, and she's just getting started.

Until next week, thanks for listening, and God bless you.

Note: The President spoke at 12:06 p.m. from Camp David, MD.

Proclamation 5170—National Eye Donor Month, 1984
March 31, 1984

By the President of the United States of America

A Proclamation

One of the most magnificent presents that one human being can bestow upon another is the gift of sight. Human eye tissue which is donated at death may be used in research and cornea transplant operations. Each year, thousands of Americans suffer from impaired vision caused by congenital defects, injuries, and diseases. Cornea transplant surgery can improve or restore the sight of many of these people. Unfortunately, all too many people are unable to retain their sight because there is not enough corneal tissue available.

Through the efforts of 93 eyebanks across the Nation, these problems are being alleviated. The eyebanks help coordinate the nationwide distribution of donated eye tissue for use in medical education, continuing research efforts, and cornea transplants. Developing from a single institution in 1944, the eyebanks have greatly encouraged research into the prevention and treatment of eye disease and helped increase national awareness of the urgent need for more eye donations, so that others may receive the gift of sight.

The Congress, by Senate Joint Resolution 225, has designated March 1984 as "National Eye Donor Month" and has authorized and requested the President to issue a proclamation in observance of that occasion.

Now, Therefore, I, Ronald Reagan, President of the United States of America, do hereby proclaim the month of March 1984 as National Eye Donor Month. I urge all citizens, health care professionals, educators, and other public and private organizations concerned with vision and vision research to join with the Nation's eyebanks in recognizing this humanitarian cause with appropriate activities.

In Witness Whereof, I have hereunto set my hand this thirty-first day of March, in the year of our Lord nineteen hundred and eighty-four, and of the Independence of the United States of America the two hundred and eighth.

RONALD REAGAN

[*Filed with the Office of the Federal Register, 11:31 a.m., April 2, 1984*]

Letter to the Speaker of the House and the President of the Senate on United States Policy on Arms Control for Antisatellite Systems
March 31, 1984

Dear Mr. Speaker: *(Dear Mr. President:)*

I am pleased to transmit this report on my Administration's policy on arms control for antisatellite systems as required in the Conference Report for the Department of Defense Appropriations Act for Fiscal Year 1984.

The United States is committed to the exploration and use of space by all nations for peaceful purposes and for the benefit of mankind. Among the activities conducted by the United States in space is the pursuit of fundamental national security objectives. Arms control arrangements for space would serve these objectives if they contributed to our overall deterrence posture and reduce the risk of conflict.

With this in mind, I announced on July 4, 1982, the basic posture of this Administration which I now reaffirm:

"The United States will continue to study space arms control options. The United States will consider verifiable and equitable arms control measures that would ban or otherwise limit testing and deployment of specific weapons systems, should those measures be compatible with United States national security."

Guided by these criteria, the United States has been studying a range of possible options for space arms control, with a view to possible negotiations with the Soviet Union and other nations, if such negotiations would serve U.S. interests. Within the U.S. Government, this work is being conducted by an Interdepartmental Group chaired by the Office of the Secretary of Defense and the Arms Control and Disarmament Agency. The United States is also prepared to examine space arms control issues in the Conference on Disarmament (CD). However, no arrangements or agreements beyond those already governing military activities in outer space have been found to date that are judged to be in the

overall interest of the United States and its Allies. The factors that impede the identification of effective ASAT arms control measures include significant difficulties of verification, diverse sources of threats to U.S. and Allied satellites, and threats posed by Soviet targeting and reconnaissance satellites that undermine conventional and nuclear deterrence.

Notwithstanding these difficulties, the United States is continuing to study space arms control, in search of selected limits on specific types of space systems or activities in space that could satisfactorily deal with problems, such as those described above. Until we have determined whether there are, in fact, practical solutions to these problems, I do not believe it would be productive to engage in formal international negotiations. The United States remains ready, however, to examine the problems and potential of space arms control at the Conference on Disarmament in Geneva.

The attached Report on U.S. Policy on Antisatellite Arms Control sets forth in greater detail the views of my Administration on this important issue. It is unclassified and is suitable for general release. As you are aware, information regarding certain U.S. and Soviet space activities involves sensitive information. Accordingly, I am also transmitting a classified Report providing such information under separate cover. In preparing both Reports, every effort was made to respond to the questions asked by various Committees and Members of Congress.

Sincerely,

RONALD REAGAN

Note: This is the text of identical letters addressed to Thomas P. O'Neill, Jr., Speaker of the House of Representatives, and George Bush, President of the Senate.

The text of the letters was released by the Office of the Press Secretary on April 2.

Remarks on Meeting the Cherry Blossom Festival Princesses
April 2, 1984

Well, I'm delighted to welcome you all here. This is the 57th year of this event, and it's the oldest and largest event that is held annually here in the Capital. I'm very proud, and Nancy is very proud that she is the honorary chairman. And I'm glad to see you all. I've never seen the Rose Garden look lovelier. [*Laughter*]

You're a sure sign of spring; the arrival of the princesses here makes that positive. The festival symbolizes the spirit of friendship between the United States and Japan, as well as the beginning of spring.

And it gives me particular pleasure to welcome the 1983 Cherry Blossom Queen from Japan, Etsuko Kobayashi. And we have with us our own queen, Lynn Ridgley, and the 56 princesses chosen by the State societies and the territories.

And as I said, this is a longtime event here. You're, all of you, most welcome, and I can assure you that after the winter we've had, believe me, if you're bringing spring, you are welcome. [*Laughter*]

Now, I'm going to say some "hellos," if I can.

Note: The President spoke at 11 a.m. in the Rose Garden at the White House.

Appointment of Five Members of the Board of Foreign Scholarships
April 2, 1984

The President today announced his intention to appoint the following individuals to be members of the Board of Foreign Scholarships for terms expiring September 22, 1986:

Marvin Howard Alisky would succeed Mario A. Anglada. Mr. Alisky is currently a professor of political science at Arizona State University. He is married, has two children, and resides in Tempe, AZ. He was born March 12, 1923, in Kansas City, MO.

Brigitte Berger would succeed H. Brandt Ayers. Mrs. Berger is currently a professor of sociology at Wellesley College. She is married, has two children, and resides in Brookline, MA. She was born August 8, 1928, in Hildburghausen, Germany.

Milorad M. Drachkovitch would succeed Adelaide Cromwell Gulliver. Mr. Drachkovitch is currently senior fellow at the Hoover Institution. He is married, has two children, and resides in Stanford, CA. He was born November 8, 1921, in Belgrade, Yugoslavia.

Nathan Glazer would succeed Harrison E. Salisbury. Mr. Glazer is currently a professor of education and sociology at Harvard University Graduate School of Education. He is married, has three children, and resides in Cambridge, MA. He was born February 25, 1923, in New York, NY.

Richard Anderson Ware would succeed Jean J. Smoot for the remainder of the term expiring September 22, 1985. Mr. Ware is currently president of the Earhart Foundation, which maintains a philanthropic program of research and educational support for institutions and individuals in the fields of economics, political science, international studies, and national security affairs. He is married, has three children, and resides in Ann Arbor, MI. He was born November 7, 1919, in New York, NY.

Proclamation 5171—Pan American Day and Pan American Week, 1984
April 2, 1984

By the President of the United States of America

A Proclamation

The nations of the Western Hemisphere have been blessed with a common heritage that has bound them together in the pursuit of peace and harmony within the framework of democratic institutions. The annual proclamation of Pan American Day and Pan American Week has for 53 years stressed our unity of purpose and drawn the attention of the world to the significant achievements of the Inter-American system and the Organization of American States.

Through the OAS, the nations of the Americas have worked to fulfill their shared aspirations for peace, prosperity, and freedom. These goals form the cornerstone of the OAS and find eloquent expression in the OAS Charter. While other areas of the world have been fraught with strife, the OAS has been instrumental in maintaining the peace in this hemisphere. The peacekeeping mechanisms available to OAS member nations have proved responsive in a multitude of tests in the past, including those posed by the subversion and indirect aggression of Cuba and its partners. The continued strength and resilience of these peacekeeping mechanisms should be of primary importance to all the nations of the Americas as we deal with the current challenges to peace, prosperity and freedom, especially in Central America.

Because in this century our hemisphere has been spared the violence other regions have had to endure, we have been fortunate to be able to dedicate our energies to the important tasks of economic, social, scientific, educational, and cultural development of our nations. In this effort to better the lives of our people, the OAS, through its technical councils and specialized Inter-American agencies, has served as a model for others.

Consistent with the spirit of the Inter-American system as expressed in the OAS Charter, the peoples of this hemisphere are turning more and more to democratic institutions as a means of solving the difficult problems we face. This is a vote of confidence in democracy as an effective means of governing—a practical problem-solving mechanism—not just an abstract political ideal. The trend reinforces the bonds which unite us and strengthens our capacity for cooperation.

During the bicentennial year of the birth of the great Liberator, Simon Bolivar, it is appropriate that we rededicate ourselves to the spirit of hemispheric solidarity that he symbolized. His example serves as an inspiration for all Americans to face the difficult challenges of our time. Bolivar believed that diversity does not preclude unity. The kind of cooperation the Pan American nations enjoy today is based on mutual respect for the individual characteristics that distinguish us, as well as the long-standing ties that unite us. Pan American Day is a welcome opportunity to recognize this cooperation and the impressive progress we have made together.

On this Pan American Day of 1984, the people of the United States extend warm greetings to all of their neighbors in the Americas, and reaffirm their active support for the Organization of American States and the principles for which it stands.

Now, Therefore, I, Ronald Reagan, President of the United States of America, do hereby proclaim Saturday, April 14, 1984, as Pan American Day, and the week beginning April 8, 1984, as Pan American Week. I urge the Governors of the fifty States, and the Governor of the Commonwealth of Puerto Rico, and officials of the other areas under the flag of the United States of America to honor these observances with appropriate activities and ceremonies.

In Witness Whereof, I have hereunto set my hand this 2nd day of April, in the year of our Lord nineteen hundred and eighty-four, and of the Independence of the United States of America the two hundred and eighth.

RONALD REAGAN

[*Filed with the Office of the Federal Register, 10:37 a.m., April 3, 1984*]

Statement on the Nomination of Edwin Meese III To Be Attorney General of the United States
April 3, 1984

I am pleased that the judicial panel has acted promptly in responding to the Attorney General's request to name an independent counsel. The counsel's responsibilities are to assure the full and impartial investigation of the allegations concerning Ed Meese that have been raised in connection with his confirmation hearings. This will provide an opportunity to determine the facts in a fair and expeditious manner.

I have instructed all members of the administration to cooperate fully with the independent counsel. Pending completion of his inquiry, the White House will have no further comment on this matter.

Nomination of Joseph F. Dennin To Be an Assistant Secretary of Commerce
April 3, 1984

The President today announced his intention to nominate Joseph F. Dennin to be an Assistant Secretary of Commerce (International Economic Policy). He would succeed Alfred Hugh Kingon.

Mr. Dennin is currently Deputy Assistant Secretary of Commerce for Africa, the Near East and South Asia. Previously, he was Deputy Assistant Secretary, Department of Commerce, Finance and Investment Services (1981–1982); Deputy Associate Attorney General, Department of Justice (1979–1981); Director of Operations, U.S. International Trade Commission (1978–1979); Counsel to the Intelligence Oversight Board, the White House Office (1976–1977); and counsel, Senate Select Committee on Intelligence (1975–1976).

Mr. Dennin graduated from Stanford University (B.A., 1965; J.D., 1968) and attended the University of Helsinki (1968–1969). He is married, has three children, and resides in Washington, DC. He was born June 9, 1943, in New York, NY.

Appointment of Four Members of the Presidential Commission for the German-American Tricentennial
April 3, 1984

The President today announced his intention to appoint the following individuals to be members of the Presidential Commission for the German-American Tricentennial. These are new positions.

Robert E. Evans is currently chairman of the board of Evans Industries, Inc. He is also chairman and chief executive of 23 personally owned manufacturing companies. Mr. Evans resides in Detroit, MI, and was born March 19, 1906, in Richmond, VA.

Carlota Giersch is currently a special consultant to Anheuser-Busch for Grant's Farm of St. Louis, as well as the company's breweries in 10 United States cities and its theme parks. Ms. Giersch resides in Pasadena, CA, and was born July 19, 1927, in St. Louis, MO.

Noel Gross is currently president and chief ad-ministrative officer of the Hudson Landing Corp. She resides in Saddle River, NJ, and was born December 25, 1938, in New York, NY.

Arthur Spitzer is currently director of Tesoro Petroleum Corp. He resides in Beverly Hills, CA, and was born August 3, 1912, in Czernowitz, Austria.

Proclamation 5172—National Child Abuse Prevention Month, 1984
April 3, 1984

By the President of the United States of America

A Proclamation

Abuse of children occurs in all segments of our society, in rural, suburban, and urban areas and among all racial, ethnic, and income groups. The time has come for Americans to unite in an all-out effort to eradicate child abuse, both physical and sexual, from the Nation.

Child abuse is a national concern, but it is a community and family problem first, and the answers must be found at the community level. Most physical and emotional violence takes place within the family. All Americans aware of the problem of child abuse must work for an end of this tragedy.

There is a place for everyone in this effort. By being a good neighbor to the family next door who may be under stress, Americans can be an enormous help. Our schools have an important role to play by educating children about parental roles and responsibilities, values, and appropriate behavior in the family setting. We must do what we can to reverse the trend of abused children becoming abusive parents. In addition, voluntary community self-help groups such as Parents Anonymous are taking positive steps to break this cycle.

In recognition of the need to find ways to prevent the agony of child abuse from continuing in future generations, the Congress, by Senate Joint Resolution 161, has designated the month of April 1984 as "National Child Abuse Prevention Month" and has authorized and requested the President to issue a proclamation in observance of this period.

Now, Therefore, I, Ronald Reagan, President of the United States of America, do hereby proclaim the month of April 1984, as National Child Abuse Prevention Month. We must find a way to leave our future generations a priceless legacy—the confidence and trust resulting from a secure childhood.

In Witness Whereof, I have hereunto set my hand this third day of April, in the year of our Lord nineteen hundred and eighty-four, and of the Independence of the United States of America the two hundred and eighth.

RONALD REAGAN

[*Filed with the Office of the Federal Register, 4:45 p.m., April 3, 1984*]

Photographic
Portfolio

Overleaf: At University College in Galway, Ireland, June 2. *Left:* Meeting with Chinese officials in Beijing, China, April 27. *Below left:* Touring an archeological site in Xi'an, China, April 29. *Above right:* Participating in an arrival ceremony at Guam International Airport, April 25. *Below:* With Pope John Paul II upon his arrival at Fairbanks International Airport, AK, May 2.

Left: At the opening of the 1984
International Games for the
Disabled in Uniondale, NY, June 17.
Above: Participating in
commencement exercises at the
U.S. Air Force Academy in
Colorado Springs, CO, May 30.
Right: On the South Lawn,
presenting an award to singer
Michael Jackson in recognition of
his efforts in the campaign against
drunk driving, May 14.

Left: At the U.S. Olympic Training Center in Colorado Springs, CO, May 29. *Below:* With allied leaders at a ceremony commemorating the 40th anniversary of D-day at Utah Beach in Normandy, France, June 6. *Above right:* With Secretary of Defense Weinberger at Memorial Day ceremonies honoring an unknown soldier of the Vietnam conflict at Arlington National Cemetery, May 28. *Below right:* Luncheon with workers at the Ford Claycomo Assembly Plant in Kansas City, MO, April 11. *Overleaf:* Waving to participants in the March for Life rally on the Ellipse, January 23.

Proclamation 5173—Mother's Day, 1984
April 3, 1984

By the President of the United States of America

A Proclamation

By tradition, the second Sunday in May is designated as Mother's Day, a day on which we honor and think about our mothers.

Almost every woman in our Nation looks forward to the rewards and joys of motherhood without overlooking the long-term effort that raising children demands. We are grateful to mothers for their willingness to give of themselves for their children's well-being, for their wholehearted belief in their offspring, for their love, for being wellsprings of hope, and for all the support they lend to us throughout life.

Motherhood is both a great responsibility and one of the most unique, rewarding, and pleasurable experiences life has to offer. Just as the family is the basis of a strong nation, so dedicated mothers are frequently the key to strong families. The quality and scope of their activities, as well as their overriding concern for the well-being of their families and the future of our country, inspire and strengthen us as individuals and as a Nation.

In recognition of the contributions of all mothers to their families and to the Nation, the Congress, by a joint resolution approved May 8, 1914 (38 Stat. 770), designated the second Sunday in May each year as Mother's Day and requested the President to call for its appropriate observance.

Now, Therefore, I, Ronald Reagan, President of the United States of America, do hereby request that Sunday, May 13, 1984, be observed as Mother's Day. I direct Government officials to display the flag of the United States on all Federal government buildings, and I urge all citizens to display the flag at their homes and other suitable places on that day.

In Witness Whereof, I have hereunto set my hand this 3rd day of April, in the year of our Lord nineteen hundred and eighty-four, and of the Independence of the United States of America the two hundred and eighth.

RONALD REAGAN

[*Filed with the Office of the Federal Register, 4:46 p.m., April 3, 1984*]

Executive Order 12472—Assignment of National Security and Emergency Preparedness Telecommunications Functions
April 3, 1984

By the authority vested in me as President by the Constitution and laws of the United States of America, including the Communications Act of 1934, as amended (47 U.S.C. 151), the National Security Act of 1947, as amended, the Defense Production Act of 1950, as amended (50 U.S.C. App. 2061), the Federal Civil Defense Act of 1950, as amended (50 U.S.C. App. 2251), the Disaster Relief Act of 1974 (42 U.S.C. 5121), Section 5 of Reorganization Plan No. 1 of 1977 (3 C.F.R. 197, 1978 Comp.), and Section 203 of Reorganization Plan No. 3 of 1978 (3 C.F.R. 389, 1978 Comp.), and in order to provide for the consolidation of assignment and responsibility for improved execution of national security and emergency preparedness telecommunications functions, it is hereby ordered as follows:

Section 1. The National Communications System. (a) There is hereby established the National Communications System (NCS). The NCS shall consist of the telecommunications assets of the entities represented on the NCS Committee of Principals and an administrative structure consisting of the Executive Agent, the NCS Committee of

Principals and the Manager. The NCS Committee of Principals shall consist of representatives from those Federal departments, agencies or entities, designated by the President, which lease or own telecommunications facilities or services of significance to national security or emergency preparedness, and, to the extent permitted by law, other Executive entities which bear policy, regulatory or enforcement responsibilities of importance to national security or emergency preparedness telecommunications capabilities.

(b) The mission of the NCS shall be to assist the President, the National Security Council, the Director of the Office of Science and Technology Policy and the Director of the Office of Management and Budget in:

(1) the exercise of the telecommunications functions and responsibilities set forth in Section 2 of this Order; and

(2) the coordination of the planning for and provision of national security and emergency preparedness communications for the Federal government under all circumstances, including crisis or emergency, attack, recovery and reconstitution.

(c) The NCS shall seek to ensure that a national telecommunications infrastructure is developed which:

(1) Is responsive to the national security and emergency preparedness needs of the President and the Federal departments, agencies and other entities, including telecommunications in support of national security leadership and continuity of government;

(2) Is capable of satisfying priority telecommunications requirements under all circumstances through use of commercial, government and privately owned telecommunications resources;

(3) Incorporates the necessary combination of hardness, redundancy, mobility, connectivity, interoperability, restorability and security to obtain, to the maximum extent practicable, the survivability of national security and emergency preparedness telecommunications in all circumstances, including conditions of crisis or emergency; and

(4) Is consistent, to the maximum extent practicable, with other national telecommunications policies.

(d) To assist in accomplishing its mission, the NCS shall:

(1) serve as a focal point for joint industry-government national security and emergency preparedness telecommunications planning; and

(2) establish a joint industry-government National Coordinating Center which is capable of assisting in the initiation, coordination, restoration and reconstitution of national security or emergency preparedness telecommunications services or facilities under all conditions of crisis or emergency.

(e) The Secretary of Defense is designated as the Executive Agent for the NCS. The Executive Agent shall:

(1) Designate the Manager of the NCS;

(2) Ensure that the NCS conducts unified planning and operations, in order to coordinate the development and maintenance of an effective and responsive capability for meeting the domestic and international national security and emergency preparedness telecommunications needs of the Federal government;

(3) Ensure that the activities of the NCS are conducted in conjunction with the emergency management activities of the Federal Emergency Management Agency;

(4) Recommend, in consultation with the NCS Committee of Principals, to the National Security Council, the Director of the Office of Science and Technology Policy, or the Director of the Office of Management and Budget, as appropriate:

a. The assignment of implementation or other responsibilities to NCS member entities;

b. New initiatives to assist in the exercise of the functions specified in Section 2; and

c. Changes in the composition or structure of the NCS;

(5) Oversee the activities of and provide personnel and administrative support to the Manager of the NCS;

(6) Provide staff support and technical assistance to the National Security Telecommunications Advisory Committee established by Executive Order No. 12382, as amended; and

(7) Perform such other duties as are from time to time assigned by the President or

his authorized designee.

(f) The NCS Committee of Principals shall:

(1) Serve as the forum in which each member of the Committee may review, evaluate, and present views, information and recommendations concerning ongoing or prospective national security or emergency preparedness telecommunications programs or activities of the NCS and the entities represented on the Committee;

(2) Serve as the forum in which each member of the Committee shall report on and explain ongoing or prospective telecommunications plans and programs developed or designed to achieve national security or emergency preparedness telecommunications objectives;

(3) Provide comments or recommendations, as appropriate, to the National Security Council, the Director of the Office of Science and Technology Policy, the Director of the Office of Management and Budget, the Executive Agent, or the Manager of the NCS, regarding ongoing or prospective activities of the NCS; and

(4) Perform such other duties as are from time to time assigned by the President or his authorized designee.

(g) The Manager of the NSC shall:

(1) Develop for consideration by the NCS Committee of Principals and the Executive Agent:

a. A recommended evolutionary telecommunications architecture designed to meet current and future Federal government national security and emergency preparedness telecommunications requirements;

b. Plans and procedures for the management, allocation and use, including the establishment of priorities or preferences, of Federally owned or leased telecommunications assets under all conditions of crisis or emergency;

c. Plans, procedures and standards for minimizing or removing technical impediments to the interoperability of government-owned and/or commercially-provided telecommunications systems;

d. Test and exercise programs and procedures for the evaluation of the capability of the Nation's telecommunications resources to meet national security or emergency preparedness telecommunications require-

ments; and

e. Alternative mechanisms for funding, through the budget review process, national security or emergency preparedness telecommunications initiatives which benefit multiple Federal departments, agencies, or entities. Those mechanisms recommended by the NCS Committee of Principals and the Executive Agent shall be submitted to the Director of the Office of Management and Budget.

(2) Implement and administer any approved plans or programs as assigned, including any system of priorities and preferences for the provision of communications service, in consultation with the NCS Committee of Principals and the Federal Communications Commission, to the extent practicable or otherwise required by law or regulation;

(3) Chair the NCS Committee of Principals and provide staff support and technical assistance thereto;

(4) Serve as a focal point for joint industry-government planning, including the dissemination of technical information, concerning the national security or emergency preparedness telecommunications requirements of the Federal government;

(5) Conduct technical studies or analyses, and examine research and development programs, for the purpose of identifying, for consideration by the NCS Committee of Principals and the Executive Agent, improved approaches which may assist Federal entities in fulfilling national security or emergency preparedness telecommunications objectives;

(6) Pursuant to the Federal Standardization Program of the General Services Administration, and in consultation with other appropriate entities of the Federal government including the NCS Committee of Principals, manage the Federal Telecommunications Standards Program, ensuring wherever feasible that existing or evolving industry, national, and international standards are used as the basis for Federal telecommunications standards; and

(7) Provide such reports and perform such other duties as are from time to time assigned by the President or his authorized designee, the Executive Agent, or the NCS

Committee of Principals. Any such assignments of responsibility to, or reports made by, the Manager shall be transmitted through the Executive Agent.

Sec. 2. Executive Office Responsibilities. (a) *Wartime Emergency Functions.* (1) The National Security Council shall provide policy direction for the exercise of the war power functions of the President under Section 606 of the Communications Act of 1934, as amended (47 U.S.C. 606), should the President issue implementing instructions in accordance with the National Emergencies Act (50 U.S.C. 1601).

(2) The Director of the Office of Science and Technology Policy shall direct the exercise of the war power functions of the President under Section 606 (a), (c)–(e), of the Communications Act of 1934, as amended (47 U.S.C. 606), should the President issue implementing instructions in accordance with the National Emergencies Act (50 U.S.C. 1601).

(b) *Non-Wartime Emergency Functions.* (1) The National Security Council shall:

a. Advise and assist the President in coordinating the development of policy, plans, programs and standards within the Federal government for the identification, allocation, and use of the Nation's telecommunications resources by the Federal government, and by State and local governments, private industry and volunteer organizations upon request, to the extent practicable and otherwise consistent with law, during those crises or emergencies in which the exercise of the President's war power functions is not required or permitted by law; and

b. Provide policy direction for the exercise of the President's non-wartime emergency telecommunications functions, should the President so instruct.

(2) The Director of the Office of Science and Technology Policy shall provide information, advice, guidance and assistance, as appropriate, to the President and to those Federal departments and agencies with responsibilities for the provision, management, or allocation of telecommunications resources, during those crises or emergencies in which the exercise of the President's war power functions is not required or permitted by law;

(3) The Director of the Office of Science and Technology Policy shall establish a Joint Telecommunications Resources Board (JTRB) to assist him in the exercise of the functions specified in this subsection. The Director of the Office of Science and Technology Policy shall serve as chairman of the JTRB; select those Federal departments, agencies, or entities which shall be members of the JTRB; and specify the functions it shall perform.

(c) *Planning and Oversight Responsibilities.* (1) The National Security Council shall advise and assist the President in:

a. Coordinating the development of policy, plans programs and standards for the mobilization and use of the Nation's commercial, government, and privately owned telecommunications resources, in order to meet national security or emergency preparedness requirements;

b. Providing policy oversight and direction of the activities of the NCS; and

c. Providing policy oversight and guidance for the execution of the responsibilities assigned to the Federal departments and agencies by this Order.

(2) The Director of the Office of Science and Technology Policy shall make recommendations to the President with respect to the test, exercise and evaluation of the capability of existing and planned communications systems, networks or facilities to meet national security or emergency preparedness requirements and report the results of any such tests or evaluations and any recommended remedial actions to the President and to the National Security Council;

(3) The Director of the Office of Science and Technology Policy or his designee shall advise and assist the President in the administration of a system of radio spectrum priorities for those spectrum dependent telecommunications resources of the Federal government which support national security or emergency preparedness functions. The Director also shall certify or approve priorities for radio spectrum use by the Federal government, including the resolution of any conflicts in or among priorities, under all conditions of crisis or emergency; and

(4) The National Security Council, the Director of the Office of Science and Technology Policy and the Director of the Office of Management and Budget shall, in consultation with the Executive Agent for the NCS and the NCS Committee of Principals, determine what constitutes national security and emergency preparedness telecommunications requirements.

(d) *Consultation with Federal Departments and Agencies.* In performing the functions assigned under this Order, the National Security Council and the Director of the Office of Science and Technology Policy, in consultation with each other, shall:

(1) Consult, as appropriate, with the Director of the Office of Management and Budget; the Director of the Federal Emergency Management Agency with respect to the emergency management responsibilities assigned pursuant to Executive Order No. 12148, as amended; the Secretary of Commerce, with respect to responsibilities assigned pursuant to Executive Order No. 12046; the Secretary of Defense, with respect to communications security responsibilities assigned pursuant to Executive Order No. 12333; and the Chairman of the Federal Communications Commission or his authorized designee; and

(2) Establish arrangements for consultation among all interested Federal departments, agencies or entities to ensure that the national security and emergency preparedness communications needs of all Federal government entities are identified; that mechanisms to address such needs are incorporated into pertinent plans and procedures; and that such needs are met in a manner consistent, to the maximum extent practicable, with other national telecommunications policies.

(e) *Budgetary Guidelines.* The Director of the Office of Management and Budget, in consultation with the National Security Council and the NCS, will prescribe general guidelines and procedures for reviewing the financing of the NCS within the budgetary process and for preparation of budget estimates by participating agencies. These guidelines and procedures may provide for mechanisms for funding, through the budget review process, national security

and emergency preparedness telecommunications initiatives which benefit multiple Federal departments, agencies, or entities.

Sec. 3. Assignment of Responsibilities To Other Departments and Agencies. In order to support and enhance the capability to satisfy the national security and emergency preparedness telecommunications needs of the Federal government, State and local governments, private industry and volunteer organizations, under all circumstances including those of crisis or emergency, the Federal departments and agencies shall perform the following functions:

(a) *Department of Commerce.* The Secretary of Commerce shall, for all conditions of crisis or emergency: (1) Develop plans and procedures concerning radio spectrum assignments, priorities and allocations for use by Federal departments, agencies and entities; and

(2) Develop, maintain and publish policy, plans, and procedures for the control and allocation of frequency assignments, including the authority to amend, modify or revoke such assignments, in those parts of the electromagnetic spectrum assigned to the Federal government.

(b) *Federal Emergency Management Agency.* The Director of the Federal Emergency Management Agency shall:

(1) Plan for and provide, operate and maintain telecommunications services and facilities, as part of its National Emergency Management System, adequate to support its assigned emergency management responsibilities;

(2) Advise and assist State and local governments and volunteer organizations, upon request and to the extent consistent with law, in developing plans and procedures for identifying and satisfying their national security or emergency preparedness telecommunications requirements;

(3) Ensure, to the maximum extent practicable, that national security and emergency preparedness telecommunications planning by State and local governments and volunteer organizations is mutually supportive and consistent with the planning of the Federal government; and

(4) Develop, upon request and to the extent consistent with law and in conso-

nance with regulations promulgated by and agreements with the Federal Communications Commission, plans and capabilities for, and provide policy and management oversight of, the Emergency Broadcast System, and advise and assist private radio licensees of the Commission in developing emergency communications plans, procedures and capabilities.

(c) *Department of State.* The Secretary of State, in accordance with assigned responsibilities within the Diplomatic Telecommunications System, shall plan for and provide, operate and maintain rapid, reliable and secure telecommunications services to those Federal entities represented at United States diplomatic missions and consular offices overseas. This responsibility shall include the provisions and operation of domestic telecommunications in support of assigned national security or emergency preparedness responsibilities.

(d) *Department of Defense.* In addition to the other responsibilities assigned by this Order, the Secretary of Defense shall:

(1) Plan for and provide, operate and maintain telecommunications services and facilities adequate to support the National Command Authorities and to execute the responsibilities assigned by Executive Order No. 12333; and

(2) Ensure that the Director of the National Security Agency provides the technical support necessary to develop and maintain plans adequate to provide for the security and protection of national security and emergency preparedness telecommunications.

(e) *Department of Justice.* The Attorney General shall, as necessary, review for legal sufficiency, including consistency with the antitrust laws, all policies, plans or procedures developed pursuant to responsibilities assigned by this Order.

(f) *Central Intelligence Agency.* The Director of Central Intelligence shall plan for and provide, operate, and maintain telecommunications services adequate to support its assigned responsibilities, including the dissemination of intelligence within the Federal government.

(g) *General Services Administration.*

Except as otherwise assigned by this Order, the Administrator of General Services, consistent with policy guidance provided by the Director of the Office of Management and Budget, shall ensure that Federally owned or managed domestic communications facilities and services meet the national security and emergency preparedness requirements of the Federal civilian departments, agencies and entities.

(h) *Federal Communications Commission.* The Federal Communications Commission shall, consistent with Section 4(c) of this Order:

(1) Review the policies, plans and procedures of all entities licensed or regulated by the Commission that are developed to provide national security or emergency preparedness communications services, in order to ensure that such policies, plans and procedures are consistent with the public interest, convenience and necessity;

(2) Perform such functions as required by law with respect to all entities licensed or regulated by the Commission, including (but not limited to) the extension, discontinuance or reduction of common carrier facilities or services; the control of common carrier rates, charges, practices and classifications; the construction, authorization, activation, deactivation or closing of radio stations, services and facilities; the assignment of radio frequencies to Commission licensees; the investigation of violations of pertinent law and regulation; and the initiation of appropriate enforcement actions;

(3) Develop policy, plans and procedures adequate to execute the responsibilities assigned in this Order under all conditions or crisis or emergency; and

(4) Consult as appropriate with the Executive Agent for the NCS and the NCS Committee of Principals to ensure continued coordination of their respective national security and emergency preparedness activities.

(i) All Federal departments and agencies, to the extent consistent with law (including those authorities and responsibilities set forth in Section 4(c) of this Order), shall:

(1) Determine their national security and emergency preparedness telecommunica-

tions requirements, and provide information regarding such requirements to the Manager of the NCS;

(2) Prepare policies, plans and procedures concerning telecommunications facilities, services or equipment under their management or operational control to maximize their capability of responding to the national security or emergency preparedness needs of the Federal government;

(3) Provide, after consultation with the Director of the Office of Management and Budget, resources to support their respective requirements for national security and emergency preparedness telecommunications; and provide personnel and staff support to the Manager of the NCS as required by the President;

(4) Make information available to, and consult with, the Manager of the NCS regarding agency telecommunications activities in support of national security or emergency preparedness;

(5) Consult, consistent with the provisions of Executive Order No. 12046, as amended, and in conjunction with the Manager of the NCS, with the Federal Communications Commission regarding execution of responsibilities assigned by this Order;

(6) Submit reports annually, or as otherwise requested, to the Manager of the NCS, regarding agency national security or emergency preparedness telecommunications activities; and

(7) Cooperate with and assist the Executive Agent for the NCS, the NCS Committee of Principals, the Manager of the NCS, and other departments and agencies in the execution of the functions set forth in this Order, furnishing them such information, support and assistance as may be required.

(j) Each Federal department or agency shall execute the responsibilities assigned by this Order in conjunction with the emergency management activities of the Federal Emergency Management Agency, and in regular consultation with the Executive Agent for the NCS and the NCS Committee of Principals to ensure continued coordination of NCS and individual agency telecommunications activities.

Sec. 4. General Provisions. (a) All Executive departments and agencies may issue such rules and regulations as may be necessary to carry out the functions assigned under this Order.

(b) In order to reflect the assignments of responsibility provided by this Order,

(1) Sections 2–414, 4–102, 4–103, 4–202, 4–302, 5–3, and 6–101 of Executive Order No. 12046, as amended, are revoked;

(2) The Presidential Memorandum of August 21, 1963, as amended, entitled "Establishment of the National Communications System", is hereby superseded; and

(3) Section 2–411 of Executive Order No. 12046, as amended, is further amended by deleting the period and inserting ", except as otherwise provided by Executive Order No.   " and inserting the number assigned to this Order.

(c) Nothing in this Order shall be deemed to affect the authorities or responsibilities of the Director of the Office of Management and Budget, or any office or official thereof; or reassign any function assigned any agency under the Federal Property and Administrative Services Act of 1949, as amended; or under any other law; or any function vested by law in the Federal Communications Commission.

Sec. 5. This Order shall be effective upon publication in the *Federal Register.*

RONALD REAGAN

The White House,
April 3, 1984.

[*Filed with the Office of the Federal Register, 4:47 p.m., April 3, 1984*]

Appointment of Michael Dennis Antonovich as a Member of the Presidential Commission on the Conduct of United States-Japan Relations
April 4, 1984

The President today has appointed Michael Dennis Antonovich to be a member of the Presidential Commission on the Conduct of United States-Japan Relations.

Mr. Antonovich is currently chairman of the board of supervisors, fifth district, county of Los Angeles. Previously, he was a vice president and project director, J. Phil Johnson Corp. (1979–1980); instructor, California State University and Pepperdine University (1979); member of the board of regents for Christ Lutheran College (1978–present); and he served in the California State Assembly (1972–1978).

Mr. Antonovich graduated from California State University (B.A., 1963; M.A., 1967). He resides in Glendale, CA, and was born August 12, 1939, in Los Angeles, CA.

Appointment of James Andrew Dorn as a Member of the Commission on Presidential Scholars
April 4, 1984

The President today announced his intention to appoint James Andrew Dorn to be a member of the Commission on Presidential Scholars. This is an initial appointment.

Mr. Dorn is currently associate professor of economics at Towson State University. He is also editor of the Cato Journal of Public Policy at the Cato Institute. Previously he was a lecturer at Goucher College (1976–1980) and a graduate assistant instructor at the University of Virginia (1968–1971).

Mr. Dorn graduated from Canisius College (B.S., 1967) and the University of Virginia (M.A., 1969; Ph.D., 1976). He is married, has two children, and resides in Lutherville, MD. He was born August 26, 1945, in Buffalo, NY.

The President's News Conference
April 4, 1984

U.S. Proposal for Ban on Chemical Weapons

The President. Good evening. I have an important announcement. In 2 weeks, I will send Vice President Bush to Geneva to present to the 40-nation Conference [Committee] on Disarmament a bold American initiative for a comprehensive, worldwide ban on chemical weapons. Our proposal would prohibit the production, possession, and use of chemical weapons.

The shortcomings of early chemical weapons treaties have been made tragically clear in recent years. Chemical weapons have been used against defenseless peoples in Afghanistan, in Southeast Asia, and in the conflict between Iran and Iraq. The use of these terrible weapons also has serious implications for our own security.

The Soviet Union's extensive arsenal of chemical weapons threatens U.S. forces. It requires the United States to maintain a limited retaliatory capability of its own until we achieve an effective ban. We must be able to deter a chemical attack against us or our allies. And without a modern and credible deterrent, the prospects for achieving a comprehensive ban would be nil.

Our comprehensive treaty proposal can bring the day closer when the world will prohibit all chemical weapons, but verification of a chemical weapons ban won't be easy. Only an effective monitoring and enforcement package can ensure international confidence in such an agreement. The United States is, therefore, developing bold and sound verification procedures.

This latest initiative reflects my continuing strong commitment to arms control. Our administration seeks to move forward in several areas. I'm pleased, for example, that the United States is also participating in a promising new multilateral negotiation dealing with confidence building measures in Europe, and in the recently resumed East-West talks on reducing conventional forces in Europe.

We're working closely with our NATO allies to try to make progress in all these areas. I can't report these promising developments, however, without expressing my deep, personal regret that the Soviet Union still has not returned to the two negotiations on nuclear arms reductions—the START and the INF talks which it walked away from late last year.

The United States and many other countries have urged repeatedly that the Soviets return to these talks. So far, they've ignored the will of the world. I hope that the Soviet leadership will respond to our new initiatives, not only by negotiating seriously on chemical weapons but also by joining us in the urgent task of achieving real reductions in nuclear arms.

The Vice President's mission is a vital one, and we wish him Godspeed.

And now, Helen [Helen Thomas, United Press International].

Military Strength and Space Weapons

Q. Mr. President, Secretary of State George Shultz is advocating a wider, greater use of military force, a show of force, around the world and, also, preemptive strikes against potential terrorists. And this week you slammed the door on negotiations for killer satellites, which could lead to an arms race in space. My question is, how do these moves serve the cause of peace, and

do you think that the country is really ready for wider involvement, military involvement around the world?

The President. I don't think that George meant to imply anything of that kind or that we're going to get more militant or anything. I think he was trying to express to those people that have been so concerned about arms and whether there's an arms race, and that is that your military strength is a definite part of diplomacy. And I think this is what he was trying to explain.

With regard to the space weapons, this is a situation in which the Soviet Union is ahead of us and already has—and has in place—such a weapon. We are still in the stage of studying such a thing. The great problem that we have—and we're very willing to enter into a treaty with regard to outlawing such weapons, except that it so far seems almost impossible to verify such a weapon, if not actually impossible. And if that's true, then we, again, must have a deterrent.

Q. Mr. President, you're one who always says nothing is impossible and you're going to try on chemical weapons. Why don't you on the killer satellites?

The President. Well, in both of them we're trying, but we, as we say, we have to face the reality that before you can place any confidence in such a treaty, you must be confident that you have the one thing that the Soviets have been the most reluctant to give in any treaties that we've ever had, or that we have with them, and that is verification procedures.

Ethics in Government

Q. Mr. President, more than a dozen members of your administration have left under some sort of a cloud, and this is what the Democrats are calling the sleaze factor. Are you concerned that voters might think there's a lack of integrity in the people that you've hired, and how are you going to deal with this as a campaign issue?

The President. Well, in the first place, I reject the use of the word "sleaze," and I don't think that it fits any situation that we have here. I'll repeat what I have said many times before, and over a period of years. I believe the halls of government are as

461

sacred as our temples of worship, and nothing but the highest integrity is required of those who serve in government. But at the same time, I also respect very much something that is very typically American, and that is you are innocent until proven guilty. And we're having an awful lot—and have for the past several years—of guilt by accusation. And I intend to protect that particular American tradition, and I would think that you would all feel a shared responsibility in doing the same thing—that you're not guilty simply because you've been accused.

Now, I will be the first to remove anyone in the administration that does not have the highest integrity, and I adhere to that. At the same time, however, I'm not going to take any action that is based on accusation without proof, and I'm not going to take any action in any case for political expediency.

Q. So, is this all politics that's behind this? And if that's the case, why have you let some of these people leave?

The President. Well, some of these people have simply—they have left on their own, and they have left simply because they recognize that while they remain a part of the administration the accusations and the charges will continue. Now, others have not felt that way, and a great many have been cleared. But it's a strange thing that their names keep popping up again by the same ones who were the first to throw the accusations out.

Bill [Bill Plante, CBS News]?

Ban on Chemical Weapons

Q. Mr. President, with regard to your proposal to ban chemical weapons, isn't this proposal another way to get Congress— what they've failed to do for the last 3 years, which is appropriate money for chemical weapons? And what do we say if our adversaries accuse us of talking peace but preparing for war?

The President. Well, I don't think the accusation would stand up if they said that. The situation is that we haven't produced any such weapons for 15 years. The Soviet Union has a massive arsenal and is ahead of us in many areas having to do with chemical warfare.

Now, if there is ever one example—or

one place where there is an example—of the power of a deterrent force, it is in the field of chemical weapons. And I hand you World War II, when all the nations had them and no one used them even in the most desperate moments when defeat was staring at them because they knew that the others had them and could use them in return.

The second thing is, if we're going to have a chemical warfare ban or a treaty banning them, you've got to have something to bargain with. And, therefore, it's just the same as it is with the other weapons. They must know that the alternative to banning them is to then face the fact that we are going to build a deterrent.

Effects of Budget and Tax Cuts

Q. Mr. President, the Congressional Budget Office has just released a study on the impact of your budget and tax cuts that have been enacted since you took office, and it found that the poorest families lost the most and the richest families gained the most. For instance, families earning under $10,000 a year lost almost $400, and families earning over $80,000 a year gained more than $8,000. Is that fair?

The President. It not only wouldn't be fair, but I don't think it's true. You know, as Disraeli once said, "There are lies, blankety-blank lies, and statistics."

We have a tax program that was a 25-percent cut across the board. Now, that's 25-percent reduction in the tax burden of everyone. If you have someone whose tax burden is $20, that cut means that they saved $5, and they still owe $15. But someone who owes a hundred times as much, who pays a hundred times as much tax, $2,000, gets $500 but still owes $1,500. In other words, the progressivity of the tax program stays the same. So, there is no way that the tax program could have benefited someone at one end of the scale and not the other. It's based on proportions.

The other thing is—that makes me doubtful of those figures—is what we have done for everyone with regard to inflation. And here you do benefit the people at the lower end of the scale more than you do at the top. Now, the fact of that is someone that—

the beginning of 1979, with an $8,000 income, they were about $500 or so above the poverty-level income. By the end of 1980, 2 years later, with that same income they were some $500 below the poverty-level income in purchasing power.

Maybe some of the things they were talking about is that in our program—and it wasn't an Executive order; it was passed by Congress and signed by me—with regard to some cuts, for example, in the aid for dependent children program—now every protection was made for all of those totally dependent on welfare. There are some 3 million of them still there. There were 943,000 families that were removed, but they were families that had considerable outside earnings, plus their welfare grants.

Now, we were told when we did this that, oh, these people would quit their jobs just to take the security of being on welfare. Well, only a very few did. And two-thirds of the people that did not, then sizably increased their actual earnings and became independent of welfare.

Q. Mr. President, just to follow up, whatever the interpretation of this particular report, are you concerned that the perception that your administration has been a friend of the wealthy at the expense of the poor is going to be a political problem for you this year?

The President. Oh, I'm concerned about it. It's a political problem if people believe it, but there's absolutely no truth in it. It's probably the most glaring example of political demagoguery that our friends have been engaging in.

Yes, Sam [Sam Donaldson, ABC News].

Situation in Lebanon

Q. Mr. President, last October you said the presence of U.S. Marines in Lebanon was central to our credibility on a global scale. And now you've withdrawn them and terminated our presence in the MNF. To what extent have we lost credibility—[inaudible]?

The President. We may have lost some with some people, but situations change, Sam. It was true when I said that, but I can, I think, explain, and I'll try to make it as brief as I can what the situation, or what the change was.

We and three of our allies—our four governments—decided that in an effort to straighten out the situation that was so out of control in Lebanon, that we would send in a combination force, a multiple force, not to participate in a war but to be on hand to help provide stability while the Lebanese were allowed, then, to create a government.

You will remember a civil war had been going on there for about 10 years. And at the time this was decided, the Israelis were at the border of Beirut; the PLO, 10 to 15 thousand of them, were fighting from within the heart of Beirut; the Syrians were also involved.

The idea was that if a government could be created in Lebanon, and then we could help them re-create their military, and the foreign forces withdraw, then, as their military moved out into the areas previously occupied by the foreign powers to hopefully pacify some of the internecine fighting groups—the militias that were fighting each other as well as the official forces of Lebanon—that the multinational force would be a kind of stable peacekeeping force behind keeping order while they went out to do that job, because they wouldn't have the manpower to do both.

Now, this was the task. The first success was the leaving Lebanon of some 10 to 15 thousand PLO who, up until then were unwilling to surrender even though they faced defeat, because they feared a massacre at the hands of those that were fighting them. So, with the multinational force there to guarantee against that, they were ushered out.

Now, the Government was formed—of Lebanon. The same Government that today is negotiating and has been holding meetings in Geneva and elsewhere to bring about a peaceful settlement.

We did train—and there was no attention paid to this—our army had a unit in there training the Lebanese military and equipping them, and made a very capable military. What did happen, with the deterioration when Syria insisted on staying in and backing some of the rebel radical forces there, was that with religious and ethnic differences, some units of the army refused to take up arms against some of their same ethnic background, or religious background. Now, the Government of Lebanon went forward, then, in trying to bring together the kind of a consensus government—of the radical elements and all—and take them into a broadened based government.

In the meantime, because the multinational force had been successful, to that extent, it was determined by those who don't want that kind of a solution in Lebanon that they had to put the pressure on to get our forces and the others out. And with the terrorist attacks that brought such tragedy, our forces dug in. But once dug in, while this was offering security to them from the kind of attacks they'd been subjected to, they were no longer visible as the kind of force they were supposed to be.

And so with agreement with our allies, we redeployed; some of them redeployed to other areas. But then as these efforts went forward on their own for peace, it was agreed that there was no longer any point in the four governments keeping their forces there, and we withdrew.

We are still engaged diplomatically with anything that we can do to help. And there are those in the area who say that they doubt that there can be any solution or peace without our help. And so we'll do that.

Q. If I may, you began your answer by saying we lost some credibility. Are you to blame for that? Or, like Secretary Shultz, do you blame Congress?

The President. I have to say this, Sam, and then I'll move on to another subject. I have to say that this was one of the things—and they must take a responsibility. When you're engaged in this kind of a diplomatic attempt, and you have forces there, and there is an effort made to oust them, a debate as public as was conducted here, raging, with the Congress demanding, "Oh, take our, bring our men home, take them away"—all this can do is stimulate the terrorists and urge them on to further attacks, because they see a possibility of success in getting the force out which is keeping them from having their way. It should come to the—it should be understood by everyone in government that once this is committed, you have rendered them ineffective when

you conduct that kind of a debate in public.

U.S. Aid to El Salvador

Q. Mr. President, the Senate today unanimously adopted a proposal to withdraw U.S. military aid from El Salvador if the government there is overthrown by a military coup. Some people have suggested that that might happen if Mr. Duarte is elected. Do you support the proposal that passed the Senate today? And would you veto it if it came to your desk?

The President. Well, I'm not going to talk about whether to veto or not, but I think here, again, this is not helpful in what we're trying to accomplish. And I think it's something that—I just don't think they should be doing it at this time.

Chris?

Q. So, does that mean you don't support it, sir?

The President. No.

Chris [Chris Wallace, NBC News]?

The War Powers Act and the Conduct of Foreign Policy

Q. I'd like to follow up on Sam's question, if I could, Mr. President. Secretary of State Shultz says one of the problems in Lebanon is the War Powers Act and that Congress is always meddling in foreign policy; that neither our foes nor our friends know who's in charge. How much of a problem do you have with the War Powers Act, and would you like to see a Supreme Court test of whether or not it's constitutional?

The President. Well, there's been no talk of such a test or doing anything of that kind but, Chris, I do have to say this. In the last 10 years the Congress has imposed about 150 restrictions on the President's power in international diplomacy, and I think that the Constitution made it pretty plain way back in the beginning as to how diplomacy was to be conducted. And I just don't think that a committee of 535 individuals, no matter how well intentioned, can offer what is needed in actions of this kind or where there is a necessity.

Do you know that prior to the Vietnamese war, while this country had only had four declared wars, Presidents of this country had found it necessary to use military forces 125 times in our history?

Q. But let me, if I could follow up on that, people do cite Vietnam, where a President waged an undeclared war for years, and they say without the War Powers Act that's going to continue.

The President. Well, I'll tell you, Chris, this is the time for me to say, "I told you so." For a long time, and even before I became Governor [President], I was saying that the war in Vietnam had reached a position or a state in which we should have asked for a declaration of war and called it a war.

Yes?

Public Opinion Polls and the Proposed School Prayer Amendment

Q. Mr. President, while you were lobbying for the school prayer amendment recently, the gist of one of your arguments was that Congress should pass it because polls showed the American people were overwhelmingly in favor of it. Public opinion polls, sir, also show that Americans favor stricter control of handgun sales and an immediate, verifiable U.S.-Soviet nuclear freeze. In light of that and in light of your argument, do you see any change in your position on these two issues?

The President. No, I don't. And I think that calling attention to the fact that the overwhelming majority of the people favored prayer being permitted in schools was a logical thing to say to the Members of Congress when I was trying to get that amendment passed.

My only regret is that the debate was never on the real issue. I don't know how to explain it, but for them to sit there and debate hour after hour, as they did, that somehow we were asking for prayer to be mandated on schools—we were asking nothing of the kind. Quite the contrary, we were asking that the Constitution be restored to neutrality with regard to religion.

The government is to neither be an advocate of, nor a controller of, or preventer of the practice of religion. And all the amendment would do is say, if someone wants to pray in schools, they can, under the Constitution. And then we did add some provisions that no one could mandate, no one could write or prepare any prayer for them.

And they didn't debate that at all. They debated openly all the time, in spite of a few people trying to bring them back on track, that, no, this would be a government mandate that the schools the very next day would have to wake up and say, "All right, how are we going to plan the prayers?"

Well, I was in—I've told many of the Congressmen—I was in more elementary schools than most people. My father moved around a great deal. I was in five of them before I got out of eighth grade. And I don't recall there ever being a mandatory— or a prayer session in any of the schools. But we all knew that prayer was not denied in schools.

Public Opinion Polls and Handgun Control

Q. Well, sir, if I could just follow up, I understand your disappointment in the Senate debate and the vote, but I guess what I'm trying to ask you is why are the public opinion polls a valid argument for the school prayer amendment, which you do favor, and not a valid argument for the handgun control and the nuclear freeze issues which you do not?

The President. Well, there are methods of handling it. I have always preferred a different method with regard to handguns, and one that we used in California.

In California, knowing that the wrong people would probably never have any problem getting a gun and the law-abiding citizen would be denied the right to have one, we simply passed a law that said that anyone who commits a crime, is convicted of a crime and had in his or her possession a gun at the time of the commission of the crime, whether they used it or not, add 5 to 15 years to the sentence by virtue of their having carried—or carried a gun in the commission of a crime. You'd be surprised how effective it became.

Lou [Lou Cannon, Washington Post]?

U.S. Policy Toward Nicaragua

Q. Mr. President, recently the U.S.-backed opponents of the Sandinista regime have gone beyond their warfare on land to mining ports off the Nicaraguan coast. Are you concerned that these mines there, which neutral freighters or others could hit, run a risk of widening the war in Central America? And do you think that there's any point in which we ought to try to call a halt to the activities of the contras?

The President. No, our interest in Nicaragua—I'm not going to comment on that one way or the other, or the tactics that are used in a war of that kind. Our interest in Nicaragua is one and one only. The present Government of Nicaragua is exporting revolution to El Salvador, its neighbor, and is helping, supporting, arming, and training the guerrillas that are trying to overthrow a duly elected government. And as long as they do that, we're going to try and inconvenience that government of Nicaragua until they quit that kind of action.

U.S. Military Exercises in Honduras

Q. If I could follow up, sir, we are training troops down there in Honduras. Do you see, from your perspective, a danger of a wider war in Central America at this point?

The President. No, I think these maneuvers are something we've done before. They're not something unusual or aimed at anyone down there. They are combined exercises that we hold with our own units and when we have—one unit goes through some of these and gets the training, we send another one down to do the same thing. And that's all they are is war games.

Trade With Japan

Q. Mr. President, until recently your administration had handled trade disputes with Japan with relatively little public fanfare. But over the last few days, three of your Cabinet members and several other administration officials have spoken out publicly and firmly in criticizing Japan. Why the change in strategy?

The President. Well, maybe it's not a change in strategy, it's just talking frankly about what's going on. It's like any government with its various interests and its bureaucracies and so forth. We're not making as much progress as we would like to make with regard to the things that I had discussed in Japan with Prime Minister Nakasone and here at the Williamsburg summit. I know where he stands. And I know that he sincerely and honestly wants better trade relations and some of the obstacles removed that are impairing free and fair trade between us. But then there are other elements, and they're subject to political pressure and public opinion pressure the same as we are in our own country. And I think what you've been hearing are some complaints about those who are trying to negotiate these things.

Jerry?

Q. Sir, you mentioned the public pressure. Is there any difference between your position on these trade disputes and the position of the Democratic Presidential candidates?

The President. I'm not going to comment on them, other than to say that I think there's a difference with them on almost everything.

Jerry [Jeremiah O'Leary, Washington Times]?

Statement by Governor Lamm of Colorado

Q. Mr. President, some people might say that you're a man who's approaching the Golden Years, and I'd like to know what your reaction is to Governor Lamm of Colorado who said that some elderly people have a duty to die and get out of the way and fall like leaves to provide humus for the younger generation. What is your reaction to that statement?

The President. Well, I think I was as shocked as anyone was to hear such a statement. I since, however, have seen reports that that was not exactly the way it was said, and that he was referring to outright terminal cases of the kind that have been under so much discussion over recent years, of someone who had a very limited time and was, for example, in a coma and simply being artificially kept alive, that this is what he was talking about. I don't know. All I know is the way the stories were carried. I have not had anyone fill me in on the actual case and how he said it. And having been interpreted incorrectly myself sometimes, I'm going to—I'm not going to speak out until I know.

Ralph [Ralph Harris, Reuters]?

The Middle East

Q. Mr. President, you've been saying recently that you're trying to encourage moderate Arab leaders to join the Middle East peace process. Yet, King Hussein, the key moderate Arab, seems to have shut the door rather firmly. In view of that, what is your future course for guiding your '82 peace plan, and how do you intend to try to remove the obstacles on that course?

The President. That continues to be our plan, and I believe that King Hussein still feels and believes that he would have to be an important part, being the next door neighbor to Israel, in bringing about such negotiations. And I continue to believe in this. This is the answer. It's what started us from the very beginning in the Middle East—to continue the Camp David process, to persuade other nations to do what Egypt did in making that peace.

At the present moment you have a group of Arab nations who still are of that—have never retreated from their position that Israel does not have a right to exist as a nation. And we're trying to persuade them that we can be evenhanded and that we're not trying to dictate any peace of any kind, that we simply want to be of help if we can, an intermediary in bringing about a negotiation that will erase the issues and the problems that have kept them apart, so that they can settle back and live in peace together. And we're going to continue to try to do that.

Dean [Dean Reynolds, Cable News Network], and then I'll take you.

Soviet Military Exercises

Q. Mr. President, the Soviet Union is currently engaged in perhaps its largest military exercise ever in the Atlantic Ocean— an exercise that involves some 40 vessels, including submarines, destroyers, and a nuclear-powered battle cruiser. I wonder if you could tell us what you think the Soviet Union is up to in all of this?

The President. I think it's spring in Russia as well as in the United States, and that's when you have war games and maneuvers. We've been having some of our own. We always tell them when we're going to have them; we wish they'd tell us.

But I think this is nothing more than that. Your war games are actually—whoever's conducting them—based on your own thoughts as to what contingencies could

arise that would find you in an emergency situation, and so you set out to train or practice for that.

Some 40 ships, I know, sounds like an awful lot, but when you stop to think that we're talking about a navy of almost 1,000 ships, it kind of comes down in size a little bit.

No, I think these are regular and routine maneuvers that usually begin in the spring of the year for most of us.

Q. So you don't think that the Soviet Union is trying to send us any particular signal?

The President. No, I really don't. Nor are we trying to send them a signal with our own war games.

The Vietnam Conflict

Q. Mr. President, getting back to your earlier statement that you felt for sometime that we should have declared war during the Vietnam period, against whom would we have declared war? And if we had done so, wouldn't that have widened the war and gotten us stuck into an even greater quagmire?

The President. Well, I can only say, with regard to that, I said that at a time when it was going on because of what was going on here in our own country, in which none of the rules of warfare could apply with regard to lending comfort and aid to the enemy.

Who we would have declared war against would have been a country, North Vietnam. The settlement of French Indochina created two nations—South Vietnam and North Vietnam. They were two separate nations. In fact, back through history they had pretty much been separate countries before. You say that because of the situation at the time; whether I would still feel the same way or not. I know that there was great concern about the possibility of a war widening, just as there was in Korea that prevented us from allowing General MacArthur to lead us to a victory in Korea. Everyone thought that you have to fight a war without winning it, or you might find yourself in a bigger war. Well, maybe General MacArthur was right. There is no substitute for victory.

Ms. Thomas. Thank you, Mr. President.

The President. [*Laughing*] You all had followups again.

Mr. Donaldson. Why are you doing it this way?

The President. Our people, Sam, just got tired of seeing me in the old set. [*Laughter*]

Mr. Donaldson. Goodbye.

Note: The President's 23d news conference began at 8:01 p.m. in the East Room at the White House. It was broadcast live on nationwide radio and television.

The final question referred to the fact that the President faced the reporters and cameras from the west side of the East Room, rather than the customary east side.

Remarks at the Conference Luncheon of the Women Business Owners of New York
April 5, 1984

Good afternoon, and thank you for that warm reception. I'm delighted to be back in the Big Apple. And I've been eager to get to one of these conferences for women in business ever since the Small Business Administration's office of women's business ownership, under Carolyn Gray, started cosponsoring them.

It's a special honor to be here with you, the members and friends of Women Business Owners of New York. You and your firms make up a vibrant part of the New York economy, employing thousands of men and women, providing goods and services that range from bookbinding to financial consulting. Each of you knows from personal experience that American women have the vision, the talent, and the determination to make great contributions to our nation's economy. And you're serving as role models for a new generation of women—women for whom participating in the economy will be much easier because of your efforts. On behalf of all Americans, I commend you.

In our lifetime, America has begun an historical social change that offers women exciting new opportunities. Just 35 years ago, only a third of adult women held jobs outside the home. Today more than two-thirds of the women between the ages of 25 and 44 are in paid positions. Growing numbers of women are doctors, military officers, police, and firefighters; more than a third of our law students are female; and women business owners represent the fastest growing segment of the small business community.

On a personal level, I've seen these changes clearly in the lives of the women closest to me. My mother, Nelle, never had the chance to go beyond elementary school. All her life she devoted herself to our family and held us together both emotionally and financially. For a while during the depression, she helped make ends meet by working in a dress shop for $14 a week.

My wife, Nancy, belongs to a later generation of women, in which many were raised with society expecting one thing of them, only to discover years afterward that society had come to expect something else. Like so many women, Nancy's had both the challenges and the rich rewards of adapting. She pursued a successful career as an actress, and today she gracefully combines her role as a loving wife and mother with her many duties as First Lady.

And, you know, the Government gets quite a bargain with First Ladies. They aren't on the payroll, but Nancy's office hours and duties run about even with mine. That's why she's not here at this moment. No words can express how proud I am to be the man in her life.

And my daughters, Patti and Maureen, belong to a new generation. And Maureen, as you've heard, has worked in radio and television, promoted overseas trade, run for political office. And today she's giving advice to her dad on something she understands very well: how to communicate to women what the administration is working to accomplish. My younger daughter, Patti, seeks a career in the entertainment world. When certain people for political reasons claim that I don't understand the modern woman, I'm tempted to say, "Then how come I have two very independent daughters? [*Laughter*]

But in my mother's time and throughout our history, women were always hard at work, seeking self-fulfillment, giving of themselves to their families, and building a better nation. Today women in our country are just as hardworking and giving as ever. It's America that has changed and grown, giving women increased chances to reach for the stars and go as far as their God-given talents can take them.

Women in the eighties are a diverse majority with varied interests and futures. Some seek to pursue their own careers, some run for political office, some focus on the home and family, and some seek to do all these things. No role is superior to another. What's important is that each woman must have the freedom to choose her path for herself, and I'm committed to just that. The simple truth is I've been frustrated by the perception that's been created about my supposed lack of interest in the welfare of women, and I'm going to take advantage of this opportunity to reveal some things our administration has been doing and that seem to have been closely guarded secrets up till now.

Once, after making a speech, a minister, the late Bill Alexander of Oklahoma, took it upon himself to tell me the story of his first sermon. I've never forgotten it. I always suspected maybe it had something to do with the length of my speech. He said that he had worked for weeks after his ordination on this first sermon and had been asked to speak—or to pray or preach at a small country church in Oklahoma, an evening service. And he arrived after working all these weeks on that first sermon that he was going to preach as a minister and looked out at a church that was empty except for one lone little fellow sitting out there amongst all the empty pews.

And Bill went down, and he said, "My friend, you seem to be the only member of the congregation that showed up. I'm just a young preacher getting started. What do you think? Should I go through with it?" And the fellow said, "Well, I wouldn't know about that sort of thing. I'm a little old cowpoke out here in Oklahoma. But I do know this. If I loaded up a truckload of hay, took it out in the prairie, and only one cow showed up, I'd feed her." [*Laughter*]

Well, Bill took that as a cue, got back up on the pulpit, and an hour and a half later said, "Amen." [*Laughter*] And he went down and said, "My friend, you seem to have stuck with me and, like I told you, I'm a young preacher getting started. What do you think?" And he says, "Well, like I told you, I'm just a little old cowpoke out here in Oklahoma. I don't know about that sort of thing. But I do know this. If I loaded up a truckload of hay, took it out in the prairie, and only one cow showed up, I sure wouldn't give her the whole load." [*Laughter*]

Now, I'm not going to miss an opportunity like this, and I'm going to take a certain advantage of the situation. [*Laughter*] I'm not going to talk an hour and a half, but you're going to get the whole load. [*Laughter*] Because during the past 3 years, I've appointed more than 1,400 women to top government positions, not because of their sex, but because they were the best people for the jobs.

Now, among many other firsts, our administration has Susan Meredith Phillips, the first woman head of the Commodity Futures Trading Commission; Elizabeth Jones, the first woman Chief Engraver of the United States Mint; and Janet McCoy, the first woman High Commissioner of the U.S. Trust Territories. And today, I'm delighted to announce that I'm sending to the Senate the nomination of Rosemary Collyer to be General Counsel of the National Labor Relations Board, and that will be another first.

For the first time in history, our nation has three women in the Cabinet—Margaret Heckler, who as Secretary of Health and Human Services is in charge of the third largest budget in the world; Elizabeth Dole, who as Secretary of Transportation oversees matters ranging from expendable rocket launches to revisions of our maritime laws; and Jeane Kirkpatrick, who as Ambassador to the United Nations plays a crucial role—she does play a crucial role in our country's foreign policy.

I must tell you, shortly after she had arrived there, she informed some of her colleagues from other countries that there was going to be a change. And one of them jokingly said, "Well, you mean you're not going to stand for being kicked around?" She said, "No, we're just going to take off the 'kick me' sign."

Well, one of my proudest days in office came when I appointed Sandra Day O'Connor to be the first woman in history on the United States Supreme Court.

To aid women in business, our administration has put together the three-point National Initiative Program to assist women business owners. The first of the three components is the Advisory Committee on Women's Business Ownership. Now, this Committee is made up of 12 women and 3 men, all very successful in the business and professional world.

I had lunch with the Committee last week, and they told me about the hearings they're holding to learn about the problems that women business owners encounter. And if you have any suggestions for the Committee, please write to me at the White House, and I'll pass your letters on to them.

The second part of our initiative for women business owners is the Interagency Committee on Women's Business Enterprise. This Committee is composed of high-level Federal officials representing the various departments and agencies of the Federal Government. I've charged that Committee with making certain that in dealing with women-owned businesses, the Federal Government sets an example for private enterprise.

A series of conferences like this one is the final part of initiative for women business owners. In addition to this New York conference, conferences for women in business have been held in places ranging from Somerset, New Jersey, to San Francisco, as you've been told—and many more are planned. The conferences are designed to help women acquire management skills and compete more effectively, and they're all cosponsored by private sector groups to make sure that we get private enterprises in the act.

In Atlanta, for example, local private firms responded to the conference enthusiastically. A group of businesses agreed to publish a women business owners directory for the State of Georgia at their own expense, and a group of banks established a hotline—one number for women to call to find out about everything from the availability of venture capital to where to get help in drawing up a contract.

Now, just as we're supporting you as you make gains in private enterprise, we're making certain that women receive fair treatment under the law. Our administration has moved to amend or eliminate statutes that discriminate on the basis of sex. At my direction, the Justice Department conducted a review of Federal statutes and found 140 that give different treatment to men and women. We have already proposed legislation to correct 122 of them. Of the remaining 18, 6 are still under study, the rest favor women and will remain unchanged. [*Laughter*] Like the law that—well, it's like the law that establishes a Women's Bureau in the Department of Labor. And I want to mention the superb job that Dr. Lenora Cole-Alexander is doing in heading that Bureau.

At the same time, the Task Force on Legal Equity for Women has begun a thorough review of nonstatutory rules, practices, and procedures throughout the Federal Government. Whenever it finds women treated unfairly, the Task Force works with the agencies or departments to ensure changes will be made.

To reach laws and procedures beyond the Federal level, we've established the Fifty States Project, a program that's working with Governors to help them find the areas where their State codes, regulations, and administrative rules treat women unfairly. I'm delighted to say that 42 States have already begun reviews of their laws and procedures, and more than half our States are already amending their laws to ensure equal treatment for women.

At the same time, the Department of Justice has been hard at work to fight discrimination in individual cases. The Department has filed the first seven suits in its history to enforce the Pregnancy Discrimination Act of 1978, and one of those suits involve the rights of some 9,000 women. Just last year, the Justice Department won a record-breaking $2¾ million discrimination case dealing with the rights of 685 women and blacks. Perhaps most important, the Department of Justice has so far filed more charges—or cases charging sex discrimination in employment than did the last administration during a comparable time.

Let there be no doubt, this administration considers discrimination based on sex just as great an evil as discrimination based on religion or race, and we will prosecute cases of sex discrimination to the full extent of the law.

Now, just as we're joining you in your efforts for legal equity, we're helping in a number of ways as American women work for economic self-reliance.

For those whose former spouses are delinquent in child support payments, we've moved to strengthen the Federal child support enforcement system. The year we took office, some $4 billion were owed to the children of America. Since then, our measures have raised child support collections by two-thirds. Improvements still need to be made in this area. So, we proposed new legislation that would further improve collection of child support for both welfare and nonwelfare families.

For those receiving Aid to Families with Dependent Children, the majority of whom are women, we've increased training opportunities that will help them secure permanent, productive employment, because no government handout can give a woman who's supporting her family the same sense of dignity as a job. Now, our Job Training Partnership Act specifically targets these women as a group that must be served.

For workers in the Federal Government, I signed into law a bill that extends flexible work hours. This applies to both men and women, but it's of particular importance to women who are holding down a job while raising a family. Now they'll be better able to structure their working hours to do things like spend more time with their families and perhaps be at home when their children come home from school.

For all women, we're working with the Congress and women's groups to provide several forms of tax relief—relief, by the way, which could and should have been passed long ago by those in Washington who had a monopoly on power and who still claim a monopoly on compassion.

Our administration has greatly reduced the income tax marriage penalty. We've eliminated estate tax that's levied on a surviving spouse, giving significant benefits to those with family farms and small businesses where women have long been hard-working partners. We've put social security back on a firm footing and made reforms that help many divorced spouses and disabled widows. And we've expanded participation in IRA accounts, helping women whether they work at home or in paid jobs.

Nothing is more important to parents than knowing their children are being taken good care of while they're on the job. So, we've almost doubled the maximum child care tax credit. In other moves to make child care more available and affordable, we proposed tax relief for organizations that care for the dependents of working people, and we're pressing for a restructuring of the dependent care tax credit to make more benefits available for low- and middle-income taxpayers.

We're also working with the Congress to pass historic legislation that will reform inequities that women suffer in some private pension plans. This legislation has passed the Senate, and we're awaiting a vote on the floor of the House, in case you'd like to call or write someone. [*Laughter*] I have often said it is not only necessary to make the legislators see the light; it's better to make them feel the heat. [*Laughter*] The reforms will lower the age at which employees can participate in company pension plans; protect nonworking spouses from losing death benefits without their knowledge; coordinate State and Federal laws so divorced spouses can collect court-awarded pension benefits more easily; require pension plans to offer survivor's benefits protection to workers after they reach 45; and permit a break in service of up to 5 years without loss of pension credit, a change that would help women take time to start a family but still go back to their careers.

Despite the importance of all these reforms, I've always believed the most important step we can take for women is the most important step that we can take for all our people—a dynamic, sustained economic expansion. Economic growth will provide more opportunities for women than if all the promises made in the history of Washington, DC, were enacted into law.

Think back just 3 years. Raging inflation, the highest prime interest rate in more than a century, an ever-growing tax burden, government regulations that were out of control—all these had stifled investment, smothered productivity, and brought growth to a virtual standstill.

The economic crisis hit women especially hard. Elderly women living on fixed incomes found their purchasing power eaten up by inflation. Working women saw jobs become more and more scarce. Homemakers found that 12½-percent inflation made it harder and harder to buy the groceries and pay the bills. And the thousands of women who wanted to start their own businesses saw 21½-percent prime interest rates slam the door in their faces.

When we took office, we made restoring economic vitality our top priority. We cut the growth of government spending. We pruned needless regulations. We chopped tax rates and enacted an historic reform called tax indexing. Indexing means that government will never again profit from inflation at your expense. And today, less than 3 years after we set our program in place, we're seeing a surging economic expansion.

The prime interest rate has fallen to about half what it was when we took office. Inflation has plummeted some two-thirds to about 4 or 4½ percent. Housing starts, factory orders, and retail sales are up. Compared to the last quarter of 1982, net private savings during the same period in 1983 shot up nearly 50 percent to over $230 billion, providing new funds to fuel innovation and spur growth.

In the 15 months since the recovery began, nearly 5 million Americans have found work, and the overall unemployment rate has fallen to 7.7 percent, marking the steepest drop in more than 30 years. And just last month it was announced that

during the first quarter of 1984 our gross national product grew at the robust annual rate of more than 7 percent, proving that expansion is here to stay.

Now, just as the economic crisis hit women hard, today's expansion is giving them a powerful lift. The unemployment rate among adult women has dropped from 9.1 percent to 6.9 percent. More women have jobs today than ever before in our nation's history. Just as important, the jobs women hold are getting better and better. In 1983 women filled almost three-quarters of all the new jobs in managerial, professional, and technical fields. And the number of women-owned businesses is growing four times faster than the number of those owned by men.

Entrepreneurs like you, who own their own, mostly small businesses, are playing a special part in this expansion. Last year alone, there were almost 600,000 new business incorporations. That's an all-time high in our history and half again the number of incorporations each year during the early seventies. At the same time, bankruptcies declined some 30 percent in the second half of 1983 compared with the same period in 1982. And small business income, as measured by proprietorships and partnerships, grew by a remarkable 18 percent. Perhaps most important, during this expansion small businesses, like the ones that many of you own, provided the most new jobs, gave the most employees the freedom to work part-time, and hired the most young people, senior citizens, and women. The American entrepreneur is building a dazzling new future, and she's just getting started.

We must and will go forward to keep opportunities expanding for you and all Americans. To prevent the nightmare of inflation from ever coming back, we must enact constitutional reforms like the line-item veto and the balanced budget amendment. Please, I'd like both of those. And to provide new incentives for growth, make taxes more simple and fair, I believe we must design and enact a program of tax simplification; not tinkering here and there, but a sweeping, comprehensive reform of the entire tax code. We must and will enact these measures. And I'm convinced that when we do, the American economy will reach new heights of prosperity.

When I look at America, I see our basic industry making striking gains, and new industries, like robotics and bioengineering, gathering strength. I see America leading the world in a technological revolution that's putting men and women into space and adding years to life here on Earth. I see a country of open, self-confident people, serving as a force for peace among nations. And I see women, who are holding families together, entering the work force, starting new enterprises, and doing it all with courage and confidence. America is back.

And now, I know that many of your companies gross millions of dollars a year, but I'd like to share a letter I received that tells about a woman who started a business that's more modest. The letter comes from a person called Betty Lou, and I believe it shows the enterprising spirit of American women. She wrote, "Mr. President, I'm a simple person in that I have simple needs . . . . My husband, a Vietnam veteran of the Marine Corps, is a union steamfitter. When we got married, he was out of work for 2 years, but we learned how to budget around it and still were able to save money . . . . Now that construction work is available in our area, we know we still have to save . . . . We both know that nothing comes from nothing—you make your own fortune, so to speak."

To help make ends meet, Betty Lou writes, ". . . with only $530 and a big smile, I began a new venture. I . . . had no previ-

ous business management experience, and didn't know exactly where I'd end up. But I had the chance. Now, 3 years later, I own and operate (my own word processing company) . . . . It has grown from that initial $530 to an annual income for 1983 of $41,000; from an older-technology machine costing $3,000 to a new . . . system costing $22,000; from one person logging a huge number of hours to two full-time employees each logging over 40 hours a week . . . . We have pride in the work we do and are even more proud of the fact that we're being given the chance to do it. And, who knows what goals can be achieved in 1984." She closed, adding that they're a young couple in their early thirties, and they've already built a new home for themselves.

Well, whether founding their own companies like Betty Lou and so many of you, or holding down any of the millions of jobs our economy provides; or devoting themselves to caring for their loved ones and raising happy, healthy children; or doing all these things, I know that women will play a vital part in leading our nation into the future—and that there will always be American women who are American heroes.

Thank you, and God bless you.

Note: The President spoke at 1:13 p.m. in the Empire State Ballroom at the Grand Hyatt Hotel in New York City.

Following his appearance at the luncheon, the President visited the Hudson Guild Day Care Center on the Lower West Side of Manhattan. He then went to the Plaza Hotel, where he held a meeting with local Jewish community leaders.

Nomination of Rosemary M. Collyer To Be General Counsel of the National Labor Relations Board
April 5, 1984

The President today announced his intention to nominate Rosemary M. Collyer to be General Counsel of the National Labor Relations Board for a term of 4 years. She would succeed William A. Lubbers.

Mrs. Collyer is currently Chairman of the

Federal Mine Safety and Health Review Commission. Previously, she was senior associate with the firm of Sherman & Howard in Denver, CO (1977–1981); instructor, Personnel Prediction and Research, Inc. (1973–1974); creative director, Pennington and

Richard Associates (1972–1973); director of public relations, Manlius Pebble Hill School (1971–1972); and reporter with the Canadian Register, Toronto (1969–1970).

Mrs. Collyer graduated from Trinity College (B.A., 1968) and the University of Denver College of Law (J.D., 1977). She is married, has one child, and resides in Chevy Chase, MD. She was born November 19, 1945, in Port Chester, NY.

Remarks to the New York State Federation of Catholic School Parents
April 5, 1984

Thank you all very much for a very wonderful and warm welcome. And of course I realize, now, that I, in addition to everything else, will be held responsible for the cross-town traffic in New York. [*Laughter*]

Americans are always thrilled to come to this city, and believe me, for a midwesterner from a small town in Illinois, the sidewalks of New York still evoke that sense of romance and excitement that is unique to this city and this State.

Now, whether it's that towering lady out there in the harbor, or the memory of your first Catholic Governor, Al Smith, New York City and New York State symbolize America—its togetherness, its openness, its opportunity, its hope.

And like so many other Americans, I was thrilled a few weeks ago by the sights at Archbishop O'Connor's installation at St. Patrick's Cathedral—the rabbis standing there in the front pews, the Greek Orthodox bishop approaching the altar, St. Thomas Episcopal Church holding hundreds who watched the proceedings on a video screen, and that homily of welcome and humor and love from Archbishop O'Connor.

I've been accused of liking a good story, but I really did love the one the Archbishop told about the second-grader who wrote him and asked if he held down a job before this one. [*Laughter*] The same young man also wanted to know if the Archbishop had any children. [*Laughter*] Well, he's spoken to that tonight. I think we're aware that he does—the thousands and thousands of children who are in the schools that bring us to this gathering here tonight.

But who can forget the substance of your new Archbishop's sermon? How many fewer accounts of violence, heartbreak, and tragedy would there be, especially in places like the Mideast, if all the people of the world could take his words to heart? How valid, how meaningful those words are for this season of Lent, this time of reflection and renewal.

"Whether or not you are of my religious faith or my moral convictions," Archbishop O'Connor said, "whether you accept the teaching of the Church or reject it on any issue, I see you as sacred persons to be loved, persons of priceless dignity and worth."

Your Excellency, I know how excited you are about your new work here in the Archdiocese of New York, and with a beginning like that, I can't help but think your success here is assured. You have the prayerful best wishes of all of us here tonight and of all America. But, Your Excellency, just one word of advice about living here in New York. Be careful what you say around Mayor Koch—[*laughter*]—I know I am. [*Laughter*] I learned this morning he's working on another book. And if the mayor would permit me, I'd like to mention that in the city of Scranton, Pennsylvania, where Archibishop O'Connor previously served, Mayor James Barrett McNulty, who's no amateur himself, called the Archbishop the "best politician I've ever seen." [*Laughter*] So, I intend to warn the mayor to be careful, too. [*Laughter*]

But I want, honestly, all of you to know I really was a little nervous about speaking to you here tonight, especially on issues like education. When I look around this room and see the distinguished members of the hierarchy and many prominent educators, not to mention you parents who've given so much time and effort to improving Catholic schools, I have to think of a story that kind of fits the position that I'm in tonight, and particularly having to follow the Archbishop up here at this podium.

There was a fellow who, for very many years, had been quite a celebrity in his end of the country up in Pennsylvania, because he was in great demand as a speaker—he was the last living survivor of the Johnstown flood. And so in telling and retelling his adventures, as I say, he was in great demand. Finally, however, the day came when he passed on to a better life and wasn't in heaven very long before St. Peter told him that newcomers there were expected to sort of bring the others there up-to-date on what was going on. And he said, "Oh, that's great," and he told them about what he'd been doing on Earth.

So he said, "Yes, I'd be very happy to." Well, St. Peter put the group together, and he said, "I'm sure they'll be interested in what you have to say." And then as he introduced him, and as the man stepped toward the lectern, St. Peter just quietly said to him, "That fellow second from the aisle in the front row is named Noah." [*Laughter*]

But actually, the fact that so many of you are activists for education is not a reason for concern, but for pride. Not long ago, opinion polls showed the confidence of average Americans for our governmental institutions had declined to new lows. Many Americans simply believed that government belonged now to politicians and bureaucrats, not to the people. Well, there was a reason for this. After years of listening to the bromides and aphorisms of liberal government, the people felt they'd been had. Federal spending had skyrocketed—it tripled in the seventies—and taxation doubled between 1976 and 1981. Yet far from solving anything, all this government only made our problems worse. It fueled inflation, it drained energy and wealth from the private sector, it halted economic growth, and it eventually put millions out of work.

But at the root of this spend-and-spend, and tax-and-tax, and borrow-and-borrow philosophy was the belief that solving our social problems was simply a matter of allocating resources rather than exerting moral leadership. There were those who thought, and still do, that by changing man's material environment we could perfect human nature and usher in a brave new world. So they favored gigantic government programs and social engineering schemes run by a tiny elite of experts. And that's why they frequently saw traditional values like family, work, neighborhood, religion, as obstacles. In their view, the solutions to America's problems were no longer in her homes, her churches, her schools, or her work places, but in a bureaucrat's budget and a social worker's files.

Much of this was well intentioned. In fact, a book about what liberalism did to even this great city of New York was called just that: "The Cost of Good Intentions." Well today, under the courageous leadership of Mayor Koch, New Yorkers have brought their city back from bankruptcy and disorder. I think you can be proud of that, and you can be proud of your mayor. I bet he wishes now he was here. [*Laughter*]

But on the national level, the fight goes on. One example is the question of tuition tax credits. As you know, we've submitted a bill to the Congress that would make such credits available to parents like yourselves. And the bill that we proposed does not violate the separation of church and state. And it's certainly no threat to public education. What it would do is give hard-working Catholic and other private school parents a break, while increasing diversity and excellence in both public and private schools. And I want to compliment you on your efforts in the past for this bill and pledge again my strongest efforts on its behalf.

I quoted from a Scottish ballad when we were defeated on that. The ballad goes, "I am wounded, but I am not slain. I will rest a bit and fight again." Together, we can uphold and reinforce the basic right of all parents to educate their children in the way that best meets their children's needs.

But opposition to tuition tax credits isn't the only roadblock those in Washington have put in our way. They also managed during the past generation to construct a tax system that excessively burdens the

475

family and actually discriminates against those traditional family values. For example, the dependency exemption on your income tax—the money you can deduct for raising a child or caring for an elderly relative—was $600 in the late forties. That has been increased to $1,000 now. But if that deduction had been indexed to keep pace with inflation, today you would be deducting more than $3,000 for every one of your children. So, you can see that in the very time that the cost of raising a family has gone up, the tax treatment of families has actually worsened. Is it any wonder that American parents feel so much financial pressure today and that such pressure sometimes contributes to family breakups?

I want you to know I've told the Treasury Department to come up with recommendations to make your taxes more simple, fair for families and for all Americans, and to increase incentives for economic growth by broadening the base and bringing your income tax rates down, not up.

On this issue of tax fairness for families, or other issues like the prayer amendment, stricter laws against the criminals that prey on our young people, greater discipline in our schools, and our pro-life amendment, there is more at stake here than just one administration's political agenda. Our goal is to make this nation's traditional values a reality in our daily life.

When I visited His Holiness Pope John Paul II in Rome—and I'm pleased to say I will have the privilege of visiting with him soon again when our paths cross in Alaska—he spoke about the importance of these values. He said it was his profound hope "that the entire structure of American life will rest ever more securely on the strong foundation of moral and spiritual values. Without the fostering and defense of these values," he said, "all human advancement is stunted and the dignity of the human person is endangered."

Respect for the dignity of life, concern for our fellow man, extraordinary acts of charity and mercy—this is our heritage as Americans. And how profoundly this heritage has been enriched by the Catholic experience here in New York.

There are so many examples that come to mind. In my State of the Union Message I mentioned a man known to many of you, the guardian of homeless youth in Times Square, Father Bruce Ritter, who has saved so many young, formerly lost lives at Covenant House. I know that Father Ritter and all who want to see stronger efforts to combat child abduction and child exploitation will be pleased to learn some good news: Within a week, the Justice Department will sign a $3.3 million grant to create the National Center for Missing and Exploited Children. This Center will help educate parents to prevent abductions and runaways, assist parents whose children are missing, and give technical assistance to local law enforcement agencies in their efforts to find missing children. Let's win these children back.

Or, I wonder how many of you remember the daughter of one of America's most famous novelists, a young woman who came from New England to New York before the turn of the century? Her beauty, her own literary skill, and that of her husband's, made the young couple the toast of society here. But with the death of an infant son and the unavoidable breakup of her marriage, tragedy struck. The young woman, a convert to Catholicism, sought again the meaning and purpose of life, and somehow she found herself on Cherry Street in lower Manhattan. And from that little dilapidated house in New York's slums grew a nursing order of Dominican nuns with hospitals throughout the United States. For cancer patients, shunned in those days like the lepers of another age, the odyssey of Nathaniel Hawthorne's beautiful daughter, Rose Hawthorne Lathrop, would become a blessing beyond all description. Hundreds, then thousands, would find treatment and solace and hope, and they were welcome whether they could afford it or not.

The work of Mother Alphonsa of the Hawthorne Dominicans goes on today in two hospitals here in this State and five other hospitals in other States. It's a perfect example of how "sorrow built a bridge into the infinite," of how generous and giving have been the hearts of New York Catholics. It's been a tradition carried right up until our own time. Rarely has the world seen a more magnificent display of the cardinal virtues of faith, hope, and charity than in the manner in which your own beloved Terence Cardinal Cooke met death last year. It was a fitting and inspiring climax to a life of holiness and service to others.

And tonight, ladies and gentlemen, it is my privilege to present posthumously the Nation's highest civilian award, the Medal of Freedom, to Terence Cardinal Cooke. Accepting the medal for Cardinal Cooke will be Archbishop O'Connor.

Thank you for having me as your guest tonight. I know of no better way to close than by reading this inscription.

[*At this point, the President read the citation which accompanied the medal. The text of the citation follows:*]

A saintly man and a great spiritual leader, Terence Cardinal Cooke inspired his countrymen with his dedication to his Church, devotion to his flock, and service to his country. As the Military Vicar to our Nation's Armed Forces, Cardinal Cooke worked tirelessly on behalf of those who serve their country in uniform. As a patriot and national leader, he preached the love of country and championed the cause of human freedom. He will live in the memory of his countrymen as a man of compassion, courage, and personal holiness.

Note: The President spoke at 8:32 p.m. in the Grand Ballroom at the New York Hilton Hotel in New York City.

Following his remarks at the dinner, the President returned to Washington, DC.

Remarks at the National Leadership Forum of the Center for International and Strategic Studies of Georgetown University
April 6, 1984

Thank you very much, Ann Armstrong. Thank you, Cochairman Sam Nunn. I am honored to have this opportunity to take part in your National Leadership Forum. The CSIS reputation for distinguished scholarly research is well deserved, and your organization rightly enjoys that great respect.

I'd like to address your theme of bipartisanship with a view toward America's foreign policy—the challenges for the eighties.

All Americans share two great goals for foreign policy: a safer world, and a world in which individual rights can be respected and precious values may flourish. These goals are at the heart of America's traditional idealism and our aspirations for world peace. Yet, while cherished by us, they do not belong exclusively to us. They're not made in America. They're shared by people everywhere.

Tragically, the world in which these fundamental goals are so widely shared is a very troubled world. While we and our allies may enjoy peace and prosperity, many citizens of the industrial world continue to live in fear of conflict and the threat of nuclear war. And all around the globe terrorists threaten innocent people and civilized values. And in developing countries, the dreams of human progress have too often been lost to violent revolution and dictatorship.

Quite obviously the widespread desire for a safer and more humane world is, by itself, not enough to create such a world. In pursuing our worthy goals, we must go beyond honorable intentions and good will to practical means.

We must be guided by these key principles:

Realism—the world is not as we wish it would be. Reality is often harsh. We will not make it less so, if we do not first see it for what it is.

Strength—we know that strength alone is not enough, but without it there can be no effective diplomacy and negotiations, no secure democracy and peace. Conversely, weakness or hopeful passivity are only self-defeating. They invite the very aggression and instability that they would seek to avoid.

Now, economic growth—this is the underlying base that ensures our strength and permits human potential to flourish. Neither strength nor creativity can be achieved or sustained without economic growth, both at home and abroad.

Intelligence—our policies cannot be effective unless the information on which they're based is accurate, timely, and complete.

Shared responsibility with allies—our friends and allies share the heavy responsibility for the protection of freedom. We seek and need their partnership, sharing burdens in pursuit of our common goals.

Nonaggression—we have no territorial ambitions. We occupy no foreign lands. We build our strength only to assure deterrence and to secure our interests if deterrence fails.

Dialog with adversaries—though we must be honest in recognizing fundamental differences with our adversaries, we must always be willing to resolve these differences by peaceful means.

Bipartisanship at home—in our two-party democracy, an effective foreign policy must begin with bipartisanship, and the sharing of responsibility for a safer and more humane world must begin at home.

During the past 3 years, we've been steadily rebuilding America's capacity to advance our foreign policy goals through renewed attention to these vital principles. Many threats remain, and peace may still seem precarious. But America is safer and more secure today because the people of this great nation have restored the foundation of its strength.

We began with renewed realism, a clear-eyed understanding of the world we live in and of our inescapable global responsibilities. Our industries depend on the importation of energy and minerals from distant lands. Our prosperity requires a sound international financial system and free and open trading markets. And our security is inseparable from the security of our friends and neighbors.

I believe Americans today see the world with realism and maturity. The great majority of our people do not believe the stark differences between democracy and totalitarianism can be wished away. They understand that keeping America secure begins with keeping America strong and free.

When we took office in 1981, the Soviet Union had been engaged for 20 years in the most massive military buildup in history. Clearly, their goal was not to catch us, but to surpass us. Yet the United States remained a virtual spectator in the 1970's, a decade of neglect that took a severe toll on our defense capabilities.

With bipartisan support, we embarked immediately on a major defense rebuilding program. We've made good progress in restoring the morale of our men and women in uniform, restocking spare parts and ammunition, replacing obsolescent equipment and facilities, improving basic training and readiness, and pushing forward with long overdue weapons programs.

The simple fact is that in the last half of the 1970's, we were not deterring, as events from Angola to Afghanistan made clear. Today we are. And that fact has fundamentally altered the future for millions of human beings. Gone are the days when the United States was perceived as a rudderless superpower, a helpless hostage to world events. American leadership is back. Peace through strength is not a slogan. It's a fact of life. And we will not return to the days of handwringing, defeatism, decline, and despair.

We have also upgraded significantly our intelligence capabilities, restoring morale in the intelligence agencies and increasing our capability to detect, analyze, and counter hostile intelligence threats.

Economic strength, the underlying base of support for our defense buildup, has received a dramatic new boost. We've transformed a no-growth economy, crippled by disincentives, double-digit inflation, 21½-percent interest rates, plunging productivity, and a weak dollar, into a dynamic growth economy bolstered by new incentives, stable prices, lower interest rates, a rebirth of productivity, and restored our confidence in our currency.

Renewed strength at home has been accompanied by closer partnerships with America's friends and allies. Far from buckling under Soviet intimidation, the unity of the NATO alliance has held firm, and we're moving forward to modernize our strategic deterrent. The leader of America's oldest ally, French President Francois Mitterrand, recently reminded us that peace, like liberty, is never given. The pursuit of both is a continual one. In the turbulent times we live in, solidarity among friends is essential.

Our principles don't involve just rebuilding our strength; they also tell us how to use it. We remain true to the principle of nonaggression. On an occasion when the United States, at the request of its neighbors, did use force in Grenada, we acted decisively, but only after it was clear a bloodthirsty regime had put American and Grenadian lives in danger, and the security of neighboring islands in danger. As soon as stability and freedom were restored in the island, we left. The Soviet Union had no such legitimate justification for its massive invasion of Afghanistan 4 years ago. And today, over a hundred thousand occupation troops remain there. The United States, by stark contrast, occupies no foreign nation, nor do we seek to.

Though we and the Soviet Union differ markedly, living in this nuclear age makes it imperative that we talk with each other. If the new Soviet leadership truly is devoted to building a safer and more humane world, rather than expanding armed conquests, it will find a sympathetic partner in the West.

In pursuing these practical principles, we have throughout sought to revive the spirit that was once the hallmark of our postwar foreign policy: bipartisan cooperation between the executive and legislative branches of our government.

Much has been accomplished, but much remains to be done. If Republicans and Democrats will join together to confront four great challenges to American foreign policy in the eighties, then we can and will make great strides toward a safer and more humane world.

Challenge number one is to reduce the risk of nuclear war and to reduce the levels of nuclear armaments in a way that also reduces the risk they will ever be used. We have no higher challenge, for a nuclear war cannot be won and must never be fought. But merely to be against nuclear war is not enough to prevent it.

For 35 years the defense policy of the United States and her NATO allies has been based on one simple premise: We do not start wars; we maintain our conventional and strategic strength to deter aggression by convincing any potential aggressor that war could bring no benefit, only disaster. Deterrence has been and will remain the cornerstone of our national security policy to defend freedom and preserve peace.

But as I mentioned, the 1970's were marked by neglect of our defenses, and nuclear safety was no exception. Too many forgot John Kennedy's warning that only when our arms are certain beyond doubt can we be certain beyond doubt they will never be used. By the beginning of this decade, we face three growing problems: the Soviet SS–20 monopoly in Europe and Asia; the vulnerability of our land-based ICBM, the entire force; and the failure of arms control agreements to slow the overall growth in strategic weapons. The Carter administration acknowledged these problems. In fact, almost everyone did.

There is a widespread, but mistaken, impression that arms agreements automatically produce arms control. In 1969, when SALT I negotiations began, the Soviet Union had about 1,500 strategic nuclear weapons. Today the Soviet nuclear arsenal can grow to over 15,000 nuclear weapons and still stay within all past arms control agreements, including the SALT I and SALT II guidelines.

The practical means for reducing the risks of nuclear war must, therefore, follow two parallel paths—credible deterrence and real arms reductions with effective verification. It is on this basis that we've responded to the problems I just described. This is why we've moved forward to implement NATO's dual-track decision of 1979. While actually reducing the number of nuclear weapons in Europe, it is also why we have sought bipartisan support for the recommendations of the Scowcroft commission and the builddown concept and why we've proposed deep reductions in strategic forces at the strategic arms reduction talks.

Without exception, every arms control proposal that we have offered would reverse the arms buildup and help bring a more stable balance at lower force levels. At the START talks, we seek to reduce substantially the number of ballistic missile warheads, reduce the destructive capacity of nuclear missiles, and establish limits on bombers and cruise missiles, below the levels of SALT II. At the talks on intermediate-range nuclear forces, our negotiators have tabled four initiatives to address Soviet concerns and improve prospects for a fair and equitable agreement that would reduce or eliminate an entire class of such nuclear weapons. Our flexibility in the START and INF negotiations has been demonstrated by numerous modifications to our positions. But they have been met only by the silence of Soviet walkouts.

At the mutual and balanced force reduction talks in Vienna, we and our NATO partners presented a treaty that would reduce conventional forces to parity at lower levels. To reduce the risks of war in time of crisis, we have proposed to the Soviet Union important measures to improve direct communications and increase mutual confidence. And just recently, I directed Vice President Bush to go to the Conference [Committee] on Disarmament in Geneva to present a new American initiative, a worldwide ban on the production, possession, and use of chemical weapons.

Our strategic policy represents a careful response to a nuclear agenda upon which even our critics agreed. Many who would break the bonds of partisanship, claiming they know how to bring greater security, seem to ignore the likely consequences of their own proposals.

Those who wanted a last-minute moratorium on INF deployment would have betrayed our allies and reduced the chances for a safer Europe. Those who would try to implement a unilateral freeze would find it unverifiable and destabilizing, because it would prevent restoration of a stable balance that keeps the peace. And those who would advocate unilateral cancellation of the Peacekeeper missile would ignore a central recommendation of the bipartisan Scowcroft report and leave the Soviets with little incentive to negotiate meaningful reductions. Indeed, the Soviets would be rewarded for leaving the bargaining table.

These simplistic solutions and others put forward by our critics would take meaningful agreements and increased security much further from our grasp. Our critics can best help us move closer to the goals that we share by accepting practical means to achieve them. Granted, it's easy to support a strong defense. It's much harder to support a strong defense budget. And granted, it's easy to call for arms agreements. It's more difficult to support patient, firm, fair negotiations with those who want to see how much we will compromise with ourselves first. Bipartisanship can only work if both forces, both sides, face up to real world problems and meet them with real world solutions.

Our safety and security depend on more than credible deterrence and nuclear arms reductions. Constructive regional development is also essential. Therefore, one—or our second great challenge is strengthening the basis for stability in troubled and strategically sensitive regions.

Regional tensions often begin in longstanding social, political, and economic inequities and in ethnic and religious disputes. But throughout the 1970's, increased Soviet support for terrorism, insurgency, and aggression coupled with the perception of weakening U.S. power and resolve greatly exacerbated these tensions.

The results were not surprising: the massacres of Kampuchea followed by the Vietnamese invasion, the Soviet invasion of Afghanistan, the rise of Iranian extremism and the holding of Americans hostage, Libyan coercion in Africa, Soviet and Cuban military involvement in Angola and Ethiopia, their subversion in Central America, and the rise of state-supported terrorism.

Taken together, these events defined a pattern of mounting instability and violence that the U.S. could not ignore. And we have not. As with defense, by the beginning of the eighties, there was an emerging consensus in this country that we had to go do better in dealing with problems that affect our vital interests.

Obviously, no single abstract policy could deal successfully with all problems or all regions. But as a general matter, effective, regional stabilization requires a balanced approach—a mix of economic aid, security assistance, and diplomatic mediation—tailored to the needs of each region.

It's also obvious that we alone cannot save embattled governments or control terrorism. But doing nothing only ensures far greater problems down the road. So, we strive to expand cooperation with states who support our common interests, to help friendly nations in danger, and to seize major opportunities for peacekeeping.

Perhaps the best example of this comprehensive approach is the report and recommendations of the National Bipartisan Commission on Central America. It is from this report that we drew our proposals for bringing peaceful development to Central America. They are now before the Congress and will be debated at length.

I welcome a debate, but if it's to be productive, we must put aside mythology and uninformed rhetoric. Some, for example, insist that the root of regional violence is poverty, but not communism. Well, three-fourths of our requests and of our current program is economic and humanitarian assistance. America is a good and generous nation, but economic aid alone cannot stop Cuban- and Soviet-inspired guerrillas determined to terrorize, burn, bomb, and destroy everything from bridges and industries to electric power and transportation. And neither individual rights nor economic health can be advanced if stability is not secured.

Other critics say that we shouldn't see the problems of this or any other region as an East-West struggle. Our policies in Central America and elsewhere are in fact designed precisely to keep East-West tensions from spreading, from intruding into the lives of nations that are struggling with great problems of their own.

Events in southern Africa are showing what persistent mediation and ability to talk to all sides can accomplish. The states of this region have been poised for war for decades, but there is new hope for peace. South Africa, Angola, and Mozambique are implementing agreements to break the cycle of violence. Our administration has been active in this process, and we'll stay involved, trying to bring an independent Namibia into being, end foreign military interference, and keep the region free from East-West conflict. I have hope that peace and democratic reform can be enjoyed by all the peoples of southern Africa.

In Central America we've also seen progress. El Salvador's Presidential election expresses that nation's desire to govern itself in peace. Yet the future of the region remains open. We have a choice. Either we help America's friends defend themselves and give democracy a chance, or we abandon our responsibilities and let the Soviet Union and Cuba shape the destiny of our hemisphere. If this happens, the East-West conflict will only become broader and much more dangerous.

In dealing with regional instability, we have to understand how it is related to other problems. Insecurity and regional violence are among the driving forces of nuclear proliferation. Peacekeeping in troubled regions and strengthening barriers to nuclear proliferation are two sides of the same coin. Stability and safeguards go together.

Now, no one says this approach is cheap, quick, or easy. But the cost of this commitment is bargain-basement compared to the tremendous sacrifices that we will have to make if we do nothing, or do too little. The Kissinger commission warned that an outbreak of Cuban-type regimes in Central America will bring subversion closer to our own borders, and the specter of millions of uprooted refugees fleeing in desperation to the north.

In the Middle East, which has so rarely known peace, we seek a similar mix of economic aid, diplomatic mediation, and military assistance and cooperation. These will, we believe, make the use of U.S. forces unnecessary and make the risk of East-West conflict less. But, given the importance of the region, we must also be ready to act when the presence of American power and that of our friends can help stop the spread of violence. I have said, for example, that we'll keep open the Straits of Hormuz, the vital lifeline through which so much oil flows to the United States and other industrial democracies. Making this clear beforehand and making it credible makes a crisis much less likely.

We must work with quiet persistence and without illusions. We may suffer setbacks, but we mustn't jump to the conclusion that we can defend our interests without ever committing ourselves. Nor should other nations believe that mere setbacks will turn America inward again. We know our responsibilities, and we must live up to them.

Because effective regional problemsolving requires a balanced and sustained approach, it is essential that the Congress give full, not piecemeal, support. Indeed, where we have foundered in regional stabilization, it has been because the Congress has failed to provide such support. Halfway measures, refusing to take responsibility for means, produce the worst possible results. I'll return to this point when I discuss the fourth challenge in just a few minutes.

Expanding opportunities for economic development and personal freedom is our third great challenge. The American concept of peace is more than absence of war. We favor the flowering of economic growth and individual liberty in a world of peace. And this, too, is a goal to which most Americans subscribe. Our political leaders must be judged by whether the means they offer will help us to reach it.

Our belief in individual freedom and opportunity is rooted in practical experience. Free people build free markets that ignite dynamic development for everyone. And in America, incentives, risktaking, and entrepreneurship are reawakening the spirit of capitalism and strengthening economic expansion and human progress throughout the world. Our goal has always been to restore and sustain noninflationary worldwide growth, thereby ending for good the stagflation of the 1970's, which saw a drastic weakening of the fabric of the world economy.

We take our leadership responsibilities seriously, but we alone cannot put the world's economic house in order. At Williamsburg, the industrial countries consolidated their views on economic policy. The proof is not in the communique; it's in the results. France is reducing inflation and seeking greater flexibility in its economy. Japan is slowly, to be sure, but steadily, we will insist, liberalizing its trade and capital markets. Germany and the United Kingdom are moving forward on a steady course of low inflation and moderate, sustained growth.

Just as we believe that incentives are key to greater growth in America and throughout the world, so, too, must we resist the sugar-coated poison of protectionism everywhere it exists. Here at home we're opposing inflationary, self-defeating bills like domestic content. At the London economic summit in June, I hope that we can lay the groundwork for a new round of negotiations that will open markets for our exports of goods and services and stimulate greater growth, efficiency, and jobs for all.

And we're advancing other key initiatives to promote more powerful worldwide growth by expanding trade and investment relationships. The dynamic growth of Pacific Basin nations has made them the fastest growing markets for our goods, services, and capital. Last year I visited Japan and Korea—two of America's most important allies—to forge closer partnerships. And this month I will visit the People's Republic of China, another of the increasingly significant relationships that we hold in the Pacific. I see America and our Pacific neighbors as nations of the future going forward together in a mighty enterprise to build dynamic growth economies and a safer world.

We're helping developing countries grow by presenting a fresh view of development—the magic of the marketplace—to spark greater growth and participation in the international economy. Developing nations earn twice as much from exports to the United States as they received in aid from all the other nations combined.

And practical proposals like the Caribbean Basin Initiative will strengthen the private sectors of some 20 sectors—or I should say, 20 Caribbean neighbors, while guaranteeing fairer treatment for U.S. companies and nationals and increasing demand for American exports.

We've recently sent to the Congress a new economic policy initiative for Africa. And it, too, is designed to support the growth of private enterprise in African countries by encouraging structural economic change in international trade. We've also asked the Congress to increase humanitarian assistance to Africa to combat the devastating effects of extreme drought.

In building a strong global recovery, of course, nothing is more important than to keep the wheels of world commerce turning and create jobs without renewing the spiral of inflation. The International Monetary Fund is a linchpin in our efforts to restore a sound world economy, resolve the debt problems of many developing countries. With bipartisan support, we implemented a major increase in IMF resources. In cooperation with the IMF, we're working to prevent the problems of individual debtor nations from disrupting the stability and strength of the entire international financial system. It was this goal that brought nations of north and south together to help resolve the debt difficulties of the new democratic Government of Argentina.

Because we know that democratic governments are the best guarantors of human rights, and that economic growth will always flourish when men and women are free, we seek to promote not just material products but the values of faith and human dignity for which America and all democratic nations stand—values which embody the culmination of 5,000 years of Western civilization.

When I addressed the British Parliament in June of 1982, I called for a bold and lasting effort to assist people struggling for human rights. We've established the National Endowment for Democracy, a partnership of people from all walks of life dedicated to spreading the positive message of democracy. To succeed we must oppose the double speak of totalitarian propaganda. And so, we're modernizing the Voice of America and our other broadcasting facilities, and we're working to start up Radio Marti, a voice of truth to the imprisoned people of Cuba.

Americans have always wanted to see the spread of democratic institutions, and that goal is coming closer. In our own hemisphere, 26 countries of Latin America and the Caribbean are either democracies or formally embarked on a democratic transition. This represents 90 percent of the region's population, up from under 50 percent a decade ago.

Trust the people—this is the crucial lesson of history and America's message to the world. We must be staunch in our conviction that freedom is not the sole possession of a chosen few, but the universal right of men and women everywhere.

President Truman said, "If we should pay merely lip service to inspiring ideals, and later do violence to simple justice, we would draw down upon us the bitter wrath of generations yet unborn." Well, let us go forward together, faithful friends of democracy and democratic values, confident in our conviction that the tide of the future is a freedom tide. But let us go forward with practical means.

This brings me to our fourth great challenge. We must restore bipartisan consensus in support of U.S. foreign policy. We must restore America's honorable tradition of partisan politics stopping at the water's edge, Republicans and Democrats standing united in patriotism and speaking with one voice as responsible trustees for peace, democracy, individual liberty, and the rule of law.

In the 1970's we saw a rash of congressional initiatives to limit the President's authority in the areas of trade, human rights, arms sales, foreign assistance, intelligence operations, and the dispatch of troops in time of crisis. Over a hundred separate prohibitions and restrictions on executive branch authority to formulate and implement foreign policy were enacted.

The most far-reaching consequence of the past decade's congressional activism is this: Bipartisan consensus-building has become a central responsibility of congressional leadership as well as of executive leadership. If we're to have a sustainable foreign policy, the Congress must support the practical details of policy, not just the general goals.

We have demonstrated the capacity for such jointly responsible leadership in certain areas, but we've seen setbacks for bipartisanship, too. I believe that once we established bipartisan agreement on our course in Lebanon, the subsequent second-guessing about whether we ought to keep our men there severely undermined our policy. It hindered the ability of our diplomats to negotiate, encouraged more intransigence from the Syrians, and prolonged the violence. Similarly, congressional wavering on support for the Jackson plan, which reflects the recommendations of the National Bipartisan Commission on Central America, can only encourage the enemies of democracy who are determined to wear us down.

To understand and solve this problem—this problem of joint responsibility—we have to go beyond the familiar questions as to who should be stronger, the President or the Congress. The more basic problem is, in this post-Vietnam era, Congress has not yet developed capacities for coherent, responsible action needed to carry out the new foreign policy powers it has taken for itself. To meet the challenges of this decade, we need a strong President and a strong Congress.

Unfortunately, many in the Congress seem to believe they're still in the troubled Vietnam era, with their only task to be vocal critics and not responsible partners in developing positive, practical programs to solve real problems.

Much was learned from Vietnam—lessons ranging from increased appreciation of the need for careful discrimination in the use of U.S. force or military assistance, to increased appreciation of the need for domestic support for any such military element or policy. Military force, either direct or indirect, must remain an available part of America's foreign policy. But clearly the Congress is less than wholly comfortable with both the need for a military element in foreign policy and its own responsibility to deal with that element.

Presidents must recognize Congress as a more significant partner in foreign policymaking and, as we've tried to do, seek new means to reach bipartisan executive-legislative consensus. But legislators must realize that they, too, are partners. They have a responsibility to go beyond mere criticism to consensus-building that will produce positive, practical, and effective action.

Bipartisan consensus is not an end in itself. Sound and experienced U.S. foreign policy leadership must always reflect a deep understanding of fundamental American interests, values, and principles. Consensus on the broad goals of a safer and more humane world is easy to achieve. The harder part is making progress in developing concrete, realistic means to reach these goals. We've made some progress, but there is still a congressional reluctance to assume responsibility for positive bipartisan action to go with their newly claimed powers.

We've set excellent examples with the bipartisan Scowcroft commission, bipartisan support for IMF funding, and the bipartisan work of the Kissinger commission. But it's time to lift our efforts to a higher level of cooperation, time to meet together with realism and idealism, America's great challenges for the eighties.

Distinguished ladies and gentlemen, we have the right to dream great dreams, the opportunity to strive for a world at peace enriched by human dignity, and the responsibility to work as partners so that we might leave these blessed gifts to our children and to our children's children.

We might remember the example of a legislator who lived in a particularly turbulent era, Henry Clay. Abraham Lincoln called him "my beau ideal of a statesman." He knew Clay's loftiness of spirit and vision, never lost sight of his country's interest, and, election year or not, Clay would set love of country above all political considerations.

The stakes for America, for peace, and for freedom demand every bit as much from us in 1984 and beyond. This is our challenge.

I can't leave without a little lighter note that maybe points to some of the intricacies of diplomacy and how seemingly small they can be. I just, in leaving, want to give you a little experience that occurred and could have been a diplomatic crisis at the recent state dinner for President Mitterrand.

Nancy and the President started toward their table in the dining room with everyone standing around their tables waiting for us. Mrs. Mitterrand and I started through the tables, the butler leading us through the people. And suddenly Mrs. Mitterrand stopped and she calmly turned her head and said something to me in French, which, unfortunately, I did not understand. [*Laughter*] And the butler was motioning for us to come on, and I motioned to her that we should go forward, that we were to go to the other side of the room. And, again, very calmly she made her statement to me. And then the interpreter caught up with us. She was telling me that I was standing on her gown. [*Laughter*]

Thank you all, and God bless you.

Note: The President spoke at 9:57 a.m. at the International Club.

Remarks on Meeting the University of Southern California Women's Basketball Team
April 6, 1984

The President. [*Inaudible*]—before we're through here. But I just looked forward to this, to welcome you all to the White House. Now, you're across the street from it, but this is considered part of the White House, too. And I want to congratulate you on the magnificent season that you had and in winning the second consecutive—for the second consecutive year, the NCAA's women's basketball national title.

I know that you came from behind last Sunday against Tennessee and won in the second half. And being a southern Californian, why, I can say that this is the kind of performance that made USC a giant in the sports world. And now you're part of that impressive sports tradition.

You've not only won another title for the school, you've done a great deal, I think, for women's sports, women's athletics. There was a time when the only jumping that was done at an athletic contest by women was by the cheerleaders—[*laughter*]—and there's nothing wrong with that. I—having been in athletics and played football, not basketball, myself—I know it means a great deal to have that kind of support, so there's an honorable place for the cheerleaders.

But you are proving that women can make their mark as well in the field of athletics out there on the floor of the arena. It's pretty hard not to recognize players like Pam and Paula McGee who've scored almost 5,000 points between them. Where are you? There. Must be pretty hard—a guard every once in awhile must think that he's seeing double when—[*laughter*]——

Well, and also then congratulate Cheryl Miller.

Ms. Miller. [*Inaudible*] [*Laughter*]

The President. All right. She was named the most valuable player in that title tournament and also this year's top collegiate women's basketball player.

But then I can also add a congratulation to all of you as a team, because it was a great team effort. And I think that your coach, the university, and your friends and families all must be very proud of you, and they have every reason to be. And you have a reason to be proud of yourselves and what you've accomplished. I think you're an inspiration to athletes all over America.

So, I think, simply put, "well done." And now I'd like to say hello to each one of you, if I could meet each of you.

Ms. Sharp. Mr. President, nice to meet you.

The President. Nice to see you. Maybe I should start over here. Should—oh, do you have something?

Ms. Sharp. I'd like to say a few words.

The President. Yes.

Ms. Sharp. Mr. President, on behalf of the University of Southern California, the women's athletic program, and the women's basketball team, we would like to thank you for honoring us here today. We were very excited when we got the call, and we're going to have a wonderful time while we're here. And on behalf of you, we'd like to thank you very much.

We've also brought some gifts for you and Nancy. And I'd like to present those to you.

When you want to shoot hoops. [*Laughter*] And I hope this fits.

The President. Thank you very, very much.

Note: The President spoke at 11:35 a.m. in the Indian Treaty Room of the Old Executive Office Building. Linda Sharp, the team's coach, presented the President with a USC sweatshirt and a basketball that had been autographed by members of the team.

Nomination of Robert S. Cooper To Be an Assistant Secretary of Defense
April 6, 1984

The President today announced his intention to nominate Robert S. Cooper to be an Assistant Secretary of Defense (Research and Technology). This is a new position.

Mr. Cooper is currently Director of the Defense Advanced Research Projects Agency at the Department of Defense. Previously, he was vice president for engineering, Satellite Business Systems, Inc. (1979–1981); Director, NASA Goddard Space Flight Center (1975–1979); Assistant Director of Defense Research and Engineering, Department of Defense (1972–1975); staff member, group leader, and division director at MIT Lincoln Laboratory (1968–1972); and assistant professor of electrical engineering at MIT, and staff member in the Research Laboratory for Electronics (1963–1968).

Mr. Cooper graduated from the University of Iowa (B.S.E.E.), Ohio State University (M.S.E.E.), and the Massachusetts Institute of Technology (D.Sc.). He resides in McLean, VA, and was born February 8, 1932, in Kansas City, MO.

Nomination of James H. Webb, Jr., To Be an Assistant Secretary of Defense
April 6, 1984

The President today announced his intention to nominate James H. Webb, Jr., to be an Assistant Secretary of Defense (Reserve Affairs). This is a new position.

Mr. Webb is an author and journalist; he recently wrote "A Country Such as This," which has been nominated for the Pulitzer and Pen-Faulkner awards. He was assistant minority counsel to the House Committee on Veterans Affairs in the U.S. Congress in 1977–1978. In 1979 he became the first visiting writer at the United States Naval Academy. He returned to the Congress in 1979 to become the chief minority counsel for the Veterans Affairs Committee. Since 1981 he has been a full-time writer.

Mr. Webb graduated from the United States Naval Academy (B.A., 1968) and from the Georgetown University Law Center (J.D., 1975). He is married, has three children, and resides in Arlington, VA. He was born February 9, 1946, in St. Joseph, MO.

Nomination of Donald Ian Macdonald To Be Administrator of the Alcohol, Drug Abuse and Mental Health Administration
April 6, 1984

The President today announced his intention to nominate Donald Ian Macdonald to be Administrator of the Alcohol, Drug Abuse and Mental Health Administration, Department of Health and Human Services. He would succeed William E. Mayer.

Since 1962 Dr. Macdonald has been a pediatrician in Clearwater, FL. Previously, he was a clinical associate professor of pediatrics, College of Medicine, University of South Florida (1980); and president, Scientific Advisory Board, American Council for Drug Education (1981). Dr. Macdonald is president of the Florida chapter of the

American Academy of Pediatrics and the Florida Pediatric Society.

Dr. Macdonald graduated from Williams College (B.A., 1952) and Temple University School of Medicine (M.D., 1958). He is married, has four children, and resides in Pinellas, FL. He was born April 15, 1931, in New York, NY.

Radio Address to the Nation on United States Foreign Policy
April 7, 1984

My fellow Americans:

Yesterday I spoke here in Washington about America's foreign policy challenges and what we're doing to meet them. Well, I'd like to continue talking about those challenges today.

All Americans long for a safer world in which individual rights are respected and precious values flourish. But we're also realistic. We know we live in a troubled world and that we have global responsibilities. Our industries depend on energy and minerals from distant lands. Our prosperity requires a sound financial system and markets open to our goods. And our security is linked with the security of our allies and trading partners.

When I took office, we faced the greatest foreign policy challenges since World War II. Challenge number one was reducing the risk of nuclear war. Second, we had to try to help bring greater stability to regions riddled by terrorism and revolutionary violence that threatened our interests and, ultimately, our security. Third, we had to deal with an international economy that was crippled by soaring inflation rates, low growth, and predictions of an imminent global depression. Finally, we had to restore bipartisan support for a foreign policy that would meet our responsibilities.

How is America meeting her foreign policy challenges today? Well, much better. We've regained our strength and confidence. We're a leader again for peace and progress.

Reducing the risk of nuclear war means maintaining a secure military balance and pursuing every opportunity to reduce weapons by agreement. Today America is safer because our defenses are stronger. We're offering the most sweeping arms control proposals in history, from reducing nuclear arms to banning chemical weapons.

Does the new Soviet leadership truly want to reach agreements that can make the world safer? Well, they'll never convince the world they're sincere with harsh rhetoric and walk-outs. We do know they respect strength. And in time, we should expect that they will return to the negotiating table where all of us hope and pray that a safer world can be secured.

Our second challenge, peacemaking in troubled regions, has demanded a new direction. We're trying to bring all our strengths to bear. Economic aid alone won't stop Soviet-sponsored guerrillas, and individual rights aren't secure without peace. We need all the tools we have—diplomatic mediation, economic help, security assistance, and promotion of democratic reforms—to address complex regional problems. The recent Presidential elections in El Salvador probably couldn't have been held if we'd followed any other approach. And for democracy to have a chance in the future, the Congress must pass the plan we've proposed, which follows the recommendations made by the National Bipartisan Commission on Central America.

Our third challenge, expanding opportunities for economic development and personal freedom, is also being met. America's powerful expansion is pulling the international economy forward. As we buy more from our friends, they buy more from us. Jobs, income, and opportunities increase for all. We've developed creative initiatives to spark private enterprise in the Caribbean. We're expanding our economic relationships with the growing nations of the Pacific Basin. And we're shoring up the international financial system.

You hear about the economic upturn. You don't hear enough about the democratic upturn. Ten years ago, fewer than half the people of Latin America and the Caribbean lived in democracies or countries embarked on a democratic transition. Today 90 percent of the people do. The tide of the future is a freedom tide.

Finally, our fourth challenge, restoring bipartisan consensus to our foreign policy, is urgently needed. The Congress has given itself many new powers in foreign policy. Over 100 separate restrictions on executive authority were enacted in the 1970's, but the Congress hasn't yet accepted an equal sense of responsibility. We've had some successes in bipartisanship. The Scowcroft commission helped create a consensus on arms control policy, and the bipartisan Kissinger commission gave us a comprehensive set of recommendations on Central America. But we must go beyond recommendations to action. I applaud the Senate's approval this week of emergency security assistance to El Salvador, and I hope the House will give its approval. When we develop a problem-solving plan to help build a safer world and a better world, there must be no Republicans or Democrats, just Americans pulling together.

Until next week, thanks for listening, and God bless you.

Note: The President spoke at 12:06 p.m. from the Oval Office at the White House.

Remarks on Meeting the Georgetown University Hoyas, the National Collegiate Athletic Association Basketball Champions
April 7, 1984

The President. Coach Thompson and members of the Hoyas, welcome to the White House, and congratulations on a magnificent job.

I know your victory Monday night represents not just a single effort, but is the result of countless hours of conditioning, training, and practicing by each of you individually, all of which is part of making a truly great team.

You're the first team from the northeast to win the NCAA championship in 30 years, and you have every reason to be proud, as I know you must be. You came close 2 years ago. Now, you've made it. And we're all happy for you and, I think, understand a little of how you all must feel.

I'd like to congratulate Pat Ewing, as tournament and Big East Conference Most Valuable Player. You had a great season, Pat, and you know you and all your teammates are going to remember this for the rest of your lives.

And, Coach, you not only put together and directed a fine team, but you've watched out in the long run for the interests, the true interests of these young men.

I think they'll remember you for a long time, and they'll be most grateful as the years go by.

During your time at Georgetown in coaching, the overwhelming majority of your players have graduated, which is also something of a record in intercollegiate athletics in these days. But it also says something about the coach's priorities.

Now, I understand there's been some criticism, Coach Thompson, that maybe your coaching was a little too stringent or almost military. I wouldn't let that bother me at all. It's results that pay off and certainly this has been a result.

You've won the title. You've never let—and this, I think, is vitally important, as much so as the title—you have never let these young men forget that there is something more important for their being at Georgetown than basketball. And that isn't always true.

So, again, just a hearty "well done" from all of us. And I think all of us feel a great pride in what you've accomplished.

And now I'd like to—well, Coach?

Coach Thompson. Mr. President, certainly

we do appreciate you taking the time in your busy schedule to honor us. And I've got to say that that's got to be one of the highlights in these young men's lives, to have an opportunity to meet you.

And I'd just like to say if the worst thing that could ever be said about us is that we're military, I feel very honored. [*Laughter*]

And I do want to give you a little token so that you can remember our team, and I also have a shirt. It should have "Hoya Par-anoia" on it, because that's what they called us all year. But I'd like to give you this shirt to make you our official member.

The President. Thank you very much. Thank you.

Note: The President spoke at 1:13 p.m. in the Rose Garden at the White House. Coach John Thompson presented the President with a shirt and a basketball that had been autographed by members of the team.

Statement on the Death of Senator Frank Church of Idaho
April 7, 1984

Nancy and I were saddened today to learn of the death of former Senator Frank Church of Idaho. Senator Church served his nation with distinction and dedication. His abiding interest in foreign policy made an important intellectual contribution to our country. We send our sympathy to his family and friends.

Remarks at a Ford's Theatre Benefit Gala
April 8, 1984

The President. Nancy and I are honored to be here tonight. And I know I speak for everyone in the audience when I thank Bill Schustik, the playwright, for the play, and the entire cast of "On Shiloh Hill" for that magnificent performance.

Ford's Theatre opened in 1863. I wasn't here at that point but—[*laughter*]—but it was a year when most Americans were farmers, and people still sang folk songs like "Shoofly." The street outside was a dirt road, and America was locked in a Civil War that ravaged thousands of acres and tens of thousands of lives. In one titanic struggle that gave tonight's play its name, the Battle of Shiloh, more than 20,000 soldiers were cut down.

Few burdens can compare with those that were borne by the men and women who lived in this city during those bitter years. And yet even then, Washingtonians could gather at Ford's Theatre as we've gathered tonight to see the latest play, to enjoy relief from the troubles of the day. Congressmen, Senators, Mr. Lincoln, himself, found their duties easier because they could seek an evening of entertainment at Ford's.

This theatre demonstrated during the years that whatever events demand the Nation's attention, the arts must always have their place. Today Ford's Theatre is still giving Americans uplift and inspiration. And in keeping Ford's an active, vibrant institution, all of you testify to the importance of remembering our own history and witness the central place of the arts in our lives and set a fine example of the kind of private support that we've given in this country to such rich—given it such a rich cultural life.

Hundreds of people deserve thanks, as you were told. But as executive producer of Ford's, Frankie Hewitt, of course, played the central role in making possible this wonderful evening and every evening in this theatre.

Then there are the board of governors, the sponsors, the patrons, and the contributors. But tonight does belong to one woman who has given of herself to Ford's, to the city, and to everyone fortunate enough to know her—Mildred O'Neill.

Now, Mildred, you may have suspected now and then that from time to time your husband and I find something about which we disagree. [*Laughter*] But there is one thing that we sure agree on—he's lucky, mighty lucky, to be the man in your life. On behalf of everybody with whom you work, your work for this grand, old theatre has meant so much, Millie, that we all thank you from the bottom of our hearts.

And now, the lady—the man whose life I'm lucky to be in—[*laughter*]—has a word to say.

Nancy?

Mrs. Reagan. Thank you, Mr. President. [*Laughter*]

It's always such a special pleasure to be in Ford's Theatre, and tonight I feel doubly honored to have the privilege of giving a unique award to a wonderful lady. Millie O'Neill, as most of us know, moved to Washington permanently when her husband was elected as Speaker of the House. Ford's Theatre was the first organization she became involved with in our Nation's Capital, and 7 years later she's been unanimously chosen to receive the Lincoln Medal for her generous support of the Theatre.

It would be impossible to tell you every-thing that Millie has done for Ford's, but I do want to make special mention of her help in raising almost $4 million for the Theatre over the last 5 years.

On behalf of the board of trustees of Ford's Theatre and everyone who applauds the live theater program at Ford's, I'm honored to present the Lincoln Medal to Mrs. Thomas P. O'Neill, Jr.

Mrs. O'Neill. Thank you, Nancy, very much. And, Mr. President, I want to thank you so much for sharing your very precious time with Ford's Theatre to make our gala so successful. Thank you.

Mr. Speaker, thank you. [*Laughter*]

I'm delighted to receive this award and be included in the very prestigious group who have been honorees before me. I am just delighted. But I have said many times before that anything that I have done for Ford's Theatre has been a labor of love. I've enjoyed every minute of it.

There aren't enough medals around for everyone that should be awarded. I would like to share this and accept it in the name of all the very wonderful men and women who have performed here at the galas, and also to the wonderful friends of Ford's who have been so very generous and gracious when I came begging—and I came begging very often.

I thank you all, and I'm truly very gratefully yours. Thank you.

Note: The President spoke at 9:58 p.m. at the theatre following the performance and remarks by Frankie Hewitt.

Proclamation 5174—National Mental Health Counselors Week, 1984
April 8, 1984

By the President of the United States of America

A Proclamation

Mental health counselors use special counseling skills and understanding of human development to help their fellow Americans cope with problems of adjustment, the pain of illness, and the stresses of life. They provide 50 percent of the mental health services delivered in this country, working with the chronically mentally ill, the depressed, the anxious, the abused, and others, who, through no fault of their own, cannot fully meet their daily obligations or experience life's pleasures.

Through a variety of techniques, mental health counselors assist people to attain self-understanding and skills needed to solve problems, make decisions, and successfully deal with others in an increasingly complex world. Mental health counselors work in hospitals, community agencies, clinics, and the private practice sector and with all types of health professionals, applying the expertise gained through their many years of education and training.

In recognition of the important services that these counselors perform for others to save lives and reduce suffering, the Congress, by Senate Joint Resolution 203, has designated the week beginning April 8, 1984, as National Mental Health Counselors Week and has authorized and requested the President to issue a proclamation in observance of this event.

Now, Therefore, I, Ronald Reagan, President of the United States of America, do hereby proclaim the week beginning April

8, 1984, as National Mental Health Counselors Week. I call upon health care professionals, educators, the media, individuals, and public and private organizations concerned with mental health to observe this week with appropriate ceremonies.

In Witness Whereof, I have hereunto set my hand this 8th day of April, in the year of our Lord nineteen hundred and eighty-four, and of the Independence of the United States of America the two hundred and eighth.

RONALD REAGAN

[*Filed with the Office of the Federal Register, 4:09 p.m., April 9, 1984*]

Note: *The text of the proclamation was released by the Office of the Press Secretary on April 9.*

Remarks on Signing the Law Day Proclamation
April 9, 1984

Today's ceremonies mark the 27th year that we've set aside May 1st as Law Day, a day to reflect on and give thanks for a constitutional system that has, just as its Framers dreamed, secured the blessings of liberty through the rule of law. And so, I'm delighted that we could be joined today by so many who represent that continuing tradition of law and liberty—Chief Justice Burger, the Attorney General, Senator Thurmond, and Director Webster, distinguished members of the judiciary, the presidents of the American Bar Association, the National Bar Association, the Federal Bar Association, and the other distinguished representatives of our legal profession, present for these Law Day proclamation ceremonies.

The theme of this year's Law Day observance is a simple phrase, but one that goes to the heart of a philosophy that has kept us both strong and free: "Law Makes Freedom Work." Our Founding Fathers knew that law and freedom must be linked if both were to survive, and they knew, as the proclamation I'm about to sign states, that

without law there can be no freedom, only chaos and disorder. And without freedom, law is but a cynical veneer for injustice and oppression.

In too many countries around the globe today the truth of that warning is all too evident. In America on May 1st, free men and women will commemorate Law Day, celebrating a two-century-old partnership between law and liberty. But in those other lands men and women will be summoned to state-sponsored commemorations of May Day—sad and artificial celebrations of a revolution that enslaved the very people it promised to liberate.

In these nations, as in ours, one can find constitutions and written guarantees of fundamental rights. But the freedom that would bring these guarantees to life is systematically denied.

I, some time ago, was interested and took it upon myself to read some of those constitutions I've just referred to. And I saw phrases very similar to the same phrases in ours regarding the fundamental rights. But there was one subtle difference. It might seem small, but it told the whole story. All of those other constitutions said these were the rights that the government was granting to the people, and our Constitution says these are the things that the people will grant to the government.

We in the United States have been blessed to live in a land where law and freedom are found not simply in a Constitution and a Bill of Rights, but in our daily lives. This is cause not for complacency and self-congratulation, but for profound gratitude—a gratitude that's best expressed in the lives of responsible citizenship.

In particular, those of us who are gathered here today in this historic place have a special responsibility as leaders of our government and our legal profession to be worthy of the citizens we serve. To the degree that we're faithful to this trust through lives marked by public virtue and personal honor, so, too, will we be worthy of the precious gifts of law and freedom that are the unique heritage we celebrate as Americans this Law Day.

And having said that, I will now sign the proclamation.

Note: The President spoke at 11:30 a.m. in the Rose Garden at the White House.

Proclamation 5175—Law Day U.S.A., 1984
April 9, 1984

By the President of the United States of America

A Proclamation

May 1, 1984 is Law Day U.S.A., a time to affirm the essential role of the rule of law in the development and preservation of our free society.

This year's Law Day theme, "Law Makes Freedom Work," captures the essence of our heritage as a Republic. Our unique experience demonstrates that law and freedom must be indivisible partners. For without law, there can be no freedom, only chaos and disorder; and without freedom, law is but a cynical veneer for injustice and oppression.

The guarantees of freedom embodied in our Constitution and the Bill of Rights are a continuing legacy, enhancing the lives of our citizens and serving as an inspiration to people around the world. One of our Nation's strongest principles is that voluntary adherence to the rule of law expands, rather than limits, the opportunities for freedom.

For twenty-seven years, we have set aside this day as a time for reflection upon and celebration of the vital bond between liberty and the rule of law that gives life to our national goals and ideals. It is also an opportunity for all Americans to improve their understanding and appreciation of the contribution law makes to the preservation of freedom.

Now, Therefore, I, Ronald Reagan, President of the United States of America, in accordance with Public Law 87–20 of April 7, 1961, do hereby proclaim Tuesday, May 1, 1984 as Law Day U.S.A. I urge the people of the United States to use this occasion to renew their commitment to the rule of law and to reaffirm our dedication to the partnership of law and liberty. I also urge the legal profession, schools, civic, service and fraternal organizations, public bodies, libraries, the courts, the communications media, business, the clergy, and all interested individuals and organizations to join in efforts to focus attention on the need for the rule of law. I also call upon all public officials to display the flag of the United States on all government buildings open on Law Day, May 1, 1984.

In Witness Whereof, I have hereunto set my hand this ninth day of April, in the year of our Lord nineteen hundred and eighty-four, and of the Independence of the United States of America the two hundred and eighth.

RONALD REAGAN

[*Filed with the Office of the Federal Register, 10:58 a.m., April 10, 1984*]

Remarks at a White House Ceremony Honoring the National Teacher of the Year
April 9, 1984

The President. Well, it's a pleasure to see you—and I'm going to say "again" to some old friends and meet some new ones. And I'm especially happy to see the students here from Ballard High. It was very kind of all of you students to chaperone Mrs. Sisney and make sure that she doesn't get into any trouble while she's here. [*Laughter*]

This is the 33d White House ceremony honoring the National Teacher of the Year and the State Teachers of the Year. And always, in all those years since Harry Truman, the President himself or a member of his family has personally given the award. And I think it's a clear expression that—the high regard in which you're all held.

You hold a critically important place in the life of our nation, not just because of the skills you impart, though that in itself would be enough, but because you shape the future by shaping the adults of the future. And you do this by being the kind of people that we would want our children to become. I'm not sure that yours is the most unsung profession, but you work with quiet confidence and little fanfare, and so many teachers do not receive the praise they deserve.

I remember a scene from Robert Bolt's play, "A Man for All Seasons," that speaks of this. Sir Thomas More is talking to his friend, Richard Rich, a bright young man who's full of ambition and eager to make a name for himself, and he ponders going into law or politics. Sir Thomas tells him, "Be a teacher. You'd be a great one." "And if I was, who would know it?" the young man asks. And Sir Thomas answered, "You, your pupils, your friends, and God. Not a bad public, that." Well, I'm here to let you know that the President's part of the public, too.

In an important way, teachers set the tone for society. I don't think there's one of us in the country who doesn't remember a teacher who made a difference in our life, one who steered us in the right direction or showed faith in us early on or encouraged us when things weren't going well. It was a teacher who steered me into acting, an English teacher named B.J. Fraser, back in Dixon, Illinois. He's gone now, but I somehow can imagine him standing back there someplace and saying, "But I take no responsibility for his going into politics." [*Laughter*]

I noted, by the way, in her biographical sketch that Sherleen Sisney became a teacher partly because of the influence of one of her high school teachers, also an English teacher. And, now, Mrs. Sisney is America's Teacher of the Year.

There's another way you set the tone. When children are just starting grade school, teachers are the first representatives they meet of the world outside the family. And when these teachers are gifted, when they encourage and communicate the excitement of learning, then children learn to be eager about the world and optimistic toward it.

There's another thing that teachers do, a quiet thing that isn't usually noted. For lonely children, children from troubled families who don't get enough attention at home, for them the classroom becomes a kind of family and the teacher their parent—sometimes, the only parent from whom they receive affection and understanding.

You know how it is with young children when they aren't loved. They think themselves unlovable, and that's the beginning of trouble. But when a teacher comes along and gives that child attention, shows him or her kindness and makes them feel special, then for the first time, the child feels self-esteem and self-worth. And they blossom in the warmth.

Your kindness and the values you live by echo down the decades, shaping the adults, the citizens they'll become. And that's why, as Henry Adams said, "A teacher affects eternity; he can never tell where his influence—or her influence—stops."

All of this puts great demands on you, and I just hope that you know how much this administration is on your side and eager to help. But right now, I want to stop for a moment because I want you to hear a few words from another president.

Tracy Wright is the president of the senior class at Ballard High School. Tracy?

Ms. Wright. Thank you. Mrs. Sisney is most deserving of this award, not only because she's an outstanding teacher in the professional sense but also in the human sense. She's a caring teacher who wants only the best for her students. By using such techniques as "learning by doing," Mrs. Sisney causes students to think for themselves and to rationalize certain situations. Possessing strong leadership abilities and commitment in the school and also in the community, Mrs. Sisney is respected by both her colleagues and her students. On behalf of the Ballard student body, it is with much pride that I congratulate you, Mrs. Sisney, on this great accomplishment. We love you.

The President. Thank you very much.

Ms. Wright. Thank you.

The President. When I first came into office, I was very disturbed by what teachers were being forced to contend with in America's schools. Somehow in the sixties and seventies, people decided that discipline was old fashioned and high standards unnecessary. It made teaching so difficult that I admire all of you who endured all of that and held on.

Secretary Bell and others have been working long and hard to turn it around. And we're still a long way from where we want to be, but already the indications are good, and working together with State and local governments, we are turning it around. Since 1980 more than half the school districts in the country have moved to tighten course requirements. Forty-six States are making graduation requirements tougher, and now all 50 States have special task forces in education.

We want most of all to restore all honor to this profession and to all who are among America's most overburdened and underpaid professionals. So, we're working on merit pay for teachers, because they deserve to have their excellence rewarded and because the decision to become a teacher shouldn't be a decision to endure financial sacrifice for the rest of your life.

And now as I end these remarks in this great, old garden, I realize I haven't even touched on the part that you play, the vital part in keeping democracy and the democratic spirit alive. Thomas Jefferson noted this when he said, "If you expect the people to be ignorant and free, you expect what never was and never will be." The ongoing experiment called democracy, the longest continuing experiment in human history, cannot exist without an informed citizenry, and cannot exist, therefore, without you.

We owe all of the teachers of America a debt we can never pay, but I mean to honor all of them today by honoring you. And so, I may say to you, Mrs. Sherleen Sisney of Ballard High School in Kentucky, and to all the State Teachers of the Year, may I say what Presidents say when they give medals for courage and extraordinary contributions: I thank you on behalf of a grateful nation.

And now, it's been a long time since I've been able to bring an apple to the teacher. [*Laughter*] Mrs. Sisney, congratulations.

Mrs. Sisney. Thank you so much. We appreciate all you're doing for children. That's just beautiful.

The President. Well, our pleasure. Congratulations, again.

Mrs. Sisney. Thank you.

The President. I think that concludes the ceremony.

Note: The President spoke at 2:05 p.m. in the Rose Garden at the White House.

Statement on the Final Report of the President's Commission on Strategic Forces
April 9, 1984

On January 3, 1983, I established a bipartisan Commission to examine issues raised by the Congress concerning the strategic modernization program, especially the Peacekeeper (MX) missile. On April 19, 1983, I was very pleased to report to the Congress and the American people that the Commission unanimously agreed on strategic force modernization recommendations, which I strongly endorsed. Secretary Shultz, Secretary Weinberger, the Joint Chiefs of Staff, the Director of the Arms Control and Disarmament Agency, and the National Security Council also endorsed the recommendations of the Commission. At that time, I affirmed my commitment to pursue ambitious arms reduction negotiations as an integral part of the package.

Despite the range of views which existed in the past, the Congress joined us in supporting this bipartisan effort to modernize our strategic deterrent. This consensus was a major accomplishment in our common effort to enhance national security. The willingness of all parties to reexamine their previous positions allowed us to end a decade of political paralysis over arms control and modernization.

Last week the Commission issued its final report. The report focuses on the arms control portion of its earlier recommendations. Once again, the Commission members and their counselors have performed a tough job extraordinarily well. Again, we all owe this distinguished group of Americans special thanks.

This final report reiterates the original recommendations, that is, an integrated strategic program consisting of an arms control structure with incentives to enhance stability at reduced levels of strategic arsenals; deployment of 100 MX missiles; and development of a small, single warhead ICBM; as well as other elements. The Commission again emphasizes that each element is essential to the overall program it outlined.

After noting the disappointing history of U.S.-Soviet arms control negotiations, the Commission emphasizes the importance of keeping expectations within bounds. In particular, arms control can make a substantial contribution to U.S. security by increasing strategic stability, allowing some types of defense expenditures to be avoided, and offering a useful forum for dialog on strategic concepts and priorities. The Commission stresses, however, that arms control alone cannot end the threat of nuclear war, reduce the casualties and damage in the event of such a war, or automatically permit deep or early defense budget cuts.

On related issues, the Commission confirms the need for effective verification and satisfactory compliance to sustain the arms control process. The Commission recognizes the significance of the 1972 Anti-Ballistic Missile Treaty and notes that research permitted under the treaty is important to ascertain realistic, technological possibilities as well as to guard against Soviet ABM breakout. The Commission also recommends extreme caution in proceeding to engineering development of an active strategic defense system.

Our proposed strategic defense initiative is limited to technology research. The initiative also includes continued study of strategic policy and arms control implications of strategic defense concepts. The program is consistent with all treaty obligations and there is no conflict between our initiative and the recommendations made by the Commission.

Finally, the Commission notes the importance of measures to reduce the risk of nuclear war and makes clear the serious flaws of a nuclear freeze.

I am pleased to announce that I, along with Secretary Shultz, Secretary Weinberger, the Joint Chiefs of Staff, the Director of the Arms Control and Disarmament Agency, and the National Security Council, strongly endorse the Commission's final report.

I urge continuing support by the Congress and the American people for this bipartisan consensus which unites us in our common objective of strengthening our national security and moving toward significant reductions in nuclear arms.

Letter to the Speaker of the House and the President of the Senate on the Export-Import Bank of the United States
April 9, 1984

Dear Mr. Speaker: *(Dear Mr. President:)*

This report is being submitted pursuant to Section 7(a) (2) of the Export-Import Bank Act of 1945, as amended. I have determined that the authority available to the Bank for fiscal year 1984 is sufficient to meet the needs of the Bank. This determination was based upon the transactions already approved, applications received by the Bank and estimates of the level of business likely for the remainder of the fiscal year.

Sincerely,

RONALD REAGAN

Note: This is the text of identical letters addressed to Thomas P. O'Neill, Jr., Speaker of the House of Representatives, and George Bush, President of the Senate.

Proclamation 5176—Parkinson's Disease Awareness Week, 1984
April 9, 1984

By the President of the United States of America

A Proclamation

For most of us, movement is part of our lives which, though essential, we often take for granted. But for nearly half a million Americans, every step, every gesture is fraught with apprehension. These people suffer from Parkinson's disease, a movement disorder that affects people as they grow older.

We now know that the tremor and rigidity characteristic of Parkinson's disease are caused by a chemical deficiency in the part of the brain that controls movement. Through research, scientists have discovered that certain drugs can help overcome this deficiency. Many Americans with Parkinson's disease have found that with medication, physical therapy, and emotional support from families and friends, they can lead normal and productive lives.

Superbly trained scientists are hard at work trying to solve the problems caused by Parkinson's disease. Many of these scientists are supported by the Federal government's National Institute of Neurological and Communicative Disorders and Stroke and by four national voluntary health organizations: the American Parkinson Disease Association, the National Parkinson Foundation, Inc., the Parkinson's Disease Foundation, and the United Parkinson Foundation.

While these medical advances are encouraging, it is important that there be greater public awareness of what it means to have Parkinson's disease. We must let people with Parkinson's disease know that we understand when they have trouble walking through a doorway or when the disorder causes their hands or their heads to shake uncontrollably. A smile may be all the encouragement they need to relax enough to resume normal movement. I commend the courage of Americans who refuse to be vanquished by Parkinson's disease. And I applaud the resourcefulness of the families and friends who provide them with sustained affection and encouragement.

The Congress, by Senate Joint Resolution 263, has designated the week of April 8–14, 1984, as "Parkinson's Disease Awareness Week" and has authorized and requested the President to issue a proclamation in observance of that week.

Now, Therefore, I, Ronald Reagan, President of the United States of America, do hereby proclaim the week of April 8–14, 1984, as "Parkinson's Disease Awareness Week," and I call upon Government agencies and the people of the United States to observe this week with appropriate ceremonies and activities.

In Witness Whereof, I have hereunto set my hand this ninth day of April, in the year of our Lord nineteen hundred and eighty-four, and of the Independence of the United States of America the two hundred and eighth.

RONALD REAGAN

[*Filed with the Office of the Federal Register, 10:59 a.m., April 10, 1984*]

Note: The President signed the proclamation at a ceremony in the Oval Office at the White House.

Remarks at the Welcoming Ceremony for President Salvador Jorge Blanco of the Dominican Republic
April 10, 1984

President Reagan. President and Mrs. Jorge Blanco, it's indeed an honor for me to welcome you, the first President of your country to make a state visit to the United States. This is a special visit. The people of our countries are both friends and neighbors, and we're pleased to have this opportunity to express our good will to neighbors who reflect the same love of liberty in which we take such pride.

The Dominican Republic today shines as a beacon of freedom-loving people everywhere. Your people have shown the spirit, courage, and perseverance necessary to build, in your words, "a true functional democracy in the Caribbean." Democracy, as all free people have found, is not the easiest path, but it is the best one. It is the way most consistent with the spirit of the New World, with the values of which all Americans from one end of the hemisphere to the other can claim as their birthright.

As such, it is fitting that the Dominican Republic, with its stability and political liberty, now shows others the way. Your nation, after all, was the beachhead of Western civilization in the New World. Christopher Columbus, the great discoverer, landed on your shores during his first voyage of exploration. In your country still stands the first cathedral of America, built in 1540. The hopes and dreams of all the Americans once focused on those hardy souls who left the Old World and entered the New through the doorway of Santo Domingo.

Today, as you strive to increase the opportunity of all your citizens, you follow in the spirit of those who came before you. You face many challenges in invigorating your economy and improving the standard of living of your people. Yet even in the days of Columbus, the magnificent beauty and vast potential of your land were evident. In early 1493 Columbus wrote, "In that island . . . we named Española, there are mountains of very great size and beauty, vast plains, groves, and very fruitful fields . . . . The convenience and excellence of the harbors in this island and the abundance of the rivers . . . surpass anything that would be believed by one who had not seen it." Well, that beauty and that potential still remain. Coupled now with freedom, your people have every reason to expect that great things can be accomplished.

President Jorge Blanco, it is propitious that your visit coincides with Pan American Week, a time when we have for the last 53 years celebrated the ties between the peoples of the Western Hemisphere. The people of the United States place great value on the special ties that we have with friends close to home. And while the progress of any country depends most heavily on the freedom, the hard work, and ingenuity of its own people and government, the United States is committed to healthy cooperation with our Caribbean Basin neighbors for the betterment of all our peoples.

Combined with your own domestic reforms, which we heartily applaud, the trade and commerce unleashed by the Caribbean Basin Initiative should bring vast new opportunities to Dominicans and to other Caribbean people. Your country and some two dozen others will now have for most of your products virtually unrestricted duty-free entry until 1996 into the world's largest market. Never before has the United States or any other nation offered one-way free trade to any regional group of countries. It's a revolutionary step based on the conviction that enterprise, investment, and job creation will elevate the quality of life while preserving the freedom and independence so cherished by both our peoples.

There is a Caribbean country on a much different path. Instead of economic freedom, it imposes heavy-handed controls, denying for people, for example, the right of private ownership and the right to organize independent unions. Instead of seeking mutual respect and friendly commerce with its neighbors, it exports violence and hatred. Instead of enjoying democratic liberties as are guaranteed in the Dominican Republic and most other Caribbean countries, its people are denied freedom of the press, speech, and religion. This tyranny has brought little hope for economic progress, providing its people only shortages and foodlines. Cuba is now dependent on a far-away totalitarian power without whose subsidy its dictatorial government could not export aggression or, indeed, survive.

Such serfdom and bowing to the interests of faraway masters is not consistent with the legacy of the people of this hemisphere. Our history is that of breaking away from such tutelage, and in this all Americans have a common vision. Your proud independence and the continuing strength of democracy in the Dominican Republic is a tremendous inspiration here and to other people in the hemisphere who are now battling to establish their own democracies.

President Jorge Blanco, we in the United States are fully aware that the success of democratic institutions in your country is due to the good will and strenuous efforts of individuals like yourself. You and your fellow countrymen have our respect. As we work to build a more prosperous and happy future, let us continue to open the doors of commerce and social interaction between our peoples.

In less than a decade we will be celebrating the 500th anniversary of a history-shattering event—Columbus' first great voyage of discovery. We look forward to commemorating this, one of mankind's greatest leaps, with the free people of the Dominican Republic.

Mr. President, Pedro Henriquez Ureña, a renowned literary figure as well as a great Dominican patriot, once wrote, "Words are like empty sacks. One must fill them with true human feeling." Well, I hope today that you can sense the feeling, the warmth, and admiration behind these words of welcome. President and Mrs. Jorge Blanco, we're proud to have you visiting with us.

President Jorge Blanco. President Reagan, Mrs. Reagan, ladies and gentlemen, my greetings to you, President Reagan, to your distinguished wife, and to the representatives of your government—and greetings, also, to the generous people of the United States.

I am very pleased with this state visit, made at your invitation and which begins at the doorstep of the majestic White House, which represents and symbolizes the prestigious image of the United States all over the world.

Since the Pilgrims arrived on the shores of Massachusetts in search of a safe haven in order to freely exercise their religious and political ideas; through the heroic struggles which culminated in independence and the establishment of the first democracy in the Americas; and then on to the emancipation of the slaves proclaimed by the eminent Abraham Lincoln, your people have been and are a model for men who join together in support of the eternal ideals of human freedom and dignity. These common efforts have created the great melting pot of races and cultures which is the United States of America.

As President and as jurist, I must recall with admiration the important documents which sustain the institutional history of the great American people, and which have established landmarks in the upward climb of humanity—the Mayflower Compact, the Declaration of Independence, the Bill of Rights, Lincoln's Gettysburg Address, the Proclamation of the Four Freedoms by Roosevelt, among many others, have been and shall always be the most outstanding example of this nation's contributions to equality, democracy, and social progress.

We represent a Dominican democracy which is nourished, among other sources, by the old teachings which came precisely from this great nation when it proclaimed its independence on the 4th of July of 1776. Since that time, freedom has had its most immediate origin on these American lands.

In the Dominican Republic, we have always fought for freedom, and our recent history increasingly has enhanced this struggle, which is the mainstay of our democracy, playing a vital role within the inter-American system, whose principles have been incorporated into the fundamental charter of our Organization of American States.

I am particularly grateful, Mr. President, for the reference you made to my political role of responsibility for the destinies of my country, and of the difficult task that I face in strengthening our democracy, while at the same time facing the dire effects of an international economic crisis which has dealt harsh blows to the weak economies and fragile political institutions of developing countries. And I want to express my appreciation for the Caribbean Basin Initiative, which has opened new possibilities for the development of our countries in the Caribbean.

We are pleased with the certainty that our efforts will always receive the encouragement and cooperation of friendly peoples, particularly the people of this great nation which never falters in its resolve to provide necessary and important solidarity.

I accept your words of praise towards me as a recognition of the values of the Dominican people, firmly resolved to enrich its political democracy with economic and social development and to strengthen peace throughout the hemisphere. I hope that our visit will serve to strengthen even more the firm bonds of friendship and of mutual cooperation between our governments and between our peoples.

And now I would hope that our visit will be able to provide us, a visit which we are making at your kind invitation, with a way to increase even more the very strong bonds of friendship that exist between your people and mine.

Thank you very much, Mr. President.

Note: President Reagan spoke at 10:10 a.m. on the South Lawn of the White House, where President Jorge Blanco was accorded a formal welcome with full military honors. President Jorge Blanco spoke in Spanish, and his remarks were translated by an interpreter.

Following the ceremony, the two Presidents, together with U.S. and Dominican officials, met together, first in the Oval Office and then in the Cabinet Room.

Remarks by Telephone With Crewmembers on Board the Space Shuttle *Challenger*
April 10, 1984

The President. Hello, Bob. These calls——

Commander Crippen. Good afternoon, Mr. President. Thank you very much for speaking with us.

The President. Well, these calls between the two of us are becoming a habit. I promise you, though, I won't reverse the charges. Over.

Commander Crippen. I don't think I could afford them, Mr. President. [*Laughter*]

The President. Well, once again, I'm calling to congratulate you and the rest of the crew aboard the *Challenger* there on an historic mission. The retrieval of the Solar Max satellite this morning was just great. And you and the crew demonstrated once again just how versatile the space shuttle is and what we can accomplish by having a team in space and on the ground. I know you'll agree that those folks at the Goddard Space Flight Center did a fantastic job maneuvering the satellite for you.

And, Terry, I guess you made one long reach for man this morning when you snapped that satellite with the 50-foot robot arm. And George and Jim, you've done fine work as well. The pictures sent back of you working in space are spectacular. They're also a little scary for those of us that are sitting comfortably anchored to the Earth.

But, Bob, I understand that satellite you have on board would cost us about $200 million to build at today's prices, so if you can't fix it up there, would you mind bringing it back? Over.

Commander Crippen. Well, we're going to do our best to repair it tomorrow, sir, and if for some reason that is unsuccessful, which we don't think it will be, we will be able to return it.

We certainly concur with all of your remarks. The *Challenger* and its sister ships are magnificent flying machines, and I think that they can make a significant road into space with regard to repair and servicing of satellites. And we believe this is the initial step.

I would also like to concur with your remarks regarding the people up at Goddard who managed to put this satellite back in a configuration that we could retrieve it after the little problem we ran into the other day. Those people and the people in Houston and everybody that worked on it truly made this recovery possible. It is a team effort all the way.

It so happens we get to do the fun part.

The President. Well, let me tell you, you're all a team that has made all Americans very proud of what you're doing up there and what the future bodes for all of us with regard to this opening up of that great frontier of space.

And, seriously, I just want to again say how proud we all are of all of you, and congratulations to you all. Have a safe mission, a safe trip home, and God bless all of you.

I'll sign out now and let you get on with your chores.

Commander Crippen. Thank you, sir.

The President. Bless you. Thank you.

Note: The President spoke at 12:01 p.m. from the Oval Office at the White House to the Challenger's *crew, astronauts Robert L. Crippen, Francis R. Scobee, Terry J. Hart, George D. Nelson, and James D. Van Hoften.*

The primary mission of the flight was the repair of the Solar Maximum Observatory, a satellite orbiting the Earth.

Remarks at a White House Ceremony Marking the Observance of Fair Housing Month
April 10, 1984

Secretary Pierce and ladies and gentlemen, I'm delighted to join you today as our nation observes the 16th anniversary of the law that guarantees one of the most basic American rights—the right to fair housing.

Just a generation ago, nearly 1 in 10 Americans were forced to live lives that were separate and unequal. Most black Americans were taught in segregated schools. Many could find only poor jobs and toiling for low wages. They were refused entry into hotels and restaurants. And across the country, when they wanted to buy a house or rent an apartment, they were too often told they weren't welcome.

That glaring injustice gave rise to a dramatic movement for civil rights. Men and women of integrity and courage organized boycotts and rallys and marches. And often they were beaten and imprisoned, but they remained devoted to their cause. "Work with the faith," Dr. Martin Luther King, Jr., told his followers, "that unearned suffering is redemptive."

The struggle for equality of rights moved our nation to the very depths of its soul. Throughout the land, people began to treat each other not as blacks and whites, but as fellow Americans. In 1968 an historic civil rights bill was passed, and it is title VIII of that act that we honor here today.

The opening words of title VIII were simple, but profound. "It is the policy of the United States to provide, within constitutional limitations, for fair housing throughout the United States." From Maine to Hawaii, title VIII made it unlawful to discriminate in housing on the basis of race, color, religion, or national origin. No American could ever again be denied housing because of the color of his skin. The law was soon amended to prohibit discrimination on the basis of sex as well. And it became crucial in protecting the rights not only of black Americans but of all minorities, including Hispanics, Native Americans, Asians, single mothers, and others.

And today our country is more commit-ted to fair housing than ever. State and local fair housing laws that are substantially equivalent to the Federal law have increased from 23 in 1979 to 82 today. At the national level, the Department of Housing and Urban Development under Secretary Pierce is aggressively investigating complaints of housing discrimination.

Perhaps most important, our administration has proposed legislation to give the fair housing law tougher enforcement. Among other changes in the present law, our legislation would impose civil penalties of up to $50,000 for a first housing discrimination offense and of up to a hundred thousand dollars for a second offense; allow individual as well as pattern or group complaints to be referred to the Attorney General; allow complaints to be filed up to 2 years after the alleged offense; and would extend the protection of the Fair Housing Act to the handicapped and disabled.

Despite the importance of these government efforts, fair housing can never become a permanent way of life without the involvement of thousands of contractors, realtors, building managers, and others who make up the housing industry. And that's where HUD's Public-Private Partnerships for Fair Housing programs comes in.

In partnerships in housing, local realtors, chambers of commerce, and other committed groups and citizens are conducting fair housing campaigns at their own expense. On behalf of all Americans, I want to give my heartfelt thanks to those Secretary Pierce has presented with awards and to everyone who has participated in the Public-Private Partnerships for Fair Housing program.

Celebrities for Fair Housing is another program that's going to have a powerful impact. When people like Phyllis Hyman, Arthur Ashe, Melba Moore, Harry Belafonte, and so many others talk about the importance of fair housing, the whole Nation listens. I know something about that, because I found out years ago in Hollywood that if you don't sing or dance, you wind up as an after-dinner speaker. [*Laughter*] To all these well-respected and well-loved celebrities who are going to give so freely of their time and talents to the cause of fair housing, I want to say a heartfelt "thank you."

Ever since the passage of the Fair Housing Act during this month in 1968, April has traditionally been Fair Housing Month. This April let us once again dedicate ourselves to the great work of assuring fair housing for all. And let us continue that work until fair housing becomes a permanent reality in our national life.

I think that's all I want to say. And thank you, and God bless you.

Note: The President spoke at 1:30 p.m. in Room 450 of the Old Executive Office Building.

Remarks on Signing the Agricultural Programs Adjustment Act of 1984
April 10, 1984

In my State of the Union Address this year, I called on the Congress to join me in cutting projected deficits significantly over the next 3 years. I said at the time that deficit reductions should be a bipartisan effort, bringing representatives of both parties in the Congress together with the top officials of the administration to develop specific proposals. I'm delighted to report that the first result of that effort has finally reached—well, not my desk, but that table. H.R. 4072, the Agricultural Programs Adjustment Act of 1984, will reduce Federal spending by $3.2 billion over the next 3 fiscal years.

Seldom do I receive legislation that will reduce government spending and at the same time help improve conditions for farmers. This new law will help reduce excessive wheat supplies. At the same time, it'll keep the production of other major crops from growing too fast by establishing more reasonable target price levels—price levels that discourage excessive production both here and abroad.

In addition, during negotiations on this legislation we were able to provide additional funding for farm exports and for farm disaster assistance programs, both high priorities for farmers. In recent years, farmers have gone through some hard times because of a weak demand in export markets and unusually large harvests of certain crops that resulted in weak prices. In addition, farmers went through a particularly

wrenching transition from the very high inflation and interest rates of the late 1970's to today's more restrained inflation. Now that the cost of fuel, fertilizer, equipment, and the other items that farmers depend on has stopped rising at double-digit rates, I believe that we're poised for a more stable and secure recovery in the farm economy.

When the Congress passed the 1981 farm bill, few people thought that inflation would come down as fast as it did. That law, therefore, mandated large automatic increases in farm price supports, a desperate effort to keep farmers' heads above water in a rising tide of inflationary pressures. Well, with our success in controlling inflation, those mandated increases are no longer needed to offset costs; indeed, instead of improving conditions in the farm sector, the mandated target price increases threatened to further depress commodity prices by creating too great an incentive for increased production at the same time that they were adding to the deficits. H.R. 4072 makes much needed reductions in the increases mandated by the 1981 farm bill.

I want to commend the fine bipartisan effort of the chairman of the Senate Committee on Agriculture, Nutrition, and Forestry, Jesse Helms, and the chairman of the House Committee on Agriculture, Kika de la Garza, and thanks as well to Secretary of Agriculture, John Block for his fine leadership. Their work was vital in moving H.R. 4072 through the Congress quickly.

This bill was the product of some tough head-to-head negotiations. Like any compromise, it's far from perfect, but it demonstrates that a good-faith effort by all parties can produce results. As I sign this first installment of the deficit downpayment, I want to give a word of encouragement to those who are working on the remaining proposals still under consideration by the Congress. The skeptics who claimed that the Congress and the administration would be unwilling to take any tough steps to reduce the deficit were just plain wrong. And now that we've shown we can do it, we must go on to take the other tough steps that the good of the country demands.

So, I thank all of them, thank you. God bless you, and now I should do what I've been talking about and sign that bill.

Note: The President spoke at 3:53 p.m. in the Rose Garden at the White House.

As enacted, H.R. 4072 is Public Law 98–258, approved April 10.

Statement by Principal Deputy Press Secretary Speakes on United States Policy in Central America
April 10, 1984

The following statement is concurred in by Secretary of State George Shultz, Secretary of Defense Caspar Weinberger, Director of the Central Intelligence Agency William Casey, and Assistant to the President for National Security Affairs Robert McFarlane:

In recent days a shrill and often confusing debate has developed over our goals, plans, and activities in Central America. Because this debate, much of it uninformed and unattributed, is obscuring the real situation, we believe it in the public interest to set the record straight on our objectives, our policy, and our actions—*on the record.*

First, allegations have been made that we are planning for U.S. combat troops to conduct an invasion in Central America. We state emphatically that we have not considered nor have we developed plans to use U.S. military forces to invade Nicaragua or any other Central American country. Secretary Weinberger made this point in his television appearance on Sunday. Some have chosen to disbelieve him—consciously or unconsciously confusing what they call "invasion" plans with our longstanding obligations under the 1947 Rio Treaty, our treaty obligations to defend the Panama Canal, or military contingency plans for disaster relief, humanitarian assistance, or emergency evacuations. For over a generation, as prudence would dictate, we have maintained and updated plans for these contingencies. We have *not*, however, planned to use our forces to invade any country in the region.

Second, some have indicated that we are planning to conduct a postelection military enterprise in Central America. This quite simply is not the case. As stated before, we are not planning for such action now nor are we planning for it after our election.

Third, it has been alleged by critics of the administration that certain activities in the Central American region have not been adequately briefed to appropriate committees of the Congress. To the contrary, all U.S. activities in the Central America region have been fully briefed in detail to the committees of the Congress which exercise jurisdiction in full compliance with the law. Further, last week (April 4) the President sent a letter to the majority leader of the Senate, Howard Baker, assuring him that our objectives and goals in the region had not changed—specifically, "the United States does *not* seek to destabilize or overthrow the Government of Nicaragua."

Fourth, and perhaps most significantly, the current debate has tended to confuse the improvements that we have helped make in El Salvador with what is really going on in Nicaragua:

—Our policy toward Nicaragua has been consistent in that we have supported the multilateral dialog in what is known as the Contadora process. We have endorsed the 21 Contadora objectives which would require that Nicaragua terminate the export of subversion, reduce the size of its military apparatus, implement its democratic commitments to the OAS, and remove Soviet bloc and Cuban military personnel.

—Nicaragua's response throughout has been fraudulent and cynical. They have tried to avoid a comprehensive solution for the region by seeking to reduce all diplomacy to bilateral questions. They have tried to bypass regional and hemispheric efforts by making propaganda at the United Nations. Now they have cynically attempted to sidetrack negotiations by going to the International Court of Justice. A government fanatically dedicated to intervention beyond its borders thus seeks to use an honorable international institution to protect it from its own citizens who are rising up against it. This administration will not be deceived nor will it play that game. Following the example of other nations, the United States has checked this maneuver by a temporary and limited modification of our acceptance of the court's jurisdiction.

—Nicaragua continues to be the source of regional subversion and insurgency. In May 1983, the House Permanent Select Committee on Intelligence, itself, concluded that "the Sandinista Government of Nicaragua is helping train insurgents and is transferring arms and financial support from and through Nicaragua to the insurgents. They are also providing the insurgents bases of operations in Nicaragua. Cuban involvement—especially in providing arms—is also evident."

—In El Salvador, on the other hand, we have witnessed an inspiring display of courage and commitment to the democratic process by the people of El Salvador. At the end of last month, these courageous people again braved guerrillas' violence and sabotage to vote for their next President.

The courage and confidence in democracy that the Salvadoran people are demonstrating deserve our admiration and full support. Now more than ever, our backing for the democratic process must go beyond mere words. Recent uninformed comment on these matters has diverted attention from the central issue. The administration has proposed a long-term program based on the recommendations of the National Bipartisan Commission on Central America. We have also presented our case for urgent military assistance to El Salvador. That case is sound, and the ongoing Salvadoran election process about to enter a runoff requires our support so that El Salvador can ensure its safe conduct.

It is critical that the American people understand what is at stake in the Central American region. Central America is strategically important to the United States. It not only contains the Panama Canal but sits astride some of the most important sealanes in the world. Most importantly, it contains millions of people who want to be free and who crave democracy. The recent elections in El Salvador prove that. The real issues are whether we in the United States want to stand by and let a Communist government in Nicaragua export violence and terrorism in this hemisphere and whether we will allow the power of the ballot box to be overcome by the power of the gun. There is no doubt that the Soviet Union and Cuba want to see communism spread further in Central America. The question is: Will the United States support those countries that want democracy and are willing to fight for their own freedom?

Toasts of President Reagan and President Salvador Jorge Blanco of the Dominican Republic at the State Dinner
April 10, 1984

President Reagan. President and Mrs. Jorge Blanco, ladies and gentlemen, it's a pleasure to have you as our guests this evening.

President Jorge Blanco and his lovely wife represent a country rich in history, blessed with natural beauty, and filled with creative and robust people. This morning at the welcoming ceremony, I mentioned the great accomplishments of your people. And, Mr. President, you can be rightfully proud of your country's freedom.

Eugenio Maria de Aostos, a writer from the last century, truly a man of the hemisphere, once wrote, "No one knows better the meaning of justice and freedom than those who have lived under despotism." Well, such is the case of those who lead the Dominican Republic today. In our lifetime, through your efforts and those of good people like you, the Dominican Republic has been rescued from tyranny and brought safely into the family of free nations. Your personal commitment to the high ideals of liberty, Mr. President, is exemplary.

There can be no greater vocation for any statesman than to lead his people to a more free, just, and humane society. In pursuit of that vocation, you have set a standard of statesmanship and patriotism which is a model not only for the Caribbean but for the Western Hemisphere—indeed, for the leader of any country seeking to create a climate of dignity and freedom in which the human spirit can flourish.

This is not to suggest that under a free government there are no problems. One of the perplexing difficulties, as we're both fully aware, Mr. President, is ensuring economic growth and progress. World events totally beyond our control can dramatically change the rules of the game. Such was the case with energy costs during the last decade. Maintaining healthy economic growth in the face of rising energy costs has been a major challenge to democratic governments throughout the world. Progress can no longer be taken for granted, but, instead, requires constant diligence and a commitment to the long-run well-being of a country.

Yet there's no reason that, working together, free people cannot triumph over adversity today just as we have in the past. Juan Pablo Duarte, the great Dominican patriot, said it well: "Let us work for the country," he wrote, "for in so doing we work for ourselves and for our children."

President Blanco, your government is today ensuring a better tomorrow. You're meeting the challenge head on, working diligently to rebuild your economy through fiscal responsibility and courageous reform in public administration. You've improved your country's business and investment climate. And by stressing the importance of the private sector, and by providing practical incentives for investment, you've made certain the Dominican Republic will be part of the economic upsurge now taking place in the United States, as it spreads throughout the global economy.

Some of you may not be aware that President Blanco, in his country, has established enterprise zones to encourage investment and commerce. Mr. President, perhaps you've got some tips on how to get great ideas like that—[*laughter*]—through the legislative process here in Washington. Seriously, though, Mr. President, the strength of Dominican democracy have not gone unnoticed by our Congress. Your support and the example of a strong Dominican democracy deserve credit for helping assure the passage of the Caribbean Basin Initiative. You proved that there is a better way, and it works.

Together we can show the world that, indeed, freedom works. Together—well, it's up to us. President Jorge Blanco, we honor you tonight for the part that you and your country are playing in the cause of human freedom.

Now, if you will all join me in a toast to President and Mrs. Jorge Blanco, and to the Dominican Republic.

President Jorge Blanco. President Reagan, Mrs. Reagan, ladies and gentlemen:

This dinner will be permanently engraved in my memory, as it will be in that of my wife and of the members of our delegation. Henceforth, we can include it among the most stellar moments of our lives.

Over and above protocol, we feel the warmth and affection of President Reagan, his gracious wife, Nancy, and the high officials of this nation who receive us as emissaries of the democracy which we represent with genuine pride.

We are pleased to see once again that the

Dominican democracy is respected and admired by the great democracy of the United States of America. We are both associated with and agree upon the defense of the human values which gave birth to our respective nations. We share a common past of ideals and principles, and a present full of responsibilities which must contribute to the building of a more promising future for our people.

I appreciate your recognition of the democratic vocation of our people and of the firm resolve of the government we are fortunate to head to fight tenaciously, with unswerving faith and will, for maintenance of a democratic system, in spite of the adversities of an unprecedented world economic crisis which affects all of the international community, but more so the developing countries.

From the very moment I took office I set a clear and precise target: to restore the economy and the finances of the Dominican nation to health. We are devoting major efforts and sacrifices to this unpostponable objective, conscious of the fact that a house in order and the adoption of policies that are conducive to sustained development and of reform measures that will ensure a true system of social justice, are indispensable prerequisites for the strengthening and full effectiveness of our democratic institutions.

The Presidency of a country, be it large or small, is a forge where leadership is hammered out, in the awareness of the resources and aspirations of their peoples. That is why we do not hesitate to support and defend the generous program of the Caribbean Basin Initiative, which has already become reality and serves as a means to expand our markets, at the same time that it constitutes a great stimulus for private enterprise, a constant and necessary engine for the development of our societies.

I sincerely hope that our talks will lead to appropriate and fair solutions to common problems and will guarantee positive achievements for the development of our economies and the prosperity of our nations.

[*At this point, President Jorge Blanco departed from the prepared text of his re-*

marks. He then proposed a toast as follows.]

Let us drink a toast to the personal good fortune of the President and his distinguished wife. Let us drink a toast to the happiness of our respective peoples.

Interpreter. There was a part of the President's remarks that were improvised, and I'd like to transmit, to those of you who didn't understand, the English—what he said.

"President Reagan, I have been deeply moved by your mention of Eugenio Maria de Aostos and Juan Pablo Duarte. Eugenio Maria de Aostos was the teacher par excellence of all successive generations of Dominicans as the years have gone by. Juan Pablo Duarte, together with other two great patriots, was the founder of our modern republic. But the mention of the name of Juan Pablo Duarte here in this room at the White House is an extraordinary recognition of the ideals that have shaped our nation throughout the years, and which led to the independence movement which led, in turn, to our independence declared on the 27th of February of 1844.

"Into this beautiful room have come men. They have come to share the warmth with the beautiful ladies who've accompanied them, and with all of their beautiful dresses. And this, undoubtedly, will be an indelible part of the recollection that we have of this evening. But above all, Mr. President, the warm welcome that you have given us, on behalf of the great American democracy of which you are a worthy leader and to which you bring so much prestige, fills every one of the aspirations that we might have had when we came to this city. And the fruitful results of our conversations will be the golden touch that will accompany us upon our return to our country."

Thank you.

Note: President Reagan spoke at 9:52 p.m. in the State Dining Room at the White House. President Jorge Blanco spoke in Spanish, and a text of his remarks in English was provided to the dinner guests. As printed above, the remarks follow that text, except where the modification was made by President Jorge Blanco's interpreter.

Remarks at the Ford Claycomo Assembly Plant in Kansas City, Missouri
April 11, 1984

Thank you, Phil Caldwell, Mr. Nolan, Governor Bond, Congressman Coleman, and you ladies and gentlemen. And thank you all for welcoming me here today and showing me Kansas City's Claycomo plant.

I've heard enough since I've been here to know something that Mr. Caldwell was talking about, and that is the relationship—the communication that takes place here. And you know, I've always believed that a lot of the troubles in the world would disappear if we were talking to each other instead of about each other. And communication really means people having something to say and then the manner in which it's done.

And a favorite story of mine about communication was told to me by Danny Villanueva. You younger ones won't remember, but he once was the placekicker for the Los Angeles Rams and then he became a sports announcer. And Danny told me that one night he was over having dinner at the home of one of the ballplayers with the Dodgers. The young wife was bustling about getting dinner ready. They were talking sports, and the baby started to cry. And over her shoulder, she said to her husband, "Change the baby." And he was embarrassed, being a young fellow, in front of Danny. And he said, "What do you mean, change the baby? I'm a ballplayer. That's not my line of work." She turned around, put her hands on her hips, and she communicated. [*Laughter*]

She said, "Look, buster, you lay the diamond out like a diaper, you put second base on home plate, put the baby's bottom on the pitcher's mound, hook up first and third, slide home underneath. And if it starts to rain, the game ain't called. You start all over again." [*Laughter*]

Well, you communicated since I've been here. You've shown me an exciting success story and given me a glimpse of America's future. And it looks mighty good. In this place, in one of our country's basic industries, we can see where America's headed and what lies in store for all our people.

Each of you can rightly take pride in helping make us all that we are and all that we can be.

You've also made me remember how far we've come. And speaking for myself, that's a long way, because when I think back to my first car—I bet it isn't the same as yours, a Model-T. Well, as I toured part of your assembly plant just for a short time here and watched how busy the assemblers and the other workers are, I couldn't help but think back to the days when America's economy had sputtered and stalled. Only a few years ago this industry and all America were in the worst economic mess in decades.

It didn't matter who you were or where you came from, double-digit inflation was slamming shut the doors of opportunity. And if you dreamed of owning a home or buying a new car, 21½-percent interest rates were closing the doors on those dreams, too. And that's what we faced in January of 1981.

An industry which burst onto the scene in the early days of the 20th century and became a vital part of our existence found itself crippled by too much regulation, too much government interference, and too much backseat driving by Washington. In 1980 alone, the Big Three lost $4.2 billion. Plant closings across the country plunged businesses and families into desperate financial straits. Many of those families were uprooted, as workers set out across the country looking for jobs.

1980—I happened for a particular reason to be in a number of cities at that time and a number of them where automobiles were assembled and made. And in city after city, I was told when I arrived that the inflation rate was 20 percent—or I mean inflation—I mean the unemployment rate was 20 percent or more.

It was time for a change. So, we charted a new course to rebuild America from the bottom up. And we knew that to do that, government had to get its own house in

507

order. And at the same time we knew that government needed to get out of the way of the people and the spirit of enterprise that encourages risk taking and rewards innovation. And we knew it wouldn't be easy.

Both the economy and the auto industry were in recession, the culmination of years of overtaxing, overspending, and overpromising by those who claimed they could spend your earnings better than you could. We knew that progress would come in inches, not miles, but we knew that if we worked together, progress would come.

It hasn't been easy. Times have been rough and, yes, the recession was much deeper and longer than anyone had predicted. But these problems had been building up for 20 years, and we were determined to find a real economic cure, not just resort, as they had so often in the past, to another political quick fix. There have been eight recessions since World War II, and seven of those were the political quick fix. There's no compassion in snake oil cures.

We weathered the storm together, and now the sun is shining on a strong economy and an American automobile industry that's moving forward again. Inflation, once out of control, has plummeted by nearly two-thirds. For 2 years it's been under 4 percent. Right now it's in the neighborhood of 4 percent or a little above, probably because of some weather conditions that changed food prices and so forth. The prime rate is down by nearly half from when we came to office. And a few weeks ago, we learned that last quarter's gross national product grew at a healthy 7.2 percent.

At the same time—and this is the greatest figure of all—5.1 million more Americans have jobs today than had jobs just 16 months ago. We've had the steepest drop in unemployment in over 30 years. Factory orders, housing starts, and retail sales are up, and—listen closely to this one—auto sales are up dramatically. More than 100,000 of you auto workers went back to work in 1983, with more expected back this year. And right now there are 85,000 more people working in the automobile industry in general than were working there in 1980 in that period I was telling you about. The unemployment rate, we know, in America

across the country, the average is 7.7 percent. I think you'd be happy to know that in the automobile industry, the unemployment rate is down to 5.5 percent. And I hope it's going down lower than that.

Here at Ford, because of your determination, dedication, and hard work, you sold more cars last year than any time since 1979. All of us, working together and ignoring the gloom criers and the pundits who said it couldn't be done, all of us have hung tough. And today, as we see the auto industry and the economy humming with activity, aren't we glad we did?

There was a time when Claycomo nearly had to shut down. But today almost 5,000 people—4,500 or more—are working two 10-hour shifts, producing 86 cars and trucks an hour, 1,600 a day. You're continuing a Ford tradition that began here in Kansas City, as Chairman Caldwell told you, in 1906 with nearly 7 million cars built in all. And whatever you may have heard about my age, I wasn't here at that time. [*Laughter*] But you're not getting older, you're getting better.

Your industry and many others have begun to shape up. You're getting lean and mean and ready to face the challenge of the future. By the end of this year, some $50 billion will have been invested in the 1980's by American automobile companies to modernize plants and design and produce attractive, fuel-efficient cars. At this plant, Ford has invested almost $200 million to modernize and refurbish for the future.

And best of all, the quality of American automobiles has never been better, reflecting the pride and determination of employees at every level. Your success story is so widespread that industry leaders from Europe, China and, yes, even Japan, have come halfway around the world to see for themselves. Everyone can see these Tempo/Topaz cars rolling off the line with that sticker on the front window: "Jointly Dedicated to Quality—Built with Missouri Pride."

Now, we all know that government and management and labor had a role to play in the industry's problems that developed during the seventies. And all three have played a role in its resurgence.

I think government did its part by reducing regulations and getting the economy rolling again. Shortly after we came into office, our administration discussed the auto industry's problems with the Japanese. They offered to voluntarily restrain auto exports to the United States. And this gave the domestic auto industry the breathing room it needed to build new plants and products, improve quality, increase productivity, and participate in the economic recovery.

Now, some advocate far harsher methods. They believe we should run up the flag in defense of our markets, embrace protectionism, and insulate ourselves from world competition. But we'll never meet the challenge of the eighties with that kind of defeatist mentality.

In there having lunch, I told just a few of you my own experience when I entered the job market back in the early thirties at the very depths of the Great Depression. Twenty-six percent unemployment; the government putting radio ads on—don't leave home looking for work, there is none—and a great deal of that was due to what somebody thought might be an answer to our Depression problems, the Smoot-Hawley tariff bill, which literally destroyed free trade worldwide and perpetuated the Depression at that time—which, incidentally, was only cured then by World War II.

I believe if Americans work together to improve quality, become more productive, hold down costs, and invest in tomorrow's technology, then we can out-compete, outperform, and out-sell the pants off anybody. And echoing Mr. Caldwell, I believe in America being first, because America is best.

You know, if the dream of America is to be preserved, we mustn't waste the genius of one mind, the strength of one body, or the spirit of one soul. We need all our people, men and women, young and old, individuals of every race to be healthy, happy, and whole. This is our goal. And we won't rest until all Americans can reach as high as their vision and God-given talents take them.

I thank you again for inviting me, and God bless all of you.

Don't worry, I'm not going to do an encore, but one of the things that I enjoy most in this job is the opportunity to get out of Washington and to meet people from every walk of life and from every corner of the world. But I have to tell you that no matter where I go, there are no more finer people than those men and women who raise our food and patrol our streets and man our mines and factories and teach our children, keep our homes, and heal us when we're sick. These people are everyday Americans, but they're heroes in their own right. They're the unsung heroes of America.

And today I'd like to honor one such hero. Barney Maxon, could you and your wife, Jewell—I thought your daughter, Carol, was with you. Carol, come on up here. Today I'd like to honor one of those heroes I was talking about, Barney Maxon. Barney's someone who's always been there, given above and beyond what was required of him. And, Barney, Chairman Caldwell and I would like to present you with a plaque in honor of the 50 years of loyal and dedicated service you've given to the Ford Motor Company.

Congratulations, Barney, and thank you, again.

Well, again, God bless you, and thank you all. It's good to be here.

Note: The President spoke at 12:21 p.m. in the finished product auto assembly line area of the plant. He was introduced by Phillip Caldwell, chairman of the board of the Ford Motor Co. In his opening remarks, the President also referred to Paul Nolan, manager of the plant.

Prior to his remarks, the President had lunch in the cafeteria with plant workers and executives and then toured the assembly line. Following his remarks, the President went to a conference room at the plant for a meeting with labor and managment leaders.

At the conclusion of his visit to the plant, the President left Kansas City and went to the AM-FAC Hotel in Dallas, TX, where he remained overnight.

Remarks at the Oak Hollow Housing Development in Grand Prairie, Texas
April 12, 1984

Good morning. Hey, that came on loud, didn't it? Maybe I'm speaking to the group down the street there.

Well, I just wanted to say good morning, and I've been seeing this and hearing about this construction and all. And, of course, you all know that one of the reasons for coming here is that in this industry, in the housing industry, you're out in front of the rest of the United States as to the comeback—and more going on here than—and a higher percentage than any place else.

This is an industry that can cause a depression when things are bad all by itself. But it's also an industry that can lead, as this one has been leading, in a recovery from the recession that we've had. And I just have to say, from what I've seen here—now, I don't know exactly when I'll be in the market. It could be several years; it could be next year. [*Laughter*] But I've been watching with great care, because I'll probably be in the house market, having sold the one we owned due to the change in locale.

Now, all those people that are covering this here, they're all speculating as to what I'm doing on trips like this and why I'm doing this. You know, the truth of the matter is, it's just good to get out of Washington every once in a while. [*Laughter*]

But I have to tell you, I'm so pleased about the recovery that we have and what has happened with this industry, and that at last, a dream is restored that probably is more prevalent here than in any other country in the world. And that is everyone's dream of wanting to own their own piece of ground and their own house.

And I have a little confession to make to you also. I was sort of in this business from the hammer-and-nail side and pick-and-shovel side. One of the first jobs I ever got—summer jobs—was I was 14 years old, and it was with an outfit that wasn't building new ones, but they were buying old ones and remodeling. And before the summer was over, I laid hardwood floor, I shingled roof, I painted. But I do remember also, I started—some of these houses, they wanted to add basements and so forth, and didn't have the tools and equipment that we have today. It was pick and shovel. And I was on the pick and shovel.

And I remember one hot day, just approaching noon, and I'd been swinging that pick all day—you know, a lot of hard clay and rock. And I had the pick right up over my shoulder ready for another blow when the noon whistle blew. And I just didn't even finish the blow. I just let go and stepped out from underneath it. And then, behind me, I heard some very firm and not polite conversation aimed at me, and I turned around. And there was the boss, and the pick was embedded in the ground right between his feet. I didn't have any answer to any of the things that he was saying to me. [*Laughter*]

Well, I just, again, I just want to commend you for all of this. I think this is a picture of what's happening all over America, and you can be very proud that you're out in front on it here. Thank you for letting me come in and stop production for a while.

Note: The President spoke at 9:45 a.m. to construction workers following a tour of the construction site.

Remarks During a Roundtable Discussion With Housing Industry Representatives in Arlington, Texas
April 12, 1984

Mr. Wood. Well, we understand you've been visiting a nearby housing subdivision, and we're very interested to hear your reactions to it. But we thought before that you might like to know what we've been talking about here.

The map in front of us, the topographical map, is a new town in this area about 25 minutes from here called Las Calinas. And it has commercial buildings, as you can see, and ultimately will house fifty to sixty thousand people. It's being developed by the Southland Financial Corporation. Many of the biggest homebuilders in the country have bought pieces of land and are building their own developments there.

We're in Dallas for the roundtable because Dallas is the number one city in the country for housing starts, and Las Calinas is one of the best examples in the country of new homebuilding development.

The President. Well, that's remarkable. I don't suppose where I was was part of that.

Mr. Wood. I don't think you were at this development, but it is in this area.

The other thing I thought I'd tell you before asking for your response to the trip that you took this morning, the panel—and I know, rather than take the time to introduce them all, I know you've seen the list, and you know that we have representatives here from——

The President. Yes.

Mr. Wood. ——from the homebuilders and the realtors and the savings and loan league. We have some major publicly held homebuilding companies. We have building product manufacturers. And before you came, we went around and introduced ourselves and talked about how business was, and the consensus was that business right now is good. Eleven of the 12 people on the panel mentioned concerns about interest rates.

The President. Well, I can't understand why. [*Laughter*]

Well, I know, too, that I'm going to have an opportunity later to greet each one of you, so that's why I didn't take time here in the beginning. It was most interesting and enjoyable, the project that I just—and the fine homes that are being built there. And I had an opportunity to tell them a little bit about, in my boyhood, having a job with a unit that was building. But it was a little different then. We didn't have the machinery and skiploaders, and things weren't around—you did it with a pick and shovel.

But you also weren't limited to just one type of work. As I explained to them, before the projects were over, why I would end up laying hardwood floor and shingling roofs, and even painting, and so forth. But today, the improvement in tools and productivity and all—although if you see a slowdown in the Dallas area, why it's because I slowed it down by being there. Everyone stopped work. [*Laughter*] That happens in government, too. I don't even have to be around. [*Laughter*]

But it's certainly a pleasure for me to get out of Washington and to be with all of you today. It helps to get a fresh perspective. You know, if you stay in Washington too long, the world begins to look like "The Twilight Zone." And I have, as I say, just come from that site in Grand Prairie, and I'm interested with what I saw and the people I met.

Far too many in our Nation's Capital have come to believe that progress is the result of passing laws and regulations. But I think this group knows better than most that that isn't so. It's opportunities for hard work and risktaking by people like yourselves that keeps this country building and growing. And more often than not, you're doing it in spite of the roadblocks put in your way by government.

For the last 3 years, we've been busy trying to remove roadblocks and create a stable economic environment in which enterprise can flourish. Irresponsible taxing and spending policies in the years prior to this administration gave us double-digit inflation and economic stagnation. You saw firsthand the failure of the liberal tax, spend, and inflate policies. Your industry had its legs knocked out from under it by ruinous inflation and killer interest rates.

It takes time to put a program in place, and it takes time for it to start working, and working its magic throughout the economy. But I think even the skeptics are admitting that our reforms are working. The American economy as a whole, and your industry in particular, are coming back strong.

Overall economic growth last year was a robust 6 percent. And the first quarter growth this year suggests the recovery is going to continue at a healthy rate. But I'm also encouraged by the fact—and this may sound strange—that the figures that were released this morning by the Commerce Department suggest that there is some slowing of that first quarter growth. And I think that's fine, because I think it indicates that this is a sustainable expansion, not just a quick fix or a splurge.

And when our program was put in place in the fall of '81, housing starts were at an annual rate of 840,000 annual. Now they've jumped to almost 2.2 million. That's the highest rate in 6 years. Building permits which were only 730,000 in the fall of '81 have risen to nearly 2 million. That's a 166-percent increase. In February, 721,000 new homes were sold as compared with 338,000 in September of '81. And that makes a 113-percent increase.

But the strength surging through your industry and the rest of our economy is no accident, and it's not a reflection of some uncontrollable cycle. They used to try to explain inflation away like a plague of locusts that we didn't know where it came from and it just was there. Well, when the last administration took over, inflation was running at 5 percent, and the prime interest rate—and it hurts to say this—was 7 percent. And after just 4 years, we were left with double-digit inflation, 21½-percent prime interest rates, and spiraling mortgage rates, of course.

The average monthly mortgage payment rose from $256 to $598, and that $342-a-month increase in the cost of buying a home made all the difference, as you all well know. Since our economic recovery program took effect, the decline in mort-gage rates from a peak of about 18 down to 13½ translates into a typical savings of $225 in the monthly payment for families that are now buying homes.

Inflation has been reduced by around two-thirds. Home ownership is an essential part—as I told these people out there today—of the American dream. It strengthens the family. It's fundamental to our way of life, and we want to build an opportunity society where more and more families from all walks of life can afford to buy their own homes.

But, you know, one of the strangest things to me has been listening to people suggest that we should be frightened because the economy's growing too fast, that too many people are finding jobs, and this will push up interest rates. Well, no one will ever convince me that economic growth is bad for us. I think it's good for everybody, especially the homebuilding industry.

I believe there are three keys to bringing interest rates down further and keeping them down: first, real and lasting spending restraint by the Congress; second, an overhaul of our tax system to make taxes more simple, more fair, and to provide greater incentives for growth; and third, confidence that the Federal Reserve Board will provide sufficient liquidity to finance economic growth while maintaining long-term price stability.

The progress that we've made can't be taken for granted. We can't go back to the same taxing and spending patterns of the last decade and expect that we will not also fall into the pit of recession, inflation, and stagnation from which we're now just emerging. How we come to grips with the Federal deficit will set the tone. We can try to balance up by increasing taxes, undercutting economic growth and investment. Or we can try to balance down with lower spending and tax rates, permitting our economy to break free.

Now, let me interject here that when I talk about simplifying taxes, I don't want to go the route of the form that I saw the other day that someone sent in as a sample of simplified taxes. It only had two lines on it. The top line said, "How much did you make?" and the second line said, "Send it." [*Laughter*]

But we've heard considerable talk about crowding out, about government borrowing too much of the funds in the private credit markets. Well, that is indeed a threat and one of which you're keenly aware. Yet even with all the attention that's focused on this issue, not one of the advocates of raising taxes has ever answered a challenge that I have issued—I've made it over and over again. Explain why taxing the money out of the private system will not eliminate money from the private credit market every bit as much as if the Federal Government borrows it.

The same amount of money is going to be taken, whether the government takes it in taxes or the government borrows to fund the present activities of government. The problem is government is taking too big a share from the private sector, and we're not going to answer our economic problems until we harness government and bring it back down to within a reasonable percentage of the gross national product.

The answer to the deficit, as I say, is not raising taxes and pushing us back into recession, nor is the answer to sabotage the defense rebuilding program we've begun and which is so long overdue. The answer's economic growth and a responsible program to control Federal spending.

We've made a proposal, as you know, for a downpayment on the deficit that would be a good first step. And yesterday the Finance Committee in the Senate passed that. In 1982 an agreement was made with me—and I'm remembering this to this day—that the Congress would provide $3 in savings for every additional dollar of revenue that we would agree to. Well, it was against my grain, but I went along with a tax reform package that was designed to raise about a hundred billion dollars over 3 years, thinking that there would be a $300 billion cut in spending. Well, I haven't seen any serious effort to cut spending; in fact, there are even proposals to increase spending in certain areas. So, there's a great deal of politicking going on about the deficit. People are going to have to judge for themselves who's serious about the problem.

Now, I'm willing to do my part, but I will not simply give in to those who would take

us back into recession and/or play fast and loose with the security of our country. You can expect some progress in the areas where the executive branch can act on its own. The Grace commission provided us with a great number of suggestions being evaluated through the departments and agencies right now. But for tangible progress to be made, we need commitment from the Congress, which until now has not been forthcoming.

I'm not pessimistic about the deficit or any of the challenges we face. And I was only joking when at the Gridiron the other night I said I wouldn't worry about it because it's big enough to take care of itself; that was a joke. [*Laughter*] But already the deficit has been coming down from the economic growth that we've been seeing throughout the country.

And I also think that the Members of Congress who are out seeking votes are finding that their constituents are concerned about the deficit, but at the same time opposed to raising taxes. Members of Congress don't have to see the light. We just have to make them feel the heat.

And now, I've gone on long enough, so I think I'll hear more from what's on your mind and what you have planned here.

Mr. Wood. Thank you, Mr. President. We do have a short 3-minute presentation for you from the leadership of the National Association of Home Builders, the National Association of Realtors, and the U.S. League of Savings. So, if it's all right with you, I'll introduce the first of those three speakers——

The President. Fine.

Mr. Wood. ——who is Dave Smith, who'll be the president of the NAHB in 1986.

Mr. Smith. Mr. President, we thank you for this opportunity to brief you this morning on the housing industry and the current market conditions.

As you told our board of directors last May, homebuilders are leading the recovery by the sweat of their brow and the strength of their nerve. That is still true today. Last year, we built about 1.7 million housing units, an increase of 60 percent from the previous year. This year, we expect to start 1.8 million units. During February, new homes were being started at an annual rate of 2.2 million, and new homes are selling at their fastest pace in 4 years.

Looking back, this recovery represents a major triumph for your administration. You put America back on its feet. You put Americans back to work. You licked inflation and helped create an economic climate in which it was possible for small builders like myself to build affordable housing for young people just starting families and careers.

But the recovery, Mr. President, has reached a critical turning point. Looking ahead and beyond today's robust economic news, there's a great deal of uncertainty in the marketplace. This uncertainty is being expressed by the typical member of our association who constructs fewer than 20 houses per year. Builders are the ones out in front of this economic recovery. They are the ones that are taking the risk. Builders are the ones who'd live and die with the ups and downs in interest rates. And interest rates, Mr. President, are rising. That has the builders worried.

When mortgage rates were in the 13-percent range a few months ago, we had a strong market. Now mortgage rates are approaching 14 percent and still rising. That's too high for millions of potential home buyers. Unless this upward trend in interest rates is reversed, it is only a matter of time before home sales drop, new construction declines, and unemployment rises.

Can another economic crisis touched off by rising interest rates be avoided? The answer is yes. But to do so requires your bold, demonstrated, decisive leadership. It requires immediate action on the Federal budget that would cut the deficit in the neighborhood of 150 to 200 billion over the next 3 fiscal years.

Builders view the deficit as the single greatest threat to the Nation's economic recovery. Deficits keep interest rates high. Deficits are inflationary. Deficits compete with investments. Deficits reduce our ability to compete in the world market. And deficits threaten to upset the current economic recovery.

Mr. President, the time is running out. The bipartisan program now in Congress appears to be our last chance of cutting the deficit during this election year. We appreciate your work on the bipartisan effort, and we hope you will continue to take a leadership in this deficit reduction program. By using your office to negotiate a consensus on the budget, you will be sending a powerful message throughout this land. Interest rates would decline or at least settle down. Confidence would be restored. The American dream of owning a home would be preserved. And the economic recovery we worked for so hard to get off the ground would be sustained.

We certainly appreciate your being with us today, Mr. President.

The President. Thank you.

Mr. Wood. Do you want to respond, or shall I ask the next man to——

The President. Well, whichever is suitable here. I would like to comment this with regard to the interest rates and what you just said here with regard to the connection to the deficit. As I hope I've made clear, deficits are something—we shouldn't have had them for the last 50 years as a part of our regular policy, and we shouldn't continue having them.

But I think that there are two other reasons for the interest rates right now and one of them, in one way, is a sign of the progress that we've made. The other one is a pessimism that, because of the past experiences going back to the time of the Second World War, the seven previous recessions, that the market isn't quite convinced that inflation is going to stay down where it is. And so they're protecting themselves before they lend that money out for fear it'll go back up. That's one.

The thing that is born out of the encouragement is that, yes, this last flurry of a little bit of climbing interest rates, I think, is more due to the fact that the robust economy saw a great upsurge—we've gone to 12-something percent over about 5 percent of business investment in new plant and equipment, and so forth, and at the same time, the great upsurge in consumer buying. Now, that's the thing that as of this morning we find, there's been some slowdown in that, particularly in those areas that are tied to interest rates, such as appliances, the durable goods, and automobiles.

And there we've just run in temporarily, I'm sure, to supply and demand. There's more market for the money out there than there is money. I believe that we're going to see before long that beginning to come down.

Now, if I could respectfully suggest that with no retreat from going after the deficits, I think that there it's more that they contribute to the pessimism of the people in the marketplace that would account for the interest rates than having any direct tie, because let me point one significant thing. When we started, and the interest rates were coming down from that 21½ down to that 11-percent prime, in that same period our deficit was doubling. So, obviously with the interest rates coming down at the same time that the deficit was going up indicates that there isn't that tie.

And the same thing is true if we look at foreign countries. If we look at our deficits on the basis of percentage of gross national product, we find that this great growth in them in the number of dollars is not as severe, that there are other countries among our industrial allies out there that have the same percentage of deficit in their gross national product, but they don't have the high interest rates we have.

But you are right that it is a problem, that in solving it I think we can restore the confidence in the market. And I am going to say that I believe that before the warm weather's left us, I think we're going to see some settling down of the interest rates.

Mr. Wood. Now I'll call on Jack Carlson, Mr. President, who's representing the National Association of Realtors.

Mr. Carlson. Mr. President, we appreciate your proclamation of this being Private Property Week. 625,000 realtors across the country are joined together with 60 million families that own their own home to celebrate private property in this country. And home ownership is, of course, the most important part of private property.

Mr. President, we're concerned about the deficit, and we agree with you: The primary cause of a high deficit is inflationary expectations, and we have to move that out of the marketplace.

We're also concerned about how we go about to bring down the deficit. As you've said, if we tax investment on the front end to lower interest rates on the back end, we will have already taken taxes away from investment if the tax is paid on investment. So, we will not have any gain at all by bringing down the deficit by taxing investment.

That's why we're particularly concerned, not with what happened in the House, as you indicated passed yesterday, but also what's happening in the Senate Finance Committee. They want to erase away your accelerated cost-recovery program, going from 15 years to 20 years. And this would be primarily for rental housing. And the impact upon it when it's fully effective will mean rent increases for those in rental housing, $25 a month. And, as you know, that affects the safety net, that's a lower income part of the market. And we would hope that you would not favor the increase of the depreciation life or the accelerated cost-recovery period going from 15 to 20 years, because that's a huge increase. Also, we end up with about a million fewer rental housing units than we would otherwise have in this country.

The second point: There has been rumors, as there always will be, about your suggestion of a study to be made, a report to be made to you in December as to what an overall tax reform and simplification program might be. There are rumors that are starting to abound—and some of them deal with some of your assistants, who, I'm sure, are not reflecting your viewpoint, but, nonetheless, cause some concern—that increased taxation on homeownership is being considered, such as doing away with interest deductibility on home mortgages, while allowing deductibility of interest on all the other kinds of investments. That would increase taxes on the average homeowner, and there are 60 million households who are homeowners in this country, two-thirds of Americans. That would increase it by $2,500, a very large increase, if it was totally removed, or a smaller amount, if it was eliminated on a small basis.

And there is concern, because since 1980 the homeownership rate has gone down. And we've washed away half the gain that we got in the 1970's already during the

1980's. And clearly, as you have indicated in your proclamation on Private Property Week and also right here, that we want to move in the opposite direction because of the fundamental values that homeownership has. I would hope that you would disavow any effort to increase taxation on homeownership or increase taxation on rental units in this country.

Mr. Wood. And our third prepared speaker is Paul Prior, who represents—he's the national chairman of the U.S. League of Savings. Mr. Prior's on the other end—there he is.

The President. All right.

Mr. Prior. Mr. President, I thank you for giving the opportunity once again to talk with you personally, as you have three previous times, and to discuss with you concerns of our savings institutions in the country.

Savings and loan associations and savings banks are the main sources of financing of all this activity, the real estate sales and new homebuilding that we're talking about this morning. We have been in that position of market dominance in the past, and despite some of what has been written and said in recent years—some of which was just said on my starboard side before you got here this morning—we remain the primary mortgage lending source today.

In 1983 we had an alltime record lending year in our institutions—$137 billion in mortgage loans by savings institutions. Now, what made this volume possible is the increasing acceptance of the adjustable rate mortgage; 60 to 75 percent of our lending was represented by this flexible interest.

The financial institutions industry has also just gone through the very gratifying experience of more than recapturing the deposit base that we had lost to the money market funds, and that has helped to make the strong housing recovery possible.

But we're concerned about what lies just ahead, and what you said a minute ago is most encouraging. The fear that looms in people's minds today is, are we going to be hit again with higher and higher interest rates? And underlying that, will Washington be able to get these huge deficits under control?

Now, I manage a small financial institu-

tion in the cornfields of Indiana. And I talk to men and women every day when I'm in my office who wonder whether they'll ever be able to afford a house with the interest rates as high as they are and seeming to be headed still higher.

The U.S. League, 2 days ago, released a survey showing home buying patterns last year, and the good news is that more first-time buyers got into the home buying market than ever before. And home prices were not spiraling upward as they had been. In fact, to the surprise of many people, home prices were actually lower, our study showed, in 1983 than in 1981. That is median prices.

But we should not be misled by the recent strong showing of housing markets, because the fear of inflation and high interest rates is decidedly back in people's minds. Some of us here and our customers have been through a couple of very difficult years with high interest rates. And just as you have pointed out to us, Mr. President, we see the Federal Government at the core of the problem. Federal borrowing to cover Federal spending takes so much of the credit pool that businesses and families are shortchanged. We simply can't bid competitively for it.

Now, there's also an important new factor that we're confronting with the deregulation of the rates that lenders pay to depositors. The rates to borrow are also floating in the marketplace. There's no longer an insulation of borrowers from the impact of the money markets, because adjustable mortgages let that rise in market interest rates pass through to the borrower. This is one big reason why more and more people are becoming sensitive to these interest rate moves. A rate increase will cost them money every month, once their mortgage is adjusted. This time around it'll not be just the financial institutions and business borrowers that feel the pinch; it will be many families as well.

So, we in the savings institutions want to be sure the deficit problem is dealt with now, while there is still time to bring it under control. And we are hopeful as you are, Mr. President, and as you have said many times, that a nonpartisan approach will, in fact, get something done. We're not concerned with who gets the credit for bringing the deficit down as long as we get the job done.

Mr. Wood. If you have some time left, Mr. President, we have some other members of the panel who would like to ask you questions.

The President. Fine.

Mr. Wood. And the first one is to your immediate left, Barbara Ann Kirk from this area.

Ms. Kirk. Thank you, Mr. President. Our question: The deficit, as you've heard, is a major concern to all of us, and especially to the building industry. We know that Congress is currently working on a number of proposals to control the deficit. Mr. President, what steps are you willing to take in this effort?

The President. Well, there virtually aren't any steps that I won't take if they can be taken without punishing any particular segment of our society. And apropos of some of the things that you were saying, sir, in this year—and I know there's a lot of talk that, "Well, everybody's waiting until the election year is over because of the threat of votes" and so forth. Actually, one of the main problems is that in an election year like this, the Congress time is restricted. There is so much time that is now going to be taken out—and understandably—for campaigning that there's a limit to how much you can put on their plate. This is why we've called what we're asking for a downpayment.

But in the meantime, as I've said before, we have to and are looking at the whole structure. And I have to say we're all and should be indebted to Peter Grace and the more than 2,000 business and professional people in this country who not only volunteered their services, free time to go in and look at government but who also, for whatever financial overhead there was, contributed the money for that.

But they came back—this idea had come to me when I was first elected Governor of California and the State was almost in as bad a shape as the Federal Government is. And only there we had a constitutional requirement that in the first 6 months that I was in office, I had to restore the balance

that had been lost in the previous administration out there. And I called on business and the private sector in California to do what the Grace commission has done.

They came in, some 250 there, average giving 114 days full-time away from their own activities and their own businesses and professions, came back with about 1,800 recommendations. We implemented more than 1,600 of those and restored California to the point that, over the next few years, we would come to such surpluses that I was able to restore them to the people as one-time tax rebates come income tax collection time.

And I remember about the third time that we did that, a long-time senator, State senator, came into my office one day outraged about our giving that money back to the people. And he said he considered giving that money back to the people an unnecessary expenditure of public funds. [*Laughter*] I think it revealed a difference in philosophy there.

But we have some 2,470 recommendations from the Grace commission, and we have a task force now within government looking at these. A number of them can be done administratively, many of them will take legislation, but we're going to go—just one simple example I used this morning that can show. Government is so hidebound. It gets into the habit of doing things the way they've always been done. And they don't realize, as business has to, that there are new ways and that there're improvements and efficiencies.

For example, one agency of our government—that it cost them $4.20 to process a paycheck for an employee; every paycheck cost $4.20. Out in business it costs around a dollar, on the average. Well, why should government not be doing it the way business is doing it?

In the Defense Department, with all the complaints that people may want to make because we're trying to restore defenses, the percentage of the budget that goes to defense now is smaller than it historically has been back through the years. Defense, being the prime responsibility, used to take half the Federal budget. Well, it's down to a little less than 30 percent now of the Federal budget.

But there they found that they were putting out, due to the things of the day and the machinery of the day, they were putting out paychecks that were on a kind of cardboard type of paycheck. And they're now putting them out on the regular kind of paper paycheck, and it costs about half as much as it used to cost.

But we are going to continue. We're going to do everything we can, and it's going to take aiming down the road at a balanced budget. And I'm going to continue to insist on an amendment that demands a balanced budget in the Federal Government.

And if any of you are talking to any of your Congressmen also, one of the best tools that I had as Governor that I would like to have as President—line-item veto. Let a President be able to veto out that item that was tied into a necessary bill in order to get it passed because they knew they couldn't get it passed on its own.

As Governor of California, I vetoed 943 of those and was never overridden once. Even though the budget had to be passed by a two-thirds majority, the same as is required for overriding a veto, they would not stand up and vote for that single item out there exposed for what it was in order to override the veto. So, that is a tool we must have.

Some of the things in the tax that you're talking about—deduction of interest on home mortgages and all—I have told them I want them to look in the area of simplification at everything, but study everything that can be done. Now, would there be any harm if—and this is theoretical; I don't know anything that so far has—that we're engaged in in the study—but if we could have a tax simplification that was so constructed that you could then actually reduce the individual's rates because of the simplification of the tax structure, and if that included such things as eliminating some things that today are deductibles, would that not resolve the problem, if we had an entirely different type of tax structure with a quite low rate?

Mr. Carlson. I would argue, Mr. President, that investment can be found in the home as well as in the commercial part of the economy. If we have deductibility elsewhere as to investments, we certainly ought to have it for homeownership. I would argue that that should be excluded.

The President. I won't argue with you on that. I believe very strongly in what you say. But I was just hypothesizing that suppose they came in with some entirely different form of taxation aimed at something different than income as a method of taxing. I don't know, but I've told them I want them to look at everything there is in that structure.

Now—I'm trying to answer three questions here, and I forget where I started. [*Laughter*] Yours was on the deficit.

Ms. Kirk. Right.

The President. Yes, we have to. I remember being told more than 20 years ago when I was out on the mashed-potato circuit and didn't think I'd be doing anything like this, but speaking about things and criticizing government. And I remember then, the defense of the deficit spending was that, well, the national debt didn't mean anything because we owed it to ourselves.

Well, today, when you stop to think about it—that the interest on the national debt is more than the total Federal budget of some 20 years ago—there's no way to explain how far we've gone and what we're doing there. And the answer has to be that I would think that today, we are sophisticated enough in our knowledge of business and finance to know what is the optimum point, the percentage level that government can take from the private sector before government becomes a roadblock or a drag on the economy, which it is now. And once you've established that point, then we should see that government never spends above that percentage of the gross national product. So, if there's a second term, that's what I'm going to be doing in the second term.

Mr. Wood. Several of the members of the panel were hoping to get a chance to ask you a question. I think we'll have time for one more if it's okay with you.

The President. I'll try to make the answers shorter. [*Laughter*]

Mr. Wood. And if it's okay with Lloyd Bowles, I'm going to skip your question, because it was, as I remember, interest rate related, and I think the President has answered that. And I was going to go to Joe Howell, who has a question about—well, you ask it.

Mr. Howell. Mr. President, I think everyone has agreed that the housing industry lives and dies by interest rates, and my question is, with the progress that has been made in lowering the inflation rate, why do we still have these historically high spreads between the interest rate and the inflation rate?

The President. I have to say that I'm convinced that it is nothing but a pessimism out there. We've had—well, this was the eighth recession since World War II, and in seven of those, we always resorted to the quick fix, artificial stimulant of the money supply. And what happened was, yes, you cured that present recession, and some, people—the unemployment rate went down; but you wound up about 2 or 3 years later with another recession, and this time you started with inflation higher than it had been. And I think that they just—and particularly with the opposition that we're having in getting, say, this downpayment, if we get this, I think this could be a great measure of reassurance out there. They just are not convinced yet that government is going to be serious about keeping inflation down.

And if I could cite myself as an example, again, I remember once back in those motion picture days, I knew that some day they'd come to an end, and I bought a retirement policy. And I wanted to think that I could retire and continue to live the same way I was living. So, I bought the policy on that basis. Well, the policy finally came to the payment date, retirement age, and the policy by that time wouldn't pay the prop-

erty tax on the house that we lived in. So, I think that inflation is the biggest single enemy of it all.

There is no way that you can have a sound economy where a person is expected to invest or put money away and know that at the payoff time the dollar's only going to be worth half what it was or less when it comes time to pay out. So, the people with the money to loan, they're going to have to have more of a guarantee that it isn't going to happen again.

Mr. Wood. Well, thank you very much, Mr. President, for being with us today. It's been a terrific thrill for all of us in the industry and those of us at Builder magazine, who sponsored the roundtable. And I don't know if you had any final remarks you wanted to make.

The President. Well, no more than just to thank you all for having me here. And I'm sorry that I did take so long on some of those answers. I would have liked to have answered the others. Maybe we'll have a chance walking out or something to hear some of them. But I am more confident than ever—I'm an optimist generally and normally—but I'm more confident than ever, after what I've seen this morning and after meeting with all of you, that we're going to continue.

And I will quote to you a very renowned economist who wrote to me the other day and castigated me for continuing to call this a recovery. He said, "We have passed the recovery stage; we are now in legitimate expansion." [*Laughter*]

Mr. Wood. Thank you, Mr. President.

The President. All right.

Note: The panel discussion began at 10:15 a.m. in the ballroom of the Arlington Hilton Hotel. Michael Wood, publisher of Builder magazine, was the moderator.

Following his appearance at the panel, the President returned to Washington, DC.

Appointment of Charles D. Hobbs as Deputy Assistant to the President for Policy Development
April 12, 1984

The President today announced his appointment of Charles D. Hobbs to be Deputy Assistant to the President for Policy Development. He assumed his duties on April 1, 1984.

Mr. Hobbs, for the past 10 years, has been president and principal consultant of Charles D. Hobbs, Inc., a California-based public policy and management consulting firm. His company has served a wide variety of Federal, State, and local government agencies in the development of public service programs and management plans.

Mr. Hobbs was chief deputy director of social welfare in California from 1970 to 1972 and also served on then-Governor Reagan's Tax Limitation and Local Govern-ment Task Forces in 1973 and 1974. He was delegate to the Economic Summit Conference on Inflation in 1975. He designed and managed the development of computer-based information and command/control systems from 1958 to 1970.

Mr. Hobbs received his B.S. degree, with honors in English, from Northwestern University in 1955, and was a Woodrow Wilson Fellow at UCLA in 1958 and 1959. He was the distinguished military graduate at Northwestern in 1955 and served 3 years as an officer in the United States Air Force. He was born on September 2, 1933, in Kansas City, MO. He is married to Joan Resag Hobbs. They have three sons: Charles, Jonathan, and Jeremy.

Remarks of the President and Prime Minister Prem Tinsulanonda of Thailand Following the Signing of a United States-Thailand Science and Technology Agreement
April 13, 1984

The President. Ladies and gentlemen, our Foreign Ministers are here to sign the science and technology agreement between Thailand and the United States. And the agreement represents another new area of cooperation and furthers the close ties that historically marked our relationship.

And with me now is Prime Minister Prem, who is visiting here for the second time, and we're very pleased to have him here.

Mr. Prime Minister.

The Prime Minister. Thank you. Mr. President, Mr. Secretary, distinguished guests, the agreement on cooperation in science and technology just concluded constitutes a new dimension in the long established relationship and cooperation between our two nations.

As the United States is the world leader in science and technology, Thailand stands to benefit significantly from the transfer of your ingenuity. As a strong and unwavering friend and ally of the United States in Southeast Asia. Thailand—[*inaudible*]—has prosperity generated by the scientific and technological cooperation with the United States—will complement American long-term interest in the region.

We look forward to an active cooperation in the field of science and technology, and this agreement is an important first step in that direction.

Note: The President spoke at 12:15 p.m. in the Rose Garden at the White House. The agreement was signed for the United States by Secretary of State George P. Shultz and for Thailand by Siddhi Savetsila, Minister of Foreign Affairs.

Prior to the ceremony, the President and

the Prime Minister met in the Oval Office. Following the ceremony, they went to the *State Dining Room for a working luncheon with U.S. and Thai officials.*

Nomination of Victor M. Rivera To Be an Assistant Administrator of the Agency for International Development
April 13, 1984

The President today announced his intention to nominate Victor M. Rivera to be an Assistant Administrator of the Agency for International Development (Latin America and the Caribbean), United States International Development Cooperation Agency. He would succeed Otto J. Reich.

Since 1981 Mr. Rivera has been serving as Director of the Minority Business Development Administration. Previously, he was Senior Advocate, Office of Chief Council for Advocacy, Small Business Administration, in 1977–1981, Regional Director (1975–1977), and District Director (1973–1975) for the Small Business Administration; and deputy finance administrator for the New York City Finance Administration in 1968–1973. He was with the Puerto Rico Economic Development Administration in 1960–1968, serving as director of the Office of Economic Research (1960–1967) and director of the Office of Tourism Development (1967–1968).

He graduated from New York University (B.A., 1959). He is married, has three children, and resides in Vienna, VA. He was born July 27, 1937, in Brooklyn, NY.

Remarks of the President and Prime Minister Prem Tinsulanonda of Thailand Following Their Meeting
April 13, 1984

The President. I'm delighted to have this opportunity to exchange views with Prime Minister Prem and to discuss with him events in Southeast Asia and in other parts of the world.

This is the Prime Minister's second visit with me, and on both occasions he's provided valuable counsel. And I am particularly happy to renew our personal relationship, because it mirrors the deep friendship between the Thai and American people. Thailand and the United States have a history of friendship and cooperation going back to 1833, when we signed the Treaty of Amity and Commerce.

Today we took our relationship one step further with the signing of a science and technology agreement. The 150 years of our relations have seen many changes, yet throughout this time the fundamental determination of that and American people to—of Thai, I should say, and American people to live their lives in freedom is unchanged.

Whatever our differences of climate or culture, in our love of liberty we're the same. This is the unchanging basis of our friendship. The economic vitality found in Thailand is something else with which Americans identify. American investors and traders are proud of the part that they're able to play in Thailand's growth. Working together, Americans and Thais are building a better quality of life for both our peoples.

Prime Minister Prem will return to his country confident in our friendship and assured that America's commitments remain sound and solid. As treaty allies of the Manila Pact, the United States fully appreciates the situation in Southeast Asia and Thailand's key role in ASEAN's effort to promote peace and stability in that vital area.

In response to Thailand's immediate security requirements, I'm happy to announce that the United States will make available immediately a sizable number of M–48 tanks. We'll also request the Congress to extend the repayment terms of our security assistance to Thailand. High-level defense consultations between our countries will continue. We'll discuss Thailand's overall defense needs, including its requirement for advanced aircraft, something we fully support. The administration will confer with the Congress on these defense matters, as appropriate.

Thailand today will be celebrating, by the old lunar calendar, the beginning of the new year. So, may I wish you, Mr. Prime Minister, and all the people of Thailand, a very fine *Songkran* holiday and, for all the Thai people, prosperity, health, and peace. We're pleased to have had you as our guest, again.

The Prime Minister. Thank you.

The President. Thank you.

The Prime Minister. I was most pleased and honored to be invited to meet with President Reagan for the second time since my last visit 3 years ago. My discussion with the President on issues of mutual concern and interest were most constructive and fruitful. Together we have decided on ways and means to strengthen our bilateral ties and to enhance our cooperation.

The relationship between our two countries spans over one century-and-a-half. Over the years this relationship has increased in strength and expanded in dimension. Under the leadership of President Reagan, the United States has returned to the traditional values and demonstrated a determination in the pursuit of real peace. On our part, Thailand and the other ASEAN partners have distinguished themselves as a moderating influence on the international economic and political issues. Our collective efforts have served to enhance security in Southeast Asia, which is vital to the stability and prosperity of the East-Asian Pacific region and beyond.

Later on today I will meet members of the U.S. business community to explore opportunities for expanding trade and business ties for mutual benefits. Thailand shares with you the faith in the dynamism of economic relationships between countries in the Pacific community, the dynamism which has become more evident and which represents great economic potential for further development.

The recovery of your economy, which is undoubtedly the largest single economy of the world, is most welcome. For this to be longlasting, the recovery must generate prosperity of the wider front, particularly in the free-market economies such as that of Thailand.

Finally, on behalf of the Thai nation, I would like to express our heartfelt gratitude for the administration's full support to the modernization of Thailand's defense. This gesture reaffirms the United States commitment to Thailand's security in recognition of our role in strengthening the fabric of peace in the area, which the United States considers to be vital to her interests.

Note: The President spoke at 1:26 p.m. in the East Room at the White House.

Proclamation 5177—National Hearing Impaired Awareness Week, 1984
April 13, 1984

By the President of the United States of America

A Proclamation

More than fifteen million Americans of all ages experience some degree and form of hearing impairment. These hearing-impaired Americans continue to share in the life of the Nation, contribute to family life and the home, and provide civic support to their communities. They have steadfastly striven not only to overcome their handicaps, but also to assist other members of our society. In so doing, the deaf and hearing impaired have made significant contributions to society, science, the arts and industry in virtually every field.

Research has shown us that hearing loss can sometimes be alleviated, corrected, or best of all, prevented. Scientific investigators supported by the Federal government's National Institute of Neurological and Communicative Disorders and Stroke and by professional societies and voluntary health organizations are learning more about how the auditory system works, and what can go wrong and why. Innovative programs in research, education, and prevention have long been conducted and supported by many voluntary agencies working on behalf of the hearing impaired. I commend their dedication to this important service.

The Congress, by House Joint Resolution 407, has designated the week beginning April 8, 1984, as "National Hearing Impaired Awarenesss Week," and has authorized and requested the President to issue a proclamation in observance of that week.

Now, Therefore, I, Ronald Reagan, President of the United States of America, do hereby proclaim the week beginning April 8, 1984, as National Hearing Impaired Awareness Week. I call upon the people of the United States to observe this week with appropriate activities in their homes, offices, schools, and communities, and I urge all Americans to reflect upon the important contributions made by the hearing-impaired citizens to the progress and well-being of our country.

In Witness Whereof, I have hereunto set my hand this 13th day of April, in the year of our Lord nineteen hundred and eighty-four, and of the Independence of the United States of America the two hundred and eighth.

RONALD REAGAN

[*Filed with the Office of the Federal Register, 4:05 p.m., April 13, 1984*]

Proclamation 5178—Asian/Pacific American Heritage Week, 1984
April 13, 1984

By the President of the United States of America

A Proclamation

The great strength of America lies in the determination and caring hearts of our people. Reflecting diverse backgrounds and the experiences of all our citizens, this Nation is a hearty amalgam of individuals united in their commitment to freedom.

Americans who have come from Asian and Pacific countries have added a special quality to the United States. They have made outstanding contributions to our Nation's progress in a wide range of fields, including science, the arts, medicine, law, literature, agriculture, industry and commerce, and government. Bringing with them the strong and varied traditions and heritages of their Asian and Pacific homelands, they have greatly enriched America's culture and institutions.

This Nation owes a debt of gratitude to the Asian and Pacific immigrants. Their desire for liberty strengthens and underscores our own.

As we celebrate the accomplishments of Asian and Pacific Americans, we dedicate ourselves to overcoming the legacy of past discrimination, knowing that the struggle for full participation and equal opportunity goes on. We are grateful to Asian and Pacific Americans for their enduring belief in the inalienable rights to life, liberty, and the pursuit of happiness.

Now, Therefore, I, Ronald Reagan, President of the United States of America, do hereby proclaim the week beginning May 5, 1984, as Asian/Pacific American Heritage Week and call upon all the people of the United States to observe this week with appropriate ceremonies and activities.

In Witness Whereof, I have hereunto set my hand this 13th day of April, in the year of our Lord nineteen hundred and eighty-four, and of the Independence of the United States of America the two hundred and eighth.

RONALD REAGAN

[*Filed with the Office of the Federal Register, 4:06 p.m., April 13, 1984*]

Proclamation 5179—National Maritime Day, 1984
April 13, 1984

By the President of the United States of America

A Proclamation

On March 20, 1984, I signed into law the Shipping Act of 1984. This important legislation removed several burdensome and unnecessary Government regulations restricting both United States-flag and foreign-flag ocean common carriers operating in the foreign commerce of the United States. This is the most significant ocean regulatory legislation since the enactment of the Shipping Act in 1916.

The United States is the greatest trading nation in the world, and this landmark legislation will provide for more flexible and responsive ocean transportation services, including intermodal service, that will benefit both our exporters and importers. United States flag-ocean carriers will benefit by being assured evenhanded regulatory treatment with foreign competitors. The Shipping Act of 1984 represents but one part of my Administration's commitment to foster and maintain the United States-flag merchant marine required by this great Nation for our national security and economic benefit.

In recognition of the importance of the American merchant marine, the Congress, by joint resolution of May 20, 1933, designated May 22 as National Maritime Day and requested the President to issue annually a proclamation calling for its appropriate observance. This date was chosen to commemorate the day in 1819 when the SS SAVANNAH departed Savannah, Georgia, on the first transatlantic steamship voyage.

Now, Therefore, I, Ronald Reagan, President of the United States of America, do hereby proclaim May 22, 1984, as National Maritime Day, and I urge the people of the United States to observe this day by displaying the flag of the United States at their homes and other suitable places, and I request that all ships sailing under the American flag dress ship on that day.

In Witness Whereof, I have hereunto set my hand this 13th day of April, in the year of our Lord nineteen hundred and eighty-four, and of the Independence of the United States of America the two hundred and eighth.

RONALD REAGAN

[*Filed with the Office of the Federal Register, 4:07 p.m., April 13, 1984*]

Proclamation 5180—Prayer for Peace, Memorial Day, May 28, 1984
April 13, 1984

By the President of the United States of America

A Proclamation

In the course of America's existence, our citizens too often have been called upon to make the ultimate sacrifice for the cause of peace, freedom, and justice. From Bunker Hill to Beirut, these brave men and women have passed into the hands of our Creator so that we may enjoy the fruits of liberty. As Americans gather this Memorial Day to pay homage to their sacred memory and selfless commitment, we can offer no higher praise than that these patriots defended the high ideals bestowed upon this Nation by our Founding Fathers.

Today, as we commend their deeds, we also bear a heavy burden of responsibility to ensure that their sacrifice was not in vain by never wavering in our dedication and determination to maintain the peace, to safeguard human rights, and to protect the economic well-being of our Nation for future generations.

In honor and recognition of those Americans to whom we pay tribute today, the Congress, by joint resolution of May 11, 1950 (64 Stat. 158), has requested the President to issue a proclamation calling upon the people of the United States to observe each Memorial Day as a day of prayer for permanent peace and designating a period on that day when the people of the United States might unite in prayer.

Now, Therefore, I, Ronald Reagan, President of the United States of America, do hereby designate Memorial Day, May 28, 1984, as a day of prayer for permanent peace, and I designate the hour beginning in each locality at 11 o'clock in the morning of that day as a time to unite in prayer. I urge the press, radio, television, and all other information media to cooperate in this observance.

I also request the Governors of the United States and the Commonwealth of Puerto Rico and the appropriate officials of all units of government to direct that the flag be flown at half-staff during this Memorial Day on all buildings, grounds, and naval vessels throughout the United States and in all areas under its jurisdiction and control, and I request the people of the United States to display the flag at half-staff from their homes for the customary forenoon period.

In Witness Whereof, I have hereunto set my hand this 13th day of April, in the year of our Lord nineteen hundred and eighty-four, and of the Independence of the United States of America the two hundred and eighth.

RONALD REAGAN

[*Filed with the Office of the Federal Register, 4:08 p.m., April 13, 1984*]

Executive Order 12473—Manual for Courts-Martial, United States, 1984
April 13, 1984

By virtue of the authority vested in me as President by the Constitution of the United States and by Chapter 47 of Title 10 of the United States Code (Uniform Code of Military Justice), I hereby prescribe the following Manual for Courts-Martial to be designated as "Manual for Courts-Martial, United States, 1984."

This Manual shall take effect on August 1, 1984, with respect to all court-martial processes taken on and after that date: *Provided,* That nothing contained in this Manual shall be construed to invalidate any restraint, investigation, referral of charges, designation or detail of a military judge or counsel, trial in which arraignment had been had, or other action begun prior to that date, and any such restraint, investigation, trial, or other action may be completed in accordance with applicable laws, Executive orders, and regulations in the same manner and with the same effect as if this Manual had not been prescribed; *Provided further,* That Rules for Courts-Martial 908, 1103(j), 1105–1107, 1110–1114, 1201, and 1203 shall not apply to any case in which the findings and sentence were adjudged by a court-martial before August 1, 1984, and the post-trial and appellate review of such cases shall be completed in accordance with applicable laws, Executive orders, and regulations in the same manner and with the same effect as if this Manual had not been prescribed; *Provided further,* That nothing contained in this Manual shall be construed to make punishable any act done or omitted prior to August 1, 1984, which was not punishable when done or omitted; *Provided further,* That nothing in part IV of this Manual shall be construed to invalidate the prosecution of any offense committed before the effective date of this Manual; *Provided further,* That the maximum punishment for an offense committed prior to August 1, 1984, shall not exceed the applicable limit in effect at the time of the commission of such offense; *Provided further,* That for offenses committed prior to August 1, 1984, for which a sentence is adjudged on or after August 1, 1984, if the maximum punishment authorized in this Manual is less than

that previously authorized, the lesser maximum authorized punishment shall apply; *And provided further,* That Part V of this Manual shall not apply to nonjudicial punishment proceedings which were initiated before August 1, 1984, and nonjudicial punishment proceedings in such cases shall be completed in accordance with applicable laws, Executive orders, and regulations in the same manner and with the same effect as if this Manual had not been prescribed.

The Manual for Courts-Martial, 1969, United States (Revised edition), prescribed by Executive Order No. 11476, as amended by Executive Order Nos. 11835, 12018, 12198, 12233, 12306, 12340, 12383, and 12460 is hereby rescinded, effective August 1, 1984.

The Secretary of Defense shall cause this Manual to be revised annually and shall recommend to the President any appropriate amendments.

The Secretary of Defense, on behalf of the President, shall transmit a copy of this Order to the Congress of the United States in accord with Section 836 of Title 10 of the United States Code.

RONALD REAGAN

The White House,
April 13, 1984.

[Filed with the Office of the Federal Register, 1:53 p.m., April 16, 1984]

Note: The Manual for Courts-Martial, United States, 1984, is printed in the Federal Register *of April 23, 1984.*

Message to the Senate Transmitting the United States-Thailand Treaty on Extradition
April 13, 1984

To the Senate of the United States:

With a view to receiving the advice and consent of the Senate to ratification, I transmit herewith the Treaty on Extradition between the United States of America and Thailand, signed at Washington on December 14, 1983.

I transmit also, for the information of the Senate, the report of the Department of State with respect to the Treaty.

The Treaty will facilitate United States efforts to prosecute narcotics conspiracies by expressly providing that conspiracies and attempts to commit extraditable offenses constitute extraditable offenses.

The Treaty follows generally the form and content of extradition treaties recently concluded by this Government.

Upon entry into force, it will terminate and supersede the existing Extradition Treaty between the United States and Thailand.

This Treaty will make a significant contri-

bution to international cooperation in law enforcement. I recommend that the Senate give early and favorable consideration to the Treaty and give its advice and consent to ratification.

RONALD REAGAN

The White House,
April 13, 1984.

Nomination of Two Members of the National Advisory Council on Women's Educational Programs
April 13, 1984

The President today announced his intention to nominate the following individuals to be members of the National Advisory Council on Women's Educational Programs for terms expiring May 8, 1986:

Naomi Brummond serves on the State board of directors of the Nebraska Farm Bureau Federation. She has been actively involved with the Nebraska Farm Bureau since 1978, serving as chairman of the State Affairs Conference and of the Safemark Study Committee. She has been on the board of directors of the County

Farm Bureau since 1974. She is married, has three children, and resides in Rosalie, NE. She was born May 9, 1933, in Marquez, TX. She would succeed Mary Jo Arndt.

Peter Douglas Keisler is a student at Yale Law School in New Haven, CT. He received his bachelor of arts degree from Yale College in 1981. He served as executive vice president of the Leadership Institute in 1981–1982. He was born on October 13, 1960, in Hempstead, NY, and now resides in New Haven, CT. He would succeed Virginia Gillham Tinsley.

Nomination of Six Members of the National Council on the Humanities
April 13, 1984

The President today announced his intention to nominate the following individuals to be members of the National Council on the Humanities, National Foundation on the Humanities, for terms expiring January 26, 1990:

William Barclay Allen, of Claremont, CA, is associate professor of government at Harvey Mudd College in Claremont, CA. He is married and has two children. He was born March 18, 1944, in Fernandina Beach, FL. He would succeed Charles V. Hamilton.

Mary Josephine Conrad Cresimore, of Raleigh, NC, was founding chairman of the City of Raleigh Arts Commission and served as president of the Raleigh Chamber Music Guild (1983–

1984). She was a founding member of the Friends of the John F. Kennedy Center for the Performing Arts. She is married and has three children. She was born February 11, 1936, in Chicago, IL. She would succeed Louis J. Hector.

Leon Richard Kass, of Chicago, IL, is professor of the liberal arts of human biology, the College of the Committee on Social Thought, the University of Chicago. He is married and has two children. He was born February 12, 1939, in Chicago. He would succeed M. Carl Holman.

James Vincent Schall, of Washington, DC, is associate professor of the department of government at Georgetown University. He was ordained a Roman Catholic priest in 1963. He was born January 20, 1928, in Pocahontas, IA.

Father Schall would succeed Leon Stein.

Kathleen S. Kilpatrick, is president of the American Literary Society and publisher of the Yale Literary Magazine in New Haven, CT. She is married and resides in New Haven. She was born May 12, 1952, in Portsmouth, VA. She would succeed Harriet Morse Zimmerman.

Helen Marie Taylor, of Richmond, VA, has been active in the performing arts as a producer, director, actress, teacher, and lecturer. She is also an architectural and planning consultant. She is married and has four sons. She was born November 17, 1923, in Waco, TX. She would succeed Mary Beth Norton.

Proclamation 5181—Education Day, U.S.A., 1984
April 13, 1984

By the President of the United States of America

A Proclamation

Throughout our history, Americans have recognized that education is vital to our Nation's future. Our educational system has always done far more than simply train people for a given job or profession; it has equipped generation upon generation of young men and women for lives of responsible citizenship, by helping to teach them the basic ethical values and principles that are both our heritage as a free people and the foundation of civilized life.

As the beneficiaries of that heritage, we bear a corresponding responsibility to ensure that the moral values on which freedom rests continue to be transmitted to each successive generation of Americans. If our educational efforts are rooted in first principles—that human life is sacred; that men and women should be treated as individuals, with certain fundamental rights and responsibilities; that respect for law is crucial to the survival of freedom—then our children and our children's children will share, as we have, in the blessings of liberty.

The Lubavitch movement, headed by Rabbi Menachem Mendel Schneerson, has provided people of all faiths a shining example of the true value of education. The Lubavitcher Rebbe's work is a living reminder that knowledge is worthy only when accompanied by moral and spiritual wisdom and understanding. In fostering and promoting a tradition of ethical values that can trace its roots to the Seven Noahide Laws, which have often been cited as universal norms of ethical conduct and a guarantee of fundamental human rights, the Lubavitch movement and its greatly respected leader have shown Americans of every faith that true education involves not simply what one knows, but how one lives.

In recognition of Rabbi Schneerson's contributions and in honor of his 82nd birthday on the 11th day of the Jewish month Nisan, which falls this year on April 13, the Congress, by House Joint Resolution 520, has designated April 13, 1984, as "Education Day, U.S.A.," and has authorized and requested the President to issue an appropriate proclamation.

Now, Therefore, I, Ronald Reagan, President of the United States of America, do hereby proclaim April 13, 1984, as Education Day, U.S.A., and I call upon the people of the United States, and in particular our teachers and other educational leaders, to observe that day with appropriate ceremonies and activities.

In Witness Whereof, I have hereunto set my hand this 13th day of April, in the year of our Lord nineteen hundred and eighty-four and of the Independence of the United States of America the two hundred and eighth.

RONALD REAGAN

[*Filed with the Office of the Federal Register, 10:57 a.m., April 16, 1984*]

Proclamation 5182—Crime Victims Week, 1984
April 13, 1984

By the President of the United States of America

A Proclamation

As citizens of this free Nation, we support a system of justice which protects the rights of the accused by ensuring them due process of law, a just and fair guarantee inscribed into our Constitution. Yet, through ignorance and insensitivity, our criminal justice system has often failed to provide the victims of crime the compassionate treatment they deserve. These persons too often have had to endure alone the physical and emotional pain that crime inflicts upon its victims. Victims of crime have had their lives threatened and disrupted, and their families have been subjected to unnecessary strains. Victims sometimes fear the loss of their livelihood, health, or life, and, most importantly, their cries for elementary justice too frequently go unheard.

Among the essential reasons governments are instituted among peoples is to establish a system of justice for the protection of their citizens. Justice is a primary goal and responsibility of government. As a country founded with the noble purpose of protecting and defending its people, our society cannot ignore the pleas of crime victims. Guided by recommendations of the President's Task Force on Victims of Crime, my Administration is working to implement much-needed changes throughout our criminal justice system to respond to the concerns of crime victims.

The national movement seeking more compassionate treatment for the victims of crime is led in large part by the victims themselves. I commend these courageous men and women who have overcome their pain and despair and are working to help ease the trauma of other victims. But it is crucial to remember that no segment of our society should refuse to recognize its responsibility to help in this most worthy endeavor. We must all strive to preserve the principles of justice on which our free society depends.

Now, Therefore, I, Ronald Reagan, President of the United States of America, do hereby proclaim the week beginning April 15, 1984, as Crime Victims Week. I urge officials at all levels of government to pay special attention to the burdens crime victims face. I ask that all Americans listen and respond to the needs of crime victims, who urgently require and deserve our support.

In Witness Whereof, I have hereunto set my hand this 13th day of April, in the year of our Lord nineteen hundred and eighty-four, and of the Independence of the United States of America the two hundred and eighth.

RONALD REAGAN

[*Filed with the Office of the Federal Register, 10:58 a.m., April 16, 1984*]

Note: The President signed the proclamation at a ceremony in the Oval Office at the White House.

Statement by Principal Deputy Press Secretary Speakes on United States Aid to El Salvador
April 13, 1984

On February 17 of this year, the President submitted a plan to the Congress based on the work of the Bipartisan Commission on Central America—the "Scoop Jackson plan"—to advance democracy, peace, and development in Central America. It included a request for $178 million in supplemental military aid for El Salvador in FY 1984.

Early last month, the President asked that

about half of that money ($93 million) be appropriated immediately to meet urgent security requirements until the Congress could act on the whole plan in the summer.

Two weeks ago, to help get things moving, the President authorized reducing our request to $62 million. This lower sum would have met only minimal medical, supply, and ammunition requirements. Our proposal passed the Senate with broad bipartisan support. Unfortunately, the two Houses were unable to meet and complete action before leaving for the 2-week Easter recess.

Meanwhile, in El Salvador a tragic irony is at hand. At the very moment when the people have turned out in massive numbers to register dramatically their hopes and beliefs in democracy, their armed forces are running out of means to defend against Marxist violence. We must not let that happen.

For the past 10 days, officials from State, Defense, and the White House have worked with bipartisan leaders of both Houses to secure the necessary funding. We would have preferred that the Congress complete its processes before the congressional recess. Congress will, of course, have that opportunity upon its return. In the interim, in order to prevent unnecessary loss of life and to assure security required for the run-off election, the President is today exercising authorities provided in law to deliver the essential materials to El Salvador.

We look forward to continuing discussions with the Congress on this matter when the Congress returns.

Remarks at the Baptist Fundamentalism Annual Convention
April 13, 1984

Reverend Falwell, ladies and gentlemen, thank you very much, for there are no words to describe a welcome such as you've given me here. It's a real pleasure to be with so many who firmly believe that the answers to the world's problems can be found in the Word of God.

I'm only sorry I can't spend the entire evening with you, but I'm expected across town. [*Laughter*] But tonight, believe me, I came here with some trepidation, and your warm welcome didn't exactly make me feel any easier, because I'm going to do something that I haven't done before. I'm not going to talk to you about some of the things we've talked about before and some of the things that we've tried to accomplish and that we haven't yet. With regard to that, I will only say let us all heed the words of an old Scotch ballad, "For those defeats that we've had so far, we are hurt; we are not slain. We'll lie us down and rest a bit, and then we'll fight again."

What I'm going to do—and I know you're not supposed to apologize any time you start speaking for what you're going to say—but I know that even you, whose call-ing it is to keep the rest of us, if possible, on the right path, in these days of cynicism, in these days when there are people that in the guise of separating church and state would go so far as to say we should not even have chaplains in the military serv-ice—I know that there are times when all of us wonder whether we're being effec-tive. And tonight, I'd like to share an ac-count that I received that shows how God works in our lives even in the darkest of hours.

This report concerns the marines in Beirut, brave men who believed that the goal we sought in that place was worthy of their best and gave their best. In the end, hatred centuries old made it impossible for Lebanon to achieve peace when we and so many others hoped it would. But while they were there, those young men of ours pre-vented widespread killing in Beirut, and they added luster, not tarnish to their motto, "Semper Fidelis."

I'm going to read to you another man's words. And they're words that, perhaps, answer what I said a moment ago about whether we sometimes were shaken in our faith and in our beliefs. On that October day when a terrorist truck bomb took the lives of 241 marines, soldiers, and sailors at the airport in Beirut, one of the first to reach the tragic scene was a chaplain, the chaplain of our 6th Fleet, Rabbi Arnold E. Resnicoff. And here is what he finally felt urged at the end of that day to put down in writing of the experiences of that day.

He said, "I along with Lieutenant Commander George 'Pooch' Pucciarelli, the Catholic chaplain attached to the marine unit, faced a scene almost too horrible to describe. Bodies and pieces of bodies were everywhere. Screams of those injured or trapped were barely audible at first, as our minds struggled to grapple with the reality before us—a massive four-story building, reduced to a pile of rubble; dust mixing with smoke and fire, obscuring our view of the little that was left.

"Because we'd thought that the sound of the explosion was still related to a single rocket or shell, most of the marines had run toward the foxholes and bunkers while we, the chaplains, had gone to the scene of the noise, just in case someone had been wounded. Now, as the news spread quickly throughout the camp—news of the magnitude of the tragedy, news of the need for others to run to the aid of those comrades who still might be alive, marines came from all directions. There was a sense of God's presence that day in the small miracles of life which we encountered in each body that, despite all odds, still had a breath within. But there was more of His presence, more to keep our faith alive, in the heroism and in the humanity of the men who responded to the cries for help. We saw marines risk their own lives again and again as they went into the smoke and the fire to try to pull someone out or as they worked to uncover friends, all the while knowing that further collapse of huge pieces of concrete, precariously perched like dominos, could easily crush the rescuers.

"There was humanity at its best that day and a reminder not to give up the hope and dreams of what the world could be in the tears that could still be shed by these men, regardless of how cynical they had pretended to be before, regardless of how much they might have seen before.

"Certain images will stay with me always," he writes. "I remember a marine who found a wad of money amidst the rubble. He held it at arm's length as if it were dirty and cried out for a match or a lighter so that it could be burned. No one that day wanted to profit from the suffering of catastrophe. Later the chaplains would put the word out that the money should be collected and given to us, for we were sure that a fund for widows and orphans would ultimately be established. But at that moment, I was hypnotized with the rest of the men and watched as the money was burned."

"Working with the wounded—sometimes comforting, simply letting them know help was on the way; sometimes trying to pull and carry those whose injuries appeared less dangerous in an immediate sense than the approaching fire or the smothering smoke—my *kippa* was lost. That is the little headgear that is worn by rabbis. The last I remember it, I'd used it to mop someone's brow. Father Pucciarelli, the Catholic chaplain, cut a circle out of his cap—a piece of camouflaged cloth which would become my temporary headcovering. Somehow he wanted those marines to know not just that we were chaplains, but that he was a Christian and that I was Jewish. Somehow we both wanted to shout the message in a land where people were killing each other—at least partially based on the differences in religion among them—that we, we Americans still believed that we could be proud of our particular religions and yet work side by side when the time came to help others, to comfort, and to ease pain.

"Father Pucciarelli and I worked that day as brothers. The words from the prophet Malachi kept recurring to me—words he'd uttered some 2,500 years ago as he had looked around at fighting and cruelty and pain. 'Have we not all one Father?' he had asked. 'Has not one God created us all?' It was painfully obvious, tragically obvious, that our world still could not show that we had learned to answer, yes. Still, I thought, perhaps some of us can keep the question alive. Some of us can cry out, as the marines did that day, that we believe the answer is yes.

"Before the bombing, Pooch—that's his name for the other chaplain with him—and I had been in a building perhaps a hundred yards away. There'd been one other chaplain, Lieutenant Danny Wheeler, a Protestant minister who'd spent the night in the building which was attacked. Pooch and I were so sure that he was dead that we had promised each other that when the day came to return to the States we would visit his wife together. Suddenly, Pooch noticed Danny's stole, what he used to call his Protestant tallith. Because it was far from the area Danny was supposed to have been in, there was cautious hope that perhaps he had been thrown clear, that perhaps he had survived. Later, Danny would tell the story of his terror. He was under the rubble, alive, not knowing what had happened and not knowing how badly he was hurt. Then he heard voices of the marines searching near his stole. And his cry for help was answered with digging, which lasted 4 hours before he was dragged out alive.

"Danny told me later that I treated him like a newborn baby when he came out; that I counted his fingers and toes, trying to see that he was whole. I didn't realize that I was so obvious, but the truth is that we couldn't believe that he was in one piece. I hugged him as they brought over a stretcher. I can still hear his first words. Wracked with pain, still unsure of his own condition, he asked how his clerk was. Like so many of the men we would save that day, he asked first about others.

"These men, the survivors, still had no idea of the extent of the damage. They still thought that perhaps they'd been in the one area of the building hit by a rocket or mortar. We would wait until later to sit with these men and tell them the truth, to share with them the magnitude of the tragedy. After the living were taken out there was much more work to be done. With the wounded, with those who had survived, there was the strange job of trying to ease a gnawing feeling of guilt that would slowly surface, guilt that they——"

[At this point, the President was interrupted by persons chanting, "Bread, not bombs!"]

Wouldn't it be nice if a little bit of that marine spirit would rub off, and they would listen about brotherly love? *[Applause]*

[The chanting continued.]

I was talking about the guilt that was felt by the men who were alive; the guilt that they had somehow let down their comrades by not dying with them. That is something that happens a great deal in combat.

"So, our job," he said, "was to tell them how every life saved was important to us; how their survival was important to our faith and our hope. They had to give thanks with us that they still had the gift and the responsibility of life which would go on——"

[The chanting continued.]

I've got more decibels at work for me than they have. *[Applause]*

[At this point, there was some commotion in the audience.]

I think they're leaving. *[Applause]* Well, back to the chaplain. *[Laughter]*

"With others, the marines who stayed behind to continue the job of digging—a terrible, horrifying job of collecting human parts for identification and for eventual burial—there was the job of comforting them as they mourned.

"Thankfully, the self-defense mechanism within us took over from time to time and we were able to work without reacting to each and every horror that we would encounter. But suddenly something would trigger our emotions, something would touch our humanity in a way impossible to avoid. For some it would be the finding of a friend's body, someone filled with life only days before. For others, it would be a scrap of paper or a simple belonging, a birthday card or a picture of someone's children which would remind them that this was no abstract body count of 240 military casualties. This was a tragedy of people where each was unique and each had a story. Each had a past and each had been cheated of a future. As the Mishnah puts it, 'Each was a world.' We were not digging up 240. We were digging up one plus one plus one.

"I have a personal memory of two things which brought to my mind images of life, images which haunt me still. One was a packet of three envelopes tied together with a rubber band. On top, under the band, was a note which read, 'To be mailed in case of death.' The other was a Red Cross message delivered the next morning. The American Red Cross is the agency used by many Navy families to communicate medical news from home. This message was a birth announcement. A baby had been born, and we were to deliver the good news. Only now, there was no father whom we could congratulate, no father to whom the news could be conveyed. That message stayed on the chaplains' desk for days. Somehow we couldn't throw it away, so it stayed on the desk and without mentioning it, we all seemed to avoid that desk.

"I stayed in Beirut for 4 more days before finally returning to Italy and to my family. During those days, as the work went on, a marine here or there would send a silent signal that he wanted me, that is, a chaplain, near. Sometimes it was to talk. Sometimes it was so that he could shrug his shoulders or lift his eyes in despair. Sometimes it was just to feel that I was near. For despite the struggles I might be feeling on a personal level, I was a chaplain and, therefore, a symbol that there was room for hope and for dreams, even at the worst of times.

"In our tradition, of course, when we visit the home of a mourner during Shiva, the first week following the death of a loved one, visitors follow a simple rule: If the mourner initiates the conversation, the visitor responds. Otherwise, you sit in silence, communicating concern through your very presence, even without words. Somehow I applied those rules during those days of digging. When a soldier or sailor said something, I responded. Otherwise, I stood by.

"During all of my visits to Beirut, I, along with the other chaplains, spent much time simply speaking with the men. Informal discussions, whether going on while crouched in a foxhole or strolling toward the tents set up for chow, were just as important as anything formal we might set up.

"I remember the first time I jumped in a foxhole, the first time the shells actually fell within the U.S. area. Looking around at the others in there with me, I made the remark that we probably had the only interfaith foxholes in Beirut. The Druze, the Muslims, Christians, all had theirs. The Jewish forces

in the Israeli Army had theirs. But we were together. I made the comment then that perhaps if the world had more interfaith foxholes, there might be less of a need for foxholes altogether.

"To understand the role of the chaplain—Jewish, Catholic, or Protestant—is to understand that we try to remind others, and perhaps ourselves as well, to cling to our humanity even in the worst of times. We bring with us the wisdom of men and women whose faith has kept alive their dreams in ages past. We bring with us the images of what the world could be, of what we ourselves might be, drawn from the visions of prophets and the promises of our holy books. We bring with us the truth that faith not only reminds us of the holy in heaven, but also of the holiness we can create here on Earth. It brings not only a message of what is divine, but also of what it means to be truly human.

"It's too easy to give in to despair in a world sometimes seemingly filled with cruelty and brutality. But we must remember not just the depths to which humans might sink, but also the heights to which they may aspire.

"That October day in Beirut saw men reach heroic heights—indeed, heights of physical endurance and courage to be sure, but heights of sacrifice, of compassion, of kindness, and of simple human decency as well, and, even if the admission might bring a blush to the cheeks of a few of the marines, heights of love.

"Long ago the rabbis offered one interpretation of the Biblical verse which tells us that we're created in the image of God. It does not refer to physical likeness, they explained, but to spiritual potential. We have within us the power to reflect as God's creatures the highest values of our Creator. As God is forgiving and merciful, so can we be; as He is caring and kind, so must we strive to be; as He is filled with love, so must we be.

"Because of the actions I witnessed during that hell in Beirut, I glimpsed at least a fleeting image of heaven, for in the hearts and hands of men who chose to act as brothers, I glimpsed God's hand as well. I did not stand alone to face a world forsaken by God. I felt I was part of one created with infinite care and wonderful, awesome potential.

"We live in a world where it's not hard to find cause for despair. The chaplain has the challenge to bring to those who often see terror at its worst, some reason for hope. We need to keep faith and to keep searching, even in the worst of times. Only then may we find strength enough to keep believing that the best of times might still be."

These were the words of Lieutenant Commander Resnicoff. I read them because

I just felt that all of us—and I know how much you do of this—let us strive to live up to the vision of faith that Chaplain Resnicoff saw that day, and let us never stop praying and working for peace.

Thank God, and thank you, and God bless you all.

Note: The President spoke at 6:50 p.m. at the District of Columbia Convention Center. He was introduced by the Rev. Jerry Falwell.

Remarks at the Annual Dinner of the White House Correspondents Association
April 13, 1984

Well—*[laughter]*—let's get one thing over with right away. I know all of you are uptight—asking yourselves, "Is he going to say anything about Fritz Mondale?" Well, Fritz'll do all right. If he doesn't get the nomination, he can always do perfume commercials—"Promise them anything but give them Arpege." *[Laughter]* I hope you'll forgive me—look, if some of these aren't funny. I asked Congress—they only gave me a third of all the ones I asked for. *[Laughter]*

But I hope you'll forgive me if I say that I'm filled with mixed emotions. I didn't know there were so many of you that couldn't get tickets to the Gridiron. *[Laughter]* And I appreciate your inviting me, but I do get a little nervous at a ceremony where the new president is replacing the old one. *[Laughter]*

Incidentally, I know that some of you—you talk a little bit, and you're critical about what you say is my "living in the past." But I think that's because a lot of you don't just realize how good the old days were. You know, then you looked forward to seeing Lana Turner in a sweater, not Dan Rather. *[Laughter]* But you all have given me some problems at home. Nancy's taken to watching the press conferences, and now every time I answer a question, she says, "I have a followup." *[Laughter]*

And I hear that Lesley Stahl has been asking if anything can be done to improve my answers. Yes, ask better questions. *[Laughter]* But do you know what it's like to have Chris Wallace and Bill Plante screaming questions in your ear when you're only about 10 feet from the helicopter with the motor roaring, and you realize they're asking, "What's wrong with your hearing, Mr. President?" *[Laughter]*

The other day the Washington Post ran a story heralding the return of spring, and I thought it was just another one of the reports on the political campaign. The headlines said, "The Sap Is Running Again." *[Laughter]*

You know, I think it's interesting—your new president's been out covering Gary Hart, and I understand that he's come up with yet another new idea about the future: Avoid Roger Mudd. *[Laughter]* Every time he thinks about that interview, Ted Kennedy's entire life flashes before his eyes. *[Laughter]* He got so rattled with some of Roger's questions that he gave his right age. *[Laughter]* And of course, about that name thing—the other day he said that the name, as far as he knows, goes as far back as the Revolutionary War. Well, I wouldn't know about that far back, but I do feel that I remember running across somebody by the name of Hartpence at San Juan Hill. *[Laughter]*

You guys and gals are always trying to pin me down as to which candidate worries me the most—Mondale, Hart, or Jackson. None of those. The guy that scares me is Governor Dick Lamm. [*Laughter*]

But I've been enjoying this, and yet sometimes I find myself thinking about what it would be like to have a steady job with real job security, like managing the New York Yankees for George Steinbrenner. [*Laughter*] You've got to be a baseball fan to get that one. [*Laughter*] They're in and out in 3 weeks.

If I could just switch for a minute, I'd like to say how great it was to see and hear the great talent of Rich Little. I was a little disappointed tonight, because you should really see him when he impersonates Gary Hart imitating Jack Kennedy. [*Laughter*] I'd like to have him come up with an imitation of a balanced budget. [*Laughter*]

But, you know, I just don't understand those guys that are bellyaching about the economy and trying to make out that everything is so bad. Inflation is down. Taxes are down. Unemployment is down. Productivity is up. So, what's the beef? [*Laughter*] And what's all that talk about a breakdown of White House communications? How come nobody told me? [*Laughter*] Well, I know this: I've laid down the law, though, to everyone there from now on about anything that happens, that no matter what time it is, wake me, even if it's in the middle of a Cabinet meeting. [*Laughter*]

Another thing that needs taking care of are the leaks. And we're really going to get ahold of those. Already I have ordered that we get rid of all those White House memo pads that have a notation on the bottom of each page that says, "Courtesy copy: Lou Cannon, Steve Weisman." [*Laughter*]

And by the way, why are you all so willing to carry the bad news about the administration? Now, you all did stories about the Vice President taking a dive at the bowling alley, but no one mentioned that he knocked down nine pins. [*Laughter*] And if he had slid just a little further, he'd have caught the 10th one with his head. [*Laughter*] "Bowling for Dollars" wants him to do a guestspot. [*Laughter*]

There's just one last thing, and that's those stories—and then I'm through—about Tip O'Neill and me and as if we're having some kind of a fight or feuding. That's nonsense. Tip is really crazy about me. Just this morning he sent me a whole case of Girl Scout cookies. [*Laughter*] And he put in the cutest note. He said, "They taste better if you eat them with your eyes shut." [*Laughter*]

Well, thank you, thank you all for inviting us to be here tonight. You know, the American people need you, and they need the truth. And your challenge is to report the truth about America and about those societies where the truth is despised. And if the truth is served, then America is served, and we'll all remain free.

And, again, it's been a wonderful evening, and thank you, and God bless you.

Note: The President spoke at 10:33 p.m. in the International Ballroom at the Washington Hilton Hotel.

Radio Address to the Nation on Central America
April 14, 1984

My fellow Americans:

Much has been made of late regarding our proper role in Central America and, in particular, toward Nicaragua. Unfortunately, much of the debate has ignored the most relevant facts. Central America has become the stage for a bold attempt by the Soviet Union, Cuba, and Nicaragua to install communism, by force, throughout this hemisphere.

The struggling democracies of Costa Rica, Honduras, and El Salvador are being threatened by a Soviet bloc and Cuban-supported Sandinista army and security force in Nicaragua that has grown from about 10,000 under the previous government to more than 100,000 in less than 5 years.

Last year alone, the Soviet bloc delivered over $100 million in military hardware. The Sandinistas have established a powerful force of artillery, multiple-rocket launchers, and tanks in an arsenal that exceeds that of all the other countries in the region put together.

More than 40 new military bases and support facilities have been constructed in Nicaragua—all with Soviet bloc and Cuban support—and an investment of over $300 million. In addition to money and guns, there are now more than 2,500 Cuban and Soviet military personnel in Nicaragua, another 5,000 so-called civilian advisers, as well as PLO, East bloc [East German], and Libyan assistance to the Sandinistas.

And that's not all. Our friends in the region must also face the export of subversion across their borders that undermines democratic development, polarizes institutions, and wrecks their economies. This terrorist violence has been felt by all of Nicaragua's neighbors, not just El Salvador. There have been bombings in peaceful Costa Rica and numerous attempts to penetrate Honduras—most recently last summer, when the Sandinistas infiltrated an entire guerrilla column [colony] which had been trained and equipped in Cuba and Nicaragua.

El Salvador, struggling to hold democratic elections and improve the conditions of its people, has been the main target of Nicaragua's covert aggression. Despite promises to stop, the Sandinistas still train and direct terrorists in El Salvador and provide weapons and ammunitions they use against the Salvadoran people. If it weren't for Nicaragua, El Salvador's problems would be manageable, and we could concentrate on economic and social improvements.

Much of the Sandinista terror has been aimed at the Nicaraguan people themselves. The Sandinistas who govern Nicaragua have savagely murdered, imprisoned, and driven from their homeland tens of thousands of Miskito, Rama, and Suma Indians. Religious persecution against Christians has increased, and the Jewish community has fled the country. The press is censored, and activities of labor and business are restricted.

The Sandinistas have announced elections for November, but don't hold your breath. Will new parties be permitted? Will they have full access to the press, TV, and radio? Will there be unbiased observers? Will every adult Nicaraguan be allowed to vote? Given their record of repression, we should not wonder that the opposition, denied other means of expression, has taken up arms.

We've maintained a consistent policy toward the Sandinista regime, hoping they can be brought back from the brink peacefully through negotiations. We're working through the Contadora process for a verifiable multilateral agreement, one that ensures the Sandinistas terminate their export of subversion, reduce the size of their military forces, implement their democratic commitments to the Organization of American States, and remove Soviet bloc and Cuban military personnel.

But the Sandinistas, uncomfortable with the scrutiny and concern of their neighbors, have gone shopping for a more sympathetic hearing. They took their case to the United Nations, and now to the International Court of Justice. This does little to advance a negotiated solution, but it makes sense if you're trying to evade the spotlight of responsibility.

What I've said today is not pleasant to hear, but it's important that you know Central America is vital to our interests and to our security. It not only contains the Panama Canal, it sits astride some of the most important sea lanes in the world—sea lanes in which a Soviet-Cuban naval force held combat maneuvers just this week.

The region also contains millions of people who want and deserve to be free. We cannot turn our backs on this crisis at our doorstep. Nearly 23 years ago, President Kennedy warned against the threat of

Communist penetration in our hemisphere. He said, "I want it clearly understood that this government will not hesitate in meeting its primary obligations which are to the security of our nation." We can do no less today.

I have, therefore, after consultation with the Congress, decided to use one of my legal authorities to provide money to help the Government of El Salvador defend itself.

Till next week, thanks for listening. God bless you.

Note: The President spoke at 12:06 p.m. from the Oval Office at the White House.

Statement by Principal Deputy Press Secretary Speakes on the Visit of President Salvador Jorge Blanco of the Dominican Republic
April 15, 1984

President Salvador Jorge Blanco of the Dominican Republic this week concluded a highly successful state visit to the United States.

In his discussions with President Reagan and senior American officials, President Jorge and his delegation showed once again that the Dominican Republic is an outstanding example of a people and leadership committed to democracy and to seeking solutions to social and economic problems through democratic means. President Reagan praised President Jorge for his skillful and courageous leadership in a time of serious economic difficulties and for his role in promoting solidarity among the Caribbean Basin nations.

President Reagan expressed his strong confidence in the economic potential of the Dominican Republic. Among the first countries to be designated for participation in the Caribbean Basin Initiative (CBI), the Dominican Republic's proximity to the U.S., its installed industrial capacity, and agricultural potential make it one of the countries most likely to benefit from the CBI's trade and investment incentives.

President Jorge's announcement, during the course of his visit, of the conclusion of an agreement with the International Monetary Fund (IMF) on measures to resolve the Dominican Republic's economic problems further bolsters confidence in his government's economic program and prospects for the island nation's economic recovery. The agreement is the second President Jorge has negotiated with the IMF since taking office in 1982.

Reflecting the U.S. Government's confidence in its democratic neighbor, President Reagan informed President Jorge that U.S. assistance to the Dominican Republic will be increased during this fiscal year which ends September 30, 1984. Furthermore, as a result of the meetings between the two Presidents, the U.S. Government and the Dominican Government have already begun discussions regarding additional cooperation during the current period of economic recovery.

President Reagan told his guest that the United States is proud to have the Dominican Republic as a close friend. Wishing the departing President every good fortune, President Reagan stressed his confidence in the future of the Dominican Republic and its enlightened and capable leadership.

Remarks to Reporters on the Vice President's Trip to Geneva, Switzerland, To Present the United States Initiative for a Ban on Chemical Weapons
April 16, 1984

The President. The Vice President leaves tonight on an extremely vital mission in the cause of peace, and it's a mission which all Americans and people around the world, I'm sure, support. Our goal is to eliminate from this Earth one of the most horrible and terrifying weapons known to mankind—chemical weapons.

To most people, when we say "chemical weapons," I'm sure they realize we're talking mainly about the various poison gases. And some of us who are old enough remember the horror in World War I when only one side had those weapons and first used them against allied forces that were unable to protect themselves against them or to retaliate.

On Wednesday, in the 40-nation Conference on Disarmament in Geneva, the Vice President will present an American initiative for a comprehensive worldwide ban on chemical weapons. And we know this won't be easy to achieve. We're not the first nation that attempted to control chemical weapons; there've been previous international efforts, including the Geneva Protocol of 1925. But such efforts dealt only with the actual use of such weapons, and they lacked effective compliance provisions.

History proves that success in arms control requires ensuring that agreements are lived up to. Chemical weapons provide a sad example, as I indicated, of past arms control failures. In recent years, both combatants and noncombatants have fallen victim to them in several areas of the world. We must move to ban these weapons now, but not only their use but also the development, production, and possession of them. And each country must have confidence that a new international agreement is being complied with.

That's what our treaty proposal is designed to do. We've worked long and hard to develop it, and we think it's a first-rate proposal. Of course, there will be hard negotiations ahead, but we're ready to work side by side with the representatives of the Soviet Union and other countries to achieve the goal of an effective ban on chemical weapons. And we hope that once they've seen the full treaty proposal, the Soviet Union and others will respond seriously and negotiate in good faith.

In seeing the Vice President off, I'd like to remind him of the motto of a school that he once attended. "The end depends on the beginning." Well, these words are especially right for this occasion. The goals and standards we set now will do much to determine whether we're successful in banning chemical weapons. And that's why I've asked the Vice President to undertake this mission. His journey to Geneva with this new American treaty proposal reflects the United States commitment to eliminate forever the threat of chemical warfare.

And, Vice President Bush, we wish you Godspeed.

The Vice President. Well, thank you, Mr. President.

Let me simply add, first I'm delighted that you and the Secretary of State and others are enthusiastic about this mission. Secondly, it's a return for me, a return to Geneva after the mission you sent me on 14 months ago to explain to this Conference on Disarmament your commitment on getting rid of these chemical weapons.

While in Geneva I'll have an opportunity to, in a broad context in front of that prestigious group, to explain your commitment to talks on these other arms forums as well—MBFR, START, INF, Confidence-building.

And I hope that this trip will result in more understanding, and, I think even more important than that, I hope it will result in a first major step towards your conviction of banning these weapons. I'll sure try.

The President. I know you will.

Q. Mr. President, the Soviets have called

this a propaganda trick, and——

Mr. Speakes. Lights, please.

Q. ——say that the proposal's unacceptable on its face——

Mr. Speakes. No questions. I'm sorry, no questions.

Q. ——do you think there's any hope for a serious negotiation?

The President. He's saying, "No questions."

Q. Well, you can overrule him. [*Laughter*]

The Vice President. We'll be discussing that at length in Geneva, incidentally, that question and any others like it. It's a very serious proposal, and a good proposal—a far-reaching proposal.

Mr. Speakes. Thank you. That's it.

Note: The President spoke at 10:04 a.m. in the Roosevelt Room at the White House.

Larry M. Speakes is the Principal Deputy Press Secretary to the President.

Nomination of Everett Pyatt To Be an Assistant Secretary of the Navy
April 16, 1984

The President today announced his intention to nominate Everett Pyatt to be an Assistant Secretary of the Navy (Shipbuilding and Logistics). He would succeed George A. Sawyer.

Since 1981 he has been serving as Principal Deputy Assistant Secretary of the Navy (Shipbuilding and Logistics). Prior to joining the Department of the Navy, Mr. Pyatt was deputy chief financial officer for project and business management at the Department of Energy. In 1977–1980 he served as the Principal Deputy Assistant Secretary of

the Navy (Logistics). Previously he was in the Office of the Secretary of Defense serving as the Director of Logistics, Planning, and Analysis (1976–1977); Director of Systems Acquisition and Planning (1973–1976); and in the Office of the Director of Defense Research and Engineering.

Mr. Pyatt graduated from Yale University (B.S., B.A., 1962) and the University of Pennsylvania, Wharton School, in 1977. He is married, has three children, and resides in Arlington, VA. He was born July 22, 1939, in Kansas City, MO.

Nomination of Virgil E. Brown To Be a Member of the Advisory Board of the Saint Lawrence Seaway Development Corporation
April 16, 1984

The President today announced his intention to nominate Virgil E. Brown to be a member of the Advisory Board of the Saint Lawrence Seaway Development Corporation, Department of Transportation. He would succeed Foster S. Brown.

Mr. Brown is president of the board of commissioners of Cuyahoga County, Ohio. He was first appointed Cuyahoga County commissioner in 1979 and was elected to a

4-year term in 1980. Prior to his appointment to the board of commissioners, he served 7 years as director of the Cuyahoga County Board of Elections. Mr. Brown founded the Virgil E. Brown Insurance Agency in 1967.

Mr. Brown is married, has two children, and resides in Cleveland, OH. He was born August 12, 1920, in Louisville, KY.

Nomination of Ann S. Peterson To Be a Member of the Board of Regents of the Uniformed Services University of the Health Sciences
April 16, 1984

The President today announced his intention to nominate Ann S. Peterson to be a member of the Board of Regents of the Uniformed Services University of the Health Sciences, Department of Defense, for a term expiring June 20, 1989. She would succeed Robert Higgins Ebert.

Dr. Peterson is associate director of the division of education for the American Medical Association in Chicago, IL. Previously she served as associate dean at Cornell University Medical College. She was associate dean of Columbia University College of Physicians and Surgeons in 1972–1979; assistant dean and associate dean at the University of Illinois College of Medicine in 1969–1972; and assistant director, clinical research unit, Georgetown University, in 1962–1969.

She graduated from Cornell University (A.B., 1950), Cornell University Medical College (M.D., 1954), and Massachusetts Institute of Technology, Sloan School of Management (M.S., 1980). She was born October 11, 1928, in Rhinebeck, NY, and now resides in Chicago, IL.

Nomination of James E. Burnett, Jr., To Be Chairman of the National Transportation Safety Board
April 16, 1984

The President today announced his intention to nominate James E. Burnett, Jr., to be Chairman of the National Transportation Safety Board. This is a reappointment.

The President also today designated Mr. Burnett as Vice Chairman of the Board, which will permit him to continue to act as Chairman pending confirmation of his reappointment.

Mr. Burnett has been serving as a member of the NTSB since December of 1981 and as Chairman since March of 1982. Prior to this, Mr. Burnett was a practicing attorney in Clinton, AR, from 1973 to 1981. He served as special associate justice of the Supreme Court of Arkansas in 1981, and was a municipal judge for Clinton, AR, Van Buren County, from 1975 to 1979. He was a juvenile judge, Van Buren County, from 1973 to 1981 and city judge, Damascus, AR, from 1979 to 1981. He was the youngest judge in the State of Arkansas when elected.

Mr. Burnett graduated from the University of Arkansas with a B.A. in 1970. He received his J.D. degree from the University of Arkansas Law School in 1973. He is a resident of Clinton, AR. He was born September 20, 1947.

Remarks at a Meeting With Chinese Students Studying in the United States
April 16, 1984

I just have a few minutes, and I know you've been in good hands here with the Vice President.

You represent 11,000 students from

China who are here in our country now. And I don't know how much history you've studied, but you know, this all began many years ago in the history of your country when there was a situation—similar to something we'd had in our own country—called the Boxer Rebellion. And countries from Europe and the United States and others, we went in with armed forces to rescue our people who were there from this strife and trouble.

And as I have read history, all the other countries then imposed reparation payments on China except the United States. And the United States said, "No, use our share as a scholarship fund to send your students here and ours to your country so we can get to know each other, and never again should there be any bitterness between our two peoples."

So, you are coming along here as a very definite part of what I think is a nice note in history that hasn't too often happened between great nations. And you're certainly welcome, but we'd like to see the 11,000 become a hundred thousand. And we're going to work toward that goal.

I'll probably be getting back to your country before you are. Why do I say, "getting *back* to it"? [*Laughter*] George has been there. I've never been there. It'll be my first trip, and I'm looking forward to it very much.

But I understand that the only way we can possibly have a chance to meet is that— it's so crowded in here—is if I step outside that door in the hall and then if each of you come out one at a time, and we'll all have our pictures taken out there and I get a chance to meet you individually.

But again, welcome. And I'll send them back in here.

Note: The President spoke at 3:27 p.m. in the Roosevelt Room at the White House. The 12 students, who are studying in the Washington, DC, area, were meeting with the Vice President and members of the National Security Council staff.

Interview With Chinese Journalists on the President's Trip to China
April 16, 1984

Q. It's nice to have a chance to meet you here at the White House and to do an interview. And I think this will be the first interview given, Mr. President, to the journalists from the People's Republic of China. And I must add this will be the first press interview ever given by any U.S. President to the permanent representatives of the Chinese press in Washington.

The President. Well. Well, I'm delighted to be a first in that regard.

Q. So, with your permission, I will ask the first question——

The President. All right.

Q. ——and followed by my colleagues. Mr. President, not long ago Chinese Premier Zhao Ziyang visited the United States. Now you are about to leave here for a visit to the People's Republic of China. Would you like to comment on the significance of this visit and the impact of such mutual visits on the bilateral relationship between China and the United States, and on the world situation as a whole?

The President. Well, yes. The visits—I had been invited by the Premier to visit China; I, in turn, had invited him. And the way it had turned out between the leaders of China and of the United States, we felt was proper that our invitation to him that he come here, and I would wait and take my turn after his visit.

As to the importance of it, I think our countries are friends. We recognize the nonaligned status of the People's Republic and respect that, but also, I know it has been my thinking for a long time that the United States is truly a nation of the Pacific Basin. And certainly the largest and most important state in that Pacific Basin is the People's Republic of China. I think that these visits are a sign of maturing our friendship, our relationship. There are some differences between us, but there are many more things that we have in common that can be mutually beneficial.

And I believe that the entire Pacific Basin is the world's future. It is the fastest growing area. And we can cooperate in some of the modernization that is going on in industry in the People's Republic. They, in turn—well, the benefits would be mutual.

Just a few minutes ago, before you came in, I met with a little group of the students from China who are here in the United States. There are some 11,000 here, but this was just a small group representative of them. And I told them how we would hope to see that expand with more of our students going there, more young students from China coming here.

We have a long history of friendship between our two peoples. It began 200 years ago when an American clipper ship visited China and trade began—farm products mainly from our part; Chinese arts, textiles, handiwork from China's part in the trade. Now, while some of those same things are the basis of the trade, we've added high technology. And I think the future in trade and development for both of us holds out a great promise for our people.

I'll try to make some of my answers shorter, but you asked a kind of a question that couldn't be answered short.

Q. Mr. President, in a couple of days, you'll be on your way to China for a friendly visit, and observers describe your visit—trip—historical. And I believe you'll be warmly welcomed in our country. My question is, how would you assess the present state of Chinese-American relations, and what is your view of the prospects of these relations? And, finally, what results are you going to achieve from your scheduled trip?

The President. Well, as I said in answer to the first question, it is, I think, a maturing of the relationship between us. I do believe that there is a friendship between our two peoples that's historic. There are a number of areas having to do with trade that we're going to discuss. I know there are certain things that we hope we can come to agreement on with regard to trade matters. I know at the ministerial level we've been

discussing a tax treaty that would protect China's people and our own from the penalty of double taxation.

There are a number of things in which we can come to agreement. We've been discussing nuclear relations and—well, I've always believed that people only get in trouble when they're talking about each other, not talking to each other. So, I think this will be a time for talking to each other, as it was when the Premier was here.

Q. Mr. President, this is going to be your first visit to the People's Republic of China. Would you tell us how you feel and what kind of message are you bringing to the Chinese people?

The President. I think it could be summed up that I know I'm going to be addressing students at the university. I'm going to be speaking to the nation on television. I'm going to speak of our desire for increased friendship and relations with the People's Republic.

Q. Mr. President, one outstanding problem in the China-U.S. relations is the difference in dealing with the Chinese territory of Taiwan. As President of the United States, what measures are you prepared to take in eliminating this difference?

The President. I realize there is a difference there and it's been discussed, and on the recent visit here this was one of the subjects of discussion. I think our position is pretty well known to the leaders of the People's Republic, that we have a long and historic friendship with the Chinese people on Taiwan. We are not going to turn our back on old friends in order to, let's say, strengthen or make new friends. And all this I have made clear.

The problem between the People's Republic and the people on Taiwan is one for the Chinese to settle between themselves. We will do nothing to intervene; we will do nothing to pressure one side or the other. The only thing is, as I have stated many times, we believe that the solution must be peaceful in settling whatever differences there may be, and we look forward to and hope that there will be a peaceful settlement of that issue.

Q. Could I follow up with a little question on this? You said you are going to have continued friendly people-to-people relationships with Taiwan. I understand it's a people-to-people friendship, not in the sense of any relationship between governments. I want to ask whether am I right?

The President. We have diplomatic relations with the People's Republic. We have an unofficial relationship with the people on Taiwan, and it is one that is based on friendship and based on trade, things of that kind. And we have been perfectly frank about that, and I don't think that it is an obstacle to improved friendship between ourselves and the People's Republic.

Q. Mr. President, you will be the first incumbent U.S. President to visit the Chinese ancient capital city of Xian. Why have you made this choice?

The President. Oh, my goodness, that's an easy one to answer. That was the capital for 2,000 of the last 3,000 years. It has been the scene of some of the great and most historic excavations, archeological excavations, in the world. I've seen pictures, photos. I've read some of the discoveries there and the historic significance of that, and we want to see for ourselves, we want to visit.

Q. Thank you. Now would you tell us what kind of preparations are you making to prepare for the visit—for instance, what kind of books and articles you and Mrs. Reagan have been reading and what kind of movies about China you have seen?

The President. Well, let me say, as to the first part of your question—and the other one that I just answered also—let me express my appreciation for the effort and the arrangements that the Government of the People's Republic has made in order for us to be able to visit that site.

But now, as to the overall visit, I, of course, have been reading many briefing tomes that have been provided, both with regard to the People's Republic and the matters that we're going to discuss. But also I have been trying to indoctrinate myself. I have met with scholars; I have met with—who have been there. I have seen a number of books, and, well, the National Geographic has put together, as you know, a whole volume on China itself. Believe me, I have gone through that. And I don't know why I didn't know enough about China to be as aware, as I am now, of the great scenic

beauty of the land.

You see normally in a newspaper pictures of cities or something—and all cities have a certain amount of looking alike—but in these other things that I've seen, the magnificent scenery, the beauty of the land, we're looking forward to that very much.

But I have been—well, I've had available a great deal of information that has increased my interest in getting there.

Q. You're well prepared?

The President. Yes.

Q. Any movies you have seen about China?

The President. I've just seen some film that our own people put together on the various locations of where we will be, in discussing the schedule and the trip itself. I can't—well, I've seen some reruns of tapes of President Nixon's visit, first visit, there.

I have to tell you, you should have asked the question of Mrs. Reagan, though, because she has more time for reading. And she has been reading a number of accounts of people there, and stories and background—more than I have. So, I'll ask her questions if I need to.

Q. Thank you.

Q. Mr. President, did you practice using chopsticks?

The President. Because I have had other trips to Asia, if not to the People's Republic—Korea, to Japan, and, too, Taiwan—I've—it's been a while yet, but I think I still remember how. And I don't think I'll have any trouble with that.

You know, this is the second trip to Asia in 6 months, the last one to Japan and Korea. And now this one. But I mention that because it is an indication of how strongly I feel that the Pacific Basin is the future.

Q. Well, thank you very much, Mr. President. We have enjoyed your conversation and, as I say, it is the first, and we hope, and I'm sure, it won't be the last.

The President. Well, I hope not.

Q. And we wish you a very happy journey to China. And *bon voyage* to you.

The President. Well, thank you very much. I am looking forward to meeting the other leaders that I have not yet met—of the government there. And also I'm going to extend some invitations for them to visit our country.

Now, will any of you—you're all based here as I understand.

Q. Yes, we are.

Q. Yes.

The President. Will any of you be making the trip?

Q. No. Not for this time, no.

The President. You mean you're going to have to read the Washington Post to find out what I'm doing? [*Laughter*]

Q. Watch the television. [*Laughter*]

The President. All right.

Q. We're going to rely on you for a big press conference. [*Laughter*]

Q. To see the response in this country.

The President. Well, all right.

Q. Thank you again, Mr. President.

Q. Thank you very much.

The President. Thank you.

Note: The interview began at 3:49 p.m. in the Oval Office at the White House. Participating in the interview were Peng Di of the Xinhua News Agency, Zhang Yunwen of the People's Daily, Lian Xingqian of the Wen Hui Bao Daily, Xue Fukang of the Guang Ming Daily, and Ma Ruiliu of Radio Beijing.

The transcript of the interview was released by the Office of the Press Secretary on April 17.

Proclamation 5183—Older Americans Month, 1984
April 16, 1984

By the President of the United States of America

A Proclamation

As our Nation prepares to celebrate Older Americans Month, we can take heart from several significant and encouraging developments.

Americans are living longer than ever before. Today, record numbers of men and women are living full and productive lives well into their seventies, eighties, and nineties. Indeed, some 32,000 Americans have celebrated their one hundredth birthdays.

Lengthened life spans are tributes to the achievements of modern science and medical progress and reflect the positive individual lifestyles that can help to maintain and improve health.

But such progress is far from universal. Too many older Americans still suffer from health problems that are attributed, mistakenly, to the process of aging. Far from being "normal" aspects of aging, many health problems can be prevented.

Regular medical examinations can prevent serious illnesses by discovering problems when they are small. Physical exercise is also good preventive health care. If done on a regular basis, exercise aids the body's ability to maintain, repair, and improve itself at any age.

Preventive health care also includes eating a proper diet, paying special attention to safety in the home, being careful with drugs, and avoiding extreme heat and cold.

While recognizing the importance of prevention for the maintenance of good health, we also acknowledge that some illnesses are associated with advancing age.

Prolonging health throughout life takes many kinds of efforts. While science continues its search for better ways to prevent and treat health problems associated with aging, we can increase our own efforts to maintain our health and prolong our lives.

As we acknowledge the theme for this year's Older Americans Month—"Health: Make It Last a Lifetime"—I urge all Americans, regardless of age, to resolve to follow good health practices so that still greater numbers of us can enjoy our older years.

Now, Therefore, I, Ronald Reagan, President of the United States of America, do hereby proclaim the month of May 1984 as Older Americans Month. I ask public officials at all levels, community agencies, educators, the clergy, the communications media, and the American people to take this opportunity to honor older Americans and to encourage them to do everything they can to make their health last a lifetime.

In Witness Whereof, I have hereunto set my hand this 16th day of April, in the year of our Lord nineteen hundred and eighty-four, and of the Independence of the United States of America the two hundred and eighth.

RONALD REAGAN

[*Filed with the Office of the Federal Register, 4:06 p.m., April 17, 1984*]

Note: The text of the proclamation was released by the Office of the Press Secretary on April 17.

Message to the Senate Transmitting the United States-Jamaica Treaty on Extradition
April 17, 1984

To the Senate of the United States:

With a view to receiving the advice and consent of the Senate to ratification, I transmit herewith the Treaty on Extradition between the United States of America and Jamaica, signed at Kingston on June 14, 1983.

I transmit also, for the information of the Senate, the report of the Department of State with respect to the Treaty.

The Treaty is the first modern United States extradition treaty within the Caribbean region. The Treaty will facilitate United States efforts to prosecute narcotics conspiracies by expressly providing that conspiracies and attempts to commit extraditable offenses constitute extraditable offenses.

The Treaty follows generally the form and content of extradition treaties recently concluded by this Government. Upon entry into force of this Treaty, the Extradition Treaty between the United States and the United Kingdom signed on December 22, 1931, shall cease to have effect between the United States and Jamaica.

This Treaty will make a significant contribution to international cooperation in law enforcement. I recommend that the Senate give early and favorable consideration to the Treaty and give its advice and consent to ratification.

RONALD REAGAN

The White House,
April 17, 1984.

Nomination of S.L. Abbott To Be United States Ambassador to Lesotho
April 17, 1984

The President today announced his intention to nominate S.L. Abbott, of Texas, to be Ambassador to the Kingdom of Lesotho. He would succeed Keith Lapham Brown.

Dr. Abbott served in the United States Army in 1943–1945. In 1953 he began his practice as doctor of optometry in El Paso, TX. In 1965–1982 he was president of Sunland Management Co., Inc., in El Paso and in 1972–1983 director of Valley Bank of El Paso. He was president of Sunland Optical Co., Inc., in 1976–1983, and presently serves as chairman of the board of directors. He was a self-employed rancher from 1976 to 1983. In 1979 he served as director of the Continental National Bank in El Paso, and in 1980–1982 served as director of Pan American Savings and Loan, and president of Sunland Builders, Inc.

Dr. Abbott's government service includes serving as regional director of the American Revolution Bicentennial Administration in Dallas in 1973–1976 and as a member of the Texas House of Representatives in Austin in 1977–1979. In 1979–1983 he was honorary vice consul of Spain in El Paso.

Dr. Abbott graduated from Pacific University (B.S., 1952; O.D., 1953). His foreign language is Spanish. He was born July 23, 1924, in Fairview, OK.

Statement on the Death of General Mark Clark
April 17, 1984

I join all Americans in mourning the death of a true American hero, General Mark Clark. As a young officer of infantry on the battlefield in World War I, as one of America's top-ranking commanders in World War II, and as commander in chief of United Nations forces during the Korean conflict, General Clark proudly wore the uniform of an American soldier—with courage, dignity, integrity, and, above all, honor.

General Clark's memory will live forever in the hearts of his countrymen. We are free because of men like him. His professionalism and dedication will be the standard of every soldier who takes the oath to defend our nation.

Nancy and I extend to General Clark's family our deepest sympathies.

Statement by Principal Deputy Press Secretary Speakes on International Terrorism
April 17, 1984

Acts of terrorism continue to plague us and our friends and allies. The toll of bombings, assassinations, and kidnapings bears terrible witness to the indiscriminate attacks and lawlessness that rules the behavior of terrorist groups. It is also apparent that several states have adopted these lawless acts as instruments of state policy. While we diligently seek the means to control this scourge, we must also take the steps that are necessary to protect our citizens, our institutions, and our friends and allies.

We have, in the course of a detailed review, reached some conclusions on what we must do to protect ourselves, and to assist others in protecting themselves from this growing threat. Our actions will be guided by the following principles: First, no nation can condone international terrorism. Second, it is the right of every legitimate government to resist the use of terrorism against its people, institutions, or property by all legal means available. Third, terrorism is a problem for all nations, and this government will work as closely as possible with other governments—particularly other similarly threatened democracies—to deal with it.

While we have cause for deep concern about the states that now practice or support terrorism, our policies are directed against all forms of international terrorism. The states that practice terrorism or actively support it cannot be allowed to do so without consequence. As a first step in dealing with these states, every channel of communication that is available to us will be used to dissuade them from the practice or support of terrorism. We will increase our efforts with other governments to obtain and exchange the information needed about states and groups involved in terrorist activities in order to prevent attacks, warn our people, our friends and allies, and reduce the risk. We will also do everything we can to see that acts of state-supported terrorism are publicized and condemned in every appropriate forum. When these efforts fail, however, it must be understood that when we are victimized by acts of terrorism we have the right to defend ourselves—and the right to help others do the same.

Finally, it should be noted that our paramount interest is in improving our ability to prevent terrorist attacks on our citizens, installations, and those foreign persons and facilities in the U.S. we are obligated to protect. We believe we can best achieve these results through a combination of improved information and better security and protection. This does not present any change in U.S. policy—rather, a refocused emphasis.

Remarks at a White House Luncheon for the National Hispanic Leadership Conference
April 17, 1984

Buenas tardes, and welcome to the White House. You know, I'm delighted to have had this chance to break bread with you. I met with many of the organizations represented here today during my first weeks in office, and I had the pleasure of renewing that acquaintance at a roundtable discussion in El Paso.

And I have a special word of congratulations to Jose Cano and Raul Yzaguirre. [*Laughter*] How am I doing? [*Laughter*] [*Applause*] Thank you. But I really mean it, congratulations for all that they have accomplished in putting this third National Hispanic Leadership Conference together.

I think being a Californian, even though some people may doubt this, I've always appreciated our country's rich Hispanic tradition. And I remember an incident I'm going to tell you about—back when I was Governor. I remember visiting the site, it was just outside of Santa Barbara, where there'd been a truly national disaster—or natural disaster, I should say—our typical mudslides when it rains too much. And I visited an area there, an area of nice—modest but very nice homes, but all of them had been inundated by the mud and water that came down from the hills.

And I had just arrived and started down this street and then went into one home. And there was an elderly man of Hispanic descent, standing knee-deep in mud in what had been his living room. And the furniture had all been carried by the mud and piled up against one wall, and it was pretty obvious from looking at it that it was rather new. And this man, with that characteristic dignity and courtesy, greeted me and said, *"Mi casa es su casa,"* standing there in the mud of his home. I never forgot him. It struck me that here was an individual, that amidst all his trials, having just lost so many of the things he dearly loved, still maintained his pride and composure enough to offer me that most traditional of Hispanic greetings.

So, let me say welcome, and *mi casa es su casa.* And in this case, it really is your house. [*Laughter*]

Americans of Hispanic descent have every right to be proud of the contributions that they've made and are making to our way of life. The strength of your values, even in the face of discrimination and hardship, is an inspiring story of dignity and courage. The emergence of Americans of Hispanic descent in business and government proves that the American dream is alive and well if we just give it a chance. And we're going to keep on giving it a chance. Providing more opportunity to all our citizens through a strong and growing economy has been priority number one of this administration.

Four years ago, talk about economic advancement and increasing opportunity was, I think, a cruel hoax. Economic stagnation and murderous inflation were destroying the dream of a better life. A spirit of pessimism, not in keeping with the American character, was rising. And even our leaders were throwing up their hands and saying that there was a "malaise" throughout the land.

Well, by stopping people from being mauled by higher and higher taxes, decreasing the regulatory burden, and bringing down inflation, we've set this country back on the road to real economic growth. We've broken the grip stagnation had on our throats during the 1970's. And from the pit of pessimism, a stronger and more vital America is emerging. The gross national product was up 6 percent last year. This year's first quarter growth rate was 7.2 percent, suggesting that this recovery is continuing at a good clip. And in the last 16 months, 5.1 million people have found jobs, bringing employment to its highest level in our history—more people working than have ever worked in the history of this country.

The unemployment rate is declining faster than anyone predicted. In 1982 we passed the Job Training Partnership Act to help those who need it the most to develop marketable skills. Of all the job training and employment programs in the Department of Labor, and there are many, some of the most effective are sponsored by Hispanic organizations. Ranking among the top in placement and cost-effectiveness is the American GI Forum's National Veterans Outreach Program. Similar to the GI Forum is the well known SAIR—Jobs-for-Progress Program. These organizations, both of which were helping people even before the legislation, have used this opportunity to do even more. And I want you to know how much I appreciate and applaud your good citizenship.

Of course, training would be useless unless jobs are available. And three out of four new jobs are created by small business. With a recovery gaining steam, 548,000 new businesses were incorporated last year. I believe that was a record in our history. Americans of Hispanic descent already own some 363,000 businesses, generating about $18 billion in sales per year. The small business surge is good news to your community.

Now, I know that education, the doorway to opportunity, has always been a major concern to all of you. Indeed, we were talking about it at our table here. When we

arrived in Washington, educational standards had been falling for nearly 20 years. So our administration appointed the National Commission on Excellence in Education, and we've been mobilizing support across the country to implement its recommendations.

We're turning the situation around, and I'm absolutely determined to provide opportunities for all American children to develop the skills they need in this society. One way to do that is through bilingual education.

The immigration legislation that's now being debated on the Hill is also important to you and, I know, is a source of concern to some of you. Well, let me assure you, I will insist that any immigration legislation passed by the Congress provides for fair and effective enforcement.

A rising economy and greater opportunities give us confidence, but America doesn't exist in a vacuum. Today, a faraway totalitarian power is committing enormous resources to change the strategic balance of the world by turning Central America into a string of anti-American, Soviet-style dictatorships. And when I use the term anti-American, I'm not using it "anti-United States," because we're all Americans—from Tierra del Fuego in the south to the North Pole. And it is all of America that this assault is aimed at.

If we do not have the courage and the political will to help them counter this power play, our friends will lose their freedom, and America's security from pole to pole will be threatened. We've made an ambitious economic effort in that region with the Caribbean Basin Initiative and an expanding aid program. But economic assistance, as much as some people on Capitol Hill would like to think otherwise, will not overcome the military threat.

Nicaragua, with the full support of its Cuban and Soviet allies, is arming, supplying, and directing an insurgency operation in El Salvador. If they succeed, it will set the course for the rest of Central America.

The United States has a balanced policy—supporting democracy, effective negotiations, economic aid, and security assistance. The focus of our commitment is countering aggression. We face one of the major challenges to democracy in our time. Debate on this issue has strayed too far from reality. If we mean to oppose Communist aggression, then we cannot throw every possible roadblock in the way of helping our peaceloving friends defend themselves. We cannot ignore the consequences of passively watching guerrillas force Communist dictatorships down the throats of the people of Central America. If Central America is lost, then our own borders will be threatened. And that's why this issue is so important to the security of our people.

There's still time to defend freedom. But to do so, we can't stand as a house divided against itself. We must recognize our common values. We must take a no-nonsense approach to protecting our vital interests. President Kennedy demonstrated this kind of determination when he said, "I want it clearly understood that this Government will not hesitate in meeting its primary obligations, which are to the security of our Nation."

We Americans carry a heavy burden. Free people everywhere look to us. If freedom is to survive, much depends on what we do, on our courage, and on our strength of character.

Now this, of course, is not new. A few weeks ago, I was honored to meet in the Roosevelt Room with 10 American heroes, Medal of Honor winners who represent the best of our country. And it was a privilege to be in their company. More than any others I've met here in the White House, I felt that this, indeed, was their house. They paid for it with their courage and service above and beyond the call of duty. Their valor kept this country free, and I was truly awed by them.

Now, it just so happens that these American heroes, each proudly wearing his Medal of Honor around his neck, were all Americans of Hispanic descent. And, as I say, we *are* all Americans.

You realize that the Medal of Honor, the Congressional Medal of Honor isn't just given for someone who was brave in battle or did something exceptional in that regard. To win that honor, you must have performed a duty above and beyond the call of duty, the call of what could be expected of even the bravest person. And all 10 of these Americans of Hispanic descent were wearing, very proudly, that honor.

Together, united in purpose, we can meet the challenges to our liberty.

You know, having talked about those, I'm going to take just a second. I have to tell you one of them was, of course, from down in Texas, Roy Benavidez. I had the pleasure of giving him his medal. I don't know what had stalled it. It had been lying there, not being delivered to him, which he had earned in Vietnam—wounded four times, going back and forth to a patrol in which every man was wounded, and he had been carrying these men to the helicopter for evacuation.

And I had asked him to tell me, and he was telling it in very simple terms, kind of minimizing all that he had done. Shot four times! Then, with one of the men over his shoulder, carrying him to the helicopter, he was attacked by a Vietnamese with a rifle and bayonet. And he told me, he said, "I know that we're taught to fend the bayonet aside, but you don't think very fast in circumstances like that." So, he said when he thrust the bayonet, he grabbed it under his arm, holding it here. And that arm is totally disabled now, as the man tried to saw back and forth and get that bayonet loose. And the only reason I'm telling you this is because at that point in the story, he said to me, "That's when I got mad." [*Laughter*]

But together we can make certain that America fulfills its historic responsibilities and remains the land of opportunity and freedom that God intended it to be. So, I thank you for being here today. Good luck, and *vaya con Dios*.

Note: The President spoke at 1:04 p.m. in the State Dining Room at the White House.

Executive Order 12474—Agreement on Government Procurement
April 17, 1984

By the authority vested in me as President by the Constitution and statutes of the United States of America, including Title III of the Trade Agreements Act of 1979 (19 U.S.C. 2511 *et seq.*) and Section 301 of Title 3 of the United States Code (3 U.S.C. 301), the Annex to Executive Order No. 12260 is amended as follows to reflect changes in the name or the status of agencies to which the Agreement on Government Procurement applies:

Section 1. "8. Community Services Administration" is deleted and the subsequent items are renumbered.

Sec. 2. "National Tool Center", in the parenthetical expression in renumbered item 31, is replaced by "Tools Commodity Center".

Sec. 3. "54. The Peace Corps" is added to the list.

RONALD REAGAN

The White House,
April 17, 1984.

[Filed with the Office of the Federal Register, 4:07 p.m., April 17, 1984]

Letter to the Speaker of the House and the Chairman of the Senate Foreign Relations Committee Reporting on the Cyprus Conflict
April 17, 1984

Dear Mr. Speaker: (Dear Mr. Chairman:)

In accordance with Public Law 95–384, I am submitting herewith a bimonthly report on progress toward a negotiated settlement of the Cyprus question.

Since my last report to you of January 24, 1984, President Kyprianou met with the U.N. Secretary General in Paris on February 4. Shortly thereafter, State Department Counselor Edward Derwinski and Special Cyprus Coordinator Richard Haass paid separate visits to the region to discuss developments with the governments of Greece, Turkey and Cyprus and to urge their cooperation with the Secretary General. In March, Turkish Cypriot community leader Denktash visited New York for discussions with the Secretary General and with Messrs. Derwinski and Haass. Also in March, Cypriot Foreign Minister Iacovou met with both the Secretary General and with Secretary Shultz.

These meetings have been held to discuss the proposal made by the two sides in early January, as described in my previous report, and to support the efforts of the Secretary General to promote negotiations between them in accordance with his Security Council mandate.

We are pleased to report at this time that the Committee on Missing Persons has met and agreed on the procedure it will follow at future meetings. We expect the committee to begin its first working session shortly.

We are encouraged by the Secretary General's active involvement in seeking common ground for progress, and we continue to offer him our support. We are hoping for positive results from this intensive diplomatic activity.

Sincerely,

RONALD REAGAN

Note: This is the text of identical letters addressed to Thomas P. O'Neill, Jr., Speaker of the House of Representatives, and Senator Charles H. Percy, chairman of the Senate Foreign Relations Committee.

Message to the Senate Transmitting the United States-Costa Rica Treaty on Extradition
April 17, 1984

To the Senate of the United States:

With a view to receiving the advice and consent of the Senate to ratification, I transmit herewith the Treaty on Extradition between the United States of America and Costa Rica, signed at San Jose on December 4, 1982, together with a related exchange of notes signed on December 16, 1982.

I transmit also, for the information of the Senate, the Report of the Department of State with respect to the Treaty.

The Treaty will facilitate United States efforts to prosecute narcotics conspiracies by expressly providing that conspiracies and attempts to commit extraditable offenses constitute extraditable offenses. The Treaty also provides a legal basis for temporarily surrendering prisoners to stand trial for crimes which occurred in the requesting State.

The Treaty follows generally the form and content of extradition treaties recently concluded by this Government. Upon entry into force, it will terminate and supersede the existing extradition treaty between the United States and Costa Rica.

This Treaty will make a significant contribution to international cooperation in law enforcement. I recommend that the Senate give early and favorable consideration to the Treaty and give its advice and consent to ratification.

RONALD REAGAN

The White House,
April 17, 1984.

Statement on Signing a Bill Appropriating Funds for the Clement J. Zablocki Outpatient Facility at the Children's Hospital in Krakow, Poland
April 17, 1984

I am pleased to sign H.R. 4835, a bill authorizing the appropriation of $10 million dedicated to the equipping and furnishing of the Clement J. Zablocki Outpatient Facility at the Children's Hospital in Krakow, Poland, as well as the provision of medical supplies to the people of Poland. This is a fitting tribute to a man who meant so much to the people of both the United States and Poland.

Note: As enacted, H.R. 4835 is Public Law 98-266, approved April 17.

Proclamation 5184—Military Spouse Day, 1984
April 17, 1984

By the President of the United States of America

A Proclamation

Since the early days of the Continental Army, the wives of our servicemen have made unselfish contributions to the spirit and well-being of their fighting men and the general welfare of their communities.

Throughout the years, as the numbers of our married men and women in uniform have grown and as their military missions have become more complex and dispersed, their spouses have made countless personal sacrifices to support the Armed Forces. In many instances, they subordinated their personal and professional aspirations to the greater benefit of the service family. Responding to the call of duty, they frequently endured long periods of separation or left familiar surroundings and friends to reestablish their homes in distant places. And there they became American ambassadors abroad.

As volunteers, military spouses have provided exemplary service and leadership in educational, community, recreational, religious, social and cultural endeavors. And as parents and homemakers, they preserve the cornerstone of our Nation's strength—the American family.

Now, Therefore, I, Ronald Reagan, President of the United States of America, do hereby proclaim May 23, 1984, as Military Spouse Day, in recognition of the profound importance of spouse commitment to the readiness and well-being of service members on active duty and in the National Guard and Reserve, and to the security of our Nation. I invite all the Armed Forces, the Army, Navy, Marine Corps, Air Force and Coast Guard, the Departments of Defense and Transportation, the Governors of the several States, the chief officials of local governments, and the people of the United States to observe this day in an appropriate manner.

In Witness Whereof, I have hereunto set my hand this 17th day of April, in the year of our Lord nineteen hundred and eighty-four, and of the Independence of the United States of America the two hundred and eighth.

RONALD REAGAN

[*Filed with the Office of the Federal Register, 10:22 a.m., April 18, 1984*]

Letter to Konstantin U. Chernenko on His Election as Chairman of the Presidium of the Supreme Soviet of the Soviet Union
April 11, 1984

Dear Mr. Chairman:

Please accept my congratulations upon your election as Chairman of the Presidium of the Supreme Soviet of the Union of Soviet Socialist Republics.

Our two countries bear a special responsibility toward our fellow human beings, both of this generation and of generations yet to come. We must ensure that our differences, however large, are resolved without the use of force and we must seek to build a better set of relationships based on those values that are common to all mankind. As you assume your new duties, I want to assure you that the United States remains ready to pursue a constructive dialogue aimed at reducing the risks of war and the levels of armaments, resolving regional conflicts peacefully and promoting trust and confidence which will enable the people of our two countries, and of the world, to live freer and more prosperous lives.

Sincerely,

/S/ RONALD REAGAN

Note: The text of the letter was released by the Office of the Press Secretary on April 18.

Nomination of Harold Peter Goldfield To Be an Assistant Secretary of Commerce
April 18, 1984

The President today announced his intention to nominate Harold Peter ("H.P.") Goldfield to be Assistant Secretary of Commerce (Trade Development). He would succeed Richard L. McElheny.

Since September 1983 Mr. Goldfield has served as Deputy Assistant Secretary of Commerce for Trade Development. Prior to this appointment, he served at the White House as Associate Counsel to the President.

Mr. Goldfield was formerly associated with the New York City law firms of Cadwalader, Wickersham & Taft and Shulte, Roth & Zabel. From 1975 to 1977, he served as assistant and law clerk to Philip W. Buchen, Counsel to President Ford.

Mr. Goldfield graduated from Georgetown University Law Center in 1977 and holds a masters degree in urban studies from Occidental College. He was awarded a CORO Foundation Fellowship in Public Affairs during 1973–1974. Mr. Goldfield graduated cum laude from Connecticut College in 1973 with a B.A. in Asian studies. He graduated from Kingswood School in West Hartford, CT, in 1969.

Mr. Goldfield was born August 5, 1951, in Hartford, CT, and now lives in Washington, DC.

Nomination of William W. Hoover To Be an Assistant Secretary of Energy
April 18, 1984

The President today announced his intention to nominate William W. Hoover to be an Assistant Secretary of Energy (Defense Programs). He would succeed Herman W. Roser.

General Hoover is currently Deputy Assistant Secretary for Military Application and Director of Military Application at the Department of Energy. Previously he was Commander of the Lowry Technical Training Center, Lowry Air Force Base, CO (1978–1979); Military Assistant to the Secretary of the Air Force (1976–1978); Executive Officer to the Command's Chief of Staff, Operations, Supreme Headquarters Allied Powers Europe (1974–1976); Executive Officer to the Assistant Chief of Staff, Operations, Supreme Headquarters Allied Powers Europe (1973–1974); and Commander of the 6498th Air Base Wing (1972–1973).

General Hoover graduated from the U.S. Naval Academy (B.S., 1954) and from the Air Force Institute of Technology (M.S., 1960). He also attended the Air Command and Staff College, Maxwell Air Force Base, AL. (1965), and the National War College, Fort Lesley J. McNair (1971). He is married, has three children, and resides in Gaithersburg, MD. He was born March 30, 1932, in St. Joseph, MO.

Nomination of Clyde A. Bragdon, Jr., To Be Administrator of the United States Fire Administration
April 18, 1984

The President today announced his intention to nominate Clyde A. Bragdon, Jr., to be Administrator of the United States Fire Administration, Federal Emergency Management Agency. He would succeed Bobby Jack Thompson.

Since 1977 Mr. Bragdon has been serving as county forester, fire warden, and fire chief for the county of Los Angeles. Previously he was division fire chief in 1973–1977; division assistant fire chief in 1970–1973; battalion chief in 1964–1970; and fire captain, fire apparatus engineer, and fireman in 1956–1964.

He graduated from the University of California, School of Public Administration (B.S., 1963). He also attended Loyola University and the University of the Redlands. He is married, has five children, and resides in Newhall, CA. He was born July 20, 1929, in Boston, MA.

Nomination of Eric Reichl To Be a Member of the Board of Directors of the United States Synthetic Fuels Corporation
April 18, 1984

The President today announced his intention to nominate Eric Reichl to be a member of the Board of Directors of the United States Synthetic Fuels Corporation for the remainder of the term expiring September 14, 1986. He would succeed C. Howard Wilkins.

Mr. Reichl is an engineering consultant. He was president of Conoco Coal Development Co. in 1974–1978. In 1948–1974 he was with Consolidation Coal Co. serving as vice president for research (1962–1974), director of research (1954–1962), and research manager (1948–1954). He was with California Research Corp. in 1946–1948 and Stanolind Oil & Gas Co. in 1944–1946.

He is a member of the American Chemical Society, the American Institute of Chemical Engineering and the National Academy of Engineers. He was chairman of the Coal Task Group, National Petroleum Council Energy Study in 1972.

He is married, has two children, and resides in Greenwich, CT. He was born December 3, 1913, in Vienna, Austria.

Nomination of Jacqueline E. Schafer To Be a Member of the Council on Environmental Quality
April 18, 1984

The President today announced his intention to nominate Jacqueline E. Schafer to be a member of the Council on Environmental Quality. She would succeed Nancy A. Maloley.

Ms. Schafer is currently Regional Administrator of the U.S. Environmental Protection Agency, Region II, in New York, NY. Previously, she was a professional staff member, U.S. Senate Committee on Environment and Public Works (1977–1982); legislative assistant to U.S. Senator James L. Buckley (1971–1976); and analyst, Banking Studies Department, and research assistant,

Research Department, Federal Reserve Bank of New York (1967–1970).

Ms. Schafer graduated from Middlebury College (A.B., 1967). She resides in New York, NY, and was born October 12, 1945, in Greenport, NY.

Nomination of Aulana L. Peters To Be a Member of the Securities and Exchange Commission
April 18, 1984

The President today announced his intention to nominate Aulana L. Peters to be a member of the Securities and Exchange Commission for the remainder of the term expiring June 5, 1984, vice Bevis Longstreth, and for a term expiring June 5, 1989, reappointment.

Mrs. Peters is currently an attorney with the law firm of Gibson, Dunn & Crutcher in Los Angeles, CA. Previously she was administrative assistant (1966–1967) and English correspondent and speechwriter (1965–1966) for the Organization for Economic Cooperation and Development.

Mrs. Peters graduated from the College of New Rochelle (B.A., 1963) and from the University of Southern California (J.D., 1973). She is married and resides in Los Angeles, CA. She was born November 30, 1941, in Shreveport, LA.

Nomination of Bernadine Healy Bulkley To Be an Associate Director of the Office of Science and Technology Policy
April 18, 1984

The President today announced his intention to nominate Bernadine Healy Bulkley to be an Associate Director of the Office of Science and Technology Policy (Life Sciences). This is a new position.

Dr. Bulkley is currently director, coronary care unit, at the Johns Hopkins Hospital and has served on active staff, medicine and pathology, at the hospital since 1976. She is also assistant dean for postdoctoral programs and faculty development, associate professor of pathology, and professor of medicine at the Johns Hopkins University School of Medicine. Dr. Bulkley has been associated with the Johns Hopkins School of Medicine since 1974, serving as associate professor of medicine (1977–1982); assistant professor of medicine and pathology (1976–1981); fellow, department of pathology (1975–1976); and fellow, cardiovascular division, department of medicine (1974–1976).

Dr. Bulkley graduated from Vassar College (A.B., 1965) and Harvard Medical School (M.D., 1970). She resides in Baltimore, MD, and was born August 2, 1944, in New York, NY.

Message to the Senate Transmitting a Protocol to the United States-France Convention on Taxation
April 18, 1984

To the Senate of the United States:

I transmit herewith for Senate advice and consent to ratification a Protocol to the Convention between the United States of America and the French Republic with respect to taxes on income and property of July 28, 1967, as amended by the Protocols of October 12, 1970, and November 24, 1978. The present Protocol was signed at Paris on January 17, 1984. I also transmit the report of the Department of State on the Protocol.

The principal reason for further amending the Convention is the recently enacted French wealth tax which could adversely affect Americans living in France. The Protocol exempts from this tax foreign assets owned by United States citizens temporari-

ly resident in France. The Protocol also provides an exemption from tax at source on interest, and it includes rules for limiting the benefits of the Convention to residents of the United States or France.

I recommend that the Senate give early and favorable consideration to the Protocol and give advice and consent to its ratification.

RONALD REAGAN

The White House,
April 18, 1984.

Message to the Senate Transmitting the United States-Ireland Treaty on Extradition
April 18, 1984

To the Senate of the United States:

With a view to receiving the advice and consent of the Senate to ratification, I transmit herewith the Treaty on Extradition between the United States of America and Ireland, signed at Washington on July 13, 1983.

I transmit also, for the information of the Senate, the Report of the Department of State with respect to the Treaty.

The Treaty is the first law enforcement treaty directly negotiated between the United States and Ireland. It fills a gap resulting from a 1965 change in Irish law which precludes the implementation of any

applicable extradition agreements between the United States and Great Britain. The Treaty follows generally the form and content of extradition treaties recently concluded by this Government.

This Treaty will make a significant contribution to international cooperation in law enforcement. I recommend that the Senate give early and favorable consideration to the Treaty and give its advice and consent to ratification.

RONALD REAGAN

The White House,
April 18, 1984.

Message to the Senate Transmitting the United States-Italy Treaty on Extradition
April 18, 1984

To the Senate of the United States:

With a view to receiving the advice and consent of the Senate to ratification, I transmit herewith the Treaty on Extradition between the United States of America and Italy, signed at Rome on October 13, 1983.

I transmit also, for the information of the

Senate, the Report of the Department of State with respect to the Treaty.

The Treaty will facilitate United States efforts to prosecute narcotics conspiracies by expressly providing that conspiracies and attempts to commit extraditable offenses constitute extraditable offenses. The Treaty also provides a legal basis for temporarily surrendering prisoners to stand trial for crimes which occurred in the requesting State.

The Treaty follows generally the form and content of extradition treaties recently concluded by this Government. Upon entry into force, it will terminate and supersede the existing extradition treaty between the United States and Italy.

This Treaty will make a significant contribution to international cooperation in law enforcement. I recommend that the Senate give early and favorable consideration to the Treaty and give its advice and consent to ratification.

RONALD REAGAN

The White House,
April 18, 1984.

Statement on Signing the Omnibus Budget Reconciliation Act of 1983
April 18, 1984

I have today approved H.R. 4169, the Omnibus Budget Reconciliation Act of 1983.

A key provision of this bill, which is a vital part of the deficit reduction downpayment, is to shift the annual cost-of-living adjustments (COLAs) in government retirement programs to the same timing and method of computation as is used in the social security system. In enacting this provision, which will produce budgetary savings of $5.6 billion over fiscal years 1984–1989, we are asking Federal retirees to accept a delay in their next COLA payment until December 31, 1984, in the case of military retirees and January 1, 1985, for civilian retirees. A similar delay has already been enacted for persons receiving other Federal benefits such as social security, veterans pensions and compensation, and supplemental security income.

To ensure timely, proper benefit payments to Federal retirees, action on the COLA delay must be taken immediately. That is why I have signed H.R. 4169 despite misgivings about other parts of this bill. For example, the bill, which was developed last year, will increase from 3½ percent to 4 percent the pay raise already granted to Federal civilian employees as of January 1984. Although I consider this increase undesirable, the additional budgetary costs are far less than the savings that will be achieved from the COLA provision.

The bill also has an obsolete provision

calling for a domestic economic summit conference consisting of the President, congressional leaders, and others responsible for economic policy development, to develop a comprehensive deficit reduction plan within 45 days. In light of the extensive discussions that have been held between the executive branch and the Congress this year on ways to reduce the projected budget deficits and the proposals already under active consideration by the Congress, I believe we should view the required conference as having taken place and therefore unnecessary.

The most serious problem I have with H.R. 4169 concerns its amendments to loan programs of the Small Business Administration. These amendments could result in unacceptably large increases in Federal budgetary costs unless both the administration and the Congress are prepared to take steps necessary to avoid that contingency.

Specifically, by substantially lowering interest rates for SBA's disaster loans, H.R. 4169 will have the effect of making farm enterprises once again eligible for them instead of their relying on loans available from the Farmers Home Administration. This reverses reforms that have resulted in significant budget savings in recent years.

H.R. 4169 also reauthorizes a nonphysical disaster lending program and expands it to authorize loans to small businesses adversely affected by the Payment-in-Kind (PIK) program and currency devaluations.

Although these programs are subject to ceilings on the total amount of loans that may be made, actual demand for such loans may well exceed those ceilings. I am, therefore, directing the Small Business Administration to control the costs associated with these programs to the maximum extent possible through its implementing regulations.

In addition, if necessary to constrain the budgetary impact of these programs, the administration will work with the Congress to enact appropriate modifications of the small business loan provisions.

Note: As enacted, H.R. 4169 is Public Law 98–270, approved April 18.

Nomination of James Paul Wade, Jr., To Be an Assistant Secretary of Defense
April 18, 1984

The President today announced his intention to nominate James Paul Wade, Jr., to be an Assistant Secretary of Defense (Development and Support). This is a new position.

Since 1968 Mr. Wade has been at the Department of Defense and is presently serving as Principal Deputy Under Secretary of Defense for Research and Engineering. Previously he was Assistant to the Secretary for Atomic Energy in 1978–1981. In 1974–1977 he was Deputy Assistant Secretary of Defense for Policy Plans and National Security Council Affairs and also was Director, Department of Defense Strategic Arms Limitation Talks (SALT) Task Force. Dr. Wade holds the Department of Defense Distinguished Civilian Service Medal and the Department of Defense Medal for Distinguished Public Service with Bronze Palm.

He graduated from the United States Military Academy (B.S., 1953) and the University of Virginia (M.S., 1959; Ph.D., 1961). He is married, has three children, and resides in Reston, VA. He was born December 26, 1930, in St. Louis, MO.

Nomination of John R. Wall To Be a Member of the Advisory Board of the Saint Lawrence Seaway Development Corporation
April 18, 1984

The President today announced his intention to nominate John R. Wall to be a member of the Advisory Board of the Saint Lawrence Seaway Development Corporation, Department of Transportation. He would succeed Joseph N. Thomas.

Mr. Wall is currently retired. He was associated with Republic Steel Corp. of Cleveland, OH, from 1956 to 1982, serving as assistant general traffic manager (1956-58); general traffic manager (1958–67); director of personnel (1967–70); and vice president-personnel (1970–82).

Mr. Wall graduated from Georgetown University (B.S., 1939) and Georgetown University Law School (J.D., 1942). He is married, has three children, and resides in Bratenahl, OH. He was born November 6, 1917, in Lynchburg, VA.

Proclamation 5185—Father's Day, 1984
April 18, 1984

By the President of the United States of America

A Proclamation

Each year this Nation sets aside a special day on which to honor fathers for their many contributions to the strength and well-being of their children and families.

Through acts of courage, of selflessness, and of love fathers have lifted, inspired, and blessed the lives of those around them. It is fathers who have such a major role in giving their children guidance, leadership and direction and teaching them integrity, truth, and humility.

Children will forever remember the father who is devoted to his family, anxious for their welfare, proud of their successes, and whose example is a beacon to them. He has left them with memories that have enriched and molded their lives.

The love fathers express involves friendship, compassion, partnership, and unity. It inspires affection, confidence, trust, and self-control. It can never be separated from character, from devotion, from good humor, and from every tender virtue.

Fathers also provide that discipline that begins with concern and commitment and example. Children have the right to learn that love is the foundation of a good family, and that love cannot exist apart from such qualities as respect, consideration, responsibility, and loyalty. Fathers provide for their loved ones in an atmosphere of warmth and kindness that accepts and preserves the uniqueness of each as an individual person while building the unity of the home.

Every father rises to his tallest stature as he selflessly cares for his family, his wife, and his children. Our finest fathers have come to know what Martin Buber meant when he wrote that our treasure is hidden beneath the hearth of our own home.

Now, Therefore, I, Ronald Reagan, President of the United States of America, in accordance with the joint resolution of the Congress (36 U.S.C. 142a), do hereby proclaim Sunday, June 17, 1984, as Father's Day. I invite the States and communities and the people of the United States to observe that day with appropriate ceremonies as a mark of gratitude and abiding affection for their fathers. I direct government officials to display the flag of the United States on all Federal government buildings, and I urge all Americans to display the flag at their homes and other suitable places on that day.

In Witness Whereof, I have hereunto set my hand this eighteenth day of April, in the year of our Lord nineteen hundred and eighty-four, and of the Independence of the United States of America the two hundred and eighth.

RONALD REAGAN

[*Filed with the Office of the Federal Register, 11:25 a.m., April 19, 1984*]

Message to the Senate Transmitting a Protocol to the United States-Canada Convention on Taxation
April 18, 1984

To the Senate of the United States:

I transmit herewith, for Senate advice and consent to ratification, a Second Protocol, signed at Washington on March 28, 1984, Amending the Convention between the United States and Canada with Respect to Taxes on Income and on Capital, signed at Washington on September 26, 1980, as amended by a Protocol signed at Ottawa on June 14, 1983. I also transmit the report of the Department of State with respect to the second protocol.

The Social Security Amendments of 1983 were enacted since the negotiation of the convention and first protocol. They provide in part that social security benefits paid to nonresident aliens henceforth will be subject to an effective 15 percent withholding tax. The Canadian Government has requested that the pending convention be amended to exempt Canadian residents from such withholding.

The second protocol would amend Article XVIII (Pensions and Annuities) of the convention, so as to provide that social security benefits paid by one party to residents of the other "shall be taxable only in that other State." However, United States citizens resident in Canada will continue to be taxable to the extent provided under United States law.

It is most desirable that this second protocol, together with the convention and first protocol, be considered by the Senate as soon as possible and that the Senate give advice and consent to ratification of the convention and two amending protocols.

RONALD REAGAN

The White House,
April 18, 1984.

Note: The text of the message was released by the Office of the Press Secretary on April 19.

Informal Exchange With Employees at the Weyerhaeuser Industries-Port of Tacoma Log Export Shipping Facility in Tacoma, Washington
April 19, 1984

The President. Well, this is a first for me. This is the first time I've ever seen anything, and while I knew I was going to see a ship being loaded here, I hadn't quite pictured what it was like. And I just speculated here to Dick, in showing us around, if somebody punched a hole in the bottom of that, it still wouldn't sink—[*laughter*]—not with the load it's got here.

You know, coming in here I happened to remember a lot of years back that the first time that I came to Tacoma was for the premiere of a movie that I was in called "Tugboat Annie Sails Again." And I remember they brought us in the last stretch on a yacht. And they had fireboats out there, putting on a display and everything, and then that night they saw the movie. And the next morning, there we were all alone, out on a curb, trying to flag down a cab. [*Laughter*] Kind of a change of attitude—probably correctly.

Listen, I'm not going to stand here and try to make a speech or anything. I know we've only got a few minutes to visit, and it's just occurred to me there must have been some times when you've said, "If I had a chance to ask him, would I . . . ." Well, go ahead. If you've got a question or something on your mind, maybe we could have a dialog instead of a monolog.

Q. When do you plan to leave for China, Mr. President?

The President. What's that?

Q. When do you plan to go to China?

The President. Leaving Sunday morning. The reason is, I'm, from here, going down to the ranch and have a couple of days on horseback. But it's all a thing of trying to break the change to the time zone difference. You see there are 13 hours time difference between there and our Washington time. Now here, it's 10 hours difference. And what we're going to do is have a couple of days there to get changed—this, 3 hours of it—and then we're going to stop in Honolulu for two overnights there and then one in Guam, and hope by that time that we're getting closer to their time. [*Laughter*] These last several days, you know, every once in a while I'd stop and think—you know here it is the middle of the afternoon, and what time is it in China? Well, it's the middle of the night. And I've been wondering about when I'm going to find my eyes closing, and it'll be at the wrong time. So, I think that everyone that's been there before says this is the way to do it.

Somebody with something else?

Q. What will you be doing in China?

The President. Oh, an awful lot of meetings. It's really a working trip. Premier Zhao was in Washington, you know, and we made an exchange that after his visit I would go there. We'll be taking up matters that have to do with just what's happening here—in the dock trade matters—with them; negotiating out some tax differences so that back and forth, people not only working there but investment and so forth that they've opened up to American investment there won't be taxed double. We're hoping to negotiate out a number of things—and trade agreements that will build up more trade.

They have now become our third largest trading partner in the world. And I know I was just talking here that 5 years ago, they didn't import any lumber from the United States. In 1983 it was almost 800,000 board feet. And I think we can get that even bigger—increase it more.

So, the schedule is very tough, a very minimum of sightseeing. At least we'll get to see the Great Wall and a couple of things like that. But the rest of it is very lengthy meetings.

Q. Are you going to visit several cities while you're there?

The President. We'll mainly be in Beijing. We'll go up—among the sightseeing things, we'll go up to that 3,000-year-old capital where they've uncovered all those terra cotta soldiers and all, life-size figures. But that's just for a visit of that kind—and the Great Wall.

But then we'll go to Shanghai, where there's a lot of American investment now. In fact, I'll be going through a company there that is half and half. It's a partnership deal with an American private company and the Chinese Government. And also, visit a university outside Shanghai, and from there, home by way of Alaska.

Q. You'll be away for how long?

The President. Well, it's about 15 days from the start this morning from Washington. Now, the fourth day we'll be leaving—

actually, we'll be 7 days in China.

Q. Is Nancy going with you?

The President. Yes. I'll meet her down in California. She left early to stop and visit her mother in Phoenix. Yes, we'll be going together.

Anything else?

Q. I also understand we're going to be exporting to Korea.

The President. Yes. Yes, and we've been dealing with Japan on more open trade and some changes in tariffs and so forth, particularly with regard to wood and paper products that they've kind of had a restricted market to us. We were there some time ago, and Prime Minister Nakasone is all—he really, honestly, and sincerely wants to have better trade relations with us. He's got some political problems, and I can understand that. I've got some, too. [*Laughter*]

Q. Mr. President, we've got time for about one more question, I think, and then——

The President. One more.

Q. Did you order this nice weather for today?

The President. I'll take it, though. [*Laughter*]

Q. Our jobs rely pretty heavily on the housing industry, and some of us younger guys are still trying to figure out how to afford our first house—[*inaudible*].

The President. Yes, and I know I'm going to be talking about that at this next meeting that I go to here. Yes, we know that this interest rate is still a problem. You do know, though, that the housing industry has staged a comeback that is unbelievable, almost, the rate. Now, there was a drop in March, but that drop was only down to about 1,600,000 starts, where the previous month it had been about 1,900,000. And so the whole average for this last year, since the recovery started, is very good. As a matter of fact, February was, I think, a record, an all-time record for housing starts.

There's no question that this is still a problem. Right now, those interest rates— there are two explanations for them staying where they are. One of them is on the positive side. They're up there because of the recovery, the old law of supply and demand. There is so much recovery going, and business investment in plant and equipment and so forth, consumer borrowing to buy, installment purchases and so forth, automobiles, heavy appliances and so forth, that that has kept it up. But the other one, I think, is just plain pessimism. The money market out there still isn't willing to let the money go on loan at a lower rate until they're sure that we really have got control of inflation. Well, inflation is now—this is going into the third year that we've had it down below 4 percent, and I think that they're being unnecessarily pessimistic.

I have a hunch that when the Congress comes back from this recess, if they'll go forward with this cut in spending that we want, this program to start whittling away at that deficit, I think maybe this could reassure the market, and we would see before too long the rates coming down again.

But I know what they mean to the housing industry, and I can only tell you that it is—right now, it's very healthy. And there's been a great surge, I think, because of the number of years in this recent recession that people have been standing by waiting to buy.

And, of course, I know your interest is only just passing in the housing industry. It doesn't mean anything to you. [*Laughter*]

Q. I'm afraid we're going to have to drag the President away.

The President. All right.

Q. Thank you.

The President. Okay. Well, it's nice to see all of you. Thank you very much; appreciate it.

Note: The President spoke at 12:03 p.m. following a tour of the facility. He was accompanied on the tour by George Weyerhaeuser, president and chief executive officer of Weyerhaeuser Industries, and Richard McLean, manager of the facility.

Remarks During a Roundtable Discussion With Export Trade Industry Representatives in Tacoma, Washington
April 19, 1984

The President. I thank you for the warm greeting that you've given us already, and I want to thank George Weyerhaeuser in particular for his generosity and for letting us have the use of this hall.

I know that we're going to talk about foreign trade this afternoon, and I'd like to begin by pointing out that the backdrop for all these issues is the economic climate here in our own country. And I know you're all familiar with the turnaround that we've accomplished. We're enjoying an economic revival here in the States, and I think we've got a lot to be proud of.

Inflation has dropped very definitely. Industrial production is surging to the point where we're creating an average of some 300,000 jobs a month.

I thought it was very telling when for the month of March, the figures on unemployment came in and it had not changed in the percentage. We still had 7.7 percent unemployment, but there were 248,000

more people working than had been working in the previous month. And I'm not adept enough to figure how all that can take place and not change the percentage, but I know there's a reason for it. We're creating, in other words, the new jobs that we need to accommodate our growth.

Factory orders and retail sales are strong. Housing starts are still strong despite last month's drop. And I've often wondered, sometimes, the way last month's drop was treated, what the reporting would have been like on the evening news if they'd been around at the time of the 1929 stock crash.

But in the past year and a half, we've enjoyed the steepest drop in unemployment in over 30 years. Prime rate is nearly down to the halfway point from when we came into office. But we know we have much more to do with regard to interest rates.

That's the backdrop, or real American

comeback story, and I think it's just begun.

I know you're eager to talk about trade with the Asian nations, especially China and Japan. And I just saw that big ship down there being loaded with logs and lumber for China, and that's as good an illustration as any of the big increase in U.S.-China trade over the past few years. The United States is now China's third largest trading partner. We have over a hundred American companies with offices there, and the United States is now China's leading foreign investor.

We want to further improve the investment climate. We've already signed a series of bilateral agreements with China covering trade and financial matters. And when we arrive in Beijing next week, I'll continue our talks on agreements involving taxes and financial investment.

There are other trade issues that we're still resolving with China, and I know that as in any relationship, there are going to be some growing pains. You know, as I do, that occasionally the interests of diplomacy and the interests of American industry sometimes seem to collide. Well, I see it as our job to reconcile the two and to make it easier for American businessmen to open up new markets on a fair footing.

We've begun some initiatives in that direction. Two years ago, after the preceding administration tried, we passed the Export Trading Company Act aimed at opening up new foreign trade opportunities for medium- and small-sized businesses. The bill removed impediments to trade and permitted companies to sell American products overseas more efficiently, more effectively.

We're also implementing our international investment policy to lessen the number of government measures that distort or impede the international investment flows.

Now, these are just some of the efforts. I know that you're good traders, but I know you have problems, too, including the continuing problem of state-subsidized goods from other nations, some of which are doing this in violation of international agreements.

And then there's Japan. Japan's been a fine friend of the United States in many respects. We still have a lot of trade questions to work out with Tokyo, but we've

made some major progress in the last 2 years. Just a few weeks ago, Japan agreed to virtually double the beef quota. And they also dramatically eased restrictions on the import of various citrus projects—or products.

And Japan helped our automobile industry get enough breathing room to recover from the siege of double-digit inflation and record interest rates that nearly destroyed us. As a matter of fact, today, the entire automobile industry, as an industry, has an unemployment rate of only 5½ percent. There are 85,000 more people working in the automobile plants—manufacturing plants and assembly plants—than there were back in 1980.

We're pushing hard for tariff cuts and to lower nontariff trade barriers. And by the way, George, I know, as we've discussed, your keen interest in limiting Japan's tariffs on forest products. Well, we're hoping that very soon we'll have progress to report on that.

But I want you to understand that this administration is on your side and is sensitive to your concerns. I think there's been too long a period in which our government had virtually an adversarial relationship with its own business community. And that doesn't make sense at all as far as we're concerned.

So, I spent a good many years out on the mashed-potato circuit telling people that the only American—that only American business can give us the jobs and prosperity of the future. And we're going to address that future these next several days in China, and in Washington next month when our U.S. Trade Representative, Bill Brock, meets informally with 13 key Ministers from around the world to see what we can do to raise our collective will to do better.

But now, I think I should go back to listening to you and hearing your concerns and questions.

[At this point, George Taylor, president of the Washington Council on International Trade, made brief remarks. A slide show sponsored by the council was then viewed by the panel. Jack Barrington, president of the Washington State China Relations Council, then made a presentation on trade

between the State and China. Following the presentations, George Weyerhaeuser served as moderator of the panel discussion.]

Mr. Weyerhaeuser. Richard Robbins of Robbins Company.

Mr. Robbins. Thank you, Mr. Weyerhaeuser. Mr. President, it's a delight for us to have this discussion with you. We had a little discussion here, just before you arrived, among a number of the people from the business community. And one of the gentlemen pointed out that his firm spent 5 years cultivating a relationship with the People's Republic of China before they actually converted this into a business opportunity, which became a very important business thing for them. That's been a similar experience with us.

I speak from the perspective of small business, which is somewhat unusual in trade with China. I must say I'd like to compliment the Department of Commerce for the work, particularly, that they have been doing here in the State of Washington with ourselves and with other small businesses, helping us come together and deal as a group with possibilities in China.

We've had a couple of problems which perhaps the government could be helpful in dealing with in developing this trade. We find that when we are in Beijing, for example, trying to do business there, it's very difficult to communicate properly with home office and perhaps even other countries in which we have to communicate. Some facilities could perhaps be made available to us which could be in the form of secretarial services, meeting rooms, Telex, telephones, facts, et cetera, which would make it easier for us to do business.

Another point, which is more a comment than a question—but you may comment if you'd like—is that we've found that from the point of view of the small business, it's very difficult to handle the big expenses. With the sales and marketing expenses, it takes years to develop, and particularly in dealing with Chinese delegations that are coming to the United States and other countries in which our people have to travel with them and be with them and in which we are expected to go and attend

seminars and training programs in China—whether the government could provide some kind of funding or aid in some respect that would make it easier for small business to approach that type of expense and develop a business relationship.

The President. Well, both of those points are—they're both something that I think—I don't know that we've given as much thought as we should to those—the communications and so forth. I can only tell you on that, look into that. You know that we have, with regard to small business, particularly, we have started holding some seminars and some meetings with our AID Agency—Agency of International Development—to work with small businesses and let them know that—because the bulk of our foreign aid is spent for American products—to let them know that there is a potential there for small business in America to participate. So far, it's been rather successful. And I will take these matters up with them, as well as with others, to see if there are some areas here where we can be of help.

I know, when you speak about the communications problems and so forth back and forth, believe it or not, in arranging the Presidential visit to China, we found that there are certain procedures that took a great deal more negotiation than we had expected with regard to our own transportation, communication, and so forth. But everything was worked out very well.

And I just—from all that you're saying here, I think the potential is so great. The change that has occurred there in, now, their willingness for American investment, their willingness to collaborate with private enterprise, free enterprise, is an amazing change and offers not only a great hope for us but, I think, a great hope for them and their own people.

And the purpose of this meeting is to see that all the doors are as wide open as they can be and what we can do to make some agreements. When the grain deal was mentioned a moment ago, and wheat—we know that we had a grain deal with them, and in 1983, they failed to buy their quota. They have promised that this will be different in '84, and that they will even make up this slack.

We were in a kind of period of strain there, having to do with textiles and high technology. And fortunately, we've been working that out, too.

Ms. Jacobs. Mr. President——

Mr. Weyerhaeuser. Nancy Jacobs——

Ms. Jacobs. Thank you.

Mr. Weyerhaeuser. ——dean of the University of Washington Business School.

Ms. Jacobs. What implications do you see for the potential for a growing relation between Japan and China for our own trade with the PRC and for our foreign policy?

The President. Oh, I don't think there's any question but that we're going to find Japan a competitor in many areas there. And yet, if we believe in free enterprise, as we do, there's nothing we can do about that. We also have competition right now, here in our own continent, with Canada, and in the very field that we've been talking about—your field.

But I think that—and this does not mean that in what we're doing that we're going there with any intention of slackening our efforts in our relationship with Japan—I think we've made great headway there, also. Prime Minister Nakasone has been most forthcoming and, as I said earlier today, he has some political problems, of course, that have kept him from moving as fast as he might like. I've got some political problems, too, that slowed some things down. But I think that all of this is leading toward a greater development as a market in the People's Republic.

Mr. Weyerhaeuser. I have another question. Mr. [T.A.] Wilson, chairman of Boeing Company.

Mr. Wilson. Mr. President, the United States has had a very good relationship with China in the sale of our aircraft products, not only Boeing Company but also McDonnell Douglas. The point I would like to make with you is that we're in competition now with a consortium in Europe. And I know that President Mitterrand has pleaded their case on his visit to China, and I would hope that you—and this is in the area of medium-range airplanes—I would hope that when you're there, you would point out that you would recommend they make their choice on the basis of technical and economic performance and not be swayed by other extraneous factors. [*Laughter*]

The President. Emblandishments? [*Laughter*] Let me tell you, I go as something of a salesman, and I'll do everything I can up to the limit of not putting a "Buy American" sticker on my bag. [*Laughter*]

Mr. Wilson. Mr. President, the fact that you would just indicate a knowledge and interest would be most helpful. And incidentally, dealing with those people has been fun, and I think you're going to enjoy yourself.

Mr. Weyerhaeuser. Have another question?

Mr. Lelli.[1] Mr. President, George Weyerhaeuser's been a good friend of labor in this area, and if you could help him export some of his wood products, it would certainly help the longshoremen in the city of Tacoma. [*Laughter*]

Mr. Weyerhaeuser. Phil, you and I are in this together. [*Laughter*]

Q. Right. We're in the same boat with two plugs. [*Laughter*]

The President. Yes, if one of them pulls one plug, don't make the mistake of thinking you'll get even by pulling the other. [*Laughter*]

Well, I can assure you that strikes a note that's warm to my heart, too, because I'm the first fellow that's ever held this job who's a lifetime member of a union and was six times president of his own union. So, I have long believed that what the founder of the AFL–CIO said is the truest thing in the world, and that is that labor and management are partners and one can't profit without the other. And he, Samuel Gompers, also said that the greatest sin that management can commit is to not make a profit.

No, I believe that none of us can measure yet what the changes are that are taking place in that great continent with virtually a fourth of the world's population—the difference in—as to what it set out to be when it first adopted its ideology, modern ideology. And labor has to be a great consideration in anything that we propose.

---

[1] *Philip M. Lelli, president of Tacoma Local 23, International Longshoreman's and Warehousing Union.*

You know, one thing we mustn't fall into: When there was talk, also, of protectionism and what its faults can be—that Smoot-Hawley tariff back in the Great Depression when I was looking for my first job, I remember the effect of that. But I also remember how we cannot see the whole picture.

When I was Governor, driving home one afternoon from the office in the time of one of those several recessions that we had between World War II and the present—and ahead of me was a car, fellow driving a pickup. And on his bumper he had a bumper sticker—"Buy American." He was driving a Toyota. [*Laughter*]

So, I think we're all in this to sink or swim.

Mr. Weyerhaeuser. I've time for one more question.

Q. Mr. Weyerhaeuser, sir.

Mr. Weyerhaeuser. Mr. [Richard] Smith, who's chairman—or head of the Port of Tacoma.

Mr. Smith. Thank you. Mr. President, this is a rare honor to have you visit our port, certainly, this morning. And I would like to bring up a couple of other, sort of housekeeping items.

We've heard rumors recently, Dick Ford and I, that they were going to cut back in Customs services. And at a time when we are expanding our port export and import businesses rapidly in the Puget Sound and northwest area, this is a very troublesome idea for us to accept, both in the maritime port and, as Dick would tell you, in his excellent international airport. And we have a little rule of thumb that we've worked on out here that says that every dollar spent on augmenting Customs personnel comes back 17 times—17 dollars for each one. So, I hope you would be able to persuade the Customs services, sir.

In the meantime, we need to be ready in the port systems. I'm against speaking—let Dick speak for himself on this—but all the indications are this vast increase of trade in the Pacific Ocean areas, some as much as 250 percent from some of the national concerns that have been studying this, we in the port system must be ready. It means we've got giant facilities to develop, and fast tracking of permit systems is absolutely essential, sir.

The President. This particular issue has not come before our Cabinet or Cabinet Councils, and so I actually can't comment here on what is back of that move or how they felt that they—that it would be justified, unless it was an agency that thought that it was overstaffed, and there aren't very many government agencies that volunteer that kind of information. [*Laughter*] But I can promise you that we will deal with that, and we'll deal with it in a way that we're not going to shoot ourselves in the foot.

Mr. Weyerhaeuser. Unfortunately, we're out of time for the panel questions and comments, and I'd like to call on the President to—if he would—to make any concluding remarks.

The President. Well, I wish we could sit around and visit longer and more on this. As I said earlier, I believe in the partnership of government and business and these various things that have been suggested here. I am definitely opposed to protectionism. It has failed whenever it has been tried. And the purpose of these meetings in China is going to be—again, and with regard to Mr. Weyerhaeuser's business here—we're going to deal very decisively with regard to certain tariffs. And I, again, realize that this is almost historic, because of the great turn to private investment that we're seeing in the People's Republic and be prepared to deal with that. I don't think that I ever anticipated that I would be going to discuss with them problems of eliminating the danger of dual taxation on our people and their people coming here. But that is going to be one of the subjects that we'll be talking about.

And we just—we have—well, I'm scolded by some economists when I say we have a recovery. They have written me, several of them, to tell me to stop using the word recovery. We have passed that point. We are now in a full-blown expansion. And we're going to keep it that way. And we're going to continue doing the things that we think brought this recovery around—about—and keep the expansion going without inflation, and my hope is that with a further reduction of the percentage of the gross national product and the peoples' earnings that government is taking for itself, because I think that has been the cause of our economic problems. Government must be taking a smaller share. And we shall continue to work at that.

We'll continue, also, to broaden our markets to encourage export wherever we can. We're not only the biggest buyer and the biggest market in the world for other people's goods, we also can be far more productive and able to compete. And we're going to do everything to get government out of the way to make sure that we have the best means of competing in a world market.

Mr. Weyerhaeuser. Thank you very much, Mr. President. I would say on behalf of all of us, this is a red letter day for the State of Washington. It surely is for Weyerhaeuser Company our pleasure to lease the hall.

It's much more than that. When the President of the United States is both actively informed, fully involved, fully supportive of, and acting as the lead trader for the country, I truly believe it augurs well for this country. I think that we have tremendous opportunities facing the Pacific. And to have a Western President come up here into the Northwest, the leading trading area, and spend time with us and try to listen to some of our ideas and problems is really unique.

I was delighted to have him see some very, very high-quality products on their way to China today. And I can assure you that he is well informed and that we're well served to have him leading the charge for us.

And it's been a pleasure to have you stop by here on your way on a long and arduous trip. And I'd like to thank you on behalf of everybody here and for the Northwest.

The President. Well, thank you very much.

You know, it still sounds strange to my ears to be saying I'm glad to be back in Washington again. [*Laughter*] And then I have to say, "but *this* Washington." [*Laughter*]

Note: The panel discussion began at 12:42 p.m. in the conference room at the Weyerhaeuser corporate headquarters. The President was introduced by Robert Kapp, executive director of the Washington State China Relations Council.

Following the panel discussion, the President left Washington and went to Rancho del Cielo, his ranch near Santa Barbara, CA, where he remained until his departure for Hawaii, Guam, and China on April 22.

Statement Announcing a Major United States Initiative in the Mutual and Balanced Force Reductions Negotiations
April 19, 1984

I am very pleased to announce another major initiative in arms control. Earlier today in Vienna, the U.S. and our NATO allies tabled a new proposal aimed at breaking the impasse that has long stalled the negotiations between NATO and the Warsaw Pact on reducing conventional forces in Europe. This important initiative in the talks on mutual and balanced force reductions, known as MBFR, was developed in close consultations with our allies, and it reflects their significant contributions.

Since the MBFR talks began in 1973, we have sought an agreement to reduce to equal, verifiable levels the conventional force personnel of the two sides which face each other in Central Europe. Although the Warsaw Pact has a significant manpower advantage in Europe, it has been unwilling to acknowledge the imbalance. Without agreement on the total number of forces on each side, there can be no agreement on the number that must be reduced to obtain equal levels.

This data issue is one major unresolved problem in the MBFR negotiations. The other issue is the continuing unwillingness of the Eastern side to agree on effective verification provisions. Today's proposal is designed to move the talks forward in both areas.

This new proposal in the MBFR negotiations comes just a day after the American initiative for a comprehensive, worldwide ban on chemical weapons. This was presented personally by Vice President Bush yesterday in Geneva to the 40-nation Conference on Disarmament. I hope these twin initiatives will lead to real progress in both negotiations.

We are bargaining in good faith. With equal willingness on the other side, real progress can be achieved quickly. I have no higher priority than reducing arms to equal and more stable levels and, where we can,

banning them altogether.

Having made these significant new moves this week in chemical and conventional arms control, I want to emphasize once again my strong desire to get on with the urgent business of reducing nuclear arms. We call upon the Soviet Union to respond to the repeatedly expressed desire of the world community by returning to the two nuclear negotiating tables, START and INF, which they left 5 months ago. When they do this, they will find the United States to be an accommodating and creative partner in seeking nuclear reductions, just as we and our allies have shown ourselves to be in the negotiations on chemical and conventional forces.

Message on the Observance of Secretaries Week, April 22–28, 1984
April 20, 1984

Each year during Secretaries Week, we have an opportunity to express our appreciation to the thousands of individuals who play such an important part in the efficient operation of offices around the country.

Over the years, the role of secretaries has changed considerably. New technologies and innovation have added more complex assignments to traditional responsibilities. All Americans owe a great deal to secretaries for the outstanding job they do and for the dedication they demonstrate every day of the year.

In all facets of our society, whether in business, education, labor, industry, or government, secretaries perform tasks and bring a sense of coordination that is essential to the success of our economic system. Their cooperation and loyalty make our offices a more pleasant place to be. Their professionalism and expertise are worthy of the highest commendation.

I am proud to salute the secretaries of America and wish them the very best for an enjoyable week.

RONALD REAGAN

Appointment of Martin L. Duggan as a Member of the Advisory Committee on Federal Pay, and Designation as Chairman
April 20, 1984

The President today announced his intention to appoint Martin L. Duggan to be a member of the Advisory Committee on Federal Pay for a term expiring January 20, 1990. He will succeed Jerome M. Rosow. The President also intends to designate him as Chairman.

Mr. Duggan recently retired as editorial page editor of the St. Louis Globe-Democrat. He is active in community affairs and serves as president of Dismas House, a rehabilitation center for former convicts. He is a director of Downtown St. Louis, Inc., president of the Society of Jesus, and a member of the advisory board of the Salvation Army.

He is a founder of the Mid-America Press Institute and is an active member of the American Society of Newspaper Editors.

He is married, has four children, and resides in St. Louis, MO. He was born June 3, 1921, in St. Louis.

Designation of Jean F. Ross as the United States Commissioner of the Upper Colorado River Commission
April 20, 1984

The President today announced his intention to designate Jean F. Ross as the United States Commissioner on the Upper Colorado River Commission. He will succeed Hugh P. Dugan.

Mr. Ross is a partner in the law firm of Saunders, Snyder, Ross & Dickson in Denver, CO. Prior to joining the firm in 1966, he was staff attorney for the board of water commissioners of the city and county of Denver.

He is a member of the National Water Resources Association, the American Bar Association, National Resources Law Section, and the Colorado Bar Association, water section. Since 1959 he has been a member of the Colorado Water Congress.

Mr. Ross graduated from Yale College (A.B., 1953) and the University of Michigan Law School (LL.B., 1956). He is married, has two children, and resides in Littleton, CO. He was born January 1, 1931, in Colorado Springs, CO.

Radio Address to the Nation on the Economic Recovery Program and on Tax Reductions
April 21, 1984

My fellow Americans:

As a boy growing up in Illinois, swimming was an important part of my life. Pools weren't very common or affordable in those days, so my swimming was done in the Rock River.

I soon learned that swimming with the current downstream was a lot easier than swimming upstream. Nevertheless, today I'm going to swim against the current. The current I'm talking about is a riptide of criticism that claims this administration's economic policies impoverish the poor and bestow benefits on the rich. This distorted view was created by special interest demagoguery and political-year oratory, dutifully reported by a goodly portion of the press.

A week or so ago there was a report, complete with impressive figures, showing that our economic policy has punished people at the poverty level. The report was accurate that in 1978 an income of 6,662 was the poverty level. It is also accurate that inflation has now pushed the poverty level up to $10,180. In other words, it takes that much to buy what 6,662 would buy in 1978. Critics have concluded on the basis of this report that because of our economic program, those at that level were much poorer than they had been in 1978. Well, they're right that those at the poverty level have not kept up, but wrong as to what is to blame. It certainly isn't our tax cut, which is helping low-income earners keep more of their hard-earned dollars.

Part of it was caused by the biggest single tax increase in history, which had been passed back in 1977, calling for several successive increases in the social security payroll tax to take place between 1977 and 1990. During that same period, by the way, there will be increases in the amount of earnings subject to the tax up to more than 52,800.

But this is only part of the reason those people at the poverty level are having trouble keeping up, and it hasn't anything to do with our across-the-board, 25-percent cut in the income tax. The simple truth is the income tax does not take into account the value of your dollars. It's based on the number of dollars you earn. So, even though $10,180 is only worth as much in purchasing power as 6,662 was a few years ago, you have to pay income tax on those 3,500 additional dollars just as if you gained that much in purchasing power.

Now, let's take a look at that other drumbeat that our tax cut is designed to help the rich get richer and either does nothing for the low- or middle-income earners or, even worse, adds to their burden, and how they arrive at that conclusion. Well, it's true that if your tax burden is $100, your tax cut is only $25. But if your tax is $1,000, your saving is $250, 10 times as much. But the ratio stays the same. If your tax burden was 10 times as much before, you're still paying ten times as much tax.

There's a better test of whether one group benefits more than another: Did the tax cut increase or decrease the share of the total tax paid by the earners at various levels? In 1982, the last year for which we have complete figures, all those with incomes below $20,000 a year paid a 10-percent smaller share of total income tax revenue than they did in 1981. From $20,000 to $50,000, the share only dropped by 1 percent. From $50,000 and up, the share of total tax increased by 7 percent. And if you break that group down to those earning $500,000 and up, their share of the total income tax burden increased by 43 percent.

This, then, is the best kept secret about our tax cut. The wealthiest Americans are carrying a higher share of the total tax burden after our tax cut than they were before.

Next year, another part of our tax program will go into effect. It's called indexing and will begin on January 1st. Very simply, it means you will no longer pay an income tax on inflation, which you've done every time a raise or cost-of-living increase pushed you into a higher tax bracket. The greatest beneficiaries of indexing will be those in the lower and middle-income tax brackets. It will do little for the so-called rich, because they're already in top tax brackets.

Many of those who were the loudest in declaring our tax program unfair want to cancel indexing before it goes into effect. Canceling indexing would increase the tax burden for lower and middle-income earners by three times as large a percentage as it would for the rich.

And one last point—perhaps the most important. Our program is stimulating strong economic growth, creating more jobs and opportunity than ever before.

Well, so much for swimming upstream. Until next week, thanks for listening. God bless you.

Note: The President spoke at 9:06 a.m. from Rancho del Cielo, his ranch near Santa Barbara, CA.

Remarks on Arrival at Hickam Air Force Base in Honolulu, Hawaii
April 22, 1984

Governor and Mrs. Ariyoshi, Admiral and Mrs. Crowe, and fellow Americans, Nancy and I want to thank you for your warm and very generous welcome. To all the people of Hawaii, we want to convey our thanks for the aloha spirit of your greeting and to say how thrilled we are to begin a long journey for peace in this place of overpowering beauty and tranquillity.

It is also appropriate that this journey should begin on Easter Sunday—a day of peace proclaimed, a day of triumph over evil and suffering. In a short time, we will be worshiping at St. Andrew's Cathedral, and I can assure you that our prayers this afternoon will not just be for the success of this mission, but for an enduring peace among the peoples of all nations.

On this Easter, in the year of our Lord 1984, I ask for the prayers of all Americans and the peoples of the world for peace among men and peace among nations. Let the nations and the peoples of the world renounce war, and let us pledge ourselves to its permanent abolition. Let us forsake its anguish and agony and live in love with one another.

Like all Americans, the people of these islands cherish peace. Unlike most of their countrymen, the people of Hawaii have known firsthand the destruction wrought by nations that take up arms against each other. As we passed over Pearl Harbor this afternoon, I don't have to tell you of our silence as we reflected on the Arizona Memorial beneath us. The building that is now the Pacific Air Force's headquarters is still pockmarked with bullets from that fateful Sunday almost 43 years ago. And 32 years later, it was here to this airport that our first prisoners of war returned from an awful captivity in North Vietnam.

The American people have never sought war nor the test of arms. And yet in my lifetime I have seen four such wars—none of them because the United States was too strong or too ready. The United States is resolved to avoid war, pursue peace, and to do so by remaining strong and remaining ready.

Hawaii remains key to this resolve and readiness. To our men and women in uniform today, I bring the greetings and gratitude of your country. In these islands there is testimony to the heroism and courage of others who've worn their country's uniform before you. And today you continue in that valiant tradition. Your vigilance makes peace possible; your readiness protects freedom and brings closer the day when mankind will renounce forever the use of force.

It's our fervent hope that the events of this coming week will also bring us closer to that day. One of the critical developments in our country's postwar foreign relations is

our opening to China and the establishment of diplomatic relations with that nation of a billion people. Today in the economic, educational, and cultural areas we have a wide range of agreements with the Chinese, and the United States is now China's third leading trade partner. And we share similar concerns on many critically important geopolitical situations, such as our disapproval of the aggression waged against the peoples of Kampuchea and Afghanistan.

Our shared progress did not happen instantly; it took more than a decade to build. This week, we hope to continue the process of reconciliation. I believe the mission that we undertake is another careful yet sure step toward peace and friendship between the Chinese and American people.

While our friendship is vital to the cause of world peace, we should also acknowledge that our vital national interests are at stake. The Pacific Basin is one of the fastest growing markets for American goods, services, and investments. To a great extent, our nature's [nation's] future is in the Pacific.

And this is why we're especially glad to begin our journey here in Hawaii, the crossroads of the Pacific. All Americans are proud of Hawaii, proud of her 25 years of statehood, proud of her history, her people, and proud of the role that she's played in the struggle for progress and human freedom. In the years and decades to come, Hawaii's importance will continue to grow. And it is America's great, good fortune that Hawaii is her 50th and youngest State. We're grateful to you for your hospitality, for this chance to rest and relax, to enjoy Hawaii's beauty and the warmth of her people.

So, again, I'll just say Happy Easter, and thank you, and God bless all of you. Thank you.

Note: The President spoke at 1:05 p.m. at the base. He was greeted by Gov. George Ariyoshi, and Mrs. Ariyoshi; Adm. William J. Crowe, Jr., Commander in Chief, U.S. Pacific Command, and Mrs. Crowe; and Sfc. and Mrs. Gregory Lee Emfinger.

Remarks on Departure From Hickam Air Force Base in Honolulu, Hawaii
April 24, 1984

Ladies and gentlemen, Nancy and I have greatly enjoyed our brief stay here in Hawaii. And we wish to thank Governor and Mrs. Ariyoshi, the superb staff here at Hickam, and all the people of Hawaii for their warm and generous hospitality.

We're about to embark on the next important phase of our relations with the nations of the Pacific Basin with this second visit to Asia in 6 months. From here we go on to Guam, where we will meet with the Governors of Guam, American Samoa, and the Northern Mariana Islands and the Presidents of the Marshalls, the Federated States of Micronesia, and Palau. These islands occupy a broad expanse of the Pacific Ocean equivalent in size to the continental United States.

From Guam, we'll go on to China—first to the capital, Beijing, where I will meet with Chinese leaders; afterward, we will visit Xi'an to see something of ancient China and also the Chinese countryside; then on to Shanghai, China's largest city, busiest seaport, and commercial center.

Our trip will reciprocate the visit paid to our country 3 months ago by Chinese Premier Zhao, which began right here in Honolulu. This will be the first visit to China by an American President since 1975. Our trip symbolizes the maturing of the United States relationship with China, which was given a new beginning 12 years ago by President Nixon after more than two decades of isolation, and then carried forward by Presidents Ford and Carter.

It's fitting that we should depart for China from these enchanting islands. Residents of Hawaii are keenly aware of the great stake that America has in Eastern Asia. From your unique viewpoint, you see the importance of America's responsibilities as a Pacific power—both for our security and for our own economic well-being.

The Pacific Basin is one of our fastest growing markets. America and her Pacific neighbors are nations of the future. We must work with our friends to keep the Pacific truly peaceful—an ocean for commerce, not conflict.

Together, we can go forward in a mighty enterprise to build dynamic growth economies and make the world safer by working for peace and opposing expansionist aggression. And that's what our trip to China is all about. We journey to China in a spirit of peace and friendship, realistic about our differences, but desiring to build upon our common interests.

The American people have always held the achievements of Chinese civilization in the highest esteem, and we have the warmest feelings of friendship for the Chinese people. Last January, when Premier Zhao traveled around America, he said he was struck by the warmth the Americans feel toward the Chinese. Well, we go to China to convey this respect and friendship directly to the Chinese people, to hear their hopes and concerns, and to express our readiness to cooperate with China in its ambitious efforts to modernize its economy.

In the days ahead, I'll be holding a number of significant meetings with China's leaders. We will have the chance to review our respective positions on a variety of international concerns and to discuss the state of our bilateral relations. We hope to chart the direction of our relationship for the months and years to come.

U.S.-China relations are good. I believe they can and will be better. Close ties between our countries serve the interests of both our peoples. A stable and enduring U.S.-China relationship provides a vital contribution to the peace and well-being of all the peoples of East Asia and an important building block on the structure of world peace. We will carry with us your good wishes and those of all the American people.

I have to take a moment and say to you here, in this particular place, what it means to me to be here with you men and women in uniform and with all of those who are not in uniform but who also serve; those who know some of the privations and hardships, the inconveniences—your families, your wives, your children—they, too, serve.

There are some among us who say that the military is one of the causes of war. I'm sure they're sincere in their belief, but they're dead wrong to believe that the uniform, that the military could be among the causes of war is like believing that the police department is responsible for crime. You are the peacemakers. The better you perform, the less likely it is that we will ever see combat or hostilities directed against our nation.

You know, many years ago in one of the four wars in my lifetime, an admiral stood on the bridge of a carrier watching the planes take off and out into the darkness, bent on a night combat mission, and then found himself asking with no one there to answer, just himself, to hear his own voice, he said, "Where do we find such men?" A

decade or so ago, after spending an evening with the first returning POW's from Vietnam, Nancy and I found ourselves—as the evening ended, having heard the stories of horror and brutality by men who had been confined as prisoners of war longer than any other fighting men in America's history—found ourselves asking that same question, "Where do we find such men?" We find them where we've always found them when we need them. We find them where we found you—on the main streets and the farms of America.

You are the product of the freest, the fairest, the most generous and humane society that has ever been created by man. God bless you all, and thank you. Thank you very much.

Note: The President spoke at 10:50 a.m. at the base. Following the departure ceremony, the President boarded Air Force One for his trip to Guam.

Remarks on Arrival at Guam International Airport in Agana
April 25, 1984

Governor and my fellow citizens and honored guests, thank you, and a warm *hafa adai* [hello].

I'm delighted to be here on Guam where you're fond of saying that the rays of each sunrise first touch the Stars and Stripes, and that's a great way to start the day.

It's an honor to be with all of you who've worked so hard to make this visit possible. My special thanks to Congressman Won Pat, to Governors Bordallo, Coleman, and Tenorio, and to President Nakayama of the Federated States of Micronesia, President Kabua of the Marshall Islands, and President Remeliik of Palau.

It's good to see that Assistant Secretary of the Interior Richard Montoya, High Commissioner Janet McCoy, and Ambassador Fred Zeder are also here today.

Guam, the hub of the Pacific, is easily within range of almost all major cities in the Far East. For many people, Guam is a convenient stop on the way to someplace else,

but for us, Guam means a great deal more. We may be nearly 9,000 miles from our Nation's Capital, but it's a real pleasure to know that we're among fellow Americans.

Governor and Mrs. Bordallo, thank you very much for such a warm and wonderful welcome. There has been so much history and greatness on this sparkling island of democracy. And this July, Guam will commemorate the 40th anniversary of its liberation. Together, we returned peace and freedom to this beautiful land; and together, we'll keep it that way.

The men and women who serve on Guam are carrying on in the finest tradition of those before them. At Andersen Air Force Base and Agana Naval Air Station and on bases and ships all over the world, Americans in uniform are going about their duties with dedication, valor, and skill. And their mission is peace today, tomorrow, and for always.

This morning as we left the base in Honolulu—Hickam Airfield there—and I had the pleasure of speaking to those young men and women of ours in uniform—and there are so many here today—and I reminded them that at a time—and I thought it should be said to them, that at a time when there are people who would link the uniform and the military with the other causes of war and say that that is one of the reasons for war, let it be said here and now that those who wear the uniform are the peacemakers. And blessed are the peacemakers. And the better they perform their tasks, the greater is our chance of not seeing war again. There have been four wars in my lifetime—none of them started because America was too strong.

Incidentally, I might say, of all the things that go with the position I now hold, nothing, nothing has made me more proud than the young men and women, the people that are in the Armed Forces of all our branches. I am so proud of them, I can't look at them without getting a lump in my throat.

The United States is proud to be part of the Pacific community. Pacific Americans have always lived up to the values that make us a good and worthy people, values that begin with the sacred worth of human life, religious faith, family, community spirit, and hard work.

I see some of you expected this. They told me that it really doesn't get you wet when it rains out here—[*laughter*]—so I'll just keep on going.

In times of crisis, few Americans have been more steadfast in the defense of our shared values and few have made more sacrifices to preserve them. Together, we have built an enduring partnership for freedom, peace, and prosperity. And once again, America's new strength, confidence, and purpose are carrying hope and opportunity to people far from the mainland.

While each island is proud of its own culture, economy, and history, all share the desire for a brighter future for their people. We have a natural interest in the progress of all the island peoples of the Pacific. We want to help the development of their economies, and we will help keep the region free from tension and rivalries. With our partnership, much can and will be accomplished.

We're looking forward to expanding and improving our ties with the island nations of the Pacific. We've reached an important milestone in the relationship between the Trust Territory and the United States. You're right, Governor, 14 years of negotiations on the future political status of the Trust Territory are drawing to a close.

In 1975 the people of the Northern Marianas voted for commonwealth status with the United States. And last year, the people of the Federated States of Micronesia, the Marshall Islands, and Palau voted for a compact of free association, defining a new relationship with the United States. Because the compact reflects the will of the people, I hope that both the United States Congress and the international community will recognize that complete self-government for the peoples of the Trust Territory should not be delayed.

We have submitted the compact to the Congress and have urged full consideration and approval as soon as is feasible. In the meantime, we will continue negotiations in order to resolve the constitutional issues holding up resolution of Palau's future political status.

The United States Government will work closely with the Micronesian Governments as they move forward in their new direction. We want to build on our shared values and develop an even better relationship. We're your close friends, and we will be reliable partners.

In closing, let me echo the noble sentiment expressed in the Constitution of the Federated States of Micronesia: "The Micronesian nation is born in an age when men voyage among stars; our world itself is an island. We extend to all nations what we seek from each—peace, friendship, cooperation, and love in our common humanity."

Well, I know that those eloquent words express the feelings of all Americans. And again, Nancy and I, from the bottom of our hearts, thank you for your very beautiful welcome here. God bless you all. Thank you.

Note: The President spoke at 3:49 p.m. in response to remarks by Gov. Ricardo J. Bordallo.

Message to the Congress Transmitting Proposed Legislation To Combat International Terrorism
April 26, 1984

To the Congress of the United States:

I am sending to the Congress today four separate bills to attack the pressing and urgent problem of international terrorism.

In 1983 more than 250 American citizens were killed in terrorist attacks, the largest number in any year of record. In the wake of the tragic deaths of our diplomats and Marines, as well as French and Israeli soldiers in Lebanon, in light of the cynical murder of four South Korean cabinet officers and many others by North Korean terrorists in Burma, and as a result of the attack on our embassy in Kuwait, it is essential that we act immediately to cope with this menace and to increase cooperation with other governments in dealing with this growing threat to our way of life.

In the past fifteen years, terrorism has become a frightening challenge to the tranquility and political stability of our friends and allies. During the past decade alone, there have been almost 6,500 terrorist incidents. Over 3,500 people have been killed in these incidents, and more than 7,600 people have been wounded. American citizens have been the victims of more than 2,500 terrorist incidents. Of special concern to me has been the toll inflicted on our diplomats and members of the Armed Forces. I am also deeply concerned, however, about attacks against other American citizens, who have been the victims of forty percent of the terrorist incidents over the past decade.

In recent years, a very worrisome and alarming new kind of terrorism has developed: the direct use of instruments of terror by foreign states. This "state terrorism," starkly manifest in the recent dreadful spectacles of violence in Beirut, Rangoon, and Kuwait, accounts for the great majority of terrorist murders and assassinations. Also disturbing is state-provided training, financing, and logistical support to terrorists and terrorist groups. These activities are an extremely serious and growing source of danger to us, our friends and our allies, and are a severe challenge to America's foreign policy.

The protection of our citizens, our official personnel, and our facilities abroad requires the close cooperation and support of other governments. We depend on other governments to provide security protection to more than 250 United States diplomatic and consular posts abroad. We look to other governments to maintain the normal protections of law in their countries for our citizens living and traveling abroad and for our business representatives and business properties.

In 1983, this Administration sent to the Congress legislation to enable us to provide adequate protection for foreign officials in the United States. Not only is their protection essential to meet the obligations of the United States under international treaties, it is equally important to demonstrate to officials of other governments that they can count on full protection while they are in the United States.

I also asked the Congress to provide legislative authority for anti-terrorism training, and in some cases equipment, to foreign governments in order to enhance cooperation with governments on whom we must depend for protection abroad. In my view, the more effective and knowledgeable local law enforcement officials and officers are, the greater will be their ability to provide the kind of security both they and we need. I commend the Congress for providing a two-year authorization for this program and an appropriation of $2.5 million for 1984.

I am determined that my Administration will do whatever is necessary to reduce the incidence of terrorism against us anywhere in the world and to see that the perpetrators of terrorist acts are brought to justice. I believe it is essential, however, that the Executive branch, the Congress and the public clearly understand that combatting terrorism effectively requires concerted action on many different fronts. With trained personnel, effective laws, close international cooperation, and diligence, we can reduce the risks of terrorism to our people and increase the deterrent to future acts of terrorism.

Dealing with the immediate effect of terrorist violence is only part of the challenge, however. We must also assure that the states now practicing or supporting terrorism do not prosper in the designs they pursue. We must assure that international forums, such as the United Nations, take a balanced and practical view of who is practicing terrorism and what must be done about it. We must assure that governments that are currently passive—or inactive—respecting this scourge understand the threat that terrorism poses for all mankind and that they cooperate in stopping it. We must work to assure that there is no role in civilized society for indiscriminate threatening, intimidation, detention, or murder of innocent people. We must make it clear to any country that is tempted to use violence to undermine democratic governments, destabilize our friends, thwart efforts to promote democratic governments, or disrupt our lives that it has nothing to gain, and much to lose.

The legislation I am sending to the Congress is an important step in our war against terrorism. It will send a strong and vigorous message to friend and foe alike that the United States will not tolerate terrorist activity against its citizens or within its borders. Our legislative package consists of four separate bills, each of which is outlined below.

Act for the Prevention and Punishment of the Crime of Hostage-Taking

In September 1981, I signed the instrument ratifying the International Convention Against the Taking of Hostages, which was adopted by the United Nations on December 17, 1979. The convention has not been implemented domestically through enabling legislation, however. This legislation would implement the 1979 convention. It would amend the Federal kidnapping statute to provide for Federal jurisdiction over any kidnapping in which a threat is made to kill, injure, or continue to detain a victim in order to compel a third party to do or to abstain from doing something. This is a common ploy of terrorists. At the time I

signed the instrument of ratification, the Congress was informed that the instrument of ratification would not be deposited with the United Nations until enabling legislation had been enacted. To demonstrate to other governments and international forums that the United States is serious about its efforts to deal with international terrorism, it is essential that the Congress provide the necessary enabling legislation, so that we may fully implement the Hostage-Taking Convention.

Aircraft Sabotage Act

The United States became a party to the Tokyo Convention, which covers certain offenses or acts committed aboard aircraft, in 1969 and the Hague Convention, concerning the suppression of unlawful seizure of aircraft, in 1971. The Convention for the Suppression of Unlawful Acts Against the Safety of Civil Aviation was adopted at Montreal in 1971 and ratified by the United States in November 1972. The Montreal Convention requires all states party to it to establish jurisdiction over certain offenses affecting the safety of civil aviation.

The Congress has approved enabling legislation for the first two of these conventions but not for the Montreal Convention. This means that certain criminal acts related to aircraft sabotage or hijacking are not adequately covered by United States law. This gap in the law sends a false signal to terrorists, and it also indicates to other governments that we may not be as serious as we should be, and as in fact we are, in our efforts to combat international terrorism. Action by the Congress now would provide the basis for long-overdue implementation of this convention.

Act for Rewards for Information Concerning Terrorist Acts

Current law authorizes the payment of rewards for information concerning domestic crimes but is outdated. Maximum rewards are inadequate, and terrorism is not specifically included as a basis for paying a reward. Moreover, there is no authority for the payment of rewards for information on acts of terrorism abroad.

The proposed legislation, which is modelled on an existing statute that allows payment of rewards for information concerning the unauthorized manufacture of atomic weapons, recognizes that payment of a reward in connection with acts of domestic terrorism raises a matter of law enforcement that is properly within the jurisdiction of the Attorney General, but that the payment of a reward in connection with an act of terrorism abroad poses a political and foreign relations problem within the jurisdiction of the Secretary of State. By increasing the amounts of fines that may be paid, and by authorizing rewards for information concerning terrorist acts committed abroad, this Act would markedly improve the ability of the Departments of Justice and State to obtain information leading to the freeing of hostages or the capture of the perpetrators of acts of terrorism. In passing this legislation, the Congress can further underscore the intent of the United States to take every appropriate and necessary step to protect its citizens and property from terrorist acts.

Prohibition Against the Training or Support of Terrorist Organizations Act of 1984

The training and support of terrorist groups and activities by a number of countries has reached alarming proportions. In addition, the number of states now using terrorism as an instrument of foreign policy is both increasing and highly disturbing. The provision of assistance to countries that support terrorism and use terrorism as a foreign policy tool has thus become a matter of grave concern to national security. This Act, together with revised and strengthened regulations that the Department of State intends to issue shortly, would enhance the ability of the Department of Justice to prosecute persons involved in the support of terrorist activities and of states using terrorism. Enactment of this legislation would be a strong contribution to the effort to combat terrorism.

We must recognize that terrorism is symptomatic of larger problems. We must dedicate ourselves to fostering modernization, development, and beneficial change in the depressed areas of the world. We must renew our commitment to promoting and assisting representative and participatory governments. We must attack the problem of terrorism as a crime against the international community whenever and wherever possible, but we must strive to eradicate the sources of frustration and despair that are the spawning places and nutrients of terrorism.

The legislative proposals that I am sending to the Congress today will, when approved, materially benefit our Nation and help us to assist friendly countries. I believe that they are extraordinarily important, and I strongly urge that the Congress undertake their timely consideration and speedy passage.

RONALD REAGAN

The White House,
April 26, 1984.

Toast at a Dinner Hosted by President Li Xiannian of China in Beijing
April 26, 1984

President Li, Premier Zhao, distinguished ladies and gentlemen, it's a pleasure to be here with you tonight. Nancy and I are most grateful for the warmth of the reception that you've given us. I'm certain I speak for everyone in our entourage when I say we are overwhelmed by the loveliness of this hall, the gardens. The setting is certainly a tribute to the richness and depth of your culture.

And might I add, this meal appears to be a tribute to your culinary arts, as well.

You've made us feel welcome after a long journey. And this, even more than the grandeur of the surroundings and the grace of the meal, is appreciated.

Premier Zhao's recent trip to the United States and our visit, as well, demonstrate how technological leaps in communications and transportation are changing our perceptions of the world. Yet, even as technology catapults us into the future, making possible in our travel that once took months or even years, ancient truths are reconfirmed. Many centuries ago, Wang Po, a famous Chinese poet-philosopher, wrote, "Although we reside in far corners of the world, having a good friend is akin to having a good neighbor."

The essence of that observation is as true today as it was when it was penned. In that spirit, President Li, I come to China representing the sincere desire of the American people to be good neighbors to the Chinese people.

It was just 200 years ago when the first American merchant ship called on a Chinese port. Two hundred years seems like the blink of an eye to Chinese civilization; yet, for Americans, this spans almost the entire history of our Republic. Looking back, President Li, we can see that at times the relationship between our two nations was not what it should have been. But thanks to the hard work and determination of farsighted leaders of both of our countries during the last 12 years, our future is bright with potential.

There are differences between us, yes, differences that should be neither glossed over nor dented—denied, I should say. Yet we, the people of China and the United States, share a sincere desire for peace and prosperity, and we understand that by working together, emphasizing our areas of agreement, everyone will benefit.

Premier Zhao's visit to the United States was the first visit ever by a Chinese Premier. And now this marks the first visit by an American President since our countries formally established diplomatic relations in 1979.

The travel of government leaders is symbolic of the surge of activity, of the exchange and cooperation going on between our peoples at all levels. Whether in commerce, the arts, science, or industry, our citizens are establishing personal bonds of trust and friendship that mirror the good will found at the highest levels.

This healthy intercourse is encouraged because our countries, our people as a whole, have determined that what we have in common, what we can accomplish working and building together, is vastly more significant than those things that separate us. This, of course, does not mean progress will be easy. Few things worthwhile ever happen without commitment and effort by good people. We can be proud, considering our differences, of how much has already been accomplished.

If you'll permit me, we believe even greater progress can be made if our future efforts are based on *hu jing hu hui*—mutual respect and mutual benefit. If we have the will to live up to it, *hu jing hu hui* can make our countries more prosperous and more secure. It can keep us friends, even while recognizing that we do not totally agree on some things which we believe important. There is every reason for optimism about the continuing peaceful evolution of relations between our two countries.

I would hope in the not too distant future that you, President Li, as I have already expressed to you earlier, will come and be our guest in the United States, so that you can meet and talk with the American people.

Nancy and I are now looking forward with great anticipation to the rest of our visit to your country. We're especially pleased to see Premier Zhao again. I'm also eager to make the personal acquaintance of Chairman Deng and General Secretary Hu.

This, our first day, was even more gratifying than expected. Meeting you and having the opportunity for open and constructive dialog was an excellent way to inaugurate this trip.

During our stay, Nancy and I hope to see and learn much about China and its people. The history, the beauty, and the culture of your country is legend throughout the world. I first learned about it as a boy in a small school in the farm country of America. I never dreamed back then that I'd have the opportunity to come and see these things for myself.

Now, as I suggested a moment ago, technology has made us neighbors. Neighbors are not family, but they can be dear and trusted friends. And that is the spirit I sense already. It's something upon which weighty accomplishments can be built. In that spirit, I invite all of you to join me in a toast.

To your health, Mr. President, and that of Mrs. Li, and to the health of Premier Zhao and of China's other distinguished leaders, and to further success in advancing the relations of our two countries.

Note: The President spoke at 7:30 p.m. at Yang Yuan Hall in response to a toast by President Li.

In his opening remarks, the President also referred to Premier Zhao Ziyang.

Remarks to Chinese Community Leaders in Beijing, China
April 27, 1984

Thank you very much, Dr. Zhou Peiyuan, and all of you distinguished ladies and gentlemen. I'm honored to come before you today, the first American President ever to address your nation from the Great Hall of the People.

My wife, Nancy, and I have looked forward to visiting the people and treasures of your great and historic land, one of the world's oldest civilizations. We have marveled at Beijing's sweeping vistas, and we have felt the warmth of your hospitality touch our hearts. We only regret that our visit will be so brief. I'm afraid it will be as a Tang Dynasty poet once wrote, "looking at the flowers while riding horseback." But you have another saying from the book of Han which describes how Nancy and I feel: "To see a thing once is better than hearing about it a hundred times."

Twelve years ago former President Nixon arrived in Beijing, stepped down from Air Force One, and shook hands with former Premier Zhou Enlai. Premier Zhou would later tell him, "Your handshake came over the vastest ocean in the world—25 years of no communication." With one handshake, America and China each turned a new page in their histories.

I believe that history beckons again. We have begun to write a new chapter for peace and progress in our histories with America and China going forward hand in hand—*xieshou bingjin* [walk together hand in hand].

We must always be realistic about our relationship, frankly acknowledging the fundamental differences in ideology and institutions between our two societies. Yes, let us acknowledge those differences. Let us

never minimize them. But let us not be dominated by them.

I have not come to China to hold forth on what divides us, but to build on what binds us. I have not come to dwell on a closed-door past, but to urge that Americans and Chinese look to the future, because together we can and will make tomorrow a better day.

When Premier Zhao was in the United States, he told us, "China has opened its door and will never close it again." Permit me to assure you today, America's door is open to you, and when you walk through, we'll welcome you as our neighbors and our friends.

We may live at nearly opposite ends of the world. We may be distinctly different in language, customs, and political beliefs. But on many vital questions of our time, there is little difference between the American and Chinese people. Indeed, I believe if we were to ask citizens all over this world what they desire most for their children, and for their children's children, their answer, in English, Chinese, or any language, would likely be the same: We want peace. We want freedom. We want a better life. Their dreams, so simply stated, represent mankind's deepest aspirations for security and personal fulfillment. And helping them make their dreams come true is what our jobs are all about.

We can work together as equals in a spirit of mutual respect and mutual benefit. I believe in Chinese you say *hu jing hu hui.*

Well, America and China are both great nations. And we have a special responsibility to preserve world peace.

To help fulfill that responsibility, the United States is rebuilding its defenses, which had been neglected for more than a decade. Our people realize this effort is crucial if we're to deter aggression against America, our allies, and other friends. But we threaten no nation. America's troops are not massed on China's borders. And we occupy no lands. The only foreign land we occupy anywhere in the world is beneath gravesites where Americans shed their blood for peace and freedom. Nor do we commit wanton acts, such as shooting 269 innocent people out of the sky for the so-called cause of sacred airspace.

America and China both condemn military expansionism, the brutal occupation of Afghanistan, the crushing of Kampuchea; and we share a stake in preserving peace on the Korean peninsula.

I think our two peoples agree there can be only one sane policy to preserve our precious civilization in this modern nuclear age: A nuclear war cannot be won and must never be fought. And that's why we've proposed to the Soviet Union meaningful negotiations that go beyond rhetoric to actual arms reductions and why we must all work for the day when nuclear weapons will be banished from the face of the Earth.

America's interest in China, our friendship for your people, and our respect for China's many contributions to the progress of civilization date back to the beginning of our own history. You might be interested to know that personal dinner settings used by our first three Presidents—George Washington, John Adams, and Thomas Jefferson—were of Chinese origin, evidence of our Founding Fathers attraction for your country's high artistic standards.

Back in 1784, when the first American trading ship, the *Empress of China*, entered your waters, my country was unknown to you. We were a new republic, eager to win a place in international commerce. A slightly homesick American sailor recorded that first day in a letter home.

"My dear father," he wrote, "if ever you receive this letter, it will acquaint you, that after a passage of 6 months and 7 days we came to anchor at Wampoo . . . The Chinese had never heard of us, but we introduced ourselves as a new nation, gave them

our history with a description of our country, the importance and necessity of a trade here to the advantage of both, which they appear perfectly to understand and wish."

Well, since those early days, our countries have both profited from the exchange of people, goods, and ideas. Chinese settlers helped tame our continent during the 19th century. Today their families' descendants join other Americans in cooperating with you to build a new prosperity in China.

How did America, which began as an impoverished country and a melting pot, attracting immigrants from every corner of the globe, pull together and become the leading economic nation in the world? How did we go in so short a time from living by candlelight to exploring the frontiers of the universe by satellite, from each farmer laboring with horse and hoe for an entire year just to feed four people, to running his farm with the most modern machinery and producing enough to feed 75 people, making America the breadbasket of the world?

Well, we're people who've always believed the heritage of our past is the seed that brings forth the harvest of our future. And from our roots we have drawn tremendous power from two great forces: faith and freedom. America was founded by people who sought freedom to worship God and to trust in Him to guide them in their daily lives with wisdom, strength, goodness, and compassion.

Our passion for freedom led to the American Revolution, the first great uprising for human rights and independence against colonial rule. We knew each of us could not enjoy liberty for ourselves unless we were willing to share it with everyone else. And we knew our freedom could not truly be safe unless all of us were protected by a body of laws that treated us equally.

George Washington told us we would be bound together in a sacred brotherhood of free men. Abraham Lincoln defined the heart of American democracy when he said, "No man is good enough to govern another man without that other's consent. . . ." These great principles have nourished the soul of America, and they have been enriched by values such as the dignity of work, the friendship of neighbors, and the warmth of family. Like China, our people see the future in the eyes of our children. And like China, we revere our elders. To be as good as our fathers and mothers, we must be better.

"Trust the people"—these three words are not only the heart and soul of American history but the most powerful force for human progress in the world today. Those who ignore this vital truth will condemn their countries to fall farther and farther behind in the world's competition for economic leadership in the 1980's and beyond, because look around us, the societies that have made the most spectacular progress in the shortest period of time are not the most rigidly organized nor even the richest in natural resources. No, it's where people have been allowed to create, compete, and build, where they've been permitted to think for themselves, make economic decisions, and benefit from their own risks, that societies have become the most prosperous, progressive, dynamic, and free. Nothing could be more basic to the spirit of progress for a farmer, laborer, or merchant than economic reward for legitimate risk and honest toil.

A little over a century ago, Ulysses S. Grant, who was then a former President, visited your country and saw China's great potential. "I see dawning . . ." Grant wrote, "the beginning of a change. When it does come, China will rapidly become a powerful and rich nation . . . The population is industrious, frugal, intelligent, and quick to learn."

Well, today, China's economy crackles with the dynamics of change: expansion of individual incentives for farmers in your new responsibility system; new bonuses for workers and more disciplined management in terms of profits and losses; improved methods of market distribution; opening your economy to the world through China's membership in the International Monetary Fund, the World Bank, and through your invitation to trade and invest, especially in your four Special Economic Zones; and your commitment to attract capital and scientific knowledge to create a high technology base for the future. All this reflects China's new role in the international eco-

nomic community and your determination to modernize your economy and raise the standard of living of your people.

Unlike some governments which fear change and fear the future, China is beginning to reach out toward new horizons, and we salute your courage.

"Progress," Premier Zhao has told us, "lies in our efforts to emancipate our thinking in a bold way—to carry out reform with determination, to make new inventions with courage, and to break with the economic molds and conventions of all descriptions which fetter the development of the productive force." Well, we Americans have always considered ourselves pioneers, so we appreciate such vitality and optimism.

Today I bring you a message from my countrymen. As China moves forward in this new path, America welcomes the opportunity to walk by your side.

Incidentally, I know Premier Zhao has demonstrated mastery of his subject. When he was directing agricultural policies in Sichuan, the peasants went from food shortages and forced imports to bumper harvests and rising exports. In fact, I'm told that because of the work he did, it is said in Sichuan Province, "If you want rice, go see Zhao."

Well, China's growth is in China's hands. You will choose your own path to development. But we're not surprised to see the fresh breezes of incentives and innovation sweeping positive changes across China. And behind the statistics of economic growth are reports of personal success stories pointing to a new spirit of progress. Chairman Deng has a saying, "Seek truth from facts." Well, today in China, the reality of more small enterprises doing a thriving business, more families profiting from their own hard work and the bigger harvests they produce, and more investment in science and technology points to more opportunity for all. President John Kennedy often used a metaphor to describe such progress: "A rising tide lifts all boats."

In the United States, as I mentioned earlier, we've always believed deeply that incentives are key and that free people build free markets that ignite dynamic development for everyone. For a time, America's government had drifted away from this key principle, and our economic growth suffered.

When we took office, in January 1981, we said to the people, "Let us make a new beginning. From now on, if you work harder and earn more than before, your reward will be greater than it was. We're putting America's future in your hands. You can spark the spirit of enterprise. You can get America moving again." And they have.

In 3 short years, the American people have revived a dynamic growth economy bolstered by incentives of lower tax rates, stable prices, reduced interest rates, a rebirth of productivity, and restored confidence in our currency.

Hope is high. Confidence is strong. America's future looks bright again. With a strong technological base, pioneering sunrise industries and modernizing older ones, the United States is beginning an economic renaissance and helping pull other nations toward worldwide recovery.

I see America and our Pacific neighbors going forward in a mighty enterprise to build strong economies and a safer world.

The United States and China have an historic opportunity. We can expand our economic and scientific cooperation, strengthen the ties between our peoples, and take an important step toward peace and a better life. And there is much we can share.

We think progress in four areas is particularly promising: trade, technology, investment, and exchanges of scientific and managerial expertise.

In a few short years, two-way trade has risen sharply. The United States is now China's third largest trading partner. Our bilateral trade shows great promise for the future, particularly in areas such as machinery, technology, oil equipment, petroleum, agricultural and manufacturing products.

Last June, I instructed our government to liberalize controls over the export to China of high technology products, such as computers and laboratory instruments. Our policies on technology transfer will continue to evolve along with our overall relationship and the development of broader cooperation between us. May I emphasize to the members of the scientific community here today: The relaxing of export controls reflects my determination that China be treated as a friendly, nonallied nation and that the United States be fully prepared to cooperate in your modernization.

During Premier Zhao's visit to our country, we took another step forward, signing the United States-China Industrial and Technological Cooperation Accord. Our Joint Commission on Commerce and Trade will discuss implementation of the Accord during their next meeting in Washington in May. We will focus our efforts on the sectors to which China has attached greatest priority. Our trade and development program will facilitate our progress.

Expanding cooperative ventures is another area of promising growth: American firms have invested almost $700 million in joint ventures and offshore oil exploration in China, making the United States your largest foreign investor. We welcome your determination to improve conditions for foreign business in China. Streamlining bureaucratic procedures, establishing a more predictable system for investment through domestic legislation and international agreements, reforming prices to make them internationally competitive, and providing foreign business people with the offices, housing, and schools they and their families need to work effectively, will stimulate more American investment.

For your part, some 50 Chinese firms have established offices or branches in the United States, and China has invested in several joint ventures in our country.

We intend to strengthen these trends. When Treasury Secretary Regan was here last month for the meeting of the Joint Economic Committee, he concluded a bilateral tax agreement. Monday, our two countries will sign this agreement, which, I'm pleased to report, will increase incentives for even closer cooperation between American and Chinese firms. And we're continuing to work toward conclusion of bilateral agreements on greater investment protection and many other areas of cooperation.

I am particularly proud that the United States and China have reached agreement on cooperation in the peaceful uses of atomic energy. As many of you know, the negotiations between our two countries go back almost to the beginning of my administration. We have held a total of six sessions in Washington and Beijing. We made great progress during Premier Zhao's visit, and our negotiations have just now concluded successfully. The result: an agreement for cooperation in peaceful uses of nuclear energy.

I understand that several of the people here made major contributions to this effort, which meets the requirements of both sides. Once approval is complete, it will open broad opportunities for joint work in development of the energy base which China needs for her modernization. Scientists, engineers, business leaders, and officials of both countries interested in peaceful nuclear energy will welcome this agreement. China has one of the world's most ambitious programs for expansion of electric power generation, and I believe that America's energy technology—not just in nuclear energy but across the board—is second to none, and perhaps most suitable for China's varied needs.

Our agreement is founded on important nonproliferation standards. We have noticed recent statements of China's nonproliferation policies, particularly those by Premier Zhao in Washington and Beijing over the past several months. Premier Zhao and I have discussed these matters directly. I can tell you that our countries share the same basic principles of preserving world peace and preventing the destabilizing spread of nuclear explosives. Neither of us will encourage proliferation nor assist any other country to acquire or develop any nuclear explosive device. Our cooperation in the peaceful uses of nuclear energy will be based on shared principles of nonproliferation.

There is also great potential in our joint efforts to increase managerial and scientific expertise. I know that many of you have heard through the Chinese press about the good work of the 9-month Dalian program of management training for industry, science, and technology. More than 750 graduates have received training in modern methods of industrial management. And I'm told some of you are graduates of that program. Well, I'm delighted to announce that we have agreed to establish a special new

program there offering a full 3-year master's degree in business administration. The degree will be awarded by the State University of New York. We're to share with you the knowledge that is America's key technology—management and science skills to develop a nation.

Under our Joint Commission on Science and Technology, we have a very productive agreement with exchange programs in 21 specific areas. We're sharing the benefits of research in medicine, energy, and other technical fields. Our scientists are learning a great deal from each other in public health, agricultural sciences, and many other areas.

Men and women of vision already see that working in the zero gravity environment of space offers dazzling opportunities to improve life on Earth. Experiments done on our space shuttle have shown that life-saving medicines can be manufactured in space with four times the purity of the same medicines on Earth. And they can be made over 400 times more rapidly, so 1 month's production of medicines in space yields as much as 30 years' production on the ground.

We also look forward to being able to manufacture large crystals of exceptional purity in space. These crystals are the basis of the semiconductor chips which run modern computers. By manufacturing them in zero gravity, we can make new strides toward producing larger, faster computers, the so-called supercomputers, and ultimately reduce the cost of computer manufacturing. We look forward to exploring with China the possibilities of cooperating in the development of space on behalf of all our fellow citizens.

In the humanities and social sciences, hundreds of American and Chinese scholars have visited each others' countries to teach and study subjects ranging from law and economics to poetry and history. For our part, we welcome this new Pacific tide. Let it roll peacefully on, carrying a two-way flow of people and ideas that can break down barriers of suspicion and mistrust, and build up bonds of cooperation and shared optimism.

The future is ours to build. Surmounting the risks and the fears of some may be difficult, but I'm convinced the challenge is worth it. The greatest victories come when people dare to be great, when they summon their spirits to brave the unknown and go forward together to reach a greater good.

So often, we see individual actions of courage and love in everyday life that give us faith to believe in ourselves and hope for a better future. In 1981 a bright, young American student, John Zeidman, came here to study China and to seek new friends. He was a boy of great heart and enthusiasm, and riding his bicycle on Beijing's streets, conversing and camping with artists and students, he fell in love with your country. Tragically, he was struck ill on his 20th birthday and later died. But his tragedy brought forth new life.

John's family and friends have established a Chinese studies program at the Sidwell Friends School in Washington. Hundreds have contributed, and the program now attracts young people from public and private schools and serves as a model for other schools all across America. Earlier this year, Premier Zhao visited the school. This summer the entire class will come to China as his guests to meet their student contemporaries.

From the great grief of one boy's death came a seed. And from that seed has grown a tree of understanding, a tree that now blossoms with the beauty of friendship and cooperation. If our people could go forward in this same spirit, planting not one tree, but millions, and then tending each so it may grow sturdy and tall—then the dream of a single youth might grow into the golden dreams of all mankind.

Thank you very much.

Note: The President spoke at 1:20 p.m. in the auditorium at the Great Hall of the People. Zhou Peiyuan, a Chinese scientist, hosted the event, which was attended by Chinese citizens who either have been involved in the various aspects of U.S.-China cooperation directly related to China's modernization program or who study Sino-U.S. relations.

Toast at a Welcoming Banquet Hosted by Premier Zhao Ziyang of China in Beijing
April 27, 1984

Premier Zhao, ladies and gentlemen, since we arrived yesterday, the graciousness with which we have been received has been truly heartwarming. A Chinese proverb best describes my feelings: "When the visitor arrives, it is as if returning home."

Having already known Premier Zhao, one of the purposes of my visit was to make new friends. But I find, especially after meeting President Li and General Secretary Hu, that instead of making friends, I am among friends.

Mr. Premier, this has been a stimulating day. Much was accomplished, not the least of which was the renewal of the personal rapport we established during your memorable visit to the United States. Your visit permitted you to judge for yourself the intentions of the American people. I hope the good will you experienced, just as I enjoyed from your people today, confirmed to you that our citizens want our countries to work in harmony.

The American and Chinese Governments have responded to that wish in a series of formal communiques which set forth the fundamental principles of our relationship— the 1972 Shanghai communique, the January 1, 1979, communique establishing diplomatic relations, and the August 17, 1982, communique negotiated by my administration.

Mr. Premier, by any accounting the cooperation between China and the United States already has been a boon to our people. We have both gained. In the last few years, two-way trade has taken off. There has been a veritable explosion of student, science, business, and tourist exchanges between our peoples. Joint business ventures which profit all concerned are multiplying.

We would be less than candid if we minimized the significance of the benefits we each receive from our good relations. Standing together, we can expand the trade and commercial ties that increase the quality of life in both countries. Standing together, we can further peace and security. Great nations, if adversaries, cannot draw from each other's strength.

The commitment to stand as friends has been made. The promise is solid. The challenges that remain, however, will take both patience and mutual understanding. I have suggested and, with your permission, say again this evening: Let us use as our guide the principle of *hu jing hu hui*—mutual respect, mutual benefit. This principle has within it both dignity and fairness.

Another source from which to draw is our knowlege of each other, a well of familiarity which increases in depth with every passing day.

We are each working hard to learn more about the delicate and detailed workings of the other's system—ours with its complex legal procedures based on the separation of powers, and yours with its own intricate patterns. Insights into why and how decisions are made can help both of us appreciate our agreements and accept in good faith our disagreements.

From what we see, Premier Zhao, my countrymen are enthused by what is happening in China. Your modernization program, an ambitious undertaking, makes our future relationship even more promising. You are striving to quadruple your production by the year 2000, and the eyes of the world are watching as you progress on this peaceful and productive course. The American people wish you success and offer you our cooperation in this great endeavor.

Americans, more than others, admire those who set great goals and strive to improve their lot. When that first American merchant ship set sail for China 200 years ago, our Forefathers were citizens of a weak republic living in an unexplored and undeveloped land. We Americans are proud of our accomplishments in these last 200

years, just as you are rightfully proud of the enormous contributions Chinese civilization has made to mankind.

As China moves forward to modernize and develop its economy, the United States is eager to join in a cooperative effort to share the American capabilities that helped turn our country from a vast wilderness into an industrial giant. Those American capabilities flow from the creative enterprise our society encourages. Our progress is based on what we have found to work. If it did not work, the American people, who are pragmatic by nature, would likely have abandoned it long ago.

China today, I understand, is taking its own practical approach. By increasing incentives and decentralizing decisionmaking, you are promoting innovation, creativity, and a better ability to adapt to local conditions. The responsibility system in agriculture has spurred increases in food production throughout China, and the special economic zones are providing dramatic examples of how incentives can raise productivity and offer bountiful opportunities for a better life.

In your drive for modernization, you have our best wishes. If you ask our advice, we can only answer with truth as we see it. But let me assure you, we want you to succeed. Having 1 billion people—nearly a quarter of mankind—healthy, well fed, clothed, and housed, educated, and given the opportunity for a higher standard of living, is in the interest of good and decent people everywhere. It is certainly in the interest of the American people, who wish to trade and be friends with the Chinese people.

Premier Zhao, as we're all well aware, our cooperation is based on more than simply the desire to improve our economies. Today the peace of the world is threatened by a major power that is focusing its resources and energies not on economic progress but, instead, on military power.

The shift in military might of the last decade has made trust and friendship between us even more vital. I know it is your desire, and that of the United States as well, that peace be preserved. We seek to better the quality of life of our people, and that can be done only in a peaceful environment. War is the great destroyer of all the hopes of mankind.

To preserve the peace and protect our own sovereignty and independence, we stand together in opposing expansionism and hegemony. We stand together in support of the independence of Afghanistan and Kampuchea. Both of us seek to promote peace and reconciliation through dialog between South and North on the Korean Peninsula. Both of us seek the early independence of Namibia and an end to outside interference in the affairs of southern Africa. Although our prescriptions for getting there are quite different, we share a common desire for a resolution of the turmoil in the Middle East and Central America. Both of us seek an end to the use of chemical weapons and agree on the necessity of reducing nuclear arms.

A strong China, dedicated to peace, clearly is in the best interest of international stability and in the best interest of the United States. A robust and enduring friendship will bolster the security of both our countries without compromising the independence of either. It will be the trust between us that will keep us and the world at peace. In this, let us be of the same mind. And as a saying from "The Book of Changes" goes, "If two people are of the same mind, their sharpness can cut through metal."

It is the hope and prayer of the American people that someday there will no longer be a need for our nation to use any of its resources to produce weapons of any kind. The Chinese and American people are now showing the world by our example that there is a better way than hatred and violence.

Many of us in this room have seen much history in our lifetime. My own lifetime spans one-third of the history of the American Republic. Over the many years that God has permitted me to live, I have observed the changing nature of the relationship between our two countries.

At times, our feelings toward each other were hostile and negative. Today, we have the opportunity to keep our countries on a path of genuine good will that will reap rewards for generations to come. Let us not shy from the task. It will not be easy; yet, let us move forward so that someday when the young people of our countries reach a ripe old age, they will look back, and there will be no memory of a time when there was anything else but friendship and good feelings between the Chinese and American people. That is a gift we can give to them.

In our shared spirit of friendship, peace, and cooperation, I am delighted to note that both President Li and General Secretary Hu have accepted our invitation to visit the United States. We look forward to reciprocating the warm hospitality that we've been shown in your beautiful country.

And in that same spirit, permit me, Premier Zhao, to propose a toast. To your health, Mr. Premier, to the health of President and Mrs. Li who so graciously acted as our hosts yesterday, to the health of Chairman Deng, General Secretary Hu, and the other distinguished Chinese citizens it is my privilege to meet this week, and to the friendship and cooperation between our two countries.

Note: The President spoke at 7:23 p.m. in the Banquet Hall at the Great Hall of the People in response to a toast by Premier Zhao.

Statement by Principal Deputy Press Secretary Speakes on the Broadcast of the President's Remarks to Chinese Leaders
April 28, 1984

On Thursday we were informed by the Information Department of the Ministry of Foreign Affairs that Chinese Central Television would carry the President's Friday speech to Chinese leaders in full in a taped program in prime-time evening television Friday night. Late in the day Friday, Mr. Qi Huaiyuan, Director of the Information Department of the Ministry of Foreign Affairs, advised me that portions of the speech dealing with the Soviet Union would not be broadcast.

Last night we learned that the broadcast also omitted several other segments of the speech, including key passages dealing with the President's view of values that Americans cherish, including religion and democracy. We had made it clear to the Chinese Government prior to the trip that we hoped for an opportunity for the President to communicate with the Chinese people on the American approach to world affairs, its bases in our system, and the goals we

seek in our relationship with the People's Republic.

The Chinese Government, which controls information in the country, has given the President extensive news coverage; certainly more than we would consider likely for most foreign leaders visiting the United States. The decision to delete material from the President's speech from the Chinese television broadcast and from other Chinese news media is an internal matter for the Chinese to decide, and we understand that. We, nevertheless, regret the fact that statements by the President which would have given the Chinese people a better understanding of our country and its people were not included in Chinese media coverage of the speech.

Interview With Representatives of Chinese Central Television in Beijing, China
April 28, 1984

Q. Mr. President, this year marks the bicentennial of the beginning of Sino-U.S. contacts and the fifth anniversary of the establishment of diplomatic relations between China and the United States. Mr. President, this visit at this time is, therefore, of exceptional significance. This is your first visit to China. Would you please, Mr. President, tell us your impression of the visit?

The President. Well, thank you, and may I say how pleased I am to visit your great and historic country. As a boy going to school in a small town in our Midwest, I used to dream of coming here. In those days China seemed a million miles away, and today modern jet travel gives us the privilege of seeing China, meeting your hard-working people and learning more about the progress that you're making, and visiting the many treasures of your civilization—one of the oldest in the world.

Permit me first to thank you on behalf of Nancy and myself for the warmth of your welcome. We journey to your country to make friends, but already you've made us feel that we are among friends, and you

have touched our hearts. Our only regret is our visit will be so brief. It's a little like, as a Tang Dynasty poet once wrote, "looking at the flowers while riding on horseback." But I mentioned at the Great Hall yesterday that you have another saying from the book of Han that describes how Nancy and I feel: "To see a thing once is better than hearing about it a hundred times."

Our visit this year marks the 200th anniversary since the first American merchant ship called at a Chinese port. Two hundred years for your civilization seems like the blink of an eye, but for Americans they span the entire history of our Republic. Yes, your country is old while ours is young, and, yes, we speak different languages, have different customs, and our governments hold different political beliefs. But I believe if you could look beyond labels and into the homes and hearts of our people, you'd find they share many basic values, values with your own—values like the dignity of work, the importance of opportunity, the love and strength of family, reverence for elders, the dream of leaving a better life for our children and our children's children, and finally our simple, heartfelt desire to be friends and to live together in peace.

Americans are people of peace. It's important you know that. We pose no threat to China or any nation. We have no troops massed on your borders. We occupy no lands. After World War II, we were the only undamaged industrial power, the only nation to harness the atom, and the only people with the power to conquer the world. But we didn't conquer anybody. We used our power to write a new chapter in history by helping rebuild the war-ravaged economies of both friends and foes. We love peace, and we cherish freedom, because we've learned time and again in place after place that economic growth and human progress make their greatest strides when people are secure and free to think, speak, worship, choose their own way, and reach for the stars.

We admire the progress your government has made in opening China's economy to the world and in providing more opportunities for your people to better their lives. And we've told your leaders that as the world's leading economy, the United States welcomes the chance to walk by China's side, sharing our technology and encouraging a greater flow of people, products, and ideas between our two countries.

Like China, the United States is a Pacific nation. A prosperous future is being built in the Pacific, and we're now your nation's third largest trading partner. We're working together to improve industrial, technological cooperation, increased trade and investment, and expand educational and cultural exchanges.

Let us resolve that communication, not confrontation, and commerce, not conflict, will always govern Chinese-American relations. If we do, there is no limit to the progress we can make by going forward hand in hand—*xieshou bingjin* [walk together hand in hand].

And now I'd be delighted to answer any more of your questions.

Q. Mr. President, the Chinese public expect that your visit will give an impetus to the steady and the sustained growth of Sino-U.S. relations. In your view, what concrete steps the Chinese and American sides should take to promote the further development of Sino-U.S. relations?

The President. Well, we've taken a number already. The progress that we have made with regard to trade agreements, that we're discussing right now with regard to protecting your people and ours against double taxation. We have arrived at an agreement on nuclear cooperation for peaceful energy, and at the same time we have agreed to prevent as much as we can by ourselves nuclear proliferation of weapons to other countries.

But we've had, I believe, five members of our Cabinet here in the last several months meeting with their counterparts in your government, working out everything from commerce and trade relations. Our Secretary of Defense has been here, our Secretary of State. We're discussing energy problems.

So, we'll continue along that path, finding all these areas of agreement and cooperation. And, as I say, we've made great progress already.

Q. Mr. President, both you and the Chinese leaders have expressed the desire for further development of Sino-U.S. relations. Everyone knows that the issue of Taiwan is a major obstacle to the development of our bilateral relations. It is also an important matter affecting the national feelings of 1 billion Chinese people. Could you please tell us how the United States intends to gradually remove this obstacle?

The President. Well, we believe that this is a problem of Chinese people on both sides of the straits to work out for themselves. It is true that we have a long historical relationship, a friendship with the people on Taiwan. We believe that the solution when it comes should be peaceful, and we do not believe that we should involve ourselves in this internal affair.

Our position, however, has been with the utmost sincerity. We want to go forward with friendship for the people of the People's Republic of China. At the same time, we don't believe that it would be right to cast aside longtime old friends in order to make new friends. But we will do anything we can to encourage the peaceful solution of this problem by the peoples of China.

Q. Mr. President, there is a great potential for Sino-U.S. economic cooperation. What measures the U.S. Government is prepared to adopt to promote further economic and technological cooperation between the two countries?

The President. Well, I believe I answered that in part on your previous question here. We are going forward. We have made great strides in providing high technology information and high technology itself in trade with the People's Republic of China, and we have an agricultural agreement now with regard to our grain sales to you. But we also have worked out agreements covering other forms of trade.

There are still some leftover prohibitions in some of our own laws, but we are working with the Congress—our own Congress—to eliminate those and have made great progress with that. And so, again, it's a case of continuing on the path that has already been started.

Q. For the last question, Mr. President, we would like to invite you to speak about your—perhaps your prediction for the prospects for the growth of Sino-U.S. relations in the future.

The President. Well, I am very optimistic about this growth of the relations that have already been started. And I think in my two previous questions—or your two previous questions—I left out one of the most important things that should be mentioned, and that is the development of relations in education, the exchange of students.

Just before I left the United States to come here, I met with a group of your students who are attending our colleges in the United States. There are some 12,000 in all, and we, at the same time, are looking forward to an exchange—our own students coming here. Of course, we also have a visitation in which roughly a hundred thousand of our people visit your country now with great interest and enjoyment.

So, this, I think, is one of the great things for the future, as our young people get to know each other. I have always said that our troubles begin when people are talking *about* each other instead of *to* each other. And if we can have our young people talking to each other, I'm very optimistic about the future.

Q. Thank you, Mr. President, for your accepting my interview.

The President. Well, it has been a great pleasure. I've enjoyed it. Thank you.

Note: The interview began at 9:14 a.m. in the Garden Room at the Diaoyutai State Guest House. It was taped for later use on Chinese television.

Remarks at a Reception for Members of the American Community in Beijing, China
April 28, 1984

And they thought I couldn't erase the deficit. [*Laughter*] Well, thank all of you for a very warm welcome. Nancy and I are delighted to be with you this evening. We've come to Beijing to strengthen America's ties, as you know, with China, something that each one of you has been doing very well already.

Now, about this honorary presidency: I greet it with mixed emotions—[*laughter*]—because once about 25 years after I'd gotten out of my alma mater, they had me back at commencement and gave me an honorary degree. And on that occasion, a sense of guilt that I'd been nursing for 25 years rose up and almost choked me, because I'd figured the first one they gave me was honorary. [*Laughter*] Now, if it's this easy, where will you all be along about next November? [*Laughter*]

Well, I'm sure that sometimes life as an American in Beijing can present challenges. But whatever difficulties you may face here, each of you is making history.

For more than two decades, as you know, the United States and China had no relations whatsoever. And then in 1972, President Nixon's trip to China and the Shanghai Communique broke that long silence. Our relationship since that time has been a force for peace in the world and will continue to serve that end. But at the same time, China and the United States recognize that we have many other areas of mutual interest, particularly since 1978, when Chinese leaders decided to foster the growth of the Chinese economy and open more to the West.

Since then, we've expanded our cultural exchanges. Last year, 150,000 Americans, as you probably know better than I do, visited China, and today more than 10,000 Chinese students are studying in the United States. And I had the pleasure of meeting with a small group of those just before coming here, and they were fine young people.

Just as significant, we've begun to form new economic bonds. Today more than a hundred American firms have offices in Beijing, and the Bank of China has an office in Manhattan. Just a few years ago, both would have been unthinkable.

Our visit here is intended to demonstrate the maturing of U.S.-China relations through four American administrations, and I think it's doing just that. Thursday, I met President Li; Friday, I had meetings with Premier Zhao and General Secretary Hu. And earlier today, I had extensive discussions with Chairman Deng.

While respecting the differences between us, the Chinese leaders and I have agreed to focus on all that unites us—our determination to resist foreign threats, the fundamental desire of our people to earn their livings and raise their families in prosperity and peace. The Chinese have made it clear that they want to multiply the economic ties between us. And we, in turn, have sought ways to promote the equitable export of high technology to China and work to promote more Chinese-American joint ventures.

When I return to the Great Hall on Monday morning, we'll have important new agreements to sign. And when I leave this country on Tuesday, the U.S.-China partnership will be stronger than ever.

Each of you is playing a vital role in this new and historic relationship. The diplomats among you are seeking new areas of agreement between our two countries and implementing the many agreements that we've already made. And those of you in business are making possible the export of raw materials and manufactures from China to America and the shipment to China of many American goods including products of our technology.

Many business people are involved in joint ventures like this dazzling new hotel. The expansion of these commercial ties is due in no small part to the efforts of the National Council for U.S.-China Trade.

Those of you who are teachers or students are helping the Chinese to understand not just the strength and prosperity of the United States but the open and peace-loving character of the American people. Day by day, each of you is helping to build a firm friendship between the most prosperous nation and the most populous nation on Earth. On behalf of all Americans, believe me, I thank you.

Now, I know that many of you haven't been home in some time, so I thought you'd like to hear that it's beautiful springtime in America. The magnolias are out in Washington. The azaleas are in full bloom in California. Of course, you know that that doesn't mean all that it sounds like, because those of us who are Californians know the truth of a statement made by the great comic, Joe Friscoe, once. Joe said that "California is the only place in the world," he said, "where you can fall asleep under a rosebush in full bloom and freeze to death." [*Laughter*]

Well, earlier this month, I threw out the first ball at the opening game of the Orioles in Baltimore. Then the Orioles lost the game. [*Laughter*] Since then, I haven't had any offers to turn pro. [*Laughter*]

The economy is still expanding briskly with leading indicators showing the expansion is here to stay. And polls tell us the national mood is the brightest that it's been in 5 years. Americans this springtime are proud of themselves, their jobs, and their country, and they're facing the future with confidence and courage.

So, as you go about your work here in this great city, you can rest assured that folks back in the States are doing just fine. And you can take pride in the knowledge that, although you're far from home, you're advancing the causes of world peace and international prosperity that are so close to your country's heart.

Before I leave, I just have to tell you a little incident. You all know, of course, about the Grenada rescue mission. And, incidentally, to those who have been trying to call it something ulterior like an invasion or something else, we had the great thrill—Nancy and I—of having several hundred of those medical students from Grenada who were rescued by our Armed Forces at the South Lawn of the White House and some of the first returnees among the troops of all four branches who were part of that rescue mission there.

And it would have put a lump in your throat to see these young people—and many of them frankly telling you that they were from an era where they didn't look with kindliness on the uniform; they didn't take to it. But they couldn't keep their hands off those youngsters their own age there on the South Lawn, and they would come hug them, come back and tell us, "They saved our lives" and all.

Well, some days later, I got a message from the Armed Forces Journal in the Pentagon. They'd received a letter from a young marine pilot of a Cobra helicopter who had been at Grenada and then went on to Beirut. And after he got there, he wrote back to the Armed Forces Journal. And he said that every story that he read in the press about that incident, in every story, they said Grenada produces more nutmeg than any other spot on Earth. And

he decided it appeared so often, it was a code. And he was going to break the code.

So, he wrote back to say he had broken the code. He said Grenada does produce more nutmeg than any other spot on Earth. The Soviets and the Cubans are trying to take Grenada. He said, "You can't have good eggnog without nutmeg." [*Laughter*] And he said, "You can't have Christmas without eggnog. So, the Soviets and the Cubans were out to steal Christmas." [*Laughter*] And his sixth and final point was, he said, "We stopped them." [*Laughter*]

I know that we have to move on here, but this has been most wonderful, and I thank you very much for the honor that you've done me and for giving me the seal. And now, just as soon as I find out from the Treasury, I'll settle some other problems—[*laughter*]—that have been bothering us.

Thank you all very much, and God bless you.

Note: The President spoke at 7:10 p.m. in the atrium at the Great Wall Hotel. Attending the reception were members of the American Club, a group of Americans living in China. The President was introduced by William Clarke, president of the club, who presented the President with a chop bearing the official American Club seal.

The President's opening comment regarding the deficit was in response to Mr. Clarke's remark that the President could issue orders and have access to the club's treasury with the chop.

Toast at a Dinner Honoring Premier Zhao Ziyang of China in Beijing
April 28, 1984

Premier Zhao, ladies and gentlemen, Nancy and I are delighted to welcome you here tonight. We hope to return in at least a small way the kind hospitality that has been extended to us since we set foot in this magnificent city.

For Americans, Mr. Premier, the very

mention of China holds a sense of allure. It conjures up images of the Yangtze River alive with traditional *fanchuan* [sailboat] and modern steamers, with the wide deserts of the north, of the bamboo forests in the southwest that are home to pandas, golden monkeys, and so many other animals native only to China, of the rich, productive fields and farmlands of the east, and of the huge cities like Beijing and Shanghai.

All these provide a sharp contrast with America and remind us of China's sweep and vitality. Yet what strikes us most, perhaps, is the sense of China's history. Chinese records date back 3,500 years. Kingdoms rose and fell in China long before we in the West saw the rise and fall of Rome. And your people were creating and building architectural wonders more than a thousand years before Christopher Columbus discovered America.

By contrast, Mr. Premier, it was barely four centuries ago that the first European settlers landed on our eastern coast. These hardy men and women and those who followed them came from virtually every nation in Europe. They felled trees, planted crops, built towns, and established legislatures. Later, many thousands came from China and joined the pioneers who were establishing farms and towns in the American West.

I have to interject here and think if they had only come earlier and the earliest had come from across the Pacific instead of the Atlantic, the Capitol would now be in California. [*Laughter*]

But together these diverse peoples built a great and free nation. Today that nation represents a powerful force for peace in the world and is leading a technological revolution that ranges from tiny microchips to voyages through the vastness of space.

Our national experience has instilled in all Americans certain fundamental beliefs. It has taught us that for a nation to prosper there must be peace, and that for men and women to work together, they must respect each other's rights. And just as these beliefs guide our dealings with one another, they've guided us from the first in our dealings with other nations.

Just over a century ago, Ulysses S. Grant, then a former President, came to China and described America's foreign policy goals to the Chinese leaders of that time. "We believe," he said, "that fair play, consideration for the rights of others, and respect for international law will always command the respect of nations and lead to peace. I know of no other consideration that enters into our foreign relations."

Well, the policy that President Grant described then remains our policy now. For nearly four decades, the United States and her allies have kept the peace in Europe. Throughout the world, the United States is supporting the causes of national self-determination and economic progress. And in the interest of peace for our children and our children's children, we're working to achieve an equitable and balanced reduction of nuclear arms.

Our aims and commitments are fully consistent with the sovereignty, independence, and economic development of all nations, including China. We seek no expansion but the expansion of good will and opportunity; no victory but the victory of peace.

China and the United States, Mr. Premier, differ markedly in their values, forms of government, and economic systems. To ignore or understate our differences would be to do an injustice to both. But we both believe that despite our differences our people are united in their desire to resist foreign threats, raise their families in prosperity and peace, and go as far in this life as their intelligence and imagination might take them. We hold more than enough in common to provide firm ground on which we can work together for the benefit of both.

In the 12 years since the long silence between our nations was broken by the signing of the Shanghai Communique, China and America have begun a productive partnership. Our cooperation has helped to provide a counterbalance to aggressive world forces. In recent years, we have formed new and important bonds in other fields as well, expanding our cultural and academic exchanges.

One figure tells a big part of the story. Just 5 years ago, there were no more than a handful of Chinese and Americans studying in each other's countries. Since then, several hundred American scholars have come to China, and more than 10,000 Chinese students have gone to America. These students are forming the ties of friendship and understanding on which the future of our relationship depends.

At the same time, our two nations have

begun economic exchanges that are growing in importance every day. Today China exports tons of foodstuffs, raw materials, and manufactured goods to the United States each year. America in turn supplies China with grain, transportation equipment, and scientific instruments, and the United States is helping China to acquire the capital and technology so vital to a growing economy. Already, some of the many joint Chinese-American business ventures have begun to bear fruit. This magnificent hotel is the outcome of just such a joint venture.

As our relationship has matured, Mr. Premier, both our nations have undergone important changes. In the past 12 years, we in the United States have had four Presidential administrations. Each has worked steadfastly to improve the Chinese-American friendship. Here in China, you, too, have had changes in leadership. But you, too, have remained firmly committed to the friendship between our nations. We in the United States are particularly pleased by the new emphasis on economic development. We congratulate you, Mr. Premier, and the other Chinese leaders who have worked so diligently and boldly to improve the lives of the Chinese people. We recognize that it took courage to set these policies in place.

And you have our pledge to give you our full cooperation as you modernize your nation's economy.

To view China and the United States as immense lands a world apart is to see one aspect of the truth. But in this century, there's another view that is even more meaningful. It is the view of a small green and blue ball spinning in the darkness of space—a sight that has so deeply moved all who have seen it. That view is a view of the future, for it shows one planet, our planet, where all nations seem as close neighbors. Our two nations, Mr. Premier, are firmly committed to that future.

So, ladies and gentlemen, please join me in a toast. To your health, Mr. Premier; to the health of President Li, General Secretary Hu, Chairman Deng, and the other Chinese leaders I've been privileged to meet; and to the everlasting friendship of the Chinese and American people.

And if I say the final word that I was going to say, with the glass that I will hold in my hand—I'm afraid we can't do it. I was going to say *gan bei* [bottoms up]. [*Laughter*]

Note: The President spoke at 9:28 p.m. in the Grand Ballroom at the Great Wall Hotel.

Radio Address to the Nation on the Trip to China
April 28, 1984

My fellow Americans:

I'm sure you've heard that Nancy and I are traveling a long way from home this week. We've already flown more than 9,000 miles, stopping off in the beautiful islands of Hawaii to visit the citizens of our 50th State; and then across the International Dateline to Guam, where the rays of each sunrise first touch the Stars and Stripes; and then on to our primary destination, China, one of the world's oldest civilizations and a country of great importance in today's Pacific community of nations.

This is our second trip to Asia in the last 6 months. It demonstrates our awareness of

America's responsibility as a Pacific leader in the search for regional security and economic well-being. The stability and prosperity of this region are of crucial importance to the United States. The nations comprising the Pacific Basin represent our fastest growing trading markets. Many say that the 21st century will be the century of the Pacific.

Our relations with China have continued to develop through the last four administrations, ever since President Nixon made his historic journey here in 1972. In 1978 the Chinese leadership decided to chart a new course for their country, permitting more economic freedom for the people in an effort to modernize their economy. Not surprisingly, the results have been positive.

Today China's efforts to modernize, foster the spirit of enterprise, open its doors to the West, and expand areas of mutual cooperation while opposing Soviet aggression make it a nation of increasing importance to America and to prospects for peace and prosperity in the Pacific.

When Nancy and I arrived in Beijing, we were touched by the friendly hospitality of the Chinese people, and we've been delighted to see the sweeping vistas, the bustling activity, and the many hallmarks of history in this great, old city.

In Beijing, narrow residential streets, traditional one-story houses, and treasures like the Forbidden City, a former Imperial Palace, first erected in 1420, are interspersed with modern highrises and wide avenues. The streets are normally filled with people riding bicycles. All of you who like bikeriding would love Beijing.

From the first moment, our schedule has been fully packed. I've already had extensive meetings with the Chinese leaders—President Li, Prime Minister Zhao, General Secretary Hu, and Chairman Deng. I had the honor of addressing a large group of Chinese and American leaders in science and industry in the Great Hall of the People, and I've spoken to the people of China over Chinese television.

We've also squeezed in some side trips—first, to the magnificent Great Wall, built by the Chinese more than 2,000 years ago to protect their country from outside invaders; and tomorrow, to the ancient city of Xi'an, an archeological treasure considered the cradle of Chinese civilization and located in a fertile plain near the Yellow River.

In all of our meetings and appearances, I've stressed one overriding point—different as to our two forms of government—different as they may be, the common interests that bind our two peoples are even greater. Namely, our determination to build a better life and to resist aggressors who violate the rights of law-abiding nations and endanger world peace.

When people have the opportunity to communicate, cooperate, and engage in commerce, they can often produce astonishing results. We've already agreed to cooperate more closely in the areas of trade, technology, investment, and exchange of scientific and managerial expertise. And we've reached an important agreement on the peaceful uses of nuclear energy for economic development.

Our last stop in China will be Shanghai, a center of culture and commerce. We plan to visit the Shanghai Foxboro Company, where Americans and Chinese are making high technology equipment to help advance China's industries. And I'll also visit with the students at Fudan University and speak to them about the meaning of America, the challenges our people face, and the dreams we share.

We can learn much from the rich history of China and from the wisdom and character of her people. And I've told the Chinese that Americans are people of peace, filled with the spirit of innovation and a passion for progress to make tomorrow better than today.

Our two nations are poised to take an historic step forward on the path of peaceful cooperation and economic development. I'm confident that our trip will be a significant success, resulting in a stronger U.S.-China relationship than before. For Americans, this will mean more jobs and a better chance for a peaceful world.

Until next week, thanks for listening, and God bless you.

Note: The President recorded his address at the Diaoyutai State Guest House on Saturday, April 28, Beijing time, for broadcast on Saturday, April 28, in the United States.

As printed above, this item follows the text of the White House press release, which was released by the Office of the Press Secretary in Beijing on April 29.

Remarks at a Signing Ceremony for Four United States-China Agreements
April 30, 1984

Thank you, Premier Zhao.

The developing relationship between China and the United States has been one of the principal events of postwar diplomacy. And today we're taking further steps to broaden and strengthen the ties based on shared principles of mutual respect and mutual benefit. We're concluding new accords that will facilitate trade and investment, enhance the exchange of people and ideas between our countries, expand the prospects for cooperation in developing China's nuclear energy capability, and help address China's critical need for developing skilled managers.

First, we're signing a tax agreement that will make it easier for Chinese and American firms to engage in trade and cooperate in joint ventures. With this agreement, private investors in professional exchanges can make a stronger contribution to Chinese development and to the benefit of both of our nations.

We're also signing the implementing accord for the Cultural Agreement between the United States and China. Our visit has reinforced our appreciation for Chinese hospitality and for China's ancient and honorable culture. I'm delighted that now millions of other Americans will be able to see the artistic and cultural achievements of the Chinese people.

This accord will open my own country's rich heritage to the Chinese people. And under the terms of the agreement, an exhibit from the Brooklyn Museum of Art is just now opening here in Beijing. We're pleased that many Chinese people will be able to see more American art and culture and learn more about our people and our country.

Ambassador Richard Kennedy and State Science and Technology Commissioner Jia Weiwen are initialing the text of an agreement, as the Premier told us, for cooperation between the United States and China in the peaceful use of nuclear energy. We congratulate the negotiators for their hard work and diligence. This agreement will permit American firms and experts to help China meet the ambitious energy goals of its modernization program. Our agreement is based on our shared desire to prevent the proliferation of nuclear explosives in the world. And it brings a new dimension of peaceful cooperation to our relationship.

Finally, we are signing a protocol which extends the successful Dalien Program and creates a special new 3-year course in management.

The Chinese people are known to Americans as people of admirable patience and endless courtesy. Throughout our stay here, we have seen both of those virtues. Let us hope that as contacts grow between the Chinese and American people, each of us will continue to learn about the other, and this important, new friendship of ours will mature and prosper.

Note: The President spoke at 9:03 a.m. in the Western Hall at the Great Hall of the People in Beijing, China.

Premier Zhao Ziyang also made remarks.

Text of the United States-China Accord for Cultural Exchange
April 30, 1984

Implementing Accord for Cultural Exchange in 1984 and 1985 Under the Cultural Agreement Between the Government of the United States of America and the Government of the

People's Republic of China

The Government of the United States of America and the Government of the People's Republic of China (hereafter referred to as "both sides"), desirous of enhancing friendly relations between the peoples of the two countries, and strengthening cultural cooperation between the two countries, based on the principles of mutual respect for sovereignty, of equality, reciprocity and mutual benefit, and in accordance with the Cultural Agreement signed on January 31, 1979, by the two governments, have agreed on the following program of cultural exchange between the two countries for the period 1984 and 1985.

I. CULTURE AND THE ARTS

1. An official American Cultural Delegation, which might include but would not be limited to participants from the United States Information Agency, will visit China.

2. An official Chinese Cultural Delegation will visit the United States in the fall of 1985 to discuss and sign the 1986–1987 Implementing Accord to the U.S.-China Cultural Agreement.

3. Both sides will send one high quality small scale performing arts group to the other country for visits and performances during the life of the Accord. During such visits, artists may participate in workshops and give demonstrations and master classes. The specifics for sending performing arts groups will be decided through specific agreements signed by relevant organizations designated by each side respectively. Both sides agree to exchange views and propose suggestions on the types of performing arts groups to be exchanged during the life of the next implementing accord, so that preparations can begin early.

4. Both sides will hold one high quality art exhibit in the other country during the life of the Accord. This will be carried out by the U.S. side with the exhibit "Town and Country: Images of Urban and Rural Life in America, Paintings from the Brooklyn Museum" in China in 1984, and by the Chinese side with the exhibit "Chinese Traditional Painting: Five Modern Masters" in the United States in 1984 and 1985. The specifics for sending art exhibits will be decided through specific agreements signed by relevant organizations designated by each side respectively. Both sides agree to

exchange views and propose suggestions on the types of art exhibits to be exchanged during the life of the next implementing accord, so that preparations can begin early.

5. Both sides will encourage the exchange of films, including the exchange of Film Weeks and film delegations to participate in Film Week activities. Both sides agree that exchange projects in this field will be decided through specific agreements signed by relevant organizations designated by each side respectively.

6. Both sides will encourage the sending of artists and experts in fields such as music, dance, drama, painting, sculpture, arts and crafts, photography and film to the other country for visits, short-term lectures, professional exchanges and possible performances and exhibits.

II. JOURNALISM, BROADCASTING, AND TELEVISION

1. Both sides will continue to encourage personnel and professional exchanges and facilitate the exchange of scripts and materials between the Voice of America and Radio Beijing.

2. The Director of the Voice of America and the Director of Radio Beijing will each lead a delegation for an exchange of visits and the Voice of America and Radio Beijing will exchange broadcasters for visits and professional exchange during the life of the Accord.

3. Both sides will encourage and facilitate the exchange of personnel and materials in the fields of print journalism, television, and radio. Both sides agree that exchange projects in these fields will be decided through separate discussion between relevant organizations from both countries.

III. LITERATURE, TRANSLATION AND PUBLICATION

Both sides will encourage the exchange of writers, translators and publishers in order to further mutual understanding of each other's culture, history and society.

IV. LIBRARIES AND ARCHIVES

1. Both sides will continue to facilitate the exchange of personnel, publications, and library materials between the Library of Congress and the National Library of

China, as well as between other libraries in the two countries.

2. Both sides will continue to facilitate the exchange of personnel and archival materials between the National Archives and Records Service of the United States and other American archival organizations and the Chinese National Archives Bureau.

V. EDUCATION, SOCIAL SCIENCES, AND SPORTS

Both sides agree that exchange projects in education, the social sciences and sports will be decided through separate discussions between relevant organizations from both countries.

VI. PARKS AND RELATED MATTERS

Both sides will encourage continued exchange of personnel and professional cooperation between the National Park Service of the United States and the Bureau of Landscape Architecture under the Ministry of Urban and Rural Construction and Environmental Protection of China. Both sides agree that specific exchange projects will be decided through separate discussions between the two above-mentioned organizations.

VII. PRIVATE EXCHANGES

Both sides will encourage and promote the expansion of non-governmental cultural exchanges to facilitate the future development of friendly relations between the peoples of the two countries.

VIII. FINANCIAL PROVISIONS

1. Both sides agree that the necessary expenses for mutual visits by official delegations or individuals for official projects under this Accord will be borne as follows:

(A) The sending side will bear the two-way international travel expenses of the delegations or individuals.

(B) The receiving side will bear the expenses of board and lodging, transportation, and medical care or medical insurance, necessary to ensure the continuation of the program, when the delegation or individual is in its territory.

2. Both sides agree that payment of expenses for exchanges under this Accord involving exhibits, such as works of art, handi-

crafts, historical or archaeological objects, space objects, and other objects of special value or artistic interest, including expenses for accompanying staff, will be decided through specific agreements signed separately and based on the differing conditions in the two countries.

3. Both sides agree that the financial provisions for official projects under this Accord which involve mutual exchange of delegations of performing artists, including staff accompanying the delegations, will be as follows:

(A) The sending side will bear the delegations' two-way international travel expenses or the expenses from the receiving side to a third country, as well as the international transportation expenses of the properties, costumes, musical instruments, etc.

(B) The organization or organizations designated by the receiving side as host organization(s) will bear the expenses of the delegations' board and lodging, travel, and medical care or medical insurance necessary to ensure the continuation of the program within the receiving country, and transportation expenses of the properties, costumes, musical instruments, etc., while in the receiving country, and provide the necessary interpreters.

(C) Other financial matters will be negotiated separately.

4. If either side encounters financial difficulties in the course of carrying out an individual project, a suitable adjustment or postponement of the project will be decided upon by consultation between the two sides.

IX. ENTRY INTO EFFECT

The present Accord will enter into effect on the day of signature.

Done in duplicate at Beijing on this 30th day of April 1984, in the English and Chinese languages, both texts being equally authentic.

For the Government of the United States of America:

/s/RONALD REAGAN

For the Government of the People's Republic of China:

/s/ZHAO ZIYANG

Remarks at the Shanghai Foxboro Company, Ltd., in Shanghai, China
April 30, 1984

Mr. Qin, Mr. Sorterup, and distinguished guests and workers of Shanghai Foxboro, thank you for the opportunity to visit this fine company.

Yesterday, in Xi'an, I had the privilege of seeing some of the wonders and majesty of China's ancient civilization. Your past achievements, illustrious history, and rich culture testify to the spirit and determination of the Chinese people. And today we're witnessing that same spirit and determination being carried forward into the world of high technology. I'm delighted that American businessmen are working side by side with their Chinese partners to develop new technologies for China's industries.

Shanghai Foxboro is one of the first of a growing number of joint ventures between Chinese and American firms. The Shanghai Instrumentation Corporation brings to this new venture a proud record as one of China's leading suppliers of automation products. And the advanced technology of the Foxboro Company will help open new horizons. Your pioneer efforts demonstrate that a promising future beckons for expanded cooperation between our people.

We both understand that the capabilities and requirements of our two countries complement each other. We both can be confident that our relationship is based on equality, cooperation, and mutual respect. And we both can be satisfied that the results provide mutual benefits. We're striking a balance between the needs of the Chinese economy and the principles that make for successful business relationships in America.

As you know, last year the United States liberalized controls on the export of high technology to China. Today it was our honor to renew an agreement between our two governments that extends and expands our management cooperation, including the training center in Dalian. I'm delighted to learn that Shanghai Foxboro has on its team a graduate of the Institute, engineer Shen Guozuo.

Business partnerships between Chinese and American companies are bound to succeed. The bonds of friendship and partnership in this fine company are a wellspring of hope and progress, of modernization and prosperity.

Opportunity has brought results. Shanghai Foxboro is a fine beginning. And now it's time to go forward and to build on this promising foundation. We can make tomorrow even better. And with the skill and cooperation I'm seeing here today, I am sure that we will.

Thank you very much, and good luck.

Note: The President spoke at 12:59 p.m. in the ground floor display room at the plant.

In his opening remarks, the President referred to Qin Fu Xiang, general manager of the joint venture, and Donald N. Sorterup, vice president for foreign affairs and trade of the Shanghai Instrumentation and Telecommunications Bureau. Following his remarks, the President viewed equipment in the display room and then went to the assembly building, where he joined Chinese women who were soldering chips onto panelboards for electronic circuitry.

The joint venture is composed of the Foxboro Company of Massachusetts and the Shanghai Instrumentation Corp.

Remarks and a Question-and-Answer Session With Students at Fudan University in Shanghai, China
April 30, 1984

The President. Madam President and all of you—please, be seated—I'm delighted to be with you today. I'm especially pleased to be here because, as I have already told Madame Xie, I feel I have a family tie to Fudan University. You see, the president of this university and my wife, Nancy, both earned degrees from Smith College in America.

As an avid sports fan and one-time sports announcer on radio, I want to use this opportunity to express my admiration for Fudan University's championship men and women's volleyball teams. And before I say anything else, I want to congratulate Fudan University on acquiring a powerful American Honeywell computer.

As students, you may be asking yourselves some of the same questions that American students ask, questions I asked when I was in college myself: "What kind of a world am I preparing myself for? Will I be able to raise my own family as well as, or maybe better than, my parents raised me?"

My own college days, years, took place some 50 years ago. It was a difficult time in America then. We were in a great worldwide depression, and I used to wonder what kind of place I could find for myself after graduation. But here we are 50 years later, and our people, the American people, enjoy a standard of living that was undreamed of back then.

Each decade during those past 50 years, real income per person in America rose an average of nearly 30 percent. And today, in America, we have taken—or things we take for granted that didn't even exist 50 years ago—television, computers, space flights, and so many more things, including the very means of travel—space or the jet travel brought me here to this country.

Yes, hunger and sickness still exist in many parts of the world and in our own land. But thanks to breakthroughs in agriculture and medicine, today more people on Earth eat better and live longer than ever before in the history of our planet. As

a matter of fact, I have lived some 20-odd years longer than my life expectancy when I was born. Now, that's a source of annoyance to a number of people in my own country. [*Laughter*]

But the key to all this progress has not been minerals, electricity, or building materials, but the human capacity for intelligence, imagination, and wonder and the opportunity to put all of them to use.

Here in China, for example, centuries ago wood was used only for our most basic needs like keeping warm. It was the ingenuity of the human mind that devised methods of turning wood into paper, transforming civilization by making it possible to store and exchange the written word. In the United States just a few years ago when we thought of sand, we thought of little more than deserts and beaches. And today we use that sand to make the computer chips that guide satellites through space.

I'm convinced that each of you stands at a great beginning. The Chinese people have skill, ingenuity, and a rich heritage. And those of you who are privileged to come to this university will help lead your country to new prosperity. If I could offer one piece of advice to remember in the years ahead, I would suggest this: It's not so much what's inside the Earth that counts but what's inside one's heart and mind, because that's the stuff that dreams are made of. And China's future depends on your dreams and your faith and determination to make your dreams come true.

And now I thank you again for my being here, and I'd be very happy to entertain a few questions in the limited time that we have, if you have some.

Q. Respected Mr. President, just now you recalled your life 50 years ago when you were young. So, now could you specify which aspects of your university life impressed you most and which of these experiences turned to be most helpful to your later political career?

The President. All right. Well, you know, I

went not to a large university like this. I went to a small liberal arts college similar to Smith College. And the funny thing is it was literally all of it. I majored in economics, and so, therefore, my studies certainly have played a part in what I'm doing now. [*Laughter*] I had two other great interests in addition. One was athletics, and I played football, basketball, ran on the track team, swam. And when I got out of school in that Great Depression, when even our own government was telling people on the radio not to go leave home looking for work because there was none—more than a fourth of our work force unemployed—believe it or not, it was the athletics that got me my first job in radio as a sports announcer.

And from there I went to Hollywood, because the other great interest that I'd had besides going to the classes in the college was in student theatricals, acting in plays and dramas. So, I wound up in Hollywood. And I have to say that today, while not only the economics and the athletics still serve me in good stead in the job I'm in. You'd be surprised how much being a good actor pays off. [*Laughter*]

Someone else?

Q. Mr. President, in recent years, Fudan has been developing academic exchange with a number of American universities, and we're looking forward to the further expansion of such exchange and collaborations. So, my question is, what do you think are the prospects of the further promotion of such ties?

The President. I think the prospects are very good. Indeed, I have been talking to your national leaders about that very thing. We have more than 10,000 of your students in our universities and colleges in America right now. A lesser number of ours are here. But we discussed this whole thing of making this exchange even better and more even and definitely want to continue it. And I had the opportunity just before leaving to come here of meeting with about a dozen of those 10,000 who came to the White House, and we had an opportunity to visit. And they're fine young people. And you'll be very proud of them when they come home.

Q. Mr. President, just now you mentioned the role of young people in the progress of

the world. And I think the future of the world belongs to the youth. And we Chinese young people are confronted with the task of realizing our modernization program and maintaining a world peace. So, I'd like to know how the American young people are preparing themselves for such a changing world.

The President. I think they're doing it very much the same as you are right here. There was a period when there was a kind of rebellious spirit in our land, and many young people—not a majority, but enough of them to make quite a crowd—were somewhat disillusioned, and they wanted to throw away all the values of the past, all the things that we've learned to believe in. And, you know, this is true of every generation. We all think that the generation that went before us didn't quite do things right, and we were going to make some changes and all. But be very careful. Don't throw away the values that have been tested through time and that have proven over the centuries that they are basic values essential to civilization and to what we call civilization.

There's since that time—and I see it here also—there has been a change. And our young people all over America are determined to make a place for themselves in the world of tomorrow. They're working hard. They're serious about it. And I think there's been a return now to acceptance of the basic values that have always made for civilization. And you have to remember this also: Every generation stands on the shoulders of the generation that went before. And so, you see farther because you're standing taller than we did and can look farther. But at least give us the credit that you're seeing farther because you're standing on our shoulders. Don't settle for the same level of view that we have. Realize that you are to look on and beyond and progress.

Q. Mr. President, I'm a student of international politics. So, I would like to know, after your trip to China, what measures are you going to take to further improve Sino-American relations?

The President. Well, this, too, was the subject of the discussions that I have had with

Chairman Deng and Premier Zhao, President Li, others in your government.

We signed this morning some agreements that had to do with commerce and trade and broadening the ability for exchange and for partnerships such as the one that I just visited here in Shanghai when I arrived, before I came here, the Foxboro Company, which is a partnership between the People's Republic and the Foxboro Company of Massachusetts in our own country. We talked of all these things, as to how we can broaden the base of friendship and understanding and knowledge of each other. And this includes that part with the exchange of students and all.

We have signed an agreement with regard to double taxation and eliminating the unfairness of double taxation so that there can be a better opportunity for the people of your country and ours. We are continuing to negotiate on a number of issues that are of concern. Cultural exchange—right now in Beijing, and then I understand it's going to go to other cities— is an art exhibit from one of our art museums in Brooklyn, New York. You, in turn, are going to send your art treasures to our country for our people to understand better.

So, I guess it comes down to something that's a favorite saying of mine: We only get in trouble when we're talking *about* each other, not when we're talking *to* each other. So, we're going to be talking to each other a great deal.

Q. Mr. President, what part do you think the American universities have been playing in the development of science and technology in United States? And in face of the new technological revolution, what are they doing about it now?

The President. I didn't hear the last part of the question—the last part.

Q. In face of the new technological revolution, what are they doing about it now? What are the universities—of the American are doing about it now?

The President. Oh, well, our universities have played a fantastic role in this development. The research that is conducted in our universities—and there is someone right near to me right now who knows a great deal about that, because in addition to

Smith, she also went to the Massachusetts Institute of Technology, one of our great technical engineering schools——

Madam Xie. Thank you.

The President. ——and I think could give you all the information that you would need about the research—*[laughter]*—that is going on in our universities. They have been the center of research in our country. And the future is unlimited.

Well, I was talking to the mayor on the way over here today about his generation and mine—he's a few years younger than I am, but we're still of the same generation— and our generation, you are going to see marvelous things. I'm not sure that you will see the great change or transition that we did in our single lifetime, because when I was very young, living in a small town in America, you traveled in horse and buggy.

I can remember my first automobile ride. There were no airplanes then, there was no television, there was no radio, and there was certainly no travel in space. But we have—in one generation, we have gone from horse and buggy to the Moon in a spaceship. And all of that—those are the building blocks that you have with which to go forward from here. And don't be afraid to dream and make your dreams come true.

Someone else?

Q. Mr. President, your China trip will soon come to its end. Could you tell us what impresses you most during this visit, and what impressions you especially want to convey to American young people when you are back home?

The President. What impressed me most? I'm still sorting it out. *[Laughter]* It's a kaleidoscope.

One thing above all that impressed me almost before we got to the Guest House in Beijing when we flew in the other day was the warmth and the friendliness of you, the Chinese people, toward us. It was a most and has been a most heartwarming experience ever since we've been here. We shall remember it for a long, long time.

But then was the vitality, the changes that are taking place—the program of modernization itself, the courage that it took to embark on that, and then the manner in which it's succeeding. And coupled with that, which helps make it a kaleidoscope, was then also the few glimpses that we had of the great heritage, a civilization that began here long before it had begun anyplace in the world. You had gone through so much of civilization before, in the West, the Roman Empire ever even came into being or fell.

And the first was the trip to the Wall. Now, I've seen pictures of it on television; I've seen motion pictures and everything. I wasn't quite prepared for the feeling that I had standing there and looking at the almost impossibility of that structure, and then to think that a people did it several thousand years ago. And I was getting a little bit weak in the knees from climbing one of the steep slopes. [*Laughter*] And then I said to myself, but a few thousand years ago, people were climbing this slope carrying rocks. [*Laughter*]

And then yesterday, we go to Xi'an and go down in the pit and stand there with the terra cotta warriors—and to think in terms of all this. And you know—well, you probably know this already, but there were no two of them alike. You know, you could think of 800 terra cotta warriors, and they would all be the same. No, they all had different faces; they had different hair combs, and I almost had an eerie feeling that they might speak to me. [*Laughter*]

But the mix of the great civilization and heritage that you have—and today, of the speed and drive of your modernization program. And I just go home with a dream in my heart that we perhaps have started a friendship here between two great peoples—not an alliance; I admire the position of being nonaligned that you have—but being friends and neighbors, and that we will be friends and neighbors. And we can be such a force for good in the world if we are.

Q. Thank you for your kind audience, Mr. President. Please take back best regards from us, the students of Fudan University, to the American people, especially to American students. Thank you.

The President. Thank you.

Mr. Liu. Well, on behalf of the students and in my own name, I should like to thank Mr. President again for having come over to our classroom and talk to us. And we all appreciate your beautiful speech, the gracious things you said about China and Fudan University, and your superb answers to our questions.

Thank you.

The President. Well, thank you very much. Thank you all.

Can I take just a second for something? The press will get very annoyed with me; they've heard me tell this so often. But just a few weeks ago, we had a visitor in our land—the President of France and his wife, Madam Mitterrand. And in the White House at a state dinner, Nancy was accompanying the President, I was accompanying Mrs. Mitterrand, into the dining room—everyone standing around the tables. And Nancy and the President stayed on this side of the room, and Mrs. Mitterrand and I start at the other side of the room—and I tell this just as an example of how close you can come to a diplomatic crisis.

Suddenly, Madam Mitterrand stopped. And we had the room to cross yet. And I leaned forward to tell her that we were to go on over there. And the butler ahead of her was motioning her on. And she said something very quietly and calmly over her shoulder to me in French, which I did not understand. [*Laughter*] And, again, I gave the signal. And, again, she repeated what she'd said to me. And then the interpreter caught up with us and told me what she was saying. I was standing on her gown. [*Laughter*] She couldn't move. [*Laughter*]

Thank you very much.

Note: The President spoke at 3:10 p.m. in a classroom at the university, where approximately 170 students from the international politics, foreign language, electrical engineering, physics, and biology departments had assembled for the event. Liu Gou Seng, an associate professor of English, was conducting a class on Shakespeare as the President entered the room.

Remarks at Fudan University in Shanghai, China
April 30, 1984

We've been in your country only 5 days, but already we've seen the wonders of a lifetime—the Great Wall of China, a structure so huge and marvelous that it can be seen from space; the ancient city of Xi'an; and the Tomb of the Great Emperor and the buried army that guards him still. These are the wonders of ages past. But today I want to talk to you, the young people of a great university, about the future, about our future together and how we can transform human life on this planet if we bring as much wisdom and curiosity to each other as we bring to our scholarly pursuits.

I want to begin, though, with some greetings. I bring you greetings not only from my countrymen but from one of your countrymen. Some of you know Ye Yang, who was a student here. He graduated from Fudan and became a teacher of English at this university. Now he is at Harvard University in the United States, where he is studying for a doctorate in comparative literature.

My staff spoke to him before we left. Mr. Ye wants you to know he's doing fine. He's working hard on his spring term papers, and his thoughts turn to you often. He asked me to deliver a message to his former students, colleagues, friends, and family. He asked me to say for him, and I hope I can, *"Wo xiang nian da jia"* [I am thinking of all of you].

He wants you to know that he looks forward to returning to Fudan to teach. And President Xie, he said to tell you he misses your friendship and encouragement. And Mr. Ye says you are a very great woman and a great educator. You will be proud to know that he received straight A's last term. And when we congratulated him, he said, "I have nothing to be proud of myself; I am so proud of my university."

I'd like to say a few words about our China-U.S. educational exchange programs. It's not entirely new, this exchanging of students. Your President Xie earned a degree from Smith College in the United States. Smith is also my wife Nancy's alma mater.

And President Xie also attended MIT, Massachusetts Institute of Technology, one of our greatest universities of science, engineering, and technology.

But in the past few years, our two countries have enjoyed an explosion in the number of student exchanges. Five years ago you numbered your students studying abroad in the hundreds. Since then, 20,000 Chinese scholars have studied throughout the world, and more than half of them have come to American schools. More than 100 American colleges and universities now have educational exchanges with nearly as many Chinese institutions.

We have committed more resources to our Fulbright program in China than in any other country. Two of the American professors teaching here at Fudan are Fulbright professors. And there are 20 American students studying with you, and we're very proud of them.

American students come to China to learn many things—how you monitor and predict earthquakes, how you've made such strides in researching the cause and treatment of cancer. We have much to learn from you in neurosurgery and in your use of herbs in medicine. And we welcome the chance to study your language, your history, and your society.

You, in turn, have shown that you're eager to learn, to come to American schools and study electronics and computer sciences, math and engineering, physics, management, and the humanities. We have much to share in these fields, and we're eager to benefit from your curiosity. Much of this sharing is recent, only 5 years old. But the areas of our mutual cooperation continue to expand. We've already agreed to cooperate more closely in trade, technology, investment, and exchanges of scientific and managerial expertise. And we have just concluded an important agreement to help advance our technological and economic development through the peaceful use of nuclear energy.

That term "peaceful use of nuclear

energy" is key. Our agreement rests upon important principles of nonproliferation. Neither of our countries will encourage nuclear proliferation nor assist any other country to acquire or develop any nuclear explosive device.

We live in a troubled world, and the United States and China, as two great nations, share a special responsibility to help reduce the risks of war. We both agree that there can be only one sane policy to preserve our precious civilization in this modern age: A nuclear war cannot be won and must never be fought. And no matter how great the obstacles may seem, we must never stop our efforts to reduce the weapons of war. We must never stop at all until we see the day when nuclear arms have been banished from the face of this Earth.

With peaceful cooperation as our guide, the possibilities for future progress are great. For example, we look forward to exploring with China the possibilities of cooperating in the development of space on behalf of our fellow citizens.

Our astronauts have found that by working in the zero gravity environment of space, we will be able to manufacture lifesaving medicines with far greater purity and efficiency, medicines that will treat diseases of heart attack and stroke that afflict millions of us. We will learn how to manufacture Factor 8, a rare and expensive medicine used to treat hemophiliacs. We can research the Beta Cell, which produces insulin, and which could provide mankind's first permanent cure for diabetes.

New satellites can be launched for use in navigation, weather forecasting, broadcasting, and computer technology. We already have the technology to make the extraordinary commonplace. We hope to see the day when a Chinese scientist working out an engineering problem in Fudan will be able to hook into the help of a scientist at a computer at MIT. And the scientist in Boston will be able to call on the expertise of the scientist in Shanghai, and all of it in a matter of seconds.

My young friends, this is the way of the future. By pooling our talents and resources, we can make space a new frontier of peace.

Your government's policy of forging closer ties in the free exchange of knowledge has not only enlivened your economy, it has opened the way to a new convergence of Chinese and American interests. You have opened the door, and let me assure you that ours is also open.

Now, all of this is particularly exciting in light of the recent history of our two countries. For many years, there was no closeness between us. The silence took its toll. A dozen years ago, it began to change. Together, we made it change. And now in the past 5 years, your policy of opening to the outside world has helped us begin to know each other better than we ever had before.

But that process has just begun. To many Americans, China is still a faraway place, unknown, unseen, and fascinating. And we are fascinated. [*Laughter*]

I wonder if you're aware of the many ways China has touched American life? The signs of your influence and success abound. If I were spending this afternoon in Washington, I might look out the window and see a man and woman strolling along Pennsylvania Avenue wearing Chinese silk. They might be on their way to our National Portrait Gallery to see the Chinese art exhibit. And from there, perhaps they would stroll to our National Gallery to see the new building designed by the Chinese American architect, I.M. Pei. After that, they might end their day dining in a restaurant that serves Chinese cuisine. [*Laughter*]

We associate China with vitality, enormous vitality, and something that doesn't always go along with that—subtlety, the subtlety of discerning and intelligent minds.

Premier Zhao saw something of the American attitude toward China when he visited us in January. He said after a few days in our country that he never expected such profound feelings of friendship among the American people for the Chinese people.

Well, let me say, I'm happy to return the compliment. I have found the people of China to be just as warm and friendly toward us, and it's made us very glad.

But meeting you and talking to you has only made me want to know more. And I sense that you feel the same way about Americans. You, too, wish to know more.

I would like to tell you something about us, and also share something of my own values.

First of all, America is really many Americas. We call ourselves a nation of immigrants, and that's truly what we are. We have drawn people from every corner of the Earth. We're composed of virtually every race and religion, and not in small numbers, but large. We have a statue in New York Harbor that speaks of this, a statue of a woman holding a torch of welcome to those who enter our country to become Americans. She has greeted millions upon millions of immigrants to our country. She welcomes them still. She represents our open door.

All of the immigrants who came to us brought their own music, literature, customs, and ideas. And the marvelous thing, a thing of which we're proud, is they did not have to relinquish these things in order to fit in. In fact, what they brought to America became American. And this diversity has more than enriched us; it has literally shaped us.

This tradition—the tradition of new immigrants adding to the sum total of what we are—is not a thing of the past. New immigrants are still bringing their talents and improving the quality of American life. Let me name a few—I think you'll know their names.

In America, Wang computers have become a fixture in offices throughout the country. They are the product of the energy and brilliance of Mr. An Wang, who himself is the product of a Shanghai university.

The faces of our cities shine with the gleaming buildings of Mr. I.M. Pei, who first became interested in architecture as a student here in Shanghai.

What we know of the universe and the fundamental nature of matter has been expanded by the Nobel Prize winning scientist, Dr. Lee Tsung-Dao, who was born in Shanghai.

We admire these men; we honor them; and we salute you for what you gave them that helped make them great.

Sometimes in America, some of our people may disagree with each other. We are often a highly disputatious nation. We

rather like to argue. We are free to disagree among ourselves, and we do. But we always hold together as a society. We've held together for more than 200 years, because we're united by certain things in which we all believe, things to which we've quietly pledged our deepest loyalties. I draw your special attention to what I'm about to say, because it's so important to an understanding of my country.

We believe in the dignity of each man, woman, and child. Our entire system is founded on an appreciation of the special genius of each individual, and of his special right to make his own decisions and lead his own life.

We believe—and we believe it so deeply that Americans know these words by heart—we believe "that all men are created equal, that they are endowed by their Creator with certain unalienable Rights, that among those are Life, Liberty and the pursuit of Happiness." Take an American student or teacher aside later today and ask if he or she hasn't committed those words to memory. They are from the document by which we created our nation, the Declaration of Independence.

We elect our government by the vote of the people. That is how we choose our Congress and our President. We say of our country, "Here the People Rule," and it is so.

Let me tell you something of the American character. You might think that with such a varied nation there couldn't be one character, but in many fundamental ways there is.

We are a fairminded people. We're taught not to take what belongs to others. Many of us, as I said, are the children and grandchildren and great-grandchildren of immigrants, and from them we learned something of hard labor. As a nation we toiled up from poverty, and no people on Earth are more worthy to be trusted than those who have worked hard for what they have. None is less inclined to take what is not theirs.

We're idealists. Americans love freedom, and we've fought and died to protect the freedom of others. When the armies of fascism swept Europe four decades ago, the

American people fought at great cost to defend the countries under assault.

When the armies of fascism swept Asia, we fought with you to stop them. And some of you listening today remember those days, remember when our General Jimmy Doolittle and his squadron came halfway around the world to help. Some of those pilots landed in China. You remember those brave young men. You hid them and cared for them and bound up their wounds. You saved many of their lives.

When the Second World War was won, the United States voluntarily withdrew from the faraway places in which we had fought. We kept no permanent armies of occupation. We didn't take an inch of territory, nor do we occupy one today. Our record of respect for the freedom and independence of others is clear.

We're a compassionate people. When the war ended we helped rebuild our allies—and our enemies as well. We did this because we wanted to help the innocent victims of bad governments and bad policies, and because, if they prospered, peace would be more secure.

We're an optimistic people. Like you, we inherited a vast land of endless skies, tall mountains, rich fields, and open prairies. It made us see the possibilities in everything. It made us hopeful. And we devised an economic system that rewarded individual effort, that gave us good reason for hope.

We love peace. We hate war. We think—and always have—that war is a great sin, a woeful waste. We wish to be at peace with our neighbors. We want to live in harmony with friends.

There is one other part of our national character I wish to speak of. Religion and faith are very important to us. We're a nation of many religions. But most Americans derive their religious belief from the Bible of Moses, who delivered a people from slavery; the Bible of Jesus Christ, who told us to love thy neighbor as thyself, to do unto your neighbor as you would have him do unto you.

And this, too, has formed us. It's why we wish well for others. It's why it grieves us when we hear of people who cannot live up to their full potential and who cannot live in peace.

We invite you to know us. That is the beginning of friendship between people. And friendship between people is the basis for friendship between governments.

The silence between our governments has ended. In the past 12 years, our people have become reacquainted, and now our relationship is maturing. And we're at the point where we can build the basis for a lasting friendship.

Now, you know, as I do, that there's much that naturally divides us: time and space, different languages and values, different cultures and histories, and political systems that are fundamentally different. It would be foolish not to acknowledge these differences. There's no point in hiding the truth for the sake of a friendship, for a friendship based on fiction will not long withstand the rigors of this world.

But let us, for a moment, put aside the words that name our differences and think what we have in common. We are two great and huge nations on opposite sides of the globe. We are both countries of great vitality and strength. You are the most populous country on Earth; we are the most technologically developed. Each of us holds a special weight in our respective sides of the world.

There exists between us a kind of equipoise. Those of you who are engineering students will perhaps appreciate that term. It speaks of a fine and special balance.

Already there are some political concerns that align us, and there are some important questions on which we both agree. Both the United States and China oppose the brutal and illegal occupation of Kampuchea. Both the United States and China have stood together in condemning the evil and unlawful invasion of Afghanistan. Both the United States and China now share a stake in preserving peace on the Korean Peninsula, and we share a stake in preserving peace in this area of the world.

Neither of us is an expansionist power. We do not desire your land, nor you ours. We do not challenge your borders. We do not provoke your anxieties. In fact, both the United States and China are forced to arm themselves against those who do.

The United States is now undertaking a

major strengthening of our defenses. It's an expensive effort, but we make it to protect the peace, knowing that a strong America is a safeguard for the independece and peace of others.

Both the United States and China are rich in human resources and human talent. What wonders lie before us if we practice the advice, *Tong Li He Zuo*—Connect strength, and work together.

Over the past 12 years, American and Chinese leaders have met frequently to discuss a host of issues. Often we have found agreement, but even when we have not, we've gained insight into each other, and we've learned to appreciate the other's perspectives on the world.

This process will continue, and it will flourish if we remember certain things. We must neither ignore our problems nor overstate them. We must never exaggerate our difficulties or send alarms for small reasons. We must remember that it is a delicate thing to oppose the wishes of a friend, and when we're forced to do so, we must be understanding with each other.

I hope that when history looks back upon this new chapter in our relationship, these will be remembered as days when America and China accepted the challenge to strengthen the ties that bind us, to cooperate for greater prosperity among our people, and to strive for a more secure and just peace in the world.

You, the students at Fudan University, and the scholars at all the universities in China and America have a great role to play in both our countries' futures. From your ranks will come the understanding and skill the world will require in decades to come. Today's leaders can pave the way of the future. That is our responsibility. But it is always the younger generation who will make the future. It is you who will decide if a continuing, personal friendship can span the generations and the differences that divide us. In such friendship lies the hope of the world.

When he was a very young man, Zhou Enlai wrote a poem for a schoolmate who was leaving to study abroad. Zhou appreciated the responsibilities that separated them, but he also remembered fondly the qualities that made them friends. And his poem ends:

Promise, I pray, that someday
When task done, we go back farming,
We'll surely rent a plot of ground
And as pairing neighbors, let's live.

Well, let us, as pairing neighbors, live.

I've been happy to speak to you here, to meet you in this city that is so rich in significance for both our countries. Shanghai is a city of scholarship, a city of learning. Shanghai has been a window to the West. It is a city in which my country and yours issued the communique that began our modern friendship. It is the city where the Yangtze meets the East China Sea, which, itself, becomes the Pacific, which touches our shores.

The Yangtze is a swift and turbulent river, one of the great rivers of the world. My young friends, history is a river that may take us as it will. But we have the power to navigate, to choose direction, and make our passage together. The wind is up, the current is swift, and opportunity for a long and fruitful journey awaits us.

Generations hence will honor us for having begun the voyage, for moving on together and escaping the fate of the buried armies of Xi'an, the buried warriors who stood for centuries frozen in time, frozen in an unknowing enmity.

We have made our choice. Our new journey will continue. And may it always continue in peace and in friendship.

Thank you very much.

Note: The President spoke at 3:40 p.m. in the auditorium at the university.

Toast at a Banquet Hosted by Mayor Wang Daohan of Shanghai
April 30, 1984

Mayor Wang, distinguished guests, it's a pleasure to be here in Shanghai, a center of culture and commerce where enterprising men and women look to the future with confidence and hope.

Twelve years ago, as we've been told, in this city, the American and Chinese Governments issued the Shanghai Communique. And this agreement pledged to broaden the understanding between our peoples. We agreed that cooperation in trade, science, and culture would benefit both nations. And we announced that normalization of relations between China and the United States would advance the interests of all countries.

We've come a long way since February 1972. And I'm honored to commemorate tonight this historic reconciliation and to mark the progress that we've made.

Twelve years ago, America and China each turned a new page in their histories. Today, America and China share the commitment to go forward together to write a new chapter of peace and progress for our people.

My trip to China has been as important and as enlightening as any I've taken as President. My discussions with your leaders—President Li, Premier Zhao, General Secretary Hu, and Chairman Deng—were productive and far-ranging. I welcome the opportunity to make new friendships and to enhance the personal relationship we have already established. Only through such steps can we deepen the understanding between our two great countries, broaden our political, economic, and cultural relations, and stand firm against expansionist aggression.

China is a fabled land in America. Schoolchildren across our country have read about your ancient history, the Great Wall, and the discovery of the treasures at Xi'an. To see these wonders in person is a moving and impressing experience. To me, it is even more impressive to meet the Chinese people of today. To see and feel your energy, vitality, and hopes for a better to-morrow gives me confidence in China's future.

Earlier today I had the opportunity to meet with students and faculty members of Fudan University. The students I talked to are serious about their learning. They want to know more, not just about my country but about the world that we all inhabit together. They're serious about their responsibility for their country's development and well-being. China is fortunate to have such talented young people to be its leaders for tomorrow.

This afternoon I also met with the workers and managers of the Shanghai Foxboro Company, a joint venture between an American and a Chinese company. There, Americans and Chinese are working side by side to make high technology equipment that will help advance China's industries, just as these new technologies are helping advance America's industries.

I'm greatly encouraged to note that the factory I visited today represents only one of the many forms of economic and technological cooperation between American and Chinese firms here in Shanghai. We're seeing cooperative activities in such diverse fields as advanced technology, glassmaking, civil aircraft parts assembly, athletic shoe production, pharmaceuticals, essential oils, offshore petroleum, and engineering, electrical machinery, and audiovisual products. Soon, with the support of both Shanghai and national authorities, we can expect our cooperation to increase.

My visit to China leaves me confident that U.S.-China relations are good and getting better. Our relationship is firmly grounded on realism, mutual respect, and a shared determination to expand our economies, provide greater opportunities for our people, and resist those who threaten peace.

Tomorrow, we leave to return to the United States. The famous poet Alfred Lord Tennyson wrote, "I am a part of all that I have met." Well, the people and places of China that Nancy and I have met and seen will always remain a part of us. May I thank the leaders and the people of China for your warm hospitality and offer this toast: To the health of Mayor Wang, to the health of the other distinguished guests here this evening, and to enduring friendship be-

tween the Chinese and American people. *Gan bie* [Bottoms up].

Note: The President spoke at 7:28 p.m. at the Shanghai Industrial Exhibition Hall in response to a toast by Mayor Wang.

Letter to the Chairman of the Commission on Civil Rights Concerning the President's Views on the Ku Klux Klan
April 30, 1984

Dear Morris:

While in China, I have been distressed to learn that some individuals back home have questioned whether my views on the Ku Klux Klan have somehow changed since 1980. Nothing could be further from the truth.

In 1980, I said that I have no tolerance for what the Klan represents, and would have nothing to do with any groups of that type. If anything, my feelings on this subject have only grown stronger. The politics of racial hatred and religious bigotry practiced by the Klan and others have no place in this country, and are destructive of the values for which America has always stood. Those of us in public life can only resent the use of our names by those who seek political recognition for the repugnant doctrines of hate they espouse.

I firmly believe that there is no room for partisanship on this question. Democrats and Republicans alike must be resolute in disassociating ourselves from any group or individual whose political philosophy consists only of racial or religious intolerance, whose arguments are supported only by intimidation or threats of violence.

We must, and will, continue our unified rejection of such elements of hate in our political life, for while there are many issues which divide us, it is fundamental principles such as this which will always draw us together.

Sincerely,

RONALD REAGAN

[The Honorable Morris B. Abram, U.S. Commission on Civil Rights, 1121 Vermont Avenue, N.W., Washington, D.C. 20425]

Remarks by Telephone With Premier Zhao Ziyang of China Upon Returning to the United States
May 1, 1984

The Premier. Mr. President, you will be ending your visit to China soon and before you go home, I would like to once again express my greetings and best wishes. Also on behalf of President Li, General Secretary Hu, and Chairman Deng, I would like to express how they were happy to have the opportunity to once again get to know you and to have had cordial meetings with you. Before you leave, I would like also to

convey their best wishes to you.

As for myself, I am very happy that we were able to exchange views sincerely and frankly on international and bilateral problems. And I think that your visit has enhanced understanding and improved relations between our two countries. So, I would like to congratulate you on the success of your visit.

The President. Hello. Yes. Mr. Premier,

Mr. Zhao, let me just echo what you have said about the great pleasure in this exchange and our hopes for the future. Mrs. Reagan and I couldn't be happier. We enjoyed meeting and being with you, and our discussions, and with our colleagues there. Please extend to them our warmest regards. We leave with many warm memories and a warm feeling for you and your people, and we shall do our utmost to continue the relationship that we feel has been established.

The Premier. Thank you, Mr. President, and please once again convey my best wishes to Mrs. Reagan, and we welcome you and Mrs. Reagan to come back to visit us again. And I would like to wish you, Mr. President, Mrs. Reagan, and American friends good health and a good journey back.

The President. Premier Zhao, again our regards to you. And I convey to you Mrs. Reagan's warmest regards. And we will look forward to one day visiting again, and we would come with great pleasure, believe me. Thank you for all that you have done for us and for making this trip so enjoyable and so fruitful.

Note: Premier Zhao called the President from Beijing at 8:30 a.m. Shanghai time. The Premier's remarks follow an unofficial translation which was included in the White House press release.

Question-and-Answer Session With Reporters on the Trip to China
May 1, 1984

Q. What do you think of communism?

The President. Why am I still working and everybody's still eating?

Q. The Chinese Communists, what was your impression of them?

The President. Well, any communism—I obviously have never approved of the system, and they understand that we have our differences about it. However, I must say there—I think here—the modernization program, the thing we saw this morning and the indication of results are very—I was impressed with them, with what they are accomplishing with this modernization.

Q. How far do you think that can go?

The President. That's up to them, whether it runs into ideology or not.

Q. We asked Premier Zhao how he felt having you in his midst being such a virulent anti-Communist, someone in the past who has denounced his government. He said that you knew that ideology was not the basis for establishing relations one way or the other. What do you say?

The President. Well, I say that, too. And I tell you something that I think we ought to get clear about my position in the past on China. When Richard Nixon went there and made the opening, I immediately supported him in that and publicly went to bat for the value in doing what he was doing. And I think that we—there have been now three Presidents who—he opened it; two others have carried on, trying to further this relationship. And I think frankly that we arrived at a new level and a new stage now in the relationship. They understand where—how we feel—or where we feel about that system, but we understand how we feel about ours. But we still found there are areas of agreement with regard to peace, opposition to expansionism and hegemony, and we found we could agree on a great many things.

Q. How did they like preaching—your preaching at them about democracy, God, capitalism, freedom?

The President. They never said any word about that, and I never put it as preaching to them. I—that was part of—I felt that if we're to get along, they've got to understand us and what we believe. That's why I did that.

Q. Do you think that they thought that you were trying to propagandize their people?

The President. I wasn't, and I and—evidently they took care of that in their own way. They just did not repeat that to their—to their people.

Q. What did Deng tell you about their relations with the Soviets? And there's a report that he said to you he understood our military buildup because of the problem with the Soviets. What did he say?

The President. Well, there's no question but there is—we've reached an understanding. There were some areas where they had misunderstandings, and we cleared those up. In these meetings today—in these last few days, why I say we reached a new plateau—we went beyond the nuts and bolts of a tax agreement or the things that we signed the other day—that was valuable. They are things that we—practical things that need to be done. But we moved into a level of general understanding about international relations there on the global level, regional spots of possible trouble, and so forth, and found ourselves in—in great agreement on many of those.

Q. What about the Russians? What did he say about the Soviets, their attitudes toward them and what we are doing in the way of buildup?

The President. Well, Sam [Sam Donaldson, ABC News], he certainly had no disagreement with us on what we're doing in our buildup. He was in agreement with that. I would rather not quote him on anything he might have said about another—about another government. That's up to them to keep their relations.

Q. You are always saying, Mr. President, that it's better to talk to people than about them.

The President. Yes.

Q. Will you talk to Castro, and will you talk to the Sandinistas, and will you talk to other Communist leaders?

The President. I, uh, no, I explained our Central America situation to them, and they understood—all of them that I talked to understood very well—when I pointed out that you had a reverse situation between the two countries there. You had one country in which the government was trying to help the guerrillas overthrow a duly elected government on the other side—and this is what we're objecting to—and the fact that the El Salvador Government has offered amnesty to the guerrillas and asked for them to participate in the electoral process. And the guerrillas have refused. On the other side in Nicaragua, the guerrillas, the *contras*, have asked to lay down their arms and participate in the democratic process, and the Government of Nicaragua has refused. It's a complete opposite situation in, in the two countries.

Q. What was your overall impression of the trip, your real feelings?

The President. Very good. I think they have an understanding and a confidence in us. They might not have had that confidence if I had backed down and not said things that I believed—and they likewise—and we went forward from there. I feel very good about it. I really believe we've reached a new level of understanding.

Q. They put you on television live in Shanghai but with no translation. You had to be able to speak English to understand you. [*Laughter*]

The President. I don't know whether they have any plans—I've heard that there's some speculation as to whether they have any plans to——

Q. Your speech to the university. They carried it live.

The President. Yes, Helen [Helen Thomas, United Press International]?

Q. How did you feel personally, and were you able to carry on all the meetings and never get sleepy? And were you able to handle all that vigorous talking?

The President. You mean physically? Yes, I have to give—pay my compliments to that doctor who has written the book about conquering jet lag. We followed that program, and I have never made a trip across several time zone changes as successfully as this one has been with regard to instantly being on their time when we arrived. You see, under this doctor's plan, by the time we arrived in China, for 2 days we had been eating our meals on China time, so that it makes a great difference that when you get off, dinnertime is the dinnertime that you've been on, and thus bedtime kind of automatically becomes the normal.

Q. By the way, there's a report that you're considering moving the U.S. Embassy in Israel to west Jerusalem, sort of as a compromise. Are you considering such a change?

The President. I read these and was surprised, myself, to hear that there were some recommending that. No, I feel very strongly that this is not something we should do. This should be part of the negotiation. Jerusalem has to be part of the negotiations if we're to have peace talks.

Q. Did the trip change your thinking about China in any way?

The President. Not particularly. I've always had an admiration for the Chinese people no matter where they live. They've proven their great capabilities, their industry, and all of that. I was gratified by the warmth of the reception by all of the people.

Q. Tell us some of your thoughts about your discussion with Deng.

The President. What?

Q. Your thoughts about your discussion with Chairman Deng.

The President. Well, we moved right in, and I—we both expressed our feelings. And it was there particularly that I had an opportunity to correct some misapprehensions they had about us and what we were doing here or there in the world. I think the greatest indication of success was that the luncheon was supposed to be a working luncheon, that we were to continue. By the time we got to lunch we had closed out the agenda, and we had a social lunch.

Q. What were some of the misapprehensions you corrected?

The President. Well, things having to do with—such as our attitude in the Middle East and what our goals were. I don't think they quite understood how far we have gone in our relations with the Arab States in trying to bring about peaceful negotiations and so forth. And I think they were very pleased to hear that.

Q. Are you contemplating a speech to the American people on Central America? This keeps coming up.

The President. We've been talking about—no date or anything has been set. And I haven't put anything down on paper yet.

Q. Was there any mention of President Nixon in your meetings with the Chinese leaders? Did they say anything about him?

The President. Oh, I gave them orally his regards and greetings that he—I had talked to him as well as others before I came here, and he, knowing all of them—as you recall, Premier Zhao called on him while he was in America—and so I relayed his greetings to him.

Q. I know that you told them we would not abandon Taiwan, but did you give them any belief that we would reduce the arms sales to Taiwan at a quicker pace?

The President. No. No.

Q. I didn't see you.

Mrs. Reagan. I saw you.

Q. Did you buy anything for him yesterday?

Mrs. Reagan. No, I didn't, because you wouldn't give me the money, Sam.

Q. I always have had a *yuan* for you. [*Laughter*]

Mrs. Reagan. Oh, oh.

The President. Sam, wow! [*Laughter*]

The President. I have to tell you, though, speaking of quiet diplomacy, right in front of me, Chairman Deng invited her back to China—without me.

Q. I saw you sitting there feeling ignored while the two of them were having a tete-a-tete.

The President. Oh, they were having—yes, he made it very specific. Not me.

Q. Are you going to let her go?

Mrs. Reagan. That's all right, that's all right, honey. I'll tell you all about it. [*Laughter*]

Q. Are the Chinese people of their word—they went back on their word in terms of letting you project yourself to the people?

The President. Well, evidently, our people tell me there was never any negotiations about that or whether I would, whether anything they carried—whether it would be word for word or not. I don't feel—I feel that was their right to do, whatever their reasons may have been, and, uh, just as it was my right to say what I wanted to say when I was over there.

Q. Had you always intended to do it that way, because it was considered very bold to go into a country and say this is the way we are?

The President. Well, I thought that was part of the trip.

Mr. Speakes.[1] Thank you, sir.

The President. Frankly, I think it had something to do with a very favorable outcome. I think they believe in me, and they have confidence in me they might not have had if I had kind of tried to pretend I was something I wasn't.

Q. And do you think this will help your reelection?

The President. What?

Q. Your reelection?

The President. I would like to make one thing clear about this trip, Helen. Almost from the very first of my administration, there was an invitation to Zhao, and my statement—because there had been an invitation to me, immediately—and I said that I thought that after three Presidents—that protocol suggested that they come here, and then I would return the visit there. And the date for this thing was set a year ago or more, so, uh——

Q. Then in terms of serendipity, do you think it will help? If it does, so be it?

The President. Well, I—I don't think it can hurt. But there certainly was never any consideration of this before, or with regard to election, because all of this was being arranged and was going on long before I'd ever got around to saying what I was going to do.

Mr. Speakes. Thank you, sir.

Q. What about Vice President Mondale's statement then this is a belated coming to grips with the Chinese problem on your part, that you're 25 years late in your coming to these views?

The President. Twenty-five years late? Would he suggest that we should have sat back and approved when they were calling us imperialist running dogs? You've got to remember that this has been a great change in the leadership and a change in the last 12 years in their position towards us.

Q. There's another report——

Mr. Speakes. Thank you.

Q. ——that we are trying to get together with our allies to put more pressure on Qadhafi in some way to put him further back in that box.

The President. I don't know what's going on on the diplomatic level here, but I know that there are discussions going forward on this whole problem.

Mr. Speakes. Thank you.

Q. I thought you were conscious of saying what you wanted to say, that the speech you gave—you thought that out quite deliberately, about saying precisely what you wanted to say about America and so forth?

The President. Yes.

Q. And wrote a lot of that yourself?

The President. I've always had a hand in what I say.

Mr. Speakes. Thank you, sir.

The President. All right, all right, it's lunchtime for me.

Note: The question-and-answer session was held on board Air Force One as the Presidential party was enroute to Fairbanks, AK, from Shanghai, China.

As printed above, this item follows the text of the White House press release.

Remarks Upon Returning From China
May 1, 1984

Thank you very much, Frank. Let me just say I'm proud of Alaska's congressional delegation and grateful for their help and support and for the way they represent their State in Washington. And on behalf of

Nancy and myself, and from the bottom of our hearts, thank you all for your very warm welcome.

It's been a fascinating and rewarding 10 days, and now our long journey is nearly over. I was interested to read one report on whether the meetings were a success or not this morning. It seems that TASS, the Russian news agency, says that I was a failure at

---

[1] *Larry M. Speakes, Principal Deputy Press Secretary to the President.*

trying to eat a pigeon egg with my chopsticks. [*Laughter*] And as usual, TASS was wrong. [*Laughter*] It wasn't a pigeon egg; it was a quail egg. And I got it on the second stab. [*Laughter*]

But we traveled almost 20,000 miles to Hawaii, Guam, and finally, China—to the cities of Beijing, Xi'an, and Shanghai. We saw the wonders of that country and the fine antiquities of the old civilization. But I think the best moment was late last night—or I should say, early this morning.

Now, I had it all in mind that I was going to talk about coming through the darkness and then finally seeing the lights of the coast of Alaska down below—[*laughter*]—and the coastline there, and that we knew that we were seeing America again, and we were home. Well, there was a cloud cover all the way over the Pacific Ocean. [*Laughter*] So, the lights that we saw were the lights of Fairbanks, and believe me, we knew we were home, and it was just fine.

There's a poem that was popular when I was a boy. It was a poem about the American soldiers returning from the trenches in the First World War. They admired the grandeur and the oldness of Europe, but their hearts longed for the newness of their own country. And upon their return, in that poem they said:

So it's home again and home again, America for me.
My heart is turning home again and there I long to be.
The blessed land of room enough beyond the ocean bars,
Where the air is full of sunlight and the flag is full of stars.

Well, it's good to be back in our blessed land.

We went to China to advance the prospects for stability and peace throughout the world. And we went to illustrate, by our presence, our sincere desire for good relations. We went to meet again with the Chinese and review our concerns and our differences. And we went to China to further define our own two countries' relationship—and, by defining it, advance it.

And I feel that we have progress to report. I had long and thoughtful meetings with the Chinese leadership, comprehensive meetings. We each listened carefully to what the other had to say. We discussed and agreed to cooperate more closely in the areas of trade, investment, technology, and exchanges of scientific and managerial expertise. We concluded an important agreement on the peaceful uses of nuclear energy. We agreed that in this imperfect world, peace in its most perfect form cannot always be reached—but it must always be our goal. And we, the people of China and the United States, must make our best efforts to bring greater harmony between our two countries.

It's a good thing for the world when those who are not allies remain open to each other. And it's good to remember that competitors sometimes have mutual interests, and those interests can make them friends.

I told the Chinese leaders, as I told the students at Shanghai University yesterday, that we must continue to acknowledge our differences, for a friendship based on fiction will not long withstand the rigors of the world. But we agreed that there is much to be gained from mutual respect. And there's much to be gained on both sides from expanded opportunities in trade and commerce and cultural relations.

I was heartened by some of the things that we saw. The Chinese have begun opening up their economy, allowing more farmers and workers to keep and sell on their own some of the fruits of their labor. The first injection of free market spirit has already enlivened the Chinese economy. I believe it has also made a contribution to human happiness in China and opened the way to a more just society.

Yesterday, before we left, we sat in a Chinese home at one of the now-called townships—they were once called communes—the farm communes where they raise the foodstuffs for all of China, but now there is a difference. They owe a portion of what they produce to the government, but then over and above that they can produce on their own and sell in a free marketplace. And in this home, it was most interesting. This young couple, their little son, his mother and father living with them, and he was telling us all the things—and he built that home himself, and a very fine job it was—and then told us of how they're saving and what they're saving to buy next. It could have been in any home in America, talking about the problems of making ends meet and that they were saving for this or that for their future.

And I was also impressed—not only by them but by all of the Chinese that we met—by their curiosity about us. Many of the Chinese people still don't understand how our democracy works or what impels us as a people. So, I did something unusual. I tried to explain what America is and who we are—to explain to them our faith in God and our love, our true love, for freedom. They'll never understand us until they understand that.

It was a breathtaking experience and in some ways, I think, a groundbreaking experience. But for us now, it's very fitting that we return home here to Alaska—the only one of our States that is equidistant to Asia and Washington, a westward facing State, and a State, may I say, from which we've received strong support.

When I was in Beijing, I explained to the Chinese that our attempt to build up our defenses, after more than a decade of almost constant neglect, is an attempt to preserve the peace and preserve freedom in the world. No one has helped us more in our efforts to rebuild our strength than the members of your Alaskan congressional delegation. And I thank them, as always, for their efforts and their good sense.

It's been good to talk to you and to see you and to be welcomed by you. Every time I come to Alaska I think of Robert Service, and I always threaten to recite "The Shooting of Dan McGrew"—[*laughter*]—which I can do, believe it or not. But I won't subject you to it or those tired and bedraggled persons over there—my friends in the press. They've been working very hard the past 10 days to bring you at home the look and sound of China; and they're tired, so we'd like to give them a chance to rest. Maybe at the next press conference I'll recite it. [*Laughter*]

But it's wonderful to be here, and I thank you again for your very warm greetings. We'll take them with us tomorrow when we meet here in Fairbanks with a great man of peace—Pope John Paul II, who is also on his way to Asia, to South Korea. His continuing mission of peace is a service to all humanity, and I look forward to seeing and having a few moments with him again, as we had once before in Rome.

But again, God bless you all. It's just wonderful to be here, to see you all again. And all I can say, as far as Nancy and I are concerned, we'll be back.

Note: The President spoke at 12:23 p.m. in the Patty Athletic Center at the University of Alaska in Fairbanks. He was introduced by Senator Frank H. Murkowski, at whose home he and Mrs. Reagan had stayed upon arrival in Fairbanks earlier that day.

Remarks at a Luncheon With Community Leaders in Fairbanks, Alaska
May 1, 1984

Governor Sheffield, thank you very much. Reverend clergy, Senator Murkowski, and the distinguished mayors and the officials of the university, the lovely ladies here at the head table, and all of you, Nancy and I thank you very much for this welcome.

I couldn't help but think when the president of the university was speaking here about this institution that yesterday I was on another campus in Shanghai, Fudan University, speaking to several hundred students, all of whom spoke English. There are a number of American professors there, some American students, but also there are some 10,000 Chinese students attending colleges and universities here in our country. And I took questions in one class from some of the young people there. And I couldn't help but think that if we, in our generation, can continue and hold this peace and do what we're doing, there is the hope—because I looked at them and I saw the president of the university, Chinese, but a graduate of Smith College and MIT in America; head of the economics department—I met another professor, Chinese, his degree was from Columbia University. Those young people, they are growing up and learning and having a compatibility with each other across the oceans that can mean peace for the future if we, when we turn it over to them, if we have managed to preserve the peace and give them that kind of a start. And to look at them, it was almost like being home.

But now we are home. And we enjoyed our visit to China, but it's great to be back in the U.S.A. And we couldn't be happier than to have our first stop here in Alaska.

Your State, Governor, is contributing so much to our national well-being. And without Alaska's oil and mineral wealth the United States would be in a far more vulnerable position than it is. The strategic role that you play in our defense is invaluable. And if your congressional delegation and the President have anything to say about it, you bet it's going to continue being a part of Alaska's life. But even more, the spirit that you represent reinforces our self-image as a nation. To most of your fellow Americans, you exemplify that frontier spirit, strength of character, and sense of adventure that all of us claim as our own.

My visit to China has bolstered my belief that our future is bright. And I'm more convinced than ever that we're living in an incredibly exciting time. America is on the edge of a new era of peace, prosperity, and commerce—and you Alaskans will be playing a major role in shaping this bright future.

The region of the Pacific Basin is expanding with commerce and creative energy. If we can maintain the peace—and if we're diligent, there's no reason why peace should not prevail—then the people of our country can expect great leaps in their quality of life in the next century, just as we've enjoyed in this 20th century.

Our trip to China demonstrates how much progress is really possible. Who would have thought that 20 years ago genuine friendship would be developing between our two countries? And I can't help but believe—after the many hours of meetings that we've had with the Chinese leaders, with the attitude that we saw on the part of people on the street—that we have that friendship started. Certainly there are fundamental differences that still exist. We recognize them and so did the Chinese. But with the hard work of American and Chinese leaders in the last 12 years, we've put those differences in perspective.

During our visit, I was impressed with the sincere desire of the Chinese people to strengthen our cooperation for the mutual benefit of both our peoples. And I expressed to them on your behalf and on behalf of all the people of the United States our commitment to a more peaceful and prosperous world. And I told them that we're anxious to live and trade together as friends. I found that same sentiment true with the Chinese people everywhere we traveled.

Instead of the points of difference that some might suspect in the meetings, that this kept us at edge—no. We frankly recognized and from both sides we said and they said, "But let's talk about the things that we have in common and where we can agree."

Now, I know there's been much said about my anti-communism. Well, I'm an anti-Communist if you talk about communism for the United States. And in some Communist regimes, I'm very critical of their violation of human rights and so forth. But I have never thought that it was necessary for us to impose our form of government on some other country. The Communists don't share that view; they do seem to be expansionist. Except that I found that our Chinese leaders I was talking with have no expansionist ideas at all. They're resistant to that.

So, as far as I'm concerned, we can live at peace in the world together. If they prefer socialism or communism and we prefer the democracy that we have—we may know that ours is best, but—[*laughter*]—we won't say that to them. But the very fact that today—yesterday in Shanghai I went through a business concern manufacturing high technology equipment, but as a partnership between Foxboro Company of Massachusetts and the People's Republic of China. And, more than that, they are opening up now that American concerns can create branches of their own in China, in this so-called Communist China, and they don't have to be in partnership with anyone. And capitalism will be there in these plants. So, I think that great progress was made.

I took a step backward and realized that I was back in the United States today when the previous remarks just earlier at the ceremony I called Xi'an, the old capital of China, where we journeyed—I opened my mouth and it came out "Zian." I know better than that. It's Xi'an.

But if our economy is to be vibrant enough to take full advantage of the future opportunities, if we're to compete with the economic powers now emerging in the Pacific, we must follow responsible taxing and spending policies here at home. We have a few things to do.

Four years ago, the people of the United States were not quite as optimistic as they are today. With murderous inflation, economic stagnation beating us down, a spirit of pessimism totally inconsistent with our national character permeated the land. Our ills were not a product of some uncontrollable cycle. And they were not, as some suggested, a symptom that America was in decline. Our woes were a direct result of going extremely wrong in our taxing policies, big taxing, big spending, and inflation, policies that we have been attempting to change.

By bringing down the rate of growth in Federal spending, by preventing our people from being mauled with higher and higher taxes, by relieving the regulatory burden and by bringing inflation down and keeping it down, we've put our country back on the road to growth and progress.

From the darkness of pessimism, a new, more vital and confident America is emerging. The gross national product was up a healthy 6 percent last year, up at an annual 8.3 percent the first quarter of 1984. Productivity, which will keep us competitive and add to our standard of living, jumped

3½ percent last year. It fell in the 2 years before we took office. Another signpost of future growth is venture capital. It rose at less than a billion dollars in 1980, and last year it shot up by $4 billion.

John Naisbitt, author of "Megatrends," is so excited by what he sees that he's been telling people, "1984 has arrived just in time to witness an explosion of bottom-up entrepreneurialism and the dawn of an era that may offer our best hope yet." It is the American entrepreneur, the so-called small business man or woman, who are responsible for 80 percent of the new jobs that are created in our country. That is really the heart and soul of capitalism. And last year, there were six hundred-and-some thousand new incorporations of new businesses starting up.

There are still challenges to meet. How we come to grips with the deficit problem means a great deal. Any solution that places the emphasis on raising taxes is no solution at all. It's a formula for failure, because we'd be taxing ourselves right back into a recession. If we become overconfident and permit the Congress to fall back into the same "something for everyone" spending habit, then we will also end up in the same boat.

I want to take this opportunity to give a special word of congratulations to the members of your congressional delegation—one of them with us today; the other two, I guess, are tending the store—Senators Stevens and Murkowski and Congressman Young have been fighting the good fight. And I want to thank all Alaskans for sending them to us.

In the international arena, we face great challenges. We're trying to restore a balance of military power, making up for more than a decade of almost constant neglect of the defense needs of our country. We would rather negotiate agreements with the Soviets than build new weapons, but we cannot negotiate with empty chairs when the Soviets walk away, as they have, from the bargaining table.

In Central America, our friends are not only struggling for democracy; they're battling for their lives against a Soviet-sponsored Nicaraguan power play. Our nation cannot afford to permit Soviet-sponsored guerrillas to shoot their way into power and turn Central America into a string of Marxist-Leninist dictatorships.

All of these are part of the ever-evolving problems that we must, as free people, face together. But we can and we will meet our responsibilities.

Tomorrow I am meeting with Pope John Paul II, a man and spiritual leader for whom I have enormous respect and affection. Pope Pius XII, Eugenio Pacelli, has noted the burdens that we Americans carry. He was the Pope at the time of World War II. And right after that war, he said of us, "The American people have a genius for splendid and unselfish action." And he added, "Into the hands of America God has placed an afflicted mankind." Well, we're proving to the world that the American spirit is alive and well. Together we'll keep America the land of freedom and opportunity that God intended it to be.

And I thank you for having us with you today. We are looking forward to joining you, as I say, for that welcome to the Pope tomorrow. And God bless all of you, and God bless America.

Thank you.

Note: The President spoke at 1:49 p.m. in the William Wood Student Center at the University of Alaska. He was introduced by Gov. William Sheffield.

Following the President's remarks, he and Mrs. Reagan returned to the home of Senator Frank H. Murkowski, where they remained overnight.

Statement on the Soviet Occupation of Afghanistan
May 1, 1984

We strongly condemn the current Soviet escalation of warfare in the Panjshir Valley of Afghanistan. These new Soviet military actions are unprecedented in several respects, including the large force levels being employed in the Panjshir Valley against the Afghan resistance and the use for the first time in Afghanistan of high altitude bombing, which will bring untold new suffering to the civilian population.

This new Soviet offensive, the most massive in the 4-year history of the Soviet occupation of Afghanistan, further highlights the brutal anticivilian tactics being used by the Soviet Union in its efforts to subjugate an independent country. It worsens the instability of the region and raises serious questions concerning the sincerity of Soviet statements that nations should undertake not to use force against each other.

These new Soviet actions seriously undermine the search for a negotiated political settlement, based on the four elements of the repeated U.N. General Assembly resolutions on Afghanistan:

(1) withdrawal of Soviet forces;

(2) restoration of the independent and nonaligned status of Afghanistan;

(3) self-determination for the Afghan people; and

(4) permitting the Afghan refugees who have been forced to flee their own country to return with safety and honor.

The U.S. remains committed to achieving these internationally agreed objectives. It is past time that the Soviet Union respect the wishes of the world community and bring to an end the terrible ordeal which they have imposed on the Afghan people.

Remarks at the Welcoming Ceremony for Pope John Paul II in Fairbanks, Alaska
May 2, 1984

The President. Well, now, I want to welcome Your Holiness to the United States and, on behalf of the American people, say how pleased and privileged we are to have you among us. We're just returning from a mission of peace, and I can think of no more fitting close to this journey than to be here in the presence of Your Holiness, who has worked so diligently for recognition of the rights and dignity of the individual and for peace among nations.

I can assure you, Your Holiness, the American people seek to act as a force for peace in the world and to further the cause of human freedom and dignity. Indeed, an appreciation for the unalienable rights of every human being is the very concept that gave birth to this nation. Few have understood better than our nation's Founding Fathers that claims of human dignity transcend the claims of any government, and that this transcendent right itself has a transcendent source. Our Declaration of Independence four times acknowledges our country's dependence on a Supreme Being, and its principal author and one of our greatest Presidents, Thomas Jefferson, put it simply: "The God who gave us life, gave us liberty at the same time."

But no one knows better than Your Holiness that the quest for human rights and world peace is a difficult, often disheartening task. In the face of turmoil and tragedy in our world we must always remember the central message of your own ministry—that the quest for peace begins with each of us. When I began this journey on Easter Sunday, I asked the American people to join me in a prayer for peace, a prayer that the nations of the world would renounce the agony and heartbreak of war and learn to live in love with each other. We must never underestimate such efforts. Far more can be accomplished by the simple prayers of good people than by all the statesmen and armies of the world. Only when the fellowship of all men under the Fatherhood of God is recognized and acknowledged, only then will the world finally know true peace and understanding.

To us, Your Holiness, the Holy See and your pastorate represent one of humanity's greatest moral and spiritual forces. And your visit is particularly significant, coming as it does soon after the reestablishment of relations between the Holy See and the United States. For over a century we maintained warm and fruitful, but informal relations. Now we have exchanged Ambassadors, and we hope to build on this new relationship to our mutual benefit and to the benefit of peace-loving people everywhere.

In a violent world, Your Holiness, you have been a minister of peace and love. Your words, your prayers, your example have made you—for those who suffer oppression or the violence of war—a source of solace, inspiration, and hope. For this historic ministry the American people are grateful to you, and we wish you every encouragement in your journeys for peace and understanding in the world. I also want to say how grateful I am for this opportunity to meet personally with you to discuss matters of vital concern to the Holy See and to the United States. We deeply value your counsel and support and express our solidarity with you. On behalf of the American people, I welcome you, and I extend to you our warmest greetings.

The Pope. Praised be Jesus Christ.

Mr. President, dear people of Alaska, esteemed citizens of America, it gives me great pleasure to visit Alaska once again and from this northern State to send a greeting of special warmth and affection to all the citizens of the United States of America. As you know, today I have begun a pastoral journey that will take me to Korea, Papua New Guinea, the Solomon Islands, and Thailand. And I am delighted that this pilgrimage enables me to stop here in Fairbanks and to be among you.

I am deeply honored by the presence of President Reagan who, himself, is just returning from an important trip to China. Mr. President, I thank you for your kind welcome on my arrival, and I wish to reaffirm, through you, my friendship and esteem for all the citizens of your great nation.

My thanks go as well to Bishop Whelan for his much appreciated invitation to the Diocese of Fairbanks. I also extend my good wishes to Bishop Kaniecki, and I pray that the Lord will grant him many joyful years of service to the Church.

I would also offer a word of greeting to the cardinals and bishops of the United States Episcopal Conference who have shown their fraternal union with me by coming here on this happy occasion.

When I arrived on my first visit to your beautiful State, dear people of Alaska—and it is beautiful, your State—I remember being welcomed by a lovely little child, Mary, who reached out and handed me a bouquet of forget-me-nots, your State flower. Shortly afterwards that little girl was called home to her heavenly Father, but her loving gesture is not forgotten, and her memory is held in blessing.

I found in what she did at that time a living truth about the people of the vast Alaskan territory—that in your thoughts and in your prayers, you remember the Pope. Today I'm here in person to give you the assurance that I have not forgotten you. Even when I am miles away, I hold the people of Alaska and those of the whole of the United States close to me in my heart. I do not forget you, for we are linked together by bonds of friendship, of faith, and of love.

In some ways, Alaska can be considered today as a crossroads of the world. President Reagan is returning from visiting the beloved people of China, even as I am making my way to a neighboring area in the Far East.

The city of Fairbanks reminds us also of another direction, for it is called "the heart of the golden north." Here in this vast State, 65 languages are spoken, and peoples of many diverse backgrounds find a common home with the Aleuts, Eskimos, and Indians. This wonderful diversity provides the context in which each person, each family, each ethnic group is challenged to live in harmony and concord, one with the other.

To achieve this aim requires a constant openness to each other on the part of each individual and group—an openness of heart, a readiness to accept differences, and an ability to listen to each other's viewpoint without prejudice. Openness to others, by its very nature, excludes selfishness in any form. It is expressed in a dialog that is honest and frank, one that is based on mutual respect.

Openness to others begins in the heart. As I stated at the beginning of this year in my message for the World Day of Peace, if men and women hope to transform society, they must begin by changing their own hearts first. Only with a new heart can one rediscover clear sightedness and impartiality with freedom of spirit, the sense of justice with respect to the rights of man, the sense of equity with global solidarity between the rich and the poor, mutual trust and fraternal love.

Here in Fairbanks, you have the opportunity to rediscover such values and express them in your harmonious relationship with your neighbor, which reflects the stupendous harmony of nature which pervades this region. May God grant you the strength to express this harmony in your own lives, in your relationships with others. May He give you the courage to share generously and selflessly the blessings that you yourselves have received in abundance.

God bless America.

Note: The President spoke at 10:09 a.m. at the Fairbanks International Airport.

Following the ceremony, the President and the Pope met, together with U.S. and Vatican officials, in the airport terminal. The President and Mrs. Reagan then boarded Air Force One for the return to Washington, DC.

Statement by Principal Deputy Press Secretary Speakes on the President's Meeting With Pope John Paul II
May 2, 1984

In his meeting today with Pope John Paul II, the President discussed his trip to China and the Holy Father's forthcoming visit to Korea. The two engaged in an exchange of views on arms control, East-West relations, regional and humanitarian issues.

The President offered to send a Presidential mission to Rome to discuss economic development and humanitarian assistance with Vatican officials. The mission would explain U.S. foreign assistance and economic and humanitarian programs. In turn, the Vatican would brief the mission on its development and humanitarian activities throughout the world. The goal of the Presidential mission would be to begin a dialog that could lead to U.S.-Vatican cooperation in the effort to alleviate hunger and disease and to promote peace worldwide.

Note: Following the Pope's arrival at Fairbanks International Airport, AK, he and the President met, together with U.S. and Vatican officials, in the airport terminal.

Nomination of Ben C. Rusche To Be a Director at the Department of Energy
May 3, 1984

The President today announced his intention to nominate Ben C. Rusche to be Director of the Office of Civilian Radioactive Waste Management at the Department of Energy. This is a new position.

Mr. Rusche is presently serving as president of Management and Technical Resources, Inc., and also as a consultant to the Secretary of Energy. Previously, he was vice president of the Management Analysis Co., in 1982–1984; a member of the Nuclear Regulatory Commission Task Group of the President's Private Sector Survey on Cost Control in 1982; and Special Assistant for Policy and Programs in the Office of the Secretary of Energy in 1981–1982. In 1977– 1978 he was corporate director for health and safety at E.I. DuPont Co. and was Director of the Office of Nuclear Reactor Regulation at the U.S. Nuclear Regulatory Commission in 1975–1977.

He also served as executive director of the South Carolina Research Institute and, while on leave of absence, served as director, Waste Management, Three-Mile Island Recovery Operations, General Public Utilities Corp.

Mr. Rusche graduated from Tennessee Polytechnic University (B.S., 1953). He is married, has three children, and resides in Columbia, SC. He was born February 18, 1931, in Yazoo City, MS.

Appointment of Randall E. Davis as Special Assistant to the President for Policy Development and Assistant Director for Energy and Natural Resources
May 3, 1984

The President today announced his appointment of Randall E. Davis to be Special Assistant to the President for Policy Development and Assistant Director for Energy and Natural Resources.

Since January 1983, Mr. Davis has been a Special Assistant to the President for Legislative Affairs. Prior to joining the White House staff, Mr. Davis was the minority counsel and staff director of the House Committee on Energy and Commerce from January 1981 to January 1983 and was associate minority counsel of the House Interstate and Foreign Commerce Committee from July 1978 until January 1981.

In 1980 Mr. Davis served as a staff member of the Subcommittee on Energy of the Committee on Resolutions at the Republican National Convention. He was also a member of the Department of Energy transition staff, Office of the President-elect, from November 1980 to January 1981.

Mr. Davis received his juris doctor degree from the Catholic University of America in 1977 and his B.A. in economics and business administration from Wilmington College in 1973. He is a member of the Ohio and District of Columbia Bars.

Mr. Davis was born on October 20, 1951, in Piqua, OH. He is married to Kim Turpin Davis and resides in Alexandria, VA.

Proclamation 5186—Student Awareness of Drunk Driving Month, 1984
May 3, 1984

By the President of the United States of America

A Proclamation

As school sessions come to a close, students will have greater opportunities to drive on our streets and highways. Students, like all motor vehicle operators, have a responsibility to adhere to the principle of "safety first." Driving while under the influence of alcohol and other drugs is destructive not only to the irresponsible driver, but to others—those who are injured or killed in the resulting motor vehicle accidents. Whether the victims are close friends or total strangers, the injury and loss of life are tragic.

We are losing lives unnecessarily, and the economic cost to America is billions of dollars each year. These statistics cannot reflect the devastating grief of families and friends as they view the senseless loss of their loved ones. This grief is repeated many times. Alcohol-related accidents kill twenty-five thousand persons each year.

Our young people are particularly vulnerable when they combine youthful exuberance and lack of driving experience with alcohol- or drug-impaired judgment and reflexes. Alcohol-related accidents are the leading cause of death for our young people between 16 and 24 years of age.

Fortunately, there has been a ground swell of awareness and action through such initiatives as the Presidential Commission on Drunk Driving, Mothers Against Drunk Drivers (MADD), Students Against Driving Drunk (SADD), and the activities of numerous other citizens groups. Also, over the last decade the U.S. Department of Education has developed alcohol and drug abuse education programs which have reached approximately five million students and indirectly affected millions more.

To emphasize the combined efforts of the Government and private sector organizations to combat the hazards of drunk driving to the youth of our Nation, the Congress, by House Joint Resolution 443, has designated the month of June 1984 as "Student Awareness of Drunk Driving Month."

Now, Therefore, I, Ronald Reagan, President of the United States of America, do hereby proclaim the month of June 1984 as Student Awareness of Drunk Driving Month. I encourage all citizens to observe this important month by participating in appropriate ceremonies and activities planned by governmental agencies, individuals, and private associations and institutions throughout the country to educate our young people about the tragic consequences of drunk driving.

In Witness Whereof, I have hereunto set my hand this third day of May, in the year of our Lord nineteen hundred and eighty-four, and of the Independence of the United States of America the two hundred

and eighth.

RONALD REAGAN

[*Filed with the Office of the Federal Register, 4:21 p.m., May 3, 1984*]

Message to the Congress Reporting on the Declaration of a National Emergency With Respect to Iran
May 3, 1984

To the Congress of the United States:

Pursuant to Section 204(c) of the International Emergency Economic Powers Act (IEEPA), 50 U.S.C. Section 1703(c), I hereby report to the Congress with respect to developments between my last report of November 4, 1983, and mid-April 1984, concerning the national emergency with respect to Iran that was declared in Executive Order No. 12170 of November 14, 1979.

1. The Iran-United States Claims Tribunal, established at The Hague pursuant to the Claims Settlement Agreement of January 19, 1981, continues to make progress in arbitrating the claims of U.S. nationals against Iran. Since my last report, the Tribunal has rendered 36 more decisions for a total of 118 final decisions. Eighty-five of these decisions have been awards in favor of American claimants. Sixty of these were awards on agreed terms, authorizing and approving payment of settlements negotiated by the parties and 25 were adjudicated. Total payments to successful American claimants from the Security Account stood at over $193.1 million, as of March 31, 1984. Of the remaining 33 decisions, 16 dismissed claims for lack of jurisdiction, 3 partially dismissed claims for lack of jurisdiction, 11 dismissed claims on the merits, two approved withdrawal of a claim and one was an award in favor of the Government of Iran. As of March 31, the Tribunal had held 143 prehearing conferences and 88 hearings on the merits and had scheduled another 19 prehearings and 17 hearings through the end of September.

2. The Department of State continues to coordinate the efforts of the concerned government agencies in presenting U.S. claims against Iran as well as U.S. responses to claims brought by Iran. The Department continues to devote a great deal of time to responding to cases brought by Iran under Articles II(3) and VI(4) of the Claims Settlement Agreement, which establish Tribunal jurisdiction over questions of interpretation and implementation of the Algiers Accords. Since my last report, the Tribunal has issued an award in favor of the United States in one of these cases, holding that it had no jurisdiction over Iran's standby letter of credit claims except as counterclaims to claims brought on the underlying contract. The Full Tribunal has also determined that it does have jurisdiction over claims by individuals possessing both U.S. and Iranian nationality, as well as claims by nonprofit organizations. In both instances, the Tribunal's decisions largely accorded with the position taken by the United States. Although the United States has filed replies in all of the interpretive cases, Iran has failed to do so and most of the hearings scheduled for the past six months have been cancelled.

3. Since my last report, a few government-to-government claims based on contracts for the provision of goods or services have been resolved. The United States withdrew three claims following the receipt of payment from Iran for each claim. In addition, the Tribunal dismissed on jurisdictional grounds one claim filed by Iran and one claim filed by the United States, stating that neither was based on contract. It also issued an award in favor of Iran in one claim arising from monies deposited by the

Iranian Department of the Environment with the Environmental Protection Agency. In all three claims, the Tribunal based its decision solely on the pleadings. It will most likely continue this practice with most of the remaining official claims.

4. Over the last six months, the Tribunal has continued to make progress in arbitrating the claims of U.S. nationals for $250,000 or more. More than 25 percent of these claims have been disposed of through adjudication, settlement, or voluntary withdrawal, leaving 381 claims on the docket. The Tribunal has rendered a number of significant decisions for American claimants. It has held that expropriation may be either *de facto* or *de jure* and that compensation for expropriated property must be prompt, adequate and effective. It has also decided that noncontractual Iranian counterclaims based on taxes allegedly owed by the U.S. claimant are outside its jurisdiction. As I reported in my last report, the Tribunal has requested Iran to stay court proceedings in Iran against at least eight U.S. nationals who have filed claims at the Tribunal on similar issues, but to date Iran has not complied with these requests.

5. In December 1983, the Tribunal adopted a test case approach for arbitrating claims for less than $250,000 which, as a result of withdrawals, terminations, and settlements, now number 2,706. (The procedure to be used was described in my last report.) Two additional legal officers have joined the Tribunal's staff to work exclusively on these claims. The Tribunal has selected 18 test cases and has begun to set deadlines for Iran's Statements of Defense and, in some cases, has requested Supplemental Statements of Claim from the United States. In March 1984, the Tribunal selected an additional 50 claims at random for which the United States has been requested to file Supplemental Statements of Claim. The Department of State is accordingly in the process of preparing the factual and legal argumentation for all of these claims.

6. In the last six months, there have also been some changes in the composition of the Tribunal. Richard M. Mosk, one of the three U.S. arbitrators, resigned effective January 15, 1984, and Charles N. Brower has replaced him. Mr. Brower, who had

previously been named a substitute arbitrator, is a well-known international lawyer who has served as a senior member of the Office of the Legal Adviser of the Department of State. Mr. Mosk is now acting as a substitute arbitrator. In addition, Carl F. Salans and William H. Levit, Jr. have been appointed substitute U.S. arbitrators. Mr. Salans, a member of the law firm of Salans Hertzfeld Heilbronn Beardsley & van Riel in Paris, France, has an extensive background in international adjudication, arbitration and negotiation. Mr. Levit, an experienced litigator, is a senior partner in the law firm of Godfrey & Kahn, Milwaukee, Wisconsin.

7. The January 19, 1981, agreements with Iran also provided for direct negotiations between U.S. banks and Bank Markazi Iran concerning the payment of nonsyndicated debt claims of U.S. banks against Iran from the $1.418 billion escrow account presently held by the Bank of England. Since my last report, only one additional settlement has been reached. The Bank of America received $472 million in settlement of its claim, of which $289.1 million was subsequently paid to Iran, primarily for interest on Iran's domestic deposits with the bank. Thus, as of March 31, 1984, there have been 25 bank settlements, totaling approximately $1.4 billion. Iran has received $616 million in settlement of its claims against the banks. About 24 bank claims remain outstanding.

8. On December 22, 1983, the Department of the Treasury amended Section 535.504 of the Iranian Assets Control Regulations to continue in effect indefinitely the prohibition of that section on any final judgment or order by a U.S. court disposing of any interest of Iran in any standby letter of credit, performance bond or similar obligation. The prohibition was promulgated to facilitate the ongoing implementation of the Algiers Accords and, especially, to allow the resolution before the Iran-United States Claims Tribunal of the many claims and issues pending before it involving letters of credit. The prohibition was extended indefinitely because it is not possible to predict how much time will be required in order to resolve these claims.

9. Although the Tribunal has made some progress over the past six months in arbitrating the claims before it, significant American interests remain unresolved. Iran has challenged the validity of four more of the Tribunal's awards in favor of U.S. claimants in the District Court of The Hague and has attempted to delay the arbitral process through repeated requests for extensions and failure to appear at Tribunal proceedings.

10. Financial and diplomatic aspects of the relationship with Iran continue to present an unusual challenge to the national security and foreign policy of the United States. I shall continue to exercise the powers at my disposal to deal with these problems and will continue to report periodically to the Congress on significant developments.

RONALD REAGAN

The White House,
May 3, 1984.

Message to the Congress Transmitting the United States-Poland Fishery Agreement
May 4, 1984

To the Congress of the United States:

In accordance with the Magnuson Fishery Conservation and Management Act of 1976 (Public Law 94–265; 16 USC 1801), I transmit herewith an exchange of Diplomatic Notes, together with the present agreement, extending the Governing International Fishery Agreement between the United States and Poland, signed at Washington on August 2, 1976, until December 31, 1985. The exchange of notes together with the present agreement constitute a Governing International Fishery Agreement within the requirements of Section 201(c) of the Act.

Several U.S. fishing interests have urged prompt consideration of this agreement. In view of the July 1 expiration date of the current agreement, I urge that the Congress give favorable consideration to this extension at an early date.

RONALD REAGAN

The White House,
May 4, 1984.

Nomination of Edward E. Wolfe for the Rank of Ambassador While Serving as a Deputy Assistant Secretary of State
May 4, 1984

The President today announced his intention to nominate Edward E. Wolfe for the rank of Ambassador in his capacity as Deputy Assistant Secretary of State for Oceans and Fisheries Affairs. He would succeed Theodore George Kronmiller, and the rank would pertain only during periods of his representation of the United States at international conferences and meetings on fish and wildlife matters.

Mr. Wolfe served in the United States Army from 1969 to 1971. From 1972 to 1974, he was field manager at Coca Cola USA in Atlanta, GA. He was senior legislative assistant to Congressman G. William Whitehurst (1976–1978) and an associate in the firm of Steele and Utz in Washington, DC (1978–1980). In 1981 he served as policy and program consultant, National Oceanic and Atmospheric Administration, National Marine Fisheries Service, in the Department of Commerce. From 1981 to 1982, he was Washington legislative representative to the United States Tuna Foundation. In the Department of State he was Special Advisor for International Affairs in the Bureau of Oceans and International Environmental and Scientific Affairs from 1982 to 1983, and since 1983 has been Deputy Assistant Secretary of State for Oceans and Fisheries Affairs.

Mr. Wolfe received his B.A. in 1969 from West Virginia University and his J.D. in 1977 from George Mason University School of Law. He was born January 20, 1947, in Norfolk, VA.

Message on the Observance of National Volunteer Week, May 6–12, 1984
May 4, 1984

Across the broad expanse of our national history, from the earliest colonial times to the present, Americans have distinguished themselves by rising to the challenge of adversity. It is in this spirit that voluntarism has become a cornerstone of our way of life and a fundamental part of our country's continuing progress.

The American people are deeply proud of this long tradition of neighbor reaching out to neighbor with a helping hand. In the continuing need to solve community problems, the compassionate actions of the private sector reflect the sense of essential decency and concern that has so often been a hallmark of our national character. Truly there is no finer expression of the values we cherish than our united efforts to address problems through the creativity and the initiative of the private sector.

The record of achievement of government and the private sector working together inspires us to look to this source of strength in pursuing worthy goals in the future.

By acknowledging gratefully our heritage of voluntarism during National Volunteer Week, I hope all Americans will vigorously participate in their community's efforts to better the lives of their fellow citizens.

RONALD REAGAN

Written Responses to Questions Submitted by Pacific Magazine on United States Policy in the Pacific Island Region
May 4, 1984

Q. Mr. President, is it possible to state in a few concise words what the basic principles and goals are of U.S. policy in the Pacific island region?

The President. First of all, we are part of the Pacific island region. Hawaii, American Samoa, Guam, and the Northern Mariana Islands, which soon should formally acquire commonwealth status, make the United States of America a permanent part of the area. In addition, we continue to have a special relationship with the Federated States of Micronesia, the Republic of the Marshall Islands, and the Republic of Palau.

Our relationship with the Pacific island region is a partnership. We share a strong belief in freedom and democracy, respect for human rights, and faith in the power of the free market. We want to build on these values to establish even better relationships with the new nations of the Pacific. And we want to help the islanders keep the region free from tensions and rivalries as it has been since World War II.

Q. Is there any likelihood that in the future there will be more U.S. aid to the Pacific island nations, possibly on a direct bilateral basis?

The President. We intend to maintain a helpful development assistance role, supplementing the larger programs of Australia and New Zealand. We anticipate that future U.S. aid to the region will be at modestly increasing levels.

Our assistance is available indirectly through the Asian Development Bank, the United Nations, and various regional institutions. There are grants to local and U.S. private voluntary organizations for programs in the individual countries, and of course, we have the U.S. Peace Corps. This system seems to work quite well. This approach provides a broad range of U.S. assistance on a regional and individual country basis.

I should also add that private business can and will play a larger role in the economic development of the Pacific island region than aid from any government. This theme was stressed in my message to the South Pacific Conference held in American Samoa 1½ years ago. The free enterprise system is the best way to promote growth and development. As far as Micronesia is concerned, we are the primary donor, and if Congress approves, we will continue to support the economic development of the Micronesian States under the Compact of Free Association.

Q. Vanuatu has recently established full diplomatic relations with Cuba. The Solomon Islands has adopted a policy of looking to Southeast Asia for partners in its economic development. Western Samoa has full diplomatic relations with the People's Republic of China and a significant cultural exchange program. Kiribati is receiving some material aid from the People's Republic of China. Do you regard these events as a trend that may cause the United States to reassess its Pacific islands policies?

The President. As independent countries, Vanuatu, the Solomon Islands, Western Samoa, and Kiribati have the right to choose their friends. We share a community of values and interests with the islanders. We try to understand their activities in light of our common interests. We hope they take the same approach with us.

Q. Some heads of state from South Pacific nations have complained that not enough attention is paid to them in Washington. Is there still a residual attitude in Washington that writes off the islands because of their

comparatively small populations?

The President. Direct U.S. involvement in the South Pacific was very limited until the middle 1970's, since almost all of the islands were colonial dependencies of other states. Nevertheless, the United States began responding to the changing situation in the South Pacific more than a decade ago. We initiated Peace Corps programs, educational and cultural exchanges, and established consulates. As more states became independent, we upgraded the consulates to embassies and accredited ambassadors. This process is continuing. We are now considering additional diplomatic representation in the area. These posts symbolize our recognition of the importance of the Pacific island nations. Also, recently, we began a regional development assistance program and stepped up our contributions to the work of the South Pacific Commission.

I can assure you that the U.S. Government is very conscious of the island states and sensitive to their needs and aspirations.

Q. Now that the Compact of Free Association between the United States and the Federated States of Micronesia, Marshall Islands, and Palau is close to completion, do you foresee anything that could block approval of the Compact in the U.S. Congress or the United Nations?

The President. Because the Compact reflects the will of the people, I hope that both the United States Congress and the international community will recognize that self-government for the peoples of the Trust Territory should not be delayed. I have sent the Compact to Congress with a message urging its approval. We expect close examination of the Compact by the Congress. The democratic process and public review of the Compact will benefit the Compact and the people of the region.

There is an outstanding issue that could delay implementation of the Compact with respect to Palau. It is an internal constitutional problem that has prevented Palau's government from approving the Compact and implementing the mandate of the Palauan people. The primary issue has to do with nuclear materials.

Free association is a partnership. Under the Compact the United States has responsibility for regional peace and stability, while Palau would have self-government, substantial economic assistance, and autonomy in foreign affairs. This partnership requires the United States to perform a security role. Therefore, I have asked the United States Congress to approve the Compact with the Marshall Islands and the Federated States of Micronesia at this time. I will request congressional approval of the Compact with Palau only after that government has confirmed that its internal constitutional approval process is complete. We will cooperate with the Palauan Government, but ultimately it is an issue for the Palauans to decide.

Partnership requires resolution of this issue. Last October the President of Palau joined the Presidents of the Federated States of Micronesia and the Marshall Islands in signing the Saipan accords, which call for prompt approval of the Compact by the U.S. Congress and early termination of the trusteeship.

Q. Leaders in these islands—the Federated States of Micronesia, the Marshall Islands, and Palau—generally give the United States high marks for promoting democracy. However, they have often criticized its effort in promoting economic development. Is your administration addressing this issue?

The President. We are meeting that challenge head on. The United States supports the operations and economic development of these governments under U.N. trusteeship. A long-range capital improvement program devoted to basic requirements such as power, water and sewage systems, docks, roads, and airports, is near completion. Looking to the future, the Compact of Free Association provides substantial grants for government operations, social services, capital improvements, economic development programs, health, education, telecommunications, energy self-sufficiency, and other needs.

This assistance will enable the Federated States of Micronesia, the Marshall Islands, and Palau to work toward the economic goals they have established for themselves. I would like to highlight the point that the elected leaders of the Micronesians will establish the economic policies under the Compact. This will put decisionmaking au-

thority and economic resources in the hands of Micronesians and their leaders.

Q. How does your administration evaluate the prospects for economic independence of these island nations after the expiration of the U.S. Compact-related funding?

The President. During the initial term of free association, the Micronesians will have the tools and resources to make significant progress towards economic self-sufficiency. Much will depend on the priorities they establish and their ability to exercise fiscal restraint. The Compact provides an opportunity for them to move toward their goals and objectives.

Again, however, I want to stress the important role of private business. A free enterprise system offers opportunity and rewards, initiative, imagination, hard work, perseverance, and productivity. The governments of the Micronesian States will find that the private sector is the key to a promising future.

Q. Is it likely that the United States will require more naval, air, and ground force bases in the Pacific islands in the future than it now has?

The President. The short answer is no. However, it is always wise to preserve our options. The United States already has important air and naval bases on Guam. They will continue to be the principal U.S. facilities in the Central Pacific. In addition, we exercised our option for a long-term lease of land in the Commonwealth of the Northern Mariana Islands, which will ensure added flexibility to meet any change in our base and logistics requirements. Although current plans are to use the area only for training, we will also have the option, under the Compact, for limited harbor, airfield, and training sites in Palau. The only other defense installation in Micronesia is our testing facility at Kwajalein. Use of this facility is set by the Compact for 15 years, with an option for an additonal 15 years. We do not anticipate the need for any major changes.

Q. A tremendous amount of attention has been given to the Federated States of Micronesia, the Marshall Islands, and Palau during the years of negotiating the Compact of Free Association with them. In the meantime, many people in the U.S. Pacific territories of American Samoa, Guam, and the Northern Marianas are complaining that they are being overlooked—not enough U.S. private capital, not enough technical assistance. Do you think these complaints are justified?

The President. I can understand why the American territories view the negotiations in Micronesia with great interest. Guam has been a loyal part of the American political family since 1898; American Samoa since 1900. The people of the Northern Marianas chose to become Americans in 1975. The Compact of Free Association has been negotiated over the past 14 years. It is an agreement that recognizes the sovereignty of the people of Micronesia.

Although Americans in the territories have watched these negotiations with interest, I hope they share my pride in their own permanent role in America's future.

American Samoa, Guam, and the Northern Marianas are parts of the American family. We have done much to guarantee that their specific problems receive special assistance. And we will do more. We are working with the three territories to diversify and expand their economies, particularly with the help of the private sector.

The territories do need more technical assistance and a major effort is underway to establish long-range technical assistance objectives for major programs in each territory. Once the objectives are established, needed resources will be better defined. During the last 2 years the U.S. Congress has been supportive of increased technical assistance programs, and I hope this welcome trend continues.

But there still is not enough U.S. private capital available to the territories. We are exploring ways to make financial capital more available and accessible. We are working closely with the territories to identify and make changes in Federal regulations and legislation that will promote economic development.

The most important thing to remember is that the people there are our fellow U.S. citizens and nationals. They enjoy great benefits and carry the responsibilities of citizenship. They have, and should have, the full resources of the Federal Government available to them. The challenge—

and one I'm sure we can assist—is to tailor those benefits to their unique circumstances.

Q. The United States has not yet signed the Law of the Sea Convention. Why not? Is it possible that the United States would sign it if it were in any way amended?

The President. When we announced that the United States would not sign the convention, I stated that the deep seabed mining section did not meet U.S. objectives. Our problems with the deep seabed mining regime include:

—provisions that would actually deter future development of deep seabed resources, when such development should serve the interest of all countries;

—a decisionmaking process that would not give the United States or others a role that fairly reflects and protects their interests;

—provisions that would allow amendments without United States approval. This is incompatible with our approach to treaties;

—stipulations relating to mandatory transfer of private technology and the possibility of national liberation movements sharing in benefits; and

—the absence of assured access for future qualified deep seabed miners to promote the development of these resources.

In spite of our well-known objections and renewed negotiating efforts in early 1982, the Law of the Sea Conference adopted the convention on April 30, 1982, although, after nearly 2 years, it has not yet come into force. I would also point out that many major industrialized nations share our concerns. As to amending the convention, at this point it would be most difficult, and we are not aware of any move to do so.

Nevertheless, the convention contains many positive and significant accomplishments. We are prepared to accept and act in accordance with international law as reflected in the Law of the Sea Convention that relates to traditional uses of the ocean. We are willing to respect the maritime claims of others, including economic zones, that are consistent with international law as reflected in the convention, so long as the international rights and freedoms of the United States and others in such areas are respected.

Q. The nuclear issue is a big one in the Pacific. Could you clarify the U.S. position on the testing of nuclear weapons and on the dumping of nuclear waste in the South Pacific?

The President. The United States is sensitive to the nuclear concerns of the island people. We share the desire to protect the ocean from pollution. The United States is a party to the London Dumping Convention and other international agreements aimed at protecting the health of the oceans. Our domestic laws regulating ocean dumping are even more stringent and are vigorously enforced. The United States is also a member of the Nuclear Test Ban Treaty, which bans nuclear weapons tests in the atmosphere, in outer space, and under water.

Q. The passage of U.S. Navy ships that are nuclear powered and that are capable of carrying nuclear weapons is also of concern to the people of the South Pacific. Can you clarify the U.S. position in this regard?

The President. U.S. nuclear powered warships have an unparalleled record of safe operation since the first nuclear-powered ship became operational in 1955. U.S. nuclear-powered ships have accumulated over 2,700 reactor years of operation without a single nuclear mishap. This record reflects the very strict control exercised over the design, construction, operation, maintenance, and repair of our nuclear-powered ships and the careful selection, training, and qualification of the personnel manning the ships.

Over 40 percent of our Navy's major ships are nuclear powered, and they are among our most effective ships. Access to all areas of the oceans by U.S. nuclear-powered warships is essential to maintain the peace.

The ability of the United States to deter aggression and to help maintain peace throughout the world depends on the ability of its ships and aircraft to travel the ocean spaces, including the South Pacific. The presence of the U.S. Navy ships does not pose a danger to the interests of the people of the South Pacific; rather, it helps guarantee their continued peace and freedom.

Q. You are a man from California—the Pacific State. What would you like the Pacific people to remember you and your administration for having accomplished in the Pacific?

The President. As a Californian, I am particularly aware of our Pacific interests. I would like to have our administration remembered as one which fully recognized the importance of Asia and the Pacific. Focus is shifting increasingly to the Pacific, which is now—as I said earlier—the fastest growing economic region of the world. We want to build on the good relations we already have and make them stronger. We want to do our part to encourage regional cooperation. And we want to continue our security role, a role that permits the islands to develop politically and economically according to the wishes of the islanders themselves.

Recently, meeting at the White House with a group of Americans of Asian and Pacific heritage, I had a chance to reflect on the contributions to American society that derive from the people of this region. It's part of what you might call "the spirit of America." Back in the fall of 1980, I attended a rally held in the shadow of the Statue of Liberty. And there were many nationalities and ethnic groups there, all reminding us that we're all descendants from immigrants who came here looking for freedom and opportunity. And, while our country had its flaws and we still have them, the American dream was real.

Asian and Pacific Americans have helped preserve that dream by living up to the bedrock values that make us a good and a worthy people. I'm talking about principles that begin with the sacred worth of human life, religious faith, community spirit, and the responsibility of parents and schools to be teachers of tolerance, hard work, fiscal responsibility, cooperation, and love. After all, it is values, not programs and policies, that serve as our nation's compass. They hold us on course. They point the way to a promising future.

America needs its Asian and Pacific

American citizens. They've enriched our national culture and our heritage. They've held the beliefs that account for so much of our economic and social progress. They've never stopped striving for excellence, despite times in the past when they experienced terrible discrimination. We will continue to fight against discrimination, wherever there are any vestiges of it remaining, until we've removed such bigotry from our entire land.

And when we look toward that great and grand Pacific Basin, there's a promising future. Americans may not hear much about our Pacific and Asian foreign policy, but then there's a lot of good news that they don't seem to hear about.

Our relations with our Pacific and Asian friends and allies have never been better.

First of all, as I indicated in answering your first question, it's not all foreign policy. The United States of America is part of the Pacific. There's Hawaii, American Samoa, Guam, and the soon-to-be commonwealth status of the Northern Mariana Islands and our special relationship with the Federated States of Micronesia and the Republics of the Marshall Islands and Palau. It is my hope that our administration will be remembered as helping the people of the Pacific Basin achieve their hopes and aspirations, and that together, we will bring a pacific, tranquil future to the region.

Note: As printed above, the questions and answers follow the text of the White House press release.

Radio Address to the Nation on Waste, Fraud, Abuse, and Mismanagement in the Federal Government
May 5, 1984

My fellow Americans:

When I spoke to you a week ago we were in China working to strengthen cooperation between our two countries, increase opportunities for jobs and a better life for our people, and improve the prospects for a more peaceful world. As I told the citizens of Alaska when we arrived back in the States, I feel we made significant progress.

Today I'd like to speak about our efforts toward another goal, one that might not get the headlines of a trip to China, but that nonetheless has an important impact on our lives. I'm talking about reducing waste, fraud, abuse, and mismanagement in government—problems that for too long were permitted to grow and spread like an unchecked cancer, plundering your pocketbooks and hindering government's ability to provide essential public services in an efficient and timely manner.

Our administration is determined to reverse the years of neglect and get this monster under control so we can have a government of, by, and for the people again, not the other way around. That's why we're

pushing comprehensive measures like Reform '88, which involves over 1,000 different projects to upgrade the management of the Federal Government; and why we're moving to implement recommendations of the Grace commission, which I established and which has identified billions of dollars in wasteful government spending.

Let me give you some specific ways in which we've begun to make progress in improving government's management practices—doing what others said couldn't be done.

First, debt collection: For too long Washington seemed only to care about handing money out, not collecting debts owed. In fact, collection practices were so bad the Federal Government didn't even know how much was owed and how much was overdue. We inherited a delinquency rate that was growing at the shocking rate of almost 30 percent a year. In the $8 billion guaranteed student loan program, 1 student out of 10 defaults on his or her loan. These defaults each year equal enough money to give loans to about 700,000 eligible students.

Well, with support from the Congress, we're taking a tough new stance on collections. We're not singling out any individuals or groups, but we can, we must, and we will go after the cheaters who profit from the system at the expense of honest citizens like yourselves who live by the rules.

For instance, one military surgeon in Hawaii refused to pay his student debt, even though he made over $50,000 a year and owned seven pieces of real estate. After being threatened with litigation, he paid in one lump sum the $11,500 that he owed.

Tens of thousands of Federal employees have been reneging on their student loans. They will get one last chance to pay up before finding their July paychecks smaller. Call it enforced repayment through cuts in take-home pay.

Justice Department officials are now aggressively pursuing those who default on loans by putting new emphasis on collection of debts and fines. Our U.S. attorneys collected $201 million last year, a return of $24 for every dollar invested.

The second area—waste, fraud, and abuse—is the byproduct of mismanagement. Our management improvements, together with the tremendous accomplishments of our Inspectors General, are a one-two punch taking steam out of the waste and fraud that was eroding faith in our government.

Not only have billions in waste and fraud been rooted out, but preventive actions are nipping problems in the bud before they occur. We're making a very determined effort to crack down on white-collar crime, those who abuse positions of power for their own benefit. Both the Department of Transportation and the Environmental Protection Agency are pushing nationwide investigations of bid rigging in the awarding of contracts for Federal highway and wastewater treatment facility construction. The Justice Department has already initiated 270 criminal prosecutions in highway bid rigging involving 255 corporations and 256 individuals in 20 States.

You've all heard of the problems at the Pentagon with spare parts suppliers charging outrageous prices. Well, what you haven't heard is that this waste was actually uncovered by Department of Defense auditors working for the Inspector General I appointed. We are the first administration which has faced up to these abuses and taken action to correct them.

The progress we've made is a good start, but it's little more than a ripple in the river of waste, fraud, and abuse that's been rising for years. That's why it's clear the way to reduce the deficit is by strong economic growth and by reducing wasteful bloated government, not by raising taxes on you, the people.

Until next week, thanks for listening, and God bless you.

Note: The President spoke at 12:06 p.m. from Camp David, MD.

Statement on the Second Round of the Conference on Confidence and Security Building Measures and Disarmament in Europe
May 5, 1984

The second round of the Conference on Confidence and Security Building Measures and Disarmament in Europe, known as CDE, will begin in Stockholm next Tuesday, May 8, 1984.

The CDE arises out of the "Helsinki process," in which we and our allies seek balanced progress in both the security and human rights areas. The CDE negotiations began last January and are a promising new part of the dialog on European security issues. The participating countries include the United States, Canada, our European allies, the European neutral states, and the members of the Warsaw Pact.

The CDE is an essentially new approach to European security. We and our allies seek an agreement on practical, meaningful ways to reduce the risk of surprise attack and to reduce the uncertainty and potential for misunderstandings over military activity in both the East and West. Western unity has been and will continue to be a crucial factor in the progress we achieve.

During the recess, we have consulted closely with our allies and other participating nations. At my request, our Ambassador to the CDE, James Goodby, has just completed senior level consultations in several capitals, including Moscow. He had a full and useful exchange of views with Soviet officials.

It is important now to engage in serious negotiations on the concrete proposals which the West presented during the first round. Those proposals are designed to increase mutual knowledge and understanding of military forces and activities in Europe; reduce the chance of war by miscalculation; enhance the ability of all to deal with potential crises; and minimize the possibility that military activities could be used for political intimidation. The Western nations are ready for a serious dialog on these issues. We hope this is true of the East as well.

Our proposals in the Stockholm Confer-

ence are part of our larger efforts to move forward, in a spirit of genuine cooperation, on arms control and East-West relations. Two weeks ago, at the Committee on Disarmament in Geneva, Vice President Bush presented a new American proposal for a comprehensive worldwide ban on chemical weapons. The same week, we and our NATO allies presented a new proposal at the MBFR talks in Vienna. This initiative is designed to break the impasse in the negotiations on reducing conventional forces in Central Europe.

We are striving hard for real progress in all three negotiations. But it is also vitally important to get on with the urgent business of reducing nuclear arms. I strongly hope that the Soviet Union will heed the wishes of the international community—and of its own people—and return to the negotiations on strategic and intermediate-range nuclear forces.

The opportunity for meaningful progress in arms control exists. The Soviet leaders should take advantage of it. Our representatives are ready to return to the two negotiating tables on nuclear arms, and we will negotiate in good faith. As I have said before, whenever the Soviet Union is ready to do likewise, we will meet them halfway.

Proclamation 5187—National Correctional Officers Week, 1984
May 5, 1984

By the President of the United States of America

A Proclamation

Correctional officers have the difficult and often dangerous assignment of ensuring the custody, safety and well-being of the over 600,000 inmates in our Nation's prisons and jails. Their position is essential to the day-to-day operations of these institutions; without them it would be impossible to achieve the foremost institutional goals of security and control.

Historically, correctional officers have been viewed as "guards," occupying isolated and misunderstood positions in prisons and jails. In recent years, the duties of these

officers have become increasingly complex and demanding. They are called upon to fill, simultaneously, custodial, supervisory and counseling roles. The professionalism, dedication and courage exhibited by these officers throughout the performance of these demanding and often conflicting roles deserve our utmost respect. The important work of correctional officers often does not receive the recognition from the public it deserves. It is appropriate that we honor the many contributions and accomplishments of these men and women who are a vital component of the field of corrections.

In recognition of the contributions of correctional officers to our Nation, the Congress, by Senate Joint Resolution 132, has designated the week beginning May 6, 1984, as "National Correctional Officers Week," and authorized and requested the President to issue an appropriate proclamation.

Now, Therefore, I, Ronald Reagan, President of the United States of America, do hereby proclaim the week beginning May 6, 1984, as National Correctional Officers Week. I call upon officials of State and local governments and the people of the United States to observe this week with appropriate ceremonies and activities.

In Witness Whereof, I have hereunto set my hand this fifth day of May, in the year of our Lord nineteen hundred and eighty-four, and of the Independence of the United States of America the two hundred and eighth.

RONALD REAGAN

[*Filed with the Office of the Federal Register, 12:50 p.m., May 7, 1984*]

Note: The text of the proclamation was released by the Office of the Press Secretary on May 7.

Proclamation 5188—National Photo Week, 1984
May 5, 1984

By the President of the United States of America

A Proclamation

Photography, the prime visual recorder of human events, preserves memories, emotion, and sentiment for virtually all Americans. It is an established and growing art form which communicates the beauty and diversity of America as well as the vitality of its culture and its people.

Photography has played an important role in our commercial and artistic lives and in the process of government through motion pictures, video cameras, and still shots. Photographs preserve the history of the Nation and the changing panorama of American landscape and culture. Visual records also contribute to the advancement of many fields of science, technology, and inquiry, including communications, meteorology, geography, medicine, justice, astronomy and agriculture.

To honor the invaluable contribution that photography has made to the quality of our life, the Congress has, by Senate Joint Reso-

lution 250, designated the week of May 7 through May 13, 1984, as "National Photo Week" and has authorized the President to issue a proclamation in honor of that occasion.

Now, Therefore, I, Ronald Reagan, President of the United States of America, do hereby proclaim May 7 through May 13, 1984, as National Photo Week, and I call upon the American people to engage in appropriate observances to reflect our appreciation and understanding of the value of photography to the Nation.

In Witness Whereof, I have hereunto set my hand this fifth day of May, in the year of our Lord nineteen hundred and eighty-four, and of the Independence of the United States of America the two hundred and eighth.

RONALD REAGAN

[*Filed with the Office of the Federal Register, 12:51 p.m., May 7, 1984*]

Note: The text of the proclamation was released by the Office of the Press Secretary on May 7.

Proclamation 5189—National Defense Transportation Day and National Transportation Week, 1984
May 5, 1984

By the President of the United States of America

A Proclamation

America's transportation systems are a mainstay of our economy, an essential component of our commerce, an important part of our defense and the means by which our citizens and visitors alike enjoy the freedom to travel throughout our land.

Historically, transportation has opened America's frontiers. Transportation gave our Nation's territorial and industrial pioneers access to the country's resources. More than any other element of our society, transportation has been a vibrant economic catalyst, building cities, generating new industries, spurring ambitions, providing jobs and linking us to the peoples of the world. Our transportation systems and facilities, including America's merchant fleet and road, rail and aviation networks, support the Nation's defense readiness and emergency response capabilities.

As our transportation systems have developed, they have become increasingly safe. The constant commitment to safety, shared by the government and the private sector, is reducing fatalities and accident rates to the lowest levels in our history, saving lives and preventing injuries.

As we vigorously pursue safety efforts, the Federal government is relaxing the constraints of economic regulation, enabling the Nation's rail, airline, trucking and interstate bus companies to compete more aggressively and operate more efficiently. Economic deregulation is a gateway for new carriers entering the transportation field. It is generating new competition, providing lower fares and more choices for consumers, and competitive rates for shippers. America's transportation industries stand today on the threshold of an era of broader opportunities and greater prosperity. We stand, as well, at the beginning of a new era of space transportation, in which the Federal government is fully prepared to assist the private sector in development of a commercial space industry.

In recognition of the importance of transportation in America and to honor the millions of Americans who serve and supply our transportation needs, the Congress, by joint resolution approved May 16, 1957, has requested that the third Friday in May of each year be designated National Defense Transportation Day; and by a joint resolution approved May 14, 1962, that the week in which that Friday falls be proclaimed National Transportation Week.

Now, Therefore, I, Ronald Reagan, President of the United States of America, do hereby designate Friday, May 18, 1984, as National Defense Transportation Day and proclaim the week beginning May 13, 1984, as National Transportation Week. I urge the people of the United States to observe these occasions with appropriate ceremonies which will give full recognition to the importance of our transportation system and the maintenance of its facilities.

In Witness Whereof, I have hereunto set my hand this fifth day of May, in the year of our Lord nineteen hundred and eighty-four, and of the Independence of the United States of America the two hundred and eighth.

RONALD REAGAN

[*Filed with the Office of the Federal Register, 12:52 p.m., May 7, 1984*]

Note: The text of the proclamation was released by the Office of the Press Secretary on May 7.

Proclamation 5190—Jewish Heritage Week, 1984
May 7, 1984

By the President of the United States of America

A Proclamation

Through both its spiritual ideals and its significant practical efforts, the Jewish community has contributed much to our country's greatness. So many of the values and ethics we proudly espouse in America are derived from the laws and traditions of the Jewish people: That there should be one law for the homeborn and the foreigner; that education and self-discipline are to be continually cultivated; and that family and community are the cornerstones of society. And individually—as committed citizens, soldiers in the armed forces, laborers and professionals, artists and entrepreneurs— American Jews have given of their heart, soul and might so that this Nation may prosper.

Each spring, Jews all over the world celebrate Passover, when the story of the Exodus from Egypt is retold, and the holiday of Shavuot, commemorating the giving of the Law at Mount Sinai. Traditionally, Jews spend that seven-week period between these festivals reflecting on their history and heritage. During this period, American Jews also join with their brethren throughout the world in observance of the National Days of Remembrance, honoring the victims and survivors of the Holocaust, the anniversary of the Warsaw Ghetto Uprising, and Solidarity Day for Soviet Jews. Celebration of joyous occasions like Israel's Independence Day also occur at this season.

In recognition of the special significance of this time of year to America's Jews, in tribute to the important contributions they have made to American life, and in an effort to foster understanding and appreciation of the cultural diversity that has made America such a special and unique society, the Congress, by Senate Joint Resolution 241, has authorized and requested the President to proclaim May 6 through May 13, 1984, as "Jewish Heritage Week."

Now, Therefore, I, Ronald Reagan, President of the United States of America, do hereby proclaim May 6 through May 13, 1984, as Jewish Heritage Week. I call upon the people of the United States, Federal, State and local government officials, and interested organizations to observe that week with appropriate ceremonies and activities.

In Witness Whereof, I have hereunto set my hand this 7th day of May, in the year of our Lord nineteen hundred and eighty-four, and of the Independence of the United States of America the two hundred and eighth.

RONALD REAGAN

[*Filed with the Office of the Federal Register, 4:06 p.m., May 7, 1984*]

Nomination of Charles G. Untermeyer To Be an Assistant Secretary of the Navy
May 7, 1984

The President today announced his intention to nominate Charles G. Untermeyer to be an Assistant Secretary of the Navy (Manpower and Reserve Affairs). He would succeed Chapman Beecher Cox.

Since 1983 Mr. Untermeyer has been serving as Deputy Assistant Secretary of the Navy for Installations and Facilities. Previously, he was Executive Assistant to the Vice President of the United States in 1981–1983; a member of the Texas House of Representatives in 1977–1981; fellow at the Institute of Politics at Harvard University in 1980; and executive assistant to the county judge of Harris County, TX, in 1974–1976.

He graduated from Harvard University (B.S., 1968). He was born March 7, 1946, in Long Branch, NJ, and now resides in Washington, DC.

Nomination of Richard Schifter To Be Deputy United States Representative in the United Nations Security Council
May 7, 1984

The President today announced his intention to nominate Richard Schifter, of Maryland, to be Deputy Representative of the United States of America in the Security Council of the United Nations, with the rank of Ambassador. He would succeed William Courtney Sherman.

Mr. Schifter served in the United States Army in 1943–1946. Since 1951 he has been with the law firm of Fried, Frank, Harris, Shriver, and Kampelman in Washington, DC, and has been a partner since 1957. He served in Government as economic investigator of the Office of Military Government for Germany in Berlin in 1946–1948. He was an attorney on the President's Materials Policy Commission (1951) and counsel for the Office of Food for Peace (1961). In 1966–1967 he was a member of the President's Task Force on American Indians. Since 1980 he has been a member of the United States Holocaust Council. He has served on the Human Rights Commission of the United Nations as Alternate United States Representative in 1981–1982 and since 1983 as Representative of the United States of America. He was United States Representative on the Committee on Conventions and Recommendations of UNESCO in 1981–1983. In 1984 he served as head of the United States delegation to the United Nations Human Rights Commission with the personal rank of Ambassador for the meeting held in February and March.

Mr. Schifter graduated from the College of the City of New York (B.S., 1943) and Yale University (LL.B., 1951). His foreign language is German. He was born July 31, 1923, in Vienna, Austria, and became a naturalized United States citizen in 1943.

Accordance of the Personal Rank of Ambassador to Robert W. Searby While Serving at the 1984 International Labor Conference
May 7, 1984

The President today accorded the personal rank of Ambassador to Robert W. Searby, of Virginia, in his capacity as Chairman of the United States Delegation to the 1984 International Labor Conference.

Since 1981 Mr. Searby has been Deputy Under Secretary of Labor for International Affairs, and also United States Representative on the Governing Body of the International Labor Office. He is presently serving as the chairman of the United States delegation to the 1984 International Labor Conference. This Conference will be held in Geneva, Switzerland, June 6–27, 1984.

In 1974–1978 he was executive director of Walter Bagehot Research Council, Inc. In 1978–1981 he was a consultant to several corporations, including Westinghouse and the Edison Electric Institute; executive director of the New York State Committee for Jobs and Energy Independence, Inc.; and professor of government and politics and administrator of criminal justice programs at St. John's University and the New

York Institute of Technology.

Mr. Searby graduated from Iona College (B.S., 1968) and St. John's University (M.A., 1973). He is married and has six children. He was born November 2, 1946, in New York, NY.

Message to the Senate Transmitting the Convention on the Transfer of Sentenced Persons
May 7, 1984

To the Senate of the United States:

With a view to receiving the advice and consent of the Senate to ratification, I transmit herewith the Convention on the Transfer of Sentenced Persons drawn up within the Council of Europe by a committee of experts from member States and observers from the United States and Canada, as adopted by the Council of Ministers, and signed on behalf of the United States at Strasbourg on March 21, 1983.

The provisions of the Convention are explained in a report of the Acting Secretary of State which accompanies this letter. The major advantages of a multilateral treaty on this subject are that it provides uniform procedures for transfer of sentenced persons and saves the resources that would be required to negotiate and bring into force bilateral treaties with a substantial number of member States of the Council of Europe in whose jails approximately one fourth of our citizens imprisoned abroad are serving sentences.

I recommend that the Senate give favorable consideration to this treaty at an early date.

RONALD REAGAN

The White House,
May 7, 1984.

Nomination of Weston Adams To Be United States Ambassador to Malawi
May 7, 1984

The President today announced his intention to nominate Weston Adams to be Ambassador to the Republic of Malawi. He would succeed John A. Burroughs, Jr.

Mr. Adams was a clerk in the law office of Louis W. Ingram, Columbia, SC, in 1963. From 1963 to 1966, he was Assistant Staff Judge Advocate, United States Air Force. He was a trust officer, South Carolina National Bank in Columbia, from 1966 to 1970. He served as associate counsel on the Select Committee on Crime, United States House of Representatives, in Washington, DC, 1970–1971. From 1971 to 1972, he was an associate attorney in the law office of Albert Watson in Columbia, SC, and from 1972 to 1974 was a member of the South Carolina House of Representatives. From 1972 to the present, he has been self-employed as an attorney in Columbia.

Mr. Adams received his A.B. in 1960 from the University of South Carolina and his LL.B. in 1962 from the University of South Carolina Law School. He attended the University of South Carolina Graduate School in 1962–1963 and the American Institute of Banking in 1968. His foreign languages include reading comprehension in French and German. He was born September 16, 1938, in Columbia, SC. Mr. Adams is married to the former Elizabeth N. Nelson, and they have four children.

Remarks at the Presentation Ceremony for the President's Volunteer Action Awards
May 7, 1984

Well, thank you very much for the applause, but, believe me, today it's the other way around. I'm here to applaud you. And this is a particularly fitting time to be holding this luncheon—today is the first working day of National Volunteer Week, and we've just ended a National Year of Voluntarism.

Now, I want to begin by expressing my thanks here to some volunteers who've made this occasion possible. I'm talking, of course, about George Romney and Clem Stone. I remember from our days as Governor, how much interest George took in voluntarism, and fortunately for all of us, it's an interest that he's continued with up until this day. And what can you say about Clem Stone? If he doesn't qualify for most generous American, who can?

Now, there's one lady here today who isn't getting an award, but is someone who really ought to be mentioned. Her name is Edith Westerman. And she volunteers full-time and sometimes works a lot more than full-time in our private sector initiatives office here at the White House. And, Edie, from all of us, thanks for your help in today's event and throughout the year.

You know, there's a fair amount of paperwork in this job that I'm currently holding. Homework, too. You ought to see the stacks of stuff that I lug upstairs every night. It's a good thing that I go home from work in an elevator. [*Laughter*]

Some of it—in fact, a lot of it—is not exactly the sort of thing that would be your first choice for bedtime reading. But I want you to know that recently I've had a chance to do some reading that not only riveted my attention but filled my heart with pride. It's a feeling I know all Americans would share if they, too, had a chance to see what I see. I'm referring to the citations for the awards that you're receiving today and the descriptions of the incredible work that you've done through your organizations or as individuals to better the lot of others.

What magnificent stories there are to tell about each of you. You've run jobs in health programs; you've helped the unemployed and the handicapped; you held out a helping hand to those who are forgotten or shunned or can't help themselves—drug addicts and prostitutes and convicts. You've started worldwide relief agencies and community colleges. You've run Vietnam veterans hiring programs and Indian culture schools. You've helped provide orthopedic shoes and braces for crippled children. You've donated clothes and school supplies for underprivileged children.

In fact, I can assure you that every time my staff and I thought we would single out a person or an organization for these citations, we came across somebody else who was just as worthy of mention. Each one of you has made a personal sacrifice to do the work that you did. None of you ever expected any rewards for what you did. Many times I'm sure there were doubts and lots of discouragement, and it took real courage to carry on.

We've had a lot of heroes at ceremonies here at the White House during the past few years—our shuttle astronauts, for example, or our marines and rangers from the Grenada expedition. But, believe me, you stand as tall in your own way as any of them. What you've done is in the finest traditon of your country.

You know, it was that Frenchman, de Tocqueville, so often quoted by after-dinner speakers, who, when he came here in the 1830's, reflected in awe about American voluntarism. He said, "These Americans are the most peculiar people in the world. You'll not believe me when I tell you how they behave. In a local community in their country, a citizen may conceive of some need which is not being met. What does he do? He goes across the street, discusses it with his neighbor. And then what happens? A committee comes into existence. [*Laughter*] And the committee begins functioning in behalf of the need." And he went on to say that no bureaucrats were involved at all, just the people did it. [*Laughter*]

Well, each of you here today has demonstrated this unique American spirit of voluntarism, partnership, and innovation. In your own way, you're working to resolve issues in a more effective manner than we could do with large Federal programs. Personal dedication and commitment seem to be the underlying key to success in all of your efforts. And in the 3 years since we started these awards, we've seen an ever-increasing rise in people actively helping their neighbors.

So, I want to applaud you today and thank you on behalf of all your fellow Americans. Every one of us is grateful to you. As members of your families and communities and citizens of our country, you've been an inspiration and an example to us. But most of all, we're grateful for the people you've helped, for the people whose lives you've touched and whose burdens you've lifted because you cared enough to extend a helping hand and a warm heart.

And now, with the assistance of Tom Pauken of ACTION and George Romney, I'd like to have the pleasure of handing out your awards.

[*At this point, Thomas W. Pauken, Director of ACTION, announced the award winners and read the citations accompanying the awards. Recipients included James F. "Buck" Burshears, LaJunta, CO; Nick Monreal, San Antonio, TX; Friends of Cooper Mountain College, Twentynine Palms, CA; Elizabeth Copper Terwilliger, Mill Valley, CA; Bill and Pat Barton, Naples, FL; Ray G. Villarreal, El Paso, TX; Corporate Angel Network, White Plains, NY; Children of the Night, Hollywood, CA; Americares Foundation, New Canaan, CT; Irene Auberlin, Detroit, MI; Delaware Vietnam Veterans Leadership Program, Wilmington, DE; Chris Stout, Lynnwood, WA; Knights of Columbus Supreme Council, New Haven, CT; Volunteer for Minnesota, St. Paul, MN; Tom Rader, Dos Palos, CA; Glenn Williams, Seattle, WA; San Diego & Imperial Counties Labor Council, AFL–CIO, CA; Laid-Off Employees Assistance Program, Armco Corp., Middletown, OH; and Levi Strauss & Co., San Francisco, CA. The President then resumed speaking.*]

I was supposed to be through now, but I just have one word that I just can't help but say here. I asked a question once—it wasn't original with me. It had first been asked by an admiral standing on the bridge of a carrier at the time of the Korean war when planes were taking off on a night mission. And as he watched them go, he asked, "Where do we find such men?"

I asked the question after an evening some years ago while I was still in California when we had been in the company of the first of the returning POW's from Vietnam. And I said it to Nancy—where did we find them?—after hearing them all evening. And the answer came to me as quickly as I'd asked the question.

I have only repeated it or told this with regard to incidents of that kind, but believe me, it fits today. Where do we find such people as you? And the answer is just as it was with those others—where we've always found them, the product of the freest, the most generous, the greatest social structure that has ever been devised by man. Just the product of Main Street and the farms and the cities and towns of America.

All of you, God bless you all for reaffirming what this country is all about. Thank you.

Note: The President spoke at 1:05 p.m. in the East Room at the White House.

Message to the Congress Transmitting an Extension of the United States-Soviet Union Fishery Agreement
May 8, 1984

To the Congress of the United States:

In accordance with the Magnuson Fishery Conservation and Management Act of 1976 (Public Law 94–265; 16 USC 1801), I transmit herewith an exchange of Diplomatic Notes, together with the present agreement, extending the Governing International Fishery Agreement between the United States and the Soviet Union, signed at Washington on November 26, 1976, until December 31, 1985. The exchange of notes together with the present agreement consti-

tute a Governing International Fishery Agreement within the requirements of Section 201(c) of the Act.

Several U.S. fishing interests have urged prompt consideration of this agreement. In view of the July 1 expiration date of the current agreement, I urge that the Congress give favorable consideration to this extension at an early date.

RONALD REAGAN

The White House,
May 8, 1984.

Message to the Congress Reporting Budget Deferrals
May 8, 1984

To the Congress of the United States:

In accordance with the Impoundment Control Act of 1974, I herewith report one new deferral of budget authority totaling $101,999,550 and one revision to a previously reported deferral increasing the amount deferred by $778,000. The total for the previously deferred deferral is now $55,850,019.

The deferrals affect Funds Appropriated to the President and the Department of Ag-

riculture.

The details of the deferrals are contained in the attached reports.

RONALD REAGAN

The White House,
May 8, 1984.

Note: The attachments detailing the deferrals are printed in the Federal Register *of May 11, 1984.*

Statement on the Situation in Cyprus
May 8, 1984

At the end of this month I will meet with the Foreign Ministers of all the NATO countries to mark the 35th anniversary of NATO's founding. The alliance is sound. But continuing disagreements between two vital members of the alliance, Greece and Turkey, are of great concern. Because our friendship with each country is so important, and because their need for one an-

other is so great, special efforts must be made to reduce disagreements and promote harmony—particularly on the island of Cyprus, which has become a focal point of tension.

Successive administrations have tried unsuccessfully to solve the painful dispute which has divided Cyprus into separate Greek and Turkish communities. Over the last several years the Secretary General of the United Nations has worked painstakingly to keep the parties talking to one another. In November, after the Turkish Cypriot declaration of independence, the United States condemned the action and called for its reversal, while also working to encourage the parties to move forward in making real progress. On January 2 the Turkish Cypriots responded by proposing a series of goodwill measures, offering among other things to turn over part of the coastal city of Varosha to the United Nations for eventual Greek settlement. A few days later the Government of Cyprus proposed new guidelines for a comprehensive settlement. Turkey itself announced the removal of 1,500 troops from northern Cyprus. And the Secretary General of the United Nations was preparing to meet with the parties to discuss his own plan. We welcomed these developments as positive steps. Movement was at last occurring.

At this point, less than 2 months ago, Secretary Shultz wrote leaders of the Congress to caution that cuts in the Turkish assistance program could risk endangering this progress. Unfortunately, important NATO-related funding for Turkey was nonetheless cut in committee, no doubt in the mistaken hope that this would somehow stimulate progress on Cyprus. As a result, diplomatic efforts quickly ground to a halt.

We are now working to get diplomacy back on track. We have assured U.N. Secretary General Perez de Cuellar of our continuing support for his efforts to bridge the gaps between the Greek and Turkish communities of Cyprus.

I understand the frustration in the Congress and elsewhere about the need for progress. Indeed, I believe the time has come to try a new and more positive approach. Rather than punishing Turkey, let us focus constructive energy on ways of encouraging the parties on Cyprus itself, for it is here, ultimately, that differences must be resolved.

The administration and the Congress need to work together to re-create conditions conducive to successful diplomacy. We ask the Congress to work with us by supporting my request for security assistance for our Greek and Turkish allies, and by removing punitive conditions on that assistance. In return, I am prepared to work with the Congress in committing now to a special Cyprus peace and reconstruction fund of up to $250 million. Specific authorizations would be requested at such time as a fair and equitable solution acceptable to both parties on Cyprus is reached, or substantial progress is made toward that end. I intend this commitment to be a symbol of the shared concern of the administration and the Congress for promoting genuine results on Cyprus.

Peace cannot be bought. But peacemakers should know that the United States is prepared to go to great lengths to ensure that their labors are transformed into an enduring achievement. A reunified, stable, and secure Cyprus would be such an achievement.

We need to recognize, however, that our security assistance to Greece and Turkey is not given as a favor, but rather to deter aggression upon NATO. U.S. national interests are at stake. Greek security needs deserve to be fully met. And Turkey—working to strengthen democracy, curb terrorism, and defend NATO along its vast common border with the Soviet Union—also deserves every penny we have requested.

The path ahead will not be easy. But bringing harmony to NATO's southern flank and to the troubled island of Cyprus is a goal worthy of our most special efforts.

Nomination of June Q. Koch To Be an Assistant Secretary of Housing and Urban Development
May 8, 1984

The President today announced his intention to nominate June Q. Koch to be an Assistant Secretary of Housing and Urban Development (Policy Development and Research). She would succeed Emanuel S. Savas.

Since 1981 she has been serving as Deputy Under Secretary for Intergovernmental Relations. Previously, she was president of Koch & Associates in 1976–1980; director of Federal liaison for the Philadelphia Bicentennial Corp. in 1973–1975; and assistant professor of English, Bryn Mawr College, in 1967–1973.

She graduated from Brooklyn College (B.A., 1958), Temple University (M.A., 1959), and Columbia University (Ph.D., 1965). She is married, has five children, and resides in Potomac, MD. She was born January 18, 1933, in Brooklyn, NY.

Nomination of Mae Neal Peden To Be an Assistant Administrator of the Agency for International Development
May 8, 1984

The President today announced his intention to nominate Mae Neal Peden to be an Assistant Administrator of the Agency for International Development (Bureau for Private Enterprise), United States International Development Cooperation Agency. She would succeed Elise R.W. du Pont.

Since 1981 she has been director of administration for the Republican National Committee. Previously, she was comptroller of the Reagan-Bush transition in 1980–1981; deputy treasurer for the Reagan-Bush campaign and administrative assistant to the national political director, Reagan for President, in 1979–1980; and administrative assistant to the political director of the Republican National Committee in 1977–1979.

She attended Mississippi State College for Women. She has one son and resides in Alexandria, VA. She was born June 20, 1930, in Leakesville, MS.

Nomination of Marianne Mele To Be a Commissioner of the Copyright Royalty Tribunal
May 8, 1984

The President today announced his intention to nominate Marianne Mele to be a Commissioner of the Copyright Royalty Tribunal for the unexpired term of 7 years from September 27, 1982. She would succeed Katherine D. Ortega.

Since 1978 she has been an associate professor at Northern Virginia Law School. She also serves as a trust business development officer for NS&T Bank. Previously, she was an equal employment specialist for Riggs National Bank in 1979–1980; a member of the general counsel staff for the Copyright Office, Washington, DC, in 1977; campaign cochairman for the New Jersey 9th congressional election in 1976; and a special services agent for Eastern Airlines in 1972–1975.

She graduated from Northeastern University (B.S., 1972) and Rutgers School of Law (J.D., 1978). She has one child and resides in Falls Church, VA. She was born July 8, 1950, in New York City.

Appointment of V. Kim Hoggard as Assistant Press Secretary to the President
May 8, 1984

The President today announced his intention to appoint V. Kim Hoggard to be Assistant Press Secretary to the President.

Ms. Hoggard has served as Staff Assistant in the Office of the Press Secretary since January 20, 1981. From December 1979 through January 1981, she served as assistant to the press secretary in the press offices of the Reagan for President Campaign Committee, the Reagan-Bush Campaign Committee, and in the office of the President-elect.

From August 1978 to December 1979, she was assistant to the managing director of the Radio-Television News Directors Association, and from June 1977 to February 1978, she was a traffic assistant for WJLA–TV in Washington, DC.

Ms. Hoggard received her B.A. in 1978 from the University of Maryland. She was born December 14, 1956, in Oahu, HI. She is married and resides in Washington, DC.

Appointment of Robin C. Gray as Assistant Press Secretary to the President
May 8, 1984

The President today announced his intention to appoint Robin C. Gray to be Assistant Press Secretary to the President.

Mr. Gray has served in the Office of the Press Secretary as staff assistant since January 20, 1981. He was assistant to the press secretary of the Reagan for President Committee in Los Angeles, CA, and Washington, DC, in 1979–1980. He later served in the office of the President-elect during the Presidential transition period.

Mr. Gray was communications assistant at Citizens for the Republic, a political action committee formed by former Gov. Ronald Reagan, in Santa Monica, CA, in 1977–1979. He was previously a courier with the Central Intelligence Agency in Washington, DC, in 1976–1977. During the summer of 1974 Mr. Gray participated in the Lyndon B. Johnson Congressional Intern Program as an intern to Representative Donald G. Brotzman (R-CO). He later joined the Congressman's staff until January 1975.

Mr. Gray attended the University of Colorado in Boulder. He was born August 24, 1955, in Elmira, NY. He resides in Purcellville, VA.

Statement by Principal Deputy Press Secretary Speakes on Soviet Withdrawal From the 1984 Summer Olympic Games
May 8, 1984

The decision by the Soviet Union means that they have disregarded the feelings of most nations and millions of people the world over that the Olympics will be conducted in a nonpolitical atmosphere. It is a decision that will disappoint many.

The allegations contained in the statement by TASS are totally unjustified. The U.S. Government and the Los Angeles Olympic Organizing Committee have done everything possible to facilitate the participation of all nations in the 1984 Olympic Games. We have made exhaustive efforts to meet Soviet concerns about arrangements in Los Angeles, and we have met those concerns.

Note: Larry M. Speakes read the statement to reporters assembled in the Briefing Room at the White House during his daily press briefing, which began at 12:30 p.m.

Remarks at a White House Luncheon Commemorating the Centennial of the Birth of Harry S. Truman
May 8, 1984

Well, ladies and gentlemen and honored guests, thank you for joining us today. And may I say to Margaret Truman Daniel that it's good to have you back in this house in which you lived, and we thank you and your husband, Clifton Daniel, and your sons for adding to this occasion by your presence.

We have some other honored guests here today, some old friends who served on the staff of the Truman White House. We even have some current members of the White House staff who served under President Truman. And I think they all deserve a round of applause. [*Applause*]

We are here today to honor Harry S. Truman. A long century has passed since he was born a hundred years ago today, but he's still a vital presence. He lives on in the American consciousness. He is a shared memory. Harry Truman in the pearl-grey Stetson and the light-grey suit and the round-rimmed glasses and the walking stick. Harry Truman on his morning stroll, the brisk cadence of his walk matched by the blunt rhythm of his speech. Plain-spoken, plain-talking, no-nonsense Harry.

"Little Harry," some people called him when he first took Roosevelt's place. "Little man," they called him the day F.D.R. died. Funny that "Little Harry" looms so large in our memories. He was in many ways the quintessential American. He was a patriot. He loved his country. He was an unpretentious man who esteemed common sense and common wisdom. And he was most American in this: Imbedded in his heart, like a piece of gold, was a faith that said that the ideals that shape this country are enduring, that they are continually reborn as we live our lives every day.

Once at a White House luncheon very much like this one, a big lunch with the leaders of his party in attendance, Harry Truman was criticized for one of the many good but controversial things that he'd done. He had recently put forward a 10-point plan to outlaw racial segregation. And a Democratic committeewoman from Alabama stood up and said, "Mr. President, I want to take a message back to the South. Can I tell them you're not ramming miscegenation down our throats?"

Harry Truman looked at her, and then he recited the Bill of Rights. And when he was done he said, "I'm everybody's President. I take back nothing of what I propose, and I make no excuse for it." A White House waiter became so excited listening to the argument that he accidentally knocked a cup of coffee out of the President's hands. [*Laughter*]

He was born in the center of the continent. Lamar, Missouri, was farm country, and as a young man, Harry worked the family farm. It was a hard life, up at the first light working the fields. But there must have been a part of Harry Truman that even then was working on silent dreams. In the summer of 1912, he kept stopping his plow and walking into town to go to the telegraph office to keep up with what was happening at the Democratic Convention. He had great hopes for Woodrow Wilson.

He left the farm to fight in the First World War. About a month after he landed in France they made him a captain and put him in charge of a battery that had already broken four commanders. Captain Truman called the sergeants and corporals together and said, "It's not my job to get along with you. It's your job to get along with me. And let me know if you don't think you can, so I can bust you back right now." [*Laughter*] They knew they had a leader. They adored Captain Harry for the rest of their lives. And many of them were still writing to him when he lived in this house.

When he returned to the States, he made what I suspect he would call the most important decision of his life. He married his beloved Bess. She was, in the deepest sense, his soul mate, as Margaret was his joy.

He opened a haberdashery in Kansas City, did well for a while, and then lost everything. He refused to declare bankruptcy and spent the next 15 years working off his debts. Harry Truman's life found its true purpose when he went into politics. History records his first political job. He was appointed Postmaster of Grand View, Missouri. But he passed the job on to a widow, who needed the money.

On the day he became President, he said, "I felt like the moon, the stars and all the planets had fallen on me." And in a way they had. History handed him the toughest of all tasks—to explain to his troubled countrymen that all their efforts in 4 years of war had not assured the victory of freedom, that the struggle against totalitarianism would have to continue, and that the victories would not be as clear cut as those of World War II and the battlelines would keep moving.

He led the fight to save Greece, which was threatened by a vicious Communist takeover attempt. He saved Berlin, which Stalin threatened to starve, encircle, and squeeze to death. He saved South Korea when it was threatened by Communist expansionism. He tried to protect the West. He protected it wherever he had to.

He was often criticized for his decisions, and he was sometimes alone. Later, after listening to attacks on what was called "Trumanism," he took to his diary and wrote, "Let us define Trumanism. We have built up our Armed Forces. We prevented Tito from taking Trieste. We forced Stalin out of Iran. We saved Greece and Turkey. We stayed in Berlin. We knocked the socks off the Communists in Korea. We gave the Philippines free government. And we gave Puerto Rico home rule. If that's Trumanism, I confess I'm proud to have my name attached to it."

He could have added that he showed the world the depth of America's commitment to freedom when he started NATO. He could have added that when the war was over, he and General Marshall considered the burned-out rubble of Europe and put together a plan to put our former allies and our former enemies back on their feet. And the Marshall plan saved Europe. It was in its way the most stunning act of American idealism since Lincoln declared his policy of "malice toward none; and charity for all." And you have to go back to Grant telling Lee to keep his sword to find another such moment of American grace.

None of his decisions were made without cost. By 1948 the joke of the day was, "To err is Truman." Tom Dewey was picking his Cabinet. At the Democratic Convention, they carried signs that said, "We're just mild about Harry." Even the symbolism was against him. When he walked into the Convention Hall, they released 50 doves that had been hidden under a liberty bell as a symbol of peace. The doves were weak from the heat and the long confinement. The first one one fell dead to the floor. Another circled frantically looking for a landing place, a safe place—finally spotted a smooth and shiny perch, and it was Sam Rayburn's head. [*Laughter*] Truman recounted the scene for years and couldn't control his laughter. [*Laughter*]

Harry Truman won the nomination and went to the people on a whistlestop tour, going from point to point throughout the country and bringing his message, explaining what he was doing and why and how the Congress was thwarting his efforts. Everyone knew he'd lose. The commentators said so, and the polls and the politicians. But a funny thing happened. Everywhere his train went, the people went, thronging the platforms and spilling onto the grass and the sidewalks. They cheered him on. "Give 'em hell, Harry," they'd say. "Pour it on." And Truman said, "I never give 'em hell. I just tell the truth and they think it's hell." [*Laughter*]

I have, if you'll permit me, a personal recollection. It was in California, and I was just a Hollywood character at the time. And he came to Hollywood to speak at an outdoor rally at one of those dirt tracks for the midget automobile races that were so popular at the time. And Georgie Jessel—whom, I believe, if my memory is correct, it was Harry Truman had named him as the "Toastmaster General of the United States"—and I rode in the open car to that meeting, in the back seat with President Truman. Open car. Those were a different time than they are today. [*Laughter*]

But I remember on the way over, he and Jessel had known each other for quite some time, and George was asking him—because this was when all the talk was going on how he was conducting a lost cause—and George asked him about the election. And I shall never forget—that not as a kind of a campaign declaration or anything else, just very quietly, Harry Truman said, "George, I'm going to win." He just said, "I've been out and across the country," and he said, "believe me, I'm going to win reelection." And—had occasion to remember that a few months later. [*Laughter*]

Election night, the returns came in, and when it was over, Harry Truman had won by 2 million votes. He held aloft a newspaper headline, smiled his great smile, and gave us a picture we'll never forget, because there just aren't that many photographs of greatness triumphant.

Well, that's the way a lot of us remember him. And that's where I'll end my remarks. But I ask you to join me in a toast to his memory.

One hundred years ago today was born Harry S Truman, first child and eldest son of John and Martha Truman of Independence, Missouri. He was a great man, a patriot, an idealist, and he understood the world. May the heartland of this country ever yield his kind.

Now, may I say one more thing from my heart. I have lauded Harry Truman for his profound resolve to stop Communist expansionism and for trying to protect the freedom of the West. May I say that in this effort, he received the essential support of a Congress that understood that freedom is not negotiable. And the only response to expansionism is bipartisan agreement to stop it. And in those days, Democrats and Republicans alike were united in their opposition to tyranny. And seeing this unity, the Soviet Union was forced to back down.

The bipartisan spirit is still desperately needed in our times to face challenges to freedom ever closer to home, and I pray that it is still awake and will prevail.

Thank you all very much.

Note: The President spoke at 2:07 p.m. in the State Dining Room at the White House.

Remarks at a Meeting of the Council of the Americas
May 8, 1984

I appreciate this opportunity to be with you today. You may have heard that I will be speaking to the American people tomorrow evening on the very subject that you are discussing here, our responsibilities in this hemisphere. As members of the Council of the Americas, you've fostered cooperation and understanding between the United States and our neighbors in the south.

Having been Governor of California, I've long been aware of the rich Hispanic heritage of our country. The Hispanic heritage that we appreciate so much in our Southwestern States reflects not just our traditions but on the many things which all the peoples of this hemisphere share.

Simón Bolívar, the Great Liberator, saw this natural bond between all Americans. Early in the last century, he said of us, "We are a special kind of human being. We have a world apart." Well, building the ties between our people and the 380 million people in the 33 countries of Latin America has been of utmost importance to this administration.

Our policies toward Latin America are aimed at achieving three consistent and mutually enforcing goals. First, we seek to encourage the development of democratic political institutions. Second, we want to see all the peoples of the Americas better their standard of living and improve the vitality of their economies. Third, we want to help our friends defend themselves from Soviet bloc and Cuban-sponsored subversion.

Some of the most inspirational heroes of human liberty emerged from the struggles for freedom and independence in Latin America. One of them, Jose Marti, a Cuban patriot who found refuge in the United States from a despotic regime in his native land, once said, "Like bones to the human body, the axle to the wheel, the wing to the bird and the air to the wing, so is liberty the essence of life. Whatever is done without it is imperfect."

Well, that spirit is alive and growing in Latin America today. Right now, of Latin America's 33 countries, 26 with about 90 percent of the region's population, are either democratic or in transition to democracy. A decade ago, less than 40 percent of Latin America's population was so fortunate.

Transition to democracy in Peru, Ecuador, and the Dominican Republic has been followed more recently by Honduras and Argentina. All of this should give us tremendous hope for the future. No longer can Communist dictatorship be juxtaposed against rightist dictatorship as the only alternative.

In June of 1982, I was honored to speak before the British Parliament, the living monument to democracy. I proposed that the people of free countries take a more active role in encouraging and aiding in the development of democratic institutions such as political parties and civic groups throughout the world. For many years, we'd been doing something similar to that by helping build democratic trade unions. Well, with congressional enactment of the National Endowment for Democracy, another little noticed yet, nevertheless, giant step forward has been made. The National Endowment is now working to strengthen democratic parties, trade unions, business and civic associations, and other democratic institutions.

The times we live in are as challenging and as exciting as any in history. There are people in Latin and Central America who are fighting for their freedom every bit as much as our own forefathers. Last Sunday, this struggle for freedom took the shape of Presidential elections in Ecuador, Panama, and El Salvador.

In El Salvador, unofficial results indicate the winner will be Napoleón Duarte, a Christian Democrat who for more than two decades has been in the forefront of democratic reform and in opposition to the Communist left and the violent right.

We look forward to a cordial and productive working relationship with El Salvador. The fact that the Salvadoran election was held at all rejects the—or reflects, I should say, the dedication to democracy and personal courage of the people of that troubled land.

The Communist guerrillas warned people not to vote, yet the people defied the threat. The guerrillas mined roads, and still many thousands walked miles to mark their ballots. Each one of these people who braved such threats deserves our greatest respect and admiration.

A member of my National Security Council staff, Jackie Tillman, was down there last Sunday. She was accompanying Members of the Congress and others who were there to witness the elections. She met a young 15-year-old poll watcher and asked him—15-year-old—asked him how he felt about the voting, half expecting a typical, nonchalant, adolescent reply. And instead, he pointed to his heart and very quietly said, "I feel this voting right here. Well, this is what my country needs," he said, "to defeat the guerrillas and bring peace." That lad, and the millions of other courageous individuals like him, people who've maintained their dignity and honor in the face of such adversity, are, indeed, heroes of democracy.

The economic challenges faced in the southern half of this hemisphere appear as monumental as those in the political arena. Yet there's reason for hope. For the three decades after the Second World War, substantial economic progress was made in Latin America. Growth rates, in fact, matched those in the industrialized democracies and improved the standard of living of a significant proportion of the population. At the same time, however, a rapid increase in the population strained resources and left many in dire poverty. The leap in energy prices and the onset of global recession in 1979 was felt the world over. Few places experienced more pain than Latin America and the Caribbean.

While coping with worldwide economic currents must be the primary responsibility of each country, we're doing what we can to help. We increased by over 50 percent the level of bilateral economic assistance over the previous administration. We've continued to support contributions to the World Bank, the Inter-American Bank, and IMF programs, all of which are vital to

Latin America. Discreetly, with much care and consideration for political, social, as well as economic consequences, we worked with leaders in government and the private sector to encourage the refinancing of international debts. And your cooperation has been indispensable in this effort.

And last year, the Congress enacted our Caribbean Basin Initiative, a dramatic and innovative approach to progress in Central America and the Caribbean. By opening up one-way free trade to the United States, the world's biggest market, we're bringing the vast resources of the private sector to play in our efforts to improve the lot of 165 million hemispheric neighbors.

There is no magic or instant solution to the economic woes that plague our neighbors to the south, but we can be confident because in the long run, freedom works. During the last century, a Venezuelan intellectual, Andrés Bello, noted that "liberty gives wings to the spirit of enterprise wherever it meets it." Well, I believe that. That's what America—and I mean, when I say "America," from the North Slope of Alaska to the tip of Tierra del Fuego—what it is all about.

Liberty is, of course, something we can't take for granted. One of the greatest challenges faced by this generation of Americans is in Central America today. If we act responsibly, there's no reason we will not meet this challenge.

As you're aware, a bipartisan commission on Central America, headed by Henry Kissinger, came to that conclusion when they reported in mid-January. In Central America today, freedom-loving people, our friends, are under attack by Soviet bloc- and Cuban-backed insurgents. We're trying our best to help these courageous and decent people develop their democratic institutions and better their economic lot. But if we do nothing or not enough to help them protect themselves, there will be grim consequences to pay. It's not only their security; it's our security.

If the Communists succeed, if we face a flood of refugees and a direct threat on our own southern border, it will not be because we acted, but because we refused to do what was necessary to avert the crisis. And make no mistake, further Communist inroads in Central America will undermine stability in the entire region and make financial problems far more severe. Together, we can make sure that doesn't happen. I'll be speaking more about that tomorrow night.

What a mighty force for good we, the citizens of all this hemisphere, can be. What a potential we have from pole to pole. And yet one should never expect anything worthwhile to come easy. It'll take all of us working together, acting responsibly, and having the courage to face challenges head-on. But have no worry, in the end we can, with God's help, accomplish great things.

I thank you for letting me be with you today. God bless you, and carry on in what you're doing.

Note: The President spoke at 3:15 p.m. in the Loy Henderson Auditorium at the Department of State.

Appointment of Theodore Alfred Burtis as the United States National Chairman for United Nations Day, 1984
May 8, 1984

The President today announced his intention to appoint Theodore Alfred Burtis to be the United States National Chairman for United Nations Day, 1984.

Mr. Burtis is chairman and chief executive officer of the Sun Co., Inc. Previously, he was with the Sun Co. as president in 1976–1981; executive vice president and director in 1975; president, products group in 1974–1975; vice president for marketing in 1972–1974; and vice president for research and development in 1970–1972.

He graduated from Carnegie Institute of Technology (B.S., 1942) and Texas A & M University (M.S., 1946). He is married, has three children, and resides in Villanova, PA. He was born May 17, 1922, in Jamaica, NY.

Remarks on Presenting the Small Business Person of the Year Award
May 9, 1984

I'm delighted to welcome you, the representatives of small business all across America, to the White House and to this East Room. Today we pay tribute to the small business owners of our nation. And in a few minutes, it'll be my great pleasure to announce the 1984 Small Business Person of the Year.

You know, not too long ago, I was asked to explain the difference between a small businessman and a big businessman. And my answer was that a big businessman is what a small businessman would be if only the government would get out of the way and leave him alone. [*Laughter*] But that's what we're trying hard to do—help the small business men and women of America make it big.

Before the founding of our great Republic, entrepreneurs led the rebellion against excessive taxation and regulation. And with your help, we're doing it again. We're trying to put this economy back in the hands of the people and to give you the incentives to save, invest, and take risks so that you can go as far as your God-given talents will take you and more wealth can be created at every level of our society.

I just have to interject and tell you that on this recent trip, there in the Communist Government of the People's Republic of China, they have recognized the value of incentive. And it was amazing to see what just allowing a certain amount of private entrepreneurism to their people, what it has accomplished and how far they've gone. And it was most encouraging, and I had to believe that things are going to get better as they—to stand there in the house of a young man with his wife and small son, his parents living with them, and have him tell me how he saved and was able to build his own home there in a Communist country. And we, of course, know an awful lot about that in America.

But one of the great cornerstones of our way of life is our right to openly and critically discuss the policies of government. And there's a story about a Russian and an American who were talking about the freedoms in their countries; and the American said, "Listen, in America," he said, "I can stand on any street corner or out in the park or anyplace I want and openly criticize the President of the United States." And the Russian said, "We have that same privilege in the Soviet Union." And the American was pretty surprised. He says, "I can stand on any street corner in any park in Russia, and I can openly criticize the President of the United States." [*Laughter*]

But in some quarters, we still hear a lot of criticism about our economic policies. And I just can't help wondering what the critics—why they haven't heard about our recovery. In fact, some pretty renowned economists have been lecturing me recently and sending me letters complaining that I'm talking about economic recovery. And they say that we've passed that stage; we're now in economic expansion. And I'm glad to be corrected. [*Laughter*]

But from the mess that we inherited just 3 years ago, a strong and a more vibrant America is taking shape. Inflation, once out of control, has plummeted by nearly two-thirds. We're going to keep it down for good. Productivity, after falling for 2 years before we took office, rose 3½ percent last year, and it's still rising. Economic growth in 1983 was a robust 6 percent, and for the first quarter of 1984, it grew at an amazing 8.3 percent. Venture capital, which lays the foundation for a better tomorrow, rose less than a billion dollars in 1980. It shot up $4 billion last year. That's the money that's

there and available for people who want to do what you're doing, to start up—go into business and have to borrow to do so.

And lo and behold, the deficit, which all the pessimists predicted would keep going up, is now coming down, and it's coming down because of economic growth. And the deficit will keep coming down if the Congress would start devoting more energy to government spending than to raising your taxes, to reducing government spending.

The best news is that we've had the steepest drop in unemployment in over 30 years. Some 5.4 million more Americans have jobs today than just 17 months ago; 106 million Americans are employed, and that's the highest number ever in the history of our country.

Last year alone, almost 600,000 new businesses were incorporated, and that's an all-time high in our history. Now, most of those were small business ventures, spearheaded by individuals like yourselves, proud and independent, taking risks and putting in long, hard hours to earn a living and be your own boss. Each one is just a tiny piece of the economy. But together, America's small business owners represent a dynamo of energy and creativity that can take our country toward unprecedented levels of opportunity and freedom. And perhaps most importantly during this expansion, small businesses, like the ones you own, provided the most new jobs, gave the most employees the freedom to work part-time, and hired the most young people, senior citizens, and women. And that's why we must go forward toward new goals, so this economic expansion can last.

Small business and large industries aren't moving forward again because some big-spending bureaucrats handed out more subsidies. This expansion was created by bringing down inflation and tax rates. We don't need less of a good thing. We need more of a good thing. And that's why I favor—I'll put in a plug right here—a line-item veto, the balanced budget amendment, and a sweeping comprehensive reform of the entire tax code.

In California, as Governor, I had line-item veto. And in 8 years I vetoed 943 spending items that had been attached to otherwise necessary legislation. And they never overrode one of those 943 vetoes. Presidents should have that, too.

Well, you can bet that I'm going to continue to press for these reforms, and they'll do wonders for small business.

I'm pleased to tell you that just yesterday I signed legislation authorizing a second White House Conference on Small Business. We'll soon begin the conference process, and I call on all small business owners to participate in State and regional conferences leading to the final session at the White House that will take place in 1986.

Small business employs about half of our private work force, contributes 42 percent of sales, and generates about 38 percent of our gross national product. So, America is small business. Small firms are on the cutting edge of innovation, providing products, ideas, and opportunities for the future. Small business is dreaming impossible dreams and making those dreams come true.

This week, National Small Business Week, provides an excellent opportunity to salute some of our most successful small firms and the men and women who are the real heroes behind America's success. The entrepreneurs here today, you, are from every State and the District of Columbia and Puerto Rico. You represent industries as diverse as printing, nursing home care, furniture, electronics, lumber, seafood, and professional baseball. And they're all pioneers

in America's continuing frontier of opportunity—the free market system.

And now for the most pleasant job that I've had all week, and I'm sure that it wasn't up to me to pick the winners because, believe me, every one of you is a winner, and we're very proud of what you're doing.

The three top award winners are: Robert Battles of Gulfport, Mississippi, who started a small company in 1980, and last year his sales totaled almost $4 million; Frederic Starrett, Jr., of Belfast, Maine—in the past 3 years, his frozen food company has tripled sales, and employment has risen from 70 to 270 workers; and finally, William Fuldner of Monett, Missouri; 32 years ago, he started to make aluminum windows in the basement of a laundry. Today Mr. Fuldner's EFCO Corporation employs 410 workers and is the second largest producer of nonresidential aluminum windows in the United States.

And the 1984 Small Business Person of the Year is Mr. William Fuldner.

Well, thank you all again, and God bless you all. And now, they told me I have to do what the little girl told me in a letter when I first got here. She wrote me a letter, told me everything that I should do, and then said, "Now, get over to the Oval Office and get to work." [*Laughter*]

Note: The President spoke at 10:47 a.m. in the East Room at the White House.

Proclamation 5191—National Tuberous Sclerosis Week, 1984
May 9, 1984

By the President of the United States of America

A Proclamation

Few Americans have heard of tuberous sclerosis, but for an estimated 10,000 of us, this disease and its devastating effects are all too real. For these people, life is a perpetual struggle with convulsive seizures, mental retardation, tumors throughout the body, and other physical handicaps. Be-

cause tuberous sclerosis is hereditary, its threat extends to future generations; children of those afflicted with it stand a 50 percent chance of developing the disease themselves.

Tuberous sclerosis has no known cause or cure. Early detection, accurate diagnosis, careful use of anticonvulsant drugs, and support of family and friends can go far in helping a victim cope with the disease. Research to help us learn how to treat, cure, and prevent this dread disease is being supported by the National Institute of Neurological and Communicative Disorders and Stroke and by two voluntary health agencies—the National Tuberous Sclerosis Association and the Tuberous Sclerosis Association of America. Through this sponsorship, scientists across America are working diligently to find a way to track down the gene responsible for the disease, to develop more effective drug therapies for patients, and to discover ways to improve diagnosis.

I urge all Americans to become aware of the pressing national need to overcome the scourge of tuberous sclerosis. In doing so, we can all help our courageous fellow citizens to lead more comfortable and productive lives at home, at school, or in the workplace.

To enhance the public's understanding of the seriousness of this disease, the Congress, by Senate Joint Resolution 148, has author-

ized and requested the President to designate the week of May 6 through 13, 1984, as "National Tuberous Sclerosis Week."

Now, Therefore, I, Ronald Reagan, President of the United States of America, do hereby proclaim the week of May 6 through 13, 1984, as National Tuberous Sclerosis Week. I call upon all government agencies, health organizations, communications media, and the people of the United States to observe this week with appropriate ceremonies and activities.

In Witness Whereof, I have hereunto set my hand this ninth day of May, in the year of our Lord nineteen hundred and eighty-four, and of the Independence of the United States of America the two hundred and eighth.

RONALD REAGAN

[*Filed with the Office of the Federal Register, 11:48 a.m., May 9, 1984*]

Letter Accepting the Resignation of Martin S. Feldstein as Chairman of the Council of Economic Advisers
May 9, 1984

Dear Marty:

It is with regret that I accept your resignation as Chairman of the Council of Economic Advisers, effective July 10, 1984.

In agreeing to come to Washington at my request, you were required to interrupt a distinguished academic career, and I can understand the necessity that impels you to return to Harvard this summer. During the past two years, you have given me the benefit of your great knowledge and experience, and I want to thank you personally for the job you have done.

I know that you share my belief that we must return to the wisdom of the free market in determining the allocation of our nation's human and material resources. You have worked with great dedication for this goal while serving in my Administration, and I am certain you will continue to do so as you return to academic life.

Nancy and I send you our best wishes for

every future success and happiness.

Sincerely,

RONALD REAGAN

[The Honorable Martin Feldstein, Chairman, Council of Economic Advisers, The White House, Washington, D.C. 20500]

May 8, 1984

Dear Mr. President:

As I told you when you first asked me to serve as Chairman of the Council of Economic Advisers, Harvard University has an absolutely inflexible rule limiting leaves of absence to two years. In order to have adequate time to prepare for my teaching before the September term begins, I would like to leave my position on July 10th. By that date I will have completed my work for the midsession budget review.

Although I look forward to my return to research and teaching, I am very sorry that

I cannot stay for another year to work with you on your post-election economic program. I would be pleased to help you and my successor and other members of the Administration in any way that I can.

It has been a great honor for me to serve as Chairman of your Council of Economic Advisers and a great pleasure to be able to work closely with you. In the past three years, you have changed the course of America's economic history. Inflation is down sharply and monetary policy is following a course that should prevent a return to increasing inflation. The reduction in government domestic spending that you have achieved distinguishes your Administration from any that has come before. The 1981 Tax Act not only reduced high distortionary tax rates but specifically strengthened incentives for saving and investment.

All of these accomplishments reflect your personal vision of a good society: low inflation, a less intrusive government, less burdensome taxation, and maximum scope for the potential contribution of the free market. I am proud to have been associated with you in your pursuit of these economic goals.

I know that the achievements of your first term will be preserved and extended in your next four years. Thank you for giving me the opportunity to work with you and thank you for all that you are doing for our country.

Sincerely,

MARTIN
Martin Feldstein

[The President, The White House, Washington, D.C.]

Nomination of Ralph E. Kennickell, Jr., To Be Public Printer
May 9, 1984

The President today announced his intention to nominate Ralph E. Kennickell, Jr., to be Public Printer, Government Printing Office. He would succeed Danford L. Sawyer, Jr.

He is presently serving as Special Assistant to the Administrator of the Small Business Administration. Previously, he was Special Assistant to the Deputy Administrator, Small Business Administration in 1982–1984; Special Assistant to the Associate Administrator for Management Assistance,

Small Business Administration in 1982; Special Consultant to the Assistant Secretary for Administration, U.S. Department of the Treasury in 1981–1982; vice president and manager of Kennickell Printing Co. in 1971–1981; and staff officer and Artillery Battery Commander, U.S. Army Field Artillery, West Germany, in 1967–1971.

He graduated from The Citadel Military College (B.S., 1967). He is married, has two children, and resides in Reston, VA. He was born October 21, 1945, in Savannah, GA.

Nomination of Charles L. Marinaccio To Be a Member of the Securities and Exchange Commission
May 9, 1984

The President today announced his intention to nominate Charles L. Marinaccio to be a member of the Securities and Exchange Commission for the remainder of the term expiring June 5, 1985. He would succeed Barbara S. Thomas.

Since 1975 Mr. Marinaccio has been serving as minority general counsel, Committee on Banking, Housing, and Urban Affairs, United States Senate. Previously, he was Director, Executive Secretariat, Law Enforcement Assistance Administration in 1973–

1975; adviser to the Division of Supervision and Regulation and senior attorney at the Federal Reserve Board in 1969–1973; and trial attorney for the Antitrust Division (1965–1969) and the Criminal Division (1963–1965) at the United States Department of Justice.

He graduated from the University of Connecticut (B.A., 1957) and George Washington School of Law (J.D., 1962). He is married, has two children, and resides in Crofton, MD. He was born December 10, 1933, in Stratford, CT.

Nomination of Clint Arlen Lauderdale To Be United States Ambassador to Guyana
May 9, 1984

The President today announced his intention to nominate Clint Arlen Lauderdale, of California, a career member of the Senior Foreign Service, Class of Minister-Counselor, as Ambassador to the Cooperative Republic of Guyana. He would succeed Gerald E. Thomas who is serving as Ambassador to the Republic of Kenya.

Mr. Lauderdale served in the United States Army in 1951–1954. He began his government service in 1956 as a policeman with the city of Albany, CA. He was an employment interviewer with the State of California (1957–1958) and deputy clerk of the United States Tax Court (1958–1959). In 1959–1962 he was a personnel specialist with the Department of Health, Education, and Welfare in Washington, DC, and Boston, MA. In 1962 he entered the Foreign Service and served as Foreign Service

officer-general in Mexico City, personnel officer in Rio de Janeiro (1964–1966), and general services officer in Brussels (1967–1970). He attended the University of Michigan in 1970–1971. In the Department he was administrative officer in the Bureau of European Affairs in 1971–1972. He was administrative officer in Bonn (1972–1975) and counselor for administration in Madrid (1975–1979). In the Department he was Director of Recruitment, Employment, and Examination in the Bureau of Personnel in 1979–1980, and since 1980 has been Deputy Assistant Secretary of State for Personnel.

Mr. Lauderdale received his B.A. in 1957 from the University of California at Berkeley. His foreign languages are German and Spanish. He was born September 14, 1932, in Ackerly, TX.

Nomination of Peter Sebastian To Be United States Ambassador to Tunisia
May 9, 1984

The President today announced his intention to nominate Peter Sebastian, of Maryland, a career member of the Senior Foreign Service, Class of Minister-Counselor, as Ambassador to the Republic of Tunisia. He would succeed Walter Leon Cutler, who is serving as Ambassador to the Kingdom of Saudi Arabia.

Mr. Sebastian served in the United States Army in 1944–1946. He was translator at

the Chase Manhattan Bank in 1950–1951, and was owner-director of Peter Sebastian, Consultant Linguist, in 1951–1957 in New York City. In 1957 he entered the Foreign Service and served as consular and political officer in Rabat. In 1960–1961 he was intelligence research specialist in the Bureau of Intelligence and Research in the Department. He was political officer in Bangui

(1961–1963) and in Paris (1963–1967). He was international relations officer in the Department in 1967–1969 and attended the National War College in 1969–1970. In the Department he was political-military affairs officer in 1970–1972. He was counselor for political affairs in Addis Ababa in 1972–1976 and deputy executive secretary in the Department in 1976–1977. In 1977–1978 he attended the executive seminar in national and international affairs at the Foreign Service Institute. He was Consul General in Casablanca (1978–1980), and Deputy Chief of Mission in Rabat (1980–1982). Since 1982 he has been Director of the Office of North African Affairs in the Department.

Mr. Sebastian graduated from the University of Chicago (B.A., 1950). He also attended Roosevelt University (1947–1948), Université d'Aix-Marseille (1948–1949), and the New School for Social Research (1951). His foreign languages are French, German, Italian, Spanish, and some knowledge of Russian and Arabic. He was born June 19, 1926, in Berlin, Germany, and became a naturalized United States citizen in 1944.

Remarks of President Reagan and President Quett K.J. Masire of Botswana Following Their Meetings
May 9, 1984

President Reagan. It's been my very great pleasure to meet today with President Masire of Botswana.

The President's leadership as Vice President and President has been important to his nation since its independence over 17 years ago. He follows in the distinguished footsteps of Seretse Khama, a friend of the United States and a tireless worker for peace in Africa and progress for Botswana. Botswana's success as a free and democratic nation owes much to the wise leadership of President Masire and his predecessor.

I've enjoyed the opportunity to exchange views on matters of mutual interest to our two nations. Our discussions covered a wide range of topics, including bilateral and regional issues. And it goes without saying, our exchange was open and friendly.

I appreciate the President's insights into the issues of importance to the African continent. We admire the economic strides that Botswana has made since independence. It has managed its resources with skill and improved the standard of living of its people. And that progress, due in large part to prudent financial planning and receptivity to investment, is an example to others in Africa who seek to better the lives of their people.

President Masire described to me the serious problems Botswana is facing as a result of the severe drought that has plagued southern Africa for 3 years now. And I, of course, expressed my heartfelt concern and that of the American people for the tragedy wrought by this natural disaster. Together, we explored ways that American aid can alleviate at least some of this suffering.

We have also used this occasion to discuss the political situation in southern Africa, and I assured President Masire that the United States will continue to seek peaceful solutions to the problems of that volatile part of the world. This will not be an easy task. However, we believe that the recent accord between South Africa and Mozambique, as well as the disengagement of forces in Angola, are encouraging signs. Both Botswana and the United States want peace among the nations of the region, internationally recognized independence for Namibia, self-determination for the people of the area, and a peaceful change in South Africa.

Botswana, which has long lived in peace with its neighbors without compromising its democratic and nonracial principles, has proven how much can be accomplished. Its democratic standards have served Botswana and the region well. As a leader of one of the frontline states, President Masire's views have been particularly instructive to me.

Mr. President, the United States and Botswana are tied by our dedication to democracy and respect for individual rights. These are the bonds that unite all good and decent people. I would like to offer my best wishes and those of the American people for the peace and prosperity of the people of Botswana. And I'm pleased that you were able to accept our invitation to come to Washington, and I look forward to meeting with you again.

Thank you for being here.

President Masire. Mr. President, honorable ministers, and members of the press, we are here at the invitation of the President and the people of the United States. We are very grateful that this invitation has been extended to us because, as the President has said, this has given us the opportunity to talk together on matters of mutual interest and to brief the President and his colleagues on some of the goings on in our part of the world.

Ours is a long association. Since independence, Botswana has had very amicable relationship with the United States. We have had Peace Corps volunteers who have worked there. Some of them initially went there for 2 years, but ended up staying for 10 years or so. We have found not only Peace Corps but other American personnel to be very useful in our development effort.

As you know, we are a democracy. Perhaps we are a little too democratic, because while here, you have only the Republican Party and the Democratic Party, back home, we have something like six parties. And we, much as people have said democracy cannot work in Africa, I think we

should thank God that in Botswana so far it has worked. And I think one of the reasons it has worked is that there has been mutual trust and mutual respect. The opposition is treated seriously, because we see it as the means to be a multiparty state. And we know if we treated the opposition shabbily, we will be in trouble when it is their turn to run the show. [*Laughter*] We, unlike elsewhere, consult on matters of national interest, national security and—with the opposition. And so far, as I said, we have found this to be perhaps the best of running a country.

We are an open economy, market-led economy. People are free to invest. That's one of the things we have talked about, that if there are American investors who would like to come over to Botswana and invest, they must know they are very much welcome. There are no problems about capital repatriation. There are no problems about repatriation of any, so far, of expatriate stuff. There are no problems of racial discrimination, because, being next to South Africa and knowing just how bad racial discrimination is, we know is just as bad when practiced by whites as when practiced by blacks. And, therefore, we avoid at all cost to be discriminatory.

We have enjoyed our stay here. We have tasted of the traditional American hospitality, and we go back home very pleased with the outcome of our visit.

They say, "Least said, soonest mended."

I thank you, Mr. President.

Note: President Reagan spoke at 1:15 p.m. at the South Portico of the White House.

Earlier, the two Presidents met in the Oval Office and then attended a meeting with U.S. and Botswana officials in the Cabinet Room. They then held a working luncheon in the State Dining Room.

Informal Exchange With Reporters on Soviet Withdrawal From the 1984 Summer Olympic Games
May 9, 1984

Q. Mr. President, could you give us a little preview of what's going to be in your speech tonight?

The President. I wouldn't spoil the surprise for anything in the world. [*Laughter*]

Q. Is it going to be a surprise?

The President. No. I just think it's some things that need to be made a little more clear.

Q. Mr. President, you haven't spoken out yet personally on the Soviets not attending the Olympics. What was your reaction when you heard that yesterday?

The President. Well, now, I'm not supposed to answer any questions here in the press photo opportunity, but I think I can't let that go by without saying that, like so many, I have a great feeling of disappointment. I'm sorry that they feel that way, and I think it's unfair to the young people that have been waiting for so long to participate in those games.

And it ought to be remembered by all of us that the games more than 2,000 years ago started as a means of bringing peace between the Greek city-states. And in those days, even if a war was going on, when Olympic year came, they called off the war in order to hold the games. I wish we were still as civilized.

Note: The exchange began at 2:05 p.m. in the Cabinet Room at the White House as reporters observed the beginning of the President's meeting with members of an American team of observers of the Salvadoran Presidential election, which took place May 6.

Appointment of Karen Hanson Munro as a Member of the President's Committee on the Arts and the Humanities
May 9, 1984

The President today announced his intention to appoint Karen Hanson Munro to be a member of the President's Committee on the Arts and the Humanities. She would succeed Ignacio Lozano.

She is a member of the board of trustees of the Washington Commission for the Humanities. She served as president of the board in 1980 and 1981. In 1982 she was elected to be a member of the board of directors of the National Federation of State Humanities Councils, on which she still serves. She was administrative assistant for the Washington Council for the Humanities in 1973–1976.

Mrs. Munro graduated from the University of Washington (B.A., 1965). She is married, has one child, and resides in Olympia, WA. She was born July 9, 1943, in Seattle, WA.

Appointment of James Berry Hill as a Member of the Cultural Property Advisory Committee
May 9, 1984

The President today announced his intention to appoint James Berry Hill to be a member of the Cultural Property Advisory Committee for a term of 2 years.

Mr. Hill is president and director of Berry-Hill Galleries, Inc., in New York City. He is a member of the National Antiques and Art Dealers Association of America and is former secretary and director of the Association. He is also a member of the Art Dealers Association of America, Inc., and the Appraisers Association of America. He also serves as a consultant to several major American collections and museums.

He is married and has two children. Mr. Hill was born June 24, 1945, in New York City, where he now resides.

Address to the Nation on United States Policy in Central America
May 9, 1984

My fellow Americans:

Last week I was in Beijing and Shanghai—3 weeks from now, I'll be preparing to leave for Dublin, Normandy, and the annual economic summit in London.

I'm pleased that our trip to China was a success. I had long and thoughtful meetings with the Chinese leadership. Though our two countries are very different, we are building a strong relationship in a genuine spirit of cooperation, and that's good for the cause of peace.

This was our second trip to Asia in the last 6 months. It demonstrates our awareness of America's responsibility for leadership in the Pacific Basin, an area of tremendous economic vitality. I believe our relations with our Asian allies and friends have never been better.

But that isn't what I want to talk to you about.

I asked for this time to tell you of some basic decisions which are yours to make. I believe it's my constitutional responsibility to place these matters before you. They have to do with your national security, and that security is the single most important function of the Federal Government. In that context, it's my duty to anticipate problems, warn of dangers, and act so as to keep harm away from our shores.

Our diplomatic objectives will not be attained by good will and noble aspirations alone. In the last 15 years, the growth of Soviet military power has meant a radical change in the nature of the world we live in. Now, this does not mean, as some would have us believe, that we're in imminent danger of nuclear war. We're not. As long as we maintain the strategic balance and make it more stable by reducing the level of weapons on both sides, then we can count on the basic prudence of the Soviet leaders to avoid that kind of challenge to us.

They are presently challenging us with a different kind of weapon: subversion and the use of surrogate forces, Cubans, for example. We've seen it intensifying during the last 10 years, as the Soviet Union and its surrogates move to establish control over Vietnam, Laos, Cambodia, Angola, Ethiopia, South Yemen, Afghanistan, and recently, closer to home, in Nicaragua and now El Salvador. It's the fate of this region, Central America, that I want to talk to you about tonight.

The issue is our effort to promote democracy and economic well-being in the face of Cuban and Nicaraguan aggression, aided and abetted by the Soviet Union. It is definitely not about plans to send American troops into combat in Central America. Each year, the Soviet Union provides Cuba with $4 billion in assistance, and it sends tons of weapons to foment revolution here in our hemisphere.

The defense policy of the United States is based on a simple premise: We do not start wars. We will never be the aggressor. We maintain our strength in order to deter and defend against aggression, to preserve freedom and peace. We help our friends defend themselves.

Central America is a region of great importance to the United States. And it is so close: San Salvador is closer to Houston, Texas, than Houston is to Washington, DC. Central America is America. It's at our doorstep, and it's become the stage for a bold attempt by the Soviet Union, Cuba, and Nicaragua to install communism by force throughout the hemisphere.

When half of our shipping tonnage and imported oil passes through Caribbean shipping lanes, and nearly half of all our foreign trade passes through the Panama Canal and Caribbean waters, America's economy and well-being are at stake.

Right now in El Salvador, Cuban-supported aggression has forced more than 400,000 men, women, and children to flee their homes. And in all of Central America, more than 800,000 have fled—many, if not most, living in unbelievable hardship. Concerns about the prospect of hundreds of thousands of refugees fleeing Communist oppression to seek entry into our country are well-founded.

What we see in El Salvador is an attempt to destabilize the entire region and eventually move chaos and anarchy toward the American border.

As the National Bipartisan Commission on Central America, chaired by Henry Kissinger, agreed, if we do nothing, if we continue to provide too little help, our choice will be a Communist Central America with additional Communist military bases on the mainland of this hemisphere and Communist subversion spreading southward and northward. This Communist subversion poses the threat that a hundred million people from Panama to the open border of our South could come under the control of pro-Soviet regimes.

If we come to our senses too late, when our vital interests are even more directly threatened, and after a lack of American support causes our friends to lose the ability to defend themselves, then the risks to our security and our way of life will be infinitely greater. But there is a way to avoid these risks, recommended by the National Bipartisan Commission on Central America. It requires long-term American support for democratic development, economic and security assistance, and strong-willed diplomacy.

There have been a number of high-level, bilateral meetings with the Nicaraguan Government, where we presented specific proposals for peace. I have appointed two Special Ambassadors who have made more than 10 trips to the region in pursuit of peace during the last year. And Central America's democratic neighbors—Mexico, Venezuela, Colombia, and Panama—have launched a comprehensive initiative for peace through what is known as the Contadora process. The United States fully supports the objectives of that process.

We can and must help Central America. It's in our national interest to do so, and morally, it's the only right thing to do. But helping means doing enough—enough to protect our security and enough to protect the lives of our neighbors so that they may live in peace and democracy without the threat of Communist aggression and subversion. This has been the policy of our administration for more than 3 years.

But making this choice requires a commitment from all of us—our administration, the American people, and the Congress. So far, we have not yet made that commitment. We've provided just enough aid to avoid outright disaster, but not enough to resolve the crisis, so El Salvador is being left to slowly bleed to death. Part of the problem, I suspect, is not that Central America isn't important, but that some people think our administration may be exaggerating the threat we face. Well, if that's true, let me put that issue to rest.

I want to tell you a few things tonight about the real nature of the Sandinista regime in Nicaragua.

The Sandinistas, who rule Nicaragua, are Communists whose relationship and ties to Fidel Castro of Cuba go back a quarter of a century. A number of the Sandinistas were trained in camps supported by Cuba, the Soviet bloc, and the PLO. It is important to note that Cuba, the Sandinistas, the Salvadoran Communist guerrillas, and the PLO have all worked together for many years. In 1978 the Sandinistas and elements of the PLO joined in a "declaration of war" against Israel.

The Cuban-backed Sandinistas made a major attempt to topple the Somoza regime in Nicaragua in the fall of 1978. They failed. They were then called to Havana, where Castro cynically instructed them in the ways of successful Communist insurrection. He told them to tell the world they were fighting for political democracy, not communism. But most important, he instructed them to form a broad alliance with the genuinely democratic opposition to the Somoza regime. Castro explained that this would deceive Western public opinion, confuse potential critics, and make it difficult for Western democracies to oppose the Nicaraguan revolution without causing great dissent at home.

You see, that's how Castro managed his revolution. And we have to confess he fooled a lot of people here in our own country, or don't you remember when he was referred to in some of our press as the "George Washington of Cuba?"

The Sandinistas listened and learned. They returned to Nicaragua and promised to establish democracy. The Organization of American States, on June 23, 1979, passed a resolution stating that the solution for peace in Nicaragua required that Somoza step down and that free elections be held as soon as possible to establish a truly democratic government that would guarantee peace, freedom, and justice. The Sandinistas then promised the OAS in writing that they would do these things. Well, Somoza left, and the Sandinistas came to power. This was a negotiated settlement, based on power-sharing between Communists and genuine democrats, like the one that some have proposed for El Salvador today. Because of these promises, the previous U.S. administration and other Western governments tried in a hopeful way to encourage Sandinista success.

It took some time to realize what was actually taking place, that almost from the moment the Sandinistas and their cadre of 50 Cuban covert advisers took power in Managua in July of 1979, the internal repression of democratic groups, trade unions, and civic groups began. Right to dissent was denied. Freedom of the press and freedom of assembly became virtually nonexistent. There was an outright refusal to hold genuine elections, coupled with the continual promise to do so. Their latest promise is for elections by November 1984. In the meantime, there has been an attempt to wipe out an entire culture, the Miskito Indians, thousands of whom have been slaughtered or herded into detention camps, where they have been starved and abused. Their villages, churches, and crops have been burned.

The Sandinistas engaged in anti-Semitic acts against the Jewish community, and they persecuted the Catholic Church and publicly humiliated individual priests. When Pope John Paul II visited Nicaragua last year, the Sandinistas organized public demonstrations, hurling insults at him and his message of peace. On this last Good Friday, some 100,000 Catholic faithfuls staged a demonstration of defiance. You may be hearing about that demonstration for the first time right now. It wasn't widely reported. Nicaraguan Bishop Pablo Antonio Vega recently said, "We are living with a totalitarian ideology that no one wants in this country"—this country being Nicaragua.

The Sandinista rule is a Communist reign of terror. Many of those who fought alongside the Sandinistas saw their revolution betrayed. They were denied power in the new government. Some were imprisoned, others exiled. Thousands who fought with the Sandinistas have taken up arms against them and are now called the *contras.* They are freedom fighters.

What the Sandinistas have done to Nicaragua is a tragedy. But we Americans must understand and come to grips with the fact that the Sandinistas are not content to brutalize their own land. They seek to export their terror to every other country in the region.

I ask you to listen closely to the following quotation: "We have the brilliant revolutionary example of Nicaragua . . . the struggle in El Salvador is very advanced: The same in Guatemala, and Honduras is developing quickly . . . very soon Central America will be one revolutionary entity. . . ." That statement was made by a Salvadoran guerrilla leader in March of 1981.

Shortly after taking power, the Sandinistas, in partnership with Cuba and the Soviet Union, began supporting aggression and terrorism against El Salvador, Honduras, Costa Rica, and Guatemala. They opened training camps for guerrillas from El Salvador so they could return to their country and attack its government. Those camps still operate. Nicaragua is still the headquarters for Communist guerrilla movements. And Nicaraguan agents and diplomats have been caught in Costa Rica and Honduras supervising attacks carried out by Communist terrorists.

The role that Cuba has long performed for the Soviet Union is now also being played by the Sandinistas. They have become Cuba's Cubans. Weapons, supplies, and funds are shipped from the Soviet bloc to Cuba, from Cuba to Nicaragua, from Nicaragua to the Salvadoran guerrillas. These facts were confirmed last year by the House Intelligence Committee.

The Sandinista regime has been waging war against its neighbors since August of 1979. This has included military raids into Honduras and Costa Rica, which still continue today.

And they're getting a great deal of help from their friends. There were 165 Cuban personnel in Nicaragua in 1979. Today that force has grown to 10,000. And we're being criticized for having 55 military trainers in El Salvador. Manpower support is also coming from other parts of the terror network. The PLO has sent men, and so has Libya's dictator, Qadhafi. Communist countries are providing new military assistance, including tanks, artillery, rocket-launchers, and help in the construction of military bases and support facilities.

Just last week a Soviet ship began unloading heavy-duty military trucks in Nicaragua's Corinto Harbor. Another Soviet ship is on its way with more trucks and 155 Soviet jeeps.

Nicaragua's own military forces have grown enormously. Since 1979 their trained forces have increased from 10,000 to over 100,000. Why does Nicaragua need all this power? Why did this country of only 2.8 million build this large military force?

They claim the buildup is the result of the anti-Sandinista forces. That's a lie. The Sandinista military buildup began 2½ years before the anti-Sandinista freedom fighters had taken up arms.

They claim the buildup is because they're threatened by their neighbors. Well, that, too, is a lie. Nicaragua's next-door neighbor Costa Rica dosen't even have an army. Another neighbor, Honduras, has armed forces of only 16,000.

The Sandinistas claim the buildup is in response to American aggression. And that is the most cynical lie of all. The truth is they announced at their first anniversary, in July of 1980, that their revolution was going to spread beyond their own borders.

When the Sandinistas were fighting the Somoza regime, the United States policy was hands off. We didn't attempt to prop up Somoza. The United States did everything to show its openness toward the Sandinistas, its friendliness, its willingness to become friends. The Carter administration provided more economic assistance to the Sandinistas in their first 18 months than any other country did. But in January of 1981, having concluded that the Sandinistas were arming the Salvadoran guerrillas, the Carter administration sent military aid to El Salvador.

As soon as I took office, we attempted to show friendship to the Sandinistas and provided economic aid to Nicaragua. But it did no good. They kept on exporting terrorism. The words of their official party anthem describe us, the United States, as the enemy of all mankind. So much for our sincere but unrealistic hopes that if only we try harder to be friends, Nicaragua would flourish in the glow of our friendship and install liberty and freedom for their people. The truth is, they haven't.

Back in 1958 Fidel Castro pledged that, once his revolution had triumphed, he would start a much longer and bigger war—a war against the Americans. "That war," Castro said, "will be my true destiny."

For 26 years, during Republican and Democratic administrations, Castro has kept to his own path of revolutionary violence. Today, Cuba even provides safe passage for drug traffickers who poison our children. In return, of course, Cuba gets hard cash to buy more weapons of war.

We're in the midst of what President John F. Kennedy called "a long twilight struggle" to defend freedom in the world. He understood the problem of Central America. He understood Castro. And he understood the long-term goals of the Soviet Union in this region.

Twenty-three years ago, President Kennedy warned against the threat of Communist penetration in our hemisphere. He said, "I want it clearly understood that this government will not hesitate in meeting its primary obligations which are to the security of our nation." And the House and Senate supported him overwhelmingly by passing a law calling on the United States to prevent Cuba from extending its aggressive or subversive activities to any part of this hemisphere. Were John Kennedy alive today, I think he would be appalled by the gullibility of some who invoke his name.

I've told you that Cuba's and Nicaragua's present target is El Salvador. And I want to talk to you about that country, because there's a lot of misunderstanding about it.

El Salvador, too, had a revolution several years ago, and is now struggling valiantly to achieve a workable democracy and, at the same time, to achieve a stable economic system and to redress historical injustices. But El Salvador's yearning for democracy has been thwarted by Cuban-trained and -armed guerrillas, leading a campaign of violence against people and destruction of bridges, roads, power stations, trucks, buses, and other vital elements of their economy. Destroying this infrastructure has brought more unemployment and poverty to the people of El Salvador.

Some argue that El Salvador has only political extremes—the violent left and the violent right—and that we must choose between them. Well, that's just not true. Democratic political parties range from the democratic left to center to conservative. Trade unions, religious organizations, civic groups, and business associations are numerous and flourishing. There is a small, violent right-wing as opposed to democracy as are the guerrillas, but they are not part of the government. We have consistently opposed both extremes, and so has the Government of El Salvador. Last December I sent Vice President Bush to El Salvador with a personal letter in which I again made clear my strong opposition to both violent extremes, and this had a positive effect.

Land reform is moving forward. Since March of 1980 the program has benefited more than 550,000 peasants, or about a quarter of the rural population. But many can't farm their land; they'll be killed by the guerrillas if they do.

The people of Central America want democracy and freedom. They want and hope for a better future. Costa Rica is a well-established and healthy democracy. Honduras made a peaceful transition to democracy in 1982. And in Guatemala, political parties and trade unions are functioning. An election is scheduled for July there with a real prospect that that country can return to full constitutional government in 1985. In fact, 26 of 33 Latin American countries are democracies or striving to become democracies. But they are vulnerable.

By aiding the Communist guerrillas in El Salvador, Nicaragua's unelected government is trying to overthrow the duly elected government of a neighboring country. Like Nicaragua, the Government of El Salvador was born of revolution, but unlike Nicaragua it has held three elections, the most recent a Presidential election last Sunday. It has made great progress toward democracy. In this last election, 80 percent of the people of El Salvador braved Communist threats and guerrilla violence to vote for peace and freedom.

Let me give another example of the difference between the two countries, El Salvador and Nicaragua. The Government of El Salvador has offered amnesty to the guerrillas and asked them to participate in the elections and democratic processes. The guerrillas refused. They want to shoot their way into power and establish totalitarian rule.

By contrast, the *contras,* the freedom fighters in Nicaragua, have offered to lay down their weapons and take part in democratic elections, but there the Communist Sandinista government has refused. That's why the United States must support both the elected government of El Salvador and the democratic aspirations of the Nicaraguan people.

If the Communists can start war against the people of El Salvador, then El Salvador and its friends are surely justified in defending themselves by blocking the flow of arms. If the Soviet Union can aid and abet subversion in our hemisphere, then the United States has a legal right and a moral duty to help resist it. This is not only in our strategic interest; it is morally right. It would be profoundly immoral to let peace-loving friends depending on our help be overwhelmed by brute force if we have any capacity to prevent it.

If our political process pulls together, Soviet- and Cuban-supported aggression can be defeated. On this, the centennial anniversary of President Harry Truman's birth, it's fitting to recall his words, spoken to a Joint Session of the Congress in a similar situation: "The free peoples of the world look to us for support in maintaining their freedoms. If we falter . . . we may endanger the peace of the world, and we shall surely endanger the welfare of this nation."

The speech was given in 1947. The problem then was 2 years of Soviet-supported indirect aggression against Greece. The Communists were close to victory. President Truman called on the Congress to provide decisive aid to the Greek Government. Both parties rallied behind President Truman's call. Democratic forces succeeded, and Greece became a parliamentary democracy.

Communist subversion is not an irreversible tide. We've seen it rolled back in Venezuela and, most recently, in Grenada. And were democracy flourishes, human rights and peace are more secure. The tide of the future can be a freedom tide. All it takes is the will and resources to get the job done.

In April 1983 I addressed a Joint Session of the Congress and asked for bipartisan cooperation on behalf of our policies to protect liberty and democracy in Central America. Shortly after that speech, the late Democratic Senator Henry Jackson encouraged the appointment of a blue-ribbon bipartisan commission to chart a long-term course for democracy, economic improvement, and peace in Central America. I appointed 12 distinguished Americans from both political parties to the National Bipartisan Commission on Central America.

The Bipartisan Commission rendered an important service to all Americans—all of us from pole to pole in this Western hemisphere. Last January the Commission presented positive recommendations to support democratic development, improve living conditions, and bring the long-sought dream for peace to this troubled region so close to home. The recommendations reinforced the spirit of our administration's policies that help to our neighbors should be primarily economic and humanitarian, but must also include sufficient military aid.

In February I submitted a comprehensive legislative proposal to the Congress which would implement the Commission's recommendations. And because this report presented a bipartisan consensus, I'm hopeful that the Congress will take prompt action. This proposal calls for an increased commitment of resources beginning immediately and extending regularly over the next 5 years. The program is a balanced combination of support for democracy, economic development, diplomacy, and security measures, with 70 percent of the dollars to be used for economic and social development. This program can get the job done.

The National Bipartisan Commission on Central America has done its work. Our administration has done its work. We now await action by the Congress. Meanwhile, evidence mounts of Cuba's intentions to double its support to the Salvadoran guerrillas and bring down that newly-elected government in the fall. Unless we provide the resources, the Communists will likely—to succeed.

Let's remember the Soviet bloc gave Cuba and Nicaragua $4.9 billion in assistance last year, while the United States provided all its friends throughout all of Central America with only a fraction of that amount.

The simple questions are: Will we support freedom in this hemisphere or not? Will we defend our vital interests in this hemisphere or not? Will we stop the spread of communism in this hemisphere or not? Will we act while there is still time?

There are those in this country who would yield to the temptation to do nothing. They are the new isolationists, very much like the isolationists of the late 1930's who knew what was happening in Europe, but chose not to face the terrible challenge history had given them. They preferred a policy of wishful thinking, that if they only gave up one more country, allowed just one more international transgression, and surely sooner or later the aggressor's appetite would be satisfied. Well, they didn't stop the aggressors; they emboldened them. They didn't prevent war; they assured it.

Legislation is now before the Congress that will carry out the recommendations of the National Bipartisan Commission. Requests for interim appropriations to give the soldiers fighting for their country in El Salvador and the freedom-loving people of Central America the tools they need also— that awaits action by the House of Representatives.

For the last 4 years, only half of the military aid requested for El Salvador has been provided, even though total aid for El Salvador is only 5 percent of our worldwide assistance. I'm asking the Congress to provide the funds I requested for fiscal year 1984 and, also, to enact the entire National Bipartisan Commission plan for democracy, economic development, and peace in Central America.

As I talk to you tonight, there are young Salvadoran soldiers in the field facing the terrorists and guerrillas in El Salvador with the clips in their rifles the only ammunition they have. The lack of evacuation helicopters for the wounded and the lack of medical supplies if they're evacuated has resulted in one out of three of the wounded dying. This is no way to support friends, particularly when supporting them is supporting ourselves.

Last week, as we returned across the vast Pacific to Alaska, I couldn't help being struck again by how blessed has been our land. For 200 years the oceans have protected us from much that has troubled the world, but clearly our world is shrinking. We cannot pretend otherwise if we wish to protect our freedom, our economic vitality, and our precious way of life.

It's up to all of us—the administration, you as citizens, and your representatives in the Congress. The people of Central America can succeed if we provide the assistance I have proposed. We Americans should be proud of what we're trying to do in Central America, and proud of what, together with our friends, we can do in Central America to support democracy, human rights, and economic growth while preserving peace so close to home. Let us show the world that we want no hostile Communist colonies here in the Americas—South, Central, or North.

Thank you, God bless you, and good night.

Note: The President spoke at 8 p.m. from the Oval Office at the White House. His remarks were broadcast live on nationwide radio and television.

Written Responses to Questions Submitted by the Far Eastern Economic Review
May 9, 1984

President's Trip to China

Q. How would you sum up the achievements of your recent visit to China and your meetings with the Chinese leaders?

The President. Well, we all feel very good about the trip, and I do particularly. Granted there are differences between us—in our styles and kinds of government and all—yet there was a friendliness. We found they and we had the same idea. The things that were important were not the differences, but the things we had in common.

They are as opposed to expansionist policies as we are, attempts to dominate or have hegemony over other areas or other countries. We made it plain to them that we respected their nonaligned situation. They're very serious about wanting to be nonaligned, and we agreed with that, but said that didn't mean that we could not work together on things as two independent countries with the same interests.

I happen to be a believer in the Pacific Basin as the place of the future. An American once said: "Go west, young man." Well, we're still going west.

And I think between us, the two biggest nations—the United States and China—can contribute a great deal to stability in the whole Pacific Basin and East Asia. I was struck by the changes the Chinese are making as part of their modernization, including their welcome to outside capital. It was pretty unusual after recent years actually to go through a plant that was a partnership between a Massachusetts company and the People's Republic, to know that they have now also opened up to investments without partnership, involving the outright ownership of concerns and industries by foreign firms. I think it all was a most successful trip. We found ourselves in agreement on so many things.

Q. Are they moving closer to our way of life?

The President. Well, in the sense of believing in incentives for the people, yes. The last day we were there, we visited what a few years ago was a commune—now they call them townships. They are set up virtually as a township, with autonomous government, local control and all, with their own schools and so on. There are production quotas which they must meet which go to the government. But over and above that, they can sell their surplus produce in the marketplace. We visited the home of a young couple, with their son and his father and mother living with them. He had a new home—and he had built it. He spoke of how they were able to save money to do this and of how they were now saving for further furnishings for the home. It sounded very American.

Q. Do you feel as a Californian who has just quoted the saying "Go west, young man" that you have a more positive view of the Pacific than someone from, say, the eastern seaboard, who still tends to look towards the Atlantic?

The President. I think that's only natural in the Western States of the United States. We started our trip with a visit to the State of Washington, seeing the lumber industry there. Much of their foreign trade—as far as I could see, all of it is across the Pacific to the west. Yes, we do have that. It does not mean that we downgrade in any way our Atlantic relations or our participation in the North Atlantic alliance. Actually, our parentage, you might say, is basically European. But you cannot help but feel that the great Pacific Basin, with all its nations and all its potential for growth and development—that is the future.

Q. When you campaigned for the Presidency back in 1980, did it ever occur to you that in 1984 you would make a "red carpet" tour of China?

The President. I have always recognized the importance of good U.S.-China relations. From the very outset of my administration, I was determined to place this relationship on a more stable and enduring footing. I think we have succeeded. We have had some problems and some differences over the past 3½ years, but we have never stopped communicating with each other.

Improving U.S.-China relations is in the best interests of the American people, the Chinese people, the peoples of the East Asian region, and the cause of world peace. We made substantial progress in working out some difficult problems and then proceeded to advance the relationship in a number of important areas—technology transfer, trade, student exchanges, and so on.

The exchange of high-level visitors during our administration has been intense, leading to the visit to the United States in January by Premier Zhao and my visit to China. The Vice President, Secretary of State Shultz, Secretary of Defense Weinberger, Secretary of the Treasury Don Regan, and Secretary of Commerce Baldrige all visited China for substantive talks prior to our recent visit. We look forward to continuing this exchange with visits to the United States by Chinese President Li Xiannian, General Secretary Hu Yaobang, and Defense Minister Zhang Aiping.

We went to China to advance the prospects for stability and peace throughout the world. And we went to illustrate, by our presence, our sincere desire for good relations. We went to meet again with the Chinese to review our concerns and our differences. And we went to China to further define our own two countries' relationship—and, by defining it, advance it. And I feel that we made progress.

I had long and thoughtful meetings with the Chinese leadership, comprehensive meetings. We each listened carefully to what the other had to say. We agreed that in this imperfect world, peace in its most perfect form cannot always be reached—but it must always be our goal. And we, the people of China and the United States, must make our best efforts to bring greater harmony between our two countries.

I told the Chinese leaders that we must continue to acknowledge our differences, for a friendship based on fiction will not last. But we agreed that there is much to be gained from mutual respect. And there is much to be gained on both sides from expanded opportunities in trade and commerce and cultural relations, and much to be gained through stability and economic progress throughout the entire Pacific Basin.

Q. Your administration has categorized China as "friendly" for export control purposes. Do you think that China's status under COCOM should be changed?

The President. COCOM is a cooperative organization of many countries, and any changes would need the careful consideration and approval of all its members. COCOM has been processing cases for China expeditiously and has approved many exports to China at higher technical levels than exports to the U.S.S.R.

The steps we have taken on export licensing take into account China's needs and capabilities by providing support for China's modernization programs. We still maintain some controls, as we do for many friendly countries, on very sophisticated items which are essential to our national security interests. But very few exports to China—less than 1 percent last year—have been denied.

Taiwan

Q. You have always been known as a friend and supporter of Taiwan, arguing for official recognition during your campaign for the Presidency. What are your feelings about the island today, and do you expect that any agreement reached on the future of Hong Kong will augur well or ill for Taiwan?

The President. My longstanding, personal friendship and deep concern for the people of Taiwan are steadfast and unchanged. I am committed to maintaining the full range of contacts between the United States and the people of Taiwan—commercial, cultural, and other contacts—which are compatible with our unofficial relationship. As I have often said, we will not abandon old friends to make new friends.

The British and Chinese are continuing discussions on Hong Kong. I hope the two sides will reach an agreement which preserves the prosperity and stability there. We have an interest in such a settlement, particularly in light of our significant business and investment presence in Hong Kong.

Trade With Japan

Q. Your administration has emphasized a closer relationship between Japan and the United States as a vital link between the world's two most powerful economies, both married to the principle of free trade. However, during this election year, Tokyo has come under increased pressure from the United States to internationalize and revalue the yen, open its markets to U.S. goods, and limit exports to the U.S. (a strong theme in the Mondale campaign). Are you satisfied with Tokyo's moves to liberalize its market, and can Japan expect a softening of U.S. pressure next year?

The President. Our trade policy toward Japan this year is the same one we have been pursuing all through my administration. It is a simple and, we believe, fair policy. We would like our companies to have the same access to Japan's market that Japanese companies have to ours. During the past 2 years, Japan has made considerable progress in opening its markets further to American products, and we are confident we'll see more progress in the months ahead.

Now, as you pointed out, this is an election year, and there are those who would like to take the easy way out and throw up protectionist barriers around our country. This may seem like good politics in an election year, but I can assure you that it is bad economics, and bad for our country and the world trading system. We are determined to resist this, but we need progress in foreign markets opening to our products.

As for internationalizing the yen, I gave my view in my speech to the Diet last November. Here you have a country that has the world's second largest free market economy and tremendous political stability. We believe that its currency should reflect this and play the same role in the world economy that other major currencies do. Our Treasury Department and the Japanese Finance Ministry have been meeting on this issue since February, and I believe that we have been making steady progress.

Economic Recovery

Q. Your administration continually exhorts other countries, particularly in the developing world, to practice fiscal and monetary discipline. But would you not agree that it is the United States own unmanageable budget and current account deficits which endanger the world economic recovery and its (still historically high) interest rates which result in the undervalued yen, increase the debt burdens of borrowing countries, and inhibit investment worldwide?

The President. By reviving strong economic growth, while reducing the rate of growth of government spending more than in half, we are beginning to make real progress in reducing the Federal deficit. With cooperation from Congress, we expect further reductions. Meanwhile, the rest of the world is benefiting greatly by the rapid recovery in the United States, which has led to a sharp increase of American orders for foreign goods and services.

The strength of the dollar results from a number of powerful market forces, including the strength of our economic recovery and the confidence of foreign investors who see the United States as the safest and most attractive country in which to invest. It is true that our interest rates are still high by historical standards, but they have been cut nearly in half since the beginning of this administration. And now that we have succeeded in bringing inflation down, we are determined to keep it down. Once this commitment becomes clear, we expect interest rates to decline even further.

Southeast Asia

Q. On the Cambodian issue, the U.S. policy of passively supporting ASEAN is seen, even in ASEAN, as reflecting a less positive commitment to the region and even as a willingness for China to play a larger role in Southeast Asia (while the United States confronts the Soviet Union in Northeast Asia). Is there any justification for the feeling that, faced with the problems of relations with the Soviet Union, the Middle East, Central America, and Europe, the United States accords low priority to the former "dominoes" of Southeast Asia?

The President. Not at all. The United States has very important economic and security interests in Southeast Asia, particularly in the ASEAN [Association for South East Asian Nations] countries. ASEAN, as a group, is our fifth largest trading partner and the site of some $10 billion in U.S. investment. We have bilateral security commitments to two ASEAN members, Thailand and the Philippines. If our involvement appears to be less than in other areas of the world, it is only because of the success the ASEAN countries have had in managing the economic and political issues they face, independent of a heavy U.S. presence.

United States support for ASEAN's efforts to achieve a just political solution to the problem of Kampuchea, which will restore to the Khmer people control over their own destiny, has been vigorous. It is, however, ASEAN's security which is most directly threatened by Vietnam's occupation of Kampuchea; therefore, ASEAN should continue to take the lead on this issue.

ASEAN, the United States, and China have a common interest in restoring peace to Southeast Asia. China's role in the area will be determined by the state of its relations with the region's governments, not by the United States. We will continue to manage our relationship with China so that the interests of our friends in Southeast Asia are not disadvantaged.

Q. In supporting ASEAN, China and the Khmer coalition in exile (which includes, of course, the Khmer Rouge), U.S. policy increases Vietnam's dependency on Moscow and thus Moscow's leverage over Hanoi, resulting in Soviet naval and air force units using the bases at Cam Ranh and Danang. Just as former President Nixon once helped to open China up, is there any possibility of a Reagan initiative to Vietnam designed to break the Cambodian deadlock?

The President. First, the United States does not recognize the Khmer coalition as a government. We welcomed it as a vehicle to press for a settlement based on the ICK (International Conference on Kampuchea) principles. We provide moral and political support to the non-Communist resistance groups, as evidenced by my meeting last September with Prince Sihanouk and Son Sann in New York. We give no support to and have no contact with the Khmer Rouge, whose record of atrocities we have always condemned.

Second, it is not the United States which has isolated Vietnam. Hanoi's policies in Kampuchea have isolated it internationally and left it with almost no friends outside the U.S.S.R. and its most obedient followers. The Soviet Union has been able to trade on its massive military and economic assistance to obtain access to air and naval facilities in Vietnam. Hanoi has chosen its present isolation. It can choose to end it by negotiating a comprehensive political solution to the problem of Kampuchea.

At the same time, we and the Vietnamese have agreed that the question of Americans missing from the Indochina war is a humanitarian matter separate from other issues. Our discussions with Hanoi on this question continue and resolution of this issue could only help to improve the American people's image of Vietnam.

Q. Vice President George Bush, visiting Manila, once praised President Marcos' "commitment to democracy." Marcos has recently quoted excerpts from a letter from yourself, which, at least out of context, appear to be supportive. Will the U.S.A. continue to support Marcos with money and good will if he fails to deliver free and fair elections? How would you view the emergence of a military regime? Are you worried about the anti-U.S. base position of the non-Communist opposition to Marcos?

The President. We have recently underscored to President Marcos the deep commitment to representative government and a democratic electoral process which all Americans share. Various steps had been taken in the Philippines to encourage fair and open legislative elections in May. Continued movement toward fully functioning democratic institutions appropriate to the Philippines is the key to rebuilding both economic and political confidence after the difficulties of the last months.

I'm not in the habit of commenting on events that haven't yet occurred, but I would point out that the United States and the Philippines are treaty allies. The United States, through both Republican and Democratic administrations, has had very good relations with the Philippines. We expect to continue these relations in the years to come.

Your question about the emergence of a military regime is highly speculative when we consider the unbroken Philippine tradition of civilian authority over the military. To my mind, the whole point of elections in the Philippines is to strengthen their political institutions, to assure that they reflect and are responsive to the will of the people, and to enable the country to meet the serious political and economic challenges that it faces.

The U.S. military presence is not a campaign issue in the Philippine elections. Thanks in part to the vast reservoir of good will that exists between the American and Filipino peoples, there seems to be an appreciation by the majority of Filipinos that the U.S. military facilities serve the security interests of both countries and of the region as a whole.

669

U.S.-India Relations

Q. Despite its anti-American stance and its close relations with the Soviet Union, do you not feel that past and present U.S. administrations could have done more to improve relations with the world's most populous democracy, India?

The President. Well, I do not consider India to be anti-American. It is certainly true that India has close relations with the Soviet Union, but this has not prevented us and other Western nations from developing our own relations with India. Mrs. Gandhi has said that India is not pro or anti any other country, but is instead pro-India. We accept that position.

In this administration, we have taken a number of steps to strengthen our bilateral relationship. Recognizing that India is a very important country both in the South Asian region and globally, I have met with Mrs. Gandhi three times. During her 1982 visit to Washington, we agreed that there must be a regular dialog between us. This process is continuing. Secretary Shultz visited India in 1983, and Vice President Bush will be visiting India this month. In addition, we have taken steps to strengthen business and commercial relations between India and the United States, which I believe is a very important factor in building a long-term relationship. Furthermore, we are making efforts to increase understanding between India and the United States through major cultural exchanges this year and in 1985.

We have our differences with India, certainly. But I truly believe that India and the United States have reached a point where we can pursue a mature and constructive relationship, based on the values and interests we share rather than on points of difference.

U.S. Foreign Policy

Q. In its past efforts to contain Communist expansion in Asia, America allied itself with many corrupt dictators unworthy of the support of the world's most powerful democracy. This allowed the Communists to claim to represent the "people" (although in fact they were manipulating the forces of nationalism). Is not America in danger of repeating these mistakes in backing the present regime of El Salvador and in undermining that of Nicaragua, forfeiting in the process the revolutionary idealism in which America was born and which remains its greatest international appeal?

The President. I think your question can best be answered by describing current U.S. policy and the situation on the ground in Central America.

The image of an area ruled by corrupt dictators simply does not reflect current circumstances. Today there are four practicing democracies in the area: Costa Rica, El Salvador, Honduras, and Belize. Two of the remaining three countries, Guatemala and Panama, are committed to an early return to full democracy. Only in Nicaragua is there a serious exception to this area wide norm, and there the people face a dictatorship of the left.

Those who would look for simple one-sided solutions to the problems of Central America will be disappointed. The issues are complex, and during the past year, the United States has pursued a policy designed to deal with many aspects of the constantly evolving situation. That policy is based on four elements: support for political reform, support for economic development, support for dialog within and among the countries of the region, and security assistance to provide a shield behind which reforms, development, and negotiations can take place.

This balanced, comprehensive policy recognizes the deep-rooted economic, social, and political problems which are the fundamental cause of the current instability in Central America. It also addresses the external sources of the conflict: attempts by Marxist-Leninist forces to exacerbate indigenous problems.

The situation in El Salvador is frequently portrayed as your question implies: a clash between extremes of left and right—the forces of oppression versus the forces of violent revolution. But this view omits a vital new element: The reformist coup of October 1979 and subsequent coalition governments have created an alternative that offers the prospect of genuinely democratic and progressive reform. A new, liberal constitution was passed by the Salvadoran Legislative Assembly in December 1983, and on June 1, a democratically elected President will be inaugurated. Since 1979 the history of El Salvador has been fundamentally the story of these kinds of efforts for change and reform.

In Nicaragua, when the Sandinistas came to power in 1979, they pledged to the Organization of American States to establish a democratic, pluralistic, and nonaligned regime. The United States took a leading role in the international effort to assist the new government in Nicaragua, and the first 21 months after the fall of Somoza, we authorized 117.2 million dollars in economic assistance.

Despite the promises, what we see today are Sandinista leaders who have succeeded in removing from influence everyone who disagreed with them, who have built an army four times the size of Somoza's who have developed close ties with Cuba and the Soviet Union, and who have continued to support subversion in neighboring states, particularly El Salvador. Today there is no longer any serious dispute that Nicaragua is a major source of instability in Central America.

The Contadora peace process offers the opportunity for Nicaragua to address the legitimate concerns of the United States and its neighbors. The United States supports the comprehensive, verifiable implementation of the Contadora Document of Objectives, agreed to by the five Central American states and the Contadora Four countries—Colombia, Mexico, Panama, and Venezuela—last September. The principles identified in the Document of Objectives, which include the reciprocal, verifiable withdrawal of foreign military advisers, an end to arms trafficking and support for subversion, and national reconciliation through the democratic process, are the issues which must be treated if there is to be a sincere and lasting peace in Central America.

Afghanistan

Q. Your administration has been giving active support to the opponents of the left-ist Nicaraguan regime, but little direct help to the Afghani resistance to Soviet occupation. Is the difference a matter of geography or of a willingness to confront Soviet "proxies," but not the Soviets themselves?

The President. I think your question mixes apples and oranges a bit, but you seem to be suggesting that we have not been supportive of the Afghans who are resisting Soviet efforts to take over their country. If that's the implication, I'm afraid I'd have to disagree. The United States has been active, along with the vast majority of the free nations of the world, in trying to help the Afghan people win back their independence. Such support has taken many forms—diplomatic activity within the United Nations, making Afghanistan an important part of our bilateral agenda with the Soviets, substantial aid for the refugee communities, and firm backing for Pakistan in its efforts to resist Soviet intimidation.

The general point is that there is more than one effective response to Soviet-backed aggression. These problems are complex and vary from region to region. So do our responses. But one thing should be clear: Soviet actions in Afghanistan, including recent escalation of warfare there, seriously undermine the search for a negotiated political settlement, based on the four elements of the repeated U.N. General Assembly resolutions: withdrawal of Soviet forces; restoration of the independent and nonaligned status of Afghanistan; self-determination for the Afghan people; and permitting the Afghan refugees who have been forced to flee their own country to return with safety and honor.

The United States remains committed to achieving these internationally agreed objectives. It is past time that the Soviet Union respect the wishes of the world community and bring to an end the terrible ordeal which they have imposed on the Afghan people.

Note: As printed above, the questions and answers follow the text of the White House press release.

Proclamation 5192—National P.O.W./M.I.A. Recognition Day, 1984
May 9, 1984

By the President of the United States of America

A Proclamation

Ever since the Revolutionary War, America's men and women have heroically served their country in times of conflict. In each of America's wars, our prisoners of war have been required to make special sacrifices, serving their country under conditions of hardship. Their burden greatly increased when they were treated in violation of the fundamental standards of morality and international codes of conduct for the treatment of prisoners of war.

Our P.O.W.s and M.I.A.s have earned a very special place in the hearts of all Americans because of their selfless devotion to duty and unflinching courage. We must not forget or fail to honor those who have served their country so faithfully.

Our Nation deeply appreciates the acute suffering and pain experienced by the families of our servicemen held captive or missing in action. The loss of a loved one is a tragic situation under any circumstance, but that burden is magnified when the fate of the loved one is unknown. All Americans fully support efforts to end the uncertainties with which they continue to live.

We accept and remember our obligation to these missing servicemen. Until the P.O.W./M.I.A. issue is resolved, it will remain a matter of the highest national priority. On July 20, 1984, the P.O.W./M.I.A. Flag will fly over the White House, the Departments of State and Defense, and the Veterans' Administration as a symbol of our unswerving commitment to achieve the fullest possible accounting for the servicemen and civilians.

By Senate Joint Resolution 171, the Congress has designated July 20, 1984, as "National P.O.W./M.I.A. Recognition Day." On this day, I firmly believe that we should recognize the special debt all Americans owe to our fellow citizens who gave up their freedom in the service of our country and to the families who have undergone a great travail.

Now, Therefore, I, Ronald Reagan, President of the United States of America, do hereby proclaim Friday, July 20, 1984, as National P.O.W./M.I.A. Recognition Day. I call on all Americans to join in honoring all former American prisoners of war, those still missing, and their families who endured the uncommon sacrifices on behalf of this country. I also call upon State and local officials and private organizations to observe this day with appropriate ceremonies and activities.

In Witness Whereof, I have hereunto set my hand this 9th. day of May, in the year of our Lord nineteen hundred and eighty-four, and of the Independence of the United States of America the two hundred and eighth.

RONALD REAGAN

[*Filed with the Office of the Federal Register, 12:23 p.m., May 10, 1984*]

Note: The text of the proclamation was released by the Office of the Press Secretary on May 10.

Executive Order 12475—Textile Import Program Implementation
May 9, 1984

By the authority vested in me as President by the Constitution and laws of the United States of America, including Section 204 of the Agricultural Act of 1956, as amended (76 Stat. 104, 7 U.S.C. 1854), and Section 301 of Title 3 of the United States Code, and in order to prevent circumvention or frustration of multilateral and bilateral agreements to which the United States is a party and to facilitate efficient and equitable administration of the United States Textile Import Program, it is hereby ordered as follows:

Section 1. (a) In accordance with policy guidance provided by the Committee for the Implementation of Textile Agreements (CITA), through its Chairman, in accordance with the provisions of Executive Order No. 11651, as amended, the Secretary of the Treasury shall issue regulations governing the entry or withdrawal from warehouse for consumption of textiles and textile products subject to Section 204 of the Act.

(b) Initial regulations promulgated under this section shall be promulgated no later than 120 days after the effective date of this order.

(c) To the extent necessary to implement more effectively the United States textile program under Section 204, such regulations shall include:

(i) clarifications in, or revisions to, the country of origin rules for textiles and textile products subject to Section 204 in order to avoid circumvention of multilateral and bilateral textile agreements;

(ii) provisions governing withdrawals from a customs bonded warehouse of articles subject to this Order transformed, changed or manipulated in a warehouse after importation but prior to withdrawal for consumption; and

(iii) any other provisions determined to be necessary for the effective and equitable administration of the Textile Import Program.

(d) Any such regulations may also include provisions requiring importers to provide additional information and/or documentation on articles subject to this order which are determined to be necessary for the effective and equitable administration of the Textile Import Program.

Sec. 2. (a) The Commissioner of Customs shall establish Textile and Apparel Task Force (the Task Force) within the United States Customs Service to coordinate enforcement of regulations concerning importation under the Textile Import Program.

(b) CITA, through its Chairman, shall, in accordance with the provisions of Executive Order No. 11651, as amended, provide information and recommendations to the Task Force, through the Department of the Treasury, on implementation and administration of the Textile Import Program.

(c) The Department of Treasury shall, to the extent practicable, inform the Chairman of CITA of the progress of all investigations concerning textile imports; provide notice to CITA of all requests for rulings on matters that could reasonably be expected to affect the implementation of the Textile Import Program; and take into consideration any comments on such requests that CITA, through its Chairman, timely submits.

Sec. 3. This order supplements, but does not supersede or amend, Executive Order No. 11651 of March 3, 1972, as amended.

Sec. 4. This order shall be effective upon its publication in the *Federal Register.*

RONALD REAGAN

The White House,
May 9, 1984.

[*Filed with the Office of the Federal Register, 11:50 a.m., May 10, 1984*]

Note: The text of the Executive order was released by the Office of the Press Secretary on May 10.

Message to the Senate Transmitting the United States-Morocco Convention on Mutual Assistance in Criminal Matters
May 10, 1984

To the Senate of the United States:

With a view to receiving the advice and consent of the Senate to ratification, I transmit herewith the Convention between the United States of America and the Kingdom of Morocco on Mutual Assistance in Criminal Matters, signed at Rabat October 17, 1983.

I transmit also, for the information of the Senate, the report of the Department of State with respect to the treaty.

The treaty is one of a series of modern mutual assistance treaties being negotiated by the United States. The treaty is self-executing and utilizes existing statutory authority.

The new treaty provides for a broad range of cooperation in criminal matters. Mutual assistance available under the treaty includes: (1) executing requests relating to criminal matters; (2) taking of testimony or statements of persons; (3) effecting the production, preservation of documents, records, or articles of evidence; (4) serving judicial documents; (5) facilitating the appearance of a witness before a court of the requesting Party; (6) locating persons; and (7) providing judicial records, evidence, and information.

I recommend that the Senate give early and favorable consideration to the treaty and give its advice and consent to ratification.

RONALD REAGAN

The White House,
May 10, 1984.

Message to the Congress Transmitting the United States-United Kingdom Social Security Agreement
May 10, 1984

To the Congress of the United States:

Pursuant to section 233(e)(1) of the Social Security Act as amended by the Social Security Amendments of 1977 (P.L. 95–216, 42 U.S.C. 433(e)(1)), I transmit herewith the Agreement between the United States of America and the Government of The United Kingdom of Great Britain and Northern Ireland which consists of two separate instruments. The Agreement was signed in London on February 13, 1984.

The U.S.-U.K. agreements are similar in objective to the social security agreements already in force with Italy, the Federal Republic of Germany and Switzerland and to proposed agreements with Canada, Belgium and Norway which are expected to enter into force later this year. Such bilateral agreements, which are generally known as totalization agreements, provide for limited coordination between the United States and foreign social security systems to overcome the problems of gaps in protection and of dual coverage and taxation for workers who move from one country to the other.

I also transmit for the information of the Congress a comprehensive report prepared by the Department of Health and Human Services, which explains the provisions of the Agreements and provides data on the number of persons affected by the Agreements and the effect on social security financing as required by the same provision of the Social Security Act.

The Department of State and the Department of Health and Human Services join with me in commending the U.S.-U.K. Social Security Agreement and related documents.

RONALD REAGAN

The White House,
May 10, 1984.

Nomination of Charles G. Stalon To Be a Member of the Federal Energy Regulatory Commission
May 10, 1984

The President today announced his intention to nominate Charles G. Stalon to be a member of the Federal Energy Regulatory Commission, Department of Energy, for a term expiring October 20, 1987. He would succeed John David Hughes.

Since 1977 Dr. Stalon has been commissioner of the Illinois Commerce Commission. He also serves as a member of the following organizations: the gas committee of the National Association of Regulatory Utility Commissioners; the Advisory Council of the Gas Research Institute; the National Society of Rate of Return Analysts; the Advisory Committee of the Institute for Study

of Regulation; and the panel on gas statistics at the National Academy of Science. He was president of the Mid-America Regulatory Commissioners in 1983–1984; research economist for the Federal Power Commission in 1969–1980; and associate professor at Southern Illinois University in 1963–1977.

Dr. Stalon graduated from Butler University (B.A., 1959) and Purdue University (M.S., 1963; Ph.D., 1966). He is married, has two daughters, and resides in Carbondale, IL. He was born October 29, 1929, in Cape Girardeau, MO.

Nomination of Joseph Wentling Brown To Be a Member of the Foreign Claims Settlement Commission of the United States
May 10, 1984

The President today announced his intention to nominate Joseph Wentling Brown to be a member of the Foreign Claims Settlement Commission of the United States, Department of Justice, for the term expiring September 30, 1986. This is a reappointment.

Mr. Brown is a partner with the law firm Jones, Jones, Bell, Close & Brown, Ltd., in Las Vegas, NV. Previously he served as associate attorney with the firm of Laxalt,

Bell, Berry, Allison & LeBaron in 1969–1971. He has been a member of the board of litigation for the Mountain States Legal Foundation since 1978. He served as commissioner of the Nevada Department of Wildlife in 1979–1982.

He graduated from the University of Virginia (B.A., 1965) and Washington & Lee University (LL.B., 1968). He is married, has four children, and resides in Las Vegas, NV. He was born July 31, 1941, in Norfolk, VA.

Remarks at the Midyear Meeting of the National Association of Realtors
May 10, 1984

Anybody that was in a meeting at 7 o'clock this morning shouldn't have to stand up now. [*Laughter*] And, of course, having just returned from China, I'm not sure what time 7 o'clock in the morning is anymore.

[*Laughter*] But I thank you for your warm welcome.

And President Donald Treadwell and President-elect David Roberts, members of the board of directors, before I say any-

675

thing, I want to take this opportunity to thank all of you for the support that you've given our efforts over the last 3 years to cut spending and get taxing under control. You were rock solid even when the going got rough. I'll never forget your encouragement and support here in Washington and throughout the cities and towns of America.

And I guess nothing less can be expected from individuals who represent the best of our country. When it comes to free enterprise and competition, you represent the innovation, creativity, energy, and community spirit so much a part of small and independent business in America. The principle of private property and its relationship to personal liberty is not theory with you. It's everyday business.

Small business today, as it has always been, is the mainspring of American well-being. And, of course, there are a few individuals in small business who aren't as efficient as we'd like them to be. There's the story of a fellow—and if I've told this story to you before, just be kind—[*laughter*]—remember that when you pass 40, you begin to have a tendency toward lumbago and telling the same story over and over again. [*Laughter*]

But this fellow was so successful that he was opening a branch office, and he decided to order a floral decoration for the occasion. When he got to opening, he was shocked to see that the inscription on the flowers read, "Rest in peace." [*Laughter*] On his way home, he stopped at the flower shop to register a complaint. And the shopowner heard him out and then said, "Well, take it easy. Things aren't that bad. Just remember that someplace today there's somebody opening something up, and its says, 'Good luck in your new location.'" [*Laughter*]

But America's greatest assets are among the men and women who manage private sector businesses of every kind. And the profit motive to spur them on—they, or I should say, you are providing this country with goods and services with a higher quality and a lower price than ever imagined by the central planners of socialist economies.

There's been talk about having more centralized planning for our economy. Well, that's not the American way, and it doesn't work. The American miracle is a product of freeing the energies of our people, not harnessing them to some central plan or bureaucratic program.

Jefferson once said, "Were we directed from Washington when to sow and when to reap, we would soon want for bread." The Founding Fathers were right. As far as I'm concerned, the best thing the Government can do to keep our country growing is get out of the way and let the people run their own affairs.

You know, my favorite story having to do with your business came from a fellow that was building his own home, and it happens to be right near my own neighborhood in California. And he got so fed up one day that he took all the various forms that he had had to fill out with regard to all the regulations all the way up through the branches of government, pasted them all together, and strung them in front of his half-built house on two poles. The ribbon was 250 feet long. You know all about that.

Well, during the last decade, we strayed far from the principles that built our great nation. By the end of the 1970's, we were overtaxed and overregulated. The policies of tax, tax, spend and spend gave us economic stagnation and ruinous double-digit inflation. A spirit of pessimism, totally inconsistent with the American character, permeated the land. And by the time we got to Washington, the prime interest rate was shooting through the roof at 21½ percent, knocking the legs from under our basic industries. Being in the industry you're in, I don't have to remind you of that.

When we got here, the pressure was on. We didn't go for a quick, short-lasting fix, as you've been told. Instead, I think we've made some fundamental changes in direction. The funny thing was to hear our opponents labeling our efforts a failure and blaming us for America's economic difficulties even before our program went into effect, had time to work.

Well, I'd listen to them, and then I'd remember that old Robert Frost saying: "The brain is a wonderful organ. It starts working the moment you get up in the morning and doesn't stop until you get to the office." [*Laughter*]

Seriously, though, the first 2 years of my or any Presidency is spent, to one degree or another, in transition from a predecessor's policies. It isn't until the third year that the seeds planted by a new administration begin to bloom. And if you will forgive me for saying this, I think I've been seeing a few economic blossoms springing up here and there.

By keeping taxes stable with a 25-percent across-the-board cut in income tax rates, by reducing the growth rate of Federal spending, by chipping away at the heavy burden of excessive Federal regulation, and by bringing inflation under control, we put our country back on the road to stable progress. Overall economic growth last year was a robust 6 percent. After a burst of economic activity in the first quarter, we believe America is well on the road this year to lasting expansion.

The savings rate is on the way up again, which will make available new funds for investment. In contrast to the gloom and doom of 4 years ago, there's a spirit of optimism alive in the land. And why not?

Real wages rose for the first time—1982—for 3 years and continued to rise in 1983. Productivity, which also fell in the years before we took office, rose over 3 percent last year. Laying the foundation for future prosperity, venture capital, which only rose a billion dollars in 1980, shot up to $4 billion last year.

The economic expansion is bringing unemployment down and generating unprecedented new opportunities in small business, where two out of three new jobs are created. Last year, 600,000 new businesses were incorporated—an all-time high. Each one of these is a tiny part of the economy, but together, they represent a dynamo of energy and innovation that is opening a whole new era of opportunity and freedom.

The housing industry, building and selling, is an integral part of the progress that we're witnessing. First, reinvigorated companies, after a period of entrenchment, are beginning to move employees to different parts of the country. The Employee Relocation Council says that 35 percent of its member companies are expecting a higher transfer volume in 1984 over 1983. The

ERC predicts transfer volume will be up at least 10 percent. I know that that is music to your ears.

There is also good news in new housing. When our program was put in place in the fall of 1981, housing starts were at an annual rate of 840,000. Now they've jumped to more than 1.6 million. Building permits were only 730,000 back in the fall of '81. They've risen to more than 1.7 million.

The rebound in your industry, as in the rest of the economy, is no accident. When the last administration took over, inflation was running at about 5 percent, and the prime interest rate—and, my, it's painful to say this—was under 7 percent. But then everything went haywire. You can't have policies that run 5 percent inflation up to 12.4 and take the prime from 7 to 21½ percent and expect that housing or any other business, or the country, for that matter, is going to prosper. In the case of the housing industry, the average monthly mortgage payment rose from $256 to 598 during the 4 years of the previous administration.

I firmly believe that the opportunity to own a home is part of the American dream. Almost a hundred years ago, the poet Walt Whitman knew this when he wrote: "The final culmination of this vast and varied republic will be the production and perennial establishment of millions of comfortable city homesteads . . . healthy and independent, single separate ownership, fee simple, life in them complete but cheap, within reach of all." Well, our country was moving toward the fulfillment of that vision when the policies of tax, spend, and inflate destroyed the dream for millions of Americans.

I pledge you today that this administration will continue working tirelessly to create an expanding economy in which, as Walt Whitman said, "ownership of one's home is in reach of all."

We've made progress. Bringing inflation under control has helped. The increase in personal income has helped. A trimming of Federal regulations has helped. And—I bet you didn't think I was going to mention this—and we all know the overall decline of interest rates, notwithstanding the recent upticks, has also helped. But let me assure you, we are not pleased with the recent increases in interest rates, and, frankly, there is no satisfactory reason for them.

Of course, our economic problems have to be attacked from many directions. I believe institutional reforms are badly needed. We can start with something that will give the Chief Executive the power to cut pork-barrel projects that have been attached to needed legislation. Forty-three Governors have, and I think the Chief Executive of this country should have, a line-item veto. *[Applause]* The Capitol dome just shook. *[Laughter]*

We could also use an amendment to the Constitution that requires a balanced Federal budget. Do you know that as long ago as right after the adoption of the Constitution, Thomas Jefferson, who had so much to do with it, said it had one glaring lack. "A constitution," he said, "should have an article prohibiting the federal government from having the right to borrow."

Well, one basic reform that's long overdue is a complete overhaul of our tax system to make it more fair and provide greater incentives for everyone to work, save, and invest. We need to broaden the base so we can bring income tax rates down. In that connection, I know some of you've heard questions raised about whether there might be some plan to do away with the home mortgage interest deduction, which has played such an important role in helping Americans fulfill their dream of homeownership. I'm afraid that story was just another example of someone trying to read into my remarks things that weren't there.

At that time, I was trying to emphasize that the Treasury Department's study of ways to simplify and reform the tax code, which I consider a real priority, is supposed to look at every aspect of the tax structure. However, in saying that, I also stressed that I strongly agreed with the home mortgage interest deduction, which is so vital to millions of hard-working Americans. And in case there's still any doubt, I want you to know we will preserve that part of the American dream. I could've said that first and saved you listening to a lot of speech, couldn't I? *[Laughter]*

Well, that is the thing, that deduction, that symbolizes, I think, that American dream. And I'll be the first one to admit that there are good ways and bad ways of simplifying the tax code. Not long ago, someone sent me a proposed new tax form which wasn't exactly to my liking. It had two lines on it. The first one said, "What did you make last year?" And the second one said, "Send it." *[Laughter]*

We aren't waiting for the Congress or for institutional change. In the executive branch, we're already moving forward where we can. The Grace commission, for example, provided us with 2,478 cost-saving suggestions, brought in by more than 2,000 businessmen who volunteered their help. Many of these are being evaluated right now throughout the departments and agencies.

We also have gone a long way to clean up what was an unacceptable level of waste in the Department of Defense. Now, let me mention here that many of you are aware of the horror stories emerging from the Department of Defense about the incredible high cost of certain items, like a single bolt that maybe cost a hundred dollars. Well, these, for the most part, are not stories originating from investigative journalists. These are our figures. These are success stories on where our antiwaste program is uncovering and correcting these wasteful situations. And more progress can and will be made. But don't let anyone tell you that it is business as usual in any department, especially the Department of Defense. They are the ones who found out that that other thing had been going on and are correcting it. There have been hundreds of indictments. There have been refunds of hundreds of millions of dollars. There have been convictions for fraud.

Recently, I accepted a compromise in reducing defense spending. I did this reluctantly and in good faith that substantial cuts in other areas will be made. Those pushing for further defense cuts are rolling dice with the security needs of this country and, at the same time, undercutting any chance for tangible arms reduction agreements with the Soviets.

The Congress is now facing a decision on

Central America that could well chart our country's future for decades to come. As I mentioned last night on television, if we are to avert a monumental crisis in Central America, a crisis that would affect the lives of each and every American citizen, we must act. The flood of refugees and loss of innocent life that always results from Communist takeovers can be averted. With the balanced program we've proposed of supporting the economic progress, democratic development, and security needs of our neighbors and friends, we can succeed. And now is the time for the Congress to act. We can prove democracy works and that when it comes to our country's safety, there are no Republicans or Democrats, just Americans.

If we're to have peace, we must stand together in the face of the threats to our freedom and security. We must act responsibly when it comes to allocating our resources. After all, today's expenditures pay for tomorrow's security—the security of our children and our children's children.

We're now living with—or, more accurately, I'd say, making up for decisions made during the last decade. We should do better by our next generation than what was passed to us. The 1970's, in many ways, was a period of irresponsibility. Basic American values were made light of and spoken of as if they were relics of the past. Things like family, God, and love of country were mocked. Well, I think some of those who were so flippant about our traditions have grown up a bit in the last few years. America is finding itself again, and we've got every reason to hold our heads high.

Our greatest strength, the most powerful force for good on this planet, is the character of the American people. And I'd like to take this opportunity to thank you, all of you, for all that you're doing in the many cities and towns from coast to coast, to make this a better country.

I know about your many "Make America Better" projects. And I'm proud of each of you. I know about the realtors in Raleigh who are responsible for putting smoke detectors in the homes of the elderly. I know about the Dogwood Trail Days project, with which Birmingham realtors beautified their city; about the help of Manchester, New Hampshire, realtors have been to the Junior Olympics; about the emergency food and shelter the Asheboro-Randolph realtors have provided to people in distress; about the help the Fond du Lac, Wisconsin, realtors have been to the Toys for Tots program; about all the help the Baton Rouge, Louisiana, realtors have been in establishing a home for abused children in their community; about the patriotism projects and the nonpartisan voter registration drive you're planning.

I've often described America as a compact of good and decent people who came here from every corner of the world to live together in freedom. In a free country, what kind of society it is does not depend on the government; it depends on we, the people. Your good citizenship is showing others what Americanism is all about.

Recently, I met with Pope John Paul II on my way back from China. And there in the chilled air of the Fairbanks Airport, he spoke to me and the other citizens who had gathered there to greet him—some of them Eskimos from faraway villages, some of them city dwellers, others frontiersmen and women from many parts of our country who were there living on the last American frontier. And this Polish Pope, a symbol of courage and conviction to so many millions, knows how important our country is to the future of human liberty. And his parting words to the crowd were, "God bless America."

Working together and standing together, we will and we can keep America the shining light of liberty and opportunity that God intended it to be—the last, best hope of mankind.

Thank you, really, for all that you're doing. And thank you for having me with you again, and God bless you.

Note: The President spoke at 1:32 p.m. in the International Ballroom at the Washington Hilton Hotel.

Nomination of M. Robert Hill, Jr., To Be a Member of the Board of Regents of the Uniformed Services University of the Health Sciences
May 10, 1984

The President today announced his intention to nominate M. Robert Hill, Jr., to be a member of the Board of Regents of the Uniformed Services University of the Health Sciences, Department of Defense, for a term expiring June 20, 1989. He would succeed Eugene M. Farber.

Dr. Hill is a general and vascular surgeon in Concord, CA. He is also assistant clinical professor of surgery at the University of California at Davis and attending consultant to Martinez VA Hospital in Martinez, CA. He is a member of the American Medical Association, the California Medical Association, and the American College of Surgeons.

He graduated from La Sierra College (B.S., 1945) and Loma Linda University (M.D., 1947). He is married, has three children, and resides in Walnut Creek, CA. He was born June 1, 1923, in Los Angeles, CA.

Appointment of E. Charles Fullerton as a United States Member of the International Pacific Salmon Fisheries Commission
May 10, 1984

The President today announced his intention to appoint E. Charles Fullerton to be a member on the part of the United States of America of the International Pacific Salmon Fisheries Commission. He would succeed Herbert A. Larkins.

Since 1983 Mr. Fullerton has been director of the National Marine Fisheries Service's Southwest Region. Previously he was director of California's Department of Fish and Game. He joined the department in 1947 and served as warden, patrol captain, and patrol inspector until his appointment as chief of the law enforcement branch in 1964. He became chief of operations in 1969 and served as deputy director in 1972–1975. He is past president of the International Association of Fish and Wildlife Agencies.

He is married and resides in Sacramento, CA. He was born August 22, 1922, in Los Angeles, CA.

Statement by Principal Deputy Press Secretary Speakes on Approval by the House of Representatives of an Amendment Authorizing Military Assistance for El Salvador
May 10, 1984

The President is extremely pleased at this example of cooperative spirit between the Congress and the executive branch. He expresses his deep respect to Congress and particularly to the House for their action, which sends a solid signal of U.S. resolve to support friends in this hemisphere. The President looks forward to working with Congress to take the next step in the process, which is to appropriate the funds this vote authorizes.

Remarks at the Annual Senate-House Fundraising Dinner
May 10, 1984

Thank you, Dick, and thank you, everyone, you know, hearing others here tonight tell of what you have done and what you've accomplished in this gathering, I kept remembering back in World War II when someone asked General Marshall if we had a secret weapon. And he said, "Yes, the best damn kids in the world." Well, now, if anyone asks me if we, on our side, have a secret weapon, I'm going to say those best damn kids grew up into the best damn people— [*laughter*]—and you're all here tonight.

You know, this has been a wonderful time. Oh, I had a little difficulty with a knife and fork. [*Laughter*] Nancy wasn't here to help me cut my meat. [*Laughter*] I didn't have chopsticks, but we're delighted to be with you this evening.

Drew Lewis, Dick Lugar, Guy Vander Jagt, Ted Welch, Jack McDonald, you've done a superb job of putting this event together. To the Members of the House and Senate here tonight, you have my heartfelt thanks for all that you've done over these past 3 years to help put America back on course. And a special thanks to Howard Baker and Bob Michel for your outstanding leadership on the Hill. We saw an example of that in one of the Houses there today.

And to those of you who've come here tonight from across the country, you have my deepest gratitude for your generous support of the cause that unites us. With your help, we're making history.

Now, it's no secret that this is an election year. And we've already begun to hear talk about various political strategies—the Northern strategy, the Western strategy, the Sunbelt strategy. My favorite is the Rose Garden strategy—a sure winner if all you want is the horticulture vote. [*Laughter*]

But I want you all to know that I've already decided on my strategy. We'll stand on the record.

Think back just 3 years ago. Big taxing and spending had led to soaring interest rates and inflation. Our defenses had grown weak. All over the world, America's reputation was no longer one of strength and resolve, but of vacillation and self-doubt. Many in Washington seemed to forget that the bedrock values of faith, freedom, and family were what made us a great and good people. It seemed for a season as though any sense of justice, self-discipline, and duty was ebbing out of our national life and that our nation was in an inevitable decline.

But on this Earth, there's no such thing as inevitable. And the American people decided it was time to put a stop to that decline, time to give our country a rebirth of feedom and faith, time for a great national renewal. Well, we Republicans took office determined to make a new beginning. And today, America is back.

We've knocked inflation down to about a third of what it was. The prime rate has fallen 9 percentage points since its peak the month we took office. And all across the country, a surging economic expansion is taking place.

As a matter of fact, I've been getting letters from some prominent economists who are asking me to stop calling it an economic recovery. They said we've passed that point. It is now an economic expansion. And all across the country, a surging economic expansion is taking place.

Retail sales and factory orders are up. And tomorrow morning at about 8:30, the figures will be released, and you'll find they're up some more. The stock market has shown new strength. Since the expansion began 16 months ago, 5.4 million Americans have found jobs, and the unemployment rate has shown the steepest drop in 30 years. Today more Americans have jobs than at any other time in our history— 106 million.

Despite the overwhelming success of our economic program, the opposition won't rest. They'll never stop calling our tax cuts unfair. Now, that just shows how the Democrats think. When inflation pushes Americans into higher tax brackets year after year, taking more and more money away from the people who earned it, giving it instead to big government, the Democrats think everything's hunky-dory. But when we pass through a long overdue, 25-percent, across-the-board, personal income tax rate cut, the Democrats scream foul play and say that we gave a windfall to the rich. Well, with regard to fairness, let's take a look at the facts.

In 1982, the last year for which we have complete statistics, people with incomes below $20,000 a year contributed 10 percent less to tax revenues than they did a year before, in large part because of our tax cuts. For those with incomes from $20,000 to $50,000, their tax payments as a share of the total tax return dropped by 1 percent. But those with incomes of $50,000 and up contributed not less, but 8 percent more to the total tax revenues. And if you go one step further and narrow that group down to those earning $500,000 and up, the share of taxes paid by them increased by a whopping 41 percent.

1982 wasn't a fluke. History has shown again and again that when high marginal tax rates are cut and the economy expands, revenues actually rise. In the 1920's, Treasury Secretary Andrew Mellon instituted a series of tax cuts that reduced the top rate from 73 percent to 25 percent. The cuts increased revenues from the rich by 186 percent between 1921 and '28. The share of total income taxes paid by those with net incomes over $50,000 rose from under a half to more than three-quarters.

Just 20 years ago, the Kennedy tax cuts reduced marginal rates on personal income by an average of 20 percent. Did the rich pay less? No, they paid more. And overall revenues rose. The plain fact is that while our tax cuts spurred the economy on to new vigor, they actually shifted a larger percentage of the tax burden from the middle class to the rich. Today our tax code is fairer than it was under the Carter-Mondale administration.

And now, if you'll just bear with me, for all the Capitol Hill Democrats who'll read this with disbelief in tomorrow's papers, let me say that again—[*laughter*]—today our tax code is fairer than it was under Carter and Mondale.

The opposition needs to spend less time carping and more time supporting things like tax cuts that really, truly help the American people.

Earlier this month, liberal Democrat Paul Tsongas put it well when he rose on the floor of the Senate to say this to his fellow Democrats: "The weakness that we have is that we, as Democrats, have never convinced the country we know how to run the economy; that Democrats are viewed as people who care less about how well the economy is doing and spend all of their time worrying about how you distribute the golden eggs. The goose's health is irrelevant." [*Laughter*] You know—and then this liberal Democrat added, "You know, the funny thing about it is we deserve it because it's true." Isn't it funny how a fellow will get religion when he's decided to quit running for office? [*Laughter*]

But just as we've moved ahead on the economy, our administration has taken vigorous action against waste and fraud in the Federal Government. We've taken aim at crime, increasing drug-related arrests, more than doubling organized crime convictions, and setting up drug task forces across the country.

And we moved education to the very top of the national agenda. When we took office, only a handful of States had task forces on education. Today that number is 50.

At the same time, we've begun rebuilding our defenses and given our foreign policy a new sense of direction. In Grenada, we set a nation free. In Europe, we and our NATO allies went through months of Soviet bluff and bluster and came out of it more firmly united than ever.

I'd like to pause right here and just tell you something about those—when every time I see those young men and women in uniform that we have today and remember back to when I was Governor, and young people that age, if I got any place around them, I started a riot—[*laughter*]—but I see them, and I know they weren't conscripted. They're in those uniforms because they chose to be in them. And let me just tell you one little thing out of a letter that I got from an ex-marine, a Vietnam veteran, now a man with a grown son who is in the service.

He wrote a letter, and it was tragic. He told me of how, on Christmas Day, his wife passed away from cancer, and his son was home from his boot training with the Rangers and had to leave to go back to camp. And this former ex-marine, this bereaved husband, said that he actually toyed with the idea of suicide, that it seemed that life held nothing for him. And then he said one day the mail arrived and, he said, "from young men that I have never known or never seen, the members of my son's platoon." He said, "I received these letters telling this old marine to stand up and fight back, that there were people that cared" about him. And he said, "All of a sudden," he said, "I thought I was back on the drill field. I could hear the marine hymn. I thought I could feel the breeze on the deck of the *Midway* where I was stationed." And he said, "all from a bunch of young fellows that I've never known." And I thought there sure has been a change. They are the best damned kids in the world today again.

In the Pacific, a trip to Korea and Japan strengthened our ties with our Asian allies. Our recent visit to China improved the prospects for a continued development of this important relationship and produced agreements to cooperate more closely on trade, investment, technology, nuclear energy, and scientific and managerial exchanges. No one should underestimate the differences between China and the United States, and yet the Chinese have chosen not to threaten our interests, but to follow the path of cooperation.

In Central America, our administration has firmly supported the forces of democracy and economic progress. Three out of four American dollars—or of dollars of American aid to that region have not been military, but economic. And as I said last night on TV, the United States must not allow the free governments of this vitally important region to be overrun by Soviet- and Cuban-backed guerrillas.

And while I'm on this subject, I want to ask those who seem ready to desert the forces of democracy in Central America, name one totalitarian country where the people can practice the freedom of speech

that these critics themselves value so highly and that people in free Central American nations now enjoy. Name one country that was taken over by Marxist guerrillas that has held a truly democratic election like the one that just took place last Sunday in El Salvador. And name one Communist country where the people are as free to worship their God as the millions of faithful are in El Salvador, Honduras, and the other free Central American nations. They can't do it, because no such country exists. And that's why I, for one, refuse to sell out the liberty of our hemisphere.

Yes, from the economy to foreign policy we have made a new beginning. It's a record we can take to the people with pride. But we must give the people more than our record; we must give them our vision. We Republicans see America forever free from the evils of inflation. To make that dream a reality, we will enact structural reforms like the line-item veto and the balanced budget amendment.

We see an America with a fair and simple tax code that allows the American people to keep a greater share of their earnings. To bring that about, we'll design a major tax reform, not tinkering here and there, but a sweeping and comprehensive reform of the entire tax code. We won't accept that one plan that was sent in to me the other day. It was a tax form with only two lines on it. The top line said "How much did you earn last year?" And the second line said "Send it." [*Laughter*]

We see a world of peace and ever-growing freedom, so we'll keep our defenses strong, support the forces of progress in Central America and elsewhere, and remain eager to negotiate equitable and verifiable nuclear arms reductions—not just limitations, an actual reduction. The Democrats can run on gloom, if they want to; we'll run on reality, and the American reality is good.

Our basic industries are gaining new strength, and we're leading the world in a dazzling technological revolution. Our people are once again self-confident, and polls show that Americans are more optimistic about the future of this nation than at any time in the past 5 years. Together we're building an opportunity society here at home and making America a powerful force for peace among nations throughout the world.

The Republican message is simple: Our country's best days are still to come. And with faith, freedom, and courage, there's no limit to what the American people can accomplish. If we do everything in our power to carry that message to the voters on November 6th, they'll respond by keeping Republicans where we belong: on the job, in the House, in the Senate, and in the administration.

I know I should say "thank you and good night" right here, but I told my two charming dinner partners here at the table a little incident that happened a week or so ago, and I just think I'll share it with you just to finish.

I've talked here about diplomacy and trips to foreign governments, and everything, but diplomacy can be very treacherous. And a week or so ago, a couple of weeks ago—well, no, before the China trip—we had the President of France and Mrs. Mitterrand as our guests at a state dinner. And after all the guests had gone into the State Dining Room and were standing around the tables, similar to these, then the four of us, Nancy and Mrs. Mitterrand and the President and I followed. And Nancy and the President turned to go to their table, and the diplomatic crisis began right then.

Nancy tripped over a TV wire and lost a shoe. The President was holding her. Mrs. Mitterrand got to the first row of tables and stopped, absolutely motionless. And the butler ahead was motioning to come on, and I leaned up and said, "We can go on." She said something very calmly in French, which I didn't understand—[*laughter*]—and then I again motioned, and she again said the same thing in French. I still didn't understand. And, fortunately, just then the interpreter arrived. She was telling me I was standing on her gown. [*Laughter*] One more step and diplomatic relations with France would have ended. [*Laughter*]

Well, this has been just wonderful and what you're doing—and we've got to have that majority back, as you've been told, in the Senate. We couldn't have done anything we've done without having that one House, but what a wonder it would be if, for the first time in 26 years, Republicans once again had a majority in both Houses of the Congress. It hasn't happened since then.

Thank you for all you've done. God bless you. Thank you.

Note: The President spoke at 9:27 p.m. in the International Ballroom at the Washington Hilton Hotel. He was introduced by Senator Richard G. Lugar of Indiana, chairman of the National Republican Senatorial Committee, one of the sponsoring organizations for the dinner.

Earlier in the evening, the President attended a reception for the dinner committee members on the State Floor of the White House.

Remarks at a White House Ceremony Marking the First Anniversary of the Report of the National Commission on Excellence in Education
May 11, 1984

Well, ladies and gentlemen, Secretary Bell and Dr. David Gardner and distinguished guests and, most especially, distinguished students, I want to thank all of you for coming here today on this beautiful day. We arranged this just particularly. We always like to plan nice weather for these things so you can have a good time while you're cutting school. [*Laughter*]

We did a little checking the other day and found out that this is the 43d time that I have spoken on education in the past 3½ years. And that doesn't include such things as White House meetings on education and talks with reporters. And I've given education so much time and used the—what Teddy Roosevelt said was the "bully pulpit" of this office to discuss this issue for a very clear and simple reason: It's because we in this administration view education as central to American life.

It is central as the family is central, as the towns we live in are central, and as our churches are central. If a modern de Tocqueville came searching for the heart of this country today, I would tell him to go to those junctions where family, church, town, and school meet, for that's where America is.

We came to Washington believing that education was key to the American comeback that we wanted to bring about. And one of the first things we did was appoint a National Commission on Excellence in Education. And I asked them to study our schools, define their problems, and come up, if they could, with solutions. And I can say "you" because the Commission is right here—you did just that.

Last spring in your report, you documented 20 years of decline, 20 years of declining academic standards and declining discipline. And you were very blunt. You said, "If a foreign nation had done to our schools what we ourselves have done to them, we would be justified in calling it an act of war." Well, you don't get much blunter than that.

But you spoke of hope, too. You outlined the reforms needed to put us back on the path of excellence. And you gave us old but enduring advice: Get back to basics. And the public response to your report was electrifying. There is a huge and growing public mandate for change. And it's not overstating things at all to say that your report changed our history by changing the way we look at education and putting it back on the American agenda.

Virtually every major national organization in this country has supported some aspect of the reform movement. State leadership has been clear and strong. In this past year alone, 35 States raised high school graduation requirements. Twenty-one States are reviewing steps to make text-

books more challenging. Eight States have lengthened the school day, and seven have lengthened the school year. Many legislatures are carefully—or currently, I should say, developing workable and fair merit pay plans, and 47 States are studying improvements in teacher certification.

The private sector, too, is doing its part. We have new partnerships between community businesses and community schools. Some businesses are adopting local schools, working with students and teachers to make education more rewarding and more exciting.

The Federal Government is doing its part. We're taking a new look at violence in the schools and how to restore the peace and order without which no teacher can instruct and no student can learn. We're taking a new look at the national dropout rate. Estimates show that we're losing roughly a million students a year in the high schools. Now, that will surely erode our ability to compete in business, and it could lead to a permanent underclass of unskilled new workers who don't have much hope in the job market.

We're taking a new look at truancy. And across the country, there are efforts to cut back on it by using everything from greater discipline to new incentives.

Now, you may have heard about one such case in Indiana. The local schoolboard wanted to encourage better high school attendance, so they offered a $100 reward for any student who graduated with a perfect attendance record their senior year. Well, word got around, and the kids stopped cutting classes. And now the schoolboard has found that close to 200 students made perfect attendance records, and they'll have to come up with $20,000 before graduation day.

I've been watching our young students over there. They're looking like they think this is a pretty good idea. I hope I'm not contributing to a number of schoolboard bankruptcies with that story. [*Laughter*]

The point I'm making is that education is back on the agenda. All over this country, there has been a renaissance of interest in and involvement with the schools. And so much of the spirit of this renewal is directly traceable to your report last year.

And, Dr. Gardner, as head of the National Commission on Excellence in Education, I just want to say thank you on behalf of your country and on behalf of the generations that will benefit from your great work.

And now the high point of my day. One of the things we did this past year was start a new award for students who have strived to reach their potential and worked hard to learn, study, and get good marks. You remember that some years back, President Kennedy was concerned about the physical fitness of all Americans. And a few years later, President Johnson followed up that concern by creating the President's Physical Fitness Award. Well, this year, we instituted the President's Academic Fitness Award. And I am pleased to announce that more than 220,000 graduating high school seniors are recipients of the first awards.

And today, we have here around 60 representatives of all the winners from all the States, and I'm aware of how hard you worked for these awards. You are meeting your potential through your scholarly attainments. You are leaders, good students, and you've worked hard to learn and study. As a matter of fact, I happen to believe you're the most priceless asset this country has.

You are America's future. You've made us very proud. And I'm not only delighted to give these awards, I feel deeply honored to be the first President to do so.

And now, Secretary Bell, will you be so good as to help us begin, and I'll go over on my mark. [*Laughter*]

[*As Secretary Bell read their names, the 60 students approached the platform and received their certificates from the President. After the last award was presented, he resumed speaking.*]

I'll bring home one thing from our trip to China, and that is that after applause of that kind, I applaud you.

Thank you.

Note: The President spoke at 11:32 a.m. on the South Lawn of the White House. Prior to the ceremony, he met with Secretary of Education Terrel H. Bell and members of the Commission in the Oval Office.

Proclamation 5193—National Asthma and Allergy Awareness Week, 1984
May 11, 1984

By the President of the United States of America

A Proclamation

Asthma and allergic diseases annually result in physical, emotional, and economic hardship for more than thirty-five million Americans and their families. Even though sufficient medical knowledge and resources exist to prevent many asthma-related deaths, thousands of Americans die each year from asthma. Indeed, student absenteeism is due in significant part to asthma and allergic diseases. Furthermore, in some instances, medical patients suffer unfortunate allergic reactions to prescribed medicines.

It is estimated that the American people pay $2 billion per year in medical bills directly attributable to the treatment and diagnosis of asthma and allergic diseases and another $2 billion per year as a result of the indirect social costs of such illnesses.

Recent developments in the study of immunology enable health care providers to diagnose and treat asthma and allergic diseases more effectively. Increased public awareness of these scientific advances in immunology will help dispel many of the common misconceptions concerning these diseases and their victims. With the determination and support of our citizens, scientists hope that continuing progress will eventually lead to the control and prevention of these life-limiting and sometimes life-threatening diseases.

In recognition of the significant importance of increased public awareness of recent advancements in the study of immunology to the health and well-being of millions of American children and adults, the Congress, by Senate Joint Resolution 244, has designated the week beginning on May 6, 1984, as "National Asthma and Allergy Awareness Week," and authorized and requested the President to issue an appropriate proclamation.

Now, Therefore, I, Ronald Reagan, President of the United States of America, do hereby proclaim the week beginning May 6, 1984 as National Asthma and Allergy Awareness Week. I call upon the people of the United States to observe such week with appropriate ceremonies and activities.

In Witness Whereof, I have hereunto set my hand this 11th day of May, in the year of our Lord nineteen hundred and eighty-four, and of the Independence of the United States of America the two hundred and eighth.

RONALD REAGAN

[*Filed with the Office of the Federal Register, 4:07 p.m., May 11, 1984*]

Executive Order 12476—Presidential Commission on the Conduct of United States-Japan Relations
May 11, 1984

By the authority vested in me as President by the Constitution and laws of the United States of America, including the Federal Advisory Committee Act, as amended (5 U.S.C. App. I), it is hereby ordered that Executive Order No. 12421 of May 12, 1983, is amended as follows:

Section 1. Sections 1(b), 2(b) and 2(d) are amended by deleting the phrase "Advisory Group on United States-Japan Relations" in each Section and inserting instead the phrase "United State-Japan Advisory Commission." Section 2(b) is further amended by deleting the phrase "This group" and inserting instead the phrase "This bi-national group."

Sec. 2. Section 2(c) shall read: "To pursue its goals in connection with participation in the United States-Japan Advisory Commission, the Commission may conduct studies, hearings, and meetings as it deems necessary; assemble and disseminate information; and issue reports and other publications."

Sec. 3. Section 4(b) shall read: "In accordance with the Federal Advisory Committee Act, as amended, the Commission shall terminate on October 31, 1984, unless sooner extended."

RONALD REAGAN

The White House,
May 11, 1984.

[*Filed with the Office of the Federal Register, 4:08 p.m., May 11, 1984*]

Message on the Observance of National Nursing Home Week, May 13–19, 1984
May 11, 1984

As we observe National Nursing Home Week, let us remember that nursing home residents need more than the quality medical and social services nursing homes provide. They also need contact with the people and activities in their communities.

Living in our modern world, we often feel troubled by the rapid pace of social change. Yet, as a society, we tend to ignore one of our most valuable reservoirs of strength, comfort and stability: our older citizens. Their lives, their conversation, and their companionship can give us new perspectives and new insight into events known to us only through books but to them through personal experience.

When our younger and older generations share their understanding, we all benefit. I hope you will visit a nearby nursing home this week and return often. By keeping in touch with our elders, we enlarge our own lives as well as theirs.

RONALD REAGAN

Message on the Observance of Police Week and Police Officers' Memorial Day, May 1984
May 11, 1984

Each year at this time we pause to remember those law enforcement officers who gave their lives in the line of duty.

The job of police officers is perhaps the most difficult and challenging one of all in our free society. They must protect society from those who would violate its laws, while scrupulously observing the rights of everyone.

All too often, these disciplined and courageous men and women give their lives to the cause of justice. As we pause to remember and reflect upon those who have made the ultimate sacrifice for the good of their fellow citizens, let us pray that no more names are added to the list.

All Americans are thankful that there are those willing to risk injury and death so that the rest of us can live in a nation of greater safety and security. It is our responsibility to continue to strive for a society which will lessen the risks of such tasks. For we are committed to a vision of justice that will ensure that those who have been lost will not have died in vain.

RONALD REAGAN

Note: Police Week is observed May 13–19, and Police Officers' Memorial Day is observed May 15.

Appointment of Three Members of the National Advisory Committee for Juvenile Justice and Delinquency Prevention
May 11, 1984

The President today announced his intention to appoint the following individuals to be members of the National Advisory Committee for Juvenile Justice and Delinquency Prevention for terms expiring January 17, 1987. These are reappointments:

Allan B. Moore is a student at Harvard University in Cambridge, MA. He graduated from Groton School in 1982. He was born July 21, 1964, in Boston, MA.

Donna M. Smith is a student at George Mason University in Fairfax, VA. She graduated from Kempsville High School in Virginia Beach, VA. She was born July 6, 1963, in San Diego, CA.

Sylvester E. Williams IV is a law clerk with the firm of Raby & Stafford of Alexandria, VA. He is a law student at Stanford University. He was born May 24, 1961, in Chicago, IL.

Radio Address to the Nation on Education
May 12, 1984

My fellow Americans:

I want to talk to you today about a wonderful thing that's happening in our country. It began a year ago, so it's only just begun. But already it's changing our country, and I think it may change it forever. I'm talking about the recent progress in America's schools.

You may remember the day a year ago when the National Commission on Excellence in Education came out with its report on what was wrong with the Nation's schools. The Commission documented 20 solid years of decline—decline in academic standards and discipline, decline in authority and in scholastic results. The Commission said a rising tide of mediocrity was wiping out America's reputation for the best education system in the world. That report was electrifying, and its current swept the country.

Parents and teachers got together, marshaled their resources, and began to turn the situation around. So now, 1 year later, we can report that together we have met the rising tide of mediocrity with a tidal wave of school reforms.

Those reforms reflect the Commission's advice: Get back to basics, tighten standards, heighten academic requirements, and remember discipline in the classroom is vital. In short, make sure that Johnny and Mary can read and write, and make sure their school is allowed the peace without which no student can learn and no teacher can instruct.

I want you to listen to some of the things that have happened since the Commission made its recommendations. Thirty-five States have raised high school graduation requirements. Twenty-one States are reviewing steps to make textbooks more challenging. Eight States have lengthened the school day; seven have lengthened the school year. And every State in the Union has put together a task force to improve its educational system. School districts across the country are moving toward requiring 4 years of English in high school and 3 solid years each of math and science. Many legislatures are currently developing workable and fair merit pay plans. Many States have increased teachers' salaries.

The private sector, too, is playing a big part in the reforms. Local businesses are adopting local schools, sending in their executives and employees to work with students and teachers to make education more exciting and more pertinent to the 1980's.

We're seeing a willingness to reconsider what our schools should be teaching. In the State of Maryland, a commission concluded students aren't being taught enough about American traditions of freedom and liberty. A bipartisan panel came up with a plan to teach students that most basic of democratic arts, the art of citizenship. In New Jersey Governor Tom Kean had another creative idea—give scientists and mathematicians in private industry a form of teaching accreditation so they can go into the schools and teach what they know.

Last year, as part of our program to encourage academic excellence, we began the President's Academic Fitness Awards, a scholastic version of the Physical Fitness Awards. Well, participation in the program exceeded our estimates by 400 percent.

This month 220,000 high school seniors, who had maintained high marks and achieved high scores on scholastic aptitude tests, won the Academic Fitness Awards. And yesterday, on the South Lawn of the White House, I personally gave the awards to 60 students from around the country. Just seeing their proud faces spoke a world of words about the importance of education to our country's future and the spirit of renewal that's underway.

This entire reform movement proves how wrong the people are who always insist money is the only answer to the problems of our schools. Well, leaving aside the fact that the 20 years they kept shoveling money in was the same 20 years in which the schools deteriorated, I think it's fair to say they missed the essential point. Money was never the problem. Leadership was—

leadership in getting the schools back to basic values, basic traditions, and basic good sense.

With the leadership of plain American citizens, we're getting back on track. Much remains to be done. Our administration will go forward with our efforts to control school crime, pass tuition tax credits and school vouchers as well. And, once again, I'll continue working for the restoration of voluntary school prayer, for nothing is as basic as acknowledging the God from whom all knowledge springs.

But we can be proud of the progress we're making. And I think this is only the first chapter of a marvelous story about how the people of America came together to re-create a school system that was once the envy of the world. Let's all write the next chapter together.

Until next week, thanks for listening, and God bless you.

Note: The President spoke at 12:06 p.m. from Camp David, MD.

Remarks During a Visit to the Jeanne Jugan Residence on Mother's Day
May 13, 1984

Mother Mary Agnes, thank you for inviting us here today.

Since the Little Sisters of the Poor was founded in 1839, the order has spread to 34 countries on 5 continents and cared for more than a million of the elderly today, of my generation. And here in Washington, although this home is only a year old, it replaced one that was operated by the Little Sisters of the Poor for more than a century.

And throughout all these decades, you've cared for the elderly in our Capital City who had nowhere else to go. You've brought them into a warm and happy home. And you've given them, in addition to the necessities, the thing that only the love of others can bestow: dignity.

I know that for your financial support, you depend on individual donations, and I can't think of any worthier cause than the Little Sisters of the Poor. And on behalf of all those you've done so very much to help, I thank you.

You know, Nancy and I, coming down here from Camp David on the helicopter, we couldn't help but be thinking about this particular day and what it was. I think in hindsight, perhaps, I realize more about my mother than—and as so many of us do, did

not at the time—Nelle was a little woman, auburn hair, and, I realize now, had a strength through some very trying times that held our family together. We were poor, but the government didn't come around and tell us we were, so—[*laughter*]—we didn't know it. And probably we didn't know it because Nelle was always finding someone that was worse off then we were that needed help.

And my father was hard-working. He had a sense of humor. He also had a very great problem, but my mother saw that my brother and I, from the time we were children, understood that problem and that it was something—a sickness, and that he was not to be blamed, but to be loved.

And she taught us about life, I think, by her deeds as well as her words. She had never gone beyond—in education—beyond elementary school, but she had a different kind of education that I think has been imprinted and a faith that I know now has been bestowed on me.

I'd like to just tell a little anecdote about it. Some years after I was in Hollywood, I was able to bring my parents out there, and she immediately started finding people. And one she found was a county tubercular sanitarium that could provide, as a public institution could of that kind, the necessary care, but certainly failed in some of the homelike atmosphere that was necessary.

And my mother went to work, and she visited that place regularly. She arranged for movies to be shown and for television and things of that kind that they had never had before. And one night—and she has left us now—but one night I was at a banquet. I was the speaker at a banquet. And a few years ago, banquet food wasn't of the same quality that it is today. And the waiter that was coming along leaned down to me and whispered and said, "Would you rather have a big steak than what we're serving here?"

"Well," I said, "if that's possible, yes,"— [*laughter*]—because I did a lot of banquet speaking in those days, and I'd had enough of banquet food. Well, he arrived back with the nicest, big T-bone steak you ever saw and put it in front of me.

Now, in the meantime, I had decided that he had to be a motion picture fan, and he must have liked my pictures. And I was basking in that kind of reflected glory. And as he put the steak down, he leaned down and whispered in my ear, "Anytime, for a relative of Nelle Reagan's. I used to be a patient at Olive View Sanitarium." [*Laughter*]

But Nancy, at the same time—and this is a coincidence—thank heaven, Nancy's mother is still with us—Nancy's mother, living in Chicago, was one of a kind also. I don't think there was a policeman or a doorman or a cabdriver or anyone like that in Chicago that didn't know Edith Davis, because she, too, was always engaged in good works. And we saw a classic example of that.

Nancy and I got off the train, the New York Twentieth Century Limited in Chicago, in the midst of a blizzard and laden with bags and baggage and so forth from the trip we'd been on. Everyone else—and not a redcap, not a porter in sight and ev-

eryone struggling with their bags and everything. And we—this whole length of the train to go—and all of sudden looked down, and here came Nancy's mother, arm in arm with two redcaps. [*Laughter*]

And as she got closer, we could hear, she was asking the one about his children. She knew his children's names, knew all about them, what grade they were in, and was talking to him. The other one, asked about his wife's operation. She knew all about that, too. And just happened to stop by us and say, "Oh, these are my children. Could you give them a hand with their bags?" [*Laughter*] And a whole trainload of people saw us stride down the platform with Nancy's mother and with the two porters, and they were still trying to manage with their bags, and we had plenty of help.

But I think things like this make me understand what Abe Lincoln was feeling when he said, "All that I am or hope to be, I owe to my mother."

And I know there are many of you mothers in this room. I also know that there are others who live as mothers live, the Little Sisters of the Poor, 17 who are residents in this home and together with the 4,500 Little Sisters around the world who have chosen to give of themselves completely in humble service to their fellow men and women. The residents are your family. Your prayers and hard work have made this a very friendly and, it's very obvious, a joyful home.

And thank you all for allowing us to share this special day with you. And we wish each one of you a very happy and rewarding Mother's Day and the blessings of our beloved God.

Thank you.

Note: The President spoke at 2:20 p.m. in the home's auditorium. Prior to his remarks, the President and Mrs. Reagan attended the home's Mother's Day dinner for its residents and their families.

Remarks at a White House Ceremony Marking Progress Made in the Campaign Against Drunk Driving
May 14, 1984

The President. Well, isn't this a thriller? [*Laughter*] I'm delighted to see all of you here today. We haven't seen this many people since we left China. And just think, you all came to see me. [*Laughter*]

No, I know why you're here, and with good reason—to see one of the most talented, most popular, and most exciting superstars in the music world today—Michael Jackson.

And, Michael, welcome to the White House. I hope you'll forgive me, but we have quite a few young folks in the White House who all wanted me to give you the same message. They said to tell Michael, "Please give some TLC to the PYTs." [*Laughter*] Now, I know that sounds a little off-the-wall, but you know what I mean. [*Laughter*]

And, Michael, I have another message from our fans in the Washington, DC, area. They said, we want you back. So, when you begin your greatly awaited crosscountry tour, will you please be sure to drop off here in the Nation's Capital?

Well, down to business. We're gathered here to mark the progress of a shared endeavor and to commit ourselves to an even greater national effort, as Elizabeth told you. On April 14th of 1982, I created a Presidential Commission on Drunk Driving. And since that date, real progress has been made. States have passed tougher laws, arrests and enforcement have been stepped up, and citizens across our country are taking a stronger stand against the tragedies caused by drinking and driving.

Another milestone resulted in the Commission's work—the creation of a National Public Service Campaign to make more Americans aware of solutions to this national problem. Our campaign will marshal the power of the media, with the help, as you've been told, of the Advertising Council, our Private Sector Initiatives Office, and the Department of Transportation, under the strong leadership of Secretary Elizabeth Dole. This private sector-government partnership brings a message to young people that will touch many lives and change them for the better.

Today we recognize all these fine efforts of voluntarism by the Commission members as well as those of the Ad Council. Helping one another for the good of this country and its citizens and without concern for reward or payment, this is the heart of America—strong, good, and true.

I want to recognize another volunteer effort made for the good of our country, especially our nation's youth, and it is, as you've been told, none other than Michael Jackson's effort.

At this stage of his career, when it would seem he's achieved everything a musical performer could hope for, Michael Jackson is taking time to help lead the fight against alcohol and drug abuse.

Michael, you've made it possible for us to warn millions of young Americans about the dangers of drinking and driving. You've done this with your music you've provided to the public service messages as well as through your own personal example. And thanks to your help, Michael, young people from virtually every family in America will hear these messages on television and radio. And they will hear them at one of the most criticial times of the year, when graduations and vacations are fast approaching. Thanks to your help, lives will be saved. And no one can put a dollar value on the precious life of one boy or girl.

Michael Jackson is proof of what a person can accomplish through a lifestyle free of alcohol or drug abuse. People young and old respect that. And if Americans follow his example, then we can face up to the problem of drinking and driving, and we can, in Michael's words, beat it.

Nancy spends a great deal of her time with young people talking about the problems of drug and alcohol abuse, so I speak for both of us when I say, thank you, Michael, for the example that you're giving to millions of young Americans who look up to you.

And let me just say as one who spent a certain part of his life in the entertainment business, what Michael Jackson has achieved is a tribute to 20 years of hard work, energy, tireless dedication, and a wealth of talent that keeps on growing. Your success is an American dream come true.

And now, if you'd permit me, I would like to present you with this award. And I would like to read what it says: "To Michael Jackson, with appreciation for the outstand-ing example you have set for the youth of America and the world. Your historic record-breaking achievements and your preeminence in popular music are a tribute to your creativity, dedication, and great ability. The generous contribution of your time and talent to the National Campaign Against Teen-age Drunk Driving will help millions of young Americans learn that drinking and driving can kill a friendship."

Michael Jackson. I'm very, very honored. Thank you very much, Mr. President and Mrs. Reagan.

Note: The President spoke at 11:01 a.m. on the South Lawn of the White House.

Remarks and a Question-and-Answer Session With Reporters on Foreign and Domestic Issues
May 14, 1984

Production of the MX Missile

The President. Our defense policy is based on a simple premise—I stated it the other night—that we do not start wars. We maintain our strength to deter aggression and preserve peace. Since the dawn of the nuclear age, we've sought to reduce the risk of war by maintaining a strong deterrent and by seeking genuine arms control. And after close bipartisan coordination with the Congress, the Scowcroft Commission on Strategic Forces last year reaffirmed that we must continue the Peacekeeper program as part of an overall strategic modernization program that includes ambitious arms control negotiations.

There is no more compelling priority on my agenda, and that is why we've been working so hard to convince the Soviet Union to join us in a spirit of genuine cooperation to achieve real and equitable reductions in the levels of nuclear arms. And that's why the United States is continuing to carry out its own obligations and commitments under previous agreements as we call upon the Soviet Union to demonstrate equal restraint.

It's important to remember that since the December 1979 NATO decision on longer range, intermediate nuclear forces, the United States has already withdrawn over 1,000 nuclear weapons from Europe. We will continue to withdraw one additional nuclear weapon for each Pershing II and ground-launched cruise missile deployed. We and our allies have also announced plans to withdraw an additional 1,400 nuclear weapons from Europe. In sum, the United States will withdraw five times as many nuclear weapons as are planned for deployment in the ground-launch cruise missiles and Pershing II programs.

In five rounds of START, the United States has been flexible in exploring all avenues to achieve verifiable arms reductions. The U.S. position was adjusted to reflect the Scowcroft Commission's recommendations to incorporate a proposed mutual guaranteed build-down, and to include trade-offs between the interests and advantages of each side. Negotiations on mutual balanced force reductions resumed March 16th. We tabled a new initiative to break the deadlock with the Soviets over existing force levels. And in the Conference on Disarmament, we're pressing for a total ban on chemical weapons.

Despite all our initiatives, the Soviet

693

Union walked out of the Intermediate Nuclear Force talks and has still failed to agree to resume the START talks. We regret this Soviet action, and we remain prepared to resume negotiations immediately, without preconditions. We must not cast doubt on U.S. and allied reserve [resolve] nor reward the Soviets for their current belligerent behavior towards arms control.

In the early 1970's, the United States expected to field a modernized ICBM system by the end of the seventies. We didn't make it. The Peacekeeper will not be deployed, in even limited numbers, until late 1986. The Soviet Union, however, deployed over 800 SS–17's, SS–18's, and SS–19's, missiles that are similar to or even larger than the MX. Also, the Soviet Union is now flight-testing two new ICBM's—the MIRVed SS–X24 and the SS–X25—and have others under development.

The U.S.S.R. has a comprehensive program to strengthen their strategic force. We cannot afford to delay any longer. Without Peacekeeper, the MX, the incentive for the Soviets to return to the negotiating table is greatly reduced. The Soviets hope that, once again, our modernization efforts will be curtailed. To falter now would only encourage the Soviet Union to ignore our arms control efforts. For our own security and the cause of world peace, we must support the bipartisan national program that we approved last year.

Yeah, Bill [Bill Plante, CBS News].

U.S.-Soviet Relations

Q. Mr. President, why would you expect the Soviets to come back to the arms talks after the way you talked about them over in China? What incentive do they have, sir?

The President. What did I actually talk about over in China? I have thought back on the remarks that were supposedly—or were censored out or at least, removed. What I said about them was I was contrasting what we have—we obviously differ in many ways from the Chinese, but I was saying we have many things in common. And I pointed out that on our own behalf, we didn't have any troops massed on their border. We were not pursuing an expansionist policy. We were not invading another country, such as Afghanistan or doing

what they're doing in Kampuchea. Now, is that harsh rhetoric, or is that telling the simple truth?

Q. Mr. President, relations between the U.S. and U.S.S.R. have really hit a new low, almost cold war dimensions in the eyes of some experts. What is the real reason for this? What are you going to do about it? Do you think that your rhetoric—you say no now—and/or your actions have contributed to this? Or is it all their fault? What are they up to?

The President. Well, Helen [Helen Thomas, United Press International], sometimes I wonder why we don't ask those questions of them. Why is it that it's almost a pattern that the United States is possibly doing something that might cause the threat of war or that—what should we—we didn't walk away from the table. In fact, we made some efforts to bring them back to the table by showing them how flexible we were willing to be in these discussions. And they didn't come back. It was my—there were people who said that my rhetoric wasn't harsh enough after they shot down a civilian airliner with 269 innocent people aboard.

Soviet Boycott of the Olympics

Q. Well, what's the reason for the boycott?

The President. What?

Q. The real reason for the boycott?

The President. Again, you'd have to ask them. The reasons they have given are absolutely false—and we've been able to prove it—the reasons that there might not be sufficient security for their visitors, their athletes, and so forth. And we were able to prove no one in the history of the Olympics has ever done as much as we're doing to ensure that.

Andrea [Andrea Mitchell, NBC News]? And then I'll come across——

Q. Mr. President, you have said in the past—in 1980 you said that you supported the boycott. This year, you're saying that politics have no place in an Olympic boycott. Why have you changed your position?

The President. Well, let's remember the different situation. The Soviets have now announced that they are not going to come because they don't believe that we can offer protection to their athletes. And, as I say, we have been given—we've given them chapter and verse on what we have done, and there had never been anything like it.

Now, in 1980, the reason for the boycott that was given by the then administration was because the Soviets had invaded—openly invaded with their own forces—a neighboring country, Afghanistan, that hadn't done any thing to them or lifted a finger against them.

I think this was a completely different situation. It is true, however, that I went through several stages of thinking then. It wasn't just an automatic accepting of the politicizing of that. I was as angry as anyone, I'm sure, as we all were, and as disapproving of the invasion of Afghanistan—and still am. But at the time, I did voice a question as to—I questioned our government setting a precedent of denying the right of our own citizens to leave our borders and go someplace else.

I then thought in terms of shouldn't this decision be made by the free American citizens, the Olympic Committee, the athletes themselves? I went through a stage of thinking in which I said it wasn't so much of their not participating as, I said, shouldn't we—since the Olympics traditionally were born in and exist on the basis of trying to provide peace between nations—they, the host nation, having done what they did, should we not consider removing the Olympics from that country and staging them someplace else? And from that I went to exploring what so many have and are exploring now: possibly having the Olympics from now on be in the home of their origin, Greece, and not have them move around the world.

Q. But, sir, your final decision, your final statement back in 1981, that you supported the boycott—now Jesse Jackson and some others have said that you should personally intervene and try to intercede with the Soviets. The government position has been that it's not a government-to-government problem; it should be handled by the Olympic Committee. Would you consider taking some action to intervene?

The President. I don't think there's any action that I could take that would be prudent. I would—naturally, I would do anything if I thought it could have a result, and I have encouraged citizens groups and our people to do this. It is not a government relation problem.

El Salvador Election

Q. Mr. President, to switch the subject for a moment, Senator Helms has said that the United States bought the election in El Salvador. Could you tell us, please, exactly what was the financial involvement of the CIA and other Government agencies?

The President. I don't think that there was any attempt by any agency of the United States Government to participate in a partisan fashion in that election. There has been overtly, not covertly, aid given to labor unions, to trade associations, within the very framework of the program that I announced before the British Parliament a couple of years ago, and that is the idea of trying to help democracy by strengthening those organizations within a country that lead toward democracy, such as free labor unions, and so forth. And we have helped finance those.

Now, it's possible that some of those groups then, just as our own do, decide to take a partisan stand in support of someone in an election. But that had nothing to do with the helping to fund those organizations, nor do we intervene with what they may want to do.

Q. Have you talked to Senator Helms about his remarks?

The President. No, I've had no conversation with him.

Q. Mr. President, so you're saying that the reports or allegations that the CIA covertly gave money to some of the parties or are involved is untrue?

The President. What I'm saying is that I'm not going to discuss intelligence matters of that kind or what an agency like the CIA may do. But I'm here to tell you that I am assured that we have not tried to participate as a government in any way in the elections in El Salvador.

And I'd like to call to your attention that the group that just went down there to observe this election—and we've done this every election—but this last group, completely bipartisan and with some people who admittedly went down there with a different idea, came back and reported to me—and you can check with any of them—that they made every effort to view this from the standpoint of eligibility to vote right on up to the counting. And they were totally enthused and convinced that this election was fair, that the people were enthusiastically in support of it, and that they found no evidence of anything, even judging to the point of the suspected thing of the military may be influencing people. They saw only the military in protection of the right of the people to vote. They reported that they were very courteous about answering questions or directing people to where they needed to go and so forth.

They found not a thing wrong or any hint of any dishonesty or fraud in the election.

U.S.-Soviet Relations

Q. Mr. President, many observers think the Soviets have boycotted the Olympics to make a political point—the point being that they can't do business with you, that you are a dangerous man, and thus, apparently try to hurt your reelection chances. Do you think that's their motive?

The President. I don't know. You'd have to ask them about that. But, Sam [Sam Donaldson, ABC News], I have to tell you—a little thing with you. The other day, I had in my possession a kind of a scholarly type magazine—I can't even give you the name of it now—that had been given to me, dated April 1980. And on the plane over in China, I gave it to George Shultz, because I thought he would be interested. It was one of those where there are a whole series of essays in the magazine on various national and international topics. And I gave it to him, because one of the essays was on Soviet-American relations.

And there hasn't been an adjective used or a word spoken with regard to our relations now that I did not see in that article—where the relations were at the lowest ebb they had ever been. They were frozen tight, and the President—the then President of the United States, according to the essay, was to blame for this terrible relationship.

What have we done to the Soviets that can compare with any of the things that they are presently doing except tell them that we're not going to let them get so powerful that they can impose nuclear blackmail on us and that we are willing to meet them in arms reductions to the point of total disarmament, if they would be willing to meet in that?

Q. But, sir, if they are trying to influence our election, do you think it would backfire?

The President. I don't know how to assess that. I don't know. It might.

Q. Say, yes. [*Laughter*]

Q. Mr. President——

Mr. Speakes.[1] That's all we have time for, Mike [Michael Gelb, Reuters].

I'm sorry. Ten minutes is up.

Q. He wants to go on.

Q. You can—you can take the question.

Q. This is a very important question.

Mr. Speakes. How do you know?

Federal Reserve Board

Q. Mr. President, could you tell us if you think the Federal Reserve Board is responsible for the rise in interest rates and what sort of policies the Fed should be following?

The President. I've got to answer that one, Larry. And that's it then. I was—I was going to walk out on it, but you've just asked a touchy one.

Q. [*Inaudible*]—preview of the Michael Jackson—Michael Jackson album that—preview of that? It's a new album that's yet to be released.

The President. No. The question on the Fed is—I think that one of the reasons for the interest rates is still a lack of confidence out there that we do have inflation under control. What we want from the Fed is for the—we want the money supply to be increased at a range that is commensurate with the increase in the growth in the economy and that will thus make possible the continued growth of the economy without a return to inflation. So, therefore, we want no great big upsurges, nor do we want any string-tightening down to the point that

---

[1] *Larry M. Speakes, Principal Deputy Press Secretary to the President.*

there is not enough money supply in the economy.

Now, I have to say also, in behalf of the Fed, we must recognize these tools are not all that accurate that they have to work with. It is possible for there to be for limited times an inadvertent upsurge or an inadvertent decline that the Fed doesn't have anything to do with. They do as well as they can in trying to keep this projected growth.

Q. Well, are you backing off of the criticism by Secretary Regan?

The President. I think that that was what Secretary Regan was also trying to say. There was a downsurge recently. And that slump could have been—what I say—inadvertent. But as far as we know, they are within the two brackets. They have an upper line and a lower line, and they try to keep the increase within those lines.

Q. That was his hidden message.

Q. Are you sorry you appointed Volcker—reappointed him?

Q. How about a glove? Have you considered a glove?

Q. Special Prosecutor, Mr. President? What about the Special Prosecutor in the Carter briefing papers?

Mr. Speakes. That's all we've got——

The President. Just lead off with all of your articles and reporting that the Congress should approve the funding for MX, and I'll be happy.

Q. As Michael Jackson would say, beat it. [*Laughter*]

Note: The President spoke at 1:01 p.m. in the Briefing Room at the White House.

Announcement of Proposed Legislation To Reduce Funding for the National Synthetic Fuels Program
May 14, 1984

The President announced today that he will transmit legislation to the Congress that would reshape the Nation's synthetic fuels program while reducing its estimated total cost by $9.5 billion.

The legislation would rescind $9.5 billion of the $19 billion appropriated by Congress in 1980 for support of synthetic fuels. It would also limit the use of the remaining funds to those projects whose products will not cost significantly more than the projected market price of competing fuels.

The President's proposal is the result of careful review within the administration and reflects an effort to strike a balance between avoiding unnecessary and wasteful expenditures of scarce Federal dollars and preserving a sound, sensibly scaled national synthetic fuels program.

The administration also announced the President's intent to nominate three individuals to fill the current vacancies on the Board of Directors of the Synthetic Fuels Corporation. A fourth nomination is currently in progress.

Enactment of the proposed legislation would leave the Synthetic Fuels Corporation with approximately $4.6 billion in unobligated funds that could be used to support a wide array of carefully selected private synthetic fuels projects. These projects would be in addition to the four major synthetic fuels projects and other alternative energy grants totaling approximately $5 billion that have received Federal support from the funds appropriated to the Energy Security Reserve in 1980.

The Synthetic Fuels Corporation was established in 1980 with the enactment of the Energy Security Act of 1980 for the purpose of providing financial assistance to commercial-scale synthetic fuels projects.

Remarks at a White House Ceremony on the 1984 Olympic Torch Relay
May 14, 1984

Members of the Congress, distinguished guests, and friends of the Olympics, it's a pleasure to welcome you and to have this opportunity to take part in this ceremony.

The 1984 Olympic Torch Relay carries on in the footsteps of 10 previous Olympics. By the time the torch reaches the Los Angeles Coliseum on July 28th, it will have passed through 33 States, more than a thousand communities, and, as you've probably guessed, through the District of Columbia.

But I believe this year's relay is truly special, because it's giving something back to our young people. Thanks to the generosity of thousands of Americans, we now have a multimillion-dollar fund to promote and expand amateur sport training. I'm so pleased that the Legacy for Youth Program will help the Special Olympics, the family YMCA's, Boys' Clubs and Girls' Clubs of America strengthen their commitment to the growth and well-being of young people all across America.

The Olympic torch, the symbol of continuity between the ancient and modern Olympic games, was a proud tradition. It is now in our hands, and the United States is totally committed to upholding the Olympic Charter and the traditions which this torch represents. As the host nation for the games of the 23d Olympiad, we will fulfill our responsibilities. Athletes and Olympic officials of all countries will find a warm welcome in Los Angeles and will be treated equally and without discrimination.

As you know, the Los Angeles Olympic Organizing Committee and the International Olympic Committee have done everything possible to create a hospitable climate in which all participants will be able to perform to the best of their ability. And I have instructed agencies of the Federal Government to cooperate fully with Olympic and local officials to ensure the safety of all participants.

We consider sport to be one of the finest opportunities for people of all nations to come and to know and to understand each other. And in sport, nothing can match the competition of the Olympics. The Olympics provide the ultimate experience in watching athletes strive through honest effort, fair play, discipline, and determination to reach the top. Athletes know better than anyone that there is more, much more, to the Olympic experience than winning medals. It's the personal striving, the ability to achieve the fullest measure of human potential that counts most. Athletes look to their sport with a common mind, knowing that they will never go fast enough to say, "This is as fast as we can go." There will always be a new standard to aim for—that last fraction of an inch, that extra second.

Athletes all over the world live by the Olympic motto: Swifter, higher, stronger. Olympics breed inspiration. Who will ever forget Jesse Owens' achievements in 1936; Bob Beamon's 29-foot, 2½-inch broadjump in Mexico City? The thrill of striving for excellence in sports, as in other areas of our lives, fires our imagination, stirs us to dream great dreams, and often enables us to achieve them. By embracing the Olympic tradition, we have reason to look to the future with optimism and hope because the Olympic spirit carries beyond the field of competition.

Do we place too much emphasis on sports or expect too much of them? I don't think so. The Olympics were started more than 2,000 years ago to hopefully offer a substitute to the constant warfare between the city-states of Greece. They were revived on an international basis nearly a century ago, and again, the goal was peace and understanding. Let us keep that Olympic tradition alive in Los Angeles and resolve that the Olympic flame will burn ever brighter.

And now, let's get that Olympic torch on to Los Angeles. I'll see you all there, and thank you, and God bless you all.

Note: The President spoke at 5:14 p.m. on the South Lawn at the White House.

Following the President's remarks, Kurt

Thomas, a former Olympic gymnast, passed the flame from his torch to that of Char- *lotte Pearson, a member of the Special Olympics team.*

Remarks at the Welcoming Ceremony for President Miguel De la Madrid Hurtado of Mexico
May 15, 1984

President Reagan. Mr. President, it's an honor and a pleasure for Nancy and me to welcome you and Mrs. De la Madrid to Washington. We welcome you with the respect and admiration due to the leader of a great nation. We welcome you also with the warmth and good will with which one greets a friend.

A special relationship between the Presidents of our countries is becoming somewhat of a tradition, and the rapport we build as individuals is in keeping with the finest sense of that valuable tradition. Our ability to meet and, face to face, discuss the issues of the day, honestly and without reservation, is beneficial to both our countries. The trust between us is something of great value which should never be taken for granted.

Mr. President, I well recall first making your acquaintance in June of 1981 at Camp David. And the next time we met, you were President-elect of Mexico, and we agreed then, even before you were sworn into office, to maintain a continuing dialog and to meet and confer often. Your visit today builds upon the professional and personal bonds about which I'm speaking.

We have much to discuss. That is as one would expect between the elected leaders of two countries whose people, by the millions, interact with each other on a daily basis. Not only are our destinies tied, but in ways too numerous to count, our present as well.

Mr. President, we're fully aware of your commitment to overcoming Mexico's current economic difficulties. We applaud your dedication and wish you success in your drive to invigorate your economy and better the lives of your people. Our support represents the best wishes of a friend and more.

Mexico is now the third largest trading partner of the United States. We, on the other hand, are the world's largest market for Mexican goods. The prosperity and happiness of our peoples are inexorably linked by these bonds of commerce and friendship. I hope when you return home that you will bring the message to your citizens that the American people are on your, the people of Mexico's side.

The United States and Mexico have a common border and a common American heritage as well. The people of our countries—Spanish- and English-speaking alike—represent the values and culture of the New World, a bond shared by 650 million Americans from the North Slope of Alaska to the tip of Tierra del Fuego. It behooves all of us to work together to ensure the peace and stability of our hemisphere.

That is especially true in regard to Central America. Mr. President, I understand your deep concerns about the turmoil plaguing that region. We do not agree on everything concerning this situation. Yet, the level of respect in our relationship remains high, and that is the way it should be between neighbors who trust each other.

Where we do disagree is not on goals or principles. Instead, it is on the means by which to achieve our goals. The magnitude of our agreement, on the other hand, is substantial and should not be underestimated. Both the United States and Mexico are motivated by a love of liberty and independence inherent in our systems of government and embedded in the souls of our people.

As you said in your book on constitutional law while assessing Rousseau's influence, "Liberty and equality are values incompatible with despotism, and mankind will not benefit from them while there may be oppressors and oppressed." Our fundamental beliefs suggest that a lasting peace for Central America must be based on the principles of democracy, on economic development that expands opportunity for all people, on noninterventionism, and on the avoidance of military cooperation with Communist and other aggressor regimes.

We appreciate the creative and energetic efforts to bring peace to the region by the Contadora group, in which Mexico has participated. The Contadora's 21-point document of objectives enunciates the goals we both support. We pray that the consensus that produced the document of objectives can translate what has already been done into sound treaty provisions that can be monitored, verified, and enforced on a reciprocal basis.

For the United States, the conflagration in Central America appears too close to ignore. Like a fire in one's neighborhood, this threat should be of concern to every nation in the hemisphere. We can and should work together to save lives and prevent further destruction.

Complicating the situation and making it even more dangerous has been the intervention of a totalitarian coalition which has undermined what we had hoped would be a democratic revolution. These totalitarians have been pouring gasoline onto the fire by pumping massive supplies of weapons into Central America and encouraging tyranny and aggression. Thousands of Cubans and Soviet-bloc military personnel have accompanied this flow of weapons and equipment into the region.

Responsible governments of this hemisphere cannot afford to close their eyes to what is happening or to be lulled by unrealistic optimism. I look forward to discussing with you, Mr. President, this issue of utmost importance.

President De la Madrid, earlier this year, you visited Buenos Aires where you said, "We do not want new conflicts and wars in our vast territory. We need peace and well-being. We do not want martyrs from warlike confrontations. We are civilian heroes." Well, I agree with that sentiment completely.

Let me reaffirm today that the United States will do what it can. It will go the extra mile to find peaceful solutions and to protect democracy and independence in the hemisphere.

Cooperation and respect between the United States and Mexico will do much in our efforts to promote peace and improve the standard of living of our people. As adversaries, our horizons would be limited. As friends, equal in each other's eyes and drawing from each other's strength, a universe of opportunity awaits.

Mr. President, I speak for all the citizens of my country when I say your friends welcome you to the United States.

President De la Madrid. Mr. President, I thank you and your distinguished wife for your cordial welcome.

I have come here to continue a personal dialog that we began in San Diego in 1982 and continued in La Paz in 1983. Being constantly in touch has allowed us to become better acquainted and, in our friendly and honorable dealings, to more effectively meet our responsibility to solve the problems and overcome the obstacles in the wide-ranging and complex relations between our two countries.

It is with great pleasure that I transmit through you warm greetings from the people of Mexico to the great people of the United States of America. We Mexicans wish to continue building not only peaceful and dignified neighborly relations but also a fruitful and positive friendship. Our two countries are reliable neighbors and friends, and we know how to conduct our relations in mutual respect for our independence and our cultural and political concepts.

We have learned to solve our problems with serenity and realism. Two peoples with different histories and cultures with imbalances and disparities have found the path of dialog and communication to be the basis for their understanding. The wide range and diversity of our bilateral relations highlight our dialog.

Our talks will cover trade and tourism, financing and investment, the very close relationship between our border zones, and human and labor aspects of the Mexican workers who migrate to the United States, to name only some of the most important topics. Progress has been made in several of these areas since the last time we spoke to each other. In others, solutions are pending, as will always be the case in our dynamic relations. The important thing, Mr. President, is that we must continue to tackle our problems frankly and in good faith, and that we, with imagination and determination, seek the best possible solutions for the benefit of our countries.

I must acknowledge, Mr. President, that I have always found this to be your attitude and that of your associates. Your government has supported various financial programs for overcoming our economic problems, and it has also been willing to help surmount difficulties in our trade relations. We must broaden and enhance this open attitude to dialog and negotiation.

Our exchange of ideas goes beyond solely bilateral matters. Both countries are members of the international community, and we share responsibilities on the American Continent. We are all concerned about threats to peace, the problem of the arms race, and the severe economic crisis that is hampering the efforts of developing countries to pursue their goal of economic and social progress in order to satisfy their people's legitimate ambitions and to banish hunger, unhealthy conditions, ignorance, and poverty.

The United States and Mexico should be concerned, as well, about the specially serious difficulties that Latin American countries are experiencing. Peace has been disrupted in Central America, and the risk of a generalized war, the scope and duration of which no one can foresee, is growing. Every country on the continent must do its utmost to restore peace and avoid war by respecting and upholding the sovereign right of its people to decide their own destiny and by rejecting interventionist solutions of any kind.

In peacetime, we must also support the Central Americans in their social and economic development programs and encourage their efforts to build democracy and respect human rights. To that end, let us apply the principles and rules of international law established by the countries of the American Continent: self-determination, nonintervention, equality of states before the law, peaceful solution of conflicts, and international cooperation for development.

Latin America is suffering the most severe economic crisis of modern times. Its peoples and governments have been obliged to implement harsh economic programs to cope with the situation. We are correcting the internal imbalances that come under our responsibility: the reduction of fiscal deficits and the imbalance in our commercial and financial accounts with foreign countries. The Mexican people are giving ample proof of their vigor and responsibility.

Nonetheless, our determined efforts require international understanding and cooperation in the field of trade and finance so that international conditions do not frustrate domestic actions. The crucial point is external debt servicing and the high and rising interest rates. In the short term, it is necessary to take effective action on the cost of money. The broadest and most far-reaching solution is to recover our payment capacity so that we can meet our debt obligations to regain our purchasing power abroad, to renew the process of economic growth, and to generate employment, thereby strengthening the basis of stability.

Solutions are not easy. It is we who must make the basic effort. We have already shown that we are both willing and able to do so. Now we ask the international community and essentially the industrialized countries to accept that. Since interdependence is an irreversible fact, the imperative of solidarity is a duty based not only on ethics but also on expedience.

Mr. President, I have no doubt that in a climate of frankness and friendship our talks will enhance our understanding of these topics, and we will be able to find new solutions to the problems that concern us. Mr. President, I thank you very much for your warm welcome.

Note: President Reagan spoke at 10:10 a.m. on the South Lawn of the White House, where President De la Madrid was accorded a formal welcome with full military honors. President De la Madrid spoke in Spanish, and his remarks were translated by an interpreter.

Following the ceremony, the two Presidents met privately in the Oval Office.

They then joined U.S. and Mexican officials for a meeting in the Cabinet Room.

Nomination of James Henry Quello To Be a Member of the Federal Communications Commission
May 15, 1984

The President today announced his intention to nominate James Henry Quello to be a member of the Federal Communications Commission for a term of 7 years from July 1, 1984. This is a reappointment.

Since 1974 Mr. Quello has been a member of the Federal Communications Commission. In 1972–1974 he was a communications consultant in Michigan. In 1947–1972 he was vice president and station manager for Goodwill Stations, Inc., in Detroit, MI.

While in Michigan, Mr. Quello served as a member of the Governor's Special Commission on Urban Problems, the Governor's Special Study Committee on Legislative Compensation, the Mayor's Committee on Human Relations, and as assistant national public relations chairman for the VFW.

He graduated from Michigan State University (B.A., 1935). He is married, has two children, and resides in Alexandria, VA. He was born April 21, 1914, in Laurium, MI.

Proclamation 5194—Missing Children Day, 1984
May 15, 1984

By the President of the United States of America

A Proclamation

Each year hundreds of thousands of American families face the stark terror of a unique tragedy—that of a missing child. Our children are our most precious resource—they are the bond that binds our past with the future. It is for them that we struggle to build a better world. They are the embodiment of our hopes and dreams. To have a child simply disappear strikes an incalculable blow against the spirit and soul of any family so afflicted.

In our efforts to address the nightmare of missing children, 1984 marks the year of a significant step forward. The Department of Justice has awarded a $3.3 million grant to establish a National Center for Missing and Exploited Children. Its purpose is to aid parents and law enforcement agencies in locating missing youngsters and preventing the exploitation of children. By collecting and disseminating information regarding missing young people, the Center will lend major support to those searching for their children.

As a Nation committed to the worth of every individual, there can be no more imperative goal for our society than the protection and safety of our young people. It is hoped that these new efforts combined with the increasing awareness of the seriousness of this problem will encourage greater vigilance by the agencies that work to solve this singular type of crime.

As a Nation and as individuals, we all have a responsibility to direct our resources and our efforts to this worthy goal.

Now, Therefore, I, Ronald Reagan, President of the United States of America, do hereby proclaim May 25, 1984, as Missing Children Day. I urge officials at all levels of government to take decisive action to ensure the safety and protection of the children in their respective jurisdictions, and I urge all our law enforcement agencies to take particular notice of the danger that threatens any child who has lost his or her home. I urge every American family to take the proper precautions to protect their children.

In Witness Whereof, I have hereunto set my hand this 15th day of May, in the year of our Lord nineteen hundred and eighty-four, and of the Independence of the United States of America the two hundred and eighth.

RONALD REAGAN

[*Filed with the Office of the Federal Register, 10:55 a.m., May 16, 1984*]

Appointment of Five Members of the National Cancer Advisory Board
May 15, 1984

The President today announced his intention to appoint the following individuals to be members of the National Cancer Advisory Board for terms expiring March 9, 1990:

Roswell K. Boutwell is director of research for the Radiation Energy Research Foundation in Hiroshima, Japan. He is on leave from McArdle Laboratory for Cancer Research at the University of Wisconsin, where he is a professor of oncology. He is married and has three children. He was born November 24, 1917, in Madison, WI. This is a reappointment.

Helene G. Brown is director for community applications at Jonsson Comprehensive Cancer Center at the University of California at Los Angeles. Since 1977 she has served as chairman of the education committee for the American Cancer Society. She is married, has two children, and resides in Sherman Oaks, CA. She was born May 3, 1929, in New York City. She will succeed Morris M. Schrier.

Gertrude B. Elion is scientist emeritus, Wellcome Research Labs, Research Triangle Park, NC, and serves as research professor of pharmacology and medicine at Duke University Medical Center. Dr. Elion resides in Chapel Hill, NC. She was born January 23, 1918, in New York City. She will succeed Janet Davison Rowley.

David Korn is professor and chairman of the department of pathology at Stanford Medical School in Stanford, CA. He was chairman of the board of scientific counselors, division of cancer biology and diagnosis, National Cancer Institute in 1980–1982. He is married, has three children, and resides in Stanford. He was born March 5, 1933, in Providence, RI. He will succeed Sheldon W. Samuels.

Louise Connally Strong is associate professor of medical genetics, associate geneticist, and associate professor of pediatrics and biology at the University of Texas System Cancer Center, M.D. Anderson Hospital and Tumor Institute in Houston, TX. She is married, has two children, and resides in Houston. She was born April 23, 1944, in San Antonio, TX. She will succeed Maureen McGrath Henderson.

Toasts of President Reagan and President Miguel De la Madrid Hurtado of Mexico at the State Dinner
May 15, 1984

President Reagan. President and Mrs. De la Madrid, distinguished ladies and gentlemen, it's been our pleasure to have you as our guests this evening.

Being here with so many friends from Mexico, I can't help but take my thoughts back to California. Tonight is reminiscent of the gala evenings in old California, the vineyards, the music, the pride and accomplishments of the Hispanic frontier men and women, individuals who conquered a wilderness, but while doing so, maintained a phenomenal level of dignity. All of this,

703

and more, reflects the character of a people whose legacy is now shared by the citizens of our two countries.

I'm not certain it goes back as far as the *hacienda* days, but I would like to extend to you a traditional greeting that I've adopted as my own, just as I adopted California. President and Mrs. De la Madrid, *mi casa es su casa* [my house is your house].

Today we've had frank and fulfilling discussions. Mr. President, I hope you agree with me that although we do not see eye to eye on everything, it is clear that we as individuals, and our two nations as well, remain solid in our friendship and undeterred in our trust.

The good will between us goes far beyond the transitory issues of the day. Our people recognize that issues, even those that seem important at the moment, will someday pass from the scene. What will not change are the many gifts and mandates given to us by God that serve as the basis of our societies. I can't believe that the Lord brought us to this level of political, social, and economic development, that He located us—the Mexican and American people—in such proximity and did not intend us to be friends.

In the last 50 years, when people of bordering countries in so many parts of the world were killing each other, or were immersed in envy and hatred, the mutual respect and ever-increasing cooperation between our peoples and governments shined in contrast.

Our trade and commerce is a powerful engine for economic progress for both our countries. The cultural and social ties between our people enrich and add diversity and flavor to our everyday lives. Yet the cement with the strongest grip is found in the ideals and values that our people share.

President Thomas Jefferson, a man so important to the development of human liberty, outlined in his first inaugural address some of the aspirations of our new republic. Although spoken 183 years ago, the words still ring true. Our desire in foreign affairs, he said, was "equal and exact justice to all men, of whatever state or persuasion, religious or political; peace, commerce and honest friendship with all nations. . . ."

I heard an echo of these sentiments last August in La Paz when you, Mr. President, said, "Nationalism, cultural identity, freedom, democracy, economic development with social justice, an independent foreign policy, and defense of our territorial integrity are shared values embodied in our national design and vital bonds that link us all."

Mr. President, if we can be guided by these principles with our shared values and interests overshadowing momentary disagreements, surely the good will between us will endure, and our relationship will continue to shine as an example to others.

And now will all of you join me in a toast to our honored guests—to President and Mrs. De la Madrid, to their health, and to the continued good will between our two great nations.

President De la Madrid. President Reagan, Mrs. Reagan, may my first words be to express my gratitude for the kind courtesies that we have received during our visit to Washington today. Both during our work meetings and today, during this dinner, we have seen proofs of affectionate and cordial friendship that both my wife, myself, and the members of my party appreciate very much.

This kind of a dialog is also always fruitful. It makes it possible for us to compare our analysis and evaluation, our perceptions of reality, to agree on our similarities, and also to know our differences.

Geography has influenced both of us. It has led us to be neighbors, and it has led us to be friends. Neighbors we are because geography is as it is, but friends is something that comes from our own self. It is a quality of the human being.

Friends always seek to extend areas of consensus and to make their differences smaller, to seek formulas to overcome the problems that come from our close, complex, and very broad relationship. Friendship presupposes all of this. There must be sincerity and frankness, dignity and respect in our dealings, careful examination of our discrepancies and above all, it demands good will.

Differences of opinion are natural and can be explained among human beings. They can be explained among us. Even though Mexico and the United States have often traveled the same road, even though they stem from the same roots, there are differences in our culture, and these differences have made our sensibilities also different. It has come to enrich the human race, because it is variation which is needed for this enrichment. It is not good for everyone to be just the same.

In this way, Americans and Mexicans find themselves face to face with a rich culture and a rich and profound perception of our nationalities. But there are not only differences among us—or between us; analogies are also evident.

Both nations have rooted their political and social systems in the aspiration to live in freedom, to permanently build democracy, and to seek the equality of opportunity for all. Both nations postulate respect for law and justice as a norm for peaceful and dignified coexistence. And that which makes our two countries similar, Mr. President, is that we are not societies that are frozen and opposed to change. We are societies that are open to change.

We who love freedom must be open to change. We cannot freeze the human spirit. And it is for this reason that we are also obliged to be tolerant.

President Reagan, our conversations have been honorable and cordial. They reflect our common purpose: to extend the areas in which we agree and to reduce our differences. But the road to travel is a long one. The life of individuals has a limit, but the life of nations does not have a historical horizon.

The important thing about this meeting is that we have renewed our will to continue to travel that road as individuals and as nations that are living in good faith. As I said before, during the luncheon that was kindly offered me by Secretary Shultz, we know that you want to have dignified, prosperous, and strong neighbors.

It is very important that a powerful nation such as the United States, which is the most powerful nation of all, can say to the other countries, "We have neighbors who are dignified; they are not slaves." I, therefore, President Reagan, express my hope that this relationship with dignity and cordiality that has been built by the Americans and the Mexicans will always be the common denominator of our relationship, that we shall always be capable with talent and good will to continue to strengthen our friendship to our mutual benefit.

This is the thinking and the will of the Mexican people. And I am certain that there is this same thinking and this same will in the United States. That is why I express my wishes that the relations between Mexico and the United States will always be vigorous, that they may be strengthened by our will to understanding, and because friendship and cooperation is what will bring us together.

I wish to ask you to join me in a toast to the personal happiness of President Reagan and his charming wife, Nancy, to the happiness and prosperity of the American people, and to those values which we cherish, which are freedom, democracy, and justice.

Note: President Reagan spoke at 10 p.m. in the State Dining Room at the White House. President De la Madrid spoke in Spanish, and his remarks were translated by an interpreter.

Remarks at a White House Meeting With the American Retail Federation
May 16, 1984

Good afternoon, I'm glad to welcome you—I know you've probably been welcomed by others already—you, the merchants of America, back to the White House.

It's hard to believe that 2 years have passed since we last met—2 short years, but what a difference. As you probably remember, when we met in the Rose Garden, I didn't have very much good news to give you. The American people had paid a steep price for years of good intentions badly misdirected. And as a result, our national economy had nearly reached the breaking point. As a result of that crisis that faced us—well, we weren't, however, pursuing a program based on the shifting sands of government expediency. Another quick fix certainly would have failed. There was only one way to go, and that was use three simple words as our guide: Trust the people.

Lasting economic recovery had to be built on the solid rock of the American free enterprise system. And when I think back to all the critics who cynically said we couldn't possibly get it done, I find myself remembering my previous life in the entertainment world.

You know, back in the days of vaudeville, vaudevillians trying to get bookings and even young ones trying to break into the show business would go into an empty theater, and there'd be an agent sitting out there in about the third row, all alone in the theater, cigar in his mouth, wearing a check suit and—[*laughter*]—the vaudevillian would have to show his wares to this cynic. And one day a young fellow came in—the agent was sitting out there—and this young fellow who wanted to break into show business walked down to the stage and the agent said, "All right, kid, what do you do?" And the kid never answered. He just took off and flew around the ceiling of the theater, made a couple of circles right up there at the top, and then zoomed down and stopped right in front of the agent. The agent took the cigar out of his mouth and says, "What else do you do besides bird imitations?" [*Laughter*]

Well, I've felt that way quite a bit about some of the people that were so critical of what we were trying to do here. There are still some of them around, and they think what we're doing are bird imitations. [*Laughter*] But as far as I'm concerned we've passed the recovery stage; we're well into economic expansion. And from the mess we inherited just a few years ago, I think a strong and vibrant America is taking shape.

Inflation, once out of control—they said it would take 10 years, at least, to make a dent in it—it's now down by nearly two-thirds, and we're determined to keep it down.

Purchasing power is back in the hands of the consumers, and that's great news for retailers. And we're doing everything we can to keep it that way. Starting next year, tax rates will be indexed, as you know, so that the Federal Government will no longer be able to profit by inflation. And we're not finished yet.

To provide greater incentives to every hard-working American, we're going to try to make taxes more simple and fair, and we will press for a tax simplification—not just tinkering here and there—but a sweeping, comprehensive reform of the entire tax code. One thing I've had to rule out already is one proposal that was sent to me recently. It was a tax form, and it had just two lines on it. The top line said, "How much did you earn?" And the second one said, "Send it." [*Laughter*] We won't do that.

But I know there's a lot of talk about the monster, inflation, coming back. We don't think that's happening. Consumer prices rose a scant two-tenths of a percent in March, and last month the Producer Price Index didn't rise at all. The pessimists made dire predictions about the economy when it was announced that the gross national product for the first quarter this year expanded at a robust 8.3 percent. Overheating, they warned, would cause a return of inflation. But the economy isn't conforming to their fears.

Housing starts continue to be soft—or strong, I should say. I looked at the wrong word there. [*Laughter*] Somebody's probably told you, but if they have, well, I'm going to tell it to you again: At 8:30 this morning, it was announced that housing starts in April rose to an annual rate of 1.96 million, and that's an increase of 19 percent over March. And new housing permits are still holding steady at 1.7 million. New homeowners mean more retail business.

Venture capital is up to four times what it was in 1980. Real fixed business investment increased by 13 percent last year, and that's the best increase in 30 years. Bankruptcies declined some 30 percent in the second half of '83, and that was compared with the second half of '82.

The best news of all has been the steepest drop in unemployment in over 30 years— 5.4 million more Americans are working— have jobs—than just 17 months ago. And it's no wonder that the retail sales last year reached an all time high of $1.2 trillion. When *we* talk those figures, we're dealing in deficits. [*Laughter*]

We must and will go forward to keep opportunities expanding for you and for all Americans. Now, just in case you want to call or talk to someone in a nearby public building while you're in town, there are still a lot of things that we're trying to get done.

We want to see the business community grow and grow. We're working hard to be sensitive to your concerns. The Federal Trade Commission, with Jim Miller at the helm, has built a solid, balanced relationship with your industry. And we're pressing to get passage of legislation which would tighten up consumer credit provisions on Federal bankruptcy laws. I know this issue is important to you, so I hope you'll make your views known.

And we all have an interest in making sure that Federal spending is brought down into line with government revenues. And that's why I strongly favor constitutional reforms like giving the President the right to line-item veto and the balanced budget amendment. I have told repeatedly other groups that have been in here, as a Governor, in 8 years, I had line-item veto. And I line-item vetoed spending items that were attached to legitimate legislation 943 times in those 8 years, and never once when they were faced with having to vote for an override on that particular item and hold it up to view, not buried in some other legislation, they never overrode one of those 943 vetoes. And yet it took a two-thirds majority for them to send me the proposal in the first place.

So, I have no quarrel with the big spenders, so long as they spend their money at your stores. [*Laughter*] I just want them to stop spending our money on government programs that don't serve the interests of the American people.

Now, before I close, I want to take this opportunity to thank retailers all across America for the work that you're doing to help our young people find that crucial first job. When America's youth can get their feet on the first rung of the economic ladder, everybody benefits. You're taking advantage of the tax credit for hiring disadvantaged, minority youth. And I'd like to see you take even greater advantage of this program.

And while I'm at it, let me mention that more and more people recognize the problem the minimum wage causes for our unskilled young people. Our youth employment opportunity wage bill will give a much needed boost to those looking for their first summertime job, and it deserves your active support.

We can establish that the imposition of the minimum wage, and then the increases through the years, have been followed in every increase with a further decline in teenage employment in America. And so, we're trying to do something about it. And there's a lot of opposition to it, but I think it's necessary. Those unskilled young people should not have that handicap to overcome.

When it comes to the bottom line, if I can borrow a phrase that's the heartbeat of all retailers, it's a great time to be a merchant. But I believe that the best is yet to come. And I hope that your 46th meeting will be a great success, and thank you all for being here. God bless you.

Note: The President spoke at 1:20 p.m. in the East Room at the White House.

Remarks at the Annual Awards Dinner of the White House News Photographers Association
May 16, 1984

Thank you, Bob Hope—I think. [*Laughter*] Well, a special thanks to Bernie Boston, Ken Blaylock, Paul Lyons, and the dinner committee for doing such a fine job of putting all this together. And greetings to Buck May, the dean of White House photographers.

And now, I already know what's on your minds. [*Laughter*] You're all wondering whether I'm going to put my thumbs in my ears and waggle my fingers the way I did last year. [*Laughter*] Well, the answer is yes. But since, last time, Rich Lipski was quick enough with the camera to catch it, this year I'm going to make my moves a little bit faster, and I'm only going to do it once, so—what's going on back there? [*Laughter*] Well, you see, you missed it. [*Laughter*] Want to see it again? [*Laughter*]

Well, seriously, it's a pleasure to be here. You know, in Washington, there are a lot of big dinners like this, but tonight is special. I've been around photographers all my adult life, or most of it, and I think that I can say that I've developed an appreciation for your craft. So, it's as an old pro that I admire the work of each of you and that each of you performs. You demonstrate true professionalism and artistry. And time and again, I find myself pausing to admire a wonderful picture that one of you has produced.

As you record history in the making, you, yourselves, are a part of historic tradition. Ever since Mathew Brady took his stirring pictures of Abe Lincoln and the Civil War, photographs have been imparting immediacy to American news. And it isn't true that I carried Brady's camera. [*Laughter*] News photographs show us what's specific and vivid. A story might explain what happened during World War II, but it was a photo that gave us that unforgettable image of four marines struggling to hoist the Stars and Stripes on Iwo Jima.

And although news analysts might discuss the Presidency, it's your photos that show J.F.K. working in the Oval Office with John-

John playing under the desk or me giving a briefing with Nancy waiting in the wings to surprise me with a birthday cake. And pictures like that remind us the Presidency isn't an abstraction, but an office held by just ordinary men who do their job the best they can.

Often, news photos remind us of the first things, the fundamentals of human experience that make us do what we do. Living in the United States, for example, we might begin to take democracy for granted. And then we see a news photo of people lined up at ballot boxes in El Salvador—simple men and women who've braved death threats to travel into town and cast their votes. We see the care in their faces and the life of hard work in their shoulders and hands, and we remember once again why we strive for democracy and peace.

My admiration for news photographers goes to the root of my political philosophy. In too many countries, photographs of top officials are only released once in a while to show that the leaders are still healthy. But in our country, your right to snap anything you want is protected by the Constitution. And each of you represents a vital part of the great and lively American system of freedom.

Earlier this year, one event said it all—took place at an air base in South Carolina shortly after a plane had returned from Grenada carrying the medical students who'd been trapped at St. George's Medical School. As one student got off the plane, we all know he dropped to his knees and kissed the good earth of the United States, and nearby there was a news photographer, clicked his camera and caught that moment for all Americans to share. Although there will always be some hurly-burly and tugging between the White House and the press, I know that photo captured the way that all of us feel about this great land.

So, we just came by—they won't let us stay; we didn't dress. [*Laughter*] Anyway, I just want to thank you all for allowing us to

share even for a few minutes in this particular event.

God bless you, and keep up the good
work.

*Note: The President spoke at 7:54 p.m. in
the main ballroom at the Sheraton Washington Hotel.*

Remarks of President Reagan and President Miguel De la Madrid Hurtado of Mexico at the Annual Meeting of the Mexico-United States Interparliamentary Conference
May 17, 1984

President Reagan. Well, welcome. I think
it's a wonderful coincidence that these
meetings have coincided and that we have
an opportunity together to welcome you
here for your own meetings.

President De la Madrid and myself have
just concluded our second meeting. We've
had good conversations, and we both listened to what the other had to say.

I believe that we both sharpened our perceptions and, at the same time, know we
deepened our personal friendship. And like
good friends, we spoke openly and with
candor on those few issues on which there
might have been differences between us.
But let me hasten to say that we found that
the differences were not with regard to our
goals.

We both share a commitment to democracy, to the greater economic well-being,
and a secure peace in all the Americas. Our
differences, where there were any, were
only with regard to the means of reaching
the goals and objectives that we share. And
both our delegations at the ministerial level
worked very hard and, I think, have made
great progress on a number of bilateral
issues.

And let me just say to all of you here—
and I think I'm really speaking for what was
the tone of our conversations—we must remember that we are all in this Western
Hemisphere. Our nations were born of
people that were seeking the same things—
freedom, better life in this New World that
was here for our forefathers to discover.
We've been given great gifts, resources,
technology and, above all, that spirit of
freedom.

Early in my administration I made a trip

down through Central America and into
South America and in all of them said the
same thing. There have been misunderstandings between us in the past, and
maybe there's been an insensitivity on the
part of our own country, the United States.
But what I wanted to find out was, how
could we all meet as partners here in this
Western Hemisphere, recognizing that
from the tip of South America all the way
to the North Slope of Alaska, we are all
Americans. We are all related in a sense
that is not true in any other part of the
world—that when we cross a border from
one country into another, we still have that
common heritage.

And if we look at ourselves, 650 million
people in North, Central, and South America, and we look at the potential of what we
can achieve, we cannot only be a great
force for good here in the Western Hemisphere, we can be a great force for good in
the entire world.

And thank you again for being here.
Thank you very much. We're proud and
pleased to have you. Thank you.

President De la Madrid. Gentlemen, legislators of the United States and of Mexico,
it is a great pleasure for me to be able to
greet you at the beginning of a new inter-
parliamentary meeting between the United
States and Mexico.

In accordance with our constitutional
norms are the relations, the formal relations
of our countries are formed through a very
complex process that is in the hands of the
legislative and the executive bodies. It is
one of the most serious responsibilities that
this Presidential system gives the heads of

709

the executive branch, both in the United States and in Mexico. But there is no doubt that the political process through which the foreign policy is formed has as one of its basic ingredients the opinions of the Congresses and, particularly, of the Senates.

That is why it is very promising that this meeting among legislators is beginning precisely when the meeting between the Presidents has just finished. I agree with what my friend, President Reagan, has said just a few minutes back. Our dialog has progressed as it should between good friends that work with dignity. Both sides have been led by the main guideline of our conversations, which has been the interest of our peoples, mutual respect and, also, respect for one another's truth.

As President Reagan has already said, we have made progress during these conversations. We have made progress in coming to a better understanding of each other and also in keeping each other better informed and bringing about certain solutions to some of our problems, problems which are every day more complex and deeper between Mexico and the United States.

I have no doubt that the work that you will be beginning today will be another positive and constructive episode. An exchange of points of view within a framework of sincerity, of respect, and of dignity will give each one of our countries new elements of judgment in order to continue to work towards a stronger friendship and a relationship which is every day more cordial and more sincere.

Gentlemen, my best wishes for your success in your work.

Note: President Reagan spoke at 9:31 a.m. in the East Room at the White House. President De la Madrid spoke in Spanish, and his remarks were translated by an interpreter.

Prior to the meeting, the two Presidents had a breakfast meeting in the Blue Room.

Remarks at a White House Ceremony Marking the Beginning of the Summer Youth Employment Program
May 17, 1984

The President. Members of the Congress, Secretary Ray Donovan, our distinguished guests sharing the platform with me, and you ladies and gentlemen, good morning, and welcome to the White House.

I'm delighted to help kick off this 1984 summer youth employment program. And I want to congratulate all the Presidential Certificate Award winners for their dedication to the career development of America's youth and for their generous support of the 1983 private sector jobs program. It's times like this that remind us America was built by people helping people.

We're proud to honor you this morning. And I hope that next year your numbers will grow. Wouldn't it be great if we had to hold this out on the South Lawn—[*laughter*]—couldn't get it in the Rose Garden anymore.

Many of you'll recall that last July we held a similar ceremony right here in the Rose Garden. And since then, more than 3 million Americans have found jobs. In fact, since the economic expansion began 17 months ago, 5.4 million Americans have found jobs, and the unemployment rate has shown the sharpest drop—or the steepest drop in 30 years. Now, that's why when I'm asked to describe our economic program I do it with three words—jobs, jobs, jobs. But we can't rest until everyone who wants one and needs one has one.

We must and will go forward to keep opportunities expanding, particularly for the young people of America. No single sector of our nation—government, business, labor, or nonprofit organization—can solve the unemployment problem, the needs of our young people. But by working together, pooling our resources and building on our strengths, we can accomplish great things.

That's the whole idea behind our youth employment programs' public-private partnerships—to produce real, not makework, jobs.

Partnerships take advantage of opportunities to help America's youth gain a foothold on the economic ladder. Young people who want to work in the summer deserve the chance, and partnerships can make it happen.

The summer youth employment program includes a $725 million block grant to State and local governments. This grant will give 718,000 young Americans valuable work experience, but it's only part of our effort to help deserving young people get a start. Another program in place gives employers who hire economically disadvantaged teenagers a tax credit of up to 85 percent of the wages paid. The employers get a young employee the company may not be able to afford without the tax break, and the young worker gets a needed job and valuable work experience in the private sector.

Mr. Austin Cunningham of Orangeburg, South Carolina, who is with us today, can tell you how well the targeted jobs tax credit program works. After he discovered the program, Mr. Cunningham promoted the idea to 77 other small business men and women in Orangeburg. Together, they hired 264 economically disadvantaged young people. For most of these 16- and 17-year-olds it was their first real job. And when the summer was over, many of them were asked to stay on full-time even though the tax credit no longer applied. Now, that's partnership in action, and everybody's better off because of it.

What we're trying to do is help our young people find that critical first job. With experience in the workplace, America's youth can develop skills and demonstrate their qualifications and potential—permanent employers.

But far too often, inexperienced and disadvantaged young people are priced out of the labor market by the minimum wage. Well, Ray Donovan and a lot of other people here today have put together legislation that will give a much-needed boost to those looking for that first job. Today I will submit our youth employment opportunity wage act to the Congress. And Senators Percy and Hatch and Congressman Pack-

ard, who have worked hard on this bill, will introduce it on the Hill in behalf of the administration and the American people.

This legislation would allow employers to hire young people at a lower minimum wage during the summer months. The bill would increase summer employment opportunities and provide explicit safeguards to protect permanent employees and sanctions to prevent abuse.

Now, I'm delighted that the National Conference of Black Mayors has endorsed the concept of the youth employment opportunity wage. And now that Mayor Johnny Ford, the past president, and Mayor Marion Barry, the current president of the National Conference of Black Mayors, have endorsed this legislation, maybe we can help Chuck, Orrin, and Ron get this important jobs initiative approved by the Congress.

While I have the chance, I want to thank Bill Kolberg and all the other executives of the National Alliance of Business for their continuing support in coordinating the summer jobs program. The White House Office of Private Sector Initiatives and the NAB have done an outstanding job in leading this year's effort. And thanks to the support of other business, community, and State and local agencies, we're reaching out and responding to the needs of our young people.

Councils like the Greater Kansas City Alliance of Business are using innovative ideas and modern marketing techniques to develop thousands of summer jobs. Companies like Philip Morris, Coca-Cola, Chevron, the American Council of Life Insurance have donated generously to meet the challenge.

Television stations like WTVJ in Miami, KPIX in San Francisco, have held job-a-thons. WPIX–TV is leading a very successful summer jobs program for New York City. Small business men and women all across America are opening their hearts and their business doors to American youth.

And thousands of caring Americans, like Roosevelt Grier and Dave Winfield, who hit a two-run homer in the 10th last night—[*laughter*]—are with us today pitching in to help make this year's program the best ever.

711

Yes, America is reaching out with a gift of opportunity, and that's a gift that'll last a lifetime. But there are still far too many young people, particularly disadvantaged and minority youth, who cannot find summer employment. We can and must help them get the chance they so richly deserve.

Let me close by asking America's business men and women two questions. Do you remember your first job? Do you remember the lucky break you received even though you were inexperienced and the only skills you had were enthusiasm and determination?

I can remember mine. I was 14. It was summer, and there I was with a pick and shovel. And you do learn things, not only about using that pick and shovel. I remember one day, all morning, I'd been swinging that pick. And I had it up for another swing when the noon whistle blew. And I just felt, "That's it," and I just let go and stepped out from under it and let it fall behind me. And then I heard some very strong language immediately to my rear. And I turned around, and the boss was standing there, and the pick was embedded in the ground right between his feet. [*Laughter*] And I learned, if you get that thing up there, swing it. [*Laughter*]

Well, it's your turn now to offer the same opportunity, and you'll never regret it. And thank you, and God bless you all for being here.

Mr. Grier. Mr. President and distinguished people up here and you business men and women, I really love this country, and I love this spirit which we have. I know the young people sometimes think that people don't really care about them, and I think today it proves it that you really do care about them. A lot of minority youth have given up. They turn to drugs and other things. And we don't want that to happen to our young people. They have so much to contribute, and we all have so much to give them in inspiring them.

I like it when people like yourself help the young people because they think that no one really cares about them. They don't see their future as we see it. We've all grown up. And we went through our hard knocks, and they're going to do the same

thing. But with your help, they're really going to make it.

And, Mr. President, on behalf of the young people and these men here, here is an outstanding award for a job well done. [*The President was presented with an award that resembled the Motion Picture Academy's Oscar award.*]

The President. And I wasn't acting at all. [*Laughter*] But then there were some who said that I wasn't before. [*Laughter*]

Mr. Winfield. Ladies and gentlemen, most of my adult life, I've worked with young people. It's just been part of my ideological philosophy. That's just the way I basically am. And I've worked through my Winfield Foundation, and I've worked with kids in health and education and sports and recreation.

And recently—this past year—I was asked by the New York City Partnership and the Daily News in New York City to spearhead the Summer Jobs '84, the jobs for youth in the city of New York. And our plan is to get at least 25,000 jobs for the young people of New York City. So, I am here today representing those people, and I'd like to say, Mr. President, on behalf of Summer Jobs '84 and at least 25,000 youngsters in New York City, I'm happy to present this Daily News recognition of your support.

You know, we've tried to not only get the private sector involved, but, in fact, that is the main thing we're emphasizing this year, to get involved, along with the corporations. It means a lot, and I know it's encouraging me to work a little harder. But one thing I do know, aside from the clear benefits that the youngsters receive from these jobs, businesses really prosper from their help also. When given a chance, these youngsters will always do us proud.

So, once again, thanks again for your recognition of these efforts and your support. Thank you, Mr. President.

Note: The President spoke at 10:45 a.m. in the Rose Garden at the White House. Prior to his appearance before the group, Secretary of Labor Raymond J. Donovan participated in the awards ceremony for the 166 business and community leaders who had supported private sector summer jobs programs for disadvantaged youth.

Message to the Congress Transmitting Proposed Youth Employment Opportunity Wage Legislation
May 17, 1984

To the Congress of the United States:

I am pleased to transmit to you proposed legislation entitled the "Youth Employment Opportunity Wage Act of 1984."

One of the Nation's most serious and long-standing problems is providing adequate employment for our young people. The purpose of this proposal is to remove a government-created impediment that makes it difficult for young people who want to work to find jobs.

Studies over the past decade have repeatedly demonstrated that the minimum wage has reduced job opportunities for large numbers of our youth. This is particularly true for jobs involving considerable initial training. The restricted job opportunities for youth, especially minority youth, due to the minimum wage have contributed to the growing consensus on the value of a lower minimum wage for youth as a means of expanding their employment. Many organizations, large and small, including the National Conference of Black Mayors, have formally endorsed the concept of a youth employment opportunity wage.

A business cannot be expected to hire a youth unless it can reasonably anticipate that the work done by the youth will be worth the required wage. While some businesses can afford to hire unskilled youth and provide the training and experience expected to pay off in future productivity, such expectations are often unreasonable over a short summer employment span. This proposed legislation would permit employers to pay wages equal to 75 percent of the minimum wage to young people under 20 years of age hired to work between May 1 and September 30.

The proposal would enable employers to expand job opportunities for youth during the summer months. It would enable many young people to find jobs, earn money, and gain the experience and skills needed for future work and higher wages. The bill would not prevent those with work skills from getting the higher wages they are worth. It prohibits discharge, transfer, or demotion of any adult, or youth employed in order to hire a youth at the summer wage.

I urge the Congress to speedily enact this legislation.

RONALD REAGAN

The White House,
May 17, 1984.

Nomination of Donald C. Latham To Be an Assistant Secretary of Defense
May 17, 1984

The President today announced his intention to nominate Donald C. Latham to be an Assistant Secretary of Defense (Command, Control, Communications and Intelligence). This is a new position.

Since 1981 Mr. Latham has been serving as Deputy Under Secretary of Defense. Previously, he was with the Riverside Research Institute in 1980–1981; division vice president, engineering, at RCA Corp., government systems division, in Moorestown, NJ (1978–1980); director of engineering at Martin Marietta Aerospace, Orlando division, in 1977–1978; Deputy Chief, Office of Microwave, Space, and Mobile Systems, Department of Defense, in 1974–1977; Chief, Engineering Staff, National Security Agency, European Headquarters, in 1971–1974; and at Martin Marietta Aerospace, Orlando division, in 1963–1971.

He graduated from The Citadel (B.S., 1955) and the University of Arizona (M.S., 1957; E.E., 1965). He is married, has two children, and resides in Alexandria, VA. He was born December 22, 1932, in Sayre, PA.

Nomination of Frank K. Richardson To Be Solicitor of the Department of the Interior
May 17, 1984

The President today announced his intention to nominate Frank K. Richardson to be Solicitor of the Department of the Interior. He would succeed William H. Coldiron.

Judge Richardson is presently serving on the faculty of Pepperdine Law School in Malibu, CA. Previously, he was on the California Supreme Court in 1974–1983; presiding justice of the Court of Appeals, 3d District, Sacramento, in 1971–1974; and on the National Institute of Justice Advisory Board in 1966–1969. He was in private law practice in Oroville, and then Sacramento in

1939–1971, and professor of law at McGeorge School of Law in 1946–1951.

He is a member of the California Bar Association and has served on several association committees. He is also president of the board of Methodist Hospital in Sacramento.

Judge Richardson graduated from Stanford University (B.A., 1935; LL.B., 1938). He is married, has four children, and resides in Sacramento, CA. He was born February 13, 1914, in St. Helena, CA.

Nomination of Robert Laxalt To Be a Member of the National Council on the Humanities
May 17, 1984

The President today announced his intention to nominate Robert Laxalt to be a member of the National Council on the Humanities, National Endowment for the Humanities, for a term expiring January 26, 1990. He would succeed Sister Joel Read.

Mr. Laxalt is an author. His works include "Sweet Promised Land," "A Man in the Wheatfield," and "Nevada: A Bicentennial History." He is also the author of over 200 magazine articles, including a series for the National Geographic Society. He joined the University of Nevada system in 1954, serving first as director of news and publications and later as director of the University of Nevada Press, which he founded. He was

also writer-in-residence for the University system. Upon his retirement in 1983, he was designated director emeritus of the University Press.

In 1978 he received the Decade Award by the Nevada State Council on the Arts and was cited by the Governor of Nevada for exemplary service to the State. He is a member of the Author's League of America and the Western Writers of America.

He attended Santa Clara University in California and later graduated from the University of Nevada, Reno. He is married, has three children, and resides in Reno, NV. He was born September 24, 1923, in Alturas, CA.

Statement on Senate Approval of Proposed Federal Deficit Reduction Legislation
May 17, 1984

I commend the Senate for passing today the central element of the downpayment plan to cut projected deficits.

I congratulate Senate Majority Leader Howard Baker, the Senate Republican leadership, and responsible Senate Democrats for making this victory possible. And for the good of the country, I urge House Members to join their Senate colleagues in moving this package through conference so it can be enacted into law as swiftly as possible.

Letter Accepting the Resignation of Donald H. Rumsfeld as the President's Personal Representative in the Middle East
May 17, 1984

Dear Don:

I want you to know my personal appreciation for your enormous efforts and good work during the time you were able to serve as my Special Representative for the Middle East. It is unquestionably one of the most difficult of assignments and your ability, insight and contributions were invaluable during a critical period.

I very much appreciated your willingness to rearrange your many responsibilities to take this assignment and I am particularly grateful to the Board of Directors of G. D. Searle for making it possible for you to undertake this task.

I am pleased that you will be able to continue as a consultant and be available to me and to Secretary Shultz for advice and counsel in the period ahead, consistent with your other responsibilities.

Sincerely,

RONALD REAGAN

[The Honorable Donald Rumsfeld, President & Chief Executive Officer, G.D. Searle & Co., P.O. Box 1045, Skokie, Illinois 60076]

———

May 15, 1984

Dear Mr. President:

As we agreed when I undertook the assignment as your Special Representative for the Middle East, my involvement could only be for a limited period. Secretary Shultz, you and I discussed what that period could be, given my continuing responsibilities as President and Chief Executive Officer of G. D. Searle. As you know, that point has approached and I must proceed on with my other responsibilities.

As we are all aware, the problems in the Middle East are at once both exceedingly difficult and terribly important. The conflicts in the area are deep seated. While a continuation of our steady efforts is vital, you have rightly identified the growth of state-sponsored terrorism and the use of surrogates to mask accountability as profound threats to hopes for progress in the area. A broad public understanding of the nature and magnitude of these threats is necessary. Your efforts to make the world aware of and to develop effective policies for deterring such activities are important steps forward.

I am deeply grateful for your confidence in asking me to undertake the responsibilities as your Special Representative and for the support you and Secretary Shultz have given me during this assignment.

Sincerely,

DONALD RUMSFELD

[The President, The White House, Washington, D.C. 20500]

Note: The text of the letters was released by the Office of the Press Secretary on May 18.

Statement on the Election of José Napoleón Duarte as President of El Salvador
May 18, 1984

On Wednesday, May 16, the Central Elections Commission of El Salvador certified José Napoleón Duarte as the winner of the May 6 Presidential election in that country. By this act, the people of El Salvador have made clear their choice of Mr. Duarte as the first popularly elected President of that country in recent history.

The voters have chosen as President a man who had dedicated his life to achieving democracy and reform for his homeland. We congratulate President-elect Duarte on his victory and pledge that we will do all in our power to strengthen the ties of freedom and democracy that unite us.

Mr. Duarte carried with him a clear mandate from the people of El Salvador, over 80 percent of whom voted on May 6, that democracy and the vote should determine their future. The United States bipartisan observer delegation noted that, "This election was fair and honest, and . . . provided a clear and undeniable mandate to whichever candidate is elected." Election observers from other countries echoed a similar conclusion.

In protecting both rounds of the recent elections, the Salvadoran Armed Forces took more than 80 casualties, demonstrating once again their determination to defend freedom. They acted professionally and apolitically and are showing us now that they will respect the popular electoral will. In contrast, the guerrillas refused to participate in the election and intensified the combat before, during, and after the voting.

As El Salvador's voters had to brave the intimidation of the guerrillas, their newly elected President will have to face the challenges of creating a peaceful and secure framework for social and humanitarian reform, economic development, and further democratic advance.

The people of El Salvador have spoken. We, along with other nations committed to a democratic form of government, must heed their courageous action. We will support their newly elected government in the pursuit of and the opportunity for a better life.

I look forward to meeting with El Salvador's new President-elect on Monday, May 21, during his visit to Washington. In addition, I have asked Secretary of State George Shultz to head our delegation to the President-elect's inauguration on June 1 in San Salvador.

Nomination of Robert N. Broadbent To Be an Assistant Secretary of the Interior
May 18, 1984

The President today announced his intention to nominate Robert N. Broadbent to be an Assistant Secretary of the Department of the Interior (Water and Science). He would succeed Daniel N. Miller, Jr.

Since 1981 he has been serving as Commissioner of the Bureau of Reclamation, Department of the Interior. Previously he was commissioner of Clark County, Las Vegas, NV (1968–1981), and served as a trustee of the Federal Bankruptcy Court, Las Vegas, NV, in 1975–1981; mayor and council member of the city of Boulder City, NV, in 1959–1968; and chairman of Boulder City Charter Committee in 1958–1959. In 1950–1975 he also served as owner, partner, and manager of Boulder City Drug.

He graduated from Idaho State University (B.S., 1950). He is married, has four children, and resides in Springfield, VA. He was born June 19, 1926, in Ely, NV.

Radio Address to the Nation on Summer Jobs for Youth
May 19, 1984

My fellow Americans:

I want to talk to you today about our young people and what we can do to provide them an all-important opportunity—a summer job. This is a crucial time for young jobseekers, May being the month many firms make their summer hiring decisions.

Why are summer jobs so important for teenagers? Well, because when young people are exposed to the world of work, they can reap a wealth of benefits that often remain with them for a lifetime—values of personal initiative, self-reliance, and hard work; practical experience which teaches skills that impart confidence in the ability to compete in the permanent job market; the beginning of work history and references, which are vital to successful careers; and, of course, earnings, which can make the difference between going on to college and greater educational achievements or not.

I'll always remember my first job. I was 14 at the time, and I wound up finding work with a construction company that was remodeling homes. By summer's end, I was laying hardwood floors, shingling roofs, and painting houses.

I recognize that a lot of rules and regulations have changed since then. Fourteen-year-olds can't receive those kinds of opportunities today. But what of those who receive no opportunity to work at all?

That is a crushing disappointment not just for these individuals who may lose motivation and, eventually, self-respect, but also for our economy, because we're literally throwing away America's most precious resource—our next generation.

The problem of teenage unemployment is most severe among our black and other minority youth. For some time now, the unemployment rate among black youth has been more than twice as high as that for all youth. And while the current economic expansion has brought the overall unemployment rate down with record speed, the drop in black teenage unemployment has been far less dramatic.

As of April, the unemployment rate for all youth, 16 through 19 years of age, was 19.4 percent. Among black teenagers, that rate was 44.8 percent. If a 19.4-percentage unemployment rate is unacceptable—and it is—then a 44.8-percent unemployment rate is a national tragedy. And neither must be allowed to persist.

Our administration has been working hard on this problem, and we're beginning to make headway. But we want and intend to do much more. Clearly, if the dream of America is to be preserved, we must not waste the genius of one mind, the strength of one body, or the spirit of one soul. We must use every asset we have. And our greatest progress will come by mobilizing the power of private enterprise.

We're supporting an extension of the Targeted Jobs Tax Credit Program, providing major incentives for employers to hire more disadvantaged youth. Employers can receive tax credits of as much as 85 percent on the first $3,000 in wages they pay. Last year almost 300,000 young Americans were hired out of this program.

The Job Training Partnership Act is another important initiative. The act grants $1.9 billion to States, of which 40 percent must be earmarked for training youth for private sector jobs. Many private firms are cooperating in this program, and I hope many more will do so in coming weeks.

But one of the barriers to more jobs for youth is the single minimum wage system, because the cruel truth is, while everyone must be assured a fair wage, there's no compassion in mandating $3.35 an hour for startup jobs that simply aren't worth that much in the marketplace. All that does is guarantee that fewer jobs for teenagers will be created and fewer young people will be hired.

So, we're proposing youth employment opportunity wage legislation that can create more than 400,000 new summer jobs for youth. Our bill would allow employers to hire young people at a lower minimum wage during the summer months. And our legislation would do this without displacing adults. The bill explicitly prohibits employers from displacing adults in order to hire youth at the summer wage.

I'm delighted this concept has been endorsed by the National Conference of Black Mayors. Thanks to the strength of the economy, some 8½ million young people are likely to be employed this summer, an increase over last year.

But America can do better, and must do better, if we're to bring those teenage unemployment rates down further. I'm asking the Congress to pass our youth employment opportunity wage legislation. But I also want to request that all employers review their operations with the aim of creating more summer jobs. You, the business leaders of America, can make a great difference, and the time to act is now.

Until next week, thanks for listening, and God bless you.

Note: The President spoke at 12:06 p.m. from Camp David, MD.

Proclamation 5195—Return and Final Interment of Unknown American Killed in Vietnam
May 20, 1984

By the President of the United States of America

A Proclamation

On this Memorial Day, the remains of an unknown American who gave his life in service overseas in Vietnam will be interred in Arlington National Cemetery.

The casket of this unknown American will arrive in the City of Washington on May 25, 1984, to lie in state in the rotunda of the United States Capitol until final interment.

The individual who finds his last resting place at Arlington on this occasion will be nameless to the entire world. But to the generations of Americans who left their homes and families to fight and defend the freedom and independence of our Nation, he will be known well by his embodiment of that most noble of all sentiments—patriotism.

There will be families from across the land who will come to view this place. To them it will mean that their son, husband, or father rests before them. And, in spirit, it will be true. For they, as we, know him well as one who, as Lincoln said at Gettysburg, gave his "last full measure of devotion."

As we work to preserve that for which he struggled, let us equally dedicate ourselves to the peace we yearn for in our hearts.

Now, Therefore, I, Ronald Reagan, President of the United States of America, do hereby direct that the flag of the United States be flown at half-staff upon all public buildings and grounds, at all military posts and naval stations, and on all naval vessels of the Federal government in the District of Columbia and throughout the United States and its Territories and possessions, when customarily flown, on May 25, May 26, May 27, and May 28, 1984. I also direct that the flag be flown at half-staff for the same period at all United States embassies, legations, consular offices, and other facilities abroad, including all military facilities and naval vessels and stations.

As a sign of our national gratitude and concern, I also urge my fellow citizens to display our country's flag at half-staff at their homes and other appropriate places during this period.

In Witness Whereof, I have hereunto set my hand this 20th day of May, in the year of our Lord nineteen hundred and eighty-four, and of the Independence of the United States of America the two hundred and eighth.

RONALD REAGAN

[*Filed with the Office of the Federal Register, 2:59 p.m., May 21, 1984*]

Note: *The text of the proclamation was released by the Office of the Press Secretary on May 21.*

Proclamation 5196—National Arts With the Handicapped Week, 1984
May 20, 1984

By the President of the United States of America

A Proclamation

Art flows from and nourishes the human spirit. Through art, we learn to understand ourselves and our potential. For disabled people, the creative experience—whether as artists, audiences, educators, or students—is an essential part of leading a full and productive life. It is an important means for the disabled to be integrated into the mainstream of educational and cultural programs as well.

Therefore, it is critical that our cultural institutions, educators, and communities strive to assure that disabled people can participate fully in the arts. The National Committee Arts with the Handicapped, an educational affiliate of the John F. Kennedy Center for the Performing Arts, is dedicated to extending opportunities for such participation. It conducts education programs in all fifty States, the District of Columbia, and Puerto Rico. Funded by both the public and private sectors, the Committee is celebrating its tenth anniversary this year. To mark this achievement, the Committee is sponsoring a very special arts festival during the week of May 20, 1984, in Washington, District of Columbia.

In recognition of the importance of the arts in enriching the lives of disabled persons and in celebration of the work of the National Committee Arts with the Handicapped, the Congress, by Senate Joint Resolution 220, has designated the week of May 20, 1984, as "National Arts with the Handicapped Week" and authorized and requested the President to issue an appropriate proclamation.

Now, Therefore, I, Ronald Reagan, President of the United States of America, do hereby proclaim the week of May 20, 1984, through May 26, 1984, as National Arts with the Handicapped Week. I encourage the people of the United States to observe the week with appropriate ceremonies, programs and activities.

In Witness Whereof, I have hereunto set my hand this 20th day of May, in the year of our Lord nineteen hundred and eighty-four, and of the Independence of the United States of America the two hundred and eighth.

RONALD REAGAN

[*Filed with the Office of the Federal Register, 3 p.m., May 21, 1984*]

Note: *The text of the proclamation was released by the Office of the Press Secretary on May 21.*

Joint Communique Following Discussions With President-elect José Napoleón Duarte of El Salvador
May 21, 1984

President Ronald Reagan and President-elect José Napoleón Duarte have undertaken consultations together, May 21, 1984, in recognition that a new chapter in the history of El Salvador as a democratic nation is about to be enacted.

During the past three years, Salvadorans of widely differing political views have joined together in a process of building democracy which has moved successfully through the stages of elections for a constituent assembly in March 1982, approval of a new constitution and the presidential elections, just completed. The United States applauds this historic process and proudly welcomes President-elect Duarte as the first freely and directly elected leader of democratic El Salvador.

The two Presidents, having reviewed the problems of Central America, which are of concern to free people throughout our hemisphere, hereby express their joint views and conclusions regarding the future basis of understanding and collaboration between their two nations. We agree on three major objectives for Central America and El Salvador:

1. The strengthening of democratic institutions;
2. The improvement of living standards and expanded economic development;
3. The need for an increased level of U.S. assistance to obtain peace and to defend against Communist-supported guerrillas of the extreme left and the violence of the extreme right.

The peoples of both nations look forward to the coming five year term of elected government in El Salvador as a period of consolidation of bilateral relations in a spirit of deep friendship as close neighbors in our hemisphere. Both nations will take into account their common interests and problems, maintaining the fullest respect for each other's sovereignty.

Both nations share with other countries of the Americas a fundamental interest in the strengthening of democracy and the firm rejection in this hemisphere of any form of totalitarianism or outside interference in the affairs of sovereign nations. Democracy enhances their individual and collective security. Democratic neighbors are peaceful neighbors, capable of regulating their relations in a framework of cooperation, consultation, mutual respect and peaceful settlement of differences.

It is a fundamental objective of the Duarte administration to broaden and strengthen El Salvador's democratic institutions. And it is the intention of the United States to provide support and assistance to help achieve that objective.

Both Presidents proclaim that democracy, justice and the rule of law require the participation and commitment of all sectors in the political and economic mainstream of the nation. The rule of law requires protection for all against violence and criminal actions. It requires full confidence that the judicial process will produce punishment of the guilty and timely justice with due process for all. Both Presidents reaffirm their staunch commitment to the promotion of human rights, which are central to the democratic process and our freedoms. They believe that there should be greater support for genuinely democratic organizations from public and private sources in the major democracies, such as in the U.S. National Endowment for Democracy.

The two Presidents pledge to work for the achievement of economic development and growth, and increased regional cooperation, to improve the standard of living of the people of El Salvador and throughout the hemisphere. President-elect Duarte joins President Reagan in support of the comprehensive legislative proposal now before the U.S. Congress which will contribute so greatly, once enacted, to Central American peace and prosperity. The two Presidents express the view that a continuing and healthy economic assistance relationship between the two countries will be needed over the years immediately ahead.

Such a relationship will complement broader initiatives, such as the Caribbean Basin Initiative and the National Bipartisan Commission Report, so that El Salvador's interdependent economic and social objectives can be met.

The protection and promotion of a strong private sector, with opportunities for small, medium and large entrepreneurs, is an indispensable means of expanding wealth and creating employment. Close collaboration between the public and private sectors will enhance the revitalization of production, improvement in public health and education, reintegration of displaced persons, and national reconstruction. This collaboration is a basis for stimulating domestic confidence, ensuring access to international credit and attracting new international investment.

The consolidation of democracy requires social peace and the protection and improvement of basic reforms begun in El Salvador in the 1980's, including the finding of new ways to stimulate production, ensure clear titles to land, pay adequate compensation and guarantee land reform beneficiaries permanence and tranquility in their new ownership.

Democracy cannot survive or thrive without security. Military assistance and the existence of a strong well-equipped national armed force is essential to shield democratic development. All governments have the obligation to guarantee their peoples full political participation and must have the means to protect democratic institutions against those who would subvert them, be they marxist guerrillas and their external allies or violent internal extremist groups.

The two Presidents share the view that the armed conflict in El Salvador must be resolved through national reconciliation based on the full integration of all its people into the political processes of the country. This participation should take place within the democratic rule which establishes that the only access to power is in accordance with the will of the people expressed through free elections. They particularly welcome the efforts to achieve regional peace undertaken within the Contadora process and reaffirm their full commitment to the principles of the Contadora Document of Objectives.

The two Presidents reaffirm strongly that abandonment of El Salvador and Central America in the midst of a continuing armed struggle serves neither the interests of their two nations, nor those of the community of free countries. They support the development of strong democracies in all parts of Central America, the democratic forces in Nicaragua, and the objective of holding free, fair and democratic elections in each of the countries of the region. On the basis of common national interests and common belief in the principles of democracy and freedom, they pledge to work together toward peace with security and toward human betterment with freedom, for El Salvador and for all of Central America.

To achieve these objectives, the two Presidents have decided to maintain regular and frequent contact to carry out these joint principles, assuring that their relations are guided by considerations of dignity, equality, friendship and mutual respect.

Note: President Reagan met with President-elect Duarte in the morning in the Oval Office at the White House.

Remarks on Signing the Child Protection Act of 1984
May 21, 1984

Ladies and gentlemen, my remarks here will be brief, because the issue this bill deals with is so clear that it requires little elaboration. Please, sit down. [*Laughter*] You can see how much of—in a hurry I am to—

[*laughing*]—finish the remarks and get to the task.

I'm about to sign the Child Protection Act of 1984, a bill which will toughen the Federal laws dealing with the production and distribution of pornographic materials involving children. It strengthens prosecuting authority against the producers and distributors, and it creates stiffer penalties for them.

And I feel very strongly about these measures. There's no one lower or more vicious than a person who would profit from the abuse of children, whether by using them in pornographic material or by encouraging their sexual abuse by distributing this material.

For years, some people have argued that this kind of pornography is a matter of artistic creativity and freedom of expression and so on and so on, and they go on with that. Well, it's not. This pornography is ugly and dangerous. If we do not move against it and protect our children, then we, as a society, just aren't worth much.

In the last few months, we've seen news reports of cases involving child pornography and child abuse on a large scale. We've seen reports suggesting a link between child molesting and pornography. And academics' studies have suggested a link between pornography and sexual violence toward women.

Back in 1970, you may recall, a Presidential commission studied this whole issue. And its famous conclusion was that pornography has no significant effect on behavior.

I think the evidence that has come out since that time, plus the tendency of pornography to become increasingly more extreme, shows that it is time to take a new look at this conclusion, and it's time to stop pretending that extreme pornography is a victimless crime.

And so, I want to announce that the Attorney General is setting up a new national commission to study the effects of pornography on our society. The commission will study the dimensions of the problem and what we can do about it.

We've taken some other initiatives in the antipornography effort. Last year the Cus-

toms Service increased its seizures of obscene materials coming in across our borders by over 200 percent. Sixty percent of the material was child pornography. And just last week the Justice Department held a seminar for nearly 200 Federal and State prosecutors and investigators to train them on how to better deal with pornography cases, including child pornography.

So, I want to make our interests and our intentions known. We consider pornography to be a public problem, and we feel it is an issue that demands a second look.

And I am particularly happy to sign this bill in the presence of Congressman Harold Sawyer, Republican of Michigan. This bill is largely his work. He plans to retire at the end of the current term. And, Hal, I want you to know that your great efforts will be dearly missed in our nation's Congress and by this administration. And, by the way, may I also note that under your leadership this bill passed the House by a vote of 400 to 1 and enjoyed similar strong support in the Senate.

So, there are issues on which bipartisan agreement can be overwhelming. And I'm heartened by this, and I feel it bodes well for our dealings with this issue in the future.

And now, I will sign House resolution 3635, the Child Protection Act of 1984, with great satisfaction and great appreciation for the good work of the Congress on this and a declaration that this administration shares your commitment and will continue to work closely with you on this issue in the future.

[At this point, the President signed the bill into law.]

There—and high time!

Note: The President spoke at 1:16 p.m. in the Rose Garden at the White House.

As enacted, H.R. 3635 is Public Law 98–292, approved May 21.

Message to the Congress Reporting a Budget Deferral
May 21, 1984

To the Congress of the United States:

In accordance with the Impoundment Control Act of 1974, I herewith report one new deferral of budget authority for $8,000,000.

The deferral affects the Department of the Interior.

The detail of the deferral is contained in the attached report.

RONALD REAGAN

The White House,
May 21, 1984.

Note: The attachment detailing the deferral is printed in the Federal Register *of May 24, 1984.*

Proclamation 5197—Year of Excellence in Education
May 22, 1984

By the President of the United States of America

A Proclamation

We live in times that are unforgiving of mediocrity, poor citizenship and lack of interest in the world about us. Mankind has rarely faced a period in which preservation of world peace and economic vitality depend more upon the able citizenship of individuals. Our world is becoming smaller each day. Lack of understanding about technological developments or events in even the most remote corners of the globe may affect all our lives.

All Americans are aware of this tremendous responsibility, and we are proud to focus on the need for excellence in education. Every child is a precious resource whose potential should be realized to the fullest. Only informed citizens can preserve our priceless legacy of democracy, individual liberty, and the rule of law.

Our modern technological society is imposing new demands on schools. The report of the National Commission on Excellence in Education and a number of other studies urgently advocate a national effort to revitalize teaching and learning in the 15,800 local school districts and thousands of private schools in our land. Quality education for teachers, recognition of the best in their profession through merit pay, and the restoration of their authority and that of other school officials to maintain respect and discipline in the classroom are essential to guarantee quality education for our Nation's future leaders. We also need to follow a back to basics approach emphasizing fundamental scholastic achievement. Parental and community involvement must be enlarged, and there must be greater participation by business, industries, and individuals. One way to facilitate the involvement of the private sector is to widen the Adopt-a-School and partnership programs that seek to link a company or companies to an individual school.

This same report stated that the declining educational achievement of our schools had left America "a nation at risk." It went on to emphasize that our determination to address this challenge successfully would determine whether America's place in the world will be secured or forfeited.

As a free and democratic people, we depend on the sound judgment of our fellow citizens. Quality education contributes in a major way to that judgment. There are few more important issues before us, for, as Thomas Jefferson once wrote: "I know no safe depository of the ultimate powers of the society but the people themselves; and if we think them not enlightened enough to exercise their control with a wholesome discretion, the remedy is not to take it from them but to inform their discretion."

The Congress, by Senate Joint Resolution 210, has designated the period commencing April 1, 1984, and ending March 31, 1985, as the "Year of Excellence in Education," and has authorized and requested the President to issue an appropriate proclamation.

Now, Therefore, I, Ronald Reagan, President of the United States of America, do hereby proclaim the period commencing April 1, 1984, and ending March 31, 1985, as the Year of Excellence in Education. In recognition of the vital role education plays in our Nation, I encourage parents, teachers, administrators, government officials, and the people of the United States to observe the year with activities aimed at restoring the American educational system to its place of preeminence among nations of the world.

In Witness Whereof, I have hereunto set my hand this twenty-second day of May, in the year of our Lord nineteen hundred and eighty-four, and of the Independence of the United States of America the two hundred and eighth.

RONALD REAGAN

[*Filed with the Office of the Federal Register, 4:10 p.m., May 22, 1984*]

Statement on Signing a Bill Designating Certain Sections of the National Wildlife Refuge System as the Edwin B. Forsythe National Wildlife Refuge
May 22, 1984

I am honored to sign into law today H.J. Res. 537, which recognizes the late Congressman Edwin B. Forsythe's leadership in the conservation of the Nation's fish and wildlife resources. In recognition of his contributions, H.J. Res. 537 designates the Brigantine and Barnegat units of the National Wildlife Refuge System as the Edwin B. Forsythe National Wildlife Refuge.

Congressman Forsythe was an outstanding conservationist and a strong supporter of the U.S. Fish and Wildlife Service. From 1975 until his death on March 29, 1984, he served as the ranking minority member of the House Subcommittee on Fisheries and Wildlife Conservation and the Environment, and he continued to serve in this capacity after becoming ranking minority member of the full Merchant Marine and Fisheries Committee at the beginning of the 98th Congress.

In addition, he was the primary sponsor of the Fish and Wildlife Conservation Act of 1980, which recognized the importance of nongame wildlife. He was a strong defender of the Endangered Species Act and the Marine Mammal Protection Act. He had an abiding interest in the National Wildlife Refuge System and supported legislation to establish refuge units in the lower 48 States and Alaska. During this Congress, he was the primary sponsor of H.R. 3082, the Emergency Wetlands Resources Act.

During his tenure, the Subcommittee took a bipartisan approach to conservation issues. Through Congressman Forsythe's efforts, reasonable solutions were found to resolve complex legislative issues and great strides were made for the conservation of fish and wildlife resources.

Brigantine and Barnegat refuges are situated only a few miles from each other on the coast of New Jersey, Congressman Forsythe's home State. Both are primarily coastal marsh and were created for the conservation and management of waterfowl. Congressman Forsythe was instrumental recently in obtaining Migratory Bird Conservation Commission approval for a 4,000-acre addition to Brigantine.

In light of Congressman Forsythe's sponsorship of comprehensive wetlands legislation as one of his last acts in Congress, it is particularly appropriate that these two refuges be renamed in his honor. Their designation will stand as a continuing reminder of the legacy of natural beauty and wildlife

diversity that Ed Forsythe, with dedication and insight, contributed to the Nation.

Note: As enacted, H.J. Res. 537 is Public Law 98–293, approved May 22.

Nomination of Frances Todd Stewart To Be a Member of the Board of Directors of the Overseas Private Investment Corporation
May 22, 1984

The President today announced his intention to nominate Frances Todd Stewart to be a member of the Board of Directors of the Overseas Private Investment Corporation, United States International Development Cooperation Agency, for a term expiring December 17, 1986.

Since 1979 Mrs. Stewart has been president and owner of Kerr-Hays Co. in Ligonier, PA, which manufactures, exports, and imports plastic housewares and promotional products. In 1983 she also became the chief executive officer. Previously, she served on the board of directors of Marlborough Ltd. (1979–1983) and was New England sales manager for Kerr-Hays Co. (1979). In 1978 she became a member of the Young Presidents Organization, the youngest woman

ever to do so. She is a member of the Committee of 200, a group of several hundred of the Nation's top businesswomen. She also serves on the Pittsburgh Advisory Board for the National Association of Women Business Owners and the Women in Business Advisory Board for the Overseas Education Fund. Mrs. Stewart is chairman of the Management Assistance and International Trade Committee of the Pittsburgh Advisory Board for the Small Business Administration.

Mrs. Stewart graduated from Williams College (B.A., 1978). She is married to Charles P. Stewart and resides in Ligonier, PA. She was born October 5, 1956, in Pittsburgh, PA.

The President's News Conference
May 22, 1984

Central America

The President. Good evening. I have a statement.

We have an important visitor in Washington, José Napoleón Duarte, the President-elect of El Salvador. The President-elect and I yesterday issued a joint statement in which we agreed on three major objectives for Central America: the strengthening of democratic institutions, the improvement of living standards, and increased levels of U.S. security assistance to defend against violence from both the extreme left and the extreme right.

The election of José Napoleón Duarte is the latest chapter in a trend toward democracy throughout Latin America. In Central America, El Salvador now joins Costa Rica and Honduras in having a democratically elected government. Democracy in Central America is a fundamental goal of our policy in that region. But continued progress toward that goal requires our assistance.

Most of our aid, three-quarters of it, is economic assistance. But security assistance is essential to help all those who must protect themselves against the expanding export of subversion by the Soviet bloc,

Cuba, and Nicaragua.

Also, as I said in my speech to the Nation on May 9th, we must support the democratic aspirations of the people of Nicaragua and oppose the Sandinista aggression against their neighbors and who seek genuinely democratic elections in Nicaragua, as the Sandinistas promised the OAS in 1979.

Peace can only be achieved in Central America if the forces of democracy are strong. We strongly support multilateral efforts toward peace, especially the Contadora process. However, no lasting peace settlement through the Contadora process can be achieved unless there is simultaneous implementation of all the Contadora objectives, including genuinely democratic elections in Nicaragua. The freedom fighters in Nicaragua have promised to lay down their arms and to participate in genuinely democratic elections if the Sandinistas will permit them.

Our Congress faces some historic decisions this week. Those who struggle for freedom everywhere are watching to see whether America can still be counted upon to support its own ideals. The people of El Salvador are watching, the freedom fighters of Nicaragua are watching, Nicaragua's threatened neighbors are watching, and the enemies of freedom are watching as well.

Our balanced policy can succeed if the Congress provides the resources for all elements of that policy as outlined in the bipartisan recommendations of the Kissinger commission. But if the Congress offers too little support, it'll be worse than doing nothing at all. The success of communism in Central America poses the threat that a hundred million people from Panama to the open border on our south could come under the control of pro-Soviet regimes. We could face a massive exodus of refugees to the United States.

The Congress has the opportunity to reaffirm our commitment to brave people risking their lives for the cause of liberty and democracy in Central America. The Congress also has the opportunity to reaffirm our bipartisan tradition, which will tell the world that we're united when our vital interests are at stake. I'm asking the Members of the Congress to make that commitment.

And now, tonight's first question will be from Maureen Santini. And incidentally, this is a double first for Maureen—her first, first question in her new role as the AP's chief White House correspondent. Maureen?

Persian Gulf

Q. Thank you, sir. Mr. President, it's been reported that you are willing to provide U.S. air power to keep oil tankers moving through the Persian Gulf. Could you tell us what the Saudi response has been to your proposal and under what circumstances the United States could become militarily involved in that region?

The President. Well, Maureen, I've seen all the stories and a lot of them based on speculation already—no, what we have—we have kept in touch and are keeping in touch with the Gulf States and with our own allies. But we have not volunteered to intervene nor have we been asked to intervene. And we've communicated with them regarding that and so far it seems as if the Gulf States want to take care of this themselves. They're concerned, as I think we all should be, about not enlarging the war.

Q. Do we have a contingency plan for doing so if they can't take care of themselves?

The President. Well, if they ask us for help, we have—obviously we've thought in terms of what we might do. But I don't think that's something I should talk about.

Helen [Helen Thomas, United Press International]?

U.S.-Soviet Relations

Q. Mr. President, Senator Byrd says that our relations with the Soviet Union have reached the lowest point in 20 years. Did you misjudge the Russians? Are your hardline policies responsible for the boycott of the Olympics, the breakoff of the arms negotiations, stepped-up offensive in Afghanistan, more missiles off our coast?

The President. No, Helen, I don't think I'm responsible for any of those things. And if these are at the lowest state that we've had for 20 years—not too long ago, just a matter of days ago, I gave to George Shultz one of our very eminent national news magazines for him to see an article on this very subject. And the article—it was an April issue—and the article cited that we had the lowest relations we'd ever had and the President was to blame for that—his vacillation and so forth and so on—except that it was April of 1980 when they were saying that about our relations with Russia.

And I have to say that today, no, we didn't walk away from the negotiating table. We made every effort to prove that we were ready to be flexible in trying to negotiate a reduction of weapons.

And as for the Olympics, the only thing as a government that we did in the Olympics was ensure them and meet virtually every request that they made with regard to their people there of up to allowing their cruise ship to anchor, and we were going to spend about a half-a-million dollars on protection for that ship.

Q. Would you admit there's a heightened belligerency? And six eminent world leaders today said that we're headed for global suicide. What are you going to do about it with this arms race?

The President. I don't think we are, and I don't think we're any closer or as close as we might have been in the past to a possible conflict or confrontation that could lead to a nuclear conflagration. I think the very fact that we're stronger—yes, the Soviet Union is unhappy. They're unhappy because, for the first time in a couple of decades, we are preserving our security ability. We're building up our military, and we're not unilaterally disarming while they continue their massive arms buildup. And I'm sure this makes them a little unhappy about that, that things aren't as easy as they once were.

But when they're ready to come back to the table, it probably—or might not be till after the election, I don't know. But I think that the world maybe is a little safer than it has been in the past.

Persian Gulf

Q. Mr. President, on the Persian Gulf again, is it true that you have written to the Saudis saying that you should they ask the United States for aid, that we are willing to supply air cover to protect the oil tankers?

The President. We haven't specified what we would do, but we have told them, be-

cause I made a statement earlier that neither we nor the Western World as such would stand by and see the straits or the Persian Gulf closed to international traffic.

Q. Mr. President, then, in your judgment, what is the likelihood of American servicemen being involved in some kind of shooting war shortly or in the near future in the Middle East?

The President. I think very slight. I can't foresee that happening.

Now—yeah?

Q. You cannot foresee that happening?

The President. What?

Q. You cannot foresee that happening?

The President. As things stand now, no, I don't think so.

Central America

Q. Mr. President, you've said America's vital interests are at stake in Central America. What will we have to do if the Congress does deny that security assistance to stop this threat of Soviet-sponsored regimes taking over all the countries right up to our southern borders

The President. You say what do we have to do——

Q. Yes. Suppose the Congress did not vote the money that you need for the freedom fighters, as you call them? What, then, would we be required to do to prevent this scenario from developing?

The President. We'd be in the very difficult position, and so would they. But I have great hopes that after President Duarte's visit here and meeting with as many of the Congress as he did that there's some reason for optimism.

Yeah, Andrea [Andrea Mitchell, NBC News].

Q. Mr. President, there are reports that the administration has gone around Congress and continued to increase military and intelligence activities in Central America by channeling money, through accounting tactics, tricks of accounting, through the Pentagon to the CIA. While you can't discuss covert activities, can you at least assure the American people that you have not had this administration go beyond the will of Congress in increasing the spending for military activities in Central America?

The President. Andrea, we've followed no procedures that are any different from what has been done in past administrations, nor have we done anything without the knowledge of the Congress.

Q. So, can you explain then, sir, we were told, Congress was told about a month ago that if Congress didn't appropriate the money, the CIA-supported *contras* would run out of money by now. Now Congress has been told that the CIA has enough money to get through the rest of the summer. How is that possible without their getting secret funds?

The President. Well, unless they guessed wrong on the first statement—I thought that they were closer to being out of money than they apparently are. But I don't think any—well, nothing of that kind could take place without the knowledge of Congress.

Sam [Sam Donaldson, ABC News]?

The Nation's Economy

Q. Sir, interest rates are going up. The stock market is going down, and some economists say we're going to be into a recession, perhaps this fall. Do you think we're headed for a recession?

The President. Oh, I didn't think anyone would get around to some pleasant subjects. [*Laughter*]

No, I don't think we are. And there are always some pessimists out there. But I think all of the indicators show that, if anything, the economy might be getting ready to level off a little bit from that 8.8-percent bulge that we had for the first quarter, and which I think was a little out of line, but which was probably based on inventory building. The end sales figures did not keep pace with that level of growth, so a great many businesses were building up inventory which accounted for the 8.8. We're still estimating that we think for the year the economic growth will be about 5 percent.

But all the other indicators—last month, housing starts at a rate of one 1,960,000 a year; permits at 1,700,000; personal earnings up; and inflation—the Producer's Price Index just the other day that came out, which is the one that indicates what the cost price index is going to be, that was at zero increase.

Q. Well, sir, a few weeks ago in Dallas,

you predicted by the end of the summer that interest rates would begin to drop. Are you still willing to make that prediction tonight?

The President. I expressed my belief, an optimistic belief that before we were through with warm weather—we may have to have a warm September to add to that— [*laughter*]—but summer isn't over till then.

Let me go back here.

European Trip

Q. Mr. President, two questions on your upcoming trip to Europe. First, are you concerned in any way that the planned demonstrations in Ireland will mar what was supposed to be a friendly homecoming for the television cameras? And, secondly, you have gone to economic summits for 4 years now and told the allied leaders that American interest rates will be coming down and the deficit will be coming down. Given the fact that interest rates are going up, why should allied leaders believe you if you sing this same song—or say the same things this year?

The President. I think that the interest rates are one of those things that can be volatile. They slid up here this—they have, if you compare them to what they were when we started, they are well down. So, there was a little increase recently, which I think represented fear in the marketplace of possible return of inflation. I don't think it was necessary, and I still hold that those conditions or their doing that is really unwarranted.

The rate of money increase right now is well within the guidelines set by the Fed— Federal Reserve—and it's commensurate with our increased growth, and yet it is not at a point that would add to inflation. So, I am still optimistic that those interest rates— we're going to see them continue to come down.

As for the deficit, I'm also going to be optimistic and tell you that I think that everyone has been overestimating. Not that it isn't a serious problem—it is. But I think that they've been overestimating the amount in the outyears in the projections of what the deficit will be.

Q. Are you concerned about the Irish

demonstrations?

The President. Oh, the Irish demonstrations. I think that's just Irish hospitality. They know—[*laughter*]—that I haven't—I haven't gone anyplace in years that there hasn't been a demonstration, and they don't want me to feel as if I'm not at home.

Charlotte [Charlotte Saikowski, Christian Science Monitor]?

Arms Reduction Negotiations

Q. Mr. President, your administration has said that once we build up our military strength, the Russians would have an incentive to come to the negotiating table. You have said that we have built up our military defenses. Why have the Russians not returned to the negotiating table?

The President. Well, as I say, maybe they're waiting for the election to be over. But, no, we have built up. On the other hand, they can see, for example, the modernization of our strategic weapons, which are all important—the Peacekeeper, the MX—they can see the contest that is going on as to whether that's going to be built or not. And this can't help but be encouraging to them.

But I think it's true they came to the table, and I think they only came to the table because they believed in our determination to continue our military buildup. And they left because their whole propaganda campaign against the deployment of the Pershings and the cruise missiles in Europe—which was agreed to in 1979 by this country, when NATO requested it, and we're keeping that promise—but at all the time that they were negotiating with us, they kept on building and adding to their stock of SS–20's. Now, these are triple warhead missiles that are intermediate range, targeted on all the targets of Europe. But also, they have been adding them aimed at targets in Asia. And it was for this—in response to this—that NATO asked for an intermediate-range weapon that could be based in Europe, targeted on Russia. And we're providing that. It won't, in any way, match the 1,350 or so warheads that are in the SS–20's, but we believe it will be enough for a deterrent.

Use of a deterrent is to have the enemy know that if he's contemplating some rash action, the cost to him might be more than he cares to bear. So, we're going forward with this. They had waged such a campaign to stop it that I think they made this other move to, hopefully—or in the hope that our allies in Europe might change their mind and cancel out their request. Well, the allies stood firm. I don't think the alliance has ever been more solidly together than it is right now.

Q. But, Mr. President, given the coolness of our relationship right now, do you think the Russians have a problem of saving face, perhaps, in returning to the negotiations? If so, would you be prepared to offer some gesture, to make some overture that would be that positive sign that they asked for in order to come to the table without a loss of face?

The President. Well, Charlotte, I don't think it would be proper for us to do something, some concessions that would make it look that we rewarded their intransigence and their walking out of the meetings. But we have pursued—and we took the lead in this—negotiations on a number of other matters between our two countries that have nothing to do with strategic weapons, and we've been making some progress in a number of those negotiations. So, I don't think things are as bad as they're being painted.

Let me switch around a little bit here. Bob [Robert Ellison, Sheridan Broadcasting]?

Civil Rights Act of 1984

Q. Mr. President, the Civil Rights Act of 1984 is expected to go to House committees tomorrow. Because of the Supreme Court's decision in the Grove City College case, the bill restores all-inclusive prohibitions against sex, race, handicap, or age discrimination at institutions with federally assisted programs. Do you support this measure?

The President. There are some that are watching this legislation very closely. The court decision was based on the way article IX was written by Congress, and it was the way we interpreted it also. Now, if there is legislation to reverse the court decision with regard to title IX—I said "article"— title IX that will prevent discrimination against women in educational institutions that are getting funds from the government, we support that.

There is legislation that has been proposed—and I don't know just which they're going to take up tomorrow—there is legislation which is so broad that actually it would open the door to Federal intrusion in local and State governments and in any manner of ways beyond anything that has ever been intended by the Civil Rights Act. That kind of legislation we would oppose.

Yeah.

Persian Gulf

Q. Mr. President, you said earlier that if asked, the United States would assist Persian Gulf States in keeping the Strait of Hormuz open. Are there any circumstances where American interests could be so threatened that the United States would act unilaterally or without a request from those states?

The President. Well, again, I can't foresee that. We probably would be—among all the importing-of-oil nations, we would be the least hurt by any shutdown. It is our allies— it is Japan; it is our friends in Western Europe—who would really be in trouble if there was any stop to the Middle East oil.

Actually, only 3 percent of our oil supply now—thanks to decontrolling oil and increasing domestic production—only 3 percent is involved in the Persian Gulf for us. And we have increased our stockpile of oil to four times what it was when we came here. So, I can't see a kind of an emergency that would do this.

But also remember, we are in consultation also with our allies, with those nations that would be affected, because we're not contemplating anything unilaterally here. This problem is one that affects all of us.

Q. What would the United States do to help its allies in the event of an oil cutoff? Would we give them oil from the strategic reserve?

The President. We have had people in consultations with our allies, and they've been holding meetings on discussing contingencies of this kind. We would not hold back on immediately turning to our reserve, but I'm not prepared to say we've made any specific plans.

Gary [Gary Schuster, Detroit News]?

Federal Reserve Board

Q. Mr. President, some of your top advisers suggest that the interest rate question could be the cutting edge in November for the election, with some of your people saying that the Federal Reserve Board has had too much control of the interest rates, others saying that they haven't had; that they've been too harsh, the criticisms have been too harsh of the Fed. What is your position? Do you think the Fed should loosen up on the money supply?

The President. No. As I indicated earlier, Gary, I think they're right on target with it now. It is true that a short time ago there was a dip below their regular line. And I think this was one of the things that caused some panic out there in the money markets, because usually, or in the past, on a number of occasions, such as back around '79 and '80, that—such a dip was then followed by a real loosening of the strings, such a flood of money, that that's when we went to 21½-percent interest rates and double-digit inflation for 2 years, and so forth.

But it is possible—that's not an exact tool, the money supply. Sometimes, and judging on a weekly basis the way they do, sometimes there can be an inadvertent dip or an inadvertent splurge. So, I don't know whether the time when they got below their line was inadvertent or not, but they are back up on target and where they should be, with a normal rate of increase tied to the increase in economy.

Soviet Submarines

Q. Mr. President, the White House and the Pentagon worked very hard yesterday to tell people they shouldn't really worry about the new nuclear missile submarines the Soviet Union says they've placed off the American coast. Can you tell the American people that these new missile subs are not any cause for concern, and is there anything the U.S. must do to respond to the Soviets?

The President. If I though there was some reason to be concerned about them, I wouldn't be sleeping in this house tonight.

[*Laughter*] No, this isn't really anything new. They're announcing and they're publicizing, but those submarines off both our coasts—they've had submarines in and out and patrolling there for extended periods of time. Maybe there's one or two more than have been there at one time in the past, but I think it's—I think, again, it is in keeping with their talk about us putting the Pershings in Europe and that they're now going to show us that they can do something in return if we do that. So, they have the submarines offshore. But they're—no, I don't think they pose any particular threat at all.

Jerry [Jeremiah O'Leary, Washington Times]?

The Sakharovs

Q. Mr. President, if it's any consolation to you, I've written all my relations in County Kerry not to demonstrate seriously until you and I are safely out of the country. [*Laughter*] But I wanted to ask you if you have any message for the Soviet Government or for the Sakharovs about the possibility of getting them out of the country—whether there's any deal or any trade that can be made that would save their lives?

The President. Jerry, on this one I have to say we're as concerned as anyone—deeply concerned. Mrs. Bonner has a very serious heart condition. She is a physician herself. She's a war hero also. She was wounded three times in World War II. She was permitted to leave Russia once and had medical treatment for her problem outside the country, and I think it's only natural that someone would want to go back to the person that had treated them before.

But I can't go further than that, because this is a little bit like when I put a moratorium on myself before I was here in talking about our people in the Embassy in Iran. I just have a feeling that anything I might say publicly could be injurious to her chances. I just hope and pray that the Soviet Union will do the humane thing and let her go.

Yes.

Bank Failures

Q. Mr. President, after the bailout of Continental Illinois Bank, some experts are concerned about the soundness of America's banking system. You have pushed for deregulation. But are you now concerned that your administration will have to bail out more big banks because, like public utilities, for example, they cannot be permitted to fail?

The President. No, this particular bank and this so-called bailout as may be—is by the banking system itself, and it's been done before. The protection has been offered to the depositors. And obviously everyone would like to hope that there won't be any—that the bank won't fail, but if it does, the people who would be injured would be the stockholders. And, no, I do not see that this is any threat to the banking system as such. This is one bank that needs some help.

Tax Increases

Q. Mr. President, the other day Treasury Secretary Regan raised the possibility that your administration may push Congress for passage of two separate tax bills in 1985—one to simplify the current tax code and the second to raise new revenues in order to shrink the budget deficit. If you are reelected, are higher taxes a good possibility next year?

The President. I have to feel—I haven't had a chance to talk to Don about this—I have a feeling that he started probably trying to clarify that and make it plain that if we have a reform plan and a simplification of the tax structure, it won't be a gimmick in order to raise revenues. So, he was divorcing any tax increase from that.

Now, speaking of a tax increase in addition to that, the only thing I could think is that he was possibly feeling that if we get to the absolute bottom of where we can get government spending, and it still would then turn out to be a higher percentage of the gross national product than our tax structure provides, then you would have to review the tax structure to see—if you knew that you could not get any more cuts, reductions in the cost of government, you'd have to make the tax structure match that. I have said that myself. But we're not anywhere near that, and I'm not looking for any tax increase that soon. We've got a long way to go in cutting government spending.

Government is taking too big a chunk out of the gross national product, out of the private economy.

El Salvador

Q. Mr. President, you have said in the past that you have no intention of sending U.S. troops into combat in El Salvador, and President-elect Duarte said yesterday that he has no intention of asking for U.S. troops to go there. But despite these denials, the doubts linger. Walter Mondale insists that your policy will lead to U.S. involvement down there. Can you say unequivocally tonight that you would not send troops down to El Salvador, even if it appears that without them El Salvador might fall to the Communists.

The President. First of all, President Duarte made it very plain that they would never request American troops. We have never had any consideration of doing that or any thought of doing that at all. I don't know how I can convince anyone that—but all you'd have to do is look at all our friends and neighbors in Latin America, and probably as a holdover from the past, we'd lose all those friends and neighbors if we did that. They want our help. They know they have to have our help, economically, and in the manner in which we're giving it in military support—by training and supplies and equipment and so forth—but they don't want American manpower there.

Sarah [Sarah McClendon, McClendon News Service]?

Q. But if El—excuse me, if I may follow up. If El Salvador clearly were going to fall to the Communists, would you feel it's in the U.S. interest to send our troops in there and stop that, or would you allow the country to go Communist?

The President. Well, you're asking me for a hypothetical question, and one in which that I think that I would be very foolish to try and answer.

Defense Procurement

Q. Mr. President? Sir, people on your staff and people in the Justice Department are well aware of some of the shenanigans of defense contractors—I refer to General

Dynamics and some of their stablemates. If you want specific names, I can give them. But I wonder if you are going to leave this curtain down on this national scandal or you're going to see that it's brought out and that the—some of the 650 million tax money that was allowed to go in settlement from the Navy to General Dynamics a while back, if you'll see if that's collected.

The President. Sarah, I have to tell you that all of this about defense spending and the spare parts' high prices and all of that— I have said this before, I will say it again: This has been a past practice, but it's our administration, it's under Cap Weinberger, those figures are ours, because we're the ones who found out these things were going on——

Q. But, sir, you haven't revealed it. You haven't come out and told us all about it yet, and we're waiting to hear.

The President. I have told you, and there's been a report from the Defense Department. There have been hundreds——

Q. Not on this case.

The President. There have been hundreds of indictments; there have been convictions for fraud. There have been rebates from companies of all kinds.

Q. Sir, that was picayune to what I'm talking about.

The President. The what?

Q. That was picayune to what I'm talking about. That was little stuff. I'm talking about the big stuff.

The President. Sarah, you've been here longer than I have. I haven't been here long enough to call $600 million picayune. [*Laughter*]

Q. Well, I want you to collect it. [*Laughter*] I want you to get it back.

Deployment of Missiles in Europe

Q. Mr. President, I was wondering, sir, if you could give us your definition of "holding firm" in answer to Charlotte's question. You said our allies in Europe were holding firm in accepting missiles, yet the Dutch Government here is going through a little rain dance here because their people don't want to take the new missiles. Could you sort of tell me how that is holding firm?

The President. Well, the decision must be made by the Dutch Cabinet—Cabinet of the Netherlands—and the Parliament, and they have not yet taken up that issue or made a decision on it. They are slated to get some cruise missiles there. But in the other countries, basically, Italy, Germany, the other NATO countries, are all going forward; England, the bases are being erected for the missiles, including the Pershings and, as I say, not just on that issue alone.

But I have to tell you that some time ago when we came here we found there was disarray in the NATO alliance, and that no longer holds true today. I think we're closer than we've probably ever been.

Q. Well, if the Dutch Government reverses and changes their mind, are you fearful that'll set up a chain reaction among the other allies, where the situation is, at best, tenuous?

The President. No. I doubt that they would. There might be another country or so among some of the smaller allies that might follow suit, but the rest, you can rest assured, wouldn't.

Ms. Thomas. Thank you, Mr. President.

U.S.-Soviet Relations

Q. Mr. President, you said a little while ago that you felt that the world was a little more secure place since you've been in power. How do you account for the fact that so many people in so many countries think that during the last 3½ years the world has moved closer to war, rather than closer to peace?

The President. I would say that that is because that's all that most of the people have been hearing in political dialog from one side, since we've been here in the 3½ years, that I somehow have an itchy finger and am going to blow up the world. And that has all been duly reported by so many of you that, that is the tone that the people have been getting. And it doesn't do me any good to tell you that, having seen four wars in my lifetime, I don't know of

anyone, in or out of government, that is more determinedly seeking peace than I am. And my goal is the total elimination of nuclear weapons. If we can get those fellows back to the table and get them to start down that road of mutual reduction, then they might find out what common sense it would mean to eliminate them.

But I would also point out, that if we're that dangerous in 3½ years, why is it that while the Soviets are still carrying on in Afghanistan and backing the forces in Kampuchea—the North Vietnamese forces there—but all those gains that they were making in the few years before we came here—Ethiopia, South Yemen, Angola—all of those things, they haven't taken another inch of territory since we've been here.

Ms. Thomas. Thank you, Mr. President.

Q. I think, Mr. President, what the ordinary person is seeing is that the United States is re-arming heavily, the Russians are re-arming heavily, and the ordinary person says, "What is going to be the outcome of this arms race? Nobody is at any table."

The President. No, it is as simple as this, the Soviets—this isn't new for them; they're up at full pitch. I doubt if they could expand their military production anyplace beyond where it is right now, or the rate that it is.

On the other hand, they know that when for the first time in, as I say, decades, they see us determined to refurbish our defenses, they know that they can't match us in—if there is such a race, which means that the only alternative for them is to watch us catch up or to sit down at the table with us and work out something in which they won't have to run the risk of someone being superior to them militarily.

Helen's told me I'm all through. [*Inaudible*]—I'm on the wrong set.

Note: The President's 24th news conference began at 8 p.m. in the East Room at the White House. It was broadcast live on nationwide radio and television.

Remarks at the Presentation Ceremony for the President's "E" and "E Star" Awards
May 23, 1984

I don't know about you, but all morning I've been sitting in there watching the sky. [*Laughter*] I heard early predictions of rain; we'll have to get this over with.

But I thank you all very much, and it's always a pleasure to welcome the business men and women of America to the White House. I'm delighted to take part in celebrating World Trade Week, which reaffirms the importance to our well-being of trade and recognizes the need for increased export efforts.

America's future growth and prosperity depend on how well we develop and compete in foreign markets. One in eight manufacturing jobs is related to exports, and 25 percent of our farmers' cash receipts come from exports. In fact, exports account for 25 percent of the total value of all goods produced in this country.

Exports mean jobs for our people, profits for our businesses, and growth for our economy. And that's why it's going to be a pleasure to present the well-deserved "E" and "E Star" Awards for excellence in exporting.

But let me begin by pointing out the backdrop for export opportunities in the economic climate here at home. I know you're all familiar with the dramatic turnaround that has been accomplished. We're in the midst of a wonderful economic expansion, and I believe we have a lot to be proud of. Our growth is helping to pull the rest of the free world out of recession, and this will increase demand for American exports.

But occasionally the interests of diplomacy and the interests of American industry seem to conflict. Well, our administration sees it as our job to reconcile the two and make it easier for American business to open up new markets on a fair footing. And we're working hard in that direction.

In 1982 we passed the Export Trading Company Act aimed at opening foreign trade opportunities for medium- and small-sized companies. The bill removed impediments to trade, permitting companies to sell American products overseas more efficiently and more effectively. We're also implementing an international investment policy to reduce the number of government measures that distort or impede the flow of international investment. Our trade missions have been to Europe, Asia, Africa, and Latin America, seeking to develop new export opportunities.

Now, these are just several of the efforts. We're going to do everything we can to get government out of the way to make sure that you have the opportunity to compete effectively in world markets. And there's something else. Last November I visited Japan and Korea. And last month it was China. And next week it's Europe and the London Economic Summit. I'm beginning to feel a little like an export product myself. [*Laughter*] But one of the key purposes of these trips is to see that all the export trading doors are opened as wide as possible.

As I told a number of export trade industry representatives last month in Tacoma, when I go abroad I go as something of a salesman and do everything I can to promote U.S. exports except, possibly, wear a "Buy American" bumper sticker on my bag.

We're committed to keeping markets open to free trade. We oppose protectionism because, like so many other forms of government intervention, it doesn't work. Protectionism brings higher prices, it provokes retaliation, and it insulates inefficiencies in production. And we'll continue to oppose it.

Government can set the framework for expanded trade, but it can't make trade flourish. That's up to you, the private sector, to make that happen. And that's why it's my privilege to present the "E" and "E Star" Awards. Our award winners are making it happen in a fiercely competitive environment. And you have good reason to be proud, and we're proud of you.

And so now, for the awards, I shall turn this back to Secretary Brown.

[*At this point, the awards were presented.*]

Well, thank you all again for being here. And congratulations to all of you, gentlemen. Thank you very much.

And now, I'll go back to work.

Note: The President spoke at 11:45 a.m. in the Rose Garden at the White House. Following the President's remarks, Deputy Secretary of Commerce Clarence J. Brown announced the names of the award winners, and a representative of each organization was presented with a framed citation by the President.

Recipients of the "E" Award were James B. Cantrell, president, Belco Industries, Inc., Carrizozo, NM; John R. Bondhus, president, Bondhus Corp., Monticello, MN; Emery G. Olcott, president, Canberra Industries, Meriden, CT; Sergio de Armas, president, Florida Exporters and Importers Associa- tion, Miami, FL; Leonard Kunzman, direc-*tor, Agricultural Development and Marketing Division, Oregon Department of Agriculture, Salem, OR; J. Reese Phifer, president, Phifer Wire Products, Tuscaloosa, AL; Dwight F. Messinger, president, Power Curbers, Inc., Salisbury, NC; D. David Szymanek, president, REC Specialties, Camarillo, CA; Dr. Leonard Skolnick, president, Spitz Space Systems, Chadds Ford, PA; John Walker, Tennessee Department of Economic and Community Development, Nashville, TN; and Dr. Donald Tourville, president, Zeus Scientific, Inc., Raritan, NJ.*

Recipients of the "E Star" Award were Harold W. Godberson, president, GOMACO Corp., Ida Grove, IA; William Donohue, commissioner, New York State Department of Commerce; and Steve Perry, general manager, Toledo Scale Co., Division of Reliance Electric, Worthington, OH.

"Berlin—A Very Special Place for America," an Article by the President Published in Die Welt
May 23, 1984

Berlin is a very special place for me and for America.

I visited Berlin in 1978 and again, after I became President, in 1982. The first impression entering the city by air is, of course, that terrible wall which surrounds and divides Berlin. Despite its bright white paint and the flowerboxes placed here and there to soften the effect, the wall's inhuman purpose cannot be disguised.

The wall suppresses man's natural impulse to be free. The angry words of protest splashed across the western side of the wall show the frustration that Berliners feel in living with this symbol of tyranny, knowing that there are Berliners too on the other side.

Berlin is a microcosm of a greater division. The ugly slash that divides Berlin is replicated on a larger scale in a similar division of Germany and in the artificial line cutting off one part of Europe from another. In divided Berlin, as elsewhere in divided Europe, families and friends are separated; contacts severed; freedoms denied.

This first impression, however, does not tell the full story. The tragedy of Berlin is evident even from a distance. One must move closer to see the triumph as well. For Berlin *is* a triumph of the human spirit. The visitor quickly realizes and admires the enormous courage and endurance of the Berliners. They are the inheritors of a devastated city. A city the Soviet Union once tried to bring to its knees through the Berlin blockade. A city cut in two by that cruel wall. But Berliners, all the while surrounded by a hostile environment, did not succumb to threats of pressure. They have repeatedly come through adversity with bravery, dignity, and grace.

Berliners have had to struggle to maintain their liberty, and their unwavering devotion to freedom is an example for us all. This is the first lesson of Berlin: that we cannot be timid in preserving our democratic way of life. We must stand up for our freedoms. The terrible price of losing them is vividly demonstrated just on the other side of the wall.

The United States stands with Berlin. We are honored to have an important role in the preservation of Berlin's freedom. The United States has a solemn obligation to Berlin which time has only reaffirmed and strengthened. The American commitment to Berlin is firm and unshakable.

Berlin, like the rest of the West, benefits from the ability of the Atlantic Alliance to deter war. This community of free nations, dedicated to democratic ideals, has given Europe a generation of peace. The unity and strength of the Atlantic Alliance provide the protective shield that keeps us free and secure. Last fall, the Soviet Union failed to intimidate the Alliance over the NATO decision on intermediate-range nuclear forces. As in Berlin 35 years earlier, the West refused to bow to Soviet dictates and is more secure in consequence. The Soviet Union now knows that the West will do what is necessary to keep the peace.

As a testing-ground for Western strength of will, Berlin has often been at the cutting edge of East-West relations. In times past, shock waves from strife elsewhere were frequently felt in Berlin. More recently, however, Berlin has become known for a different kind of East-West relationship. It has become an example of the successful management of delicate East-West problems.

A long-standing vital function in which the Soviet Union and the Western Allies cooperate is the coordination of Berlin air traffic. The maintenance of Allied rights and responsibilities with respect to Berlin air traffic is an integral part of the working relationship between the Soviet Union and the Western Allies.

The Quadripartite Agreement of 1971 has helped Berlin become calmer, and more stable and secure. Berliners have found it easier to visit and communicate with friends and relatives in East Berlin and the German Democratic Republic. Trade and travel between Berlin and the Federal Republic of Germany have been facilitated. The Quadripartite Agreement must continue to be strictly observed and fully implemented, in all sectors of Greater Berlin.

The second lesson of Berlin is that it is possible to build constructive and practical East-West relationships on the basis of realism, strength, and dialogue. While we cannot ignore the profound differences between East and West, we can accomplish much that is in the interest of all people.

The applicability of this second lesson extends beyond Berlin—it underpins the whole East-West relationship. By remaining unified in our determination to defend freedom—in Berlin and elsewhere—while at the same time exploring reasonable avenues for improved East-West relations, the West is making an important contribution to world peace. The key is solidarity. As has been the case for more than 35 years, the entire free world maintains its support for the freedom of Berlin. Today, it is important that all of us, Berliners included, show the same support for oppressed peoples in places such as Afghanistan and Poland. If we are to maintain freedom, we must remain united.

I am optimistic about the future of Berlin. Berlin is an extraordinarily vital world city, bustling with prosperity. It has a rich culture and history. The city is blessed with great universities and scientific institutes. Most of all, Berlin is blessed with the Berliners themselves—whose strength and spirit have served it well. The security guarantee of the Western allies is inalterable and permanent, and American ties of friendship with Berlin run deep. East-West accords have led to practical improvements to make life easier in Berlin. But the barriers to the free flow of information, to human contacts, are still far too high. Even the cultural life of the city is divided—museums, theaters, symphony orchestras and operas split between two sides.

Such human divisions are intolerable. If peace is to be secured, we must increase our efforts to accommodate the human aspirations of millions of persons in Europe who are not satisfied with the conditions under which they must live. In this regard, I would like to recall my 1982 visit to Berlin. At that time, I asked the Soviet Union to join with the West in working to reduce the human barriers which divide Europe. Rather than a symbol of oppression, reflected in barbed wire and walls, would it not be better for Berlin to be the starting point for the reduction of the human and political divisions which create misery in the world?

Today, I would like to repeat that challenge. In 1987, Berlin—all of Berlin—will celebrate its 750th birthday. Would not that occasion be appropriate for celebrating the further reduction of the barriers which divide the city?

In 1984, we celebrate another anniversary—the 35th anniversary of successful conclusion of the Berlin Airlift. This historic undertaking was made possible by the close cooperation of Americans, British and French officials with their German friends. It was truly an historic turning point, and the United States will be forever proud of its role in saving the freedom of the Western Sectors of this great city. All Americans join me in the hope that it will not take another 35 years to restore the unity of Berlin and that Berliners on both sides of the wall will one day be able to live together in peace and liberty.

Note: The President's article was published in the May 23 edition of Die Welt.

As printed above, the article follows the text of the White House press release.

Proclamation 5198—Galway's Quincentennial Year, 1984
May 23, 1984

By the President of the United States of America

A Proclamation

Many Americans trace their heritage directly to Ireland. All Americans have benefitted greatly from the distinctive Irish cultural contribution, plus the creativity and enduring effort of Irish people from colonial days to the present.

Many Americans have a special affection for a city on Ireland's western shore, Galway, which this year celebrates its Quincentennial as a mayoral city. For many Americans, the song "Galway Bay" has a special place in their hearts. Even those not of Irish extraction are aware that this song encapsulates a bit of the history of Ireland and its proud culture, and serves as a reminder of what separation from a beloved land meant to many Irish emigrants in the United States.

The area of Galway has been inhabited since the thirteenth century. A Franciscan monastic centre was established in 1291 and served as a focus for scholarship and religious activities. The town grew in prominence, and its chief officer was granted the rank of Mayor in 1484. Historically, Galway's relative geographical isolation from the central seat of English power fostered a spirit of independence, which it has nurtured to this day. Galway's importance as an international trading center gave medieval Galway a cosmopolitan flavor, perhaps unique in Ireland. Tradition has it that Christopher Columbus and many other explorers visited Galway on one of their voyages.

Medieval Galway developed into a de facto city-state, ruled by a merchant oligarchy, the famous "tribes." Galway's history is a rich one involving trading and cultural contributions from many nations and the more direct impact of the Normans and the English. Pre-Cromwellian Galway became an important seat of learning, boasting the famous free school founded by the Lynch family. This was swept away in the havoc caused by Cromwell's forces in 1652 and marked the end of Galway's Golden Age.

The Williamite wars, brought to an end by the Treaty of Limerick in 1691, added further to the decline of the city. The greatest calamity of all to befall the city was the great famine of 1846–47, which seemed to mark the end and to relegate the city to the level of country town. The Seaport, which had once rung with the laughter of many tongues in better days, now echoed with the wails of country- and city-folk alike as they left the city for the last time on board the dreaded coffin ships headed for North

737

America.

The darkness of the nineteenth century gave way to a century bright with prospects for the city of Galway. The new Irish state encouraged Galway's growth as a university city and industrial center, and once again the city began to expand and develop. Today, Galway is a modern and thriving city, a center of culture, learning and industry. The "city of the tribes," which has given so much to Irish culture and history, rightly enjoys the admiration of all who have a special affection for Ireland.

Now, Therefore, I, Ronald Reagan, President of the United States of America, do hereby recognize Galway's Quincentennial

Year, 1984. I call upon the people of the United States to join in celebrating and honoring Galway's Quincentennial with appropriate ceremonies and activities.

In Witness Whereof, I have hereunto set my hand this 23rd day of May, in the year of our Lord nineteen hundred and eighty-four, and of the Independence of the United States of America the two hundred and eighth.

RONALD REAGAN

[*Filed with the Office of the Federal Register, 4:21 p.m., May 23, 1984*]

Executive Order 12477—Federal Civilian and Military Pay Increases
May 23, 1984

Adjustments of Certain Rates of Pay

By the authority vested in me as President by the Constitution and laws of the United States of America, and in accordance with section 202 of the Omnibus Budget Reconciliation Act of 1983, it is hereby ordered as follows:

Section 1. Executive Order No. 12456 of December 30, 1983, is amended by replacing the schedules attached thereto with the corresponding new schedules attached hereto.

Sec. 2. The adjustments of rates of pay

made by section 1 of this Order are effective on the first day of the first applicable pay period beginning on or after January 1, 1984.

RONALD REAGAN

The White House,
May 23, 1984.

[*Filed with the Office of the Federal Register, 4:22 p.m., May 23, 1984*]

Note: The schedules are printed in the Federal Register *of May 25, 1984.*

Executive Order 12478—Protection of Foreign Missions to International Organizations
May 23, 1984

Transfer of Authority to the Secretary of State To Make Reimbursements for Protection of Foreign Missions to International Organizations

By authority vested in me as President by the Constitution and statutes of the United States of America, and in accordance with

the provisions of the Act of December 31, 1975, Public Law 94–196 (89 Stat. 1109), codified as sections 202(7) and 208(a) of Title 3, United States Code, as amended, it is hereby ordered as follows:

Section 1. There is transferred to the Secretary of State authority to determine the need for and to approve terms and conditions of the provision of reimbursable extraordinary protective activities for foreign diplomatic missions pursuant to section 202(7), and the authority to make reimbursements to State and local governments for services, personnel, equipment, and facilities pursuant to section 208(a) of Title 3, United States Code;

Sec. 2. There are transferred to the Secretary of State such unexpended moneys as may have been appropriated to the Department of the Treasury for the purpose of permitting reimbursements to be made under the provisions of section 208(a) of Title 3, United States Code;

Sec. 3. The authority transferred pursuant

to this Order shall be exercised in coordination with protective security programs administered by the Secretary of State under the Foreign Missions Act of 1982; authority available under that Act may also be applied to any foreign mission to which section 202(7) applies; and

Sec. 4. This Order shall be effective on October 1, 1984.

RONALD REAGAN

The White House,
May 23, 1984.

[*Filed with the Office of the Federal Register, 4:23 p.m., May 23, 1984*]

Statement on the Resumption of Mutual and Balanced Force Reductions Negotiations
May 24, 1984

Today in Vienna, negotiators from East and West resume the talks on mutual and balanced force reductions, or MBFR. The purpose of these talks, in which 18 NATO and Warsaw Pact nations are participating, is to reach an agreement to reduce conventional forces in Central Europe.

On April 19, near the end of the last round, the West presented a major new initiative aimed at moving these negotiations forward. The new Western proposal seeks to overcome the longstanding disagreement over the number of Warsaw Pact soldiers in Central Europe. Our proposal will permit the two sides to focus initial attention on counting just their most highly structured and visible forces, since this is the area where East and West are already closest to agreement.

The timing of this offer gave the Warsaw Pact the opportunity to study it in their capitals during the break between rounds. We therefore hope that the Soviet Union and its allies are prepared now to respond constructively to our initiative and to move the negotiations forward. By reaching agreement on lower, equal, and verifiable levels of conventional forces in Central

Europe, we will be able to enhance the security of both sides and to strengthen peace and stability in Europe. The force reductions themselves and the associated verification measures called for in the Western proposal would enhance mutual confidence between East and West.

The MBFR negotiations resume at the same time that another part of the East-West security dialog, the Conference on Confidence and Security Building Measures and Disarmament in Europe (known as CDE), is continuing in Stockholm. There, too, the West presented a package of proposals that would enhance confidence and trust among the 35 participating countries. And in both Stockholm and Vienna, the West is fully prepared to discuss any serious counterproposals from other participants.

The West is doing its part to achieve progress in other areas of arms control as well. In the same week that we made the new MBFR proposal, Vice President Bush presented to the 40-nation Committee on Disarmament in Geneva a comprehensive U.S. proposal for a global ban on chemical weapons. This proposal will again be under discussion when the Committee on Disarmament reconvenes in June.

We are just as prepared to move forward in negotiating reductions in nuclear forces. But the Soviet Union still refuses to return to the START and INF negotiations which it left last fall. I repeat what I have said on many occasions: We are prepared to resume those negotiations at any time and without preconditions. We again invite the Soviet Union to return to the negotiating table to resume the serious work of reducing nuclear arsenals and the risks of nuclear war.

Remarks at Groundbreaking Ceremonies for an Addition to the Central Intelligence Agency Headquarters Complex
May 24, 1984

When President Eisenhower came to this place a quarter of a century ago to dedicate the cornerstone of this building, he spoke of undecorated and unsung heroes. And when I was with you here 2 years ago, I mentioned those words and noted the heroes President Eisenhower spoke about were you, the men and women of the Central Intelligence Agency.

I return to the CIA today with exactly the same thought in mind. Without you, our nation's safety would be more vulnerable and our security fragile and endangered. The work you do each day is essential to the survival and to the spread of human freedom. You remain the eyes and ears of the free world. You are the "trip wire" over which the totalitarian rule must stumble in their quest for global domination.

Though it's sometimes forgotten here in Washington, the American people know full well the importance of vital and energetic intelligence operations. From Nathan Hale's first covert operation in the Revolutionary War to the breaking of the Japanese code at Midway in World War II, America's security and safety have relied directly on the courage and collective efforts of her intelligence personnel.

Today I want to stress to you again that the American people are thankful for your professionalism, for your dedication, and for the personal sacrifice each of you makes in carrying on your work. You're carrying a great and noble tradition. And I believe that you're adding a brilliant new chapter to the annals of American intelligence services.

In 3½ years, significant changes have oc-curred at this Agency. New and vitally important missions are being performed that a few years ago many would have said were impractical or unachievable. Funding and personnel have grown substantially. The operations and analysis sections have seen increases in productivity and product. Morale has steadily improved. Recruiting is highly successful with the continuing growth in the number of talented, young Americans who want to work at CIA. Individual employees are gaining greater recognition for their work, and throughout this Agency, as well as in the Congress and our nation itself, there is a new recognition of the urgent importance of the mission of the CIA.

There are many quantitative measures of what you're achieving. You've increased the number of national intelligence estimates from 19 in 1980 to 55 in 1983, and in addition, completed 800 other special research projects. Though the specifics are classified, new stations have been opened abroad, and work with friendly intelligence and security services have been greatly expanded.

As most of you know, Bill Casey recently reported to me on all of this. And, frankly, it's a bit breathtaking. Something else equally dramatic has happened here recently. In two separate reports to you during the past 6 months, your Director has outlined an exciting new process of management reform and renewal. Your guidelines in this process are the techniques of modern management used at America's top companies, including many of the concepts outlined in the remarkable management and best seller, "In Pursuit of Excellence."

There has been a new emphasis on lean management staffs and, above all, establishing a consensus on the mission and the role of the agency. Underlying all this is a central insight: that, even more than material rewards, a chance to create, to build, and to put into action the shared values of an institution is the strongest inducement to human excellence.

Memoranda and suggestions have been asked for from all of you, suggestions and memos that have been read by the Director personally. Now, all this has meant not only a stimulating period of discussion and analysis leading to many specific reforms, but also the adoption of a new Agency credo, written by you, the personnel of the Central Intelligence Agency. I've had a chance to read the credo of CIA. It's everything such a credo should be—practical, yet idealistic; careful, but inspiring; specific, yet general enough to explain not only what it means to be a member of the CIA but what it means to be an American serving the cause of freedom in a dangerous and difficult world.

On this point, I want to stress: An intelligence agency cannot operate effectively unless its necessary secrets are maintained even in this, the most open and free country on Earth. We cannot expect you or your informants to endanger life and work because of carelessness, sensationalism, or unnecessary exposure to risk. Hostile intelligence activities conducted in this country and directed at U.S. interests abroad threaten not only our legitimate secrets and our technological advantages but also our privacy and, ultimately, our freedom. To the danger of espionage is added active measures designed to subvert and deceive, to disinform the public opinion upon which our democracies are built.

One of the greater dangers facing you is also the loss of necessary secrets through unauthorized and illegal disclosures of classified information. As I said in my memorandum last summer to all Federal employees, the unauthorized disclosure of our nation's classified information by those entrusted with its protection is improper, unethical, and plain wrong. I cite for emulation by the rest of the Government another phrase from the CIA credo: "We subordi-

nate our desire for public recognition to the need for confidentiality. We give unfailing loyalty to each other and to our common purpose."

Well, let me conclude by adding that the changes you have underway at CIA are a reflection of a larger renewal among the forces of freedom throughout the world. I think many of you realize that the days of defeatism and weakness are over for America and that in contrast to previous times the objectives of our foreign policy are being met.

Our economic recovery has strengthened the hand of the democracies, even as it has widened the economic and technological gap between ourselves and totalitarian nations. Our defense buildup has been a signal to the world that the American people remain ready to make the sacrifices necessary for the protection of human freedom.

Our alliances have been renewed and revitalized. Our support, both direct and indirect, for people whose countries are the victims of totalitarian aggression has blunted the Communist drive for power in the Third World.

The tide of the future is a freedom tide. American foreign policy has a new coherence and moral purpose. We have proposed the most extensive series of arms reduction proposals in history, and we have made it clear that we will negotiate without preconditions for as long as it takes.

We're now in a period of readjustment. Some of our adversaries who had grown used to disunity or weakness from the democracies are not enthusiastic about the success of our policies or the brightening trend in the fortunes of freedom. What is needed now is steadiness and calm and above all a quiet resolve to advance the cause of freedom as we continue to press our program for arms reductions and many other peace initiatives.

When historians look back at all of this, I'm sure they will conclude that no one has played a more important role in this exciting new era than all of you here at CIA. Your work, the work of your Director, the other top officials have been an inspiration to your fellow Americans and to people everywhere.

I wanted to come here today not only to dedicate this new building, which will assist greatly in better coordinating and consolidating CIA activities, but to pledge to you my continued support and bring to each and every one of you the heartfelt thanks of the American people.

God bless you all.

Note: The President spoke at 11:34 a.m. at the site of the new addition near Langley, VA. He then joined other officials in breaking ground for the building.

Proclamation 5199—National Farm Safety Week, 1984
May 24, 1984

By the President of the United States of America

A Proclamation

Agriculture has always been one of our most important industries. Although our ancestors were bound to the land in order to survive, the remarkable advances of science and technology have overcome most limitations that dictated scarcity. American agriculture has emerged as a marvel of efficiency and productivity. Now, fewer than five percent of our people are able to supply an abundance of high-quality but low-cost food, freeing most others for the task of providing the incredible array of goods and services we enjoy.

Unfortunately, the accident rate for people engaged in agriculture is unacceptably high. Many thousands of farm and ranch residents and workers suffer disabling, crippling, or fatal injuries each year. This unhappy toll is further compounded by many job-related illnesses. The direct economic costs of these problems exceed $5 billion annually, and there is no way to measure the pain, despair and family disruption that also result.

This regrettable situation need not continue. The waste of life, limb, property and financial resources can be sharply reduced if rural people take a decisive stand for better safety and health. Accidents and job-related illnesses can be averted by safe and proper methods, control of hazards, and use of protective equipment when appropriate. In addition, guidance in safety and health is readily available to all from the Extension Service, safety councils, volunteer safety leaders and the manufacturers of the products we use.

Now, Therefore, I, Ronald Reagan, President of the United States of America, do hereby proclaim the week of September 16 through September 22, 1984, as National Farm Safety Week. I urge every man and woman engaged in farming and ranching to make basic safety a priority in every activity and task—on the job, in the home and on the highway. I also urge those who serve and supply farmers and ranchers to encourage and support personal and community safety and health efforts in every possible way.

In Witness Whereof, I have hereunto set my hand this twenty-fourth day of May, in the year of our Lord nineteen hundred and eighty-four, and of the Independence of the United States of America the two hundred and eighth.

RONALD REAGAN

[*Filed with the Office of the Federal Register, 4:46 p.m., May 24, 1984*]

Executive Order 12479—Management Reform in the Federal Government
May 24, 1984

By the authority vested in me as President by the Constitution and statutes of the United States of America, and in order to coordinate and implement policies with respect to management reform in the Federal government, it is hereby ordered as follows:

Section 1. Establishment of the President's Council on Management Improvement.

(a) There is established as an interagency committee the President's Council on Management Improvement.

(b) The Council shall be composed of the following members:

(1) The Deputy Director of the Office of Management and Budget, who shall be Chairman of the Council;

(2) The Assistant Secretary for Administration, Department of Agriculture;

(3) The Assistant Secretary for Administration, Department of Commerce;

(4) The Assistant Secretary (Comptroller), Department of Defense;

(5) The Deputy Under Secretary for Management, Department of Education;

(6) The Assistant Secretary for Management and Administration, Department of Energy;

(7) The Assistant Secretary for Management and Budget, Department of Health and Human Services;

(8) The Assistant Secretary for Administration, Department of Housing and Urban Development;

(9) The Assistant Secretary for Policy, Budget and Administration, Department of the Interior;

(10) The Assistant Attorney General for Administration, Department of Justice;

(11) The Assistant Secretary for Administration and Management, Department of Labor;

(12) The Assistant Secretary for Administration, Department of State;

(13) The Assistant Secretary for Administration, Department of Transportation;

(14) The Assistant Secretary for Administration, Department of the Treasury;

(15) The Assistant to the Administrator for Management, Agency for International Development;

(16) The Assistant Administrator for Administration and Resources Management, Environmental Protection Agency;

(17) The Deputy Administrator, General Services Administration;

(18) The Associate Administrator for Management, National Aeronautics and Space Administration;

(19) The Associate Director for Management, Office of Management and Budget;

(20) The Associate Director for Administration, Office of Personnel Management;

(21) The Associate Deputy Administrator for Resource Management, Small Business Administration;

(22) The Associate Deputy Administrator for Information and Resources Management, Veterans' Administration;

(23) The Assistant to the President for Policy Development, or a Federal employee designated by that official, to advise on management and administration; and

(24) The Assistant to the President for Presidential Personnel, or a Federal employee designated by that official, to advise on human resource development.

Sec. 2. Functions of the Council. The Council shall:

(a) develop and oversee the implementation of improved management and administrative systems for government-wide application;

(b) formulate long-range plans to promote improvements in the management and administrative systems of the Federal government;

(c) identify specific department and agency management reforms applicable to other agencies and assist in their implementation;

(d) work to resolve intergency management problems; and

(e) work with the Office of Management and Budget, the General Services Administration and the Office of Personnel Management to ensure timely implementation and coordination of their policies.

In conducting these functions, the Council shall not interfere with existing lines of authority and responsibility in the departments and agencies.

Sec. 3. Responsibilities of the Chairman. The Chairman shall:

(a) establish, in consultation with the members of the Council, procedures for the Council and establish the agenda for Council activities;

(b) On behalf of the Council, report to the President; the goals and the results of the Council on management projects shall be reported to the President through the Cabinet Council on Management and Administration; the Chairman shall advise the Council with respect to the reaction of the President and the Cabinet Council to its activities;

(c) provide agency heads with summary reports of the activities of the Council;

(d) establish such committees of the Council, including an executive committee, as may be deemed necessary or appropriate for the efficient conduct of Council functions; committees of the Council may act for the Council in those areas that affect the membership of the committee;

(e) appoint Vice-Chairmen to one-year terms to assist the Chairman in representing the Council and perform duties as de-

termined by the Chairman;

(f) appoint other Federal officials as at-large members to one-year terms to provide special expertise to the Council and perform duties as determined by the Chairman; and

(g) be supported by the Associate Director for Management of the Office of Management and Budget, who shall advise and assist the Chairman in the execution of the entire range of responsibilities set forth above and act for the Chairman in his absence.

Sec. 4. Administrative Provisions.

(a) The Director of the Office of Management and Budget shall provide the Council with such administrative support as may be necessary for the performance of its functions.

(b) The head of each agency represented on the Council shall provide its representative with such administrative support as may be necessary, in accordance with law, to enable the agency representative to carry out his or her responsibilities.

RONALD REAGAN

The White House,
May 24, 1984.

[*Filed with the Office of the Federal Register, 4:47 p.m., May 24, 1984*]

Message to the Congress Transmitting Proposed Legislation To Implement the National Synthetic Fuels Program
May 25, 1984

To the Congress of the United States:

Today I am pleased to transmit to the Congress the "Energy Security Reserve Amendments of 1984," legislation to implement the new synthetic fuels policy that I announced on May 14, 1984.

This legislation reaffirms the Nation's commitment to a long-range program of developing a private-sector synthetic fuels industry while recognizing that improvements in the energy outlook can permit us to achieve a major reduction in Federal

spending through prudent realignments in the program.

When the Congress established the Synthetic Fuels Corporation in 1980, making available a total of $19 billion for related activities, oil prices were projected to reach $75 to $125 per barrel by 1990; America was dependent on imported oil for 18 percent of its energy supply; and the memories of gas lines lingered.

Synthetic fuels held promise as an economically competitive alternative to traditional fuel sources. Proponents of the current law argued that the Federal program would have little or no impact on the deficit and established an extremely rapid and ambitious schedule for developing a commercial synthetic fuels industry.

In the intervening years, the energy outlook has improved dramatically. The price of imported crude oil has declined more than 25 percent since I took office, and our oil imports are down 33 percent compared to 1980 levels. The Strategic Petroleum Reserve, at nearly 400 million barrels, provides more than 80 days protection against a total disruption of our imports and over 200 days if OPEC halted supplies—in 1980, it provided less than 17 days protection. The energy conservation efforts of the American people have far exceeded expectations, further enhancing our energy situation.

As a consequence of these major changes, the presumptions that underlie the current synthetic fuels program have proven at variance with the realities of the market place. It is now apparent that developing a commercial synthetic fuels industry at the pace envisioned by the Energy Security Act of 1980 would require enormous direct budget outlays that would not be offset by any economic benefits.

Proceeding down the path set by current law would thus result in the inefficient use of billions of dollars. It would also grossly distort the market place for synthetic fuels, possibly creating an industry that would be permanently dependent on government subsidies, not the commercially-viable industry envisioned by Congress in 1980.

The "Energy Security Reserve Amendments of 1984" reflect an effort to strike a balance between avoiding wasteful expenditures and preserving an appropriate national synthetic fuels program. The legislation would rescind $9 billion of the $19 billion originally appropriated. It would also require that projects supported by use of the remaining funds be limited to those that produce fuels whose prices will not be significantly above projected market prices of competing fuels.

At the same time, the legislation leaves completely intact the administrative structure for the synthetic fuels program. By continuing to use the Synthetic Fuels Corporation, we can avoid unnecessary delay and disruption in the national effort of ensuring synthetic fuels commercialization.

Swift passage of this legislation will make a major contribution to reducing the Federal deficit in the years ahead while putting the synthetic fuels program on a sounder footing.

I urge the Congress to act expeditiously in its consideration of this legislation.

RONALD REAGAN

The White House,
May 25, 1984.

Note: The text of the proposed legislation was included in the White House press release.

Proclamation 5200—National Digestive Diseases Awareness Week, 1984
May 25, 1984

By the President of the United States of America

A Proclamation

Digestive diseases rank third in the total economic burden of illness in the United States. In terms of human discomfort and pain, mortality, and burden on the Nation's economy, they represent one of our most serious health problems. Digestive diseases account for a yearly expenditure of approximately $17 billion in direct health care costs, and a total economic burden of $50 billion.

Research into the causes, cures, prevention, and clinical treatment of digestive diseases and related nutrition problems is a national concern. The week of May 20, 1984, marks the first anniversary of the initiation of a national digestive diseases education program. Its goals are to encourage the digestive diseases community to educate the public and other health care practitioners to the seriousness of these diseases and the methods available to prevent, treat, and control them, and to inform the public that diseases of the digestive system are a major health priority.

In recognition of the important efforts to combat digestive diseases, the Congress, by Senate Joint Resolution 228, has designated the week beginning May 20, 1984, through May 26, 1984, as "National Digestive Diseases Awareness Week," and authorized and requested the President to issue a proclamation calling for observance of this week.

Now, Therefore, I, Ronald Reagan, Presi-

dent of the United States of America, do hereby proclaim the week of May 20, 1984, through May 26, 1984, as National Digestive Diseases Awareness Week. I urge the people of the United States, and educational, philanthropic, scientific, medical, and health care organizations and professionals to participate in appropriate ceremonies to encourage further research into the causes and cures of all types of digestive disorders so as to alleviate the suffering of their victims.

In Witness Whereof, I have hereunto set my hand this twenty-fifth day of May, in the year of our Lord nineteen hundred and eighty-four, and of the Independence of the United States of America the two hundred and eighth.

RONALD REAGAN

[*Filed with the Office of the Federal Register, 4:52 p.m., May 25, 1984*]

Remarks at a Ceremony Honoring an Unknown Serviceman of the Vietnam Conflict
May 25, 1984

An American hero has returned home. God bless him.

We may not know of this man's life, but we know of his character. We may not know his name, but we know his courage. He is the heart, the spirit, and the soul of America.

Today a grateful nation mourns the death of an unknown serviceman of the Vietnam conflict. This young American understood that freedom is never more than one generation away from extinction. He may not have wanted to be a hero, but there was a need—in the Iron Triangle, off Yankee Station, at Khe Sanh, over the Red River Valley.

He accepted his mission and did his duty. And his honest patriotism overwhelms us. We understand the meaning of his sacrifice and those of his comrades yet to return.

This American hero may not need us, but surely we need him. In Longfellow's words:

So when a great man dies,
For years beyond our ken,
The light he leaves behind him lies
Upon the paths of men.

We must not be blind to the light that he left behind. Our path must be worthy of his trust. And we must not betray his love of country. It's up to us to protect the proud heritage now in our hands, and to live in peace as bravely as he died in war.

On this day, as we honor our unknown serviceman, we pray to Almighty God for His mercy. And we pray for the wisdom that this hero be America's last unknown.

Note: The President spoke at 3:07 p.m. in the Rotunda at the Capitol.

Nomination of Thomas H. Etzold To Be an Assistant Director of the United States Arms Control and Disarmament Agency
May 25, 1984

The President today announced his intention to nominate Thomas H. Etzold to be an Assistant Director of the United States Arms Control and Disarmament Agency (Multilateral Affairs Bureau). He would succeed James L. George.

Since 1983 he has been serving as Special Assistant to the Director for Program Coordination, Center for Naval Warfare Studies, at the Naval War College in Newport, RI. He is also presently on the visiting faculty at the Federal Executive Institute. He has been at the Naval War College since 1974, serving as Assistant Director, Center for Naval Warfare Studies (1982–1983); Director, Strategic Research, Center for Naval Warfare Studies (1981–1982); professor of strategy (1977–1981); and associate professor of strategy (1974–1977). Prior to this he was assistant professor of history at Miami University (1971–1974) and an instructor in history at Yale University (1970–1971).

He graduated from Indiana University (A.B., 1967; M.A., 1968) and Yale University (M.Phil., 1969; Ph.D., 1970). He is married, has two children, and resides in Portsmouth, RI. He was born June 2, 1945, in St. Claire County, IL.

Radio Address to the Nation on the Economy and on National Defense
May 26, 1984

My fellow Americans:

I want to talk to you today about a few elements of America's progress. First—the economy. We've seen some increases in interest rates in recent weeks, and, of course, we don't like that. But we're not about to panic or be buffaloed by the pessimists who ignore the great progress we've made during these last 3½ years.

In 1980 double-digit inflation was a silent thief of every paycheck. Today, it's been cut by nearly two-thirds. For the last 2 years, it's been under 4 percent.

I mentioned interest rates. Recently the prime rate climbed from 10½ percent to 12½ percent, and that means mortgage rates have also risen. These increases must be laid to fear that inflation is coming back. Well, we're determined to see that it doesn't.

Tax rates have also dropped by nearly 25 percent. If our tax program had not been passed, a median-income family would be paying over $900 a year more in taxes than it does today. And next year, your tax rates will be indexed. From then on, a cost-of-living raise won't bump you into a higher tax bracket. For years, government has used inflation as a silent partner to raise your taxes without having to pass a tax increase and take the heat for doing so. With indexing, you'll be protected against that kind of theft.

So, with inflation down, interest rates still down significantly, and taxes no longer rising, America is moving forward with impressive power. By virtually any yardstick, our economy is coming back. America is coming back. And for the first time in a long time, hope for the future is coming back.

The strength of the economy continues to defy the experts. Gross national product—the sum total of what our economy produces—rose 3.4 percent in 1983 and a healthy 8.8 percent in the first quarter of 1984. Back in 1980, gross national product went down by three-tenths of 1 percent.

Jobs are coming back. Nearly 5½ million Americans found work during the last 17 months—the fastest drop in unemployment in over 30 years. Today, some 106 million of us are working—more than ever before in our history. And last year, some 100,000 new businesses started up. That's a 5-year high that means more jobs for the future.

Housing is coming back. Three years ago, even the smallest house seemed completely out of reach. The median monthly mortgage payment shot up from $333 in 1977 to $688 in 1981. During that time, the median price for a home went up by $23,000. Since then monthly mortgage payments have risen only $10. Today, more Americans can afford homes, and more of us are buying homes—some 10,000 each day.

The auto industry is recovering. Domestic car sales dropped by almost 3 million units between 1977 and 1981. Since then they've increased by 1 million, and they're selling at the fastest rate in 5 years.

Past recoveries from recession were snuffed out by a rekindling of inflation. Well, this time inflation is staying down, and we mean to keep it down. In the last 12 months, the Producer Price Index for finished goods—one indicator of future inflation—has risen less than 3 percent. If inflation stays down, interest rates will come down, too, and our economy will keep expanding.

There's another area where America was weak, but is now regaining strength—national defense. Our ability to deter war and protect our security declined dangerously during the 1970's. By 1979 defense spending, as a percent of our total economy, had reached its lowest level in 20 years. Since 1981 we've begun to rebuild America's security and restore the morale, training, and readiness of our Armed Forces. Our precious freedoms are more secure today than they were 3 years ago.

A stronger economy and greater security are good news, but we still face great challenges. We must eliminate billions of dollars in wasteful government spending. We must make our tax system more simple and fair so we can bring your personal income tax rates down further and keep our economy growing. And we must keep our defenses strong, so the Soviets will decide it's time to return to the negotiating table and work with us to reduce armaments and assure a more peaceful world.

We've made a new beginning. Americans feel prouder and stronger that things are getting better, and rightly so.

Until next week, thanks for listening, and God bless you.

Note: The President spoke at 12:06 p.m. from Camp David, MD.

Remarks at Memorial Day Ceremonies Honoring an Unknown Serviceman of the Vietnam Conflict
May 28, 1984

My fellow Americans, Memorial Day is a day of ceremonies and speeches. Throughout America today, we honor the dead of our wars. We recall their valor and their sacrifices. We remember they gave their lives so that others might live.

We're also gathered here for a special event—the national funeral for an unknown soldier who will today join the heroes of three other wars.

When he spoke at a ceremony at Gettysburg in 1863, President Lincoln reminded us that through their deeds, the dead had spoken more eloquently for themselves than any of the living ever could, and that we living could only honor them by rededicating ourselves to the cause for which they so willingly gave a last full measure of devotion.

Well, this is especially so today, for in our minds and hearts is the memory of Vietnam and all that that conflict meant for those who sacrificed on the field of battle and for their loved ones who suffered here at home.

Not long ago, when a memorial was dedicated here in Washington to our Vietnam

748

veterans, the events surrounding that dedication were a stirring reminder of America's resilience, of how our nation could learn and grow and transcend the tragedies of the past.

During the dedication ceremonies, the rolls of those who died and are still missing were read for 3 days in a candlelight ceremony at the National Cathedral. And the veterans of Vietnam who were never welcomed home with speeches and bands, but who were never defeated in battle and were heroes as surely as any who have ever fought in a noble cause, staged their own parade on Constitution Avenue. As America watched them—some in wheelchairs, all of them proud—there was a feeling that this nation—that as a nation we were coming together again and that we had, at long last, welcomed the boys home.

"A lot of healing went on," said one combat veteran who helped organize support for the memorial. And then there was this newspaper account that appeared after the ceremonies. I'd like to read it to you. "Yesterday, crowds returned to the Memorial. Among them was Herbie Petit, a machinist and former marine from New Orleans. 'Last night,' he said, standing near the wall, 'I went out to dinner with some other ex-marines. There was also a group of college students in the restaurant. We started talking to each other. And before we left, they stood up and cheered us. The whole week,' Petit said, his eyes red, 'it was worth it just for that.' "

It has been worth it. We Americans have learned to listen to each other and to trust each other again. We've learned that government owes the people an explanation and needs their support for its actions at home and abroad. And we have learned, and I pray this time for good, the most valuable lesson of all—the preciousness of human freedom.

It has been a lesson relearned not just by Americans but by all the people of the world. Yet, while the experience of Vietnam has given us a stark lesson that ultimately must move the conscience of the world, we must remember that we cannot today, as much as some might want to, close this chapter in our history, for the war in Southeast Asia still haunts a small but brave

group of Americans—the families of those still missing in the Vietnam conflict.

They live day and night with uncertainty, with an emptiness, with a void that we cannot fathom. Today some sit among you. Their feelings are a mixture of pride and fear. They're proud of their sons or husbands, fathers or brothers who bravely and nobly answered the call of their country. But some of them fear that this ceremony writes a final chapter, leaving those they love forgotten.

Well, today then, one way to honor those who served or may still be serving in Vietnam is to gather here and rededicate ourselves to securing the answers for the families of those missing in action. I ask the Members of Congress, the leaders of veterans groups, and the citizens of an entire nation present or listening, to give these families your help and your support, for they still sacrifice and suffer.

Vietnam is not over for them. They cannot rest until they know the fate of those they loved and watched march off to serve their country. Our dedication to their cause must be strengthened with these events today. We write no last chapters. We close no books. We put away no final memories. An end to America's involvement in Vietnam cannot come before we've achieved the fullest possible accounting of those missing in action.

This can only happen when their families know with certainty that this nation discharged her duty to those who served nobly and well. Today a united people call upon Hanoi with one voice: Heal the sorest wound of this conflict. Return our sons to America. End the grief of those who are innocent and undeserving of any retribution.

The Unknown Soldier who is returned to us today and whom we lay to rest is symbolic of all our missing sons, and we will present him with the Congressional Medal of Honor, the highest military decoration that we can bestow.

About him we may well wonder, as others have: As a child, did he play on some street in a great American city? Or did he work beside his father on a farm out in America's heartland? Did he marry? Did he have children? Did he look expectantly to return to a bride?

We'll never know the answers to these questions about his life. We do know, though, why he died. He saw the horrors of war but bravely faced them, certain his own cause and his country's cause was a noble one; that he was fighting for human dignity, for free men everywhere. Today we pause to embrace him and all who served us so well in a war whose end offered no parades, no flags, and so little thanks. We can be worthy of the values and ideals for which our sons sacrificed—worthy of their courage in the face of a fear that few of us will ever experience—by honoring their commitment and devotion to duty and country.

Many veterans of Vietnam still serve in the Armed Forces, work in our offices, on our farms, and in our factories. Most have kept their experiences private, but most have been strengthened by their call to duty. A grateful nation opens her heart today in gratitude for their sacrifice, for their courage, and for their noble service. Let us, if we must, debate the lessons learned at some other time. Today, we simply say with pride, "Thank you, dear son. May God cradle you in His loving arms."

We present to you our nation's highest award, the Congressional Medal of Honor, for service above and beyond the call of duty in action with the enemy during the Vietnam era.

Thank you.

Note: The President spoke at 2:15 p.m. at the Amphitheater at Arlington National Cemetery.

Earlier in the day, the President returned to the White House following a weekend stay at Camp David, MD. Upon his arrival by helicopter on the South Lawn, he proceeded to the motorcade for the drive to the cemetery.

Interview With Brian Farrell of RTE-Television, Dublin, Ireland, on Foreign Issues
May 28, 1984

The President's Trip to Ireland

Mr. Farrell. Good evening. Welcome to "Today-Tonight," the Library, White House, Washington, DC. On Friday, the President of the United States, Ronald Reagan, begins his European tour with a state visit to Ireland.

Mr. President, it's not your first visit to Ireland, of course. It is your first visit as President and in an election year. So, is it a sentimental journey? Is it electioneering?

The President. Well, it is true, I have been there more than once in a previous occupation when I was a performer in the entertainment business, and then, subsequently, when I was Governor—and when you and I met, when I was sent there by President Nixon on a mission for him. Actually, I would be going even if I were not a candidate, so it isn't a part of an election process. But I'm accepting an invitation that was first made by former Prime Minister Haughey and repeated by your present Prime Minister FitzGerald when he was here.

But there is another reason, a personal reason, why I'm going, also. I have known I would be going one day because up until I became President I had no knowledge of my father's family beyond him and his parents. He was orphaned at less than 6 years of age. So, he had no knowledge of his family roots. And I must say, the people of Ireland and the Government of Ireland have been very kind and generous, and I found when I arrived here in this job that they had gone to great lengths and have traced our family roots and found that Ballyporeen is the locale and so forth.

So, I've always known I was going to have to go there. I want to go there.

Mr. Farrell. But it's not going to do you

any harm in an election year. So, how important is that Irish American constituency anymore?

The President. Well, I want the vote of all the Americans that I can get, and obviously, the Irish Americans constitute quite a sizable block in our country. There is a rich history of the millions of them that we have. I'm one of them. So, of course, I would like to have their approval, but I'm not making this trip for that purpose. I think that their votes will be based on their belief in whether I should be President for 4 more years or not.

Mr. Farrell. You're coming to us after the New Ireland Forum has finally reported. The Congress is already giving its backing to that report. What's your view of the findings of the report?

The President. Of the report?

Mr. Farrell. The Forum—The New Ireland Forum.

The President. Oh. Well, I think that Prime Minister FitzGerald said it very eloquently, and that was that it was a practical agenda for a meeting of the minds and discussion. And I think so, too. But I believe to go beyond that would be presumptuous of me.

This is a problem to be settled there between not only the Governments of England and Ireland but also of the people in the north and the people of the south. They, too, must be considered, and their wishes—and I hope and pray we can find a solution that will bring peace.

Mr. Farrell. So, you wouldn't be proposing to pick up Mr. Haughey's suggestion that, in fact, the United States might intervene at this date?

The President. I don't think it's our place to do that.

Mr. Farrell. But will you be raising it with Mrs. Thatcher, for instance, in seeking—using your good offices to encourage her at least to begin a process of further discussion?

The President. Well, I confess to a curiosity, knowing her well, about this proposal from the Forum that has been made, and a curiosity as to how she sees it and how she feels about it. And I could possibly ask a question about that.

Mr. Farrell. Mr. President, many Irish Americans still see what goes on in Northern Ireland as a freedom fight. They see the IRA not as terrorists, but as people to be supported. Can they be persuaded they're wrong on that?

The President. Well, I think that there is a fraction of the IRA that is revealed now, mainly what is called the Provisional IRA, that is not the IRA of the glorious days of the fight for freedom and that it has all the attributes of a terrorist organization. At the same time, I think that there is an element of the same on the other side of that.

I have a feeling myself that the majority of people, on both sides of the border out there would want, and do want, a peaceful solution, but that possibly, on both sides of the border, there is a problem about voicing that because of fear of the more radical elements. And that, if it's true—that's a tragedy, and there must be a solution found.

Central America

Mr. Farrell. Mr. President, as you know, there are people in Ireland who are objecting already to your visit. In particular they feel that your stand on Central America has not supported justice sufficiently. How do you feel about the likelihood of those protests?

The President. I feel that they're misinformed. We know that Cuba and the Soviet Union have vast, worldwide disinformation machineries—or machines—in which they can give out misinformation to the media, to organizations and groups and so forth. I'm sure that many of those people, if there are people demonstrating on this issue—I'm sure they're probably sincere and well-intentioned. But I don't think that they know the situation.

Now, we've had a case here in which, with the three elections that have taken place, bipartisan groups of our Congress and others have gone down there, in addition to the bipartisan commission I appointed under Dr. Kissinger, to go down to Central America. When they come back from viewing those elections—many of these Congressmen have gone down openly admitting they're like those people that would want to demonstrate, they think we're on the wrong side—they have come back completely converted by what they saw.

We've got a situation where, for decades and decades or even centuries, in Central America and Latin America, generally, we've had revolutions in which it's simply one group of leaders being overthrown by another group of leaders who want to take over and be in charge and the dictators. Some years ago, there was an overthrow of a military dictatorship in El Salvador. And the government that was set up then became kind of the same type of military thing. And then a man named Duarte, who was President after that first overthrow, was exiled, was—well, first was imprisoned, was tortured, was exiled even though he'd been chosen as President. He has now returned, and the people overwhelmingly have elected him as their choice for President.

Now, how anyone could not believe that he is going to be determined to enforce civil rights, and if there is—well, first of all, he's picking up something that has already been vastly improved under the existing government already there, which was elected by the people. We've had three elections in 26 months there, and in each one of them, a greater proportion of their people turned out for that election than turns out for an election in the United States.

Mr. Farrell. But, of course, it's mandatory to vote.

The President. Not really. As a matter of fact, they had something like about a $20 fine if you didn't vote. But these teams of observers of ours went down; they couldn't find anyone that ever worried about that or that thought that it would ever be enforced—whether they did or not.

But they did find an overwhelming enthusiasm on the part of the people. When a woman stands in the line for hours, waiting her turn to vote, and has been wounded by the guerrillas, whose slogan was, "Vote today, and die tonight," and she refused to leave the line for medical treatment of her bullet wound until she had voted—she wouldn't take the chance of missing the opportunity to vote.

Now, the guerrillas—the government offered amnesty. The government offered for them to put down their guns and come in

and participate—submit candidates for office and all—in the electoral process, and the guerrillas turned that down.

By the same token, in Nicaragua, the Sandinista government—which is as totalitarian as anything in Cuba or the Soviet Union—indeed, they are the puppets of Cuba and the Soviet Union—that government, the so-called freedom fighters there—or if they prefer to call them guerrillas—they are former revolutionaries who were aligned with the Sandinistas in the revolution to overthrow the authoritarian government of Somoza. And once they were in, the Sandinistas, which is the, as I say, totalitarian element, Communist element, they got rid of their allies in the revolution and have broken every promise that the revolutionaries—when it was still going on—made to the Organization of American States as to free elections, human rights, freedom of the press, freedom of religion.

The present Government of Nicaragua—right now, the Catholic bishops are protesting as far as they can, at the risk of great persecution—they embarrassed one bishop by parading him through the streets of the capital naked. Now, the Archbishop of San Salvador has been quoted by this disinformation network here and there as being one who wants America to stop lending aid, military aid, to the Government of El Salvador. He has refuted that. He has denied that and said no. He knows that the others—the guerrillas—are getting outside support, and he knows from whence it comes. And he has said, no, he does not want us to leave.

So, the program we have is one in which three out of four dollars will go to help establish a democratic economy and society in El Salvador, and only one dollar is going in military aid. You can't have social reforms in a country while you're getting your head shot off by guerrillas.

Mr. Farrell. But your critics, Mr. President—your critics here in the United States, your critics in Europe, your critics in Ireland—don't see, necessarily, Nicaragua and El Salvador quite in the same way. There are those who've come back and who've said Nicaragua isn't as repressive as it looks. There are those who say American aid going in to the guerrillas there strengthens and toughens that government.

The President. How do they explain, then, the Miskito Indians, which, even under the Somoza authoritarian government, were allowed to have their own communities, their own culture and religion and so forth, and almost upon taking office, the Sandinista government marched its forces into those Miskito villages, burned their crops, burned their homes, their villages, and then confined as many as they could in concentration camps? But thousands of them fled across the borders. Now, we know an awful lot about some of those Miskitos, because some of our medical personnel in our military are helping taking care of them where they are in refugee camps in Honduras.

All I can suggest to some of these people who are saying this in Europe and who have evidently been propagandized is—and I don't mean this to sound presumptuous— but is there any one of them that has access to all the information that the President of the United States has? I'm not doing this because I've got a yen to involve ourselves or spend some money. But I do know that when the Sandinista—well, the revolution won in Nicaragua, the previous administration immediately set out to help them— financial aid to that government. And it was only a few days before my inauguration when that administration had irrefutable evidence that the Nicaraguan Government was supplying arms and materiel to the guerrillas in El Salvador, attempting to overthrow a duly elected government that was trying to be a democracy. And he put a hold on any further help.

Now, we came into office a few days later, and we still had to find out for ourselves. We thought if there is a possibility of negotiating some kind of a settlement—and so, on that basis, we renewed the aid—financial aid that was going to them and tried to deal with them. By April we had found out that, no, there was no honor, no honesty. They were totalitarian, but more than that, they openly declared that their revolution knows no boundaries, that they are only the beginning of what they intend to be further revolution throughout all of Latin America.

Mr. Farrell. Would that, nevertheless, jus-

tify mining ports?

The President. Those were homemade mines that couldn't sink a ship. But let me ask you this. Right now, there is a Bulgarian ship unloading tanks and armored personnel carriers at a port in Nicaragua. That is the fifth such Bulgarian ship in the last 18 months. Just a week or two ago, there were Soviet ships in there unloading war materiel. Now, the Nicaraguan Government—the Sandinista government is funneling this through to the guerrillas in El Salvador. Indeed, the headquarters for the guerrilla movement in El Salvador is only a few miles from the capital of Nicaragua, in Nicaragua where the strategy is planned and the direction of their revolution is taking place.

Now, it seems to me that if you're going to justify people trying to bring this present Nicaraguan Government back to the original promise of the revolution, to modify its totalitarian stand, and you're going, at the same time—and one of the reasons we were offering help is to interdict those arms and weapons that were going to the El Salvador guerrillas, but you know that a flood of that materiel is coming in through the ports and being unloaded, that you're going to try to think of a way to interdict that.

And those were homemade mines, as I say, that couldn't sink a ship. They were planted in those harbors where they were planted by the Nicaraguan rebels. And I think that there was much ado about nothing.

U.S.-Soviet Relations

Mr. Farrell. Mr. President, you have an image problem, don't you? You said it in your press conference last week that people think you've got an itchy finger.

The President. Yeah.

Mr. Farrell. Many people in Europe see you as a cold warrior. They see you as the man who started your Presidential years talking about the empire of evil. They see you as the President who, at this stage, is not involved in disarmament talks with the Soviet Union.

The President. But we didn't walk away from the table, did we?—the disarmament table. They did.

And let me point something out. There

have been some 19 efforts by our country since World War II to enlist the Soviets into talks to talk about disarmament—the reduction of arms and the control of weapons. It was this country that, as far back as 1946, when we were the only ones who had a nuclear weapon, we made a proposal that an international commission be appointed to take charge of all nuclear materiel, all weapons turned over to them. The Soviet Union hadn't even completed one yet, but they turned down that proposal.

I am the first one since 1946 who has gone to the bargaining table and proposed the total elimination of the intermediate-range weapons system in Europe, and they wouldn't listen. So, we said, "All right. We still think that's the best idea—to free Europe of this threat. But we will then talk to you about what figure would you suggest that we could reduce the numbers to, to at least reduce the size of the threat." And their reponse is to walk away from the table.

Now, I think that—I know that the relations are bad right now.

Mr. Farrell. Very bad?

The President. Yes—well, not all that bad. They're maybe more unhappy than they've been in the past. But I think one of the reasons for that is that in the past, the Soviet Union has seen this country unilaterally disarm, cancel weapons systems such as the B–1 and other systems, close down our Minuteman missile assembly line. We don't even have the facility to make them anymore. And they've seen that while they were doing—while we were doing that, with some idea that maybe they would see we meant no threat and, therefore, they would follow suit—no, they continued with the biggest military buildup in the history of man.

Now, how can anyone—what I started to say, I guess, is that, sure, they're unhappy. They're unhappy because they see that we're preparing to defend ourselves if need be.

Mr. Farrell. Many West Europeans are very unhappy, though, because they see the danger that if the confrontation happens, if you don't get to talks in some shape or form, it is Europe where that war will be fought.

The President. Yes, but also there's some 300,000 American troops there which are an indication of our standing by them in the alliance.

They have lived almost 40 years now, since World War II, under an umbrella which has kept peace, and that umbrella is our nuclear capability in this country. I know that there are demonstrators, and I know that there are people that are influenced by the Soviet-sponsored World Peace Council, but I don't think our alliance in Europe has ever been stronger than it is today.

But, as I say, I think the Soviets—sure, they're unhappy because they liked it the other way when under a kind of détente, they were having things their own way. Now they know that we're not going to make ourselves vulnerable, as was done before. But they also know that we're willing anytime they want to sit down, we are willing to start reducing these weapons. And my ultimate goal is—I think common sense dictates it—the world must rid itself of all nuclear weapons. There must never be a nuclear war. It can't—shouldn't be fought, and it can't be won.

Mr. Farrell. When do you think that might happen? When do you think the process, the talks might begin?

The President. I don't know. We have kept the door open on any number of other negotiations. We've been doing business with them on some things of interest to them as well as us, and with some progress being made. It is only in this area—they did come back to the mutual balanced force— the conventional arms treaty, and we are discussing with them, as well as others, at the Stockholm disarmament talks. But it is on those two, the major nuclear weapons— the START talks, as we call them, and the intermediate-range weapons—where they are being intransigent.

Mr. Farrell. What about the boycott on the Olympics? Many people see this symbolically as just that further little bit of evidence of the Soviet Union and the United States pulling further apart.

The President. Well, I know that no one can really understand or fathom the thinking of the Politburo, the people in the Politburo of the Soviet Union, but I would hazard two ideas that stick in my mind as possibly an explanation for what they've done. One is retaliation for the boycott——

Mr. Farrell. 1980.

The President. ——President Carter, in those Olympics when it was their Olympics. Number two, frankly, I think they don't want to be embarrassed by having revered athletes in their country come to this country and decide to stay.

Persian Gulf

Mr. Farrell. Different part of the world very much in the news this week—the Gulf. We're obviously teetering into a crisis there. Do you see, Mr. President, the possibility of a direct American involvement?

The President. Well, so far, it doesn't seem to be. The Gulf States have themselves said that this is their problem, and they want to deal with it. Some have asked for some military assistance in the sense of weaponry, and this is why we are sending some weapons, some Stinger weapons, to them and possibly augmenting our little squadron of tankers that are there. We have four there presently—have had for quite some time. That could be expanded to six. But they have not asked us to intervene, and certainly, we have not offered to intervene.

Mr. Farrell. Do you see this as essentially an American problem, or is it a problem for the West? Is this something that either regionally should be picked up by the Gulf States, or is it something that the Western alliance should come in, that you should stand back from?

The President. Well, if it comes to a complete shutdown of the sources of oil in the Middle East, this is a Western problem, and far more than for us. Actually, only about 3 percent of our oil comes from the Persian— or by way of the Persian Gulf. Many of our allies are not in that advantageous a position. They are very dependent on that. And I have said previously that I don't see how the Western World could let that be closed down. But at the moment, the Gulf States who are directly involved and who are on the firing line there believe that the problem can be solved and without outside interference.

Middle East

Mr. Farrell. What about the Middle East? You, after all, tried the Reagan plan in terms of resolving the West Bank problem. Do you see now a possibility of somehow coming to a reconciliation of Israel with its Arab neighbors?

The President. This is what we have to continue to try. We have never given up on that. It was set back by the inability to get a solution in Lebanon. It seemed impossible to go forward with that while, for example, Israel itself was engaged in combat in Lebanon. But, ultimately, the solution, as I have put it, is we must find more Egypts. We must—and our job is to convince our Arab friends over there that we can be even-handed and that we're not seeking to dictate a settlement of any kind, but that they must be prepared to sit down—and the Israelis at the same time to sit down—and negotiate out an end to a war situation in which there are countries that have still said they do not recognize Israel's right to exist.

Now, we have been supportive of Israel since 1948 and continue to be, but we also believe that, rather than our Arab friends and the Israelis continuing to exist in armed camps, it is time to do what the Government of Egypt did a few years ago and make peace.

Views on the Presidency

Mr. Farrell. Mr. President, you're constantly being asked to do the impossible. You're being asked to intervene and not intervene. You're being asked, for instance, in Ireland to make an intervention in regard to the trial of a priest there in Manila. You're being asked to do something about Qadhafi. Can you do anything in these areas.

The President. Well, we can't do all of the things that people suggest. I think we've taken action with regard to Qadhafi. We removed many of our people, as you know, and recognized him for what he is. You mention the Irish priest in the Philippines. I do not know the details of that. I have only recently heard about that, but we've had a longstanding relationship, dating back to the—when we were the protector of the

Philippines, with that government. And if there is any way in which we could be of help in that, we'd be pleased to do it.

Mr. Farrell. Mr. President, we're in a library in the White House, surrounded by the lives of American Presidents. Most of them, in the long haul of history, are remembered for one thing, one speech, one decision. What do you want to go down in history for doing?

The President. I know that's a question that comes up every once in a while. I find it rather difficult to think that way or think about yourself in history. I guess, if they just said I did my best, I might be pleased with that.

Mr. Farrell. But your priorities—after all, you're expecting to run into a second term. This is the time for you to do things. You said last week that the top priority is disarmament. Do you think you can achieve action in that over the next 4 years?

The President. I have to believe I can, because I don't think the world can go on this way. And we're going to try. Yes, if I had to say one thing that we would be aiming for—that I would be aiming for as mine—it is our country continuing along the path that was set so many years ago with its goal the ultimate in individual liberty and freedom consistent with an orderly society; with a government that is the servant of the people, not the master; and with peace throughout the world.

Mr. Farrell. The United States began with a revolution, with a message for the rest of the world. Mightn't some people argue that you've run out of steam, that, when they look at Central America, they look at the North-South debate, they look at the inequality of resources, they look at your richness and what you've got—they wonder whether you can really appeal to the poor people of the world effectively?

The President. I think we can. I remember that when World War II ended, Pope Pius XII said the Americans, the American people, "have a genius for great and unselfish deeds. Into the hands of America, God has placed an afflicted mankind." And we were the only nation that was left untouched by war, that still had our industrial power and all, had not been bombed and fought over and so forth. And we turned

our resources to helping reestablish not only the wartorn countries on our side but our enemies as well. And we have lived to see those former enemies close allies with us today, and democracies, living up to all the principles that we have believed in for so long.

I don't think America's run out of gas at all. I think there are great challenges out there before us. And even though some people are criticizing what we tried to do in Beirut, we were there on an errand of peace, seeking peace, and I'm not going to be ashamed of that. We didn't succeed. There were some advances made, and maybe that was one of the reasons why the terrorism started against the multinational force was because they were succeeding.

But, no, where there's a chance to bring peace—our relationship with our Latin American neighbors—I made a trip down there shortly after I got into office to tell them that my desire was that I think we'd been insensitive in the past. We haven't recognized that maybe we looked like the big colossus; and we were suggesting ideas with the best of intentions, but it was us telling them. And I went down to tell them, "Look, we're all partners, we're all neighbors. Let's exchange ideas and find out how we can all be better neighbors here in this hemisphere."

Mr. Farrell. Finally, Mr. President, any doubts that it will be you in the White House for the next 4 years?

The President. Oh, now, you've touched on a superstitious point with me. I find it impossible to speculate or suggest that I am going to win. I think it jinxes me if I do that. So, I'm always going to behave as if I'm one vote behind. I'll run scared.

Mr. Farrell. Mr. President, thank you very kindly for talking to us.

And that's all from this edition of "Today-Tonight," from the Library, White House, Washington, DC. Good night.

Note: The interview began at 3:40 p.m. in the Library at the White House. It was recorded for broadcast in Ireland on May 29, the date the transcript was released by the Office of the Press Secretary.

Nomination of Dodie Truman Livingston To Be Commissioner of the Administration for Children, Youth, and Families
May 29, 1984

The President today announced his intention to nominate Dodie Truman Livingston to be Chief of the Children's Bureau (and Commissioner of the Administration for Children, Youth, and Families) at the Department of Health and Human Services. She would succeed Clarence Eugene Hodges.

She is presently serving as Special Assistant to the President and Director of the Office of Special Presidential Messages at the White House. Previously, she was director of the correspondence department for the Reagan-Bush committee in 1980; a consultant to the Reagan for President campaign in 1979; and a writer and researcher for the Deaver and Hannaford Co. in 1978–1979.

She also served as a communications specialist with the State Department of Finance in California in 1972–1975 and as a writer in the Governor's office, State of California, in 1972. In 1960–1968 she worked as a staff writer and investigative reporter for the Oakland Tribune in Oakland, CA, and in 1964 received the John Swett Award of the California Teachers Association for distinguished reporting on school finance issues. From 1960 to the present, she has worked as a volunteer in community service.

Mrs. Livingston attended San Jose State University in 1956–1960. She has two sons and resides in Washington, DC. She was born September 12, 1938.

Remarks During a Visit to the United States Olympic Training Center in Colorado Springs, Colorado
May 29, 1984

The President. Colonel Miller asked me if I'd like to say a few words. I'd be awful disappointed if I didn't; I had them all written out here. [*Laughter*] Well, it is a pleasure to be with you here today. This is a training facility of which I think we can all be proud, and let me add, it's being used by some of the finest athletes in the world. And we're mighty proud of them, too, which means proud of you.

By the way, where's the riding ring— [*laughter*]—to get down to my present sport. But we had the U.S.C. women's basketball team at the White House not long ago, and so I saw a couple of familiar faces here when I was watching the practice over there.

I'm planning to be at the July 28th opening ceremony, so I'll see you there along with many of your friends from around the world. It's unfortunate that not all nations will be represented at the games. I hope

you realize, however, that the success of the Olympics and your personal success in the games in no way depend on political machinations of powerbrokers in countries that are less than free. The games are moving forward, and they'll be successful.

Closer to home, the Olympic movement is alive and well in the United States. Part of the reason is because of the excellent leadership given to the United States Olympic Committee by your president, Bill Simon, by your executive director for over a decade, Colonel Don Miller.

One of the major goals of our administration has been promoting private-sector initiatives, getting people involved instead of waiting for the government to take responsibility. Well, this Olympic effort is probably the greatest private-sector initiative that's ever been undertaken.

Seventy thousand athletes have trained at

this facility since 1977. The U.S. Olympic Committee budget is increased from less than $9 billion—million dollars—during Don Miller's first year to nearly $90 million for this Olympiad. I'm particularly impressed with the job opportunity program for athletes, permitting them to train while earning a living, and that sounds like a good job to me.

A host of corporations, sponsors, and individuals have contributed time, energy, and financial support to make sure the games and our team are the best ever. This spirit is especially important in our efforts, because ours is the only major national Olympic committee out of all 158 which receives no government financial support.

We pulled out all the stops. Every State of our Union has a volunteer organization to raise money. Thirty-seven corporations and more than a million individuals are supporters of the U.S. Olympics—they're all members of the U.S. team. And thanks to this national team effort, you'll be the best prepared competitors in history, and the Olympics are going to be the best ever held.

The Los Angeles Olympic Organizing Committee has also done a terrific job. There are more Olympians involved in these games than ever before. Their "Spirit Team" has been relating their Olympic experiences to get others involved and build support and enthusiasm for the Olympics. Unlike past Olympics, which never employed Olympians in management roles, the Los Angeles Olympic Organizing Committee has Olympians participating at all levels.

One aspect of the games of special note is the new competitive events for women. These games will do more for women than has ever been done before in the Olympics. There'll be 12 new women's Olympics events.

I remember the years when I was playing some football. And then in college I got tied up between swimming and track, and I knew I couldn't do both—and a quarter mile and a 220 and the 880 relay team in track, and then the dashes up to the 220 in—now it's 200 meters, but then we did it in yards—swimming. And I finally settled on swimming.

But I know that the—well, I followed that up with being a sports broadcaster. Indeed, I was broadcasting the Drake relays when Jesse Owens broke three American records in one afternoon. It was a great day for him, and I know you all know of him and what a great Olympic star and what a great American he was.

But even back then, our Olympic team was a great morale builder for the American people. And it's something which brings all your fellow citizens together. It gives us all the chance to wave the flag together. I'd end this by saying good luck, but I know it's not luck that you're depending on, although I've said it to some of you individually. It's your skill and all the training that you've done.

We're all very proud of you, and just remember: We are with you all the way. God bless all of you.

Lynette Woodard. Mr. President, this is a very exciting day for all of us. And we're very honored that you have graced us with your presence. On behalf of the 1984 Women's Olympic Basketball Team, we would like to extend to you a very warm welcome and present you with this gift.

[*Ms. Woodard gave the President a warmup suit.*]

The President. Hey, that's great.

Ms. Woodard. At this time—excuse me?

The President. This is all the rest of it?

Ms. Woodard. Yes. [*Laughter*]

The President. Thank you.

Ms. Woodard. At this time, the other sports would like to present you with some gifts.

The President. I didn't really come here for this, but thank you very much. You said there was more. I'm not going to leave. [*Laughter*]

Mel McGinnis. Mr. President, sir, I'm a race walker. And I know you don't know much about that sport, but I'm sure glad you came, and I'll probably vote for you, too. [*Laughter*]

The President. Thank you very much.

Thank you all very much. God bless all of you again.

Note: The President spoke at 2:53 p.m. at the center. Prior to his remarks, he was given a tour of the facility.

Following his appearance at the center, the President went to the Broadmoor Hotel, where he attended several receptions for

Colorado Reagan-Bush volunteers and Republican officials. He remained at the hotel overnight.

Address at Commencement Exercises at the United States Air Force Academy in Colorado Springs, Colorado
May 30, 1984

Secretary Orr, General Gabriel, General Scott, Senator Goldwater, Congressman Kramer, and distinguished guests, officers, cadets, and friends of the Air Force:

It's an honor and a real pleasure to come to Colorado Springs and to the Pike's Peak region. I just hope all Americans have the opportunity to visit Colorado and this breathtaking campus. Like me, they'll feel a deep pride in you, the men and women of our Air Force Academy.

On the flight from Washington, I asked our Air Force pilot for a few tips on Academy tradition. Well, he talked about Cadet Nino Baldacci—[*laughter*]—and then he offered to demonstrate an Immelman and a wingover. [*Laughter*] And my Air Force aide turned pale and said, "Mr. President, it would be better if you just remember the Air Force Academy is 7,250 feet above sea level, and that's far above West Point and Annapolis." [*Laughter*]

The greatest privilege of my office has been to lead the people who defend our freedom and whose dedication, valor, and skill increase so much our chance to live in a world of peace. I believe that we've made great progress in our efforts to rebuild the morale and the readiness of our Armed Forces. Once again, young Americans wear their uniforms and serve their flag with pride, and our military forces are back on their feet and standing tall.

And now, the class of 1984 has its turn. After 4 years of hard work and dedication, you've earned the right to be saluted. It will now be your responsibility to guard the flame of peace and freedom and to keep that flame burning brightly.

Your jobs will never be easy. But I believe you're ready to meet the challenges

before you and to turn them into opportunities for America. Your experience at this magnificient institution, guided by honesty, integrity, and an abiding loyalty to our nation will serve you well.

Dedicated instructors have increased your knowledge and understanding. You've been trained to deal in facts, not wishful thinking. And in doing many things together in classrooms, squadrons, and on the playing fields, you've learned the value of leadership and discipline and the need for both.

You've lived with the traditions and pioneering spirit of Rickenbacker, Billy Mitchell, Spaatz, Yeager, Lance Sijan, and the Mercury 7. You know that without the yeast of pioneering, we cannot rise above the status quo.

Personal honor, courage, and professional competence will guide your thoughts and actions. You understand the horrors of war, and you know that peace with freedom is the highest aspiration of our time. As a matter of fact, these past 4 years have prepared you to take your place in the best darn air force in the world.

So, now that I've paid your superiors a compliment, I hope they won't mind if their Commander in Chief pulls rank just this once. I hereby direct that the Secretary of the Air Force and the Superintendent of the Air Force Academy remit all existing confinements and other cadet punishments for minor offenses, and that this order be carried out today.

By the calendar, 52 years separate my college class from yours. Yet by the changes mine has seen, it might as easily have been 520. The world which the class of '32 had grown to know would soon disappear. True,

759

America was in the midst of a great world-wide depression which all of us desperately wanted to escape. Our immediate concern was work, but our class, like every college class, also thought about the future—and what a future it has been.

The pace of change, once orderly and evolutionary, became frantic and revolutionary. A series of scientific and technological revolutions flashed past us, touching Americans everywhere and every day. A new future was discovered and then quickly rediscovered. Technological progress was a cataclysmic rush.

The armies of Napoleon had not moved across Europe any faster than Caesar's legions eighteen centuries earlier—and neither army worried about air cover. But from my college days to yours, we went from open cockpits to lunar landings, from space fiction to space shuttles. Plotted on a graph, the lines representing technological progress would leap vertically off the page, and it wouldn't matter whether you plotted breakthroughs in agriculture or medicine, communications or engineering, genetics or military capability.

During the past few decades, the way we look and think about our world has changed in fundamental and startling ways. In 1932 "splitting the atom" was a contradiction in terms. We knew the word "atom" came from the Greek "atomos," meaning indivisible and, by definition, you couldn't split anything that was indivisible. But Albert Einstein wouldn't arrive in the States until the following year, and the Manhattan Project had not yet begun. The nuclear age was more than a decade away.

So many of the things that we take for granted today didn't exist on my commencement day: transistors, computers, supersonic flight, fiber optics, organ transplants, microelectronic chips, and xerography. Yes, even the venerable Xerox machine is only 25 years old.

Our progress results from human creativity and the opportunity to put our knowledge to use to make life better. We have yet to rid the world of disease and sickness, but today more people are living longer than ever before in human history. In many ways the good old days never were. In fact, I've already lived some two decades longer than my life expectancy when I was born. That's a source of annoyance to a number of people—[*laughter*]——

But the greatest of all resources is the human mind; all other resources are discovered only through creative human intelligence. God has given us the ability to make something from nothing. And in a vibrant, open political economy, the human mind is free to dream, create, and perfect. Technology, plus freedom, equals opportunity and progress.

Now, what about your generation? Where do you go from here? The quickening pace shouldn't generate the belief that the tide of events is beyond your control. No, you should be confident that with wisdom, responsibility, and care you can harness change to shape your future.

We've only seen the beginning of what a free and courageous people can do. The bold, not the naysayers, will point the way, because history has shown that progress often takes its greatest strides where brave people transform an idea which is scoffed at by skeptics into a tangible and important part of everyday life.

Your generation stands on the verge of greater advances than humankind has ever known. America's future will be determined by your dreams and your visions. And nowhere is this more true than America's next frontier—the vast frontier of space.

The space age is barely a quarter of a century old, but already we've pushed civilization forward with our advances in science and technology. Our work on the space shuttle gives us routine access to the landscape above us, dropping off payloads, performing experiments, and fixing satellites. And I believe we've only touched the edge of possibilities in space. It's time to quicken our pace and reach out to new opportunities.

This past January, in my State of the Union Address, I challenged our nation to develop a permanently manned space station and to do so within a decade. And now we're moving forward with a strategy that will chart the future course of the U.S. space program.

The strategy establishes priorities, provides specific direction for our future efforts, and assigns responsibilities to various government agencies. Above all, America's space strategy offers a balanced program that will best serve the down-to-earth needs of our own people and people everywhere.

Our goals are ambitious and yet achievable. They include a permanently manned presence in space for scientific, commercial, and industrial purposes; increased international cooperation in civil space activities; expanded private investment and involvement; cost-effective access to space with the shuttle; and strengthened security and capability to maintain the peace.

The benefits to be reaped from our work in space literally dazzle the imagination. Together, we can produce rare, life-saving medicines, saving thousands of lives and hundreds of millions of dollars. We can manufacture superchips that improve our competitive position in the world computer market. We can rapidly and efficiently repair defective satellites. We can build space observatories enabling scientists to see out to the edge of the universe. And we can produce special alloys and biological materials that benefit greatly from a zero-gravity environment.

Let me give you just one exciting glimpse that illustrates the great potential of how working in space can improve life on Earth. There is a medicine called—and I'm not quite sure of my pronunciation—it is either "urokinase" or "urokenase", but whichever name, it is used to treat victims of pulmonary embolism and heart attacks caused by blood clots. On Earth, this medicine is very difficult and expensive to produce. About 500,000 doses are needed annually at a cost of $500 million. Dr. Robert Jastrow, chairman of the first NASA Lunar-Exploration Committee, notes that tests in our shuttle have shown that production of urokinase in zero gravity could reduce that cost by a factor of ten or more. We could make this medicine available to thousands of people who cannot afford it at today's price.

Our willingness to accept the challenge of space will reflect whether America's men and women today have the same bold vision, the same courage and indomitable spirit that made us a great nation. Where would we be if the brave men and women who built the West let the unknowns and dangers overwhelm them? Where would we be if our aviation pioneers let the difficulties and uncertainties sway them?

The only limits we have are those of your own courage and imagination. And our freedom and well-being will be tied to new achievements and pushing back new frontiers. That's the challenge to the class of '84.

If I could leave you with one final thought, it would be to remind you again: The measure of America's future safety, progress, and greatness depends on how well you hold fast to our most precious values—values that embody the culmination of 5,000 years of Western civilization. Let your determination to make this world better and safer override all other considerations.

This Academy was not built just to produce air warriors; it was also built to produce leaders who understand the great stakes involved in the defense of this country, leaders who can be entrusted with the responsibility to protect peace and freedom. You are those leaders. And while you must know better than those before you how to fight a war, you must also know better than those before you how to deter a war, how to preserve peace.

As you look to the future, always remember the treasures of our past. Every generation stands on the shoulders of the generation that came before. Jealously guard the values and principles of our heritage; they didn't come easy.

Inspiration springs from great tradition. As military officers, guard the traditions of your service built here in the foothills of the Rockies and in the air over Ploesti, Mig Alley, the Red River Valley, and a thousand other places. The traditions you hold will serve you well.

Good luck, Godspeed, and God bless you all.

[At the conclusion of his formal address, the President presented the Medal of Honor to William J. Crawford.]

Now, there's something I want to do that means a lot to me and, I'm sure, will mean a lot to you. We're graced with the company of a man who believed so much in the values of our nation that he went above and beyond the call of duty in defending them.

In July 1944 a grateful nation bestowed the Medal of Honor on a soldier, a private, for extraordinary heroism on Hill 424 near Altavilla, Italy. The soldier could not accept the award that day. He was a prisoner of war, and his father accepted in his behalf.

Since early in this century, it has been customary for the President to present the Medal of Honor. Well, nearly 40 years have gone by, and it's time to do it right. A native son of Colorado and certainly a good friend of the Air Force Academy will forever be in the select company where the heroes of our country stand.

It gives me great pleasure to ask Mr. William J. "Bill" Crawford, formerly of the 36th Infantry Division, to come forward.

Colonel Wallisch. Please rise. Attention to orders: The President of the United States takes pleasure in awarding the Medal of Honor to William J. Crawford for service as set forth in the following citation.

For conspicuous gallantry and intrepidity at risk of life above and beyond the call of duty in action with the enemy near Altavilla, Italy, 13 September 1943. When Company I attacked an enemy-held position on Hill 424, the Third Platoon, in which Private Crawford was a squad scout, attacked as base platoon for the company. After reaching the crest of the hill, the platoon was pinned down by intense enemy machine gun and small-arms fire.

Locating one of these guns, which was dug in on a terrace on his immediate front, Private Crawford, without orders and on his own initiative, moved over the hill under the enemy fire to a point within a few yards of the gun emplacement and single-handedly destroyed the machine gun and killed three of the crew with a hand grenade, thus enabling his platoon to continue its advance.

When the platoon, after reaching the crest, was once more delayed by enemy fire, Private Crawford, again in the face of intense fire, advanced directly to the front, midway between two hostile machine gun nests, located on a higher terrace and emplaced in a small ravine.

Moving first to the left, with a hand grenade, he destroyed one gun emplacement

and killed the crew. He then worked his way, under continuous fire, to the other, and with one grenade and the use of his rifle, killed one enemy and forced the remainder to flee. Seizing the enemy machine gun, he fired on the withdrawing Germans and facilitated his company's advance.

The President. Thank you. I think everyone could sit down, couldn't they?

Colonel Wallisch. Oh, yes, sir.

The President. Yes, please be seated. [*Laughter*] Sometimes I don't know my own power. [*Laughter*]

For the past 12 years, the Commander in Chief's trophy has symbolized football supremacy among the Air Force Academy, West Point, and Annapolis. I understand that it's a rotating trophy, but from the performance of the Falcon football team these last 2 years, it looks like you have other ideas. [*Laughter*]

Last year, the scores weren't even close. When I think back to my playing days at a place called Eureka College, I must tell you, I can sympathize, however, with West Point and Annapolis. [*Laughter*] I remember some rough afternoons on the gridiron, in which we were winning too many "moral victories." [*Laughter*]

But as all athletes know, character is built on the playing fields through hard work, fair play, and gritty determination to rise to the highest challenge. The Duke of Wellington once remembered that the Battle of Waterloo was won on the playing field of Eaton.

It gives me great pleasure to ask Cadets First Class Marty Louthan, Michael Kirby, and John Kershner to come forward to accept the Commander in Chief's trophy.

[*After presenting the trophy, the President was made an honorary member of the football team and was given a Falcon jersey.*]

Note: The President spoke at 9:38 a.m. at Falcon Stadium on the Academy grounds. In his opening remarks, he referred to Secretary of the Air Force Verne Orr, Gen. Charles A. Gabriel, Chief of Staff of the Air Force, and Gen. Winfield W. Scott, Superintendent of the U.S. Air Force Academy.

Following his remarks, the President was

made an honorary member of the class of 1984 and was awarded the Distinguished American Award by William Thayer Tutt, chairman of the board, U.S. Air Force Academy Foundation. The President then par-

ticipated in the awarding of the diplomas to the graduating cadets.

Following the ceremonies at the Academy, the President returned to Washington, DC.

Toasts of the President and Secretary General Joseph M.A.H. Luns at a Dinner Honoring the NATO Foreign Ministers on the 35th Anniversary of the North Atlantic Alliance
May 30, 1984

The President. Secretary General Luns, distinguished guests, and ladies and gentlemen, it's an honor and a pleasure to welcome our NATO partners to the White House. This evening has been a special opportunity to celebrate the unprecedented success of our enduring friendship, our partnership—an alliance dedicated to peace and freedom.

Thirty-five years ago, in the troubled aftermath of a tragic conflict, 12 nations met here in Washington to sign the North Atlantic Treaty. That event was an act of realism. The member nations recognized the threat to their security and undertook to meet it together.

The establishment of the North Atlantic alliance was also an act of optimism, an affirmation of the enduring vitality of Western civilization. Thirty-five years of peace with freedom testify to the wisdom and the foresight of those nations, and of the four other nations who have since joined NATO.

Although the founders could not have foreseen the dramatic changes that have taken place since 1949, their vision was right on the mark. By uniting Europe and North America, NATO has made possible the longest period of peace and prosperity in modern history. And today our proud alliance remains united in its commitment to the defense of democracy and individual liberty.

We cannot be content with the accomplishments of the past. As we look ahead, there are compelling reasons to strengthen even further our solidarity and unity. Our commitment to collective security will con-

tinue to be an indispensable bulwark against aggression, terrorism, and tyranny.

Our unity will be the essential framework for building a constructive dialog with our adversaries and reducing the risks of war and the level of nuclear arms. And I know that it will be our societies, the democracies, that will offer a bright and hopeful future for our people and for people everywhere.

We can be confident. The events of the past year challenged us, and the Western democracies stood firm in the face of an intense Soviet campaign of intimidation, aimed at undermining NATO's commitment to defend Europe and preserve peace. Today we are stronger and more conscious of our unity. And that's of crucial importance, because when the Soviet Union becomes convinced that NATO cannot be shaken it may finally realize it has a clear and compelling interest to return to the negotiating table. We will be waiting, ready to meet them halfway.

Tonight is more than a celebration of an anniversary. It's also an opportunity to recognize the special contributions of our Secretary General. Joseph Luns is a distinguished diplomat and a man of many virtues.

First as the Dutch Foreign Minister, and then at NATO's helm, he's been at the center of the transatlantic bridge for nearly 30 years. His mission—his vision, I should say—his humor, and his patience have sustained us in good times and bad. As Secretary General, he's never lost sight of the goals and objectives of our alliance, and peace has been his profession.

You have been a trusted friend, an honest broker, a respected colleague, and, above all, an invaluable leader of the Atlantic alliance. Joseph, you've said that the state of our alliance is like Wagner's music—better than it sounds. [*Laughter*] Well, I must tell you that thanks largely to your efforts I rather like the way the alliance sounds. And I hope that even in retirement you will still watch over our partnership and that you will not hesitate to share your counsel with us.

Ladies and gentlemen, in recognition of Joseph Luns uncommon dedication to the ideals of our alliance and in tribute to his outstanding service and enduring contributions to our freedom and security, it is my great privilege to bestow America's highest civilian award, the Medal of Freedom, on Secretary General Luns.

But before I invite him to receive the medal, I would ask that you raise your glasses and join me in a toast to Secretary General Joseph Luns and to the organization he has faithfully served and so ably guided.

[*The toast was offered, and the President presented Secretary General Luns with the Medal of Freedom.*]

Mr. Secretary General, it gives me great pleasure to present that to you.

The Secretary General. Thank you very, very much, indeed. Thank you.

The President. Thank you.

The Secretary General. Mr. President, distinguished guests, I feel greatly flattered, deeply honored, immensely proud by having received from your hands, Mr. President, this very special award which I value highly and for which I am very, very grateful. Thank you very much, indeed.

May I say that I have now been nearly 13 years Secretary General of this great organization, and looking back on those 13 years, I must and I want to gratefully acknowledge the immense role the United States has played in this alliance. Far from being a hegemonic power, far from imposing your wishes and your will on your allies in an alliance where every decision must be taken by unanimity, you have always taken into account the views and the opinions of your European allies. And it is simply a truism to say that without the presence of more than 300,000 of your sons in Europe, Europe—the world—would be a far worse place than it is now, and I would not be standing here, nor would be the 16 Ministers of this alliance who have gathered here in Washington to have our yearly conclave, where, I must say, we had an excellent, excellent exchange of views.

The fact that your Secretary of State, Mr. George Shultz, and Counselor Weinberger, the Secretary of Defense, are among your guests, as well as so many distinguished people whom I have known, some of whom for a long time and some who have become personal friends of mine—and I look at Tapley Bennett, who is now Under Secretary of the State Department, and so many others I could name—makes, of course, this evening even more special than it is, Mr. President.

I could go on telling you, the guests here and the Ministers of the alliance, that we have gone through somewhat difficult times and that we have gone through very good times.

Let me say that if I had left this alliance last year at this time I would be less confident, less optimistic. But the fact that the United Kingdom, the Federal Republic of Germany, and Italy have started to station on their territory the modernized missiles in order to counter the threat of the SS–20 and, thereby, restoring the credibility of our nuclear deterrence, and on that credibility, Mr. President—you have said it often, and I repeat it—on that credibility, the peace of this world rests. And the President l'honneur Monsieur Cheysson said it yesterday and has repeated it today. I therefore repeat, I go with a certain optimism.

I am not pretending that I am deliriously happy to lay down my job as Secretary General. [*Laughter*] If I were to say what I feel, I would say I am somewhat content. [*Laughter*] That is, perhaps, already an overstatement. But let me say that all the various positions I have held in life, like Secretary of State of the Netherlands—and I was for 14 years a diplomat—the most rewarding, the most rich position, rich in achievement, and important in what the alliance has done, has been that I was chosen in '71 to serve this great alliance, the greatest, the most important alliance and organization for peace the world has known. And you are quite right, Mr. President, that the peace has been preserved for a far longer period, certainly in Europe, than we could have hoped for in the days after the last war.

And, Mr. President, may I end by saying that we are all deeply grateful for your unflinching support for the alliance. You have shown it over and over again. And let me say, too, that I will always treasure this very special award, which I will, for the days which will still be with me, I hope, always see as one of the most important and the most precious awards which was ever bestowed on me.

Thank you very much, Mr. President. All the best to you and to that great nation, the United States of America.

Note: The President spoke at 8:50 p.m. in the State Dining Room at the White House.

Text of a Foreword Written for Irish Times Magazine on the President's Visit to Ireland
May 31, 1984

For many Americans, coming to Ireland is like coming home. That is certainly true in my case. My great, great grandfather, Thomas Reagan, lived in the town of Doolis, Ballyporeen, in the county of Tipperary. His youngest son Michael, and Michael's son John, who was my grandfather, emigrated to the United States.

Nancy and I look forward to visiting Ballyporeen to see the church records of my ancestors and to meet family members and friends. We hope to make new friends while enjoying traditional Irish hospitality and savoring the beauty of this precious land.

In a way, my visit to your country is the story of Irish-American relations come full circle. My ancestors, like so many of their compatriots, left Ireland to seek a new beginning in a young and growing country. These Irish immigrants helped to build America with their bodies, their intellect and their love of beauty and culture—and their sense of humor, I should add. They wrote one of the most remarkable success stories in American history. The United States owes much to these men and women for their many contributions to our society in the arts, literature, drama and countless other fields.

Today, some 40 million of my fellow Americans—including 14 other U.S. Presidents—trace their roots to Ireland. As an Irish-American, I am honored to represent the United States as I return to a dynamic and growing country that is America's gateway to Europe.

America's friendship with the people of Europe is nowhere closer than with the people of Ireland. The respect and affection that the people of America have for your country are deep and sincere, founded upon the most durable bonds of family and common values.

I can personally say that we "Sons of Ireland in America" are proud of our Irish heritage of individualism and of our tenacious love of freedom.

Our two countries share many deeply held values, not the least of which are justice and peace. We have a common heritage of government by popular consent and of respect for the rule of law. Irishmen and Americans share other values too: importance of the family, deep religious beliefs, respect for individual rights and an abiding commitment to political, social and economic opportunity.

We have learned over the centuries since the first large party of Irish immigrants arrived in America in 1621, that peace, prosperity and freedom are the keys to the future, not only for ourselves, but also for our children. Ireland can be proud of its contribution to international peacekeeping and of its role in reducing international tensions.

Speaking for my country, I can say that Americans believe that the tide of history is a freedom tide, and that the values of freedom, democracy and independence that we have developed over the centuries will endure beyond the lives of all of us here

today.

The history of friendship between the Irish and American peoples is a long one. I hope that my visit to Ireland will serve to honor and to strengthen that long tradition of friendship.

Remarks on the 35th Anniversary of the North Atlantic Alliance
May 31, 1984

It has been a pleasure and an honor to welcome the Ministers of the North Atlantic Council to the White House. And I'm so pleased that the United States is hosting this meeting, because we're also celebrating the 35th anniversary of the signing in Washington of the North Atlantic Treaty.

Last night at dinner and again this morning, we had the opportunity to discuss the major challenges facing the alliance, including the security and defense of the West, relations with the Soviet Union, and arms control.

We all recognize that there is no more important consideration than the development of a better working relationship with the Soviet Union—one marked by greater cooperation and understanding and leading to stable, secure, and peaceful relations. This has been and will continue to be a primary goal of the United States and the NATO alliance.

The alliance is dedicated to peace. And thanks to the courage and vision of our member nations and their leaders, we can reflect on the past with pride and look to the future with confidence.

For us, our NATO partnership is an anchor, a fixed point in a turbulent world. And it's our sincere hope that the Soviet Union will soon come to understand the profound desire for peace which inspires us. And I hope that the Soviet leadership will finally realize it is pointless to continue its efforts to divide the alliance. We will not be split. We will not be intimidated. The West will defend democracy and individual liberty. And the West will protect the peace.

At the same time, we remain ready to negotiate fairly and flexibly and without

preconditions. It is our hope that the Soviet Union will soon return to the negotiating table. Our commitment to dialog and arms reduction is firm and unshaken. No other step in the near term would do so much for the cause of peace and stability as a return to constructive negotiations and agreements reducing the levels of nuclear arms.

I've said many times and will say again that when the Soviet Union returns to the negotiating table, we'll meet them halfway. I also hope that the Soviet leadership will respond positively to the range of proposals which we and our allies have advanced in other areas of arms control.

Our proposals serve the cause of peace: the draft treaty to abolish chemical weapons, presented by Vice President Bush in Geneva; the recent NATO proposal seeking to break the deadlock in the conventional force talks in Vienna; and the measures introduced by NATO in Stockholm in our effort to reduce the risk of surprise attack in Europe.

Tomorrow, I will leave for Europe. I'm looking forward to the trip and the opportunity to underscore the enduring importance of the political, cultural, and economic ties that bind the industrialized democracies.

The meeting of NATO Foreign Ministers has reinforced my own confidence in the strength and durability of the alliance and the common destiny of free societies.

And, so, I want to thank all these NATO Ministers. We're pleased to have had all of you with us as our guests and proud to have you as our partners.

Thank you, and God bless you all.

Note: The President spoke at 9:22 a.m. in the Rose Garden at the White House following a meeting with the Foreign Ministers in the Cabinet Room.

Proclamation 5201—National Physical Fitness and Sports Month, 1984
May 31, 1984

By the President of the United States of America

A Proclamation

Regular, vigorous physical activity is essential to good health and effective performance of our daily responsibilities. In addition, physical activity and sports programs can provide rich sources of personal pleasure and satisfaction.

Many individuals, families, communities, and others are increasingly concerned about physical fitness, and there is a growing recognition that physical activity is an important part of daily life for people of both sexes and all ages. Americans who are not reaping the benefits and pleasures of physical activity and sports should develop a personal physical fitness program in accordance with their capability.

In recognition of the importance of physical activity as a part of our daily life, the Congress, by Senate Joint Resolution 232, has authorized and requested the President to designate the month of May 1984 as "National Physical Fitness and Sports Month."

Now, Therefore, I, Ronald Reagan, President of the United States of America, do hereby proclaim the month of May 1984 as National Physical Fitness and Sports Month and urge communities, schools, States, employers, voluntary organizations, churches, and other organizations to stage appropriate observances and special events. Furthermore, I urge individuals and families to use this occasion to renew their commitments to make regular physical activity an integral part of their lives.

In Witness Whereof, I have hereunto set my hand this thirty-first day of May, in the year of our Lord nineteen hundred and eighty-four, and of the Independence of the United States of America the two hundred and eighth.

RONALD REAGAN

[*Filed with the Office of the Federal Register, 11:56 a.m., May 31, 1984*]

Proclamation 5202—National Animal Health Week, 1984
May 31, 1984

By the President of the United States of America

A Proclamation

Unparalleled progress in agricultural production has made the United States the world's food production model. Our ability to conquer disease and advance the health and productivity of our livestock has brought animal scientists and animal production specialists from around the world to our shores to learn the secret of America's agriculture.

A major milestone in this progress was the creation of the Bureau of Animal Industry on May 29, 1884. The efforts of the Bureau, followed by its successor agencies within the United States Department of Agriculture, have resulted in great strides forward to ensure an abundant supply of safe, wholesome animal products.

In today's dynamic economy, it is difficult to remember that these high-quality, healthy animal products have not always been with us. Whenever we enjoy a meal of meat, eggs, or milk, administer a life-improving health supplement, or enjoy a fine leather or wool item, we reap the benefits of persistent hard work over the decades. Without the progress represented by the improved health and productivity of our animals, we, in the United States, would not enjoy these items as we do for a fraction of the cost often paid by the people in other nations.

On this centennial of progress in advancing the health of livestock and production of animals through research and cooperative endeavors, we salute all who have contributed to the progress we enjoy today. The sound, scientific, and humane principles which have guided those in the forefront of this century of progress continue today, not only for livestock and poultry on our farms and ranches, but also for the care and feeding of our pets and wildlife.

To emphasize the combined efforts of the Government, private sector organizations, the veterinary profession and producers to combat the health hazards experienced in the past by the animal industry, the Congress, by House Joint Resolution 526, has authorized and requested the President to issue a proclamation designating the week beginning May 27, 1984, as "National Animal Health Week."

Now, Therefore, I, Ronald Reagan, President of the United States of America, do hereby proclaim the week beginning May 27, 1984, as National Animal Health Week. I encourage all Americans to observe this week by participating in appropriate ceremonies and activities planned by government agencies, individuals, and private sector organizations and institutions throughout the country to recognize the great strides made during the past century with animal health.

In Witness Whereof, I have hereunto set my hand this thirty-first day of May, in the year of our Lord nineteen hundred and eighty-four, and of the Independence of the United States of America the two hundred and eighth.

RONALD REAGAN

[*Filed with the Office of the Federal Register, 11:57 a.m., May 31, 1984*]

Message to the Congress on Trade With Hungary, China, and Romania
May 31, 1984

To the Congress of the United States:

I hereby transmit the documents referred to in subsection 402(d)(5) of the Trade Act of 1974 with respect to a further 12-month extension of the authority to waive subsection (a) and (b) of section 402 of the Act. These documents constitute my decision to continue in effect this waiver authority for a further 12-month period.

I include as part of these documents my determination that further extension of the waiver authority will substantially promote the objectives of section 402. I also include my determination that continuation of the waivers applicable to the Hungarian People's Republic, the People's Republic of China and the Socialist Republic of Romania will substantially promote the objectives of section 402. The attached documents also include my reasons for extension of the waiver authority; and for my determination that continuation of the waivers currently in effect for the Hungarian People's Republic, the People's Republic of China and the Socialist Republic of Romania will substantially promote the objectives of section 402.

RONALD REAGAN

The White House,
May 31, 1984.

REPORT TO CONGRESS CONCERNING EXTENSION OF WAIVER AUTHORITY

Pursuant to subsection 402(d)(5) of the

Trade Act of 1974 ("The Act") I have today determined that further extension of the waiver authority granted by subsection 402(c) of the Act for twelve months will substantially promote the objectives of section 402, and that continuation of the waivers currently applicable to the Hungarian People's Republic, the People's Republic of China and the Socialist Republic of Romania will also substantially promote the objectives of section 402 of the Act. My determination is attached and is incorporated herein.

The general waiver authority conferred by section 402(c) of the Act is an important means for the strengthening of mutually beneficial relations between the United States and certain countries of Eastern Europe and the People's Republic of China. The waiver authority has permitted us to conclude and maintain in force bilateral trade agreements with Hungary, the People's Republic of China, and Romania. These agreements continue to be fundamental elements in our political and economic relations with those countries, including our important, productive exchanges on human rights and emigration matters. Moreover, continuation of the waiver authority might permit future expansion of our bilateral relations with other countries now subject to subsections 402 (a) and (b) of the Act, should circumstances permit. I believe that these considerations clearly warrant this renewal of the general waiver authority.

I also believe that continuing the current waivers applicable to Hungary, the People's Republic of China and Romania will substantially promote the objectives of section 402 of the Act.

Hungary.—Hungary continues to take a positive and constructive approach to emigration matters. The Hungarian record of the past year, during which all outstanding problem cases were resolved, was excellent. The number of Hungarian citizens who apply to leave Hungary remains small, and emigration permission is granted apparently without undue difficulty. There are no sanctions imposed on those who seek to emigrate, nor do emigration procedures appear excessive.

People's Republic of China.—China continued its open emigrations policy throughout the past year. Chinese who wish to emigrate do so with little difficulty. In FY-1983, nearly 10,000 immigrant visas were issued by our Foreign Service posts in China. This figure has increased every year since the normalization of relations with China in 1979. In addition, tens of thousands of Chinese have traveled freely abroad over the past few years to study, conduct business, or simply tour and visit family. The limiting factor on Chinese emigration remains less official constraint than the limited ability or willingness of this and other countries to receive large numbers of potential Chinese immigrants.

Romania.—Emigration from Romania to all countries has more than doubled and emigration to the United States has increased almost ninefold since 1974, the last year before MFN was granted to Romania. In 1983, about 3,500 people came to the United States from Romania, and departures of ethnic Germans to the Federal Republic of Germany reached an all-time high of nearly 14,000, while Jewish emigration to Israel declined slightly from the relatively high level of 1982. I will continue to monitor closely Romania's performance in improving its emigration procedures and in the area of Jewish emigration to Israel.

Between February and June, 1983, Romania required that all emigrants repay the state in convertible currency the cost of any education they had received beyond the compulsory ten years of schooling. However, in early June 1983 I received assurances from President Ceaușescu that Romania would no longer require reimbursement of education costs as a precondition to emigration and would not create economic or procedural barriers to emigration. Since then, we are not aware of any emigrant who has had to pay for his education. Moreover, while there still are many problems in the emigration area, Romania's overall performance has significantly improved over the past year, particularly in the numbers of people receiving exit documentation and the shorter time taken to process their passport applications. On the basis of Romania's performance and the progress it has made in the area of emigration since last year, I believe that continuation of the waiver applicable to Romania will substantially promote the objectives of the Act.

For the above reasons, I have determined that continuation of the waivers for Hungary, the People's Republic of China and Romania will substantially promote the objectives of the Act.

Memorandum on Trade With Hungary, China, and Romania
May 31, 1984

Memorandum for the Secretary of State

Subject: Determination under Subsection 402(d)(5) of the Trade Act of 1974—Continuation of Waiver Authority

Pursuant to the authority vested in me under the Trade Act of 1974 (Public Law 93–618), January 3, 1975 (88 Stat. 1978) (hereinafter "the Act"), I determine, pursuant to subsection 402(d)(5) of the Act, that the further extension of the waiver authority granted by subsection 402(c) of the Act will substantially promote the objectives of section 402 of the Act. I further determine that the continuation of the waivers applica-

ble to the Hungarian People's Republic, the People's Republic of China and the Socialist Republic of Romania will substantially promote the objectives of section 402 of the Act.

This determination shall be published in the *Federal Register*.

RONALD REAGAN

[*Filed with the Office of the Federal Register, 12:30 p.m., June 8, 1984*]

Note: The determination is printed in the Federal Register of June 12, 1984.

Message to the Congress Transmitting a Report on the Domestic Uranium Mining and Milling Industry
May 31, 1984

To the Congress of the United States:

Pursuant to the requirements set forth in Section 23(a) of P.L. 97–415, the Nuclear Regulatory Commission Authorization Act of 1983, the "Comprehensive Review on the Status of the Domestic Uranium Mining and Milling Industry" is provided to the Congress.

The report presents information on the current and projected status of the domestic uranium mining and milling industry including uranium requirements and inventories, domestic production, import penetra-

tion, domestic and foreign ore reserves, exploration expenditures, employment, and capital investment. In addition to presenting projections of industry behavior under current policy, the report provides projections under alternative policy scenarios in the event that foreign import restrictions were enacted by Congress. The anticipated effect of spent nuclear fuel reprocessing on the demand for uranium is also addressed.

RONALD REAGAN

The White House,
May 31, 1984.

Message to the Congress Transmitting the Annual Report of the National Science Foundation
May 31, 1984

To the Congress of the United States:

I am pleased to send you the annual report of the National Science Foundation for fiscal year 1983. This report describes research supported by the Foundation in the mathematical, physical, biological, social, behavioral, and information sciences; in engineering; and in education for those fields.

The National Science Foundation is a key part of the national effort to revitalize our capabilities in research, innovation, and production. Achievements such as those described here underlie much of this Nation's strength—its economic growth, military security, and the general well-being of our people.

I hope you will share my enthusiasm for this fine work.

RONALD REAGAN

The White House,
May 31, 1984.

Nomination of Owen W. Roberts To Be United States Ambassador to Togo
May 31, 1984

The President today announced his intention to nominate Owen W. Roberts, of New Jersey, a career member of the Senior Foreign Service, Class of Minister-Counselor, as Ambassador to the Republic of Togo. He would succeed Howard Kent Walker.

Mr. Roberts served in the United States Army in 1943–1946. In 1955 he entered the Foreign Service as consular officer in Cairo and was commercial officer in Leopoldville in 1958–1960. In the Department he was desk officer for Africa in the Bureau of Intelligence and Research (1961–1962) and in the Bureau of International Organization Affairs (1963–1964). He was political officer in Lagos from 1964 to 1965, and deputy chief of mission in Ouagadougou from 1966 to 1968. He attended the Air War College from 1969 to 1970. In the Department he was staff director of the Board of Examiners for the Foreign Service (1970–1971), Deputy Director for Cultural Affairs for Africa (1971–1972), a member of the policy planning staff (1973), and Executive Director of the Office of Inspector General (1974–1975). From 1976 to 1978, he was Deputy Director of the Sinai Field Mission, Sinai Desert. He was Director of the African Office at the Department of Defense (on detail) from 1978 to 1979, and deputy chief of mission in Addis Ababa from 1979 to 1982. In 1983 he served as African adviser at the United Nations General Assembly. From 1982 to 1984, he was roving Chargé in Victoria, Banjul, and then N'Djamena.

Mr. Roberts graduated from Princeton University (A.B., 1948) and from Columbia University (M.A., 1952; Ph.D., 1955). His foreign languages are French and German. He was born March 29, 1924, in Ardmore, OK.

Interview With Television Correspondents Representing Nations Attending the London Economic Summit
May 31, 1984

Mr. Bell. Mr. President, as a group of correspondents from the countries represented at the London summit, we thank you for sharing this time with us. I'm Martin Bell of the BBC, and with me are Craig Oliver of CTV of Canada, Edouard Lor of Attend Deux from France, Dieter Kronzucker of ZDF in Germany, Guiseppe Lugato of RAI, Italian television, and Toshio Hidaka of NHK, Japanese television.

Persian Gulf Conflict

Mr. President, it seems so often that these economic summits tend to get caught up in the crisis of the moment, which, at this time is clearly the situation in the Gulf. I wonder if I could ask, first, what sort of commitment are you looking for from your allies and friends on the Gulf, and how far are you willing to go, if diplomacy fails, to keep the oil flowing?

The President. Well, I made a statement once that I didn't believe that the Western World could see that area closed to traffic and a shutoff of the oil supply. It is far more important to the countries that some of you represent than it is to us, because the bulk of our import now is coming from sources here in this hemisphere. But at the same time now, we're staying in close consultation with representatives of your governments, and at the same time, we are all staying in touch with the Gulf States.

Now, the Gulf States have taken a position, very firmly, that they want to deal with the problem themselves. They do not want it to enlarge—as it might—and expand into more of a war if everyone else got involved. They've made it plain, however, as is evident in the media right now, that there is some help they need in the line of materiel—weapons. And, we have sent—we've answered their request with some. But I think that we have to stay, as I say, in that consultation and watching, in the event that there should be a complete shutdown.

However, if you look at the last few days, it appears that, rather then getting worse, the situation has quieted somewhat. I don't believe there have been any attacks to speak of in the last several days. So, maybe it's going to turn out all right.

Mr. Oliver. Mr. President, at the beginning of the Second World War in the Middle East, a United States admiral sent home a now famous telegram. He was confused and said, "Please advise, who is the enemy?" [*Laughter*] And I think that a lot of people here in Washington are asking the same things at this moment—who is the enemy in the Gulf? Iran or Iraq?

The President. Well, let's look at it this way. Iraq did confine its raids, its attacks on shipping that was vital to Iran's economy. And Iran, when it responded, however, did not respond against Iraq; it attacked ships that belonged to neutral nations that were getting oil and doing business with countries like Saudi Arabia and Kuwait and so forth. And you had to say, "What was on Iran's mind?" I think we've always recognized that in a time of war, the enemy's commerce and trade is a fair target, if you can hurt them economically. So, in that sense, Iraq had not gone beyond bounds, as Iran had done.

And now, even though Iraq, we must admit, is the one who started the war 4 years ago, Iraq now had made overtures to have a negotiated settlement and end the war. And Iran has refused to do this. So, Iran is in more or less the position of demanding unconditional victory. And if there was any way that any of the rest of us could, by appeal, bring an end to that fighting, I'm sure we would all do it, because it's a tremendous and horrible bloodletting that is going on. And Iran, as I say, is the one now who seems to resist any effort, short of a total victory, ending that war.

U.S.-France Relations

Mr. Lor. Mr. President, last month, George Shultz said that France is your best ally in Europe. Do you think so, before the London summit?

The President. Well, I think there's a little language difficulty there, in that what the Secretary of State actually said was, "We have no better ally than France," meaning that the other allies are equally good. But there's no one that we would think of as a greater ally, and certainly no one longer as an ally than France. And, as I say, I think it was a language difficulty that made it come out "best." And that would be rather unfair of us.

U.S.-Soviet Relations

Mr. Kronzucker. Mr. President, many Europeans consider the American attitude versus the Soviet Union as too uncompromising. They fear that the smaller Communist satellite states in Eastern Europe might lose the little amount of leeway and liberties they have. Especially we West Germans fear damage to the relationship to Eastern Germany. Could you elaborate on that?

The President. Yes, I can. And I don't know why it is that it's always the other fellow, never the Soviet Union. Now, we offered a treaty to the Soviet Union to totally eliminate intermediate-range nuclear weapons in Europe. At that time, they had about 800 warheads targeted on Europe, not on the United States. And in 1979, NATO allies asked us to provide the weapons—which we could, the Pershing II's and so forth, and cruise missiles, a combination—as a deterrent to the SS–20's of the Soviet Union, each with its three warheads. And my predecessor and the government at that time in this country agreed. So, I inherited this program that was underway with us building and testing the weapons to go there. And we came to deployment.

Well, the Soviet Union, when I said, "Zero-zero. There'll be no deployment of these weapons if you will agree to eliminate yours." And they refused. So, we said, "All right. If you won't go for zero-zero now, we'll hope that in the future you'll see the wisdom of it, but if not, we're willing to sit down and negotiate a reduction in numbers that would be fair to both sides." And they walked away from the table on the basis of our deployment.

At first, they did make an answer. They would reduce the number of their missiles, but we would have to have zero. In other words, they bought half my proposal of zero-zero. We'd be zero, and they'd have— well, as it stands now, about 1,350 warheads targeted on Europe. They continued adding those warheads, those missiles, all the time we were talking at the negotiating table about reductions. They were continuing to increase.

Well, now they've—the Economist Magazine has an article called, "May Hibernation." And it suggests that the Soviet Union right now maybe doesn't have any answers, so the bear has just decided to hibernate, hunker down in the cave and not say anything.

But we don't feel that we're at fault in these relations. They left the table. They left the START talks, which were based on the overall nuclear. We have repeatedly told them how flexible we are willing to be. We have recognized some of the points they made that they thought our first proposal did not meet some of their problems, and we said, "All right. Tell us what those problems are, and we'll meet."

But I happen to believe that, first of all, there is no great risk in this silence on their part. I think they're unhappy because we have refurbished our military after unilaterally disarming over the years, hoping that they would then follow suit, and they didn't. They continued the biggest buildup possible.

We're ready, and as a matter of fact, we are having negotiations with them, very quietly and on a number of subjects that are of interest to them. We have told them that we're ready to—we're willing to talk on those particular matters, and those talks are going forward. And there's some productivity in them.

But I—when I'm accused every once in a while of being guilty of harsh rhetoric—the other day we had a very moving ceremony in the burial of our unknown soldier. I thought it was going a little far when the Soviet Union publicly referred to that as a "militaristic orgy" that we were engaged in. I don't know just how you could get that out of a ceremony for a young man whose name will forever be known only to God, but who gave his life in the service of his country. And we decided to bury him at

Arlington Cemetery.

So, I think it's time for the world to begin asking the Soviet Union when are they going to move, when are they going to make some proposal.

Now, we're dealing with them in Stockholm in those meetings. We're dealing with them and with our NATO allies in the Vienna talks on conventional forces. And they just stubbornly refuse to talk the nuclear weapons.

That shouldn't surprise us. Our effort to get them engaged in nuclear talks, weapon talks is, I think, the 20th since World War II ended. And the closest they ever came to a successful agreement—well, there was the antiballistic missile treaty. But remember the significance of that. We were trying to get such a treaty for some time, and they refused. And then one day, our Congress voted an appropriation of money for us to research and build an antiballistic missile. And the Soviet Union suddenly volunteered to sit down and discuss a treaty banning the weapon.

Now I think it's their move. But we'll be ready if there's anything we can do. We're not going to offer them some great concession as a reward for walking away from the table.

North Atlantic Alliance

Mr. Lugato. Mr. President, the uneasy alliance is something that we have been hearing for several years. It's a sort of complaint, if you want, of the European—of American complaint of the European allies. Now there is a concern in Europe about the so-called shift between the Atlantic to the Pacific. What's your reaction, sir? How do you comment?

The President. Oh, well, that's very easy. Let me just say that last night in this same room we're in, we had a very enjoyable dinner with the 16 Foreign Ministers of the 16 alliance nations. I don't believe that relationship has ever been closer or better or stronger than it is right now. No concern about that.

At the same time, the United States, placed here as we are in the Western Hemisphere, we have always been a Pacific nation in that we're on the rim of the Pacific Basin. And we see no diminution in our

closeness to the European alliance. But at the same time, we recognize that we have friends and allies on the other side of the Pacific, and we're just as concerned about keeping that relationship and enhancing it to keep peace and friendly bonds in that part of the world.

So, Japan is one of our close friends and allies and certainly is a close friend and ally of the alliance, Europe. And I think the trip that we made to the People's Republic was a very fruitful one. The ASEAN nations to the south, in Southeast Asia, who are concerned there about maintaining peace and having an alliance among themselves and getting—obtaining a settlement to the Kampuchea problem. No, I think that we fought a war two-handed, in the East and the West, and certainly we could be peaceful neighbors and friends in the same way.

Trade With Japan

Mr. Hidaka. In Japan also, the 6th of Saturday is quite well welcomed, and the people like it. Here I'd like to ask you about a trade matter. I think you are surrounded by a very strong protectionism in the Congress, and we Japanese realize that and try the best effort to open the market. I'd like to have your assessment on Japanese effort to open the market. In connection with that, do you want Japan should continue self-imposed restriction of automobile import in this country after next year?

The President. I'm glad that you said what it was, because here in the treatment of our own press, they've—without really deliberately misstating, they've given an impression to the people of this country that this was something we imposed on you, that we asked for the quota on automobile imports. And it's a good opportunity for me to reiterate what you said, that this was Japan's voluntary move when our automobile industry was as hard hit by the great recession as it was, and you were selling a product that we could not match pricewise. It was Japan that voluntarily agreed to limit the number of automobiles they would sell in this market. Now, the renewal of that, or if there is to be a renewal, isn't due for some months yet, and that is strictly up to Japan and what they decide to do.

But on the general trade matters, I have to say that Prime Minister Nakasone has just been a tower of strength in his belief in trade relations between our two countries—improving them, making them more fair wherever there is an unfairness. And great progress has been made. Just previous to this last trip, as you know, I was in Japan and met with him, and since then, our other—or our Cabinet ministers—Secretary Regan and others have. And he and the Cabinet in Japan have worked with our people to bring about correction of some things that were unfair. And we've made greater progress, I believe, than has been made in the last quarter of a century as trading partners. And we're most appreciative of that fact.

U.S. Economy

Mr. Bell. Mr. President, that would seem to lead naturally into a question about the London summit, whither you're bound. We would expect the Americans to come under some pressure there on account of rising interest rates and budget deficits. Is there a message that you're carrying to London?

The President. Yes. I'd like to point out to them when I get there that if you go by deficits as a percentage of gross national product, we're not too out of line with our deficits with the deficits of our allies there in the summit. They, too, have deficits. Not all of them, but—well, I think possibly all of them do, but not to the same extent.

The deficit—and we're working hard—the message I will bring is that we now have the House and the Senate in a conference committee working out their differences on what I had asked for earlier, a downpayment on the deficit of $150 billion or so over the next 3 years. I think we're going to have that, and it's just various details that have to be worked out that they will agree to.

Then I will also be able to convey that I want a balanced budget. I'm trying to get a balanced budget amendment to our Constitution. I'm trying to get also the right of line-item veto.

This old political custom of attaching a spending bill of some kind that is lacking in merit to a good piece of legislation and then, because you want the good legislation,

you pass the bad also. As Governor of California, I had line-item veto. I could intercept and veto out of that good bill that amendment. Then the legislature, if it had the power, by a two-thirds majority, could override my veto. Well, in 8 years, I vetoed 943 times without ever being overridden, because once they have to vote for that bad bill all by itself, without it being hidden by this other legislation, they decide not to do that. Well, I want the same thing here.

But, also, once we get the downpayment, beginning next year we will begin implementing some two thousand, four hundred and—I believe it's seventy-eight recommendations that were made to us by a citizens group. More than 2,000 of the business leaders of our country voluntarily came together and, at our invitation, went into every area of government and came back with these thousands of recommendations as to how modern business practices could be put to work to make government more efficient and more effective. And the savings are astronomical if this is done.

Now, some of those we've managed to put into operation by my Executive order. Most of them would undoubtedly result in changes that would require legislation from the Congress. But we're pursuing that. We have a study group right now combing those and framing legislation to bring those. So, we're going to go to work on the deficits.

But the other part of my message will be: I don't believe the deficits have anything to do with our high interest rates, because at the very time that we were bringing the interest rates that we inherited from the previous administration down from 21½ percent, and bringing them down to half that level, at the same time the deficit was going up. Now, how could that be and now there be a connection with the lower interest rates that we've already achieved, that somehow the deficit is responsible for those?

The responsibility for those is one and one only. The money market out there is not yet convinced that we have control of inflation. We've had about eight recessions since World War II, and every time they've seen government kind of turn to a quick fix and inflation go up some more. The world has been in the longest period of sustained worldwide inflation in the world's history.

Well, for the last 2 years, from inflation being 12.4 percent, we have had inflation that is less than 4 percent. And in the first quarter of this year, it is less than 4 percent. We believe we have inflation under control. We're determined to keep it under control.

I think once the Congress passes this other legislation about the deficit and so forth and they see that we're not going to turn to flooding the market with money and the quick-fix idea, I think the marketplace will be more reasonable, and we will see a decline in interest rates. There may be a little flurry of a point or something here and there while this is going on. But I think that's based on an economic lesson I learned when I was getting my own degree in economics. There is nothing so timid as a million dollars. [*Laughter*]

U.S.-Canada Relations

Mr. Oliver. Mr. President, your Ambassador in Ottawa is a pretty outspoken fellow, Mr. Paul Robinson. And he's been outspoken lately saying—criticizing Canada's level of defense spending, saying Canada is not living up to its NATO responsibilities, and also saying that the departing Trudeau government has treated U.S. investors very badly. Are these Mr. Robinson's own views, or are they the views of your administration and you?

The President. Well, I've just heard these for the first time—[*laughter*]—so they must be his own views.

I know it is true that recently your country has done what a number of Members of our Congress would do to us if they would get away with it, and that is reduce deficit spending. If there's any opportunity to reduce spending, they'll reduce deficit spending rather than anything else.

Mr. Oliver. You mean defense spending, sir, or deficit spending?

The President. What'd I say?

Mr. Oliver. You said "deficit spending."

The President. Oh, I've been saying "deficit" so much—defense spending. I'm sorry, defense spending, yes.

Mr. Oliver. Yes, sir.

The President. And we've had discussions, and in the summit—and probably will some more—about some of the differences in our approach to outside investment. But we'll deal with them at the summit.

Mr. Oliver. So, you don't think the Trudeau government has treated investment badly from the U.S.?

The President. Well, you don't want to get me in a fight with our Ambassador, do you? [*Laughter*] Let me just say that there are some differences, different views about international investment between our two countries, but with all of that, you still remain our primary trading partner, and you still remain, I think, about as close a friend as a nation can have.

Mr. Bell. Mr. President, I say that, regretfully, our time is up. They're making signals at me. But I want to thank you for covering so much ground.

The President. Well, I'm very pleased and sorry that we couldn't go around again here. I've been running behind all day here, and with tomorrow being getaway day, I guess I better listen to those who are trying to shut us off. [*Laughter*]

Mr. Bell. Well, let us at least wish you a safe and successful journey to Europe.

The President. Well, thank you very much.

Note: The interview began at 1:58 p.m. in the State Dining Room at the White House.

Nomination of Jorge L. Mas To Be a Member of the Advisory Board for Radio Broadcasting to Cuba, and Designation as Chairman
May 31, 1984

The President today announced his intention to nominate Jorge L. Mas to be a member of the Advisory Board for Radio Broadcasting to Cuba, for a term of 2 years.

This is a new position. The President also intends to designate Mr. Mas as Chairman of the Advisory Board upon his confirmation.

Mr. Mas is currently president and chief executive officer of Church & Tower of Florida, Inc., a firm of engineering contractors. He is also editor of RECE, one of the oldest Cuban monthly publications. Previously he served as an executive member of RECE and was responsible for three weekly commentaries on WMIE Radio in Miami (1964–1968). He graduated as a second lieutenant from the Infantry School at Fort Benning, GA, in 1963. From 1960 to 1961, he made biweekly radio broadcasts to Cuba through radio stations WRUL and SWAN and served as a member of the invasion forces at the Bay of Pigs.

Mr. Mas is chairman of the Cuban American National Foundation, a nonprofit organization with offices in Washington, DC, and Miami. He also serves as a member of the Presidential Commission on Radio Broadcasting to Cuba.

Mr. Mas is married, has three children, and resides in Miami, FL. He was born September 21, 1939, in Santiago, Cuba.

Remarks Announcing the Nomination of Martha R. Seger To Be a Member of the Board of Governors of the Federal Reserve System
May 31, 1984

The President. I am delighted and honored to announce today that I am nominating Dr. Martha Seger to become a member of the Board of Governors of the Federal Reserve System.

Dr. Seger is a financial economist with extensive experience in business, banking, and government. She has served at both the State and Federal levels as the Commissioner of Financial Institutions for the State of Michigan and as a financial economist for the Federal Reserve Board in Washington, DC. And most recently, she has been a professor of finance at Central Michigan University.

Dr. Seger arrives at a time of optimism and challenge. We received more evidence this morning that our economic expansion continues steady and strong. The leading economic indicators rose again in April, the 18th increase in the last 20 months. At the same time, inflation remains low, contrary to many predictions.

We've begun a new era in America of strong growth and stable prices. And I'm convinced that it results from our program to take America in a new direction—restore incentives to people, stimulate more competition in our economy, but restrain government's ability to spend, tax, and regulate. And I believe that we should press on with even greater determination.

I'm confident that Dr. Seger can and will make a significant contribution, helping us meet challenges of keeping our economy growing and keeping inflation down.

And now, Dr. Seger, we're delighted to welcome you to Washington.

Dr. Seger. Thank you very much, Mr. President. It's really an honor for me to be here today and to be nominated for what I think is probably one of the most important jobs in the world.

Thinking back to being a kid in a small town in Michigan during World War II and having my parents tell me that I lived in the greatest country on Earth and that, while most people knew all about their rights as citizens, that we also had duties and responsibilities—then, I never dreamed that I would one day have an opportunity to serve my country in this type of job.

I'm really grateful. And again, I'd like to thank the President, because I support everything he's doing, and I think that getting our economy back on track is the best way to keep America great.

Thank you very much.

Mr. Volcker. Mr. President, if I could just add my word of welcome on behalf of the

Federal Reserve Board to Dr. Seger. We're delighted this day has come. It's a particularly appropriate day. We happened to be meeting with the Chairmen of the various Federal Reserve Banks today, so they were able to come over here and have a chance to meet Dr. Seger. Beyond that, we would be happy even if it wasn't that day. It's particularly opportune. And we are well aware of the breadth of her background, the kind of experience that she's had, that I'm sure is going to be a very fine addition to our system. And we're delighted.

The President. Lest anyone is suspicious, she was a victim recently of an unfortunate accident. This is not from twisting. [*Laughter*]

Note: The President spoke at 2:27 p.m. in the Rose Garden at the White House. His closing comment referred to the cast on Dr. Seger's left arm.

Paul A. Volcker, Chairman of the Board of Governors of the Federal Reserve System, also made remarks.

Nomination of Martha R. Seger To Be a Member of the Board of Governors of the Federal Reserve System
May 31, 1984

The President today announced his intention to nominate Martha R. Seger to be a member of the Board of Governors of the Federal Reserve System for a term of 14 years from February 1, 1984. She would succeed Nancy Hays Teeters.

Dr. Seger is a financial economist who has been serving as professor of finance at Central Michigan University since 1982. Previously she was commissioner of financial institutions for the State of Michigan in 1981–1982 and associate professor of economics and finance at Oakland University in 1980. She has also taught at the University of Michigan and the University of Windsor. Dr. Seger has had 10 years experience in commercial banking, including serving as

chief economist for Detroit Bank and Trust for over 7 years. Prior to this, she was financial economist in the capital market section at the Federal Reserve Board.

Dr. Seger is a director of Comerica, Inc., and the Comerica Bank-Detroit. She is a member of the National Association of Business Economists, the American Economics Association, the Economic Club of Detroit, and the Women's Economic Club.

She has three degrees from the University of Michigan, including an M.B.A. in finance and a Ph.D. in finance and business economics. Dr. Seger was born February 17, 1932, in Adrian, MI, and now resides in Bloomfield Hills, MI.

Memorandum on the Renewal of Trade Agreements With Romania and Hungary
May 31, 1984

Presidential Determination No. 84–10

Memorandum for the Honorable William Emerson Brock III, United States Trade Representative

Subject: Renewal of Trade Agreements with Romania and Hungary

Pursuant to my authority under subsection 405(b)(1) of the Trade Act of 1974 (19 U.S.C. 2435(b)(1)), I find that a satisfactory balance of concessions in trade and services has been maintained during the lives of the Agreements on Trade Relations between the United States and the Socialist Republic of Romania and the Hungarian People's Republic. I further determine that actual or foreseeable reductions in United States tariffs and non-tariff trade barriers are satisfactorily reciprocated by the Socialist Republic of Romania and by the Hungarian People's Republic.

This memorandum and the attached justification shall be published in the *Federal*

Register.

RONALD REAGAN

[Filed with the Office of the Federal Register, 4:36 p.m., May 31, 1984]

Note: The memorandum and justification are printed in the Federal Register *of June 4, 1984.*

Proclamation 5203—National Theatre Week, 1984
May 31, 1984

By the President of the United States of America

A Proclamation

Theatres enrich the lives of all Americans. They have pioneered the way for many performers and have given them a start in artistic careers. Theatres enable their audiences to take part in the creative process; they challenge and stimulate us and show us our world in a new light. The strength and vitality of America's theatres are proof of our dedication and commitment to this vital art form.

Americans in all parts of the country have made theatre a part of their lives. We participate as performers and audience members in schools, community theatres, and at the professional level. Through these efforts, we have nourished an art form that proudly celebrates the diversity and creativity of all our people.

In recognition of the many contributions theatres make to the quality of our lives, and in celebration of this art form which

enriches us in so many ways, the Congress, by House Joint Resolution 292, has designated the week of June 3 through June 9, 1984, as "National Theatre Week," and authorized and requested the President to issue a proclamation in observance of this week.

Now, Therefore, I, Ronald Reagan, President of the United States of America, do hereby proclaim the week of June 3 through June 9, 1984, as National Theatre Week. I encourage the people of the United States to observe the week with appropriate ceremonies, programs, and activities.

In Witness Whereof, I have hereunto set my hand this thirty-first day of May, in the year of our Lord nineteen hundred and eighty-four, and of the Independence of the United States of America the two hundred and eighth.

RONALD REAGAN

[Filed with the Office of the Federal Register, 11:58 a.m., May 31, 1984]

Proclamation 5204—Flag Day and National Flag Week, 1984
May 31, 1984

By the President of the United States of America

A Proclamation

Over two hundred years ago, in June

1775, the first distinctive American flags to be used in battle were flown by the colonists at the Battle of Bunker Hill. One flag was an adaptation of the British Blue Ensign, while the other was a new design.

Both flags bore a common device of the colonial era which symbolized the experience of Americans who had wrested their land from the forest: the pine tree.

Other flags appeared at the same time, as the colonies moved toward a final separation from Great Britain. Two featured a rattlesnake, symbolizing vigilance and deadly striking power. One bore the legend "Liberty or Death"; the other "Don't Tread on Me." The Grand Union flag was raised over Washington's Continental Army headquarters on January 1, 1776. It displayed not only the British crosses of St. Andrew and St. George, but also thirteen red and white stripes to symbolize the American colonies. The Bennington flag also appeared in 1776, with thirteen stars, thirteen stripes, and the number "76."

Two years after the Battle of Bunker Hill, on June 14, 1777, the Continental Congress chose a flag which tellingly expressed the unity and resolve of the brave colonists who had banded together to seek independence. The delegates voted "that the flag of the thirteen United States be thirteen stripes, alternate red and white; that the union be thirteen stars, white in a blue field representing a new constellation."

After more than two centuries of history, and with the addition of thirty-seven stars, the Stars and Stripes chosen by the Continental Congress in 1777 is our flag today, symbolizing a shared commitment to freedom and equality.

To commemorate the adoption of our flag, the Congress, by a joint resolution approved August 3, 1949 (63 Stat. 492), designated June 14 of each year as Flag Day and requested the President to issue an annual proclamation calling for its observance and the display of the Flag of the United States on all government buildings. The Congress also requested the President, by a joint resolution of June 9, 1966 (80 Stat. 194), to issue annually a proclamation designating the week in which June 14 occurs as National Flag Week and calling upon all citizens of the United States to display the flag during that week.

Now, Therefore, I, Ronald Reagan, President of the United States of America, do hereby designate the week beginning Sunday, June 10, 1984, as National Flag Week, and I direct the appropriate officials of the government to display the flag on all government buildings during this week. I urge all Americans to observe Flag Day, June 14, and National Flag Week by flying the Stars and Stripes from their homes and other suitable places.

I also urge the American people to celebrate those days from Flag Day through Independence Day, set aside by Congress as a time to honor America (89 Stat. 211), by having public gatherings and activities at which they can honor their country in an appropriate manner.

In Witness Whereof, I have hereunto set my hand this thirty-first day of May, in the year of our Lord nineteen hundred and eighty-four, and of the Independence of the United States of America the two hundred and eighth.

RONALD REAGAN

[*Filed with the Office of the Federal Register, 1:11 p.m., May 31, 1984*]

Proclamation 5205—Citizenship Day and Constitution Week, 1984
May 31, 1984

By the President of the United States of America

A Proclamation

September 17, 1984, marks the 197th anniversary of the signing of our Constitution. As the bicentennial of this dynamic and timeless document nears, all Americans should become reacquainted with its role as our great country's guiding beacon. With this document as its blueprint, this Nation has become the finest example in history of the principle of government by law, in which every individual is guaranteed certain inalienable rights. Exemplifying this precept, a newly naturalized citizen once wrote:

"After our arrival here we very soon realized that the U.S.A. is really a wonderland: It is the first one among the few countries in the world where liberty, justice, democracy, and happiness are not only not empty slogans, but real benefits for all; where the Constitution is still as valid as it was in those days when the people of the U.S.A. ordained and established it in order to secure the blessings of liberty for themselves and their posterity. It was just natural that our next wish could not be other than to become a citizen of this wonderful country.

"And now, a few minutes after we solemnly pledged allegiance to the flag of the United States, we have just one more wish, that may God give us a long life, and ability to help at our very best in holding this flag straight up, flying as free and clear forever as it has been doing from the beginning of this country."

The Constitution provides a framework for our continuous striving to make a better America. It provides the basic balance between each branch of government, limits the power of that government, and guarantees to each of us as citizens our most basic rights. The Constitution, however, is only the outline of our system of government. It is through each individual citizen living out the ideals of the Constitution that we reach for a full expression of those ideals. Therefore, while we celebrate Citizenship Day and Constitution Week, let us rededicate ourselves to a full realization of the potential of the great country which the Founding Fathers struggled to create more than two hundred years ago.

Once each year, on September 17, all four pages of the original signed Constitution are placed on public exhibition in the Rotunda of the National Archives building in Washington, DC. I encourage all Americans to take the opportunity to view this document, which embodies our national commitment to freedom.

In recognition of the importance of our Constitution and the role of our citizenry in shaping our government, the Congress, by joint resolution of February 29, 1952 (36 U.S.C. 153), designated September 17th of each year as Citizenship Day and authorized the President to issue annually a proclamation calling upon officials of the government to display the flag on all government buildings on that day. The Congress also, by joint resolution of August 2, 1956 (36 U.S.C. 159), requested the President to proclaim the week beginning September 17th and ending September 23rd of each year as Constitution Week.

Now, Therefore, I, Ronald Reagan, President of the United States of America, call upon appropriate government officials to display the flag of the United States on all government buildings on Citizenship Day, September 17, 1984. I urge Federal, State and local officials, as well as leaders of civic, educational and religious organizations to conduct ceremonies and programs that day to commemorate the occasion.

I also proclaim the week beginning September 17 and ending September 23, 1984, as Constitution Week, and I urge all Americans to observe that week with appropriate ceremonies and activities in their schools, churches and other suitable places.

In Witness Whereof, I have hereunto set my hand this thirty-first day of May, in the year of our Lord nineteen hundred and eighty-four, and of the Independence of the United States of America the two hundred and eighth.

RONALD REAGAN

[*Filed with the Office of the Federal Register, 1:12 p.m., May 31, 1984*]

Proclamation 5206—D-day National Remembrance
May 31, 1984

By the President of the United States of America

A Proclamation

On Tuesday, June 6, 1944, General Dwight D. Eisenhower made a dramatic announcement from London:

"People of Western Europe: A landing was made this morning on the coast of France by troops of the Allied Expeditionary Force. . . . The hour of your liberation is approaching."

Operation Overlord, the invasion of Adolph Hitler's "Fortress Europe" forty years ago, thrust approximately 130,000 American and Allied troops under General Eisenhower's command onto beaches now known to history as Utah, Omaha, Gold, Juno, and Sword along the coast of Normandy, France. Another 23,000 British and American airborne forces were parachuted or taken by glider to secure critical inland areas. Some 11,000 sorties were flown by allied aircraft, and innumerable sabotage operations were carried out by Resistance forces behind the lines.

On that day and in the ensuing weeks, the soldiers, sailors, and airmen of the assault forces, and the men and women who supported the landing, displayed great skill, unwavering tenacity, and courage. The Americans who landed at Omaha Beach—where sharp bluffs, strong defenses, and the presence of a powerful German division produced enormous difficulties—wrote an especially brave and noble chapter in the military history of the United States.

Opposed by bitter enemy resistance, the landing forces gained the beaches at great sacrifice, pushed inland, and expanded their beachheads. Feats of leadership and courage by individuals and small groups turned the tide. The great battles of 1944 that followed, from the hedgerows to the Ardennes, hold a place of highest honor in the tradition of the United States Armed Forces. The brave, often heroic deeds of our fellow Americans and others in the Allied Armed Forces set in motion the liberation of Europe and brought unity and pride to all free people.

Welded by the experiences of war, the old world and the new formed an enduring alliance which shared the rebuilding of Europe and forged a shield that has kept the peace in Europe for almost forty years. A common dedication to remain strong can continue that peace which these brave men and women fought so hard to secure.

In recognition of the fortieth anniversary of this historic event, the Congress, by H.J. Res. 487, has designated June 6, 1984, as "D-day National Remembrance" and has authorized and requested the President to issue a proclamation in observance of that day.

Now, Therefore, I, Ronald Reagan, President of the United States of America, do hereby proclaim June 6, 1984, as D-day National Remembrance, a national day commemorating the fortieth anniversary of D-day. I call upon the people of the United States to commemorate the valor of those who served in the D-day assault forces with appropriate ceremonies and observances.

In Witness Whereof, I have hereunto set my hand this 31st day of May, in the year of our Lord nineteen hundred and eighty-four, and of the Independence of the United States of America the two hundred and eighth.

RONALD REAGAN

[*Filed with the Office of the Federal Register, 4:35 p.m., May 31, 1984*]

Appointment of Willie J. Nunnery as a Member of the President's Committee on the National Medal of Science
May 31, 1984

The President today announced his intention to appoint Willie J. Nunnery to be a member of the President's Committee on the National Medal of Science for a term expiring December 31, 1986. He will succeed Sidney Topol.

Mr. Nunnery is an attorney and an energy consultant. He also serves as adjunct associate professor of civil engineering, College of Engineering, University of Wiscon-

sin—Madison. Previously, he was commissioner of the Public Service Commission of Wisconsin; deputy secretary of the Department of Administration; and State energy director in Wisconsin.

He graduated from the University of Kansas (B.S., 1971) and the University of Wisconsin (J.D., 1975). He was born July 28, 1948, in Chicago, IL, and now resides in Madison, WI.

Written Responses to Questions Submitted by Indro Montanelli, Editor of Il Giornale, on Foreign and Domestic Issues
June 1, 1984

Outlook for the Future

Q. Mr. President, my newspaper was among the few in Europe to look forward to your victory in 1980, to believe it, and to rejoice when you obtained it. I will not ask you if you think your first term was a success; if you were not convinced of that, you would not have run again. Tell me, rather, what you propose to do in the next 4 years that is different from what you have done up to now.

The President. First, I want to thank Il Giornale for its support and for its skillful efforts to explain to Italian readers the significant issues in American politics. Your newspaper has played a vital role in promoting understanding between our two countries.

But to turn to your question, my hopes for a second term must be seen in the light of our administration's accomplishments during this term. When we took office in 1980, the United States was a nation in crisis. Our defenses had grown weak. Our foreign policy lacked direction. And with inflation well into double digits and interest rates at record highs, our economy was in its worst condition in more than three decades. We took office determined to make a

new beginning, and we have managed to do just that.

Today American defenses are being rebuilt. In foreign policy, the United States is reasserting its role as a force for world peace and freedom. The American economy has recovered its vitality and is entering what we hope will be a period of sustained expansion. The inflation rate has fallen by two-thirds since we took office; prime interest rates have dropped by half; unemployment over the past year has undergone the sharpest drop in 30 years; and today more Americans have jobs than at any time in our nation's history. Perhaps most important, America has seen a rebirth of faith and hope. Polls show that our people are more optimistic about themselves and their country than at any other time in 5 years. Horace Busby, a long-time observer of the American scene, put it well when he said, "What I have begun to hear in this decade is a wonderful chorus of celebration."

A successful effort to repair past damage and a return to national strength, courage, and self-confidence—these are the achievements of the first term. The stage has now been set for a second term that will place America on a firm footing for the future.

In financial policy, our top priority during the second term will be to get the Federal budget under complete control. That will mean attacking unnecessary government spending, passing amendments to the Constitution to require balanced budgets and give Presidents a line-item veto, and it will mean a sweeping reform of the tax code, giving Americans new incentives and simpler, fairer taxes.

In social policy, my administration will work to promote the fundamental values that made America great—values like faith, family, and freedom. We will support a constitutional amendment for voluntary, vocal prayer in our schools; we will work to pass tuition tax credits and education vouchers to make it easier for hard-working parents to send their children to the schools they believe suit them best; and we will make certain that our tax reform gives families the tax relief they need.

One other issue demands attention: We cannot remain true to values based on the dignity of human life while each year allowing over a million unborn infants to be aborted. Our administration will strive to put aside rancor and bring Americans together to find positive solutions to the tragedy of abortion.

In foreign policy, we will be guided by the twin principles of peace and freedom. Our administration will continue to keep American defense strong. At the same time, we will remain ready to negotiate with the Soviets, seeking not nuclear limitations, but equitable and verifiable nuclear arms reductions.

Under Project Democracy, we will go on teaching nations in the Third World about the benefits of democratic institutions. Communism used to be called the wave of the future. But after decades of experience with communism, the world knows that Communists have nothing to offer but economic stagnation, empty slogans, and arms. The free nations of the world, by contrast, offer rising standards of living and cultural vitality. No, the rising tide in the world today is not communism; it is liberty.

The Nation's Economy

Q. Among the most debated topics in Europe is your economic policy, in particu-lar, the so-called over-valued dollar. Many maintain that this damages the European economy, keeping the prices of primary goods high and attracting to the American market capital which could otherwise be invested in Europe. Will you continue this way or will you do something to help us?

The President. Our administration's economic policies do take account of Europe's and the world's economic problems—and are contributing to their solution. Because the American economy is so large a part of the world economy, we believe our first responsibility is to get it into healthy shape and keep it that way. In this respect, our record of bringing down inflation and restoring noninflationary growth has been impressive. Today our economy is still advancing. Over the four quarters of 1983, we experienced real growth of 6.2 percent. For the four quarters of 1984, we are projecting 5-percent growth, but our achievement to date has even exceeded that. The gross national product in the first 3 months of 1984 grew at a rate of 8.8 percent. Solid real growth has been accomplished in an environment of low inflation, improved productivity, and restored business profitability. We expect this economic activity to begin to slow and proceed at a more moderate pace during the year.

Capital is attracted to the United States, and the dollar rises in value for a host of reasons, including the better investment climate in the United States and a "safe haven" effect. Of course, a stronger dollar also encourages exports from other countries. The American merchandise trade deficit in 1983 of about $70 billion and a projected trade deficit of around $100 billion in 1984, which has unfortunate effects on our own economy, is providing a tremendous stimulant to European economies. I understand that Italy's economy is beginning to experience some export-led growth, and that is partly due to the American recovery and increased American imports. I believe that our economic policies represent a major contribution to a durable recovery in the United States, Europe, and throughout the world.

Q. The American economic recovery in the last 2 years has been extraordinary;

ours, unfortunately, much less so. Do you have some secret recipe to impart to us?

The President. I can only tell you the recipe that we believe has worked best in the United States. When we took office we were determined to reduce inflation, control government spending, decrease government regulation of the economy, and encourage slow, steady monetary growth. This strategy has been successful. There has been a resurgence of private initiative, millions of new jobs, and increased optimism for the future. I know that Italy is a country of extremely resourceful people. My basic advice would be to provide the freedom for private enterprise to flourish.

Lebanon

Q. Allies for decades within NATO, the United States and Italy were also allied in the recent Lebanese adventure, which ended in failure. Where did we go wrong? Where did Ronald Reagan go wrong?

The President. The idea that we "failed" in Lebanon is simply wrong. We knew we were taking a risk when we became involved, but we and our allies thought it was important to give the Lebanese a chance to resolve their differences and begin to rebuild their country. We were right to try, even though things did not work out as we had hoped. Certainly, Italians should be proud of their peacekeeping accomplishments in Lebanon, and of the warmth with which your countrymen were received there.

The final outcome in Lebanon is still unclear. The Lebanese people may still find a way to achieve reconciliation. Meanwhile, the joint efforts of Italy, the United States, and our allied partners in Lebanon accomplished something else. On balance, we proved once more that we can cooperate effectively even in difficult and quickly evolving situations. This experience can only help us when we face future challenges together.

East-West Relations

Q. Mr. President, Soviet propaganda has, in the last few years, attempted to divide Europe and the U.S. First, it aimed at European neutralism; more recently, it seems to me, it has aimed at American isolationism,

that of the liberal-left. Europe, in spite of everything, has held firm. Are you sure that America, too, will hold fast and will not succumb to another hysterical crisis like that which caused the abandonment of Vietnam?

The President. First let me say how delighted I am that the allies have ignored Soviet efforts to divide them. Allied unity behind the 1979 two-track decision on intermediate-range nuclear weapons represented a dramatic reaffirmation of our common interests and collective strength.

As to whether America will hold fast, let's remember that the two-track decision on INF was originally a European initiative. It was intended to ensure the coupling of European and North American security. We supported that initiative unshakably because of our commitment to the security of Western Europe. That commitment will remain just as firm in years to come as it is today.

There is absolutely no possibility that America will cut its ties to Western Europe or weaken its commitment to its NATO allies. European and American security are permanently bound together.

Women

Q. Why, Mr. President, don't women like you (at least when they vote)? Is it a kind of irrational antipathy, a reflex based on a fear of war, or a more liberal orientation on the part of American women with respect to a more conservative one on the part of men?

The President. Let me begin by mentioning my two daughters, Patti and Maureen. Maureen has worked in radio and television, promoted overseas trade, and run for political office. Today she's giving advice to her dad on something she understands very well: how to communicate to women what the administration is working to accomplish. My younger daughter, Patti, is seeking a career in the entertainment world. When certain people claim for political reasons that I don't understand modern women, I'm tempted to say, "Then why do I have two of the most independent and loving daughters a father could find?"

From appointing Justice Sandra O'Connor, the first woman to sit on the United

States Supreme Court, to rewriting laws that discriminate against women, our administration has worked with American women to provide with new opportunities and to make sure each woman has the freedom to choose her own role for herself. Our Ambassador to the United Nations, Jeane Kirkpatrick, has made an enormous contribution to her country and to our international relations. And with the economic expansion our policies helped to produce, the unemployment rate among adult women has dropped steeply, businesses owned by women are multiplying, and women are rapidly moving into professional and managerial fields.

Now, I know there were polls that showed a so-called gender gap, but in other polls lately women have rated our administration ahead of my Democratic opponents. It only goes to show that there's just one poll that counts—the poll taken on election day. During the coming campaign, we'll present our record to the people. And I'm confident that on November 6, American women will give our administration enthusiastic support.

Prayer in Schools

Q. Not many among us (Italians) have understood the sense of the battle to reintroduce prayer in American public schools. You were defeated in the Congress, but you insist. Why does it seem so important to you that American children not be prohibited from morning prayer in the schools?

The President. Any serious look at American history shows that from the first, our people were deeply imbued with faith. Many of the first settlers came for the express purpose of worshiping in freedom, and the debates over independence and the Constitution make it clear that the Founding Fathers were sustained by their belief in God. It was George Washington who said, "Of all the dispositions and habits which lead to political prosperity, religion and morality are indispensable supports."

From the early days of the American colonies, prayer in school was practiced and revered as an important way of expressing that faith. Then in 1962, the Supreme Court—in a decision that many legal scholars and millions of Americans believe was sadly mistaken—declared school prayer illegal. Once that happened, the only way to reinstate voluntary, vocal school prayer was by passing a constitutional amendment. My administration firmly supports such a step, and although the Senate recently defeated our school prayer amendment, the battle is far from over.

The American people understand that no country can remain strong and free when it has lost basic values like faith. By reinstating school prayer we would be declaring—to our children, ourselves, and all the world—that we have reasserted the right to observe fundamental beliefs that make our nation great. The people are making their will known, and I'm confident that one day soon a school prayer amendment will be ratified.

Views on the Presidency

Q. You are 73 years old; if you are reelected, you will continue until age 78 to exercise a difficult job full of tension, while you could be enjoying a trouble-free life on your marvelous ranch in California. What makes you do it: ambition, a taste for power, the sense of being irreplaceable, ideological passion . . .?

The President. The answer is simple: I don't like to leave a job half done. Despite all the accomplishments of the past 3½ years, we still have a great deal to do to prepare America for the future. Besides, I have a hunch that at 78, I'll still be young enough to enjoy the ranch for quite a few years to come.

Nuclear Weapons

Q. I will ask last, Mr. President, the question that everyone asks first: What can be done to lessen nuclear fear in the world? By unilateral disarmament or throughout the interminable negotiations with the Russians? By reinforcing conventional armaments? By giving free reign to new technologies which take from nuclear arms their current invincibility?

The President. Well, unilateral disarmament is clearly *not* the answer. History teaches us that wars begin when governments believe that the price of aggression is cheap. So, all of us in the alliance must be strong enough to convince any potential aggressor that attacking would be a disastrous mistake.

But strength and dialog go hand in hand. We're ready right now to resume the talks on strategic and intermediate-range nuclear weapons that the Soviets broke off, and whenever they come back to the table, we'll be ready to meet them halfway.

What we want in all our negotiations is agreements that reduce the risk of war. A big part of that is getting real reductions in nuclear weapons. We have proposed far-reaching cuts in strategic forces. We've put forward the zero option for intermediate-range missiles, but we're ready to accept an interim agreement that is balanced and verifiable. And we have proposed a number of confidence-building measures to reduce the possibility of miscalculation between the two sides.

Someday, I hope, we'll reach the point where nuclear weapons are obsolete. As you know, I've directed that, consistent with our treaty obligations, we step up research on technology that could be used in providing a defense against ballistic missiles. We will consult closely with our allies on this program.

Meanwhile, the Soviets keep increasing their forces, nuclear and conventional. Their conventional buildup, of course, threatens to lower the nuclear threshold. The West can and must use its technological superiority to ensure adequate forces for conventional defense. At the same time, in the Vienna MBFR talks we and our allies have just offered a creative proposal for significant, verifiable reductions to equal levels of all forces in central Europe. And in April, Vice President Bush went to Geneva to propose a draft treaty to outlaw chemical weapons once and for all.

There is no more serious subject in our world today than nuclear weapons, believe me. Americans and Italians, and our other friends and allies, must constantly seek ways to reduce the number of these weapons of mass destruction. I am committed to doing that and to reducing the nuclear tensions in our world. We can have no more compelling priority.

Note: As printed above, the questions and answers follow the text of the White House press release.

Informal Exchange With Reporters on Employment Figures for May
June 1, 1984

The President. Good morning. I hope I can be heard over this.

I just wanted to say that I leave with happy news for the economic summit as far as our own situation's concerned. The figures as of 12 minutes ago were released. Unemployment has dropped—if we include the military—down to 7.4 percent, which is the level it was when we took office; 7.5 percent if you do not count the military, which I think would be dishonest, because they certainly have jobs. But the other significant thing is that there are far more people working because we have created at the same time, millions of new jobs to take care of the expanding work force.

So, I just wanted to give you that word— I'm practicing on you for what I will tell the people at the summit.

Q. What will you tell the leaders about the deficit, though?

The President. About the deficit?

Q. [*Inaudible*]

The President. Well, if you view the deficit by the percentage of gross national product—I will be talking to people who also have deficits in pretty much the same percentage range of their gross national products as ours. So, they will understand the problems.

Q. So, you're going to say it's nothing to worry about?

The President. Oh, no. I have been saying for 30 years that deficit spending is something to worry about, while the Democrats kept telling us that it didn't matter because we owed it to ourselves. Well, we don't believe that, and we're going to do something about the deficit, which should have been done 30 years ago.

Q. What about interest rates, sir?

The President. Interest rates? Well, they're not connected to the deficit. If you look closely at the statistics, you'll see why, when the interest rates came down by 9 percent, is when the deficit was increasing to its largest point. No, the interest rates are tied to the lack of confidence of so many in the market, as to whether we are determined to hold down inflation. And, believe me, with inflation having been at less than 4 percent for the last 2 years, I think there's evidence that they should have more confidence.

Q. Do you know when interest rates are coming down?

The President. What?

Q. Do you know when interest rates are coming down?

The President. There may be another flurry of a half a point or a point or something, but I believe that over the next period of months, yes, they will be coming down.

Thank you all.

Q. What's your message going to be at the summit?

The President. What?

Q. What's your message going to be at the summit?

The President. Pretty much what I've been saying right here.

Note: The President spoke at 8:40 a.m. at the South Portico of the White House as he was preparing to board Marine One for the flight to Andrews Air Force Base, MD, and his trip to Europe.

Remarks on Arrival at Shannon Airport in Shannon, Ireland
June 1, 1984

President and Mrs. Hillery, Prime Minister and Mrs. FitzGerald, distinguished guests, and I want to add with the greatest of pleasure—I'll try—*A chairde Gaeil* [Irish friends]. [*Laughter*] How did I do? [*Applause*] But on behalf of Nancy and myself, thank you very much for your warm and wonderful Irish welcome.

We're beginning a mission to strengthen ties of friendship and cooperation among the world's leading democracies. It's our deepest hope and our earnest conviction that we can make genuine progress together toward a safer world, a more prosperous world, a far better world.

To be able to begin our journey on this isle of wondrous beauty, with a countryside green as no other place seems to be, to be able to stand on the soil of my ancestors among all of you is, for me, a very special gift. I want you to know that for this great-grandson of Ireland, this is a moment of joy.

And I'm returning not only to my own roots, I'm returning to America's roots. So much of what America means and stands for we owe to you—to your indomitable spirit and generosity and to your impassioned love for liberty and independence.

There are few people on Earth whose hearts burn more with the flame of freedom than the Irish. George Washington said, "When our friendless standard was first unfurled for resistance, who were the strangers who first mustered around our staff? And when it reeled in fight, who more bravely sustained it than Erin's generous sons?"

You did.

America has always been a haven of opportunity for those seeking a new life. They, in turn, have given to us, they have shaped us and enriched us. And from the beginning, when that first large party of your ancestors arrived at Newport News in 1621, your Irish blood has enriched America.

With courage and determination, you helped our struggling colony break free. And then day by day, by the sweat of your brow and with an ache in your back, you helped turn our small, undeveloped country into a great and mighty nation. Your hearts and minds shaped our literary and cultural history. Your smiles, mirth, and song lifted our spirits with laughter and music. And always, you reminded us by your deep faith that wisdom and truth, love and beauty, grace and glory begin in Him—our Father, our Creator, our loving God.

No wonder we've been blessed all these years by what some call "the luck of the Irish."

Today, the sons and daughters of our first Irish settlers number 40 million strong. Speaking for them, and even for those not so fortunate, may I say: We're still part of you; we have and will remain true to your values; long live Irish-American friendship.

The challenges to peace and freedom that we face today are neither easy nor free from danger. But face them we must, and surmount them we can, providing that we remember the rights of individual liberty, and of government resting on the consent of the governed, are more than the sole position of a chosen few; they are universal rights, gifts from God to men and women everywhere. And those rights are a crucial anchor for stability in a troubled world, a world where peace is threatened by governments that oppress their citizens, renounce God, and prey on their neighbors. Edmund Burke's warning of nearly two centuries ago holds true today: "The only thing necessary for the triumph of evil is for good men to do nothing."

Well, Ireland today is undertaking important responsibilities in international councils, and through your peacekeeping forces, to help reduce the risks of war. The United States bears a heavy burden for strengthening economic development and preserving peace, and we're deeply grateful for Ireland's contributions.

Americans are people of peace. We've known and suffered the trauma of war, witnessed the fruits of reconciliation. And that is why we pray tolerance and reconciliation will one day unite the Catholics and Protestants in Northern Ireland in a spirit of communion and community. And that is why those who advocate violence or engage in terrorism in North Ireland will never be welcome in the United States.

Looking to the future, I believe there's reason for optimism and confidence. America's economic expansion can and should bring more jobs and opportunities to your people. And the more than 300 United States companies that are based here demonstrate our clear commitment to a future of peace and well-being for all the people of Ireland, North and South.

So, thank you, again, for making Nancy and me feel so welcome. And may I speak for so many of your families and friends in America when I say the words:

"Ireland, oh, Ireland . . . Country of my fathers . . . Mother of my yearning, love of all my longings, home of my heart . . ."

God bless you.

Note: The President spoke at 8:37 p.m. at the airport, where he was greeted upon arrival by President and Mrs. Patrick J. Hillery, Prime Minister and Mrs. Garret Fitz-Gerald, Foreign Minister and Mrs. Peter Barry, Michael Fitzgerald, Irish Chief of Protocol, and Robert F. Kane, U.S. Ambassador to Ireland.

Following the arrival ceremony, the President and Mrs. Reagan went to Ashford Castle, in Cong, County Mayo, where they remained overnight.

Interview With Foreign Journalists
May 31, 1984

International Debt Situation

Q. Mr. President, as representative from the host country, it's been left to me to bowl the first ball.

The London Economic Summit is taking place under a number of clouds. One is the international debt crisis. So far, Western creditor nations have dealt with this problem on a case-by-case basis. However, I'd like to ask you, in light of the growing hostility of debtor nations, first of all whether a coordinated long-term solution is now essential; and second, what the U.S. can do to guarantee confidence of its banking system?

The President. Well, first of all, let me answer that by saying that I believe the five-point system—or program that we all agreed to at the summit meeting last year at Williamsburg has been working. And I'm sure there is unhappiness here and there with some. But I believe that since it is working, and it's working on a case-by-case basis, that we should continue that, and that the greatest thing we can contribute now to helping them in their problems is to do everything we can to ensure and increase, if possible, the economic recovery that is presently taking place.

Q. What about the U.S. banks? We've had two banks recently to run into trouble as a result of problems with these debtor countries.

The President. Well now, we had the Continental of Illinois—are you referring to the——

Q. Manufacturers Hanover.

The President. Well, that turned out to be quite a rumor that seemed to be believed only on Wall Street and the stock market for 24 hours and caused quite a panic, but developed that there was not the same kind of crisis involved there.

Nuclear Arms

Q. Mr. President, in the last few days you've said that the world feels a little bit more secure because of the strengthening in the American strategic and conventional posture. As paradoxical as it may seem in considering the reported widespread violations of SALT II by the Soviet Union, do you feel that the world can continue to feel a little bit more secure for an extended period of time in the absence of an agreement with the Soviet Union limiting nuclear arms?

The President. Well, I think the ultimate of what we want, of course, is for them to come back to the table and join us in not a limitation, as SALT was, that was simply legalizing an arms race in that the limitation was only a limit on how many more you could continue to build—as a matter of fact, it's interesting to note that from the time of the signing by both parties to the SALT treaty, the Soviet Union added 3,950 more warheads.

When I say more secure, I believe that the United States, basically, in recent decades, went all out in various efforts at détente and in which we unilaterally disarmed with the idea that maybe if we did this and showed our good faith, they would reciprocate by reducing their own. Well, they didn't. They've engaged in the most massive military buildup the world has ever seen. And therefore, the reason I believe that there is more security today is the redressing that we've done of our own military strength, the strength of the alliance, and the unity that we have.

And the alliance resisted all that propaganda of the Soviets with regard to the intermediate-range placement, and their efforts to divide us failed. So I think—there's an article that I could call to your attention in The Economist, called "May Hibernation." It was an idea that hadn't occurred to me, but I think it makes a great deal of sense: that they are not deviously planning something or having a great plan going forward. The author of this article said that they don't have any answers right now, so they've just hunkered down and they're hibernating, waiting until they have an answer.

Sure, they're unhappy. And all this talk about great strain in the relations—well, the unhappiness is because they're not having their way freely, as they did a short time ago.

Persian Gulf Conflict

Q. Mr. President, in the connection of this problem of the United States-Soviet relations, East-West relations, which my Italian colleague just mentioned, I'd like to ask this question. Many observers suggest that the United States and the Soviet Union have a common national interest in calming down the present gulf crisis—Persian Gulf crisis, the U.S. and the Soviet Union have a common interest. Do you agree with this view? If so, would you consider taking this crisis as an opportunity to reopen the U.S.-Soviet dialog, which so many people are anxious to have——

The President. Well, I don't see that particular issue as one lending itself to that. We are not out of touch with the Soviet Union. We have continued to negotiate with them on other matters—other than the arms treaties—that were of concern to them. And there's been some progress made on those. So, we've made it very plain that the door is open for negotiations.

On the gulf, I think the idea—none of us want to see this spread into a major conflict. And I think the fact that the gulf nations themselves have not asked for help other than wanting more weaponry for their own defense here and there, and which we've provided, and I believe that that is the course to follow. If it ever goes beyond that, then I think that the major nations—it would begin with us and our allies getting together, because basically our allies, including your own country, have a greater stake in—if that energy supply was cut off.

But, no, I don't believe that that really offers a kind of opening we're talking about.

Q. Yes, but you have direct talk with the Soviet Union on this?

The President. Oh, yes, yes.

Q. So then—this is a followup question—what initiative, if any, do you plan to take at the London summit on this gulf crisis, on this subject?

The President. That what?

Q. On the gulf—this Persian Gulf crisis in the summit meeting?

Q. Do you plan to take any——

The President. Oh, I'm quite sure we——

Q. What kind of initiative——

The President. Oh, I'm quite sure we'll be discussing that. The summit meetings, I'm proud and happy to say, since Williamsburg, are kind of planned at a more informal basis. They used to be very programmed and with subjects in advance determined on and so forth. And we didn't think, when we had the Williamsburg summit, we didn't think that that really opened the door to what everyone would like to talk about. So it's more or less an informal get-together,

and whatever subject is on anyone's mind, they can bring up, that they think is of interest to it. And I'm quite sure that we'll be discussing that.

Q. Central America?

Trade, Deficits, and Interest Rates

Q. Well, if I can come back to the economic problem, Mr. President, the latest figures on the U.S. export performance—they paint a rather grim picture. It is understood that the U.S. trade deficit—trade imbalance will reach a staggering $126 billion this year, compounding, it seems, the deficit problem that already exists. How can interest rates really come down under such auspices? And what will you tell your partners at London, who are worried stiff already about interest rates and about the high dollar that it's created and the capital that comes out of their economies into banks in this country? What are you going to tell your partners about this?

The President. Well, the trade imbalance—I don't think it has anything to do with the interest rates. The trade imbalance that you've mentioned there, as a matter of fact, is due to the value of the dollar in comparison to other currencies, and this is part of the worldwide recession that's been going on. But our imports are actually responsible for about a third of the recovery of our trading partners now. And there is another element that we don't consider in the balance of trade, but that is capital investment from outside the United States in our country. And yet, that is a kind of balance to this imbalance.

We'd like very much to be exporting more than we are, but we realize that our recovery started earlier and has been faster than it has in the other countries. And so the result is they have been less able to buy. And the very fact, as I say, that we're continuing to import is helping that recovery. And I think that this will move to change that.

Now, we get to the deficit, which is—every country has one right now—the spending over and above revenues in government functions. We have a program right now that is in conference committee before the House and Senate to work out the differences in their two versions of what I have called a downpayment. And that is a 3-year program to—certain, some revenue increases—but both domestic spending and some reductions in defense spending that will not set us back too much in our program. But this downpayment will amount to about $140 or $150 billion over the 3-year period in the reduction of our deficit.

But that's only part of it. We recognize that we have a long way to go in reducing the share of the gross national product that the Government is taking in taxes and is spending. And we had a commission from the private sector—I asked a man named Peter Grace, a businessman, to form task forces and go into every agency and department of our government. I had done this in California when I was Governor, for the State, and it worked. And some 2,000 American leaders from the private sector spent several months doing this. And they have left us with 2,000—I think it's 478 specific recommendations as to how government can be made more efficient and more economical by simply implementing modern-day business practices.

For example, when they could find that in one area of our government, it was costing us $4 and something every time we wrote a paycheck for an employee, and out in the business world that process takes less than a dollar—well, there's no reason why government shouldn't take less than a dollar in processing a paycheck—well, this kind of thing. And we now have a task force that is working on those recommendations. Many of them will require legislation by the Congress; some of them only require Executive order by me. And we have already in our planning, right now, and in this downpayment, we have already included some of their recommendations and are going forward with them.

So, we think that actually the interest rates, however, that—I'm dealing with the deficit part now—are not that closely linked to the deficit. As a matter of fact, the deficit of some of our allies as a proportion of gross national product is not too out of line as a percentage of GNP any more than ours is.

But what I stand on as evidence that it isn't the deficit that is causing the interest rates, the high interest rates, is the fact that

we brought those high interest rates down from 21½ percent down to a little more than half that at the same time that our deficit was increasing vastly over what it had been. Now, how could that be?—that interest rates were coming down while the deficit was going up, and now the deficit is responsible for interest rates not coming down any farther, or maybe, as they have, gone up a point or so recently?

We think that out there in the money market in our own country, after nearly half a century of deficit spending in this country and a growing inflation that has been worldwide for a longer period than ever in the world's history, that the money market is not yet convinced that we have control of inflation. And every move by the Federal Reserve System—they always look to see, well, does this mean that suddenly inflation is going to start?

Remember that in '79 and '80, before we came here, inflation in this country went up to double digits, and for 2 years in a row it was at double digits. One time, it was running at 17 percent. And since we've been here, it has come down to where for the last 2 years inflation has been less than 4 percent.

But I believe we're sound in thinking that it is just the lack of confidence. Now, if we pass—if the Senate and the House come together and this downpayment is made, and then, as we begin to put together the 1985 budget, which we will shortly be doing, and we begin to show in that budget the effect of the Grace commission reports and so forth, I think we will see a little more confidence out there in the business community, and I think we'll see interest rates come down a little further.

Q. Mr. President, first of all, let me say I'm disappointed you haven't offered us any of those jellybeans. But anyway——

The President. Oh, pass them around. Help yourselves. [*Laughter*]

Q. Good.

The President. They always sit there.

Prime Minister Trudeau's Peace Initiative

Q. My question: Our Prime Minister, Mr. Trudeau, set out on a personal disarmament quest last year, based on the assumption that the superpowers were deadlocked, that the world was becoming more dangerous, and that smaller powers might help to break that deadlock—and got the support and endorsement of the Commonwealth.

Now, we came to see you in December. You cooled them out with a noncommittal good will. You thanked them for suggestions, you wished them Godspeed, as I recall——

The President. Yes.

Q. ——and, in effect, you trivialized his whole undertaking. So, my question is, why did you not pick up on this initiative and give it momentum as a new run for arms control?

The President. Well, I suppose because we were convinced that it has to be the Warsaw Pact and the NATO—I won't just say the United States and the Soviet Union. Here is where the issue lies, here's where the threat, if there is one to the world, comes from. And we were busily trying to show the Soviet Union that we hadn't made any demands in which we said, "It's this or nothing." We tried to show them our flexibility.

For example, my first proposal about the intermediate-range weapons was why not 0–0? Why not leave that European area free of any intermediate-range weapons? Well, the Soviets refused to discuss that. So we said: "All right, then, whatever figure you have in mind, or whatever we have in mind, let's sit down then and see how much we can reduce the numbers of weapons." And we told them, frankly, we would always keep in mind that someday we'd still like to have 0–0, but we were willing to talk a lesser number.

Now, they walked away on the—the line that it was the—that when deployment started. Well, the request for the NATO——

Q. [*Inaudible*]—peace initiative?

The President. What?

Q. Peace initiative. You're reviewing disarmament, but this is not—as far as I can tell—nothing to do with the peace initiative.

The President. Oh. Maybe I misunderstood.

Q. Well, I was asking about Prime Minister Trudeau's peace initiative to try and break the deadlock that the two superpow-

ers were in.

The President. Oh. Listen—well, no. We encouraged him and gave him our blessing to go forward with that. I think that it's awfully easy for us in our relations with the Soviet Union to be the kiss of death, sometimes, to these things. No. The Prime Minister came here—I'm sorry, I misunderstood what you are asking.

I think the world pretty generally, with just a few exceptions, is ready for world peace. And this is our primary goal. But I don't believe that you can really—that it is really on a sound basis unless it is accompanied by a reduction, particularly in the strategic nuclear weapons. This is the threat that we cannot—the world cannot go on living under that threat. And one day, if there's any common sense left in the world, one day there will be no nuclear weapons.

Our country presented that at a time when we were the only ones who had them—1946. And we suggested an international commission to be given total control over all nuclear material. And the Soviets refused. Now, we knew they were trying to have such a weapon, and eventually did, but at that time they—all they had to do was give in, and there wouldn't be any.

El Salvador

Q. Mr. President, during his visit to Washington, President Duarte of Salvador declared that he would never ask American troops to fight in his country. And last week you have stated yourself that you had never had any thought of sending American soldiers to Central America. And what would be your reaction if next fall, for example, the Government of Salvador was seriously threatened? I mean, with collapse, by guerrilla offensive?

The President. The—and again, I have problems with those of you who are further out there. This domed room has terrible acoustics here. [*Laughter*] I think you're asking about El Salvador and Nicaragua, our Central American——

Q. Not especially about Nicaragua, but about Salvador.

The President. Yes.

Q. If there is, next fall, for example, a guerrilla offensive——

The President. Yes.

Q. ——threatening, and threatening with collapse the Government of Salvador, what would be your reaction?

The President. What would be——

Q. Your reaction?

The President. ——our reaction?

Q. Military—will you send military forces there?

The President. Well, it would not be military forces because El Salvador has not only not asked for them, but President Duarte on his visit here recently said, no, they were not wanted or needed. They will do this with their own forces but frankly admit they must have our help with regard to equipment and supplies and the help that we've been to them in training.

You know, a great many of the Central American countries, their militaries over the years have been kind of garrison troops—more concerned with internal problems than in fighting a war. And so they have been most open in their request of training.

And before we got here—the previous, under the previous administration—some of their training consisted of bringing El Salvadoran troops up here and training them at our own bases with our own men. Well, then, as the war heated up, they couldn't afford to have the men gone for that long a time. So we have 55 trainers working with their entire army.

And the guerrillas, of course, are being supplied by way of Nicaragua—through Nicaragua by Cuba and the Soviet Union—not only with weapons, but with replacements, with personnel. And now the guerrillas are resorting to kidnapping. They're rounding up—going into villages and rounding up even just youngsters off the streets and simply taking them, forcing them to be guerrillas. And as would happen—the law of averages—every once in a while some of those youngsters escape and get away, and so we know that this is the practice and what they're doing.

But, no, if this fall offensive comes, I believe we have confidence in the El Salvadoran Army. We think that the guerrillas could make things very unpleasant, and we think that they are building up the possibility of such a thing.

But now the election has taken place, the election of the President, and Duarte is very definitely dedicated to continuing to move toward democracy in El Salvador; certainly has the support of the people. And I am optimistic that we're on the right path. And our Congress has voted now to give us the appropriation we asked for further aid to El Salvador.

Irish Unity

Q. Mr. President, I want to ask a specifically Irish question, as you're going to be—the first country you're going to touch down in. And I'm familiar with what you said about Irish unity and the question—your not becoming involved, as between Ireland and England. But are there any circumstances which might change that? If, for instance, Ireland were to join NATO or such a question were muted, would that make it more attractive, for instance, for America to support the idea of Irish unity?

The President. I really believe that that is an internal problem to be worked out, first of all because there are two governments involved, and the other government is already a member of NATO. I have been impressed with the Forum and some of its recommendations, and the—as Prime Minister, your Prime Minister said, the recent finding of the Forum of recommendations certainly provided an agenda for serious thinking. If there's any way in which, without being an interferer in things going on there, but in which the people of Ireland felt that we could in any way be helpful with anything that we might do, we'd be very pleased to do it.

Irish Immigration to the U.S.

Q. I believe I'm in order in asking a supplementary. On the question of these unprecedented protests, which are unheard of in terms of an American President visiting Ireland, one of the factors in this is that there is a certain alienation between the Irish at home and the Irish here, because the quota of immigration has cut down the numbers of Irish with a day-to-day knowledge of America. Do you think that there is any likelihood that the Irish immigration quota might be increased?

The President. Well, now, the truth is—and I only just recently heard about any problem of that—the truth is that Ireland's quota is 20,000 and, based on the worldwide quotas, it is certainly equal to and proportionate to all the others. But also, the quota has not been fully used, so there isn't a waiting line there that says there's no more room for us. They haven't used the quota——

Q. I would suspect that there is a waiting line in Ireland. It mightn't have the right qualifications or so on.

The President. It might be that or it might just be the slow turning of bureaucratic wheels. But it's my understanding that the quota has not yet been filled.

Nuclear Arms

Q. Mr. President, you said the other day at your press conference you didn't expect any real progress to take place on nuclear arms talks this year. Do you think if you're reelected in November and the Soviet Union sees they're going to have to deal with you for another 4 years that we could expect a fairly early return to the negotiating table, either on INF, or START, or both?

The President. Well, I know many people who are students of Soviet history and Soviet methods feel that there's a better chance of them deciding to join us in negotiations and things after the election is over. But they're not going to do anything in the meantime to help me get reelected. Now, I hope I am reelected and look forward to dealing with them.

We have to live in the world together, and we have to seek peace together. But right now, if the Soviet Union and the men running the Soviet Union truly want peace, then there can be peace tomorrow, because none of the rest of us want war.

Q. Thank you, Mr. President. Thank you very much.

Note: The interview began at 1:22 p.m. in the Oval Office at the White House. Participants in the interview included Nicholas Ashford, the London Times; Thomas Kielinger, Die Welt, Bonn; Marino de Medici, Il Tempo, Italy; Fumio Matsuo, Kyodo News Service, Japan; William Johnson, Toronto Globe and Mail; Bernard Guetta, Le Monde, France; and Tim Pat Coogan, the Irish Press.

The transcript of the interview was released by the Office of the Press Secretary on June 2.

Remarks at University College, Galway, Ireland
June 2, 1984

A chairde Gaeil [*Irish friends*]—thank you.

I very much appreciate the honor that you've done me today. A degree, honorary though it may be, is a recognition of a certain understanding of culture and of the truths that are at the foundation of Western civilization. And a degree from an Irish university, in this respect, is of even greater significance.

I have to confess that on the 25th anniversary of my own graduation, my alma mater presented me with an honorary degree, and thereby culminated 25 years of guilt that I had nursed, because I had always thought the first one they gave me was honorary. [*Laughter*]

But I would like to take this moment to congratulate your distinguished president of University College, Galway, Dr. O'hEocha for all that he has done and is doing to overcome the spiral of violence which has plagued Northern Ireland. As chairman of the New Ireland Forum, you helped to open honors—or doors of opportunity for peace and reconciliation.

Progress will depend on other responsible leaders, in both parts of Ireland and in Great Britain, following your example. As far as the United States is concerned, we applaud all those who strove for constructive political cooperation and who renounce violence. We pray that men and women of good will in all parts of this land can, through mutual consent and consultation, find a way of bringing peace and harmony to this island that means so much to us.

It was here in Ireland that monks and scholars preserved the theological and classical achievements of the Western World during a time of darkness on the continent of Europe. With the triumph of St. Patrick and Christianity, Ireland emerged as one of the most learned countries of Europe, attracting students from distant lands and known for centuries as the Island of Saints and Scholars.

This veneration of knowledge is part of our heritage I am most proud to share. While tyrants in many nations stamped their populations into conformity and submission, our ancestors enjoyed heated exchanges of ideas as far back as in the court of good King Brian Boru. It's part of our blood. That's what I keep telling myself every time I try to iron out my differences with the Speaker of our House of Representatives, a lad by the name of Tip O'Neill. [*Laughter*]

Well, he's a great son of Ireland and America as well, and I can say that, knowing that we have heartfelt differences of opinion. Yet, in free societies, differences are expected, indeed, encouraged. It is this freedom to disagree, to question, to state one's case even when in opposition to those in authority that is the cornerstone of liberty and human progress.

When I arrived in Shannon yesterday, I mentioned that I was not only returning to my own roots but also to those of my country's freedom. Historically, of course, no one can doubt Ireland's enormous contributions to American liberty. Nine of the signers of our Declaration of Independence were of Irish ancestry; four were born in Ireland. Twenty generals in our Revolutionary Army were of Irish ancestry. Generals Montgomery, Sullivan, Wayne, and others were in the thick of the battle. On Washington's personal staff were Generals Moylan and Fitzgerald. And on the high seas, Commodore John Barry, considered by many the father of the United States Navy, was born in County Wexford.

As officers and as soldiers, sailors, and ma-

rines, Irish immigrants added fire to the American Revolution, a fire that ignited a flame of liberty as had never before been seen. This was not a result of uncontrollable historical forces, but the accomplishment of heroic individuals whose commitment and courage shook the foundations of empires. William Butler Yeats put it well: "Whatever flames upon the night, man's own resinous heart has fed." And I imagine the British weren't surprised to see just who was fanning those flames. Sir Henry Clinton wrote home to London that, "the emigrants from Ireland are our most serious opponents."

By the time of the American Revolution, Ireland was already a nation steeped in culture and historical traditions, a fact evidenced by your own city of Galway—now my own city of Galway—which is celebrating its 500th anniversary. Permit me to congratulate all of your citizens on this august occasion.

This esteemed university is only one part of the traditional educational glory of Galway. I'm told that as far back as 1580, Galway Mayor Dominick Lynch founded a free school here which became a well-known center of Catholic culture and nationalist activity, attracting pupils from near and far. By 1627 so many were flocking here, many with no means of support, that the city ordered "foreign beggars and poor scholars" to be whipped out of town. Now, considering the degree you've just bestowed on me, I can hope that that rule is no longer in effect. [*Laughter*]

I'm afraid we have no communities quite so venerable as Galway in the United States. But what we lack in years we try to make up for and try hard in spirit. From the time of our independence until the present moment, the mainspring of our national identity has been a common dedication to the principles of human liberty. Further, we believe there's a vital link between our freedom and the dramatic progress—the increase in our material well-being that we've enjoyed during these last 200 years.

Freedom motivates people of courage and creativity to strive, to improve, and to push back the boundaries of knowledge. Here, too, the Irish character has contributed so much. Galway, a city Columbus, as has been said already, is supposed to have visited on his way to the New World, is on a coast which for so long was the western edge, the frontier of the known world.

This is the 1,500th anniversary of the birth of St. Brendan, who, legend tells us, sailed west into uncharted waters and discovered new lands. This man of God, a man of learning whose monasteries were part of Ireland's Golden Age, may, indeed, have been the first tie between Ireland and America. I understand much time and effort has gone into organizing what will be an annual trans-Atlantic yacht race between Ireland and the United States commemorating Brendan's voyage. I commend those making this effort to establish what could prove to be an exciting new link between our two countries.

Whether Brendan reached the American Continent or not, there is no doubt about the Irish role in taming the wilderness of the New World and turning America into an economic dynamo beyond imagination. The Irish came by the millions, seeking refuge from tyranny and deprivation—from hunger of the body and of the soul. Irish Americans worked in the factories. They built our railroads and, as with my family, settled and farmed the vast stretches of uncultivated prairie in the heartland of America.

I have a hunch that I should be shortening my remarks.[1] [*Laughter*]

The dream of a better life brought these people to our shores and millions of others from every corner of the world. They and their descendants maintain great pride in their ancestry—but also to say thank you to your nation and to your people for all you contributed to the spirit and well-being of the United States of America.

Certainly an important part of that spirit has and must remain close people-to-people contacts. The Prime Minister and I are therefore pleased to announce our agreement to increase academic exchange programs between the United States and Ireland.

We have instructed the appropriate agencies to put this into effect as soon as possible. We have a long tradition of academic cooperation; we'll strengthen it. And for our part, we intend to triple the number of students and scholars—triple them—in participating in the programs.

America in these last four decades has assumed a heavy burden of responsibility to help preserve peace and promote economic development and human dignity throughout the world. Sometimes, as is to be expected in all human endeavors, mistakes were made. Yet, overall, I believe that we have an admirable record.

There is something very important I want you to know, and then I will hasten on. The American people still hold dear those principles of liberty and justice for which our forefathers sacrificed so much. Visiting America you understand this—and I hope that each of you will one day be able to do that.

We're still a nation comprised of good and decent people whose fundamental values of tolerance, compassion, and fairplay guide and direct the decisions of our government.

Today the free world faces an enormously powerful adversary. A visit to that country or to its colonies would reveal no public disagreement, no right of assembly, no independent unions. What we face is a strong and aggressive military machine that prohibits fundamental freedoms.

Our policy is aimed at deterring aggression and helping our allies and friends to protect themselves, while, at the same time, doing everything we can to reduce the risks of war.

We seek negotiations with the Soviet Union, but unfortunately we face an empty chair.

I'll be speaking more on this in my speech to Parliament, but right now I think that I should cut short whatever I was going to say, because I would like to bring up a proclamation in which we are congratulating Galway on its 500th anniversary.

This is our greeting on the quincentennial from our country to your city. Let it hope in our hearts that we will always stand together. Brothers and sisters of Ireland, *Dia libh go leir* [God be with you all].

Thank you.

---

[1] *It had begun to rain heavily.*

Note: The President spoke at 3:11 p.m. in the Quadrangle Square at the university.

Upon arrival at the university, the President met briefly with Dr. Colm O'hEocha, president of the university, and T. Kenneth Whitaker, chancellor of the National University of Ireland.

Prior to his address, the President received an honorary doctorate of laws degree from the National University, of which the college at Galway is a part, and was presented with the Freedom of the City and a resolution scroll by Mayor Michael Leahy.

At the conclusion of the ceremony, the President signed the university guest register and then departed Galway and returned to Ashford Castle in Cong, County Mayo, Ireland.

Radio Address to the Nation on the Trip to Europe
June 2, 1984

My fellow Americans:

Top o' the mornin' to you. I'm speaking from a small town named Cong in western Ireland, first stop on a 10-day trip that will also take Nancy and me to France and England.

We're in an area of spectacular beauty overlooking a large lake filled with islands, bays, and coves. And those of you who, like me, can claim the good fortune of Irish roots, may appreciate the tug I felt in my heart yesterday when we saw the Emerald Isle from Air Force One. I thought of words from a poem about Ireland:

A place as kind as it is green,
The greenest place I've every seen.

I told our welcoming hosts that to stand with them on the soil of my ancestors was, for this great-grandson of Ireland, a very special moment. It was a moment of joy.

Earlier today we were in Galway, a coastal city celebrating its 500th anniversary. Legend has it Columbus prayed at a church there on his way to the New World. For a thousand years, Ireland was considered the western edge of civilization and a place that continued to revere learning during a time of darkness on the continent of Europe.

That reverence earned Ireland its reputation as the Island of Saints and Scholars. I was pleased to address representatives of University College in Galway to speak to them of Ireland's many contributions to America and to give thanks for those great, great forces of faith and love for liberty and justice that bind our people.

The president of that institution, Dr.

O'hEocha, also chaired a group called the New Ireland Forum, which has sought to foster a spirit of tolerance and reconciliation in Northern Ireland, so the spiral of violence that has cast so many innocent lives there—or cost so many, I should say, can be finally ended.

Ireland is a beautiful, proud, and independent land with a young and talented population. But they have an employment problem. By the strength of our economy, and by the presence of some 300 U.S. firms here, Americans can and will help our Irish cousins create jobs and greater opportunities. And, of course, what helps them will help us, too.

Tomorrow, Nancy and I will travel to Ballyporeen for a nostalgic visit to the original home of the Reagan clan. On Monday, we'll be in Dublin, where I'll have the honor of addressing a joint session of the Irish Parliament, as John Kennedy did here 21 years ago.

When we leave Ireland, we'll be participating in two events that mark America's determination to help build a safer, more prosperous world.

On June 6th, I'll join former U.S. Army Rangers at the historic battlefield of Pointe du Hoc and, later, President Mitterrand and other American veterans at Omaha Beach and Utah Beach on the Normandy coast of France. Together we'll commemorate the 40th anniversary of D-day, the great Allied invasion that set Europe on the course toward liberty, democracy, and peace.

That great battle and the war it helped

bring to an end mark the beginning of nearly 40 years of peace in Europe—a peace preserved not by good will alone, but by the strength and moral courage of the NATO alliance. On June 6th I will reaffirm America's faithful commitment to NATO. If NATO remains strong and unified, Europe and America will remain free. If NATO can continue to deter war, Europe and America can continue to enjoy peace—40 more years of peace.

And let me make one thing very plain: A strong NATO is no threat to the Soviet Union. NATO is the world's greatest peace movement. It never threatens; it defends. And we will continue trying to promote a better dialog with the Soviet Union. The Soviets could gain much by helping us make the world safer, particularly through arms reductions. That would free them to devote more resources to their people and economy.

Growth and prosperity will occupy our attention when we return to London for the annual economic summit of the major industrialized countries. And we'll be mark-

ing another important anniversary: 50 years ago, America's leaders had the vision to enact legislation known as the Reciprocal Trade Agreements Act of 1934. It helped bring an end to a terrible era of protectionism that nearly destroyed the world's economies.

We'll talk about how best to maintain the recent progress that has lifted hopes for a worldwide recovery for our common prosperity. You can be proud that the strength of the United States economy has led the way. I believe continued progress lies with freer trade and more open markets. Less protectionism will mean more progress, more growth, more jobs, a bigger slice of the pie for everyone.

As we meet in Normandy and London, we'll have much to be thankful for, much to be optimistic about, but still much to do.

Till next week, thanks for listening, and God bless you.

Note: The President spoke at 5:06 p.m. from Ashford Castle in Cong, County Mayo, Ireland.

Remarks to the Citizens of Ballyporeen, Ireland
June 3, 1984

In the business that I formerly was in, I would have to say this is a very difficult spot—to be introduced to you who have waited so patiently—following this wonderful talent that we've seen here. And I should have gone on first, and then you should have followed—[*laughter*]—to close the show. But thank you very much.

Nancy and I are most grateful to be with you here today, and I'll take a chance and say, *muintir na hEireann* [people of Ireland]. Did I get it right? [*Applause*] All right. Well, it's difficult to express my appreciation to all of you. I feel like I'm about to drown everyone in a bath of nostalgia. Of all the honors and gifts that have been afforded me as President, this visit is the one that I will cherish dearly. You see, I didn't know much about my family background— not because of a lack of interest, but be-

cause my father was orphaned before he was 6 years old. And now thanks to you and the efforts of good people who have dug into the history of a poor immigrant family, I know at last whence I came. And this has given my soul a new contentment. And it is a joyous feeling. It is like coming home after a long journey.

You see, my father, having been orphaned so young, he knew nothing of his roots also. And, God rest his soul, I told the Father, I think he's here, too, today, and very pleased and happy to know that this is whence he came.

Robert Frost, a renowned American poet, once said, "Home is the place where, when you have to go there, they have to take you in." [*Laughter*] Well, it's been so long since my great-grandfather set out that you don't have to take me in. So, I'm certainly thankful for this wonderful homecoming today. I can't think of a place on the planet I would rather claim as my roots more than Ballyporeen, County Tipperary.

My great-grandfather left here in a time of stress, seeking to better himself and his family. From what I'm told, we were a poor family. But my ancestors took with them a treasure, an indomitable spirit that was cultivated in the rich soil of this county.

And today I come back to you as a descendant of people who are buried here in paupers' graves. Perhaps this is God's way of reminding us that we must always treat every individual, no matter what his or her station in life, with dignity and respect. And who knows? Someday that person's child or grandchild might grow up to become the Prime Minister of Ireland or President of the United States.

Looking around town today, I was struck by the similarity between Ballyporeen and the small town in Illinois where I was born, Tampico. Of course, there's one thing you have that we didn't have in Tampico. We didn't have a Ronald Reagan Lounge in town. [*Laughter*] Well, the spirit is the same, this spirit of warmth, friendliness, and openness in Tampico and Ballyporeen, and you make me feel very much at home.

What unites us is our shared heritage and the common values of our two peoples. So many Irish men and women from every walk of life played a role in creating the dream of America. One was Charles Thompson, Secretary of the Continental Congress, and who designed the first Great Seal of the United States. I'm certainly proud to be part of that great Irish American tradition. From the time of our revolution when Irishmen filled the ranks of the Continental Army, to the building of the railroads, to the cultural contributions of individuals like the magnificent tenor John McCormack and the athletic achievements of the great heavyweight boxing champion John L. Sullivan—all of them are part of a great legacy.

Speaking of sports, I'd like to take this opportunity to congratulate an organization of which all Irish men and women can be proud, an organization that this year is celebrating its 100th anniversary: the Gaelic Athletic Association. I understand it was formed a hundred years ago in Tipperary to foster the culture and games of traditional Ireland. Some of you may be aware that I began my career as a sports announcer—a sports broadcaster, so I had an early appreciation for sporting competition. Well, congratulations to all of you during this GAA centennial celebration.

I also understand that not too far from here is the home of the great Irish novelist Charles Joseph Kickham. The Irish identity flourished in the United States. Irish men and women proud of their heritage can be found in every walk of life. I even have some of them in my Cabinet. One of them traces his maternal roots to Mitchellstown, just down the road from Ballyporeen. And he and I have almost the same name. I'm talking about Secretary of the Treasury Don Regan.

He spells it R-e-g-a-n. We're all of the same clan, we're all cousins. I tried to tell the Secretary one day that his branch of the family spelled it that way because they just couldn't handle as many letters as ours could. [*Laughter*] And then I received a paper from Ireland that told me that the clan to which we belong, that in it those who said "Regan" and spelled it that way were the professional people and the educators, and only the common laborers called it "Reagan." [*Laughter*] So, meet a common laborer.

The first job I ever got—I was 14 years old, and they put a pick and a shovel in my hand and my father told me that that was fitting and becoming to one of our name.

The bond between our two countries runs deep and strong, and I'm proud to be here in recognition and celebration of our ties that bind. My roots in Ballyporeen, County Tipperary, are little different than millions of other Americans who find their roots in towns and counties all over the Isle of Erin. I just feel exceptionally lucky to have this chance to visit you.

Last year a member of my staff came through town and recorded some messages from you. It was quite a tape, and I was moved deeply by the sentiments that you expressed. One of your townsmen sang me a bit of a tune about Sean Tracy, and a few lines stuck in my mind. They went like this—not that I'll sing—"And I'll never more roam, from my own native home, in Tipperary so far away."

Well, the Reagans roamed to America, but now we're back. And Nancy and I thank you from the bottom of our hearts for coming out to welcome us, for the warmth of your welcome. God bless you all.

Note: The President spoke at 2:44 p.m. in the village square.

Following his remarks, the President left Ballyporeen and traveled to Dublin.

Toasts of the President and Prime Minister Garret FitzGerald of Ireland at a Dinner Honoring the President in Dublin
June 3, 1984

The Prime Minister. Mr. President, in accordance with long-established custom and given that it's expected of us, let me start on an historical note. We are believed, outside this country, to always plunge back into the depths of history. Well, I'm going to do so, because in the year 1029, King Reagan of Brega inflicted a crushing defeat on the Vikings of Dublin. [*Laughter*]

The victor demanded as ransom for the Viking king, Olaf Sitricsson, the following: 1,200 cows, 6 score Welsh horses—I don't know why Welsh—60 ounces of gold, 60 ounces of pure silver, and all the "Irishmen of Leinster and of the North" who were being held prisoner in Dublin on this very site, then the fortress of the Viking city.

Fortunately for us FitzGeralds, we didn't arrive for another 140 years—[*laughter*]—when the Reagans, having in the meantime failed in a bid for the High Kingship of Ireland—you made it on a second try, playing on a different field—had become less powerful. And fortunately for us, because I doubt if my family could have bought themselves out of a Reagan jail at that price. [*Laughter*]

We, the FitzGeralds, do, however, owe the Reagans one important debt. For it was one, Malachy Reagan, then Latin secretary to a rather well-known king of Leinster—whom I don't need to and would prefer not to name—who wrote to us inviting us over here in 1169. [*Laughter*] The Irish people 800 years later are, I need hardly tell you, deeply grateful. [*Laughter*] Isn't that right—[*inaudible*]? [*Laughter*]

Mr. President, your great-grandfather and my grandfather left for London from two places divided 7 miles apart a century and a quarter ago. They both married Irish wives, in the very same church in that city, Southwark Cathedral. And thereafter their paths divided, bringing us by very different routes to the leadership of our respective governments.

Since they both left Ireland, much has happened in this small country. Much of it has been good. An independent Irish State has come into existence that is now respected by the nations of the world. Literature in the English language has since been transformed by towering Irish figures such as Shaw and Wilde, Yeats, and Joyce. And the grinding poverty in which our people lived three generations back has been replaced by a modest prosperity, as you will have seen traveling through Mayo and Galway and Tipperary and flying over other counties.

This modest prosperity has not marred the beauty and calm of our countryside, which continues to draw hundreds of thousands of your compatriots as welcome visitors to our shores.

Most significantly for the future, the last decade has seen the growth in Ireland of high technology industry—the vast bulk of it the fruit of U.S. investment here, now in total amounting to over $4 billion and employing one in six of our manufacturing labor force. Ireland's share of Europe's high technology activity is now totally disproportionate to our size and population. We are well on the way to becoming a Silicon Valley in Europe, as your investors match their inventiveness with the special skills and enthusiasm of our dynamic, well-educated labor force—the youngest in Europe.

There is, of course, another side to this picture—one of heavy umemployment as the worldwide recession, now lifting in your country, continues to take its toll in Europe and, particularly, in this island. And we also have our own specific economic and financial problems. We'll have an opportunity to discuss some of these issues together tomorrow.

But worst of all, we have within this island a conflict that threatens the peace and stability of this corner of Europe, one that has brought tragedy to thousands of homes in Northern Ireland and to many here, also, and in Britain. This is a conflict of two traditions, two identities in this island, but first and foremost, within Northern Ireland.

You are aware, Mr. President, of the work of the New Ireland Forum, launched in this great hall, and you have commented supportively on it. The New Ireland Forum made only one set of proposals in its report. It used the word "proposes" only once. It proposes, as necessary elements of a framework within which a new Ireland could emerge, a set of requirements, a list of "musts," centered on the need to accommodate each of the two Irish traditions equally satisfactorily in new structures. I'm deliberately availing of this important occasion to emphasize this point, because it has, perhaps, not been fully understood.

The Forum goes on to express the belief—the belief, not the demand—of nationalists that unity offers the best solution and our further preference that the particular form of unity we would wish to see established is a unitary state, achieved by agreement and consent. That is our belief, our strong preference; it is not a demand. We set out our best arguments in favor of this preference, but we also set out the arguments in favor of two quite different alternatives that we considered: a federal-confederal state and joint authority. And most significantly of all, we committed ourselves to being open to discuss other views which may contribute to political development. Nothing, I believe, could be more open than that approach.

The report of the New Ireland Forum is, as I have said, an agenda, not a blueprint. We know that you and our European friends want, in an appropriate way, to help to end this tragedy. The people of Northern Ireland have suffered far too much. They deserve and they need our help and yours.

You will forgive me, Mr. President, for having dwelt for some minutes on a problem that is so close to our hearts, so ever-present to our minds. It is, alas, only one of the many problems of violence and threats of violence in the world today—problems to which you and I will be turning our thoughts together tomorrow morning.

Dominating everything, of course, is the issue of East-West relations, the arms race and, in particular, the nuclear menace that threatens life on this planet. Here, above all, as we have indeed been discussing together the last few minutes, there's an absolute need for dialog between the superpowers, for the reopening of channels of communication that have become clogged, for the creation, if it can be achieved, of the kind of trust and confidence upon which alone world peace can be built. We look forward to hearing you speak on aspects of these problems to the joint session of the Houses of Oireachtas [Parliament] tomorrow.

Ireland is a small country with a nightmare past. More than most people, therefore, we are deeply concerned at the violent tyranny that tears apart small countries like Afghanistan, at the repression that seeks to still the powerful instinct for freedom in Eastern European countries like Poland, and at the deprivation of human rights in so many countries of Latin America. With many of these Latin American countries our people have close emotional ties through the work of our priests and nuns and lay helpers there who seek to relieve the poverty of the people and to give them back their dignity of which they've been deprived by oppressive regimes. Our people's deep concern is that these problems be resolved peacefully by the people of the region themselves—in Central America, along the lines proposed by the Contadora countries. In this connection, I might add that many people in Ireland have been most heartened by the news of Secretary Shultz's visit to Nicaragua on Friday last and hope that this may lead to the restoration of normal relations between that small state and your great country, thus enhancing the climate for peace and democracy in that troubled region.

Mr. President, in 4 weeks time Ireland takes over the responsibilities of the Presidency of the European Community. It will be our task to bring to a conclusion the negotiations to enlarge the Community by admitting Spain and Portugal as members and to complete the negotiations for the new convention between the EEC and the African, Caribbean, Indian Ocean, and Pacific countries. We should also be seeking during this Presidency to secure agreement to a more coherent organization of the economic policies of our member States so as to take fuller advantage of the recovery that has been taking place in the United States. Hopefully, this task may be made somewhat easier by the discussions that you will be having with other major economic powers in London this week.

Mr. President, there's another task we should also tackle. Just as in our first Presidency of the European Community in 1975, it fell to me as President of the Council of Ministers of the Community to establish and get working the new system of political consultation between Europe and America that had been decided upon in the previous year, so in this new Irish Presidency we shall endeavor to reconcile economic differences between Europe and America and to secure a greater convergence of views on foreign policy issues.

There are few tasks that the Irish Government could look forward to with as much enthusiasm or commitment. After all, our own relations with your great country are based first on human considerations, on people, rather than on the cold concerns of policy. It is on that human dimension, on such old, enduring, and unquenchable friendships that the hope of our world can best rely today.

Mr. President, your visit to your homeland has reinforced and revitalized that precious bond. I ask all here to raise their glasses in a toast to the President of the United States and Mrs. Reagan.

The President. Prime Minister and Mrs. FitzGerald, my Irish friends, Nancy and I are delighted to be here in the homeland of my ancestors and delighted to be with all of you this evening. The magnificent green of your hills and meadows, likewise, the warmth and kindredship of your people during our visit has touched us deeply. May I offer in return a heartfelt thank you from both Nancy and me.

Every American, even those not lucky enough to be of Irish background, has much to be grateful for in the Isle of Erin. I think I have some firsthand knowledge of this. You see, I currently—Nancy and I reside in a house that was designed by an Irishman. [*Laughter*]

We all know the Irish names and the lists of their achievements in our government, going all the way back to our Revolutionary history. Not only have Ireland's own had great impact on America, but the opposite has also been true.

The cross-pollination of American and Irish liberty is truly an historic phenomenon. Benjamin Franklin, a preeminent influence on the course of American democracy, visited here during our Revolutionary period. As Prime Minister FitzGerald pointed out to me during his last visit to Washington, more than just a "couple" of American Presidents—and one which I will not mention—descend from this land.

On the other side of the coin, individuals significant to the development of Irish liberty were much affected by what was happening in America. Daniel O'Connell, a nationalist hero and a true humanitarian, was influenced by our great pamphleteer, Thomas Paine. And the great parliamentarian, Charles Stewart Parnell, journeyed to America as a youth, a journey which may well have colored his political views of the world. And, of course, Eamon de Valera, your third President, was actually born in the United States.

And yet, with our countries so close, there are some influences we're not so proud of. And I believe I speak for all Americans of Irish descent who now hold elected office when I join you in condemning any misguided American who supports terrorists in Northern Ireland. I want to offer my thanks to Prime Minister FitzGerald for his strong stand on this issue. When he last visited Washington, he articulated a message of conviction and courage and, by doing so, I'm sure has saved some innocent lives.

Oscar Wilde had a comment on war that is also applicable to terrorism. He said, "When it is looked upon as vulgar," Wilde said, "it will cease to be popular."

The American people overwhelmingly support peaceful efforts to reconcile the differences between the two traditions on this island. We pray there will be a new dawn, that it will come soon, when both Catholics and Protestants in Northern Ireland can live in the sunlight of a peaceful and just society.

We're following, with keen interest, the efforts that your government has been making, and we wish you success. We especially welcome the hard work and thought that went into the New Ireland Forum's report. We hope it will strengthen Anglo-Irish cooperation in resolving the Northern Ireland problem through a peaceful reconciliation.

Ireland, even with this problem at home, has been exerting an admirable influence internationally. As peacekeepers, working within the structure of the United Nations, you've taken great risks for peace. Your bilateral development assistance to less fortunate countries is a tribute to your generosity and your humanitarianism, as is the personal dedication of Irish men and women engaged in voluntary service throughout the world.

Ireland has had an active and respected role in the European Community. We look forward to consulting closely with your government during Ireland's forthcoming Presidency of the European Community Commission. Ireland has always promoted an open and meaningful dialog between the United States and the member States of the Community, and I know we can count on a continuation of that fine and very practical tradition.

We respect Ireland's independent course in international affairs. We respect Ireland's contributions, which were predicted by President Kennedy, as a maker and shaper of world peace. And we respect the democratic and humanitarian values embodied in your actions. Taoiseach [Prime Minister], our people have a common love of freedom and a sense of decency that transcends political consideration. In many respects, my journey here is a celebration of our ties and ideals, as well as of family. They are ties that secure our friendship and ensure our good will.

That Thomas Paine that I mentioned a moment ago said—and I think that all of us should take this to heart—he said that the opportunity is ours; we have it in our power to start the world over again. And I think we share another ideal. What is our goal when we talk of ideologies and philosophies? It is one, very simple: the ultimate in individual freedom consistent with an orderly society. That is our goal.

Ladies and gentlemen, please join me in a toast to the President [Prime Minister] of Ireland.

Note: Prime Minister Garret FitzGerald spoke at 10 p.m. in Dublin Castle.

Address Before a Joint Session of the Irish National Parliament
June 4, 1984

I am fully cognizant of the great honor that has been done me by your invitation for me to speak here. [*Applause*] Thank you.

And I can't help but say, I wonder if there is an awareness in some that there are countries in the world today where representatives would not have been able to speak as they have here.[1]

When I stepped off Air Force One at Shannon a few days ago and saw Ireland, beautiful and green, and felt again the warmth of her people, something deep inside began to stir.

Who knows but that scientists will someday explain the complex genetic process by which generations seem to transfer across time and even oceans their fondest memories. Until they do, I will have to rely on President Lincoln's words about the "mystic chords of memory"—and say to you that during the past few days at every stop here in your country, those chords have been gently and movingly struck. So, I hope you won't think it too bold of me to say that my feelings here this morning can best be summarized by the words "home—home again."

Now, I know some of us Irish Americans tend to get carried away with our ancestral past and want very much to impress our relatives here with how well we've done in the New World. Many of us aren't back in Ireland 5 minutes before, as the American song has it, we're looking to shake the hand of Uncle Mike and kiss the girl we used to swing down by the garden gate. [*Laughter*]

Well, I do want you to know that for Nancy and me these last few days will remain in our hearts forever. From Shannon to Galway, to Ballyporeen to Dublin, you have truly made us feel as welcome as the flowers in May, and for this we'll always be grateful to you and to the Irish people.

Now, of course I didn't exactly expect a chilly reception. As I look around this chamber, I know I can't claim to be a better Irishman than anyone here, but I can perhaps claim to be an Irishman longer than most any of you here. [*Laughter*] There are those who just refuse to let me forget that. [*Laughter*] I also have some other credentials. I am the great-grandson of a Tipperary man; I'm the President of a country with the closest possible ties to Ireland; and I was a friend of Barry Fitzgerald.

---

[1] *After he was introduced by Prime Minister Garret FitzGerald, three members of Parliament protested the President's presence and left the room.*

[*Laughter*] One Irishman told me he thought I would fit in. "Mr. President," he said, "you love a good story, you love horses, you love politics—the accent we can work on." [*Laughter*]

But I also came to the land of my forebears to acknowledge two debts: to express gratitude for a light heart and a strong constitution; and to acknowledge that wellspring of so much American political success—the Blarney Stone. I don't have to tell you how the Blarney Stone works. Many times, for example, I have congratulated Italians on Christopher Columbus' discovery of America, but that's not going to stop me from congratulating all of you on Brendan the Navigator. [*Laughter*]

I think you know, though, that Ireland has been much in our thoughts since the first days in office. I'm proud to say the first Embassy I visited as President was Ireland's, and I'm proud that our administration is blessed by so many Cabinet members of Irish extraction. Indeed I had to fight them off Air Force One or there wouldn't be anyone tending the store while we're gone. And that's not to mention the number of Irish Americans who hold extremely important leadership posts today in the United States Congress.

I can assure you that Irish Americans speak with one voice about the importance of the friendship of our two nations and the bonds of affection between us. The American people know how profoundly Ireland has affected our national heritage and our growth into a world power. And I know that they want me to assure you today that your interests and concerns are ours and that, in the United States, you have true and fast friends.

Our visit is a joyous moment, and it will remain so. But this should not keep us from serious work or serious words. This afternoon, I want to speak directly on a few points.

I know many of you recall with sadness the tragic events of last Christmas: the 5 people killed and 92 injured after a terrorist bomb went off in Harrods of London. Just the day before, a Garda recruit, Gary Sheehan, and Private Patrick Kelly, a young Irish soldier with four children, were slain by terrorist bullets. These two events, occurring 350 miles apart, one in Ireland, one in Britain, demonstrated the pitiless, indiscriminate nature of terrorist violence, a violence evil to its core and contemptible in all its forms. And it showed that the problems of Northern Ireland are taking a toll on the people of both Britain and Ireland, north and south.

Yet, the trouble in the north affects more than just these two great isles. When he was in America in March, your Prime Minister courageously denounced the support that a tiny number of misguided Americans give to these terrorist groups. I joined him in that denunciation, as did the vast majority of Irish Americans.

I repeat today, there is no place for the crude, cowardly violence of terrorism—not in Britain, not in Ireland, not in Northern Ireland. All sides should have one goal before them, and let us state it simply and directly: to end the violence, to end it completely, and to end it now.

The terrorism, the sense of crisis that has existed in Northern Ireland has been costly to all. But let us not overlook legitimate cause for hope in the events of the last few months. As you know, active dialog between the governments—here in Dublin, and in London—is continuing. There's also the constructive work of the New Ireland Forum. The Forum's recent report has been praised. It's also been criticized. But the important thing is that men of peace are being heard and their message of reconciliation discussed.

The position of the United States in all of this is clear: We must not and will not interfere in Irish matters nor prescribe to you solutions or formulas. But I want you to know that we pledge to you our good will and support, and we're with you as you work toward peace.

I'm not being overly optimistic when I say today that I believe you will work out a peaceful and democratic reconciliation of Ireland's two different traditions and communities. Besides being a land whose concern for freedom and self-determination is legendary, Ireland is also a land synonymous with hope. It is this sense of hope that saw you through famine and war, that sent so many Irish men and women abroad to seek new lives and to build new nations, that gave the world the saints and scholars who preserved Western culture, the missionaries and soldiers who spoke of human dignity and freedom, and put much of the spark to my own country's quest for independence and that of other nations.

You are still that land of hope. It's nowhere more obvious than in the economic changes being wrought here. I know Ireland faces a serious challenge to create jobs for your population, but you've made striking gains, attracting the most advanced technology and industries in the world, and improving the standard of living of your people. And you've done all of this while maintaining your traditional values and religious heritage, renewing your culture and language, and continuing to play a key role in the world community.

Based on Ireland's traditional neutrality in international affairs, you can be proud of your contribution to the search for peace. Irish soldiers have been part of eight United Nations peacekeeping operations since you joined that organization.

In the economic sphere, we Americans, too, are proud that our businesses have been permitted to prosper in Ireland's new economic environment. As you know, there are more than 300 American businesses here providing between 35,000 and 40,000 jobs. We're continuing to encourage this investment. And I assure you today that we will encourage even greater investment for the future.

I think part of the explanation for the economic progress you are making here in Ireland can be found in your nation's historic regard for personal freedom. Too often the link between prosperity and freedom is overlooked. In fact, it's as tight as ever. And it provides a firm basis for increasing cooperation, not only between our two countries but among all countries of the globe that recognize it.

Men and women everywhere in our shrinking world are having the same experience. For most of mankind the oceans are no longer the fearful distances they were when my great-grandfather, Michael Reagan, took weeks to reach America. Some men and women still set out with their children in small boats fleeing tyranny and deprivation. For most of us, though, the oceans and airways are now peaceful avenues, thronged with ideas, people, and goods going in every direction. They draw us together. Slowly, but surely, more and more people share the values of peace, prosperity, and freedom which unite Ireland and America.

In the last year, I've made two visits to America's neighbors across the Pacific in Asia. This century has brought the Pacific nations many hardships, and many difficulties and differences remain. But what I found everywhere was energy, optimism, and excitement. Some nations in Asia have produced astounding economic growth rates by providing incentives that reward initiative by unleashing freedom. More and more, there is a sense of common destiny and possibility for all the peoples of this great region. The vast Pacific has become smaller, but the future of those who live around it is larger than ever before.

Coming to Ireland, I sensed the same stirring, the same optimism toward a better future.

I believe that great opportunities do lie ahead to overcome the age-old menaces of disease and hunger and want. But moments of great progress can also be moments of great testing. President Kennedy noted, when he was here, that we live in a "most climactic period" but also, he said, "in the most difficult and dangerous struggle in the history of the world." He was talking about our century's struggle between the forces of freedom and totalitarianism, a struggle overshadowed, we all know too well, by weapons of awful destruction on both sides.

Believe me, to hold the office that I now hold is to understand, each waking moment of the day, the awesome responsibility of protecting peace and preserving human life. The responsibility cannot be met with halfway wishes; it can be met only by a determined effort to consolidate peace with all the strength America can bring to bear.

This is my deepest commitment: to achieve stable peace, not just by being prepared to deter aggression but also by assuring that economic strength helps to lead the way to greater stability through growth and human progress—being prepared with

the strength of our commitment to pursue all possible avenues for arms reduction; and being prepared with the greatest strength of all, the spiritual strength and self-confidence that enables us to reach out to our adversaries. To them, and to all of you who have always been our dear and trusted friends, I tell you today from my heart, America is prepared for peace.

What we're doing now in American foreign policy is bringing an enduring steadiness, particularly in the search for arms reduction. Too often in the past, we sought to achieve grandiose objectives and sweeping agreements overnight. At other times, we set our sights so low that the agreements, when they were made, permitted the numbers and categories of weapons to soar. For example, one nation from the time of the signing of the SALT II agreement until the present has added 3,950 warheads to its arsenal. That might be arms limitation; it certainly isn't arms reduction. The result was—it wasn't even arms control. Through all of this, I'm afraid, differing proposals and shifting policies have sometimes left both friends and adversaries confused or disconcerted.

And that's why we've put forward, methodically, one of the most extensive arms control programs in history. We believe there can be only one policy, for all nations, if we are to preserve civilization in this modern age: A nuclear war cannot be won and must never be fought.

In five areas, we have proposed substantive initiatives. In Vienna less than 2 months ago, the Western side put forward new proposals on reducing the levels of conventional military forces in Europe. In the same week in Geneva, Vice President Bush put forward a draft agreement for a worldwide ban on chemical weapons, the gases that have been used in Afghanistan and in Kampuchea. In Stockholm, we're pursuing at the Conference on Disarmament in Europe a series of proposals that will help reduce the possibility of conflict. And in Geneva—as most of you are aware—we have been participating, until recently, in arms reduction talks on two fronts: the START talks on reducing intercontinental nuclear forces, and the INF talks, which deal with the issue of intermediate-range missiles worldwide. In addition, we're working to prevent the spread of nuclear weapons and to require comprehensive safeguards on all nuclear exports.

During the months the START and INF talks were underway, the United States proposed seven different initiatives. None of these were offered on a take-it-or-leave-it basis. Indeed, we made a number of adjustments to respond to the stated concerns of the Soviet side. While Soviet flexibility did not match our own, the Soviets also made some steps of the kind required in any serious negotiations. But then, after the first deployment of intermediate-range missiles here in Europe, the Soviets quit the bargaining table.

Now, this deployment was not something we welcomed. It had been my hope, and that of the European leaders, that negotiations would make the deployments unnecessary. Unfortunately, the Soviet stance in those talks left us no alternative. Since 1977, while we were not deploying, but urging the Soviets to negotiate, they were deploying some 370 SS–20 missiles, capable of reaching every city in every country in Europe. We and our allies could not ignore this threat forever.

But I believe today it is still possible to reach an agreement. Let me assure you that in both the START and INF talks, we want to hear Soviet proposals; we want them to hear our own; and we're prepared to negotiate tomorrow if the Soviets so choose. I'm prepared to halt, and even reverse, the deployment of our intermediate-range missiles from Europe as the outcome of a verifiable and equitable agreement. But for such an outcome to be possible, we need to have the Soviets return to the bargaining table. And before this body, and the people of Europe, I call on them to do so.

Indeed, I believe we must not be satisfied—we dare not rest, until the day we've banished these terrible weapons of war from the face of the Earth forever.

My deepest hope and dream has been that if once we can, together, start down the road of reduction, we will inevitably see the common sense of going all the way, so that our children and grandchildren will not have to live with that threat hanging over the world.

In addition to the arms control negotiations, I want to stress today that the United States seeks greater dialog in two other critical areas of East-West relations. Just as we seek to reduce the burden of armaments, we want to find, also, ways to limit their use in troublesome or potentially difficult regional situations. So, we seek serious discussions with the Soviets to guard against miscalculation or misunderstanding in troubled or strategically sensitive areas of the world. I want to stress again today the serious commitment of the United States to such a process.

In the Stockholm conference I mentioned a moment ago, the United States and 34 other nations are negotiating measures to lessen East-West tensions and reduce uncertainties arising from military activities in Europe, the area with the greatest concentration of armed forces in the world. The 16 nations of the Atlantic Alliance have advanced concrete proposals which would make conflict in Europe less likely. The Soviet Union has not accepted these proposals, but has focused upon a declaration of the non-use of force.

Well, mere restatement of a principle all nations have agreed to in the U.N. Charter and elsewhere, would be an inadequate conclusion to a conference whose mandate calls for much more. We must translate the idea into actions which build effective barriers against the use of force in Europe. If the Soviet Union will agree to such concrete actions, which other countries in the Stockholm conference already seem prepared to accept, this would be an important step forward in creating a more peaceful world.

In [If] discussions on reaffirming the principle not to use force, a principle in which we believe so deeply, will bring the Soviet Union to negotiate agreements which will give concrete, new meaning to that principle, we will gladly enter into such discussions. I urge the Soviet Union now to join all other countries in the Stockholm conference to move promptly to take these steps which will help ensure peace and stability in Europe.

We seek to build confidence and trust

with the Soviets in areas of mutual interest by moving forward in our bilateral relations on a broad front. In the economic field, we're taking a number of steps to increase exchanges in nonstrategic goods. In other areas, we have, for example, extended our very useful incidents at sea agreement for another term. And we've proposed discussions for specific steps to expand and multiply contacts of benefit to our people. I might add here that the democracies have a strong mutual obligation to work for progress in the area of human rights. And positive Soviet steps in this area would be considered by the United States a significant signal.

In summary then, we're seeking increased discussion and negotiation to reduce armaments, solve regional problems, and improve bilateral relations. Progress on these fronts would enhance peace and security for people everywhere.

I'm afraid the Soviet response has been disappointing. Rather than join us in our efforts to calm tensions and achieve agreements, the Soviets appear to have chosen to withdraw and to try to achieve their objective through propaganda, rather than negotiations.

The Soviets seek to place the blame on the Americans for this self-imposed isolation. But they have not taken these steps by our choice. We remain ready for them to join with us and the rest of the world community to build a more peaceful world. In solidarity with our allies, confident of our strength, we threaten no nation. Peace and prosperity are in the Soviet interest as well as in ours. So, let us move forward.

Steadiness in pursuing our arms reduction initiatives and bettering East-West relations will eventually bear fruit. But steadiness is also needed in sustaining the cause of human freedom.

When I was last in Europe, I spoke about a crusade for freedom, about the ways the democracies could inaugurate a program promoting the growth of democratic institutions throughout the world. And now it is underway. And this can have an impact in many ways in many places and be a force for good.

Some, of course, focusing on the nations that have lost their freedom in the postwar era, argue that a crusade for democratic values is impractical or unachievable. But we must take the long view. At the start of this century, there were but few democracies. Today there are more than 50, comprising one-third of the world's population. And it is no coincidence—showing once again the link between political, economic freedom and material progress—that these nations enjoy the highest standards of living.

History is the work of free men and women, not unalterable laws. It is never inevitable, but it does have directions and trends; and one trend is clear—democracies are not only increasing in number, they're growing in strength. Today they're strong enough to give the cause of freedom growing room and breathing space, and that's all that freedom ever really needs. "The mass of mankind has not been born with saddles on their backs." Thomas Jefferson said that. Freedom is the flagship of the future and the flashfire of the future. Its spark ignites the deepest and noblest aspirations of the human soul.

Those who think the Western democracies are trying to roll back history are missing the point. History is moving in the direction of self-government and the human dignity that it institutionalizes, and the future belongs to the free.

On this point of democratic development, I think it is vital to appreciate what has been happening in the Western Hemisphere, particularly Latin America. Great strides have been made in recent years. In fact, 26 of 33 Latin American countries today are democracies, or are striving to become democracies. I think it is also vital to understand that the United States current program of assistance to several Central American countries is designed precisely to assist this spread of democratic self-rule.

Now, I know that some see the United States, a large and powerful nation, involved in the affairs of smaller nations to the south, and conclude that our mission there must be self-seeking or interventionist. Well, the Irish people, of all people, know Americans well. We strive to avoid violence or conflict. History is our witness on this point.

For a number of years at the end of the last war, the United States had a monopoly on nuclear weapons. We did not exploit this monopoly for territorial or imperial gain. We sought to do all in our power to encourage prosperity and peace and democracy in Europe. One can imagine if some other countries, possibly, had had these weapons instead of the United States, would the world have been as much at peace in the last 40 years as it has been.

In a few days in France, I will stand near the only land in Europe that is occupied by the United States—those mounds of earth marked with crosses and Stars of David, the graves of Americans who never came home, who gave their lives that others might live in freedom and peace. It is freedom and peace that the people of Central America seek today.

Three times in little more than 2 years, the people of El Salvador have voted in free elections. Each time they had to brave the threats of the guerrillas supported by the Sandinista regime in Nicaragua and by Cuba and the Soviet Union. These guerrillas use violence to support their threats. Their slogan in each one of those elections has been, "Vote today and die tonight." Yet the people of El Salvador, 1.4 million of them, have braved ambush and gunfire and trudged for miles to vote for freedom and then stood in line for hours waiting their turn to vote.

Some of our observers who went down there—many of them going down convinced that perhaps we were wrong in what we are trying to do there—came home converted. Some of them came home converted by one woman standing in the voting line—had been there for hours. She had been shot. She suffered from a rifle bullet. She refused to leave the line for medical treatment until she had had her opportunity to vote. They came home convinced that the people of El Salvador want democracy.

All the United States is attempting to do—with only 55 military advisers and $474 million in aid, three-fourths of which is earmarked for economic and social development—is give the Salvadorans the chance they want for democratic self-determina-

tion, without outside interference. But this the Government of Nicaragua has been determined not to permit.

By their own admission, they've been supplying and training the Salvadoran guerrillas. In their own country they have never held elections. They have all but crushed freedom of the press and moved against labor unions, outlawed political freedoms, and even sponsored mob action against Nicaragua's independent human rights commission and imprisoned its director.

Despite this repression, a hundred thousand Nicaraguan Catholics attended a rally on Good Friday this year to support their church, which has been persecuted by the Sandinistas' Communist dictatorship. And the bishop has now written a pastoral letter citing this persecution of the church by that government. And yet, even in our own country we didn't read anything of that demonstration. Somehow word of it didn't get out through the news channels of the world.

In a homily to 4,000 Nicaraguans packed into Don Bosco Church several weeks ago, the head of the Nicaraguan Bishops Conference, Bishop Pablo Antonio Vega, said, "The tragedy of the Nicaraguan people is that we are living with a totalitarian ideology that no one wants in this country." You may not have heard about this—again, as I say, the words of Nicaraguan Archbishop Obando y Bravo. "To those who say that the only course for Central American countries is Marxism-Leninism, we Christians must show another way. That is to follow Christ, whose path is that of truth and liberty."

Well, the vast majority of those now struggling for freedom in Nicaragua—contrary to what the Sandinistas would have the world believe—are good and worthy people who did not like the Somoza dictatorship and who do not want the Communist dictatorship. The tragedy is they haven't been given the chance to choose.

The people of Nicaragua and El Salvador have a right to resist the nightmare outside forces want to impose on them, just as they have the right to resist extremist violence from within whether from the left or right. The United States must not turn its back on the democratic aspirations of the people of Central America.

Moreover, this is a worldwide struggle. The Irish orator John [James] Philpot Curran once said, "The condition upon which God hath given liberty to man is eternal vigilance." And yes, military strength is indispensable to freedom. I have seen four wars in my lifetime, none of them came about because the forces of freedom were too strong.

In the moving words used by the Czechoslovak Charter 77 group just a week ago, in reply to supporters of nuclear disarmament in the West, they said, "Unlike you, we have personal experience of other, perhaps less conspicuous, but no less effective means of destroying civilization than those represented by thermonuclear war; some of us, at the very least, prefer the risk involved in maintaining a firm stance against aggression to the certainty of the catastrophic consequences of appeasement."

The struggle between freedom and totalitarianism today is not ultimately a test of arms or missiles, but a test of faith and spirit. And in this spiritual struggle, the Western mind and will is the crucial battleground. We must not hesitate to express our dream of freedom; we must not be reluctant to enunciate the crucial distinctions between right and wrong—between political systems based on freedom and those based on a dreadful denial of the human spirit.

If our adversaries believe that we will diminish our own self-respect by keeping silent or acquiescing in the face of successive crimes against humanity, they're wrong. What we see throughout the world is an uprising of intellect and will. As Lech Walesa said: "Our souls contain exactly the contrary of what they wanted. They wanted us not to believe in God, and our churches are full. They wanted us to be materialistic and incapable of sacrifices; we are antimaterialistic, capable of sacrifice. They wanted us to be afraid of the tanks, of the guns, and instead we don't fear them at all." Lech Walesa.

Well, let us not take the counsel of our fears. Let us instead offer the world a politics of hope, a forward strategy for freedom. The words of William Faulkner, at a Nobel prize ceremony more than three decades ago, are an eloquent answer to those who predict nuclear doomsday or the eventual triumph of the superstate. "Man will not merely endure," Faulkner said, "he will prevail . . . because he will return to the old verities and truths of the heart. He is immortal because, alone among creatures, he has a soul, a spirit capable of compassion and sacrifice and endurance."

Those old verities, those truths of the heart—human freedom under God—are on the march everywhere in the world. All across the world today—in the shipyards of Gdansk, the hills of Nicaragua, the rice paddies of Kampuchea, the mountains of Afghanistan—the cry again is liberty. And the cause is the same as that spoken in this chamber more than two decades ago by a young American President, who said, "A future of peace and freedom."

It was toward the end of his visit here that John Fitzgerald Kennedy said, "I am going to come back and see old Shannon's face again." And on his last day in Ireland, he promised, "I certainly will come back in the springtime."

It was a promise left unkept, for a spring that never came. But surely in our hearts there is the memory of a young leader who spoke stirring words about a brighter age for mankind, about a new generation that would hold high the torch of liberty and truly light the world.

This is the task before us: to plead the case of humanity, to move the conscience of the world, to march together—as in olden times—in the cause of freedom.

Thank you again for this great honor, and God bless you all.

Note: The President spoke at 12:10 p.m. in the Dáil (House of Representatives) at Leinster House in Dublin.

Toasts of President Reagan and President Patrick J. Hillery of Ireland at a Luncheon Honoring the Irish President in Dublin
June 4, 1984

President Reagan. President and Mrs. Hillery, Mr. Prime Minister and Mrs. FitzGerald, ladies and gentleman, Nancy and I are delighted to welcome you here this afternoon. We hope to return the kind hospitality that has been extended to us from the moment that we set foot on this Emerald Isle. By the way, I noticed that this house has a Blue Room, a Coral Room, and a Gold Room—and that reminds me of the White House back in Washington. As you may have seen when you visited Washington, Mr. Prime Minister, the White House is a good home for an Irishman, because every March 17th, I can honor St. Patrick by spending all day in the Green Room. [*Laughter*]

For Americans, the very mention of Ireland holds a magical sense of allure. It brings to mind images of green pastures, rugged highlands, and wide lakes—like Lough Conn, Corrib, Killarney—images of a lovely village square in Galway, or the graceful Georgian architecture here in Dublin. Perhaps what strikes Americans most when they visit Ireland is that yours is a land of many faces—a face of rich and unparalleled beauty, a face of a proud and glorious past, and a face of a young, and bright, and hopeful future.

More than eight centuries before Columbus discovered the New World, Irish monasteries were great centers of faith and learning. Scholars from all over Europe came here to study theology, philosophy, Greek, and Latin. Your ancestors created stunning illuminated manuscripts, including a book many consider the most beautiful ever made, the Book of Kells.

Today, you and your sons and daughters are making Ireland young again—young in your spirit of hope and faith in the future; young in your determination to create new opportunities and attract new technologies to help your economy along. And you're young in heart, ready to give and forgive, and ready to reach out in goodness and friendship and love.

Now, our own country of course remains a young nation simply because it is a young nation. Only a few centuries have passed since the first settlers landed on our eastern shores. And they and those who followed them came from virtually every nation on Earth. By 1900 nearly 4 million had come from Ireland alone. They cleared the land, built towns, established legislatures. They created a new and distinctly American way of life, and yet they continued to cherish memories of their homelands. Today Ireland and the United States share a living bond: the many Irish people who have cousins in America, and the 40 million Americans of Irish descent who always keep a special place for this island in our hearts.

Our two countries share a second bond— a bond of fundamental beliefs and enduring values. And as Ireland works to foster international understanding in this troubled world, you'll have the admiration, the respect, and the support of the United States. We pledge our unremitting effort for the cause of peace with freedom and human dignity.

As you may know, my own family left Ireland for the United States more than a hundred years ago. Some of the people in our country say I was with them. [*Laughter*] This homecoming to the land of my ancestors has moved me more deeply than I can say. And Nancy and I as we draw our visit to a close, we know that many Irish Americans who can't be here today will watch from home. They're with us in spirit and sharing a deep affection for Ireland and her people—an affection that's shared, as well, by your great poet, or I should say—well, he did share it when he wrote—William Butler Yeats, when he wrote: "Land of Heart's Desire, Where beauty has no ebb . . . But joy is wisdom, time an endless song."

Now, ladies and gentlemen, would you please join me in a toast to the President of Ireland, President Hillery.

President Hillery. Mr. President, somebody remarked to me that your progress in Irish was so rapid that I should begin my speech in Irish and that you would understand it.[1] [*Laughter*]

I would like to thank you for your kind words, for your invitation to Maeve and to me to be here, and to thank you and Mrs. Reagan for arranging this very happy occasion. I'm sure everybody here would wish to thank you both personally, if time allowed, because for us it is a really happy occasion.

We will, when you have left, wonder after your all too brief visit—we'll reflect on the personal and official reasons and aspects of your visit and what made it such a success. And I think I'd start off by saying that you brought to us a cheerful atmosphere, which Europe is badly in want of.

I suppose it's safe to say that if anybody in the free world has cause to look worried and overburdened, it's you, Mr. President. And still you come among us with courageous cheerfulness, showing us the way you're going and assuring and reassuring our people and the people of the world. And I thank you for doing that.

Your search for Irish roots has obviously been an important consideration for you and for us. It goes straight to the heart of the relationship between this country and the United States of America. We have our friends and relations in your country, and you have yours here.

You were here for the first time in 1948 as a private citizen, and you returned in 1972 as Governor of California. Now, 12 years later you have come again, this time as President of the United States. It is not necessary for me to say how much we welcome you.

We're not promoting the idea that every American who comes to Ireland 3 times will become President of the United States— [*laughter*]—but some among us are pointing to the wisdom of letting young people in America know that they cannot visit Ireland too early or too often. In fact, inherited wisdom has brought Ronald Reagan, Jr., here twice already. [*Laughter*]

Your visit, Mr. President, has consolidated the special friendship which exists between Ireland and the United States. Your presence among us testifies to that special friendship—a friendship which has endured and grown and become more, not less important with the passage of time, and moving away from the original links of history. It is based on blood and kinship and reinforced by the bedrock of shared beliefs and ideals.

Ireland shares with the United States of America a profound respect for the rights of the individual, for the abiding worth of democracy and for the dignity of the human person. The tyranny of flying time compels me to omit reference to very many aspects of our friendship and ties at official and unofficial levels. Some, but not all have been referred to and recalled over the past 3 days. Suffice it to say that the bonds which bind us are many and strong and enduring.

The best guarantee of ensuring the permanence of such a happy relationship is in the best tradition of old friends—is to visit more often. With that in mind, Mr. President, I hope that you and Mrs. Reagan will soon return to our shores. And you will, let me assure you, receive *céad míle fáilte* [100,000 welcomes].

I now ask those of you who are not Mr. and Mrs. Reagan—[*laughter*]—to join with me in a toast to the President of the United States of America.

---

[1] *President Hillery's opening remarks were in Gaelic. The remarks were not translated nor included in the White House press release.*

Note: The President spoke at 1:45 p.m. in the ballroom at Deerfield, the residence of U.S. Ambassador to Ireland Robert F. Kane.

Remarks on Departure From Dublin, Ireland
June 4, 1984

The President. President and Mrs. Hillery, Prime Minister FitzGerald, all our new friends, what a wonderful visit this has been for us and what a wonderful homecoming. Your country has given us a whole world of memories and images, from the gentle beauty of Galway to the busy hum of Dublin, from the peacefulness of Ballyporeen to the loveliness of sweet Shannon. You gave us "a hundred thousand welcomes." I won't try to say that in Gaelic, but I've mastered at least a bit of your native tongue. I now call Nancy, Mavoureen. [*Laughter*]

Prime Minister FitzGerald. Very good.

The President. Your warmth has touched our hearts. You've made this traveler feel like one of the family. Now it's time to say goodby, and as I leave, I feel such a tug, and I want to stay with you and laugh and talk some more. There's something in your country that makes the American Irish feel like exiles when they leave as if they're leaving a part of themselves behind.

This is my third visit to your country. I remember my first, 35 years ago. Oh, I was just a lad at the time. [*Laughter*] I walked the streets of Dublin, and I went by the Abbey Theatre. And I stayed at the Gresham, strolled down O'Connell Street, and saw the bullet marks on the old Post Office. And that night, I followed the sound of music to the entrance of a ballroom there at the hotel. And I peered in and was told that it was a university dance. And all the young men were dressed in white tie and tails, the young women were all in flowing white gowns, and they were doing a whirling waltz. And it was so graceful and so beautiful, it looked like it should have been a scene in some very expensive musical movie. And I wished the world would just slow down a little and make room—more room for such graciousness.

Well, that's how Nancy and I feel today. We wish the world would just slow down so we could have more time with all of you.

When I came back to Ireland a few years ago, I went out to the west and saw the ruins of the chapel where they say St. Patrick raised the first cross on Irish soil. And nearby, there was a well fed by underground springs from a hill far away. And they told me then, just as we were looking, our guide said it's a wishing well. Well, I should just say that Nancy and I threw in some coins and made a wish. The truth of the matter is we had been in six other countries before we got there. I had a dime and a penny in my pocket. She threw the dime and I threw the penny, and we went home with empty pockets. But we did make a wish. And a few days ago when we landed in Shannon again, our wish came true.

Nancy and I made another wish this morning. We want to come back when my work is done in Washington. By my calculations, that will be in January of 1989. [*Laughter*] Though I won't make that a promise, because I understand there is some disagreement on whether that should be the date or not. But when I come back, I'll be able to stay longer, and I hope able to see all of you again.

We will never be far apart, Ireland and America. We're tied by ties of blood, ties of history, and by a natural affinity and affection. America loves the Irish. And I hope the Irish will always love America. You're in our hearts forever. And as I leave this place, I think again of the words of a poem:

> Pearly are the skies in the country of my
> fathers,
> Purple are the mountains, home of my
> heart.
> Mother of my yearning, love of all my
> longings,
> Keep me in remembrance, long leagues
> apart.

We will keep you in our remembrance, long leagues apart, and will remember your kindness and your warmth forever.

Thank you, and God bless you.

Note: The President spoke at 3:13 p.m. at Dublin Airport. Following the ceremony, the President boarded Air Force One for the trip to London.

Text of Remarks to the French People on the 40th Anniversary of the Normandy Invasion, D-day
June 5, 1984

This year, thousands of Americans are returning to the Normandy shores to revisit the scene of that momentous landing 40 years ago. This week hundreds are, like myself, guests in your country as we join in remembering that day. On behalf of all Americans, I thank you for your gracious hospitality.

Franco-American friendship has a long and proud past. Indeed, one of the great heroes of American history is a Frenchman. Many towns, streets, and squares—even a college—in America bear his name. A beautiful park that I look out upon each day—directly across the street from the White House in Washington—is named in honor of him. He was the Marquis de Lafayette, and he served with George Washington as a general in the American Revolutionary Army. Yet despite the importance of Lafayette's military skill, he took a step as a legislator that had perhaps even greater significance for the two centuries of friendship and alliance between your country and mine.

On July 11th, 1789, as a Deputy in the French National Assembly, Lafayette introduced a bill calling for the passage of a Declaration of the Rights of Man. Formally adopted by the assembly 6 weeks later, the Declaration appeared as the Preamble to the French Constitution of 1791. This Declaration of the Rights of Man embodied the same fundamental beliefs about human liberty as those expressed in the American Declaration of Independence and Bill of Rights. Together, those French and American documents proclaim that all men are endowed with equal and sacred rights, that

among these, in the words of the American Declaration, are "Life, Liberty and the pursuit of Happiness." It is this shared commitment to human freedom that has formed the bedrock on which our fast friendship has been built. And it was in the name of this human freedom that so many brave men risked their lives on the beaches of Normandy 40 years ago.

Those courageous men, living and dead, gave us a priceless legacy of peace and prosperity in Europe—a legacy that has endured now for two generations. To preserve that legacy of peace, those of us who cherish liberty must continue to labor together.

Your country and mine belong to an alliance committed to democracy, individual liberty, and the rule of law. Of course, membership in the alliance imposes its burdens. To demonstrate the American commitment to this continent, thousands of American troops are stationed here in Europe, far from their homes and families. France, the United States, and all the alliance nations, must spend more on defense than any of us like to do in peacetime. But the burdens we bear in defending our freedom are far less than the horrors we would have to endure if we lost that freedom.

I believe that the best way we can honor those who gave so much 40 years ago, is by rededicating ourselves today to the cause for which they fought: freedom—freedom for ourselves, freedom for our children, and freedom for generations yet unborn.

Thank you, and God bless you.

Note: The remarks were broadcast on French television (FR-3).

Nomination of George Nesterczuk To Be Deputy Director of the United States Information Agency
June 5, 1984

The President today announced his intention to nominate George Nesterczuk to be Deputy Director of the United States Information Agency. He would succeed Leslie Lenkowsky.

Since 1981 he has been with the Office of Personnel Management and is presently serving as Associate Director for Workforce and Effectiveness Development. From 1977 to 1981, he was scientific consultant and senior scientist for EG & G Washington Analytical Services Center, Inc. At that time he also served as a consultant for the Ukrainian National Information Service in Washington, DC. He was vice president and chief scientist for Atlantic Science Corp. from 1972 to 1977.

He is a member of the American Astronomical Society, the American Geophysical Union, the American Association for the Advancement of Science, and the New York Academy of Science.

He graduated from Cornell University (B.A., 1967) and the University of Maryland (M.S., 1971). He is presently a candidate for a Ph.D. at the University of Maryland. He is married and resides in Greenbelt, MD. He was born May 21, 1945, in Asch, West Germany.

Remarks at a Meeting With Conservative Members of the British Parliament
June 6, 1984

[*Inaudible*]—meeting with Conservative M.P.s. I thank you, Mr. Peter Viggers, and I thank all of you for your kind words and for your strong support for our efforts to preserve peace with freedom in our troubled world.

Your remarks are particularly timely, today being the 40th anniversary of D-day, as the Ambassador said. In all the 20th century, D-day stands as the shining example of what free nations can do when united and inspired by mankind's highest ideals.

I understand that your group is composed of Members of Parliament who were elected for the first time last June. And please accept my congratulations on the honor you've been accorded in joining the Mother of Parliaments. As younger Members of the House of Commons, you've reached maturity in a divided world. You may have heard that I come from a slightly older generation. Ours lived as adults through the most severe test in history for freedom-loving people.

So, I'm very gratified to see that those vital lessons learned by my generation—lessons about the wisdom of collective defense and about the need for allied strength and unity to defend free institutions—have been learned as well by all of you.

Today in Europe, peace through strength is not a slogan; it is a fact of life. There is another important lesson we've learned: While we remain strong, we must always be ready for reconciliation, ready to resolve differences with our adversaries and resolve them peacefully at the negotiating table.

I want you and your fellow citizens in Britain to know the United States is seeking, and we will continue to seek, cooperation with the Soviet Union to make our world a safer place. Continued public support for collective security in all NATO countries is absolutely essential. I thank you for all that you're doing to foster that support. You can be proud that you're members of a fraternity within the free nations who have assumed the heavy burden of working for both peace and liberty.

Just recently in Washington, I met with 16 Foreign Ministers that make up the alliance. And I couldn't help but think, as we sat around the table, there has never in history been such an alliance, dedicated to the preservation of peace and freedom.

With wisdom and courage, peace and freedom will not be lost again. They can and will be preserved. We can live up to Winston Churchill's vision of freedom in 1941. He looked at the past and saw light which flickered; he looked at his time and saw light which flamed; but he looked at the future and saw "a light which shines over all the land and sea." He had another statement. He said that "When great forces are on the move in the world, we learn that we are spirits, not animals, and that there is something going on in time and space and beyond time and space which, whether we like or not, spells duty."

Well, I thank all of you very much, and I feel greatly honored. God bless all of you.

Note: The President spoke at 11:33 a.m. at Winfield House, where he met with a group of 25 Conservative Members of Parliament, who presented him with a letter demonstrating their support for the U.S. commitment to the NATO alliance.

Peter Viggers is the Conservative Party spokesman for defense affairs.

As printed above, this item follows the text of the White House press release.

Remarks at a Ceremony Commemorating the 40th Anniversary of the Normandy Invasion, D-day
June 6, 1984

We're here to mark that day in history when the Allied armies joined in battle to reclaim this continent to liberty. For 4 long years, much of Europe had been under a terrible shadow. Free nations had fallen, Jews cried out in the camps, millions cried out for liberation. Europe was enslaved, and the world prayed for its rescue. Here in Normandy the rescue began. Here the Allies stood and fought against tyranny in a giant undertaking unparalleled in human history.

We stand on a lonely, windswept point on the northern shore of France. The air is soft, but 40 years ago at this moment, the air was dense with smoke and the cries of men, and the air was filled with the crack of rifle fire and the roar of cannon. At dawn, on the morning of the 6th of June, 1944, 225 Rangers jumped off the British landing craft and ran to the bottom of these cliffs. Their mission was one of the most difficult and daring of the invasion: to climb these sheer and desolate cliffs and take out the enemy guns. The Allies had been told that some of the mightiest of these guns were here and they would be trained on the beaches to stop the Allied advance.

The Rangers looked up and saw the enemy soldiers—the edge of the cliffs shooting down at them with machineguns and throwing grenades. And the American Rangers began to climb. They shot rope ladders over the face of these cliffs and began to pull themselves up. When one Ranger fell, another would take his place. When one rope was cut, a Ranger would grab another and begin his climb again. They climbed, shot back, and held their footing. Soon, one by one, the Rangers pulled themselves over the top, and in seizing the firm land at the top of these cliffs, they began to seize back the continent of Europe. Two hundred and twenty-five came here. After 2 days of fighting, only 90 could still bear arms.

Behind me is a memorial that symbolizes the Ranger daggers that were thrust into the top of these cliffs. And before me are the men who put them there.

These are the boys of Pointe du Hoc. These are the men who took the cliffs. These are the champions who helped free a continent. These are the heroes who helped end a war.

Gentlemen, I look at you and I think of

817

the words of Stephen Spender's poem. You are men who in your "lives fought for life . . . and left the vivid air signed with your honor."

I think I know what you may be thinking right now—thinking "we were just part of a bigger effort; everyone was brave that day." Well, everyone was. Do you remember the story of Bill Millin of the 51st Highlanders? Forty years ago today, British troops were pinned down near a bridge, waiting desperately for help. Suddenly, they heard the sound of bagpipes, and some thought they were dreaming. Well, they weren't. They looked up and saw Bill Millin with his bagpipes, leading the reinforcements and ignoring the smack of the bullets into the ground around him.

Lord Lovat was with him—Lord Lovat of Scotland, who calmly announced when he got to the bridge, "Sorry I'm a few minutes late," as if he'd been delayed by a traffic jam, when in truth he'd just come from the bloody fighting on Sword Beach, which he and his men had just taken.

There was the impossible valor of the Poles who threw themselves between the enemy and the rest of Europe as the invasion took hold, and the unsurpassed courage of the Canadians who had already seen the horrors of war on this coast. They knew what awaited them there, but they would not be deterred. And once they hit Juno Beach, they never looked back.

All of these men were part of a rollcall of honor with names that spoke of a pride as bright as the colors they bore: the Royal Winnipeg Rifles, Poland's 24th Lancers, the Royal Scots Fusiliers, the Screaming Eagles, the Yeomen of England's armored divisions, the forces of Free France, the Coast Guard's "Matchbox Fleet" and you, the American Rangers.

Forty summers have passed since the battle that you fought here. You were young the day you took these cliffs; some of you were hardly more than boys, with the deepest joys of life before you. Yet, you risked everything here. Why? Why did you do it? What impelled you to put aside the instinct for self-preservation and risk your lives to take these cliffs? What inspired all the men of the armies that met here? We look at you, and somehow we know the

answer. It was faith and belief; it was loyalty and love.

The men of Normandy had faith that what they were doing was right, faith that they fought for all humanity, faith that a just God would grant them mercy on this beachhead or on the next. It was the deep knowledge—and pray God we have not lost it—that there is a profound, moral difference between the use of force for liberation and the use of force for conquest. You were here to liberate, not to conquer, and so you and those others did not doubt your cause. And you were right not to doubt.

You all knew that some things are worth dying for. One's country is worth dying for, and democracy is worth dying for, because it's the most deeply honorable form of government ever devised by man. All of you loved liberty. All of you were willing to fight tyranny, and you knew the people of your countries were behind you.

The Americans who fought here that morning knew word of the invasion was spreading through the darkness back home. They fought—or felt in their hearts, though they couldn't know in fact, that in Georgia they were filling the churches at 4 a.m., in Kansas they were kneeling on their porches and praying, and in Philadelphia they were ringing the Liberty Bell.

Something else helped the men of D-day: their rockhard belief that Providence would have a great hand in the events that would unfold here; that God was an ally in this great cause. And so, the night before the invasion, when Colonel Wolverton asked his parachute troops to kneel with him in prayer he told them: Do not bow your heads, but look up so you can see God and ask His blessing in what we're about to do. Also that night, General Matthew Ridgway on his cot, listening in the darkness for the promise God made to Joshua: "I will not fail thee nor forsake thee."

These are the things that impelled them; these are the things that shaped the unity of the Allies.

When the war was over, there were lives to be rebuilt and governments to be returned to the people. There were nations to be reborn. Above all, there was a new peace to be assured. These were huge and daunting tasks. But the Allies summoned strength from the faith, belief, loyalty, and love of those who fell here. They rebuilt a new Europe together.

There was first a great reconciliation among those who had been enemies, all of whom had suffered so greatly. The United States did its part, creating the Marshall plan to help rebuild our allies and our former enemies. The Marshall plan led to the Atlantic alliance—a great alliance that serves to this day as our shield for freedom, for prosperity, and for peace.

In spite of our great efforts and successes, not all that followed the end of the war was happy or planned. Some liberated countries were lost. The great sadness of this loss echoes down to our own time in the streets of Warsaw, Prague, and East Berlin. Soviet troops that came to the center of this continent did not leave when peace came. They're still there, uninvited, unwanted, unyielding, almost 40 years after the war. Because of this, allied forces still stand on this continent. Today, as 40 years ago, our armies are here for only one purpose—to protect and defend democracy. The only territories we hold are memorials like this one and graveyards where our heroes rest.

We in America have learned bitter lessons from two World Wars: It is better to be here ready to protect the peace, than to take blind shelter across the sea, rushing to respond only after freedom is lost. We've learned that isolationism never was and never will be an acceptable response to tyrannical governments with an expansionist intent.

But we try always to be prepared for peace; prepared to deter aggression; prepared to negotiate the reduction of arms; and, yes, prepared to reach out again in the spirit of reconciliation. In truth, there is no reconciliation we would welcome more than a reconciliation with the Soviet Union, so, together, we can lessen the risks of war, now and forever.

It's fitting to remember here the great losses also suffered by the Russian people during World War II: 20 million perished, a terrible price that testifies to all the world the necessity of ending war. I tell you from my heart that we in the United States do not want war. We want to wipe from the face of the Earth the terrible weapons that man now has in his hands. And I tell you, we are ready to seize that beachhead. We look for some sign from the Soviet Union that they are willing to move forward, that they share our desire and love for peace, and that they will give up the ways of conquest. There must be a changing there that will allow us to turn our hope into action.

We will pray forever that some day that changing will come. But for now, particularly today, it is good and fitting to renew our commitment to each other, to our freedom, and to the alliance that protects it.

We are bound today by what bound us 40 years ago, the same loyalties, traditions, and beliefs. We're bound by reality. The strength of America's allies is vital to the United States, and the American security guarantee is essential to the continued freedom of Europe's democracies. We were with you then; we are with you now. Your hopes are our hopes, and your destiny is our destiny.

Here, in this place where the West held together, let us make a vow to our dead. Let us show them by our actions that we understand what they died for. Let our actions say to them the words for which Matthew Ridgway listened: "I will not fail thee nor forsake thee."

Strengthened by their courage, heartened by their value [valor], and borne by their memory, let us continue to stand for the ideals for which they lived and died.

Thank you very much, and God bless you all.

Note: The President spoke at 1:20 p.m. at the site of the U.S. Ranger Monument at Pointe du Hoc, France, where veterans of the Normandy invasion had assembled for the ceremony.

Following his remarks, the President unveiled memorial plaques to the 2d and 5th Ranger Battalions. Then, escorted by Phil Rivers, superintendent of the Normandy American Cemetery, the President and Mrs. Reagan proceeded to the interior of the observation bunker. On leaving the bunker, the President and Mrs. Reagan greeted each of the veterans.

Other Allied countries represented at the

ceremony by their heads of state and government were: Queen Elizabeth II of the United Kingdom, Queen Beatrix of The Netherlands, King Olav V of Norway, King Baudouin I of Belgium, Grand Duke Jean of Luxembourg, and Prime Minister Pierre Elliott Trudeau of Canada.

Interview With Walter Cronkite of CBS News in Normandy, France
June 6, 1984

Mr. Cronkite. Mr. President, it's quite a day out here. We're observing the fact that American soldiers can do the impossible as represented here at Pointe du Hoc when they're commanded to, but, on the other hand, at a terrible cost, isn't it?

The President. Yes. As I said in my remarks, 225 of them came up those cliffs, and 2 days later, there were only 90 of them able to take part in combat.

Mr. Cronkite. Mr. President, you know, this war—World War II, that is—was called a popular war, as opposed to the actions we've had recently—Vietnam, Lebanon, Grenada, I suppose. What are the conditions it takes to have a popular war, for heaven sakes?

The President. Well, I doubt that any war can be—if we really describe it, can be popular. No one wants it. But here was a case in which the issues of right and wrong were so clearly defined and delineated before we even got into the war. And then we didn't choose to pull the trigger; the trigger was pulled at us. And we were in a war as of a Sunday morning, December 7th, in the Pacific.

And I've always remembered my first assignment as a reserve officer called to active duty was at the port of embarkation in San Francisco. And it was a job as liaison officer loading the convoys for out in the Pacific. And standing at the foot of the gangplank one day as they—coming along full pack and gear and everything, ready to go up the gangplank—and one of them— there was a pause, a hitch in the line—one standing there, just a youngster. And I said, "How do you feel?"

"Well," he said, "I don't want to go." He said, "None of us want to go." But he said, "We all know, the shortest way home is through Tokyo."

Mr. Cronkite. You know, now we're in the nuclear age, and as terrible as this war was, is it possible in a nuclear age that we would have another war that could be restricted to anything as horrible as this even?

The President. Walter, I have said, and will continue to say, a nuclear war cannot be won. It must never be fought. And this is why the goal must be to rid the world once and for all of those weapons.

Mr. Cronkite. You don't think we could fight a strategic war like this without invoking nuclear weapons?

The President. Well, this we don't know. But if it was ever to resort to those weapons—we did, in World War II, we saw the power of deterrence. All the nations had chemical warfare, had gas. But it was never used, because everyone had it. Maybe the same thing would apply in—with regard to nuclear war. But why take that chance? If everybody is having the weapons as a deterrent to the other, then let's do away with the deterrents.

Mr. Cronkite. Do you—you had some remarks prepared. I don't think you got a chance to deliver them in a foreshortened speech in Ireland in which you said that you were optimistic that perhaps we could get nuclear limitation talks going again with the Soviets. What gives you cause for that optimism?

The President. I just think common sense. I think right now the Soviet Union is—well, there was an article in The Economist that sort of described it. They're hibernating. We're so used to thinking that they're always in the midst of some kind of devious plan. I just don't think they have any answers right now, and they're sort of hunkered down trying to decide.

Mr. Cronkite. Do we have a plan?

The President. What?

Mr. Cronkite. Do we have a plan?

The President. Yes, and the plan is to—we have maintained contact. We're negotiating other things of mutual interest to the two countries, making some progress on them. But on those talks—my idea of the goal is if we can once start down the road of achieving reductions in the armaments, I just have to believe that we'll see the common sense in continuing down the road and eliminating them.

Mr. Cronkite. Have you had a chance with your busy schedule on this tour to catch up with the fact that the Soviets on this anniversary, the 40th anniversary of D-day, are making much of the fact that they've cited before—a fact, I mean, by their token, of the fiction that we deliberately delayed this landing by 2 years in order that the Germans would eat up the Soviets by attrition, and that we came ashore virtually unopposed because of connivance with the Germans. Have you heard that they're repeating that all over Europe?

The President. Oh, I know that. As a matter of fact, recently, our ceremony for the funeral of the unknown soldier from Vietnam, they referred to that as "a militaristic orgy." I sometimes wonder——

Mr. Cronkite. No reference to Afghanistan, huh?

The President. I wonder sometimes, when they talk about heated rhetoric coming from me, doesn't anyone listen to what they're saying? But how anyone could say that this was an almost unopposed landing, we know better. And the evidence is right here; and the survivors, many of them, are right here.

They had not won the war, and we had

not delayed for any reason of that kind. I have some reason for saying that, because my own war service was spent in a unit that was directly under Air Corps Intelligence, and we had access to all the intelligence information about things, even including this. And there was an awful lot of war to be fought.

Mr. Cronkite. Yes. As a matter of fact, you know, 40,000 airmen gave their lives over Europe. I covered the Air Force as a correspondent, and I think of that. When you talk about 10,000 dying here on D-day, 40,000 died in order to get the Luftwaffe out of the skies before D-day——

The President. Yes.

Mr. Cronkite. ——or this wouldn't have been possible.

Let me ask you one more question before you have to go. Speaking of wars and political campaigns, what's your plan for D-day against Mondale, Hart, or whoever it is?

The President. Just tell them what we've done and what we're going to do and pretend they're not there. [*Laughter*]

Mr. Cronkite. Well, you may have to climb a hundred-foot cliff, but I guess you've got your weapons—[*laughter*]—at your ready.

The President. Yes.

Mr. Cronkite. Thank you very much, Mr. President.

The President. Well, it's good to see you again.

Mr. Cronkite. Thank you.

Note: The interview began at 2:50 p.m. at Pointe du Hoc. At the conclusion of the interview, the President and Mrs. Reagan departed Pointe du Hoc and traveled to Omaha Beach.

Remarks at a United States-France Ceremony Commemorating the 40th Anniversary of the Normandy Invasion, D-day

June 6, 1984

Mr. President, distinguished guests, we stand today at a place of battle, one that 40

years ago saw and felt the worst of war. Men bled and died here for a few feet of—

or inches of sand, as bullets and shellfire cut through their ranks. About them, General Omar Bradley later said, "Every man who set foot on Omaha Beach that day was a hero."

No speech can adequately portray their suffering, their sacrifice, their heroism. President Lincoln once reminded us that through their deeds, the dead of battle have spoken more eloquently for themselves than any of the living ever could. But we can only honor them by rededicating ourselves to the cause for which they gave a last full measure of devotion.

Today we do rededicate ourselves to that cause. And at this place of honor, we're humbled by the realization of how much so many gave to the cause of freedom and to their fellow man.

Some who survived the battle of June 6, 1944, are here today. Others who hoped to return never did.

"Someday, Lis, I'll go back," said Private First Class Peter Robert Zanatta, of the 37th Engineer Combat Battalion, and first assault wave to hit Omaha Beach. "I'll go back, and I'll see it all again. I'll see the beach, the barricades, and the graves."

Those words of Private Zanatta come to us from his daughter, Lisa Zanatta Henn, in a heart-rending story about the event her father spoke of so often. "In his words, the Normandy invasion would change his life forever," she said. She tells some of his stories of World War II but says of her father, "the story to end all stories was D-day."

"He made me feel the fear of being on that boat waiting to land. I can smell the ocean and feel the seasickness. I can see the looks on his fellow soldiers' faces—the fear, the anguish, the uncertainty of what lay ahead. And when they landed, I can feel the strength and courage of the men who took those first steps through the tide to what must have surely looked like instant death."

Private Zanatta's daughter wrote to me: "I don't know how or why I can feel this emptiness, this fear, or this determination, but I do. Maybe it's the bond I had with my father. All I know is that it brings tears to my eyes to think about my father as a 20-year-old boy having to face that beach."

The anniversary of D-day was always spe-cial for her family. And like all the families of those who went to war, she describes how she came to realize her own father's survival was a miracle: "So many men died. I know that my father watched many of his friends be killed. I know that he must have died inside a little each time. But his expla-nation to me was, 'You did what you had to do, and you kept on going.'"

When men like Private Zanatta and all our allied forces stormed the beaches of Normandy 40 years ago they came not as conquerors, but as liberators. When these troops swept across the French countryside and into the forests of Belgium and Luxem-bourg they came not to take, but to return what had been wrongly seized. When our forces marched into Germany they came not to prey on a brave and defeated people, but to nurture the seeds of democracy among those who yearned to be free again.

We salute them today. But, Mr. Presi-dent, we also salute those who, like yourself, were already engaging the enemy inside your beloved country—the French Resist-ance. Your valiant struggle for France did so much to cripple the enemy and spur the advance of the armies of liberation. The French Forces of the Interior will forever personify courage and national spirit. They will be a timeless inspiration to all who are free and to all who would be free.

Today, in their memory, and for all who fought here, we celebrate the triumph of democracy. We reaffirm the unity of demo-cratic peoples who fought a war and then joined with the vanquished in a firm re-solve to keep the peace.

From a terrible war we learned that unity made us invincible; now, in peace, that same unity makes us secure. We sought to bring all freedom-loving nations together in a community dedicated to the defense and preservation of our sacred values. Our alliance, forged in the crucible of war, tem-pered and shaped by the realities of the postwar world, has succeeded. In Europe, the threat has been contained, the peace has been kept.

Today the living here assembled—offi-cials, veterans, citizens—are a tribute to what was achieved here 40 years ago. This land is secure. We are free. These things are worth fighting and dying for.

Lisa Zanatta Henn began her story by quoting her father, who promised that he would return to Normandy. She ended with a promise to her father, who died 8 years ago of cancer: "I'm going there, Dad, and I'll see the beaches and the barricades and the monuments. I'll see the graves, and I'll put flowers there just like you wanted to do. I'll feel all the things you made me feel through your stories and your eyes. I'll never forget what you went through, Dad, nor will I let anyone else forget. And, Dad, I'll always be proud."

Through the words of his loving daughter, who is here with us today, a D-day veteran has shown us the meaning of this day far better than any President can. It is enough for us to say about Private Zanatta and all the men of honor and courage who fought beside him four decades ago: We will always remember. We will always be proud. We will always be prepared, so we may always be free.

Thank you.

Note: The President spoke at 4:33 p.m. at the Omaha Beach Memorial at Omaha Beach, France. In his opening remarks, he referred to President François Mitterrand of France.

Following the ceremony, President Reagan traveled to Utah Beach.

Remarks by Telephone to the Crew of the U.S.S. *Eisenhower* Following D-day Ceremonies in Normandy, France
June 6, 1984

Greetings to all of you, the officers and men of the U.S.S. *Eisenhower*. Believe me, all of us up here are inspired by the sight of your magnificent ship and the battle group which accompanied you to the coast of Normandy.

We're returning from a commemoration of the 40th anniversary of the D-day landing—the heroic operation that was planned and commanded by General Dwight D. Eisenhower. The memory of "Ike," our great allied leader, still inspires heroic efforts on both sides of the Atlantic.

Today, as 40 years ago, our Navy and all of our Armed Forces are advancing the cause of peace and freedom. The dedication of you, our sailors and marines, particularly during your recent deployment in the Eastern Mediterranean, is in the highest tradition of the service.

The American people and our allies in Europe and beyond are all more secure because men of your caliber are on station when and where needed. Admiral Flatley, Captain Clexton, officers and men of the "Ike"—I salute you for your devoted service to the cause of freedom.

You know, I'm up here hoping that you've been able to hear me. I'll just say, God bless you all, and if it wouldn't be too demoralizing, wave, and I'll know whether you've heard this.

Thank you. Thank you all. Good sailing, and God bless you.

Note: The President spoke at 7:10 p.m. on board Marine One during the flight from Utah Beach, France, to London.

As printed above, this item follows the text of the White House press release.

Nomination of Erich Bloch To Be Director of the National Science Foundation
June 6, 1984

The President today announced his intention to nominate Erich Bloch to be Director of the National Science Foundation for a term of 6 years. He would succeed Edward A. Knapp.

Since 1981 Mr. Bloch has been serving as vice president for technical personnel development at IBM in White Plains, NY. He has been with IBM since 1953, when he began there as a technical engineer. He has held several managerial positions at IBM, including assistant group executive-technology, director of subsystems and technology, and vice president for operations.

He is a member of the National Academy of Engineering and a fellow of the Institute of Electrical and Electronic Engineers. He is on the board of directors of the Semiconductor Industry Association and is chairman of the Semiconductor Research Cooperative.

Mr. Bloch received his education in electrical engineering at the Federal Polytechnic Institute of Zurich, Switzerland, and his BSEE degree from the University of Buffalo in 1952. He is married, has one child, and resides in South Salem, NY. He was born January 9, 1925, in Salzburg, Germany, and became a United States citizen in 1953.

Message to the Congress Transmitting an Amendment to the United States-United Kingdom Agreement on Atomic Energy
June 6, 1984

To the Congress of the United States:

I am pleased to transmit to the Congress, pursuant to Section 123d. of the Atomic Energy Act of 1954, as amended, the text of an amendment to the Agreement Between the Government of the United States of America and the Government of the United Kingdom of Great Britain and Northern Ireland for Cooperation on the Uses of Atomic Energy for Mutual Defense Purposes of July 3, 1958, as amended, and my written approval, authorization, and determination concerning the agreement. The joint unclassifed letter submitted to me by the Secretaries of Energy and Defense which provides a summary position on the Amendment is also enclosed. A classified letter and attachments are being transmitted directly to the appropriate Congressional committees.

The Amendment extends for ten years (until December 31, 1994) provisions which permit the transfer of nonnuclear parts, source, by-product, special nuclear materials, and other material and technology for nuclear weapons and military reactors.

In my judgment, the proposed Amendment meets all statutory requirements. The United Kingdom intends to continue to maintain viable nuclear forces. In light of our previous close cooperation and the fact that the United Kingdom has committed its nuclear forces to NATO, I have concluded that it is in our interest to continue to assist them in maintaining a credible nuclear force.

I have approved the Amendment, authorized its execution, and urge that the Congress give it favorable consideration.

RONALD REAGAN

The White House,
June 6, 1984.

Proclamation 5207—Application of Certain Laws of the United States to Citizens of the Northern Mariana Islands
June 7, 1984

By the President of the United States of America

A Proclamation

The Northern Mariana Islands, as part of the Trust Territory of the Pacific Islands, are administered by the United States under a Trusteeship Agreement between the United States and the Security Council of the United Nations (61 Stat. 3301). The United States has undertaken to promote the political development of the Trust Territory toward self-government or independence and to protect the rights and fundamental freedoms of its peoples.

The United States and the Northern Mariana Islands have entered into a Covenant to Establish a Commonwealth of the Northern Mariana Islands in Political Union with the United States of America (Public Law 94–241; 90 Stat. 263; 48 U.S.C. 1681, note) pursuant to which many provisions of the laws of the United States became applicable to the Northern Mariana Islands as of January 9, 1978 (Proclamation No. 4534, Section 2).

Sections 19 and 20 of Public Law 98–213 (97 Stat. 1464) authorize the President, subject to certain limitations, to provide by proclamation that requirements "of United States citizenship or nationality provided for in any of the statutes listed on pages 63–74 of the Interim Report of the Northern Mariana Islands Commission on Federal Laws to the Congress of the United States, dated January 1982 and submitted pursuant to section 504 of the Covenant, shall not be applicable to the citizens of the Northern Mariana Islands."

Now, Therefore, I, Ronald Reagan, President of the United States of America, by the authority vested in me by sections 19 and 20 of Public Law 98–213, do hereby proclaim as follows:

1. *Statutes relating to the uniformed services.* No requirement of United States citizenship in any of the Federal laws listed below shall be applicable to citizens of the Northern Mariana Islands who declare in writing that they do not intend to exercise their option under section 302 of the Covenant to become a national but not a citizen of the United States.

(a) Sections 311, 510, 591, 2004, 2031, 2107, 4348, 6019, 6911, 6958, 6959, 8257, and 9348 of title 10, United States Code;

(b) Sections 195, 371, 706, and 823 of title 14, United States Code; and

(c) Section 313 of title 32, United States Code.

2. *Statutes relating to Federal employment.* No requirement of United States citizenship or nationality in any of the Federal laws listed below shall be applicable to citizens of the Northern Mariana Islands.

(a) Sections 5342, 5343, 5561, 5595, 5912, 5922, 6301, 7103, 7532, 8171, 8501, 8701, and 8901 of title 5, United States Code;

(b) Section 22 of title 13, United States Code;

(c) Section 2 of Public Law 86–91, 73 Stat. 213 (20 U.S.C. 901);

(d) Section 636 of Public Law 87–195, 75 Stat. 457, as amended (22 U.S.C. 2396);

(e) Sections 5 and 6 of Public Law 87–293, 75 Stat. 613, 615, as amended (22 U.S.C. 2504 and 2505);

(f) Section 15 of Public Law 90–202, as added by section 28(b)(2) of Public Law 93–259, 88 Stat. 74, and as amended (29 U.S.C. 633a);

(g) Sections 235 and 4105 of title 38, United States Code;

(h) Section 203 of the Act of July 1, 1944, c.373, 58 Stat. 683, as amended (42 U.S.C. 204); and

(i) Civil Service Rules VII and VIII (5 C.F.R. parts 7 and 8).

3. *Statutes relating to protection and services in foreign countries.* No requirement of United States citizenship or nationality in any of the Federal laws listed below shall be applicable to citizens of the Northern Mariana Islands.

(a) Section 1486 of title 10, United States Code;

(b) Section 3(g) of the Act of August 1, 1956, c.841, 70 Stat. 890 (22 U.S.C. 2670(g));

(c) Sections 1734 and 1737 of the Revised Statutes of 1878, as amended (22 U.S.C. 4217 and 4218);

(d) Sections 1305 and 3342 of title 31, United States Code;

(e) Section 4295 of the Revised Statutes of 1878 (33 U.S.C. 383); and

(f) Section 1113 of the Act of August 14, 1935, c.531, as added by section 302 of Public Law 87–64, 75 Stat. 142, and as amended (42 U.S.C. 1313).

4. *Statutes relating to commerce.* No requirement of United States citizenship or nationality in any of the Federal laws listed below shall be applicable to citizens of the Northern Mariana Islands.

(a) Sections 302, 310D, 311, and 321 of Public Law 87–128, 75 Stat. 307, as added and amended (7 U.S.C. 1922, 1934, 1941, and 1961);

(b) Section 5146 of the Revised Statutes of 1878, as amended (12 U.S.C. 72);

(c) Subsection (a) of section 25 of the Act of December 23, 1913, c.6, as added by the Act of December 24, 1919, c.18, 41 Stat. 378, and as amended (12 U.S.C. 619);

(d) Subsection (a) of section 7 of the Act of July 22, 1932, c.522, 47 Stat. 730, as amended (12 U.S.C. 1427(a));

(e) Subsection (b) of section 5.1 of Public Law 92–181, 85 Stat. 614 (12 U.S.C. 2222);

(f) Subsection (i) of section 44 of the Act of July 5, 1946, c.540, 60 Stat. 443, as amended (15 U.S.C. 1126(i));

(g) Subsection (b)(7) of section 4 of the Act of August 8, 1956, c.1036, 70 Stat. 1121, as amended (16 U.S.C. 742c(b)(7));

(h) Subsection (e) of section 4 of the Act of June 10, 1920, c.285, 41 Stat. 1065, as amended (16 U.S.C. 797(e));

(i) Section 104(b) of title 17, United States Code;

(j) Subsection (a) of section 526 of the Act of June 17, 1930, c.497, 46 Stat. 741, as amended (19 U.S.C. 1526(a));

(k) Subsection (a)(5) of section 2 of the Act of June 20, 1936, c.638, 49 Stat. 1559, as amended (20 U.S.C. 107a(a)(5));

(l) Section 238 of Public Law 87–195, as added by section 105 of Public Law 91–175, 83 Stat. 816, and as amended (22 U.S.C. 2198);

(m) Subsection (b)(7) of section 622 of Public Law 96–294, 94 Stat. 766 (30 U.S.C. 1522(b)(7));

(n) Subsection (5) of section 3 of Public Law 93–627, 88 Stat. 2127 (33 U.S.C. 1502(5));

(o) Subsection (f)(3) of section 514 of the Act of July 15, 1949, c.338, as added by subsection (a) of section 804 of Public Law 87–70, 75 Stat. 186, and as amended (42 U.S.C. 1484(f)(3));

(p) Subsection (d) of section 103 and subsection (d) of section 104 of the Act of August 1, 1946, c.724, as added by section 1 of the Act of August 30, 1954, c.1073, 68 Stat. 936, and as amended (42 U.S.C. 2133(d) and 2134(d));

(q) Subsection (b)(2)(A) of section 7 of Public Law 93–577, 88 Stat. 1884 (42 U.S.C. 5906(b)(2)(A));

(r) Subsection (p)(1) of section 19 of Public Law 93–577, as added by subsection (b) of section 207 of Public Law 95–238, 92 Stat. 61 (42 U.S.C. 5919(p)(1));

(s) Subsection (b) of section 179 of Public Law 96–294, 94 Stat. 679 (42 U.S.C. 8779(b)(4));

(t) Subsection (a)(3) of section 2, subsection (18) of section 3, section 101, and subsection (e)(2)(C) of section 108 of Public Law 96–320, 94 Stat. 974, 976, 987 (42 U.S.C. 9101(a)(3); 9102(18); 9111; and 9118(e)(2)(C));

(u) Section 4219 of the Revised Statutes of 1878, as amended (46 U.S.C. App. 121);

(v) Sections 7102 and 8103 of title 46, United States Code;

(w) Section 4377 of the Revised Statutes of 1878, as amended (46 U.S.C. App. 325);

(x) Section 36 of the Act of September 7, 1916, c.451, 39 Stat. 738 (46 U.S.C. App. 834);

(y) Sections 501, 509, 601, 809(a), of the Act of June 29, 1936, c.858, 49 Stat. 1995, 2000, 2001, 2015, as amended (46 U.S.C. App. 1151, 1159, 1171, 1213);

(z) Sections 1103 and 1104 of the Act of June 23, 1938, c.600, 52 Stat. 969, 970, as added and amended (46 U.S.C. App. 1273 and 1274);

(aa) Subsection (a) of section 203 of Public Law 96–320, 94 Stat. 992 (46 U.S.C. App. 1279c(a));

(bb) Sections 1201 and 1203 of the Act of June 29, 1936, c.858, as added by the Act of September 7, 1950, c.906, 64 Stat. 773, and as amended (46 U.S.C. App. 1281 and 1283);

(cc) Sections 1301, 1303, 1304, and 1306 of Public Law 96–453, 94 Stat. 1997, 1998, 2003, 2006 (46 U.S.C. App. 1295, 1295b, 1295c, and 1295e);

(dd) Subsection (16) of section 101, section 104, subsection (d)(4) of section 401, and section 418 of Public Law 85–726, 72 Stat. 738, 740, 754, as added and amended (49 U.S.C. 1301(16), 1304, and 1371(d)(4));

(ee) Section 418 of Public Law 85–726, as added by subsection (a) of section 17 of Public Law 95–163, 91 Stat. 1284, and as amended (49 U.S.C. 1388); and

(ff) Sections 501, 602, and 1303 of Public Law 85–726, 72 Stat. 771, 776, 801, as amended (49 U.S.C. 1401, 1422, and 1533).

5. *Statutes relating to political and civil rights.* No requirement of United States citizenship or nationality in any of the Federal laws listed below shall be applicable to citizens of the Northern Mariana Islands, provided, however, that nothing herein shall be construed to confer upon citizens of the Northern Mariana Islands the right to vote in Federal, State, or local elections outside the Northern Mariana Islands, or to serve on juries outside of the Northern Mariana Islands.

(a) Section 319 of Public Law 92–225, as added by subsection (2) of section 112 of Public Law 94–283, 90 Stat. 486, and as redesignated by subsection (5) of section 105 of Public Law 96–187, 93 Stat. 1354 (2 U.S.C. 441e);

(b) Section 552a(a)(2) of title 5, United States Code;

(c) Sections 241 and 243, subsection (b)(5) of section 245, and subsection (a) of section 4001 of title 18, United States Code;

(d) Sections 4080 and 4081 of the Revised Statutes of 1878, as amended (22 U.S.C. 257 and 258);

(e) Subsection (b)(2) of section 1 of the Act of June 8, 1938, c.327, 52 Stat. 631, as amended (22 U.S.C. 611(b)(2));

(f) Sections 1332, 1343, 1344, 1391, 1443, 1861, 1862, and 1863 of title 28, United States Code;

(g) Section 505 of the Act of June 30,

1948, c.758, as added by section 2 of Public Law 92–500, 86 Stat. 888 (33 U.S.C. 1365);

(h) Subsection (a)(1) of section 2004 of the Revised Statutes of 1878, as amended (42 U.S.C. 1971(a)(1));

(i) Section 2, subsection (b) of section 3, section 4, and subsection (a) of section 10 of Public Law 89–110, as amended, 79 Stat. 437, 438, 442 (42 U.S.C. 1973, 1973a(b), 1973b, and 1973h(a));

(j) Subsection (a) of section 201 of Public Law 89–110, as added by section 6 of Public Law 91–285, 84 Stat. 315, and as amended (42 U.S.C. 1973aa(a));

(k) Section 203 of Public Law 89–110, as added by section 301 of Public Law 94–73, 89 Stat. 402 (42 U.S.C. 1973aa–1a);

(l) Section 5 of Public Law 98–183, 97 Stat. 1304 (42 U.S.C. 1975c);

(m) Section 1979 of the Revised Statutes of 1878, as amended (42 U.S.C. 1983);

(n) Section 1980 of the Revised Statutes of 1878 (42 U.S.C. 1985);

(o) Section 702 of Public Law 88–352, 78 Stat. 255, as amended (42 U.S.C. 2000e–1);

(p) Section 717 of Public Law 88–352, as added and amended by section 11 of Public Law 92–261, 86 Stat. 111 (42 U.S.C. 2000e–16);

(q) Section 2 of the Act of March 2, 1917, c.145, 39 Stat. 951, as amended (48 U.S.C. 737);

(r) Subsection (i) of section 101 of Public Law 95–511, 92 Stat. 1783 (50 U.S.C. 1801);

(s) Subsection (b)(3) of section 10 of the Act of June 24, 1948, c.625, 62 Stat. 619, as amended (50 U.S.C. App. 460(b)(3));

(t) Section 104 of the Act of October 17, 1940, c.888, as added by section 4 of the Act of October 6, 1942, c.581, 56 Stat. 770 (50 U.S.C. App. 514); and

(u) Section 512 of the Act of October 17, 1940, c.888, 54 Stat. 1190, as amended (50 U.S.C. App. 572).

6. *Statutes relating to Federal programs and benefits.* No requirement of United States citizenship or nationality in any of the Federal laws listed below shall be applicable to citizens of the Northern Mariana Islands.

(a) Subsection (a) of section 2545 of title 10, United States Code;

(b) Subsection (m)(2) of section 2[3] of the

Act of September 21, 1950, c.967, as added by section 6(c)(4) of Public Law 95–369, 92 Stat. 614 (12 U.S.C. 1813(m)(2));

(c) Subsection (b) of section 500 of title 14, United States Code;

(d) Paragraphs (4) and (5) of subsection (a) of section 4 of Public Law 88–578, as added by section 2 of Public Law 92–347, 86 Stat. 459, as amended, and by subsection (2) of section 9 of Public Law 96–344, 94 Stat. 1135 (16 U.S.C. 460*l*–6a(a)(4) and (5));

(e) Section 29 of the Act of August 1, 1956, c.841, as added by section 2201 of Public Law 96–465, 94 Stat. 2154 (22 U.S.C. 2701);

(f) Subsection (g) of section 9 of the Act of March 4, 1927, c.509, 44 Stat. 1430, as amended (33 U.S.C. 909(g));

(g) Subsection (b) of section 624 of title 38, United States Code;

(h) Subsection (b)(12) of section 788, of the Act of July 1, 1944, c.373, as added by subsection (a) of section 801 of Public Law 94–484, 90 Stat. 2318, as amended (42 (U.S.C. 295g–8(b)(12));

(i) Subsection (b)(3) of section 2 and section 4 of the Act of August 14, 1935, c.531, 49 Stat. 620, 622, as amended (42 U.S.C. 302(b)(3) and 304);

(j) Subsection (t) of section 202 of the Act of August 14, 1935, c.531, as added by subsection (a) of section 118 of the Act of August 1, 1956, c.836, 70 Stat. 835, and as amended (42 U.S.C. 402(t));

(k) Subsection (a)(4) of section 103 of Public Law 89–97, 79 Stat. 333, as amended (42 U.S.C. 426a(a)(4));

(l) Subsection (a)(3) of section 228 of the Act of August 14, 1935, c.531, as added by subsection (a) of section 302 of Public Law 89–368, 80 Stat. 67, as amended (42 U.S.C. 428(a)(3));

(m) Subsection (b)(2) of section 1002 and section 1004 of the Act of August 14, 1935, c.531, 49 Stat. 646, as amended (42 U.S.C. 1202(b)(2) and 1204);

(n) Subsection (b)(2) of section 1402 and section 1404 of the Act of August 14, 1935, c.531, as added by section 351 of the Act of August 28, 1950, c.809, 64 Stat. 555 (42 U.S.C. 1352(b)(2) and 1354);

(o) Subsection (b) of section 2 of the Act of August 16, 1941, c.357, 55 Stat. 623 (42 U.S.C. 1652(b));

(p) Subsection (c) of section 101 of the Act of December 2, 1942, c.668, 56 Stat. 1028, as amended (42 U.S.C. 1701(c));

(q) Section 10 of the Act of May 10, 1950, c.171, 64 Stat. 152, as amended (42 U.S.C. 1869);

(r) Subsection (c) of section 2 of Public Law 86–209, 73 Stat. 431 (42 U.S.C. 1881(c)); and

(s) Section 2 of the Act of August 3, 1950, c.520, 64 Stat. 397 (42 U.S.C. 1922).

7. As used in this Proclamation:

(a) "Covenant" means the Covenant to Establish a Commonwealth of the Northern Mariana Islands in Political Union With the United States of America, approved by the Joint Resolution of March 24, 1976 (90 Stat. 263, 48 U.S.C. 1681, note).

(b) "Citizen of the Northern Mariana Islands" means a citizen of the Trust Territory of the Pacific Islands and his or her children under the age of eighteen years, who does not owe allegiance to any foreign state, and who—

(1) was born in the Northern Mariana Islands and is physically present in the Northern Mariana Islands or in the United States or any territory or possession thereof; or

(2) has been lawfully and continuously domiciled in the Northern Mariana Islands since January 1, 1974, and, who, unless then under age, was registered to vote in an election for the Mariana Islands legislature or for any municipal election in the Northern Mariana Islands prior to January 1, 1975.

(c) "Domicile" means that place where a person maintains a residence with the intention of continuing such residence for an unlimited or indefinite period, and to which such person has the intention of returning whenever he is absent, even for an extended period.

(d) "Statute which imposes a requirement of United States citizenship or nationality" includes any statute which denies a benefit or imposes a burden or a disability on an alien, his dependents, or his survivors.

8. Upon the establishment of the Commonwealth of the Northern Mariana Islands pursuant to section 1002 of the Covenant, the benefits acquired under this Proclamation shall merge without interruption into

those to which the recipient is entitled by virtue of his acquisition of United States citizenship, unless the recipient exercises his privilege under section 302 of the Covenant to become a national but not a citizen of the United States.

In Witness Whereof, I have hereunto set my hand this seventh day of June, in the year of our Lord nineteen hundred and eighty-four, and of the Independence of the United States of America the two hundred and eighth.

RONALD REAGAN

[*Filed with the Office of the Federal Register, 4:13 p.m., June 11, 1984*]

London Economic Summit Conference Declaration on Democratic Values
June 8, 1984

We, the Heads of State or Government of seven major industrial democracies with the President of the Commission of the European Communities, assembled in London for the Tenth Economic Summit meeting, affirm our commitment to the values which sustain and bring together our societies.

2. We believe in a rule of law which respects and protects without fear or favour the rights and liberties of every citizen, and provides the setting in which the human spirit can develop in freedom and diversity.

3. We believe in a system of democracy which ensures genuine choice in elections freely held, free expression of opinion and the capacity to respond and adapt to change in all its aspects.

4. We believe that, in the political and economic systems of our democracies, it is for Governments to set conditions in which there can be the greatest possible range and freedom of choice and personal initiative; in which the ideals of social justice, obligations and rights can be pursued; in which enterprise can flourish and employment opportunities can be available for all; in which all have equal opportunities of sharing in the benefits of growth and there is support for those who suffer or are in need; in which the lives of all can be enriched by the fruits of innovation, imagination and scientific discovery; and in which there can be confidence in the soundness of the currency. Our countries have the re-

sources and will jointly to master the tasks of the new industrial revolution.

5. We believe in close partnership among our countries in the conviction that this will reinforce political stability and economic growth in the world as a whole. We look for co-operation with all countries on the basis of respect for their independence and territorial integrity, regardless of differences between political, economic and social systems. We respect genuine non-alignment. We are aware that economic strength places special moral responsibilities upon us. We reaffirm our determination to fight hunger and poverty throughout the world.

6. We believe in the need for peace with freedom and justice. Each of us rejects the use of force as a means of settling disputes. Each of us will maintain only the military strength necessary to deter aggression and to meet our responsibilities for effective defence. We believe that in today's world the independence of each of our countries is of concern to us all. We are convinced that international problems and conflicts can and must be resolved through reasoned dialogue and negotiation and we shall support all efforts to this end.

7. Strong in these beliefs, and endowed with great diversity and creative vigour, we look forward to the future with confidence.

Lancaster House
8 June 1984

London Economic Summit Conference Declaration
June 9, 1984

We, the Heads of State or Government of seven major industrialised countries and the President of the Commission of the European Communities, have gathered in London from 7 to 9 June 1984 at the invitation of the Rt Hon Margaret Thatcher FRS MP, the Prime Minister of the United Kingdom, for the tenth annual Economic Summit.

2. The primary purpose of these meetings is to enable Heads of State or Government to come together to discuss economic problems, prospects and opportunities for our countries and for the world. We have been able to achieve not only closer understanding of each other's positions and views but also a large measure of agreement on the basic objectives of our respective policies.

3. At our last meeting, in Williamsburg in 1983, we were already able to detect clear signs of recovery from world recession. That recovery can now be seen to be established in our countries. It is more soundly based than previous recoveries in that it results from the firm efforts made in the Summit countries and elsewhere over recent years to reduce inflation.

4. But its continuation requires unremitting efforts. We have to make the most of the opportunities with which we are now presented to reinforce the basis for enduring growth and the creation of new jobs. We need to spread the benefits of recovery widely, both within the industrialised countries and also to the developing countries, especially the poorer countries who stand to gain more than any from a sustainable growth of the world economy. High interest rates, and failure to reduce inflation further and damp down inflationary expectations, could put recovery at risk. Prudent monetary and budgetary policies of the kind that have brought us so far will have to be sustained and where necessary strengthened. We reaffirm the commitment of our Governments to those objectives and policies.

5. Not the least of our concerns is the growing strain of public expenditure in all our countries. Public expenditure has to be kept within the limits of what our national economies can afford. We welcome the increasing attention being given to these problems by national governments and in such international bodies as the Organisation for Economic Co-operation and Development (OECD).

6. As unemployment in our countries remains high, we emphasise the need for sustained growth and creation of new jobs. We must make sure that the industrial economies adapt and develop in response to demand and to technological change. We must encourage active job training policies and removal of rigidities in the labour market, and bring about the conditions in which more new jobs will be created on a lasting basis, especially for the young. We need to foster and expand the international trading system and liberalise capital markets.

7. We are mindful of the concerns expressed by the developing countries, and of the political and economic difficulties which many of them face. In our discussion of each of the issues before us we have recognised the economic interdependence of the industrialised and developing countries. We reaffirm our willingness to conduct our relations with them in a spirit of goodwill and co-operation. To this end we have asked Ministers of Finance to consider the scope for intensified discussion of international financial issues of particular concern to developing countries in the IBRD Development Committee, an appropriate and broadly representative forum for this purpose.

8. In our strategy for dealing with the debt burdens of many developing countries, a key role has been played by the International Monetary Fund (IMF), whose resources have been strengthened for the purpose. Debtor countries have been increasingly ready to accept the need to adjust their economic policies, despite the painful and courageous efforts it requires. In a climate of world recovery and growing world trade, this strategy should continue to enable the international financial system to

manage the problems that may still arise. But continuously high or even further growing levels of international interest rates could both exacerbate the problems of the debtor countries and make it more difficult to sustain the strategy. This underlines the importance of policies which will be conducive to lower interest rates and which take account of the impact of our policies upon other countries.

9. We have therefore agreed:—

(1) to continue with and where necessary strengthen policies to reduce inflation and interest rates, to control monetary growth and where necessary reduce budgetary deficits;

(2) to seek to reduce obstacles to the creation of new jobs:

—by encouraging the development of industries and services in response to demand and technological change, including in innovative small and medium-sized businesses;

—by encouraging the efficient working of the labour market;

—by encouraging the improvement and extension of job training;

—by encouraging flexibility in the patterns of working time;

—and by discouraging measures to preserve obsolescent production and technology;

(3) to support and strengthen work in the appropriate international organisations, notably the OECD, on increasing understanding of the sources and patterns of economic change, and on improving economic efficiency and promoting growth, in particular by encouraging innovation and working for a more widespread acceptance of technological change, harmonising standards and facilitating the mobility of labour and capital;

(4) to maintain and wherever possible increase flows of resources, including official development assistance and assistance through the international financial and development institutions, to the developing countries and particularly to the poorest countries; to work with the developing countries to encourage more openness towards private investment flows; and to encourage practical measures in those countries to conserve resources and enhance indigenous food and energy production. Some of us also wish to activate the Common Fund for Commodities;

(5) in a spirit of co-operation with the countries concerned, to confirm the strategy on debt and continue to implement and develop it flexibly case by case; we have reviewed progress and attach particular importance to:

—helping debtor countries to make necessary economic and financial policy changes, taking due account of political and social difficulties;

—encouraging the IMF in its central role in this process, which it has been carrying out skilfully;

—encouraging closer co-operation between the IMF and the International Bank for Reconstruction and Development (IBRD), and strengthening the role of the IBRD in fostering development over the medium and long term;

—in cases where debtor countries are themselves making successful efforts to improve their position, encouraging more extended multi-year rescheduling of commercial debts and standing ready where appropriate to negotiate similarly in respect of debts to governments and government agencies;

—encouraging the flow of long-term direct investment; just as there is need for industrial countries to make their markets more open for the exports of developing countries, so these countries can help themselves by encouraging investment from the industrial countries;

—encouraging the substitution of more stable long-term finance, both direct and portfolio, for short-term bank lending;

(6) to invite Finance Ministers to carry forward, in an urgent and thorough manner, their current work on ways to improve the operation of the international monetary system, including exchange rates, surveillance, the creation, control and distribution of international liquidity and the role of the IMF; and to complete the present phase of their work in the first half of 1985 with a view to discussion at an early meeting of the IMF Interim Committee. The question of a further allocation of Spe-

cial Drawing Rights is to be reconsidered by the IMF Interim Committee in September 1984;

(7) to carry forward the procedures agreed at Versailles and at Williamsburg for multilateral monitoring and surveillance of convergence of economic performance toward lower inflation and higher growth;

(8) to seek to improve the operation and stability of the international financial system, by means of prudent policies among the major countries, by providing an adequate flow of funding to the international financial institutions, and by improving international access to capital markets in industrialised countries;

(9) to urge all trading countries, industrialised and developing alike, to resist continuing protectionist pressures, to reduce barriers to trade and to make renewed efforts to liberalise and expand international trade in manufactures, commodities and services;

(10) to accelerate the completion of current trade liberalisation programmes, particularly the 1982 GATT work programme, in co-operation with other trading partners; to press forward with the work on trade in services in the international organisations; to reaffirm the agreement reached at the OECD Ministerial Meeting in May 1984 on the important contribution which a new round of multilateral trade negotiations would make to strengthening the open multilateral trading system for the mutual benefit of all economies, industrial and developing; and, building on the 1982 GATT work programme, to consult partners in the GATT with a view to decisions at an early date on the possible objectives, arrangements and timing for a new negotiating round.

10. We are greatly concerned about the acute problems of poverty and drought in parts of Africa. We attach major importance to the special action programme for Africa, which is being prepared by the World Bank and should provide renewed impetus to the joint efforts of the international community to help.

11. We have considered the possible implications of a further deterioration of the situation in the Gulf for the supply of oil. We are satisfied that, given the stocks of oil presently available in the world, the availability of other sources of energy, and the scope for conservation in the use of energy, adequate supplies could be maintained for a substantial period of time by international co-operation and mutually supportive action. We will continue to act together to that end.

12. We note with approval the continuing consensus on the security and other implications of economic relations with Eastern countries, and on the need to continue work on this subject in the appropriate organisations.

13. We welcome the further report of the Working Group on Technology, Growth and Employment created by the Versailles Economic Summit, and the progress made in the eighteen areas of co-operation, and invite the Group to pursue further work and to report to Personal Representatives in time for the next Economic Summit. We also welcome the invitation of the Italian Government to an international conference to be held in Italy in 1985 on the theme of technological innovation and the creation of new jobs.

14. We recognise the international dimension of environmental problems and the role of environmental factors in economic development. We have invited Ministers responsible for environmental policies to identify areas for continuing co-operation in this field. In addition we have decided to invite the Working Group on Technology, Growth and Employment to consider what has been done so far and to identify specific areas for research on the causes, effects and means of limiting environmental pollution of air, water and ground where existing knowledge is inadequate, and to identify possible projects for industrial co-operation to develop cost-effective techniques to reduce environmental damage. The Group is invited to report on these matters by 31 December 1984. In the meantime we welcome the invitation from the Government of the Federal Republic of Germany to certain Summit countries to an international conference on the environment in Munich on 24–27 June 1984.

15. We thank the Prime Minister of Japan for his report on the Hakone Conference of

Life Sciences and Mankind, organised by the Japan Foundation in March 1984, and welcome the intention of the French Government to sponsor a second Conference in 1985.

16. We believe that manned space stations are the kind of programme that provides a stimulus for technological development leading to strengthened economies and improved quality of life. Such stations are being studied in some of our countries with a view to their being launched in the framework of national or international programmes. In that context each of our countries will consider carefully the generous and thoughtful invitation received from the President of the United States to other Summit countries to participate in the development of such a station by the United States. We welcome the intention of the United States to report at the next Summit on international participation in their programme.

17. We have agreed to meet again next year and have accepted the Federal Chancellor's invitation to meet in the Federal Republic of Germany.

Lancaster House
9 June 1984

Note: Prime Minister Margaret Thatcher of the United Kingdom read the declaration to reporters assembled in the Great Hall of the Guildhall. Also present for the reading were President Reagan, President François Mitterrand of France, Prime Minister Pierre Elliott Trudeau of Canada, Chancellor Helmut Kohl of the Federal Republic of Germany, Prime Minister Yasuhiro Nakasone of Japan, Prime Minister Bettino Craxi of Italy, and Gaston Thorn, President of the Commission of the European Communities.

London Economic Summit Conference Declaration on East-West Relations and Arms Control
June 9, 1984

1. We had a substantial discussion of East-West relations. We stressed that the first need is for solidarity and resolve among us all.

2. At the same time, we are determined to pursue the search for extended political dialogue and long-term co-operation with the Soviet Union and her allies. Contacts exist and are being developed in a number of fields. Each of us will pursue all useful opportunities for dialogue.

3. Our aim is security and the lowest possible level of forces. We wish to see early and positive results in the various arms control negotiations and the speedy resumption of those now suspended. The United States has offered to re-start nuclear arms control talks anywhere, at any time, without preconditions. We hope that the Soviet Union will act in a constructive and positive way. We are convinced that this would be in the common interest of both East and West. We are in favour of agreements which would build confidence and give concrete expression, through precise commitments, to the principle of the non-use of force.

4. We believe that East and West have important common interests: in preserving peace; in enhancing confidence and security; in reducing the risks of surprise attack or war by accident; in improving crisis management techniques; and in preventing the spread of nuclear weapons.

London Economic Summit Conference Declaration on International Terrorism
June 9, 1984

1. The Heads of State and Government discussed the problem of international terrorism.

2. They noted that hijacking and kidnapping had declined since the Declarations of Bonn (1978), Venice (1980) and Ottawa (1981) as a result of improved security measures, but that terrorism had developed other techniques, sometimes in association with traffic in drugs.

3. They expressed their resolve to combat this threat by every possible means, strengthening existing measures and developing effective new ones.

4. They were disturbed to note the ease with which terrorists move across international boundaries, and gain access to weapons, explosives, training and finance.

5. They viewed with serious concern the increasing involvement of states and governments in acts of terrorism, including the abuse of diplomatic immunity. They acknowledged the inviolability of diplomatic missions and other requirements of international law: but they emphasised the obligations which that law also entails.

6. Proposals which found support in the discussion included the following:

—closer co-operation and co-ordination between police and security organisations and other relevant authorities, especially in the exchange of information, intelligence and technical knowledge;

—scrutiny by each country of gaps in its national legislation which might be exploited by terrorists;

—use of the powers of the receiving state under the Vienna Convention in such matters as the size of diplomatic missions, and the number of buildings enjoying diplomatic immunity;

—action by each country to review the sale of weapons to states supporting terrorism;

—consultation and as far as possible cooperation over the expulsion or exclusion from their countries of known terrorists, including persons of diplomatic status involved in terrorism.

7. The Heads of State and Government recognised that this is a problem which affects all civilised states. They resolved to promote action through competent international organisations and among the international community as a whole to prevent and punish terrorist acts.

Statement by the Chair of the London Economic Summit Conference on the Iran-Iraq Conflict
June 9, 1984

1. We discussed the Iraq/Iran conflict in all its various aspects.

2. We expressed our deep concern at the mounting toll in human suffering, physical damage and bitterness that this conflict has brought; and at the breaches of international humanitarian law that have occurred.

3. The hope and desire of us all is that both sides will cease their attacks on each other and on the shipping of other states. The principle of freedom of navigation must be respected. We are concerned that the conflict should not spread further and we shall do what we can to encourage stability in the region.

4. We encourage the parties to seek a peaceful and honourable settlement. We shall support any efforts designed to bring this about, particularly those of the United Nations Secretary-General.

5. We also considered the implications for world oil supplies on the lines set out in the

834

Economic Declaration. We noted that the world oil market has remained relatively stable. We believe that the international system has both the will and the capacity to cope with any foreseeable problems through the continuation of the prudent and realistic approach that is already being applied.

Radio Address to the Nation on the Trip to Europe
June 9, 1984

My fellow Americans:

Greetings from London. As you probably know, Nancy and I have been in Europe for 8 days, visiting Ireland, commemorating the 40th anniversary of D-day at Normandy, and now meeting with the leaders of the major industrialized democracies at the economic summit to strengthen the basis for freedom, prosperity, and peace.

Change comes neither easily nor quickly in foreign affairs. Finding solutions to critical global problems requires lengthy and sustained efforts, the kind we've been making ever since my first economic summit in Ottawa in 1981. Those efforts are now paying off as we reap the benefits of sound policies. Think back 4 years—America was weak at home and abroad. Remember double-digit inflation, 20-percent interest rates, zero growth, and those never-ending excuses that such misery would be part of our lives for years to come. And remember how our foreign policy invited Soviet aggression and expansion in Afghanistan, Central America, and Africa. Entire countries were lost. Doubts spread about America's leadership in defense of freedom and peace. And so, freedom and peace became less secure.

Well, a lot has changed. Today America stands taller in the world. At home we've made a fundamental change in direction— away from bigger and bigger government, toward more power and incentives for people; away from confusion and failure, toward progress through commitment to the enduring values of Western civilization; away from weakness and instability, toward peace through strength and a willingness to negotiate.

Together with our allies, we've tried to adopt a similar strategy for progress abroad—guided by realism, by common values and interests, and by confidence that we will not remain prisoners of fear and a disappointing past. We can and will move forward to better days.

Last year the United States hosted the Williamsburg summit. It had been an active year for allied relations as we grappled with economic and security problems, but we didn't dwell on differences. We joined in a peace and security statement and a blueprint for world economic recovery. Williamsburg was an unprecedented endorsement of Western values. Our alliance emerged stronger and more united than ever. Peace and prosperity were made more secure.

Later in the year I traveled to Japan and Korea to emphasize the importance we attached to the dynamic Pacific region. Here too, we faced tough problems, particularly in trade with Japan. But Prime Minister Nakasone is a man of vision and strength, who has worked hard with me to iron out our differences, and we've made progress. Japan has opened up its trading and financial markets and moved to increase its defense expenditures, so vital to preserving peace and freedom in the Pacific Basin. This will mean more U.S. jobs and greater security for both our nations.

In April I returned to the Pacific region to visit China. Our relations have steadily improved and our visit capped important agreements that will stimulate U.S. exports to China as we cooperate with them to modernize their economy.

Now, here in London at this year's economic summit, it's clear we've made impressive gains. In 1981 our economies had an average growth rate of only 1.8 percent and 8½-percent inflation. Today our average growth rate has risen to 4 percent, while inflation has been cut in half. Stronger growth means more jobs with the U.S. economy leading the way. We've created more than 6 million jobs in the last 18 months, and we're venturing into new, promising areas. We've offered our summit partners the opportunity to participate with us in the development of our manned space station. An international space station will stimulate technological development, strengthen our economies, and improve the quality of life into the next century.

I've stressed in London that continued progress will require new determination to carry out our common strategy for prosperity and peace. We must summon courage. We must continue with action to curb inflation by reducing unnecessary spending, spur greater growth by reducing regulation,

trade barriers, and personal income tax rates. And, yes, we must be prepared for peace by strengthening NATO's ability to deter war, while making clear we're prepared to reduce nuclear weapons dramatically as soon as the Soviets are ready to work with us on this all-important goal.

This has been a year of progress, a year when we and our friends in Europe and the Pacific set aside differences and united as great democracies should be with shared vision and values. That progress, stretching beyond America from the Pacific Basin to a strengthened Atlantic Alliance, is a source of hope for a more prosperous and safer world.

Until next week, thanks for listening, and God bless you.

Note: The President recorded the address for broadcast in the United States at 12:06 p.m.

Remarks and a Question-and-Answer Session With Reporters on the London Economic Summit Conference
June 10, 1984

London Economic Summit

The President. Good morning. I just have a brief statement here, and then I imagine you've got something to say.

This has been a productive week and, looking back, a particularly busy year for the Atlantic alliance, and a most successful one. Despite Soviet propaganda and attempts at intimidation, NATO has remained unified and strong. And we can be thankful and proud that NATO's determination to defend Europe, defend our freedom, and, yes, defend the peace.

The summit that we just concluded demonstrates the unity of the Western industrialized nations, the enduring strength of our shared vision and values, and our resolve to advance our common interests. And so, today I leave London; I am leaving with renewed confidence that the future belongs to the free and that our great democracies can meet the challenges before us. Together, we can protect peace with liberty, create greater prospects for growth, move

toward more free and open trading markets, and build an era of progress for the eighties, spreading opportunities and benefits to people throughout the world.

Sometimes people become so absorbed in day-to-day problems they forget the big picture. But step back a moment and consider the progress that we've made. In '81, the economies of the seven major industrialized nations represented here at the summit had an average growth rate of 1.8 percent, with an 8½-percent inflation. Today, our average growth rate has risen to 4 percent, while inflation has been cut in half. And in our own country, we've created more than 6 million jobs in the last 18 months.

We are succeeding. And thanks to closer cooperation, closer coordination, and thanks to steady adherence to policies that have proven to be sound, that is why we are succeeding.

And now, because by some inadvertence, I may have missed a point that you wanted to hear about.

Yes, Lou [Lou Cannon, Washington Post].

U.S.-Soviet Relations

Q. Mr. President, in the big picture of our relations with the Soviet Union, you've made a lot of appeals for them to come back to the table; you embraced a new proposal at Stockholm—but there doesn't seem to be any movement at all. What evidence is there that the Soviets are prepared in any way to negotiate with the United States or with any of the Western powers?

The President. Well, we're so accustomed to viewing the Soviets as engaged in various kinds of machinations and so forth, it's beginning to occur to some of us that maybe the silence is because they don't know what to say right now. So, we'll let them—after all, you know, this is the third leader in the period that I've been in office here. Let them make up their minds what it is, and we will keep the door open for anytime that they want to come back.

Q. Could I follow up, sir? Do you believe that they will take a different attitude if you are reelected to a second term?

The President. Well, I think there's probably more chance that we'll be talking to each other if I am than there is before.

Helen [Helen Thomas, United Press International]?

Q. Mr. President, the communique says that you'll go anywhere anytime with no preconditions to negotiate with the Soviet Union. Does that mean you will negotiate underground testing, antisatellite treaties, and the Star Wars shield?

The President. Well, Helen, I think that when you negotiate—and from my own experience back in the labor-management days of doing that—both sides, whatever is on their mind that they think are problems or facets of the problem that brings you to the table, get them all out on the table and see what the solutions might be. Yes, if this is what they want to talk about, we're very willing to talk about——

Q. But we have refused——

The President. What?

Q. We have refused to talk about the underground testing——

The President. No. What we——

Q. ——and antisatellite.

The President. There is one thing we

have that we want on the table, and that is also that there will be a recognition of the need for adequate verification. Now, the antisatellite thing is one that is the easiest thing to hide in the world—and it's going forward in that—with the possible exception of chemical warfare. So, on our part, they know that we want to be sure that we can come together on some reasonable verifications so we won't live in suspicion of each other. And whatever they want to bring up in these others, we'll be happy to see it.

Chris [Chris Wallace, NBC News]? And then I'll——

Nuclear Missiles

Q. Mr. President, everywhere you went on this trip there were big crowds supporting you, but there were also tens of thousands of demonstrators opposing your policy on nuclear arms. Why, despite all of your efforts and all of your speeches in recent months, do so many people still oppose your policies in this area?

The President. Well, I don't take credit for all of the demonstrators being there for me. I don't think yesterday picked out any single individual. I think we all felt that we were being—but isn't that sort of—doesn't that go with the territory anymore, that wherever we go or governmental people go, figures go, or even if they don't go there, demonstrations have become a fact of life. Somehow people have felt that that's the way to express their ideas in a democracy. In spite of all of the legitimate channels that are open to them, they take to the streets.

And I wasn't too conscious of them—here and there, yesterday was the major demonstration, of course, but I don't think they're speaking for a majority. And I think sometimes they're unreasoning, in that as yesterday, hadn't any of them stopped to think that no one is demonstrating and they're not demonstrating in the nation that has the most nuclear weapons of all.

Q. If I may follow up, though, sir. Why do you think it is that they oppose your policies?

The President. Well, they seem to think they have a simple answer to warfare: that if we just lay down our weapons and stand back emptyhanded that somehow peace will come to the world. They haven't stopped to figure it might be the peace of the grave.

London Economic Summit

Q. Mr. President, the summit leaders, you and the other leaders, confronted three very urgent economic problems—high American interest rates, the threat of default by debtor countries, and the possibility of an oil cutoff—and came up with solutions for none of these three. Couldn't the American taxpayers wonder whether this was really worth the time and money you spent?

The President. Oh, I disagree with that, that we didn't come up with answers for any of them. We had very thorough discussions of all of these problems, and we came to great agreement about how you go forward now in dealing with these problems. They aren't problems that you suddenly say, here, we will automatically do this if something else happens. We have a general agreement about the necessity of us all staying together in the event of another oil crisis for two reasons: not only to see that we don't have economic breakdowns in countries because of the lack of energy, but also that we do not see the panic increase in prices, that has occurred before, which could set back the recovery that's taking place in every one of our countries. But all of those things we dealt with.

Q. Well, sir, just to follow—you said that there was agreement. But there was certainly no agreement on interest rates. You were the only one of the seven who said that they were not linked to budget deficits. Do you feel that possibly you could be wrong about that?

The President. No, because I'm the only one there that with figures proved it. Right now our deficit as a percentage of gross national product is lower than that of three other nations that were present, and one nation alone was lower than ours, and one nation was tied with ours. But if you lump them all together—and roughly their combined gross national products are about equivalent to ours—and you would find that their percentage of deficit in toto was great-

er in regard to gross national product than ours.

What I was able to establish is that the connection between deficit and interest rates cannot be established at all. When we made our greatest cut in interest rates, from 21½ down to 11, the deficit was going up. But you go on to the next column of inflation in all of those countries, and you find that that's what the interest rates are tied to, is inflation or the fear of inflation. And in our country, because we've been so successful with curbing inflation, I have to say it is the fear that we still are going to let inflation get out of hand.

U.S.-Soviet Relations

Q. Mr. President, when you say that the Soviets don't really know what to say right now, are you indicating that perhaps Mr. Chernenko is in over his head or maybe just too old to do the job? [*Laughter*]

The President. No, I'm——

Mr. Speakes.[1] Last question.

The President. But wait a minute. I was really pointing at someone else. So, after his, I'll take hers back there.

But, no, I think that there come times when—since they sort of rule by committee, the Politburo, that there isn't a consensus there on the course that they should be taking right now. And this was presented in a very fine article in the Economist a short time ago that said that maybe the bear is hibernating.

Terrorism

Q. Mr. President, the statement on terrorism that was issued here outlines some proposed actions but, apparently, not a coordinated plan for action. What do you think the significance of that statement is, and what kind of discussions were held on cooperation on preemptive strikes?

The President. I don't think anything came in the nature of thinking in terms of attacking someplace if we believed—but we did discuss thoroughly the problems of terrorism, the fact that—actually the greatest defense against it is to try and know in

---

[1] *Larry M. Speakes, Principal Deputy Press Secretary to the President.*

advance what some of the plans are and what they're going to do. And for that reason, we've come to great agreement on the sharing of intelligence information of all kinds between us.

It isn't the kind of problem that you come down with a hard and fast plan, which you then discuss publicly. You come to an agreement about, number one, the necessity of dealing with it; number two, then, what together we can do to better deal with it. But you don't spread the details of that around.

Mr. Speakes. Thank you, Mr. President.

Q. Well, just to follow up. Secretary of State Shultz said there were a great many ramifications that go beyond defensive measures. What kind of a signal are you trying to send here?

The President. Well, I think what the Secretary was probably referring to is the fact that more and more we are seeing certain countries in the world more or less endorse openly the use of terrorism. And that is a separate problem also to deal with.

Mr. Speakes. Thank you, sir.

The President. Well, they've told me——

President's Family

Q. When are you going to Scotland, Mr. President? The Scots say you really belong there. [*Laughter*]

The President. Well, on my mother's side, her father came from Scotland. We didn't know much more about his line than we had about my grandparents on my father's side. But then on the maternal side, my mother's family, the family came from Epsom in County Surrey, just south of London here. And we do know something about them, how they got together and baked bread in the backyard in a brick oven that they built and—to get enough money to come to America.

Q. Are you going there next year, sir?

The President. What?

Q. Are we going there next year, sir?

Q. No, before the election.

The President. What?

Q. Before the election, you've got to go there. [*Laughter*]

Q. How many Scottish voters? [*Laughter*]

The President. I know you would never believe this—[*laughter*]—but the decision to go to Ballyporeen was in response to a long-standing invitation from them once they had established and told me what I did not know about my family. And I also had an invitation from the previous Prime Minister of Ireland and from the present Prime Minister of Ireland, and this date was set a long time ago—[*laughter*]—for the summit. And I didn't see why I could fly over Ireland to England without stopping by and accepting those invitations.

Note: The President spoke at 9:45 a.m. outside Winfield House in London, England.

Remarks to Members of the American Community Following the London Economic Summit Conference
June 10, 1984

The President. Mr. Ambassador and Mrs. Price and members of the Embassy staff, the Navy, and the students from the American school, Nancy and I are grateful that so many of you could be here today. And we would like to express our heartfelt thanks for your warm welcome and for all that you've done to make our visit a success.

Now, you could have stopped short of organizing that crowd that turned up in the streets yesterday, but—[*laughter*]—and if you get too lonely maybe you could find how to put them together again. But somehow your Embassy always rises to the challenge, no matter how many demands you have to contend with. Your good work and cheerful hospitality are legend in Washington, and I'm sure that helps explain why you see so many of us so frequently. And I don't mind telling you that we're also delighted with the job that is being done by Ambassador Charlie Price and his very talented and lovely partner Carol.

Charlie, as I look out on this beautiful lawn, I can appreciate what a delight living here must be—especially for a fine golfer like you. But then, as I look behind me at all these windows, I'm reminded that you hit one that went astray. And forgive me for asking, but how was that paid for, or did we add it to the deficit? [*Laughter*]

I know how much you all must enjoy working and living in this wonderful city. Great Britain and the United States are kindred nations of like-minded people. We defend the same values; we face the same dangers and cherish the same friendships. We look to our British cousins with a very warm and special affection. These bonds must never be broken, and I don't believe they ever will be.

We've had a wonderful and, I think, very productive 10 days—visiting some of my ancestors' homeland in Ireland, commemorating the 40th anniversary of D-day at Normandy, and then meeting with my fellow leaders at the economic summit here in London. We leave today with renewed confidence that we can and will strengthen the freedoms, prosperity, and peace that we share.

But I cannot say goodbye without thanking our Foreign Service nationals, who serve us so well. As American diplomats come and go, it's your professionalism that keeps everything running smoothly. All of you make an invaluable contribution to our Anglo-American partnership, and nobody knows that better than Miss Joan Auten. Miss Auten, would you please join me up here for a minute?

Ms. Auten. Mr. President, how nice to see you.

The President. Nice to see you.

Miss Auten's distinguished career spans nearly 44 years. She has served 14 American Ambassadors to the Court of Saint James. And during World War II, when London was under siege, she helped evacuate children to the safety of our shores in the United States. Since those early days of service, Joan Auten has played a leading role in promoting friendship and dialog between our two democracies.

And, Joan, I'm delighted to honor you with the Presidential Special Award for Exceptional Service.

Ms. Auten. Thank you, Mr. President. Thank you from the bottom of my heart.

The President. Well, thank you, for all those years.

Well, we return to the States with gratitude for all you've done. We've had a good visit. And for all that you'll continue to do, we thank you. And we'll take with us warm and lasting memories of your friendship.

I can't help but go without telling a little incident that I've told to some of the people we've been meeting with here. When we had the summit in Williamsburg, in Virginia, last year—that was the British capital at one time of the Colonies—and the first dinner meeting between the seven leaders was around a dinner table in what had been the residence of the British Colonial Governor. And I thought I was all set with quite a witticism. When we finally sat down, I would say to the Prime Minister, "Margaret, if one of your predecessors had been a little more clever, you would be hostessing this gathering."

I underestimated her. I got out—of my line, I said, "Margaret, if one of your predecessors had been a little more clever"—— She turned to me and said, "Yes, I know. I would have been hosting this gathering." [*Laughter*]

I learned then that—I'm very careful. You're very fortunate, and she conducted magnificently the meetings that we've had for the last few days, and they were productive.

And now, again, I know that you'll have to rejoice a little, because we must have caused you a great deal of trouble; but, we're most grateful to you. And we'll now go—and fly away.

Thank you all very much.

Note: The President spoke at 10:08 a.m. outside Winfield House. Following his remarks, he left London for the return to Washington, DC.

Appointment of the 1984–1985 White House Fellows
June 11, 1984

The President today announced the appointments of the 1984–1985 White House fellows. This is the 20th class of fellows since the program began in 1964.

The 13 fellows were chosen from among 1,247 applicants and screened by 11 regional panels. The President's Commission on White House fellowships, chaired by Vice Adm. James B. Stockdale, USN (Ret.), interviewed the 33 national finalists before recommending the 13 persons to the President. Their year of government service will begin September 1, 1984.

The 1984–1985 White House fellows are:

Lew W. Cramer, 35, of Glendale, CA; attorney and partner, Argue, Freston, Pearson, Harbison & Myers; and adjunct professor, Graduate School of Business Administration, University of Southern California, Los Angeles;

MacArthur Deshazer, 38, of Hollandale, MS; major, United States Army, Deputy Commanding Officer, the School Brigade, Fort Bliss, TX;

Jose C. Feliciano, 34, of Cleveland, OH; chief police prosecutor of Cleveland;

Charles L. Hirsch, 26, of Pennington, NJ; director, division of economic development, New Jersey Department of Commerce, Trenton;

Thomas C. Leppert, 29, of Los Angeles, CA; engagement manager, McKinsey & Co., Inc., Los Angeles;

Stephen C. Mott, 34, of Stamford, CT; director of marketing, MCI International, Rye Brook, NY;

Patrick A. Putignano, 32, of Park Ridge, NJ; major, United States Army, assistant professor, department of social science, United States Military Academy, West Point, NY;

Bruce K. Scott, 33, of Falls Church, VA; major, United States Army; Olmsted Scholar, John F. Kennedy School of Government, Harvard University, Boston, MA;

Teresa B. Smith, 27, of Baltimore, MD; senior electrical engineer, Westinghouse Electric Corp., Defense Center Advanced Technology Laboratories, Baltimore;

Richard D. Stamberger, 25, of Washington, DC; director of special projects, the National Cable Television Association, Washington, DC;

J. Scott Wheeler, 36, of Harker Heights, TX; major, United States Army, aide to the Commanding General of III Corps and Fort Hood, Fort Hood, TX;

Linda C. White, 27, of Richmond, VA; supervisor of cost accounting, Philip Morris U.S.A., Richmond;

J. Robert Wood, 34, of Davenport, IA; major, United States Army, assistant professor of economics, United States Military Academy, West Point, NY.

Fellows serve for 1 year as special assistants to the Vice President, members of the Cabinet, and the President's principal staff. In addition to the work assignment, the fellowship includes an education program which parallels and broadens the unique experience of working at the highest levels of the Federal Government.

The program is open to U.S. citizens in the early stages of their careers and from all occupations and professions. Federal Government employees are not eligible, with the exception of career Armed Forces personnel.

Leadership, character, intellectual and professional ability, and commitment to community and nation are the principal criteria employed in the selection of fellows.

Applications for the 1985–1986 program are available from the President's Commission on White House Fellowships, 712 Jackson Place NW, Washington, DC 20503.

Message to the Senate Transmitting the United States-Italy Treaty on Mutual Assistance in Criminal Matters
June 11, 1984

To the Senate of the United States:

With a view to receiving the advice and consent of the Senate to ratification, I transmit herewith the Treaty between the United States of America and the Italian Republic on Mutual Assistance in Criminal Matters, together with a related Memorandum of Understanding, signed at Rome on November 9, 1982.

I transmit also, for the information of the Senate, the report of the Department of State with respect to the Treaty.

The Treaty is one of a series of modern mutual assistance treaties being negotiated by the United States. This Treaty contains two major innovations: compulsory testimony in the requesting State in appropriate cases and the immobilization and forfeiture of assets. The former is of great importance in insuring complete trials in an age of rapidly increasing levels of international criminal activity. The latter is of great importance in depriving international criminals of the fruits of their crimes. The Treaty pri-

marily utilizes existing statutory authority, but will require implementing legislation for the provision concerning forfeiture of assets.

The Treaty provides for a broad range of cooperation in criminal matters. Mutual assistance available under the Treaty includes: (1) executing requests relating to criminal matters; (2) taking of testimony or statements of persons; (3) effecting the production and preservation of documents, records, or articles of evidence; (4) serving judicial documents; (5) requiring the appearance of a witness before a court of the requesting Party; (6) locating persons; and (7) providing judicial records, evidence, and information.

I recommend that the Senate give early and favorable consideration to the Treaty and give its advice and consent to ratification.

RONALD REAGAN

The White House,
June 11, 1984.

Message to the Senate Transmitting the United States-Canada Treaty on Construction of the High Ross Dam
June 11, 1984

To the Senate of the United States:

With a view to receiving the advice and consent of the Senate to ratification, I transmit herewith a Treaty between the United States of America and Canada relating to the Skagit River and Ross Lake in the State of Washington, and the Seven Mile Reservoir and the Pend d'Oreille River in the Province of British Columbia, together with a report of the Department of State.

The primary purpose of this Treaty is to provide the necessary legal bases for an arrangement under which the City of Seattle, Washington will refrain from raising the

Ross Dam on the Skagit River, thus avoiding additional flooding of the Skagit Valley in the Canadian Province of British Columbia, and will receive in return a guaranteed long-term supply of electrical power from British Columbia. Through this arrangement a longstanding dispute between Seattle and British Columbia over the construction of the High Ross Dam has been constructively and ingeniously settled, and a difficult and potentially divisive bilateral problem between the United States and Canada positively resolved. The British Columbia-Seattle Agreement and the United States-Canada Treaty that provides the necessary legal bases for the Agreement represent both a significant substantive achievement in terms of power provision and environmental conservation, and a model for the orderly and amicable settlement of international issues.

I recommend that the Senate give early and favorable consideration to the Treaty, and give its advice and consent to ratification.

RONALD REAGAN

The White House,
June 11, 1984.

Nomination of Katherine M. Bulow To Be an Assistant Secretary of Commerce
June 12, 1984

The President today announced his intention to nominate Katherine M. Bulow to be an Assistant Secretary of Commerce (Administration). She would succeed Arlene Triplett.

Since 1983 she has been serving as Deputy Assistant Secretary for Administration at the Department of Commerce. In 1981–1983 she was at the Department of Commerce as Special Assistant to the Assistant Secretary. Previously she was director of the building management division at the Republican National Committee in 1977–1981 and administrator for the petrochemical energy group in 1973–1975. She served in the Office of Congressional Affairs at the White House in 1969–1973 and at the Federal Reserve System in 1962–1967.

She has one son and resides in Bowie, MD. She was born October 4, 1943, in Kansas City, MO.

Nomination of John William Shirley To Be United States Ambassador to Tanzania
June 12, 1984

The President today announced his intention to nominate John William Shirley, of Illinois, a career member of the Senior Foreign Service, Class of Career Minister, as Ambassador to the United Republic of Tanzania. He would succeed David Charles Miller, Jr., who is now Ambassador to Zimbabwe.

Mr. Shirley served in the United States Air Force in 1952–1956. In 1957 he began his service with the United States Information Agency as intelligence research officer. In 1958–1959 he was assistant cultural officer in Zagreb and assistant cultural attaché in Belgrade in 1959–1960. He was public affairs officer in Trieste (1960–1963), press attaché in Rome (1963–1965), and press officer in New Delhi (1965–1968). In 1968–1969 he was policy officer in the Near Eastern and South Asian affairs in the Agency. He attended Polish language training at the Foreign Service Institute in 1969–1970. In 1970–1972 he was press and cultural affairs officer in Warsaw. In the Agency he was Deputy Director and then Director for East European and Soviet Affairs and Director for European Affairs (1972–1977). He was Counselor of Embassy for Public Affairs in Rome in 1977–1980. In the Agency he was Associate Director for Programs (1980–1981), Acting Director of the Agency (1981), Counselor of Agency (1981–1983), and Deputy Director ad interim (1983). Since 1983 he has been diplomat in residence at Wesleyan University in Middletown, CT.

Mr. Shirley received his B.S.F.S. in 1957

from Georgetown University. His foreign languages are Hungarian, Italian, French, German, Polish, and Serbo-Croatian. He

was born in August 18, 1931, in England, of American parents.

Nomination of Diana Lady Dougan To Be Coordinator for Communications and Information Policy at the Department of State
June 12, 1984

The President today announced his intention to nominate Diana Lady Dougan, of Utah, as Coordinator for Communications and Information Policy, Department of State, with the rank of Ambassador. This is the first such appointment to be made under the provisions of Section 124, Public Law 98–164 of November 22, 1983.

Mrs. Dougan was assistant chief clerk of the Maryland State Legislature in 1964–1965. In 1964–1966 she was telecommunication and public relations consultant in Washington, DC, and New York. She was CATV marketing and promotion director at Time, Inc., in New York City (1964–1968) and did personal investments and consulting work (primarily pro bono) and was a partner with Dougan Associates in Salt Lake City, UT (1969–1983). In 1976–1983 she served in a Presidential appointment as

Director of the Corporation for Public Broadcasting in Washington, DC, and also as a member of the Utah State Telecommunications Task Force. In 1978–1983 she was a member of CER Gubernatorial Commission to reorganize the executive branch of the Utah State government. Since 1983 she has been Coordinator for International Communications and Information Policy (accorded the personal rank of Ambassador in April 1983), Department of State. This position was a Secretarial appointment until established as Presidential with Senate confirmation.

Mrs. Dougan graduated from the University of Maryland (B.A., 1964). She attended the University of Utah (1969–1970) and Harvard University (1979). Her foreign languages are some knowledge of French and Spanish. She was born January 13, 1943, in Dayton, OH.

Remarks at a White House Ceremony Marking the Opening of the National Center for Missing and Exploited Children
June 13, 1984

Thank you for a very warm welcome, and especially from one young lady up here. But Attorney General Smith, distinguished Members of the Congress, and honored guests and ladies and gentlemen, good morning, and welcome to the White House.

I'm delighted to have the opportunity to help launch the National Center for Missing and Exploited Children, and to tell you that the safety and protection of our children is a top priority on the national agenda. All Americans, and especially our youth, should have the right and the opportunity to walk

our streets, to play and to grow and to live their lives without being at risk.

Sadly, our children are at risk. Johnny Gosh, age 12, Des Moines, Iowa, vanished from his paper route in September of 1982. He's still missing. Kevin Collins, a 10-year-old lad from San Francisco, disappeared last February after basketball practice. Ann Gotlib, 12, of Louisville, Kentucky, has been gone without a trace since last summer. And then there was Adam. America knows Adam Walsh and of his tragic story—an innocent victim of a cruel, predatory crime.

There are too many children like Adam: too many stolen each year from loved ones; too many who feel pain and suffering; too many who fall prey to exploitation and death. We don't know the exact number of victims, but it certainly numbers in the thousands.

When Adam Walsh, a bright, happy, 6-year-old boy disappeared in the summer of 1981, John and Reve Walsh found themselves alone in their crisis. They were thwarted by jurisdictional tangles and foot-dragging, and the heartbreak of the moment became a chilling nightmare of terror and unbelievable frustration.

Our commitment to criminal justice goes far deeper than a desire to punish the guilty. Our laws represent the collective moral voice of a free society. And right now that voice is crying out to protect our children and keep them safe.

I hope we can mark the opening of the National Center for Missing and Exploited Children by redoubling our efforts to do just that. We must and will continue cracking down on career criminals, drugpushers, and the pornographers. We must and will continue working to protect the interests of our children and their families.

But make no mistake, the strongest guardian against crime, and particularly crime against children, is we, the people. Helen Kromer wrote, "One man awake can waken another. The second can awaken his next door brother. The three awake can rouse the town by turning the whole place upside down. And the many awake make such a fuss they finally awaken the rest of us."

The courage of John and Reve Walsh in the face of the most difficult grief imaginable awakened our nation to the tragedy of America's missing children. Thanks to their efforts and those of Senator Paula Hawkins and many others, I was able to sign the Missing Children Act into law in October of 1982. The act established a system allowing parents, under certain circumstances, access to a central computer file to help trace missing children. The act also aids in identifying deceased children and adults and at least eases the pain of not knowing.

We've also recently signed into law child pornography legislation which will assist law enforcement agencies in their war against the exploitation of children.

And let me take this opportunity to salute a related effort aimed at helping children who become wards of the court. The Court-Appointed Special Advocate program, CASA, as it's called, is a new community-based effort of trained volunteers serving as advocates of abused and neglected children. CASA is already working in several States, giving America's discarded children the protection they need.

And now we're launching an effort to extend the program all across America. But, as you know, these efforts are only the essential first steps, and formidable challenges remain. Meeting them is what the National Center for Missing and Exploited Children is all about.

Starting with a $3.3 million Justice Department grant, the Center will have three divisions. The Division on Missing Children will assist parents and citizens groups in locating and safely returning missing children. It will give technical assistance to law enforcement agencies, and it will help coordinate the efforts of community organizations all across America that are involved in the missing children activities. And later this summer, the Center will open a toll-free 800 telephone number to handle inquiries and accept information on sightings.

The Division on Exploited Children will provide valuable support and technical assistance to the professionals who deal with these difficult missing children cases every day.

The Division on Education, Prevention, and Public Awareness will collect and distribute information on the most effective ways to address and prevent the problem of the estimated 1.8 million children missing from their homes each year.

What we're doing is launching a public-private partnership. Partnerships can take advantage of every opportunity available, and they can use these opportunities in a most efficient and productive way to protect our children and keep them safe.

No single sector of our nation can solve the problem of missing and exploited children alone. But by working together, pooling our resources, and building on our strengths, we can accomplish great things.

Three weeks ago we signed a Missing Children's Day proclamation and urged the private sector to help. And America is responding. Trailways Corporation and the International Association of Chiefs of Police have established Operation Home Free, a program that provides runaway children a ride home. Television stations are broadcasting photographs of missing children. And now it's time to do even more.

Now, before I close, I want to take this opportunity to thank Bill Smith, the Walshes, Lois Herrington, Jay Howell, the executive director of the center, and the many other concerned Americans, for all

that you're doing. America's future is in the hands of our children. Your dedication and hard work will give our children a chance to live well and live full, healthy, and happy lives.

And I want you to know that all of us in the administration stand behind you, eager to assist in any way we can. Together we can turn the tide on these hateful crimes, and, knowing what you have accomplished already, I'm confident we will.

I thank you, and God bless you all. And now, I'd like to ask John Walsh to say a few words.

Note: The President spoke at 11:35 a.m. in the East Room at the White House.

Nomination of Howard Bruner Schaffer To Be United States Ambassador to Bangladesh
June 13, 1984

The President today announced his intention to nominate Howard Bruner Schaffer, of New York, a career member of the Senior Foreign Service, Class of Minister-Counselor, as Ambassador to the People's Republic of Bangladesh. He would succeed Jane Abell Coon.

Mr. Schaffer served in the United States Army in 1951–1953. He was sales correspondent at I.M. Schaffer Co., Inc., in Brooklyn, NY, in 1950–1951. In New York City he was a research assistant at McCann-Erickson Advertising Agency (1953–1954), and marketing researcher at Lever Brothers Co. (1954–1955). In 1955 he entered the Foreign Service and served as political officer in Kuala Lumpur. He was political officer in Seoul in 1958–1960. In 1960–1961 he attended Hindi language training at the Foreign Service Institute. He was economic officer (1961–1963) and political officer

(1963–1967) in New Delhi. In the Department he was international relations officer in the Bureau of Near Eastern and South Asian Affairs in 1967–1969 and was a Woodrow Wilson fellow at Princeton University in 1969–1970. In the Department he was personnel officer in the Bureau of Near Eastern and South Asian Affairs (1970–1972) and in the Bureau of Personnel (1972–1974). He was counselor for political affairs in Islamabad (1972–1977) and in New Delhi (1977–1979). In the Department he was Director for India, Nepal, Sri Lanka, Bhutan, and Maldives Affairs in 1979–1982 and since 1982 has been Deputy Assistant Secretary of State for Near Eastern and South Asian Affairs.

Mr. Schaffer graduated from Harvard University (B.A., 1950). He attended Columbia University in 1953–1955. His foreign languages are Hindi, Urdu, and French. He was born July 21, 1929, in New York, NY.

Nomination of Paul Fisher Gardner To Be United States Ambassador to Papua New Guinea and the Solomon Islands
June 13, 1984

The President today announced his intention to nominate Paul Fisher Gardner, of Texas, a career member of the Senior Foreign Service, Class of Minister-Counselor, as Ambassador to Papua New Guinea and to the Solomon Islands. He would succeed M. Virginia Schafer, who is retiring from the Foreign Service.

Mr. Gardner was an English teacher at Asherton High School in Asherton, TX, in 1953–1954, and served in the United States Air Force in 1954–1956 as first lieutenant. In 1956 he entered the Foreign Service as intelligence analyst in the Department. He was consular officer in Tananarive (1959–1961) and political officer in Vientiane (1961–1963). He attended Indonesian language training at the Foreign Service Institute in 1963–1964. In 1964–1968 he was political officer in Jakarta, and Indonesian desk officer in the Department in 1968–1971. He was counselor for political-military affairs in Phnom Penh (1972–1974), and counselor for mutual security in Ankara (1974–1976). In Jakarta he was counselor for political affairs (1976–1978) and then Deputy Chief of Mission (1978–1981). Since 1981 he has been Director of Regional Affairs in the Bureau of East Asian and Pacific Affairs in the Department.

Mr. Gardner graduated from the University of Texas (B.A., 1952; M.A., 1956). In 1952–1953 he attended the University of Bordeaux in France. His foreign languages are French and Indonesian. He was born October 31, 1930, in San Antonio, TX.

Remarks on Meeting the Boston Celtics, the National Basketball Association World Champions
June 13, 1984

Well, I thank you, and by the way, I'd like to let you in on a little secret. I wanted to welcome all of you in the Oval Office, and then I found out the ceiling is too low. [*Laughter*]

But from the Boston Garden to the Rose Garden, it's been quite a year for the Celtics, the team Boston loves and all the world admires. Over the regular season you all lived up to your awesome reputation by compiling a 62–20 record, the best in the NBA. And then came victory in the playoffs, finally the ultimate test, the championship series against the superb Los Angeles Lakers. They weren't just as superb as they should have been. [*Laughter*]

But the battle for the title turned into a spectacular, stretching over three weekends. Both teams were great, with stars on each side rising to peak performances that dazzled and thrilled the country. And last night the whole season came down to one game.

Six times before, the Boston Celtics had played in a championship series that went to seven games. Six times before, the Celtics won. And we watched, holding our breath, wondering if you'd beat the odds again, do it again. You threw yourselves into that final battle with all the pride and determination and heart that have made you a legend in basketball history. And time and again, you came down with key rebounds, shutting off the Lakers fast break. "You can't run without the ball," said Magic Johnson, "and the Celtics seemed to rebound it every time."

On the defensive boards you were a cascade, shooting again and again, and scoring: Cedric Maxwell, 24 points; Dennis Johnson, 22; and Larry Bird, 20. And the final score: 111 to 102, the Celtics had done it again.

So many people ask, how do the Celtics

do it? How do you keep coming back? How, during that crucial moment of the seventh game of a championship series, do they always manage to reach within, to find that spark that's needed for victory?

Well, Cedric Maxwell put it quite simply last night: "How could anyone have thought we'd lose? We are the Celtics, you know." Well, you are the Celtics, and like the original Celtics, the great Irish warriors in olden times, you have fought for and won great victories and great glory.

They have won, this team, 15 championships; 8 of them since 1959. And if I have my information correct, all 8 of those were with the Los Angeles Lakers, since 1959.

Well, yours is a tradition of hard work, of teamwork, of dedication, a tradition of "Celtics pride." But aren't you afraid you might be getting in a rut? [*Laughter*]

We've seen that winning tradition carried forth again and again down through the years by some of the greatest heroes in basketball history: Cousey, Sharman, Ramsey, Russell, Sam and Casey Jones, Heinsohn, Havlicek, Cowens, and White. I may have mispronounced some of those names in there—I hope not.

Casey Jones was not only a great player; this year, he proved he's an equally great coach. He's one of only a few to have won a championship as both a player and a coach.

As the leaders of your organization changed, as one group of stars was replaced by another group, the Celtics not only survived; they maintained their championship form, because always, the Celtics have been a team of champions, larger and greater than any one player, coach, or manager. And in celebrating your championship, we see how America can be a nation of champions as well.

Red Auerbach, Coach Jones, members of this proud team—high in the rafters of Boston Garden hang 14 green and white banners proclaiming the Celtics the national champions of 14 seasons past, and sometime this summer, a 15th banner is going to be hoisted into place, as I said. That banner will belong to you, and it'll remind all who see it of the way each of you have lived up to the tradition of the Boston Celtics.

So, I thank you, and congratulations, and God bless all of you.

Note: The President spoke at 1:43 p.m. in the Rose Garden at the White House.

Remarks on Presenting a Flag to the United States Olympic Committee
June 14, 1984

The President. Well, welcome to the White House. I know we were supposed to be outdoors, but the weather wouldn't cooperate with us.

It gives me great pleasure today to present a flag to Bill Simon, president of the United States Olympic Committee, to be carried by our Olympic team in Los Angeles.

The outpouring of support for our Olympic team—voluntary and springing up all across our country—makes us happy and proud. The team, walking behind the banner, our flag, in the opening ceremonies will truly be our team, America's team. And I can't help believing that on that day, July

28th, the members of our team will feel all of us there with them—all of us behind them. They'll feel our pride in them, and they'll feel the unity, the patriotism, and the deep love we share for America, for our land of the free.

On August 3d, 1949, the Congress, by a joint resolution, designated June 14th of each year as Flag Day. And the flag is the symbol of our way of life and a reminder of those things that we stand for as a people.

Ours is a beautiful flag. It always has been, ever since Betsy Ross sewed our first flag with its 13 stars in a perfect circle. But its glory is not just in its colors or design. We salute this banner because it represents the struggle of our forefathers to build a land of freedom and opportunity.

It flew over lonely outposts when pioneers tamed our wilderness. It beckoned with a spirit of hope to the tens of millions who came here from every corner of the world to better their lot and that of their families, and to live together in freedom. Brave men and women risked their lives under this flag whenever our liberty was in peril. And many, whose names we never knew, gave their lives to ensure our country's survival so that freedom, our most precious gift, would be passed on to the next generation.

In saluting this flag, we salute them too—courageous individuals to whom we owe so much. When we salute "Old Glory," how can we not remember those words of Francis Scott Key, where the glare of the rockets "gave proof through the night that our flag was still there"?

It's always been there for us. It is always there for us. It's the one symbol of all that we are and all that we hope to be. And I now give it to you, Bill, to take to Los Angeles as proof not only of our thanks to you

and to the members of our team but also of our great hopes for you.

And just remember: No matter what happens, each and every member of the United States of America Olympic team is a champion in our eyes.

Mr. Simon. God bless you, Mr. President. Thank you. Let me say a word here.

Thank you very much, Mr. President. I'm honored on behalf of the United States Olympic Committee to accept this flag. You'll see this at the head of our delegation when we march into the stadium on opening day in Los Angeles a month and a couple of weeks hence.

We're going to have a great Olympic games. We're going to have the best team in our history, in my opinion, and more countries than ever before, more athletes than ever before. We'll treasure this.

God bless you, and we look forward to welcoming you in Los Angeles. Thank you, Mr. President.

The President. All right. Thank you all.

Note: The President spoke at 2:42 p.m. in the Roosevelt Room at the White House.

Proclamation 5208—Family Reunion Month, 1984
June 14, 1984

By the President of the United States of America

A Proclamation

The family is the cornerstone of American society. As individuals and as a people, we are nurtured by our families from birth until the ends of our lives. Families link past, present, and future generations. Family members share our joys, comfort us, and help us celebrate life's milestones.

In our mobile society, great distances often separate people from their loved ones, making frequent visits difficult or impossible. Consequently, many families hold periodic reunions. At these special times, they come together to renew and refresh their relationships. They share the accomplishments and changes in their lives. They

honor those who have passed on, and they celebrate their continuing renewal through new marriages and the birth of new babies.

Unfortunately, thousands of American families experience sorrow each year because of runaway, missing or estranged members. An estimated 700,000 children between the ages of 11 and 18 are runaway or homeless youth. Many organizations have been formed in recent years to help families and missing family members establish contact with each other while respecting the right of individuals to privacy. Nonetheless, this problem is a very serious and heartbreaking one.

This Nation treasures its families and family life. All Americans should encourage families and missing family members to get in touch with each other and, if possible, to solve the problems which brought about their separation. We should encourage missing family members to make direct contact with their families or to use the organizations which offer their support and assistance. We also should encourage families whose ties are weak to seek out the programs which offer counseling and support to keep families together.

The Congress, by Senate Joint Resolution 94, has authorized and requested the President to issue a proclamation designating the period between Mother's Day, May 13, 1984, and Father's Day, June 17, 1984, as "Family Reunion Month."

Now, Therefore, I, Ronald Reagan, Presi-

dent of the United States of America, do hereby proclaim the period between May 13 and June 17, 1984, as Family Reunion Month. I call upon all Americans to celebrate this month with appropriate ceremonies and activities.

In Witness Whereof, I have hereunto set my hand this 14th day of June, in the year of our Lord nineteen hundred and eighty-four, and of the Independence of the United States of America the two hundred and eighth.

RONALD REAGAN

[*Filed with the Office of the Federal Register, 1:36 p.m., June 14, 1984*]

Appointment of Two Members of the National Institute of Justice Advisory Board
June 14, 1984

The President today announced his intention to appoint the following individuals to be members of the National Institute of Justice Advisory Board:

Joan Lipsky, for a term expiring November 6, 1986. She will succeed Pierce R. Brooks. Mrs. Lipsky is an attorney with the firm of Shuttleworth & Ingersoll in Cedar Rapids, IA. She also serves on the board of directors for Smulekoff Investment Co. and Smulekoff Furniture Co., Inc. She graduated from Northwestern University (B.S., 1940) and the University of Iowa (J.D., 1980). She is married, has three children, and resides in Cedar Rapids, IA. She

was born April 9, 1919, in Cedar Rapids.

Roberta Rose Roper, for a term expiring January 11, 1987. She will succeed Leo F. Callahan. In 1982 she became founder and spokesperson of the Stephanie Roper Committee, an all-volunteer citizens group that is now the largest victims rights organization in the United States. She is also an art teacher at St. Ambrose School in Cheverly, MD. She attended the College of William and Mary and graduated from Monterey Peninsula College (A.A., 1959) and the University of Maryland (B.S., 1979). She is married, has four children, and resides in Upper Marlboro, MD. She was born May 17, 1937, in Passaic, NJ.

Proclamation 5209—Baltic Freedom Day, 1984
June 14, 1984

By the President of the United States of America

A Proclamation

It has been over 40 years since invading Soviet armies, in collusion with the Nazi regime, overran the three independent Baltic Republics of Estonia, Latvia, Lithua-

nia and forceably incorporated them into Moscow's expanding empire. The new regime then ordered the illegal deportation, murder, and imprisonment of tens of thousands of Baltic peoples whose only "crime" was to resist foreign tyranny and to defend their liberties and freedoms.

Oppression and persecution continue to

this day, but despite this long dark night of injustice, the brave men and women of Estonia, Latvia, and Lithuania have never abandoned the battle for their national independence and God-given rights. Although the full measure of their struggle and sacrifice is screened by the oppression and censorship under which they live, the friends and families of the Baltic peoples all over the world are aware of their heroic endeavors and aspirations.

Their peaceful demands for their rights command the admiration of everyone who loves and honors freedom. All the people of the United States of America share the just aspirations of the Baltic nations for national independence, and we uphold their right to determine their own national destiny free of foreign domination. The United States has never recognized the forceable incorporation of the Baltic States into the Soviet Union, and it will not do so in the future. The Congress of the United States, by

Senate Joint Resolution 296, has authorized and requested the President to issue a proclamation for the observance of June 14, 1984, as "Baltic Freedom Day."

Now, Therefore, I, Ronald Reagan, President of the United States of America, do hereby proclaim June 14, 1984, as Baltic Freedom Day. I call upon the people of the United States to observe this day with appropriate remembrances and ceremonies and to reaffirm their commitment to the principles of liberty and freedom for all oppressed people.

In Witness Whereof, I have hereunto set my hand this fourteenth day of June, in the year of our Lord nineteen hundred and eighty-four, and of the Independence of the United States of America the two hundred and eighth.

RONALD REAGAN

[*Filed with the Office of the Federal Register, 10:35 a.m., June 15, 1984*]

The President's News Conference
June 14, 1984

London Economic Summit

The President. I have a brief opening statement, besides saying good evening.

One week ago today in London, I joined the leaders of six major industrialized democracies for the annual economic summit. And we met to take the pulse of the world economy, to measure the impact of the policies that we've been implementing during the past 3 years, and to continue strengthening the freedom, prosperity, and peace that we share.

Change comes neither easily nor quickly in foreign affairs. But there was recognition in London that, while we continue to face pressing challenges, we are on the right track. By working together, by sticking to our policies, we've made impressive progress since 1981. The Western democracies have been moving from weakness to strength, from disappointment and pessimism to confidence and hope for a better future.

In 1981 our economies had an average growth of only 1.8 percent and 8½-percent inflation. But led by the recovery, and now the expansion in the United States, our average growth today is up to 4 percent, while inflation has been cut in half. There was recognition that the incentives of America's recovery program, which sparked our economic takeoff and the creation of more than 6 million jobs in the last 18 months, have made a major contribution to the improvement in both the performance and the outlook for the world economy.

I reaffirmed to our allies America's bedrock commitment to the NATO alliance and to its mission to protect peace and freedom in the West. Europe and America have enjoyed nearly 40 years of peace. If NATO remains strong and unified—and I believe NATO is stronger and more unified today than ever before—then Europe and America will remain free and secure.

We have reestablished strength and confidence stretching beyond America's shores to Europe and the Pacific Basin, and we're trying, as well, to promote a better, more realistic, long-term relationship with the Soviet Union. And that's why we and our allies have made so many initiatives to reduce nuclear arsenals, ban chemical weapons, break the impasse in the East-West conventional force negotiations, curb nuclear proliferation, and reach agreement on proposals for increasing confidence and reducing the risk of surprise attack in Europe. The West is doing its utmost, but to date, we have met with continued Soviet unwillingness to return to the nuclear arms negotiating tables.

America's standing taller in the world today, but if we're to continue on course toward a more prosperous, peaceful world, then we need the full cooperation of the Congress. The Congress must support our strategic modernization program to keep America strong and convince the Soviets it is in their best interest to choose the course of negotiation, not confrontation, so we can safely reduce arms while preserving peace and stability.

The Congress must pass the recommendations of the bipartisan commission on Central America and the two supplemental requests now before it to promote democracy, economic development, and greater security in that vital region to our south. And the Congress must promptly pass our deficit-reduction program to help ensure that our economic recovery remains strong.

And now, Helen [Helen Thomas, United Press International], you're number one.

U.S.-Soviet Relations

Q. Mr. President, no matter what you say you've done so far, two Republican leaders don't think you've done enough, and they are urging you to hold regular summit meetings, for fear we'll blow each other up, with the Soviets without any conditions as to issues or outcome. Both you and the Soviets have said you will go to a summit, if it's carefully prepared. My question is, where do we stand now? Are you willing to go for a summit, start the ball rolling?

The President. Well, Helen, in the first place, with regard to the two Senators—and I did talk to them—they were talking about

a goal that would be desirable, that I think we all share, and we were agreed on that. And I told them some of the difficulties and problems that we've been having. But, yes, I am willing to meet and talk anytime. So far they have been the ones not responding, but we have kept in communication. There are a number of issues other than arms reductions that we have suggested talking to them about, and we're going to continue in the area of quiet diplomacy to bring that about.

Q. Well, are you going to make an affirmative move for a summit and to try to clear away some of these stumbling blocks that have really caused great East-West tensions?

The President. Well, this is what I meant with my remarks, that we are continuing to keep communication with the idea leading toward that very thing.

Q. Mr. President, do we understand you to say that you're willing now to drop your long-held view that a summit would have to be carefully prepared in advance and hold the prospect for reasonable success?

The President. Well, it wouldn't really be necessary for me to drop that, since the Russians say that that's exactly what they feel must happen before there can be a meeting, that it must be carefully prepared and—let me explain, maybe, a little more fully what, when I say that, what I have in mind.

There've been a couple of times in the past in which representatives from the Free World and from our own country have gotten into things simply to get acquainted or say hello. And they have led to great expectations, and they've led to great disappointment. And I don't think that we ought to go into something of that kind.

But at the same time, I'm not talking about, oh, a preconstructed meeting in which you've got a list of points. You can have an agenda in which it is the general area of the things that you think could lead to better understanding. And that's good enough for me.

But right now, we're getting a response from them that they want a very carefully prepared agenda. Now, if they agree with me that there are things we can talk about that might clear the air and create a better understanding between us, that's fine.

Q. Sir, if I could follow up, are you willing to take steps now to begin the process of working on an agenda so that a summit could ultimately occur?

The President. Well, we are taking steps. This is what I mean by quiet diplomacy. And I have been in communication, myself—written communication with the Soviet leadership.

There is one thing that I think—I've said this before, but that I think many of you fail to recognize, and that is, there have been three Russian heads of state since I became President. One of them I knew personally. The second one was, we now know, in ill health because he was virtually incommunicado to anyone during his period. And now this newest one is setting up an administration and so forth. So, it isn't as if we've been sitting here for 3½ years arguing with someone or not arguing with someone. There have been a lot of changes over there. But we're ready, willing, and able.

Yes?

Carter Campaign Documents

Q. Mr. President, nearly a year ago you said that you wanted to get to the bottom of the matter of the so-called briefing papers that went from the Carter White House into your 1980 campaign. I wonder, sir, if, in that year, you have ever talked to Mr. Baker and to Mr. Casey and asked them precisely what their roles were in that matter?

The President. Yes, and I think they're easily understandable. One has no recollection—and I can understand that—from a campaign of something that might come through his office and been passed on. That goes on.

I think there is one thing that ought to be cleared up about this whole case. And I did give orders to the FBI to make this investigation thorough, and I made orders—gave orders to all of our people to cooperate to the fullest extent, and they did. And the Justice Department and the FBI were satisfied that it was no criminal intent of any kind. But the thing that I want to make clear is, we still keep calling it the briefing book. Now, it was established quite a while

ago that so-called debate briefing book, the Carter team, never has been in our possession, that all that was uncovered were some position papers, the type of things that were issues during the campaign. And all of it had been out in the open and made public as the campaign went on, before the debate. But the briefing book, if you will remember, the briefing book, it was pointed out, finally someone located on the other side, and there it was and no one on this side ever saw it, nor was it ever in our hands.

Q. If I may follow up, sir, there still seems, however, to be some conflict in the matter because, although the Justice Department said no crime had been committed, a Democratic-controlled committee on the Hill says—suggests that there may have been a crime committed. In view of the fact that there is this conflict, the Democrats don't believe your Justice Department and the Republicans don't believe the Democratic committee. Wouldn't it be better to have a special prosecutor to resolve the matter once and for all?

The President. Well, that matter is in a court now, and if that is decided by the court, I will give the same orders with regard to cooperation.

Frankly, based on that Democratic committee report, it didn't make any sense at all. This has been investigated thoroughly.

Sam [Sam Donaldson, ABC News]?

U.S.-Soviet Relations

Q. Sir, in recent speeches this year about the Soviets, you have held out an olive branch to them. But at the same time, you usually either denounce their system or their actions. Would it be better, in an attempt to get this dialog started again, whether at the summit or back in Geneva, if you simply held out the olive branch without also taking a shot at them?

The President. Well, I don't think I've gone out of my way to just call them names or anything. I've usually pointed to something that is counter to their protestations of wanting peace and cooperation, such as walking away from the arms talks. I don't think that I've said anything that was as fiery as them referring to the funeral service for the unknown soldier as "a militaristic orgy." If we're going to talk about comparisons of rhetoric, they've topped me in spades.

Lesley [Lesley Stahl, CBS News]?

Q. Sir, if I may——

The President. You want——

Q. It's up to you.

The President. You know, you shorten the number of questions we get in with all these followups.

Q. All right. [*Laughter*]

The President. All right. Thank you.

Q. Anytime, sir.

Q. I don't know if everyone else is left as unclear as I am on where we stand with a summit with the Soviets. Are you inviting Mr. Chernenko to come and have a summit with you? And are you willing to have your advisers sit down with his advisers to work out the preplanning that you both say is necessary?

The President. We have been in contact with them on a number of issues that we think—bilateral issues that should be discussed between us. Of course, there is the matter of the arms talks, also, although we've not been talking about that since they have simply walked away. All I can tell you is that, in what I call quiet diplomacy we are in contact with their people trying to establish a basis for talks.

Q. Is this an invitation, though?

The President. What?

Q. Is this an invitation?

The President. We haven't reached that point yet.

Q. I'd like to join Lesley in not being quite sure here. There seems to be a change or something that we have at least not known before. Your communication with the Soviet leadership—has that been with Mr. Chernenko, and has the subject been a summit, a meeting between you and Mr. Chernenko?

The President. No, much of the communication has been simply on the broad relationship between our two countries. And my communication, by writing, has been with Mr. Chernenko.

Q. If I could just follow up, would you be willing to meet with Mr.—sorry, Sam— [*laughter*]—I guess he's much more gentlemanly. Would you be willing to meet with

Mr. Chernenko even if he won't send his delegation back to the nuclear arms talks?

The President. Yes. Yes, I'm willing to meet with him.

Chris [Chris Wallace, NBC News]?

Q. Mr. President, you have said recently that you think that U.S.-Soviet relations would improve in a second Reagan term. But several other people who have been in Moscow quote officials there as saying that isn't true, that they're not going to ever deal with you—they feel you have been too harsh. What hard evidence do you have that relations would improve after the election?

The President. Well, I've been too harsh— maybe if I apologize for shooting down the KAL 707 and some things like that then maybe they'll warm up and be willing to talk. No, I think it's very obvious that—and I wouldn't expect them to do anything that might help me in the coming election—but I think when it's over, and they know that 4 years lie out ahead, if I'm here for 4 years, I think they'll talk.

Q. Well, that brings up the question, do you think that the Soviets could get a better deal from your Democratic opponent than they could from you?

The President. Oh, I'm not going to comment on that. [*Laughter*] No, I——

Q. Mr. President, as I recall, one of your previous formulations about a summit was that you would have to have something concrete to show for it. Are you willing to have a summit that does not have a concrete agreement or piece of paper like the new SALT or START treaty or a new initiative toward a SALT or START treaty?

The President. Well, Lars [Lars-Erik Nelson, New York Daily News], I've never thought about it in a specific of that kind. As I've said, there should be an agenda, a subject that both sides want to talk about and have some desire to get a settlement. And that holds out the promise then that something might be accomplished.

When you don't plan that well, if I could recall—and I don't mean this to be critical of my predecessors—but there was a get-acquainted meeting with Lyndon Johnson, and it was nothing more than that. Then there was a meeting with Kennedy and

Khrushchev, and it didn't ease tensions or make things any better. This was the meeting in Vienna. It led to even more strains.

So, it is a two-edge sword—such a meeting. Yes, you want to accomplish something, but you want to be sure that you aren't going to lead to more trouble.

Q. My point was, you're willing to have a summit that does not end in the signing of a treaty on arms control?

The President. Oh, yes, I've said that once already here.

Yes?

Q. What is your time frame on this if you are now willing to negotiate the possibility of a summit? Do you think it could be held before the election?

The President. Whenever the conditions that lead to having one would be fine. But one thing—let me say and make clear—I'm not going to play political games with this subject and go rushing out for some kind of political advantage to announce that I have asked for a summit meeting. That wouldn't do either one of us any good and certainly wouldn't be fair to them.

But this is legitimate. The door is open. And every once in a while, we're standing in the doorway, seeing if anyone's coming up the steps.

Q. What's your estimation, sir, on a time frame?

The President. I couldn't give you one.

Q. Mr. President, some of your advisers are saying privately that the Soviet leadership now is actually so divided and uncertain that there's really not much hope of progress at this time, and you seem to hint that when you say that there've been three leaders since you've been in office. Is that your view? And what are the implications of that?

The President. Well, we don't know. There's been the theory advanced that they're kind of marking time, and, perhaps, in some disagreement about what course they should follow. But there's no way to know that. So, we'll just keep on trying.

Dean [Dean Reynolds, Cable News Network]?

Presidential Campaign Debates

Q. Mr. President, if I could get back to political games for a second, former Presi-

dent Carter said earlier this month that despite your statements—generally in favor of a debate with your opponent—that he thinks you're going to duck your Democratic opponent and will never face him in a face-to-face debate. Now that former Vice President Walter Mondale is the apparent Democratic nominee, can you now promise that you will participate in a Presidential debate with him?

The President. President Carter said that I would hide? There he goes again. [*Laughter*] I would look forward to a debate.

Lou [Lou Cannon, Washington Post]?

U.S.-Soviet Relations

Q. Mr. President, today the chief Kremlin spokesman said, "We want to have negotiations with the United States on a whole complex of issues," which is certainly something different than Mr. Chernenko said the day before. Do you read this as a change in Soviet policy or tactics? Is there something going on there that is happening very quickly in relations between our two countries?

The President. We'll give them—we'll take a chance on finding out on that, because, as I say, we are in communication. And if they're ready to talk, we are too.

Eleanor [Eleanor Clift, Newsweek]?

Q. Mr. President——

The President. Wait a minute, I called on Eleanor.

Affirmative Action Programs

Q. Mr. President, do you interpret the Supreme Court decision this week in the Memphis firefighters case as the death knell of affirmative action as we have known it in hiring and promotion?

The President. No, I don't think that at all. I think the Supreme Court was interpreting—giving an interpretation of what the law actually says. And as a matter of fact, I think, in the discussion, up came the point that back when that was being discussed, Hubert Humphrey, in the debate in the Senate, said that the law did not provide for quotas; the law is to prevent discrimination against individuals. And this was what the Supreme Court has said in that case.

President's Commission on Organized Crime

Q. Mr. President, last year you set in action a commission on organized crime. Could you tell me why, as the first part of a two-part question, why this commission refuses to say whether it is investigating Louis Farrakhan despite seven Hanafi Muslims and Malcolm X being shot by Mr. Farrakhan's accomplices?

The President. I would have no way of knowing, but a commission that is engaged in a study, I'm quite sure that they're not going to talk about things that they are currently doing. I think the very nature of that kind of investigation would indicate that they will report when they have everything wrapped up and tied up and all the evidence that they need for any conclusions they come to.

Q. To follow up, sir, in your setting up this commission under Judge Kaufman of New York, you specified drugs. Are you at all concerned about Bob Woodward's reports of widespread cocaine use at the Washington Post, or do you kind of "shuff" it off and explaining that this illustrates a lot about why the Post publishes some of the things that it does. [*Laughter*]

The President. I'll only say, and with regard to that question, is that you are tempting me beyond my strength. [*Laughter*]

Q. Yield!

Federal Deficit

Q. You noted in your opening remarks the debate on the Hill about the deficit-reduction package. Given some problems we're having with the spending side but not on the tax side, would you be willing to sign a tax package without a spending package attached?

The President. Only if I had assurance that the spending package was coming along. There would be no point in the other. This triad that was worked out, this three-legged stool of domestic spending, defense cuts that we finally agreed to, and some changes, some reforms, in the tax structure that closed some certain loopholes, and so forth—this has to go together.

I made the mistake of going along with the tax increase in the guise of the same kind of treatment on the promise of cuts that I never then obtained. And the deficit would be considerably smaller if I had gotten those cuts that I has asked for. This time I'm going to be pretty sure——

Q. Does that mean, then, you might want them to wait from sending a tax package up until they've actually completed the spending package?

The President. No, as I say, if there is assurance that the appropriation bills are going to come up, that they're working on that also, I'm prepared to look them in the eye and say all right.

Yes?

Immigration Legislation

Q. Mr. President, you and your campaign organization have spent a lot of time trying to increase your support among Hispanic voters, yet you continue to support the controversial immigration bill on the Hill now. Will that not hurt you with Hispanic voters in the fall?

The President. Well, I know that there are people—I can understand their concern and their fear. I think that if we take every precaution we can in that immigration bill to make sure that there is not discrimination simply based on the not wanting to bother as to whether an individual is legal or not, I think we can protect against that.

But the simple truth is that we've lost control of our own borders, and no nation can do that and survive. And I think the thing that they should be looking at, that should be of the greatest appeal to them is the very generous amnesty, that all the way up to 1982, we're ready to give those people permanent residency.

Q. Mr. President——

The President. No—you. Andrea [Andrea Mitchell, CBS News]?

U.S.–Soviet Relations

Q. Mr. President, you've said tonight that you're ready and willing to talk to the Soviets. But Mr. Chernenko has proposed negotiating a ban on antisatellite weapons and other space weapons. Can you tell us why, beyond the fact that you believe there can't be verification, as you said last weekend, why can't verification be negotiated once you sit down with the Soviets to discuss those weapons?

The President. Well, there are a number of things, and we are studying that. We don't have a flat "no" on that yet. We're studying that whole situation.

The Soviets are way ahead of us in that field. They've been at this for about 10 years or more. And we are just in the field of beginning research. And I think we've got some definite reasons there for wanting to know our way before we talk. But we haven't slammed the door on that at all.

Q. Well, can you also confirm reports about the verification issue, that there has been significant Soviet violations of all of the treaties going back to 1958?

The President. We turned over a 200-page report to the Congress that was classified. We made public a summary of that, declassified in a summary. The other lengthy report is still classified because of the risk of exposing sources. But it was a report on outright violations of many of the treaties in the past, and also some ambiguities in which—maybe based on language differences or not—they claim a different interpretation of the treaty and that, therefore, they're not violating it. They have this—they're doing what they think the treaty prescribes.

But between those two things, yes, there have been those violations.

Yes?

Q. Mr. President, before you came along, in recent years, the talk had been between the two governments of parity in force between the United States and the Soviet Union. Your supporters who wrote the 1980 Republican platform called for military superiority over the Soviet Union. It's been a little bit fuzzy since, although you, in a couple of speeches, I think, starting with the Star Wars speech, have gone back to using the parlance of parity. How do you feel the Republican platform this year would handle that issue? And between those two key words, "superiority" and "parity," where should that platform go and your administration go?

The President. My own view is that we should maintain the strength and deterrent that is necessary to assure, as much as you can have such assurance, that there won't

be a confrontation, because the price would be too high, but, at the same time, emphasizing that we want more than anything else to join with them in reducing the number of weapons.

We've had arms limitation dealings and treaties and so forth, even such as the SALT treaties. All of those simply legalized an arms race. They were limitations or rules and regulations as to how many more weapons you could have. As a matter of fact, the Soviet Union added almost 4,000 warheads after the two sides had signed the SALT II agreement. That's not my idea of what we really need if we're to reduce the tensions in the world. What we need is to reduce, and, hopefully, to eliminate, the strategic nuclear weapons.

Q. If I may follow up, you're on record, and I think at least twice, of saying that we do not seek anything more than parity in the long run. Would not a platform that goes further than that and repeats the call for superiority give a wrong signal to the Soviet Union?

The President. I would prefer that we not ask for superiority now that we've entered into and started this whole area. We are negotiating with them with other countries in two negotiations that are going on that they did not leave or walk away from. And, yes, I believe that it could be counterproductive now to ask for that.

President's Second Term

Q. Mr. President, if you win a second term, are you absolutely committed to serving all 4 years? I ask the question only because of a Washington magazine reporting—I don't know how they knew—that you and the First Lady had discussed the possibility of, if you win again and if the economy's in good shape, when you're 75 or 76 years old, possibly turning over power. Have you ever thought about that? Have you considered it or discussed with the First Lady that in any case? [*Laughter*]

The President. What the devil would a young fellow like me do if I quit the job? [*Laughter*]

Q. You have not discussed it with the First Lady?

The President. No, there's never been any

such talk at all.

Employment Rights for Homosexuals

Q. Mr. President, there is a move afoot in the Congress that has the support of many of the Democratic Presidential candidates to change the Federal civil rights law to prohibit job discrimination against homosexuals. Is that something that you would favor?

The President. Now, I was so—you're going to have to start again here for—first few words. I missed them. I was so confused about three of you——

Q. There's a measure before the Congress to change the Federal civil rights law to specifically prohibit job discrimination against homosexuals. Is that something that you would favor?

The President. Well, I just have to say I am opposed to discrimination, period. Now——

Q. Well, would you support the measure, Mr. President?

The President. What?

Q. Will you support that measure, putting it into——

The President. I want to see—I want to see what else they have there.

Yes? No, her.

Civil Rights

Q. Mr. President, the Kerner report said that the United States is moving towards two societies, one black and one white, separate and unequal. Now, with the outcries from blacks, Hispanics, American Indians, and women against your civil rights policies, aren't you moving this country into two separate societies—one of white males, and the other of blacks, Hispanics, American Indians, and women—separate and unequal?

The President. I don't believe there's been any violation of either the letter or the spirit of the civil rights laws—nor would I stand for such a thing.

There has been no discrimination of any kind in this administration—nor would I stand for that—on the part of anyone. And I think that what we have done—if we will get our information from the horse's mouth, our administration, and not from the political rhetoric that has been so prevalent in

the last year, I think we can establish that no administration has done more than we have done with regard to any of these people that you speak of.

With regard to women—I think our appointments, themselves—but, I think, more than that, no government, no administration has done what we have done in the cleaning out of laws and eliminating statutes that have discriminatory language; our work with the States on the same thing, the same basis. And the same thing would go with regard to minorities and blacks and their place in the government itself. But everything that we have done—we haven't done anything that in any way discriminated against any of those people. We have done things that we think are helpful.

Q. I want to follow on that. The leadership conference, which met this past week, said that you are the greatest opponent to civil rights, as a President, in the last two decades. And they gave—very specific showing—that your policies are attempting to reverse the civil rights gains. And now these grassroots people believe that you have been blaming the leaders, and Brad Reynolds has been blaming the media. But aren't you underestimating the intelligence of the grassroots people if you think that they don't know what they're suffering from? And this is going to be—isn't this going to really cause a division in this country rather than a unified country unless you can convince these people, who are the victims of these policies? If you can't convince them that their conditions are better, then you're working toward a disunified country, aren't you?

The President. Well, I think the reduction in inflation certainly has got to help people. I'm sure you're talking about people at the lower end of the earning scale.

Our tax policies have been more beneficial to them than to anyone else. This idea that we hear on Capitol Hill all the time that our tax programs benefited the rich—the figures belie that. The people in the upper-income brackets are paying a greater percentage of the overall income tax than they were paying before our tax program went into effect. The people at the bottom of the scale are paying less, a lower percentage.

But now the other point, the inference that programs of a welfare nature—social programs and benefits have been reduced to the place that people dependent on them are now suffering—that is not true. We are helping more people and paying more money than ever in the history of this country in all of those social programs. The Government is providing 95 million meals a day. I could go on with the others.

Some of the things that have led perhaps to confusion—is taking something like the educational programs. We found out that people were eligible when we came here for college grants and loans for their children, and their income level was too high for this to be warranted. So, yes, we changed the income level, but this allowed us to increase further down to the people with real need and do more for them.

For example, we probably eliminated 850,000 people from food stamps. But we increased the number of people who were getting food stamps, because we transferred this from people who were at a higher level. Our level now of income for most of these programs, if not all, is 130 percent of the poverty level. If you're below that,

you're eligible. And most families would find themselves eligible for three or four of the programs at the same time. And it is a falsehood that is being purveyed to people that their problems, whether through unemployment or whatever—look at what we've done by the increase in unemployment. And, granted, that blacks in this country had a higher rate of unemployment than whites at the time of the recession; their rate of recovery is faster than the rate of recovery for whites.

Ms. Thomas. Thank you, Mr. President.

The President. Thank you, Helen.

Q. Are you willing to separate these job programs, summer job programs from the Nicaragua aid, covert aid?

The President. I want both these programs. I want jobs for the young people, the summer jobs, and I want the Nicaraguan aid.

Q. Did you drink your wine yet? [*Laughter*] Your summit wine, did you drink it?

The President. No. I'm aging it. [*Laughter*]

Note: The President's 25th news conference began at 8:01 p.m. in the East Room at the White House. It was broadcast live on nationwide radio and television.

Nomination of Alberto Martinez Piedra To Be United States Ambassador to Guatemala
June 15, 1984

The President today announced his intention to nominate Alberto Martinez Piedra, of Maryland, as Ambassador to Guatemala. He would succeed Frederic L. Chapin.

Mr. Piedra was a professor at the University of Villanova, in Havana, Cuba, in 1958 (April-December) and in 1959 (June-September). In 1959 he was Director General of Exports and Imports of the Ministry of Commerce in Havana. He was staff economist with the Organization of American States in Washington, DC, in 1960–1964, and associate professor at the Catholic University of America in 1964–1982. Since

1982 he has been with the Department of State as United States Representative to the Inter-American Economic and Social Council of the Organization of American States and senior policy adviser.

Mr. Piedra received his doctor of law in 1951 from the University of Havana (Cuba), his doctor in political economy in 1957 from the University of Madrid (Spain), and Ph.D. in 1962 from Georgetown University. His foreign languages are Spanish, French, German, Italian, and Portuguese. He was born January 29, 1926, in Havana, Cuba, and became a United States citizen in 1969.

Appointment of George B. Price as a Member of the Board of Visitors of the United States Military Academy
June 15, 1984

The President today announced his intention to appoint George B. Price to be a member of the Board of Visitors to the United States Military Academy for a term expiring December 30, 1986. He will succeed Patrick Caddell.

General Price is special assistant to the president of Unified Industries, Inc., and executive vice president of Southern Brand Snacks, Inc. Previously he was Chief of Staff and Chief Operations Officer of the 1st U.S. Army located in Ft. Meade, MD, (1976–1978) and city manager for an American city located in Nürnberg, Germany, in 1971–1976. General Price retired from the U.S. Army after 28 years in the grade of brigadier general.

He graduated from South Carolina State College (B.S., 1951) and Shippensburg State College (M.S., 1971). He also attended the Army War College and the United States Army Command and General Staff College. He is married, has four children, and resides in Columbia, MD. He was born August 28, 1929, in Laurel, MS.

Radio Address to the Nation on the American Family
June 16, 1984

My fellow Americans:

Tomorrow is Father's Day, so naturally our thoughts turn to them and to the well-being of family life in America. Families have always stood at the center of our society, preserving good and worthy traditions from our past, entrusting those traditions to our children, our greatest hope for the future.

Family life has changed much down through the years. The days when we could expect to live in only one home and hold only one job are probably gone forever. Perhaps we will not go back to the old family ways, but I think we can and should preserve family values—values of faith, honesty, responsibility, tolerance, kindness, and love. And we'll keep on trying to do better, trying to create a better life for those who follow.

This hasn't been easy to do in the last decade. It's become more difficult to raise children than it once was. For example, the dependency exemption on your income tax: The money you can deduct for raising a child or caring for an elderly relative was $600 in the late forties. That's been increased to a thousand dollars now. But if that deduction has been indexed to keep pace with inflation, today you would be deducting more than $3,000 for every one of your children.

Housing became harder to afford. And the cost of private education also became too expensive for millions of middle-income families. By 1980 American families felt the full shock of runaway taxes, inflation, record interest rates, and soaring prices for housing, education, food, and other necessities of life. They saw the golden promise of the American dream disappearing behind storm clouds of economic misery.

Liberals urged huge government subsidies, paying parents for expenses they used to handle themselves. But big government becoming Big Brother, pushing parents aside, interfering with one parental responsibility after another, is no solution. It only makes bad situations worse, raising prices and taxes for everyone.

We came to Washington with a better idea—help working parents to better provide for themselves and their children by enabling them to keep more of their earnings and help them by making government do its job so the terrifying specter of runaway price increases never returns.

Our tax rate reductions have helped parents, reducing the tax bill that would have been owed by a typical family by over $900 a year. And we've helped parents by reducing the inflation rate by nearly two-thirds since 1980 and by creating more than 6 million new jobs. Things are getting better for American families, but much remains to be done. That's why the Treasury Department is making greater tax fairness and greater tax incentives for families a central consideration in the tax reform proposals they're developing.

We're trying hard to help fathers and mothers in other ways, too. Many innocent children are exploited by those who traffic in the gutter of drugs, child pornography and prostitution. Last month I signed the Child Protection Act of 1984, a key part of our determination to crack down hard on the smut merchants. And this past week, we opened a National Center for Missing and Exploited Children to help educate parents and authorities on how to protect their loved ones.

We've just launched a nationwide citizen effort to encourage volunteer, court-appointed special advocates in legal cases of neglect and child abuse. Soon, we'll start up a sophisticated detective program to help law enforcement officers identify and capture the so-called serial killers who prey upon women and children. And we've urged the Congress to pass a law that will strengthen and improve child support from absent parents. Children should not be financially abandoned just because they're separated from one of their parents.

We're trying hard to make two other changes. We want to see fewer abandoned, handicapped, or underprivileged children left in perpetual foster care. And we want to see the unborn child given his or her chance to live and to know the joys of life. Adoption is often the best option. Too often, it's been the forgotten option.

We're seeing hopeful signs that our policies are paying off. Family income is improving; infant mortality rates continue to drop. And the crime rate has taken a steep dive. The outlook for families in America is better today than in 1980. And we're determined to make it better still.

Happy Father's Day. Until next week, thanks for listening, and God bless you.

Note: The President spoke at 12:06 p.m. from Camp David, MD.

Remarks at the Opening of the 1984 International Games for the Disabled in Uniondale, New York
June 17, 1984

Thank you, Fran. Governor Cuomo, Senator D'Amato, the Representatives here— Lent and McGrath and Mrazek—ladies and gentlemen and honored athletes:

Today we mark a dramatic and meaningful event, the opening of the 1984 International Games for the Disabled. The first games took place in Canada in 1976, the second in 1980 in Holland. This year, it is America's turn to host disabled athletes from around the world. I know I speak for the American people when I say that this is a great honor for our country.

The setting for the games could hardly be more spectacular. The new Mitchell Park Athletic Complex features superb facilities for competitors and spectators alike, including one of the finest tracks in the world. Nearby schools like Hofstra University and Nassau Community College are providing sites for a number of competitions and housing hundreds of the athletes. Scores of individuals and businesses have been generous in sponsoring these games. Thousands of volunteers have already been at work for months coordinating events and helping with athletes' travel arrangements.

As the games themselves take place, the volunteers will work even harder, keeping score, looking after equipment, helping to provide medical attention, and translating for competitors who speak a dozen foreign languages. As far as I can see, just about everybody in Nassau County has lent a hand.

I know that you're in for a glorious time, and I want to thank you for all your hard work and dedication. Yet all of us agree that these games belong to one group alone—the athletes.

Nearly two thousand of you have come here today from some 54 countries. From Africa, Europe, Australia, South America, Asia, and North America, you have gathered here, a group of indomitable men and women. During the next 2 weeks, you'll test your endurance in swimming and running. You'll prove your strength in weightlifting. You'll show your speed and agility in basketball and high jumping. And in the equestrian events, you'll show the beautiful teamwork that can take place between man or woman and horse.

Sports have always been an important part of my life. As a matter of fact, I just was reminded as I sat down here that Fran and I played against each other during World War II, on a couple of Army teams—basketball teams—back in 1944. I don't mind telling you—his team won. [*Laughter*]

I think I can appreciate—and I know he can, at least a little—what these games must mean to you. There will be the comradery of teamwork, the thrill of competition, the sheer joy of meeting other athletes who love the sport as much as you do. Roger Bannister, the first runner in history to break the 4-minute mile, once said, "Running has given me a glimpse of the greatest freedom that a man can ever know, because it results in the simultaneous liberation of both body and mind." Exhilaration of mind and body, that's something that all athletes understand. Yet there's something each of you understands that no one else can ever fully appreciate, something that has to do with courage, with willpower, and with the utter refusal to give up that has enabled you to rise above your disabilities and compete.

Each of you is a remarkable person, a person like Canadian Arnie Boldt. Arnie lost one leg above the knee, but when he high jumps, he can take his body farther into the air than most people are tall. Trischa Zorn, of Mission Viejo, California, is legally blind. But that didn't keep her from winning an athletic scholarship to the University of Nebraska and becoming one of the fastest backstroke swimmers in the world. Harri Juahiainew of Finland is an amputee, but he can run 400 meters in less than 50 seconds. And then there's Charlie Reid. Charlie works out twice a week with the New York Knights, a sports group run by United Cerebral Palsy of New York City. Today, Charlie can bench press 480 pounds, 2½ times his own weight and there's a good chance that at these games, Charlie will set a new world record.

By competing in these games, each of you is sending a message of hope throughout the world. You're proving that a disability doesn't have to stand in the way of a full and active life, and you're showing all of us just how far a man or woman can go if only they have the dedication and the will.

A month after these games end, another great sporting event will begin, the Olympic games in Los Angeles. Athletes from all over the world will gather for those games just as you've gathered here today. Those athletes may post faster times or lift heavier weights, but sports has less to do with things like times and weights and distances than with something very simple, the human heart. And when it comes to that, the athletes in Los Angeles will have to tip their hats to you, because you are the champions of the world.

And now it is my honor to declare the 1984 International Games for the Disabled officially open.

Thank you, and God bless you all. Thank you. Begin the games.

Note: The President spoke at 4:26 p.m. at Mitchell Park Field. He was introduced by Francis T. Purcell, county executive of Nassau County.

Following his appearance at the games, the President returned to Washington, DC.

Remarks at the Welcoming Ceremony for President J.R. Jayewardene of Sri Lanka
June 18, 1984

President Reagan. President Jayewardene, Nancy and I are very pleased to have this opportunity to welcome you and Mrs. Jayewardene to the White House.

Although our two countries are on opposite sides of the globe, we share a common bond in the great institution of democracy. Sri Lanka, Mr. President, has a remarkable record among nations which won their independence in the aftermath of World War II. You've held elections at regular intervals, and with almost equal regularity, your own hard-fought reflection—or reelection in 1982, as a notable exception, your people, through their votes, have removed from power the governing party. And in what distinguishes Sri Lanka as a truly democratic country, losers as well as winners accept the verdict of the people. The true winners are, of course, the people of Sri Lanka.

I'm told, Mr. President, that in your embassy here in Washington, pictures of every Sri Lanka head of government since independence—those from your own party, as well as the opposition—are respectfully displayed. This is the kind of democratic spirit essential to the success of human liberty, the hallmark of democratic societies.

Understanding and appreciating your personal commitment to democratic ideals, Mr. President, it is a pleasure for us to have you as our guest. You underscored this heartfelt commitment during your first visit here in September of 1951, during a gathering of the representatives of nations who had fought in the Pacific war. Some at that San Francisco conference insisted that Japan should not be given its full freedom. They argued that Japan should remain shackled as a punishment for its role in World War II. As the representative of Sri Lanka, you spoke out for the principle of freedom for all people, including the Japanese. You quoted Buddha, the great teacher, and said that "hatred ceases not by hatred, but by love."

Mr. President, we share your dedication

to freedom and good will. This is more than political theory; it's a way of life. This spirit makes it natural that our two nations should be friends.

Unfortunately, not everyone shares these values. Recently, we were reminded of the menace of those who seek to impose their will by force and terror. Two American citizens were kidnaped in Sri Lanka and threatened with death. I want to take this opportunity, Mr. President, to thank you personally for your diligence and for your resolute handling of this difficult situation. The skill and courage that you demonstrated helped free our countrymen and, at the same time, prevented the terrorists from achieving their goal.

During that time of tension, you wrote to me, and I want you to know how much I appreciated your sharing your thoughts. You wrote, "I hope that the international community will be able to eradicate terrorism, which has become a major challenge to those of us who believe in the democratic process." Well, I speak for all my countrymen—and after the economic summit I recently attended in London, I know this sentiment is shared by the people of all the democracies—when I say the free men and women of this planet will never cower before terrorists. Human liberty will prevail and civilization will triumph over this cowardly form of barbarism.

Mr. President, we applaud your determination not to yield to terrorism in your own country, as well as your efforts to find through the democratic process a peaceful resolution of communal strife. There is no legitimate excuse for any political group to resort to violence in Sri Lanka, a country with a strong democratic tradition and peaceful means to resolve conflict.

As a nation of many races, religions, and ethnic groups, we Americans know from experience that there is room for all in a democracy. Dividing your country into separate nations, as some would have you do, is not the solution. Instead of separating people, now is the time to bring them together. In the same spirit you spoke about in San Francisco three decades ago, of love, not hatred, a united, progressive Sri Lanka can flourish and live in peace with itself and the rest of the world.

Mr. President, we wish you every success in your search for reconciliation and a better life for all your people. And their lives are improving. Your leadership has increased productivity and brought down unemployment, has created exciting, new opportunities for your citizens. Sri Lanka is among those enlightened nations that understand incentives hold the key for greater economic growth and personal opportunity. I believe your people and their children will reap rewards for many years to come, thanks to the bold economic steps that you've taken.

We're pleased that Americans are playing a part in this effort. Your endeavors to improve your people's economic well-being continues to have our solid support. Your country has vast potential.

Mr. President, Sri Lanka is an example of independent people determining their own destiny and a country which the United States is proud to count among its friends.

Mr. President and Mrs. Jayewardene, welcome to America.

President Jayewardene. President Reagan, Madam Reagan, ladies and gentlemen, I'm glad that Mrs. Jayewardene and I were able to accept the invitation extended by Mrs. Reagan and you to visit your great country.

We have come a very long way from home. Yet already we feel we are among friends who believe and try to follow common ideas for the welfare of humanity.

This is not our first visit. We came in September 1951 to your west coast to attend the Japanese peace treaty conference held at San Francisco. I came as my country's representative. I received then a full measure of praise and gratitude from members of the United States Government of the day—Dean Acheson, John Foster Dulles, and others who attended the conference—for helping to secure the acceptance by the conference of the peace treaty with Japan. The Japanese leaders, Prime Minister Yoshida and others, were equally grateful. Those alive are still so.

I mention that because the thinking of the people of my country, which was expressed by me on that occasion, was that we should not ask for reparations from a fallen foe who had harmed our land and people also; that we should forgive those who were our enemies, quoting the words of the Buddha that "hatred ceases not by hatred, but by love," which you, also, Mr. President, just quoted. I pleaded that we should restore to Japan the freedoms of democracy. Those were the ideals which inspired us then and inspire us now.

Our history and civilization have survived in an unbroken sequence from the fifth century B.C. for 2,500 years. There were glimpses of modern democracy even then, as in the appointment of mayors to our ancient cities. The ruins of state buildings still contain carvings in stone where the cabinet of the kings and their ministers sat. We were the first in Asia in 1865 to select members to the municipalities that governed our major cities and, in 1931, under universal franchise, to exercise our right to elect the government of our choice.

We also have, in our country, an unbroken, historical record, extending over the same long period, of a line of heads of state, monarchies of different dynasties from Sri Lanka and abroad, including India and the United Kingdom, of two Presidents, one selected and one, myself, elected by the whole country. I happen to be the 193d in the line of heads of state from 483 B.C. to date.

In our modern history, we cannot forget the contribution made by an American, Colonel Olcott, when he helped the Buddhist leaders of Sri Lanka a hundred years ago to establish a movement for the revival of education, through schools owned and managed by the Buddhists themselves, and thus laid the foundation for the revival of Buddhism and the movement for freedom.

The United States of America, since it was born out of a revolution which freed it from foreign rule, has not been known to be hankering after territory or supporting imperialism. Sri Lanka has been for 53 years a practicing democracy, where the freedoms of speech and writing, of electing governments by universal franchise at regular intervals, and the independence of the judiciary and of the opposition are safeguarded.

Fundamental rights which are justiciable are guaranteed under the constitution. Though there are occasions when emergency powers have had to be exercised, fundamental freedoms remain intact. Democracy, Mr. President, cannot, however, live and survive on a diet of words alone. The people require food for their stomachs, clothing for their bodies, and roofs over their heads.

In the nonaligned world of developing nations, which covers the whole of Central and South America, the whole of Africa, the whole of Asia from the Mediterranean Sea to the seas of China and Japan, there are very few countries which could be called a democracy, such as is your country. Ours is one. That is why the assistance that developing nations of the world receive from the World Bank and the International Monetary Fund is appreciated, though there are many matters on which we feel there should be change to help them to exist as free countries.

We the developing world have problems similar to those who live in the developed world. We have deficit budgets, high interest rates, old valued currencies, and unstable exchange rates. These are the classical examples of the symptoms that affect both the developed and developing nations.

Those who speak so eloquently on behalf of the developing nations have been pressing for the opening of commodity markets of the developed world for their manufacturers without protective laws, stable prices for all products, and rescheduling of debts borrowed for development. Consider these requests, Mr. President, with sympathy and generosity.

In our own case, with the aid received we have been able to commence and have almost completed the largest development program, which in our long history has ever been attempted by king or president, a program possibly unequalled in magnitude by any development program in any country in the contemporary world or early. This was possible due to the effects of my government, which was elected to office in 1977 in an election conducted by our oppo-

nents, the previous government. We obtained 51 percent of the votes and won five-sixths of the seats in the legislature. And subsequently since then, we have won five elections, including the Presidential election, byelections, district council elections, local elections, and a referendum.

We have, however, our problems. Some of them are unique to our country—excessive rains, sometimes floods, landslides, cyclones—some common to all countries, but still difficult for us to bear.

Another and a modern problem, and one of universal occurrence today, is terrorism. This happened in the extreme north of our country, where a group of misguided people of Tamil birth, who were favored by the American people in the latter half of the 19th century by the erection of schools and hospitals, seek separation from a united Sri Lanka. There are more Tamils living in the east and among the Sinhalese, the major community, than in the regions that seek separation who do not support them. My party holds 10 out of 12 seats in the eastern province, which separatists seek to join to the north.

The terrorists are a small group who seek by force, including murder, robberies, and other misdeeds, to support the cause of separation, including the creation of a Marxist state in the whole of Sri Lanka and in India, beginning with Tamil Nadu in the south. Since we assumed office in 1977, members of the armed services and police, politicians who leave the ranks of the separatists and join us, and others, and innocent citizens numbering 147 have been murdered in cold blood.

I'm glad, Mr. President, that your country is taking a lead in creating an international movement to oppose terrorism. If I may suggest, it may be called a United Nations antiterrorism organization. It is vital—it is essential that the developed world helps us with finances, that we help each other in this sphere, and that all nations cooperate to eliminate the menace of terrorism from the civilized world.

I was very happy when I read your address to the Irish Parliament on June 4th. You made an appeal to nations to reform the principle not to use force in their dealings with each other. You said the democracies could inaugurate a program to promote the growth of democratic institutions throughout the world. You spoke on behalf of hundreds of millions who live on the borderline of starvation while nations will spend next year a trillion dollars on the manufacturing of armaments for destruction of human beings and their products.

At meetings of members of the Commonwealth in Sydney, in New Delhi, at meetings of nonaligned nations in Havana and in Goa, New India, I have never failed to express similar ideas. Nonviolence is "Maithri" compassion, and the great teacher whom I follow, Gautama Buddha, and the great teacher you follow, Jesus Christ, and India's great son, Mahatma Gandhi, preached and practiced the doctrine of nonviolence successfully.

Let your great and powerful nation take the lead in implementing these ideals, and the world will remember that the President of the United States of America, Ronald Reagan, preached the laying down of arms

not through fear, but by the strength of the conviction that to follow right for right is right, without fear of consequence, is a way for civilized man to adopt. The voice of America will then become the voice of righteousness.

I thank you, Mr. President and Madam Reagan, for inviting us and giving me this opportunity of speaking to you, and for entertaining us so hospitably. Thank you.

Note: President Reagan spoke at 10:05 a.m. on the South Lawn of the White House, where President Jayewardene was accorded a formal welcome with full military honors.

Following the ceremony, the two Presidents met privately in the Oval Office. They then joined U.S. and Sri Lankan officials for a meeting in the Cabinet Room.

Prior to President Jayewardene's arrival at the White House, the President greeted Col. Robert G. Krause, Commander, 3d, United States Infantry (the Old Guard), on the South Lawn. Colonel Krause is Commander of Troops for the White House welcoming ceremonies.

Remarks on Accepting a Gift From the People of Sri Lanka
June 18, 1984

President Jayewardene. Mr. President Reagan, ladies and gentlemen, on behalf of the Government, the people of Sri Lanka, Mrs. Jayewardene, and myself, I have great happiness in presenting to President Reagan and Mrs. Reagan and the people of the United States of America, a friendly country, small baby elephant.

It's a female. Its name is Jayathu, meaning "Victory." The elephant is my party symbol. And it's a very intelligent kind of animal, never forgets a wrong. It always remembers a right done to it.

May it live long in your country. May it, in its own way, help your people. Thank you.

President Reagan. Mr. President, I am exceptionally pleased to make the acquaintance of our new friend—am I pronouncing it right?—Jayathu. And Jayathu, as you've

been told, means victory. And I know that it is the symbol of your own political party, and as you say, it is the symbol of our Republican Party. And I appreciate, in view of her name, I appreciate your fine sense of timing. [*Laughter*]

I understand now that Jayathu, until now, has lived in the baby elephant orphanage in the pleasant hill country of Sri Lanka. And her survival is testimony to the traditional respect which your people have for their environment and for wildlife. We Americans admire you and your government's dedication to preserve God's gifts of nature.

And we like to think in the United States that the elephant is an animal with a good memory. Now, Jayathu is very young and can look forward to a long and happy life here in Washington where she will have a home in our National Zoo. And she will continue to remind us of the friendship between the people of Sri Lanka and the people of the United States.

And I hope to have a little more time to be on hand to watch her grow. [*Laughter*]

President Jayewardene. Undressing, Jayathu, is not a habit to be followed. [*Laughter*]

Reporter. He won't work for peanuts, you know. [*Laughter*]

President Reagan. Maybe the zoo will let her come to the ranch and visit a few times. [*Laughter*]

Q. So cute.

Q. How old will she get to be?

President Jayewardene. 18 months.

Q. How old will she get?

President Jayewardene. Well, can live to my age—76. [*Laughter*]

Q. 76? Are you really 76?

President Jayewardene. I think so.

Q. He's 73, you know.

Q. How big will she get?

President Jayewardene. Well—[*indicating size*]——

Q. I mean, how big will she grow?

President Jayewardene. Well, about this size.

Q. Oh, really?

President Jayewardene. 14 feet.

Q. Elephants still do work in your coun-try?

President Jayewardene. Oh, yes, They work for their living.

Q. Bring your friend over, Mr. President. [*Laughter*]

Q. Bring your friend over, Jayathu.

Q. Can we meet her?

President Jayewardene. Yes, why not. Come, come.

Q. Hello, Jayathu. Hello.

Q. Can I touch her?

President Jayewardene. Oh, yes.

Q. He may touch you.

Q. Hello, baby.

Q. Who's going to win the election here this fall? [*Laughter*]

Q. Is this a good omen for the party?

President Reagan. Well, of course. [*Laughter*] She has lots of time to grow, be around.

President Jayewardene. Everything he does with the trunk. He smells, he feels.

Q. Will that cut the grass? [*Laughter*]

President Reagan. No, I think the zoo will probably handle that. [*Laughter*] That trunk business is really pulling to see if there's something in your hand. [*Laughter*]

Note: President Reagan spoke at 11:30 a.m. on the South Lawn of the White House.

Nomination of Leonardo Neher To Be United States Ambassador to Upper Volta
June 18, 1984

The President today announced his intention to nominate Leonardo Neher, of Maryland, a career member of the Senior Foreign Service, Class of Counselor, as Ambassador to the Republic of Upper Volta. He would succeed Julius Waring Walker, Jr.

Mr. Neher served in the U.S. Army in 1943–1946. He was a personnel technician at the Department of the Navy in 1952–1954. In 1954 he entered the Foreign Service as consular officer in Ankara. He was economic and political officer in Tangier (1957–1961), commercial officer in Saigon (1962–1964) and in Damascus (1964–1968).

In 1966–1968 he was arms policy officer in the Bureau of Political-Military Affairs in the Department. He was on detail to the Department of Defense as assistant, foreign military rights affairs, international security affairs, in 1968–1970. He was principal officer in Lubumbashi (1970–1972), deputy chief of mission in N'Djamena (1972–1974), and counselor for political affairs in Santo Domingo (1974–1977). In 1977–1979 he was on detail to the Environmental Protection Agency as assistant for plans and policies. In the Department he was Staff Director of the Board of Examiners for the Foreign

Service (1979–1981), Inspector in the Office of the Inspector General (1981), and Deputy Director of the Office of Analysis for Africa (1981). Since 1982 he has been Director of the Office of Analysis for Africa.

Mr. Neher graduated from Bowling Green State University (B.A., 1948) and the University of Chicago (M.A., 1952). He attended Akron University in 1940–1941. His foreign languages are Spanish and French. He was born December 5, 1922, in Cincinnati, OH.

Proclamation 5210—National Child Passenger Safety Awareness Day, 1984
June 18, 1984

By the President of the United States of America

A Proclamation

Now that school sessions have come to a close and many families are preparing for summer vacations, it is especially appropriate to remind all Americans of the importance of child passenger safety. Children who are not buckled into child safety seats or safety belts are subject to great risks of serious injury in motor vehicle accidents because their less developed bodies afford them little protection.

It is a tragic fact that motor vehicle collisions are the primary cause of death and crippling injuries for children in the United States. From 1978 through 1982, nearly 3,400 children under five years old were killed in motor vehicle collisions, and more than 230,000 others were seriously injured. All Americans must do their best to reduce these senseless tragedies.

Fortunately, in the last few months, much has been done to protect young children travelling by car. We know that the proper use of child safety seats reduces the risk of death by up to 90 percent and can prevent up to 67 percent of all injuries. Through the voluntary efforts of many individuals and citizens groups, 47 States and the District of Columbia have recently enacted mandatory child restraint laws. Unfortunately, surveys show that only 40 percent of children under five years old are being protected by child safety seats and that 70 percent of the seats are not being used properly. In order to emphasize the importance of correct installation and use of child safety seats, many private and public organizations alike are initiating educational programs to achieve that end. For example, the National Automobile Dealers Association, the National Child Passenger Safety Association, and the American Academy of Pediatrics are currently sponsoring child safety clinics throughout the Nation to check on and demonstrate the correct use and installation of child restraint systems.

It is particularly vital for parents to understand the special risk which their children face as motor vehicle passengers and to educate their children about the importance of child safety seats each time they ride in the car. As adults, we all should remember that our own use of safety belts in our car can be a particularly good lesson for our children.

To emphasize the combined efforts of government and private sector organizations to promote child passenger safety throughout our Nation, the Congress, by Senate Joint Resolution 289, has authorized and requested the President to issue a proclamation designating June 18, 1984, as "National Child Passenger Safety Awareness Day."

Now, Therefore, I, Ronald Reagan, President of the United States of America, do hereby proclaim June 18, 1984, as National Child Passenger Safety Awareness Day. I encourage all Americans to observe this occasion by participating in appropriate programs, ceremonies and activities to educate motor vehicle drivers about the tragic consequences of neglecting the safety of our children when they travel by automobile.

In Witness Whereof, I have hereunto set my hand this 18th day of June, in the year of our Lord nineteen hundred and eighty-

four, and of the Independence of the United States of America the two hundred and eighth.

RONALD REAGAN

[Filed with the Office of the Federal Register, 4:23 p.m., June 18, 1984]

Proclamation 5211—Federal Credit Union Week, 1984
June 18, 1984

By the President of the United States of America

A Proclamation

This year marks the fiftieth anniversary of the passage of the Federal Credit Union Act of 1934 which enabled credit unions to be organized throughout the United States under charters approved by the Federal government.

Credit unions are uniquely democratic economic organizations, founded on the principle that persons of good character and modest means, joining together in cooperative spirit and action, can promote thrift, create a source of credit for productive purposes, and build a better standard of living for themselves. Because credit unions exemplify the traditional American values of thrift, self-help and voluntarism, they have carved a special place for themselves among the Nation's financial institutions.

Today, Federal credit unions are at their strongest point in history. They enter this, their 50th anniversary year, as the Nation's fastest-growing financial institutions. As member-owned cooperatives, credit unions operate with the credo, "Not for profit, not

for charity—but for service." Credit unions have maintained allegiance to this ideal and as a result have consistently reflected the philosophical tradition and the cooperative spirit of people helping people that prompted passage of the Federal Credit Union Act.

The Congress, by House Joint Resolution 139, has designated the week beginning June 24, 1984 as "Federal Credit Union Week" and has authorized and requested the President to issue a proclamation calling for the observance of this occasion.

Now, Therefore, I, Ronald Reagan, President of the United States of America, do hereby proclaim the week beginning June 24, 1984, as Federal Credit Union Week. I call upon the people of the United States to celebrate this week with appropriate ceremonies and activities.

In Witness Whereof, I have hereunto set my hand this eighteenth day of June, in the year of our Lord nineteen hundred and eighty-four, and of the Independence of the United States of America the two hundred and eighth.

RONALD REAGAN

[Filed with the Office of the Federal Register, 4:24 p.m., June 18, 1984]

Proclamation 5212—Harmon Killebrew Day, 1984
June 18, 1984

By the President of the United States of America

A Proclamation

On August 12, 1984, Harmon Killebrew will be inducted into the Baseball Hall of Fame in Cooperstown, New York. As a seventeen-year-old, Harmon Killebrew signed with the late Washington Senators and played with that franchise in the Nation's Capital and after its transfer to Minnesota. In an illustrious career, he hit 573 home runs, second only to Babe Ruth among all players in American League history. Harmon Killebrew was a member of the American League All-Star team on eleven occasions, and in 1969, he hit 49 home runs and batted in 140 runs and was named the American League's Most Valuable Player.

In honoring Harmon Killebrew, we recognize the accomplishments of the other baseball immortals enshrined in Cooperstown and the many contributions the sport has made to American culture and myth. Harmon Killebrew is the latest in a lengthy list of players who, in the words of Justice Harry Blackmun of the United States Supreme Court, "have sparked the diamond and its environs and that have provided tinder for recaptured thrills, for reminiscence and comparisons, and for conversation and anticipation . . . and all other happenings, habits, and superstitions about and around baseball that have made it the 'national pastime' or, depending upon the point of view, 'the great American tragedy'."

The Congress, by Senate Joint Resolution 285, has designated June 13, 1984, as "Harmon Killebrew Day" and authorized and requested the President to issue a proclamation in observance of this event.

Now, Therefore, I, Ronald Reagan, President of the United States of America, do hereby proclaim June 13, 1984, as Harmon Killebrew Day, and I call upon the people of the United States to observe that day with appropriate ceremonies and activities.

In Witness Whereof, I have hereunto set my hand this eighteenth day of June, in the year of our Lord nineteen hundred and eighty-four, and of the Independence of the United States of America the two hundred and eighth.

RONALD REAGAN

[*Filed with the Office of the Federal Register, 10:31 a.m., June 20, 1984*]

Toasts of President Reagan and President J.R. Jayewardene of Sri Lanka at the State Dinner
June 18, 1984

President Reagan. Mr. President, Mrs. Jayewardene, distinguished guests, and ladies and gentlemen, it's a special pleasure to have you with us. Sri Lankan leaders, including yourself, Mr. President, have been to our country before. Tonight, however, is the first time that a Sri Lankan chief of state has been an official guest at the White House. It's our honor to have you with us, and Nancy and I hope your visit will be followed by many more.

Our talks this morning reflected the cordial and cooperative relationship which exists between our two democracies. When your government was first elected in 1977, Mr. President, Americans were excited by your bold program for economic development. And you've led your country in a new direction, and by doing so, you've created new opportunities for your people and expanded the potential of every Sri Lankan.

The accelerated Mahaweli River project is part of your effort, as is freeing the Sri

Lankan economy from the controls and red-tape that stifled progress and economic expansion. One innovation of particular interest to me, Mr. President, is the creation of a free trade zone. This practical approach to development with its open market is attracting investment and unleashing the energy of the private sector. And I hope those over on Capitol Hill who claim enterprise zones won't work here in our country will take notice of the progress that you've made.

We in the United States are happy that we've been able to contribute to your progress. Our Agency for International Development is working with you in the river program and encouraging Sri Lanka's private enterprise sector. With the incentives that you now offer to investors, your country is attracting business and capturing the attention of American entrepreneurs and investors. And I think we can look forward to growing cooperation between our governments and our people on many levels.

U.S.-Sri Lankan cooperation comes in many forms. Last year the Peace Corps began a program to assist in the upgrading of Sri Lanka's English language teaching skills. And today we signed a science and technology agreement which provides an umbrella for increased collaboration. And we look forward to the early completion of negotiating on a tax treaty and on a bilateral investment treaty. All this reflects the extraordinary relationship that we're building, a relationship of trust and trade that will benefit both our peoples.

Mr. President, we understand Sri Lanka's choice, as a small developing country, to remain nonaligned in matters of foreign policy. We respect genuine nonalignment. Your country consistently has been a forceful voice for reason and moderation in non-aligned councils. Your strong opposition to unprovoked aggression in Afghanistan and Kampuchea has swelled the international chorus calling for restoration of independence for these two brutalized countries. We hope that Sri Lanka will remain a strong moral force in world politics.

And today, Mr. President, we came to know one another better and to understand more fully our objectives and concerns. Your visit has undoubtedly strengthened the bond between our two countries, and it's laid a basis for even closer, more cooperative relations between Sri Lanka and the United States in the future.

And finally, Mr. President, I'd like to thank you again for the elephant—[*laughter*]—a magnificent present that you gave us today. The elephant happens to be the symbol of the President's political party, and by coincidence—[*laughter*]—we happen to be also that smart. [*Laughter*]

Ladies and gentlemen, may I ask you to join me in a toast to President and Mrs. Jayewardene, and the prosperity of our relationship with Sri Lanka.

President Jayewardene. Mr. President, Madam Reagan, ladies and gentlemen, I don't mind, President Reagan telling the public that the gift of the elephant was accidental. [*Laughter*] But privately I know it's something else. [*Laughter*] The elephant led my party to victory in 1977. I received 51 percent of the votes. Any party that gets 51 percent of the votes must win an election. And I hope you will have the same luck in the months to come.

I came here as a stranger, but I find—already I feel I am among friends. I've heard that the American people are very friendly people, hospitable people. Both qualities have been proved during the last few days. I'm surrounded, I understand, by film stars. Those whom I saw in my youth were rather different. They were Charlie Chaplin, Laurel and Hardy, Fatty Arbuckle—[*laughter*]—and Mary Pickford.

I remember a story about Laurel and Hardy. They joined the French Legion. They were waiting in the inspecting line. The sergeant came and said, "What are you doing here? Why do you join the French Legion?" They said, "We joined the French Legion to forget." "To forget what?" "We've forgotten." [*Laughter*]

I haven't forgotten about the help your country has given us during the last few years. But I didn't come here to ask for help. That's not my way. I'm waiting to hear Mr. Frank Sinatra sing "My Way." [*Laughter*] That's one of my favorite songs, but I understand he didn't like it. [*Laughter*] I used it in part of my election campaign and asked the people to vote for my way, which they did.

Your country is, as far as the Americans go, young. Our country is old, very old. We go back to the fifth century before Christ. We had Ambassadors at the court of Claudius Caesar. You'll find it recorded in Pliny's letters. He even mentions the name of the Ambassadors. We had sent delegations to China in 47 A.D. and I understand the gift sent by our king to the Emperor of China were water buffalos and hump cattle. The great Chinese pilgrims Hsüan-tsang and Fa-Hsien came to our country in the fourth century A.D. and the sixth century A.D. So did Sinbad the Sailor, Marco Polo, and Ibn Batuta.

For the first time, Westerners came in the 16th century and the Portuguese came as tourists but stayed for 150 years. After that came the Dutch and then came the English. And we are now, once again, a free country. We wish to be friendly with all and the enemies of none. That is my policy and the policy of our people.

We would like the people of America to understand us. In the long history of Sri Lanka, there have been difficult periods. There have been murders; there have been assassinations; there have been riots; there have been good deeds and bad deeds. Last July we had one of those bad periods. But in time to come, it will be forgotten.

I see in one of your newspapers there is an advertisement in which some people are trying to make us remember that day. It was a fatal day; several people were killed. It was not done by the government; it was done by a gang of hooligans, about which we are very, very sorry. I'm trying to forget it. I'm trying to make our people not commit—some of them—such incidents again. I hope we will succeed.

I remember when one of your representatives came to see me and had lunch with me. I told her—she is your representative

in the United Nations organization—"A leader must know only two words." She said, "What's that?" I said, "Yes and no." And I think President Reagan knows those two words very well. Once you say yes or once you say no, stick by it. Whatever happens, never change. That has been my policy, and it has succeeded.

Therefore, Mr. President, we're surrounded by friends. We've been very happy the last few days. I have a few more days to spend. I hope to spend some time in the Indian settlements at Santa Fe, not for any other reason but because those were the stories I read in my youth, about Buffalo Bill and the various tribes. I'm fascinated by the fact they were the oldest human settlements, as far as I know, in the continent of America, and a great people. And we must give them a helping hand as we must give every race, every tribe, every human being, whatever his caste, religion, or race, a helping hand.

We're all human beings. We extend our affection, not only to human beings but even to animals; to the little elephant that we have gifted to you. That is the philosophy which we have learned in our country; that is. the philosophy which, if I can, I'll spread throughout the world. And I find in you, Mr. President and Madam Reagan, two very good disciples.

Thank you very much for entertaining us. May your country prosper. May, in the morning and in the evening, at nightfall, may the name of President Reagan and Madam Reagan, never be forgotten. Thank you.

May I drink to the health of President Reagan, Madam Reagan, the Government and people of the United States of America.

Note: President Reagan spoke at 9:45 p.m. in the State Dining Room at the White House.

Remarks at Dedication Ceremonies for the New Building of the National Geographic Society
June 19, 1984

Thank you, Mr. Chief Justice. There are so many people I want to say hello to here today: Dr. Payne, Reverend Harper, and enough members of the Cabinet and the executive branch and from up on the Hill that I'm wondering who's watching the store. [*Laughter*]

But of course, there's also your distinguished board member Lady Bird Johnson. Lady Bird, it's always wonderful to see you and to be able to say in public what is often said in private, that you were a great First Lady of this nation, and your beautification program is a lasting improvement on the American landscape. You can't be thanked enough for your great and good work.

And it's good to see Gil Grosvenor again. The first time I met him, I gave him quite a start. It was just before I took office, and we were having a reception at Blair House. Gil introduced himself and told me where he worked, and I informed him that he was responsible for one of the biggest problems that Nancy and I were having in the transition. And he looked at me a little wide-eyed, and I told him—being in the middle of a big move from the West to the East—I said, "Gil, I have hundreds of National Geographics at the ranch, and I don't know how the heck I'm going to haul them all to the White House." [*Laughter*]

Well, I'm very happy to be here today to help you dedicate your new building, as President Johnson did just 20 years ago when you opened your last new building.

I guess you have some trouble storing your old National Geographics, too. [*Laughter*] You know, it's something, when you stop to think about it—we were just talking outside before we came in—I don't know of anyone I've ever known who could throw away a National Geographic. [*Laughter*] A lot of others go in the wastebasket when you finish reading what you want to read, but not these.

In the ceiling outside this room, there's a dome showing the stars as they were that night in the winter of 1888 when a group of public-spirited scholars, scientists, and adventurers came together to start a society aimed at institutionalizing the study of science in this new experiment called America. And it occurs to me that that little firmament is an appropriate symbol for this building. It reflects the outward reaching, no-boundaries impulse that has shaped your Society. It reflects the great respect that you have for specifics, for exactitude, for recreating things as they were, dot for dot and star for star. And it reflects the spirit of inquiry that has directed your studies up to the stars, out to the continents, and into the heart of man's experience on Earth.

In a world that sometimes seems to have grown sated with all it knows, you still discover; you fund expeditions; you help researchers; you encourage impossible dreams. And then you share the results with all the Society's members in your magazine. I think one of the great reasons for your magazine's success is that it's infused with the romance of discovery, the romance of history, of seeking out the past and discovering places man has never seen before.

Sometimes we think that there are no journeys anymore, that, yes, man goes places, even into space, but it's done with a kind of clockwork perfection, with our technology clicking away and bringing us from Plainfield, New Jersey, to the Himalayas in less than a day of a man's life. But it sometimes seems that there are no journeys anymore, no more great treks.

Remember how in the movies they made when we were young—well, the movies they made when you were young. [*Laughter*] Remember how they'd show a map unfolding, and they'd have arrows showing the journey as it progresses; our hero started here, visited there, and now he's just landed in his destination, fade in on hero. And there was the sense of a long journey unfolding. Well, that sense still exists in National Geographic. And somehow you take your readers along on the ride as you climb mountains and cut your way through jun-

873

gles.

There is another thing, the special sensitivity you bring to your quest. I'm thinking here of a small item in your May issue, a picture of the frozen remains of a woman who died in the eruption of Mount Vesuvius. An anthropologist [archeologist] who studied the skeleton was quoted as saying, "She was very homely, but someone cared enough to give her beautiful things, delicate gold bracelets and jewels." A small observation, perhaps, but it carries a whole world of inference. It evokes. You bring history to life, and you remind us all that civilizations are born and die and are rediscovered in an endless continuum.

I think it should be noted that the National Geographic Society is the kind of organization that a nation like ours and a world like ours can produce. We provide the fuel upon which societies such as this one grow.

You tell your stories straight and with a rigorous objectivity. There is a fine, implicit respect for your readers in that, and it's a public service.

Throughout its history, the National Geographic Society has brought home the profound truth that we are, with all our differences, a human family living together on a tiny blue and green planet. For the past 25 years, our space program has reinforced this perspective of the world, helping us realize that we are all riders of the Earth together. As we dedicate this new home for the Society, I think it fitting that we rededicate ourselves to the pursuit of knowledge and excellence which has so long characterized our space program.

Accordingly, today I am pleased to report that NASA is beginning a new program aimed at achieving that goal. For more than 25 years, NASA has pioneered on the cutting edge of science and technology and has stimulated our young people to strive for excellence in all they do. Now NASA, in cooperation with the private sector, will expand its educational outreach program to our very young people in more than 75,000 elementary schools throughout the country. NASA will be able to share its engineering know-how, scientific discoveries, and sow the seeds of future progress by stimulating our young people to study science and engineering.

We call this new program Operation Liftoff, and it will incorporate such advanced instructional tools as computer software, laser discs, audiovisual materials, and other techniques. It will also involve, as I said, private enterprise. I've asked NASA to reinforce its ties with the aerospace industry and with private citizen's groups to expand this effort to the fullest.

In this connection, I was particularly pleased to learn of the efforts of the National Space Institute to develop and support a new national Young Astronauts Program to involve young Americans more directly in our space program. This new organization will expand their appreciation of space as a place in which people can live and work and learn. I've asked NASA to work directly with the NSI to develop this project in the context of our Private Sector Initiatives Program.

And I want to personally thank Jim Beggs of NASA for his leadership and great support in the creation of these new programs.

Now, I know as we near the end of this amazing and troubled century that you, as all of us, are looking to the future. And I know that one of your great interests and concerns is the environment—conservation and ecology. You are worried about what man has done and is doing to this magical planet that God gave us. And I share your concern.

What is a conservative after all but one who conserves, one who is committed to protecting and holding close the things by which we live. Modern conservatives in America want to protect and preserve the values and traditions by which the Nation has flourished for more than two centuries.

We want to protect and conserve the idea that is at the heart of our national experience, an idea that can be reduced to one word: freedom. And we want to protect and conserve the land on which we live— our countryside, our rivers and mountains, our plains and meadows and forests. This is our patrimony. This is what we leave to our children. And our great moral responsibility is to leave it to them either as we found it or better than we found it.

But we also know that we must do this

with a fine balance. We want, as men on Earth, to use our resources for the reason God gave them to us—for the betterment of man. And our challenge is how to use the environment without abusing it, how to take from it riches and yet leave it rich.

But I think the whole idea of conservation has often been obscured these past 20 years by some who've attempted to seize it as an issue, politicize it, and claim it as their own. I think there have been some who use the conservation movement as an excuse for blind and ignorant attacks on the entrepreneurs who help the economy grow—the farmers who make our food, the businesses that give us heat in winter and coolness in the summer. This kind of antagonism to all things that speak of business has tended to confuse the issue, blur responsibility, and overshadow sincere concern.

As I said in my last State of the Union message: "Preservation of our environment is not a liberal or conservative challenge—it's common sense."

Our nation has taken great strides in the decades since an old conservative named Teddy Roosevelt led the charge to create the National Park System. From that great beginning step, we have steadily expanded efforts to protect our heritage of land and water. We've been proud to pick up the mantle and move forward in a number of important areas.

We've spent $737 million since 1981 as part of a billion-dollar plan to repair and replace national park facilities that were designed to correct years of neglect. Even as we grapple with getting Federal spending under control, the 1985 budget request proposed that almost $160 million be made available to acquire new lands for our national park and wildlife refuge system.

We're keeping a close watch on endangered species. With the leadership of Secretary Clark, the Interior Department has listed 23 species so far this fiscal year, including the wood stork and the woodland caribou—maybe even some of us. [*Laughter*]

Together, the Federal Government and Ducks Unlimited have created a new program to ensure the protection of American waterfowl nesting areas. This, by the way, reflects our attempts to work closely with the private sector. The nonprofit Ducks Unlimited will work with the Fish and Wildlife Service and fund the protection of the waterfowl areas.

Now, just this past April, the Prudential Insurance Company donated more than a hundred thousand acres of wetlands and forest areas to the National Wildlife Refuge System. That's a $50 million gift. And we rely on private volunteers in our national parks. Last fiscal year, we had the help of more than 22,000 volunteers who, in all, donated more than a million hours of their own time. And that was a taxpayer savings of about $7 million.

Creating parks and wildlife refuges is only a part of protecting our environment, of course. I'm proud to report that the most recent studies of the Environmental Protection Agency show that we've made great progress in cleaning up the air and water. Hundreds of lakes and streams have joined the Potomac River in being declared open for fishing and swimming, after being closed to a whole generation. EPA tells us that after a national expenditure of $150 billion on air pollution controls, concentrations of all the major pollutants are on a downward trend.

We're moving forward in responding to new challenges as well. In just 3 years, we have tripled funding for the cleanup of abandoned hazardous waste dumps from $210 million in 1983 to $640 million proposed for 1985. We have doubled funding for acid rain research in each of the past 2 years. We're trying to get a clear, scientific understanding of its causes and effects. And what we're aiming at is a policy of common sense.

We have, all of us, over the past 20 years, reached consensus on the need to conserve our environment. Now we must come to agreement on how to do it. And in coming together on that, we must keep in mind the word "balance"—a balance between the desire to conserve and protect, and the desire to grow and develop; a balance between concern for the good earth, and concern for the honest impulse to wrest from the earth the resources that benefit mankind; a balance between the overall demands of society, and the individual demands of the free citizen.

If we rid our minds of cant, of empty rhetoric, of mere politics, we'll strike that balance naturally and together. This is my great hope, and in this you have my complete commitment.

And I thank you all for inviting me here today, and may you do great new work in this, your fine, new building. God bless you all.

Note: The President spoke at 11:28 a.m. in the new building's auditorium. He was introduced by Chief Justice of the United States Warren E. Burger.

Nomination of Robert J. Ryan, Jr., To Be United States Ambassador to Mali
June 19, 1984

The President today announced his intention to nominate Robert J. Ryan, Jr., of the District of Columbia, a career member of the Senior Foreign Service, Class of Minister-Counselor, as Ambassador to the Republic of Mali. He would succeed Parker W. Borg.

In 1960 Mr. Ryan entered government service with the Department of State. He was consular officer in Ponta Delgada (1961–1963) and assistant commercial attaché in Rio de Janeiro (1964–1966). He attended economic training at the Massachusetts Institute of Technology from 1966 to 1967. From 1967 to 1969, he was an economic officer in Pretoria and was a member of the National Security Council at the White House from 1969 to 1971. He was economic officer in Paris (1971–1973) and counselor for economic and commercial affairs in Rabat (1973–1974). In the Department he was Director of the Office of Monetary Affairs in the Bureau of Economic and Business Affairs from 1974 to 1977, and a member of the executive seminar in national and international affairs at the Foreign Service Institute from 1977 to 1978. From 1979 to 1981, he was Deputy Representative to the United States Mission to the Organization for Economic Cooperation and Development in Paris. In the Department he was Director of the Office of Regional Economic Policy (1981–1982) and Deputy to the Assistant Secretary for Inter-American Affairs, and Coordinator of the Caribbean Basin Initiative (1983). Since 1984 he has attended refresher language courses at the Foreign Service Institute.

Mr. Ryan received his B.A. (1960) from Johns Hopkins University and his M.A. (1967) from the Massachusetts Institute of Technology. He attended George Washington University from 1960 to 1961. His foreign languages are French and Portuguese. He was born August 11, 1939, in Washington, DC.

Appointment of Judith D. Moss as a Member of the National Advisory Council on Women's Educational Programs
June 19, 1984

The President today announced his intention to nominate Judith D. Moss to be a member of the National Advisory Council on Women's Educational Programs for a term expiring May 8, 1987. This is a reappointment.

Mrs. Moss is currently president of the law firm of Barrett & Barrett in Columbus, OH. She has been with the firm since 1975, serving as office manager (1975–1976), paralegal (1977–1978), and administrative attorney (1978–1981).

Mrs. Moss graduated from Ohio State University (B.S., B.A., 1975; J.D., 1977) and holds an associate degree (1968) from the Electronic Computer Programming Institute. She resides in Columbus, OH, and was born June 2, 1945, in Indianapolis, IN.

Appointment of R. Charles Gentry as a Member of the President's Commission on White House Fellowships
June 19, 1984

The President today announced his intention to appoint R. Charles Gentry to be a member of the President's Commission on White House Fellowships. He would succeed John D. Saxon.

Mr. Gentry is currently a partner with the law firm of Shank, Irwin & Conant in Dallas, TX. Previously, he was chief legislative assistant to United States Senator Pete V. Domenici (1973–1979); Director of the Office of Special Projects, U.S. Environmental Protection Agency (1971–1973); White House fellow assigned as special assistant to the Attorney General (1970–1971) and law clerk to the Honorable Halbert O. Woodward, District Judge, U.S. District Court, Northern District of Texas (1969–1970).

Mr. Gentry graduated from New Mexico Military Institute (B.A., 1956), the Missouri School of Mines and Metallurgy (B.S., 1962), and Texas Tech University School of Law (J.D., 1969). He is married, has two children, and resides in Dallas, TX. He was born August 10, 1935, in Dexter, NM.

Nomination of Margaret Phelan To Be a Member of the National Commission on Libraries and Information Science
June 19, 1984

The President today announced his intention to nominate Margaret Phelan to be a member of the National Commission on Libraries and Information Science for a term expiring July 19, 1988. She would succeed Philip A. Sprague.

Mrs. Phelan is currently owner of Phelan Business Research in Shawnee Mission, KS. Prior to this, she was research manager for Heidrick and Struggles, Inc., for almost 17 years.

Mrs. Phelan graduated from Kansas State University (B.S., 1945) and Rosary College (M.A., 1969). She resides in Overland Park, KS, and was born July 8, 1924, in Kansas City, MO.

Remarks at the Presentation Ceremony for the Presidential Scholars Awards
June 19, 1984

It's just occurred to me that with this blistering weather, maybe I could do something that might set a style you'd appreciate. [*Laughter*]

[*The President removed his jacket.*]

It does feel better, doesn't it? [*Laughter*]

Well, I'm delighted to be here. There, I started it out again—I was just with Rich

Little last night—and here I am again saying, "well" to start things out. [*Laughter*] In his imitations of me, he says that's a characteristic.

But I'm delighted to be here today. This is a great day for each one of you. And I hope you'll treasure this day all through your lives.

As you know, this is the 20th anniversary of the Presidential Scholars program, a program that has done much to reward initiative and encourage excellence in America's schools. It's also the second opportunity that I've had to host a gathering like this. And I have to confess I'm always a bit uneasy in the midst of all this scholarly achievement. I guess it's because I start thinking back to my own days as a student.

In fact, sometime ago my alma mater, Eureka College, gave me an honorary degree, and I thanked them profusely. But I had to admit that they had compounded a sense of guilt I'd nursed for about 25 years, because I always thought the first one they gave me was honorary. [*Laughter*]

So, I congratulate all of you today on taking advantage of the tremendous educational opportunities you've been offered and encourage you to keep up the good work. I don't think it's too optimistic to say that you can look forward to an age where a great value will be placed on your obvious capacity for achievement and excellence, an age that will be rife with opportunity.

In many ways, the things that we've been doing here in Washington the last few years have been part of this effort to open up new opportunities for all Americans. As you know, that means cutting back on the size and scope of government, reducing its drag on the private economy.

You know, it's one of the oldest lessons of history, but one that mankind always seems to forget: Too much government has always meant the oppression of the human spirit and the stultification of human progress. As Jefferson once said, "I am not a friend to a very energetic government. It is always oppressive."

Now, you think about that sometimes when you read some of those hostile columnists that say I spend a lot of time napping. [*Laughter*] I really don't. [*Laughter*]

But I think that our own time is increas-

ingly going to realize this truth. Repelled by the suffering caused by aggressive totalitarianism, our century seems to be awakening to the great prospects of human freedom and the democratic way of life.

That's why I've always believed a truly American foreign policy means more than the pragmatic business of getting along with other nations. It also means standing up for values like human freedom and our own obligation to see that freedom is spread someday to all the nations of the Earth. In a few short years, this will be the task before you, and I think you're preparing yourself well for it.

I'm especially encouraged by some of the fundamental changes that we see in American education today. We're beginning to realize, once again, that education at its core is more than just teaching our young the skills that are needed for a job, however important that is.

It's also about passing on to each new generation the values that serve as the foundation and cornerstone of our free democratic society—patriotism, loyalty, faithfulness, courage, the ability to make the crucial moral distinctions between right and wrong, the maturity to understand that all that we have and achieve in this world comes first from a beneficent and loving God.

So, we're gathered here to congratulate all of you on your success, on the credit that you've brought to yourselves, to your schools, and to your communities. We're here, too, to congratulate a select group of teachers for the enormous and unselfish dedication that they've shown to your welfare and to the highest standards of their own profession.

I had a teacher one day in a high school and on a visit to the principal's office—he was also the principal—make a very wise remark. He said, "It isn't very important what you think of me now." He said, "What I'm concerned with is what you're going to think of me 15 years from now." And even before 15 years was up, I knew I'd been in the hands of a very good friend and a very fine teacher.

But I think we also do well today to reflect on the fact that education and learning, success and power are only relative values; that they must be grounded first in the higher values of right and morality if they're to have any meaning at all.

You know, being President, and—there's a word here for the—someone in their seventies, but I am not sure that I can pronounce it. [*Laughter*] So, anyway, being in that range—[*laughter*]—I've discovered, for example, that people do tend to let you get away with giving them some advice. So, while I want to extend my congratulations to all of you, I hope you'll also permit me a few words of counsel and advice.

Thomas Jefferson, whom I mentioned a few minutes ago on the business of governing, also had some wise things to say about the business of living. When he was advising his nephew what path he should follow to find success, he reminded him that he must pursue his own and his country's best interests with what he called the "purest integrity, the most chaste honor. Make these then," he said, "your first object. Give up money, give up fame, give up science, give the earth itself and all it contains

rather than do an immoral act. And never suppose that in any possible situation or under any circumstances that it is best for you to do a dishonorable thing, however slightly so it may appear to you."

Well, I think that's good advice for all of us. And once again, congratulations to all our Presidential Scholars, their families, and our distinguished teachers who are here today. And, now, Secretary Bell is going to do the honors for me and distribute these awards.

And I'm going back to the Oval Office and do what a little girl told me to do who wrote me a letter one day and told me all the problems that she thought I should solve and then said, "Now, get back to the Oval Office and go to work." [*Laughter*] And I'll do just that.

Thank you all, and God bless you all.

Note: The President spoke at 1:20 p.m. on the South Lawn of the White House. Following his remarks, Secretary of Education Terrel H. Bell presented 141 graduating high school seniors with the Presidential Scholar medallion.

Remarks on Signing Four Bills Designating Wilderness Areas
June 19, 1984

Well, I'm glad to welcome all of you to the White House. And I know that all of you here today will agree that God has blessed the American people with a vast and beautiful land, a land of mountains and prairies, lakes and forests that reach from sea to shining sea. And no task facing us is more important than preserving the American land.

Our administration has undertaken this high task with energy and vision. And this year—well, the year we took office, we began a billion-dollar program to restore and improve our national parks. Our 5-year effort is the largest commitment to the renovation of our national parks that has ever been made. And I might add that it's running a year ahead of schedule.

We've enacted this historic Coastal Bar-

rier Resources Act also. That legislation will help to protect dunes, marshes, and other coastal formations from Maine to Texas, lands that provide irreplaceable feeding and nesting grounds for hundreds of species of fish and waterfowl. And we've made certain that State governments are involved in Federal land management as never before.

We've given our support to legislation that would create some 5 million acres of new wilderness areas. Each of these has been a significant step in the effort to preserve the American land for our children and grandchildren. And today we take another important step forward in this effort.

The legislation that I am about to sign will designate thousands of acres of wilderness area in North Carolina, New Hampshire, Vermont, and Wisconsin.

Each of these areas is intended to be completely natural—no housing developments, no powerlines, just forest, rock, wind, and sky. And because of this legislation, these wilderness areas will remain just as they are, places of beauty and serenity for hikers, campers, and fishermen. Generations hence, parents will take their children to these woods to show them how the land must have looked to the first Pilgrims and pioneers. And as Americans wander through these forests, climb these mountains, they will sense the love and majesty of the Creator of all of that.

Everyone here today had a hand in the passage of these bills. And special thanks go to all who—hard work and dedication made a critical difference. Each of you has my heartfelt thanks. But more important, you have the gratitude, I think, of the American people.

So, thank you. God bless you.

And now I'm going to sign some legislation—four bills.

Note: The President spoke at 3:03 p.m. in the Rose Garden at the White House.

As enacted, H.R. 3578, the Wisconsin Wilderness Act of 1984, is Public Law 98–321; H.R. 4198, the Vermont Wilderness Act of 1984, is Public Law 98–322; H.R. 3921, the New Hampshire Wilderness Act of 1984, is Public Law 98–323; and H.R. 3960, the North Carolina Wilderness Act of 1984, is Public Law 98–324. All were approved on June 19.

Proclamation 5213—Minority Enterprise Development Week, 1984
June 19, 1984

By the President of the United States of America

A Proclamation

America's growth and prosperity depend on the full participation of all its citizens. If we as a Nation are to remain the world's leader in innovation, technology and productivity, we must ensure that all Americans are involved in our economic progress.

The fulfillment of this challenge has become more realistic today, because of the significant contributions of minority American entrepreneurs to our economy. The Nation's 600,000 minority-owned businesses reveal the true meaning of entrepreneurship. They have emerged as a dynamic force in the marketplace, bringing innovative products and services to our economy, and constituting the principal source for jobs and training for thousands of American workers.

As we enter an era of greatly expanded opportunities in economic growth and development, it is appropriate that we encourage minority business owners by recognizing their tremendous contributions toward the continued economic development of our Nation.

Now, Therefore, I, Ronald Reagan, President of the United States of America, do hereby proclaim the week of October 7 through October 13, 1984, as Minority Enterprise Development Week, and I urge all Americans to join together with the minority business enterprises of our Nation in appropriate observances.

In Witness Whereof, I have hereunto set my hand this nineteenth day of June, in the year of our Lord nineteen hundred and eighty-four, and of the Independence of the United States of America the two hundred and eighth.

RONALD REAGAN

[*Filed with the Office of the Federal Register, 11:44 a.m., June 20, 1984*]

Informal Remarks to Reporters on the Nation's Economy
June 20, 1984

The President. That's making it a little difficult. What?

Q. Are you going to talk to us about the GNP and your reactions?

The President. That's what I was just going to do is make a statement here.

I'm sure you've all heard, but if you haven't, the remarkable good news from the Department of Commerce, that they have readjusted the figures for the first quarter. And the growth in the first quarter was 9.7 percent in the gross national product.

The inflation, the GNP deflator, was 3.9 percent for that first quarter. Now the estimate for the second quarter is growth of 5.7 percent and an inflation rate of 2.8. And all of this is remarkable good news and is evidence that we have a solid recovery that is

going forward without a renewal of inflation.

We're all very pleased.

Q. From the Russians on the summit, have you heard anything new since your news conference? Have you heard anything new on the summit?

The President. No, no, we're still, as I say, communicating, and—but, we haven't got anything new to say.

Q. Will there be a summit this year?

The President. I couldn't say. I really don't know.

Okay? Well, I'm off to Connecticut and New Jersey.

Note: The President spoke at 9:02 a.m. at the South Portico of the White House as he was departing for a trip to Oradell, NJ, and Hartford, CT.

Remarks at River Dell High School in Oradell, New Jersey
June 20, 1984

Thank you, Mr. Panico, the principal here; Governor Kean; Congresswoman Roukema; and longtime old friend, Don Newcombe—it's been too long between meetings. But all the others here—and this very courageous and fine young man [1]—all the others here, I can't tell you how much I appreciate your warm welcome and how impressed I am by what I have seen here today.

Almost 4 years ago when I accepted the nomination of my party to run for the Presidency, I talked about our nation's future. And I remember saying we need a rebirth of the American tradition of leadership at every level of government and in private

---

[1] *The President was referring to 19-year-old Hector del Valle, who had spoken to the audience about his automobile accident, caused by drinking, which left him permanently paralyzed below the neck.*

life as well. The United States of America is unique in world history, because it has a genius for leaders, many leaders on many levels. Well, today, I'm seeing that genius. I've seen real leaders and real leadership.

You in this audience—parents and teachers, public officials, students, and local groups—have fused your creativity and concern to deal with a great national problem. And in doing this, you've become part of a movement that has literally swept this country, the movement against drinking and driving.

This is community leadership and community involvement at its best. And I don't mind saying that it isn't Washington that led the way; it was a grassroots movement. Well, so was the Boston Tea Party; so was the abolitionist movement; so was the tax-cutting movement that swept across this country in the past few years. The history of our country is the history of grassroots movements, because Americans know that the purest form of law is one that springs directly from the desire of the people.

You led the way, and in leading, you've changed this country. You've saved lives. And you've shown us what you are doing.

If you'll permit me to tell you a little bit about what we're doing in Washington—and I know there must be some times when you ask. [*Laughter*] Two years ago, I appointed a Presidential Commission on Drunk Driving, and the Commission laid out in irrefutable detail the scope and the extent of the problem.

They told us that alcohol-related automobile accidents are the leading cause of teenage deaths in this country. In fact, in the past few decades, more people have died in alcohol-related auto accidents than in any war since World War II. And the Commission strongly urged Federal action to require a 21-year-old drinking age.

Now I want to talk to you about why the age-21 law is good and why we're supporting it. We know that as you've been told so eloquently here, drinking and driving is a killer. And we know that people aged 18 to 20 are more than twice as likely to be involved in an alcohol-related accident as any other age group. Society has a clear stake in seeing that these young lives, so full of promise, are not ended, or crippled. So, we know what the problem is. We know that society has a stake in solving it, and we know of a solution: raising the drinking age to 21.

Now, this isn't some fad or some experiment. It's a demonstrable success. In States in which the drinking age has been raised, teenage driving fatalities have gone down significantly. Here in New Jersey, with the support of my good friend and yours, your Governor, Tom Kean, you raised the drinking age to 21 in 1983. And you know what happened. You had a 26-percent reduction in nighttime, single-vehicle fatalities among 19- and 20-year-olds in the first year alone.

Well, when you're talking about a 26-percent decrease in the number of teenagers needlessly killed on the highways, then you're talking about something that works. And you're talking about something that's needed.

Last year when the Presidential Commis-

sion on Drunk Driving recommended that every State raise its drinking age to 21, I was delighted and hopeful. I made speeches to support it. And there was momentum, fed in part by groups such as M.A.D.D., and more States started raising the drinking age. I was delighted, again, because I hoped that the States would, as they should, take this action themselves without Federal orders or interference. Well, in the past 8 or 9 months, 4 States have done it, and in all, 23 States now have age-21 laws.

But now it appears that things have slowed down. Things have stalled. And at this point, less than half the States have the age-21 laws, and more than half don't. And it's led to a kind of a crazy-quilt of different State drinking laws. And that's led to what's been called "Blood Borders"—with teenagers leaving their homes to go to the nearest State with a lower drinking age. And they drink, get drunk, careen on home, and get into trouble of all sorts, including auto accidents.

Now, this slaughter hurts us as a people. It tears up the fabric of society by bringing grief to families, guilt to friends, and loss to the community. And we just can't tolerate this anymore. So, I want you to know that I've decided to support legislation to withhold 5 percent of a State's highway funds if it does not enact the 21-year-old drinking age. The carnage must end, and now.

Now, some feel that my decision is at odds with my philosophical viewpoint that State problems should involve State solutions and it isn't up to a big and overwhelming government in Washington to tell the States what to do. And you're partly right. But the thing is, this problem is much more than a State problem. It's a national tragedy involving transit across State borders. Beyond that, there are some special cases in which overwhelming need can be dealt with by prudent and limited Federal action. And in a case like this, where the problem is so clear-cut and the benefits are so clear-cut, then I have no misgivings about a judicious use of Federal inducements to encourage the States to get moving, raise the drinking age, and save precious lives. The choice remains with the States. I hope they'll act wisely and soon.

Let me remind you there are 23 States that haven't needed this inducement, and New Jersey is a stunning example. Your Governor, Tom Kean, has provided terrific cooperation and leadership so that New Jersey is leading the way on solving the drunk driving problem. [*Applause*] That applause is for you.

You've raised the penalties against drunk drivers, you've increased arrests and convictions, and you've added tough new legal and financial sanctions against drunk drivers, and you raised the drinking age. And what you got in return is clear and undisputed. Between 1981 and 1983, drunk driving fatalities declined almost 31 percent. You have saved lives. And all of your efforts have qualified your State for almost $800,000 in Alcohol Incentive Grant funds to pay for programs that give your State new tools to combat drunk driving and ensure highway safety. So, you have a lot to be proud of. But the battle isn't over.

I'm going to depart from the main theme here to tell you that Nancy and I discussed what I would be saying here today. And we want you to know that we're aware that the problem we have on our highways isn't just drinking and driving. It's also drinking and drugging.

You know, we know a lot of alcohol-related accidents involve drugs, too. And I know that you're aware—I'm sure you are—of Nancy's concern about this. She wanted to be here today, but she's at a big meeting out in Nevada, where she's discussing drug abuse with parents and teachers. I'm rattling around in that big house down there. I don't like it. [*Laughter*] I know what she's doing is worthwhile.

Our administration has taken many actions to combat drug abuse and drug use among children—and it occurs to me that drug use is drug abuse, so we might as well just call it that. But we know that no matter how effective we are against the pushers and drug smugglers, it all comes down to you.

And there's one thing I want to say to the students here today, and I speak as one who has lived 73 years—I don't mind saying it, because the press will never let you forget it. [*Laughter*] And I guess I've seen a lot. I lived a good part of my adult life in Holly-wood and Los Angeles. And I saw a lot of people who were living fast lives. And I just want to tell you—don't take drugs. Don't abuse your mind and body that way.

You know, I know it's hard for you young people to believe that any of the rest of us remember what it was like or know what you're thinking or feeling. But we do. And one day you're going to be very much surprised to learn how clear your memories will always be of these particular days and how much they mean to you. And, as you were told by the chief, we also remember that when we were sitting where you're sitting, we didn't think anything bad could happen to us. Death was always for someone else—and all the bad things of that kind.

Now, as your lives go on, you're going to buy a number of automobiles; you're going to trade in a number, get new ones. You've got one set of machinery you can't trade in—the one inside you. And you may not think about it now, but many of the things that you do now will affect how well you're going to be able to get around in later years, and whether you're going to be able to enjoy life as you're presently enjoying it. And I just have to tell you—believe me, it is worthwhile to take care of that particular set of machinery. Don't put any sugar in the gastank. Remember to do all the things that keep it fine-tuned. And you'll find that it really pays off.

Now, don't fall for the line that drug use is daring and fun and fearless. It's stupid. It's flirting with addiction, flirting with sickness, and a waste of your own life. Don't fall for that stuff about "life in the fast lane." That's where all the accidents take place.

Many of us who are older have lost friends to one addiction or another. And some of you have lost or will lose friends to drugs, to the addictions that will squeeze them to death, or the impairment that will make them make the wrong move in a fast car. Your generation has lost some of its favorites, like John Belushi and so many others.

I look out, and I see your bright, young faces, and I just want to say: Don't waste the health and the youth that God gave you. Don't take drugs.

But I don't want to end on a sad note. For every person who falls in this country, there are a hundred people there to pick him up. And that's one fact that's at the heart of the American experience. And I want to say to all of you, to M.A.D.D. and to C.A.A.R.D. and the others that are involved in this great national effort against drunk driving, you are all the grassroots. You are the people who change this country and always have. You're the makers of change, the improvers of our national life. And you deserve an awful lot of credit.

And so, let me say to you as I leave here today, I tip my hat. You're terrific. God bless you, and may your good work continue. And just look at who you'll be working for up here in these stands, these young people.

Thank you very much.

Note: The President spoke at 11:14 a.m. in the high school gymnasium. He was introduced by Anthony Panico, principal of the school.

Prior to his remarks, the President went to a classroom at the school for a demonstration and briefing on the school's alcohol reaction time simulator program. He then attended a meeting with alcohol awareness officials, including community leaders and representatives of Students Against Drunk Drivers (S.A.D.D.), Mothers Against Drunk Drivers (M.A.D.D.), and the Committee for Alcohol Awareness in the River Dell Communities (C.A.A.R.D.).

Following the meeting, the President traveled to Hartford, CT.

Remarks at the Annual Conference of the National Sheriff's Association in Hartford, Connecticut
June 20, 1984

Mr. Chairman and ladies and gentlemen, I want to begin by saying how much I've looked forward to this chance to be with you today.

You know, in America's frontier days the sheriff's badge was the symbol of our nation's quest for law and justice. And today that badge still stands for commitment to the law and dedication to justice. Those of you in the Sheriff's Association are in the forefront of America's law enforcement community. All of you have firsthand experience with the problem of crime and lawlessness in our society. And the jobs you hold are dangerous and difficult ones. And believe me, I know.

I mean no irreverence when I mention that back in those days when I was doing television, I once played a sheriff, a western sheriff, in a TV drama. And the gist of the story was that the sheriff thought he could do the job without a gun. It was a 30-minute show. I was dead in 27 minutes. [*Laughter*]

So, may I say to all of you today what millions of Americans would say if they had

the chance: Thank you for standing up for this nation's dream of personal freedom under the rule of law. Thank you for standing against those who would transform that dream into a nightmare of wrongdoing and lawlessness. And thank you for your service to your communities, to your country, and to the cause of law and justice.

Now, I know that many of you at this conference have served the public interest for lengthy periods of time, and that you lived through the grim years of the sixties and the seventies, when crime became an epidemic in America. In those decades, serious crime more than tripled. By the start of the eighties, crime was costing more than $10 billion in financial losses, touching 30 percent of America's homes, and taking the lives of almost 25,000 Americans a year.

Along with the rise in crime came a dangerous, widespread loss of faith by the American people in their criminal justice system. Eighty-five percent of Americans were saying the courts in their home areas weren't tough enough on criminals, and 75 percent were saying our criminal justice system just wasn't deterring crime.

Well, the reason was simple: The American criminal justice system was failing and failing badly. While our justice system was weighed down with excessive litigation and the courts were becoming arbiters of disputes they were never intended to deal with or to handle, the criminal justice system wasn't carrying out its most important function, the punishment of the guilty and protection of the innocent. In some jurisdictions and major cities, 3 percent or less of reported crimes were ending in prison terms for offenders. A small percentage of repeat offenders were responsible for a large percentage of crimes committed. One study showed that 23 percent of all male offenders accounted for 61 percent of all violent felony crimes.

This rise in crime, caused by a hardened criminal class, was fostered partly from a liberal social philosophy that too often called for lenient treatment of criminals. Because this misguided social philosophy saw man as primarily the creature of his material environment, it thought that through expensive government social programs it could change that environment and usher in a great new egalitarian utopia. And yet even while government was launching a rash of social engineering schemes in a vain attempt to remake man and society, it wasn't dealing with the most elementary social problems like rising crime.

Individual wrongdoing, they told us, was always caused by a lack of material goods, and underprivileged background, or poor socioeconomic conditions. And somehow, and I know you've heard it said—I heard it many times when I was Governor of California—it was society, not the individual, that was at fault when an act of violence or a crime was committed. Somehow, it wasn't the wrongdoer but all of us who were to blame.

Is it any wonder, then, that a new privileged class emerged in America, a class of repeat offenders and career criminals who thought they had the right to victimize their fellow citizens with impunity. And today we still pay the price for those years of liberal leniency—I mean the growth in the ranks of career criminals, criminals who

are contemptuous of our way of justice, who do not believe they can be caught and, if they are caught, are confident that once the cases against them enter our legal system, the charges will be dropped, postponed, plea-bargained away, or lost in a maze of legal technicalities that make a mockery of our society's longstanding and commendable respect for civil liberties.

Well, at last we're making progress against these criminal predators in our midst. Reported crime dropped 4.3 percent in 1982. That was the first decline since 1977. And reported crimes for last year showed an even more remarkable 7-percent decrease, and this was the sharpest decrease since 1950. Indeed, it was the first time since 1950 that the serious crime index declined for 2 years in a row.

Now, I know there are a few people who want to attribute the encouraging downward trend in crime to a statistic—the fact that fewer members of the population are now in the crime-prone age group. Well, a coincidence isn't a correlation. The truth is that crime sometimes has risen with population growth and sometimes not; there's nothing historically inevitable about it. For example, between 1970 and 1982, the numbers in the crime-prone age group did drop slightly by about 1 percent, but serious crime went up 40 percent.

So, I think the real explanation for the recent drop in crime lies elsewhere than in mere statistics. To tell you the truth, that explanation is right here in front of me today. I don't think there's any question that America's law enforcement community and her courts are now carrying out a new mandate from the American people. Throughout the Nation, there's a new consensus on the crime issue, which you've helped form. It's a consensus that utterly rejects the counsels of leniency toward criminals and the liberal philosophy that fostered it.

The increase in citizen involvement in fighting crime through such initiatives as the Neighborhood Watch programs, spearheaded by the Sheriff's Association; the tough, new State statutes directed at repeat offenders; the widespread public outcry against leniency in our court system; and the sweeping new steps we've taken at the Federal level show that the years of the pseudo-intellectual apologies for crime are now over.

This morning in New Jersey I witnessed a grassroots movement against drunk driving, and I said to the group that the history of our country is a history of such movements, because Americans know that the purest form of law is one that springs directly from the people. It is this surge of public opinion that has brought us initiatives like those I've just described, which were long overdue. The American people today insist that judges and government officials recognize what common sense has always taught: that right and wrong matters; that individuals are responsible for their actions; that retribution must be swift and sure for those who prey on the innocent.

It's interesting, too, to note that common sense about crime is making its impact in the very field which once accounted for so much of the misguided advice about crime, that of the social sciences. The work of one psychologist, Stanley Samenow, for example, has won wide attention and confirms what many of us have been saying about the crime problem for many years: Choosing a career in crime is not the result of poverty or of an unhappy childhood or of a misunderstood adolescence; it's the result of a conscious, willful, selfish choice made by some who consider themselves above the law, who seek to exploit the hard work and, sometimes, the very lives of their fellow citizens.

One very important reason for the decrease in crime, then, is tied directly to this growing toughness toward criminal offenders. In the sixties, the probability of being arrested for a crime fell off dramatically. And in the sixties and most of the seventies, the probability of being sent to jail for a crime also fell off dramatically. But in the eighties, these two critical trends have been reversed. For the last few years, both the probability of arrest and the probability of incarceration have been increasing. So, crime is coming down because—and thank heaven for this—the public's demands for justice are finally being heeded. More criminals are being arrested; more career criminals are being put behind bars. And

let's not forget that taking these career criminals off the streets doesn't just mean they're prevented from committing other crimes; it also means that their punishment acts as a strong deterrent to others who might choose a life of crime.

Now, obviously, those statistics are hardly worth celebrating. None of us likes the idea that our prison population is increasing. But we can and we must take legitimate satisfaction in the fact that more wrongdoers are being brought to justice—not out of a sense of vindictiveness or revenge, but because incarcerating these criminals means that fewer and fewer innocent Americans are being victimized by criminal wrongdoing.

I believe our administration's commitment to the war on crime has definitely helped to bring down the crime rate, and I assure you today, our commitment to fighting crime will continue to grow. Let me just briefly report to you on our efforts at the Federal level and why I think they've helped to complement your crucial work at the State and local levels.

First, from day one of our administration, the Attorney General and I have emphasized the importance of appointing responsible judges to the Federal bench, including the Supreme Court. I'm talking about judges who will not only uphold the rights of the accused but the rights of the innocent and the right of society to protect itself from criminal wrongdoers. I know all of us have been pleased by recent court decisions that show common sense once again returning to legal deliberations on criminal justice matters.

In addition to helping bring sanity back to the courtroom by appointing sound judges, we've also moved to strengthen cooperation with local and State law enforcement agencies. Our U.S. attorneys have set up law enforcement coordination committees in every Federal district. And I'm proud that some of you are now serving on them. Through our surplus Federal property program, we've helped States and localities in expanding prison space. We've strengthened and broadened training for State and local law enforcement agents, both at the FBI Academy and at a Federal facility in Glynco, Georgia.

And today I'm pleased to announce two new initiatives to assist local law enforcement. First, the Department of Justice is establishing with the FBI a new National Center for the Analysis of Violent Crime, whose mission will be to work with law enforcement agencies to identify and track repeat killers, the so-called serial killers who prey on innocent citizens. This means the latest computerized technology for detective work is moving from the research phase to the operational phase.

And second, in order to help eliminate a threat to the lives of America's sheriffs and policemen, legislation was introduced last week to ban the manufacture and importation of bullets designed to penetrate the soft-body armor worn by law enforcement officers. We worked hard on that one, and in the end, we produced a bill which has broad bipartisan and increasing support. I expect to be signing a cop-killer bullet bill before this Congress adjourns.

Our third major effort against crime has been a full-scale offensive against illegal drug trafficking. For the first time, we brought the FBI into this fight. We've increased our law enforcement budget by 50 percent and added 1,768 new investigators and prosecutors, most of this as a result of our efforts in drug-related fields. Our highly successful South Florida Interdiction Task Force has led to the establishment of investigative task forces in 12 other regions throughout the country. And those 12 task forces have already initiated some 620 cases and indicted more than 2,600 individuals. And 140 of these indictments have been under the new "Drug Kingpin" law, which carries a maximum penalty of life imprisonment without the possibility of parole.

And fourth, we've declared war on organized crime in America. I'm proud to tell you that organized crime convictions are up from 515 in fiscal '81 to 1,331 in 1983. We're getting longer prison sentences and, for the first time, making a serious effort to confiscate the financial assets of the mobsters. Our new organized crime commission has begun its investigation of the structure of the mob today in America, its money-laundering techniques. And its work will be greatly broadened when it receives subpoe-

na powers in this session of the Congress.

I repeat what I've said before: We have it within our power to shatter the regional and national syndicates that make up organized crime in America. This administration seeks no negotiated settlement, no détente with the mob. Our goal is to cripple their organization, dry up their profits, and put their members behind bars where they belong. In this effort, State and local law enforcement must play a critical role. For only when the mob is being hurt at the local level, when the revenue from illegal gambling, pornography, drug pushing, and other kinds of racketeering is dried up will the mob be permanently put out of business.

And fifth, through a series of Presidential task forces, we've brought much needed attention to critical law enforcement problems. Our task force on violent crime in 1981 led to a widespread series of proposed reforms, most of which have now been implemented. Similarly, we've appointed a Task Force on Family Violence, a problem that's been badly in need of full national airing for many years.

And sixth, this administration has brought long-overdue attention to the plight of the victims of crime. I was sure—I know that this is an area of special interest to all of you, and I commend you on the special attention you've been paying this week to ways of aiding victims of crime. Many of you have seen our Victims of Crime Task Force report, and you've heard Assistant Attorney General Lois Herrington report on how our administration has implemented many of the commission's recommendations. Well, we're especially proud that our victims of crime assistance act is now approaching passage in the Senate. This is an act that will assist the States in helping compensate the victims of crime, but—and this is very important—this assistance will be paid for by criminal fines, not by hard-earned tax dollars.

The mention of this legislation brings me to the seventh and final point about this administration's crime program, our all-out legislative effort to get those in Federal law enforcement the tools they need to deal with the criminal threat. We've already scored some important breakthroughs. We've succeeded in modifying tax laws that made it difficult for the IRS to assist in organized crime and drug trafficking investigations. We've changed the posse comitatus law to permit the military to assist us in cracking down on the drug smuggling. And, as I just mentioned, we're pushing ahead with victims of crime legislation.

But our largest and most important initiative remains where it's been for the last 3 years—becalmed in the House of Representatives. This vital crime package includes bills calling for bail reform, tougher sentencing, justice assistance to States and localities, improvement in the exclusionary rule and the insanity defense, and major reforms affecting drug trafficking, prison crowding, capital punishment, and forfeiture. All of these reforms are badly needed and constitutionally sound. In fact, our core crime package has already passed the Senate once by a vote of 91 to 1, but in the House of Representatives the liberal leadership keeps it bottled up in committee. One member of the Judiciary Committee there even claimed the package was "dead on arrival."

Well, forgive me, but those who are holding this up in the House are out of touch with reality, and they're out of touch with the American people. This is a perfect example of how Americans are forced to suffer ill effects of crime because too many of our political leaders stick to old, discredited, liberal illusions about crime.

Americans overwhelmingly favor changes in the exclusionary rule, the insanity defense, the reinstitution of capital punishment, and the tightening up of parole and bail procedures. And of all places the people's voice deserves to be heard, it is in the House of Representatives. So, today I'm asking you to continue to use your influence with your elected representatives. Let them know that you're tired of waiting and that, at a very minimum, the liberal leadership in the House owes the American people a floor debate and vote out in the open on this crime package.

Now, if the Members of the House feel our package is unwise legislation, let them have the courage to stop hiding behind parliamentary maneuvers and say so publicly.

Let them vote against these measures in full view of the people, and let them explain what gives them the right to ignore the will of the people. This they should have the courage to do.

And now, ladies and gentlemen, during the last 3½ years this administration has faced the serious problems of rebuilding America's economic strength here at home and restoring our prestige and stature abroad. Today we're in the midst of a sound and strong economic expansion, and America's national security has been restored and enhanced. But I also believe that the record I've just presented to you shows that, while this administration was coping with the crises of our economy and our national security, we were also making great efforts to help you and all our fellow citizens deal with the problem of crime in American society.

I believe I can say that in doing this, all of us sought only to speak for a new consensus in American politics—a consensus that said government had involved itself in areas where it was neither competent nor needed, while it had wrongly ignored its traditional and most fundamental obligation: the maintenance of public order and the preservation of public tranquillity.

Today the fight against crime continues, but for the first time in years, we can say that we're starting to make headway. There's still a long way to go; there still is much to do. But on behalf of all America, I want to thank all of you again for all that you are doing to make possible a safer society. And I pledge to you my continued support, even as I seek your assistance in continuing to eradicate the drug menace, fight organized crime, make our streets and homes safe again, and return America to the days of respect for the law and the rights of the innocent.

Thank you, and God bless you all.

Note: The President spoke at 2 p.m. in the main ballroom at the Park View Hilton Hotel. He was introduced by Richard Elrod, president of the association.

Following his remarks, the President returned to Washington, DC.

Message to the Congress Transmitting the Annual Report on Federal Advisory Committees
June 20, 1984

To the Congress of the United States:

As provided by the Federal Advisory Committee Act, I am pleased to transmit the Twelfth Annual Report on Federal Advisory Committees.

In fiscal year 1983, Federal advisory committees contributed significant expertise to the discussion of important issues facing our Nation. With the assistance of these committees major initiatives were undertaken in areas such as social security reform, national security, and government efficiency. Other committees furnished valuable advice to Federal agencies concerned with scientific research, health programs, environmental issues, international diplomacy, as well as economic, social and cultural affairs.

Since 1981, Federal agencies have achieved substantial overall savings in advisory committee program costs while continuing to make active use of committees in the government decision-making process. These savings have been achieved without the sacrifice of the quality advice the agencies have required. The participation of the best possible members on a voluntary basis where possible, but on a compensatory basis where appropriate, must continue to be the goal. I plan to issue shortly a memorandum to Executive branch agencies providing further guidance to sustain and improve upon these accomplishments.

The efficient and selective use of advisory committees was one of the major objectives of the Congress in enacting the Federal Advisory Committee Act. I am particularly concerned that advisory committees be established only when they are necessary, that they be carefully supported and monitored during their existence, and that they be promptly terminated when their mission is completed.

I commend the members who have served on advisory committees and thank them for sharing their experience, knowledge and advice. Advisory committees can and have demonstrated the value of a continuing partnership between citizens and their government.

RONALD REAGAN

The White House,
June 20, 1984.

Note: The 130-page report is entitled "Federal Advisory Committees: Twelfth Annual Report of the President—Fiscal Year 1983."

Message to the Congress Reporting Budget Deferrals
June 20, 1984

To the Congress of the United States:

In accordance with the Impoundment Control Act of 1974, I herewith report three new deferrals of budget authority totaling $1,850,000 and five revised deferrals of budget authority which now total $98,533,000. The deferrals affect the Department of Energy.

The details of the deferrals are contained in the attached reports.

RONALD REAGAN

The White House,
June 20, 1984.

Note: The attachments detailing the deferrals are printed in the Federal Register *of June 25, 1984.*

Executive Order 12480—Establishment of Emergency Board No. 202 To Investigate a Railroad Labor Dispute
June 20, 1984

Establishing an Emergency Board To Investigate a Dispute Between The Long Island Rail Road and the Brotherhood of Locomotive Engineers

A dispute exists between The Long Island Rail Road and the Brotherhood of Locomotive Engineers representing employees of The Long Island Rail Road.

The dispute has not heretofore been adjusted under the provisions of the Railway Labor Act, as amended ("the Act").

A party empowered by the Act has requested that the President establish an emergency board pursuant to Section 9A of the Act.

Section 9A(c) of the Act provides that the President, upon such a request, shall appoint an emergency board to investigate and report on the dispute.

Now, Therefore, by the authority vested in me by Section 9A of the Act, as amended (45 U.S.C. 159a), it is hereby ordered as follows:

Section 1. Establishment of Board. There is established, effective June 20, 1984, a board of three members to be appointed by the President to investigate this dispute. No member shall be pecuniarily or otherwise interested in any organization of railroad employees or any carrier. The board shall perform its functions subject to the availability of funds.

Sec. 2. Report. The board shall report its findings to the President with respect to the dispute within 30 days after the date of its creation.

Sec. 3. Maintaining Conditions. As provided by Section 9A(c) of the Act, as amended, from the date of the creation of the board, and for 120 days thereafter, no change, except by agreement of the parties, shall be made by the carrier or the employees in the conditions out of which the dispute arose.

Sec. 4. Expiration. The Board shall terminate upon the submission of the report provided for in Section 2 of this Order.

Ronald Reagan

The White House,
June 20, 1984.

[*Filed with the Office of the Federal Register, 10:46 a.m., June 21, 1984*]

Executive Order 12481—Establishment of Emergency Board No. 203 To Investigate a Railroad Labor Dispute
June 20, 1984

Establishing an Emergency Board To Investigate a Dispute Between The Long Island Rail Road and the Brotherhood of Railway, Airline and Steamship Clerks, Freight Handlers, Express and Station Employes

A dispute exists between The Long Island Rail Road and the Brotherhood of Railway, Airline and Steamship Clerks, Freight Handlers, Express and Station Employes, representing employees of The Long Island Rail Road.

The dispute has not heretofore been adjusted under the provisions of the Railway Labor Act, as amended ("the Act").

A party empowered by the Act has requested that the President establish an emergency board pursuant to Section 9A of the Act.

Section 9A(c) of the Act provides that the President, upon such a request, shall appoint an emergency board to investigate and report on the dispute.

Now, Therefore, by the authority vested in me by Section 9A of the Act, as amended

(45 U.S.C. 159a), it is hereby ordered as follows:

Section 1. Establishment of Board. There is established, effective June 20, 1984, a board of three members to be appointed by the President to investigate this dispute. No member shall be pecuniarily or otherwise interested in any organization of railroad employees or any carrier. The board shall perform its functions subject to the availability of funds.

Sec. 2. Report. The board shall report its findings to the President with respect to the dispute within 30 days after the date of its creation.

Sec. 3. Maintaining Conditions. As provided by Section 9A(c) of the Act, as amended, from the date of the creation of the board, and for 120 days thereafter, no change, except by agreement of the parties, shall be made by the carrier or the employees in the conditions out of which the dispute arose.

Sec. 4. Expiration. The board shall terminate upon the submission of the report provided for in Section 2 of this Order.

RONALD REAGAN

The White House,
June 20, 1984.

[*Filed with the Office of the Federal Register, 10:47 a.m., June 21, 1984*]

Announcement of the Establishment of Emergency Boards Nos. 202 and 203 To Investigate Railroad Labor Disputes
June 20, 1984

The President announced today the creation of Presidential Emergency Boards Nos. 202 and 203 to investigate and make recommendations for settlement of current disputes between the Long Island Rail Road (LIRR) and employees represented by the Brotherhood of Locomotive Engineers and the Brotherhood of Railway, Airline and Steamship Clerks, Freight Handlers, Express and Station Employes, respectively.

The President, by Executive orders, created the Emergency Boards pursuant to appropriate requests as mandated by the Railway Labor Act. The LIRR is the largest commuter railroad in the United States, transporting 283,000 passengers each week day over a 330-mile system extending from Manhattan to the end of Long Island. In addition, LIRR provides the only rail freight service on Long Island and connects with the Nation's rail system through New York City.

The emergency board procedures of the Railway Labor Act applicable to commuter railroads provide that the Boards will report their findings and recommendations for settlement to the President within 30 days. The parties must then consider the recommendations of the Emergency Boards and endeavor to resolve their differences without engaging in self-help during a subsequent 90-day period.

Message to the Congress Transmitting the Annual Reports on Highway Safety, Traffic, and Motor Vehicle Safety Programs
June 21, 1984

To the Congress of the United States:

The Highway Safety Act and the National Traffic and Motor Vehicle Safety Act, both enacted in 1966, initiated a national effort to reduce traffic deaths and injuries and require annual reports on the administration of the Acts. This is the 15th year that these reports have been prepared for your review.

The report on motor vehicle safety includes the annual reporting requirement in Title I of the Motor Vehicle Information and Cost Savings Act of 1972 (bumper standards). An annual report also is required by the Energy Policy and Conservation Act of 1975 which amended the Motor Vehicle Information and Cost Savings Act and directed the Secretary of Transportation to set, adjust and enforce motor vehicle fuel economy standards. Similar reporting requirements are contained in the Department of Energy Act of 1978 with respect to the use of advanced technology by the automobile industry. These requirements have been met in the Sixth Annual Fuel Economy Report, the highlights of which are summarized in the motor vehicle safety report.

In the Highway Safety Acts of 1973, 1976 and 1978, the Congress expressed its special interest in certain aspects of traffic safety which are addressed in the volume on highway safety.

For the first time since 1974, fatalities resulting from motor vehicle accidents showed a significant change. A total of 49,301 persons lost their lives in traffic accidents in 1981, a 3.6 percent decrease over the preceding year.

In addition, despite large increases in drivers, vehicles and traffic, the Federal standards and programs for motor vehicle and highway safety instituted since 1966 have contributed to a significant reduction in the fatality rate per 100 million miles of travel. The rate has decreased from 5.5 in the mid-60's to the present level of 3.18. This means that motorists can drive more miles today with less risk. If the 1966 fatality rate had been experienced in 1981, more than 85,000 persons would have lost their lives in traffic accidents.

Although we can be proud of these accomplishments, the number of people meeting violent deaths in traffic accidents each year remains unnecessarily high. In 1981, an average of 135 lives were lost every day. Compounding the tragedy is the fact that most of the victims were young people, killed at a time when they had the most to contribute to society and the most to gain from life.

Given the magnitude of the problem, protecting motorists and pedestrians from the kinds of dangers they face as a result of motor vehicle travel continues to be an important national priority.

The overall regulatory framework established since 1966 has clearly enhanced motor vehicle safety in this country. At a minimum, Federal motor vehicle safety standards have accelerated the introduction of needed safety improvements. However, we must take care to see that new regulations enhance traffic safety without producing unnecessary costs for consumers and manufacturers. Where the marketplace can be made to work to provide improved automobile safety, such approaches must be sought and developed. In any case, we are convinced that needed reform can be achieved without jeopardizing the safety and consumer goals and policies established by the Congress.

In the highway safety area, we will continue to work closely with the States on priorities such as safety belts and child safety seats, alcohol safety, motorcycle safety, police traffic enforcement, traffic records and emergency medical services. Highway safety grant programs will be simplified and Federal aid directed to activities that achieve verifiable results in terms of reduced deaths and injuries, and to ones that are truly national in scope.

Continued reductions in the annual traffic death toll will not be easy. Motorists today are better informed and driving in safer vehicles and on safer roads. But they are still victims of habit and of human nature. They choose not to wear a safety belt because they do not expect to be in an accident. They drink and drive because alcohol is part of our social mores. And they sometimes speed and take unnecessary chances because being in a hurry is an unfortunate fact of modern life. Changing these driving behaviors is the traditional challenge to improving traffic safety.

We will continue to pursue a variety of approaches to increasing highway safety, including widespread public education efforts and a national traffic safety commitment that involves government, industry and the public. We are convinced that significant progress can be made and that American motorists and pedestrians will ultimately enjoy a greater level of personal safety as a result.

RONALD REAGAN

The White House,
June 21, 1984.

Remarks to Participants in the National YMCA Youth Governors' Conference
June 21, 1984

The President. It's a privilege to welcome such a distinguished group of—I was going to say high school students, but they're governors and chief justices, all of them, right now—and to welcome all of you to the White House, and the Rose Garden in particular. I know you must be very proud of the offices you've been elected to, and we're proud of you.

Several weeks ago, there was a very famous young man—visited the White House. Considering the reception that he received, I was tempted to wear a white glove this morning. [*Laughter*] But it's obvious that you and I both have some things in common. We both like Michael Jackson, and we've been involved now in the political process.

In fact, whenever someone says "Governor" within my hearing, I turn around—[*laughter*]—have to catch myself. Used to be kind of funny at the Governors' conferences. In the hotels, you'd be in the lobby or something and there'll be 50 Governors present, and you'd hear the word, "Governor," and 50 heads would turn, each one thinking it was for him.

But after I looked over your Washington schedule and the questionnaire listing your interests, I decided to talk about an issue that seems to be on many of your minds, and with good reason. I know you and young people generally are interested in United States relations with the Soviet Union.

We all recognize that there is no more important foreign policy goal than the building of a more peaceful world in which liberty and prosperity can flourish. And we want to develop a more realistic working relationship with the Soviet Union, one marked by greater cooperation and understanding and by progress in arms reductions.

Real progress requires honest efforts on both sides, and unfortunately, it appears that the Soviet Union is unwilling to make that commitment as yet. As you may know, during the months that the START and the INF talks were underway, we proposed seven different initiatives. None were offered on a take-it-or-leave-it basis. Indeed, they were the result of many adjustments to respond to the concerns of the Soviet side. But the Soviet Union insisted on preserving their monopoly on medium-range missiles in Europe. I'd proposed zero-zero, that we eliminate all such missiles in Europe—zero on their side, zero on our side. Well, they met me halfway. They were willing to have it be zero on our side. Then when the nations of the West made it clear that a Soviet monopoly was not acceptable, that's when they walked away from the negotiating table.

But despite this disappointment, we shouldn't lose sight of the bigger picture. In a quiet way, we're trying to talk and negotiate with the Soviet Union on many fronts. Just 2 months ago in Vienna, we and our Western partners put forward new proposals on reducing the levels of conventional military forces in Europe. And those MBFR talks, as we call them, are continuing.

In the same week, at the 40-nation Conference on Disarmament in Geneva, Vice President Bush offered a draft agreement on a worldwide ban on chemical weapons. And as I'm sure you all know, chemical weapons now is the euphemism for poison gas. And at the Conference on Disarmament in Europe in Stockholm, we're pursuing a series of proposals that will help reduce the chance of conflict in Europe.

We're also trying to move forward on bilateral relations. And the latest round of negotiations on upgrading the hotline ended less than 2 months ago. In the economic field, we're making a number of steps—or taking a number of steps, to increase exchanges in nonstrategic goods. We've extended our very useful incidents-at-sea agreement for another term. And we've also proposed discussions to expand and multiply contacts of benefit to both our peoples.

But here, too, the Soviets have made things very difficult. And I need only mention the tragedy of the KAL flight 007 and the plight of Andrei Sakharov.

So, if you look at the big picture, it's clear that we in the West are doing our utmost to establish a cooperative, stable, and peaceful relationship. But it's also clear that the Soviet Union has not yet made the decision to join us in that effort. We'll keep trying, and we'll keep hoping that they'll realize it's in their best interests to join with us and the rest of the world community to build a more peaceful world. We're ready, willing, and able.

And I know you've been hearing and many people insist on saying that these are the most dangerous of times that we've ever known, that there's the greater tension and the greater hostility and danger between our two nations than any time since the Cuban missile crisis. Well, actually, these are not the most dangerous times. As a matter of fact, quite to the contrary.

I think with regard to the fact that they're being a little hard to talk to at the moment—there have been many worse times in recent years, and there is less of a threat simply for the reason that the United States, for the first time in a number of years, has enough deterrent capability that the Soviet Union, I don't think, would decide that it would be in their best interests to take any action.

And if you really want to get some history on this, so that I won't have to keep you standing here while I talk about it, when you leave here, get a copy of the Los Angeles—Los Angeles, the Washington Times. In the commentary section today there happens to be two columns. One is by William Rusher, who is the publisher of the conservative magazine National Review, and the other is by Morton Kondracke, who is the executive editor of the quite liberal publication the New Republic. And those two men, coming from those two opposite viewpoints, are on that page together, because each of them has done a column on disabusing our minds of this very idea that we're living in the most dangerous of times. And there's some—you'll find some very interesting reading, and at the same time, you'll have a complete knowledge of what the history of our attempts have been down through the years. So, I'm grateful to both of them.

You know, you can be on one side or the other, but you know you really must be close to right when you're standing against a cellophane wall and you're getting thrown rocks at from both sides. [*Laughter*] But here they weren't throwing rocks; they were on our side.

Well, in the meantime, we're going to continue our commitment to peace with freedom. And, believe me, because we're prepared with the strength of our allies to deter aggression, as I said, and pursue all possible avenues for arms reductions; and because we're prepared with our economic strength to achieve greater stability throughout the world; and because we have the spiritual strength and self-confidence to reach out to the Soviet Union, we're prepared to sustain peace with freedom—and, my young friends, we will.

Well, I've gone on long enough, but I do want to congratulate all the governors and chief justices for your noteworthy achievements. I am a firm believer, and I hope you'll continue to believe, that this nation is strongest when it realizes that it is a federation of sovereign States and that Washington is not the fount of all wisdom and authority in the Nation.

I urge you to use your leadership positions to get involved and get others involved in public life. And, remember, those words by one of our Founding Fathers, Thomas Paine, at the beginning of this nation—and it is still true—that we have it within our power to begin the world over again.

So, thank you. Good luck. And now, I'm going to try to say hello to each one of you individually. I'll start over there.

Gordon P. Hardey. [1] We have a gift for you. It's a surprise.

The President. I was running away. [*Laughter*]

Mr. Hardey. Okay. Being here today, Mr. President, is an honor for all of us Youth Governors. We represent 25,000 youths all over America combined, but you represent 230 million, so it's quite a difference. But we would like to tell you that we appreciate having you spend your time, your effort, and your ideas with us. And we know that time is a precious commodity that you can give out.

But we would like to say—is that we are all here in Washington to learn about government. And you are everything that we are hoping to see. You represent what we believe in, in democracy and freedom. And we hope you the best of luck in September.

But from the YMCA of the U.S.A. and the Youth Governors, we have a present for you from the Dixon, Illinois, YMCA Boys Band, performed in 1924. We have a picture. Fifth from the left, in the front row, is Ronald Reagan, who becomes the 40th President of the United States.

The President. Well, for heaven's sake. [*Laughter*] Thank you.

Actually, I was the drum major, and my older brother—he played the bass horn. And I had an incident when we were in a neighboring town on Decoration Day—we were leading the parade. And the marshal of the parade, on his horse, had ridden back to see how everything was coming. And he didn't get back quite up to the head of the parade in time. And there I was, waving that baton. I knew that the music was sounding further and further away. He had come in time to turn the band, but not me. [*Laughter*] And I was walking down the street all by myself, and the band had turned the corner. [*Laughter*] I had to cut across lots.

---

[1] *Youth Governor from California.*

My brother also had an incident when we were in college. And the bass player in the college band didn't show up for a basketball game. And so, my brother volunteered, and they accepted him. And so, he was playing, and everything was going fine, until there was one number that just sounded terrible. And the end of that one, the director rapped on the music stand, and he said to the band, " 'On the Mall,' 'On the Mall.' " And I saw my brother's face get red. And he said, "What did we just play?" [*Laughter*] He was one number ahead of them. [*Laughter*]

But to have this, this picture of our band—well, thank you very much. Very proud to have it, and proud to have you all here.

Mr. Hardey. Thank you. And here's a thing on the YMCA, also.

The President. I see. Thank you very much.

Mr. Hardey. You fly over me when you fly over Santa Barbara. I wave. [*Laughter*]

The President. Well—and I hope I'll be doing that soon. I don't do it often enough. All right.

[*At this point, the President greeted individual Youth Governors.*]

Reporter. Mr. President——

Q. What about the threshold test ban treaty? Are you going to go along with that sense of the Senate resolution?

The President. I can't take any of those questions right now.

Let me know—am I running in to some meeting or something?

Mr. Fischer. You're due in the Cabinet Room.

The President. In the Cabinet Room. Can these young people make a circular trip—go in and out? Would you all like to see the Oval Office? [*Applause*]

Q. Threshold test ban treaty?

Q. Wait, what about the Soviets? They've said there was no change in your policy that would warrant a summit.

The President. They don't know what they're talking about.

Q. Is that a complete rejection, Mr. President?

The President. I do not think so, no.

Note: The President spoke at 11:15 a.m. in the Rose Garden at the White House. Fol- *lowing his remarks, he led the students into the Oval Office for a brief tour.*

David C. Fischer is Special Assistant to the President.

Appointment of Victor George Atiyeh as a Member of the Advisory Council on Historic Preservation
June 21, 1984

The President today announced his intention to appoint Victor George Atiyeh, Governor of Oregon, to be a member of the Advisory Council on Historic Preservation for the remainder of the term expiring June 10, 1985. He will succeed Gov. Joseph Garrahy.

He has been Governor of Oregon since 1979. Previously, he was president of Atiyeh Brothers, Inc., in Portland, OR; a member of the Oregon Senate in 1965–1978, serving as minority leader in 1971–1978; and a member of the Oregon House of Representatives in 1959–1965. He is past director of Equitable Savings & Loan and past president of the Columbia-Pacific Council of the Boy Scouts of America.

Governor Atiyeh attended the University of Oregon. He is married, has two children, and resides in Salem, OR. He was born February 20, 1923, in Portland, OR.

Remarks at a Congressional Fish Fry
June 21, 1984

It may be hard for some of us to agree on some things, but I think I speak for everyone here when I say that Charlie Daniels, we thank you for sharing your talent with us.

Now, Charlie came here on very short notice, and he couldn't bring his band with him. But you know we're always prepared. We flew them in from the Persian Gulf.[1] [*Laughter*]

For those who may not know, Charlie does have a band that has walked away with dozens of awards, including Grammys, and he has performed in 50 States and a number of foreign lands. He's been named Instrumentalist of the Year more than once by the Academy of Country Music. And this isn't the first benefit he's done. [*Laughter*] He has made his talent available for worthy causes, including the fact that he has been

---

[1] *The President was referring to members of the Navy's Cross Current Band, who performed with Mr. Daniels.*

heard by an audience estimated at a hundred million people on the Voice of America in which his music has been played.

Now, this has been a fine evening, and I also want to express thanks to some generous folks from the seafood industry. We've had quite a meal. Back when I was a kid in the middle of the country, out there in the Midwest, the only fish you had was what you could catch down at the river. Life was uncomplicated then, like dealing with the Congress. [*Laughter*]

Seriously, though, I want to thank each one of you for being here. This democratic system of ours relies on good will between those of differing political opinions. This year, we go out to do battle in the political arena, and I know we will, in keeping with the finest traditions, we'll do that—the finest traditions of the democratic government. That, of course, is democrat with a small "d." [*Laughter*]

But it's been a pleasure to have all of you as our guests. And, once again, I want to thank the one and only Charlie Daniels for giving of his time to come here and entertain us as royally as he has and to thank these gentlemen from the Navy for what they have contributed also.

Thank you again. God bless you.

Note: The President spoke at 7:25 p.m. on the South Lawn of the White House.

Executive Order 12482—President's Advisory Committee on Women's Business Ownership
June 21, 1984

By the authority vested in me as President by the Constitution of the United States of America, and in order to extend the life of the President's Advisory Committee on Women's Business Ownership, in accordance with the provisions of the Federal Advisory Committee Act, as amended (5 U.S.C. App. I), it is hereby ordered that Executive Order No. 12426 of June 22, 1983, is amended as follows:

(a) Section 2(a) is amended by striking "foster" and inserting in lieu thereof "study methods of obtaining".

(b) Section 4(b) shall read: "The Committee shall terminate on December 31, 1984, unless sooner extended."

RONALD REAGAN

The White House,
June 21, 1984.

[Filed with the Office of the Federal Register, 4:19 p.m., June 22, 1984]

Note: The text of the Executive order was released by the Office of the Press Secretary on June 22.

Remarks to Representatives of the United States International Youth Year Commission
June 22, 1984

It's getting a little warm out here, isn't it? *[Laughter]*

Well, I do thank you. And first, I want to welcome you and thank you for taking the time to come to Washington to begin the activities for our national celebration of International Youth Year, 1985. I believe you all know—or you wouldn't be here— the importance of our youth to the future peace, security, and well-being of our nation and the world. And I'm certain that by working together, the youth organizations represented here today, our government, and America's private sector, Youth Year, 1985, will be a resounding success.

There's a spark in all of us which, if struck early enough, can light up our lives, elevate our ideals, and deepen our toler-

ance and strengthen our determination to make this world a better place. You couldn't make a better investment in America's future.

I've always believed that a lot of the problems in the world come from people talking past each other instead of to each other. And during Youth Year, 1985, we'll be making a special effort to help our young people reach out to each other and to their counterparts all over the world. And they will be able to build new bridges of understanding.

Understanding begins with the knowledge that the most powerful force for progress in this world comes not from government bureaucracies, nor public programs, nor even valuable resources like gold or oil. True wealth, and the real hope for the future comes from the heart—from the treasure of ideas and spirit, from free people with a vision of the future, trust in their fellow men, and faith in God. The better future that we all yearn for will not be built by skeptics who spend their lives admiring the complexity of the problems. It'll be built by free men and women who believe in themselves.

History shows that progress takes its greatest strides when people are free to worship, create, and build—when they can decide their own destiny and benefit from their own risks. The dream of human progress through freedom is still the most revolutionary idea in the world today. And it's also the most successful.

Two weeks ago today, the leaders of seven major industrial democracies issued a Declaration of Democratic Values at the London Economic Summit, and it concluded with these words: Strong in our beliefs, and endowed with great diversity and creative vigor, we look forward to the future with confidence. Well, we should be confident. The summit demonstrated the enduring strength of our shared vision and values, our resolve to sustain peace with freedom, and our desire to assist those who are seeking a better life.

You, too, should be confident—confident that if you prepare for International Youth Year, 1985, with wisdom and responsibility, you can shape a future of freedom, peace, and prosperity that can be shared by the whole world.

And that's why I'm so pleased that Prime Minister Seaga of Jamaica has proposed an International Conference of Democratic Youth during 1985. We believe that his conference, the first meeting of its kind, merits strong support of freedom-loving people everywhere. It will give young people all over the world a chance to examine and share their democratic values and principles, and to speak out for human rights and the three themes of International Youth Year: participation, development, and peace.

I hope that some of the young people from other countries have a chance to visit us as well and see our spiritual and economic vitality so that they will understand America better. And we, in turn, will learn much of value from them.

I think one of the most wonderful and rewarding experiences I had in all the trip to China recently, was one day—the day before we were to leave—in Shanghai, visiting Fudan University and going into one classroom where I was assured that all of those Chinese students could speak English. So, we didn't require translation.

And I opened it up to questions and answers. And I was amazed at the questions from those young Chinese students about you, the young people who are here in this audience, and young people all over America—really a deep and sincere interest and a curiosity in what I could tell them about how you were approaching life, and what your thoughts and dreams were. And it was a great pleasure to answer to the best of my ability. Sometimes I had to call on memory, but I thought I'd spoken to enough of you here that I was pretty much speaking your views. But it was so wonderful to see their honest and sincere desire to know you—and know you better.

The U.S. Youth Year Commission has accepted a worthy and important challenge, and you have our support. Our task force on Youth Year, under the leadership of Greg Newell, will do everything it can to help. And together, I'm certain that we will achieve great success in reaching out to America's young people and, through them, to the youth of the world.

So, I've kept you sitting out here in the sun long enough. I thank you all, and God bless you. And forward.

Yes, miss? I know this wasn't scheduled, but somebody here very appealingly says she has a question. What?

Q. President Reagan, how can we as youth help you stop the nuclear arms race—*[inaudible]*?

The President. How can American youth help us stop the arms race?

Well, I have to tell you that not through some of the demonstrations that are going on. And some of those things are so sincerely meant, but they don't realize that the two so-called superpowers in the world today must come to a meeting of the minds and an understanding that there is a better way than a continued arms race on down through the years. And this is why we have tried to open negotiations.

I still am optimistic that we're going to succeed. But we must sit down with the Soviet Union and make them understand that we mean them no harm. And then it is up to them to give some proof in line of some of the many statements they've made over the years that they mean no harm to us or to the rest of the peace-loving in the Western World.

But in order to do that, we have to have some tools. And when I can quote one Russian leader of a few years ago who said of détente—when we were all saying, "Well, we're pleased we have détente"—and his declaration to his own people as to what benefited them from détente was, that, he said, the most they got was our letting our strength erode and decline. They have to sit at the table and know that as far as strength is concerned we're nearly enough equal that we'd better discuss how we can go down.

Now, what can you do about that? You can evidence your support for legitimate arms reductions—not arms limitations that only regulated how fast and how far you could increase the weapons, which we've had too much of. But support us in our efforts to maintain our strength and to continue to give them a reason for wanting to sit down at the table with us. And you can be most helpful in that.

Well, thank you all very much. I know I've got some people in there that are looking at their clocks now and worrying about my schedule for the rest of the afternoon, but there was one more hand. I'll take this one more, and then I must go.

Q. Mr. President, I would just like to say the prosperity and progress of this nation depends on this youth, the ability of this youth to understand the plan for tomorrow's world. And I would just like to appreciate you for giving us this National Youth Day, because as Robert Kennedy once said, "Our future may lie beyond our vision, but not beyond our control." And if we can work to make this country better, it'll be better for everybody because the opportunities are here for us, and we just—[*inaudible*]——

The President. Thank you very much. Well, that wasn't a question, but I thank you for that statement. And let me just say in return: If there is anything that is the real responsibility of people in public life and holding office in this country, it is to realize and recognize the obligation to, if at all possible, when the time comes, to hand over to you—to hand you over maybe a little bit better world than was handed over to us. And I pledge to you we're going to try awfully hard to do that.

All right. Thank you all.

Kelly Alexander, Jr.[1] Thank you, Mr. President. On behalf of the 173, and growing, member organizations of the U.S. International Youth Year Commission, and over 50 million young people that we represent, I would like to express our deep appreciation for your invitation to the White House this afternoon. Before you are the leaders of the United States of tomorrow, doing what has to be done today, to assure that there will be a peaceful tomorrow.

For over 3 years, the members of our commission—reflecting the pluralistic diversity of our nation—have been discussing what we mean by the three U.N.-designated IYY themes of participation, development, and peace—subjects which we know are of particular interest to you. I am happy to say that we have reached a consensus. We believe—and I think that you would agree—that these concepts, these values, are interdependent—that true peace requires democratic participation and democratic development. And that democratic participation requires lasting peace. These objectives and their attainment serve as a cornerstone of all our IYY activities.

Mr. President, on behalf of the U.S. IYY Commission, I'm most honored to present to you our definition of the IYY themes. We very much hope that we will have an opportunity in the coming months to discuss these themes with you in more detail and that these themes will play an important role in the development of any international conferences or domestic programs that will come out of this year.

---

[1] *President of the U.S. International Youth Year Commission.*

The President. Thank you very much. [*Applause*]

Audience. [*Chanting*] Four more years! Four more years!

Reporter. Optimistic about the Russians?—can you sit down, please? Mr. President, can you tell us what makes you optimistic about the Russians?

The President. Common sense. They've got to have some concerns for the future, too.

Q. Chernenko told Mitterrand "no" to a summit, Mr. President.

The President. Well, maybe we can get that around to a "maybe" pretty soon.

Q. Do you agree with the general who says and thinks war is inevitable with the Russians—today's paper? American general——

Q. General Trainor, sir.

The President. No, I don't. And I think one of the most dangerous things in the world is for anyone to get in their—fixed in their mind the inevitability theory, because then, that very thing being in their minds, can bring about that. My theory is that there doesn't have to be a war. We're going to do everything we can to see that it doesn't.

Q. Mr. President——

Q. ——speak to General Trainor about that, sir? Will you discipline this Marine Corps general?

Mr. Speakes. Sorry, no more questions.

Q. I'm not speaking to you, Mr. Speakes, I'm speaking to the President. Sir, will you discipline General Trainor?

Note: The President spoke at 1:01 p.m. in the Rose Garden at the White House.

Larry M. Speakes is Principal Deputy Press Secretary to the President.

Proclamation 5214—Helen Keller Deaf-Blind Awareness Week, 1984
June 22, 1984

By the President of the United States of America

A Proclamation

Our eyes and ears provide vital ways of interacting with the world around us. The lilt of laughter, the beat of a brass band, the smile of a friend, and the poetry of a landscape are but a few of the life blessings that our senses of sight and hearing help us to enjoy. But for some 40,000 Americans who can neither see nor hear, the world can be a prison of darkness and silence.

Inadequate education, training, and rehabilitation for those who are deaf and blind may prevent these Americans from becoming independent and self-sufficient, thereby greatly limiting their life potential and imposing a high economic and social cost on the Nation.

We must prevent such problems among our deaf-blind citizens by fostering their independence, creating employment opportunities, and encouraging their contributions to our society. Crucial to fulfilling this urgent national need is research on the disorders that cause deafness and blindness. Toward this end, the National Institute of Neurological and Communicative Disorders and Stroke and the National Eye Institute as well as a number of voluntary health agencies are supporting a wide range of investigative projects that one day may provide the clues to curing and preventing these devastating disorders.

On June 27 we commemorate the 104th anniversary of the birth of Helen Keller, America's most renowned and respected deaf-blind person. Her accomplishments serve as a beacon of courage and hope for our Nation, symbolizing what deaf-blind people can achieve.

In order to encourage public recognition of and compassion for the complex problems caused by deaf-blindness and to emphasize the potential contribution of deaf-blind persons to our Nation, the Congress, by Senate Joint Resolution 261, has authorized and requested the President to issue a proclamation designating the last week in June 1984 as "Helen Keller Deaf-Blind Awareness Week."

Now, Therefore, I, Ronald Reagan, President of the United States of America, do hereby proclaim the week beginning June 24, 1984, as Helen Keller Deaf-Blind Awareness Week. I call upon all government agencies, health organizations, communications media, and people of the United States to observe this week with ap-

propriate ceremonies and activities.

In Witness Whereof, I have hereunto set my hand this twenty-second day of June, in the year of our Lord nineteen hundred and eighty-four, and of the Independence of the United States of America the two hundred and eighth.

RONALD REAGAN

[*Filed with the Office of the Federal Register, 4:20 p.m., June 22, 1984*]

Appointment of Armand Hammer as a Member of the President's Cancer Panel, and Designation as Chairman
June 22, 1984

The President today appointed Armand Hammer to be a member of the President's Cancer Panel for the term expiring February 20, 1987. This is a reappointment. The President also intends to designate him Chairman.

Dr. Hammer acquired the Occidental Petroleum Corp. in 1957 and currently serves as chairman of the board and chief executive officer. Previously Dr. Hammer was involved in the distilling and cattle businesses.

He is active in community and civic affairs and has been a strong supporter of cancer research. He serves on the board of

directors of the Eleanor Roosevelt Cancer Foundation and is a trustee of the Eleanor Roosevelt Memorial Foundation. In 1969 he established the Armand Hammer Center for Cancer Biology at the Salk Institute in California. He is an art patron and founded the Hammer Galleries, Inc., in New York City, and continues to be a major supporter of the Los Angeles County Museum of Art.

Dr. Hammer graduated from Columbia University (B.A., 1919; M.D., 1921). He is married, has one son, and resides in Los Angeles, CA. He was born May 21, 1898, in New York City.

Appointment of the Membership of Emergency Boards Nos. 202 and 203 To Investigate Railroad Labor Disputes
June 22, 1984

The President today appointed the members of the Presidential Emergency Boards Nos. 202 and 203, created by Executive Orders Nos. 12480 and 12481 of June 20, 1984, to investigate and make recommendations for settlement of current disputes between the Long Island Rail Road and employees represented by the Brotherhood of Locomotive Engineers and the Brotherhood of Railway, Airline and Steamship Clerks, Freight Handlers, Express and Station Em-

ployes, respectively.

Richard R. Kasher of Bryn Mawr, PA, will serve as Chairman. He is an attorney and arbitrator with extensive experience in the rail and airline industries. He was born May 30, 1939, in New York, NY.

Rodney E. Dennis of New York, NY, is an arbitrator and serves as permanent arbitrator for New York State and numerous local contracts. He was born January 26, 1928, in Sayre, PA.

Margery F. Gootnick of Rochester, NY, is a

901

lawyer; labor arbitrator, mediator; administrative law hearing examiner and university lecturer. She was born October 24, 1927, in Rochester, NY.

Radio Address to the Nation on the Economy
June 23, 1984

My fellow Americans:

This week, we had some more good economic news. The economy grew by a revised 9.7 percent in real terms for the first quarter and an estimated 5.7 percent for this quarter. Both figures are better than had been predicted.

The strength of our expansion continues to surprise experts and outperform past recoveries. The curious thing is that some experts treat this good news—strong economic growth—as a cause for worry. Well, the commonsense reaction is right. Good news is not bad, it's good.

In some key ways this expansion is both different and more durable than those in the past. Stronger growth has enabled more people to find work and bring home paychecks, and it's improved the job outlook for the future. More people are working in America today than ever before. And the United States is creating more jobs at a faster rate than any other major industrialized country in the world, well over 6 million jobs in the last 18 months. In fact, we created more jobs in the month of May alone than all the Common Market countries created in the last 10 years.

I remember back in 1983 when a bill was introduced in Congress aimed at creating 300,000 jobs a year by spending $3½ billion of your tax money. Now, I said, "No, the private economy will do the job better." And it has done better, much better. Since the recovery began, our economy has been creating, on average, more jobs every month than that government program promised to create in 12 months. And the jobs are benefiting everyone. Nearly 3 million women, a million blacks, and 650,000 Hispanics have found new jobs.

Recently, the National Federation of Independent Business said that among its small business membership, the percentage planning to hire new workers is the highest in 4 years. Since most new jobs are created by firms with a hundred employees or less, that small business survey bodes well for continued job gains in the future. So, economic growth is stronger than before, stronger than anyone expected, and jobs are being created at record rates.

But something else makes this expansion different. Inflation is staying down, and we mean to keep it down. It was up only two-tenths of 1 percent in May and only 4.2 percent over the last 12 months, barely a third of 1980's 12.4-percent rate. We've reduced inflationary pressures by reducing government spending growth, by promoting greater production through lower tax rates, and by spurring greater competition through the deregulation of key industries. Nor do we see signs that runaway price increases will reappear. This is the first time since the 1960's that we'll be able to enjoy strong and steady growth without high inflation.

Another characteristic of this expansion gives it extra power while helping us fight inflation. Investment by U.S. businesses in new plants and equipment, so crucial to helping workers be more productive and to helping our industries better compete in world markets, has been rising at the fastest rate since 1949. We're witnessing an historic surge of innovation, risk taking, technological development, and productivity growth. American economic leadership is back.

Now the question is why, and why here in America to a greater degree than anywhere else? Well, America began a fundamental change in direction in 1981; a change from a policy of government promises, a change from taxing you more no matter how hard you tried, to rewarding you for working harder and producing more than before. Personal incentives are changing America, restoring our spirit, strengthening our economy, giving us the opportunity and confidence to shape our future and make it work for us.

And that's why I'm determined to finish the job we've begun by simplifying our tax system and broadening the base so we can bring personal income tax rates down further. If we can do that while keeping Federal spending under control, there'll be no stopping the United States.

We all have a job to do to protect this expansion and keep the lid on inflation, which is the best guarantee against rising interest rates. The Congress must cooperate and restrain spending by passing the downpayment deficit reduction package. The Federal Reserve must assure enough liquidity to finance the expansion without raising expectations of new inflation. And we must all work to make government live within its means.

If we meet these responsibilities, today's good news will be here to stay, and America's best days will lie ahead.

Until next week, thanks for listening. God bless you.

Note: The President spoke at 12:06 p.m. from Camp David, MD.

Remarks at a White House Briefing for Black Administration Appointees
June 25, 1984

Well, thank you, and good morning. And I know that you've been listening to a lot of reports, and I hope mine'll be shorter than what you've had to listen to, because I don't imagine they've left me very much to talk about.

But I am proud to welcome to the White House so many of our partners in this administration. Special thanks goes to my friend Mel Bradley [1] for organizing this event. Mel was with us in the California Governor's office, and he's doing a fine job here in the White House.

You serve in positions of genuine importance in every branch of this government, from Secretary of Housing and Urban Development Sam Pierce, to Ambassador Alan Keyes, a member of our delegation to the United Nations, to Assistant Secretary of the Navy David Spurlock, to Mary Bush, one of our representatives at the International Monetary Fund, and to all of you who are here today.

Your jobs aren't easy. Long hours and constant criticism—some of it from the very people we're trying to help—are the rule, not the exception. But I know we all agree that the sacrifices and the trials are worth the rewards. Together, we're putting America back on the high road of progress, and in doing that, we're assembling a record that we can take to all Americans with pride.

Let me mention these three points of special concern.

First, education: This is the crucial tool that black Americans need to make progress. In the years before we took office, our nation's schools had begun to show unmistakable signs of crisis. From 1963 to '83—or to '81, college entrance examination scores underwent a virtually unbroken decline. Science achievement scores of 17-year-olds showed a similar drop. And most shocking, the National Commission on Excellence in Education reported that more than one-tenth of our 17-year-olds can be considered functionally illiterate.

We took office determined to change that. And since our administration put education at the top of the national agenda, we've seen a dramatic turnaround. In 1980 only a handful of States had statewide task forces on education. Today they all do. In addition, 47 States are considering new graduation requirements; 47 are studying improvements in teacher certification; and

---

[1] *Special Assistant to the President for Policy Development.*

17 are exploring merit pay for teachers. It all adds up to the most far-reaching education reform and renewal movement since the turn of the century.

In large part, because of our efforts, black children are beginning to get the educations they need to participate fully in American life. And as we go forward, let me assure you that we will remain committed to the future of our historically black colleges and universities.

These schools were very much on my mind when we started here, because they meant so much at a time when it would have otherwise been very difficult for so many to get higher education. And I was determined that they should not be left withering on a vine.

Back in September '81, I directed Federal agencies to increase the ability of these fine schools to participate in federally sponsored programs. And we've made significant progress. In the past 2 years, funding to these 103 schools has risen to $606 million. That's an 11.3-percent increase. Research and development grants and contracts have increased $282 million. And last fall we amended title III of the Higher Education Act so we can provide matching funds to help build college and university endowments. And I want you to know that we're working right now with Fisk University to help it find a way through its current economic difficulties.

Now, the second concern I want to mention lies at the very heart of the black experience in America—the struggle for equal rights. Contrary to a lot of demagoguery that we're hearing, our administration has moved with vigor and vision on this front.

In the enforcement of criminal, civil rights statutes, the Justice Department has filed 149 cases, including 24 against perpetrators of racial violence. We're energetically enforcing fair housing provisions and have proposed legislation to strengthen enforcement still further. Under our administration the Equal Employment Opportunity Commission is collecting record amounts of back pay. And since we took office, the percentage of minorities and women serving as military officers or holding white-collar jobs has risen.

I believe these figures demonstrate a commitment to civil rights that is firm and far-reaching. But let me go beyond statistics to speak from my heart. I still believe in a simple principle I learned from my mother and father: Black or white, young or old, every human being is a sacred child of God, a person of infinite dignity and worth.

All Americans have the right to be judged on the sole basis of individual merit and to go just as far as their dreams and hard work will take them. And we won't have finished the job until, in this country, whatever is done to or for someone is done neither in spite of nor because of their religion or their color, their difference in ethnic background, or anything else; that we will—*[applause]*. In this job, I have no higher duty than to defend the civil rights of all the citizens of this country.

And last, I want to mention the economy. Here, again, we in this administration are acting with energy and determination. We've helped disadvantaged and dislocated workers by enacting the Job Training Partnership Act. Indeed, in our last budget, I requested $3.6 billion for the JTPA, money that during 1985 will serve some 2.2 million individuals. We've supported minority businesses, establishing a program that over the next 10 years will call for the purchase of $22 billion in goods and services by the Government from minority firms. For the truly needy, we've enlarged the safety net, increasing spending for such items as medicare and medicaid and food stamps and housing.

To bring jobs to economically troubled places like inner cities, we've proposed a fresh idea. It's called enterprise zones. But some Democrats are blocking this proposal in the Congress, even though many State and local governments have established their own enterprise zones after they saw us trying for 2 years or more to get this program through the present Congress. Now, these zones have created thousands of new jobs. They've shown what a big success our own enterprise zones can and will be if only those do-nothing Democrats in Congress will step aside and let us get on with the job. They may have successfully blocked us so far, but we're not going to give up. They'll find we're still around.

To reduce teenage unemployment, especially black teenage unemployment, which is the highest segment of unemployment in the country, we've proposed a youth employment opportunity wage for the summer months. When I think back to my own boyhood, I remember how each summer I used to look for a job and get a job, and starting when I was 14 years old. And there wasn't anyone around to tell them that if I was willing to accept the pay that was offered that I couldn't take the job. Of course, I didn't earn as much as a full-time working man, but it was good money to me. And I was providing genuine service to my employers.

I'm convinced that it's only common sense to enact this opportunity wage and help young people get summer jobs, needed discipline, and experience. And they won't be taking jobs away from permanent, adult workers. But they will be, as unskilled and new in the job market, working at a rate that I think would be commensurate and fair for their position in the work force. Today they're unemployed because many of the jobs that would be available do not afford the minimum wage and what it has risen to. After all, why should the Federal Government stand in the way of a young man or a woman who is finding their first job? I might add that at their recent conference, America's black mayors gave our opportunity wage proposal a firm endorsement.

Despite the importance of all these efforts, one change our administration has brought about is doing more to help black Americans than all of the programs put together, and I'm talking about economic expansion. Today, inflation is less than half. As a matter of fact, it's down to about a third of what it was when we took office. Retail sales and factory orders are up. Since the expansion began, the unemployment rate has shown the steepest drop in 30 years, and over 6 million Americans have found jobs. And more Americans are working now than ever before in our history, and more jobs are being created at a faster rate here than in any other major industrialized nation.

Yes, black employment is still—or unemployment is still too high. But as I pledged last year to the National Council of Negro Women, I intend to see to it that every American regardless of race, religion, or gender benefits from this recovery. Today black unemployment is dropping even more quickly, I'm glad to say, than white unemployment. And our economic program will go on creating jobs if we control government spending and if we keep taxes where they belong, which is down.

Together, we've begun to create a genuine opportunity society, a nation where every citizen has the chance to do good, honest work and prosper. Last November when I signed into law the national holiday commemorating the birth of Dr. Martin Luther King, Jr., I quoted his stirring words about the fate of black and white Americans: "Their destiny is tied up with our destiny, and their freedom is inextricably bound to our freedom. We cannot walk alone."

Well, no, we cannot walk alone. And that's why you and I are working to improve the destiny of all Americans—to make it possible for our people to walk together into a glorious future of freedom and prosperity. I'm convinced that if each of us gives this great cause our best efforts, then our dream will come true, and in Dr. King's words, "All of God's children will be able to sing with new meaning, 'Land where my fathers died, Land of the pilgrims' pride, From every mountain-side Let freedom ring.' " [*Applause*] Thank you very much.

Now, I know we're running into lunch hour. We shouldn't do that, but I just have one last thing. First of all, I thank you for all you're doing for the country. God bless all of you. And if you didn't mind taking a few more minutes, I'm going into the Blue Room there, and then you can come through, and I can get to say hello to each one of you individually, and we can have our picture taken. All right.

Note: The President spoke at 11:45 a.m. in the East Room at the White House.

905

Message to the Senate Transmitting the Inter-American Convention on Letters Rogatory and a Protocol
June 25, 1984

To the Senate of the United States:

I transmit herewith the Inter-American Convention on Letters Rogatory, adopted at Panama City, Panama, on January 30, 1975, and the Additional Protocol, adopted at Montevideo, Uruguay, on May 8, 1979, with a view to receiving the advice and consent of the Senate to ratification. The Convention and the Additional Protocol were signed on behalf of the United States on April 15, 1980.

When ratified, the Convention with its Additional Protocol will comprise the first multilateral agreement among the United States and other members of the Organization of American States (OAS) in the field of international judicial cooperation. The provisions of the Convention and Additional Protocol are explained in the report of the Department of State that accompanies this letter. In broad terms, the purpose of the Convention is to facilitate the service in the territory of one Contracting State of documents emanating from civil and commercial proceedings in another Contracting State.

The Convention will, in effect, establish a level of international judicial cooperation among the contracting OAS States analogous to that which now exists among the 24 Contracting States to the Hague Convention on the Service Abroad of Judicial and Extrajudicial Documents in Civil or Commercial Matters. Although the latter convention entered into force for the United States on February 10, 1969, following Senate advice and consent to ratification, only one other OAS member State has become a party to it. Ratification of the Inter-American Convention on Letters Rogatory and the Additional Protocol will thus constitute a significant step in filling the void that now exists in the area of judicial cooperation with other OAS countries. Henceforth, litigants before United States courts or other adjudicatory bodies will be able to avail themselves of a number of improved and simplified procedures for the service of process in OAS countries, with consequent savings of time, effort and expense.

I recommend that the Senate of the United States promptly give its advice and consent to the ratification of this Convention and Additional Protocol, subject to two reservations which are described in the accompanying report of the Department of State and which should be made at the time of the deposit by the United States of the instruments of ratification.

RONALD REAGAN

The White House,
June 25, 1984.

Remarks to Participants in the Agricultural Communicators Congress
June 25, 1984

Hello there. Good afternoon. I'm delighted—please, sit down—I'm delighted to welcome you, America's agricultural communicators, to the White House—or, as Jack Block calls this, the South Forty. [*Laughter*]

And I'd like to congratulate you for holding your first Agricultural Communicators Congress. Your desire to work together and to share ideas and to help each other is in the fine tradition of America's farm community.

Agriculture has always been a sharing society. Pioneers helped each other cross uncharted lands and establish homesteads. In time of need a neighbor was always willing to step in and give a helping hand, and

America's farmers and ranchers have never lost that wonderful spirit. You're carrying it forward.

Through you, farmers and ranchers share know-how and business concepts. You concentrate on what is right with agriculture and how to make it better. You're problem-solvers, community builders, and information sharers. And the accent is on the positive, on success. I don't mind telling you you're my kind of communicators.

You're helping to increase yields, develop new marketing strategies, improve agricultural services, and make genetic improvements in plants and livestock. In fact, you did it so well that the American agricultural community has a record of productivity and efficiency unmatched by any other in the world. Agriculture is a driving force in our nation's economy, and you can be very proud of what your industry has accomplished.

Our administration will continue doing all we can to help the farm community recover from past policy mistakes and economic difficulties. One of my first actions, as you know, in this job was to lift the Soviet grain embargo. And last August, we signed a new 5-year grain agreement with the Soviet Union. The Soviet Union has agreed to purchase 9 million tons annually and can purchase up to 12 million tons without consultation. That's a 50-percent increase over the previous agreement. And this year, we've offered to sell them at least 22 million tons. As long as I'm President, our farmers will never again be asked to bear alone the brunt of our foreign policy.

What we're doing, and what we'll continue to do, is to pursue new export markets and work to remove export barriers. To promote exports, our administration, in the first 2 years, has authorized the largest credit guarantees in our history—over $9 billion. Export trade leads are being sent electronically to U.S. exporters.

Our trade teams have been continuously on the go in search of new markets. Jack Block has been knocking on doors all over the world, and he's going to keep on knocking. And I know that all of you join me in wishing Jack a very speedy and complete recovery and that he'll be soon—either here or back out there on the road again.

But I believe these efforts are paying off. We've negotiated new import quotas with Japan that will lead to a near doubling of citrus and beef exports over the next 4 years. And just last month, we reached agreement on internationalization of the yen, an accord that should make our exports more competitively priced.

Last year we demonstrated our determination to counter export subsidies and recovered a 1 million ton wheat flour market in Egypt. As a result, the European Community has joined us in serious discussions in an effort to solve some of the problems caused by their subsidized exports. And, as you know, I signed contract sanctity legislation that gives farmers additional assurances that existing export contracts will not be abrogated. Let me assure you, now that we've regained our reputation as a reliable supplier, we intend to maintain that reputation.

At home we tackled the price-depressing surplus of 1981 and '82 that could have hung over the market for years by quickly stepping in with that Payment-in-Kind Program. We've moved closer to the point where the market, not the government, will be sending production signals to our producers.

On another front, we've doubled the funds provided for the Farmers Home Administration operating loans and have helped some 270,000 farm borrowers who couldn't get credit through commercial sources. Our Federal Crop Insurance Program dealt with 1983's severe weather problems by paying out $580 million—that's an all-time high. And the Farmers Home Administration also provided emergency disaster loans at low interest rates and extended filing application deadlines. And we're determined to do all we can for the farmers hit hard by recent flooding in the Midwest. In fact, Secretary Block sent a team out this morning to assess the damage, and they're on site, right now, even as we meet here today.

And today we're hard at work on the 1985 farm bill. The Department of Agriculture is, and will continue, to actively solicit farmers' views on this bill. So far, they've accepted hundreds of pages of written recommendations and held listening sessions in Chicago, Atlanta, Syracuse, and Riverside, California. And I'm pleased to announce that the next session will be held on July 19th in Dallas, Texas.

All of these efforts are important, but not as important as our economic expansion. The month we took office, the prime interest rate was at the highest level since the Civil War.

They're all Democrat. Run! [*Laughter*] Every time I come here, they [*referring to the noise made by an airplane taking off from Washington National Airport*] take off. [*Laughter*]

But considering that a fifth of farmers' cash outlays are for interest expenses—that 21-percent rate that we inherited when we took office was a devastating blow. And inflation was just as cruel. In the 3 years before 1981, farm costs jumped an outrageous 45 percent. That was at $39.7 billion, and that was the largest 3-year increase in our history. And today the prime interest rate has fallen by nearly half; and we've knocked inflation down to around 4 percent—well, as a matter of fact, for the last 3 months, it's been 3.6 percent.

But don't get me wrong, interest rates are still higher than you and I would like, and we're going to continue. And I think that to get them down, they just have to finally realize that we're serious about keeping inflation under control. There is no excuse for the interest rates being at the level they are right now, other than just fear of the future.

But we've restored our nation's basic economic health. And if we continue to pursue a sound monetary policy and work to put the Federal budgeting process in order, interest rates will drop more, and inflation will stay down. We all have a stake in making sure that government spending is brought down in line with government revenues. And that's why I strongly favor constitutional reforms to give the President a line-item veto and to mandate, by the Constitution, a balanced Federal budget.

Now, the critics are still with us, but they're the same critics who were wrong on inflation. They were wrong on unemployment; they were wrong on real wages; they were wrong on interest rates; and they were wrong about whether there'd be a recovery or not. In fact, everytime I hear them, I remember Robert Frost saying: "The brain is a wonderful organ. It starts working the moment you get up in the morning, and doesn't stop until you get to the office." [*Laughter*]

Am I optimistic? Well, you bet I am. I believe our best days are yet to come. With faith, freedom, courage, there's no limit to what the American people can do and will accomplish. And that's always been the way of the American farmer.

So, once again, I want to congratulate you on your Congress and to thank you for what you're doing. I may beat this one [*referring to the noise from another airplane taking off from the airport*]. [*Laughter*] By sharing ideas with farm audiences, you're helping to keep our great nation and our farm community strong, prosperous, and free. And as I recently told the National Council of Farmer Cooperatives, America's farmers have my pledge to see to it that the dream of a successful family farm remains a living part of the American dream.

Thank you again, and God bless you all. Thank you.

Note: The President spoke at 1:32 p.m. on the South Lawn of the White House.

Executive Order 12483—Amending the Generalized System of Preferences
June 25, 1984

By the authority vested in me as President by the Constitution and statutes of the United States of America, including Title V of the Trade Act of 1974, as amended (19 U.S.C. 2461 *et seq.*), as amended (the "Trade Act"), and sections 503 and 604 of the Trade Act (19 U.S.C. 2463 and 2483), and in order to adjust the original designation of eligible articles for purposes of the Generalized System of Preferences (GSP), it is hereby ordered as follows:

Section 1. The articles provided for in item 706.39 of the Tariff Schedules of the United States (TSUS) are hereby removed from the list of eligible articles for purposes of the GSP.

Sec. 2. Annex III of Executive Order No. 11888 of November 24, 1975, as amended, listing articles that are eligible for benefits of the GSP when imported from all designated beneficiary developing countries except those specified in general headnote 3(c)(iii) of the TSUS, is further amended by deleting item 706.39.

Sec. 3. General headnote 3(c)(iii) of the TSUS, listing articles that are eligible for benefits of the GSP except when imported from the beneficiary developing countries listed opposite those articles, is modified by deleting the following TSUS item number and countries: "706.39 . . . Hong Kong, Republic of Korea, and Taiwan".

Sec. 4. The amendments made by this Order shall be effective with respect to articles both: (1) imported on and after January 1, 1976, and (2) entered, or withdrawn from warehouse for consumption, on or after June 25, 1984.

RONALD REAGAN

The White House,
June 25, 1984.

[*Filed with the Office of the Federal Register, 10:44 a.m., June 26, 1984*]

Note: The text of the Executive order was released by the Office of the Press Secretary on June 26.

Remarks at a White House Ceremony Honoring Senior Citizen Volunteers
June 26, 1984

The President. My greetings to all of you—octogenarians, nonagenarians, and, of course, the kids and my fellow septuagenarians. [*Laughter*] It's a pleasure to welcome you all here to the East Room, some of the most important members of the American family, the senior citizen volunteers.

I've been taking a look at some of the things that you have been doing, and I can tell you from your accomplishments that your attitude toward life is just like Bernard Baruch's, who once said, "Old age is always 15 years older than I am." [*Laughter*] I like that attitude. I think the thing about getting older is that you'll never grow old as long as you're still interested in the world and still eager to help it.

And I'm aware of all your great volunteer efforts, not only of the people in this audience but of senior citizens as a whole. There has been, for some time, a stereotype abroad in the land that senior citizens don't do much to contribute to society, don't do much to improve the quality of American life. Well, nothing could be further from the truth. No stereotype is as ill-deserved as that one. The truth is, volunteer work is the most prevalent outside-the-home activity for Americans 65 and over. The vast majority of older people are ready to serve.

A recent poll shows 36 percent of the 65-and-older group are involved in charitable activities. They work in the Veterans Administration giving one-on-one help to patients. They work for the Red Cross. They join the Peace Corps. They become Foster Grandparents. In fact, over 18,000 Foster Grandparents are now helping kids who are mentally retarded, autistic, and abused. Thousands of senior citizen companions are helping the elderly, their fellow citizens, and the handicapped. And across the country, over 350,000 senior citizens work about half a day a week as members of the Retired Senior Volunteer programs. They deliver meals to those who can't leave their homes and provide transportation and friendship for the incapacitated.

The fact is that more and more senior citizens in America are becoming part of a big, unsung, unknown army that is dedicated to making life better for all of us. And in doing this, they and all of you have learned the secret of everlasting youth: Stay involved. Keep taking your place at the table of life. Keep going out there into the world, making new friends, and helping people out. Keep giving and keep taking.

That was the secret of some great men and women of Western civilization. Grandma Moses was doing brilliant work well into her eighties. Verdi composed the opera "Falstaff" at 79. Adenauer was guiding the German economic miracle when he was in his eighties. Churchill was at retirement age when he began to lead Britain through World War II. And, of course, "Old Hickory," Andrew Jackson, was actually 70 years old when he left the White House. Can you imagine that? [*Laughter*] And he felt pretty trim and fit and vigorous when he left. I know—he told me. [*Laughter*]

They always talk about Presidents aging in office, and of course, like everyone else we do. But I also think that if you enjoy this office and the great debates of the day, then you'll always stay pretty young. That's the key, I think, loving your work—either the work you do for a living or the work you choose to do when you've retired. But I know I have nothing to tell you about that, because I know that in this group there are some great contributors, some great givers and takers from life.

Now, I'm aware that the aged in our society have some special problems. The world moves so fast these days, and so much of our society is geared to the young that the aged sometimes can feel left out, as if they're no longer in style, and as if they should feel some shame about having grown old. And the greater scourge of old age—the greatest of all—is loneliness. And that's why we in this administration have been trying to work closely with national, regional, and local private sector programs and civic and religious groups to help out where and when we can, and to let you know you're deeply appreciated.

I have to inject in here, if I could, a little personal experience. I've told it before, but I want to tell it again.

I refuse to be apologetic about our generation. There are few generations in the history of mankind who have lived through great transition periods. These young people today will see marvelous things that we've not seen and will not see. But, few generations have ever spanned a great transition period in history. And ours is one of those few generations.

We have literally gone from the horse and buggy to travel to the Moon and in outer space. And we have survived four wars in our lifetime; one of the greatest depressions that has ever hit—that makes this recent recession look like child's play, compared to what we went through. And we have nothing to apologize for—for what we have done.

But the incident I wanted to remind— was back when I was Governor of California. And you know the riotous days on the campuses. And one day a group of student leaders demanded a meeting with me—the nine campuses of the University of California. Well, I was delighted to meet with them, because if I went to the campus, I'd start a riot. [*Laughter*] So, they came in— some of them were barefoot, torn T-shirts, the jeans, the—that was the uniform of the day—and they sat down, and one spokesman immediately teed off.

And he said, "Governor, it is impossible for you to understand our generation." And I tried to pass it off. I said, "Well, we know more about being young than we do about being old." And he said, "No, I mean it. You cannot understand your own sons and daughters." And he went on. He said, "You didn't grow up in a world of instant electronics, of instant communication, of travel into space, of nuclear energy, and jet travel." And he went on with all these things.

Well, usually, you know, the answer comes to you 2 hours later when the meeting is over. But he talked just long enough that the answer came to me—[*laughter*]—as he listed all these things, and I was hearing what he was talking about that they were living with as if we didn't know anything about them. And he paused for breath, and I interrupted him. And I said, "You're absolutely right. We didn't have any of those things when we were your age. We invented them." [*Laughter*]

So, all of you in this audience deserve our thanks, our appreciation, and our attention. You're burying old stereotypes, and you're contributing to the world at a time in life when you've earned the right to just sit back and let someone else do it. Well, you're not sitting back, you're leading, and we owe you our thanks.

And now I want to mention someone, Clarence Nash. Ducky is a wonderful man. He's been the voice of Donald Duck at the Walt studios—Disney studios, for a long time. In fact, this is his 50th anniversary as Donald's voice. And I want to congratulate him and wish him many years of good work.

Ducky, your talents have delighted millions, and I want to mark your anniversary by giving you an award for 50 years of entertainment. Now, someone is approaching with it—yes. Thank you very much.

This reads: "To Clarence Ducky Nash, in recognition of his outstanding volunteer service to the Nation as the voice of Donald Duck. For years, Ducky Nash has given generously of his time, energy, and talent to bring pleasure and laughter to those in hospitals and institutions around the country. This commendation recognizes that unselfish commitment."

Mr. Nash. Thank you, Mr. President. It's really a great pleasure to be here today among all of us senior citizens. It's just great to come here for many reasons, too. I like to share some of my experiences in my work with children.

One time, I was in a hospital entertaining children. There was a boy that was crying. He was in pain, and a doctor was attending him. And the gentleman who was managing me, I told him, "I think I should take Donald down and talk to this boy." And he said, "No, you'll get in the doctor's way." Well, a nurse overheard this. She said, "You go right down there." So I did.

And what did you say to the boy, Donald? You put your face right in front of him.

Donald Duck. Shut up! [*Laughter*]

Mr. Nash. That boy shut up. [*Laughter*] And Donald talked to him for over 5 minutes. And the doctor—he was through—he said, "Thanks. This is one time a quack really helped a doctor." [*Laughter*]

Mr. President, I want to thank you again. You know, you and I both shared something at Disneyland in 1955. And it's wonderful that you would invite us here, too. Thank you again.

The President. Well, pleased to see you.

And now, thank you all, and God bless all of you for what you're doing. Thank you.

Note: The President spoke at 11:50 a.m. in the East Room at the White House.

Nomination of Richard Wood Boehm To Be United States Ambassador to Cyprus
June 26, 1984

The President today announced his intention to nominate Richard Wood Boehm, of the District of Columbia, a career member of the Senior Foreign Service, Class of Minister-Counselor, as Ambassador to the Republic of Cyprus. He would succeed Raymond C. Ewing.

Mr. Boehm served in the United States Army in 1944–1946. In 1950–1951 he was a proofreader and editor with the Prentice-Hall Publishing Co., and was in junior management with the Mutual Life Insurance Co. of New York in 1951–1955. In 1955 he entered the Foreign Service as press officer in the Department. He was consular officer in Naha (1956–1958), economic officer, staff officer, then political officer at the United States Mission in Berlin (1958–1962). In the Department he was intelligence and research analyst (1962–1965) and NATO political affairs desk officer (1965–1966). In 1966–1968 he was deputy chief of mission in Luxembourg. He attended the National War College in 1968–1969 and was in the Department as public affairs adviser in the Bureau of Economic Affairs in 1969–1971. He was Embassy counselor for mutual secu-rity (political-military) affairs in Ankara (1971–1974), and Embassy counselor for political-military affairs in Bangkok (1974–1976). In 1976–1977 he was diplomat in residence at Hamilton College in Clinton, NY. He was a foreign service inspector in the Department in 1977–1978. He was deputy chief of mission in Kathmandu (1978–1980), and in Ankara (1980–1983). In 1983 he was an adviser with the United States Delegation to the United Nations General Assembly in New York City. Since 1984 he has been Deputy Examiner of the Board of Examiners for the Foreign Service in the Department.

Mr. Boehm graduated from Adelphi University (A.B., 1950), George Washington University (M.A., 1969), and received a diploma from the University of Paris in 1949. His foreign languages are German and French. He was born June 25, 1926, in New York, NY.

Nomination of Paul H. Boeker To Be United States Ambassador to Jordan
June 26, 1984

The President today announced his intention to nominate Paul H. Boeker, of Ohio, a career member of the Senior Foreign Service, Class of Career Minister, as Ambassador to the Hashemite Kingdom of Jordan. He would succeed Richard N. Viets.

Mr. Boeker entered the Foreign Service in 1961 as consular officer in Ponta Delgada. He was assistant commercial attaché in Bogotá in 1964–1966. In 1966–1967 he attended economic studies at the University of Michigan. In the Department he was financial economist (1967–1970) and Director (1970–1971) of the Office of Development and Finance. He was economic officer in Bonn in 1971–1973. In the Department he was a member of the policy planning staff (1974), Deputy Assistant Secretary for International Finance and Development (1974–1976), and Deputy Assistant Secretary for Economic and Business Affairs (1976–1977). He was Ambassador to Bolivia in 1977–1980. In 1980–1982 he was Director of the Foreign Service Institute. On a leave of absence from the Department of State, he served as director of analysis for International Reporting Information Systems in Alexandria, VA, in 1981–1983. Since 1983 he has been a member of the Policy Planning Council in the Department.

Mr. Boeker graduated from Dartmouth College (A.B., 1960) and the University of Michigan (M.A., 1967). He attended graduate studies at Princeton University in 1960–1961. His foreign languages are German, Spanish, and French. He was born May 2, 1938, in St. Louis, MO.

Remarks on Presenting the Presidential Medal of Freedom to the Family of the Late Senator Henry M. Jackson of Washington
June 26, 1984

The President. Well, ladies and gentlemen, honored guests, and Mrs. Helen Jackson, thank all of you for coming here today. Won't you please be seated?

We're here to honor Henry "Scoop" Jackson, who was one of the great Senators in our history and a great patriot who loved freedom first, last, and always.

It's less than a year since his death, but already we can define with confidence the lasting nature of his contribution. Henry Jackson was a protector of the Nation, a protector of its freedoms and values. There are always a few such people in each generation. Let others push each chic new belief or become distracted by the latest fashionable reading of history. The protectors listen and nod and go about seeing to it that the ideals that shaped this nation are allowed to survive and flourish. They defend the permanent against the merely prevalent. They have few illusions.

Henry Jackson understood that there is great good in the world and great evil, too, that there are saints and sinners among us. He had no illusions about totalitarians, but his understanding of the existence of evil didn't sour or dishearten him. He had a great hope and great faith in America. He felt we could do anything. He liked to quote Teddy Roosevelt: "We see across the dangers the great future, and we rejoice as a giant refreshed . . . the great victories are yet to be won, the greatest deeds yet to be done."

Scoop came to the Congress in 1941, a year when the locomotive of history seemed wrenched from its tracks. In Europe, the ideals of the West were under siege; in America, isolationists warned against involvement. Scoop watched history unfold. He watched Norway, the country of his immigrant parents, fall to Hitler. He came to see [some] conclusions about the world. And from then until the day he died, he rejected isolationism as an acceptable way for a great democracy to comport itself in the world. This view sprang from the heart of the F.D.R. tradition of foreign policy: We accept our responsibilities in the world; we do not flee them.

Henry Jackson absorbed within himself the three great strains of thought that go to the making of a noble foreign policy: a love of freedom; a will to defend it; and the knowledge that America could not and must not attempt to float along alone, a blissful island of democracy in a sea of totalitarianism.

Scoop Jackson was convinced that there's no place for partisanship in foreign and defense policy. He used to say, "In matters of national security, the best politics is no politics." His sense of bipartisanship was not only natural and complete; it was courageous. He wanted to be President, but I think he must have known that his outspoken ideas on the security of the Nation would deprive him of the chance to be his party's nominee in 1972 and '76. Still, he would not cut his convictions to fit the prevailing style.

I'm deeply proud, as he would have been, to have Jackson Democrats serve in my administration. I'm proud that some of them have found a home here.

Scoop Jackson believed in a strong defense for only one reason: because it would help preserve the peace by deterring military violence. He believed in arms control, because he wanted a more secure world. But he refused to support any arms control initiative that would not, in his judgment, serve the security interests of the Nation and ensure the survival of the West. His command of the facts and his ability to grasp detail were legendary. At congressional hearings, people often learned more from his questions than they did from anyone else's answers.

It was very much like Scoop to see that there was a growing problem in Central America—and to see that the challenge of protecting freedom and independence there would require the commitment of Democrats and Republicans alike. He conceived the Bipartisan Commission on Central America and became one of its most active leaders. He knew that stable, democratic institutions cannot be achieved in that region without the security that American assistance can provide. He saw the Commission's work completed, and if he were alive today, he would be working tirelessly to get its recommendations accepted by the Congress.

Scoop helped shape national policy on dozens of complex issues—on strategic planning and arms control, on the Soviet Union and Central America, on human rights and Israel, and the cause of Soviet Jewry.

His support for Israel grew out of his knowledge that political decisions must spring from moral convictions. It wasn't some grand geopolitical abstraction that made him back the creation of Israel; it was seeing the concentration camps firsthand at the end of the war. At Buchenwald he saw the evil, as he said, "written on the sky," and he never forgot.

He said the Jews of Europe must have a homeland. He did everything he could to strengthen the alliance between the United States and Israel, recognizing that we are two great democracies, two great cultures, standing together. Today both nations are safer because of his efforts.

He never stopped speaking out against anti-Semitism in the Soviet Union. And he was never afraid to speak out against anti-Semitism at home. And Scoop Jackson just would not be bullied. He conceived and fought for the Jackson amendment to the Trade Act of 1974. There's hardly a soul among the hundreds of thousands of Soviet Jews who later found freedom in the West who was not sustained in the struggle to emigrate by the certain knowledge that Scoop was at his side.

Scoop was always at the side of the weak and forgotten. With some people, all you have to do to win their friendship is to be strong and powerful. With Scoop, all you had to do was be vulnerable and alone. And so when Simas Kudirka was in jail in Moscow, it was Scoop who helped mobilize the Congress to demand his release. When Baptists in the Soviet Union were persecuted, it was Scoop who went again and again to the floor of the Senate to plead their

cause. When free trade unionists were under attack in Poland, Scoop worked with the American labor movement to help them.

A few years ago, he was invited to visit the Soviet Union. The invitation was withdrawn when he said he could not go without calling on Andrei Sakharov. If Scoop were here today, I know he would speak out on behalf of Sakharov, just as Sakharov, a man of immense courage and humanity, stood up in Moscow and hailed the Jackson amendment as a triumph of "the freedom loving tradition of the American people."

Scoop Jackson was a serious man—not somber or self-important, but steady and solemn. He didn't think much of the cosmetics of politics. He wasn't interested in image. He was a practitioner of the art of politics, and he was a personage in the affairs of the world. But there was no cause too great or too small for his attention.

When he wasn't on the floor of the Senate or talking to the leaders of the world, he was usually in his office on the phone—consoling a constituent in a moment of grief, tracking down a lost social security check, congratulating an honor student, or helping a small businessman who was caught up in redtape.

The principles which guided his public life guided his private life. By the time he died, dozens of young men and women had been helped through school by a scholarship fund that he established and sustained. No one knew the money came from Scoop, until a change in the financial disclosure laws many years later forced him to 'fess up. He had never told the voters; he'd never even told his own staff.

Other people were embarrassed when the disclosure laws revealed their vanities. Scoop was embarrassed when it revealed his virtues.

One night last September, Scoop worked a long day and went home with a cold. There he fell into the sleep from which he never emerged. The next day, it was as if Washington had changed. Something was missing, some big presence.

A few days later, in a eulogy for Scoop, it was pointed out that there's a room in the Senate where members of the public are greeted. And on the walls of that room are the portraits of five of the greatest U.S. Senators, men chosen by the members of the Senate to reflect the best that chamber ever knew. There's Robert Taft, who, like Scoop, was Mr. Integrity, and LaFollette, who, like Scoop, often swam against the tide. There's Calhoun, who loved the South as Scoop loved the West, and Webster, who tried, like Scoop, to be a force to hold the Nation together, in spite of its differences. And there's Henry Clay, a gifted man, who, like Scoop, would have been a great president.

It happens that there is no appropriate space on the walls of that room for another portrait. So, I'm joining those who would suggest to the majority leader that the Senate make room and commission a portrait so that Scoop Jackson can be with his peers. And when it's all done and in place, I'd be very proud to be among those who would go to the Senate and unveil it, Republicans and Democrats alike, a bipartisan effort in memory of the great bipartisan patriot of our time.

And now I am deeply honored to present to you, Mrs. Helen Jackson, the Medal of Freedom in honor of your husband, Senator Henry Jackson of the State of Washington.

Let me read the citation.

Representative and Senator for more than four decades, Henry Martin Jackson was one of the greatest lawmakers of our century. He helped to build the community of democracies and worked tirelessly to keep it vigorous and secure. He pioneered in the preservation of the Nation's natural heritage, and he embodied integrity and decency in the profession of politics. For those who make freedom their cause Henry Jackson will always inspire honor, courage, and hope.

Mrs. Jackson. Mr. President, I'm proud to accept this great honor the Nation has bestowed on my husband.

I accept this award not only on behalf of Anna Marie, Peter, and myself but also on behalf of all those who worked with Scoop and shared his causes and convictions over the years. As Scoop used to say, "If you believe in the cause of freedom, then proclaim it, live it and protect it, for humanity's future depends upon it."

Mr. President, we thank you for today from the bottom of our hearts.

Note: The President spoke at 1:32 p.m. in the Rose Garden at the White House.

Appointment of Maynard W. Glitman as the United States Representative for the Mutual and Balanced Force Reductions Negotiations
June 26, 1984

The President today announced his intention to appoint Maynard W. Glitman, of Vermont, a career member of the Senior Foreign Service, Class of Minister-Counselor, to be the Representative of the United States of America for Mutual and Balanced Force Reductions Negotiations, and his intention to nominate Mr. Glitman for the rank of Ambassador. He would succeed Morton I. Abramowitz.

Mr. Glitman entered the Foreign Service in 1956 as economic officer in the Department and was fiscal and financial officer in 1957–1959. He was consular and economic officer in Nassau (1959–1961) and economic officer in Ottawa (1961–1965). He attended Atlantic affairs studies at the University of California in 1965–1966. In 1966–1968 he was international relations officer in the Department, and he was political officer in Paris in 1968–1973. In the Department he was Director of the Office of International Trade Policy (1974–1976). He was on detail as Deputy Assistant Secretary of Defense for International Security Affairs in 1976–1977. In 1977–1981 he was deputy chief of mission at the United States Mission to the North Atlantic Treaty Organization in Brussels. Since 1981 he has been Department of State Representative and Deputy Head of

915

the United States Delegation to the Inter-mediate-range Nuclear Force negotiations, with the rank of Ambassador, in Geneva.

Mr. Glitman was born December 8, 1933, in Chicago, IL. He graduated from the Uni-versity of Illinois (B.A., 1955) and the Fletcher School of Law and Diplomacy (M.A., 1956). His foreign language is fluent French.

Nomination of Wanda L. Forbes To Be a Member of the National Commission on Libraries and Information Science
June 26, 1984

The President today announced his inten-tion to nominate Wanda L. Forbes to be a member of the National Commission on Li-braries and Information Science for a term expiring July 19, 1988. She would succeed Francis Kepple.

Mrs. Forbes is a candidate for the South Carolina House of Representatives. Previ-ously she was an instructor at Winthrop College in 1981; a member of the South Carolina Commission on Higher Education in 1975–1978; and a media specialist at Gaston Day School in Gastonia, NC. (1972–1975). She served on the Advisory Commit-tee of the Museum of Education at the Uni-versity of South Carolina in 1981.

She graduated from Queens College (B.A., 1947) and Winthrop College (M.A., 1969). She is married, has three children and resides in Clover, SC. She was born July 21, 1925, in Keyser, WV.

Remarks to Participants in the Conference on United States-Soviet Exchanges
June 27, 1984

Well, Drs. Billington, Hamburg, Ellison, and Johnson, thank you for bringing your distinguished group to the White House. When I heard that you would be meeting at the Smithsonian to discuss U.S.-Soviet ex-changes, I was eager to share my thoughts with you on this timely and important topic.

First, I want to congratulate the Wood-row Wilson Center and the Carnegie Cor-poration of New York; certainly nothing is more worthy of our attention than finding ways to reach out and establish better com-munication with the people and the Gov-ernment of the Soviet Union.

For many months, I have encouraged the Soviet Union to join with us in a major effort to see if we could make progress in these broad problem areas: reducing the threat and use of force in solving interna-tional disputes, reducing armaments in the world, and establishing a better working re-lationship with each other.

At the United Nations, at the Japanese Diet, at Georgetown University, and at the Irish Parliament I have explained our ef-forts to reduce arms, particularly nuclear arms, and to establish a useful dialog on regional issues. Let me describe to you some of the many efforts that we're making to establish a better working relationship with the Soviet Union.

We've informed the Soviet Government that we're prepared to initiate negotiations on a new exchanges agreement, and we've completed our preparations for these nego-tiations. We've proposed to resume prep-arations to open consulates in New York and Kiev. We've taken steps to revive our agreements for cooperation in environmen-tal protection, housing, health, and agricul-ture. Activities under these agreements have waned in recent years, because there've been no meetings of their joint committees to plan projects. We've proposed that preparations begin for such meetings in order to increase the number of active projects.

We're in the process of renewing several bilateral agreements that otherwise would have expired this year. And we've agreed to extend our fishing agreement for 18 months, and we're looking at possibilities to increase cooperation under the terms of the agreement.

We've proposed that our Agreement to Facilitate Economic, Industrial and Technical Cooperation be renewed for another 10 years and that preparations begin for a meeting of our Joint Commercial Commission.

The U.S. Navy delegation held talks last month with their Soviet counterparts in accord with our agreement on avoiding incidents at sea. And we've agreed to extend this useful agreement for another 3 years.

We're reviewing the World Oceans Agreement, which has been useful in promoting joint oceanographic research, and we'll give careful thought to renewing the agreement prior to its expiration. And we've made proposals in several other areas to improve dialog, foster cooperation, and solve problems.

We've proposed a fair and equitable resolution of our differences on the maritime boundary off Alaska. We've proposed a joint simulated space rescue mission in which astronauts and cosmonauts would carry out a combined exercise in space to develop techniques to rescue people from malfunctions in space vehicles. And we're currently conducting another round of talks on consular matters, trying to improve visa procedures and facilitate travel between our two countries.

We've suggested discussions between the U.S. Coast Guard and the Soviet Ministry of Merchant Marine on search and rescue procedures to assist citizens of all countries lost at sea. And we've made progress in our talks on upgrading the hotline, proposing discussions on potential nuclear terrorist incidents, on establishing a joint military communications line, and on upgrading embassy communications in both countries. We've

also suggested regular high-level contacts between military personnel of our two countries.

So, as you can see, we've offered comprehensive and sensible proposals to improve the U.S.-Soviet dialog and our working relationship. And if the Soviets decide to join us, new avenues would open, I think, for your efforts.

It's still too early to judge the results. A few proposals are near agreement. Many others are still under discussion, and some have been rejected—at least for now.

Meaningful contact with a closed society will never be easy. And I'm as disturbed as you are by recent reports of new measures taken by Soviet authorities to restrict contacts between Soviet citizens and foreigners. These restrictions come on top of intensified repression of those brave Soviet citizens who've dared to express views contrary to those of the Soviet political elite.

The people of the Soviet Union pay a heavy price for the actions of their government. In fact, we all pay a price. When the Soviet Government takes repressive actions against its people and attempts to seal them off from the outside world, their own intellectual and cultural life suffers. At the same time, the rest of the world is deprived of the cultural riches of the Soviet people. What would classical music be without a Tchaikovsky or literature without a Tolstoi or chemistry without a Mendeleev.

Civilized people everywhere have a stake in keeping contacts, communication, and creativity as broad, deep, and free as possible. The Soviet insistence on sealing their people off and on filtering and controlling contacts and the flow of information remains the central problem.

When Soviet actions threaten the peace or violate a solemn agreement or trample on standards fundamental to a civilized world, we cannot and will not be silent. We cannot—well, to do so would betray our deepest values. It would violate our conscience and ultimately undermine world stability and our ability to keep the peace. We must have ways short of military threats that make it absolutely clear that Soviet actions do matter and that some actions inevitably affect the quality of the relationship.

917

These reactions do lead to a decrease in contacts with the people of the Soviet Union, and this is a dilemma. However, our quarrel is not with the Russian people, with the Ukrainian people, or any of the other proud nationalities in that multinational state. So, we must be careful in reacting to actions by the Soviet Government not to take out our indignations on those not responsible. And that's why I feel that we should broaden opportunities for Americans and Soviet citizens to get to know each other better.

But our proposals to do that are not a signal that we have forgotten Afghanistan. We'll continue to demonstrate our sympathy and strong support for the Afghan people. The United States will support their struggle to end the Soviet occupation and to reestablish an independent and neutral Afghanistan.

Nor do our proposals mean that we will ignore violations of the Helsinki Final Act or the plight of Andrei Sakharov, Yelena Bonner, Anatoly Shcharanskiy, Yuriy Orlov, and so many others. The persecution of these courageous, noble people weighs very heavily on our hearts. It would be wrong to believe that their treatment and their fate will not affect our ability to increase cooperation. It will, because our conscience and that of the American people and freedom-loving people everywhere will have it no other way.

Now, I know these thoughts do not resolve the dilemma we face. But it is a dilemma for all of us. And I'll value your advice.

You know, I don't think there's anything we're encouraging the Soviet leaders to do that is not as much in their interest as it is in ours. If they're as committed to peace as they say, they should join us and work with us. If they sincerely want to reduce arms, there's no excuse for refusing to talk, and if they sincerely want to deal with us as equals, they shouldn't try to avoid a frank discussion of real problems.

Some say for the Soviet leaders peace is not the real issue; rather, the issue is the attempt to spread their dominance by using military power as a means of intimidation, and there is much evidence to support this view. But it should be clear by now that such a strategy will not work. And once they realize this, maybe they'll understand they have much to gain by improving dialog, reducing arms, and solving problems.

The way governments can best promote contacts among people is by not standing in the way. Our administration will do all we can to stay out of the way and to persuade the Soviet Government to do likewise. Now, we know this won't happen overnight, but if we're to succeed, you must stay involved and get more Americans into wider and more meaningful contact with many more Soviet citizens.

It may seem an impossible dream to think there could be a time when Americans and Soviet citizens of all walks of life travel freely back and forth, visit each other's homes, look up friends and professional colleagues, work together in all sorts of problems, and, if they feel like it, sit up all night talking about the meaning of life and the different ways to look at the world.

In most countries of the world, people take those contacts for granted. We should never accept the idea that American and Soviet citizens cannot enjoy the same contacts and communication. I don't believe it's an impossible dream, and I don't think you believe that, either.

So, let me just conclude by saying thank you, and God bless you for what you're doing.

Note: The President spoke at 1:30 p.m. in the East Room at the White House.

Remarks to Members of the National Association of Minority Contractors
June 27, 1984

The President. Well, John Cruz, Jim Chandler, Dewey Thomas, Raymon Dones, and all of you very distinguished ladies and gentlemen, good afternoon and a warm welcome to you. Believe me, I extend that welcome with a very special pleasure, because when it comes to lifting human hearts with the spirit of hope and hard work, when it comes to building progress with a spirit of enterprise, and when it comes to building America by serving the Nation with pride, then, yes, we're talking about members of the National Association of Minority Contractors.

You understand so well a central truth of human progress: The struggle by all Americans for freedom from discrimination must be a spiritual struggle for brotherhood, must be a political struggle for full participation at the ballot box; but just as important, it must be an economic struggle for opportunity in a growth economy that creates jobs, not welfare; wealth, not poverty; and freedom, not dependency. And this is a lesson America has been taking too long a time to learn.

We know that prior to the 1960's it was an accepted and sometimes legal practice to discriminate in housing, education, public accommodations, and in employment. Then, in the wake of the Kennedy tax cuts, the economy began growing rapidly, but still minorities did not benefit as fully as they should have. Yet we will always remember the historic achievements of great Americans who have managed to overcome such discrimination—Americans like Andrew Brimmer, the first black ever to be appointed as a Governor of the Federal Reserve System; Ralph Bunche, the first American black to win the Nobel Peace Prize; and Benjamin Banneker, who contributed to the original design and great beauty of our Nation's Capital.

The civil rights movement of the 1960's helped start the repeal of the unjust system of discrimination. But beginning in 1966, on the very heels of the breakdown of these legal barriers, the economy entered a period of disappointing performance that lasted through the decade of the seventies. Black Americans had seen the economic train moving and had fought for and won the right to purchase a ticket. But as they came aboard, the train began to slow down, and then it stopped altogether.

Many of those big government programs had compassionate, indeed, noble intentions, but they also had serious adverse consequences. They marked a departure from creating wealth to creating dependency. I believe what black Americans need more, or most, is more opportunity, more enterprise, a bigger cash box, and economic emancipation. And to paraphrase, Thomas Wolfe, to every man and woman, regardless of their birth, their shining, golden opportunity to live, to work, to be themselves and to become whatever their vision can combine to make them—that is the promise of America. And that promise is what we came to Washington to restore.

When we arrived here we found the worst economic crisis since the Great Depression. And I know to many of you the Great Depression is just something you've read about. But take it from one who lived through it as an adult—[*laughter*]—trying to get a job and working, the most recent recession, bad as it was, there was just no comparison with that Great Depression. And we must never have anything like that happen again in our land.

Double-digit inflation though, 4 years ago, was destroying people's savings and brutally attacking the elderly and others on fixed incomes. Overregulation, high taxes, and record interest rates were destroying a dream of minority business ownership and home ownership for all but a select few. So, we went to work to make a fundamental change in direction—a change from control *by* government to control *of* government; a change from taxing you more, no matter how hard you tried, to rewarding you for your work and for your working harder and

919

producing more than ever before.

We said we couldn't change more than a decade of mistakes overnight, that our progress would come in inches and feet, rather than miles, but that progress would come. And now I know the concerns expressed about this administration's programs, and, frankly, if I believed the things that I've heard and read, I'd be concerned, too. But when we look at America, I think we can see a much different picture.

We can see inflation down from 12.4 percent to 3.6 percent for the last 3 months, interest rates down significantly, and the growth of regulations cut by a third. And that's progress.

We can see an American economic expansion, led by a surge of productivity, innovation, the fastest rising rate of business investment since 1949, and a record number of business incorporations. And that's progress.

And we can see more jobs created in the last 18 months than in any other country, including millions of jobs for minorities and women. And that's progress, too.

The overall black unemployment rate has fallen more sharply than the white unemployment rate; but it's still much too high, and it's needlessly high. For 2 years, a cruel charade has been perpetuated by some in the Congress on people at the bottom of the income scale, the very people who most desperately need opportunities to better themselves, to develop their skills, and to become productive, self-reliant members of the American mainstream.

As you know, we've proposed an innovative idea that's called enterprise zones to begin providing opportunities in some of the most destitute areas of the country and in our inner cities. But today, areas that could have become new sites for development and economic growth, pockets of enterprise, jobs, and a bright and hopeful future, remain vacant, neglected, and impoverished. Despite more than 2 years of waiting, despite support from over a hundred Democrats in the Congress and the great majority of Republicans, and despite a track record of success with many State and local governments who've already moved ahead in that area, the liberal leadership in the House has deliberately blocked our en-

terprise zones proposal from coming to a vote. And I think that's more than a tragedy; it's an outrage.

And let me just say to them today: Please spare us their sermons on fairness and compassion. If they want minority Americans to have more opportunity, doing nothing isn't doing enough. Give enterprise zones a fair debate out there on the floor and then a chance for the representatives in government to vote on it. In the name of growth, let's stop talking billions for dependency and start creating opportunity [enterprise] zones for opportunity. And in the name of America, let's stop spreading bondage and start spreading freedom.

Now, we hope to have a vote today—but certainly before the Congress goes home—on another important issue which could provide opportunities, experience, discipline, and greater self-esteem for teenagers. I'm talking about our youth employment opportunity wage proposal, which I'm sure you support—and we're very grateful for your support.

We've seen that one of the greatest barriers to more jobs for youth, and especially for minority young people, is the single minimum wage system. The truth is, while everyone must be assured a fair wage, there's no sense in mandating $3.35 an hour for startup jobs that simply aren't worth that much in the marketplace, the kind of jobs that young people can get in the vacation months of the summer or after school and weekend jobs. All that does is guarantee that fewer jobs for teenagers will be created and fewer people will be hired. So, in the time remaining, we hope you'll help persuade the Congress to pass our youth unemployment [employment] opportunity wage [bill].

We can create more than 400,000 new summer jobs for American youth. We can do it without displacing existing workers, and that should be a goal everyone supports, Republicans and Democrats alike. It is a lower minimum wage for young people who are still getting an education and who'll be going out there looking for their first jobs.

And while I'm on the subject of bipartisanship, I want to urge the Congress to pass the deficit downpayment measures that have been approved by the House-Senate conference last weekend. And let's be clear on one thing; those measures are only a part of what the Congress must achieve in spending restraint. We'll be watching the appropriations process with an eagle eye, and I stand ready to use my veto pen to make sure that spending growth by government continues to come down.

If the dream of America is to be preserved, we must not waste the genius of one mind, the strength of one body, or the spirit of one soul. We must use every asset we have, and our greatest progress will come by mobilizing the power of private enterprise. I don't think anything could better show our commitment to minority business development than the actions that we've taken in your own area of minority contracting.

We presented our program in December of 1982, and some of the results are beginning to show. The major points of that initiative were a program to form 6,000 new minority businesses a year for the next 10 years; a commitment to expand, with Federal help, at least 60,000 existing minority business enterprises; and a commitment by which the Federal Government intends to procure some $15 billion in minority business goods and services over the 3 fiscal years.

To get things rolling, Federal agency MBE procurement objectives were to be increased by at least 10 percent over fiscal year '82 levels, and I'm delighted to report that we succeeded. We've also been successful in our efforts to increase minority vending by recipients of Federal grants and cooperative agreements, increase credit assistance, and maintain the level of management and technical assistance.

About a year ago, on July 14th, 1983, I signed an Executive order to improve Federal planning for minority business programs. Department and agency heads were directed to develop and implement incentives to encourage greater minority business subcontracting by Federal prime contractors. I directed SBA, the Small Business Administration, to make special efforts to expand the number of minority firms participating in Federal procurement pro-

grams. And I'm delighted to report that from March of '83 to March of this year, SBA added 588 firms to their programs.

We encouraged American business leaders to expand their business transactions with minority firms. And the Surface Transportation Assistance Act has resulted in an additional $1 billion in new minority contracting opportunities for both this year and last year.

Now, here's what meeting our goal will mean to you. Nearly $3 billion more in contracting will be provided for minority businesses in 3 years than was provided in all the 12 years during the last three administrations. And just so no one forgets these commitments and the need for continued growth, we've started a new tradition: Beginning last year, and from now on, the first full week in October has been designated Minority Enterprise Development Week.

Now, I know that some of you may have questions about our policy in light of events in Dade County. Well, the Justice Department's position in that case resulted from the technical wording of that particular ordinance, which allowed bids by only one minority group to the exclusion of all others.

And this administration has strongly supported programs to provide special assistance to minority businesses, as evidenced by our active minority procurement program. And I assure you today, we're going to continue to do so.

Given opportunities, we know that minority firms can prevail in fair and open competition. And we will keep supporting, at every level of government, a broad range of programs to reach out to disadvantaged sectors of the community and to increase their opportunities to participate in government contracting.

We're trying to provide the broadest possible range of opportunities to all Americans without regard to race, creed, color, or sex. And sometimes it makes your day when you hear from people that understand this and agree.

I received a letter from a 39-year-old black man who said, "Your policies are not in the least bit anti-black or anti-poor. As a matter of fact," he said, "it's my opinion that your fight against inflation, your war on the drug traffic, your tough stand against street crime, your effort in revitalizing the nation's economy, are all of great importance to us poor people and us black people in America." Well, he brightened my day. To people like him and to all of you, I can only say thank you for what you give to America. Thank you for keeping her strong, for keeping her free, and for keeping our dream alive.

Together we can make our beloved land the source of all dreams and opportunities that she was placed on this good Earth to provide. I can't help but believe that we are on the good path and that if we continue on that path, our children will walk together into a glorious future and prosperity.

Let me just say one thing, that you're contributing—perhaps it hasn't struck you yet—but the contribution you're making. One of the contributing factors to poverty is, in a community or a neighborhood, dollars that come in there. How many times do they revolve before they move out of that community to do business elsewhere? And for too long a time your neighborhoods have been ones where the dollars didn't even rotate once before they went out into the other communities.

But you, by creating the businesses that you have, you are going to change that factor, and prosperity for all people will come more and more as you see that those dollars are spent within the neighborhood several times before they find their way out to somebody in the outside.

So, God bless you for what you're doing.

And we're going to continue to try and help in any way we can, and we'll heed your suggestions and advice whenever you feel that you'd like to offer it. Thanks very much.

Mr. Cruz. Mr. President, on behalf of the National Association of Minority Contractors, its board of directors, and its membership, we'd like to present you with, first, a memento of our association's national convention that's taking place here and, secondly, a symbolic NAMC hardhat, which symbolizes the contributions that minority contractors have made in the past and will continue to make in the future to building and making America great, strong, and free.

The President. Well, thank you very much. Thank you. You may not think I have any place to wear this—*[laughter]*—but you don't know how many times I have to go up on the Hill and meet with the Congress. *[Laughter]*

Ms. Clarke. Mr. President, can I say one word, please?

The President. Yes.

Ms. Clarke. I just want to take this opportunity to shake your hand. I am a black businesswoman here in the United States and a proud American and proud that you are our President and are helping us to do what is right, for leading us in the right direction.

The President. Thank you very much.

Ms. Clarke. My name is Sheryl Clarke.

Note: The President spoke at 2:12 p.m. in Room 450 of the Old Executive Office Building.

Proclamation 5215—1992 Chicago-Seville International Exposition
June 27, 1984

By the President of the United States of America

A Proclamation

In 1992, the United States and Spain will host an unprecedented joint world's fair, the Chicago-Seville International Exposition. The exposition will celebrate the 500th anniversary of Christopher Columbus' voyage of discovery from Spain to the Americas and will be the first world's fair to be conducted simultaneously in two countries.

The theme of the world's fair is the "Age of Discovery." The exposition will showcase the immense social, economic, scientific and cultural achievements which have changed the world since 1492 and will preview the discoveries anticipated in the century to come. The event also will serve to symbolize the indomitable nature of the human spirit which fired Columbus to pursue his dream of a New World and which continues to inspire us as Americans in pursuit of our dream of democracy and freedom.

Chicago is an excellent site for this historic exposition. A global crossroads, Chicago already has hosted two successful world's fairs—the World's Columbian Exposition of 1893, which became the standard of comparison for subsequent fairs, and a Century of Progress Exposition of 1933–34, which helped lift the spirits of a battered people during the most severe depression in our history. The choice of Seville as a site is especially appropriate, for without the foresight and adventurous spirit of the King and Queen of Spain, Columbus would never have had an opportunity to undertake his catalytic voyage which changed the course of history.

The unique relationship between this great American city and Seville underlines the continuity of history in a new age of communications and transportation. By bridging the seas in 1992, Chicago and Seville once again will link the New World with the Old in the dawning of a truly new "Age of Discovery."

The 1992 Chicago-Seville International Exposition thus promises to become a symbol of international peace and process, illuminating our past and our future. With its many splendid opportunities for the stimulation of trade and for cultural and technological exchange, the exposition has the enthusiastic support of the United States Government. This Administration will extend the fullest possible recognition to the event in accordance with the Paris Convention of November 22, 1928, as modified, and United States law.

Now, Therefore, I, Ronald Reagan, President of the United States of America, in recognition of the 1992 Chicago-Seville International Exposition, do hereby invite the several States of the Union and its Territories to participate in the exposition, and authorize and direct the Secretary of State to invite, on my behalf, such foreign countries as he may consider appropriate to participate in this event.

In Witness Whereof, I have hereunto set my hand this twenty-seventh day of June, in the year of our Lord nineteen hundred and eighty-four, and of the Independence of the United States of America the two hundred and eighth.

RONALD REAGAN

[*Filed with the Office of the Federal Register, 3:36 p.m., June 28, 1984*]

Note: The text of the proclamation was released by the Office of the Press Secretary on June 28.

Nomination of Robert A. Rowland To Be an Assistant Secretary of Labor
June 28, 1984

The President today announced his intention to nominate Robert A. Rowland to be an Assistant Secretary of Labor (Occupational Safety and Health). He would succeed Thorne G. Auchter.

Since 1981 Mr. Rowland has been serving as Chairman of the Occupational Safety and Health Review Commission in Washington, DC. Previously, he was a partner in the law firm of Mueller and Rowland in Austin, TX,

in 1962–1981 and assistant attorney general for the State of Texas in 1958–1962. He is a member of the American Bar Association and the Texas Bar Association.

Mr. Rowland graduated from the University of Texas (B.A., 1958; LL.B., 1958). He is married, has two children, and resides in Washington, DC. He was born March 23, 1932, in Houston, TX.

Nomination of Carol Gene Dawson To Be a Commissioner of the Consumer Product Safety Commission
June 28, 1984

The President today announced his intention to nominate Carol Gene Dawson to be a Commissioner of the Consumer Product Safety Commission for the remainder of the term expiring October 26, 1985. She would succeed Samuel D. Zagoria.

Ms. Dawson is the Deputy Special Assistant to the Secretary of Energy. Previously she served as Deputy Press Secretary at the Department of Energy. In 1977–1980 she was with Latham Realtors in Maryland. In 1971–1977 she was a writer for several publications including Human Events, New Guard, and the Easton Star-Democrat. She was news analyst for the White House News Summary in 1969 and director of information and publications for the American Conservative Union in 1966–1967.

She graduated from Dunbarton College (B.A., 1959). She was born September 8, 1937, in Indianapolis, IN, and now resides in Vienna, VA.

Nomination of Tony E. Gallegos To Be a Member of the Equal Employment Opportunity Commission
June 28, 1984

The President today announced his intention to nominate Tony E. Gallegos to be a member of the Equal Employment Opportunity Commission for the term expiring July 1, 1989. This is a reappointment.

Currently Mr. Gallegos is a Commissioner on the Equal Employment Opportunity Commission. Previously he was manager of the Douglas Aircraft Co. (1952–1982).

Mr. Gallegos graduated from the Bisttram Art Institute (B.A., 1951). He is married, has two children, and resides in Washington, DC. He was born February 13, 1924.

Nomination of Melvin A. Ensley To Be a Member of the Federal Farm Credit Board
June 28, 1984

The President today announced his intention to nominate Melvin A. Ensley to be a member of the Federal Farm Credit Board, Farm Credit Administration (District 12), for a term expiring March 31, 1990. He would succeed George Warren Lacey.

Mr. Ensley operates a 2,000-acre farm in Colfax, WA. He previously served as director of the Farm Credit Board of Spokane (1965–1980).

Mr. Ensley attended the University of Washington. He is married, has three children, and resides in Colfax, WA. He was born March 4, 1915, in Colfax.

Nomination of Lando W. Zech, Jr., To Be a Member of the Nuclear Regulatory Commission
June 28, 1984

The President today announced his intention to nominate Lando W. Zech, Jr., to be a member of the Nuclear Regulatory Commission for the term of 5 years expiring June 30, 1989. He would succeed Victor Gilinsky.

In October 1983 he retired as vice admiral of the Navy after 39 years of commissioned service. Prior to his retirement, Admiral Zech served as Deputy Chief of Naval Operations for Manpower, Personnel and Training/Chief of Naval Personnel. He was Commander of the U.S. Naval Forces in Japan in 1978–1980; Chief of Navy Technical Training at Memphis, TN, in 1976–1978; and Commandant Thirteenth Naval District

at Seattle, WA, in 1974–1976. In 1970 he was assigned to the Secretary of the Navy's Office of Program Appraisal and served as Deputy Chief of Legislative Affairs, Navy Department. In 1972–1974 he was Deputy Commander of the Navy Recruiting Command and was selected for flag rank.

His citations include the Distinguished Service Medal, two Legion of Merit Awards and Navy Commendation Medal, American Defense Service Medal, American Campaign Medal, and World War II Victory Medal.

He is married, has five children, and resides in Falls Church, VA. He was born June 29, 1923, in Astoria, OR.

Nomination of Tex Lezar To Be an Assistant Attorney General
June 28, 1984

The President today announced his intention to nominate Tex Lezar to be an Assistant Attorney General (Office of Legal Policy), Department of Justice. He would succeed Jonathan C. Rose.

Mr. Lezar is presently serving as Counselor to the Attorney General, Department of Justice. Previously, he was Special Counsel to the Attorney General in 1981–1983; attorney at law and consultant in private practice in Houston, TX, in 1980–1981; general counsel to Texas Secretary of State George W. Strake, Jr., in 1979–1980; trial

lawyer for the firm of Mandell & Wright in 1977–1979; staff assistant and speechwriter to the President, the White House, in 1971–1974; and assistant to William F. Buckley, Jr., at the National Review in 1970–1971.

He graduated from Yale College (B.A., 1970) and the University of Texas School of Law (J.D., 1976), where he was editor in chief of the Texas Law Review. He is married to Merrie Spaeth, and they reside in Rosslyn, VA. He was born September 30, 1948, in Dallas, TX.

Nomination of James B. Burnham To Be United States Executive Director of the International Bank for Reconstruction and Development
June 28, 1984

The President today announced his intention to nominate James B. Burnham to be United States Executive Director of the International Bank for Reconstruction and Development for a term of 2 years. This is a reappointment.

Since 1982 he has been serving as U.S. Executive Director of the International Bank for Reconstruction and Development at the World Bank. Previously he was special assistant to the Chairman of the Council of Economic Advisers in 1981–1982; vice president of the Mellon Bank, N.A., in 1971–1981; and special assistant to Governor Maisel at the Board of Governors of the Federal Reserve System in 1969–1971.

He graduated from Princeton University (A.B., 1961) and Washington University in St. Louis (Ph.D., 1970). He is married, has four children, and resides in Washington, DC. He was born October 22, 1939, in New York, NY.

Nomination of Alan Wood Lukens To Be United States Ambassador to the Congo
June 29, 1984

The President today announced his intention to nominate Alan Wood Lukens, of Pennsylvania, a career member of the Senior Foreign Service, class of Minister-Counselor, as Ambassador to the People's Republic of the Congo. He would succeed Kenneth Lee Brown.

Mr. Lukens served in the United States Army in 1942–1946. He was a teacher at Southern Arizona School in Tucson, AZ (1949–1950), and at St. Alban's School in Washington, DC (1950–1951). In 1951 he entered the Foreign Service as assistant cultural affairs officer in Ankara. He was cultural affairs officer in Istanbul (1952–1953) and public affairs officer in Martinique (1954–1956). In the Department he was press officer of the news division in 1956–1958. He was on detail in 1957 to the United Nations General Assembly in New York, NY, as press officer. He was committee secretary of international staff at NATO/Paris (1958–1960), American Consul, then Chargé d'Affaires in Brazzaville (1960–1961), Chargé d'Affaires in Bangui (1961), special assistant to the Ambassador and political officer in Paris (1961–1963), and political-military officer in Rabat (1963–1965). In the Department he was personnel officer in the Bureau of African Affairs in 1965–1967. He was deputy chief of mission in Dakar (1967–1970) and in Nairobi (1970–1972). In the Department he was Chief of the Junior Officer Division in the Bureau of Personnel (1972–1974), and Director of the Office of Iberian Affairs in the Bureau of European and Canadian Affairs (1974–1975). In 1975–1978, he was deputy chief of mission in Copenhagen and consul general in Cape Town in 1978–1982. Since 1982 he has been Director of the Office of Analysis for Western Europe in the Department.

Mr. Lukens graduated from Princeton University (A.B., 1948). He attended Georgetown University (1950–1951), École des Science Politiques in Paris (1948), the University of Madrid (1948–1949), and the University of Paris (1959). His foreign languages are French, Spanish, and Danish. He was born February 12, 1924, in Philadelphia, PA.

Remarks and a Question-and-Answer Session With Elected Republican Women Officials
June 29, 1984

The President. Good afternoon, and welcome. And it's always good to see so many old friends and have the chance to make new ones. And it's always a pleasure for me to be joined by two of the most important women in my life, Nancy and Maureen.

Today we're lucky to have with us some of the very capable women in our administration. You've already heard from the Director of the Women's Bureau at the Department of Labor, Lenora Cole-Alexander; the Staff Director of the U.S. Civil Rights Commission, Linda Chavez; and the Assistant Attorney General for Justice Assistance, Lois Herrington. And this afternoon you will have the chance to listen to the Director of the Export-Import Bank of the United States, Rita Rodriguez; Peace Corps Director Loret Ruppe; and the Consumer Product Safety Commission Chairman, Nancy Steorts.

In addition, here at lunch we've been joined by two other outstanding women in our administration, the Under Secretary for Travel and Tourism at the Department of Commerce, Donna Tuttle, and the Department of Education's General Counsel, Maureen Corcoran. And I see we've been joined—you've probably noticed that there were some here that seemed out of place— [*laughter*]—a few of the men in the administration. And in this crowd they do sort of stand out.

But permit me to begin by giving each of you high praise and heartfelt thanks for all you've done for our Republican cause. Politics has its share of fun and glamour, but in the end it's sheer, unrelenting hard work from people like you that makes it possible for us to put our beliefs into practice. And the role you play is especially important, because you demonstrate the Republican commitment to American women.

The GOP commitment to women runs deep. Some people have tried to keep that a secret. First, the GOP gave its backing to women's suffrage. Then our party became the first to elect a woman to the United States Congress and the only party ever to elect women to the United States Congress and the only party ever to elect women to the United States Senate who were not first filling unexpired terms. And today the two women in the Senate, my friends Nancy Kassebaum and Paula Hawkins, are Republicans. And we have nine outstanding Republican women in the House of Representatives. Now, I think you'll agree with me; it's time to give them more company.

Now, in this administration, we've appointed women to positions of top responsibility, women like our United Nations Ambassador, Jeane Kirkpatrick; our Secretary of Health and Human Services, Margaret Heckler; our Secretary of Transportation, Elizabeth Dole; Assistant to the President for Public Liaison, Faith Whittlesey; and many other women on the White House staff. And one of my proudest days in office was when I appointed Sandra Day O'Connor to be the first woman in history on the United States Supreme Court.

Just as important, today there are scores of able Republican women like you seeking—or serving, I should say, in public office outside Washington. Recently, Maureen gave me some impressive figures about Republican women candidates. In the 23 State primaries that have been held this year to select candidates for State and Federal offices, in addition to incumbents, the Grand Old Party fielded over 200 women. And more than 150 of you came out of your primaries victorious.

Now, those of you that are in or are running for State legislatures and other State and local offices, you're on the front lines of democracy. You have the chance to put your beliefs into practice close to the people, and Washington can't match that. We look on you as the eyes and ears, the leaders who truly know what the American people think and need. And just as we're eager to see the number of Republican women officeholders grow at the national level, we're determined to see these numbers grow in every American town, city, and State.

I want to be very clear on this: There's no place in the Republican Party for those who would discriminate against women. And let me say there is no place in the Republican Party for those who would exhibit prejudice against anyone. There's no place in our party for the kind of bigotry and ugly rhetoric that we've been hearing outside our party recently. We have no room for hate here, and we have no place for the haters.

We Republicans are working to reshape America's destiny. Everyone who takes part—from stuffing envelopes to running for a position on the town council to holding national office—is making history.

Now, I know you're having briefings all day, but if I could just take a moment, I'd like to give you an overview of what we've been trying to do. I may be plowing some ground that's been well plowed already.

But on the legislative front, we've made proposals to toughen child support enforcement significantly. These proposals would improve State collection of child support payments and require the adoption of proven, effective enforcement techniques. One version passed the House in November, and in April, the Senate passed a similar bill. And we trust that a conference now to resolve any differences will meet very soon.

In pension reform, we have legislation well on its way to enactment. Our bill would provide protection for widowed and divorced spouses and help women earn their own pension credits. Recently, I heard about a 62-year-old woman in Rhode Island whose husband, unbeknownst to her, dropped the survivor coverage in his company's pension plan. So, when he died, she was left with virtually nothing. Now, that's the kind of tragedy our pension reform will prevent.

Tax equity for women is another vital field. Many of our tax equity proposals are contained in the deficit reduction act that the Congress passed just this week. Of course, we're disappointed that the Congress dropped our proposal to raise the spousal IRA limit from $2,250 to $4,000, and we intend to go on pushing for its adoption. But the Congress did adopt a number of our proposals, including one that will permit contributions to thousands of nonprofit dependent care organizations like day-care centers to be treated as tax exempt. Another will remove current restrictions which keep women from treating taxable alimony as compensation in determining IRA contributions.

These measures represent a significant advance for American women. And despite the importance of these efforts, however, one step we've made possible has done more to give American women opportunity and independence than all the others combined. It's called economic expansion.

Just 3½ years ago, you remember, we inherited an economic disaster—soaring inflation and interest rates with declining productivity. The month that I stood on the steps of the Capitol to take my oath of office, inflation was in double digits, growth was disappearing, and the prime interest rate had hit the highest peak since the Civil War.

The economic crisis struck women particularly hard. Most elderly Americans living on fixed incomes are women, and they found their purchasing power eaten up by inflation. Women saw jobs become more and more scarce. They found that 12½-percent inflation made it a nightmare to buy groceries and pay the bills. And the thousands of women who wanted to start their own businesses saw a 21-percent prime interest rate slam shut the doors of opportunity.

When we took office, the economy was priority number one. With Republicans in control of the Senate, we moved quickly and boldly to get our program in place. We reduced the growth of Federal spending; we pruned needless regulation; we reduced personal income tax rates and passed an historic reform called tax indexing, a reform that means government can never again use inflation to profit at your expense. We reduced the marriage tax penalty, almost doubled the maximum child-care credit, increased the limits for IRA and Keogh contributions, and eliminated estate taxes on family farms and businesses for surviving spouses.

Today, from Maine to California a powerful economic expansion is taking place. Inflation has plummeted by more than two-thirds since we took office to under 3.6 percent for the last 3 months. Retail sales are up. The American worker's real wages are rising. Investment by U.S. businesses in new plants and equipment—that has risen at the fastest rate since 1949.

The best news of all: Since the expansion began, more than 6 million Americans have found jobs, making for the steepest drop in unemployment rate in more than 30 years. Just as the economic crisis hit women hard, today's expansion is giving them new opportunities. The unemployment rate among adult women has dropped from 9.1 to 6.8 percent, and today, more women have jobs than ever before in our nation's history—more than 50 percent—and that has never occurred before.

And we can see that the jobs the women hold are getting better and better. In 1983 women filled almost three-quarters of all the new jobs in managerial, professional, and technical fields. And the number of women-owned businesses is growing four times faster than the number of those owned by men.

Just as we've acted decisively here at home, in foreign relations, I think, the United States is demonstrating new firmness and a new sense of purpose. From the Pacific Basin to Western Europe to Central America to an island called Grenada, we're working to defend freedom and peace.

In our dealings with the Soviets, we're strengthening our defenses while proving our willingness to negotiate in good faith. Because we've been doing this, the prospects for world peace stand on a new and firm footing. It isn't true, as you've heard in the demagoguery that is being uttered today, that we are in greater danger than we've ever been. No, we aren't, because we're stronger than we've been in a great many years.

I believe our trip to Japan and Korea and our visit to China markedly improved our relations with those important nations in Asia. And our recent trip to Europe showed all the world that 40 years after so many gave their lives on the beaches of Normandy, the West remains unshakably committed to the defense of human freedom.

We Republicans have more than a good record; we have a vision. We see an America forever free from the evils of inflation. To make that dream a reality, we must enact structural reforms like the line-item veto and the balanced budget amendment. We see an America with a simple and fairer tax code that provides the American people with new incentives to work, save, and invest. And we intend to design a major tax reform in which we broaden the tax base and lower personal income tax rates for all who work and earn, and that will be a great step forward for America.

The Republican message is simple: Our country's best days are still to come, and with faith and courage, we can build a genuine opportunity society, a nation where all women and men have the chance to go forward just as far as their dreams and talents will take them. I just have to believe that if we did everything in our own power to carry our message to the voters, then November 6th they'll respond by keeping Republicans where we belong, on the job.

Now, I know that we're running late, and I only have time just for two or three questions, but—well, yes?

Taxes

Q. Mr. President, my name is Lois Eargle, and I'm running for Congress in the Sixth Congressional District in South Carolina. I have served for the past 8 years in the South Carolina Legislature as a Democrat. [*Laughter*] However, like you, Mr. President, I have chosen to become a Republican.

My question is, how can we, as Republicans, get the message across to the voters that the Republican Party represents the best interests for the working men and women, black and white, for this country?

The President. I think the message—and you're right, many of the things that we've done and that we believe in are very deeply held secrets. But I do believe that we've got the facts. And you can—we've got to see that you get the information that counters the arguments of whether we're fair or unfair.

For example, our tax program, the tax cut that we put in, which was the basic stimulant for the present economic recovery. And we're supposed to have—we're not the friends of the poor, we benefited the rich. Well, let them explain then why the people with incomes above $50,000 a year are paying a higher percentage of the total income tax burden than they have ever paid before and the people below $20,000 a year are paying a smaller percentage of the tax than they ever paid before.

There wasn't anything unfair in our tax. But there was something unfair about giving, for example, people on Aid to Dependent Children, on welfare, giving them three raises in just a brief period of a few years before we got here. And at the end of the three raises, because of their inflation, those people had purchasing power that was $43 a month less than they'd had before they got the raises because inflation was raised far faster than they were raising the taxes.

So, we've got a good argument. But you need the facts and figures. And it's our responsibility to see that you get them.

Now, I know that you had your hand up over——

Nicaragua

Q. Mr. President, I'm Mary Mochary from New Jersey.

Congress recently decided that they were not going to fund the aid to the Nicaragua *contras* that you were looking for. How will that affect your Central American policy?

The President. It would affect it dramatically and drastically, and we're not going to give up on that fight. We have a totalitarian government in Nicaragua that took power out of the barrel of a gun, then did what Castro did in Cuba when he won the revolution—kicked out of the revolution all the people who honestly wanted true democracy.

Most of the *contras* we were trying to support are people who were once part of the revolution, but who were ousted, and the Communist element took over. And there is a totalitarian government now in Nicaragua. And the Nicaraguan Government is supporting and providing ammunition and weapons to the guerrillas in El Salvador who are trying to overthrow a government that was duly elected by the people, and it's had three elections since that is democratic and not totalitarian at all.

And we're just going to have to keep fighting and convince the people of this country that to listen to those who would shut off Nicaragua is to listen to people—the same people who criticize and say that we're willing to support rightwing dictatorships, but never do we see anything from the left. Well, we're supporting people who are fighting for democracy and freedom. And those people who shut off that aid are supporting a totalitarian dictatorship in Nicaragua.

Yes?

The Nation's Economy

Q. Mr. President, Michelle Golden, from West Virginia. I was nominated Secretary of State 3 weeks ago, a Republican nomination.

When you were campaigning in 1980 to be our President, the country was loaded with doubting Thomases who refused to believe you when you promised to turn our economy around, to beat inflation, reduce unemployment and taxes, to put new millions of workers to work, and restore a widely felt sense of national security. You have kept your promises, and it borders on being miraculous. Now, we all know you have a wonderfully engaging personality, and everybody loves you. But you certainly didn't accomplish this with your charisma. Now, what is your secret? [*Laughter*]

The President. Well, if I have one secret, it is that I like people, and I believe in people. And I believe, and have always believed—even when I was Governor, holding that office—I've believed sometimes that if those of us in government would lock the door and quietly slip away for a few days, we'd be surprised how long it took the people to miss us. [*Laughter*]

No, it is giving more back to the people. And if there's one thing that, again, has not been treated as widely as it should with regard to credit—when we started our private sector initiative and encouraged people at the private level to find areas where they could be of help that, for many years, we've assumed now were government's functions, that government should take care of these. This has been so wide-spread—every major charity is collecting, even in the depths of the recession, was collecting more money than they ever had before. But the programs—we have over 3,000 programs computed over here in the West Wing in the private sector initiative place, where people all over the country can call in with some problem, and we can tell them how some community, some private group has found an answer, has put together a package at the private level with no government involvement to take care of this. And we can give them the phone numbers and the addresses of the people to get in touch with and find out how it was done.

An example, if I could—and I know I've got to run, I'm way past time here. But down in Texas, one town in Texas had a thing called "Christmas in April." And all year long, in that town, they kind of keep their eyes open. They spot the homes of people that are poor or elderly or disabled, and so forth. They see things that need doing, whether it's new plumbing or painting or a new roof, or whatever it might be. And then come April, these volunteers—and this includes the professional people, doctors and lawyers and judges and merchants and people of that kind—they put on their old clothes and out they go. And they've all been assigned to a task. They put on new roofs for these people, they do all these things.

And here I was with all of this private sector thing. And to show you how fast it all happened, I'm looking at television one day up there while I was getting dressed, upstairs, and I saw a television program and a fellow there with a painter's cap and a paint brush in his hand. And, yes, he was a judge. And what was he doing? Well, this

"Christmas in April" and so forth. And I started to yell to Nancy that, "Hey, they've got that town in Texas on the air." I found out it was Washington, DC. [*Laughter*] They've adopted the program here, too, and all over the country.

But, as I said, the main thing, I think, that's been wrong—we've had seven recessions before this last one since World War II. All of them have been cured by the Government artificially stimulating the money supply, bringing on more inflation and bringing on, within 2 or 3 years, another recession. And I have believed that we have had our business troubles and our recessions because the Government is taking too high a percentage from the gross national product for Government functions and not leaving it out there at the private sector.

So, by way of the tax cut, by George Bush heading up a task force to reduce and eliminate needless regulations—they eliminated enough regulations to reduce the paperwork burden on the American people by 300 million man-hours—and doing that so that it was a real stimulant to the economy, all of a sudden, we find we're getting more money at the lower tax rates than we were getting at the higher tax rates. And the economy is showing the result.

And I've said this before—and I should quit saying it—but one of my great happinesses is that when the program hadn't been put into effect yet, we were just getting it, our opponents named it "Reaganomics." Now that it's working, they don't call it Reaganomics anymore. [*Laughter*]

Thank you.

Note: The President spoke at 1:13 p.m. at a luncheon for the officials in the State Dining Room at the White House.

Statement by the Assistant to the President for National Security Affairs on United States-Soviet Arms Control Negotiations
June 29, 1984

The United States Government has taken note of the statement by the Soviet Government proposing a meeting of delegations in September to begin negotiations on "preventing the militarization of outer space." The militarization of space began when the first ballistic missiles were tested and when such missiles and other weapons systems using outer space began to be deployed. The United States Government therefore draws attention to the pressing need for the resumption of negotiations aimed at a radical reduction of nuclear weapons on a balanced and verifiable basis.

Therefore, the United States Government has informed the Government of the Soviet Union that it is prepared to meet with the Soviet Union in September, at any location agreeable to the Soviet Union and the government of the country where the meeting is held, for the following purposes: (1) to discuss and define mutually agreeable arrangements under which negotiations on the reduction of strategic and intermediate-range nuclear weapons can be resumed, and (2) to discuss and seek agreement on feasible negotiating approaches which could lead to verifiable and effective limitations on antisatellite weapons. We will also be prepared to discuss any other arms control concerns or other matters of interest to both sides.

We will continue contacts with the Soviet Union through diplomatic channels on arrangements for these September talks.

Appendix A—Digest of Other White House Announcements

The following list includes the President's public schedule and other items of general interest announced by the Office of the Press Secretary and not included elsewhere in this book.

January 1

The President and Mrs. Reagan spent New Year's Day in Palm Springs, CA, at the residence of Walter and Lenore Annenberg. At noon, the President telephoned Senator Barry Goldwater of Arizona on the occasion of the Senator's 75th birthday.

January 2

The President returned to the White House from Palm Springs.

January 3

The President met at the White House with:
—members of the White House staff;
—the Cabinet Council on Human Resources and the Cabinet Council on Natural Resources and the Environment, to discuss violence and discipline in schools;
—Senators Howard H. Baker, Jr., of Tennessee, Robert Dole of Kansas, and Pete V. Domenici of New Mexico, to discuss the budget.

January 4

The President met at the White House with:
—members of the White House staff;
—Representatives John N. Erlenborn of Illinois, Steve Bartlett of Texas, William F. Goodling of Pennsylvania, Mickey Edwards of Oklahoma, and Vin Weber of Minnesota, who are members on the Education Policy Task Force of the Republican Research Committee.

The President recess appointed Elliot Ross Buckley, of Virginia, to be a member of the Occupational Safety and Health Review Commission for the term expiring April 27, 1989. He will succeed Bertram R. Cottine, term expired.

January 5

The President met at the White House with:
—members of the White House staff;
—a group of his foreign policy advisers;
—leaders of agricultural organizations, to discuss food and agriculture policy, including price support programs and international trade of agricultural products;
—the Vice President, for lunch;

—the Cabinet Council on Management and Administration, to discuss paperwork reduction goals and the semiannual report of the President's Council on Integrity and Efficiency;
—Mrs. America of 1984, Susan Goodman of Waverly, TN.

January 6

The President met at the White House with:
—members of the White House staff;
—Dr. Henry A. Kissinger, Chairman of the National Bipartisan Commission on Central America, for an update on the progress of the Commission's report.

The White House announced that President Reagan has invited President Mika Spiljak of Yugoslavia to make an official working visit to the United States. President Spiljak has accepted the invitation and will meet with President Reagan at the White House on February 1.

In the afternoon, the President left the White House for a weekend stay at Camp David, MD.

January 8

The President returned to the White House from Camp David.

January 9

The President met at the White House with:
—members of the White House staff;
—U.S. business leaders who are traveling to Grenada;
—the National Security Council;
—members of the American Legislative Exchange Council;
—Julie Hayek, Miss U.S.A. 1983, and Lorraine Downes, Miss Universe 1983.

In an Oval Office ceremony, the President received diplomatic credentials from Ambassadors Thierno Habib Diallo of Guinea, Eigil Jorgenson of Denmark, Valeriano Inocencio de Araujo Ferrao of Mozambique, Federico Fahsen Ortega of Guatemala, George Toe Washington of Liberia, Rafael Garcia Velasco of Ecuador, Dato' Lew Sip Hon of Maylaysia, and Mico Rakic of Yugoslavia.

The President attended a reception for members of the President's Commission on Executive Exchange and participants in the Executive Exchange Program in the Indian Treaty Room at the Old Executive Office Building.

The White House announced that the President has declared a major disaster for the State of Texas because of the impact of severe freezing temperatures on the State's agricultural industry and the resultant unemployment in agriculture and related industries.

January 10

The President met at the White House with:
—members of the White House staff;
—Senators John Tower of Texas and John W. Warner of Virginia, who reported on their recent trip to the Middle East.

January 11

The President met at the White House with:
—members of the White House staff;
—the President's Economic Policy Advisory Board.

January 12

The President met at the White House with:
—representatives of the Small Business Legislative Council;
—William A. Wilson, U.S. Ambassador-designate to the Holy See, and Archbishop Pio Laghi, Apostolic Delegate to the United States;
—the Vice President, for lunch;
—the Cabinet Council on Economic Affairs, to discuss Federal audit activities, monetary policy, and financial market developments.

In the evening, the President attended a performance of "The Hasty Heart" at the John F. Kennedy Center for the Performing Arts.

January 13

The President met at the White House with:
—members of the White House staff;
—Minister of Foreign Affairs Giulio Andreotti of Italy;
—the National Security Council.

The President announced his intention to designate Richard L. McElheny, an Assistant Secretary of Commerce (Trade Development), to serve as a member of the Board of Directors of the Overseas Private Investment Corporation. He would succeed Raymond J. Waldmann.

The President recess appointed Paul H. Nitze to be Special Representative for Arms Control and Disarmament Negotiations and announced his intention to nominate him for the rank of Ambassador while serving in this position.

The President left the White House for a weekend stay at Camp David, MD.

January 15

The President returned to the White House from Camp David.

January 16

The President met at the White House with:
—members of the White House staff;
—the National Association of Arab Americans.

The President announced his intention to appoint Elizabeth Hanford Dole, Secretary of Transportation, to be a member of the Advisory Council on Historic Preservation. She will succeed Andrew L. Lewis, Jr.

January 17

The President met at the White House with:
—members of the White House staff;
—a group of private sector leaders, for a luncheon meeting to discuss family-related issues;
—Ambassador Paul H. Nitze, Special Representative for Arms Control and Disarmament Negotiations, to discuss the negotiations;
—the Cabinet Council on Natural Resources and the Environment, to discuss environmental issues which will be reflected in the budget.

In the afternoon, the President went to the Hay-Adams Hotel to attend a reception for the Citizens for the Republic.

January 18

The President met at the White House with:
—members of the White House staff;
—the U.S. Advisory Committee on Public Diplomacy, to receive the Committee's annual report, which presents an overview of the work of the United States Information Agency;
—Senator John C. Danforth of Missouri, who reported on his recent trip to Africa.

January 19

The President met at the White House with:
—members of the White House staff;
—Prime Minister Ruud Lubbers of the Netherlands;
—the Vice President, for lunch.

January 20

The President met at the White House with:
—members of the White House staff;
—Governors Thomas Kean of New Jersey, J. Joseph Garrahy of Rhode Island, John H. Sununu of New Hampshire, James R. Thompson of Illinois, and John Carlin of Kansas, to discuss acid rain.

In the afternoon, the President left the White House for a weekend stay at Camp David, MD.

January 22

The President returned to the White House from Camp David.

January 23

The President met at the White House with:
—members of the White House staff;
—leaders of the "March for Life" rally which took place in Washington, DC, later in the day.

The President spoke by telephone with, first, House Majority Leader Jim Wright and House Republican Whip Trent Lott; and then, Senate Majority Leader Howard H. Baker, Jr., and Senate Minority Leader Robert C. Byrd on the convening of the second session of the 98th Congress.

The White House announced that the President has invited Chancellor Helmut Kohl of the Federal Republic of Germany to make a working visit to the United States. Chancellor Kohl has accepted the invitation and will meet with the President at the White House on March 5.

The White House announced that the President has invited Prime Minister Prem Tinsulanonda of Thailand to make an official working visit to the United States. The Prime Minister has accepted the invitation and will meet with the President at the White House on April 13.

January 24

The President met at the White House with members of the White House staff.

January 25

The President met at the White House with:
—members of the White House staff;
—bipartisan congressional leaders, to receive a briefing from Secretary of State George P. Shultz on the situation in Central America and Lebanon.

The White House announced that at the request of the President, the Vice President, accompanied by Mrs. Bush, will travel to Europe February 8–12 to participate in the Wehrkunde Conference in Munich, Federal Republic of Germany, and to conduct discussions in several European capitals. Prior to his address at the Conference on February 11, the Vice President will visit Luxembourg and Bonn, Federal Republic of Germany. Following the Conference, the Vice President will visit London, England. The Vice President's visit to Luxembourg will underscore U.S. interest in close consultation with all members of the NATO alliance, and his visits to Bonn and London will continue the process of close consultations with the Governments of the Federal Republic of Germany and the United Kingdom, which the Vice President had during his previous visits.

January 26

The President met at the White House with:
—members of the White House staff;

—the Vice President, for lunch.

The President attended the third inaugural anniversary dinner of the Republican National Committee at the Pension Building.

The President designated John J. Franke, Jr., Assistant Secretary of Agriculture, Administration, as a member of the Board of Directors of the Rural Telephone Bank. He will succeed Seeley G. Lodwick.

The White House announced that the President has accepted British Prime Minister Margaret Thatcher's invitation to attend the economic summit in London, June 7–9. At the invitation of Prime Minister Garret FitzGerald, the President will visit the Republic of Ireland June 2–4 before traveling to London. The President has also accepted President François Mitterrand's invitation to travel to Normandy on June 6 to participate in the ceremonies celebrating the 40th anniversary of the Normandy D-day landings. The President will depart London for Washington, DC, on June 10.

The White House announced that President Reagan has invited President Salvador Jorge Blanco of the Dominican Republic to make a state visit to the United States. President Jorge Blanco has accepted the invitation and will meet with President Reagan at the White House on April 10.

January 27

The President met at the White House with Minister of Foreign Affairs Shintaro Abe of Japan, the Vice President, and Secretary of State George P. Shultz.

The President attended a reception for the National Conference of Republican Mayors and Municipal Elected Officials in the State Dining Room at the White House.

The President transmitted to the Congress the following reports:
—the second annual report of the Tourism Policy Council, covering fiscal year 1983; and
—the 37th annual report on United States participation in the United Nations.

January 28

In the evening, the President attended the Alfalfa Club dinner at the Capital Hilton Hotel.

January 29

Early in the evening, the President attended a Republican Party reception in the East Room at the White House.

January 30

The President met at the White House with:
—members of the White House staff;
—Ambassador Edward L. Rowny, Special Representative for Negotiations, U.S. Arms Con-

trol and Disarmament Agency, to discuss the strategic arms reduction talks with the Soviet Union;

—the executive committee of the American Hospital Association.

The President transmitted to the Congress the following reports:

—the 12th annual report on the administration of the Federal Railroad Safety Act of 1970; and

—the annual report on pipeline safety, covering calendar year 1982, as required by the Natural Gas Pipeline Safety Act of 1968 and the Hazardous Liquid Pipeline Safety Act of 1979.

The President designated the following-named persons to be members of the United States delegation to attend the inaugural ceremonies of His Excellency Dr. Jaime Lusinchi as President of the Republic of Venezuela, scheduled to be held at Caracas on February 1 and 2:

Personal Representative of the President, with the rank of Special Ambassador, to head the delegation:

George P. Shultz, Secretary of State.

Representatives of the President, with the rank of Special Ambassador:

George W. Landau, U.S. Ambassador to the Republic of Venezuela;

Langhorne A. Motley, Assistant Secretary of State for Inter-American Affairs.

January 31

The President met at the White House with:
—members of the White House staff;
—Republican Members of the House and Senate, to discuss the 1985 Federal budget.

February 1

The President met at the White House with:
—members of the White House staff;
—the Cabinet, to discuss political issues;
—a group of trade association leaders, to discuss the 1985 Federal budget.

The President transmitted to the Congress the fourth annual report of the Federal Labor Relations Authority, covering fiscal year 1982.

February 2

The President met at the White House with:
—members of the White House staff;
—Richard Schifter, U.S. Representative on the Human Rights Commission of the United Nations Economic and Social Council.

In an Oval Office ceremony, the President met with representatives of the Boy Scouts of America and received the Scouts' annual report to the Nation.

The White House announced that the President has invited Prime Minister Garret FitzGer-

ald of Ireland to make an official working visit to the United States. The Prime Minister has accepted the invitation and will meet with the President at the White House on March 16.

February 3

The President met at the White House with:
—members of the White House staff;
—Alois Mock, leader of the opposition party in Austria, to discuss his recent trip to Central America;
—Vice President Kurt Furgler of Switzerland;
—Prime Minister Eugenia Charles of Dominica.

In the afternoon, the President left the White House for a weekend stay at Camp David, MD.

February 5

The President returned to the White House from Camp David.

February 6

The President left the White House for visits to Illinois, Nevada, and California.

The White House announced that the President will meet with King Hussein of Jordan at the White House on February 13. The President extended the invitation to the King while the King was on a private visit to the United States.

The White House announced that the President will meet with President Mohammed Hosni Mubarak of Egypt in Washington on February 14. President Mubarak will be coming to the United States on February 13 and will meet with senior U.S. officials prior to his meeting with President Reagan.

February 8

The President announced his intention to appoint Secretary of the Interior William P. Clark as a member of the Delaware River Basin Commission and a member of the Susquehanna River Basin Commission and Representative of the United States.

February 9

The White House announced that the President has requested the Congress to provide $90 million in fiscal year 1984 for 245,000 tons of emergency food aid for the drought-stricken nations of Africa. Additionally, $200 million in fiscal year 1984 is requested for low-income home energy assistance. An unexpectedly severe winter has increased the need for this assistance. Also included in this proposal are requests by the legislative branch for additional appropriations totaling $6.6 million in fiscal year 1984 and $3.7 million in fiscal year 1985 and an appropriation language request to enable the Department of Defense to proceed with a classified project.

February 10

The President asked the Vice President to be his personal representative to the funeral of Soviet President Yuriy V. Andropov. The President has asked the Vice President, when in Moscow, to extend the condolences and best wishes of the American people to the people of the Soviet Union and to express to them our strong desire for peace. The President also requested the Vice President to convey to the new Soviet leadership our hope for an improved dialog and cooperation which can lead to a more constructive relationship between our two countries.

February 11

The President asked Senate Majority Leader Howard H. Baker, Jr., and U.S. Ambassador to the Soviet Union Arthur A. Hartman to accompany the Vice President in the delegation to the funeral of Soviet President Yuriy V. Andropov. The Vice President will head the delegation.

February 12

The President returned to the White House following his stay at Rancho del Cielo, his ranch near Santa Barbara, CA.

February 13

The President met at the White House with members of the White House staff.

In the afternoon, the President went to the Soviet Embassy to sign the book of condolences on the death of President Yuriy V. Andropov.

The White House announced that the President has invited Prime Minister Mário Soares of Portugal to make an official working visit to the United States. Prime Minister Soares has accepted the invitation and will meet with the President at the White House on March 14.

The White House announced that President Reagan has invited President J.R. Jayewardene of Sri Lanka to make a state visit to the United States. President Jayewardene has accepted the invitation and will meet with President Reagan at the White House on June 18.

February 14

The President met at the White House with:
—members of the White House staff;
—the Cabinet Council on Legal Policy, to discuss legislation concerning victims of crime;
—Neil Kinnock, British Labor Party leader.

In the afternoon, the President telephoned congratulations to Debbie Armstrong and Christin Cooper in Sarajevo, Yugoslavia. Ms. Armstrong won the gold medal and Ms. Cooper won the silver medal in the women's giant slalom event of the 1984 winter Olympic games.

In an Oval Office ceremony, the President met with 8-year-old Stephanie Swiney, of Lexington,

NC, the 1984 National Easter Seal Child. Stephanie presented the President with the 50th edition of Easter Seals. Other participants in the ceremony included entertainer Pat Boone, the National Easter Seal chairman and telethon host, members of Stephanie's family, and representatives of the National Easter Seal Society.

February 15

The President met at the White House with:
—the Godfrey Sperling Group, for a breakfast meeting;
—members of the White House staff;
—representatives of the United Way of America, to receive the report on the 1983 fund drive;
—Secretary of the Treasury Donald T. Regan, Chairman of the Board of Governors of the Federal Reserve System Paul A. Volcker, and Assistant to the President and Chief of Staff James A. Baker III.

February 16

The President met at the White House with:
—members of the White House staff;
—the Vice President, Secretary of State George P. Shultz, and Assistant to the President for National Security Affairs Robert C. McFarlane, for a luncheon meeting to discuss the Vice President's recent trip to the Soviet Union and Europe and the redeployment of U.S. marines in Lebanon;
—the Cabinet Council on Food and Agriculture, to discuss Federal farm programs;
—the Cabinet Council on Commerce and Trade, to discuss international trade;
—Simon Weisenthal.

Late in the morning, the President met in Room 450 of the Old Executive Office Building with the Emergency Committee for American Trade, a group of chief executive officers and senior executives interested in international trade.

The President transmitted to the Congress the annual report of the National Endowment for the Arts and the National Council on the Arts, covering fiscal year 1983.

The President declared a major disaster for the State of Idaho because of the impact of ice jams, ice, and flooding, which caused extensive property damage.

The President announced his intention to nominate four space shuttle astronauts for promotion. Comdr. Daniel C. Brandenstein, U.S. Navy, will be nominated for promotion to captain; Lt. Comdr. Dale A. Gardner, U.S. Navy, will be nominated for promotion to commander; Lt. Col. Guion S. Bluford, Jr., U.S. Air Force, will be nominated for promotion to colonel; and Maj.

Brewster H. Shaw, Jr., will be nominated for promotion to lieutenant colonel. This is the result of a policy established by President Johnson in 1965 to promote an astronaut one grade after the astronaut's first successful space flight. The last previous promotion under this policy was made in 1974.

February 17

The President met at the White House with:
—members of the White House staff;
—David C. Jordan, U.S. Ambassador to Peru, and Thomas W.M. Smith, U.S. Ambassador to Nigeria, prior to their departure for their overseas posts.

The White House announced that the President has accepted the resignation of Ambassador Richard B. Stone as Special Representative of the President to Central America. He will be replaced by Ambassador Harry W. Shlaudeman, who will be nominated as Special Presidential Envoy and Ambassador at Large for Central America.

The President announced that Dorcas R. Hardy, Assistant Secretary for Human Development Services, Department of Health and Human Services, will chair the Task Force on Legal Equity for Women.

In the evening, the President and Mrs. Reagan hosted a reception at the White House for the Princess Grace Foundation. Guests included Prince Rainier III of Monaco, Prince Albert, Princess Caroline, Princess Stephanie, and Princess Caroline's husband, Stefano Casiraghi.

February 19

The President officially began the Daytona 500 auto race in Daytona Beach, FL, by telephone from the Residence.

February 20

During his visit to Waterloo, IA, the President spoke by telephone with Phil and Steve Mahre in Zurich, Switzerland. He called to congratulate them for winning the gold and silver medals, respectively, in the men's slalom event in skiing in the 1984 winter Olympic games.

February 21

The President met at the White House with:
—members of the White House staff;
—Republican congressional leaders, to discuss proposals for reducing the 1985 Federal budget deficit and also the situation in Lebanon.

The President requested the Congress to provide $659 million in fiscal year 1984 and $735.3 million in fiscal year 1985 for economic and military assistance to various nations in Central America. These requests respond to the recommendations of the National Bipartisan Commission on Central America.

February 22

The President met at the White House with members of the White House staff.

The President transmitted to the Congress the annual report for fiscal year 1983 of the Administration on Aging of the Department of Health and Human Services.

February 23

The President met at the White House with:
—members of the White House staff;
—a group of national school leaders, to discuss discipline in schools;
—the Cabinet Council on Management and Administration, to discuss Reform '88, Federal field structure reform, consulting services control, and a review of advisory committees;
—Secretary of State George P. Shultz, Secretary of Defense Caspar W. Weinberger, Ambassador Donald H. Rumsfeld, the President's Personal Representative in the Middle East, and Assistant to the President for National Security Affairs Robert C. McFarlane, to discuss current issues pertaining to the Middle East;
—artist Olaf Wieghorst, who presented the President with the first print of a limited edition of his picture "Nomads of the Plains."

The President announced the following individuals as members of the United States delegation to attend the independence celebrations of Brunei on February 23 in the capital city of Bandar Seri Begawan:

Personal Representative of the President, with the rank of Special Ambassador, to head the delegation:

Deputy Secretary of State Kenneth W. Dam

Representatives of the President, with the rank of Special Ambassador:

Dr. Alfred Balitzer, of Claremont, CA.

Mary Davis, of Los Angeles, CA.

John C. Fitch, of Houston, TX.

John H. Schoettler, of Parker, CO.

William R. Sutton, of Fair Oaks, CA.

February 24

The President met at the White House with:
—members of the White House staff;
—Ambassador Donald H. Rumsfeld, the President's Personal Representative in the Middle East, and other foreign policy advisers.

The President left the White House for a weekend stay at Camp David, MD.

February 26

In the afternoon, the President returned to the White House from Camp David.

February 27

The President met at the White House with:

—members of the White House staff;

—the National Governors' Association;

—the Vice President, for a luncheon meeting;

—Walter Leon Cutler, U.S. Ambassador to Saudi Arabia, prior to departure for his overseas post.

Late in the afternoon, the President held a series of meetings in the Oval Office with Members of Congress and their constituents. Among the visitors was former baseball player Carl Yastrzemski, of the Boston Red Sox, who conducted a short interview with the President and presented him with a baseball commemorative ring.

The President transmitted to the Speaker of the House and the President of the Senate the report on the activities of countries within the United Nations and its specialized agencies, pursuant to Public Law 98–151. The report assesses the degree of support of United States foreign policy in the United Nations context by the governments of countries which are members of the United Nations.

February 28

The President met at the White House with:

—members of the White House staff;

—the Cabinet, for a discussion of consulting services controls, a review of advisory committees, and a report on the current status of efforts to obtain a constitutional amendment on prayer in schools;

—actress Shelley Long, 1984 chairperson of the Interagency Committee for the Purchase of U.S. Savings Bonds.

The President transmitted to the Congress the 17th annual report on the operation of the Automotive Products Trade Act of 1965.

February 29

The President met at the White House with:

—members of the White House staff;

—members of the House Republican Whip organization;

—Foreign Minister Hans van den Broek of The Netherlands.

March 1

The President met at the White House with:

—members of the White House staff;

—the Cabinet Council on Economic Affairs, to discuss youth unemployment.

Late in the afternoon, the President attended a reception in the East Room for participants in the Vietnam Veterans Leadership Program.

March 2

The President met at the White House with members of the White House staff.

March 5

The President met at the White House with:

—members of the White House staff;

—Senate Majority Leader Howard H. Baker, Jr., and Senator Paul Laxalt of Nevada, to discuss Federal budget issues.

March 6

The President met at the White House with:

—members of the White House staff;

—Senator Bob Kasten of Wisconsin, to discuss the Central American aid package;

—Senators Joseph R. Biden, Jr., of Delaware and William S. Cohen of Maine, to discuss their recent trip to the Soviet Union.

March 7

The President met at the White House with:

—members of the White House staff;

—officials of the National Association of State Departments of Agriculture;

—editors of business trade publications.

March 8

The President met at the White House with:

—members of the White House staff;

—a group of Republican Senators and administration officials, to discuss Federal budget issues and appropriations for El Salvador;

—Senator John Tower of Texas, to discuss the Senator's recent trip to the Middle East;

—the Cabinet Council on Economic Affairs, for a Commerce Department briefing on demographic changes and their economic impact;

—Timothy Diakis, of Newport News, VA, and his family. The 11-year-old boy had recently risked his life rescuing Sarah Sherman, an 83-year-old woman, from a fire.

The President hosted a reception for members of the National Newspaper Association in the State Dining Room.

The White House announced that the President requested the Congress to provide $21 million in additional funding for fiscal year 1984 for activities of the Central Intelligence Agency. The request will provide funds necessary to continue certain activities of the Central Intelligence Agency which the President has determined are important to the national security of the United States. The appropriate committees of the Congress have been thoroughly briefed on these classified activities and will be fully briefed on this request.

March 9

The President met at the White House with:

—members of the White House staff;

—a group of Republican Senators and administration officials, to discuss Federal budget issues.

The President attended a luncheon honoring the 72d anniversary of the Girl Scouts of America in the State Dining Room.

The President left the White House for a weekend stay at Camp David, MD.

March 11

The President returned to the White House from Camp David.

March 12

The President met at the White House with:
—members of the White House staff;
—members of the House Republican leadership, to discuss the status of the budget deficit reduction discussions;
—Foreign Minister Carlos José Gutiérrez Gutiérrez of Costa Rica and Foreign Minister Edgardo Paz Barnica of Honduras;
—David Rockefeller and Archibald Roosevelt, who reported on their recent trip to the Middle East.

March 13

The President met at the White House with:
—members of the White House staff;
—Thomas R. Pickering, U.S. Ambassador to El Salvador;
—Abdelaziz Khellef, Minister of Commerce of Algeria;
—Narciso Serra i Serra, Minister of Defense of Spain.

The President participated in the swearing-in ceremony in the Oval Office for Maureen E. Corcoran as General Counsel of the Department of Education.

The President met in the Oval Office with John and Reve Walsh, parents of Adam Walsh, who was abducted and murdered. He was the subject of the NBC television film "Adam." Other participants in the meeting included Linda Otto, producer of the film, and Kiki Vandewegh, basketball player for the Denver Nuggets. The meeting underscored the President's support for the forthcoming National Center for Missing and Exploited Children, sponsored by the Office of Juvenile Justice and Delinquency Prevention in the Department of Justice.

In an Oval Office ceremony, the President received diplomatic credentials from Ambassadors Doulaye Corentin Ki of Upper Volta, Marcos Martinez Mendieta of Paraguay, Wafula Wabuge of Kenya, Pengiran Haji Idriss of Brunei, William Valentine Herbert of St. Christopher-Nevis, Kayatyani Shankar Bajpai of India, and Walter Ravenna of Uruguay.

The President transmitted a report to the Speaker of the House and the chairman of the Senate Foreign Relations Committee concerning the late transmittals of certain international agreements.

March 14

The President met at the White House with:
—members of the White House staff;
—Senate Republican leaders, to discuss the budget deficit reduction package.

March 15

The President met at the White House with:
—members of the White House staff;
—John D. Negroponte, U.S. Ambassador to Honduras, and Robert C. McFarlane, Assistant to the President for National Security Affairs;
—Republican leaders of the House of Representatives, to discuss the budget deficit reduction package;
—the Vice President, for a luncheon meeting.

The White House announced that President Reagan has invited President Quett K.J. Masire of Botswana to make an official working visit to the United States. President Masire has accepted the invitation and will meet with President Reagan at the White House on May 9.

March 16

The President met at the White House with:
—members of the White House staff;
—Members of Congress, to discuss the proposed constitutional amendment on prayer in schools;
—U.S. Ambassador to Lebanon Reginald Bartholomew and Mrs. Bartholomew.

In the morning, the President telephoned Bishop John J. O'Connor of Scranton, PA, to congratulate him on his installation as Archbishop of the New York Archdiocese. The President expressed his regret that he would not be able to attend the Pontifical Mass on March 19, and conveyed his very best wishes.

In the afternoon, the President left the White House for a weekend stay at Camp David, MD.

March 18

Following his return from Camp David, the President met with Edwin Meese III, Counsellor to the President, and Fred F. Fielding, Counsel to the President, to discuss Mr. Meese's nomination to be Attorney General of the United States.

March 19

The President met at the White House with:
—members of the White House staff;
—the Joint Chiefs of Staff;

—Members of the Senate, to discuss the proposed constitutional amendment on prayer in schools.

The President transmitted to the Congress the sixth annual report on Federal energy conservation programs undertaken during fiscal year 1982.

March 20

The President met at the White House with:
—members of the White House staff;
—Vice President Antônio Aureliano Chaves de Mendonça of Brazil.

The President signed S. 47, the Shipping Act of 1984, at a ceremony in the East Room. As enacted, S. 47 is Public Law 98–237.

March 21

The President met at the White House with members of the White House staff.

The White House announced that the President has designated Michael Kelly as Chairman of the Cultural Property Advisory Committee. He has served as a member of the Committee since January 3.

March 22

The President met at the White House with:
—members of the White House staff;
—the Vice President, for lunch;
—the Cabinet Council on Natural Resources and the Environment, to discuss energy issues;
—Costa Rican businessmen Jaime Gutierrez Gangora, Armando Guardia Vaillalaz, and Orlando Castro Murillo, Langhorne A. Motley, Assistant Secretary of State for Inter-American Affairs, and Curtin Winsor, Jr., U.S. Ambassador to Costa Rica. They presented the President with a petition signed by 300,000 Costa Ricans supporting his policies in Central America.

The President announced the following individuals will travel to El Salvador as official United States observers of the March 25 elections. The delegation will be cochaired by Senator Roth and Representative Wright. U.S. Ambassador W. Tapley Bennett will be the senior administration official accompanying the delegation. Additional observers may be added to the following list.

Following are the members of the delegation:

Senator William V. Roth, Jr., of Delaware
Senator Pete Wilson of California
Senator Jeremiah Denton of Alabama
Senator Paula Hawkins of Florida
Senator David L. Boren of Oklahoma
Senator Walter D. Huddleston of Kentucky
Representative Jim Wright of Texas
Representative Manuel Lujan, Jr., of New Mexico
Representative Jack F. Kemp of New York

Representative Ed Zschau of California
Representative Olympia J. Snowe of Maine
Representative Solomon P. Ortiz of Texas
Representative E. de la Garza of Texas
Representative John P. Murtha of Pennsylvania
Representative Bob Livingston of Louisiana
Representative Dick Cheney of Wyoming
Representative Robert J. Lagomarsino of California
Representative John McCain of Arizona
Representative Tom Loeffler of Texas

Howard Penniman, American Enterprise Institute, Washington, DC

John Carbaugh, attorney, Washington, DC

William Perry, professor, Georgetown University, Washington, DC

Rev. Ira Galloway, minister, United Methodist Church, Peoria, IL

Luis Aguilar, professor, Georgetown University, Washington, DC

Jorge Mas, cofounder, Cuban-American National Foundation, Miami, FL

Walter Shea, vice president, International Brotherhood of Teamsters, Annapolis, MD

Al Keller, Jr., former commander, American Legion, Kankakee, IL

Msgr. John P. Foley, editor, Catholic Standard and Times, Philadelphia, PA

James R. Currieo, former commander, Veterans of Foreign Wars, Tucson, AZ

March 23

The President met at the White House with:
—members of the White House staff;
—members of the Tau Kappa Epsilon fraternity, for lunch.

The President announced the names of two additional members of the delegation of official United States observers who will travel to El Salvador for the March 25 elections:

Michael Novak, lay religious leader and resident scholar at the American Enterprise Institute, Washington, DC
Leonard Sussman, Freedom House, New York, NY

March 24

In the afternoon, the President and Mrs. Reagan went to Charlottesville, VA, where they toured Monticello, the home of Thomas Jefferson.

In the evening, the President attended the Gridiron Dinner at the Capital Hilton Hotel.

March 26

The President met at the White House with:
—members of the White House staff;
—a group of State attorneys general, to discuss crime control legislation;
—the Cabinet Council on Natural Resources and the Environment, for a report on energy policy;
—representatives of the National Cattlemen's Association;

—a group of the official U.S. observers of the March 25 elections in El Salvador, to discuss the elections.

In an Oval Office ceremony, the President signed S. 912, which authorizes the Corps of Engineers to provide hydropower to the city of Abbeville, SC, and deauthorizes a breakwater at Eastport Harbor, ME. As enacted, S. 912 is Public Law 98–243.

In the evening, the President attended the National Republican Senatorial Committee reception at the Shoreham Hotel.

March 27

The President met at the White House with:
—members of the White House staff;
—Secretary of the Treasury Donald T. Regan, who reported on his visit to China, Japan, and the Republic of Korea;
—a group of Hispanic Medal of Honor recipients who are members of the selection committee for a stamp honoring Hispanics in service to the country.

In the morning, President Reagan telephoned President Alvaro Alfredo Magaña Borja of El Salvador. President Reagan told President Magaña that the Salvadoran Presidential elections on March 25, reflected the commitment of the people of El Salvador, the Government, and their military to the democratic process. He expressed his congratulations on the first round of elections and noted that he met with our observers and expressed their laudatory comments. He paid tribute to the courage of the Salvadoran people in casting their votes, despite guerrilla violence and sabotage.

In an Oval Office ceremony, the President signed H.J. Res. 454, which honors the contributions of blacks to American independence. Attendees at the ceremony included the cosponsors of the legislation, Senators Strom Thurmond of South Carolina and Joseph R. Biden, Jr., of Delaware, and Representatives Katie Hall of Indiana, Jim Courter of New Jersey, and Nancy L. Johnson of Connecticut. As enacted, H.J. Res. 454 is Public Law 98–245.

March 28

The President met at the White House with:
—members of the White House staff;
—Harry W. Shlaudeman, Special Presidential Envoy and Ambassador at Large for Central America, prior to Ambassador Shlaudeman's departure for a trip to Central America;
—Arthur A. Hartman, U.S. Ambassador to the Soviet Union.

The White House announced that, at the request of the President, the Vice President would head the United States delegation to the funeral of President Sékou Touré of Guinea on March 30.

James D. Rosenthal, U.S. Ambassador to Guinea, and Frank G. Wisner, Deputy Assistant Secretary of State for African Affairs, will also serve in the official delegation.

March 29

The President met at the White House with:
—members of the White House staff;
—the Vice President, for a luncheon meeting;
—presidents of historically black colleges and universities, to discuss the Annual Federal Performance Report on Executive Agency Actions To Assist Historically Black Colleges and Universities for Fiscal Year 1983, which was prepared in accordance with Executive Order 12320 of September 15, 1981;
—Representative Andy Ireland of Florida, who recently changed his political party affiliation from Democratic to Republican;

In an Oval Office ceremony, the President presented the Cancer Courage Award to actress Amanda Blake.

The President declared an emergency for the State of Florida because of the impact of severe freezing temperatures on the State's agricultural industry and the resultant unemployment in agriculture and related industries.

March 30

The President met at the White House with:
—members of the White House staff;
—members of the President's Advisory Committee on Women's Business Ownership, for a luncheon meeting;
—New York AFL–CIO union officials who endorse the President's reelection.

The White House announced that the President requested the Congress to provide $235 million in fiscal year 1984 for emergency food aid to drought-stricken nations of Africa and for other emergencies. The President has also asked the Congress to consider appropriations requests for the legislative branch, the Inter-American Development Bank, the Department of Energy, the Department of State, and various other independent Federal agencies.

In the afternoon, the President left the White House for a weekend stay at Camp David, MD.

April 1

Following his return from Camp David, the President hosted a reception for members of the Trilateral Commission on the State Floor of the White House.

April 2

The President met at the White House with:
—members of the White House staff;
—Helmut Schmidt, former Chancellor of the Federal Republic of Germany;

—Eisenhower Exchange fellows.

The President attended the opening day of the 1984 baseball season at Memorial Stadium in Baltimore, MD. He threw the first pitch of the game between the Baltimore Orioles and the Chicago White Sox and watched 1 inning of the game before returning to the White House.

April 3

The President met at the White House with:
—members of the White House staff;
—Republican congressional leaders, to discuss the situation in Central America and the Federal budget;
—Ambassador James E. Goodby, Chief of the U.S. Delegation to the Conference on Confidence and Security Building Measures and Disarmament in Europe, to discuss the first session of the Conference;
—members of the President's National Security Telecommunications Advisory Committee.

The White House announced that during a meeting in the Oval Office with Attorney General William French Smith, the President asked the Attorney General to remain in office until a successor has been approved. The Attorney General, who had announced his intention to resign on January 23, agreed and will remain until a new Attorney General has been confirmed by the Senate.

The President designated Joseph V. Charyk as Chairman and Theodore F. Brophy as Vice Chairman of the President's National Security Telecommunications Advisory Committee for terms of 1 year.

In the evening, the President attended a lamb roast in honor of Senator Paul Laxalt of Nevada at the Georgetown Club.

April 4

The President met at the White House with:
—members of the White House staff;
—members of the Catholic Health Association.

The President transmitted to the Congress the 17th annual report of the U.S.-Japan Cooperative Medical Science Program, covering calendar year 1983.

April 5

The President met at the White House with members of the White House staff.

April 6

The President met at the White House with:
—members of the White House staff;
—members of the National Conference of Lieutenant Governors.

The President announced that he has nominated Gen. John W. Vessey, Jr., for reappointment as Chairman of the Joint Chiefs of Staff for an additional 2-year term. General Vessey, 61, was appointed Chairman in 1982. He was previously Vice Chief of Staff of the United States Army. General Vessey's present term is due to expire June 18.

April 9

The President met at the White House with:
—members of the White House staff;
—Mayor Hans Diepgen of West Berlin;
—Brent Scowcroft, Chairman of the President's Commission on Strategic Forces, who discussed his recent visits to China and the Soviet Union, as well as the final report of the Commission.

The President announced his intention to designate Francis X. Lilly, Solicitor for the Department of Labor, to serve as a member of the Board of Directors of the Overseas Private Investment Corporation. He would succeed T. Timothy Ryan, Jr.

In the evening, the President went to the Fort McNair Officers Club to attend the 35th anniversary dinner of the Chowder and Marching Society.

April 10

The President met at the White House with:
—members of the White House staff;
—members of the board of directors of the Electronic Industries Association;
—Emil Verban, former Chicago Cubs baseball player.

In an Oval Office ceremony, the President signed into law H.R. 4206, which amends the Internal Revenue Code of 1954 to exempt from Federal income taxes certain military and civilian employees of the United States who have died as a result of injuries sustained overseas. As enacted, H.R. 4206 is Public Law 98–259.

The White House announced that the President has asked Secretary of the Interior William P. Clark to head the U.S. delegation to the May 12 ceremony in Berlin commemorating the 35th anniversary of the Berlin Airlift.

The President transmitted to the Congress the fiscal year 1985 budget of the District of Columbia.

April 11

Prior to his departure for Kansas City, MO, the President met at the White House with members of the White House staff.

April 12

The President declared a major disaster for the State of New Jersey as a result of the impact of severe storms, coastal storms, and flooding, beginning on or about March 28, which caused extensive property damage.

April 13

The President met at the White House with:
—members of the White House staff;
—a group of Hispanic appointees in the administration;
—Stephen W. Bosworth, U.S. Ambassador to the Philippines, and David C. Miller, Jr., U.S. Ambassador to Zimbabwe, prior to their departure for their overseas posts.

In an Oval Office ceremony, the President received diplomatic credentials from Ambassadors Renagi Renagi Lohia of Papua New Guinea, Sonatane Tu'a Taumoepeau-Tupou of Tonga, Pio Laghi of the Holy See, and Serara Tsholofelo Ketlogetswe of Botswana.

The White House announced that President Reagan has invited President Miguel De la Madrid Hurtado of Mexico to make a state visit to the United States. President De la Madrid has accepted the invitation and will meet with President Reagan at the White House on May 15.

The President transmitted to the Congress the 18th annual report of the National Endowment for the Humanities, covering fiscal year 1983.

The White House announced that at the request of the President, the Vice President will fly to Geneva, Switzerland, on April 16, to address the plenary session of the Committee on Disarmament. He will return to the United States on April 18.

In the evening, the President attended the White House Correspondents Dinner at the Washington Hilton Hotel.

April 16

The President met at the White House with:
—members of the White House staff;
—the Cabinet, to discuss the Federal budget.

April 17

The President met at the White House with:
—members of the White House staff;
—Mexican officials, including Secretary of Foreign Relations Bernardo Sepúlveda Amor, Secretary of the Treasury Jesús Silva-Herzog Flores, Secretary of Commerce and Industrial Development Héctor Hernández Cervantes, and Ambassador to the United States Jorge Espinoza de los Reyes, and U.S. officials, including Secretary of State George P. Shultz, Secretary of the Treasury Donald T. Regan, and Secretary of Commerce Malcolm Baldrige, to discuss the upcoming visit to the United States of President Miguel De la Madrid Hurtado;
—the Cabinet Council on Food and Agriculture, to discuss the economic situation in the agricultural sector.

In an Oval Office ceremony, the President presented the Presidential Citizens Medal posthu-

mously to Leamon (Ray) Hunt, Director General of the Multinational Force and Observers in the Sinai, who was assassinated by terrorists in Rome on February 15. Mrs. Leamon Hunt accepted the medal.

The President hosted a reception for the Reagan-Bush '84 Finance Committee in the State Dining Room at the White House.

The President transmitted to the Congress the following reports:
—the fifth annual report of the Federal Labor Relations Authority, covering fiscal year 1983; and
–the 27th annual report on the trade agreements program for 1983.

The President declared a major disaster for the State of New York as a result of the impact of severe storms, coastal storms, and flooding, beginning on or about March 28, which caused extensive property damage.

April 18

The President met at the White House with:
—members of the White House staff;
—a group of Catholic clerical leaders, for lunch.

April 19

The President left the White House for a trip to the western United States and China.

The President announced that he has designated Secretary of the Army John O. Marsh, Jr., as his personal representative to the funeral of Gen. Mark Clark, to be held at West Point, NY, on April 19.

April 22

The President arrived at Hickam Air Force Base, Honolulu, Hawaii, where he was greeted by Gov. George Ariyoshi and Mrs. Ariyoshi; Adm. William J. Crowe, Jr., Commander in Chief, U.S. Pacific Command, and Mrs. Crowe; and Sfc. and Mrs. Gregory Lee Emfinger.

Later in the day, the President and Mrs. Reagan went to St. Andrew's Episcopal Cathedral, where they attended an Easter service. Following the service, they went to Washington Place, the Governor's Mansion, for tea with Governor and Mrs. Ariyoshi. The President and Mrs. Reagan then went to the Kahala Hilton Hotel, where they stayed during their visit to Hawaii.

April 23

The President met at the Kahala Hilton Hotel, his residence during his visit to Hawaii, with:
—members of the White House staff;
—Adm. William J. Crowe, Jr., Commander in Chief, U.S. Pacific Command, who provided the President with a general overview of the Pacific Theater from the perspective of his

assignment as the senior military person in the region;

—a group of Hawaii Republican leaders.

The President and Mrs. Reagan went to the home of Mrs. Cecily Johnston, which is located on the beach, for swimming.

The White House announced that the President has named Attorney General and Mrs. William French Smith to be the official U.S. representatives to the celebration of Australia-American Friendship Week. This national annual event in Australia commemorates the Battle of the Coral Sea and celebrates Australia-American friendship. A distinguished American citizen is customarily the guest of honor. Past guests have included the Vice President (1982), other members of the Cabinet, astronauts, senior military officers, and prominent Americans from the private sector. This year's observance will be between May 1–8. Attorney General and Mrs. Smith, who will be guests of the Government of Australia, will participate in major events in Canberra, Sydney, and Melbourne between May 2–5.

April 25

In the afternoon, the President arrived at Guam International Airport, where he was greeted by Gov. Ricardo J. Bordallo. Following an arrival ceremony, the President and Mrs. Reagan attended a reception with Trust Territory leaders at the airport terminal. They then went to Nimitz House, located on the grounds of the U.S. naval base, where they remained overnight.

April 26

The President and Mrs. Reagan left Guam and traveled to Beijing, China. Upon arrival at the Capitol Airport in Beijing, the President and Mrs. Reagan were greeted by Foreign Minister Wu Xueqian and several other Chinese officials. The President and Mrs. Reagan went from the airport to the Great Hall of the People, Tianamen Square, East Court, for an arrival ceremony.

Following the arrival ceremony, the President and Mrs. Reagan met with President Xiannian Li and his wife, Lin Jiamei, in the Hebei Room at the Great Hall. There, the two Presidents had a meeting. During the meeting, President Reagan extended an invitation to President Li to visit the United States at a time to be agreed upon by the two countries. President Li accepted the invitation, and on the diplomatic level, a mutually acceptable date will be worked out.

Following the meeting at the Great Hall, the President and Mrs. Reagan went to the Diaoyutai State Guest House, Villa 12, their residence during their visit to Beijing.

The President declared a major disaster for the State of Mississippi as a result of the impact of severe storms and tornadoes beginning on April 21, 1984, which caused extensive property damage.

April 27

The President met at the Diaoyutai State Guest House, his residence during his visit to Beijing, China, with Secretary of State George P. Shultz and members of the White House staff. He then went to the Great Hall of the People, where he and his advisers met with Premier Zhao Ziyang and Chinese officials. Following the meeting, the President returned to the Diaoyutai State Guest House for a private luncheon.

In the afternoon, the President met again with Premier Zhao and U.S. and Chinese officials at the Great Hall. It was agreed during the meeting that the Chinese Minister of Defense would travel to Washington in June to meet with Secretary of Defense Caspar W. Weinberger. Following the meeting with Premier Zhao, the President remained at the Great Hall and met with Hu Yaobang, General Secretary of the Chinese Communist Party. The President then returned to the Diaoyutai State Guest House for the remainder of the afternoon.

In the evening, the President and Mrs. Reagan attended a banquet hosted by Premier Zhao at the Great Hall of the People. Following the banquet, they returned to the Diaoyutai State Guest House.

The White House announced that the President has designated Wilford W. Johansen, of California, to serve as Acting General Counsel of the National Labor Relations Board.

The White House announced that the President has nominated Carol E. Dinkins, of Texas, to be Deputy Attorney General. She will succeed Edward C. Schmults.

April 28

The President met at the Diaoyutai State Guest House, his residence during his visit to Beijing, China, with Secretary of State George P. Shultz and members of the White House staff. Later in the morning, the President and Mrs. Reagan went to the Great Hall of the People, where they were greeted by Deng Xiaoping, Chairman of the Central Military Commission. Following a short visit, Mrs. Reagan departed, and the President and Chairman Deng held a meeting with their advisers. The meeting was followed by a working luncheon.

At the conclusion of the luncheon, the President was rejoined by Mrs. Reagan. They left the Great Hall of the People and went by motorcade to the Great Wall. The President and Mrs. Reagan were escorted on their tour of the Great Wall by Zhu Muzhi, Minister of Culture, and his wife.

Following their visit to the Great Wall, the President and Mrs. Reagan returned to the Diaoyutai State Guest House.

In the evening, the President and Mrs. Reagan attended a reception for members of the American community at the Great Wall Hotel. Following the reception, the President and Mrs. Reagan, accompanied by Premier Zhao Ziyang, greeted Chinese guests and then proceeded to the Grand Ballroom for a dinner hosted by the President.

Following the dinner, the President and Mrs. Reagan returned to the Diaoyutai State Guest House.

April 29

In the morning, the President met briefly at the Diaoyutai State Guest House, his residence during his visit to Beijing, China, with a group of U.S. marines who were guarding the residence of the official party. The President and Mrs. Reagan then went to Capitol Airport and flew to Xi'an. There they toured the site of ancient Chinese archaeological treasures surrounding the tomb of Qin Shihuangdi, the Qin dynasty emperor who lived from 221–210 B.C. The site includes life-sized terra cotta figures of soldiers and horses facing east in rectangular battle formation. Before returning to Beijing, the President and Mrs. Reagan also visited a facsimile of a "free market" on the outskirts of the Xi'an excavation site. Upon their return to Beijing, the President and Mrs. Reagan went to the Diaoyutai State Guest House.

April 30

Following a signing ceremony for four U.S.-China agreements, the President and U.S. officials took part in a farewell ceremony with Premier Zhao Ziyang, President Li Xiannian, and other Chinese officials at the Great Hall of the People. The President and Mrs. Reagan then went to Capitol Airport for the flight to Shanghai.

Upon arrival at Hongquiao Airport in Shanghai, the President was greeted by Mayor Wang Daohan and Deputy Mayor Yuan Chongwu of Shanghai, Xie Xide, president of Fudan University, and several municipal officials. He then went to visit the Shanghai Foxboro Co., Ltd., a joint venture composed of the Foxboro Co. of Massachusetts and the Shanghai Instrumentation Corp. Following his visit to the Shanghai Foxboro Co., the President and Mrs. Reagan went to the Jing Jang Hotel, where they stayed during their visit to Shanghai.

In the afternoon, the President attended a tea reception and later addressed students and faculty at Fudan University. The reception was hosted by Xie Xide, president of the university.

In the evening, the President attended a banquet hosted by Mayor Wang at the Shanghai Industrial Exhibition Hall. He then returned to the Jing Jang Hotel.

The White House announced that at the request of the President, the Vice President, accompanied by Mrs. Bush, will visit Japan, India, Pakistan, and Oman between May 7 and May 20. The Vice President will pay a working visit to Japan to meet with Prime Minister Yasuhiro Nakasone and to review progress made in resolving economic and trade problems between the two nations. The official visit to India, Pakistan, and Oman will underline the continuing interest of the United States in these three important nations and the region they represent. The Vice President looks forward to discussing matters of mutual interest with Prime Minister Indira Gandhi, President Mohammad Zia-ul-Haq, and Sultan Qaboos bin Said and continuing the close relationship already established with each of these distinguished leaders.

May 1

In the morning, the President and Mrs. Reagan left the Jing Jiang Hotel, their residence during their visit to Shanghai, and went to Rainbow Bridge Township, where they attended a briefing on the commune given by Jin Yong Quan, acting township head, in the administration room. Following the briefing, they visited with schoolchildren at the kindergarten. They then toured a private home, the residence of farmer Bao Hong Yuan, who escorted the President on a short tour of the eggplant fields.

The White House announced that the President telephoned William H. Webster, Director of the Federal Bureau of Investigation, to express his and Mrs. Reagan's personal condolences on the death of Mrs. Webster.

May 2

The White House announced that within the framework of their Asian tour, Vice President and Mrs. Bush will visit the Republic of Indonesia on May 10–12. The Vice President looks forward to deepening and extending our warm friendship with Indonesia through discussion with President Soeharto, Vice President Wirahadikusumah Umar, and other Indonesian leaders.

May 3

The President met at the White House with:
—members of the White House staff;
—Coach Eddie Robinson of Grambling University;
—the Vice President, for a luncheon meeting.

The President declared a major disaster for the State of Oklahoma as a result of the impact of severe storms and tornadoes beginning on April 26, which caused extensive property damage.

The President transmitted to the Congress the annual report of the Commodity Credit Corporation, covering the fiscal year ending September 30, 1983.

In the afternoon, the President left the White House for a weekend stay at Camp David, MD.

May 4

The President transmitted to the Congress the 1983 annual report of the Federal Council on the Aging.

May 6

Following his return to the White House from Camp David, MD, the President hosted a dinner for members of the Board of Regents of the Smithsonian Institution.

May 7

The President met at the White House with:
—members of the White House staff;
—Minister of Foreign Economic Relations & Trade Chen Muhua of China and Secretary of Commerce Malcolm Baldrige;
—Minister of Foreign Affairs Hans-Dietrich Genscher of the Federal Republic of Germany.

The President requested the Congress to provide $15 million in fiscal year 1985 to the U.S. Customs Service for the Air Interdiction Program. This program is combating the illegal entry of narcotics and other goods into the United States. This increase would be fully offset by reductions in other Department of the Treasury programs. Also included in this proposal are requests by the legislative branch for additional appropriations totaling $12.3 million in fiscal year 1984 and $4 million in fiscal year 1985 and an appropriation language request to enable the Federal Home Loan Bank Board to hire additional examiners to monitor the thrift industry.

May 8

The President met at the White House with:
—members of the White House staff;
—the bipartisan congressional leadership;
—Juan Antonio Samaranch, president of the International Olympic Committee, Peter V. Ueberroth, president of the Los Angeles Olympic Organizing Committee, and other Olympic officials.

The White House announced that the President has invited Grand Duke Jean of Luxembourg to make a state visit to the United States. The Grand Duke has accepted the invitation and will meet with the President at the White House on November 13.

The White House announced that at the request of the President and the invitation of vari-

ous countries, Ambassador Jeane J. Kirkpatrick, U.S. Representative to the United Nations, will make an official visit to China and several other Southeast Asian countries, including Malaysia, Thailand, Singapore, and the Philippines. She will leave May 11 and return May 31, and she will be meeting with the leaders of those countries during her visit.

May 9

The President met at the White House with:
—members of the White House staff;
—members of the American team of observers of the May 6 Presidential election in El Salvador;
—Representatives Marvin Leath of Texas and Beryl Anthony, Jr., of Arkansas;
—Republican leaders of the House of Representatives, to discuss Department of Defense appropriations legislation.

May 10

The President met at the White House with:
—members of the White House staff;
—Susumu Nikaido, vice president of the Liberal Democratic Party in Japan;
—Enrico Fermi Award winners Alexander Hollaender and John H. Lawrence;
—the Cabinet, to discuss his recent trip to China.

May 11

The President met at the White House with:
—members of the White House staff;
—U.S. Ambassador to the Soviet Union Arthur A. Hartman;
—the 1984 Mrs. America, Deborah Wolfe, and her family;
—Robert Miller Howard, Jr., the Goodwill Industries Graduate of the Year;
—leaders of conservative organizations, to discuss Central America.

In an Oval Office ceremony, the President presented the Congressional Gold Medal to Mrs. Joe Louis in recognition of her late husband's accomplishments.

The President declared an emergency for the State of Alabama as a result of severe storms and tornadoes on May 2, which caused extensive property damage.

The President declared an emergency for the State of Georgia as a result of severe storms, tornadoes, and flooding, beginning on May 4, which caused extensive property damage.

The President left the White House for a weekend stay at Camp David, MD.

May 13

The President returned to the White House from Camp David.

May 14

The President met at the White House with:
—members of the White House staff;
—U.S. officials involved in the planning of the London Economic Summit;
—Mexican-American leaders, to discuss the visit of President Miguel De la Madrid Hurtado of Mexico.

May 15

The President met at the White House with:
—members of the White House staff;
—the Cabinet Council on Human Resources, to discuss matters of concern to American families;
—Members of the House of Representatives, to discuss production of the MX missile.

The President declared an emergency for the State of Louisiana as a result of severe storms and tornadoes on May 2, which caused extensive property damage.

The White House announced that in order to carry forward U.S.-Salvadoran cooperation on bilateral and regional matters, President-elect José Napoleón Duarte will visit the United States next week for talks with administration and congressional leaders. The President will meet with President-elect Duarte on May 21.

May 16

The President met at the White House with:
—members of the White House staff;
—Members of the House of Representatives, to discuss production of the MX missile.

The White House announced that on May 30, the President will host a working dinner at the White House for Foreign Ministers of the North Atlantic Treaty Organization. They will be in Washington, DC, for the North Atlantic Council meeting on May 29–31. The occasion will also commemorate the signing of the North Atlantic Treaty 35 years ago. The President will take the opportunity at the dinner to bestow the Medal of Freedom on Joseph M.A.H. Luns, the Secretary General of NATO.

The White House announced that the President has declared a major disaster for the State of West Virginia as a result of severe storms and flooding, beginning on May 3, which caused extensive property damage.

The White House announced that the President has declared a major disaster for the State of Kentucky as a result of the impact of severe storms, tornadoes, and flooding, beginning on May 6, which caused extensive property damage.

May 17

The President met at the White House with:

—representatives of the National Conference of Black Mayors, to discuss the 1984 Summer Jobs for Youth Program;
—the Cabinet Council on Legal Policy, to discuss the scope of title IX of the Civil Rights Act and guidelines for law enforcement activities carried out by Federal agencies.

The President transmitted to the Congress a report on offshore safety and health regulations and technology in accordance with the Outer Continental Shelf Lands Act Amendments of 1978.

May 18

The President went to Bethesda Naval Hospital for a physical examination. From there he went to Camp David, MD, for a weekend stay.

May 20

In the afternoon, the President returned to the White House from Camp David.

In the evening, the President attended a reception at the White House for the National Republican Heritage Groups Council.

May 21

The President met at the White House with:
—members of the White House staff;
—the Duke of Edinburgh, for a luncheon meeting.

The President met with a group of Cuban-American leaders in Room 450 of the Old Executive Office Building.

In an Oval Office ceremony, the President met with actress Victoria Principal, national campaign chairperson for the Arthritis Foundation, and 7-year-old Amy Smith, of Redding, CA, the Foundation's poster child. Ms. Principal and Amy presented the President with a specially made 2-foot-high hourglass to mark May as National Arthritis Month and to symbolize the Foundation's current theme that "It's time we took arthritis seriously."

The President participated in a Rose Garden ceremony for the Olympic Coin Program. He presented a $10 gold coin, the first gold coin minted under the authority of the Olympic Commemorative Coin Act, to the U.S. Olympic Committee for display in their new museum. The act was designed to provide financial support for the Los Angeles games this summer and for future Olympic games, through the sale of the commemorative coins.

May 22

The President met at the White House with members of the White House staff.

The President transmitted to the Congress, as required by the Powerplant and Industrial Fuel Use Act of 1978, the fifth annual report describing Federal actions with respect to the conservation and use of petroleum and natural gas in Federal facilities.

The President transmitted to the Congress, in accordance with the Public Health Service Act, the report of the Department of Health and Human Services regarding the administration of the Radiation Control for Health and Safety Act during calendar year 1983.

The President announced his intention to designate David Campbell Mulford, Assistant Secretary of the Treasury (International Affairs), to serve as a Government member of the Board of Directors of the Overseas Private Investment Corporation. He would succeed Marc E. Leland.

May 23

The President met at the White House with members of the White House staff.

The President declared a major disaster for the Commonwealth of Virginia as a result of the impact of severe storms and flooding beginning on May 6, which caused extensive property damage.

May 24

The President met at the White House with:
—members of the White House staff;
—Kristine Holderied, the U.S. Naval Academy's top-ranking midshipman in the class of 1984;
—the Vice President, for a luncheon meeting;
—Secretary of the Interior William P. Clark, William D. Ruckelshaus, Administrator of the Environmental Protection Agency, and Jay Hair, executive vice president of the National Wildlife Federation, to discuss environmental concerns;
—the Cabinet Council on Management and Administration, to discuss cost control measures.

In an Oval Office ceremony, the President met with 28-year-old Diane Victor, of Rockford, IL, the Multiple Sclerosis Mother of the Year, and 37-year-old Phil Krieg, of Warsaw, IN, the Multiple Sclerosis Father of the Year. The President presented them with plaques recognizing their exemplary courage as citizens and parents in spite of their handicap.

In the evening, the President and Mrs. Reagan went to the residence of Clare Boothe Luce for a private dinner.

May 25

The President met at the White House with members of the White House staff.

The President declared a major disaster for the State of Tennessee as a result of the impact of severe storms and flooding beginning on May 6, which caused extensive property damage.

In the afternoon, the President left the White House for a weekend stay at Camp David, MD.

May 28

The President returned to the White House from Camp David.

May 29

The President met at the White House with members of the White House staff.

May 31

The President met at the White House with:
—members of the White House staff;
—Robert T. Hennemeyer, U.S. Ambassador to The Gambia, Thomas H. Anderson, Jr., U.S. Ambassador to Barbados, S.L. Abbott, U.S. Ambassador to Lesotho, and Peter Sebastian, U.S. Ambassador to Tunisia, prior to their departure for their overseas posts.

The President transmitted to the Congress the following reports:
—the1983 annual report on the operation of the Alaska Railroad, covering fiscal year 1983; and
—the annual report of the Corporation for Public Broadcasting, covering fiscal year 1983.

The President declared a major disaster for the State of Oklahoma as a result of severe storms and flooding, beginning on May 26, which caused extensive property damage.

The White House announced that the following individuals will be members of the U.S. delegation to the inauguration of José Napoleón Duarte in San Salvador, El Salvador, on June 1:

Secretary of State George P. Shultz
Ambassador Thomas R. Pickering, U.S. Ambassador to El Salvador
Senator Strom Thurmond of South Carolina
Senator Jesse Helms of North Carolina
Senator Paul E. Tsongas of Massachusetts
Representative William S. Broomfield of Michigan
Representative John P. Murtha of Pennsylvania
Ambassador Harry W. Shlaudeman, Ambassador at Large and Special Presidential Envoy for Central America
Assistant Secretary of State for Inter-American Affairs Langhorne A. Motley
Max M. Kampelman, partner, Fried, Frank, Harris, Shriver & Kampelman, Washington, DC
Robert P. Griffin, counsel, Miller, Canfield, Paddock & Stone, Washington, DC

The President announced the members of the U.S. delegation to attend the 40th Commemoration of the Liberation of Rome in Rome on June 2. Senator Robert Dole of Kansas will be Chairman of the delegation. The members of the delegation will be:

Gen. John W. Vessey, Jr., Chairman of the Joint Chiefs of Staff

Secretary of the Army John O. Marsh, Jr.

Ambassador at Large Vernon Walters

Senator Patrick J. Leahy of Vermont

Maurice Britt, Medal of Honor recipient, Italian campaign, Little Rock, AR

Col. Van T. Barfoot (Ret.), Medal of Honor recipient, Italian campaign, Amelia County, VA

Peter Dalessondro, Medal of Honor recipient, Albany, NY

Louis J. Esposito, businessman, D-day veteran, Philadelphia, PA

Phillip Pistilli, businessman, Kansas City, MO

Frank Stella, president, National Italian American Foundation, Detroit, MI

Celeste Andruzzi, New York, NY

June 1

The President arrived at Shannon Airport in Shannon, Ireland, where he was greeted by President and Mrs. Patrick J. Hill and other officials. Following an arrival ceremony, the President and Mrs. Reagan went to Ashford Castle in Cong, County Mayo, where they remained overnight.

June 2

The President met with a group of Irish industrial leaders at Ashford Castle in Cong, County Mayo.

Secretary of State George P. Shultz met with the President at Ashford Castle to report on his meeting at Sandino Airport, Managua, Nicaragua, with Daniel Ortega, head of the Nicaraguan Government. Secretary Shultz met with Mr. Ortega on June 1 at the request of the President.

The President went to Galway, where he was greeted upon arrival by Mayor Michael Leahy and Foreign Minister Peter Barry. Following his remarks at the University of Galway, the President returned to Ashford Castle.

June 3

The President went to Ballyporeen, County Tipperary, and was greeted by Father Eanna Condon, curate of Ballyporeen Parish, and other county and village officials. Accompanied by Father Condon, the President and Mrs. Reagan went to the rectory of the Church of the Assumption for a visit with Father John Murphy, parish priest. The President inspected a book in which was recorded the baptism of his great-grandfather, Michael Reagan, on September 3, 1829. The President and Mrs. Reagan then attended a parish prayer service in the church.

Following the service, the President and Mrs. Reagan went to O'Farrell's Pub and Ronald Reagan Lounge, where they visited with the owners, John and Mary O'Farrell, and members of the O'Farrell family. The President and Mrs.

Reagan then proceeded to the Village Square for a cultural performance. They were accompanied by Foreign Minister and Mrs. Peter Barry.

Following the performance, the President was presented with a book from the town committee, an oak carving from Father Condon and the parish, and a coat of arms from the county council.

Following his remarks to citizens of Ballyporeen, the President went to Dublin. He was greeted upon arrival by Michael Keating, Lord Mayor of Dublin. Accompanied by U.S. Ambassador and Mrs. Robert F. Kane, the President and Mrs. Reagan then met with members of the U.S. Embassy staff at Deerfield, the residence of the U.S. Ambassador.

The President and Mrs. Reagan, Ambassador and Mrs. Kane, and Secretary of State George P. Shultz then went to Aras an Uachtaráin, the home of the Irish President. There, the President and Mrs. Reagan met with President and Mrs. Patrick J. Hillery and participated in a tree planting ceremony in the garden. Following the visit, they returned to Deerfield.

Prior to the state dinner, the President met in the Apollo Room at Dublin Castle with Prime Minister Garret FitzGerald and Foreign Minister Peter Barry. Following the dinner, the President and Mrs. Reagan returned to Deerfield, where they remained overnight.

June 4

The President met with Prime Minister Garret FitzGerald of Ireland. The meeting was followed by an expanded session which included Irish and U.S. officials. The President and the Prime Minister then went to Leinster House, where the President signed the guest book in the Senate anteroom before proceeding with Prime Minister FitzGerald, Deputy Prime Minister Dick Spring, and Charles J. Haughey, leader of the opposition, to the Dáil, where he addressed a joint session of the National Parliament. Following his address, the President returned to Deerfield, the residence of the U.S. Ambassador to Ireland, Robert F. Kane.

Later that day, the President and Mrs. Reagan left Dublin and traveled to London. Upon arrival at Heathrow Airport, they were greeted by several British officials, including Sir Geoffrey Howe, Secretary of State for Foreign and Commonwealth Affairs, and Mrs. Howe. They also were met by Charles H. Price II, U.S. Ambassador to the United Kingdom, and Mrs. Price.

After a brief stop at Winfield House, the London residence of the U.S. Ambassador to the United Kingdom, the President and Mrs. Reagan went to the Kensington Palace Gardens where they were greeted by Prime Minister Margaret

Thatcher and participated in the official welcoming ceremony. Following the ceremony, the President and Mrs. Reagan returned to Winfield House, where they remained overnight.

June 5

The President and Mrs. Reagan had lunch at Buckingham Palace with Queen Elizabeth II and Prince Philip.

In the evening, the President went to 10 Downing Street, the residence of the British Prime Minister, where he was greeted by Mrs. Thatcher. Following a private meeting, the President and the Prime Minister attended a reception and a working dinner with British and U.S. officials.

At the conclusion of the dinner, the President returned to Winfield House, the London residence of the U.S. Ambassador to the United Kingdom, where he and Mrs. Reagan remained overnight.

June 6

The President and Mrs. Reagan participated in the ceremony commemorating the 40th anniversary of D-day, which was held at Utah Beach in Normandy, France, and presided over by President François Mitterrand of France.

Upon arrival at Pointe du Hoc, the President and Mrs. Reagan were met by Evan G. Galbraith, U.S. Ambassador to France, and Mrs. Galbraith, and Leon Dilliers, mayor of Cricqueville. Then, accompanied by Phil Rivers, superintendent of the Normandy American Cemetery and Memorial, the President and Mrs. Reagan inspected a powder magazine crater and gun emplacement. They were then briefed on cliff-scaling techniques and shown the grappling hooks used in World War II.

Following the ceremonies at Point du Hoc, the President and Mrs. Reagan went to Omaha Beach. He was met at the visitors center by Ambassador Galbraith, who introduced them to French dignitaries and U.S. officials stationed in Europe. They then went to the Omaha Beach Chapel for a silent prayer and then proceeded to the Normandy American Cemetery, where they placed wreaths on the graves of two sons of President Theodore Roosevelt, Quentin and Brig. Gen. Theodore Roosevelt, Jr.

The President and Mrs. Reagan then returned to the visitors center where they greeted President and Mrs. François Mitterrand upon their arrival at Omaha Beach.

Following a ceremony at the Omaha Beach Memorial, the Presidents and their wives viewed the Garden of the Missing. The President and Mrs. Reagan bid farewell to President and Mrs. Mitterrand at the visitors center and then traveled to Utah Beach.

June 7

The President met at Winfield House, the London residence of the U.S. Ambassador to the United Kingdom, with Secretary of State George P. Shultz, Secretary of the Treasury Donald T. Regan, and members of the White House staff.

The President held a bilateral meeting in the morning with Prime Minister Yasuhiro Nakasone of Japan at Winfield House. Following the meeting, he met with Secretaries Shultz and Regan, administration officials, and members of the White House staff.

In the afternoon, the President held bilateral meetings at Winfield House with Prime Minister Bettino Craxi of Italy, Chancellor Helmut Kohl of the Federal Republic of Germany, and President François Mitterrand of France.

In the evening, the President attended a reception for summit heads and members of delegations in the Armory and Queen Anne Rooms at St. James Palace. He then attended a working dinner for heads of delegation at 10 Downing Street, the residence of the British Prime Minister. Following the dinner, he returned to Winfield House.

June 8

The President met in the morning at Winfield House, the London residence of the U.S. Ambassador to the United Kingdom, with Secretary of State George P. Shultz and Secretary of the Treasury Donald T. Regan, administration officials, and members of the White House staff.

The President went to Lancaster House for the first full day of meetings of the London Economic Summit. He participated in a meeting with summit heads of delegation in the Music Room. After a working luncheon in the Gold Room, he participated in an afternoon plenary session with other heads of delegation. Following the meetings, he returned to Winfield House.

In the evening, the President attended a working dinner with summit heads of delegation in the Tudor Room at the National Portrait Gallery. He then returned to Winfield House.

June 9

The President met in the morning at Winfield House with Secretary of State George P. Shultz and Secretary of the Treasury Donald T. Regan, administration officials, and members of the White House staff.

The President went to Lancaster House for a meeting with summit heads of delegation in the Music Room. Prior to a working luncheon in the State Dining Room, the President showed the other summit leaders a model of the manned space station that the United States plans to place in orbit in the early 1990's. The model was displayed in the Eagle Room.

Following the luncheon, the President left Lancaster House and went to the Guildhall for the reading of the final communique by British Prime Minister Margaret Thatcher. He then returned to Winfield House.

In the evening, the President and Mrs. Reagan attended the state dinner hosted by Queen Elizabeth II in the State Dining Room at Buckingham Palace for summit heads and members of delegations. They returned to Winfield House following the dinner.

June 10

The President returned to Washington, DC, from his 10-day trip to Europe.

June 12

The President met at the White House with:
—members of the White House staff;
—Republican congressional leaders, to discuss his recent trip to Europe and the congressional legislative agenda;
—Minister of National Defense Zhang Aiping of China;
—members of the National Council of Farmer Cooperatives.

The President and Mrs. Reagan attended a birthday celebration for the Vice President at his home on the grounds of the Naval Observatory.

The President declared a major disaster for the State of Wisconsin as a result of severe storms and tornadoes, beginning on or about June 8, which caused extensive property damage.

The White House announced that the President requested the Congress to reduce the request for fiscal year 1984 supplemental appropriations for the Department of Defense-Military by $243.0 million. This reduction is possible because of a provision of the Omnibus Budget Reconciliation Act of 1983 (Public Law 98–270) that delayed the implementation of the cost-of-living adjustment for military retirees from May 1984 to January 1985. The President also requested an additional $83.0 million in fiscal year 1984 for the Veterans Administration's compensation program. This is a result of the enactment of Public Law 98–223, which provided for a 3.5-percent cost-of-living increase effective April 1. This increase is offset by requested reductions to Veterans Administration programs of $30.0 million in fiscal year 1984 and $119.1 million in 1985 that are made possible by lower-than-anticipated average benefit costs and caseloads in both the compensation and pension programs.

The President has also asked the Congress to consider appropriations requests for the legislative branch, the Department of Defense, and the Department of the Interior. Funds are also re-

quested to enable various Federal agencies to cover the cost of the 0.5-percent addition to the January 1 Federal pay raise mandated by the Omnibus Budget Reconciliation Act.

June 13

The President met at the White House with:
—members of the White House staff;
—Republican Members of Congress, to discuss measures to reduce the Federal budget deficit.

June 14

The President met at the White House with:
—members of the White House staff;
—the Cabinet Council on Natural Resources and the Environment;
—the Vice President, for lunch.

June 15

The President left the White House for a weekend stay at Camp David, MD.

The White House announced that the President has designated David Korn as Chairman of the National Cancer Advisory Board for the term expiring March 9, 1986.

June 16

The President announced his intention to designate Paula Stern as Chairman of the United States International Trade Commission for the term expiring June 16, 1986, vice Alfred E. Eckes, Jr., term expired. Dr. Stern has been serving as a member of the International Trade Commission since September 29, 1978.

June 17

The President left Camp David, MD, and traveled to Uniondale, NY. Following his remarks at the International Games for the Disabled, he returned to Washington, DC.

June 18

The President met at the White House with:
—members of the White House staff;
—delegates to the 16th annual National Teen Age Republican Leadership Conference.

In an Oval Office ceremony, the President received diplomatic credentials from Ambassadors Claudio Antonio Volio Guardia of Costa Rica, Richard Hendrik Fein of The Netherlands, Klaus Jacobi of Switzerland, Valentin Hernandez Acosta of Venezuela, Hernan Felipe Errazuriz Correa of Chile, and Luis Ernesto Marchand Stens of Peru.

The President declared a major disaster for the State of Connecticut as a result of severe storms and flooding, beginning on or about May 27, which caused extensive property damage.

The President declared a major disaster for the State of Vermont as a result of severe storms and flooding, beginning on June 6, which caused extensive property damage.

The White House announced that the President called Prime Minister-elect John N. Turner of Canada to congratulate him on his selection and indicate that he looked forward to working with the new Prime Minister. It was also announced that the President would be sending a letter to Prime Minister Pierre Elliott Trudeau expressing his appreciation for Prime Minister Trudeau's contributions to Canadian-American relations during his tenure.

June 19

The President met at the White House with:
—members of the White House staff;
—Republican congressional leaders, to discuss the legislative agenda for the remainder of June.

The White House announced that the President has designated Patricia A. Goldman as Vice Chairman of the National Transportation Safety Board for a term of 2 years.

The President announced his intention to appoint the following individuals as members of the Advisory Commission on Intergovernmental Relations for terms of 2 years:

Secretary of the Interior William P. Clark will succeed former Secretary of the Interior James G. Watt;

Secretary of Labor Raymond J. Donovan will succeed Secretary of Housing and Urban Development Samuel R. Pierce, Jr.

The President announced his intention to designate David C. Scott, of New York, as Chairman of the President's Export Council. He would succeed J. Paul Lyet. Mr. Scott has been serving as a member of the Council since August 13, 1981.

June 21

The President met at the White House with:
—members of the White House staff;
—members of the National Productivity Advisory Committee, who presented the Committee's final report;
—the Vice President, for lunch;
—Brian Mulroney, leader of the Conservative Party in Canada;
—members of the board of directors of the National Association of Broadcasters.

The President declared a major disaster for the State of Missouri as a result of severe storms, high winds, and flooding, beginning on June 6, which caused extensive property damage.

June 22

The President met at the White House with:
—members of the White House staff;
—Mayor Hernan A. Padilla of San Juan, Puerto Rico, newly elected president of the U.S. Conference of Mayors.

The President went to the Pentagon for a meeting with the Joint Chiefs of Staff.

The President declared a major disaster for the State of Kansas as a result of severe storms, tornadoes, and flooding, beginning on June 7, which caused extensive property damage.

The President left the White House for a weekend stay at Camp David, MD.

June 24

The President returned to the White House from Camp David.

June 25

The President met at the White House with:
—members of the White House staff;
—members of the Reagan-Bush Advisory Council.

June 26

The President met at the White House with:
—members of the White House staff;
—President-elect Leon Febres Cordero of Ecuador;
—Fuzzy Zoeller, 1984 U.S. Open golf champion.

The White House announced that the President requested the Congress to provide $289.4 million in fiscal year 1984 supplemental appropriations, including requests for the following:
—$260.0 million for the Veterans Administration's home loan guaranty program to enable the program to operate through the fiscal year. This increase is necessary because the primary source of funding for this program is no longer available, and program changes intended to reduce costs have been delayed until fiscal year 1985.
—$35.9 million for the increase in the Federal payment to various Federal employee retirement funds. This increase is necessary because of the recent 0.5-percent addition to the 3.5-percent January 1984 Federal pay raise.

The President also requested a net reduction of $26.6 million to the fiscal year 1985 request for appropriations now pending before the Congress. These proposals include the following:
—A reduction of $57.3 million for the Department of Energy due to a reestimate of the requirements of the Naval Petroleum and Oil Shale Reserves.
—$30.5 million for the Department of Justice to activate Federal correctional facilities in Loretto, PA, and Rochester, MN, and for additional U.S. attorneys and marshals to support the District of Columbia Superior Court.

The President also transmitted appropriations proposals for the legislative branch, the Department of Health and Human Services, and the Farm Credit Administration.

June 27

The President met at the White House with:
—members of the White House staff;
—Prince Bandar bin Sultan, Saudi Arabian Ambassador to the United States, who delivered a letter from King Fahd bin' Abd al-Aziz Al Sa'ud, and the Vice President, administration officials, and members of the White House staff;
—Governors Ted Schwinden of Montana, Terry Branstad of Iowa, and Allen Olson of North Dakota, to discuss agricultural issues.

The President declared a major disaster for the State of Iowa as a result of severe storms, hail, and tornadoes, beginning on June 7, which caused extensive property damage.

June 28

The President met at the White House with:
—members of the White House staff;
—the Cabinet, to discuss Federal employment issues;
—the Vice President, for lunch;
—Mai Shanley, Miss U.S.A.;
—Reginald Smith, 1984 Asthma Allergy Foundation Poster Child;
—Maj. Gen. Billy G. Weeman, who presented the Adjutant General's Association's George

Washington Freedom Award to the President;
—members of the executive committee of the National Square Dance Convention.

The President and Mrs. Reagan attended a dinner at the home of Mr. and Mrs. George F. Will in Chevy Chase, MD.

June 29

The President met at the White House with:
—members of the White House staff;
—Ambassador Harry W. Shlaudeman, Special Presidential Envoy for Central America, who reported on his recent trip to that area, and Secretary of State George P. Shultz, Secretary of Defense Caspar W. Weinberger, other administration officials, and members of the White House staff.

The President designated Susan Wittenberg Liebler as Vice Chairman of the United States International Trade Commission for the term expiring June 16, 1986.

The President announced that Dean Burch will serve as head of the delegation to the first session of the World Administrative Radio Conference on the Use of Geostationary-Satellite Orbit and the Planning of Space Service in Geneva in August 1985.

The President left the White House for a weekend stay at Camp David, MD.

Appendix B—Nominations Submitted to the Senate

The following list does not include promotions of members of the Uniformed Services, nominations to the Service Academies, or nominations of Foreign Service officers.

Submitted January 23

William H. Taft IV,
of Virginia, to be Deputy Secretary of Defense, vice W. Paul Thayer, resigned.

Submitted January 24

A.C. Arterbery,
of California, to be a member of the Board of Directors of the African Development Foundation for a term of 6 years (new position).

John A. Bohn, Jr.,
of California, to be First Vice President of the Export-Import Bank of the United States for a term expiring January 20, 1985, vice Charles Edwin Lord, resigned.

Terry Edward Branstad,
of Iowa, to be a member of the Board of Trustees of the Harry S. Truman Scholarship Foundation for a term expiring December 10, 1987, vice Christoper S. Bond, resigned.

H. Latham Breunig,
of New York, to be a member of the National Council on the Handicapped for a term expiring September 17, 1986 (reappointment).

Priscilla L. Buckley,
of Connecticut, to be a member of the United States Advisory Commission on Public Diplomacy for a term expiring July 1, 1986, vice Leonard Silverstein, term expired.

Richard D. Erb,
of Virginia, to be United States Executive Director of the International Monetary Fund for a term of 2 years (reappointment).

William Evans,
of California, to be a member of the Marine Mammal Commission for the term expiring May 13, 1985, vice James C. Nofziger, term expired.

Richard H. Francis,
of Virginia, to be President of the Solar Energy and Energy Conservation Bank, vice Joseph S. Bracewell.

Submitted January 24—Continued

Mary A. Grigsby,
of Texas, to be a member of the Federal Home Loan Bank Board for the remainder of the term expiring June 30, 1986, vice James Jay Jackson, resigned.

Robert Michael Isaac,
of Colorado, to be a member of the Board of Trustees of the Harry S. Truman Scholarship Foundation for a term expiring December 10, 1987, vice Richard A. King, term expired.

John G. Keane,
of Illinois, to be Director of the Census, vice Bruce Chapman.

Francis X. Lilly,
of Maryland, to be Solicitor for the Department of Labor, vice T. Timothy Ryan, Jr., resigned.

Michael Marge,
of New York, to be a member of the National Council on the Handicapped for a term expiring September 17, 1986 (reappointment).

Richard Thomas Montoya,
of Texas, to be an Assistant Secretary of the Interior, vice Pedro A. Sanjuan, resigned.

Sandra Swift Parrino,
of New York, to be a member of the National Council on the Handicapped for a term expiring September 17, 1986 (reappointment).

Richard M. Scaife,
of Pennsylvania, to be a member of the United States Advisory Commission on Public Diplomacy for a term expiring July 1, 1985, vice Mae Sue Talley, term expired.

Albert Lee Smith, Jr.,
of Alabama, to be a member of the Federal Council on the Aging for a term expiring December 19, 1985, vice Jacob Clayman, term expired.

James G. Stearns,
of Nevada, to be a Director of the Securities Investor Protection Corporation for a term expiring December 31, 1985 (reappointment).

Alvis Kent Waldrep, Jr.,
of Texas, to be a member of the National Council on the Handicapped for a term expiring September 17, 1986 (reappointment).

Daniel F. Bonner,
of Maryland, to be Associate Director of the ACTION Agency, vice Lawrence F. Davenport, resigned.

Capt. John D. Bossler,
National Oceanic and Atmospheric Administration, as Director of the Charting and Geodetic Services, National Ocean Service, National Oceanic and Atmospheric Administration, in the grade of rear admiral (upper half), and as a member of the Mississippi River Commission.

Richard A. Derham,
of Washington, to be an Assistant Administrator of the Agency for International Development, vice John R. Bolton, resigned.

Charles G. Hardin,
of Maryland, to be an Assistant Secretary of Transportation, vice Judith T. Connor, resigned.

Pringle P. Hillier,
of Virginia, to be an Assistant Secretary of the Army, vice Joel E. Bonner, Jr., resigned.

Sidney Lewis Jones,
of Maryland, to be Under Secretary of Commerce for Economic Affairs, vice Robert G. Dederick, resigned.

David C. Jordan,
of Virginia, to be Ambassador Extraordinary and Plenipotentiary of the United States of America to Peru.

Robert F. Kane,
of California, to be Ambassador Extraordinary and Plenipotentiary of the United States of America to Ireland.

Jim J. Marquez,
of Kansas, to be General Counsel of the Department of Transportation, vice James H. Burnley IV.

Bessie Boehm Moore,
of Arkansas, to be a member of the National Commission on Libraries and Information Science for a term expiring July 19, 1988 (reappointment).

Herbert Schmertz,
of New York, to be a member of the United States Advisory Commission on Public Diplomacy

for a term expiring April 6, 1985, vice Olin C. Robison, term expired.

William Lee Hanley, Jr.,
of Connecticut, to be a member of the Board of Directors of the Corporation for Public Broadcasting for a term expiring March 1, 1984, vice Gillian Martin Sorensen, term expired, to which position he was appointed during the recess of the Senate from August 4, 1983, until September 12, 1983.

The following-named persons for the positions indicated, to which positions they were appointed during the last recess of the Senate:

Maurice Lee Barksdale,
of Texas, to be an Assistant Secretary of Housing and Urban Development, vice Philip Abrams.

Simeon Miller Bright,
of West Virginia, to be a Commissioner of the Postal Rate Commission for the term expiring November 22, 1988 (reappointment).

Elliot Ross Buckley,
of Virginia, to be a member of the Occupational Safety and Health Review Commission for the term expiring April 27, 1989, vice Bertram R. Cottine, term expired.

Mary Kate Bush,
of New York, to be United States Alternate Executive Director of the International Monetary Fund for a term of 2 years, vice Charles H. Dallara, resigned.

Louis Roman DiSabato,
of Texas, to be a member of the National Museum Services Board for a term expiring December 6, 1987, vice Lloyd Hezekiah, term expired.

Vernon L. Grose,
of California, to be a member of the National Transportation Safety Board for the term expiring December 31, 1987, vice Francis H. McAdams, term expired.

Stephanie Lee-Miller,
of the District of Columbia, to be an Assistant Secretary of Health and Human Services, vice Pamela Needham Bailey.

Leslie Lenkowsky,
of New York, to be Deputy Director of the United States Information Agency, vice Gilbert A. Robinson, resigned.

Submitted January 24—Continued

Dennis R. Patrick,
of the District of Columbia, to be a member of
the Federal Communications Commission for the
unexpired term of 7 years from July 1, 1978, vice
Anne P. Jones, resigned.

Ruth O. Peters,
of Virginia, to be a Governor of the United States
Postal Service for the remainder of the term expiring December 8, 1987, vice Paula D. Hughes,
resigned.

Harold K. Phillips,
of California, to be a member of the Board of
Directors of the Inter-American Foundation for a
term expiring September 20, 1988, vice Alberto
Ibargüen, term expired.

Donna F. Tuttle,
of California, to be Under Secretary of Commerce for Travel and Tourism, vice Peter
McCoy, resigned.

Ann Dore McLaughlin,
of the District of Columbia, to be Under Secretary of the Interior, vice J. J. Simmons III.

J. Bonnie Newman,
of New Hampshire, to be an Assistant Secretary
of Commerce, vice Carlos C. Campbell, resigned.

Submitted January 26

William A. Wilson,
of California, to be Ambassador Extraordinary
and Plenipotentiary of the United States of
America to the Holy See.

Submitted January 27

Irving P. Margulies,
of Maryland, to be General Counsel of the Department of Commerce, vice Sherman E. Unger,
deceased.

Walter Leon Cutler,
of Maryland, a career member of the Senior Foreign Service, Class of Career Minister, to be Ambassador Extraordinary and Plenipotentiary of
the United States of America to the Kingdom of
Saudi Arabia.

Thomas W.M. Smith,
of Maine, a career member of the Senior Foreign
Service, Class of Minister-Counselor, to be Ambassador Extraordinary and Plenipotentiary of
the United States of America to the Federal Republic of Nigeria.

Submitted January 30

James Harvie Wilkinson III,
of Virginia, to be United States Circuit Judge for
the Fourth Circuit, vice John D. Butzner, Jr.,
retired.

Pauline Newman,
of Pennsylvania, to be United States Circuit
Judge for the Federal Circuit, vice Philip Nichols,
Jr., retired.

John R. Hargrove,
of Maryland, to be United States District Judge
for the District of Maryland, vice Shirley B.
Jones, resigned.

Bruce D. Beaudin,
of the District of Columbia, to be an Associate
Judge for the Superior Court of the District of
Columbia for a term of 15 years, vice John D.
Fauntleroy, retired.

Robert C. Bonner,
of California, to be United States Attorney for the
Central District of California for the term of 4
years, vice Stephen S. Trott, resigned.

The following-named persons to be members of
the Federal Council on the Aging for the terms
indicated:

For a term expiring June 5, 1985:

Ingrid Azvedo, of California, vice Charles J.
Fahey, term expired.

For terms expiring June 5, 1986:

Nelda Ann Lambert Barton, of Kentucky (reappointment).
Edna Bogosian, of Massachusetts (reappointment).
James N. Broder, of Maine (reappointment).
Tony Guglielmo, of Connecticut (reappointment).
Frances Lamont, of South Dakota (reappointment).

Submitted January 31

Julian L. Jacobs,
of Maryland, to be a Judge of the United States
Tax Court for a term expiring 15 years after he
takes office, vice Theodore Tannenwald, Jr., retired.

Errol Lee Wood,
of North Dakota, to be United States Marshal for
the District of North Dakota for a term of 4
years, vice Kenneth B. Muir, deceased.

Appendix B

Woodward Kingman,
of California, to be an Associate Director of the
United States Information Agency, vice James T.
Hackett, resigned.

Submitted February 3

Edwin Meese III,
of California, to be Attorney General.

Submitted February 8

J.J. Simmons III,
of Oklahoma, to be a member of the Interstate
Commerce Commission for the remainder of the
term expiring December 31, 1985, vice J.J. Simmons III, resigned.

Maureen E. Corcoran,
of California, to be General Counsel, Department
of Education, vice Daniel Oliver, resigned, to
which position she was appointed during the last
recess of the Senate.

Submitted February 9

Richard H. Imus,
of California, a Foreign Service officer of class
one, for the rank of Ambassador during his
tenure of service as United States Negotiator on
Textile Matters.

Submitted February 14

Harry L. Hupp,
of California, to be United States District Judge
for the Central District of California, vice A.
Andrew Hauk, retired.

Sarah Evans Barker,
of Indiana, to be United States District Judge for
the Southern District of Indiana, vice Cale J.
Holder, deceased.

Submitted February 16

Robert H. Conn,
of Virginia, to be an Assistant Secretary of the
Navy (new position—P.L. 98–94 of September 24,
1983).

Edward J. Garcia,
of California, to be United States District Judge
for the Eastern District of California, vice Philip
C. Wilkins, retired.

Edward Noonan Ney,
of New York, to be a member of the Board for
International Broadcasting for a term expiring
April 28, 1985, vice Charles David Ablard, term
expired.

Submitted February 22

Alfred Hugh Kingon,
of New York, to be an Assistant Secretary of the
Treasury, vice Ann Dore McLaughlin, resigned.

David Campbell Mulford,
of Illinois, to be a Deputy Under Secretary of the
Treasury, vice Marc E. Leland, resigned.

Fred William Alvarez,
of New Mexico, to be a member of the Equal
Employment Opportunity Commission for the
term expiring July 1, 1988, vice Armando M. Rodriguez, term expired.

David B. Rohr,
of Maryland, to be a member of the United
States International Trade Commission for the remainder of the term expiring December 16,
1985, vice William R. Alberger, resigned.

Susan Wittenberg Liebeler,
of California, to be a member of the United
States International Trade Commission for the remainder of the term expiring December 16,
1988, vice Michael J. Calhoun, resigned.

Submitted February 29

John W. Stokes, Jr.,
of Georgia, to be United States Marshal for the
Middle District of Georgia for the term of 4
years, vice Dwayne W. Gilbert, term expired.

Submitted March 1

Harry W. Shlaudeman,
of California, a career member of the Senior Foreign Service, Class of Career Minister, to be Ambassador at Large.

Fred T. Goldberg, Jr.,
of Maryland, to be an Assistant General Counsel
in the Department of the Treasury (Chief Counsel for the Internal Revenue Service), vice Kenneth W. Gideon, resigned.

Neal B. Biggers,
of Mississippi, to be United States District Judge
for the Northern District of Mississippi, vice William C. Keady, retired.

Submitted March 2

Robert R. Beezer,
of Washington, to be United States Circuit Judge
for the Ninth Circuit, vice Eugene A. Wright,
retired.

Frieda Waldman,
of California, to be a Governor of the United States Postal Service for the term expiring December 8, 1992, vice Robert L. Hardesty, term expired, to which position she was appointed during the recess of the Senate from November 18, 1983, until January 23, 1984.

Submitted March 5

Edward Sulzberger,
of New York, to be a member of the Board of Directors of the National Corporation for Housing Partnerships for the term expiring October 27, 1986 (reappointment).

Submitted March 6

H. Russel Holland,
of Alaska, to be United States District Judge for the District of Alaska, vice James A. von der Heydt, retiring.

Edward C. Prado,
of Texas, to be United States District Judge for the Western District of Texas, vice C. Frederick Shannon, Jr., resigned.

Jack L. Courtemanche,
of California, to be Administrator of General Services, vice Gerald P. Carmen, resigned.

Submitted March 12

Thomas H. Anderson, Jr.,
of Mississippi, to be Ambassador Extraordinary and Plenipotentiary of the United States of America to Barbados, and to serve concurrently and without additional compensation as Ambassador Extraordinary and Plenipotentiary of the United States of America to the Commonwealth of Dominica, Ambassador Extraordinary and Plenipotentiary of the United States of America to Saint Lucia, Ambassador Extraordinary and Plenipotentiary of the United States of America to Saint Vincent and the Grenadines, Ambassador Extraordinary and Plenipotentiary of the United States of America to Antigua and Barbuda, Ambassador Extraordinary and Plenipotentiary of the United States of America to St. Christopher and Nevis.

Gerald P. Carmen,
of New Hampshire, to be the Representative of the United States of America to the European Office of the United Nations, with the rank of Ambassador.

Richard Fairbanks,
of the District of Columbia, to be Ambassador at Large.

Barrington King,
of Georgia, a Career Member of the Senior Foreign Service, Class of Minister-Counselor, to be Ambassador Extraordinary and Plenipotentiary of the United States of America to Brunei.

David Charles Miller, Jr.,
of Pennsylvania, to be Ambassador Extraordinary and Plenipotentiary of the United States of America to Zimbabwe.

Paul H. Nitze,
of the District of Columbia, to be Special Representative for Arms Control and Disarmament Negotiations (new position—Public Law 98-202, of December 2, 1983), to which position he was appointed during the recess of the Senate from November 18, 1983, until January 23, 1984, and to have the rank of Ambassador while so serving.

Marge Bodwell,
of New Mexico, to be a member of the National Advisory Council on Women's Educational Programs for a term expiring May 8, 1986 (reappointment).

Paul H. Lamboley,
of Nevada, to be a member of the Interstate Commerce Commission for the remainder of the term expiring December 31, 1984, vice Darius W. Gaskins, Jr., resigned.

The following-named persons to be members of the National Council on Educational Research for terms expiring September 30, 1986:

J. Floyd Hall, of South Carolina (reappointment).
Donna Helene Hearne, of Missouri (reappointment).
George Charles Roche III, of Michigan (reappointment).
Carl W. Salser, of Oregon (reappointment).

Donald D. Engen,
of Virginia, to be Administrator of the Federal Aviation Administration, vice J. Lynn Helms, resigned.

Submitted March 14

Frank C. Casillas,
of Illinois, to be an Assistant Secretary of Labor, vice Albert Angrisani, resigned.

Submitted March 19

The following-named persons to be members of the Board of Directors of the Legal Services Corporation for the terms indicated:

Submitted March 19—Continued

For the remainder of the terms expiring July 13, 1984:

William Clark Durant III, of Michigan, vice William J. Olson.

Paul B. Eaglin, of North Carolina, vice Robert Sherwood Stubbs II.

Pepe J. Mendez, of Colorado, vice Peter Joseph Ferrara.

Thomas F. Smegal, Jr., of California, vice David E. Satterfield III.

Basile Joseph Uddo, of Louisiana, vice Howard H. Dana, Jr.

Michael B. Wallace, of Mississippi, vice George E. Paras.

For the remainder of the terms expiring July 13, 1986:

Hortencia Benavides, of Texas, vice Ronald B. Frankum.

Leaanne Bernstein, of Maryland, vice Albert Angrisani.

For the terms expiring July 13, 1986:

Lorain Miller, of Michigan, vice Milton M. Masson, Jr.

Claude Galbreath Swafford, of Tennessee, vice Robert E. McCarthy.

Robert A. Valois, of North Carolina, vice Donald Eugene Santarelli.

For the terms expiring July 13, 1987:

William Clark Durant III, of Michigan (reappointment).

Paul B. Eaglin, of North Carolina (reappointment).

Pepe J. Mendez, of Colorado (reappointment).

Thomas F. Smegal, Jr., of California (reappointment).

Basile Joseph Uddo, of Louisiana (reappointment).

Michael B. Wallace, of Mississippi (reappointment).

Mario F. Aguero, of New York, to be a Commissioner of the Copyright Royalty Tribunal for the unexpired term of 7 years from September 27, 1977, vice Mary Lou Burg, deceased.

The following-named persons to be members of the Board of Trustees of the Harry S. Truman Scholarship Foundation for terms expiring December 10, 1989:

Anita M. Miller, of California (reappointment).

Elmer B. Staats, of the District of Columbia, vice John W. Snyder, term expired.

Submitted March 21

Harry E. Bergold, Jr., of Florida, a career member of the Senior Foreign Service, class of Minister-Counselor, to be Ambassador Extraordinary and Plenipotentiary of the United States of America to the Republic of Nicaragua.

John F. Scruggs, of Virginia, to be an Assistant Secretary of Health and Human Services, vice Thomas R. Donnelly, Jr.

Daniel Raul Lopez, of California, to be a Commissioner of the United States Parole Commission for a term of 6 years, vice Benjamin J. Malcolm, term expired.

John P. McTague, of California, to be an Associate Director of the Office of Science and Technology Policy, vice Ronald B. Frankum.

James W. Fuller, of California, to be a Director of the Securities Investor Protection Corporation for a term expiring December 31, 1986 (reappointment).

Submitted March 22

Bruce E. Thompson, Jr., of Maryland, to be a Deputy Under Secretary of the Treasury, vice W. Dennis Thomas, resigned.

Submitted March 26

Edward Leavy, of Oregon, to be United States District Judge for the District of Oregon, vice Robert C. Belloni, retiring.

Submitted March 29

Robert Thomas Hennemeyer, of Illinois, a career member of the Senior Foreign Service, Class of Minister-Counselor, to be Ambassador Extraordinary and Plenipotentiary of the United States of America to the Republic of The Gambia.

The following-named career members of the Senior Foreign Service, Class of Career Minister, for the personal rank of Career Ambassador in recognition of especially distinguished service over a sustained period:

Lawrence S. Eagleburger, of Florida
Arthur Adair Hartman, of New Jersey

Bohdan A. Futey, of Ohio, to be Chairman of the Foreign Claims Settlement Commission of the United States for

Submitted March 29—Continued

the remainder of the term expiring September 30, 1985, vice J. Raymond Bell, deceased.

Patricia A. Goldman,
of the District of Columbia, to be a member of the National Transportation Safety Board for the term expiring December 31, 1988 (reappointment).

Submitted March 30

Stephen Warren Bosworth,
of Michigan, to be Ambassador Extraordinary and Plenipotentiary of the United States of America to the Republic of the Philippines.

Chapman B. Cox,
of Virginia, to be General Counsel of the Department of Defense, vice William H. Taft IV.

David T. Kingsbury,
of California, to be an Assistant Director of the National Science Foundation, vice Eloise E. Clark, resigned.

Submitted April 4

William D. Browning,
of Arizona, to be United States District Judge for the District of Arizona, vice Mary Anne Richey, deceased.

Alicemarie H. Stotler,
of California, to be United States District Judge for the Central District of California, vice Robert J. Kelleher, retired.

Joseph J. Longobardi,
of Delaware, to be United States District Judge for the District of Delaware, vice James L. Latchum, retired.

Terrence W. Boyle,
of North Carolina, to be United States District Judge for the Eastern District of North Carolina, vice Franklin T. Dupree, Jr., retired.

Submitted April 5

Rosemary M. Collyer,
of Colorado, to be General Counsel of the National Labor Relations Board for a term of 4 years, vice William A. Lubbers, term expiring.

Submitted April 6

James H. Webb, Jr.,
of Virginia, to be an Assistant Secretary of Defense (new position—P.L. 98–94 of September 24, 1983).

Submitted April 6—Continued

Joseph F. Dennin,
of the District of Columbia, to be an Assistant Secretary of Commerce, vice Alfred Hugh Kingon.

Submitted April 10

Donald Ian Macdonald,
of Florida, to be Administrator of the Alcohol, Drug Abuse, and Mental Health Administration, vice William E. Mayer.

Submitted April 12

Robert S. Cooper,
of Virginia, to be an Assistant Secretary of Defense (new position—P.L. 98–94, of September 24, 1983).

Submitted April 13

Joel Gerber,
of Virginia, to be a Judge of the United States Tax Court for a term expiring 15 years after he takes office, vice C. Moxley Featherston, retired.

Submitted April 18

Lloyd D. George,
of Nevada, to be United States District Judge for the District of Nevada, vice Roger D. Foley, retired.

Submitted April 19

S.L. Abbott,
of Texas, to be Ambassador Extraordinary and Plenipotentiary of the United States of America to the Kingdom of Lesotho.

James Paul Wade, Jr.,
of Virginia, to be an Assistant Secretary of Defense (new position—P.L. 98–94, of September 24, 1983).

Everett Pyatt,
of Virginia, to be an Assistant Secretary of the Navy, vice George A. Sawyer, resigned.

Ann S. Peterson,
of Illinois, to be a member of the Board of Regents of the Uniformed Services University of the Health Sciences for a term expiring June 20, 1989, vice Robert Higgins Ebert, term expired.

Virgil E. Brown,
of Ohio, to be a member of the Advisory Board of the Saint Lawrence Seaway Development Corporation, vice Foster S. Brown, resigned.

John R. Wall,
of Ohio, to be a member of the Advisory Board of the Saint Lawrence Seaway Development Corporation, vice Joseph N. Thomas.

William W. Hoover,
of Maryland, to be an Assistant Secretary of Energy (Defense Programs), vice Herman E. Roser, resigned.

The following-named persons to be members of the National Advisory Council on Women's Educational Programs for terms expiring May 8, 1986:

Naomi Brummond, of Nebraska, vice Mary Jo Arndt, term expired.
Peter Douglas Keisler, of Connecticut, vice Virginia Gillham Tinsley, term expired.

Jacqueline E. Schafer,
of New York, to be a member of the Council on Environmental Quality, vice Nancy A. Maloley, resigned.

Bernadine Healy Bulkley,
of Maryland, to be an Associate Director of the Office of Science and Technology Policy (new position).

Clyde A. Bragdon, Jr.,
of California, to be Administrator of the United States Fire Administration, vice Bobby Jack Thompson, resigned.

The following-named persons to be members of the National Council on the Humanities for terms expiring January 26, 1990:

William Barclay Allen, of California, vice Charles V. Hamilton, term expired.
Mary Josephine Conrad Cresimore, of North Carolina, vice Louis J. Hector, term expired.
Leon Richard Kass, of Illinois, vice M. Carl Holman, term expired.
Kathleen S. Kilpatrick, of Connecticut, vice Harriet Morse Zimmerman, term expired.
James V. Schall, of California, vice Leon Stein, term expired.
Helen Marie Taylor, of Virginia, vice Mary Beth Norton, term expired.

Victor M. Rivera,
of Virginia, to be an Assistant Administrator of the Agency for International Development, vice Otto J. Reich, resigned.

Michael Hayden Armacost,
of Maryland, a career member of the Senior Foreign Service, Class of Minister-Counselor, to be

Under Secretary of State for Political Affairs, vice Lawrence S. Eagleburger, resigned.

Harold Peter Goldfield,
of New York, to be an Assistant Secretary of Commerce, vice Richard L. McElheny, resigned.

Carol E. Dinkins,
of Texas, to be Deputy Attorney General, vice Edward C. Schmults, resigned.

James Eugene Burnett, Jr.,
of Arkansas, to be Chairman of the National Transportation Safety Board for a term of 2 years (reappointment).

Weston Adams,
of South Carolina, to be Ambassador Extraordinary and Plenipotentiary of the United States of America to the Republic of Malawi.

Edward E. Wolfe,
of Virginia, Deputy Assistant Secretary of State for Oceans and Fisheries Affairs, for the rank of Ambassador.

Ben C. Rusche,
of South Carolina, to be Director of the Office of Civilian Radioactive Waste Management (new position—Public Law 97–425 of January 7, 1983).

Richard Schifter,
of Maryland, to be Deputy Representative of the United States of America in the Security Council of the United Nations, with the rank of Ambassador.

Clint Arlen Lauderdale,
of California, a career member of the Senior Foreign Service, Class of Minister-Counselor, to be Ambassador Extraordinary and Plenipotentiary of the United States of America to the Cooperative Republic of Guyana.

Peter Sebastian,
of Maryland, a career member of the Senior Foreign Service, Class of Minister-Counselor, to be Ambassador Extraordinary and Plenipotentiary of the United States of America to the Republic of Tunisia.

Charles G. Untermeyer,
of Texas, to be an Assistant Secretary of the Navy, vice Chapman Beecher Cox.

June Q. Koch,
of Maryland, to be an Assistant Secretary of Housing and Urban Development, vice Emanuel S. Savas.

Marianne Mele,
of New Jersey, to be a Commissioner of the Copyright Royalty Tribunal for the unexpired term of 7 years from September 27, 1982, vice Katherine D. Ortega, resigned.

Ralph E. Kennickell, Jr.,
of Virginia, to be Public Printer, vice Danford L. Sawyer, Jr., resigned.

Charles L. Marinaccio,
of Maryland, to be a member of the Securities and Exchange Commission for the remainder of the term expiring June 5, 1985, vice Barbara S. Thomas, resigned.

Mae Neal Peden,
of Virginia, to be an Assistant Administrator of the Agency for International Development, vice Elise R.W. du Pont, resigned.

Submitted May 10

The following-named person to be a member of the Securities and Exchange Commission for the terms indicated:

For the remainder of the term expiring June 5, 1984:

Aulana L. Peters, of California, vice Bevis Longstreth, resigned.

For the term expiring June 5, 1989:

Aulana L. Peters, of California (reappointment).

Submitted May 15

Paul G. Rosenblatt,
of Arizona, to be United States District Judge for the District of Arizona, vice William P. Copple, retired.

John M. Duhe, Jr.,
of Louisiana, to be United States District Judge for the Western District of Louisiana, vice W. Eugene Davis, elevated.

Tom S. Lee,
of Mississippi, to be United States District Judge for the Southern District of Mississippi, vice Dan Monroe Russell, Jr., retired.

James H. Quello,
of Virginia, to be a member of the Federal Communications Commission for a term of 7 years from July 1, 1984 (reappointment).

Submitted May 21

Donald C. Latham,
of Virginia, to be an Assistant Secretary of Defense (new position—Public Law 98–94 of September 24, 1983).

M. Robert Hill, Jr.,
of California, to be a member of the Board of Regents of the Uniformed Services University of the Health Sciences for a term expiring June 20, 1989, vice Eugene M. Farber, term expired.

Joseph Wentling Brown,
of Nevada, to be a member of the Foreign Claims Settlement Commission of the United States for the term expiring September 30, 1986 (reappointment).

Robert N. Broadbent,
of Nevada, to be an Assistant Secretary of the Interior, vice Daniel N. Miller, Jr., resigned.

Frank K. Richardson,
of California, to be Solicitor of the Department of the Interior, vice William H. Coldiron, resigned.

Charles G. Stalon,
of Illinois, to be a member of the Federal Energy Regulatory Commission for a term expiring October 20, 1987, vice John David Hughes, term expired.

Robert Laxalt,
of Nevada, to be a member of the National Council on the Humanities for a term expiring January 26, 1990, vice Sister Joel Read, term expired.

Submitted May 24

Jean Galloway Bissell,
of South Carolina, to be United States Circuit Judge for the Federal Circuit, vice Robert L. Kunzig, deceased.

Rudi M. Brewster,
of California, to be United States District Judge for the Southern District of California, vice Howard B. Turrentine, retired.

James M. Ideman,
of California, to be United States District Judge for the Central District of California, vice Lawrence T. Lydick, retired.

William J. Rea,
of California, to be United States District Judge for the Central District of California, vice Malcolm M. Lucas, retired.

Submitted May 25

Dominick L. DiCarlo,
of New York, to be a Judge of the United States Court of International Trade, vice Bernard Newman, retired.

Peter K. Leisure,
of New York, to be United States District Judge for the Southern District of New York, vice Milton Pollack, retired.

Franklin S. Billings, Jr.,
of Vermont, to be United States District Judge for the District of Vermont, vice James S. Holden, retired.

Layn R. Phillips,
of Oklahoma, to be United States Attorney for the Northern District of Oklahoma for the term of 4 years, vice Francis Anthony Keating II, resigned.

Submitted May 30

Thomas H. Etzold,
of Rhode Island, to be an Assistant Director of the United States Arms Control and Disarmament Agency, vice James L. George, resigned.

Submitted May 31

Dodie Truman Livingston,
of California, to be Chief of the Children's Bureau, Department of Health and Human Services, vice Clarence Eugene Hodges.

Frances Todd Stewart,
of Pennsylvania, to be a member of the Board of Directors of the Overseas Private Investment Corporation for a term expiring December 17, 1986, vice Donald Eugene Santarelli, term expired.

Submitted June 4

Owen W. Roberts,
of New Jersey, a career member of the Senior Foreign Service, Class of Minister-Counselor, to be Ambassador Extraordinary and Plenipotentiary of the United States of America to the Republic of Togo.

Robert M. Hill,
of Texas, to be United States Circuit Judge for the Fifth Circuit, vice John R. Brown, retired.

Submitted June 4—Continued

John D. Tinder,
of Indiana, to be United States Attorney for the Southern District of Indiana for a term of 4 years, vice Sarah Evans Barker, resigned.

Martha R. Seger,
of Michigan, to be a member of the Board of Governors of the Federal Reserve System for a term of 14 years from February 1, 1984, vice Nancy Hays Teeters, term expired.

Submitted June 13

John William Shirley,
of Illinois, a career member of the Senior Foreign Service, Class of Career Minister, to be Ambassador Extraordinary and Plenipotentiary of the United States of America to the United Republic of Tanzania.

Submitted June 18

Katherine M. Bulow,
of Maryland, to be an Assistant Secretary of Commerce, vice Arlene Triplett, resigned.

Alberto Martinez Piedra,
of Maryland, to be Ambassador Extraordinary and Plenipotentiary of the United States of America to the Republic of Guatemala.

Submitted June 19

Howard Bruner Schaffer,
of New York, a career member of the Senior Foreign Service, Class of Minister-Counselor, to be Ambassador Extraordinary and Plenipotentiary of the United States of America to the People's Republic of Bangladesh.

Paul Fisher Gardner,
of Texas, a career member of the Senior Foreign Service, Class of Minister-Counselor, to be Ambassador Extraordinary and Plenipotentiary of the United States of America to Papua New Guinea and to serve concurrently and without additional compensation as Ambassador Extraordinary and Plenipotentiary of the United States of America to the Solomon Islands.

Leonardo Neher,
of Maryland, a career member of the Senior Foreign Service, Class of Counselor, to be Ambassador Extraordinary and Plenipotentiary of the United States of America to the Republic of Upper Volta.

Submitted June 19—Continued

Diana Lady Dougan,
of Utah, to be Coordinator for International Communications and Information Policy, with the rank of Ambassador.

Erich Bloch,
of New York, to be Director of the National Science Foundation for a term of 6 years, vice Edward A. Knapp, resigned.

Charles A. Legge,
of California, to be United States District Judge for the Northern District of California, vice Robert H. Schnacke, retired.

Marcel Livaudais, Jr.,
of Louisiana, to be United States District Judge for the Eastern District of Louisiana, vice Fred J. Cassibry, retired.

Ilana Diamond Rovner,
of Illinois, to be United States District Judge for the Northern District of Illinois, vice Joel M. Flaum, elevated.

Anthony J. Scirica,
of Pennsylvania, to be United States District Judge for the Eastern District of Pennsylvania, vice John B. Hannum, retired.

Submitted June 25

Robert J. Ryan, Jr.,
of the District of Columbia, a career member of the Senior Foreign Service, Class of Minister-Counselor, to be Ambassador Extraordinary and Plenipotentiary of the United States of America to the Republic of Mali.

Judith D. Moss,
of Ohio, to be a member of the National Advisory Council on Women's Educational Programs for a term expiring May 8, 1987 (reappointment).

Jorge L. Mas,
of Florida, to be a member of the Advisory Board for Radio Broadcasting to Cuba for a term of 2 years (new position—Public Law 98–111 of October 4, 1983).

Margaret Phelan,
of Kansas, to be a member of the National Commission on Libraries and Information Science for a term expiring July 19, 1988, vice Philip A. Sprague, term expired.

Withdrawn June 25

Leslie Lenkowsky,
of New York, to be Deputy Director of the United States Information Agency, vice Gilbert

Withdrawn June 25—Continued

A. Robinson, resigned, to which position he was appointed during the last recess of the Senate, which was sent to the Senate on January 24, 1984.

Submitted June 28

Paul H. Boeker,
of Ohio, a career member of the Senior Foreign Service, Class of Career Minister, to be Ambassador Extraordinary and Plenipotentiary of the United States of America to the Hashemite Kingdom of Jordan.

Richard Wood Boehm,
of the District of Columbia, a career member of the Senior Foreign Service, Class of Minister-Counselor, to be Ambassador Extraordinary and Plenipotentiary of the United States of America to the Republic of Cyprus.

Maynard W. Glitman,
of Vermont, a career member of the Senior Foreign Service, Class of Minister-Counselor, for the rank of Ambassador during the tenure of his service as the Representative of the United States of America for Mutual and Balanced Force Reductions Negotiations.

Stanley Sporkin,
of Maryland, to be United States District Judge for the District of Columbia, vice June L. Green, retired.

Wanda L. Forbes,
of South Carolina, to be a member of the National Commission on Libraries and Information Science for a term expiring July 19, 1988, vice Francis Keppel, term expired.

Walter T. Cox III,
of South Carolina, to be a Judge of the United States Court of Military Appeals for a term of 15 years, vice William Holmes Cook, retired.

Robert A. Rowland,
of Texas, to be an Assistant Secretary of Labor, vice Thorne G. Auchter, resigned.

Tony E. Gallegos,
of California, to be a member of the Equal Employment Opportunity Commission for the term expiring July 1, 1989 (reappointment).

Carol Gene Dawson,
of Virginia, to be a Commissioner of the Consumer Product Safety Commission for the remainder of the term expiring October 26, 1985, vice Samuel D. Zagoria, resigned.

Appendix B

Melvin A. Ensley,
of Washington, to be a member of the Federal
Farm Credit Board, Farm Credit Administration,
for a term expiring March 31, 1990, vice George
Warren Lacey, term expired.

Lando W. Zech, Jr.,
of Virginia, to be a member of the Nuclear Regulatory Commission for the term of 5 years expiring June 30, 1989, vice Victor Gilinsky, term expiring.

James B. Burnham,
of Pennsylvania, to be United States Executive
Director of the International Bank for Recon-

struction and Development for a term of 2 years
(reappointment).

Harold J. Lezar, Jr.,
of Texas, to be an Assistant Attorney General,
vice Jonathan C. Rose, resigned.

Submitted June 29

Alan Wood Lukens,
of Pennsylvania, a career member of the Senior
Foreign Service, Class of Minister-Counselor, to
be Ambassador Extraordinary and Plenipotentiary of the United States of America to the People's
Republic of the Congo.

Appendix C—Checklist of White House Press Releases

The following list contains releases of the Office of the Press Secretary which are not included in this book.

Released January 6

Transcript:
Press briefing on the upcoming Conference on Confidence and Security Building Measures and Disarmament in Europe—by Ambassador James E. Goodby, U.S. Representative to the Conference

Transcript:
Press briefing on progress in reducing fraud, waste, and abuse in the Federal Government—by Counsellor to the President Edwin Meese III and Joseph R. Wright, Deputy Director of the Office of Management and Budget

Released January 9

Fact sheet:
Report of the Cabinet Council Working Group on School Violence and Discipline

Transcript:
Press briefing on the report of the Cabinet Council Working Group on School Violence and Discipline—by Secretary of Education Terrel H. Bell and Gary L. Bauer, Deputy Under Secretary of Education for Planning, Budget and Evaluation

Transcript:
U.S. business investment mission to Grenada—by Craig A. Nalen, President and Chief Executive Officer, Overseas Private Investment Corporation; Sheldon Weinig, Chairman of the International Committee of the President's Advisory Council on Private Sector Initiatives; and James N. Brown, director of the Hitech Engineering Co.

Released January 11

Statement:
The President's meeting with the National Bipartisan Commission on Central America to receive its report—by Larry M. Speakes, Principal Deputy Press Secretary to the President

Transcript:
Press briefing on the report of the National Bipartisan Commission on Central America—by Henry A. Kissinger, Chairman of the Commission

Released January 11—Continued

Statement:
Human rights in El Salvador—by Larry M. Speakes, Principal Deputy Press Secretary to the President

Statement:
U.S.-Soviet discussions on the improvement of the direct communications link (hotline)—by Larry M. Speakes, Principal Deputy Press Secretary to the President

Released January 12

Fact sheet:
Agreement To Extend the Agreement Between the Government of the United States of America and the Government of the People's Republic of China on Cooperation in Science and Technology

Fact sheet:
Accord on Industrial and Technological Cooperation Between the United States of America and the People's Republic of China

Released January 16

Advance text:
Address to the Nation and other countries on U.S.-Soviet relations

Released January 17

Transcript:
Press briefing on the Intermediate-range Nuclear Force negotiations—by Ambassador Paul H. Nitze, Special Representative for Negotiations, U.S. Arms Control and Disarmament Agency

Released January 20

Advance text:
Remarks to the Reagan Administration Executive Forum

Statement:
On the fourth quarter rise in the gross national product—by Larry M. Speakes, Principal Deputy Press Secretary to the President

Released January 25

Excerpts:
Selected quotations from the State of the Union Address

Released January 25—Continued

Fact sheet:
State of the Union Address

Advance text:
State of the Union Address

Released January 26

Transcript:
Press briefing on the proposed permanent space station—by James M. Beggs, Administrator of the National Aeronautics and Space Administration

Advance text:
Remarks at the Spirit of America rally in Atlanta, GA

Advance text:
Remarks at the Southern Republican Leadership Conference in Atlanta, GA

Released January 29

Advance text:
Address to the Nation announcing the Reagan-Bush candidacies for reelection

Released January 30

Announcement:
Nomination of Pauline Newman to be United States Circuit Judge for the Federal Circuit

Announcement:
Nomination of Robert C. Bonner to be United States Attorney for the Central District of California

Transcript:
Press briefing following his meeting with the President to discuss the strategic arms reduction talks with the Soviet Union—by Ambassador Edward L. Rowny, Special Representative for Negotiations, U.S. Arms Control and Disarmament Agency

Advance text:
Remarks at the annual convention of the National Religious Broadcasters

Released January 31

Advance text:
Remarks to the concrete and aggregates industries associations convention in Chicago, IL

Announcement:
Nomination of Julian L. Jacobs to be a Judge of the United States Tax Court

Released January 31—Continued

Announcement:
Nomination of Errol Lee Wood to be United States Marshal for the District of North Dakota

Released February 2

Transcript:
Press briefing on the Economic Report of the President—by Martin S. Feldstein, Chairman of the Council of Economic Advisers

Advance text:
Remarks at a luncheon with Republican Members of the House and Senate at the Russell Senate Office Building

Released February 3

Advance text:
Remarks announcing a proposed initiative for Central America

Fact sheet:
Proposed initiative for Central America

Released February 6

Advance text:
Remarks to citizens of Dixon, IL

Advance text:
Remarks to students and faculty at Eureka College, Eureka, IL

Released February 7

Advance text:
Remarks at the annual convention of the National Association of Secondary School Principals in Las Vegas, NV

Advance text:
Remarks at a Republican fundraising luncheon in Las Vegas, NV

Released February 14

Announcement:
Nomination of Sarah Evans Barker to be United States District Judge for the Southern District of Indiana and Harry L. Hupp to be United States District Judge for the Central District of California

Released February 15

Announcement:
Nomination of Edward J. Garcia to be United States District Judge for the Eastern District of California

Released February 15—Continued

Advance text:
Remarks at a fundraiser for Republican women candidates on Susan B. Anthony's birthday

Released February 16

Transcript:
Press briefing on the housing starts and personal income figures for January 1984—by Secretary of the Treasury Donald T. Regan

Released February 20

Advance text:
Remarks at a caucus rally in Waterloo, IA

Advance text:
Remarks at a caucus rally in Des Moines, IA

Released February 21

Transcript:
Press briefing on the report of the Commission on Security and Economic Assistance—by Frank C. Carlucci, Chairman of the Commission

Fact sheet:
Report of the Commission on Security and Economic Assistance

Released February 27

Text:
Letter to the Speaker of the House and the President of the Senate transmitting a report, pursuant to Public Law 98–151, on the activities of countries in the United Nations and its specialized agencies

Released February 28

Advance text:
Toast at the state dinner honoring President Rudolf Kirchschläger of Austria

Released February 29

Announcement:
Nomination of John W. Stokes, Jr., to be United States Marshal for the Middle District of Georgia

Statement:
Index of leading economic indicators for January—by Larry M. Speakes, Principal Deputy Press Secretary to the President

Released March 1

Announcement:
Nomination of Neal B. Biggers to be United States District Judge for the Northern District of Mississippi

Released March 1—Continued

Advance text:
Remarks at the American Legion Auxiliary Awareness Assembly

Released March 2

Announcement:
Nomination of Robert R. Beezer to be United States Circuit Judge for the Ninth Circuit

Advance text:
Remarks at the 11th annual Conservative Political Action Conference dinner

Released March 5

Advance text:
Remarks at the annual conference of the National League of Cities

Released March 6

Announcement:
Nomination of Edward C. Prado to be United States District Judge for the Western District of Texas and H. Russel Holland to be United States District Judge for the District of Alaska

Advance text:
Remarks at the 42d annual convention of the National Association of Evangelicals in Columbus, OH

Advance text:
Remarks at a New York Republican Party fundraising dinner in New York City

Released March 13

Advance text:
Remarks at the Young Leadership Conference of the United Jewish Appeal

Transcript:
Press briefing on his meeting with the President to discuss the current situation in El Salvador—by Thomas R. Pickering, U.S. Ambassador to El Salvador

Released March 15

Transcript:
Interview with Robert C. McFarlane, Assistant to the President for National Security Affairs, by Jane Pauley and Andrea Mitchell on NBC News "Today"

Transcript:
Press briefing following his meeting with the President to discuss the current situation in Hon-

Released March 15—Continued

duras—by John D. Negroponte, U.S. Ambassador to Honduras

Statement by the President:
Agreement with the Republican congressional leadership for a budget deficit reduction plan (as read to reporters in the Rose Garden)

Released March 16

Advance text:
Toast at a luncheon for Prime Minister Garret FitzGerald of Ireland

Released March 19

Transcript:
Press briefing on the President's Annual Report on the State of Small Business for 1983—by James C. Sanders, Administrator, and Frank S. Swain, Chief Counsel for Advocacy, Small Business Administration

Statement:
Presidential elections in El Salvador—by Larry M. Speakes, Principal Deputy Press Secretary to the President

Released March 20

Statement:
Flash estimate for first quarter 1984 figures for the gross national product—by Larry M. Speakes, Principal Deputy Press Secretary to the President

Released March 22

Statement:
Appointment of an independent counsel in connection with his nomination to be Attorney General—by Edwin Meese III, Counsellor to the President

Advance text:
Toast at the state dinner honoring President François Mitterrand of France

Released March 23

Statement:
Consumer Price Index figures for February—by Larry M. Speakes, Principal Deputy Press Secretary to the President

Announcement:
The President's visit to Ireland, which begins June 1

Announcement:
Nomination of Edward Leavy to be United States District Judge for the District of Oregon

Released March 23—Continued

Announcement:
Submission to the President of a letter report on arms control aspects of its earlier recommendations by the President's Commission on Strategic Forces (together with the text of the letter report)

Released March 26

Announcement:
Recipients and citations for the Presidential Medal of Freedom

Released March 27

Transcript:
Press briefing following his meeting with the President to report on his trip to China, Japan, and the Republic of Korea—by Secretary of the Treasury Donald T. Regan

Advance text:
Remarks at the National Legislative Conference of the Independent Insurance Agents of America

Statement:
On court approval of the Attorney General's recommendation for appointment of an independent counsel to investigate allegations concerning Edwin Meese III, Counsellor to the President—by Larry M. Speakes, Principal Deputy Press Secretary to the President

Released March 28

Transcript:
Press briefing following his meeting with the President to discuss his forthcoming trip to Central America—by Harry W. Shlaudeman, Special Presidential Envoy and Ambassador at Large for Central America

Released March 29

Transcript:
Press briefing following his meeting with the President to discuss his reelection candidacy to the U.S. Congress as a Republican—by Representative Andy Ireland of Florida

Transcript:
Press briefing on the Annual Federal Performance Report on Executive Agency Actions To Assist Historically Black Colleges and Universities for Fiscal Year 1983, which was prepared in accordance with Executive Order 12320—by Secretary of Education Terrel H. Bell

Released March 30

Transcript:
Question-and-answer session with reporters following his meeting with the President—by entertainer Mel Blanc

Released April 3

Transcript:
Press briefing on his meeting with the President to discuss the Conference on Confidence and Security Building Measures and Disarmament in Europe—by Ambassador James E. Goodby, Chief of the U.S. delegation to the Conference

Released April 4

Announcement:
Nomination of William D. Browning to be United States District Judge for the District of Arizona

Announcement:
Nomination of Alicemarie H. Stotler to be United States District Judge for the Central District of California

Announcement:
Nomination of Joseph J. Longobardi to be United States District Judge for the District of Delaware

Announcement:
Nomination of Terrence W. Boyle to be United States District Judge for the Eastern District of North Carolina

Announcement:
Appointment of Margaret Ellen Noonan as a Presidential speechwriter

Released April 5

Advance text:
Remarks at the luncheon of the Women Business Owners of New York in New York City

Advance text:
Remarks at the dinner of the New York State Federation of Catholic School Parents in New York City

Released April 6

Advance text:
Remarks at the National Leadership Forum of the Center for Strategic and International Studies of Georgetown University (2 releases)

Fact sheet:
President's remarks at the Center for Strategic and International Studies

Released April 9

Transcript:
Interview of Robert C. McFarlane, Assistant to the President for National Security Affairs, by Diane Sawyer on the CBS Morning News

Transcript:
Press briefing following his meeting with the President to discuss his recent visits to China and the Soviet Union and the final letter report of the President's Commission on Strategic Forces—by Brent Scowcroft, Chairman of the Commission

Released April 10

Advance text:
Toast at the state dinner honoring President Salvador Jorge Blanco of the Dominican Republic

Released April 11

Advance text:
Remarks at the Ford Claycomo Assembly Plant in Kansas City, MO

Released April 13

Announcement:
Nomination of Joel Gerber to be a Judge of the United States Tax Court

Copies:
1983 income tax return of the President and Mrs. Reagan

Released April 18

Transcript:
Press briefing on the President's upcoming trip to China—by Secretary of State George P. Shultz

Announcement:
Nomination of Lloyd. D. George to be United States District Judge for the District of Nevada

Released April 24

Advance text:
Remarks upon departure from Hickam Air Force Base, Honolulu, HI

Released April 25

Advance text:
Remarks upon arrival in Agana, Guam

Released April 26

Fact sheet:
Proposed legislation to combat international terrorism

Released April 26—Continued
Advance text:
Toast at a dinner hosted by President Li Xiannian of China in Beijing

Released April 27

Statements:
On the agreement between the U.S. and China on cooperation in the peaceful uses of nuclear energy (2 releases)—by Larry M. Speakes, Principal Deputy Press Secretary to the President

Advance text:
Address to Chinese community leaders in Beijing, China

Advance text:
Toast at the welcoming banquet hosted by Premier Zhao Ziyang of China in Beijing

Transcript:
Interview of Secretary of State George P. Shultz on ABC News "Good Morning America"

Transcript:
Interview of Assistant to the President James A. Baker III on the CBS Morning News

Transcript:
Interview of Robert C. McFarlane, Assistant to the President for National Security Affairs, on NBC News "Today"

Released April 28

Advance text:
Remarks at a reception for members of the American community in Beijing, China

Advance text:
Toast at a dinner honoring Premier Zhao Ziyang of China in Beijing

Released April 29

Transcript:
Interview of Secretary of State George P. Shultz on ABC News "This Week With David Brinkley"

Transcript:
Interview of Robert C. McFarlane, Assistant to the President for National Security Affairs, on CBS News "Face the Nation"

Released April 30

Advance text:
Remarks at a ceremony for the signing of four U.S.-China agreements and the President's departure from Beijing, China

Released April 30—Continued
Fact sheet:
Agreements signed or initialed during the President's visit to China

Advance text:
Remarks at the Shanghai Foxboro Co., Ltd., in Shanghai, China

Advance text:
Remarks to students preceeding a question-and-answer session at Fudan University in Shanghai, China

Advance text:
Remarks to students and faculty at Fudan University in Shanghai, China

Transcript:
Interview of Assistant to the President James A. Baker III on NBC News "Today"

Transcript:
Press briefing on the President's trip to China—by Secretary of State George P. Shultz

Advance text:
Toast at a banquet hosted by Mayor Wang Daohan in Shanghai, China

Released May 1

Advance text:
Remarks upon returning from the trip to China

Advance text:
Remarks at a luncheon with community leaders at the University of Alaska in Fairbanks

Released May 2

Advance text:
Remarks at a meeting with Pope John Paul II at the Fairbanks International Airport, Fairbanks, AK

Released May 9

Advance text:
Address to the Nation on U.S. policy in Central America

Fact sheet:
Address to the Nation on U.S. policy in Central America

Released May 10

Advance text:
Remarks at the midyear meeting of the National Association of Realtors

Released May 14

Transcript:
Press briefing on the national campaign against drunk driving—by Diane Steed, Administrator of the National Highway Traffic Safety Administration

Announcement:
Nominations of John M. Duhe, Jr., to be United States District Judge for the Western District of Louisiana, Tom S. Lee to be United States District Judge for the Southern District of Mississippi, and Paul G. Rosenblatt to be United States District Judge for the District of Arizona

Released May 15

Advance text:
Toast at the state dinner honoring President Miguel De la Madrid Hurtado of Mexico

Released May 18

Announcement:
Results of the President's physical examination

Released May 21

Transcript:
Press briefing following his meeting with the President—by José Napoleon Duarte, President-elect of El Salvador

Released May 22

Statement:
Consumer Price Index figures for April—by Larry M. Speakes, Principal Deputy Press Secretary to the President

Transcript:
Press briefing on the President's visit to Normandy, France—by Secretary of the Army John O. Marsh

Released May 24

Announcement:
Nomination of Jean Galloway Bissell to be United States Circuit Judge for the Federal Circuit

Announcement:
Nomination of Rudi M. Brewster to be United States District Judge for the Southern District of California; James M. Ideman to be United States District Judge for the Central District of California; and William J. Rea to be United States District Judge for the Central District of California

Released May 25

Advance text:
Remarks at a ceremony honoring an unknown serviceman of the Vietnam conflict

Announcement:
Nomination of Dominick L. DiCarlo to be a Judge of the United States Court of International Trade

Announcement:
Nomination of Franklin S. Billings, Jr., to be United States District Judge for the District of Vermont and Peter K. Leisure to be United States District Judge for the Southern District of New York

Announcement:
Nomination of Layn R. Phillips to be United States Attorney for the Northern District of Oklahoma

Released May 28

Advance text:
Remarks at Memorial Day ceremonies at Arlington National Cemetery honoring an unknown serviceman of the Vietnam conflict

Released May 29

Transcript:
Press briefing on issues to be discussed at the London Economic Summit—by Secretary of the Treasury Donald T. Regan

Advance text:
Remarks during a tour of the U.S. Olympic Training Center in Colorado Springs, CO

Released May 30

Advance text:
Remarks at commencement exercises at the U.S. Air Force Academy in Colorado Springs, CO

Advance text:
Toast at a dinner for the NATO Foreign Ministers

Released May 31

Statement:
Index of leading economic indicators for April—by Larry M. Speakes, Principal Deputy Press Secretary to the President

Announcement:
Nomination of John D. Tinder to be United States Attorney for the Southern District of Indiana

Released June 13

Fact sheet:
National Center for Missing and Exploited Children

Released June 17

Advance text:
Remarks opening the 1984 International Games for the Disabled in Uniondale, NY

Released June 18

Advance text:
Toast at the state dinner honoring President J.R. Jayewardene of Sri Lanka

Released June 19

Announcement:
Nomination of Charles A. Legge to be United States District Judge for the Northern District of California; Marcel Livaudais, Jr., to be United States District Judge for the Eastern District of Louisiana; Ilana Diamond Rovner to be United States District Judge for the Northern District of Illinois; and Anthony J. Scirica to be United States District Judge for the Eastern District of Pennsylvania

Advance text:
Remarks at dedication ceremonies for the new building of the National Geographic Society

Released June 20

Advance text:
Remarks at an alcohol awareness program at River Dell High School, Oradell, NJ

Advance text:
Remarks at the 44th annual conference of the National Sheriff's Association in Hartford, CT

Released June 26

Text:
Citation of the Presidential Medal of Freedom awarded to former Senator Henry M. Jackson of Washington

Released June 27

Fact sheet:
U.S.-Soviet relations

Released June 28

Announcement:
Nomination of Walter T. Cox III to be a Judge of the United States Court of Military Appeals

Announcement:
Nomination of Stanley Sporkin to be United States District Judge for the District of Columbia

Appendix D—Acts Approved by the President

Approved February 2

S. 1863 / Private Law 98–7
An act for the relief of Audun Endestad.

Approved February 14

H.R. 2727 / Public Law 98–216
An act to codify without substantive change recent laws related to money and finance and transportation and to improve the United States Code.

H.R. 3969 / Public Law 98–217
An act to amend the Panama Canal Act of 1979 to allow the use of proxies by the Board of the Panama Canal Commission.

Approved February 17

H.J. Res. 290 / Public Law 98–218
A joint resolution to permit free entry into the United States of the personal effects, equipment, and other related articles of foreign participants, officials, and other accredited members of delegations involved in the games of the XXIII Olympiad to be held in the United States in 1984.

H.R. 2898 / Public Law 98–219
An act to declare certain lands to be held in trust for the benefit of the Paiute Indian Tribe of Utah, and for other purposes.

S. 379 / Private Law 98–8
An act to cancel certain indebtedness in connection with disaster relief activities.

Approved February 21

S.J. Res. 146 / Public Law 98–220
A joint resolution to designate March 23, 1984, as "National Energy Education Day".

Approved February 22

S. 1340 / Public Law 98–221
Rehabilitation Amendments of 1984.

H.R. 1557 / Private Law 98–9
An act for the relief of William D. Benoni.

Approved February 29

H.R. 4956 / Public Law 98–222
An act to extend the authorities under the Export Administration Act of 1979.

Approved March 2

S. 1388 / Public Law 98–223
Veterans' Compensation and Program Improvements Amendments of 1984.

H.R. 4336 / Public Law 98–224
Civil Service Miscellaneous Amendments Act of 1983.

S.J. Res. 184 / Public Law 98–225
A joint resolution to designate the week of March 4, 1984, through March 10, 1984, as "National Beta Club Week".

Approved March 5

S.J. Res. 193 / Public Law 98–226
A joint resolution designating March 6, 1984, as "Frozen Food Day".

H.J. Res. 422 / Public Law 98–227
A joint resolution designating the week beginning March 4, 1984, as "Women's History Week".

Approved March 7

H.J. Res. 292 / Public Law 98–228
A joint resolution designating "National Theatre Week".

Approved March 9

H.R. 4957 / Public Law 98–229
An act to apportion certain funds for construction of the National System of Interstate and Defense Highways for fiscal year 1985 and to increase the amount authorized to be expended for emergency relief under title 23, United States Code, and for other purposes.

Approved March 12

S.J. Res. 161 / Public Law 98–230
A joint resolution to designate the month of April 1984, as "National Child Abuse Prevention Month".

Approved March 14

S. 2354 / Public Law 98–231
An act to rename the "River of No Return Wilderness" in the State of Idaho as the "Frank Church—River of No Return Wilderness".

Approved March 14—Continued

S.J. Res. 112 / Public Law 98–232
A joint resolution to proclaim the month of March 1984, as "National Social Work Month".

S.J. Res. 225 / Public Law 98–233
A joint resolution designating the month of March 1984 as "National Eye Donor Month".

H.R. 1750 / Private Law 98–10
An act for the relief of Apolonio P. Tumamao and others.

Approved March 16

S.J. Res. 205 / Public Law 98–234
A joint resolution authorizing and requesting the President to designate the second full week in March 1984 as "National Employ the Older Worker Week".

Approved March 19

H.R. 3655 / Public Law 98–235
An act to raise the retirement age for judges of the Superior Court of the District of Columbia and judges of the District of Columbia Court of Appeals.

Approved March 20

H.R. 2173 / Public Law 98–236
Contract Services for Drug Dependent Federal Offenders Authorization Act of 1983.

S. 47 / Public Law 98–237
Shipping Act of 1984.

S.J. Res. 132 / Public Law 98–238
A joint resolution to designate the week beginning May 6, 1984, as "National Correctional Officers Week".

H.R. 4194 / Public Law 98–239
An act to extend the expiration date of section 252 of the Energy Policy and Conservation Act.

Approved March 21

H.J. Res. 200 / Public Law 98–240
A joint resolution designating March 21, 1984, as "National Single Parent Day".

Approved March 22

S. 820 / Public Law 98–241
An act to authorize appropriations for the Earthquake Hazards Reduction Act of 1977 and the Federal Fire Prevention and Control Act of 1974 for fiscal year 1984 and fiscal year 1985, and for other purposes.

Approved March 22—Continued

Note: The following bill became law over the President's veto of February 21 (see page 243).

S. 684 / Public Law 98–242
Water Resources Research Act of 1984.

Approved March 26

S. 912 / Public Law 98–243
An act to modify the authority for the Richard B. Russell Dam and Lake project, and for other purposes.

H.R. 2809 / Public Law 98–244
National Fish and Wildlife Foundation Establishment Act.

Approved March 27

H.J. Res. 454 / Public Law 98–245
A joint resolution honoring the contribution of blacks to American independence.

S.J. Res. 250 / Public Law 98–246
A joint resolution declaring the week of May 7 through May 13, 1984, as "National Photo Week".

Approved March 28

S.J. Res. 241 / Public Law 98–247
A joint resolution to authorize and request the President to issue a proclamation designating May 6 through May 13, 1984 as "Jewish Heritage Week".

Approved March 30

H.J. Res. 493 / Public Law 98–248
A joint resolution making an urgent supplemental appropriation for the Department of Health and Human Services for the fiscal year ending September 30, 1984.

Approved March 31

S. 2507 / Public Law 98–249
An act to continue the transition provisions of the Bankruptcy Act until May 1, 1984, and for other purposes.

Approved April 3

S. 1530 / Public Law 98–250
An act to make technical amendments to the Indian Self-Determination and Education Assistance Act and other Acts.

Approved April 6

H.J. Res. 271 / Public Law 98–251
A joint resolution designating February 11, 1984, "National Inventors' Day".

H.J. Res. 443 / Public Law 98–252
A joint resolution designating the month of June 1984 as "Student Awareness of Drunk Driving Month".

S. 1365 / Public Law 98–253
An act entitled the "Harry Porter Control Tower".

Approved April 9

S.J. Res. 203 / Public Law 98–254
A joint resolution designating the week beginning April 8, 1984, as "National Mental Health Counselors Week".

H.J. Res. 432 / Public Law 98–255
A joint resolution designating the week of April 8 through 14, 1984, as "Parkinson's Disease Awareness Week".

Approved April 10

S. 2392 / Public Law 98–256
An act to authorize the President to appoint Donald D. Engen to the Office of Administrator of the Federal Aviation Administration.

H.R. 3249 / Public Law 98–257
An act to charter the National Academy of Public Administration.

H.R. 4072 / Public Law 98–258
Agricultural Programs Adjustment Act of 1984.

H.R. 4206 / Public Law 98–259
An act to amend the Internal Revenue Code of 1954 to exempt from Federal income taxes certain military and civilian employees of the United States dying as a result of injuries sustained overseas.

Approved April 13

H.R. 4202 / Public Law 98–260
An act to designate the air traffic control tower at Midway Airport, Chicago, as the "John G. Fary Tower".

S.J. Res. 148 / Public Law 98–261
A joint resolution to designate the week of May 6, 1984, through May 13, 1984, as "National Tuberous Sclerosis Week".

Approved April 13—Continued

S.J. Res. 171 / Public Law 98–262
A joint resolution to provide for the designation of July 20, 1984, as "National P.O.W./M.I.A. Recognition Day".

H.J. Res. 407 / Public Law 98–263
A joint resolution designating the week beginning April 8, 1984, as "National Hearing Impaired Awareness Week".

H.J. Res. 520 / Public Law 98–264
A joint resolution designating April 13, 1984, as "Education Day, U.S.A.".

Approved April 17

S. 1852 / Public Law 98–265
"Defense Production Act Amendments of 1984".

H.R. 4835 / Public Law 98–266
An act to authorize funding for the Clement J. Zablocki Memorial Outpatient Facility at the American Children's Hospital in Krakow, Poland.

H.J. Res. 466 / Public Law 98–267
A joint resolution designating May 1984 as "Older Americans Month".

S.J. Res. 173 / Public Law 98–268
A joint resolution commending the Historic American Buildings Survey, a program of the National Park Service, Department of the Interior, the Library of Congress, and the American Institute of Architects.

Approved April 18

H.R. 596 / Public Law 98–269
An act to transfer responsibility for furnishing certified copies of Miller Act payment bonds from the Comptroller General to the officer that awarded the contract for which the bond was given.

H.R. 4169 / Public Law 98–270
Omnibus Budget Reconciliation Act of 1983.

Approved April 30

S. 2570 / Public Law 98–271
An act to continue the transition provisions of the Bankruptcy Act until May 26, 1984, and for other purposes.

Approved May 3

S.J. Res. 210 / Public Law 98–272
A joint resolution to designate the period commencing April 1, 1984, and ending March 31, 1985, as the "Year of Excellence in Education".

Approved May 3—Continued

S. 1186 / Private Law 98–11
An act to clear certain impediments to the licensing of the yacht Dad's Pad for employment in the coastwise trade.

Approved May 7

H.R. 3867 / Public Law 98–273
An act to amend the Perishable Agricultural Commodities Act, 1930, by impressing a trust on the commodities and sales proceeds of perishable agricultural commodities for the benefit of the unpaid seller, and for other purposes.

H.J. Res. 478 / Public Law 98–274
A joint resolution designating the week of April 29 through May 5, 1984, as "National Week of the Ocean."

Approved May 8

S.J. Res. 136 / Public Law 98–275
A joint resolution to recognize "Volunteer Firefighters Recognition Day" as a tribute to the bravery and self-sacrifice of our volunteer firefighters.

H.R. 5298 / Public Law 98–276
White House Conference on Small Business Authorization Act.

S. 2460 / Public Law 98–277
An act to designate a Federal building in Augusta, Maine, as the "Edmund S. Muskie Federal Building."

S. 2597 / Public Law 98–278
An act to authorize the awarding of special congressional gold medals to the daughter of Harry S Truman, to Lady Bird Johnson, and to Elie Wiesel.

S. 2461 / Public Law 98–279
An act to designate a Federal building in Bangor, Maine, as the "Margaret Chase Smith Federal Building."

Approved May 9

H.R. 3555 / Public Law 98–280
An act to declare certain lands held by the Seneca Nation of Indians to be part of the Allegany Reservation in the State of New York.

Approved May 11

S.J. Res. 244 / Public Law 98–281
A joint resolution designating the week beginning on May 6, 1984, as "National Asthma and Allergy Awareness Week."

Approved May 14

H.R. 3376 / Public Law 98–282
An act to declare that the United States holds certain lands in trust for the Makah Indian Tribe, Washington.

Approved May 15

S.J. Res. 232 / Public Law 98–283
A joint resolution to authorize and request the President to designate the month of May 1984 as "National Physical Fitness and Sports Month".

S. 1212 / Private Law 98–12
An act for the relief of sixteen employees of the Charleston Naval Shipyard.

Approved May 16

H.R. 2733 / Public Law 98–284
An act to extend and improve the existing program of research, development, and demonstration in the production and manufacture of guayule rubber, and to broaden such program to include other critical agricultural materials.

Approved May 17

H.R. 3240 / Public Law 98–285
An act to authorize the President of the United States to present on behalf of Congress a specially struck medal to the widow of Roy Wilkins.

S.J. Res. 220 / Public Law 98–286
A joint resolution to designate the week of May 20, 1984, through May 26, 1984, as "National Arts With the Handicapped Week".

Approved May 21

S. 597 / Public Law 98–287
An act to convey certain lands to Show Low, Arizona.

S. 1129 / Public Law 98–288
Domestic Volunteer Service Act Amendments of 1984.

S. 64 / Public Law 98–289
Irish Wilderness Act of 1984.

H.R. 4176 / Public Law 98–290
An act to confirm the boundaries of the Southern Ute Indian Reservation in the State of Colorado and to define jurisdiction within such reservation.

S. 1188 / Public Law 98–291
An act to relieve the General Accounting Office of duplicative audit requirements with respect to the Disabled American Veterans.

Approved May 21—Continued

H.R. 3635 / Public Law 98–292
Child Protection Act of 1984.

Approved May 22

H.J. Res. 537 / Public Law 98–293
A joint resolution designating the Brigantine and Barnegat units of the National Wildlife Refuge System as the Edwin B. Forsythe National Wildlife Refuge.

S.J. Res. 198 / Public Law 98–294
A joint resolution designating April 26, 1985, as "National Nursing Home Residents Day".

S.J. Res. 228 / Public Law 98–295
A joint resolution to designate the week of May 20, 1984, through May 26, 1984, as "National Digestive Diseases Awareness Week".

Approved May 24

H.R. 4107 / Public Law 98–296
An act to designate the Federal building in Salisbury, Maryland, as the "Maude R. Toulson Federal Building".

H.R. 5576 / Public Law 98–297
An act to designate certain land and improvements of the National Institutes of Health as the "Mary Woodard Lasker Center for Health Research and Education".

S.J. Res. 252 / Public Law 98–298
A joint resolution to designate May 25, 1984, as "Missing Children Day".

Approved May 25

H.R. 2174 / Public Law 98–299
An act to extend the transition period under the Bankruptcy Reform Act of 1978.

H.R. 2211 / Public Law 98–300
An act to exempt electric and telephone facilities assisted under the Rural Electrification Act from certain right-of-way rental payments under the Federal Land Policy and Management Act of 1976.

H.R. 5515 / Public Law 98–301
An act to authorize the President to award the Medal of Honor to the unknown American who lost his life while serving in the Armed Forces of the United States in Southeast Asia during the Vietnam era and who has been selected to be buried in the Memorial Amphitheater at Arlington National Cemetery.

H.R. 5692 / Public Law 98–302
An act to provide for a temporary increase in the public debt limit, and for other purposes.

Approved May 25—Continued

H.J. Res. 526 / Public Law 98–303
A joint resolution designating the week of May 27, 1984, through June 2, 1984, as "National Animal Health Week".

Approved May 31

S. 2079 / Public Law 98–304
An act to amend the charter of AMVETS by extending eligibility for membership to individuals who qualify on or after May 8, 1975.

S. 422 / Public Law 98–305
Controlled Substance Registrant Protection Act of 1984.

H.R. 2751 / Public Law 98–306
National Foundation on the Arts and the Humanities Act Amendments of 1983.

S.J. Res. 94 / Public Law 98–307
A joint resolution to authorize and request the President to designate May 13, 1984, to June 17, 1984, as "Family Reunion Month".

S.J. Res. 211 / Public Law 98–308
A joint resolution designating the week of November 18, 1984, through November 24, 1984, as "National Family Week".

S.J. Res. 239 / Public Law 98–309
A joint resolution designating the week of October 21, 1984, through October 27, 1984, as "Lupus Awareness Week".

H.J. Res. 451 / Public Law 98–310
A joint resolution designating the month of November 1984 as "National Alzheimer's Disease Month".

H.J. Res. 487 / Public Law 98–311
A joint resolution to designate June 6, 1984, as "D-Day National Remembrance".

Approved June 12

H.R. 5287 / Public Law 98–312
An act to amend title III of the Higher Education Act of 1965 to permit additional funds to be used to continue awards under certain multi-year grants.

S. 518 / Public Law 98–313
Environmental Programs Assistance Act of 1984.

S. 2413 / Public Law 98–314
An act to recognize the organization known as the American Gold Star Mothers, Incorporated.

Approved June 12—Continued

H.R. 3547 / Public Law 98–315
An act to amend the District of Columbia Self-Government and Governmental Reorganization Act to extend the authority of the Mayor to accept certain interim loans from the United States and to extend the authority of the Secretary of the Treasury to make such loans.

H.R. 5308 / Public Law 98–316
An act to amend the District of Columbia Self-Government and Governmental Reorganization Act to increase the amount authorized to be appropriated as the annual Federal payment to the District of Columbia.

Approved June 15

S.J. Res. 285 / Public Law 98–317
A joint resolution to designate June 13, 1984, as "Harmon Killebrew Day".

S.J. Res. 296 / Public Law 98–318
A joint resolution to designate June 14, 1984, as "Baltic Freedom Day".

Approved June 18

S.J. Res. 289 / Public Law 98–319
A joint resolution to designate June 18, 1984, as "National Child Passenger Safety Awareness Day".

S.J. Res. 261 / Public Law 98–320
A joint resolution to provide for the designation of the last week in June 1984 as "Helen Keller Deaf-Blind Awareness Week".

Approved June 19

H.R. 3578 / Public Law 98–321
Wisconsin Wilderness Act of 1984.

H.R. 4198 / Public Law 98–322
Vermont Wilderness Act of 1984.

H.R. 3921 / Public Law 98–323
New Hampshire Wilderness Act of 1984.

Approved June 19—Continued

H.R. 3960 / Public Law 98–324
North Carolina Wilderness Act of 1984.

Approved June 20

S. 2776 / Public Law 98–325
An act to continue the transition provisions of the Bankruptcy Act until June 27, 1984, and for other purposes.

Approved June 22

H.R. 5517 / Public Law 98–326
An act to amend title 31, United States Code, to provide for certain additional experts and consultants for the General Accounting Office, to provide for certain additional positions within the General Accounting Office Senior Executive Service, and for the other purposes.

Approved June 25

H.R. 1723 / Public Law 98–327
An act to authorize appropriations through fiscal year 1986 for the Great Dismal Swamp, Minnesota Valley, and San Francisco Bay National Wildlife Refuges.

Approved June 26

H.R. 1149 / Public Law 98–328
Oregon Wilderness Act of 1984.

Approved June 29

H.R. 4201 / Public Law 98–329
An act to provide for the rescheduling of methaqualone into schedule I of the Controlled Sustances Act, and for other purposes.

H.R. 3131 / Private Law 98–13
An act for the relief of Marina Kunyavsky.

H.R. 3221 / Private Law 98–14
An act for the relief of Harvey E. Ward.

Subject Index

Name Index

GPO 1986 O - 485-133

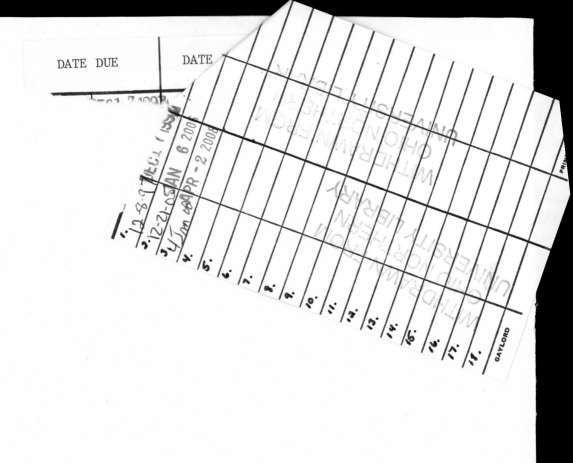